JAN '97 $ $30.85
W9-BBY-848

Police Administration

Police Administration

Structures, Processes, and Behavior

Third Edition

CHARLES R. SWANSON
University of Georgia

LEONARD TERRITO
University of South Florida

ROBERT W. TAYLOR
University of Texas, Tyler

PRENTICE HALL
Englewood Cliffs, NJ 07632

Library of Congress Cataloging-in-Publication Data

Swanson, Charles R. 1942-
Police adminstration: structures, processes, and behavior/
Charles R. Swanson, Leonard Territo, Robert W. Taylor.--3rd ed.
p. cm.--(Macmillan criminal justice series)
Includes bibliographical references and index.
ISBN 0-02-418545-0
1. Police adminstration. I. Title. II. Series
HV7935.S95 1993 92-2282
351.74--dc20 CIP

Editor: Christine Cardone
Production Supervisor: Jane O'Neill
Production Manager: Paul Smolenski
Text and Cover Designer: A Goodthing Inc.
Cover photos: Dick Luria/FPG International (background); Jean Marc Giboux/Gamma-Liaison (inset photo)
Photo Researcher: Suzanne Volkman Skloot

This book was set in Garamond Book by Americomp.

Earlier editions copyright © 1983 and 1988 by Macmillan Publishing Company.

© 1993 by Prentice-Hall, Inc.
A Simon & Schuster Company
Englewood Cliffs, New Jersey 07632

All rights reserved. No part of this book may be reproduced, in any form or by any means, without permission in writing from the publisher.

Printed in the United States of America

10 9 8 7 6 5

ISBN 0-02-418545-0

Prentice-Hall International (UK) Limited, *London*
Prentice-Hall of Australia Pty. Limited, *Sydney*
Prentice-Hall Canada Inc., *Toronto*
Prentice-Hall Hispanoamericana, S.A., *Mexico*
Prentice-Hall of India Private Limited, *New Delhi*
Prentice-Hall of Japan, Inc., *Tokyo*
Simon & Schuster Asia Pte. Ltd., *Singapore*
Editora Prentice-Hall do Brasil, Ltda., *Rio de Janeiro*

For Kittsu, Chris, and Sherri

Preface

In writing this third edition we listened to students, colleagues, reviewers, and police administrators. While it was not possible to accommodate everyone's view, we value the effort made by many people to give us their best thinking.

This edition has many new case histories, vignettes, newspaper articles, photographs, updated citations, and other related enhancements. Among the new sections are those on the pros and cons of community policing and its impact on the organizational structure, transactional versus transformational leaders, Section 1983 lawsuits with increased emphasis on excessive use of force, sexual harassment, the effect of the current fiscal environment on law enforcement agencies, police futures units, quality management, teleconferencing, local area networks, the Americans with Disabilities Act and the Civil Rights Act of 1991 and their impact on police personnel practices, police media relations, artificial intelligence applications, career ladders, and the use of surveillance in the labor–management relationship.

The three co-authors have been police officers, detectives, and administrators. Collectively, for over 65 years we have studied, practiced, researched, taught, and consulted on police administration. An inevitable by-product of these experiences is the development of certain perspectives. As these perspectives form the rationale for this book, it is important to the reader's understanding that they be stated plainly once again in this edition.

Most police administration books favor a certain point of view; the subtitle of this one, "Structures, Processes, and Behavior," effectively serves notice of our conviction that in healthy, achieving organizations the relative value of all three views is recognized and integrated. This book employs a public administration perspective and is interdisciplinary in content. It is intended for serious observers of police administration. As such, the coverage is comprehensive and analytical, and it systematically draws upon empirical literature.

The newspaper clippings, and case studies and vignettes from our own experiences—including failures—are sprinkled throughout to illustrate points discussed in the narrative and to make them concrete. We have striven to make them timely and meaningful. We have tried to communicate not only any conclusions we may have reached but also any ambiguities we might feel. The reader should be aware of our bias that police administration is a complex and dynamic process; it is always—because of the stresses, strains, and influences of the larger society—in motion and in the process of becoming. Although not without its failures and unseemly sides, the notable theme of American police administration, contrary to conventional wisdom, is its vitality and capacity for programmatic change.

Finally, the mention of a product or firm in this book is intended for illustrative purposes and does not necessarily constitute an endorsement or recommendation by the authors or the publisher.

Acknowledgments

Although it is insufficient compensation for their gracious assistance, we wish to recognize here the individuals and organizations who helped to make this book a reality. Unless asked to do otherwise, we have indicated their organizational affiliation at the time they made their contribution.

Hal Vetter, a delightful friend for some 20 years, co-authored Chapter 8, "Stress and Police Personnel." Jack Call and Donald Slesnick, a Miami attorney, co-authored Chapter 10, "Legal Aspects of Police Administration," in the first edition, while Don and Janet Ferris, Florida Department of Law Enforcement, co-authored it the second time. In this edition Bob Taylor assumed responsibility for it.

We would like to thank the following reviewers for their comments and suggestions for the third edition: James Frank, University of Cincinnati; Max Futrell, California State University-Fresno; William P. McCamey, Western Illinois University; and Mittie D. Southerland, Eastern Kentucky University. We would also like to thank Christine Cardone, Senior Editor at Macmillan, for her persistence and encouragement. Thanks are also due to Jane O'Neill for her professional production work.

Maggie Deutsch, Linda Pittman, Dwayne Shumate, Charles Keeton, Maxine Coppinger, and Donna Griffin provided typing and research assistance and made innumerable contributions.

Those who supplied photographs and written material and made suggestions about how to strengthen the book include Charlie Rinkevich and Peggy Hayward, Federal Law Enforcement Training Center, Glynco, Georgia; Chief David Coupen, Madison, Wisconsin Police Department; Scott Wofford, Radio Shack, Fort Worth, Texas; the Drug Enforcement Administration; our colleague of 20 years, Jim Campbell, East Carolina University; Chief John Kerns, Sacramento, California Police Department; the U.S. Secret Service; Willie Ellison, Bureau of Alcohol, Tobacco, and Firearms; Deputy Superintendent Jim Finley, Illinois State Police; Larry Gaines, Eastern Kentucky University; Drs. Walter Booth and Chris Hornickj, Multidimensional Research Association, Aurora, Colorado; Lieutenant Rick Frey, Broward County, Florida Sheriff's Office; Chief Jim Everett, Austin, Texas Police Department; Captain Lawrence Akley, St. Louis, Missouri Metro Police Department; Chief Lee McGehee and Captain Glenn Whiteacre, Ocala, Florida Police Department; the Maricopa, Arizona Sheriff's Office; Inspector Vivian Edmond, Michelle Andonian, and Commander Dorothy Knox, Detroit, Michigan Police Department; Major Herman Ingram, Baltimore, Maryland Police Department; Commissioner Morgan Elkins and Captain Dennis Goss, Kentucky State Police; St. Paul, Minnesota Police Department; Thomas J. Deakin, John E. Ott, editor of the FBI Law Enforcement Bulletin, and William Tafoya, a futures expert, all three with the Federal Bureau of Investigation; our longtime friend Ron Lynch, University of North Carolina; the Tigard, Oregon Police Department; the California Highway Patrol; Dr. Zug Standing Bear, Valdosta (Georgia) State University; Norma Kane, the Kansas City, Missouri Police Department; the San Diego, California Police Department; Chief Larry Robinson, Tyler, Texas Police Department; Janice Lowenberg, U.S. Probation and Parole; the Texas Department of Public Safety; the Philadelphia Police Department; Sergeant Maurice McGough, St. Petersburg, Florida Police Department; National Tactical Officers Association; Lieutenant James B. Bolger, Michigan State Police; the Denver Police Department; Colonel Carroll D. Buracker and Scott Boatright, Fairfax County, Virginia Police Department; Charles Tracy, Portland (Oregon) State University; Major Dave Sturtz, Ohio State Patrol; the National Consortium for Justice Information and Statistics, Sacramento, California; Sheriff Sherman Block and Undersheriff T. H. Von Minden, Los Angeles County, California Sheriff's Office; Phoenix, Arizona Police and Fire Departments; Deputy Chief Troy McClain, Captain Terry Haucke, Dr. S. A. Somodevilla, and Sergeants Jody Thomas and Mark Stallo, Dallas, Texas Police Department; Mary Ann Wycoff, Police Foundation; Don Fish, Florida Police Benevolent Association; Captain Keith Bushey, Los Angeles, California Police Department; Police Chief Johnny Upton and Kay Wilkenson, Personnel Director, city of Longview, Texas; Deputy Chief Kevin Stoeher, Mt. Lebanon, Pennsylvania Police Department; Karen Anderson and Lisa Bird, LAN Publications Group; Doug Hicks Minneapolis, Minnesota Police Department; Lieutenant Rex Splitt, Craig, Colorado Police Department; Joseph Scuro, attorney, Dallas, Texas; Chief Thomas Maudlin and Captain Thomas Uretsky, Pacific Grove, California Police Department; Chief R. E. Hansen and Cynthia Shaw, Fayetteville, North Carolina Police Department; Dr. Mathew Prosser, Tyler, Texas; Officer David Hoffman, Anchorage, Alaska Police Department; LaNell Thornton, ElectroCom Automation, Arlington, Texas; Chief Paul Annee and Lieutenant Michael Spears, Indianapolis, Indiana Police Department; Lexington-Fayette, Kentucky Urban County Police Department; Dr. Gary Sykes, Southeastern Law Enforcement Institute, Dallas, Texas; Environmental Systems Research Institute, Redlands, California; Nancy Brandon, Metro Software, Park City, Utah; Drs. Benjamin Ferrell and Peter Nelligen, University of Texas at Tyler; Sheriff Jim Roache and Sarah Brooks, San Diego, California Sheriff's Department; Larry Yium, Director of Budget and Finance, Houston, Texas; Lois Roethel and Leslie Doak, Las Vegas, Nevada Police Department; the Knox County, Maine Sheriff's Department; a renowned storyteller and our favorite Irishman, Major Tim Buckley, Marietta, Georgia Police Department; Chief Jim Wetherington, a mentor, and Assistant Chief Sam Woodall, Semper Fi, Columbus, Georgia Police Department; our friend Dr. Jim Sewell, Director, Florida Criminal Justice Executive Institute, who generously allowed us to draw on some of his work on stress as well as on the use of his Law Enforcement and Critical Events Scale; Richard B. Walker, Hillsborough County, Florida Sheriff's

Office, who contributed information on career tracks; and Jeffrey Higgenbotham, a Special Agent in the Legal Division, FBI Academy, Quantico, Virginia, who contributed to the discussion on sexual harassment.

Charles R. "Mike" Swanson
Leonard Territo
Robert W. Taylor

Contents

3 Organizational Theory 80

4 Concepts of Police Organizational Design 133

5 Leadership 163

6 Interpersonal and Organizational Communication 200

7 Human Resource Management 226

8 Stress and Police Personnel 296

1 The Evolution of American Policing

The police at all times should maintain a relationship with the public that gives reality to the historic tradition that the police are the public and that the public are the police.
SIR ROBERT PEEL

Introduction

If the many different purposes of the American police service were narrowed to a single focus, what would emerge is the obligation to preserve the peace in a manner consistent with the freedoms secured by the Constitution.[1] It does not follow from this assertion that our police alone bear the responsibility for maintaining a peaceful society; that responsibility is shared by other elements of society, beginning with each individual and spreading to each institution and each level of government—local, state, and federal. However, because crime is an immediate threat to our respective communities, the police have a highly visible and perhaps even primary role in overcoming the threat and fear of crime.

The preservation of peace is more complex than simply preventing crimes, making arrests for violations of the law, recovering stolen property, and providing assistance in the prosecution of persons charged with acts of criminality. In all likelihood, the police only spend something on the order of 15 percent of their time enforcing the law. The most substantial portion of their time goes toward providing less glamorous services that are utterly essential to maintaining the public order and well-being. Illustrative of these services are providing directions to motorists, mediating conflicts, evacuating neighborhoods threatened or struck by natural disasters, and serving as a bridge between other social service agencies and persons who come to the attention of the police, such as the mentally disturbed.

The degree to which any society achieves some amount of public order through police action depends in part upon the price that society is willing to pay to obtain it. This price can be measured in the resources dedicated to the public function and in the extent to which citizens are willing to tolerate a reduction in the number, kinds, and extent of liberties they enjoy. In this regard, totalitarian and democratic governments reflect very different choices. This point underscores the fact that the American police service cannot be understood properly if it is examined alone, as an island in a lake. A more appropriate and persuasive analogy is that policing is like a sandbar in a river, subject to being changed continuously by the currents in which it is immersed. As a profoundly significant social institution, policing is subject to, and continuously shaped by, a multitude of forces at work in our larger society.

The year 1890—roughly one hundred years ago—is the date normally associated with the closing of the frontier and a milestone in our transition from a rural, agrarian society to one that is highly urbanized and industrialized. This period of time is a long one to have lived by current expectancies, but as a period of history, it is brief. Still, in this historically short time span, the changes that have taken place in this country are staggering.

Inevitably any attempt to highlight this period will have some deficits. However, the balance of this chapter does so to achieve two objectives: (1) to demonstrate the impact of social forces on policing and (2) to identify and set the stage for some of the content treated in subsequent chapters. These two objectives will be met by presenting material organized under the headings of (1) politics and administration, (2) police professionalization, (3) the role of the police, (4) the impact of education, (5) research on traditional policing, (6) community policing, and (7) problems with community policing.

Politics and Administration

Politics, stated simply, is the exercise of power. As such, it is value free, its "goodness" or "badness" stemming from its application rather than from some inherent character. Although police executives can occasionally be heard avowing to "keep politics out of the department," this unqualified posture is unrealistic. Personal politics exist in every organization, and democratic control of the policing mechanism is fundamental to our society. However, policing and partisan party politics have had a long and not entirely healthy relationship in this country.

In New York City, at the middle of the nineteenth century, the approval of the ward's alderman was required before appointment to the police force, and the Tammany Hall corruption of the same period depended in part on the use of the police to coerce and collect graft and to control elections.[2] During this same time, the election of a new mayor—particularly if from a party different from the incumbent's—signaled the coming dismissal of the entire police force and the appointment of one controlled by the new mayor.

Later, at the turn of the century, our cities were staggering under the burden of machine politics, corruption, crime, poverty, and the exploitation of women and children by industry.[3] The federal government, too, was not without its woes, as illustrated by the somewhat later Teapot Dome scandal that stained Warren G. Harding's administration.

Central to the Reformation period of 1900 to 1926 was the need to arouse the public and establish a conceptual cornerstone. Steffens exposed the plight of such cities as St. Louis, Minneapolis, Pittsburgh, and Chicago in *The Shame of the Cities*

(1906); novels such as Sinclair's *The Jungle* (1906) called attention to abuses in the meat-packing industry; and Churchill addressed political corruption in *Coniston* (1911). The conceptual cornerstone was supplied by Woodrow Wilson's 1887 essay calling for a separation of politics and administration.[4] However impractical that might now seem, it is important to understand that to the reformers "politics" meant "machine politics" and all the ills associated with it.[5]

With an aroused public and a conceptual touchstone, rapid strides were made. In 1906, the New York Bureau of Municipal Research was formed, and by 1910, the city manager movement was under way. In 1911, the Training School for Public Service was established in New York, and by 1914, the University of Michigan was offering a degree in municipal administration. Further serving to strengthen the reform movement—whose center was the desire to separate politics (in the worst sense) and administration—was the issuance in 1916 of a model city charter by the National Municipal League, which called for a strict separation of these two elements. Further crystallization of the politics–administration dichotomy is found in White's *Public Administration* (1926), in which he praised the 1924 city manager's code of neutrality that stipulated that "no city manager should take an active part in politics," and in Willoughby's *Principles of Public Administration* (1927).

These events combined to produce movement toward reducing corruption, waste, fraud, and abuse in government; the desire to create a professionally qualified cadre of people committed to careers in public service; the rise of the civil service; emphasis upon proper recruitment, selection, and training of public employees; the freeing of government from the influence of machine politics; and the development of new theories, techniques, and models related to organizations. In

FIGURE 1-1. The entire Denver Police Department poses for an annual picture at the turn of the century, 1900. (Courtesy Denver, Colorado Police Department.)

short, these events were not only historical milestones; they unleased a process of improvement that is still in progress today.

Police Professionalization

The terms *profession* and *professional* are tossed around with great abandon and a conspicuous lack of definition. The general absence of attention to definition has produced endless and futile debates as to whether policing is in fact a profession. The term *profession* is derived from the Latin *pro* (forth) and *fateri* (confess), meaning to "announce a belief"; at its early use, the word referred to public or open avowals of faith.[6] Cogan[7] notes that the earliest recorded use of the word *profession* as a learned vocation was in 1541 and that by 1576 the meaning had been generalized to mean any calling or occupation by which a person habitually earned his or her living. By 1675, a refinement of the secular use of the term occurred when it was associated with the act of professing to be duly qualified.[8]

Roughly since 1920, much of the serious work on professions has centered on specifying what criteria must be met to constitute a profession. The result is not a single definition but rather a collection of similar definitions that usually approximate the following: (1) an organized body of theoretically grounded knowledge, (2) advanced study, (3) a code of ethics, (4) prestige, (5) standards of admission, (6) a professional association, and (7) a service ideal, which may also be stated alternatively as altruism.[9] In 1960 Merton[10] reduced the values that make up a profession to (1) knowing (systematic knowledge), (2) doing (technical skill and trained capacity), and (3) helping (the joining of knowing and doing). Becker[11] has reduced the argument further to the pithy observation that in a debate as to whether a particular type of work can be called a profession, if the work group is successful in getting itself called a profession, it is one.

The rise of "professional" policing is associated initially with the paid, full-time body of police that stemmed from England's Peelian Reform of 1829. Despite the existence of similar bodies in this country from 1845 onward, the genesis of American professional policing is associated with the initiatives of August Vollmer, who was chief of police in Berkeley, California, from 1902 to 1932.

Without detracting one bit from Vollmer's genius, note that his tenure as chief parallels closely the reformation movement of 1900 to 1926, which, in addition to its politics–administration dichotomy concern, also had a heavy orientation toward good, progressive government. Carte summarizes the work of this giant by noting

> The image of professional policing as we know it today is largely the creation of one man, August Vollmer. Vollmer was a tireless crusader for the reform of policing through technology and higher personnel standards. Under his direction the Berkeley department became a model of professional policing—efficient, honest, scientific. He introduced into Berkeley a patrolwide police signal system, the first completely mobile patrol—first on bicycles, then in squad cars—modern records systems, beat analysis and modus operandi. The first scientific crime laboratory in the United States was set up in Berkeley in 1916, under the direction of a full-time forensic scientist. The first lie detector machine to be used in criminal investigation was built in the Berkeley department in 1921.
>
> However, Vollmer's department was better known for the caliber of its personnel. He introduced formal police training in 1908, later encouraging his men to attend classes

FIGURE 1-2. August Vollmer, seated third from the left, at work in the Berkeley, California Police Department about 1914. (Courtesy of the Berkeley Police Department.)

> in police administration that were taught each summer at the University of California. Eventually he introduced psychological and intelligence testing into the recruitment process and actively recruited college students from the University, starting around 1919. This was the beginning of Berkeley's "college cops," who set the tone for the department throughout the 1920s and 30s and came to be accepted by police leaders as the ultimate model of efficient, modern policemen.[12]

The Pendleton Act of 1883 sought to eliminate the ills of the political spoils system in the federal government. Many states and local governments passed parallel legislation over the next 30 years, establishing civil service systems designed to protect government employees from political interference. Although these measures were intuitively attractive, their application was questioned early by one observer of the police, Fosdick, who wrote in 1920:

> In its application to a police department civil service has serious limitations. In the endeavor to guard against abuse of authority, it frequently is carried to such extremes that rigidity takes the place of flexibility in administration, and initiative in effecting essential changes in personnel is crippled and destroyed. Too often . . . civil service is a bulwark for neglect and incompetence, and one of the prime causes of departmental disorganization. Too often does the attempt to protect the force against the capricious play of politics compromise the principle of responsible leadership, so that in trying to nullify the effects of incompetence and favoritism, we nullify capacity and intelligence too.
>
> As a result of this divided responsibility between police executives and civil service commissions, there are in most large departments many men whose continuance in

> office is a menace to the force and to the community, but who cannot be dismissed because the proof of incompetence of dishonesty does not satisfy the requirements of the civil service law.[13]

It is a matter of some irony that there is a basic tension between Vollmer's trained and educated "professional" police officer and the early administration of civil service acts. The reason was that Vollmer was highly concerned with competence and performance—his notion of merit—whereas the measure of merit for many of the initial years of civil service was simply the degree to which political influence was kept out of appointments and promotions.[14]

Of significant consequence to the very structure of police organizations were the continuing efforts during the reformation period to separate politics and administration. One mechanism for doing so was to change the political structure; thus, in Los Angeles a council elected at large was substituted for the ward system.[15] Other reformers, persuaded that America was besieged by crime and that the police were our first line of defense, saw the police as analogous to the military. A second mechanism, therefore, was giving chiefs expanded powers, large and competent staffs, and the capability to actually control their departments.[16] In many cities, the precincts had previously operated largely or totally autonomously, and this second mechanism required centralization, which meant consolidating or eliminating precincts, as in New York City and elsewhere,[17] a further blow to ward boss control. The military analogy was so potent that its logical extension—recruiting military officers as police commissioners or chiefs—became a common practice for some years. Illustrative of this practice was the appointment in 1923 in Philadelphia of Marine Corps General Smedley Butler as director of public safety.

The highly centralized military analogy model (refer to Chapter 3) that became widely adopted and remains today as the dominant force of police organization is technically a bureaucratic structure that has been subjected to a number of criticisms. At the time of its adoption in American policing, it may have been an essential part of promoting police professionalism. For whatever its weaknesses, it brought with it an emphasis on discipline, inspections, improved record keeping, supervision, close-order drill, improved accountability, and other bits and pieces that contributed to the transformation of the police from semiorganized ruffians operating under the mantle of law into something entirely different.

The 1930s became a pivotal period as American police gained increasing legitimacy and authority in society.[18] Starting in 1931, the National Commission on Law Observance and Law Enforcement, popularly named after its chairman as the Wickersham Commission, presented a number of reforms for the police. Central to the commission's recommendations were provisions for civil service classification for police and enhanced support for education and training. Radelet[19] reports that "Take the police out of politics," a common slogan of the era, represented an important, first step in gaining respectability. This step was a continuation of the separation of politics and administration, which first arose during the reformation period discussed earlier in this chapter.

The emphasis on law enforcement in American society was timely, as crime was perceived to be dramatically increasing. Stimulated by celebrated cases, such as the kidnapping of Charles Lindbergh's baby, the Federal Bureau of Investigation (FBI), under the direction of J. Edgar Hoover, began to emerge as a dominant entity in American policing. In 1935 the FBI created the National Police Academy, where local police leaders and officials were educated in the "professional" and "scientific" aspects of law enforcement.[20] This move was concurrent with the first major university programs (at the University of California at Berkeley, Michigan State University, and Northwestern University) devoted to the academic study of police practices. According to Kelling and Stewart, the decade that followed concretized the "reform" period from political "patsies" to professional agencies:

> Police departments nationwide had come to embrace an integrated and coherent organizational strategy that sought authority in criminal law; narrowed police function to crime control; emphasized classical organizational forms; relied on preventive patrol, rapid response to calls for service, and criminal investigation as its primary tactics; and measured its success by crime, arrest, and clearance data. . . . Indeed, with rare exception police defined themselves as professional organizations that should be kept out of the purview of citizens, academics and researchers, and other persons with an interest in police. Police business was just that: police business.[21]

Following World War II, interest in the police seemed to wane as economic development and social mobility gave rise to new issues—urban congestion, decaying values, and ethnic/racial unrest. It was not until the 1960s that significant attention was once again brought to bear on the functions and duties of the police.

The Role of the Police

The emerging racial tensions and social unrest of the early 1960s erupted into violent confrontation between minorities and police in most major cities. Fueled in part by the U.S. involvement in Southeast Asia, the police found themselves amid a nation divided both racially and socially. Occupying a very precarious position, police agencies reacted with a "get-tough" policy. The resulting riots were often characterized by widespread violence between predominantly white police departments and black communities. The nation began to focus on the police, specifically on the role of the police in society.

For the first time, major questions were being asked concerning what the police do. The National Advisory Commission on Civil Disorders, often referred to as the Kerner Commission, as it was headed by Governor Otto Kerner of Ohio, clearly outlined the problem:

> The policeman in the ghetto is a symbol of increasingly bitter social debate over law enforcement. One side, disturbed and perplexed by sharp rises in crime and urban violence, exerts extreme pressure on police for tougher law enforcement. Another group, inflamed against police as agents of repression, tends toward defiance of what it regards as order maintained at the expense of justice.[22]

This role conflict also called into question the legitimacy of policing as a profession. Were the police viable agents capable of controlling crime and disorder, or simply "bullies" who attempted to control a culturally divided American society? Such questions led to the identification of several conflicting and ambiguous roles for the police.

As as result of the previous "crime-fighting" era, police officers were considered law enforcers, charged with fighting crime, arresting criminals, and maintaining order. This image remains today and is reinforced by the popular media as well as continued community perception. Yet, at the same time, the police were touted as conflict managers, keepers of the peace, crime prevention specialists, and, to some degree, social service agents. In other words, the police were also supposed to *assist* citizens rather than *arrest* law violators.[23] To a large extent, this role ambiguity still exists as law enforcement agencies and their communities strive to define more accurately the evolving nature of policing.

The Impact of Education

Major interest in police professionalization was renewed once again in the 1960s. During this time, the requirement of a high school diploma or a general equivalency degree became the minimum educational requirement for appointment. Character and background investigations became standard practice and increasingly more thorough. The use of the polygraph and psychological instruments to screen applicants became more widespread. Altogether, such factors signaled a shift from screening out the undesirable and hiring the rest to identifying and hiring those believed to be most able. At the state level, Police Office Standards and Training Commissions (POSTs) were created, often with the incentive of Law Enforcement Assistance Administration (LEAA) grants to initiate operations and to ensure that uniform minimum standards—including training—were met.

Training academies proliferated, and a few departments began to require a

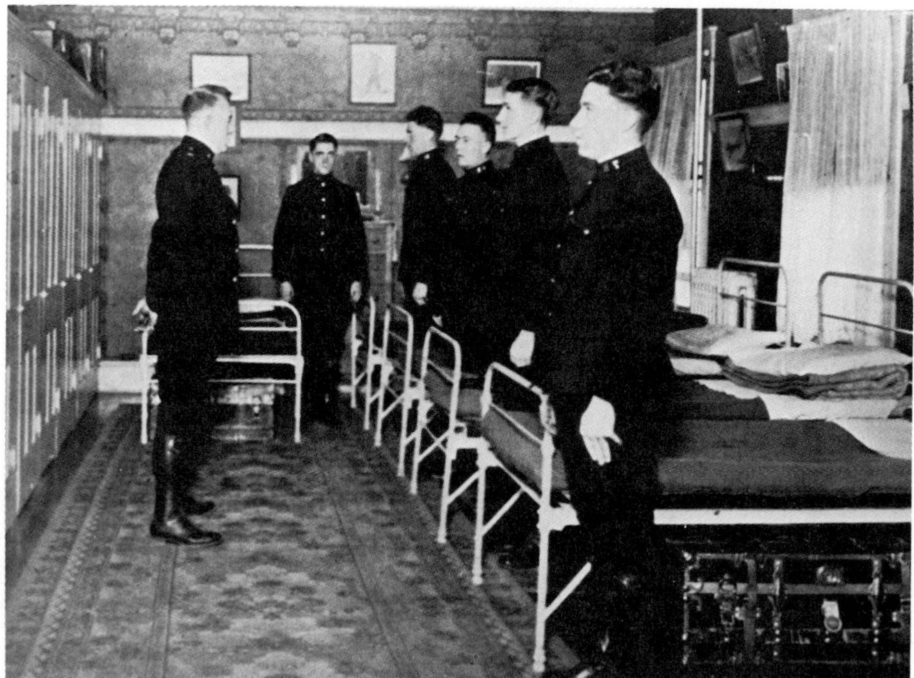

FIGURE 1-3. The military model at work in policing. A 1906 Pennsylvania State Police barracks inspection. (Courtesy of the Pennsylvania State Police.)

college degree as an entry-level educational requirement. More numerous, however, were the departments that required a few college credits, such as six or twelve, and the departments that required as a condition of employment that officers agree to obtain a certain number of college hours within a specified time after appointment. Written promotional tests gained in prominence, although many rank-and-file members objected to them, favoring seniority instead. Even some chiefs complained that written tests interfered with their ability to promote the most able persons. The length of recruit academy curricula increased steadily, and social science subjects were introduced. From 1965 on, the number of junior colleges, colleges, and universities offering police administration or criminal justice degrees grew steadily, if not exponentially, due initially to the availability of "seed money" to start such programs from the Office of Law Enforcement Assistance (OLEA), LEAA's predecessor. Law Enforcement Education Program (LEEP) funds from LEAA were offered to induce and support the studies of students with career interests in criminal justice.

Further impetus to the movement to educate in-service officers and infuse college graduates into police departments was gained by providing incentive pay for college credits, which is a supplement above the regular salary based on the number of college credits earned. "Professionalization" of the police and "education" became virtually synonymous in the eyes of many observers. Illustratively, while conspicuously failing to define professionalization, the 1967 President's Commission on Law Enforcement and Administration of Justice nonetheless clearly equated professionalism with education.

Thus, despite a variety of practices designed to foster a higher caliber of per-

FIGURE 1-4. San Francisco police recruits learning to type in a 1937 class. Note the traffic lights that were used as a training aid. The use of such training programs was a central strategy in early attempts to professionalize the police. (Courtesy of the San Francisco Archives.)

sonnel, the hallmark from 1950 to 1970—particularly after 1965—was the attempt to promote police professionalism through education. Education was seen as a means by which to improve community relations, which had suffered and contributed to the urban riots of 1965–1968; to reduce police use of violence; to promote more judicious use of police discretionary powers; to counter the problem of corruption; and to accurately define the role of police in society.[24]

Research on Traditional Policing

During the late 1970s, the issues of professionalism and the role of the police seemed to take a backseat to an ever-increasing public demand for efficiency and effectiveness. Unlike earlier years, law enforcement agencies were unable to expand their level of service delivery because of the reluctance of local officials to continually increase the police budget. This reluctance could be attributed to several factors. For example, some of the police expansion during the late 1960s and early 1970s could be traced to the creation of LEAA, which provided substantial financial resources to improve police operations. The decline of the agency during the 1970s severely cut what was once a relatively large fund for local police service improvement.

To make financial matters even worse, an inflationary economy had produced further constraints and burdens on urban police budgets. Major increases in gasoline prices and labor/personnel costs had forced many local governments to consider themselves in a state of crisis. New York City and Philadelphia laid off thousands of police officers in an attempt to recover from near economic collapse. Moreover, the social and political climate of the era focused on the scrutiny of government spending. Based in part on the public's cry for the efficient use of tax dollars, most city officials felt the need to conserve expenditures.

Still faced with rising crime and increased calls for service, police administrators looked for ways to improve the efficiency and effectiveness of existing resources. Fortunately, the ongoing research efforts of a few key institutions yielded some interesting, if not highly controversial, answers. Three important experiments once again set the stage for questioning what the police do:

The Kansas City Patrol Experiment

From October 1, 1972, to September 30, 1973, the Kansas City Police Department, along with the support of the Police Foundation, conducted a study to determine if routine patrol using conspicuously marked vehicles had any measurable impact on crime or the public's sense of security.[25] As noted in a report on the study, "police patrol strategies have always been based on two unproven but widely accepted hypotheses: first, that visible police presence prevents potential offenders; second, that the public's fear of crime is diminished by such police presence."[26]

The Kansas City experiment was conducted within fifteen beats in a 32-square-mile area with a resident population of 148,395 (see Figure 1-5). The beats were designated as reactive, proactive, and control areas. Reactive beats did not have

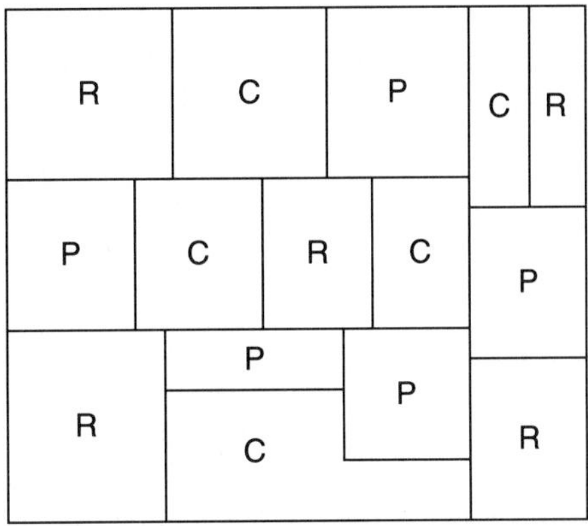

FIGURE 1-5. Schematic representation of the fifteen-beat experimental area of the Kansas City Patrol Experiment. [From George L. Kelling et al., *The Kansas City Patrol Experiment* (Washington, D.C.: Police Foundation, 1974), p. 9.]

preventive patrols; officers entered these areas only when a citizen called and requested service. When the officers were not responding to calls, they patrolled adjacent proactive beats on the boundaries of their own beats. With proactive beats, the routine preventive patrol was intensified to two to three times its usual level, whereas in control beats, the normal (usual) amount of patrolling was conducted. The following were noted in the evaluation of this experiment:

1. The amount of reported crime in the reactive, control, and proactive beats revealed only one significant statistical variation: The number of incidents under the category of "other sex crimes," including such offenses as exhibitionism and molestation (excluding rape), was higher in reactive areas than in control areas, but project evaluators felt this significance was most likely random.
2. There were no statistically significant differences found in regard to fluctuations in crimes that were not officially reported to the police.
3. No statistically significant differences in arrests among the three types of beats were found.
4. Security measures taken by citizens and businesses were not significantly altered with the variations in the level of patrolling.
5. There was little correlation found between the level of patrol and the citizens' and business persons' attitude toward the policing.
6. The citizens' fear of crime was not significantly changed by the alternations in the level of routine preventive patrol.
7. The time taken for police to answer calls was not significantly changed by variations in the level of routine preventive patrol.
8. The level of patrol had no significant effect on the incidence of traffic accidents.

The interpretations and findings of the Kansas City Patrol Experiment were highly controversial. Upon learning of the study, some local leaders felt that further increases in police manpower were not warranted and that decreases might even be justified. However, these persons failed to realize that a random moving patrol is not the only strategy of prevention available to police.

The RAND Criminal Investigation Study

In 1973, the RAND Corporation was awarded a grant by the National Institute of Law Enforcement and Criminal Justice to undertake a nationwide study of criminal investigations in major metropolitan police agencies.[27] The purposes of the study were to describe how police investigations were organized and managed and to assess the contribution of various activities to overall police effectiveness. Before the RAND study, police investigators had not been subject to the type of scrutiny that was being focused on other types of police activity. Most police administrators knew little about the effectiveness of the day-to-day activities of their investigative units, and even less about the practice of other departments.

The RAND study focused on the investigation of serious crimes against unwilling victims (index offenses), as opposed to vice, gambling, and narcotics. The information on current practice was obtained by a national survey of municipal and county police agencies who employed more than 150 officers or jurisdictions with a population over 100,000. In order to obtain a represen-

FIGURE 1-6. Based in part on the RAND Criminal Investigation Study, some departments have used a team approach to solve crimes. Here members of a crisis team help children cope with the traumatic aspects of a family crime while maintaining their roles as detectives. (Courtesy Austin, Texas Police Department.)

tative sample, interviews and observations were conducted in over 25 departments. Data on the outcome of investigations were obtained from the FBI Uniform Crime Report tapes, from internal evaluations, and from samples of completed cases. In addition, data on the allocation of investigative efforts were obtained from a computerized work-load file maintained by the Kansas City Police Department.

The data from the national survey and the Uniform Crime Reports were then combined to analyze the relationship between departmental characteristics and apprehension effectiveness. In turn, case samples were analyzed to determine how specific cases were solved.

Policy Recommendations

1. The RAND study strongly suggested that post-arrest investigation activities be coordinated more directly with the prosecutors, either by allowing prosecutors to exert more guidance over the practices and policies of investigators, or by assigning investigators to the prosecutor's office. The purpose of this recommendation was to attempt to increase the percentage of cases that could be prosecuted.
2. Patrol officers were to be given a larger role in conducting preliminary investigations—to provide an adequate basis for case screening and to reduce or attempt to eliminate redundant efforts by an investigator.
3. Additional and improved resources were to be devoted to the processing of latent prints, and improved systems were to be developed for the organizing and searching of print files.
4. The study recommended that with regard to follow-up investigations for the cases a department selected to pursue, a distinction should be drawn between cases that merely required routine clerical processing and those that required legal skills or those of a special investigative nature.

The RAND study is still a subject of controversy within the police profession. Many police officials, especially those without detective experience, were sympathetic to the study in that it supported their own impressions of how investigators functioned. Others criticized the study for "telling us what we already knew." Some police chiefs became resentful because the study was used by city officials as an excuse to cut police budgets, and others refused to accept the findings because of the limited number of departments that were studied.[28]

There have not been any major attempts to extend or replicate the findings in the RAND study; a number of reports have been published with consistent findings. Bloch and Weidman's[29] analysis of the investigative practices of the Rochester, New York, Police Department and Greenberg's[30] efforts to develop a felony investigation decision model both resulted in findings that support the idea that preliminary investigations, which are carried out in a majority of arrests, can provide adequate information for screening cases. A report by the Vera Institute on felony arrests in New York City indicated that a substantial portion of felony arrests for street crimes involve offenders who are known to their victims,[31] and a report by Forst[32] on the disposition of felony arrests in Washington, D.C., demonstrates the importance of physical evidence and multiple witnesses in securing convictions for felony street crimes. In general these studies suggest that often much of the information needed to solve a case is supplied by the uniformed officer who does the original investigation as opposed to cases solved by a detective's followup investigation.

Team Policing

Team policing was one of the most dynamic experiments that altered traditional methods of policing in both the United States and Great Britain.[33] (Table 1-1 contrasts the key features of traditional and team policing.) Team policing was an innovation that enabled police personnel from various divisions to participate as full partners in the development of a superior police service delivery system.

Generally, team policing involved combining the officers responsible for line

TABLE 1-1. Comparison of Traditional and Neighborhood Team Policing

Traditional	Neighborhood team policing
1. Smallest patrol unit (precinct or division) has 100 to 250 officers.	1. Team has 20 to 30 officers.
2. Supervision is quasi-military.	2. Supervision is professional, with consultation, setting of objectives, an in-service training program, encouraging suggestions, permitting the exercise of responsibility within necessary limits.
3. Shift responsibility includes eight-hour tours, with only unit commanders—captains or inspectors—responsible for around-the-clock operations.	3. Team commander is responsible for all aspects of police service on an around-the-clock basis.
4. Assignment is on the basis of the first available car to a call for police service—with priority for emergency calls.	4. Team provides all police service for its neighborhood. Team members are sent out of the neighborhood only in emergencies. Nonteam members take calls in the neighborhood only in emergencies.
5. Officers are rotated to new divisions or assignments.	5. Officers are given extended assignments to a neighborhood.
6. Special police units (tactical, detective, etc.) operate in local neighborhoods without informing local patrol officials.	6. Special police units inform themselves of team goals and, whenever possible, consult in advance with the local team commander.
7. Community relations is seen as "image building" (special units for community relations plus speaking engagement for officials).	7. Community relations is seen as an essential patrol function, planned by team commander and the team, and consists of good police service, friendliness on street contacts, and attendance at meetings of various community groups.
8. Reactive policing (responding to calls) or aggressive policing (stop and frisk and street interrogations) are prevalent.	8. Decentralized planning (crime analysis, use of plainclothes or special tactics, investigations, preventive programs, referral programs, service activities).
9. Planning is centralized (innovation through orders from the chief or other important officials).	9. Planning is decentralized (innovation by team commanders, subject to review by their superiors).

From Peter Block and David Specht, *Neighborhood Team Policing* (Washington, D.C.: U.S. Government Printing Office, 1973), p. 2.

operations into a team with a leader. Each officer involved in the team had an opportunity to perform the patrol, traffic, and detective functions and, where appropriate, the specialized functions of narcotics and vice and juvenile control. Community relations was not considered a specialization, because the function was the responsibility of every police officer. Each team was assigned a permanent sector or geographic area for which they were totally responsible. Authority for internal team assignments, scheduling, and complete police service was given to the team leaders. The team was held strictly accountable for police service in its assigned area.[34]

A number of police departments experimented with team policing, and the results were mixed. In New York City; Dayton, Ohio; and Holyoke, Massachusetts the programs were failures.[35] In New York City, officers continued to police in conventional ways, and low officer morale undermined the programs, as did similar problems in Dayton.[36] On the other hand, San Diego reported success in redefining the role of officers and in improving work-load management, and data from Rochester, New York, revealed improvement in crime control and investigative effectiveness. Furthermore, police from Albany, New York, and Los Angeles indicated that team policing was a qualified success in those cities in improving community attitudes about the police.[37]

A repeated theme in analyses of the failure of some attempts at team policing was the opposition of middle managers, whose importance was diminished because team policing reduces specialization and the number of levels in an organization. Wycoff and Kelling[38] report that the failures of team policing might have resulted more from implementation of change rather than from philosophy or ideas. They indicate several issues during the implementation process that deserve attention:

- Lack of planning and understanding of the change process existed throughout all levels of the organization.
- Ideas were imposed from the top or from outside the organization, often without support from the lower ranks.
- Mid-level managers and supervisors who were critical to success quickly became disaffected. They were not included in the planning nor were they prepared for the role changes the new efforts would require.
- Changes in organizational processes or structures needed to support the new programs were not made and did not evolve on their own.
- An overall organizational philosophy supportive of the new programs did not exist. In each case, the new programs were add-ons, forced to sink or swim in an unprotected organizational environment.
- The overall effort was too much too fast.[39]

Hence, although team policing lost much of its luster during the mid-1970s, some of its failure might have been the consequence of poorly conducted organizational change rather than of the concept itself. There is also some limited research evidence that suggests that the implementation of team policing in large cities, but not necessarily smaller ones, may produce short-run benefits that "wash out" over time as the latent power of bureaucracy asserts itself;[40] Michels's[41] "iron law of oligarchy" states that modern large-scale organizations tend toward centralization, even if it runs contrary to the ideals and intentions of both the leaders and the led. Large police departments require a certain amount of specialization to handle diverse tasks efficiently, such as examining various physical evidence, and the amount of hierarchy required to coordinate the various specialized parts produces a tendency toward centralization. (Refer to Chapter 4 for a more thorough discussion of organizational design.) Interestingly, similar issues concerning team policing are currently being raised regarding the implementation of community policing programs of the 1990s.

Community Policing

The failure of traditional law enforcement methods to curb rising crime rates and to reintegrate the police with society has given rise to a new movement, generally referred to as "community policing." Although Braiden[42] argues that community policing is "nothing new under the sun" because it only echoes the ideas expressed by Sir Robert Peel in the early 1800s, community policing does represent a refreshing approach to earlier problems. Community policing embraces the Peelian principle of police as members of the public giving full-time attention to community welfare and existence. Therefore, policing is linked to a myriad of social issues other than simply crime, including poverty, illiteracy, racism, teen-age pregnancy, and the like.[43]

Although precise definitions of community policing are hard to find, it generally refers to an operational and management philosophy that is uniquely identifiable.

FIGURE 1-7. Officers interact with community functions in order to provide customized police services approprite to the city area. In this case, officers on horseback patrol the extensive park areas in Portland, Oregon. (Courtesy Portland, Oregon Police Bureau.)

Primarily, community policing is characterized by ongoing attempts to promote greater community involvement in the police function. For the most part, the movement has focused on programs that foster five elements: (1) a commitment to crime prevention, (2) public scrutiny of the police, (3) accountability of police actions to the public, (4) customized police service, and (5) community organization.[44]

Community policing advocates argue that traditional policing is a system of response; that is, the police respond to calls for services *after* the activity occurs. Police response is then reactive and incident driven rather that proactive and preventive in nature. Further, a randomized motor patrol neither lowers crime nor increases the chances of catching suspects. Increasing the number of police, then, has limited impact on the crime rate because improving response time on calls for service has little relevance to preventing the original incident.[45] In addition, the role of the individual police officer is largely limited within the confines of patrol and response. Refer to Box 1-1 for a review of the research on traditional policing.

Community policing represents the emergence of a new perspective that is proactive and information based.[46] Oettmeier[47] explains that the proactive function requires accurate and timely information on which to develop directed strategies in response to identified crime and/or other disorder problems. The emphasis is placed on designing cooperative strategies within the community that interdict criminal activity before it occurs rather than on responding to the incident after it is reported. In this manner, the role of the police officer is greatly expanded with responsibility and authority to address wider social concerns and neighborhood problems. The individual officer emerges as a coordinator of municipal

BOX 1-1

Review of Research on Traditional Policing

1. Increasing numbers of police does not lower the crime rate or increase the proportion of solved crimes.
2. Randomized motor patrol neither lowers crime nor increases the chances of catching suspects.
3. Two-person patrol cars are not more effective than one-person cars in lowering of crime rates of catching criminals; they are also no safer.
4. Saturation patrol does not reduce crime; instead, it displaces crime.
5. The kind of crime that terrifies Americans most (mugging, rape, robbery, burglary, and homicide) is rarely encountered by police on patrol.
6. Improving response time on calls has no effect on the likelihood of arresting criminals or even in satisfying involved citizens.
7. Crimes are not solved through criminal investigations conducted by police—they are solved because suspects are immediately apprehended or someone identifies them (name or license number).

Source: Jerome H. Skolnick and David H. Bayley, *The New Blue Line* (New York: The Free Press, 1986).

services and neighborhood security, actively seeking ways to prevent crime and better the quality of neighborhood life rather than simply responding to calls for service and reported crimes.[48] That crime is integrally linked to other urban problems dictates that the most effective responses require the coordination of activities from private citizens, the business sector, and government agencies *outside* the traditional criminal justice system.[49] These responses must address crime as one symptom of a much broader set of social problems. Figure 1-8 compares traditional and community policing via a series of questions and answers designed to clarify their fundamental differences.

Questions	Traditional	Community Policing
Who are the police?	a government agency principally responsible for law enforcement	Police are the public and the public are the police; the police officers are those who are paid to give fulltime attention to the duties of every citizen.
What is the relationship of the police force to other public service departments?	priorities often conflict	The police are one department among many responsible for improving the quality of life.
What is the role of the police?	focusing on solving crimes	a broader problem-solving approach
How is police efficiency measured?	by detection and arrest rates	by the absence of crime and disorder
What are the highest priorities?	crimes that are high value (e.g., bank robberies) and those involving violence.	whatever problems disturb the community most
What, specifically, do police deal with?	incidents	citizens' problems and concerns
What determines the effectiveness of police?	response times	public cooperation
What view do police take of service calls?	deal with them only if there is no real police work to do	vital function and great opportunity
What is police professionalism?	swift, effective response to serious crime	keeping close to the community
What kind of intelligence is most important?	crime intelligence (study of particular crimes or series of crimes)	criminal intelligence (information about the activities of individuals or groups)
What is the essential nature of police accountability?	highly centralized; governed by rules, regulations, and policy directives; accountable to the law	emphasis on local accountability to community needs
What is the role of headquarters?	to provide the necessary rules and policy directives	to preach organizational values
What is the role of the press liaison department?	to keep the "heat" off operational officers so they can get on with their jobs	to coordinate an essential channel of communication with the community
How do the police regard prosecutions?	as an important goal	as one tool among many

FIGURE 1-8. *Traditional vs. Community Policing: Questions and Answers* [*Source:* Malcolm K. Sparrow, "Implementing Community Policing," *Perspectives on Policing* (Washington, D.C.: National Institute of Justice, November 1988) pp. 8–9.]

Several cities have implemented community policing strategies in the past decade. Three of these experiments are presented as case examples that highlight various aspects of the community policing philosophy.

Newport News, Virginia

In 1983, under the direction of a new chief, Darrel Stephens, the Newport News Police Department developed a "problem-oriented" approach to policing. This new and innovative style of community policy focused on the department's traditional response to major, recurring problems. Its goal was to reassess the traditional, incident-driven aspects of police work and fundamentally change the way the Newport News Police Department viewed its mission (see Box 1-2). The resulting self-analysis yielded an important four-step, problem-solving methodology (commonly referred to as SARA) that has become an integral part of daily operations (see Figure 1-9 on p. 20).

Scanning: Instead of relying on broad, law-related concepts such as robbery, burglary, auto theft, and the like, officers are encouraged to group individual related incidents that come to their attention as "problems" and define these problems in more precise and useful terms. For example, an incident that typically would be classified simply as a "robbery" might be seen as part of a pattern of prostitution-related robberies committed by transvestites in center-city hotels. In essence, officers are expected to look for possible problems and accurately define them as part of their daily routine.

Analysis: Officers working on a well-defined problem then collect information from a variety of public and private sources, not just traditional police data such as criminal records and past offense reports. Officers rely on problem analysis guides that direct officers to examine offenders, victims, the social and physical environment, and previous responses to the problem. The goal is to understand the scope, nature, and causes of the problem and formulate a variety of options for its resolution.

Response: The knowledge gained in the analysis stage is then used to develop and implement solutions. Officers seek the assistance of citizens, businesses, other police units, other public and private organizations, and anyone else who can help to develop a program of action. Solutions may go well beyond traditional police responses to include other community agencies and/or municipal organizations.

Assessment: Finally, officers evaluate the impact and the effectiveness of their responses. Were the original problems actually solved or alleviated? They may use the results to revise a response, to collect more data, or even to redefine the problem[50]

Goldstein[51] further explains this systematic process in his book, *Problem-Oriented Policing*. Destined to become a classic in the field, Goldstein's work attempts to give meaning to each of the four steps. For instance, a problem is expanded to mean a cluster of similar, related, or recurring incidents rather than

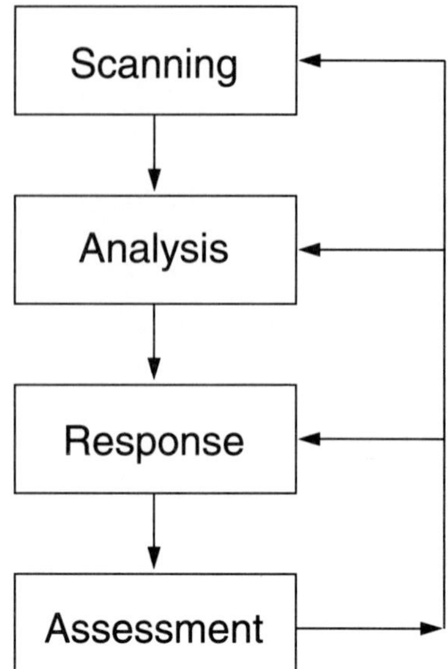

FIGURE 1-9. The problem-solving system used in Newport News, Virginia Police Department. [William Spelman and John E. Eck, "Problem Oriented Policing," *Research in Brief* (Washington, D.C.: National Institute of Justice, October, 1986), p. 4.]

a single incident. The assumption is that few incidents are isolated, as all are part of a wider set of urban social phenomena. Examples of such community problems are:

Disorderly youth who regularly congregate in the parking lot of a specific convenience store

Street prostitutes and associated "jack roll" robberies of patrons that continually occur in the same area

Drunk and drinking drivers around the skid row area of the city

Panhandlers, vagrants, and other displaced people living on the sidewalk in a business district

Juvenile runaways, prostitutes, and drug dealers congregating at the downtown bus depot

Robberies of commercial establishments at major intersections of a main thoroughfare of a suburban area that is a corridor leading out of a large central city.[52]

Note that each of these problems incorporates not only a potential or real crime, but also a wider community/social issue. Further, each problem has been identified with a specific location. Goldstein[53] emphasizes that the traditional functions of crime analysis under the problem-solving methodology take on much wider and deeper importance. The pooling of data and subsequent analysis provide the

BOX 1-2

The Problem-Oriented Approach

Midnight-watch patrol officers are tired of taking calls like Snyder's. They and their sergeant, James Hogan, decide to reduce prostitution-related robberies, and Officer James Boswell volunteers to lead the effort.

First, Boswell interviews the 28 prostitutes who work the downtown area to learn how they solicit, what happens when they get caught, and why they are not deterred.

They work downtown bars, they tell him, because customers are easy to find and police patrols don't spot them soliciting. Arrests, the prostitutes tell Boswell, are just an inconvenience: Judges routinely sentence them to probation, and probation conditions are not enforced.

Based on what he has learned from the interviews and his previous experience, Boswell devises a response. He works with the Alcoholic Beverage Control Board and local barowners to move the prostitutes into the street. At police request, the Commonwealth's Attorney agrees to ask the judges to put stiffer conditions on probation: Convicted prostitutes would be given a map of the city and told to stay out of the downtown area or go to jail for 3 months.

Boswell then works with the vice unit to make sure that downtown prostitutes are arrested and convicted, and the patrol officers know which prostitutes are on probation. Probation violators *are* sent to jail, and within weeks all but a few of the prostitutes have left downtown.

Then Boswell talks to the prostitutes' customers, most of whom don't know that almost half the prostitutes working the street are actually men, posing as women. He intervenes in street transactions, formally introducing the customers to their male dates. The Navy sets up talks for him with incoming sailors to tell them about the male prostitutes and the associated safety and health risks.

In 3 months, the number of prostitutes working downtown drops from 28 to 6 and robbery rates are cut in half. After 18 months neither robbery nor prostitution show signs of returning to their earlier levels.

Source: William Spelman and John E. Eck, "Newport News Tests Problem-Oriented Policing," *NIJ Reports* (Washington, D.C.: National Institute of Justice, January 1987).

basis for problem identification and response strategies. Therefore, the accuracy and timeliness of such information become a necessity for the department. (Refer to Chapter 12 for a more thorough discussion of information systems and crime analysis techniques.) However, the ultimate challenge in problem-oriented policing is not the identification of problems, but rather the search for the most effective ways of dealing with them.

Madison, Wisconsin

Community policing is not only a renewed emphasis on community and neighborhood involvement, but also a call for dynamic change in police organization and leadership. Community policing focuses on the quality of individual police service rather than the quantity (number) of arrests made, calls for service answered, cases cleared, and tickets written. As an example, the Madison, Wisconsin, Police Department, under the direction of Chief David Couper, has dramatically revised its mission statement and leadership principles (see Figure 1-10.) During the past seven years, the police department has slowly integrated community policing into its services.[54]

The Department's mission statement establishes several important goals: provide high quality, community-oriented police service with sensitivity; utilize problem solving techniques and teamwork; and be open to the community. Accordingly, the department has adopted new management principals and created a decentralized facility called the Experimental Police District (EPD). The EPD serves as the department's testing ground for new ideas and methods, focusing on the implementation of new management strategies, teamwork, problem solving, and other community policing techniques.[55]

The emphasis on the quality of services and the vision of a community that is an active partner in promoting safety and security is in contrast with the traditional concept of policing. (Again, refer to Figure 1-10). In the Madison Police Depart-

VISION OF THE MADISON POLICE DEPARTMENT

We are a dynamic organization devoted to improvement, excellence, maintaining customer satisfaction, and operating on the Principles of Quality Leadership.

MISSION STATEMENT

We believe in the DIGNITY and WORTH of ALL PEOPLE.

We are committed to:

- PROVIDING HIGH-QUALITY, COMMUNITY-ORIENTED POLICE SERVICES WITH SENSITIVITY;
- PROTECTING CONSTITUTIONAL RIGHTS;
- PROBLEM SOLVING;
- TEAMWORK;
- OPENNESS;
- CONTINUOUS IMPROVEMENT;
- PLANNING FOR THE FUTURE;
- PROVIDING LEADERSHIP TO THE POLICE PROFESSION.

We are proud of the DIVERSITY of our work force which permits us to GROW and which RESPECTS each of us as individuals, and we strive for a HEALTHFUL workplace.

PRINCIPLES OF QUALITY LEADERSHIP

1. IMPROVE SYSTEMS and examine processes before blaming people.
2. Have a CUSTOMER orientation and focus toward employees and citizens.
3. Believe that the best way to improve the quality of work or service is to ASK and LISTEN to employees who are doing the work.
4. Be committed to the PROBLEM-SOLVING process; use it and let DATA, not emotions, drive decisions.
5. Be a FACILITATOR and COACH. Develop an OPEN atmosphere that encourages providing and accepting FEEDBACK.
6. Encourage CREATIVITY through RISK-TAKING and be tolerant of honest MISTAKES.
7. Avoid "top-down," POWER-ORIENTED decision-making whenever possible.
8. Manage on the BEHAVIOR of 95% of employees and not on the 5% who cause problems. Deal with the 5% PROMPTLY and FAIRLY.
9. Believe in, foster and support TEAMWORK.
10. With teamwork, develop with employees agreed-upon GOALS and a PLAN to achieve them.
11. Seek employees INPUT before you make key decisions.
12. Strive to develop mutual RESPECT and TRUST among employees.

FIGURE 1-10. Mission statement and leadership principles. (Courtesy of the Madison, Wisconsin Police Department.)

FIGURE 1-11. Within the EPD, officers focus on problem solving in traditionally high crime areas such as this public housing facility. Providing quality policing and an improved image are important parts of the community policing movement. (Courtesy Madison, Wisconsin Police Department.)

ment, considerable emphasis has been given to improving the quality of management and leadership within the agency so as to highlight organizational values and the importance of individual officers (see Chapter 5 on leadership).

These principles are consistent with modern, "open-systems" thinkers who argue that improving the quality of work life for employees within large, bureaucratic agencies will subsequently improve overall organizational effectiveness.[56] (See Chapter 3 on organizational theory.) To achieve this end, the department established itself as a quality-driven, community-oriented service and developed the centralized position of quality coordinator to monitor a quality improvement process. This arrangement required continued input from members within the EPD as well as the development of an extensive internal survey. Customer surveys became an integral part of the quality improvement process, asking citizens to rate the individual officer responding to a call for service in seven areas: (1) concern, (2) helpfulness, (3) knowledge, (4) quality service, (5) solving the problem, (6) putting the caller at ease; and (7) professional conduct. The questionnaire also asked citizens for recommendations on ways to improve.[57] These surveys have continued since late 1988, providing a substantial data bank on which to evaluate the aggregate performance of officers in the EPD. In addition, the Police Foundation and the Madison Comptroller's Office have completed outside evaluations of the EPD project. Several positive findings were revealed from these evaluation studies:

Over 60% of all employees in the EPD believed that they had been more effective in solving crimes than they were in their previous assignments.

Over 80% of all employees in the EPD reported a higher level of job satisfaction compared with previous assignments.

Individual officers used considerably less sick time and earned substantially less overtime as compared to patrol officers working outside the EPD.

The top five reasons that employees chose to work in the EPD were

1. A more supportive management style
2. Less rigid structure
3. Greater input in decision making
4. More autonomy
5. A team atmosphere

Overall crime dropped 1.1 percent and violent crime decreased 9.2 percent over the past two years within the EPD while increasing 4.2 percent in other areas of the city.

Residential burglaries decreased 24 percent in the EPD since 1986, while the rest of Madison suffered a 4.2 percent increase.

EPD-patrol speeding enforcement dropped 16.6 percent in one year, possibly indicating more community adherence to traffic laws.

Finally, the most important, citizen surveys indicated a vastly improved police image (noting improved satisfaction and concern with the police) within the EPD community as compared to the rest of the city.[58]

Community policing efforts in Madison are still evolving as successful organizational and community change takes place. The department is planning to establish four additional experimental police districts within the city in an attempt to bring the entire department gradually into the community policing philosophy. Chief Couper firmly believes that successful implementation requires a strong vision of the quality of police service and the development of excellence in individual police leadership.[59] For the Madison Police Department, the resulting move to community policing has provided a vastly improved workplace, where employee growth, empowerment, and feelings of self-worth are encouraged and community support is subsequently fostered.

Houston, Texas

A discussion of community policing in the United States would be incomplete without addressing the accomplishments of the Houston, Texas, Police Department. Under the leadership of then Chief Lee P. Brown (who subsequently served as commissioner of police for New York City until August 1992), the Houston

Police Department began one of the first community policing ventures in 1982. Like other experiments in community policing, Houston's Neighborhood-Oriented Policing (NOP) concept called for a "partnership" between police officers and citizens who worked together in the prevention and control of crime.[60]

Neighborhood-oriented policing is similar to previously mentioned policing techniques in that it is information driven. Police responses are based on data collected by individual officers and citizen groups concerning the effectiveness of specific programs or the identification of community problems. According to Oettmeier and Bieck,[61] NOP is "results-oriented" and is critically dependent on individual patrol officers to understand and expand their traditional roles. Neighborhood-oriented policing attempts to combine the reactive aspects of policing (responding to calls for service) with two other perspectives: proactive and coactive patrol functions (see Figure 1-12).

The reactive function is a constant activity, representing the bulk of what the public expects police agencies to do—answer calls for service; enforce laws; arrest criminals; give traffic citations; and perform random, preventive patrol.

The proactive function requires officers to develop directed or structured patrol strategies in response to identified crime problems. Officers are empowered with new responsibilities to cope with crime. To a large extent, these new responsibilities downplay the use of random, moving patrol cars. Instead, emphasis is placed on tactical planning to develop patrol strategies for responding quickly and effectively to a myriad of crime problems (i.e., a series of street robberies in a neighborhood, a pattern of rapes at an apartment complex, or drug dealing on a school campus attributed to the actions of a juvenile gang). These types of tactical response strategies are, again, dependent on accurate and timely information from crime analysis units.

The third function is referred to as "coproduction" or "coactivity."[62] It can best be defined as an active outreach and systematic engagement between the police and the public for the purposes of identifying and addressing localized problems of crime and disorder. *Coactivity* addresses long-range, strategic problems identified through ongoing contacts between individual patrol officers and the citizens in a specific geographic area. Theoretically, officers become more familiar with a district the longer they work in their assigned areas. Therefore, officers are expected to identify what services are needed in specific areas through a self-directed effort. Through self-direction, officers are expected to contact people, explain why they are needed, seek assistance in problem identification, and learn how to coordinate police–public agency involvement to remedy the problem. As Oettmeier explains:

> It is through the responsibility of self-direction that a bond is formed between the officer and the citizens who reside and work in the officer's assigned area. This bond is characterized by a concomitant desire to identify and resolve neighborhood problems and concerns. The nature of this relation goes beyond interaction. It ascends to actual involvement and commitment of resources by the public as they work with the police. It is through this partnership that a new functional perspective begins to emerge for policing.[63]

The NOP project in Houston has been characterized by a series of individual programs that emphasize the proactive and coactive functions of policing. The first such program was the Directed Area Responsibility Team (DART) initiated in

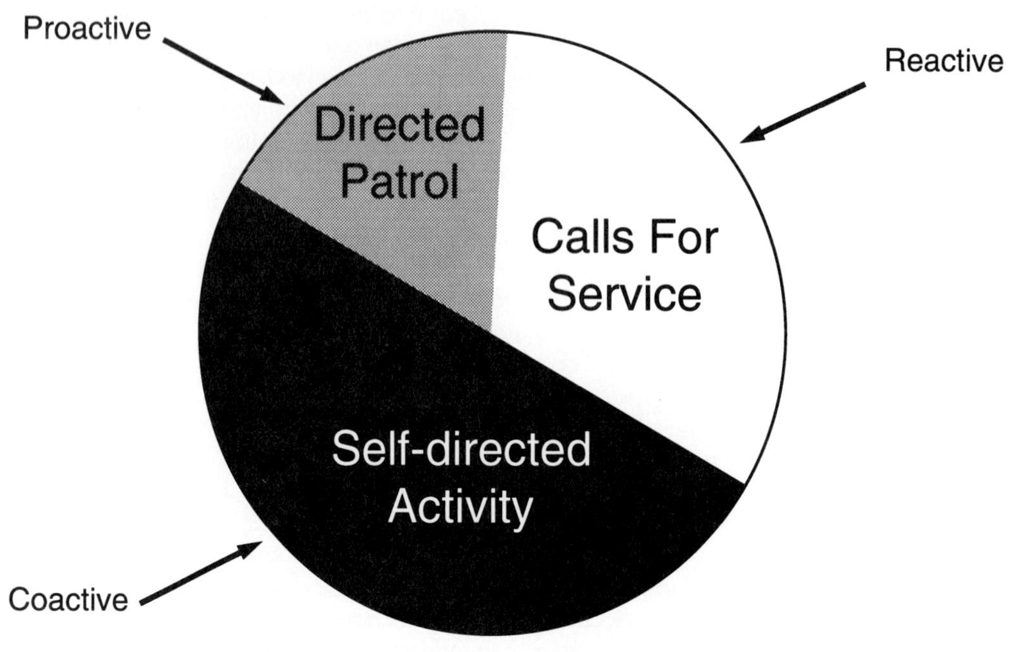

Interactive Process Linked To Community
Information Driven
Role Expansion – Increased Responsibility
Absence of Random Patrol
Planning Required
Goal/Objective/Result Oriented
Accountability Based
More Sophisticated Management System Required
Less Militaristic Structure

FIGURE 1-12. An emerging perspective for neighborhood-oriented policing (NOP) [Adapted from Timothy N. Oettmeier, "Reconfiguring Organizational Structures to Attain Functional Objectives," *Police Management Issues and Perspectives* (Washington, D.C.: Police Executive Research Forum, 1992), p. 21.]

1983, which called for the advancement of team policing concepts (as defined earlier in this chapter). Patrol officers were brought together with crime analysts, detectives, and crime prevention specialists in an attempt to address citizens' concerns and fight crime. As a result of the project, the crime rate went down, the clearance rate went up, and citizens' ratings of the quality of life in their neighborhood improved greatly.[64]

Continued program development aimed at reducing citizens' fear of crime in the Houston area. Several programs are still in existence and highlight joint police–community efforts to address crime-related problems and improve the overall police image:

Victim Recontact Program—This program was developed to focus more attention on the victims rather than the suspects of crimes. Officers were asked to recontact victims to see if additional help was needed or if additional information about the case had surfaced. The goal of the program was to lessen citizens' fear about the police and the rest of the criminal justice system.

Community Organizing Response Team (CORT)—Officers in this program focused on organizing community groups on quality of life issues. Surprisingly, residents were more concerned with the signs of neighborhood decay (e.g., vacant lots with abandoned cars, broken windows in buildings, run-down storefronts) than they were with major reported crimes (e.g., burglary, robbery, rape). As a result, officers coordinated the functions and activities of other municipal agencies in cleaning up neighborhoods.

FIGURE 1-13. Houston DART officers patrol specific neighborhoods focusing on street crime and gang activity. (Courtesy Houston, Texas Police Department.)

Neighborhood Information Network—The Houston Police Department distributed approximately 2,000 newsletters to individuals in specific neighborhoods in order to inform them accurately on criminal cases and on how to prevent such activity. With this information, direct from the police department, the individuals were able to develop a balanced picture of crime and the measures being taken to combat it. In addition, one of the first "crimestopper" bulletins was developed, asking for community assistance in solving specific crimes.

Storefront Operations—In an effort to decentralize police services, the Houston Police Department set up storefront centers throughout the city. The goals of this program were improving the perception of the police as well as providing a more intimate means to serve community needs.

Positive Interaction Program (PIP)—This program focused on the development of neighborhood associations that met monthly with local police managers. The purpose of the meetings was twofold: (1) to provide for a cooperative effort in identifying and solving specific neighborhood problems and (2) to educate the citizenry on police activities and procedures aimed at protecting wider community interests. This program has been very successful, spawning similar activities in other cities throughout the United States. Some departments have civilian police academies, where community members are taught basic police procedures and crime prevention techniques, and can even ride along in a squad car to learn more about police activities.

Project Oasis—This program is a spin-off from the original Oasis Institute in Fort Lauderdale, Florida. The basic assumption behind the technique is to replace blighted, urban decayed areas with clean, well-maintained, and freshly renovated buildings. The Houston Oasis Program targeted one of the city's worst public housing projects and required

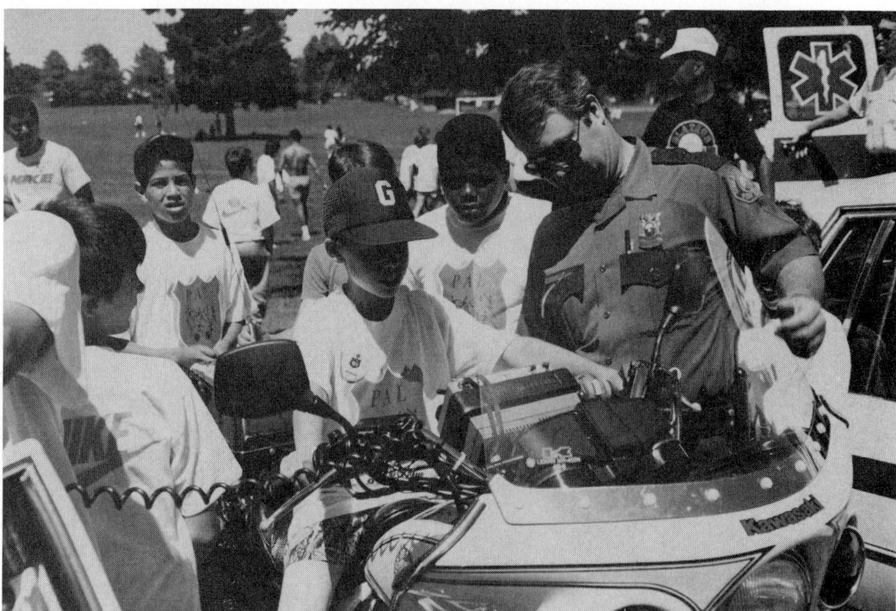

FIGURE 1-14. Police Athletic League (PAL) programs have been adopted by a number of police departments to positively improve relations with the community. Targeted youth are shown police vehicles in an attempt to close the often wide gap between police officers and juveniles. (Courtesy Portland, Oregon Police Bureau.)

that individual officers coordinate clean-up efforts on the part of the housing authority as well as other municipal agencies to remove trash/debris as well as generally renovate the area. Police officers also engaged in tactical operations that attempted to quickly eradicate visible street crime activity such as drug dealing, prostitution, vandalism, and theft.

Although these programs were originally established as part of the Houston NOP effort, similar projects have characterized community policing elsewhere (see Box 1-3), especially projects designed to curb the visible signs of drug activity such as zero-tolerance programs, "buy-and-bust" routines, decoy programs, and "drive-through" drug deal projects. The use and success of such community policing programs depend heavily on the support of the department's middle management and the initiative of individual patrol officers, as well as a partnership with the community at large.[65]

Problems with Community Policing

Community policing is a dynamic new movement expressing a bold philosophy. Its goal is to allow police to concentrate on the root causes of crime and to combine efforts with other community resources in addressing crime. Police are viewed as proactive community agents who prevent crime rather than reactive government forces that only respond to incidents and calls for service. Even considering the early successes, community policing has not been without criticism and conflict. Several academicians and practitioners have attempted to clarify some of the problems associated with the implementation of community policing efforts.[66] As mentioned earlier, many of these same issues arose during the analysis of team policing efforts during the 1970s. Some fear that the concept of community policing may be expanding too rapidly and that the agencies and officers rushing to "jump on the bandwagon" may not understand or be fully prepared for the significant changes proposed. This, in turn, will lead to partial implementation, notable failures, and permanent damage to an otherwise valuable philosophy.

This discussion explores some of the problems associated with community policing in an effort to encourage caution and avoid the setbacks experienced by earlier innovators in police management. Community policing is a valuable concept, but it is not a panacea for eliminating crime in most communities. The following issues have been identified:

Lack of definition—Despite the popularity (or perhaps because of it), the concept of community policing remains only loosely defined, referring to an array of programs as diverse as Neighborhood Watch, conflict mediation panels, buy-and-bust projects, and liaison programs to gay and other community groups. At best, community policing is a muddled term without exact meaning and precise definition. It appears that any strategy that is new is lumped within the community policing definition, regardless of how much community involvement or partnership it requires. Indeed, community policing in some departments may be more rhetoric than reality.[67]

Role confusion and low morale—Poor definition and a nontraditional approach require officers and agencies to rethink their basic philosophies of work. To the extent that officers are to become all things to all people (and communities), some degree of role conflict, confusion, and stress (refer to Chapter 8) is inevitable. For example, are police

BOX 1-3

Increasing Foot Patrols Will Keep Police in Step with Crime

George Will

New York—In 1945, this city's movie censor banned "Scarlet Street," starring Edward G. Robinson, because the ending was so shocking: a murderer remained at large. Today, in New York's enlightenment, there is no censorship. You can see any movie you can make it to through the mean streets.

In 1945, there were 292 homicides here. In 1990, there were about 2,200. In 1945, there were 1,417 armed robberies reported. In 1990, there were about 100,000, one every five minutes, and today robbery is under-reported by citizens accustomed to mayhem (such as 390 car thefts a day) as a commonplace of urban life.

A 1945 poll revealed that 90 percent of New Yorkers considered themselves happy. Today 60 percent say they plan to be living elsewhere in five years, and crime is the primary cause of flight.

Such numbers trickle across the aircraft-carrier-sized desk of Police Commissioner Lee P. Brown. Long ago that desk belonged to a peripatetic commissioner who rarely sat still behind it: Commissioner Teddy Roosevelt's midnight rambles on the city's wild side made him a rising star. Brown, a large black man with three advanced degrees, is both praised and faulted for his phlegmatic manner.

He came here from Houston, a city with 1.7 million people spread over 600 square miles. New York has 8 million in 319 square miles. New York's per capita crime statistics are not the nation's worst (for example, Washington's homicide rate is two-and-a-half times that of New York), but crime seems worse here because the density gives this city the nation's highest irritability quotient. Many New Yorkers are quick on the trigger, literally. In 1960, handguns were used in 19 percent of homicides. Today, they are used in approximately 70 percent. Until 1969, more killings were by knives.

For more than a generation, the fundamental act of American fun—watching television—has involved, for the average viewer, seeing 150 acts of violence and 15 murders a week. Is it really amazing that life seems to have been cheapened? Brown is not amazed.

On the other hand, it has been plausibly argued that Americans are not so much more violent than other people; they are only more armed. The argument is that you are more apt to see a fight in a British pub than in an American bar, but the British fight culminates in punches, the American fight in gunfire.

Brown is both proud of and appalled by the confiscation of 17,000 guns in 1990. But he is bailing an ocean—the tide of guns coming north from states (particularly Virginia, Texas, Georgia and Florida) where gun restrictions are derisory. In 1989, 80 percent of those arrested for serious crimes had drugs in their systems. Drug disputes help generate this fact: The typical homicide victim is a young black male killed by a young black male he knew. (Only about 10 percent of homicide victims are non-Hispanic whites.)

Drugs, like guns, are a tide against which no single city or state can erect a dike. But Brown, the calm at the eye of this city's storm about crime, does know what he can do: He can deploy more cops more usefully than in the recent past.

In medicine, much sophisticated research has resulted in proving that grandmother was right. The key to health is rest, exercise and nutrition. So, too, police science has lumbered laboriously to the conclusion that grandfather's generation knew a thing or two.

The newfangled notion of "community policing" is essentially the oldfangled notion that more police should get out of their cars and back on a beat. There, they can deal not just reactively with crime, but proactively with the disorders—loitering, poorly parented children, panhandling, anxiety that drives people indoors. These are early indices of neighborhood decay.

All that stands between the theory and the practice of such sensible policing is the residue of 1960s and 1970s liberalism, which considers it fascist for police to buttress bourgeois society's norms of good behavior.

Commissioner Teddy Roosevelt went prowling in the wee small hours with Jacob Riis, the journalist who wrote "How the Other Half Lives." Like the patrician Roosevelt, Brown, the product of a blue-collar family, is concerned with the social incubation of crime. When Brown was a boy, the family dinner table was where his parents "looked me in the eye to see if I had done something wrong." Now, he says, if many young men eat with their families at all, it is cafeteria style.

Brown knows that the key to fighting crime—primarily a product of young men—is in things that grandmother and grandfather took for granted.

Source: Dallas Times Herald, Feb. 14, 1991, p. A18.

agencies to merge the traditional models of law enforcement, order maintenance, and social work or are they to focus on entirely different roles such as those found in public housing, transportation, education, and/or refuse collection? This role conflict will become heightened as officers who entered policing with one set of perceptions come face to face with an entirely new array of tasks, duties and philosophies. Clearly, the resulting ambiguity is almost certain to impact employee morale. In Houston and Baltimore, two of the celebrated departments advancing community policing strategies, documented cases of low morale persist.[68]

Community policing is expensive—As the trend toward community policing has grown, few cities have looked at the costs of the programs. In Houston, for example, only 20 neighborhoods were selected for the implementation of NOP, and still the cost exceeded $250 million per year![69] Patrol beats were redefined on the basis of neighborhoods rather than on traditional crime-related factors such as calls for services, type and seriousness of calls, geographic boundaries, and the like. The police union, in turn, argued that this redistricting jeopardized officer safety, pointing to an increase in officer assaults.[70] High costs in terms of money and people may be an indicative feature of community policing, especially if the officers are to have a small enough beat to make a difference or if a department is to maintain a specific level of response while developing a new strategy for each neighborhood.

Lack of credible evaluation—Community policing can best be described as a "reform" model for urban policing having vague conceptualization and limited empirical testing.[71] Murphy writes that a combination of methodologically limited research and reform ideals has allowed community policing advocates to effectively discredit the ideology, organization, and strategies of conventional policing.[72] In reality, the empirical evidence that traditional policing methods have failed is at best mixed. Further, what are the measurable advantages of community policing? Kelling[73] argues that traditional quantitative measures such as crime statistics and police response times are inappropriate for evaluating the success or failure of community policing. Others note that the usual means of measuring more subjective goals such as reducing fear and preventing crime may be far too costly and beyond the capabilities of most police organizations. If so, then by what criteria (refer to Chapter 14) will community policing programs be accurately evaluated?

According to Elizabeth Watson, former chief of police in Houston, Texas, virtually no evaluation of the NOP experience in Houston has occurred.[74] Apparently no baseline data were ever developed previous to the implementation of NOP; no preconditional response patterns were explored; and no continuing data on changing community attitudes concerning fear, perception of crime, or feeling of security are being collected.

BOX 1-4

Houston Study Criticizes Community Policing

HOUSTON, Aug. 7—Community policing, the problem-solving philosophy that guides Commissioner Lee P. Brown's efforts to make New York City safer, has produced few tangible results in the city where he put it into effect, an independent study has concluded.

An audit by Washington consultants says that putting into action Houston's community policing program, established and heavily promoted by Mr. Brown when he was Police Chief here, has been difficult and that the department has viewed the philosophy as an "end in itself," rather than as a tool to reduce crime and improve service.

While strongly endorsing the concept of community policing, or neighborhood-oriented policing, as it is called here, the report finds that it has had limited effect on citizen's sense of security.

The report, drawn up at the request of New York City, also said that the department's emphasis on community policing had reduced overall effectiveness, including response time to reported crimes.

Bill Evans, vice president of Cresap Management Consultants, which produced the report, said the firm was not suggesting that Houston scrap community policing. Establishing the new approach "would be difficult for any large police department," he said.

Community policing is an approach that seeks to get police officers out of their patrol cars and into their neighborhoods to find ways to stop crime before it happens.

The report, released late Tuesday, recognizes Houston as a leader in community policing but details a number of problems that its police department has had in getting the system to work. Officers assigned to community beats are overwhelmed and unprepared for their new tasks, there are too few supervisors and many members of the department are skeptical of or even hostile to the program's aims, the report said.

Range of Complex Skills

Captains often have responsibility for an area of 60 or more square miles and 200,000 people, too large an area for effective crime prevention, the report found.

In addition, officers often find themselves torn between the preventive work now called for and the immediate demands of reports of crime. And the report finds that while the concept of community policing requires a range of complex skills, it is unlikely that the department can recruit a force in which most officers have these skills, particularly at current pay levels.

Police Chief Elizabeth Watson, a protégée of Mr. Brown's and a staunch advocate of community policing, declined comment today, saying she was reviewing the final report. But in a telephone interview on Monday, after she had seen an initial draft, she readily conceded the difficulty in putting community policing into place. "There's no question about it," Chief Watson said.

Doug Elder, president of the Houston Police Officers Association, agreed that many officers have had difficulty incorporating the community policing philosophy in their daily work.

"I think most officers feel it's a hoax, renaming things and using a lot of buzz words and the like," Mr. Elder said. "I think a lot of officers probably feel they're expected to be more like social workers than police officers."

Source: New York Times, Aug. 8, 1991.

Unfortunately, responses from other cities implementing facets of community policing are even less encouraging. This issue appears even more urgent as critics note that calls for police services (in Houston) have increased by over 40 percent during the effort, whereas police response times have grown considerably (see Box 1-4).[75]

Failure to understand the change process—The basic concept of community policing as an instrument of change is a valuable and noble effort. However, in the long run, community policing may prove more frustrating for the police and the community as calls for service continue to escalate. Even in cities having well-developed community policing efforts, the citizenry still expect the police to react to calls for service and reduce crime. Basically, the community perception of the police as the "thin blue line" between order and chaos still exists. Police are still expected to quell neighborhood problems; stop abusive spouses; arrest criminals; give traffic tickets; and patrol in visible, marked police units. Failing to understand the change process (see Chapter 15) as long term, ongoing, and somewhat chaotic will doom community policing (as it did team policing) if considerable effort is not given to maintaining traditional perceptions of the police. Further, community policing requires extensive changes in police recruitment, selection, training, and organizational design (refer to Chapters 4 and 7). Many of these changes simply cannot be accomplished without the involvement of police labor unions, civil service boards, and other external entities. The change process will be long and fraught with difficulty, especially if crime rates continue to escalate in areas experimenting with community policing.

Community policing advocates a necessary and important reform. Its recognition of the close relationship of crime to other social problems is a big step in the evolution of American policing (see Box 1-5). However, the implementation of community policing is a concept in vogue. As Skolnick and Bayley[76] write, "community policing represents what is progressive and forward-looking" in American policing. Unfortunately, every new technique and strategy is being lumped under the rubric of community policing. As a result, within some professional circles, those agencies not involved in the community policing movement are labeled stagnant and backward. Such generalizations are without merit, especially considering the mixed evaluations on both traditional and community policing efforts.

BOX 1-5

Community Policing and Cultural Change: An Officer's View

by Officer Wayne Kuechler, *Portland Police Bureau*

In 1990, the Portland Police Bureau and the City of Portland adopted the "Community Policing Transition Plan," whose objective is to make the transition to a "department-wide" Community Policing philosophy over the next five years. Now, a little more than one year into the transition, it has become apparent that the most difficult part is changing the way officers approach their jobs.

This resistance to change may be one of the determining reasons for adopting a smaller "project-oriented" approach like those employed by other departments (such as the Experimental Policing district in Madison, WI: Police Area Response in Auroa, CO; and Foot Patrol Districts in Baltimore County, MD). In these examples, officers volunteer to participate and are not likely to resist the modification of duties and responsibilities due to a high degree of ownership in the programs. But where these programs may be successful in one area of town or within a small group of involved officers, this encourages a separatist view by other uninvolved officers.

Total involvement

Portland was the first major city in the U.S. to involve all employes in the implementation of Community Policing. All employees have been trained on basic components of Community Policing and in problem-solving skills like those employed in Newport News, VA, and San Diego, CA. Many officers have taken this training and have solved neighborhood problems ranging from vandalism to drug dealing. The officers who have put the philosophy and the training into action have accepted the idea that what they are doing now is more like the original intent of law enforcement. They also realize that there is a great amount of similarity with what they have tried to do all along. As one of the officers said at a recent community meeting, "What I do now isn't that different . . . I'm doing what I've always done, but I'm able to get more done because of the involvement of the citizens." These officers have welcomed this approach to policing where the residents of a community take an active role with the police in solving its problems.

Resistance within the ranks

Portland's Community Officers have reaped the benefits of success through the praise of citizens, political leaders, and police officials. However, their peers have not always been supportive of Community Policing. The longstanding police culture that exists within law enforcement agencies often focuses on the failures of Community Policing rather than the successes, and conflicts develop. These may even take the form of testing, direct ridicule, and group exclusion.

Within Portland, a strong union has existed for many years. Although the union and its long-time president have worked hard to receive an excellent pay and benefit package, it has also reinforced that all officers get the same pay, regardless of how productive they may be. The union president has stated several times that Portland cannot do Community Policing until we have 300 to 400 more officers.

These kind of statements have served to reinforce the cultural belief that we don't have enough police to do good police work, let alone Community Policing. Yet the ideas behind Community Policing are still valid regardless of how many police you have. As Portland's Chief has told his officers, "You still have to do some kind of police work, why not do the most effective police work possible, Community Policing?"

Despite the resistance, there are many examples of the success and effectiveness of Community Policing, in Portland and throughout the U.S. and Canada. Hopefully, as these successes increase and more officers become involved, the culture will be modified and peer influence will reinforce the effective application of Community Policing.

Managing change

Many within law enforcement resist any change. At a recent in-service training, an officer made the comment that he thought he was going to be told that what he had done for many years was wrong. This is not the case. Rather than to admonish and abandon tradition, Community Policing seeks to expand the reach of traditional law enforcement and is not a replacement, but rather an enhancement, of the system in place. Law enforcement will always have the responsibility to protect life and property, and it will still be counted on for immediate interdiction in crisis situations.

As law enforcement seeks to improve the service we provide to the taxpayers of our communities, the question is not whether to change but how that change will take place. Most strategies for change fall into either the project-oriented model or, as in Portland, the department-wide model. Cultural resistance will exist regardless of the model chosen. The project-oriented approach may reinforce the idea that Community Policing is different from "real police work" because only some officers are involved. The uninvolved officers are left to develop their own perceptions of Community Policing. The department-wide approach is far more difficult to implement, but seeks to break down the cultural resistance by reinforcing that Community Policing is "real police work" and that all offices can do Community Policing. A project-oriented model may show faster, short-term results, but a department-wide model seeks long-term change and lasting results.

Any change is difficult to implement, particularly so with the cultural resistance that exists in law enforcement. Departments that plan to make the transition to Community Policing should be prepared for resistance and a few mistakes along the way. The foundation for change should include all employees, and the goal should be to break down the cultural resistance. When an effective strategy overcoming the resistance is developed and maintained, the change will have an opportunity to occur.

Below are some suggestions to follow when making a department-wide change to Community Policing:

- **Involve everyone**—If Community Policing is a valid approach, then it's good for everyone in the agency. Don't send the message that Community Policing is something special that only a select few can do. This includes the involvement of citizen and non-sworn employees as well.
- **Change means enhancement**—Reinforce that change doesn't mean that previous policing efforts were wasted. Traditional skills will still be needed. Community Policing should enhance the skills that they have already learned.
- **Be patient**—Don't expect things to occur overnight and don't mandate immediate change. It has taken many years for law enforcement agencies to get the way they are now, and it will take many years to change what is already in place.
- **Be consistent**—Officers look for inconsistencies and use them as justification for resistance.
- **Don't try to change everything at once**—Start at the top and work your way down. Don't expect officers to change what they do if their superiors haven't changed.
- **Expect and address resistance**—It is normal that change brings resistance, so be prepared for it and develop unique strategies to address it from the start.

Community Policing is a very effective approach to solving community problems. If your agency has not already adopted the Community Policing philosophy, you may be doing so in the future. The approach you choose can determine the success and effectiveness of Community Policing in your department. Planning strategies before making a change may minimize resistance within your agency and lead to a smoother transition for all.

Source: Footprints, Portland Police Bureau, Winter/Spring 1992, p. 12.

Summary

The role of the police is to maintain the peace within a carefully established framework of individual liberties. By devoting more resources to policing and reducing rights, we could be more effective in crime control, but our system of government is incompatible with such a choice. Policing is an institution that does not stand alone; it is part of the larger society it serves and is influenced by the issues and forces that shape that society. For present purposes, we have discussed American policing as evolving within this arena. Our exploration can be characterized by the identification of significant developments:

1. *Politics and administration,* particularly the struggle to free policing from machine politics and the improvements resulting from the reformation period from 1900 to 1926
2. *Police professionalism,* including the early work of August Vollmer through the first university programs devoted to the study of policing

3. *Role of the police,* focusing on role ambiguity resulting from the violent confrontations between police and minorities during the 1960s
4. *Impact of education,* emphasizing education as the methodology to accomplish professionalism
5. *Research on traditional policing,* highlighting three important experiments during the 1970s (the Kansas City Preventive Patrol Experiment, the RAND Criminal Investigation Study, and team policing) and the failure of traditional methods to curb crime rates and integrate the police with the community
6. *Community policing,* representing the emergence of a new perspective linking social issues to crime, advocating the police as general problem solvers in cooperation with the community, and calling for the reorganization of existing police agencies to foster improved leadership and a team atmosphere
7. *Problems with community policing,* identifying current and future problems associated with community policing changes in the 1990s.

Within the context of these headings, we have touched on some of the issues confronting police administrators. The stage is now set to explore the fundamental principles of administration more fully and identify the current challenges awaiting future police managers.

Discussion Questions

1. Whose responsibility is it for maintaining an orderly society?
2. What is the conceptual cornerstone of the separation of politics and administration?
3. Of what consequence to policing was the reformation period from 1900 to 1926?
4. What were August Vollmer's contributions to American police professionalization?
5. Why were the 1930s considered a pivotal period in American policing?
6. Discuss the conflicting roles of the police.
7. What can be gained from the research of the 1970s regarding the effectiveness of traditional policing?
8. Define community policing.
9. Describe the four-step, problem-solving system commonly referred to as SARA.
10. What were the positive findings associated with the EPD in Madison, Wisconsin?
11. Describe some of the programs that were original parts of the Houston, Texas, NOP effort.
12. What are some of the problems associated with community policing?

Notes

1. This section draws on and extends material found in the National Advisory Commission on Criminal Justice Standards and Goals, *Police,* Russell W. Peterson, chairman (Washington, D.C.: U.S. Government Printing Office,1973), p. 13.
2. Thomas A. Reppetto, *The Blue Parade* (New York: Free Press, 1978), pp. 41–42.
3. Alice B. Stone and Donald C. Stone, "Early Development of Education in Public Administration," in *American Public Administration: Past, Present, and Future,* ed. Frederick C. Mosher (Tuscaloosa, AL: University of Alabama Press, 1975), pp. 17–18. The themes in this and the subsequent paragraph are reflected in Stone and Stone's "Early Development," although they are ones sounded repeatedly in the literature. See Howard E. McCurdy, *Public Administration: A Synthesis* (Menlo Park, Calif.: Cum-

mings, 1977), pp. 19–21; William L. Morrow, *Public Administration: Politics and the Political System* (New York: Random House, 1975), p. 25; Lynton K. Caldwell, "Public Administration and the Universities: A Half-Century of Development," *Public Administration Review,* 25 (March 1965), pp. 52–60.

4. Woodrow Wilson, "The Study of Administration," *Political Science Quarterly,* 2 (June 1887), pp. 197–222.
5. Edwin O. Stene, "The Politics–Administration Dichotomy," *Midwest Review of Public Administration,* 9 (April–July 1975), p. 84.
6. E. W. Roddenbury, "Achieving Professionalism," *Journal of Criminal Law, Criminology, and Police Science,* 44 (May 1953–1954), 109.
7. Morris L. Cogan, "Toward a Definition of Profession," *Harvard Educational Review,* 23 (Winter 1953), p. 34.
8. Everette Hughes, "Professions," in *The Professions in America,* ed. K. S. Lynn (Cambridge, Mass.: Riverside Press, 1965), pp. 1–14.
9. See, for example, Ernest Greenwood, "Attributes of a Profession," *Social Work,* 2:3 (1957), p. 45.
10. Robert K. Merton, "Some Thoughts on the Professions in American Society" (Address before the Brown University graduate convocation, Providence, R.I., June 6, 1960).
11. Howard Becker, "The Nature of a Profession," in the Sixty-First Yearbook of the National Society for the Study of Education, 1962. Also Harold L. Wilensky, "The Professionalization of Everyone?" *The American Journal of Sociology,* 70:2 (1964), pp. 137–58.
12. Gene Edward Carte, "August Vollmer and the Origins of Police Professionalism, " *Journal of Police Science and Administration,* 1:3 (1973), p. 274.
13. Raymond B. Fosdick, *American Police Systems* (Montclair, N.J.: A 1969 Patterson Smith Reprint of a Century Company Work), pp. 284–85.
14. Ibid., p. 271.
15. Robert M. Fogelson, *Big-City Police* (Cambridge, Mass.: Harvard University Press, 1975), p. 76.
16. Extended treatment of this line of thinking is found in Fogelson, "The Military Analogy," pp. 40–66.
17. Ibid., p. 77.
18. George L. Kelling and James K. Stewart, "The Evolution of Contemporary Policing," in *Local Government Police Management,* ed. William A. Gellar (Washington, D.C.: International City Management Association, 1991). p. 7.
19. Louis A. Radelet, *The Police and the Community,* 3rd ed. (Encino, Calif.: Glencoe, 1980) p. 8.
20. See Kelling and Stewart, "Evolution of Contemporary Policing," for an excellent historical brief on the police
21. Ibid., p. 9.
22. U.S. National Advisory Commission on Civil Disorders. *Reports of the National Advisory Commission on Civil Disorders* (Washington, D.C.: U.S. Government Printing Office, 1968) p. 157.
23. Conflicting role expectations for police has been a historical issue. See Radelet, *Police and the Community;* James Q. Wilson, *Varieties of Police Behavior: The Management of Law and Order in Eight Communities* (Cambridge, Mass.: Harvard University Press, 1968); Michael Banton, *Policeman in the Community* (New York: Basic Books, 1964); Jerome H. Skolnick, *Justice Without Trial: Law Enforcement in Democratic Society* (New York: John Wiley & Sons, 1966); and Peter K. Manning and John Van Maanen, eds., *Policing: A View from the Street* (Santa Monica, Calif.: Goodyear Publishing, 1978).
24. James Q. Wilson, "The Police and Their Problems," *Public Policy,* 12 (1963), pp. 189–216.

25. See George K. Kelling et al., *The Kansas City Preventive Patrol Experiment* (Washington, D.C.: Police Foundation, 1974); Richard C. Larson, "What Happened to Patrol Operations in Kansas City: A Review of the Kansas City Preventive Patrol Experiment," *Journal of Criminal Justice,* 3 (Winter 1975), p. 267–97; Stephen E. Finberg, Kinley Larntz, and Albert J. Reiss, Jr., "Redesigning the Kansas City Preventive Patrol Experiment," *Evaluation,* 3:1–2 (1976), pp. 124, 131. This section is a synopsis of the Kansas City Patrol Experiment as reported by Kelling et al., *Kansas City Preventive Patrol Experiment,* and H. J. Vetter and L. Territo, *Crime and Justice in America* (St. Paul, Minn.: West, 1984), pp. 161–63.
26. Kelling et al., *Kansas City Preventive Patrol Experiment,* p. 42.
27. This section is a synopsis of the RAND Criminal Investigator Study as reported by Peter W. Greenwood, *The RAND Criminal Investigation Study: Its Findings and Impacts to Date* (Santa Monica, Calif.: The RAND corporation, July 1979), pp. 3–7, and Vetter and Territo, *Crime and Justice in America,* pp. 176–78.
28. Daryl F. Gates and Lyle Knowles, "An Evaluation of the RAND Corporation Analyses," *Police Chief,* 43 (July 1976), pp. 20–24, 74, 77.
29. P. Bloch and D. Weidman, *Managing Criminal Investigations: Prescriptive Package* (Washington, D.C.: U.S. Government Printing Office, 1975).
30. B. Greenberg et al., *Felony Investigation Decision Model: An Analysis of Investigative Elements of Information* (Washington D.C.: U.S. Government Printing Office, 1977).
31. The Vera researchers noted that in 56 percent of all felony arrests for crimes against the person, the victim had a prior relationship with the offender. In turn, 87 percent of these cases—as compared with only 29 percent of cases involving strangers—resulted in dismissals because the complainant refused to cooperate with the prosecutor. Once complainants "cool off," they are not interested in seeing the defendants prosecuted. Consequently, the Vera report recommends the use of neighborhood justice centers, rather than the courts, as the appropriate place to deal with most cases that involve prior relationships between victims and perpetrators.
32. B. Forst, *What Happens After Arrest* (Washington, D.C.: U.S. Government Printing Office, 1978).
33. Lawrence Sherman, Catherine Milton, and Thomas Kelly, *Team Policing: Seven Case Studies* (Washington, D.C.: The Police Foundation, 1973).
34. D. T. Shanahan, *Patrol Administration: Management by Objectives,* 2nd ed. (Boston Mass.: Allyn and Bacon, 1985), p. 303.
35. William G. Gay, H. Talmadge Day, and Jane P. Woodward, *Neighborhood Team Policing: Phase I Report* (Washington, D.C.: U.S. Government Printing Office, 1977), p. 40.
36. Ibid., p. 40.
37. Ibid., p. 39, from Table 15.
38. See Mary Ann Wycoff and George L. Kelling, *The Dallas Experience: Organizational Reform* (Washington, D.C.: The Police Foundation, 1978).
39. Ibid.
40. Susette M. Talarico and Charles R. Swanson, "The Limits of Team Policing," *Police Studies,* 3:2 (Summer 1980), pp. 21–29.
41. See Robert Michels, *Political Parties* (New York: Dover, 1959).
42. Chris Braiden, "Community Policing: Nothing New Under the Sun" (Edmonton, Canada: Edmonton Police Department, 1987).
43. Ibid., refer to Peel's Principle 7, as expressed on page 2.
44. Jerome H. Skolnick and David H. Bayley, *Community Policing: Issues and Practices Around the World* (Washington, D.C.: U.S. Department of Justice, 1988) pp. 67–70.
45. A number of researchers have documented the failures of traditional policing methods. Most notably, refer to A. J. Reiss, *The Police and the Public* (New Haven, Conn.: Yale University Press, 1971); Kelling et al., *Kansas City Preventive Patrol Experiment;*

M. T. Farmer, ed., *Differential Police Response Strategies* (Washington, D.C.: Police Executive Research Forum,1981); L. W. Sherman, P. R. Gartin, and M. E. Buerger, "Hot Spot of Predatory Crime: Routine Activities and the Criminology of Place," *Criminology,* 27 (1989), pp. 27–55; and W. H. Bieck, W. Spelman, and T. J. Sweeney, "The Patrol Function," in *Local Government Police Management,* ed. William A. Geller (Washington, D.C.: International City Management Association), pp. 59–95.

46. Timothy N. Oettmeier, "Endemic Issues in Policing: Matching Structure to Objectives" (Houston, Tex.: Houston Police Academy), p. 11.
47. Ibid., p. 16.
48. William Spelman and John E. Eck, "The Police and Delivery of Local Government Services: A Problem-Oriented Approach," in *Police Practice in the '90s: Key Management Issues,* ed. James J. Fyfe (Washington, D.C.: International City Managers Association, 1989), p. 56.
49. Ibid.
50. The SARA methodology was adapted from William Spelman and John E. Eck, *Newport News Tests Problem-Oriented Policing* (Washington, D.C.: National Institute of Justice, SNI 201, January/February 1987), pp. 2–3; and Spelman and Eck, "Police and Delivery," p. 61.
51. Herman Goldstein, *Problem-Oriented Policing* (New York: McGraw-Hill, 1990).
52. This list was adapted, in part, from Goldstein, *Problem-Oriented Policing,* pp. 66–67.
53. Ibid. pp. 36–37.
54. Michael A. Freeman, "Community-Oriented Policing," *Management Information Services,* 21 (September 1989), pp. 5–6.
55. "Creating a New Policing Environment in Madison: A Progress Report on the Experimental Police District" (Madison, Wis.: Madison Police Department, August, 1989), p. 1.
56. Research focusing on the improvement of quality of life for individual workers is abundant in the open system literature, as described in Chapter 3. However, for a more recent articulation on the subject matter, see Warren Bennis and B. Nanus, *Leaders* (New York: Harper Row, 1985); W. Edward Deming, *Out of the Crisis* (Cambridge, Mass.: MIT Center for Advanced Engineering Study, 1986); Thomas J. Peters, *Thriving on Chaos* (New York: Alfred Knopf, 1987); Thomas J. Peters and Nancy Austin, *A Passion for Excellence* (New York: Random House, 1985); Thomas J. Peters and Robert H. Wasserman, *In Search of Excellence* (New York: Harper & Row, 1982); John Naisbitt, *Megatrends* (New York: Warner Books, 1982); John Naisbitt and P. Auburdene, *Reinventing the Corporation* (New York: Warner Books, 1985); and John Gordon, *Leader Effectiveness Training* (New York: Bantam, 1975).
57. David C. Couper and Sabine H. Lobitz, *Quality Policing: The Madison Experience* (Washington, D.C.: Police Executive Research Forum, 1991), pp. 73–75.
58. Adapted from Couper and Lobitz, *Quality Policing,* pp. 83–88; and "Creating a New Policing Environment in Madison," (Washington, D.C.: Police Executive Research Forum, 1991), pp. 10–21.
59. Interview with Chief David Couper at the Southwestern Law Enforcement Institute Program, "Community Policing: A National Debate," Richardson, Texas, April 1991.
60. Oettmeier, p. 14.
61. See Timothy N. Oettmeier and William H. Bieck, *Developing a Policing Style for Neighborhood-Oriented Policing: Executive Session #1* and *Integrating Investigative Operations Through Neighborhood-Oriented Policing: Executive Session #2* (Houston, Tex.: Houston Police Department, 1988) p. 4.
62. The terms *coproduction* and *coactivity* frequently appear in the literature to describe the police and the community working together to solve a problem. See Wesley G. Skogan, "Making Better Use of Victims and Witnesses," in *Police Leadership in Amer-*

ica: Crisis and Opportunity, ed. William A. Geller (New York: Praeger, 1986), pp. 332–39.

63. The section on NOP defined by a reactive, proactive, and coactive function was adapted from Timothy N. Oettmeier, "Matching Structure to Objectives." For quote, see page 21.
64. Part of this section and a description of the NOP programs have been adapted from Freeman, "Community-Oriented Policing," pp. 10–12.
65. William P. Mitchell, "Problem-Oriented Policing and Drug Enforcement in Newport News," *Public Management,* 72 (July 1990), p. 15.
66. See Kenneth W. Findley and Robert W. Taylor, "Re-Thinking Neighborhood Policing," *Journal of Contemporary Criminal Justice,* 6 (May 1990), pp. 70–79. In addition, much of this material has been adapted from Dennis Jay Kenney and Robert W. Taylor, "The Problems with Community-Oriented Policing" (Paper presented at the Academy of Criminal Justice Sciences Annual Meeting, Nashville, Tennessee, March 1991).
67. Jack R. Greene and Stephen D. Mastrofski, eds., *Community Policing: Rhetoric or Reality* (New York: Praeger, 1991).
68. J. F. Persinos, "The Return of Officer Friendly," *Governing,* 21 (1989), pp. 56—61.
69. Cresap Management Audit (Washington, D.C.: Cresap, Inc., 1991), p. 10.
70. Ibid., p. 59.
71. C. Murphy, "Community Problems, Problem Communities, and Community Policing in Toronto," *Journal of Research in Crime and Delinquency,* 25 (November 1988), pp. 392–410.
72. Ibid., 392–93.
73. George Kelling, "Police and Communities: The Quiet Revolution," *Perspectives on Policing* (Washington, D.C.: National Institute of Justice, 1988), p. 6.
74. Interview with then Deputy Chief Elizabeth Watson, Houston Police Department, at the Southwestern Law Enforcement Institute, Richardson, Tex., November 15, 1989.
75. Cresap Management Audit, p. 10.
76. Skolnick and Baylay, *Community Policing,* p. 2.

2 Politics and Police Administration: External Influences and Controls

Terrifying are the weaknesses of Power
GREEK PROVERB

Introduction

In discussing the relationship between politics and police administration, it is important to distinguish between "Politics" and "politics." "Politics" means the attempts to impose external, partisan political influence on the operation of the department. For example, people are promoted because they know precinct committee persons and ward chairpersons who have influence with the party in power. The department is manipulated for partisan, political advantage and forced to make financial contributions. Justice is not dispensed evenhandedly. This use of the word is negative. However, "politics" means governance of the city. Aristotle's original understanding of the word *politics* was "science of the polis," seeking the good of both citizen and city-state. The present-day police are its practitioners, as are politicians at their best. Politics with a small *p* avoids political leveraging and supports merit and job performance—all positive connotations. The art of governing a local community requires a commitment to take bad politics out of the police department and put the right kind back in.[1]

Scrutiny of the Police

Given the authority entrusted by the public to the police in a free society, it is not surprising that there should be a variety of mechanisms through which the police are scrutinized in order to ensure that they are accountable for their actions. Therefore, some attention is given here to that scrutiny.

Differences Between Public and Private Organizations

In general, public organizations and private organizations can be differentiated on the basis of the following points:

1. Their legal bases differ.
2. What constitutes "success" for public organizations is less clearly definable and measurable than it is for private enterprise. For example, the fact that the United States has not been attacked militarily by another country may be interpreted as success in our defense policy and programs. But how do we know if entirely too much defense capability has been purchased, diverting resources from domestic needs? Also, the absence of being attacked may have nothing to do with our defense posture because other governments never considered military action against this country.
3. Public and private entities have different primary funding sources.[2]
4. The services provided by public agencies are generally of a more urgent or essential nature.
5. Traditionally, public agencies have been subject to closer scrutiny and formal criticisms than have their private counterparts.

There is no shortage of examples to illustrate the extent to which the police have been subject to scrutiny. Legislative committees at all three levels of government have held hearings on such subjects as organized crime, assaults on peace officers, and corruption. An early illustration of this type of review is the 1901 Fisk Committee, appointed by the California legislature to investigate corruption in San Francisco.[3] Another type of scrutiny by the police has been provided by a series of national commissions, including the National Commission on Law Observance and Enforcement (1931), the President's Commission on Law Enforcement and Administration of Justice (1967), the National Advisory Commission on Civil Disorders (1968), the National Commission on the Causes and Prevention of Violence (1969), the National Commission on Criminal Justice Standards and Goals (1973), and the Commission on Accreditation for Law Enforcement Agencies (1979). Parallel to these national commissions have been state-level entities, such as the Missouri and Pennsylvania crime commissions, that also have urban counterparts such as the Chicago Crime Commission and the Citizens' Crime Commission of Greater Miami, Inc., in Florida. Additionally, our cities have periodically appointed special investigative bodies such as the Knapp Commission, which investigated police corruption in New York City during the mid-1970s.

Other types of scrutiny have come from the episodic use of civilian review boards to investigate complaints against the police, a practice advocated by the American Civil Liberties Union (ACLU) during the 1950s and 1960s;[4] periodic reports such as the FBI's annual reported crime statistics in the *Uniform Crime Reports;* researchers working with and without grants to support their inquiry; and judicial review.

Police Accountability

Accountability of the police to other institutions conforms to the American notion of a system of checks and balances. There are, however, some questions about the actual means by which this accountability does occur and the degree to which it exists. It has been suggested that the degree of control over the police by political authority varies with the level of government at which the police functions take place. In this country, although cities and counties are legally creatures of the states under state constitutions, the states have traditionally divested themselves of much of their control over these jurisdictions and have allowed them to operate with considerable independence.[5] The existence of local autonomy has also been facilitated by the belief in home rule, which maintains that local government has the capability to manage its own affairs and that strong controls from the state capitol or the federal government are neither desirable nor consistent with American political philosophy. Nevertheless, the influences and controls being exerted upon local law enforcement from both the federal and state level have increased since the turbulent period of the 1960s.

Some argue that this is an encroachment of local hegemony and will eventually result in a significant shift of control and political power away from the local level. In reply, the proponents of this development argue that the traditionally strong local control of policing has resulted in a degree of parochialism that has retarded the growth of professionalism. They also maintain that the increased involvement in local law enforcement by the state and federal government has produced important qualitative improvements in such areas as personnel selection standards, training, crime laboratory capabilities, and labor–management relations, along with innovations such as community policing programs, which combine to improve the services delivered.

Federal Influence in Law Enforcement

Some authorities believe that trends occurring from the 1960s through the present have resulted in the partial nationalization of criminal justice. Up to the 1960s, it was safely said that criminal justice was almost completely the responsibility of state and local governments. Federal criminal statutes were limited in their coverage, federal assistance to local law enforcement was generally in the areas of training and the processing of evidence, and the Supreme Court concerned itself with only the most notorious violations of constitutional rights by state and local authorities.[6] This trend was reversed in no small measure by a series of opinions rendered by the U.S. Supreme Court under the strong leadership of Chief Justice Earl Warren, which greatly strengthened the rights of accused persons in criminal cases.

Supreme Court Decisions Affecting Law Enforcement: 1961 to 1966

Significant judicial review of local police actions has been a somewhat recent practice.[7] However, during the period from 1961 to 1966—a period frequently referred to as the "due process revolution"—the U.S. Supreme Court took an activist role, becoming quite literally givers of the law rather than interpreters of it. The Warren court's activist role in the piecemeal extension of the provisions of the Bill of Rights, via the due process clause of the Fourteenth Amendment, to criminal proceedings in the respective states might have been a policy decision.[8] Normally the Supreme Court will write opinions in about 115 cases during any particular term. During the 1938–1939 term, only five cases appear under the heading of criminal law; a scant three decades later, during the height of the due process revolution, about one-quarter of each term's decisions related to criminal law.[9] The

Supreme Court could scarcely have picked a worse period in which to undertake the unpopular role of policing the police; a burgeoning crime rate far outstripped population increases, and many politicians were campaigning on "law and order" platforms that all too often dissolved into rhetoric upon their election. The problem of crime increasingly came to the public's eye through the media. In sum, the high court acted to extend procedural safeguards to defendants in criminal cases precisely at a point in time when the public's fear of crime was high and there was great social pressure to do something about crime.

Fundamentally, the Supreme Court's role in the due process revolution was a response to a vacuum in which the police themselves had failed to provide the necessary leadership. The era of strong social activism by various special-interest groups was not yet at hand, and neither the state courts nor the legislatures had displayed any broad interest in reforming the criminal law. What institution was better positioned to undertake this responsibility? The Court may even have felt obligated by the inaction of others to do so. Therefore, it became the Warren court's lot to provide the reforms so genuinely needed but so unpopularly received. The high court did not move into this arena until after it had issued warnings that, to responsive and responsible leaders, would have been a mandate for reform.

Several key decisions were made by a split vote of the Court and drew heavy criticism from law enforcement officers and others as "handcuffing" police in their struggle with lawlessness. These decisions included *Mapp* v. *Ohio* (1961), which banned the use of illegally seized evidence in criminal cases in the states by applying the Fourth Amendment guarantee against unreasonable searches and seizures; *Gideon* v. *Wainwright* (1963), which affirmed that equal protection under the Fourteenth Amendment requires that legal counsel be appointed for all indigent defendants in all criminal cases; *Escobedo* v. *Illinois* (1964), which affirmed that a suspect is entitled to confer with an attorney as soon as the focus of a police investigation of the suspect shifts from investigatory to accusatory; and *Miranda* v. *Arizona* (1966), which required police officers, before questioning suspects, to inform them of their constitutional right to remain silent, their right to an attorney, and their right to have an attorney appointed if they cannot afford to hire one. Although the suspect may knowingly waive these rights, the police cannot question anyone who, at any point, asks for a lawyer or indicates "in any manner" that he or she does not wish to be questioned.[10] The impact of this court decision on police work was staggering; in an effort to curb questionable and improper tactics, a need for new procedures in such areas as interrogations, lineups, and seizures of physical evidence was created.

Although the decisions of the due process revolution initially were criticized by many law enforcement officers, over the years that view has changed as new generations of law enforcement officers come along for whom those decisions are simply the correct way to do things. Also, time has seen the exodus of some officers from the police profession who simply could not or would not adapt to a new way of "doing business." Finally, there was a growing willingness among law enforcement leaders to acknowledge not only that some of their tactics needed changing, but also that *Miranda* and other decisions had accomplished it.

In more recent years, appointments to the Supreme Court by Presidents Ronald Reagan and George Bush have provided a conservative majority who have generated decisions favorable to law enforcement. For example, in 1991 the Supreme

Court held that suspects arrested by the police without a warrant could be held for up to 48 hours before they had to be given a judicial hearing; that, contrary to the precedent decision in 1979, police officers could open and search suitcases, bags, and other containers in a vehicle if they had probable cause to believe the containers held illegal items, even if they did not have probable cause to search the vehicle itself; and that suspects in police custody who had received their *Miranda* warnings might sometimes be questioned without their attorneys being present about crimes unrelated to those for which they had been arrested, provided that the suspects waived the presence of their attorneys. Although the current members of the Supreme Court can be expected to expand police powers judiciously in such areas as search and seizure and interrogation, it is equally clear that they will produce rulings that will reverse some of the gains made since the due process revolution regarding misconduct by the police.[11]

Federal Legislation

Holten and Jones have traced the history of the federal legislation that eventually emanated from the sweeping recommendations of the President's Commission Report on Law Enforcement and the Administration of Justice. The first in this series of enactments was the Omnibus Crime Control and Safe Street Act of 1968. This act made some sweeping changes in the federal criminal justice process, but its real importance lay in the assumption of a broad federal responsibility for encouraging change in the administration of justice at the state and local levels.[12] This legislation created the Law Enforcement Assistance Administration (LEAA) within the Department of Justice to channel federal grants-in-aid to the states for use in upgrading state or local criminal justice operations. Most of the funds were to go to the states as "block grants" to be employed by the states as they saw fit, subject to federal review and approval.[13] There was great concern and some suspicion among state and local officials that the acceptance of federal monies would eventually lead to federal control of local affairs. An often heard adage during that time was "federal control follows federal money." Assurances that this would not occur were forthcoming from high offices in Washington. However, the record of federal, state, and local relations since the 1960s indicates that these fears were not groundless and once again supports the assumption that the acceptance of funding from any source generally brings with it varying degrees of control.

Juvenile Justice and Delinquency Act: 1974

In 1974, Congress passed the Juvenile Justice and Delinquency Prevention Act, which established grants for projects in juvenile justice and set up the office of Juvenile Justice and Delinquency Prevention within LEAA. This act contains one condition that goes beyond requiring generalized plans for improvements in the juvenile justice system: states that receive funds under this act must abolish the use of detention in cases involving only so-called status offenses by juveniles. The failure of states to apply for the available monies led to a recent decision that states, to be eligible, must only show good faith in trying to move toward the realization of that goal. This situation illustrates the kinds of rules that the federal government can impose as a condition of obtaining funds.[14]

National Advisory Commission on Criminal Justice Standards and Goals: 1971

This commission was created to follow up on the work done by the President's Commission on Law Enforcement and the Administration of Justice. The end results of the Advisory Commission's work were published in a series of five volumes in 1973: *A National Strategy to Reduce Crime; Criminal Justice System; Police; Courts;* and *Community Crime Prevention*. The recommendations of the Advisory Commission report, as was the case of that of its predecessor, outlined highly specific recommendations for the improvement of the various components of the criminal justice system but gave a higher priority to the crime prevention aspects of crime control at the state and local level. The Advisory Commission recommended that the federal government should continue to provide monies through various grant and revenue-sharing programs.

Civil Rights Act of 1964 and the Equal Employment Opportunity Act of 1972

The involvement of the federal government in the operations of local law enforcement has also occurred via two other pieces of important legislation, namely, the Civil Rights Act of 1964 and the Equal Employment Opportunity Act of 1972. There is little doubt that these two pieces of legislation have had a profound effect on the personnel practices and policies of police departments in the areas of recruitment, training, job assignment, and promotion.

The Civil Rights Act of 1964 is divided into a number of titles, each dealing with a particular aspect of discrimination. The entire act touches on matters concerning voting rights, public accommodations, public education, establishment of the U.S. Commission on Civil Rights, discrimination in federally assisted programs, equal employment opportunity, and a number of procedural matters. Title VII of the Civil Rights Act of 1964 has been the main body of federal legislation in the area of fair employment. Before 1972, Title VII was directed primarily toward private employers with 25 or more employees, labor organizations with 25 or more members, and private employment agencies.[15] The essence of the substantive portion of Title VII provides that

> It shall be an unlawful employment practice for an employer to (1) to fail or refuse to hire, or discharge any individual or otherwise to discriminate against any individual with respect to his compensation, terms, conditions, or privileges of employment, because of such individual's race, color, religion, sex, or national origin; (2) to limit, segregate, or classify his employees or applicants for employment in any way which would deprive or tend to deprive any individual of employment opportunity or otherwise adversely affect his status as an employee because of such individual's race, color, religion, sex, or national origin.[16]

In 1972 Congress expanded the coverage of title VII of the Civil Rights Act of 1964. On March 24, 1972, an amendment, known as the Equal Employment Opportunity Act, Title VII, was approved. It expanded coverage of Title VII to both public and private employers, including state and local governments, public and private educational institutions, labor organizations, and public and private employment agencies. In the case of government agencies, educational institutions, and labor organizations, the act applied to those organizations with 25 or more employees during the first year after the date of enactment; thereafter, it applied to agencies with 15 or more employees.[17]

Under the authority of Title VII as amended, the Equal Employment Opportunity Commission (EEOC) was designated as the regulatory agency with the function of setting standards and establishing guidelines for compliance with the requirements of the law. In 1970, the EEOC issued a set of Guidelines on Employee Selection Procedures that superseded and enlarged earlier guidelines on Employment Testing Procedures issued by the EEOC in 1966. These guidelines constitute the basic interpretation of the requirements of Title VII as it applies to state and local government, and it is these guidelines with which compliance must be shown by those involved in personnel practices. Many of the complaints filed with the EEOC and the cases that subsequently end up in court have arisen from personnel practices involving police and fire departments (see Box 2-1).[18]

BOX 2-1

Police, Fire Hiring Rules Dropped

By Dan Herbeck
News Staff Reporter

The City of Buffalo agreed late Friday to scrap its present test and selection processes for the hiring of police officers and firefighters.

An attorney for the city told U.S. District Judge John T. Curtin that the Civil Service Commission will revanp its police and firefighter hiring policies rather than proceed with two trials that would have decided whether the test and selection policies were fair.

Groups representing minorities hailed the settlement as an important victory, but the city attorney said this could be a step in the elimination of minority-hiring quotas in both departments.

"Once we get a testing and selection process that everyone can be happy with, the quotas can be lifted and we can have a test that doesn't discriminate and selects candidates based on merit," said Assistant Corporation Counsel Margaret A. Murphy.

Ms. Murphy said the city has agreed to work with an expert suggested by the U.S. Justice Department to change the city's methods of screening police and firefighter applicants.

Women and minorities have maintained that the city's hiring policies discriminate against them.

"We are ready to go back to the drawing board, to give the City of Buffalo the best testing and selection program in the country for police and firefighters," Ms. Murphy said.

The settlement occurred eight days before the scheduled start of two trials in which the city would have had to defend itself against allegations that the Civil Service Commission has been discriminating against blacks, Hispanics and women.

The agreement is the latest step in a series of legal battles and procedures dating to 1978, when Curtin ruled that both city departments had been discriminating systematically against minorities for decades.

(continued on next page)

BOX 2-1 (cont.)

Representatives of minority police officers and firefighters attended the court session, and both described the court settlement as an important victory.

"We're very pleased," said Police Officer Nadine Wilson, president of the BuffaloAfro-American Police Association. "They don't come right out and say it, but the city is admitting they have discriminated in their police and firefighter hiring for the past 12 years. This is very good news."

Firefighter Paul T. Batchelor agreed. Batchelor is president of Men of Color Helping People, an association of black city firefighters.

"There is still a long way to go. Things still have to be changed, and we are still concerned about addressing the issue of promotions," Batchelor said. "But this is a start."

Ms. Murphy vehemently denied that the city is making any admission of discrimination or acting in bad faith.

"We feel we could have proven in the trial that our selection process is fair," the city lawyer said. "We want to work with the Justice Department to develop a test that will not discriminate and will also help us to find the best candidates."

Asked why the city changed course after refusing for 12 years to change the tests, Ms. Murphy said: "We talked to our clients—the police and fire commissioner—and they felt this was what they wanted."

Judith Mathis, a Justice Department attorney from Washington, congratulated the city for "a significant change in attitude."

The hiring quotas for minorities and women will remain in effect until Curtin is satisfied that the city has enacted fair Civil Service testing and selection procedures for the jobs.

After 11 years of hiring under a program that had one minority selected for each non-minority, Curtin ruled last August that the city had met acceptable minority levels in the two departments.

But Curtin ruled in August that the city still has not proved that its testing and selection procedures were fair, so the judge kept an adjusted hiring quota in effect. Now the number of minorities and women must be determined by the percentage of minority and female applicants on each Civil Service test.

Ms. Murphy said the process of implementing court-approved new testing, test-scoring and hiring procedures will probably take two to three years.

Meanwhile, Ms. Murphy told the judge there will probably be no hiring of police officers or firefighters in the coming fiscal year because of the city's financial problems.

Source: Buffalo News (New York), Feb. 17, 1990.

The use of arrest and conviction records as a basis of employment discrimination also is subject to attack under equal opportunity laws. The EEOC has ruled that convictions may not be used in personnel selection unless the conviction is related directly to the work to be performed. Further, conviction records cannot be used as an absolute barrier to employment, but, rather, each conviction must be reviewed on the basis of its relevance to the job to be done.[19]

The 1990 Americans with Disabilities Act

The Americans with Disabilities Act (ADA) was enacted by the Congress to eradicate barriers to disabled persons in transportation, public accommodations, telecommunications, employment, and access to state and local government and its facilities. The ADA makes it unlawful to discriminate against people with disabilities in *all* employment practices, including recruitment, hiring, promotion, training, layoffs, pay, firing, job assignments, transfers, leave, and benefits.

State employers, units of state and local government, employment agencies, labor organizations, and labor–management committees are all covered under the ADA. The portion of the ADA that outlaws job discrimination is administered by the EEOC and covers

1. all employers, including state and local government employers, with 25 or more employees after July 26, 1992
2. all employers, including state and local government employers, with 15 or more employees after July 26, 1994.

Although the EEOC has responsibility for job discrimination under the ADA, other federal agencies, such as the Department of Transportation and the Federal Communications Commission, oversee the parts of the ADA that fall within their areas of specialization.

The ADA covers both *actual* and *regarded* disabilities. Briefly, a disability is defined as a "physical or mental impairment that substantially limits a major life activity." A "regarded" disability case would be exemplified by a police administrator who, believing an employee had a disability, made an adverse employment decision on that basis; the administrator would then have violated that employee's rights under the ADA even if no disability existed. For instance, assume that Chief Bob Jones transferred Officer Mary Tyler from the patrol division to a job assignment involving clerical duties in the records division because he erroneously believed she was infected with the AIDS virus and he wanted to reduce her contact with the public. If Officer Tyler learned of Chief Jones's reasons for making the transfer, she could file a complaint under the ADA. Moreover, even if she actually tested positive for the AIDS virus, such a transfer for that reason would be actionable unless she posed a significant health risk to others as determined by objective medical evidence and not through generalizations, fear, ignorance, or stereotyping. Also, if Officer Tyler had reached the point where she informed management of her disability or management reasonably determined that she could no longer perform field duties as a result of it, then reassignment to another less demanding post would be not only permissible, but actually required under the ADA as a "reasonable accommodation."

Remedies available under ADA include requiring a police department or other affected employer to hire, to promote, to reinstate, to transfer, to give back pay, to pay attorney's fees, and to make "reasonable accommodations." A reasonable accommodation is any modification or adjustment of the job or the work environment that enables a qualified applicant or an employee with a disability to perform essential job functions.

Although the actual impact of this legislation on law enforcement is presently unknown, several predictions about its future are warranted. First, as knowledge about the ADA becomes increasingly widespread there will be a sharp increase in disability discrimination complaints from prospective and current law enforcement agency employees, including those who are civilians and those who are *sworn*—that is, who have the power to arrest. Second, the complexity of the police personnel function will become even more complex and additional specialized record keeping will be required. Third, a rich body of regulations and case law will emerge over a period of years, creating another specialized area of knowledge. Fourth, because the ADA is a new law, the EEOC will very aggressively pursue complaints in order to establish a "track record." Fifth, as was the case with the

EEOC's legislation in 1972, some local government agencies are not going to be proactive in responding to ADA requirements and will become the subjects of formal complaints. Additional information about the ADA is provided in Chapter 7, "Human Resource Management."

The Civil Rights Act of 1991

In 1989, the Supreme Court issued its decision in *Wards Cove Packing* v. *Antonio,* which was widely perceived as clarifying the burden of proof in EEOC cases and making it more difficult for plaintiffs to bring adverse impact actions under Title VII of the Civil Rights Act of 1964, as amended in 1972. In 1989 the Supreme Court also decided *Martin* v. *Wilks,* which opened consent decrees favorable to the promotion of minorities to attack from majority white employees on the grounds that they had not been party to the consent and that other parties had impermissibly bargained away their rights.

In light of such developments, increasing concern was expressed by civil rights leaders and organizations, as well as by some members of both houses of the Congress, that hard-won progress was being eroded by some key Supreme Court decisions that appeared to make it more difficult for minorities to successfully challenge an employer's selection and promotion practices. As a result, the Congress passed the Civil Rights Act of 1990, but it was vetoed by President Bush, who said he wanted a civil rights bill, not a "quota bill." The following year, the Congress approved the Civil Rights Act of 1991, which President Bush signed into law.

Legal scholars and others analyzing the Civil Rights Act of 1991 see its provisions as specifically designed to obviate the impact of Supreme Court decisions perceived as pro-employer. One way of regarding the 1991 act is as legislation intended to strengthen—from a civil rights perspective—the 1972 Title VII law administered by the EEOC. It includes, in addition to the usual EEOC remedies, a new provision for punitive damages that would radically alter current practice. Many observers believe that, as a result, aggrieved employees will pursue their EEOC claims into court to obtain money settlements as well as the remedies that were available under the 1972 law.

Significant, however, for law enforcement agencies is that punitive damages may only be recovered from respondents other than a government, government agency, or political subdivision.

Commission on Accreditation for Law Enforcement Agencies

The Commission on Accreditation for Law Enforcement Agencies (CALEA) is a private, nonprofit organization. It was formed in 1979 by the four major national law enforcement associations (International Association of Chiefs of Police [IACP], National Organization of Black Law Enforcement Executives [NOBLE], National Sheriff's Association [NSA], and Police Executive Research Forum [PERF]). The Commission has developed a national set of 900 law enforcement standards for all types and sizes of state and local agencies. In some ways, CALEA can be viewed as a direct product of the reform era to professionalize the police. Nowhere is this more apparent than in the stated goals of the Commission. Its standards are designed to

- Increase agency capabilities to prevent and control crime
- Enhance agency effectiveness and efficiency in the delivery of law enforcement services
- Improve cooperation and coordination with other law enforcement agencies and with other components of the criminal justice system
- Increase citizen and staff confidence in the goals, objectives, policies, and practices of the agency.[20]

The accreditation process is a voluntary undertaking. In the last decade, significant movement toward accreditation has been spurred by two developments. First, because most of the standards identify topics and issues that must be covered by written policies and procedures, successful accreditation offers a viable defense or "liability shield" against civil litigation.[21] Second, CALEA provides a nationwide system for change.[22] One of the most important parts of the accreditation process is self-assessment. During this stage, agencies undergo a critical self-evaluation that addresses the complete gamut of services provided by law enforcement. The agency is also later assessed by an on-site team of law enforcement professionals to determine whether it has complied with the applicable standards for a department of its type and size.

CALEA enjoys wide support among police executives and community leaders. In particular, when a city manager is seeking to hire a new police chief from outside of a troubled department, experience of candidates with the accreditation process is a substantial plus. In one city, officers received information on Christmas Eve that a rapist who had beaten and cut his victims was in a house in a county outside of their jurisdiction. Without any significant evaluation of the information, without a raid plan, using personnel who were untrained or had not previously trained together for conducting raids, and without a search warrant, the officers conducted a raid, killed a 74-year-old man in his own home who had no connection with the crime, and found out the rapist had never been there. In the aftermath, the community lost confidence in its police department. A member of the grand jury asked the police chief, "How do I know that your officers won't kill me or members of my family in my home tonight?" Departmental morale plunged to an all-time low. A management study of the department revealed that written policies and procedures were virtually nonexistent and identified other deficiencies as well. The chief of police retired, and a new chief was brought in from the outside with orders from the city manager to get the department accredited. In the process of accomplishing accreditation, the department regained its esprit de corps and the support of the community. The city manager said he believed that "no other mechanism besides accreditation could have done so much good so quickly in turning the department around."

Despite similar accounts and the reduction of liability risks that typically accompanies accreditation, the process is not without its critics. Some see it as "window dressing . . . long on show and short on substance"—a reference to the fact that some departments allegedly develop the necessary policies to meet the standards and then fail to actually follow them. Some city managers are reluctant to authorize their police departments to enter a process that takes an average of 21 months to complete at an average cost of $73,708.[23] This cost includes the modest CALEA accreditation fee, which ranges from $3,800 for a department with up to nine full-time employees to $14,700 for agencies having 3,000 or more full-time employees.[24] Other components of the average cost of accreditation include direct costs, such as purchases necessary to meet standards (e.g., putting first aid kits in all cars, buying body armor for special weapons and tactics teams) and modifications to facilities or capabilities (e.g., upgrading the evidence storage area and radio communication), and indirect costs, such as the cost of personnel actually doing the work necessary to meet standards (e.g., writing policies and procedures).[25] Others have maintained that the process is control oriented and at odds with important values such as individual initiative and organizational democracy.

In balance, however, it is clear that accreditation is an important national influence because it requires both self-scrutiny and external evaluation in determining the extent to which a law enforcement agency has met the 900 standards promulgated by experts in the field. It serves as a liability shield, promotes pride among employees, and stimulates confidence among the community. Moreover, it can play an important role in the economic development of a community. Business people seeking to relocate evaluate the communities they are considering on the basis of transportation, taxation, recreational opportunities, and the ability of local government to conduct its affairs professionally. In one instance a well-managed city of 300,000 lost a major prospective employer to another city due to one salient factor: the police department in the other city was accredited. As soon as this fact became known, the mayor directed the police chief to pursue accreditation by CALEA as a "top priority."

The Roles of State and Local Government in Law Enforcement

From the outset most Americans had a firm belief that the police should be controlled by local officials organized along municipal lines. For them, a national police, such as the Italian *carabinieri,* was inconceivable, and a state police, such as the German *polizei,* was undesirable.[26] However, the history of state and local relations in the area of law enforcement has often been a rocky and tumultuous one. Fogelson, for example, has noted that

> By the mid-nineteenth century, it was plain that for most police departments local control meant Democratic control. Hence the Republican leaders, who generally spoke for the upper middle and upper classes, demanded state control, arguing that it would remove the police from partisan politics and improve the quality of law enforcement. Their Democratic opponents countered that state control would merely shift the focus of political interference and plainly violate the principle of self-government. The issue erupted in one city after another, with the Republicans usually getting their way. They imposed state control of the police in New York City in 1857, Detroit in 1865, Cleveland in 1866, New Orleans in 1868, Cincinnati in 1877, Boston in 1885, and Omaha in 1887. They also established metropolitan police departments, with jurisdiction over the central city and adjacent territory, in New York City in 1857, Albany in 1865, and a few other places thereafter.

> Under these arrangements the state authorities appointed a board to manage, or at any rate to oversee, the big-city police. But the states did not contribute anything toward the upkeep of the police departments; nor, except in a few cases, did they authorize them to operate in the metropolitan area, much less throughout the entire state. Not until the early twentieth century did Pennsylvania, New York, and a few other states form statewide constabularies; and these forces, which patrolled mainly in small towns and rural districts, supplemented rather than supplanted the municipal police. Thus despite these changes, the American police remained decentralized to a degree unheard of anywhere in Western Europe. By the late nineteenth century, moreover, state control was well on the wane. The Democrats attacked it at every opportunity; and in the face of mounting evidence that the state boards had neither removed the police from partisan politics nor improved the quality of law enforcement, the Republicans were hard pressed to defend it. The issue was soon resolved, usually when the Democrats took office. The state authorities not only abolished metropolitan policing in New York and Albany in 1870 but also reestablished local control in Cleveland in 1868, New York in 1870, New Orleans in 1877, Cincinnati in 1880, Detroit in 1891, and Omaha in 1897. By 1900 the big-city police were controlled by local officials and organized along municipal lines everywhere in urban America except for Boston, Baltimore, St. Louis, Kansas City, and a few other places.[27]

The type of direct takeover of local law enforcement by the states described by Fogelson will very likely not occur again or at least not on the grand scale of the 1800s. However, we may see some isolated cases. For example, a decade ago some public officials in Georgia were urging the state to take over the administration of the Atlanta Police Department because of dramatic political upheavals that were affecting the morale and effectiveness of that department. A takeover by the state did not occur, but the political atmosphere was conducive to such a move.

Even if a state does not exercise its official political power to intervene in local police administration, it may be called on to exercise its influence in less apparent ways, in which case the influence may not always be proper or appropriate:

> Our department was going through a major reorganization and in the process was going to have to make about 50 promotions. One of the newly created positions was deputy chief. The only requirement for the position was that you had to have been a Major for one year. "Ed Hawks" had been a Major for about 8 months and he really wanted that deputy chief's position. Nobody believed that he even had a chance. He went to his cousin, who was close to the Governor, and talked to him. The Governor called the Mayor and expressed his "confidence" in what a great deputy chief Hawks would make. The mayor's son sat as a political appointee of the Governor on one of the most important state boards. So, the Mayor sat on the reorganization plan until the day after Ed Hawks had a year in grade as a Major—which meant that 50 promotions were held up for about four months—and then approved the implementation of the plan. . . . Hawks got promoted . . . crap like that is really demoralizing.

In a positive vein, the impact of the state on the affairs of local law enforcement is continuing via the imposition of preemployment and training standards as well as through various funding formulas tied to these standards. The first state to impose minimum standards of training for police officers was California, in 1959. This move was soon followed by the states of New York, Oklahoma, and Oregon. In 1970, the LEAA did make available discretionary grants to those states that wanted to implement minimum standards programs. Today all 50 states have mandated training for law enforcement officers. It must be noted, however, that much of the impetus for the implementation of minimum standards on a statewide basis comes from the local law enforcement community. Requirements related to the minimum standards for employment as police officers are administered through state organizations, often termed Police Officers Standards and Training Commissions (POST), which generally operate under three broad mandates: (1) to establish minimum standards for employment in a state, county, or local law enforcement agency; (2) to articulate curricula of training for police officers; and (3) to conduct and encourage research designed to improve all aspects of law enforcement.[28]

In its assessment of the role of the states in criminal justice planning, in general the National Advisory Commission on Criminal Justice Standards and Goals suggested that the State Planning Agencies (SPAs), which were created by the Omnibus Crime Control and Safe Streets Act of 1968 as the state-level organizations through which federal funds were funneled from the LEAA, bear a special responsibility for the formation of minimum statewide standards.[29] However, with the demise of LEAA in 1982 there has been a reduction or total dismantling of large state planning agencies.

Local Political Forces

The special dimension of police politics varies from community to community, but law enforcement activities are governed for the most part by the dominant values of the local political culture.

James Q. Wilson, in his now-classic study of the police in eight communities, identified three distinctly different styles of law enforcement, all of which were reflective of the political culture of the communities they serve: (1) the "watchman" style of law enforcement emphasizes order maintenance and is found in economically declining cities with traditional political machines; (2) the "legalistic" style of law enforcement is found in cities with heterogeneous populations and reform-oriented, professional governments; law enforcement of both a reactive and proactive nature characterizes this style; and (3) in the homogeneous suburban communities, the "service" style of law enforcement is oriented toward the needs of citizens.[30]

In Wilson's studies, these variations in the community political culture manifested themselves in a number of ways that subsequently affected both the qualitative and the quantitative enforcement action taken by the police. Significant enforcement variations emerged in the areas of vice, juvenile offenses, order maintenance, and traffic enforcement. Numerous variations, linked to the community's political culture, also emerged in the police department's personnel entry standards, promotional policies, extent of specialization, and level of managerial skills. These, in turn, affected the overall operations of the department, which in turn impacted on the citizens' perception and confidence in its police department.

As indicated earlier, there is an unfailing, consistent, and close relationship between the type of law enforcement a community has and its dominant political culture. This is not to suggest, however, that any community's political culture is unalterably fixed. In fact, the reform movements that have been a part of the American political scene throughout much of its history have corresponded with the emergence of new political cultures. Each new dominant political culture in time leaves its own unique mark on the unit of government within its sphere of control.

Strong Mayor

To some extent, the type of local government that a community has will have impact on the way police chiefs are selected, the freedom they will enjoy in the performance of their status, and their tenure. For example, with a strong mayor form of government, the mayor is elected to office and serves as the chief executive of the city. The city council constitutes the chief legislative and policymaking body. The mayor nominates a candidate to serve as police chief, with majority approval needed from the city council. Once approved, the candidate assumes the position of police chief and serves at the discretion of the mayor.

Ideally, the person selected by the mayor as police chief should possess the full range of managerial and administrative skills necessary to operate the police department. However, to a great extent, the kind of persons selected to serve as police chief will be determined by the mayor's professional qualifications, philosophy about the role of law enforcement, and political commitments. If the mayor is endowed with sound business or public administration skills and also has a "good government" philosophy, then the chief of police will very likely be selected on the basis of professional abilities rather than extraneous political factors. Unfortunately, on too many occasions in the past, this appointment has been a method of repaying political favors. A classical case of the misuse of this appointing authority was illustrated by the Wickersham Commission in 1931:

> . . . a few years ago the mayor of Indianapolis was called upon to introduce the police chief of that city to an assemblage of police chiefs during one of their conferences. In the course of his introductory remarks, the mayor said, "I know that my man is going to be a good chief because he has been my tailor for 20 years. He knows how to make good clothes; he ought to be a good chief."[31]

No big-city mayor would make this same choice today, but the choice will nevertheless still be a reflection of the mayor's personal value system and abilities, and of the political environment of the community.

In the strong mayor form of local government, the tenure of the chief of police is often linked directly to the mayor, and the nature of the relationship is such that the chief is quite dependent on the mayor for support and guidance on budgetary matters, enforcement practices, and a multitude of other areas essential to the overall success of the police department. If there is mutual respect between the police chief and the mayor, a strong professional and political bond will be formed. If the reverse holds true, however, significant antagonisms may begin to emerge. There are too many situations to enumerate positively or negatively that can affect the working relationship between a mayor and a police chief. One finds that the important differences that do emerge are frequently those that evolve out of philosophical and ethical differences rather than questions of legality. These are differences that can occur in any form of government.

City Manager

There is no lack of supporters or detractors for every form of local government found in the United States. The proponents of the city manager form claim that it provides the most conducive atmosphere in which professional law enforcement can operate and minimizes external interference from outside controls. One of the reasons for this assessment is the balancing mechanisms developed over the years that are typically inherent in the city manager form of government: (1) the city manager is accountable to the elected members of the city council as a body rather than to any individual council member; (2) individual council members are prevented (by law of council rules) from giving administrative, operational, or policy direction to the city manager; (3) the council as a body may not give specific administrative direction to the city manager, who generally has exclusive executive authority over the city employees; (4) the city manager, consistent with civil service statutes and subject to employee appeals, has full authority to hire, promote, and discipline city personnel; (5) the city manager has broad authority within state municipal financial statutes to manage the budget and to depart from line item appropriations to meet unanticipated needs; and (6) the council as a body hires the city manager and may dismiss the city manager in its discretion without stating its cause. The city manager model is significant because it has been clearly successful in the American local political milieu and because its separation of the political policymaking body and the independent chief executive is realistically defined.[32]

The city manager more often than not is a professional administrator who is recruited for certain skills and training and appointed by the city council. A person with this background tends to make sincere efforts to select a competent individual to serve as police chief, because the manager's professional reputation is tied inextricably to the effective management of the city departments.

It is significant that city managers have sought qualified police chiefs and that they have in most instances based their selection on the professional qualifications of the candidate rather than on political or other extraneous considerations that too often have governed appointments to this position in the past.[33] This does not mean that the city manager form of government removes the chief from local politics, but it does create more distance and insulation than the one-to-one political relationship commonly found in the strong mayor form of government.

Tenure for Police Chiefs

A study conducted in California showed that police chiefs' tenure in that state approximated three years before being fired or resigning (see Box 2-2).[34]

Statutory Protections

There is considerable evidence to suggest that police executives who lack protection from arbitrary and unjustified removal will have difficulty in fulfilling their responsibilities objectively and independently. However, some states have systems offering statutory protection to police chiefs. Illinois, for example, has by statute authorized municipalities to create a board of fire and police commissioners to establish policy for these departments. The Illinois law prohibits the removal or discharge of a member of the fire or police department without cause; the individual must also be given written charges and an opportunity to be heard in his or her own defense.

BOX 2-2

Arbitrary Dismissals Shake Calif. Chiefs
Association Seeks Protection from "Volatile" Politics

Disturbed by "a volatile political environment" that has threatened the job security of several police executives, the California Police Chiefs Association is seeking enactment of state guidelines to ensure that police chiefs are "fired for cause" and not as a result of political considerations.

In recent months at least three police chiefs have faced the loss of their jobs following changes in local government administrations, said Karel Swanson, the police chief of Walnut Creek, who serves as second vice president of the chiefs association.

"We're losing police chiefs pretty fast around here and a lot of it has to do with what I would call the overall political environment," Swanson told LEN.

To rectify the situation, Swanson and other chiefs' association officials have asked the group's legislative advocate to advance a bill in the California Assembly that would specify "that police chiefs should be fired for cause," and not for personal or political reasons.

The association feels "there should be some reason that the police chief is let go," Swanson said.

Popular Chief Ousted

John Smith, the popular and highly praised police chief of Mountain View, about 10 miles northwest of San Jose, is one official who is now job-hunting. Smith, who was appointed as chief in 1984 by then-city manager Bruce Liedstrand, found himself forced to resign by Liedstrand's successor, Ralph Jaeck.

"Ralph told me that he wanted me to resign," Smith said. "If I did not, I would be terminated." Smith, a 24-year police veteran who has also served as chief in the California towns of Port Hueneme and Porterville, became jobless as of Sept. 1.

Jaeck did not return LEN's repeated telephone calls.

No reason was given for Jaeck's request, and to Smith, that hurts. Such dismissals, Smith said, "have a chilling effect on our profession."

"If there are no circumstances that show that the chief is incompetent, unethical or illegal or if they haven't created such a situation where they're incapable of working with the city staff, then I do believe that there should be some protection" against arbitrary dismissals, he said.

Chiefs Need Tenure Most

San Jose Police Chief Joseph McNamara agrees. He said that under the Peace Officers' Bill of Rights and Civil Service rules, "just about everyone but the chief has tenure in most departments, and in a way, the one who needs it the most is the chief."

McNamara said there have been a number of cases in California where chiefs have been dismissed after enforcing a law against city officials or their relatives.

"There are times when a law enforcement decision is made on a professional level. It's politically unpopular, and the next thing you know the chief is dismissed because he doesn't fit on the management team or has a different philosophy and the real reasons aren't given," McNamara said.

The public has a right to an independent police chief, McNamara said—"independent in the sense that he will enforce all of the laws without any favoritism and also will enforce department regulations without favoritism."

The California chiefs are not looking for lifetime appointments, McNamara added, but it "seems that in the interest of common sense and fair play that there should be some specific guidelines as to when a police chief is going to be removed from office."

(continued on next page)

BOX 2-2 (cont.)

Career-Ending Move

Police chiefs who are fired often find it difficult to find another job, Swanson said, "so what it means is if you become a police chief at 40 or 45 and you have a change in administration or some type of political change, you can lose your job and it's career-ending. You can't get another job in the business. I think that's the concern of the police chiefs: It's catastrophic."

Until recently, Swanson said, he felt that most chiefs felt comfortable with working "at the will" of city officials.

What is happening now, he continued, "and I think you may see this throughout the country, is a more volatile political environment. We seem to be becoming more divergent rather than convergent in a lot of things that are going on in local communities."

That has made city managers' jobs "much more unstable" and that uncertainty is carrying over to police chiefs, Swanson said.

Source: Law Enforcement News, Sept. 30, 1989, pp. 1, 5.

These protections are available to the chief of police only where there is no local ordinance creating a different procedure. If such an ordinance exists, the statute requires the municipal appointing authority to file the reasons for the chief's removal but does not require a showing of cause or a hearing.

New Hampshire affords significant protection to police chiefs. It requires written notice of the basis for the proposed termination, a hearing on the charges, and a finding of cause before the dismissal can be effected. Minnesota, on the other hand, provides no mandatory protections for police chiefs but does require that they be included in any civil service system adopted by a municipality.

A few other states have attempted to provide police chiefs with at least some job security whenever they have been promoted from within the ranks of the police department. Both Illinois and Ohio allow chiefs who resign or who are removed from their positions to return to the ranks they held within their departments before being appointed chiefs. Most states, however, offer very little protection.

Chiefs across the country are therefore forced to look for job protections in local civil service codes, local municipal ordinances, and such individual employment contracts as they are able to negotiate.[35]

Nonnegotiable and Negotiable Political Issues for Police Chiefs

A number of years ago, the highly regarded police administrator Patrick V. Murphy[36] set forth factors that in his professional judgment were nonnegotiable and factors that were negotiable for a police chief running a department. The following sections represent those views.

Non-Negotiable Issues Although the candidate's general goal should be to obtain as much independence in running the department as he can get, what should be his "deal breakers"—the minimal conditions without which he simply will not accept the job? One such condition is that the chief must have a free hand in personnel matters—as free as possible within a structured civil service system. While many departments, such as New York's and Chicago's, have "exempt" positions at the top that the chief can fill at his discretion, others have very little leeway: Everyone except the chief has tenure and cannot be replaced. This is why so many chiefs get gray hair and ulcers; they feel they can't do the job if they can't assemble their own team. Especially if he is brought in as an outsider, and it's he against everybody who has been there, the situation is impossible. Even when the top positions are civil service, it is still essential for the chief to achieve some flexibility, as Chief Lee Brown and his mayor have done in Houston by securing a change that permits the chief to select civilians for a few top-level positions. Even five or six such people give the chief a team he can work with. Otherwise, it's very lonesome at the top.

Although the mayor should not be making *decisions* about appointments, promotions, transfers, or assignments, this is not to suggest he should be deprived of a right to *input*. The key is for the chief to have some *standards* for personnel decisions and to be the one who determines when they have been met. If there is an excess of people who meet the standards, there can be some flexibility in determining which ones to select. I do not think as chief one has to be alarmed if the mayor says, "Well, if he's qualified, I'd really appreciate it if Joe Blow was one of the people who was advanced to second-grade detective." Fortunately, that was not the problem for me in New York under Mayor Lindsay nor in the other departments I headed. But I do not think serious harm would be done in my hypothetical example if the chief, in advancing 20 people to second-grade detective, included Joe Blow, so long as he was otherwise qualified and promotable.

Even with positions above lieutenant or captain, which many mayors (Lindsay included) *do* express some interest in, the point is not to deprive the mayor of an advisory role but to set minimal standards. For instance, I would not want the councilman's ignorant brother-in-law walking around in a deputy chief's uniform; a patrolman could not be made a deputy chief (which has happened); the appointee must operate within departmental policies and guidelines; the chief must have the opportunity to evaluate the person's performance; and if the person turns out to be performing unsatisfactorily, there must be some resolution of the problem—possibly that the political official could select someone else who otherwise meets the chief's criteria. The chief has to realize that, as a practical matter, the mayor sees appointments to desirable city jobs as opportunities to pay some rewards—rewards that may help him build a political coalition so that both he and the chief can survive in office. By the same token, the mayor must recognize the importance of allowing the chief to preserve ultimate control over personnel matters: It gives the chief the ability to motivate his people to work for him because they know he can reward them.

Another, closely related, power that I believe the chief candidate could not afford to bargain away is ultimate control over discipline. Who has the final administrative authority in disciplinary matters varies from city to city these days, but within the existing legal structure, the chief rather than the mayor or city manager should have the principal responsibility and commensurate authority. In matters of integrity, brutality, and misconduct the chief has to have the power to discipline, and the mayor should not override those decisions.

Also non-negotiable is the subject of partisan political activity by the chief or other members of the department. Without encroaching on First Amendment rights, I believe it would be a serious mistake for a chief to become involved in making political endorsements during civic campaigns, and if that were made a condition of employment I think it should be a deal breaker. A chief cannot be foolishly rigid about such matters, however. If the media ask me as chief what I think of the mayor, who is running for reelection, I would say, "I have the highest regard for this mayor, he's been an excellent administrator, he's been fair to me, he's lived up to the agreement we made when I was hired." If they ask, "Do you endorse him?" my answer would be, "I don't think it's appropriate for me to endorse anyone for election, so I won't endorse him."

Other matters that may not merit quite the same insistence on independence by the chief candidate but on which I would certainly try to avoid yielding ground include the chief's flexibility in being able to use his resources to best advantage, which often is related to budget authority; control over media relations; and the existence of an in-house departmental legal adviser.

Negotiable Issues Clearly, the issues that are, in varying degrees, "negotiable" are too numerous to list, let alone discuss. But some of the more important ones merit brief mention. It would be highly desirable but, I'm sorry to say, highly unlikely, for the prospective chief to secure some sort of tenure—not "chief for life" as existed until a recent change in the law in Milwaukee, but a contract for a term of, say, three to five years, during which he could only be removed for cause or by being compensated for the remainder of his contract. Among the terms some contracts cover are severance pay, work hours, moving expenses, professional expenses and travel, vacation and leave, pension, retirement, and other fringe benefits.[37] Where city ordinances provide that the chief serves at the pleasure of the mayor or city council, the candidate will not, of course, be able to secure tenure by contract. The few instances where the chief has been given reasonable job security typically involve an outsider candidate; the insiders usually have civil service protection of some sort. By contrast, it is not uncommon for city managers to have contracts of employment, and in that regard it is worth considering the recommendation that police chief independence be structured somewhat in the way a city manager's autonomy from partisan politics is structured.

Another matter that the realistic candidate has to be flexible about, within reason, is whether he has his own in-house news affairs office or handles media relations through the mayor's staff. In some cities, chiefs cannot make a speech or hold a press conference without calling city hall to get briefed by the mayor or the mayor's press person as to how to handle the situation. By contrast, the mayors of some of the smaller cities often complain at leadership institutes and other conferences that their chief is *reluctant* to talk to the media. That is not particularly surprising when one realizes that everything during the chief's police career has made him suspicious of the press and that, except in recent years, he probably has had no media relations training and little or no contact with the press on policy questions. Then there are large cities, like Minneapolis, where the mayor (Donald Fraser), although very competent, by nature is the quiet, retiring sort, and he has no problem with the chief (Tony Bouza) being out front all the time and saying flamboyant, insightful things in the media. The New York department has had its own press office for many years, so that was not much of an issue when I discussed my appointment with John Lindsay.

But where it is not clear who will handle the media, I think the chief candidate should attempt to negotiate. If the mayor says during the interview, "Look, I want the news. I want releases done through here, and I want inquiries to come through here," the applicant might respond: "Oh, is that what the *news media* expect too? Will they believe that I'm independent if I can't give an interview to one of them without saying, 'I have to call the mayor?' Will the media think I'm independent if they know, when they call the mayor, he'll tell me to give them an interview?" I think the argument the candidate needs to make is that, while arrangements should be devised to avoid substantially conflicting policy statements coming out of city hall and police headquarters, the department's image and the chief's image are very important, and the chief needs the capacity to get out the word and define the department's positions and seek citizen cooperation—all of which require that he have his own press office and not appear to be the mayor's puppet.

The mayor might say, "That's fine, except I can visualize an incident of one kind or another a few times a year where I'd like to be informed, where I'd like to know what you're planning to do." That would be fine. I think a chief can let the mayor know in advance so he doesn't hear a major story on the six o'clock news without any prior knowledge. There are ways to negotiate those arrangements and reach understandings so that if the matter to be announced is the kind of thing the mayor should know about—such as a major personnel change, a new policy on use of deadly force, a criminal investigation involving one of the mayor's staff, or long-awaited findings in a highly controversial disciplinary investigation—he is told perhaps 24 hours before releasing a statement or making an announcement. This helps the mayor because when reporters come to him it will not look like the chief is keeping him in the dark. Occasionally the chief saves himself some real headaches as well by alerting the mayor to impending announcements. For example, an outsider recently appointed as chief may learn, by virtue of sending a list of intended promotees to city hall, that his proposed deputy chief had a bloody battle with the mayor over some issue four years ago.

Yet another area that could be negotiated is the chief's role in municipal policymaking on subjects that are only indirectly related to law enforcement and order maintenance, such as zoning matters, the management of school integration, other educational issues, public health and welfare planning, traffic engineering, public works, and so forth. Chiefs could also be useful in designing buildings to improve their safety features. I think it is good practice for a mayor to have some input from the chief or one of his people early on during the planning phase on these kinds of issues.

Even on policymaking bearing directly on policing, the mayor has an appropriate role, and the prospective chief must be open to finding suitable arrangements. As an elected representative of the people, the mayor is responsible for the proper and efficient performance of the police department and has the right and the duty to oversee its policies and methods. (Although city managers are not elected officials, in my view they should be governed by the same principles as mayors because they function for the elected officials and are responsible for the performance of the police.) How much a mayor is involved in police policymaking may be determined by the size of the mayoral staff or the amount of staff time dedicated to police matters. Among the steps a mayor might properly take in performing his oversight function is the creation of a citizen committee to look into the department's conduct in some particularly controversial incident, such as a highly questionable shooting. This is not to invite city hall review in routine cases, but it is to acknowledge that sometimes the department makes mistakes in explaining its position or dealing with the community in other ways that can best be remedied by external oversight.

A final specific example of a negotiable issue might be the mayor's role in guiding the chief's deployment of personnel and organization of the agency. Ideally, the chief should retain complete control over the strategies, tactics, and management techniques for implementing the public's and the mayor's mandates concerning enforcement and service priorities. I could envision exceptions, however, such as where a senior citizens' group creates such a political clamor for establishment of a specialized departmental unit on crime against the elderly that the chief should yield to the mayor's intervention in organizational matters and create the unit. The chief should indicate to the mayor his strong feeling that in order to have credibility in directing and controlling the department he should have authority over organizational matters of that kind and should indicate that he is always happy to discuss the pros and cons of departmental reorganization but does not feel it should be imposed on the agency when he believes it would be a mistake. The chief should understand, of course, that it may be in the *department's* interest to create the unit so as to relieve the constant source of pressure from seniors and encourage them to be the allies of the police one would naturally expect them to be.

When mayoral pressure or intervention does impose a new bureau or division on the police department, however, it is essential that the personnel in the new unit report and answer to the chief, not, as occasionally happens, directly to the mayor. It may be tempting, especially for a new mayor, to place an informer or two inside the department to keep tabs on the chief's loyalty to city hall. But the mayor would be far wiser to find a way to assess the chief's performance that does not run the serious risk of undermining the chief's ability to perform well. The chief needs power not only to use himself but to delegate to his commanders so he can fairly hold them accountable for their subordinates' conduct.

City Councils

The legally defined roles of city councils are fairly consistent throughout the United States; namely, they act as the chief legislative and policymaking body. Through its ordinance power, subject to constitutional and statutory provisions, including the city charter, the council carries out its legislative function; when within its authority, its enactments have the force of law and are binding on both administration and electorate. In addition to legislative and policymaking functions, the council, in common with most legislative bodies, holds the purse strings and exercises control over appropriations.[38] Thus, the immediate impact of a council's actions on the operation of a law enforcement agency is considerable.

The record of involvement by council members and other elected officials in police operations to the detriment of both the efficiency and effectiveness of the police establishment is a well-established fact. One observer of this problem has noted that:

> Local political leaders frequently promote more abuses of police power than they deter. In seeking favored treatment for a violator of the law or in exerting pressure for police assistance in the sale of tickets to a fund-raising dinner, the politician only encourages the type of behavior he is supposed to prevent. Although such political interference into police work is not as extensive as it once was, it still exists.[39]

James F. Ahern, former chief of the New Haven, Connecticut, Police Department, discusses this issue at length in his book *Police in Trouble*. He describes as follows the extent to which political forces negatively affected the New Haven Police Department and the course of action he took to nullify them:

> There is nothing more degrading or demoralizing to a police department than the knowledge that every favor or promotion within it is controlled by hack politicians and outright criminals. And there is nothing more nearly universal. Five years ago, anyone with the most superficial knowledge of the workings of the New Haven Police Department could point to the political power behind every captain on the force. Every cop who wanted to get ahead had his "hook"—or, as they say in New York, his "rabbi." Everyone owed his success to a politician—from the Town Chairman on down—or to an influential underworld figure. Needless to say, in a situation like this there was no chance whatever of the department functioning in the public interest.
>
> A day after I had taken office, I closed the second-story back door to the Mayor's office and issued a renewal of a long-standing and long-ignored departmental order prohibiting any police officer from seeing the Mayor without the authorization of the chief.
>
> Given the incredible tangle of grimy politics that still existed in the lower levels of government and in the structures of the city's political parties, this action was largely symbolic. But as a gesture it was necessary. It would be immediately evident to everyone in the police department that if I would not permit the Mayor who had appointed me to influence departmental promotions or assignments, I certainly would allow no other politicians to influence them.
>
> Mayor Lee was aware of the connections between politics and police and was himself capable of intervening in the affairs of the police department to advance cops whom he considered honest and effective who otherwise would have been buried. Riding home with the Mayor in a car one day, I showed him a draft of my order. He frowned slightly, nodded, and then approved.
>
> But this order was only the opening shot in the war to end political interference in the police department. The far more substantive challenge was to make clear in every way possible, to every man in the department, that political influence of any kind was out. There was only one way to handle the problem, and it was somewhat heavy-handed. The men were made responsible for stopping interference themselves. They were warned that if politicians or underworld figures approached me with requests for promotions, transfers, or easy assignments for cops, the officers in question would be barred permanently from those positions.
>
> The immediate reaction among the cops was total incredulity. Political maneuvering had been the basis for advancement in the department for so long that it was doubtful whether they believed there was another way to be promoted. I would not be surprised if they thought that promotions in the department would freeze until I resigned or retired. But they did believe me. And they did convey the message to their hooks. For the time being, political interference in the department all but stopped.[40]

To suggest that the experience of New Haven is typical of most communities would be an inaccurate generalization, but there is little doubt that the council's fiscal control over the police department's budget and its legislative powers make it a political force that is never taken lightly by chiefs of police. As a matter of fact, most police chiefs will go to great lengths to maintain the goodwill and support of their council members.

State Prosecutor

The prosecutor, state's attorney, or district attorney is the chief law enforcement officer under the statutes of some states. However, despite this designation, the state prosecutor does not have overall responsibility for the supervision of the police.[41] Even so, the prosecutor's enforcement policies, procedures for review of all arrests before their presentation in court, and overall supervision of the cases prepared by the police do have an observable effect on police practices and enforcement policies. The initial contact of police officers with prosecutors occurs when the former brings a complaint to be charged. This encounter may be critical because it is an important point for making decisions about the disposition of the case and whether the complaint will be dismissed or reduced to a lesser offense. This discretionary power given the prosecuting attorney has tremendous influence on the ways and extent to which certain laws are enforced or ignored. Police chiefs who perceive that the prosecutor consistently reduces or fails to vigorously enforce certain types of violations may very likely divert their enforcement efforts and resources elsewhere. Then, again, some chiefs may decide to "go public" and try to mobilize community support for enforcing the ignored violations. However, few police chiefs take this course of action, because it could result in a serious deterioration in the working relationship with the local prosecutor, a situation most would prefer to avoid.

From the prosecutor's perspective, a cordial relationship with the police is also a desired condition. This is not, however, always possible. For example, suspicions of corruption or other illegal activity by officers from a local police department cannot be ignored by the prosecutor. When prosecutor-led investigations become public knowledge or lead to indictments, a prosecutor's rapport with the police can be severely strained, requiring years to recultivate. The resulting tension may become high if officers believe that the prosecutor is "sticking it to the police department by dragging the thing out" or by not allowing affected officers to plea bargain to lesser charges, or if the prosecutor is suspected of furthering his or her career at the officers' expense (see Box 2-3).

BOX 2-3

Santucci's Ties to Police Strained by Indicting of 5

By Dennis Hevesi

With the murder indictments of five police officers in the death of a suspect in their custody, the Queens District Attorney has once again jeopardized his rapport with the police.

BOX 2-3 (cont.)

And once again the District Attorney, John J. Santucci, finds himself in the spotlight—a glare that sometimes bares his sense of duty and just as often shines public and official scrutiny on his actions.

Mr. Santucci walked proudly alongside the New York City Police Department when his office successfully prosecuted the drug dealers who killed Officer Edward Byrne and the killers of Mildred Greene, a witness in a shooting case.

But he has also had occasion to anger police officers, particularly when he successfully prosecuted five officers three years ago in the stun-gun torturing of suspects at the 106th Precinct station house in Ozone Park.

'High' Feelings Acknowledged

"Right now, feelings are running high among members of the police force," Mr. Santucci said on Friday. "Unfortunately there will be some who, under a misguided sense of loyalty, will make life difficult for this office. But I believe the great majority of the city's policemen and women resent improper and abusive conduct."

At the age of 17, Mr. Santucci began his political career ringing doorbells to round up votes for President Harry S. Truman in Ozone Park.

Assessments of his role as District Attorney are widely divergent.

Mr. Santucci's critics, including judges, lawyers and former assistant district attorneys, have described him as a vindictive administrator who runs his office like a martinet.

Richard Emery, a civil-rights lawyer who was a member of Gov. Mario M. Cuomo's Commission on Integrity in Government, said, "I think he is a prosecutor who regrettably is motivated more by the moment than by principle."

But the 59-year-old politician also has his supporters, including Claire Shulman, the Queens Borough President, and Hyman Greenburg, a defense lawyer in Queens for 43 years.

'A Sensitive Guy'

"I have always liked John Santucci, in spite of the stuff in the press," Ms. Shulman said. "I've always found him a very caring, warm person. I think he's a sensitive guy, and I'm not sure he gets credit for that."

Mr. Greenberg said: "Mr. Santucci is one of the best district attorneys the county has ever had. He's upright, forceful and honest."

Mr. Santucci, who is married and has six children, is a graduate of St. John's University and law school. He became an assistant district attorney in 1958 and was named to the City Council in 1964. He became a State Senator in 1968 and was appointed Queens District Attorney in 1977 by Gov. Hugh L. Carey.

HIs career as District Attorney has not been without controversy.

Mr. Santucci had to defend a seven-hour luncheon in 1983 at which Salvatore Reale, an associate in the Gambino organized-crime family, was also present. The prosecutor said he had been unaware of Mr. Reale's organized-crime ties.

Mr. Santucci was also harshly criticized by some politicians for his prosecution—ultimately unsuccessful—of John Zaccaro, the husband of Geraldine Ferraro, the Democratic Vice-Presidential candidate in 1984. She was among those who complained that the District Attorney had pursued Mr. Zaccaro on extortion and bribery charges in 1987 to restore the prosecutor's image after he had failed to unearth corrupt activities by the Queens Borough President, Donald R. Manes.

Despite the controversies, Mr. Santucci—often described as quick-moving, quick-talking and always impeccably dressed—said he would leave the final assessment to the voters.

"Nobody's going to tell me when I'm through," he said in seeking a fourth term. "Only the public decides."

Source: New York Times, March 26, 1991, p. B4.

The Judiciary

Once the police have made an arrest and brought the arrestee before a judge, from pretrial release onward the case is within the domain of the judiciary (see Box 2-4). In its assessment of the relationships of the judiciary and the police, one governmental report noted that trial judges have acted as chief administrative officers of the criminal justice system, using their power to dismiss cases as a method of controlling the use of the criminal process. But, except in those rulings involving the admissibility of evidence, this has been done largely on an informal basis and has tended to be haphazard, often reflecting primarily the personal values of the individual trial judge.[42]

In contrast, the function of trial judges in excluding evidence that they determine to have been obtained illegally places them very explicitly in the role of controlling police practices. Trial judges have not viewed this role as making them responsible for developing appropriate police practices. However, many trial judges, when asked to explain their decisions, indicate that they have no more responsibility for explaining decisions to police than they have to private litigants.[43]

Occasionally, judges will grant motions to suppress evidence to dismiss cases that they feel should not be prosecuted because the violation is too minor or for some other reason. Use of a motion to suppress evidence in this manner serves to confuse the standards that are supposed to guide the police and has a disturbing, if not demoralizing, effect on them.[44]

If judges consistently interject their personal biases into the judicial process and make it very clear to police that they will dismiss certain categories of violations, the police may discontinue enforcing that particular law. This, in turn, may put the police on a collision course with certain segments of the community that favor the rigorous enforcement of those laws (see Box 2-4).

Skolnick, commenting on police-judiciary relationships, has noted that

> When an appellate court rules that police may not in the future engage in certain enforcement activities, since these constitute a violation of the rule of law, the inclination of the police is typically not to feel *shame* but *indignation*. This response may be especially characteristic of "professional" police, who feel a special competence to decide, on their own, how to reduce criminality in the community. The police, for example, recognize the court's power to bar admission of illegally seized evidence if the police are discovered to have violated the constitutional rights of the defendant. They do not, however, feel morally blameworthy in having done so; nor do they even accept such injunctions with good grace and go about their business. On the contrary, the police typically view the court with hostility for having interfered with their capacities to practice their craft. Police tend to rest their *moral* position on the argument that the "independence" and social distance of the appellate judiciary constitutes a type of government—by the courts—without the consent of the governed—the police. Thus, the police see the court's affirmation of principles of due process as, in effect, the creation of harsh "working conditions." From their point of view, the courts are failing to affirm democratic notions of the autonomy and freedom of the "worker." Their political superiors insist on "production" while their judicial superiors impede their capacity to "produce." Under such frustrating conditions, the appellate judiciary inevitably comes to be seen as "traitor" to its responsibility to keep the community free from criminality.

BOX 2-4

Police and Judges at Odds over Releases

By John Harris
American-Statesman Staff

After police arrested Steven Clark on the afternoon of October 18 on suspicion of cashing bad checks, an investigator planned to seek a warrant to search his car in hopes of recovering an estimated $51,000.

But when Sgt. Joel Thompson arrived at work the next morning, he found he had missed his chance by 35 minutes.

Clark, 29, of Austin, had been released on personal bond at 7:25 A.M. after Municipal Court Judge Nigel Gusdorf agreed the night before to release him to his attorney's custody, on the promise that he show up for arraignment later that morning.

He never showed up and has not been found. The money is missing, too.

Frustrated police say the release is the latest example of how municipal judges are too lenient in releasing suspects.

Gusdorf says there is nothing illegal or wrong with the practice, that jail officials tried to reach Thompson before personal bond was granted, and that some members of the Police Department are spreading incorrect information about court practices.

While some police officers occasionally "throw temper tantrums and act like little Saddam Husseins" over judges' actions, most officers recognize that the judges act within the law, Gusdorf said.

But similar disagreements between the judges and some police officers seem to arise every few months, signs of a lingering squabble that shows no signs of dissipating.

Part of the confusion stems from the Hobby rule, a local custom that allows people arrested for driving-while-intoxicated and misdemeanor cases to be released to their attorneys' custody overnight, if the person agrees to return to court the next morning to face charges.

Another agreement—between the Travis County Bar Association, the sheriff and the police chief—allows the jail to release inmates if no charges are filed within 24 hours of an arrest.

"The third situation is where a judge, obeying the law, has the right to (set) bail under the federal and state constitutions," Gusdorf said. That "is what happened in this case. That was me granting personal bond."

Thompson said he had planned to obtain a search warrant of Clark's car but was unable to do so after Clark was released. He had been arrested on suspicion of theft, forgery and evading detention after trying to escape from arresting officers.

"I don't know that I could have recovered the money, but I could at least have had the chance to," Thompson said. But the Travis County Central Booking Facility, where inmates usually are booked, "stays real full all the time, and they want us to process them as soon as possible."

Origins of Hobby rules

The Hobby rule got its name after the 1974 driving-while-intoxicated arrest of Lt. Gov. Bill Hobby. After Hobby was released to his attorney during the night, defense attorneys demanded their clients get the same treatment. The system was later broadened to include other non-violent misdemeanors.

But in another practice, sometimes called a "judge's Hobby," attorneys for persons accused of felonies seek personal bond from a judge, allowing their clients to be released with the understanding that they are to return the next morning for arraignment.

Gusdorf agreed that the term "Hobby" is often misunderstood and used loosely. Others say differences between the policies have grown too fuzzy.

"How do you grant personal bond when someone hasn't even been charged?" asked Senior Sgt. Sam Cox, president of the Austin Police Association. He said Clark's release shows the need for more consistency in court policies.

"We seem to be consistent in a lot of cases, but every month or two we seem to have cases that, wow, it defies common logic," Cox said. "If we have rules, we ought to stick with them."

The judges have cited a section of the Texas Code of Criminal Procedure that says a judge can assess a bail amount when a person is arrested, before a charge is filed.

But Assistant District Attorney Terry Keel said that particular statute "is just a rule of law that in determining the proper amount of bail to be set, the prisoner can ask the magistrate to look at all the available information."

"There is no interpretation of that article in the law anywhere that allows one to use that for the authority of what these municipal judges are doing, not in any way, shape or form," Keel said.

Good record for lawyer and client

Gusdorf said one reason he agreed to Clark's release on personal bond was that Clark's lawyer, Lowell Clayton, had a "perfect record" because his clients had always shown up for court the next day. Clark also had no prior criminal record, he said.

"We have to make about 4,000 bond decisions a month," Gusdorf said. "Of the municipal judges, I have the lowest bond forfeiture rate. If one of them fails to show, I'm not happy about it either.

"I did what I had to do under the law and made a judgment call," he said. "If something goes wrong, it's easy to play Monday-morning quarterback."

Betty Blackwell, vice chairwoman of the criminal law and procedures section of the county bar association, said she does not think people arrested in felony cases should be released to their attorneys as Clark was, but neither should they be placed in jail without charges being filed.

"My understanding was they were not to do that anymore," she said of Gusdorf's decision. But she said there was no formal agreement on the matter.

"I understand completely this officer's concern of people getting away and not getting to justice, but we also see regularly innocent people put in that horrible facility for 24 hours and not get released," she said.

Blackwell said part of the problem is that Austin patrol officers do not write affidavits showing probable cause for a person to be charged with a crime. That paperwork is written by sergeant-investigators.

Patrol officers could write the paperwork for approval by a judge, who then could set bail, Blackwell said. That would eliminate problems created when sergeant-investigators wait until the morning after a person is arrested to prepare charges, she said.

Gusdorf called the bail-setting procedure a "heavy responsibility" for a judge. "But you cannot have police officers leaning over judges and telling them what to do. That would be a police state."

Source: Austin American-Statesman (Texas), Nov. 11, 1990.

Antagonism between the police and the judiciary is perhaps an inevitable outcome, therefore, of the different interests residing in the police as a specialized agency and the judiciary as a representative of wider community interests. Constitutional guarantees of due process of law do make the working life and conditions of the police more difficult. But if such guarantees did not exist, the police would of course engage in activities promoting self-serving ends, as does any agency when offered such freedom in a situation of conflicting goals. Every administrative agency tends to support policies permitting it to present itself favorably. Regulative bodies restricting such policies are inevitably viewed with hostility by the regulated. Indeed, when some hostility does not exist, the regulators may be assumed to have been "captured" by the regulated. If the police could, in this sense, "capture" the judiciary, the resulting system would truly be suggestive of a "police state."[45]

Citizen Involvement

Citizen involvement in the policymaking process of law enforcement agencies is frequently met with considerable resistance from members of the law enforcement community. Many police administrators feel that their effectiveness rests on a high degree of autonomy. They view attempts to alter the way in which the law is enforced as efforts to negate the effectiveness of and to politicize the police. They argue further that during the last quarter-century law enforcement agencies have slowly but surely been successful in freeing themselves of partisan political interference and that public involvement by citizens will result in the police becoming instruments of pressure group politics and avowedly partisan to the most vocal and disruptive segments of society.[46]

One national commission took strong exception to this traditional posture of opposition to citizen involvement in the policymaking. The commission's argument was that

> In some areas of government activity, there is increasing utilization of citizen advisory committees as a way of involving members of the community in the policy making process. In some cases, the group may be advisory only, the governmental agency being free to accept or reject its advice. In other instances, the group is official and policies are cleared through the committee as a regular part of the policy making process. The advantages of both methods are that they serve as an inducement for the police administrator to articulate important policies, to formulate them, and to subject them to discussion in the advisory group. How effective this is depends upon the willingness of the group and the police administrator to confront the basic law enforcement policy issues rather than being preoccupied with the much easier questions of the mechanics of running the department. Where there is a commitment to exploring basic enforcement policy questions, the citizens' advisory group or policy making board has the advantage of involving the community in the decision making process, thus giving a broader base than would otherwise exist for the acceptance and support of enforcement policies.[47]

Citizen groups are varied, and they have different interests in police service. Chambers of commerce and service clubs generally promote police professionalism out of civic pride. Churches and church groups have historically campaigned against vice and corruption and for civil liberties and police–community relations (see Box 2-5).[48]

Box 2-5

Blacks Tell Council of Police Fear

By Richard Green
The Cincinnati Enquirer

About 300 black citizens—many representing civic, church and community organizations—crowded into City Hall on Wednesday, to demand that council act to defuse tension between police and city residents.

"We want a peaceful city," said Frank Allison, president of the local chapter of the National Association for the Advancement of Colored People. "But police must be accountable."

If they are not, "young people will be fighting the police," Allison said. "Racism is alive in Cincinnati as much as it is in Tupelo, Miss."

The Rev. Donald Tye Jr., an associate pastor of the Tabernacle Baptist Church in Lincoln Heights, said: "Taxpayers are sick and tired of the arrogance of officers. If these bad feelings persist, there will be violence and blood on city streets."

The community leaders came to council chambers in response to last week's appearance of nearly 300 officers before council.

The police were protesting City Manager Gerald Newfarmer's ruling that Officer Bruce Hoffbauer used excessive force when he fatally shot a charging, unarmed man, Walter Brown of Corryville, in a hallway outside Brown's apartment Dec. 28. Hoffbauer is white; Brown was black.

In the emotional and often heated 90-minute session Wednesday, black leaders vented their concerns and recommendations. They seek:

- The firing of Hoffbauer.
- More staff and support going for the city's Office of Municipal Investigation, a civilian investigative unit that probes alleged wrongdoing of all city departments, including the police force.
- A crackdown on police brutality.

The request that drew a standing ovation from the audience was made by Theodore M. Berry, Cincinnati's mayor from 1972–1975 and its first black mayor.

He urged council to pass a charter amendment—which must be placed before voters—giving the city manager greater authority to hire and fire the police chief, whose job is now protected by the city's civil service rules.

"The buck stops with you," Berry told council members.

Resolving the questions about the Cincinnati Police Division should be council's direct responsibility, he said.

"The president of the United States is the commander in chief of the armed forces, and he removes officers in the field when they do not perform," Berry said. "The chief operating officer of this city should be able to do the same."

After his speech, Berry said he thought council would be "reluctant" to pass such a motion in an election year.

"I haven't approached any of them individually about it," Berry said. "I just put it out there today in the arena where it needs to be done. Council is where this problem is going to have to be resolved."

Councilman Tyrone Yates—like Berry, a Charterite—said he would introduce such a motion within the next week. It would need the votes of six council members to be placed on the ballot.

While the citizens who came to the council meeting criticized Police Chief Lawrence Whalen directly, several blasted the police division.

"We do not advocate disrespect," said the Rev. Fred Shuttlesworth. "But we must demand the respect of those who are in control. And people are about ready to get back in the streets" to get that respect.

Mayor David Mann said council's Law and Safety Committee next week will begin looking into the issues raised at Wednesday's meeting.

"What we're talking about is dealing with a few bad apples," Mann said.

Source: Cincinnati Enquirer (Ohio), March 21, 1991.

Chambers of Commerce and Service Clubs

Local chambers of commerce and service clubs typically are supportive of efforts that lead toward efficient and clean government. Although such groups are characterized as being apolitical, they can exercise considerable influence. Their support for improving the quality of law enforcement in the community is frequently heard in the chambers of city hall and is demonstrated through various community projects intended to assist local law enforcement. Attuned police chiefs realize the benefit to be gained from the support of such groups, encourage personnel to become active members in these clubs, and frequently join one or two themselves. Support from these groups is not surprising when one considers that they arefrequently comprised of men and women from the middle class who are well educated and deeply involved in many aspects of community leadership. Such groups often have mobilized behind a police chief to get much-needed budget increases for salaries, additional personnel, and equipment.

Churches

The religious leaders and congregation members of a community's church groups represent one of the most potentially powerful pressure groups in the community. Their influence can, and frequently does, extend into the voting booth, which assures a high degree of responsiveness from local elected officials. Church leaders and their congregations almost always find an open door and a receptive ear at the office of their local police chief when they present their concerns. The problems that are frequently of greatest concern to such groups are vice related, such as prostitution, massage parlors, X-rated theaters, and adult bookstores. It is true that individual communities do impose different standards and have varying levels of tolerance, but, if the church leaders of a community mobilize and call on their police chief to eradicate or reduce what they perceive to be a serious problem, there is a high probability that they will receive some positive response. And, if the police chief suggests that the police department cannot cope realistically with the problem because of limited personnel and resources, these very same church groups will likely begin applying pressure on the city officials to give the police chief the needed resources. Thus, the religious leaders of the community can be powerful allies of the police chief in certain types of enforcement efforts. On the other hand, this same pressure group may force the chief to redirect resources away from areas that may have a higher priority.

News Media

It is the responsibility of the police department and especially its top leadership to establish and maintain a cordial association with all media representatives.[49] Both the electronic and the print news media can be a powerful friend or a devastating antagonist of a local police department, and to a great extent this will be determined by the attitudes, policies, and working relationships among the editors, news directors, and police chief. When friction does occur between the police and the news media, as it invariably does in every community, it frequently emanates from the events surrounding a major crime or an unusual occurrence.

Often in the case of major crimes or incidents, police departments do not want to release information that will jeopardize the safety of the public or its officers, impair the right of a suspect to a fair and impartial trial, or impede the progress of an investigation. On the other hand, the news media have a different orientation and duty: to inform the public. Although their goals are often compatible, the police and the news media frequently disagree irreconcilably:

FIGURE 2-1. The media hover while members of the Los Angeles Police Department Swat Team prepare for action as a suspected gunman emerges from cover. [Courtesy of *Police,* April 1988. Photograph by Mike Mullin.]

> In 1990, Mehrdad Dashti took 33 people hostage in a hotel bar in Berkeley, California. Dashti shot eight of his hostages, killing one of them. Police and television crews responded to the scene. Even though it was known that there was a television set in the bar on which Dashti could watch, one television station reported what the police were doing outside, including telling that an assault team had moved into position. At another time, a male hostage was shown shouting from the bar that he was about to be executed; he disappeared from the scene and a shot was heard. At the time no one knew that the bullet had missed or that the father was tuned to the station and left in turmoil. Police finally killed Dashti and freed the captives. And, the debate about real-time journalistics disclosures about sensitive police operations was on. Could not some information be held back by the news media without damage to journalistic ethics? In exercising their First Amendment rights should reporters make disclosures that could have cost the hostages their lives or needlessly endangered police officers committed to their rescue? A panel of police officials, journalists, and others discussed these and related issues at Columbia University without reaching any meeting of the minds, although television executives made a promise to "review their procedures."[50]

Another situation in which the police and other officials may be in conflict with the news media occurs when journalists uncover information that is of actual investigative or legal significance and, if police investigators, prosecuting attorneys, or defense attorneys want to confirm the information, decline to divulge from whom or how they got the information on the basis of protecting their sources. The argument of the news media is that failing to protect their sources could result in reduced information flowing to them, thus jeopardizing the public's right to know. However, a reporter's First Amendment right to protect sources is not absolute. Recognizing this, some states have enacted so-called shield laws. For both First Amendment rights and shield laws, the courts apply a "balancing test" to determine whether reporters can be required to release the identities of their sources: is there a compelling need for the information, that is, is the defendant's need for the information to make an effective defense greater than the need of a reporter to protect the identity of a source? These and related issues are framed in Box 2-6, "Law-and-Ethics Conflict Traps Karem."

Other circumstances for potential tension or conflict in police–news media relationships include "off-the-record" police information appearing in the news media; the occasional claim by a police administrator that he or she was misquoted; and the involvement of press at the scenes of bank robberies, gangland killings, and hostage situations, as well as in the sensitive investigations of kidnappings and drug rings. From a legal standpoint, the police may release relevant information about a defendant if it is not prejudicial to the defendant's right to a fair trial. Many police departments have policies that protect the defendant's rights, but those policies may obstruct the needs of reporters to gather images and information for the public. For example, with respect to pretrial suspects, Kentucky State Police policy prohibits personnel from

1. Requiring the suspect to pose for photographers
2. Reenacting the crime
3. Disclosing that the suspect told where weapons, the proceeds of a crime, or other materials were located
4. Referring to the suspect as a "depraved character," "a real no-good," "a sexual monster," or by similar terms
5. Revealing that the suspect declined to take certain types of tests or that the suspect did take certain tests, for example, a blood alcohol test to determine the degree, if any, to which the suspect was under the influence of drugs or alcohol
6. Telling the press the results of any tests to which the suspect submitted
7. Making statements as to the guilt or innocence of a suspect
8. Releasing the identities of prospective witnesses or commenting on the nature of their anticipated testimony or credibility
9. Making statements of a purely speculative nature about any aspect of the case.[51]

Despite all potential and actual conflicting interests, the fact is that both the police and the news media have profoundly important duties in a free society. In the course of day-to-day activities, people of considerable conscience in both professions go about their jobs peacefully; police–news media clashes are atypical situations. Certainly, if the local news media believe that the police are being arbitrary, high handed, uncooperative, or worst of all, untruthful, then their news stories will reflect that dissatisfaction. Moreover, their coverage may even accentuate negative stories. For example, the dismissal of a felony charge because of insufficient evidence may lead to headlines such as "Shoddy Police Work Lets Burglar Go Free" as opposed to "Attorney Successfully Defends Local Man." Another consequence of a strained relationship with the news media could be minor or no coverage of favorable stories about the police, such as an awards ceremony. Thus, police administrators should exert a great deal of effort in seeing that all personnel understand the role of the press, that the applicable police department policies are current, that those policies are followed, and that open lines of communication with the news media are maintained.

BOX 2-6

Law-and-Ethics Conflict Traps Karem

By Edward M. Sills
Staff reporter

Television reporter Brian Karem holds a unique status as he sits in the overcrowded Bexar County Jail among low-grade misdemeanants, drug users, robbers, rapists and murderers.

Unlike his fellow inmates, Karem continues to draw a paycheck for doing his job. He has no scheduled release date, facing renewable six-month terms in jail unless he agrees to turn over his notes and testify as to who arranged his exclusive jailhouse interview with an alleged police killer.

Karem's attorney says that he is "the high man on the totem pole" among wrongdoers at the jail. Attorney Larry Macon said that because Karem willfully violated a court order, he would be the last inmate to leave under early release or any other crowding-relief program.

But Karem's refusal to divulge his sources has focused attention on a clash of journalistic ethics and the law: What happens when a confidential relationship with a source runs up against a court's need for information?

The case has been chronicled in newspapers throughout the country and on Friday night was examined before the nation in a news broadcast on ABC television's Nightline.

Although reporters are ordered to turn over materials fairly often—one media representative says at least six such cases are pending in Texas now—Karem is the first journalist since 1978 to face a lengthy jail term for protecting a source. A New York Times reporter spent 40 days in a New Jersey jail for refusing to release information about his probe of a doctor in that state, later acquitted, who had allegedly killed patients.

A quick review of the facts involving Karem: A San Antonio police officer was gunned down and two brothers were arrested. Through undetermined means, Karem obtained a jail interview with one of the brothers, who said on KMOL-TV that he shot the officer in self-defense.

Prosecutors and defense attorneys for each of the brothers demanded to know who set up the interview for Karem. If jail officials were involved, it is possible the potentially damning admission would not become evidence in the trial. The courts ordered Karem to give up his notes and the names of the sources and he refused, leading to his jailing.

Karem's ethical duties are clear. Journalists have an obligation to report their sources of information when possible. But some newsworthy information—often, the juiciest news—can only be reported by offering a promise of anonymity to the source or, as in Karem's case, to a conduit.

For a reporter, protecting the identity of a confidential source is sacrosanct. Giving away a source could dry up future information, not only for a reporter but for an entire news organization.

"Anyone within our organization would say he's doing the right thing," said Ira Perry, assistant metropolitan editor of the Houston Post and chairman of Texas Media, a coalition of news groups. "If sources can't be protected, they're not going to talk to you."

Jane Kirtley, executive director of the Reporters Committee for Freedom of the Press in Washington, said, "The way around the problem is never to use confidential sources. If we do that, we might as well close down shop. The problem is prosecutors, defense lawyers and litigants in civil cases see journalists as being their investigative arm."

Perry, who himself is facing a potential contempt order for refusing to turn over to a federal court tapes of interviews he did concerning possible civil rights violations by Houston police, said of Karem's case, "There are other ways to get the same information. If they want to know who arranged the interview, they can put all the possible candidates on the witness stand. This is a fishing expedition."

(continued on next page)

BOX 2-6 (cont.)

Bexar County Sheriff Harlon Copeland said Thursday that after his own investigation, using confidential sources of his own, he now knows the names of all Karem's sources.

But Beth Taylor, the prosecutor in the capital murder case, said that only Karem can confirm who the sources were.

Karem's legal duties are also fairly clear, but what the law should be has been hotly debated. A 5–4 majority of the U.S. Supreme Court found in Branzburg vs. Hayes, a 1972 case, that reporters do not have a constitutional right to refuse to testify about violations of law that they witness.

Since then, some courts have suggested that reporters may have a limited First Amendment right to refuse to testify about confidential sources, but the right must be balanced against a criminal defendant's right to a fair trial under the Sixth Amendment.

Some judges and media groups have proposed using a three-part test suggested in the Branzburg minority opinion:

- Whether the reporter has information that is clearly relevant to a probable violation of law
- Whether the information can be obtained by alternative means
- Whether there is a compelling and overriding interest in obtaining the information.

Bexar County State District Judge Pat Priest, without using an elaborate balancing test, found Karem's rights to be outweighed by fair-trial rights. So far, a federal magistrate and district judge have agreed, and the case is pending before the 5th U.S. Circuit Court of Appeals. The U.S. Supreme Court has so far refused to get involved.

Macon said Karem's information is not relevant to the murder case.

"Initially, the public's reaction is this guy is holding back information that's stopping the trial of an alleged cop-killer," Macon said. "But I think when all the facts are explained to them, they realize that there has been no balancing of rights."

Those on the other side of the issue say a reporter's First Amendment rights to protect sources are not absolute.

"The law doesn't always protect ethical principles, so you may have to go to jail for upholding them," said Mark Stevens, the defense lawyer for the brother whom Karem interviewed.

Stevens, who has defended the First Amendment rights of numerous clients, said he, too, has an ethical obligation—to represent his client to the best of his ability.

Taylor said she does not see a reason to place Karem in a different position from any other citizen who has information relevant to a case.

"We're talking about somebody who interviewed a defendant, in custody, who has been indicted on a charge of capital murder," Taylor said. "He's gotten the glory of having an exclusive interview and now doesn't want to take the consequences."

Taylor said she could prosecute without using the interview, but has an ethical duty as a prosecutor to press for all relevant information on the crime.

One potential response to recurring Karem-like cases would be a Texas "shield-law" that would protect reporters from being compelled to reveal confidential sources.

San Antonio state Sen. Frank Tejeda sponsored a shield law when Karem was first arrested in 1989, and says he had a commitment from virtually the entire Senate to pass the measure. But Tejeda backed away after several media organizations told him of sharp disagreements within the journalism industry on the need for shield laws.

Macon said a shield law would be "vital to the press. Without protection of sources, there never would have been Watergate."

But some media groups see shield laws as dangerously resting on the premise that legislators need to grant reporters rights to protect sources because the First Amendment does not do so.

"What the Legislature gives one session they can take away the next session if you haven't been good," Kirtley said.

Stevens said he does not believe a shield law would have helped Karem, because the Sixth Amendment rights of his client would have overridden any law approved by the Legislature.

Source: San Antonio Light (Texas), July 8, 1990.

FIGURE 2-2. Public information officer being interviewed by a member of the media. [Courtesy of Scott Boatright, Fairfax County, Virginia Police Department.]

Summary

Police departments, like all administrative agencies, do not operate independently of external controls. Federal, state, and local governmental controls and influences are, in most instances, both legal and proper. The extent to which they impact on a law enforcement agency depends in part on national events and the unique political characteristics of each community.

This chapter has not identified all the possible external sources of influence and control that could affect law enforcement agencies. Instead, it has identified the most common and most influential to law enforcement agencies, categorizing them according to federal, state, or local origin. For example, the impact of decisions by the U.S. Supreme Court and local law enforcement is indisputable. Four of the most important decisions, *Mapp* v. *Ohio* (1961), *Gideon* v. *Wainright* (1963), *Escobedo* v. *Illinois* (1964), and *Miranda* v. *Arizona* (1966), have profoundly altered the police practices regarding search and seizure and interrogation. In more recent years, appointments to the Supreme Court by Presidents Ronald Reagan and George Bush have provided a conservative majority whose decisions have been favorable to law enforcement. Thus, although there may be some dispute as to whether such decisions are "good" or "bad," there is little argument that such decisions deeply affect operations of police departments at all levels of government.

Few would argue with the fact that dramatic changes have occurred in personnel practices in law enforcement agencies as a result of the Equal Employment Opportunity Act of 1972. The 1990 Americans with Disabilities Act (ADA) also will have a profound effect on personnel practices of local police departments in the future. Because federal influence and controls have been considerable, the examples provided in this chapter are not intended to be all encompassing but rather to illustrate their reach.

Even agencies without specific governmental connection can exert tremendous influence over the operations and professional image of local police departments. For example, the Commission on Accreditation for Law Enforcement Agencies (CALEA), a private nonprofit organization formed in 1979, has improved both the operations and the images of local police departments by providing the opportunity for them to become accredited and, thereby, to enjoy considerable professional status both in their local communities and at the national level with other law enforcement agencies.

The impact exerted on law enforcement by the state has increased dramatically since the 1970s, primarily via legislation that imposes pre-employment and training standards on local police agencies. Further state intervention is not expected, except in those extraordinary cases involving rampant malfeasance, misfeasance, or nonfeasance.

The greatest control of the day-to-day operations of a police department emanates from the local level but is strongly affected by the local dominant values and political culture.

Two of the principle government actors exerting influence and control over law enforcement agencies will be the mayor in a strong mayor form of government and the city manager. Because the strong mayor and city manager have hiring and firing authority over the police chief, they can, if they choose, exert considerable control and influence over that office. However, there is little evidence that any particular form of government necessarily provides greater job security to the police chief than another. There is, however, considerable evidence to suggest that police executives who lack protection from arbitrary and unjustified removal have difficulty in fulfilling their responsibilities objectively and independently. Some states have systems offering statutory protection to police chiefs, but most do not. In states that do not provide protection, police chiefs across the country are forced to look for job protection in local civil service codes, local municipal ordinances, and any individual employment contracts they are able to negotiate. Thus, although occupying highly sensitive positions that require insulation from the political process, most police chiefs have limited job protection.

The influence of city council members is somewhat less direct than that of a strong mayor and city manager, but they can be equally formidable as they control the appropriations for the law enforcement agencies. The local prosecutor can also exert considerable influence and control on the law enforcement agency because of the ultimate authority to review all arrests before their presentation in court and overall supervision of cases prepared by the police. Police chiefs who perceive that the prosecutor consistently reduces or fails to enforce certain types of violations may direct their enforcement efforts and resources elsewhere.

Similarly, police operations and enforcement efforts may be influenced by the decisions of local judges. For example, if judges consistently interject their personal biases into the judicial process and make it clear to police that they will dismiss certain categories of violations, the police may discontinue enforcing that particular law.

Discussion Questions

1. How do the authors differentiate between "Politics" and "politics"?
2. In general, public organizations and private organizations can be differentiated on the basis of which points?
3. What was the significance of the U.S. Supreme Court decision on *Mapp* v. *Ohio* (1966), *Gideon* v. *Wainright* (1963), *Escobedo* v. *Illinois* (1964), and *Miranda* v. *Arizona* (1966)?

4. Which decisions made by the Supreme Court in 1991 indicate a greater willingness to rule in favor of law enforcement?
5. What was one of the major functions of the Law Enforcement Assistance Administration (LEAA)?
6. What are the major components of the Civil Rights Act of 1964 and Equal Employment Opportunity Act of 1972?
7. Why did the Congress enact the Americans with Disabilities Act (ADA)?
8. Although the actual impact of the ADA legislation on law enforcement is unknown, several predictions about its future are warranted. Which are made by the authors?
9. Which four national law enforcement associations are credited with developing the Commission on Accreditation for Law Enforcement Agencies (COLEA)?
10. What three styles of law enforcement were described by James Q. Wilson and what are their major features?
11. How are police chiefs selected under the strong mayor and the city manager forms of government?
12. What types of statutory protections are provided to police chiefs in the United States?
13. What are the legally defined roles of city councils in most cities in the United States?

Notes

1. W. H. Hudnut III, "The Police and the Polis: A Mayor's Perspective," in *Police Leadership in America: Crisis and Opportunity,* ed. William A. Geller (Westport, Conn.: Praeger, 1985), p. 20.
2. These are, of course, quasi-private organizations, such as those in the aerospace industry that depend heavily on government contracts and are subject to considerable control.
3. Robert M. Fogelson, *Big-City Police* (Cambridge, Mass.: Harvard University Press, 1975) pp. 9–10.
4. Ibid. p. 199.
5. A. E. Bent, *The Politics of Law Enforcement* (Lexington, Mass.: D. C. Heath, 1974), p. 63.
6. N. G. Holten and M. E. Jones, *The Systems of Criminal Justice* (Boston: Little, Brown, 1978), p. 416.
7. Treatment of the Supreme Court's influence has been drawn from Thomas Phelps, Charles Swanson, and Kenneth Evans, *Introduction to Criminal Justice* (Santa Monica, Calif.: Goodyear Publishing, 1979), pp. 128–31.
8. In a legal sense, the Supreme Court opted for a piecemeal application when it rejected the "shorthand doctrine" (i.e., making a blanket application of the Federal Bill of Rights provisions binding on the states) in its consideration of *Hurtado* v. *California,* 110 U.S. 516 (1884); therefore, the statement should be read in the context that the activist role was a policy decision.
9. Fred P. Graham, *The Self-Inflicted Wound* (New York: Macmillan, 1970), p. 37. For a look at the police and due process, see A. T. Quick, "Attitudinal Aspects of Police Compliance with Procedural Due Process," *American Journal of Criminal Law,* 6 (1978), pp. 25–56.
10. T. R. Dye, *Politics in States and Communities* (Englewood Cliffs, N.J.: 1973), p. 214.
11. No author, "Supreme Court on Police Powers," *Law Enforcement News,* 17:338, 339 (June 15/30, 1991), pp. 1, 9, 10.
12. Holten and Jones, *Systems of Criminal Justice,* p. 417.

13. Dye, *Politics in States,* p. 219.
14. Holten and Jones, *Systems of Criminal Justice,* pp. 418, 419.
15. L. Territo, C. R. Swanson, and N. C. Chamelin, *The Police Personnel Selection Process* (Indianapolis, Ind.: Bobbs-Merrill, 1977), p. 22.
16. PL 92-261 Section 703(s)(1)(2).
17. *Ibid.*
18. *Ibid.*
19. Equal Employment Opportunity Guidelines, Part 1607.
20. Commission on Accreditation for Law Enforcement Agencies (CALEA) *Accreditation Program Overview* (Fairfax, Va.: CALEA, 1990), p. 4.
21. Gary W. Cordner, "Written Rules and Regulations: Are They Necessary?" *FBI Law Enforcement Bulletin* Vol 58, No. 7, p. 18.
22. Russell Maas, "Written Rules and Regulations: Is the Fear Real?" *Law and Order* (May 1990), p. 36.
23. Gerald Williams, *Making the Grade: The Benefits of Law Enforcement Accreditation* (Washington, D.C.: Police Executive Research Forum, 1989), pp. xv and xvii.
24. *Ibid.,* pp. xv and xvii.
25. *Ibid.,* pp. xvii and xviii.
26. Fogelson, *Big-City Police,* pp. 14, 15.
27. *Ibid.,* p. 14.
28. Information provided by the National Association of State Directors of Law Enforcement Training.
29. The National Advisory Commission on Criminal Justice Standards and Goals, *A National Strategy to Reduce Crime* (Washington, D.C.: U.S. Government Printing Office, 1972), p. 149.
30. James Q. Wilson, *Varieties of Police Behavior* (New York: Atheneum, 1973).
31. The President's Commission on Law Enforcement and Administration of Justice, *Task Force Report: The Police* (Washington, D.C.: U.S. Government Printing Office, 1967), p. 127.
32. A. H. Andrews, Jr., "Structuring the Political Independence of the Police Chief," in *Police Leadership in America,* ed. Geller, pp. 9, 10.
33. V. A. Leonard and H. W. Moore, *Police Organization and Management* (Mineola, N.Y.: Foundation Press, 1971), p. 21.
34. J. J. Norton and G. G. Cowart, "Assaulting the Politics/Administration Dichotomy," *Police Chief,* 45:11 (1978), p. 26.
35. Janet Ferris et al., "Present and Potential Legal Job Protections Available to Heads of Agencies," *Florida Police Chief* (Vol. 14, No. 5), pp. 43–45.
36. P. V. Murphy, "The Prospective Chief's Negotiation of Authority with the Mayor," *Police Leadership in America,* ed. Geller, pp. 31–38.
37. M. J. Kelley, "Police Chief Selection: A Handbook for Local Government," *Police Foundation* (Washington, D.C.: 1975), p. 50.
38. G. E. Berkeley et al., *Introduction to Criminal Justice* (Boston: Holbrook Press, 1976), p. 216.
39. Leonard and Moore, *Police Organization and Management,* p. 15.
40. J. F. Ahern, *Police in Trouble* (New York: Hawthorn Books, 1972), pp. 96–98.
41. The President's Commission, *Task Force Report: The Police,* p. 30.
42. *Ibid.,* p. 31.
43. *Ibid.,* p. 31.
44. *Ibid.,* p. 31.
45. J. H. Skolnick, *Justice Without Trial: Law Enforcement in a Democratic Society* (New York: John Wiley & Sons, 1966), pp. 228–29.
46. H. W. More, Jr., ed., *Critical Issues in Law Enforcement* (Cincinnati, Ohio: Anderson, 1972), p. 261.

47. The President's Commission, *Task Force Report: The Police,* p. 34.
48. Bent, *Politics of Law Enforcement,* p. 72.
49. E. M. Davis, "Press Relations Guide for Peace Officers," *Police Chief,* 39:3 (1972), p. 67.
50. Walter Goodman, "How Much Should TV Tell, and When?" *New York Times,* Oct. 29, 1990.
51. See General Order OM-F-4, "Release of Information to the News Media" issued by the Kentucky State Police, January 1, 1990.

3 Organizational Theory

Theory and practice are inseparable.
Douglas McGregor

Introduction

Formal organizations can scarcely be conceived of as a recent innovation.[1] Alexander the Great and Caesar used them to conquer; the pharaohs employed them to build pyramids; the emperors of China constructed great irrigation systems with them; and the first popes created an organization to deliver religion on a worldwide basis.[2] The extent to which contemporary America is an organizational society is such that:

> We are born in organizations, educated by organizations, and spend most of our lives working for organizations. We spend much of our time . . . playing and praying in organizations. Most of us will die in an organization and when the time comes for burial, the largest organization of all—the state—must grant official permission.[3]

The basic rationale for the existence of organizations is that they do those things that people are unwilling or unable to do alone. Parsons notes that organizations are distinguished from other human groupings or social units in that to a much greater degree they are constructed and reconstructed to achieve specific goals; corporations, armies, hospitals, and police departments are included within this meaning, whereas families and friendship groups are not.[4] Schein defines an organization as:

> the rational coordination of the activities of a number of people for the achievement of some common explicit purpose or goal, through division of labor and function, and through a hierarchy of authority and responsibility.[5]

Blau and Scott identify four different types of formal organizations by asking the question of *cui bono* or who benefits: (1) mutual benefit associations, such as police labor unions, where the primary beneficiary is the membership; (2) business concerns, such as International Business Machines, where the owners are the prime beneficiary; (3) service organizations, such as community mental health centers, where a specific client group is the prime beneficiary; and (4) commonweal organizations, such as the Department of Defense and police departments, where the beneficiary is the public at large.[6]

These four types of formal organizations each has its own central issues.[7] Mutual benefit associations, such as police unions, face the crucial problem of maintaining the internal democratic processes—providing for participation and control by their membership. For businesses, the central issue is maximizing profits in a competitive environment. Service organizations are faced with the conflict between administrative regulations and providing the services judged by the professional to be most appropriate. In the case of a community mental health center, an illustration is that, following a reduction in funding, a regulation is placed into effect that requires all clients to be treated in group sessions when the psychiatric social worker believes the only effective treatment for a particular client is to be seen individually. The core reason that police managers must have a working knowledge of organizational theory stems from the fact that police departments are commonweal organizations.

The key issue for a police department and other types of commonweal organizations is finding a way to accommodate pressures from two different sources, external and internal. The public, through its elected and appointed representatives, must and does have the means of controlling the ends served by its police department. This external democratic control feature also has the expectation that the internal workings of the police department will be bureaucratic, governed by the criterion of efficiency, and not also democratic. This is because democratic control by the members of a police department might be at the expense of lessening the police department's ability to affect the will of the community. Simultaneously, the large numbers of officers at the lower levels of the police department do not want to be treated like "cogs in a machine" and desire some voice in how the department operates. Thus, the challenge for police managers is how to maintain an organization that meets society's needs and the needs of the officers who work in it. This requires an understanding of such things as the different ways there are of organizing and the contrasting assumptions that various organizational forms make about the nature of people. Such knowledge is found within organizational theory.

This chapter consists of three major areas; each deals with different ways of thinking about how to organize work and work processes. Discussed more fully as they arise, the three major streams of thinking about work structures and processes to be treated are: (1) traditional organizational theory, upon which most police departments are based; (2) open systems theory, which represents a direct counterpoint to traditional theory; and (3) bridging theories, which to some greater or lesser degree show concern for the issues reflected both in traditional and open systems theories. Bridging theories do not fall neatly into either the traditional or the open systems category, yet reflect consideration of each, thus constituting a distinctly unique category. Within each of the three major streams of thinking about work structures and processes there are illustrations of some of the specific techniques associated with various theorists as well as examples that are cast in a police context.

Traditional Organizational Theory

Traditional theory is associated with organizations described as mechanistic, closed systems, bureaucratic, and stable. This body of knowledge evolved over centuries and crystallized between 1900 and 1940. The three stems of traditional organizational theory are (1) scientific management, (2) the bureaucratic model, and (3) administrative or management theory.

Taylor: Scientific Management

The father of scientific management was Frederick W. Taylor (1856–1915), and the thrust of his thinking was to to find the "one best way" to do work. In addition to its being a theory of work organization, Taylor's scientific management is a theory of motivation in its belief that employees will be guided in their actions by what is in their economic self-interest.

A Pennsylvanian born of Quaker-Puritan parents, Taylor was so discontent with the "evils" of waste and slothfulness that he applied the same careful analysis to finding the best way of playing croquet and of taking a cross-country walk with the least fatigue that was to be the hallmark of his later work in factories.[8] From

Frederick W. Taylor. (Courtesy of the Library of Congress.)

1878 to 1890, Taylor worked at the Midvale Steel Company in Philadelphia, rising from the ranks of the laborers to chief engineer in just six years.[9] Taylor's experience at Midvale gave him insight into the twin problems of productivity and worker motivation. He saw workers as deliberately restricting productivity by "natural soldiering" and "systematic soldiering."

Natural soldiering came from the natural inclination of employees not to push themselves; systematic soldiering came from workers not wanting to produce so much as to see their quotas raised or other workers thrown out of their jobs.[10] To correct these deficiencies, Taylor called for a "complete mental revolution"[11] on the part of both workers and managers, although it seems certain that he faulted management more for its failure to design jobs properly and to give workers the proper economic incentives to overcome soldiering than he did workers for not producing.[12]

Taylor's scientific management is only loosely a theory of organization because its focus was largely upon work at the bottom part of the organization rather than being a general model. Scientific management's method was to find the most physically and time efficient way to sequence tasks and then to use rigorous and extensive controls to enforce the standards.

Taylor's conversation with "Schmidt" illustrates this:

> "Schmidt, are you a high-priced man?"
>
> "Vell, I don't know vat you mean."
>
> "Oh yes, you do. What I want to know is whether you are a high-priced man or not."
>
> "Vell, I don't know vat you mean."
>
> "Oh, come now, you answer my questions. What I want to find out is whether you are a high-priced man or one of these cheap fellows here. What I want to find out is whether you want to earn $1.85 a day or whether you are satisfied with $1.15, just the same as all those cheap fellows are getting."
>
> "Did I vant $1.85 a day? Vas dot a high-priced man? Vell, yes, I vas a high-priced man."
>
> "Oh, you're aggravating me. Of course you want $1.85 a day—every one wants it! You know perfectly well that that has very little to do with your being a high-priced man. For goodness sake answer my questions, and don't waste any more of my time. Now come over here. You see that pile of pig iron?"
>
> "Yes."
>
> "You see that car?"
>
> "Yes."
>
> "Well, if you are a high-priced man, you will load that pig iron on that car tomorrow for $1.85. Now do wake up and answer my question. Tell me whether you are a high-priced man or not."
>
> "Vell—did I got $1.85 for loading dot pig iron on dot car tomorrow?"
>
> "Yes, of course you do, and you get $1.85 for loading a pile like that every day right through the year. That is what a high-priced man does, and you know it just as well as I do."
>
> "Vell, dot's all right. I could load dot pig iron on the car tomorrow for $1.85, and I get it every day, don't I?"
>
> "Certainly you do—certainly you do."
>
> "Vell, den, I vas a high-priced man."
>
> "'Now, hold on, hold on. You know just as well as I do that a high-priced man has to do exactly as he's told from morning till night. You have seen this man here before, haven't you?"
>
> "No, I never saw him."
>
> "Well, if you are a high-priced man, you will do exactly as this man tells you tomorrow, from morning till night. When he tells you to pick up a pig and walk, you pick it up and you walk, and when he tells you to sit down and rest, you sit down. You do that

> right straight through the day. And what's more, no back talk. Now a high-priced man does just what he's told to do, and no back talk. Do you understand that? When this man tells you to walk, you walk; when he tells you to sit down, you sit down, and you don't talk back to him. Now you come on to work here tomorrow morning and I'll know before night whether you are really a high-priced man or not."[13]

Taylor also made other contributions, including the concept of functional supervision, the exception principle, and integrating cost accounting into the planning process.

For Taylor, authority was based not upon position in a hierarchy but, rather, upon knowledge; functional supervision meant that people were responsible for directing certain tasks despite the fact this meant that the authority of the supervisor might cut across organizational lines.[14] The exception principle meant that routine matters should be handled by lower-level managers or by supervisors and that higher-level managers should only receive reports of deviations above or below standard performances.[15] The integration of cost accounting into the planning process became part of some budgeting practices treated in Chapter 13.

Despite the success of scientific management in raising productivity and cutting costs, "Taylorism" was attacked from a variety of quarters. Union leaders saw it as a threat to their movement because it seemed to reduce, if not eliminate, the importance of unions. The management of Bethlehem Steel ultimately abandoned task management, as Taylor liked to refer to his system, because they were uncomfortable with such an accurate appraisal of their performance[16] and some liberals saw it as an exploitation of workers. Upton Sinclair charged that Taylor had given workers a 61 percent increase in wages while getting a 362 percent increase in work.[17] Taylor replied to this charge by saying that employees worked no harder, only more efficiently. In hearings before the U.S. House of Representatives in 1912, Taylor's methods were attacked thoroughly and he died three years later a discouraged man.

Scientific management did not disappear with Taylor, however. There remained a core of people devoted to its practice, including Henry L. Gantt (1861–1919); Watlington Emerson (1853–1931), also a promoter of the staff concept; Frank (1868–1924) and Lillian (1878–1972) Gilbreth; and Morris Cooke (1872–1960), who in *Our Cities Awake* (1918) called for the application of scientific management in municipal government. Gantt gained a measure of immortality by developing a basic planning chart, which is illustrated in Figure 3-1, that remains in wide use today and still bears his name. Developed during the summer of 1917, while Gantt worked at the Frankford Arsenal, the Gantt chart contained the then revolutionary idea that the key factor in planning production was not quantity, but time.[18] Some international interest in scientific management also remained after Taylor's death; in 1918 France's Ministry of War called for the application of scientific management as did Lenin in an article in *Pravda*.[19] It is, of course, ironic that a Marxist society should call for the use of a management system based on the principle that economic self-interest guides the behavior of workers.

The fact that the period when scientific management was a dominant force has "'come and gone" does not mean that it is all history. Many of the techniques associated with scientific management such as time and motion studies and work flow analysis (depicted in Figure 3-2) remain in use in what is generally called industrial engineering. Other modern successors to scientific management were developed during World War II to support of the war effort, and the refinement

State Police Testing Project

Task Name	Duration	Start	End
Order Project Equipment	18.0 d	13/Sep/93	06/Oct/93
Write Request for Computer, Printer, and Software	2.0 d	13/Sep/93	14/Sep/93
Obtain Administrative Approval for Equipment Request	3.0 d	15/Sep/93	17/Sep/93
Order Equipment & Software through Procurement	3.0 d	20/Sep/93	22/Sep/93
Equipment and Software on Order	8.0 d	23/Sep/93	04/Oct/93
Receive and Configure Equipment	2.0 d	05/Oct/93	06/Oct/93
Staff Project	14.0 d	13/Sep/93	30/Sep/93
Develop Job Description	2.0 d	13/Sep/93	14/Sep/93
Announce Positions	3.0 d	15/Sep/93	17/Sep/93
Screen Applicants	3.0 d	20/Sep/93	22/Sep/93
Interview Finalists	2.0 d	23/Sep/93	24/Sep/93
Make Hiring Decisions	1.0 d	27/Sep/93	27/Sep/93
Train Staff	3.0 d	28/Sep/93	30/Sep/93

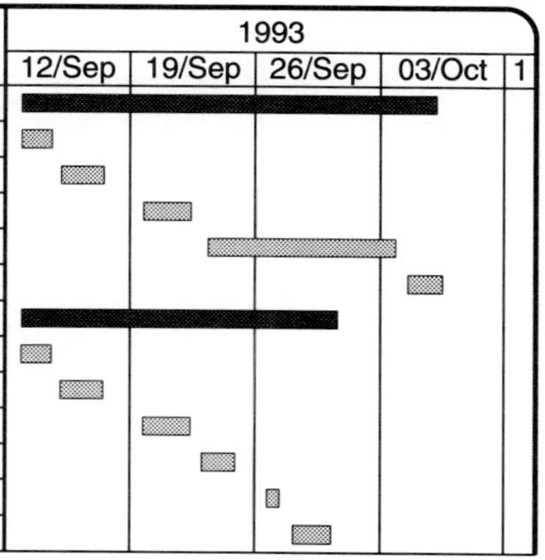

FIGURE 3-1. A portion of a Gantt Chart showing the start-up phase of a project. It was prepared using On-Target™ project planning software from Symantec which is "user friendly." The preparation of this chart only involved the use of On-Target's most basic capabilities.

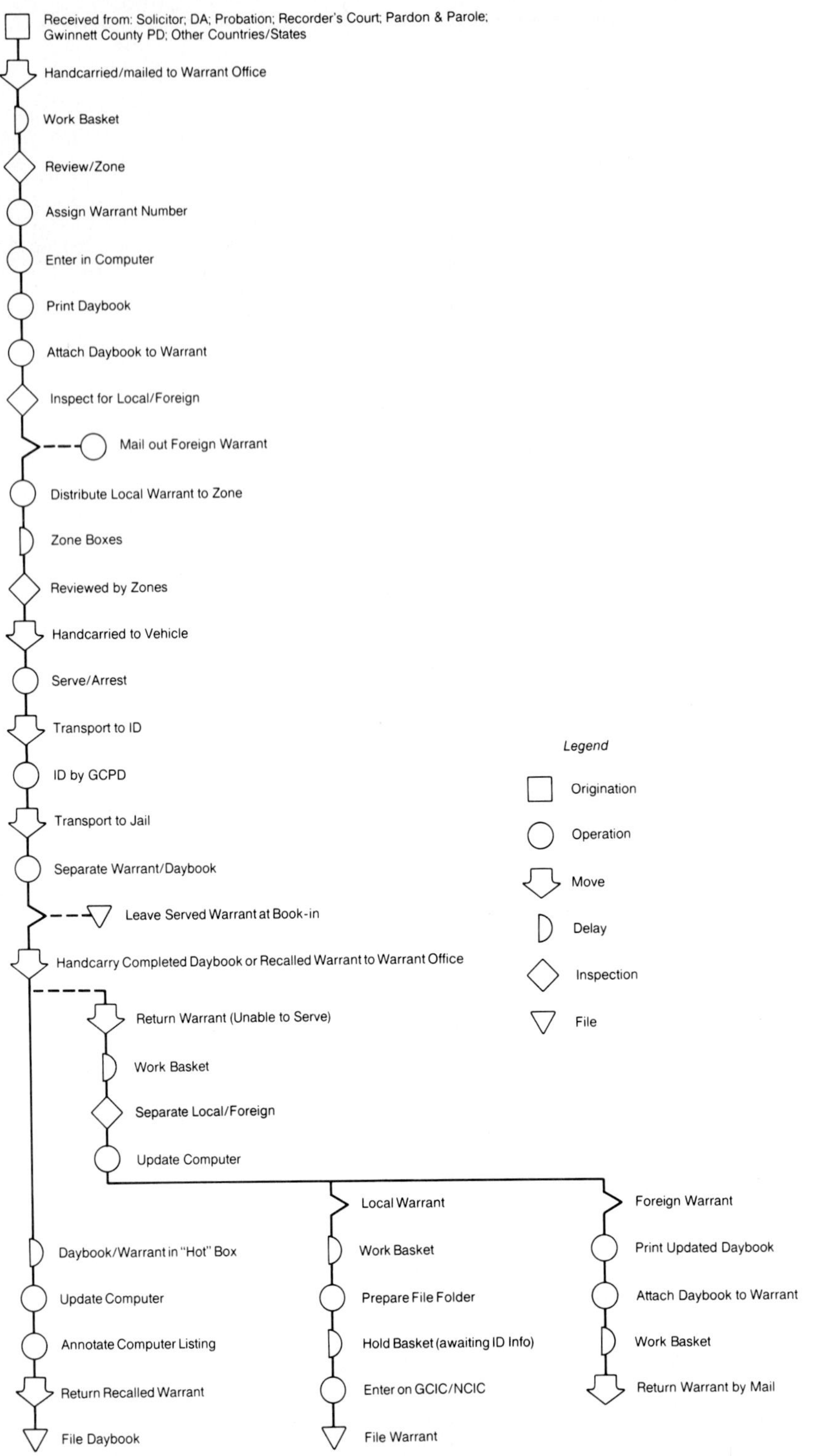

FIGURE 3-2. Analysis of sheriff's department criminal warrant work flow. [Source: Susan Reece and Charles Swanson, *Gwinnett County Sheriff's Department Workload and Staffing Analysis* (Athens: Vinson Institute of Government, University of Georgia, 1985).]

and more general application of these techniques is a post–1945 movement. The new techniques have alternatively been referred to as management science and operations research (OR), and their central orientation has been the application of quantitative and technical analysis to decision making.[20]

Weber: The Bureaucratic Model

In popular usage, bureaucracy has come to mean

> the slowness, the ponderous, the routine, the complication of procedures, and the maladapted responses of "bureaucratic" organizations to the needs which they should satisfy and the frustrations which their members, clients, or subjects consequently endure.[21]

Organizational "breakdown" (see Box 3-1) is far from the image of the ideal or pure bureaucracy developed by the towering German intellect Max Weber (1864–1920), the founder of modern sociology. For Weber, the choice was "only that between bureaucracy and dilettantism in the field of administration."[22] In this regard, Weber claimed that

> Experience tends universally to show that the purely bureaucratic type of administrative organization—that is, the monocratic variety of the bureaucracy—is, from a purely technical point of view, capable of attaining the highest degree of efficiency and is in this sense formally the most rational known means of carrying out imperative control over human beings. It is superior to any other form in precision, in stability, in the strigency of its discipline, and in its reliability. It thus makes possible a particularly high degree of calculability of results for the heads of the organization and for those acting in relation to it. It is finally superior both in intensive efficiency and in the scope of its operations, and is formally capable of application to all kinds of administrative tasks.[23]

The bureaucratic model of Weber included the following characteristics:

1. The organization of offices follows the principle of hierarchy; that is, each lower office is under the control and supervision of a higher one. There is a right of appeal and of statement of grievances from the lower to the higher.
2. Specified spheres of competence, meaning a division of labor, exist, in each of which the authority and responsibility of every organizational member is identified.
3. Official functions are bound by a system of rational rules.
4. Administrative acts, decisions, and rules are recorded in writing.
5. The "rights" associated with a position are the property of the office and not of the officeholders.
6. Candidates are appointed on the basis of technical qualifications, and specialized training is necessary.
7. Organizational members do not own the means of production.[24]

Although not all of the characteristics of Weber's bureaucratic model can be revealed by an organizational chart, Figure 3-3 does depict two important features: (1) the principle of hierarchy and (2) a division of labor that results in specialization.

BOX 3-1

"Bureaucratic Breakdown" Leaves Man Dead

By Laura Whiteside, *Tribune Staff Writer*

A judge's order to arrest an apparently suicidal man was carried out by Hillsborough County sheriffs deputies three days late—and only after the judge called a top sheriff's official—but by the time deputies showed up the man had committed suicide.

Circuit Judge Benjamin Sidwell said during an interview Wednesday, "A man's dead because of—whatever you want to call it—a bureaucratic breakdown."

Hillsborough Undersheriff John Kirk acknowledged that the order waited in the mailbox of a deputy who was out of town.

The dead man, James Trainor, Sr., died about eight hours before sheriff's deputies found him in his north Tampa apartment. He had drunk 10 to 12 ounces of insecticide, according to Hillsborough county Medical Examiner Peter Lardizabal.

Trainor's son and brother thought he was an alcoholic and was suicidal. They petitioned the court to have him treated because he wouldn't consent to treatment.

Sidwell took up the petition on April 14. Four days later, on April 18, he ordered that Trainor be arrested on April 21. He wanted to wait three days to have Trainor arrested so the man wouldn't have to spend the weekend in jail.

But Lt. Red Meighen, in charge of the warrants division of the sheriff's office, said the date on the warrant went unnoticed.

"I don't know how that was overlooked," Meighen said.

The deputy assigned to the north Tampa area where Trainor lived was on duty out of the state and, therefore, no action was taken on the order, Kirk said.

"They just put it in his box," Kirk said.

Meighen said the warrant was handled normally. Five employees in his office distribute warrants to the six deputies who cover assigned areas of the county.

"Those girls who put warrants in the boxes don't know when they (the deputies) are going to be out of town," he said.

When Trainor wasn't brought to the court Tuesday, April 22, Sidwell asked a mental health counselor to find out why. Sidwell said he thought it would be taken care of, but that Trainor still didn't show up two days later.

That's when Sidwell called Kirk.

Kirk recalled the phone call: "He asked me 'What does it take to get my papers served?' " Kirk said.

Kirk called the warrants division and deputies Wade Weatherman and Casey Wieleba. It was Wieleba's mailbox the original order was left in and the order was still there when he returned from his mission out of town.

The deputies immediately went to Trainor's apartment near Dale Mabry Highway and Waters Avenue.

"We couldn't get an answer," two knocks on the door, Weatherman said. "He didn't have a car," and the deputies visited local liquor stores looking for him.

When they returned, Wieleba was able to see through a curtain a man lying on the living room couch. The apartment manager unlocked the door and the deputies found Trainor with a bottle of insecticide and a bottle of cola nearby.

"We called patrol and turned it over to them," Weatherman said.

In seeking the court's help, Trainor's son, James, Jr., said his father's problems were serious.

"My father told me that he had attempted to commit suicide," he said in the petition. "He is unable to function and I have reason to believe he is consuming as much as two quarts of alcohol per day."

Trainor had displayed "typical and classic alcoholic" tendencies during the past few months, said another son, Michael Trainor. "He got paranoid and would only go out at night. He walked around a lot.

"We were trying to get him under psychiatric care."

There was apparently one other precaution taken to keep Trainor from killing himself, but it, too, failed. According to Sheriff's Lt. Larry Terry, Trainor's family had asked a friend of Trainor's to stay with him until April 21, when the arrest order was to be carried out, but the friend moved away the following day.
Source: Tampa Tribune, May 8, 1980, pp. 1A, 13A.

Weber's bureaucratic model rested on what he called rational-legal authority. This he contrasted to (1) traditional authority, which rested on an established belief in the sanctity of immemorial traditions and the legitimacy of the status of people exercising authority under those traditions, illustrated by kings or queens, and (2) charismatic authority, which stemmed from the exceptional sanctity, heroism, or exemplary character of an individual.[25]

There are two dimensions to Weber's work that are often not considered. First, on the one hand, he considered bureaucracy as the most efficient form of organization, and, on the other hand, he feared that this very efficiency constituted a

Max Weber (Courtesy of the Library of Congress.)

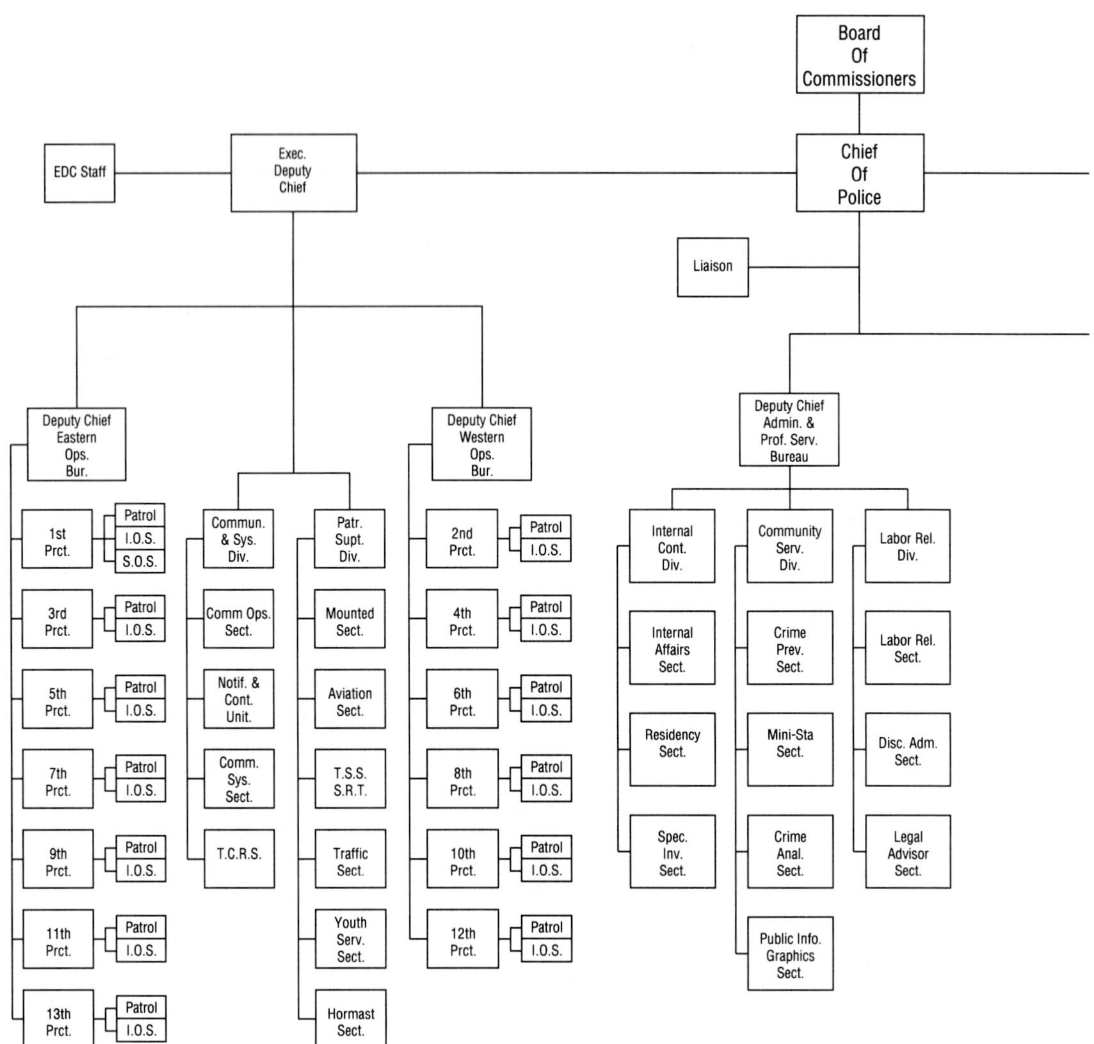

FIGURE 3-3. The organization of the Detroit Police Department.

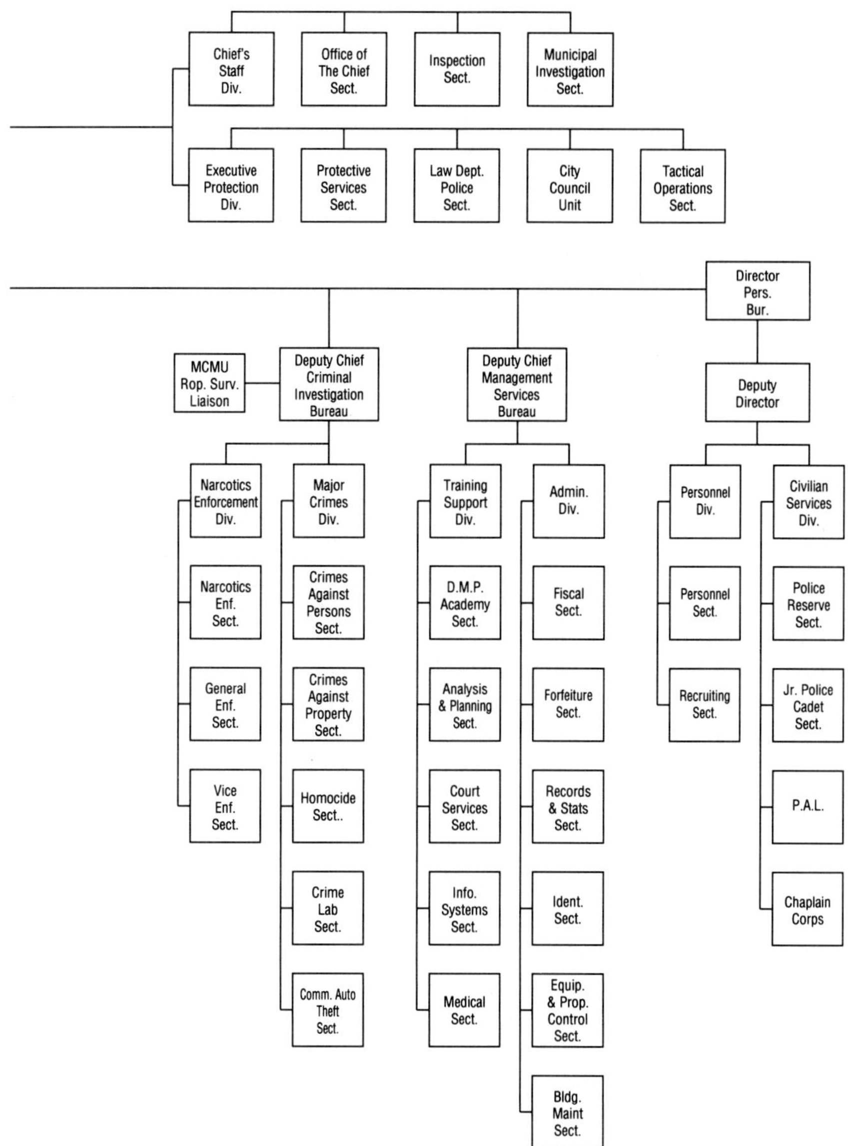

Chief's Staff Div.
Office of The Chief Sect.
Inspection Sect.
Municipal Investigation Sect.
Executive Protection Div.
Protective Services Sect.
Law Dept. Police Sect.
City Council Unit
Tactical Operations Sect.
Director Pers. Bur.
MCMU Rop. Surv. Liaison
Deputy Chief Criminal Investigation Bureau
Deputy Chief Management Services Bureau
Deputy Director
Narcotics Enforcement Div.
Major Crimes Div.
Training Support Div.
Admin. Div.
Personnel Div.
Civilian Services Div.
Narcotics Enf. Sect.
Crimes Against Persons Sect.
D.M.P. Academy Sect.
Fiscal Sect.
Personnel Sect.
Police Reserve Sect.
General Enf. Sect.
Crimes Against Property Sect.
Analysis & Planning Sect.
Forfeiture Sect.
Recruiting Sect.
Jr. Police Cadet Sect.
Vice Enf. Sect.
Homocide Sect..
Court Services Sect.
Records & Stats Sect.
P.A.L.
Crime Lab Sect.
Info. Systems Sect.
Ident. Sect.
Chaplain Corps
Comm. Auto Theft Sect.
Medical Sect.
Equip. & Prop. Control Sect.
Bldg. Maint Sect.

threat to individual freedom by its impersonal nature and oppressive routine.[26] Second, Weber deplored the career professional of moderate ambitions who craved security; this type of person Weber saw as lacking spontaneity and inventiveness, the modern-day "petty bureaucrat."[27]

As a closing note, Weber did not invent the bureaucratic model; it had existed for centuries. Thus, whereas Weber spawned the formal study of organizations, it scarcely seems fair to lay at his feet any real or fancied inadequacies of the model or its operation. Moreover, although it would be difficult to overstate Weber's contributions, it must be borne in mind that whereas some people—such as Chester Barnard—read him in the original German,[28] his work was not translated into English and was not generally available until 1947, long after the bureaucratic model was well entrenched.

Administrative Theory

Administrative or management theory sought to identify generic or universal methods of administration. Its benchmark is the 1937 publication of Luther Gulick (1892–) and Lyndall Urwick's (1891–1983) edited *Papers on the Science of Administration*. In content, administrative theory is more compatible with the bureaucratic model than with scientific management because it concentrates upon broader principles. Administrative theory, also referred to as the principles approach, is distinguished from the bureaucratic model by its "how to" emphasis. At some risk of oversimplification, the principles both operationalize and reinforce features of the bureaucratic model. Consequently, because of the continuing pervasiveness of the bureaucratic model, the principles either explicitly or implicitly continue to play an important role in organizations, including police departments. The key contributors to this school are Henri Fayol (1841–1925), James Mooney (1884–1957) and Alan Reiley (1869–1947), and Gulick and Urwick.

Henri Fayol graduated as an engineer at the age of 19 from France's National School of Mines at St. Etienne and began a 40 year career with the Commentary-Fourchambault Company.[29] His contributions are based on writings that were an outgrowth of his experiences as a manager. Fayol's fame rests chiefly on his *General and Industrial Management* (1916). The first English edition of this appeared in Great Britain in 1923, and although his "Administrative Theory of the State" appeared in *Papers on the Science of Administration,* his main work, *General and Industrial Management,* was not widely available in this country until 1949. Fayol's principles included

1. A division of work, that is, specialization
2. Authority, namely, the right to give orders and the power to extract obedience—whoever exercises authority has responsibility
3. Discipline, in essence the obedience, application, energy and behavior, and outward marks of respect in accordance with the standing agreement between the firm and its employees
4. Unity of command, with an employee's receiving orders from only one supervisor
5. Unity of direction, with one head and one plan for a group of activities having the same objective—unity of command cannot exist without unity of direction
6. Subordination of individual interest to the general interest—the interest of an individual or a group of employees does not prevail over the concerns of the firm

7. Remuneration of personnel—to be fair to the employee and employer
8. Centralization, a natural order of things—however centralization or decentralization is a question of proportion, finding the optimum degree for the particular concern
9. Scalar chain, namely, the chain of superiors ranging from the ultimate authority to the lowest ranks, often referred to as the chain of command
10. Order, that is, a place for everyone and everyone in his or her place
11. Equity, namely, the combination of kindness and justice
12. Stability of tenure of personnel, which allows employees to become familiar with their jobs and productive—a mediocre manager who stays is infinitely preferable to outstanding managers who come and go
13. Initiative at all levels of the organization—this represents a great source of strength for business
14. Esprit de corps, harmony, and union of personnel—these constitute a great strength, and efforts should be made to establish them.[30]

Fayol recognized that his scalar principle could produce disastrous consequences it if were followed strictly, since it would hamper swift action.[31] He therefore developed Fayol's gangplank, or horizontal bridge, discussed more fully in Chapter 6, as a means of combatting this issue. Fayol's belief that a mediocre manager who stays is better than outstanding ones who come and go has refound currency beginning in the late 1970s, as many city managers retreated from hiring police chiefs from outside the organization. Although it can be argued with some validity that this movement is due to the increased qualifications of internal candidates, it is also true that the frequent recruitment, screening, and selection of "'portable" police managers has been an expensive, time-consuming, and, at least occasionally in terms of results, disappointing process.

Mooney and Reiley's *Onward Industry* (1931) was generally consistent with the work of Fayol, as were the subsequent revisions of this publication, which appeared in 1939 and 1947 under the title of *The Principles of Organization*.[32]

In "Notes on the Theory of Organization," which was included in *Papers on the Science of Administration,* Gulick coined the most familiar and enduring acronym of administration, POSDCORB:

> Planning, that is, working out in broad outline the things that need to be done and the methods for doing them to accomplish the purpose set for the enterprise;
> Organizing, that is, the establishment of the formal structure of authority through which work subdivisions are arranged, defined and co-ordinated for the defined objective;
> Staffing, that is, the whole personnel function of bringing in and training the staff and maintaining favorable conditions of work;
> Directing, that is, the continuous task of making decisions and embodying them in specific and general orders and instructions and serving as the leader of the enterprise;
> Co-ordinating, that is, the all important duty of interrelating the various parts of the work;
> Reporting, that is, keeping those to whom the executive is responsible informed as to what is going on, which thus includes keeping himself and his subordinates informed through records, research and inspection;
> Budgeting, with all that goes with budgeting in the form of fiscal planning, accounting and control.[33]

Gulick acknowledged that his POSDCORB was adapted from the functional analysis elaborated by Fayol in *General and Industrial Management.* Urwick's "Organization as a Technical Problem," which appeared in the *Papers on the Science of Administration,* also drew upon the work of another Frenchman, A. V. Graicunas, for his treatment of the span of control. Urwick asserted that

> Students of administration have long recognized that, in practice, no human brain should attempt to supervise directly more than five, or at the most six individuals whose work is interrelated.[34]

Urwick, the Oxford-educated and military-career Englishman, also underscored management theory with his subsequent *Scientific Principles of Organization* (1938).

Critique of Traditional Theory

Scientific management is decried because of its "man as machine" orientation, and ample life is given to that argument by even a casual reading of the conversation between Taylor and the legendary Schmidt. On balance, although Taylor's emphasis was on task, he was not totally indifferent to the human element, arguing that

> No system of management, however good, should be applied in a wooden way. The proper personal relations should always be maintained between the employers and men; and even the prejudices of the workmen should be considered in dealing with them.[35]

The bureaucratic model has no shortage of critics; the humanist Warren Bennis levels the following specific criticisms:

1. Bureaucracy does not adequately allow for the personal growth and development of mature personalities.
2. It develops conformity and "group think."
3. It does not take into account the "informal organization" and the emergent and unanticipated problems.
4. Its systems of control and authority are hopelessly outdated.
5. It has no adequate judicial process.
6. It does not possess adequate means for resolving differences and conflicts between ranks and, most particularly, between functional groups.
7. Communication and innovative ideas are thwarted or distorted due to hierarchical divisions.
8. The full human resources of bureaucracy are not utilized due to mistrust, fear of reprisals, and so on.
9. It cannot assimilate the influx of new technology . . . entering the organization.
10. It modifies the personality structure such that each man becomes and reflects the full, gray, conditioned "organization man."[36]

Herbert Simon has mounted the most precise criticisms of the principles approach. He writes

> It is a fatal defect of the . . . principles of administration that, like proverbs, they occur in pairs. For almost every principle one can find an equally plausible and acceptable

> contradictory principle. Although the two principles of the pair will lead to exactly opposite organizational recommendations, there is nothing in the theory to indicate which is the proper one to apply.[37]

To illustrate his point, Simon notes that administrative efficiency is enhanced by keeping at a minimum the number of organizational levels through which a matter must pass before it is acted upon. Yet a narrow span of control, say, of five or six subordinates, produces a tall hierarchy. To some extent, Simon's criticism is blunted by invoking Fayol's exception principle and the gangplank, but in the main Simon's point that some of the principles contain logical contradictions is potent.

Less critical than both Bennis and Simon, Hage[38] describes bureaucracy in mixed terms and specifically as having

1. High centralization
2. High formalization
3. High stratification
4. Low adaptiveness
5. Low job satisfaction
6. Low complexity
7. High production
8. High efficiency.

In *Complex Organizations* (1972), Charles Perrow mounted a major and articulate defense of the bureaucratic model, concluding that

> the extensive preoccupation with reforming, "humanizing," and decentralizing bureaucracies, while salutary, has served to obscure from organizational theorists the true nature of bureaucracy and has diverted us from assessing its impact on society. The impact on society in general is incalculably more important than the impact upon the members of a particular organization . . . bureaucracy is a form of organization superior to all others we know or can hope to afford in the near and middle future; the chances of doing away with it or changing it are probably non-existent in the west in this century. Thus it is crucial to understand it and appreciate it.[39]

Relatedly, in *The Case for Bureaucracy* (1985), Charles Goodsell notes that denunciations of the "common hate object" are fashionable, appealing, and make us feel good; they invite no retaliation or disagreement since almost everybody agrees that bureaucracy is bad . . . but fashionable contentions are not necessarily solid ones.[40] Goodsell observes that:

> the attacks are almost always made in the tone of unremitting dogmatism. They are usually unqualified in portraying wicked behavior and inadequate outcomes. The pessimistic picture presented seems unbroken. The absolutism itself, it would seem, cannot help but strain our credulity. How can we believe that all public bureaucracies, all of the time, are inefficient, dysfunctional, rigid, obstructionist, secretive, oligarchic, conservative, undemocratic, imperialist, oppressive, alienating, and discriminatory? How could any single human creation be so universally terrible in so many ways?[41]

Purely deductive models critical of bureaucracy abound, but they are—in the words of Alvin Gouldner—"a theoretical tapestry devoid of the plainest empirical trimmings."[42] Goodsell elaborates on this theme by observing that when empirical study is taken, single cases illustrating the conclusions desired are selected, and by concentrating on the problems, disorders, and dysfunctions of bureaucracy, rather than on what is working well, academics confirm both their own diagnoses and demonstrate the need for their own solutions.[43] Interestingly, Goodsell is able to muster a number of empirical studies that reveal positive evaluations of bureaucracies, including the police, by members of the public who have had direct contact with them; in general, these favorable evaluations are at least at the two-thirds level and many go beyond the 75 percent level.[44]

Despite philosophical criticisms and practical difficulties with the stems of traditional theory, in its entirety it must be appreciated for having formed the basic fund of knowledge on which the overwhelming majority of organizations in the world rest. Knowledge of traditional theory remains as an essential part of education and training for police leaders.

Open Systems Theory

Organizations described as flexible, adaptive, and organic are associated with open systems theory. This line of thought began its development in the late 1920s and is comprised of three major divisions: (1) human relations, (2) behavioral systems, and (3) open systems theory.

Human Relations

The human relations school developed in reaction to the mechanistic orientation of traditional organizational theory, which was viewed as neglecting or ignoring the human element.

Mayo: The Hawthorne Studies

In 1927, a series of experiments, which were to last five years, began near Chicago at the Western Electric Company's Hawthorne plant.[45] This work was guided by Elton Mayo (1880–1949), a professor in the Harvard School of Business, and his associates, Fritz Roethlisberger (1898–1974) and William Dickson (1904–).[46] From the perspective of organizational theory, the major contribution of the Hawthorne experiments is the view that organizations are social systems. Two research efforts, the telephone relay assembly study and the telephone switchboard wiring study,[47] were especially important to the development of the human relations school.

In the first study, five women assembling telephone relays were put into a special room and were subjected to varying physical work conditions.[48] Even when the conditions changed unfavorably, production increased. Mayo and his associates were puzzled by these results. Ultimately, they decided that (1) when the experimenters took over many of the supervisory functions, it became less strict and less formal; (2) the women behaved differently from what was expected because they were receiving attention, creating the famous "Hawthorne effect"; and (3) by placing the women together in the relay assembling test room, the researchers had provided the opportunity for them to become a closely knit group.[49] Based on these observations, the researchers concluded that an important influence on productivity was the interpersonal relations and spirit of cooperation that had developed among the women and between the women and their supervisors. The influence of these "human relations" was believed to be every bit as important as physical work conditions and financial incentives.[50]

In the telephone switchboard wiring study, fourteen men were put on a reasonable piece rate; that is, without physically straining themselves, they could earn more if they produced more. The assumption was that the workers would behave as rational economic actors and produce more since it was in their own best interest. To insulate these men from the "systematic soldiering" they knew to exist among the plant's employees, the researchers also placed these workers in a special room. The workers' output did not increase. The values of the informal group appeared to be more powerful than the allure of financial betterment:

1. Don't be a "rate buster" and produce too much.
2. If you turn out too little work, you are a "chisler."
3. Don't be a "squealer" to supervisors.
4. Don't be officious; if you are an inspector, don't act like one.[51]

Taken together, the relay assembly study and the switchboard wiring study raise an important question. Why did one group respond so favorably and the other not? The answer is that, in the relay assembly study, the values of the workers and the supervisors were mutually supportive, whereas in the switchboard wiring study, the objectives of the company and the informal group conflicted. The harder question is: Why was there mutuality in one situation and not the other? The basis of mutuality has already been discussed; the conflict is more difficult to account for, but it may have been the interplay of some things we know and some things we must speculate about:

1. The researchers did not involve themselves in the supervision of the switchboard wiring room workers as they had with the relay assembly room employees.[52] The wiring room workers and their supervisor developed a spirit of cooperation, but it was one in which the supervisor was coopted by the informal group, which was suspicious of what would happen if output actually increased.[53]
2. The way in which the subjects for both studies were selected is suspect and may have influenced the findings. The relay assembly women were experienced operators known to be friendly with each other and "willing and cooperative" participants, whereas the men were designated by the foreman.[54]
3. The relay assembly-room workers were women and the switchboard wiring study employees were men. This difference in sexuality may have influenced the character of the responses. The studies were going on during the Depression; the women may have tried to hold onto their jobs by pleasing their supervisors, while the men restricted their output so there would be work to do and nobody would lose his job. In this context, both groups of employees can be seen as rational economic actors.

As a result of the Hawthorne studies, it was concluded that (1) the level of production is set by social norms, not by physiological capacities; (2) often workers do not react as individuals, but as members of a group; (3) the rewards and sanctions of the group significantly affect the behavior of workers and limit the impact of economic incentive plans; and (4) leadership has an important role in setting and enforcing group norms, and there is a difference between formal and informal leadership.[55]

When workers react as members of an informal group, they become susceptible to the values of that group. Thus, the informal group can be a powerful force in supporting or opposing police programs. Illustratively, a number of police unions started as an unorganized, informal group of dissatisfied officers. Although many factors contribute to the enduring problem of police corruption, such as disillusionment and temptation, an informal group that supports taking payoffs makes it more difficult to identify and prosecute "bad cops." In 1972, the Knapp Commission, investigating corruption in the New York City Police Department, distinguished between "meat-eaters" (those who overtly pursued opportunities to personally profit from their police power) and "grass-eaters" (those who simply accepted the payoffs that the happenstances of police work brought their way).[56] The behavior of the grass-eaters can be interpreted within the framework of the power that informal groups have. The Knapp Commission was told that one strong force that encouraged grass-eaters to accept relatively petty graft was their feeling of loyalty to their fellow officers. By accepting payoff money an officer could prove that he was one of the boys and could be trusted.

The foregoing discussion should not be interpreted to mean that informal groups always, or even frequently, engage in troublesome or unethical behavior, but rather as an illustration of the potency that such groups have. Astute police administrators are always alert for opportunities to tap the energy of informal groups to support departmental goals and programs.

As might be expected, the collision between the human relations school, fathered by Mayo's Hawthorne studies, and traditional organizational theory sent theorists and researchers in the various disciplines off into new and different directions. From among these at least three major themes are identifiable: (1) inquiries into what motivates workers, including the work of Maslow and Herzberg, which will be discussed shortly; (2) leadership, the subject of Chapter 5; and (3) work on organizations as behavioral systems, covered later in this chapter. As a concluding note, the term *human relations* has been used in law enforcement with two entirely different meanings. Particularly from the mid-1960s to the early 1970s, the term was used as a label for training that was basically race relations; when used in describing the major content areas of more recent police management seminars, its use denotes a block of instruction relating to individual and group relationships in the tradition of the Hawthorne studies.

Maslow: The Need Hierarchy

Abraham Maslow (1908–1970) was a psychologist who developed the need hierarchy to explain individual motivation. The model appeared first in a 1943 article[57] and later received extended coverage in Maslow's *Motivation and Personality* (1954).

Figure 3-4 depicts the need hierarchy. In Maslow's scheme, there were five categories of human needs.

1. Physiological or basic needs, such as food, shelter, and water
2. Safety needs, including the desires to be physically safe, to have a savings account for

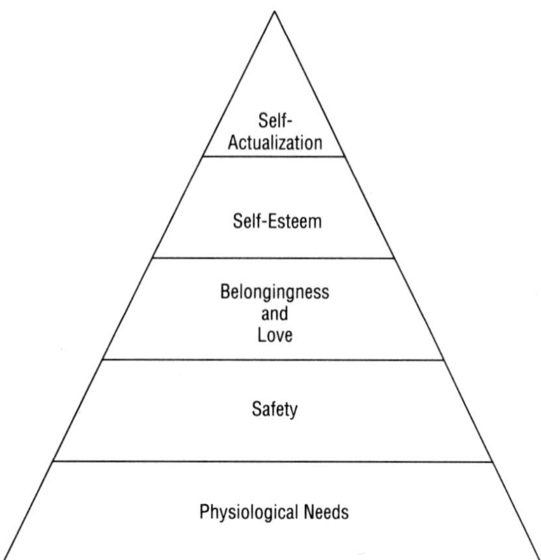

FIGURE 3-4. Maslow's need hierarchy.

financial security, and to be safe in one's job, knowing that you will not be arbitrarily fired

3. Belongingness and love needs, such as the acceptance of one's work group in the police department and the affection of one's spouse, children, and parents
4. Esteem needs, including the desire for a stable, fairly based, and positive evaluation of one's self as evidenced by compliments, commendations, promotions, and other cues
5. Self-actualization needs, such as the want to test one's self-potential and gain a sense of fulfillment.[58]

The need hierarchy is arranged, like the rungs on a ladder, from the lower-order to the higher-order needs. A person does not move from one level to the next higher one until the majority of the needs at the level one is at are met. Once those needs are met, they cease to motivate a person, and the needs at the next level of the hierarchy predominate. To illustrate this, one does not attempt to self-actualize until one has feelings of self-confidence, worth, strength, capability, adequacy, and mastery;[59] these feelings are only generated with the meeting of the esteem needs. Conversely, if people's esteem needs are unmet, they feel inferior, helpless, discouraged, and unworthwhile and are unable to move to the self-actualization level and test themselves.

It is important to understanding the need hierarchy that the character of something does necessarily not determine what need is met but, rather, to what use it is put; money can be used to buy food and satisfy a basic need, or it can be put in a savings account to satisfy safety needs. Also, any process up the hierarchy can be reversed; the police officer who is fired or is given a lengthy suspension may be thrust into a financial situation in which the physiological needs will predominate. Police agencies that are managed professionally attempt to make appropriate use of theoretical constructs. For example, the fourth level of Maslow's need hierarchy is self-esteem, which includes the need for recognition as evidenced by compliments and commendations. Faced with a significant automobile theft prob-

The Blue Max medal and its presentation at an awards ceremony. (Courtesy of the Ohio State Patrol.)

lem in their state, Ohio state patrol officials wanted to develop a strategy that would have an impact upon the problem. One of the programs they developed was the Blue Max award.[60] In the Blue Max program each time a state trooper arrested a suspect in a stolen car he or she received a lightning bolt decal to place on the side of his or her patrol car. When a trooper made his or her fifth apprehension in a year, he was given his own car for the rest of the year with a special license that read "ACE." At the end of the year the trooper who had made the most apprehensions received the coveted Blue Max award and was given a car reserved only for his use during the next year. In the first ten months in which the Blue Max program was operated, arrests of car thieves was up 49 percent as compared to the entire prior 12 months. The Blue Max program demonstrates the utility of theory and how meeting organizational goals and individual goals can be compatible.

Herzberg: Motivation–Hygiene Theory

Because of their focus, neither the need hierarchy nor motivation-hygiene are organizational theories in the larger sense; they are included here because they are part of a stream of connected thinking. Motivation-hygiene theory developed from research conducted by Frederick Herzberg (1923–), Bernard Mausner, and Barbara Snyderman on job attitudes at 11 work sites in the Pittsburgh area and reported on in *The Motivation to Work* (1959). The major statement of the theory, which evolved out of this earlier research, is found in Herzberg's *Work and the Nature of Man* (1966).

Herzberg saw two sets of variables operating in the work setting: (1) hygiene factors, which he later came to call maintenance factors, and (2) motivators. Table 3-1 identifies Herzberg's hygiene factors and motivators. The hygiene factors relate to the work environment; the motivators relate to the work itself. Herzberg borrowed the term *hygiene* from the health care field and used it to refer to factors that if not treated properly could lead to a deterioration in performance, creating an "unhealthy" organization. Hygiene factors that are not treated properly are a source of dissatisfaction. However, even if all of them are provided, a police department does not have motivated officers, just ones who are not dissatisfied. Hygiene factors and motivators operate independently of each other; the police manger can motivate subordinates if they are somewhat dissatisfied with their salaries. However, the greater the level of dissatisfaction, the more difficult it becomes to employ the motivators successfully.

Note that police managers have more control over motivators than they do over basic hygiene factors; certain policies, such as automatically placing an officer involved in a shooting incident on suspension, may be mandated by the city administrator; working conditions may be lessened if the city council refuses to buy air-conditioned cars; the chief of police has little control over the status given the officer's job by society; and a chief cannot appropriate the money for higher salaries or improved fringe benefits.

In their leadership roles, police managers can try to influence, but they do not control such matters. It is over those hygiene factors that police managers do exercise control that they can do a considerable amount of good in reducing dissatisfaction and facilitating the use of the motivators or they can cause considerable unhappiness:

> The commander in charge of the uniformed division of a 100-officer department suddenly announced that officers were going to be placed on permanent shifts. Surprised and angered by this move, the officers and their wives mobilized to oppose the plan, and after a mass meeting with the commander, the plan was abandoned. The legacy of this incident was a period of barely subdued hostility, distrust, and low morale in the police department.

TABLE 3-1 Herzberg's Motivation–Hygiene Theory

Hygiene factors	Motivators
Supervisory practices	Achievement
Policies and administration	Recognition for accomplishments
Working conditions	Challenging work
Interpersonal relationships with subordinates, peers, and superiors	Increased responsibility
Status	Advancement possibilities
Effect of the job on personal life	Opportunity for personal growth and development
Job security	
Money	

From Frederick Herzberg, *Work and the Nature of Man* (Cleveland: World, 1966), pp. 95–96.

The nature of police work is in and of itself challenging, and some motivational effect is thus naturally occurring. Police managers can build on this by varying assignments appropriately. Measures that employ various of the other motivators include an established and active commendation system, the creation of field training officer and master patrol officer designations, an annual police awards banquet, an active staff development program, and a career system with various tracks, as discussed in Chapter 7.

As a concluding comment, Maslow's need hierarchy and Herzberg's motivation–hygiene theory can be interrelated; the physiological, safety, and belongingness and love needs of Maslow correspond to Herzberg's hygiene factors; the top two levels of the need hierarchy—esteem and self-actualization—correlate with Herzberg's motivators.

Behavioral System Theory

By 1960, human relations in the tradition of the Hawthorne studies lacked vitality. Its successor, which traces its ancestry to that 1927–1932 period, was behavioral systems theory. The theorists associated with this school saw organizations as being composed of interrelated behaviors and were concerned with making organizations more democratic and participative. Behavioral systems theory is basically a post-1950 development; many of the people involved in this movement are also described in other ways. For example, Argyris, Likert, Bennis, Maslow, Herzberg, and McGregor are often referred to as organizational humanists and in one way or another are tied to organizational development, a concept treated later in this section.

Lewin: Group Dynamics

Kurt Lewin (1890–1947) was a psychologist who fled from Germany in the early 1930s.[61] His interests were diverse and included leadership; force-field analysis, a technique sometimes used in decision making; change; and group dynamics. Lewin's force-field analysis is illustrated in Figure 3-5. In force-field analysis, driving forces push for some new condition or state, and restraining forces serve to resist the change or perpetuate things as they are. In using force-field analysis, if there are exactly opposing, driving and restraining forces, the arrows of these opposing forces meet at the zero or balance line. In some instances, there might not be an exactly opposite force, in which case an arrow is simply drawn, as in Figure 3-5, to the balance line. After all entries are made and the situation is summarized, the relative power of the driving and restraining forces must be subjectively evaluated. In this regard, the zero or balance line should be regarded as a spring that will be moved in one direction or another, suggesting the action that needs to be taken or the decision that needs to be made.

Lewin is also regarded as the father of the behavioral system school and founded the Research Center for Group Dynamics at the Massachusetts Institute of Technology.[62] In the same year as Lewin died, one of his followers, Leland Bradford, established a human relations effort at Bethel, Maine.[63] This undertaking was later to be called the National Training Laboratories for Group Development, which earlier focused on stranger T-group or sensitivity training, a method whereby

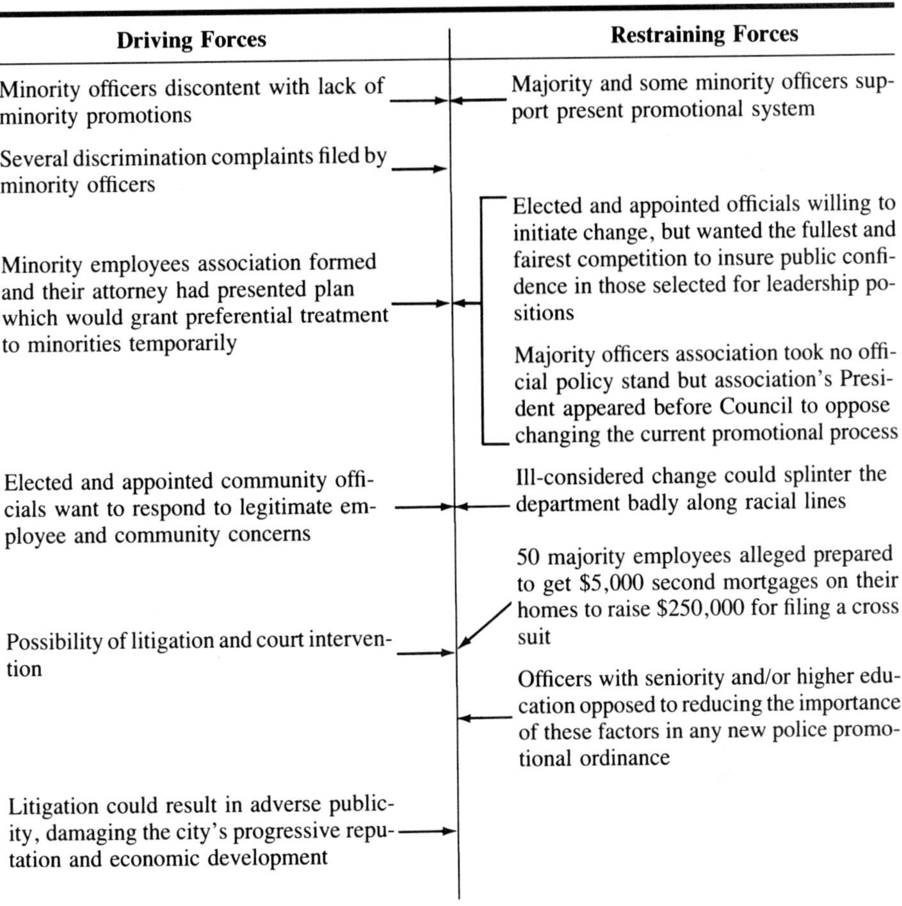

FIGURE 3-5. The use of force-field analysis regarding the decision to adopt a new police promotional ordinance.

behavior is changed by strangers in a group sharing their honest opinions of each other. The popularity of T-groups was greatest during the 1950s; its present use is diminished in large measure because some organizations that tried it were troubled by its occasional volatility and the fact that not all changes were positive:

> A division manager at one big company was described by a source familiar with his case as "a ferocious guy—brilliant but a thoroughgoing autocrat—whom everyone agreed was just what the division needed, because it was a tough, competitive business." Deciding to smooth over his rough edges, the company sent him to sensitivity training, where he found out exactly what people thought of him. "So he stopped being a beast," says the source, "and his effectiveness fell apart." The reason he'd been so good was that he didn't realize what a beast he was. Eventually, they put in a new manager.[64]

Homans: External and Internal Systems

As a contemporary of Lewin's, George Homans (1910–) did work in the tradition of group dynamics. In *The Human Group* (1950), he advanced the idea that groups have both an internal and an external system.[65] The internal system is comprised of factors that arise within the group itself, such as the feelings that members of a group develop about each other during the life of the group. In contrast, the external system consists of variables in the larger environment in which the group exists, such as the administrative policies and supervisory practices to which the group is subject. Homans saw these two systems as being in a state of interaction and influencing each other.

For example, the decision of a chief of police to suspend an officer for three days without pay because of an accident while involved in a high-speed chase might result in a group of officers who saw the suspension as being unfair agreeing among themselves not to write any traffic citations during that time. This interaction brings the formal organization of the external sytem into conflict with the informal organization of the internal system. The formal sanction of the external system is countered with the informal sanction of reducing the city's revenue by the internal system.

Both Lewin and Homans have ties to the human relations school. Homans, for instance, drew upon the switchboard wiring room study to illustrate his concept of internal and external systems. Analytically, his work falls into the behavioral systems category and foreshadowed the dynamic interaction theme of open systems theory.

Argyris: Immaturity–Maturity Theory and the Mix Model

Chris Argyris (1923–) is a critic of the mechanistic model of organization and a leading proponent of more open and participative organizations. In *Personality and Organization: The Conflict Between System and the Individual* (1957), he states a theory of immaturity versus maturity. Argyris believes that, as one moves from infancy toward adulthood in years of age, the healthy individual also advances from immaturity to maturity. The elements of the personality that are changed during this process are summarized in Table 3-2. Simultaneously, Argyris views formal organizations as having certain properties that do not facilitate the growth into a mature state:

1. Specialization reduces the use of initiative by requiring the individuals to use only a few of their skills doing unchallenging tasks.

TABLE 3-2 Argyris's Immaturity–Maturity Changes

Infancy–Immaturity →	Adulthood–Maturity
Passive →	Self-initiative
Dependent →	Relatively independent
Behaving in a few ways →	Capable of behaving many ways
Erratic, shallow, quickly changed interests →	Deeper interests
Short time perspective →	Much longer time perspective
Subordinate position in the family →	Aspirations of equality or superordinate position relative to peers
Lack of self-awareness →	Self-awareness and self-control

Data from p. 50 in *Personality and Organization: The Conflict Between System and the Individual* by Chris Argyris. Copyright © 1957 by Harper & Row Publishers, Inc., Reprinted by permission of the publisher.

2. The chain of command leaves people with little control over their work environment and makes them dependent upon and passive toward superiors.
3. The unity-of-direction principle means that the objectives of the work unit are controlled by the leader. If the goals do not consider the employees, then ideal conditions for psychological failure are set.
4. The narrow span of control principle will tend to increase the subordinate's feelings of dependence, submissiveness, and passivity.[66]

The needs of a healthy, mature individual and the properties of formal organizations therefore come into conflict; the ensuing response by the individual may take any of several forms:

1. The employee may leave the organization only to find that other organizations are similar to the one left.
2. To achieve the highest level of control over one's self permitted by the organization, the person may climb as far as possible up the organizational hierarchy.
3. The worker may defend his or her self-concept by the use of defensive mechanisms such as daydreaming, rationalizing lower accomplishments, developing psychosomatic illnesses, or becoming aggressive and hostile, attacking and blaming what is frustrating personally.
4. The individual may decide to stay in spite of the conflict and adapt by lowering his or her work standards and becoming apathetic and disinterested.
5. Informal groups may be created to oppose the former organization.
6. The employee may be nothing and remain frustrated, creating even more tension.[67]

In 1964 Argyris published *Integrating the Individual and the Organization*. The purpose of it was to present his thinking about how organizations could deal with the problem he had identified in *Personality and Organization: The Conflict Between System and the Individual*. Argyris doubted that it was possible to have a relationship between the individual and the organization that allowed the simultaneous maximizing of the values of both.[68] He did believe that it was possible to reduce the unintended, nonproductive, side consequences of formal organizations and to free more of the energies of the individual for productive purposes; Argyris's mix model was the way in which this was to be done;[69] it is basically an attempt to "mix" or accommodate the interests of the individual and the organization. The mix model favors neither people nor the organization. For example, Argyris saw the organization as having legitimate needs that were not people centered. He also believed that organizations cannot always provide challenging work. The fact, however, that some work was not challenging was viewed by Argyris as an asset to the individual and the organization; the unchallenging work provided some recovery time—for the individual and allowed the organization's routine tasks to get done.[70]

McGregor: Theory X and Theory Y

Douglas McGregor (1904–1964) believed that

> Every managerial act rests on assumptions, generalizations, and hypotheses—that is to say, on theory. Our assumptions are frequently implicit, sometimes quite unconscious,

> often conflicting; nevertheless, they determine our predictions that if we do A, B will occur. Theory and practice are inseparable.[71]

In common practice, managerial acts, without explicit examination of theoretical assumptions, lead at times to remarkable inconsistencies in managerial behavior:

> A manager, for example, states that he delegates to his subordinates. When asked, he expresses assumptions such as, "People need to learn to take responsibility," or, "Those closer to the situation can make the best decision." However, he has arranged to obtain a constant flow of detailed information about the behavior of his subordinates, and he uses this information to police their behavior and to "second-guess" their decisions. He says, "I am held responsible, so I need to know what is going on." He sees no inconsistency in his behavior, nor does he recognize some other assumptions which are implicit: "People can't be trusted," or, "They can't really make as good decisions as I can."
>
> With one hand, and in accord with certain assumptions, he delegates; with the other, and in line with other assumptions, he takes actions which have the effect of nullifying his delegation. Not only does he fail to recognize the inconsistencies involved, but if faced with them he is likely to deny them.[72]

In *The Human Side of Enterprise* (1960), McGregor stated two different sets of assumptions that managers make about people:

Theory X

1. The average human has an inherent dislike of work and will avoid it if possible.
2. Most people must be coerced, controlled, directed, and threatened with punishment to get them to put forth adequate effort toward the achievement of organizational objectives.
3. The average human prefers to be directed, wishes to avoid responsibility, has relatively little ambition, and wants security above all.

Theory Y

1. The expenditure of physical and mental effort in work is as natural as play or rest.
2. External control and the threat of punishment are not the only means for bringing about effort toward organizational objectives. People will exercise self-direction and self-control in the service of objectives to which they are committed.
3. Commitment to objectives is a function of the rewards associated with their achievement.
4. The average human learns, under proper conditions, not only to accept but to seek responsibility.
5. The capacity to exercise a relatively high degree of imagination, ingenuity, and creativity in the solution of organizational problems is widely, not narrowly, distributed in the population.
6. Under the conditions of modern organizational life, the intellectual potentialities of the average human are only partially utilized.[73]

American police departments have historically been dominated by theory X assumptions. Even police departments with progressive national images may be experienced as tightly controlling environments by the people who actually work in them:

> The person leading a training session with about thirty-five managers of a West Coast police department observed that we often react to organizations as though they were living, breathing things. The managers agreed with this and noted the use of such phrases as "the department promoted me this year" and "the department hired me in 1975." They also understood that in fact someone, not the police department, had made those decisions. The managers were then divided into five groups and asked to make a list of what they thought the police department would say about them if it could talk. When the groups reported back, they identified a total of forty-two statements, some of which were duplicates of each other. These managers, all of whom were college graduates and many of whom held advanced degrees, indicated the police department would say such things as "They are idiots"; "They don't have any sense"; "Watch them or they'll screw up royally." All of the statements reported had a theory X character to them.

Theory X assumptions are readily recognized as being those that underpin traditional organizational theory. For example, we can relate a narrow span of control to theory X's first two propositions. In contrast, theory Y is formed by a set of views that are supportive of Argyris's mix model; they postulate that the interests of the individual and the organization need not be conflictual but can be integrated for mutual benefit. The principal task of management in a theory X police department is control, whereas in a theory Y department it is supporting subordinates by giving them the resources to do their jobs and creating an environment where they can be self-controlling, mature, contributing, and self-actualizing.

The use of quality circles (QCs) or employee participation groups (EPGs) is one

A quality circle at work in the Dallas Police Department. (Courtesy of the Dallas Police Department.)

practice consistent with theory Y that is beginning to be used in police departments. Widely used in Japanese industries and such American corporations as 3M, Union Carbide, Chrysler, and Lockheed, these procedures have been credited with achieving numerous productivity and product improvements while also enjoying the support of both management and labor.[74]

Quality circles are small groups of people, roughly between five to ten with seven being regarded as ideal, who perform the same type of work, such as uniformed patrol, training, or robbery investigation. This group or QC voluntarily agrees to meet at least once a week during regular duty hours for an hour to identify, discuss, analyze, and solve specified work-related problems that the group members have identified as being important. As practiced in the Dallas Police Department, QCs also

1. Are based on the premise that all members are of equal importance in making contributions
2. Use sergeants as leaders because they can "blend" in with the group, being more readily perceived as equals than are higher ranks
3. Provide formal training to the group leader and members in analytical techniques such as problem identification, data gathering, decision making, and making presentations
4. Have access to needed information and the use of experts in areas such a budgeting and systems analysis
5. Are assigned a facilitator—a top-level manager—to serve as a "go-between" and cut through "red tape" on behalf of the QC
6. Receive the support of management to adopt all reasonable recommendations
7. Implement the solution recommended to and approved by management.

QCs can be a valuable tool for police departments. Because circle members must cost out their solutions, a greater awareness is created with respect to how a department's resources are used. The QCs' emphasis on improvement results in creative solutions that are cost effective. Each participating officer's knowledge of the department and its operating environment is enhanced and officers develop new skills such as problem identification, planning, and decision making. Although certain topics are considered beyond the legitimate scope of a QC's inquiry—such as personalities and matters of law—the available range of topics is broad. QCs also reduce the potential for dissatisfaction and conflict by providing a forum to air concerns and devise solutions, which has the additional benefit of improving communication both horizontally, among peers, and vertically, up and down the chain of command. On the down side, if police administrators create QCs as a façade of participation, officers quickly become disillusioned and withdraw. Moreover, QC leaders and facilitators must be properly trained in the interpersonal and group dynamics and must themselves be genuinely committed to the process or else meetings of the group may devolve into classical, unproductive "gripe" sessions.

Likert: Systems 1, 2, 3, and 4 and the Linkpin

The work of Rensis Likert (1903–1981) is compatible with McGregor's theory X and theory Y in that fundamentally it contrasts traditional and democratic or participative management. In *New Patterns of Management* (1961), Likert identified four different management systems or climates: (1) exploitive authoritative,

(2) benevolent authoritative, (3) consultative, and (4) participative group. In a subsequent publication, *The Human Organization* (1967), Likert extended and refined his notions of management systems, dropping the earlier designations and calling them system 1, system 2, system 3, and system 4, respectively. A partial description of these systems is given in Table 3-3.

Basically, Likert's system 1 reflects the content of McGregor's theory X, whereas system 4 incorporates the assumption of theory Y; system 2 and system 3 form part of a continuum in contrast to the simple opposites of McGregor's theory X and theory Y. Likert argues that system 2 management concepts predominate in the literature and that these conceptual tools do not fit a system 4 management style, which he believes most people prefer.[75]

Assuming some linkage between what Likert saw as predominating in the literature and actual practice, one would expect to find most people reporting their

TABLE 3-3 Likert's Organizational and Performance Characteristics of Different Management Systems

Organizational variable	System 1	System 2	System 3	System 4
Leadership processes used:				Complete confidence and trust in all matters
Extent to which superiors have confidence and trust in subordinates	Have no confidence and trust in subordinates	Have condescending confidence and trust, such as master has to servant	Substantial but not complete confidence and trust; still wishes to keep control of decisions	Subordinates feel completely free to discuss things about the job with their superior
Extent to which superiors behave so that subordinates feel free to discuss important things about their jobs with their immediate superior	Subordinates do not feel at all free to discuss things about the job with their superior	Subordinates do not feel very free to discuss things about the job with their superior	Subordinates feel rather free to discuss things about the job with their superior	
Extent to which immediate superior in solving job problems generally tries to get subordinates' ideas and opinions and make constructive use of them	Seldom gets ideas and opinions of subordinates in solving job problems	Sometimes gets ideas and opinions of subordinates in solving job problems	Usually gets ideas and opinions and usually tries to make constructive use of them	Always gets ideas and opinions and always tries to make constructive use of them

From *The Human Organization* by Rensis Likert. Copyright © 1967 McGraw-Hill Book Company. Used with permission of McGraw-Hill Book Company.

organization to be a system 2 environment. In a study of 18 different-size local police departments in 15 different states throughout the country, Swanson and Talarico[76] asked 629 uniformed police officers actually assigned to field duties what type of management climate their department had. Some 16.6 percent of the officers reported a system 1; 42.9 percent a system 2; 35.9 percent a system 3; and only 4.6 percent a system 4. These data, then, provide some support for Likert's assertion.

Likert also contributes to the management literature by contrasting between the man-to-man and linkpin patterns or organization, depicted in Figure 3-6.[77] The man-to-man pattern is found in traditional organizations; the type of interaction characteristically is superior to subordinate, most often on an individual basis, and relies heavily on the use of positional authority. The linkpin pattern is found in the democratically and group-oriented system 4. In it, a police manager is simultaneously a member of one group, say, the chief's command staff, and the leader of another group, say, the operations bureau. The pattern of interaction is as a member of one group and as the leader of another, with the emphasis upon open, honest communications in an atmosphere of mutual confidence and trust. In a loose sense the traditional organization's managers perform a linkpin function, although it is man to man and is based on superior–subordinate interaction.

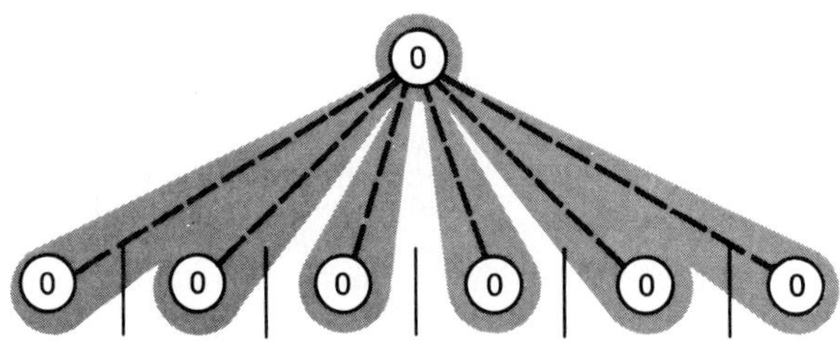

The Man-to-Man Pattern

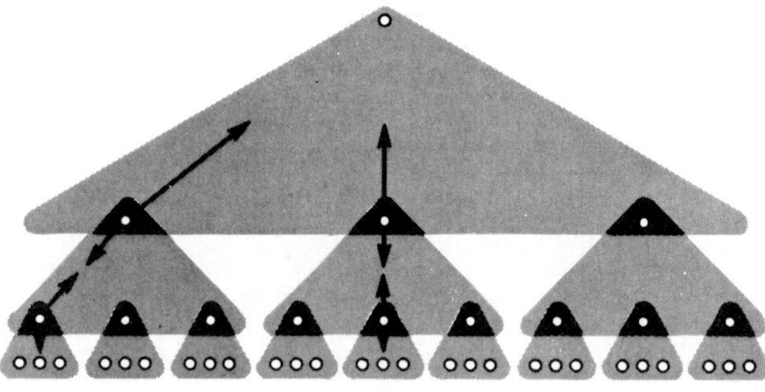

The Linkpin Pattern

FIGURE 3-6. Likert's man-to-man and linkpin patterns. [From *The Human Organization* by Rensis Likert. Copyright © 1967 McGraw-Hill Book Company. Used with the permission of McGraw-Hill Book Company.]

However, in Likert's terms the linkpin function relies more on influence than on authority and connects groups rather than individuals.

Bennis: Organizational Development

An organizational humanist, Warren Bennis's (1925–) criticisms of bureaucracy have been noted. Much of his work has been in the area of organizational development, which is

> the name given to the emerging applied behavioral science discipline that seeks to improve organizations through planned, systematic, long-range efforts focused on the organization's culture and its human and social processes.[78]

Organizational development has two separate, but entwined, stems: the laboratory training stem and survey research feedback stem.[79] The laboratory approach involves unstructured experiences by a group from the same organization, the successor to stranger-to-stranger T-groups whose popularity had waned by the late 1950s. Laboratory training grew out of the work of Lewin and his Research Center for Group Dynamics.[80] The survey research feedback stem makes attitude surveys within an organization and feeds it back to organizational members in workshop sessions to create awareness and to promote positive change.[81] The survey research stem also grew out of Lewin's Research Center for Group Dynamics from which the senior staff—which had included McGregor—moved to the University of Michigan following Lewin's death in 1947. There they joined with the university's Survey Research Center to form the Institute of Social Research, where some of Likert's work was done.

In a sense, organizational development began as a result of people rejecting stranger-to-stranger T-groups.[82] The laboratory stem began working with groups from the same organization, and the survey research feedback stem began using measurements. Fairly quickly, the focus spread from groups in the same organization to entire organizations. To illustrate the earlier point that many of the behavioral system theorists are tied to organizational development, note that McGregor employed such an approach with Union Carbide in 1957 and Argyris used it with the U.S. Department of State in 1967.

Organizational development as we know it today is an early 1960s movement. In his classic *Changing Organizations* (1966), Bennis describes it as having the following objectives:

1. Improvement in the interpersonal competence of managers
2. A change in values so that human factors and feelings come to be considered legitimate
3. Increased understanding between and within groups to reduce tensions
4. Development of more effective team management, meaning an increased capacity for groups to work together
5. Development of better methods of resolving conflict, meaning less use of authority and suppression of it and more open and rational methods
6. Development of open, organic management systems characterized by trust, mutual confidence, wide sharing of responsibility, and the resolution of conflict by bargaining or problem solving.[83]

Chapter 15, "Organizational Change and the Future," draws upon the literature of organizational development. To produce the types of climates Argyris, McGregor, Likert, and Bennis favor is hard work, and, despite good intentions by the organization at the outset, there is always the prospect of failure:

> The director of public safety in a major city wanted to implement a management by objectives (MBO) system. After discussions with the consultant who later directed the effort, it was agreed that this would take a long-term intervention. This effort focused on MBO as a rational management tool that had to be accompanied by behavioral shifts to be successful. The approach involved a survey research feedback component, training in MBO, and technical assistance in implementing it. After one year, the work had produced a good deal of paperwork, no small amount of confusion, and more than a little anger.
>
> The intervention failed because (1) the organization had not been prepared properly for change; (2) the project was seen as the director's "baby" and there was never widespread support for it; (3) many managers were threatened, denouncing it as "fad" or as an attempt by top management to find a way to evaluate them unfavorably; (4) not all managers were trained due to cost and scheduling difficulties; (5) success in part depended upon people in the organization taking responsibility for training lower-level managers and supervisors, a feat they did not accomplish; (6) the consultant's reservations about the likelihood of success given the specifics of the situation were never given sufficient weight by him or by others at the times they were voiced; (7) the timelines for the project were too ambitious; and (8) the resources dedicated to change were not sufficient.

Organizations as Open Systems

Systems theory concepts have been discussed since the 1920s, but they came into general use only as recently as 1960. A system is a grouping of separate but interrelated components working together toward the achievement of some common objective. General systems theory (GST), on which the biologist Ludwig von Bertalanffy and the sociologist Talcott Parsons have written, is a broad conceptual framework for explaining relationships in the "real world" without any consideration of the specifics of a given situation.

Organizations may be characterized as closed or open systems. In actuality, there are no entirely closed or open organizations; these are only terms used to describe the extent to which an organization approximates one or the other.

The closed system view of an organization assumes complete rationality, optimizing performances, predictability, internal efficiency, and certainty.[84] Because all behavior is believed to be functional and all outcomes predictable and certain, the closed organization can ignore changes in the larger environment, such as political, technological, and economic.[85] Thus, the closed system organization sees little need for interaction with its environment. The police chief who denies that he needs an automated management information system (MIS) prohibits subordinates from talking with politicians, prefers the "tried and true" over recent innovations, and refuses to justify budget requests carefully in a tight economic environment is reflecting a closed system view. Traditional organizational theory and the closed system fall into the same stream of thinking and are compatible.

The police department as an open system is depicted in Figure 3-7. Open systems are described by Katz and Kahn as having the following characteristics:

1. Open systems seek and continuously import sources of energy, including money, recruits, and information as inputs.
2. Once imported, the energy is transformed by the subsystems comprising the throughput function. For example, recruits are trained.

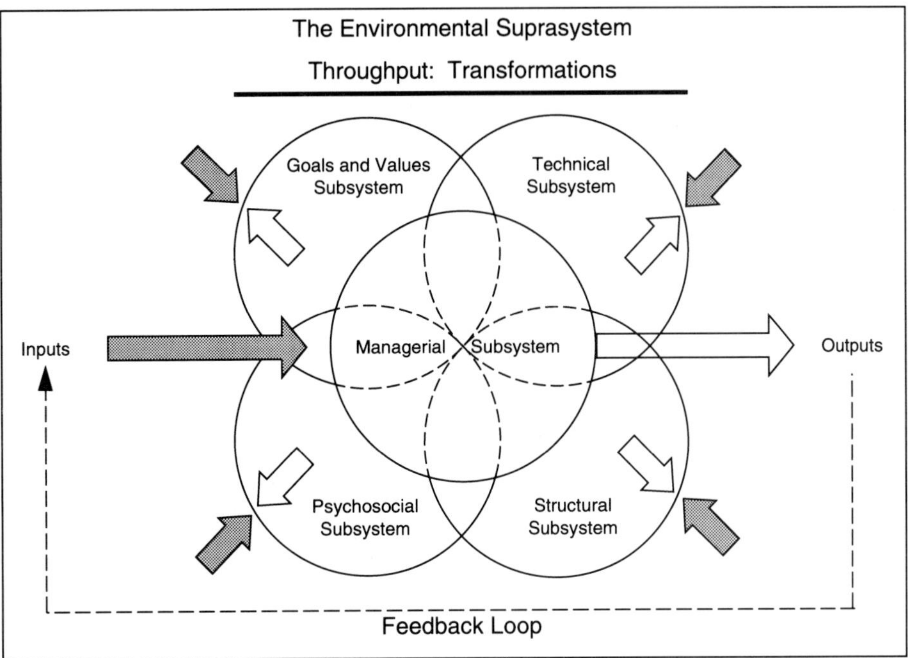

FIGURE 3-7. The police department as an open system. [From *Contingency Views of Organization and Management* by Fremont E. Kast and James E. Rosenzweig. © 1973, Science Research Associates, Inc. Reprinted by permission of the publisher with modifications.]

3. Although some energy is used by the subsystems in the throughput function, such as the efforts associated with training recruits, open systems export the bulk of the energy transformed into the environment as products, services, such as the trained recruits who are now assigned to patrol and respond to calls, and other forms.
4. There is a cyclical relationship between the inputs, the throughput, and the outputs as the services exported into the environment furnish the source of energy to repeat the cycle. Outputs both satisfy needs and create new demands for outputs.
5. All forms of organization move toward disorganization or death; this entropic process is a universal law of nature. To survive, open systems reverse the process by acquiring negative entropy. The cyclical character of open systems allows them to develop negative entropy by having energy flow continuously through them. Additionally, because open systems can import more energy than is expended, they have a storage capacity that allows them to survive brief interruptions of inputs. This may occur as one budget year ends and it is a short while until the city council enacts the new budget. Typically, the police department will have sufficient gasoline and other supplies to remain operational.
6. Open systems receive informational feedback as inputs from the larger environment in which they operate. As suggested by Figure 3-7, an open system has multiple points at which inputs occur. These inputs take place both through formal and informal exchanges. Police departments have a formally structured feedback loop to make them more responsive to control, and through it flows such things as technical evaluations of their programs and directions from the city council and the city manager. Open systems cannot absorb all informational and other inputs; excesses of inputs would overwhelm them. Therefore, open systems have a selective mechanism called "coding," which filters

out some potential inputs and attunes them to important signals from the environment. A simple illustration of this principle is that, from among the dozens of daily telephone callers asking to talk to the chief of police, only a few actually get to do so. Switchboard operators, secretaries, and aides are taught to refer most callers to the appropriate department, handle the calls themselves, or connect them with someone empowered to deal with such matters. Yet the telephone calls of the city manager and certain other people will invariably find their way through these filters.

7. The continuous cycle of inputs, transformations, outputs, and feedback produces a steady state in an open system. A steady state is not a motionless or true equilibrium but a dynamic and continuous adjusting to external forces and of internal processes to ensure the survival of the system.
8. Over time open systems develop specialized subsystems, as shown in Figure 3-7, to facilitate the importation and processing of energy and to enhance its survival.
9. As specialization proceeds, its fragmenting effect is countered by processes that bring the system together for unified functioning, the purpose of the managerial subsystem depicted in Figure 3-7.
10. Open systems can reach the same final state even though they started from different sets of initial conditions and proceeded down different paths; this is the principle of equifinality.[86]

The subsystems identified in Figure 3-7 have been discussed in various ways; more specifically these overlapping subsystems have the following functions:

1. The managerial subsystem plays a central role in establishing goals, planning, organizing, coordinating, and controlling activities and in relating the police department to its environment.
2. Organizational goals and values represent an important subsystem; while the police department takes many of its values from the broader environment, such as the content of statutory law and appellate court decisions, it also influences society. An example illustrates the interplay between the police department's subsystems and the larger environment. Conditioned by the conservative nature of the organization in which they operate, which is reflected in the police department's goals and values subsystem, the top leadership of the managerial subsystem—in relating the police department to its environment—may take positions against abortions and the legalization of marijuana and for gun control and mandatory sentences.
3. The technical subsystem refers to the means required for the performance of tasks, including the knowledge, equipment, processes, and facilities used to transform inputs into outputs.
4. Individual behaviors, motivations, status and role hierarchies, group dynamics, and influence systems are all elements of the psychosocial subsystem.
5. The structural subsystem is concerned with the ways in which tasks are divided and how they are coordinated. In a formal sense, structure can be set forth by organizational charts, job descriptions, policies, and rules and regulations. Structure is therefore also concerned with patterns of authority, communication, and work flow. Also, the structural subsystem provides for a formalization of relationships between the technical and the psychosocial systems. However, many interactions that occur between the technical and psychosocial subsystems bypass the formal, occurring informally.[87]

Knowledge of open systems theory is important to the manager because it provides a view of the police department that is more consistent with reality; the police department is not a closed system but, rather, an open one having many dynamic interactions with the larger society in which it is embedded. This interactive nature of policing is part of the core of the community police movement; thus, open systems theory and community policing are compatible orientations. Figure 3-8 demonstrates one aspect of the dynamic interactions a police department has with its larger environment, the relationship between the police department and external bodies in the fiscal management process.

Stressing the interrelatedness of the various subsystems and the interrelatedness of the police department with the larger world, open systems theory has the potential to foster increased cooperation. Also, the emphasis of open systems theory upon achieving objectives serves to reinforce the need for purposeful behavior and may lead to greater effectiveness in achieving goals.

Critique of Open Systems Theory

Mayo's human relations school has been challenged on a number of grounds:

1. It rests on questionable research methods, a point raised earlier.[88]
2. The viewpoint that conflict between management and the worker can be overcome by

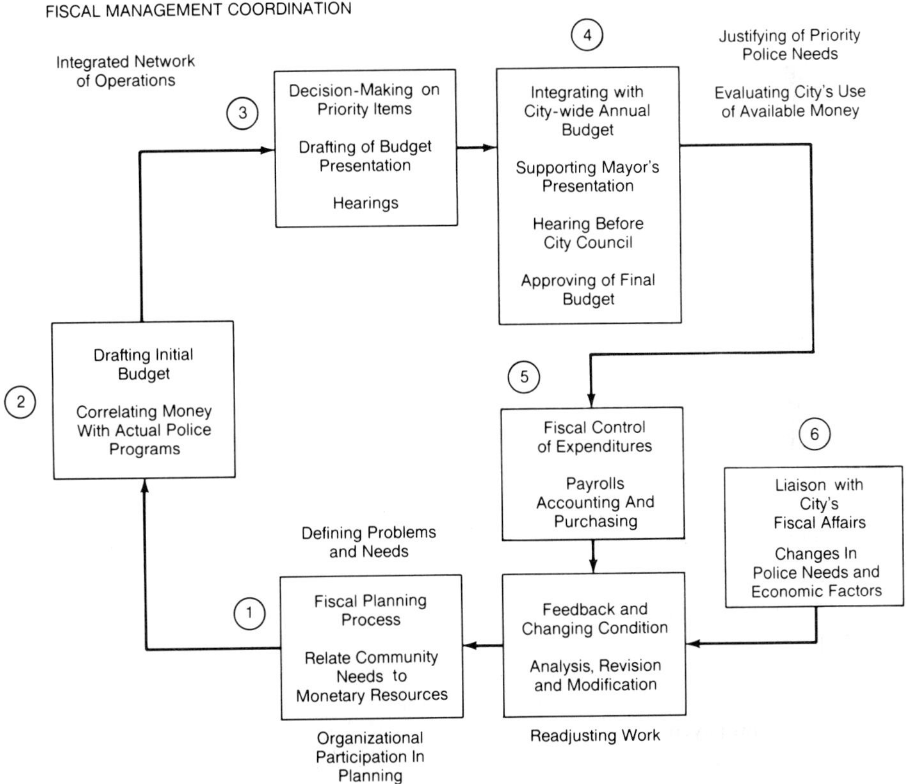

FIGURE 3-8. External relationships in the Houston Police Department's fiscal management process. [Source: Kent John Chabotar, *Measuring the Costs of Police Services* (Washington, D.C.: U.S. Department of Justice, National Institute of Justice, 1982), p. 114.]

the "harmony" of human relations attributes too much potency to human relations and ignores the potential that properly handled conflict has for being a source of creativity and innovation.

3. The single-mindedness with which advocates insisted on the importance of human relations was evangelistic.
4. Entirely too much emphasis was placed upon the informal side of organization to the neglect of the formal.
5. The attention focused on the individual and the group was at the expense of consideration of the organization as a whole.[89]

Human relations is also criticized as having a pro-management bias from several different perspectives. First, it saw unions as promoting conflict between management and labor, a condition antithetical to the values of human relations. Second, by focusing on workers, the Hawthorne studies provided management with more sophisticated means of manipulating employees. Finally, the end of human relations is indistinguishable from that of scientific management: both wanted a more efficient organization:

> Scientific management assumed the most efficient organization would also be the most satisfying one, since it would maximize both productivity and workers' pay . . . the Human Relations approach was that the most personally satisfying organization would be the most efficient.[90]

Although the Hawthorne studies never showed a clear-cut relationship between satisfaction and job performance,[91] the human relations position that satisfied people are more productive has become a widely held and cherished belief. It is a logically appealing and commonsense position whose endless repetition has accorded it the status of "fact." However popular this "fact," the unqualified assertion that satisfied people are more productive is at odds with the research findings; there is no consistent relationship between job satisfaction and productivity.[92]

This does not mean that police managers should be unconcerned about any possible consequences of job satisfaction and disatisfaction. Quite to the contrary, there are profoundly important organizational and humane reasons that they should be very concerned. On the positive side, job satisfaction generally leads to lower turnover, less absenteeism, fewer cases of tardiness, and fewer grievances and was the best overall predictor of the length of life in an impressive long-term study.[93] Conversely, job dissatisfaction has been found to be related to various mental and physical illnesses.[94] As a final note, some work on job satisfaction and productivity reverses the usual causal relationships, suggesting that satisfaction is an outgrowth of production.[95]

Maslow used a portion of his *Motivation and Personality* to attack the scientific method, claiming that its rigors limited the conclusions one could reach.[96] In turn, the scientific method has found it difficult to state the concepts of the need hierarchy in ways that they can be measured and the theory tested. Bennis[97] reported that he was baffled to discover that little had been done to test the need hierarchy. Despite the lack of research and the fact that the few existing studies do not support Maslow, there remains an almost metaphysical attraction to the need hierarchy,[98] a condition made even more perplexing by noting that Maslow's work on motivation came from a clinical study of neurotic people.[99]

In contrast to the lack of research on the need hierarchy, there has been considerable research on Herzberg's motivation–hygiene theory; after reviewing this evidence Gibson and Teasley conclude

> It would be fair to summarize these efforts as mixed as regards the validation of the Herzberg concepts. The range of findings run from general support . . . to a vigorous condemnation of Herzberg's methodology.[100]

Behavioral systems theories have also been found wanting on a variety of grounds:

1. Insufficient attention has been paid to the organization as a whole, and too much emphasis has been placed upon the individual and groups.
2. Some theories, such as Argyris's immaturity–maturity theory, McGregor's theory X and theory Y, and Likert's systems 1, 2, 3, and 4, depend as much on setting the bureaucratic model up as a "straw man" to be knocked down as easily as they do their own virtues.
3. However attractive the arguments for organizational humanism, the data supporting them are not powerful and are sometimes suspect. For example, in commenting on McGregor's theory X and theory Y, Maslow notes that:

   > a good deal of evidence upon which he bases his conclusions comes from my research and my papers on motivations, self-actualization, etc. But I of all people would know just how shaky this foundation is as a final foundation. My work on motivations came from the clinic, from a study of neurotic people. . . . I am quite willing to concede this . . . because I'm a little worried about this stuff which I consider tentative being swallowed whole by all sorts of enthusiastic people.[101]

   Concerns have also been expressed regarding what actually is being measured. For example, Johannesson[102] claims that studies of job satisfaction and organizational climate are tapping the same dimension; critics of Johannesson term his conclusion "premature and judgmental,"[103] while others argue that job satisfaction is the direct result of organizational climate.[104] Moreover, some data suggest conclusions that differ from certain of the logical positions taken by behavioral systems theorists. Argyris's argument that the narrow span of control makes people passive and dependent is a case in point. From a study of 156 public personnel agencies, Blau[105] concluded that a narrow span of control provided opportunities for more mutuality in problem solving. Although not stated directly, this also suggests the possibility that wide spans of control may produce less collaboration, because the manager has less time to share with each subordinate, and a more directive relationship.[106]
4. In one way or another, humanistic theories depend upon open and honest communications among organizational members in an environment of trust and mutual respect. A compellingly attractive theme, it gives insufficient weight to the consequences that can and do flow when authenticity meets power. Along these lines, Samuel Goldwyn is reputed to have said to his staff one day, "I want you all to tell me what's wrong with our operation even if it means losing your job."[107] The authenticity–power dilemma is not insurmountable; but it is a tall mountain whose scaling depends in large measure upon personally secure and nondefensive people dedicated to improving the organization and how it is experienced by its inhabitants.
5. In large measure the impetus to humanize organizations has been from the academic community; its belief that employees want more rewards than money from doing the work itself does not take into account the fact that some workers have a utilitarian involvement with the job. It simply provides the money necessary to live, and they save

their energies and obtain their rewards from their families and other nonjob-related sources. Also, workers may not see attempts to broaden their jobs in the same light as theorists.[108]

Six American automobile workers spent four weeks in a Swedish Saab plant working to assemble engines as a team rather than on an assembly-line basis. Five of the six American workers reacted negatively to this experience. One of them expressed his dissatisfaction in the following way: "If I've got to bust my ass to be meaningful, forget it; I'd rather be monotonous."[109] Although neither controlling nor entirely persuasive, findings such as these at least provide another framework for thinking about theories of organization.

Despite the fact that open systems theory has enjoyed some popularity since 1960, its use has not penetrated into police departments to any discernible degree. Disarmingly straightforward as a concept, its application requires the investment of resources beyond the reach of most police departments, particularly when considered in relationship to needs perceived as more directly relevant to their mission.

Bridging Theories

As noted earlier in this chapter, bridging theories are those that display a certain degree of empathy for both the traditional and open systems perspectives. Trying to place a range of theories under the traditional or open systems streams of thinking is not unlike the experience of trying to fit a square peg in a round hole. This difficulty is created by the simple reality that the work of some theorists produces thinking that does not focus solely or even largely on a single dimension. Additionally vexing is the fact that over time the importance that theorists and others attach to their work may change. Perhaps equally perplexing to those newly introduced to organizational theory is the array of classification schemes for presenting work in this area—which also may change over time. For example, at one time organic models of organization were differentiated from general systems models, although in 1967 Buckley noted that the modern concepts of systems are now taking over the duty of the overworked and perhaps retiring concept of the organic organization.[110] All of this is by way of noting that ultimately classification becomes a matter of judgment. For present purposes, it is sufficient to understand that the designation "bridging theories" is intended to encompass a range of theories that can be conceived of as falling into the middle ground between traditional and open systems theory.

Under the broad heading of bridging theories, two subheadings of theories will be considered: general bridging theories and contingency theories. Note that, as the various theories are covered, mention is made of other ways in which these theories have been categorized.

General Bridging Theories

Within this section, the work of Chester Barnard (1886–1961), James March (1928–), and Herbert Simon (1916–) is treated. Barnard's thinking has also been identified by others as part of the human relations, social systems, and open systems schools; March and Simon's efforts are sometimes categorized as being part of a decision theory school.

Chester Barnard's principal career was as an executive with American Telephone & Telegraph, although he had other work experiences as well. During World War II, he was president of United Service Organizations, and from 1952 to 1953 he was the Rockefeller Foundation's president. In 1938, he wrote *The Functions of the Executive,* which reflected his experiences and thinking. Among his major contributions are the following ideas:

1. Emphasis is on the importance of decision-making processes and a person's limited power of choice, as opposed to the traditionalist's rational man.
2. An organization is a "system of consciously coordinated activities or forces of two or more persons," and it is important to examine the external forces to which adjustments must be made.
3. Individuals can overcome the limits on individual performance through cooperative group action.
4. The existence of such a cooperative system depends on both its effectiveness in meeting the goal and its efficiency.
5. Efficiency, in turn, depends on organizational equilibrium, which is the balance between the inducements offered by the organization and the contributions offered by the individual.
6. The role of the informal organization insofar as it aids communication, cohesiveness, and individual feelings of self-respect.
7. Authority rests upon a person's acceptance of the given orders; orders that are neither clearly acceptable nor clearly unacceptable lie within a person's zone of indifference.
8. Complex organizations are themselves composed of small units.
9. The traditional view of organizations is rejected as having boundaries and comprising a definite number of members. Included in this concept of organizations were investors, suppliers, customers, and others whose actions contributed to the productivity of the firm.
10. Executives operated as interconnecting centers in a communication system that sought to secure the coordination essential to cooperative effort. Executive work is the specialized work of maintaining the organization and its operation. The executive is analogous to the brain and the nervous system in relation to the rest of the body.[111]

These ideas of Barnard reveal an appreciation for both traditional and open systems theories. On the one hand, Barnard was concerned with formal structure, goals, effectiveness, and efficiency; on the other hand, he viewed organizations as cooperative systems, having an informal side and many relationships with the larger world. Effectively then, his thinking bridges the traditional and open systems streams of thinking.

Simon's *Administrative Behavior* has been mentioned with respect to its "proverbs" attack on the principles of organization, but it also made other noteworthy contributions. Simon believed that the "anatomy of an organization" was how the decision-making function was distributed; indeed, the central theme of *Administrative Behavior* is that organizations are decision-making entities.[112] Simon was, therefore, simultaneously interested in both structure and behavior. In *Organizations* (1958), March and Simon built on some of the ideas reflected in the earlier *Administrative Behavior. Organizations* presented March and Simon's "administrative man" who was a modification of the rational economic actor behaving in his own self-interest postulated by traditional organizational theory. Administrative man reflects the tension between the traditional theory's normative values of rationality, effectiveness, and efficiency and the open system's views of human behavior and the complexity of organizations. The administrative man

1. Lacks complete knowledge of the alternatives available to him in making decisions
2. Does not know the consequences of each possible alternative
3. Uses a simple decision-making model that reflects the main features of decision situations, but not the complexity of them
4. Make decisions characterized as "satisficing," which are short of optimizing but satisfy and suffice in that they are "good enough to get by."[113]

Contingency Theory

In the late 1950s and early 1960s, a series of studies was carried out in England and in this country that were to lead ultimately to the development of what is presently referred to as situational or contingency theory. This approach holds—with respect to organizing, managing, leading, motivating, and other variables—that there is no one best way to go about it. Contingency theory does not, however, also assume that all approaches to a situation are equally appropriate. It is a bridging theory in that it favors neither traditional nor open systems theory; rather, it is the specifics of a situation that suggest which approach should be used.

An early study important to the development of contingency theory was reported on by Burns and Stalker in 1961; as a result of their analysis of the operations of some English industries, they decided that

> we desire to avoid the suggestion that either system is superior under all circumstances to the other. In particular nothing in our experiences justifies the assumption that mechanistic systems should be superseded by the organic under conditions of stability. The beginning of administrative wisdom is the awareness that there is no one optimum type of management system.[114]

In 1965, another English researcher, Joan Woodward, confirmed and extended the work of Burns and Stalker by her finding that a traditional management system was appropriate for a mass-production technology, whereas the organic, flexible, adaptive system was better suited for handling less highly repetitive tasks.[115]

In this country, the 1966 publication of Harvey Sherman's *It All Depends* was an early major statement with a contingency theme on organizations; Sherman, an executive with the Port of New York Authority, believed in a "pragmatic perspective":

> There can be no ideal design or arrangement that will fit all times, all situations, all objectives, and all values . . . these forces are in constant flux . . . it is well to reassess the organization periodically. The very design of the organization structure is a significant force in the total situation and changes in it can alter the total situation.[116]

Forces that Sherman felt were particularly important included

1. The enterprise's objectives and purposes, stated and implied
2. The nature of the work to be done

3. Technology, technological change, and the level of technological skills available to the organization
4. The technological and formal interrelationships within the enterprise
5. The psychology, values, and attitudes that prevail within the enterprise, particularly those of top management
6. The interpersonal and sociological relationship within the enterprise
7. Outside forces, such as changes in the economy, in technology, in laws, in labor relations, in the political situation and in broad sociological and cultural patterns.[117]

In the recent past, there have been a number of examples of a contingency approach short of an entire theory of organization. In 1964, Vroom[118] developed a contingency model of motivation; Fiedler's[119] 1967 situational leadership approach is a contingency statement, as is Katzell's theory Z.[120] This last concept is basically a midpoint between McGregor's theory X and theory Y; that is, theory Z holds that, depending on the specifics of each case, it may be appropriate to employ either theory X or theory Y.

Altogether, the broad and more specific approaches to organizations and behavior, regardless of whether they were designated pragmatic, situational, or some other term, received so much attention that in 1970 Lorsch and Lawrence noted

> During the past few years there has been evident a new trend. . . . Rather than searching for the panacea of the one best way . . . under all conditions . . . investigators have more and more tended to examine the functioning of organizations in relation to the needs of their particular members and the external pressures facing them. . . . This approach seems to be leading to a "contingency" theory of organization.[121]

Before leaving contingency theory, it is appropriate to note that Burns and Stalker and Lorsch and Lawrence are also referred to in other literature as environmentalists, whereas Woodward is sometimes designated as technologist. Environmentalists are theorists who state basically that various types of environments face and interact with organizations. These environments reflect various degrees of complexity and uncertainty that impact upon the organization and its operation. In contrast the theorists such as Woodward maintain that technology—in the sense of methods used to get the work done—has a significant impact on how an organization is structured.

Critique of Bridging Theories

Bridging theories, in a sense, simultaneously confirm and disconfirm both traditional and open systems theories. In so doing, they place traditional and open systems theories into a perspective of being useful given appropriate qualifications. Barnard's and March and Simon's statements provide helpful orientations that are, however, somewhat limited by the absence of understandable guidelines as to their applications. Contingency theories of organizations rest presently on relatively limited research, often involving small samples of specific types of organizations. This, added to the fact that some of the important research has been done abroad in a similar but different culture, does not provide powerful data from which to generalize. Nonetheless, contingency theories of organizations provide an alternative and promising way in which to think about organizations as monolithic types—either closed or open.

Synthesis and Prognosis

Table 3-4 summarizes the three major streams of thought: (1) traditional theories, (2) bridging theories, and (3) open systems. Note that Table 3-4 also illustrates the interrelationships among the theories. For example, McGregor's theory Y and Likert's system 4 are consistent with each other. There is not, however, an absolute correlation among all theories found under the same major heading; whereas Argyris's state of maturity is compatible with both theory Y and system 4, it only falls within the same stream of thought as the Hawthorne studies. Thus, the use of Table 3-4 depends in some measure on knowledge gained in the preceding pages. Too, throughout this chapter, reference has been made at various points to material covered that was not a theory of organization. To repeat, the purpose of including it was to connect systems of thought as they were developed. Therefore, Table 3-4 includes macro theories of organization, along with some microlevel

TABLE 3-4 The Interrelationships of the Three Major Streams of Theories

Theorists	Traditional theories	Bridging theories		Open systems theories
Taylor	Scientific management			
Weber	Bureaucratic model			
Fayol, Mooney and Reiley, Gulick, and Urwick	Administrative theory			
Mayo				Hawthorne studies and human relations
Maslow	Bottom three levels of need hierarchy			Top two levels of need hierarchy
Herzberg	Hygiene factors			Motivators
Lewin				Group dynamics
Homans				Internal-external systems
Argyris	Immaturity			Maturity
McGregor	Theory X			Theory Y
Likert	System 1	System 2	System 3	System 4
Bennis				Organizational development
Bertalanffy, Parsons, and Katz and Kahn				Systems Theory
Barnard		Cooperative system		
Simon and March		Administrative man		
Burns and Stalker, Woodward, Sherman and Lawrence, and Lorsch		Organizational contingency theory		
Vroom		Expectancy theory		
Fiedler		Situational leadership		
Katzell		Theory Z		

statements. Altogether, Table 3-4 does provide a comprehensive and easily understood overview of the theories covered and illustrates their interconnectedness.

For the vast majority of all organizations in the world, including the police, the bureaucratic model is going to remain overwhelmingly the dominant type of structure. This does not mean that police administrators should ignore or fail to try to reduce dysfunctional aspects of bureaucracy, but rather that reform efforts will generally take the form of improvements in how the bureaucratic model operates and is experienced by both employees and clients as opposed to abandoning it altogether. As discussed more fully in the next chapter, the police have experimented with structures that are alternatives to the bureaucratic model; from the late 1960s through the middle 1970s there was extensive experimentation nationally with team policing. As depicted in Figure 3-9, the Palo Alto Police Department shifted from a bureaucratic model to a team management/team policing concept that was closely aligned with the open system stream of organizational theory. Approximately one year later the Palo Alto Police Department abandoned the team management/team policing model and returned to a traditional organizational form in which it has since remained. In 1986, one manager in the Palo Alto Police Department, who was there when all of the changes were made, stated that the abandonment of the new model was necessitated because planning for the open systems orientation went too fast and officers were not prepared for the new conditions.[122] Uniformed officers went from having to do only the initial investigation of a crime to also doing the follow-up investigation, which many officers were not sufficiently experienced to do. Additionally, the shifts in the responsibilities of many officers disrupted the patterns of communication and cooperation with other agencies, which further contributed to the decline in investigative effectiveness.

Attempts to modify bureaucracy, such as team policing, may succeed temporarily in large police departments, if only because such efforts produce a Hawthorne effect. However, in large-scale organizations over time, the latent power of bureaucracy will assert itself—because it remains a superior form of organization for which there presently is no viable long-term alternative—and efforts such as team policing will largely fall away. We have a view, which may be incorrect and is based largely on impressionistic data, that the long-term implementation of true alternative models to the bureaucratic model may be possible only in smaller police departments of something in the order of less than 100 officers. This smaller scale facilitates interpersonal and group processes, such as communication, which can help maintain and institutionalize alternatives to the bureaucratic model. This is not a call to abandon efforts or experimentation with alternative organizational structures in policing; it is a call for realism and reason. The human systems approach is flawed by its small-group orientation in what is largely a large-scale organizational world. The data supporting the humanists, who make up a good part of the behavioral system theorists, are suspect on the basis of the often deductive posturing of this approach. What is left is that police managers must accept the bureaucratic form as a fact and embrace elements of the open system perspective largely on faith. Bridging theories, particularly contingency, represent a potentially rich source of satisfying the organizational imperatives of efficiency and effectiveness and of accommodating the needs of sworn officers and civilian employees.

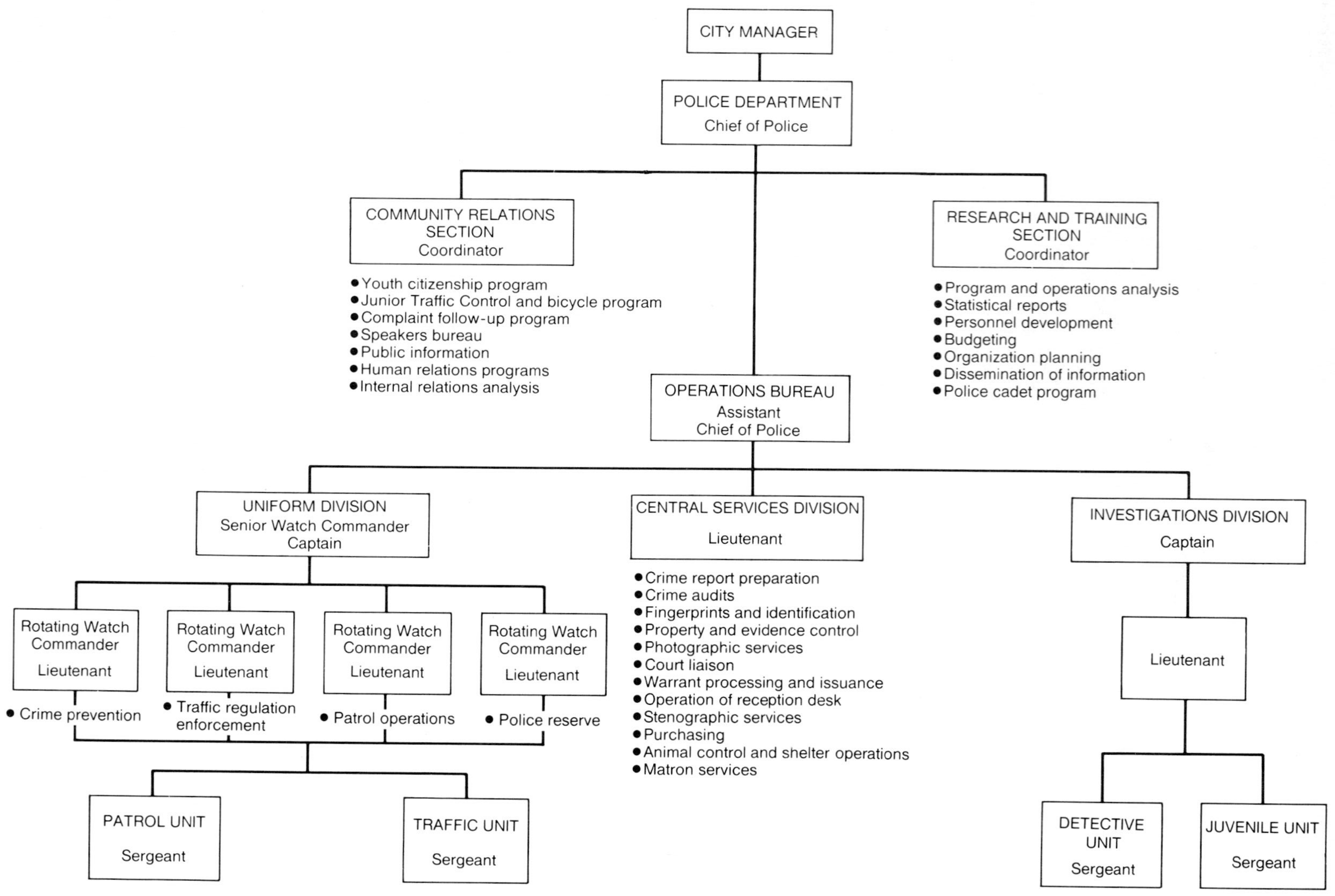

CITY MANAGER
POLICE DEPARTMENT
Chief of Police
COMMUNITY RELATIONS SECTION
Coordinator
• Youth citizenship program
• Junior Traffic Control and bicycle program
• Complaint follow-up program
• Speakers bureau
• Public information
• Human relations programs
• Internal relations analysis
RESEARCH AND TRAINING SECTION
Coordinator
• Program and operations analysis
• Statistical reports
• Personnel development
• Budgeting
• Organization planning
• Dissemination of information
• Police cadet program
OPERATIONS BUREAU
Assistant
Chief of Police
UNIFORM DIVISION
Senior Watch Commander
Captain
Rotating Watch
Commander
Lieutenant
• Crime prevention
Rotating Watch
Commander
Lieutenant
• Traffic regulation enforcement
Rotating Watch
Commander
Lieutenant
• Patrol operations
Rotating Watch
Commander
Lieutenant
• Police reserve
PATROL UNIT
Sergeant
TRAFFIC UNIT
Sergeant
CENTRAL SERVICES DIVISION
Lieutenant
• Crime report preparation
• Crime audits
• Fingerprints and identification
• Property and evidence control
• Photographic services
• Court liaison
• Warrant processing and issuance
• Operation of reception desk
• Stenographic services
• Purchasing
• Animal control and shelter operations
• Matron services
INVESTIGATIONS DIVISION
Captain
Lieutenant
DETECTIVE UNIT
Sergeant
JUVENILE UNIT
Sergeant

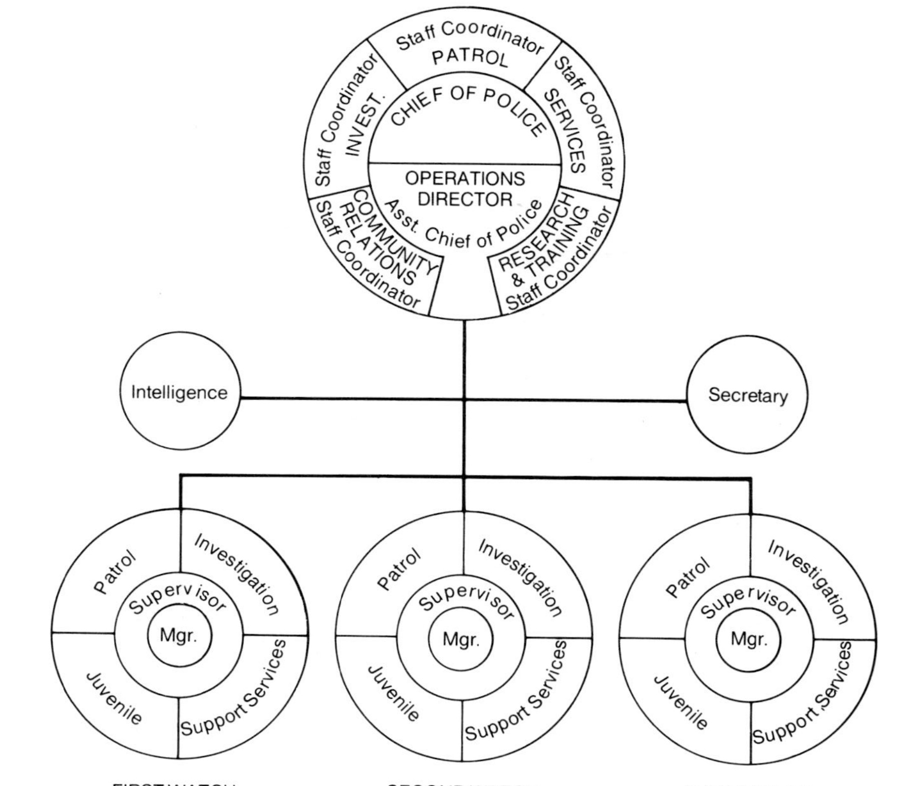

FIGURE 3-9. The shift in the Palo Alto, California, Police Department's organizational structure from the bureaucratic model (above) to a team concept (below) more closely aligned with the open system approach. [Source: Leo E. Peart, "Management by Objectives," *The Police Chief,* 38:4 (April 1971), p. 55.]

Summary

External control of police departments requires that they be responsible to the societal demands placed upon them. This requirement carries with it the expectation that police departments will be efficiency oriented, but not internally democratic. This result in a basic tension between the existing bureaucratically structured department and some number of officers who want greater input into the organization and some increased control over work conditions and environment. Although it is relatively easy to grasp the fundamentals of this issue, obtaining a solution to it has proven difficult and requires knowledge of organizational theory.

Organizational theory can be summarized as consisting of three major streams of thought: traditional organizational theory, open systems theory, and bridging theories. Traditional theory is comprised of three stems: scientific management, the bureaucratic model, and administrative or management theory. Open systems theory also consists of three divisions: human relations, behavioral systems, and open systems theory. Bridging theories in some fashion represent the difficulty associated with putting a round peg in a square hole; bridging theories do not fall into either the traditional or the open systems streams of thought, but they do show a certain affinity for both perspectives; in this sense bridging theories can be conceived of usefully as occupying the middle ground between traditional and open systems theories. The two components to bridging theories are general bridging theories and contingency theories.

Virtually all police departments rest on traditional organizational theory. Although lengthy critiques have been made of traditional theory, the data on which these critiques rest are not persuasive or powerful. Indeed, critiques have been made of all three major streams of organizational theory. For the foreseeable or near-term future—say, over at least the next three decades—significant movement away from the bureaucratic model by the police is unlikely. The police are hardly differentiated from most other organizations by this observation. The present reality is that bueaucratic organizations have achieved the very potency that Weber feared. The thorny but imminently necessary task facing police executives, perhaps their preeminent task, is to take the best features of the bureaucratic model and temper its debilitating effects with appropriate doses of other theoretical perspectives.

Discussion Questions

1. Why is knowledge of organizational theory important to police administrators and managers?
2. What is scientific management and what are three grounds on which it was attacked?
3. What are the seven characteristics of Weber's bureaucratic model?
4. Often overlooked in Weber's work on bureaucracy are two reservations that he expressed. What are they?
5. The most familiar and enduring acronym of administration was coined by Gulick. What is it and what does it mean?
6. Bennis makes certain criticisms of bureaucracy, whereas Perrow raises certain defenses. Respectively, what are they and how are they similar or dissimilar?
7. What are the major stems or divisions of traditional and open systems organization theories?
8. Elton Mayo is regarded as the father of the human relations school. With which other body of theory did human relations collide and what were the consequences?
9. How can Maslow's need hierarchy, Herzberg's motivation–hygiene theory,

McGregor's theory X and theory Y, Argyris's immaturity–maturity statement, and Likert's systems perspective be interrelated conceptually?
10. What are the characteristics of an open system, and how can they be illustrated as being present in a police department?
11. What are bridging theories?
12. Under the heading of contingency theory, one finds both technological and environmental perspectives. What do these terms mean?
13. What is the future of the police organizational structure over the foreseeable, near-term future?

Notes

1. Amitai Etzioni, *Modern Organizations* (Englewood Cliffs, N.J.: Prentice-Hall, 1964), p. 1.
2. Ibid., p. 1, with some additions.
3. Ibid., p. 1.
4. Talcott Parsons, *Structure and Process in Modern Societies* (Glencoe, Ill.: Free Press, 1960), p. 17.
5. Edgar H. Schein, *Organizational Psychology* (Englewood Cliffs, N.J.: Prentice-Hall, 1965), p. 9.
6. Peter W. Blau and W. Richard Scott, *Formal Organizations* (Scranton, Pa.: Chandler, 1962), p. 43, with some changes.
7. The treatment of the central issues of the four types of formal organizations is taken from Blau and Scott, pp. 43 and 55, with some changes.
8. Daniel A. Wren, *The Evolution of Management Thought* (New York: Ronald Press, 1972), p. 112.
9. Ibid., p. 114.
10. Ibid., pp. 114–115.
11. See the testimony of F. W. Taylor before the Special Committee of the House of Representatives Hearings to Investigate Taylor and Other Systems of Shop Management, January 25, 1912, p. 1387.
12. Wren, *Evolution of Management Thought,* p. 115.
13. Frederick W. Taylor, *Principles of Scientific Management* (New York: Harper & Row, 1911), pp. 44–47.
14. See Frederick W. Taylor, *Shop Management* (New York: Harper and Brothers, 1911), for a discussion of this concept.
15. Ibid., p. 126.
16. Wren, *Evolution of Management Thought,* p. 132. Not only did Bethlehem Steel abandon the system, but it also fired Taylor.
17. Ibid., p. 131.
18. L. P. Alford, *Henry Lawrence Gantt* (Easton-Hive Management Series: No. 6, 1972; facsimile reprint of a 1934 edition by Harper and Brothers), pp. 207, 209.
19. Sudhir Kakar, *Frederick Taylor: A Study in Personality and Innovation* (Cambridge, Mass.: M.I.T. Press, 1973), p. 2.
20. Fremont E. Kast and James E. Rosenzweig, *Contingency Views of Organization and Management* (Chicago: Science Research Associates, 1973), p. 7.
21. Michael Crozier, *The Bureaucratic Phenomenon* (Chicago: University of Chicago Press, 1964), p. 3.
22. Max Weber, *The Theory of Social and Economic Organization,* trans. A. M. Henderson and Talcott Parsons (New York: Free Press, 1947), p. 337.
23. Ibid., p. 337.

24. Ibid., pp. 330–32, with limited restatement for clarity.
25. Ibid., p. 328.
26. On this point, see Nicos P. Mouzelis, *Organization and Bureaucracy* (Chicago: Aldine, 1967), pp. 20–21 and footnote 29 of that work.
27. H. H. Gerth and C. Wright Mills, *From Max Weber: Essays in Sociology* (New York: Oxford University Press, 1946), p. 50.
28. Wren, *Evolution of Management Thought,* p. 230.
29. Henri Fayol, *General and Industrial Management,* trans. Constance Storrs (London: Sir Isaac Pitman, 1949), p. vi.
30. Ibid., pp. 19–41.
31. Ibid., p. 34.
32. The 1939 edition was co-authored, but the 1947 edition appeared under Mooney's name.
33. Luther Gulick, "Notes on the Theory of Organization," in *Papers on the Science of Administration,* ed. Luther Gulick and L. Urwick, (New York: August M. Kelley, a 1969 reprint of the 1937 edition), p. 13.
34. L. Urwick, "Organization as a Technical Problem," in *Papers on the Science of Administration,* p. 52.
35. Taylor, *Shop Management,* p. 184.
36. Warren Bennis, "Organizational Developments and the Fate of Bureaucracy," *Industrial Management Review,* 7:2 (Spring 1966), pp. 41–55.
37. Herbert A. Simon, *Administrative Behavior* (New York: Free Press, 1945), p. 20. For additional criticism of the principles approach, see Dwight Waldo, *The Administrative State* (New York: Ronald Press, 1948).
38. J. Hage, "An Axiomatic Theory of Organizations," *Administrative Science Quarterly,* 10 (1965–1966), p. 305, Table 4.
39. Charles Perrow, *Complex Organizations* (Glenview, Ill.: Scott, Foresman, 1972), pp. 6–7.
40. Charles T. Goodsell, *The Case for Bureaucracy,* 2nd. ed. (Chatham, N.J.: Chatham House Publishers, 1985), p. 11.
41. Ibid., pp. 11–12.
42. Alvin W. Gouldner, "Metaphysical Pathos and the Theory of Bureaucracy," *American Political Science Review,* 49 (June 1955), p. 501 as quoted by Goodsell at p. 12.
43. Goodsell, *Case for Bureaucracy,* pp. 12–13.
44. Ibid., p. 29.
45. As early as 1924 researchers from the National Academy of Sciences had experiments under way; for present purposes, the work at the Hawthorne plant is described following the arrival of Mayo.
46. The definitive report of this research is F. J. Roethlisberger and William J. Dickson's *Management and the Worker* (Cambridge, Mass.: Harvard University Press, 1939). Roethlisberger came from Harvard with Mayo while Dickson was a company administrator.
47. The designation of this study as the bank wiring study is also found in the literature; banks were telephone switchboards.
48. There were actually two relay assembly test room studies, one following the other. The second involved a change in the wage incentive and also confirmed the importance of the social group.
49. Roethlisberger and Dickson, *Management and the Worker,* pp. 58–59 and 180–83.
50. Bertram M. Gross, *The Managing of Organizations,* vol. I (New York: Free Press, 1964), p. 163.
51. Roethlisberger and Dickson, *Management and the Worker,* p. 522.
52. On this point, see Roethlisberger and Dickson, pp. 179–86 and 448–58.
53. During the last two weeks of the switchboard wiring room study, there was a new

supervisor, "Group Chief 2," who acted much more formally than did "Group Chief 1"; "GC-2" was regarded as a "company man." See Roethlisberger and Dickson, pp. 452–53.

54. Ibid., pp. 21 and 397.
55. Etzioni, *Modern Organizations,* pp. 34–37.
56. Whitman Knapp, chairman, Commission to Investigate Allegations of Police Corruption and the City's Anti-Corruption Procedures, *Commission Report* (New York, 1972), pp. 4, 65; also see Herman Goldstein, *Police Corruption* (Washington, D.C.: Police Foundation, 1975).
57. A. H. Maslow, "A Theory of Human Motivation," *Psychological Review,* 50 (July 1943), pp. 370–96.
58. These five elements are identified in A. H. Maslow, *Motivation and Personality* (New York: Harper and Brothers, 1954), pp. 80–92. Maslow later added a sixth category, "metamotivation," but it has never received substantial interest. See "A Theory of Metamotivation," *Humanitas,* 4 (1969), pp. 301–43.
59. Ibid., p. 91.
60. Robet M. Chiaramonte, "The Blue Max Award," *Police Chief,* 11:4 (1973), pp. 24–25.
61. Wren, *Evolution of Management Thought,* p. 324; Lewin lived in this country for the fifteen years preceding his death in 1947.
62. Ibid., p. 325.
63. Ibid., p. 325.
64. This case is reported in Paul Hersey and Kenneth H. Blanchard, *Management of Organizational Behavior,* 3rd ed. (Englewood Cliffs, N.J.: Prentice-Hall, 1977), p. 139, with credit to "The Truth Hurts" *Wall Street Journal,* no date. One of the key critics of T-groups has been George Odiorne.
65. George C. Homans, *The Human Group* (New York: Harcourt Brace, 1950), pp. 81–130.
66. Chris Argyris, *Personality and Organization: The Conflict Between System and the Individual* (New York: Harper and Brothers, 1957), pp. 58–66.
67. Ibid., pp. 76–122.
68. Chris Argyris, *Integrating the Individual and the Organization* (New York: John Wiley & Sons, 1964), p. 3.
69. For extended treatment of this subject, see Argyris, pp. 146–191.
70. Ibid., p. 147.
71. Douglas McGregor, *The Human Side of Enterprise* (New York: McGraw-Hill, 1960), p. 6. Also see Louis A. Allen, "M for Management: Theory Y Updated," *Personnel Journal,* 52:12 (1973), pp. 1061–67.
72. Ibid., p. 7.
73. Ibid., pp. 33–57.
74. The information on QCs is drawn from W. Troy McClain "Focus on 'Quality Circles': In Quest of Improved Police Productivity," *Police Chief,* 52:9 (1985), pp. 50–54 and Joyce L. Roll, and David L. Roll, "The Potential for Application of Quality Circles in the American Public Sector," *Public Productivity Review,* 7 (June 1983), pp. 122–42.
75. Rensis Likert, *The Human Organization* (New York: McGraw-Hill, 1967), p. 109.
76. Charles R. Swanson and Susette Talarico, "Politics and Law Enforcement: Implications of Police Perspectives" (Paper presented at the 1979 meeting of the Academy of Criminal Justice Sciences), Table VI of the appendix.
77. Likert, *Human Organization,* pp. 50–51.
78. Wendell L. French and Cecil H. Bell, Jr., *Organizational Development* (Englewood Cliffs, N.J.: Prentice-Hall, 1973), p. xiv.
79. Ibid., p. 21.
80. Ibid., pp. 21–25.
81. Ibid., pp. 25–26.

82. Ibid., p. 24.
83. Warren G. Bennis, *Changing Organizations* (New York: McCraw-Hill, 1966), p. 118.
84. Stephen P. Robbins, *The Administrative Process* (Englewood Cliffs, N.J.: Prentice-Hall, 1976), p. 259.
85. Ibid., p. 259.
86. Daniel Katz and Robert Kahn, *The Social Psychology of Organization,* 2nd ed. (New York: John Wiley, 1978), pp. 23–30, with some change.
87. Kast and Rosenzweig, *Contingency Views,* pp. 13–15, with changes and additions.
88. The Hawthorne studies have continued to excite the imagination. See, for instance, H. W. Parsons, "What Caused the Hawthorne Effect?" *Administration and Society,* 10 (November 1978), pp. 259–83; Henry Lansberger, *Hawthorne Revisited* (Ithaca, N.Y.: Cornell University Press, 1958).
89. These points are drawn, with change, from William H. Knowles, "Human Relations in Industry: Research and Concepts," *California Management Review,* 2:2 (Fall 1958), pp. 87–105.
90. Etzioni, *Modern Organizations,* p. 39.
91. Edward E. Lawler, *Motivation in Work Organizations* (Monterey, Calif.: Brooks/Cole, 1973), p. 62.
92. Edwin A. Locke, "The Nature and Cause of Job Satisfaction," in *Handbook of Industrial and Organizational Psychology,* ed. Marvin D. Dunnette (Chicago: Rand McNally, 1976), p. 1332.
93. In this regard, see A. H. Brayfield and W. H. Crockett, "Employee Attitudes and Employee Performance," *Psychological Bulletin,* 52 (September 1955), pp. 394–424; V. H. Vroom, *Motivation and Work* (New York: John Wiley & Sons, 1964); John P. Wanous, "A Casual-Correlation Analysis of the Job Satisfaction and Performance Relationship," *Journal of Applied Psychology,* 59 (April 1974), pp. 139–44; Niger Nicholson, Toby Wall, and Joe Lischerson, "The Predictability of Absence and Propensity to Leave from Employees' Job Satisfaction and Attitudes Toward Influence in Decision Making," *Human Relations,* 30 (June 1977), pp. 449–514; Philip H. Mirvis and Edward E. Lawler III, "Measuring the Financial Impact of Employee Attitudes," *Journal of Applied Psychology,* 62 (February 1977), pp. 1–8; Charles L. Hulin, "Effects of Changes in Job Satisfaction Levels on Employee Turnover," *Journal of Applied Psychology,* 52 (April 1968), pp. 122–126: A. H. Marrow, D. G. Bowers, and S. E. Seashore, *Management by Participation* (New York: Harper & Row, 1967); L. W. Porter and R. M. Steers, "Organizational Work and Personal Factors Related to Employee Turnover and Absenteeism," *Psychological Bulletin,* 80 (August 1973), pp. 151–76; Frederick Herzberg et al., *Job Attitudes: Review of Research and Opinion* (Pittsburgh, Pa.; Psychological Service of Pittsburgh, 1957); E. Palmore, "Predicting Longevity: A Follow-up Controlling for Age," *Gerontologist,* 9 (1969), pp. 247–50.
94. See A. W. Kornhauser, *Mental Health of the Industrial Worker: A Detroit Study* (New York: John Wiley & Sons, 1965); R. J. Burke, "Occupational and Life Strains, Satisfaction, and Mental Health," *Journal of Business Administration,* 1 (1969–1970), pp. 35–41.
95. For example, Lyman Porter and Edward Lawler, *Managerial Attitude and Performance* (Homewood, Ill.: Dorsey Press, 1967); John E. Sheridan and John W. Slocum, Jr., "'The Direction of the Causal Relationship Between Job Satisfaction and Work Performance," *Organizational Behavior and Human Performance,* 14 (October 1975), pp. 159–72.
96. Frank K. Gibson and Clyde E. Teasely, "The Humanistic Model of Organizational Motivation: A Review of Research Support," *Public Administration Review,* 33:1 (1973), p. 91. Several of the points made in the treatment of Maslow is drawn from this excellent analysis.
97. Bennis, *Changing Organizations,* p. 196.

98. Walter Nord, "Beyond the Teaching Machine: The Neglected Area of Operant Conditioning in the Theory and Practice of Management," *Organizational Behavior and Human Performance,* 4 (November 1969), pp. 375–401; also see Lyman Porter, "Job Attitudes in Management," *Journal of Applied Psychology,* 46 (December 1962), pp. 375–84; Douglas Hall and Khalil Nougaim, "An Examination of Maslow's Need Hierarchy in an Organizational Setting," *Organizational Behavior and Human Performance,* 3, (February 1968), pp. 12–35.
99. Maslow, *Motivation and Personality,* pp. 79–80.
100. Gibson and Teasley, "Humanistic Model," p. 92.
101. Abraham Maslow, *Eupsychian Management: A Journal* (Homewood, Ill.: Dorsey Press, 1965), pp. 55–56.
102. R. E. Johannesson, "Some Problems in the Measurement of Organizational Climate," *Organizational Behavior and Human Performance,* 10 (August 1973), pp. 118–44.
103. W. R. Lafollette and H. P. Sims, Jr., "Is Satisfaction Redundant with Organizational Climate?" *Organizational Behavior and Human Performance,* 13 (April 1975), p. 276.
104. J. M. Ivancevich and H. L. Lyon, *Organizational Climate, Job Satisfaction, Role Clarity and Selected Emotional Reaction Variables in a Hospital Milieu* (Lexington: University of Kentucky Press, 1972).
105. Peter Blau, "The Hierarchy of Authority in Organizations," *American Journal of Sociology,* 73 (January 1968), p. 457.
106. Perrow, *Complex Organizations,* p. 38.
107. Bennis, *Changing Organizations,* p. 77.
108. Jobs can be manipulated in three different ways: (1) jobs can be broadened by incorporating different tasks form the same skill level, referred to as "job enlargement"; (2) jobs can be made larger by giving some of the supervisor's tasks to the subordinate, called "job enrichment"; and (3) job enlargement and job enrichment may be employed simultaneously, also called "job enrichment."
109. "Doubting Sweden's Way," *Time,* Mar. 10, 1975, p. 44.
110. Walter Buckley, *Sociology and Modern Systems Theory* (Englewood Cliffs, N.J.: Prentice-Hall, 1967), p. 43.
111. This concise summary of Bernard's contributions is drawn from Dessler, *Organization and Management,* pp. 44–45.
112. Simon, *Administrative Behavior,* p. 220.
113. James G. March and Herbert A. Simon, *Organizations* (New York: John Wiley & Sons, 1958), pp. 136–71.
114. Tom Burns and G. M. Stalker, *The Management of Innovation* (London: Tavistock, 1961), p. 125.
115. Joan Woodward, *Industrial Organization: Theory and Practice* (London: Oxford University Press, 1965).
116. Harvey Sherman, *It All Depends* (University: University of Alabama Press, 1966), p. 57.
117. Ibid., pp. 56–57.
118. Vroom, *Work and Motivation.*
119. Fred E. Fiedler, *A Theory of Leadership Effectiveness* (New York: McGraw-Hill, 1967).
120. Various names have been associated with theory Z. Writing in 1962, Harold J. Leavitt called for the use of "differentiating" approaches to structure and management, based on traditional and "newer" concepts, but did not use the term theory Z; see "Management According to Task: Organizational Differentiation," *Management International,* 1 (1962), pp. 13–22. On September 4, 1961, Raymond A. Katzell gave the presidential address to the Division of Industrial Psychology, American Psychological Association and, after referring to McGregor's theory X and theory Y, called for the use of theory alpha and omega, which combined the best features of McGregor's opposites; see *American Psychologist,* 17 (February 1962), pp. 102–08. Later, Lyndall F. Urwick specifically discussed what Leavitt generally, and Katzell more specifically,

had addressed; see "Theory Z," *S. A. M. Advanced Management Journal,* 35:1 (1970), pp. 14–21.

121. Jay W. Lorsch and Paul R. Lawrence, eds., *Studies in Organization Design* (Homewood, Ill.: Irwin and Dorsey Press, 1970), p. 1.
122. Conversation of January 16, 1986, between Lt. J. Bonander, Palo Alto Police Department, and C. R. Swanson.

4 Concepts of Police Organizational Design

We trained hard . . . but it seemed that every time we were beginning to form up into teams we would be reorganized. . . . I was to learn later in life that we tend to meet any new situation by reorganizing and a wonderful method it can be for creating the illusion of progress while providing confusion, inefficiency and demoralization.

PETRONIUS, 210 B.C.

Introduction

In the previous chapter the major theoretical concepts associated with organizations and the ways in which they function were covered. In this chapter, further attention is given to how these theories actually work in police organizations and additional related concepts are presented. Attention is also focused on line and staff relationships in police departments, why they evolved as they have, some of the reasons for the dissension that results from them, and some methods by which this dissension can be eliminated or at least minimized.

Organizing: An Overview

Police administrators modify or design the structure of their organization in order to fulfill the mission that has been assigned to the police. An organizational chart reflects the formal structure of task and authority relationships determined to be most suited to accomplishing the police mission. The process of determining this formal structure of task and authority relationships is termed *organizing*. The major concerns in organizing are: (1) identifying what jobs need to be done, such as conducting the initial investigation, performing the latent or followup investigation, and providing for the custody of physical evidence seized at the scene of a crime; (2) determining how to group the jobs, such as those responsible for patrol, investigation, and the operation of the property room; (3) forming grades of authority, such as officer, detective, corporal, sergeant, lieutenant, and captain; and (4) equalizing responsibility and authority, illustrated by the example that if a sergeant has the responsibility to supervise seven detectives, that sergeant must have sufficient authority to properly discharge that responsibility or he or she cannot be held accountable for any results.[1]

Specialization in Police Agencies

Central to this process of organizing is determining the nature and extent of specialization. Some 2,300 years ago, Plato observed that "each thing becomes . . . easier when one man, exempt from other tasks, does one thing."[2] Specialization or the division of labor is also one of the basic features of traditional organizational theory.[3] As discussed more fully later in this chapter, specialization produces different groups of functional responsibilities and the jobs allocated to meet those different responsibilities are staffed or filled with people who are believed to be especially qualified to perform those jobs. Thus, specialization is crucial to effectiveness and efficiency in large organizations. Yet, specialization makes the organizational environment more complex by complicating communication, by increasing the number of units from which cooperation must be obtained, and by creating conflict among differing interests and loyalties. Also specialization creates greater need for coordination and therefore additional hierarchy and can lead to the creation of narrow jobs that confine the incumbants and stifle their willingness or capacity to work energetically in support of the police department's goals. Police departments are not insensitive to the problems of specialization and attempt through various schemes to avoid the alienation of employees. Personnel can be rotated to different jobs, they can be given additional responsibilities that challenge them, they can be involved in organizational problem solving such as through the use of quality circles, and the police department can try different forms of organizational structures. Thus, although specialization is an essential feature of large-scale organizations, any benefits derived from it have their actual or potential costs.

One of the first police executives to systematically explore the relationship between specialization and the organizational structure was O. W. Wilson.[4] He noted that most small departments do not need to be concerned with widely developed specialization because in them the patrol officer is a jack of all trades. Conversely, in large departments particular tasks (such as traffic enforcement and criminal investigation) are assigned to special units and/or individuals within the organization. There are a number of advantages to specialization in large departments.

Placement of Responsibility—The responsibility for the performance of a given task can be placed on specific units or individuals. For instance, a traffic division is responsible for the investigation of all traffic accidents and a patrol division is responsible for all requests for general police assistance.

FIGURE 4-1. Specialized patrol unit discusses geographical features of an area before saturation procedure in an effort to apprehend a rapist. [Courtesy of Maricopa County Sheriff's Office, Phoenix, Arizona.]

Development of Expertise—A narrow field of interest or attention can be the subject of specialized training; for instance, a homicide detective could be sent to a forensic pathology class to further develop his or her investigative expertise. Further, the repetition of a task can develop a high degree of skill and ability. One example of such expertise in a large police agency is the special weapons and tactics (SWAT) team that trains regularly to respond to critical incidents such as takeovers by terrorists or hostage situations.

Promotion of Group Esprit de Corps—Any group of specially trained individuals sharing similar job tasks, and to some degree dependent on each other for success, tends to form a highly cohesive unit with high morale.

Increased Efficiency and Effectiveness—Specialized units show a higher degree of proficiency in job task responsibility. For instance, a white-collar fraud unit will ordinarily be more successful in investigating a complex computer fraud than a general detective division.[5]

Specialization appears to be a sure path to operational effectiveness. It allows each employee to acquire expertise in one particular area so as to maximize his or her contribution to the overall department. However, as noted earlier, specialization has also been associated with increased friction and conflict within police departments. As units such as traffic, detective, and SWAT teams develop, an increase in job factionalism and competition also develops. The result may be a decrease in a department's overall job performance as individuals within each group show loyalty primarily or only to their own unit. This traditional problem may be observed in the relationship between patrol officers and detectives. Patrol officers are sometimes reluctant to give information to detectives because they feel detectives will take credit for their work. Specialization also increases the number of administrative and command relationships, complicating the overall organizational structure. Additionally, each unit requires a competent leader. In some instances this competent leader must also be a qualified specialist. A thorny problem here is when the specialist does not qualify for the rank usually needed to head a major unit. An example of such a problem is observed in the staffing of an air patrol unit in which the commanding officer may be a lieutenant or sergeant because that individual is the highest ranking officer with a pilot's license. In this case, the level of expertise (high) does not coincide with the level of rank (lower), which may cause difficulties when trying to deal with other commanding officers of units who hold the rank of captain or major.

Finally, specialization may hamper the development of a well-rounded police program. As specialization increases, the resources available for general uniformed patrol invariably decrease, often causing a lopsided structure wherein the need for general police services are second to the staffing of specialized programs and units (see Box 4-1).[6]

Hierarchy: Spans of Control and Grades of Authority

A police administrator's potential to direct the efforts of others personally and successfully is greater than one person and less than infinity. At the same time, the principle of hierarchy requires that each lower level of an organization be supervised by a higher level. The span of control recognizes both the limitations on potential and the importance of the principle of hierarchy. The span of control is the number of subordinates a police administrator can personally direct effectively. Depending on the nature of the activities performed by subordinates, the skills of the subordinates, their educational level, their experience, and other variables, some police administrators can effectively direct a relatively large number of officers, whereas others are fully employed supervising only a few. As a rule of thumb, seven is generally regarded as the upper limit one person can effectively supervise. Decisions regarding span of control directly influence the number of levels in the organization hierarchy and, hence, its complexity. Recently, the term *span of management* instead of *span of control* has been used to describe the number of personnel a supervisor can personally manage effectively. The term *span of management* is broader than *span of control* and also encompasses factors relating to an individual's capacity to directly oversee the activities of others, such as a police manager's ability, experience, and level of energy.[7]

The principle of hierarchy requirement that each lower level of organization be supervised by a higher level results not only in the use of multiple spans of control, but also in different grades of authority that increase at each successively higher level of the organization. This authority flows downward in the organization as a formal grant of power from the chief of police to those selected for leadership positions. These different grades of authority produce the chain of command.

BOX 4-1

At 79, an Elite Unit Finds Its Specialty Is Outdated

By Donatella Lorch

A truckload of vegetables hijacked in Brooklyn? A 15th-century Fra Angelico stolen from a gallery in Manhattan? A drug-related kidnapping in Harlem?

That's the eclectic mix of cases that for 79 years has gone to the "Tiger Unit," the oldest detective unit in the Police Department.

But the squad will soon see its last days. The unit, whose highly specialized detectives cross borough, state and international boundaries to solve cases, is being eliminated, its staff of 33 deemed needed elsewhere by the police manpower report released yesterday by Mayor David N. Dinkins.

In the one-room detective office on the 11th floor at police headquarters yesterday, there was plenty of gallows humor. A detective suggested kidnapping the captain and barricading themselves in the office. "After all, we're the kidnapping specialists!" he said.

"They Want the View"

"We've had dozens of people already coming in to look at our office space," Lieut. Joseph Pollini said. "They want the view, you can see the sunrise," he added, pointing out the window to the sweeping view of the East River and Brooklyn.

But there was also sadness and resignation. "The men are a little upset," conceded Lieutenant Pollini. "But the only certain thing about police work is that it's uncertain."

Founded in 1911, the squad—whose official name is Safe, Loft and Truck Squad—has been responsible for investigating major commercial burglaries, art thefts, truck hijackings and kidnappings. It will be eliminated gradually, Chief of Department Robert J. Johnston Jr. said. He would not say how long it would take.

According to the 535-page report released yesterday, 24 uniformed squad members will be available for reassignment to individual detective squads in the boroughs, which will take over the squad's responsibilities with two exceptions. Manhattan detectives will receive a unit of one sergeant and 10 investigators to investigate art and garment center thefts.

"We're not eliminating its functions," Chief Johnston stressed. "We're doing it a different way."

Police officials said the unit had become too specialized and many of its jobs either overlapped with other squads or were anachronistic. The squad is now investigating 100 cases.

Truck hijackings, for example, which in the 1950's and 1960's constituted the bulk of investigations have decreased significantly. This year, the squad had 22 kidnapping cases compared with 40 last year. Art thefts are also down. From a high of 35 galleries hit in 1988, only a couple were hit this year, Detective Alex Sabo, an art-theft specialist, said.

Detective Sabo, a 28-year police veteran, did not necessarily consider the squad's demise in a negative light. "Sometimes it's good to shake things up," he said. "There's always a need for expertise."

$10 Million Worth of Art

But there was also much pride in the squad. Last month, Detective Sabo and his partner busted a truck hijacking case, arresting two men who had hijacked a truck each week for 10 consecutive weeks. In April, he recovered $10 million worth of art stolen from the Colnaghi Art Gallery in Manhattan in 1988—including two Fra Angelicos valued at $5 million.

The squad is working on the William Porter kidnapping where a 12-year-old boy, the brother of a well-known drug dealer in Harlem, was kidnapped in December 1989, held for ransom, maimed and then killed.

Lieutenant Pollini said he first heard about his squad's elimination in yesterday's newspaper. "At least we still have a job," he said.

BOX 4-1 (cont.)

That also seemed to be the feeling among his detectives. But they still argued over the fate of their six-foot cardboard effigy of Tony the Tiger. It was unclear whether the smiling Bengali Tiger wearing an "I'm their leader" baseball hat would be used for target practice or decapitated.

A complicated and overlapping organizational design sometimes characterizes elite units, forcing departments to restructure as resources become scarce and the demand for general police services increases. *Source: New York Times,* October 3, 1990, p. B3.

Although there are many similarities from one department to another, the American police service does not have a uniform terminology for grades of authority and job titles.[8] In recent years some police departments have moved away from using traditional military-style ranks and have adopted, instead, alternative titles as summarized in Table 4-1. However, in many departments there remains a distinction between rank and title.[9] In these, rank denotes one's place in terms of grade of authority or the rank hierarchy, whereas title indicates an assignment. Where this distinction is made, a person holding the title of "division director," for example, may be a captain, major, or colonel in terms of the rank hierarchy.

Organizational Structure and Design

Tansik and Elliott suggest that when we consider the formal structure (or pattern of relationships) of an organization, we typically focus on two areas:

1. The formal relationship and duties of personnel in the organization, which include the organizational chart and job descriptions
2. The set of formal rules, policies, or procedures, and controls that serve to guide the

TABLE 4-1 Traditional Police Ranks Versus Alternative Titles

Traditional ranks	Alternative Titles
Chief of police	Director
Deputy chief	Assistant director
Colonel	Division director
Major	Inspector
Captain	Commander
Lieutenant	Manager
Sergeant	Supervisor
Detective	Investigator
Corporal	Senior officer/master patrol officer
Officer	Public safety officer/agent

behavior of organizational members within the framework of the formal relationships and duties.[10]

Organizational design focuses on two spatial levels of differentiation—vertical and horizontal, depicted in Figure 4-2. Vertical differentiation is based on levels of authority, or positions holding formal power within the organization; Table 4-2 on p. 148 reflects one range of vertical differentiation found in police agencies. Persons with vertical authority have the power to assign work and to exercise control to ensure job performance.[11] In Figure 4-2 the deputy chief has a span of control of three, all of whom are captains, and all to whom he or she can give assignments and control.

Horizontal differentiation, on the other hand, is usually based on activity. However, in some cases, horizontal differentiation is based on specific projects or even geographical distribution. For instance, many state police departments are responsible for large geographical areas. Their organizational structure often reflects horizontal differentiation based on location rather than function. Some of the more common ways in which activities of personnel are grouped within an organization (on a horizontal dimension) are as follows:

Grouping by Clientele—The simplest method of grouping within a police department is by clientele. Personnel are assigned by the type of client served, such as juvenile division, senior-citizen crime detail, mayor's security unit, and "gang" squad. Each group focuses on the needs of a special clientele, which may be either temporary or perma-

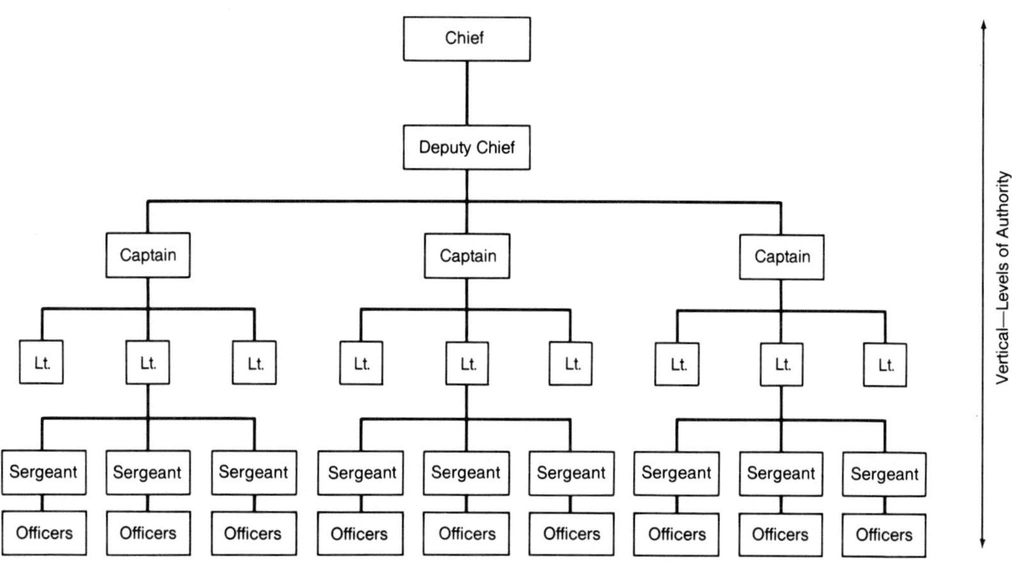

FIGURE 4-2. Organizational chart showing vertical and horizontal levels of differentiation. In some departments, especially large ones, a number of other ranks may be present within the chart.

nent. In this manner, officers become familiar with the specific enforcement problems and patterns associated with different client populations.

Grouping by Style of Service A police department usually has a patrol bureau and a detective bureau. The grouping of uniformed patrol officers on the one hand and of plainclothes investigators on the other illustrates how the former are grouped by the nature of their services (conspicuous, preventive patrol, and preliminary investigations), and how the latter are grouped also by this same principle (followup investigations). This form of grouping also takes advantage of specialization of knowledge and skill and permits the pinpointing of responsibility for results.

Grouping by Geography—Where activities are widespread over any given area, it may be beneficial to provide local command. Instances of this type of operation are large city precincts or district-type operations as well as state police posts that are located throughout a state. An example of this appears in Figure 4-4B, later in this chapter. Even in the headquarters building, activities that are related usually share the same floor. Instances of this arrangement are records, communications, and crime analysis in close proximity to each other. This permits supervisors to become familiar with operating problems of related units and to coordinate the various efforts by more direct and immediate control.

Grouping by Time—This grouping occurs when the need to perform a certain function or service goes beyond the normal work period of a single eight-hour shift. Other shifts are needed to continue the effort. The division of the patrol force into three platoons, each of which is responsible for patrolling the city during an eight-hour period, is an example of this differentiation process. This form of grouping tends to create problems of coordination and unity of direction because top administrators work normal day hours whereas many of their officers perform their functions on the evening and midnight shifts. The need to delegate authority becomes critical under these circumstances.

Grouping by Process—This involves the placing of all personnel who use a given type of equipment in one function. Examples include stenographic pools, crime laboratory personnel placed in a section to handle certain types of scientific equipment, and automotive maintenance units. This type of grouping lends itself to expertise involving a single process and makes the most efficient use of costly equipment.[12,13]

Top-Down Versus Bottom-Up Approaches

The level of complexity within a police organization is largely determined by the amount of horizontal and vertical differentiation that exists.[14] Size is often, but not necessarily, related to complexity. Some organizations, even relatively small police departments, can be highly differentiated and quite complex in organizational design.

According to Hodge and Anthony,[15] the differentiation process can occur in two basic ways in police agencies. First, the "bottom-up" or synthesis approach focuses on combining tasks into larger and larger sets of tasks. For instance, a police officer's tasks may primarily involve routine patrol, but would dramatically increase in complexity when the officer was assigned preliminary investigative duties. Tasks become more complex and therefore require additional and varied levels of supervision and accountability. The bottom-up approach is shown in Figure 4-3A. Second, the "top-down" or analysis approach looks at the overall work of the organization at the top and splits this into increasingly more specialized tasks as one moves from the top to the bottom of the organization. The top-down approach considers the overall police mission—to protect and to serve

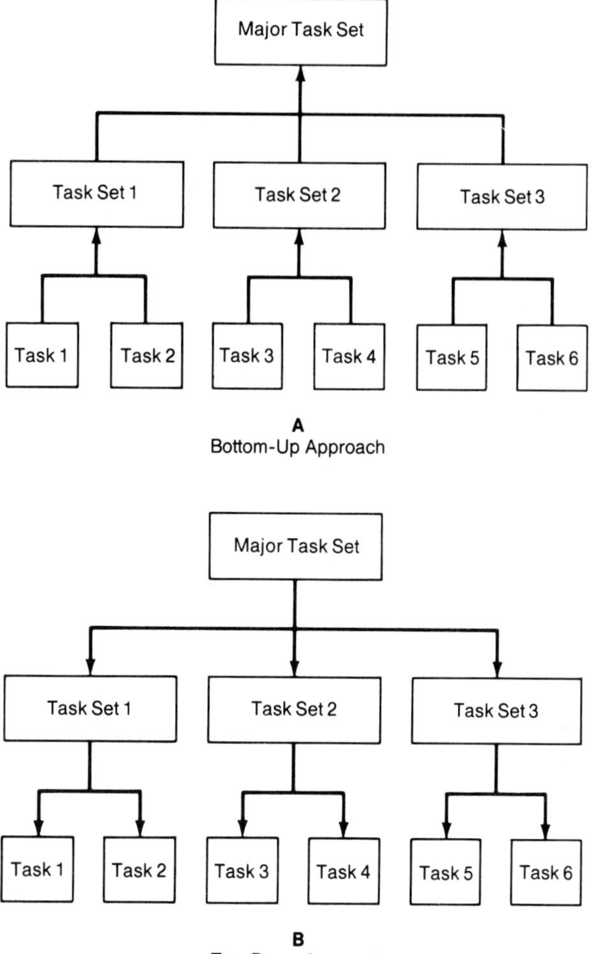

FIGURE 4-3. The bottom-up and top-down approaches to building structure around differentiation. [*Source:* B. J. Hodge and W. P. Anthony, *Organizational Theory: An Environmental Approach* Boston, Mass: Allyn & Bacon, 1979, p. 250.]

the public. At the top level of a police agency, this can be defined into various administrative tasks such as budgeting, political maneuvering, and leadership, whereas at the street level, such a mission is carried out through activities such as patrol and arrest. This type of approach is shown in Figure 4-3B.

Both approaches are commonly found in police organizations. The top-down analysis is often used in growing organizations because it is easy to visualize the set of tasks to be accomplished and then to break these sets down into specific tasks and subtasks. The bottom-up approach is often used during periods of retrenchment where organizational growth has declined, because combining tasks such as those found in patrol and detective bureaus can consolidate jobs or even units.

Flat Versus Tall Structure

Some organizations have narrow spans of management with tall structures and many levels, whereas others reduce the number of levels by widening the span of management at each level. Many narrower spans of control make a police department "taller." Shown in Figure 4-4A, the California Highway Patrol (CHP) appears to have five levels. These levels are commissioner, deputy commissioner, assistant commissioner, field division chief, and area office commander. From a more functional perspective, each area office also has a chain of command consisting of four layers—captain, lieutenant, sergeant, and officer. Thus, when the rank layers in the area offices are considered, the CHP is a tall organization with a number of different levels of authority. Seven to nine levels of rank is fairly typical of large police organizations. Figure 4-4B displays each CHP area office by geographical grouping as described earlier in this chapter.

The complexity of a police department is increased by the proliferation of levels because they can negatively affect communication up and down the chain of command. For example, during urban riots police departments found that an initially small incident grew rapidly beyond the ability of a small group of officers to control it. The process of getting approval from senior police officials to send additional officers took so long that by the time the officers arrived at the scene, the once small incident had grown into an uncontrollable riot. Thus, most departments shifted the authority to deploy large numbers of police officers downward, in some cases all the way to the individual police officer at the scene. This example illustrates several important principles:

1. Narrow spans of control make police departments taller.
2. Taller organizations are complex and may react slowly during crisis situations as effective communication is hampered by the number of different levels present within the chain of command.
3. Successful tall departments must develop policies and procedures that overcome problems created by increased complexity.

Many police agencies, such as the Dallas Police Department, have redesigned their organizations to reflect larger spans of control or management and hence flatter organizational structures. Figure 4-5 represents only three major organizational levels—chief, bureau, and division. However, although this structure is flatter than that of the CHP, traditional grades of authority, such as sergeant and other ranks, also continue to exist in the Dallas Police Department. With higher educational standards for entry-level police officers and efforts toward professionalism, police organizational structures may reflect additional changes of this nature. Ultimately, however, the capacity to flatten out police organizational structures depends to no small degree on reducing the number of traditional ranks, a movement sure to be met with resistance because it means less opportunity for upward mobility.

McFarland[16] points out that flat structures associated with wider spans of control offer numerous advantages over the more traditional tall structures. First, they shorten lines of communication between the bottom and top levels. Communication in both directions is more likely to be faster and more timely. Second, the route of communication is more simple, direct, and clear than it is in tall organizations. Third, distortion in communication is minimized by a reduced number of

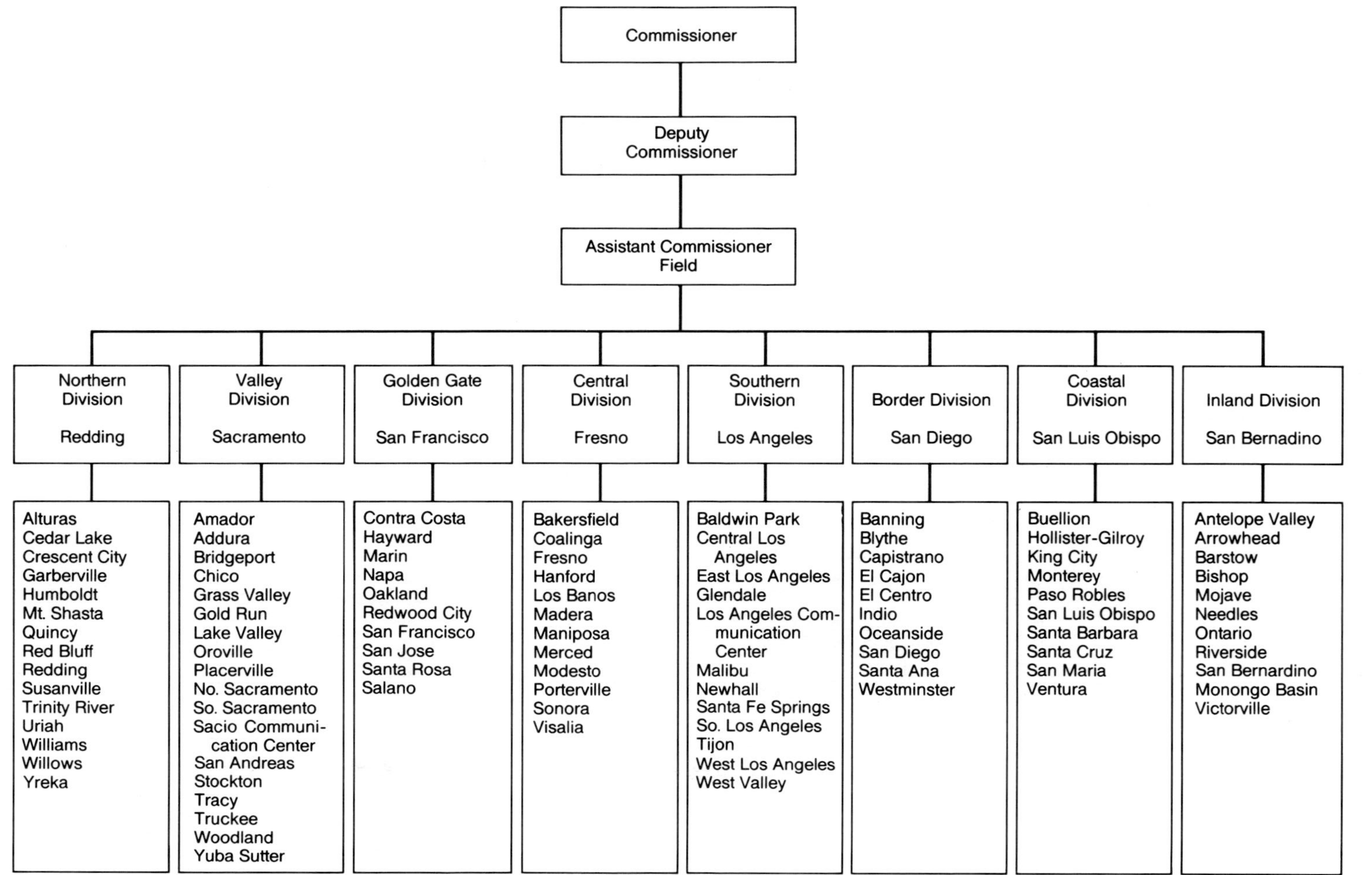

FIGURE 4-4A. Organizational chart for the California Highway Patrol (Field) with modification, showing five levels of control. [Courtesy California Highway Patrol, Sacramento, California, 1986.]

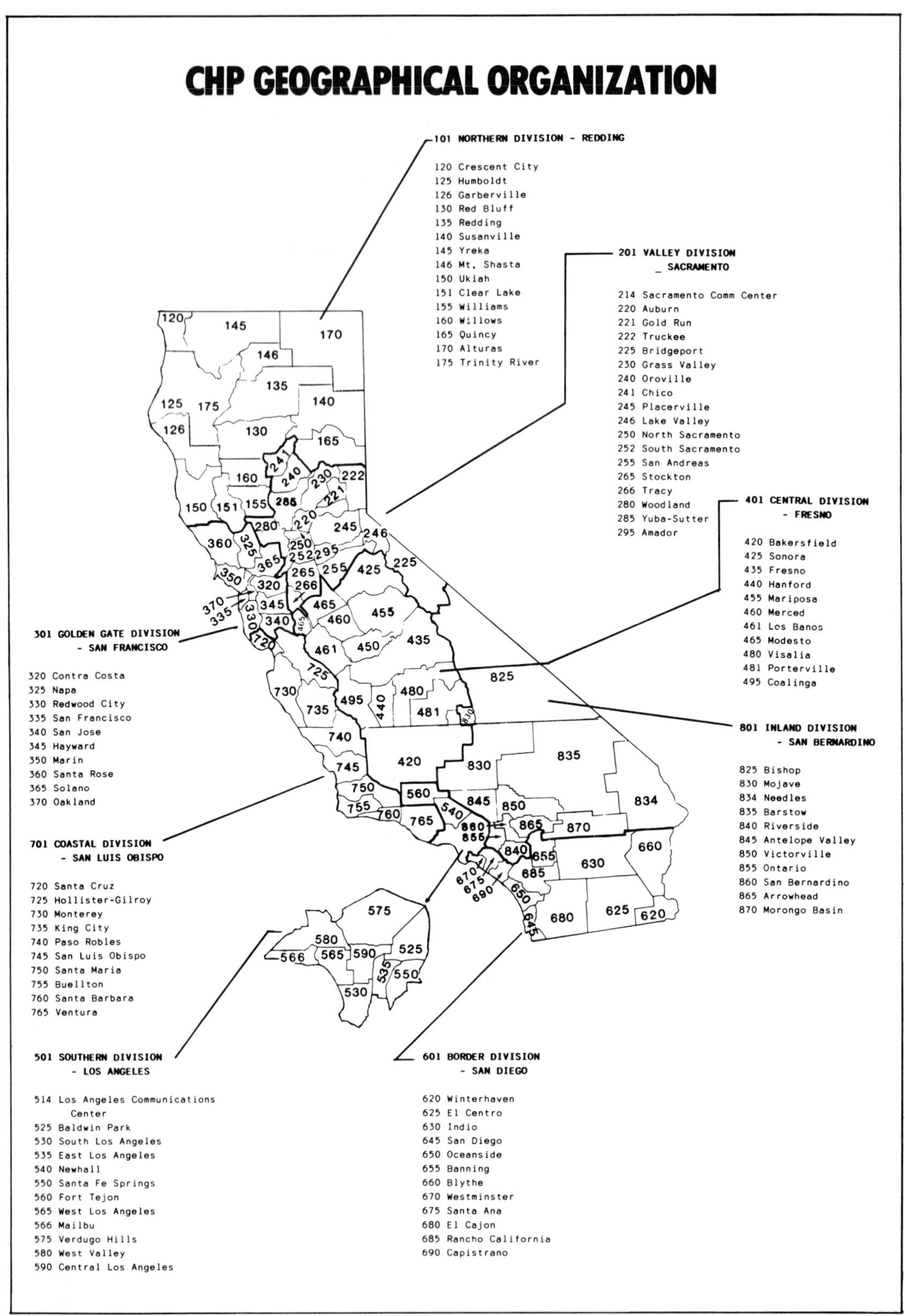

FIGURE 4-4B. Geographical organization of area offices for the California Highway Patrol. [Courtesy California Highway Patrol, Sacramento, California.]

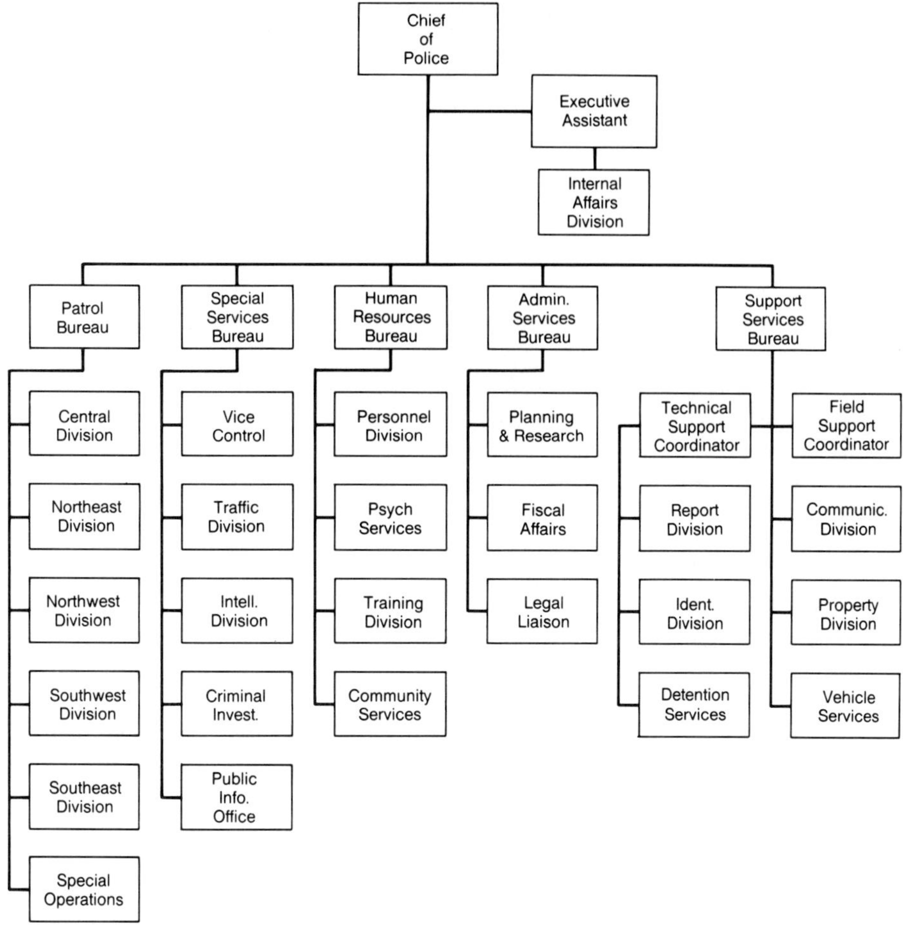

FIGURE 4-5. Flat organizational structure. [Courtesy Dallas Police Department, Dallas, Texas, 1990.]

people being involved. Fourth, and probably most important, flat structures are generally associated with employees with higher morale and job satisfaction as compared to employees in tall structured organizations.

Flat structures do, however, place demanding pressures on supervisors, require high-caliber managers, and work best in organizations in which employees are held strictly accountable for measurable and objective results. Considering the role of the police and the continuing problems associated with evaluating police services, such a structure may cause inordinate stress on personnel. Top executives can attempt to direct the development of police agencies in such a way as to maintain structural balance. Some amount of hierarchy is needed for coordination, but the extremely tall police organization is neither needed nor particularly functional. In balance, no major city has successfully flattened out both the numbers of organizational layers or units and the traditional rank structure to any significant and continuing degree. Thus, any substantial flattening of a police organization is likely to be an experimentation in organizational design rather than an institutionalized reform.

Types of Organizational Design

Four basic structural types of design may be found within organizations such as police. They are line, line and staff, functional, and matrix. These types exist separately or in combination.

Line Structure

The line structure is the oldest, simplest, and clearest form of organizational design. As illustrated in Figure 4-6, authority flows from the top to the bottom of the organization in a clear and unbroken line, creating a set of superior–subordinate relations in a hierarchy commonly called the chain of command. A primary emphasis is placed upon accountability by close adherence to the chain of command.

The term *line* originated with the military and was used to refer to units that were to be used to engage the enemy in combat. *Line* also refers to those elements of a police organization that perform the work the agency was created to handle. Stated somewhat differently, line units contribute directly to the accomplishment of the police mission. Thus, the primary line elements of a police department are uniformed patrol, investigation, and traffic. Within police agencies the line function may also be referred to as "operations," "field services," or by some similar designation.

The pure line police organization does not have any supporting elements that

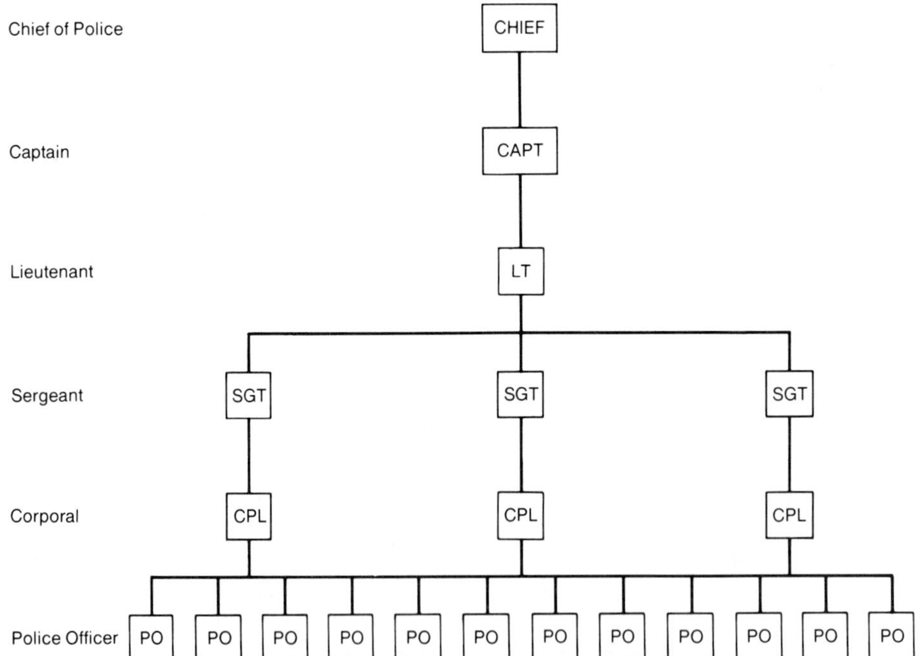

FIGURE 4-6. Line organizational structure in a small police department. [Courtesy of the Tigard Police Department, Tigard, Oregon.]

are internal or part of it such as personnel, media relations, training, or fiscal management. Instead, the line police organization totally uses its resources to provide services directly to the public. Typically found only in small towns, the line is the most common type of police organization due to the sheer frequency of small jurisdictions. However, most police officers work in larger departments that retain the basic line elements, but to which are added various types of support units. These larger police departments are often referred to as the line and staff form of organization.

Line and Staff Structure

As more demands for services are placed on police departments, there is a need to add internal support functions so that the line functions can continue to provide direct services to the public. The addition of support functions to the line elements produces a distinct organizational form: the line and staff structure. The addition of a staff component to the line structure offers a number of advantages because such units are helpful in

1. Providing expert advice to line units in special knowledge areas as demonstrated by the opinions of legal advisors
2. Relieving line managers from performing tasks they least prefer to do or are least qualified to do such as training and scientific analysis of physical evidence
3. Achieving department-wide conformity in activities that affect the entire organization such as disciplinary procedures
4. Reducing or eliminating special problems such as corruption because of the greater expertise they bring to bear on the issue and the greater amount of time they have to devote to the problem.[17]

Staff functions will sometimes be further broken down into two types: auxiliary or support and administrative staff services. Under this arrangement, auxiliary or support units, such as communications and crime laboratory services, are charged with the responsibility of giving immediate assistance to the operations of line elements. In contrast, administrative staff units, such as personnel and training, provide services that are of less immediate assistance and are supportive of the entire police department. Table 4-2 identifies typical line, auxiliary/support, and administrative staff functions. Depending on factors such as the history of the police department and the chief's preferences, there is some variation as to how functions are categorized. Less frequently, legislative enactments may establish the organizational structure, which is another source of variation in how functions are categorized.

Figure 4-7 shows a line and staff structure. In it the patrol and detective bureaus are line functions and the support services division represents staff functions, but without any of the additional breakdown shown in Table 4-2. Note in Figure 4-7 that two types of staff report directly to the chief of police: (1) the generalist, illustrated by the administrative assistant, and (2) the specialist, illustrated by personnel and internal affairs inspection. Because fiscal affairs reports directly to the administrative assistant, it is possible that the administrative assistant is actually a specialist in that area, but without more information that is by no means clear.

TABLE 4-2 Line, Auxiliary/Support, and Administrative Staff Functions

	Staff	
Line	Auxiliary/Support	Administrative
—Uniformed Patrol	—Crime Laboratory	—Personnel
—Investigations	—Detention and Jail	—Training
—Vice and Narcotics	—Records	—Planning and Research
—Traffic Enforcement	—Identification	—Fiscal/Budgeting
—Juvenile Service	—Communications	—Legal Services
—Crime Prevention	—Property Maintenance	—Media Relations
	—Transportation and Vehicle Maintenance	

Functional Structure

The functional structure is one means by which the line authority structure of an organization can be modified. Hodge and Johnson[18] state that functional structure "is a line and staff structure that has been modified by the delegation of management authority to personnel outside their normal spans of control." Figure 4-9 shows a police department in which the intelligence unit is responsible to three different captains whose main responsibility is for other organizational units.

The obvious advantage of this type of structure is in the maximum use of specialized units. Successful police work requires the coordination of various subunits or specialized resources to attain a desired objective. All too often, a coordinated effort organization-wide is prevented by competing goals, energies, and loyalties to internal subunits. A classic example can be found between patrol and investigative bureaus:

> Examples of police subunits organized on the basis of purpose of function are investigative bureaus, homicide, robbery, burglary or vice control squads, traffic enforcement details, etc. Each of these units is responsible for some function or purpose of the police mission, e.g., detection, apprehension and prosecution of robbery suspects, prevention of traffic accidents and apprehension of violators, suppression of vice activity, etc. Organization by purpose facilitates the accomplishment of certain assigned objectives by bringing trained specialists and specialized resources together under a single manager who can be held accountable for attainment of a desired state of affairs. The unit can be judged by what it accomplishes, not by its methodology. This type of organization is effective for gaining energies and loyalties of assigned officers because their purpose is clearly understood.
>
> Difficulties arise when purposes overlap or conflict. A patrol unit and a specialized investigative unit may be jointly charged responsibility for the same task. For example, a local patrol precinct and a specialized robbery squad may share responsibility for reduction of the robbery rate in a certain high-crime area. Each of the units reports to a separate commander, both of whom are at least informally evaluated by how effectively robberies in that area are reduced. Each of the commanders may have his own ideas how this might be accomplished and each wishes to receive credit for improving the crime situation. This type of core-responsibility for the same results negates the advantage of specialization by purpose. It may result in the two units working at cross-purposes, refusing to share critical leads, and duplicating efforts. In this case, competition becomes dysfunctional and cooperation and communications between the patrol and investigative units are impaired.[19]

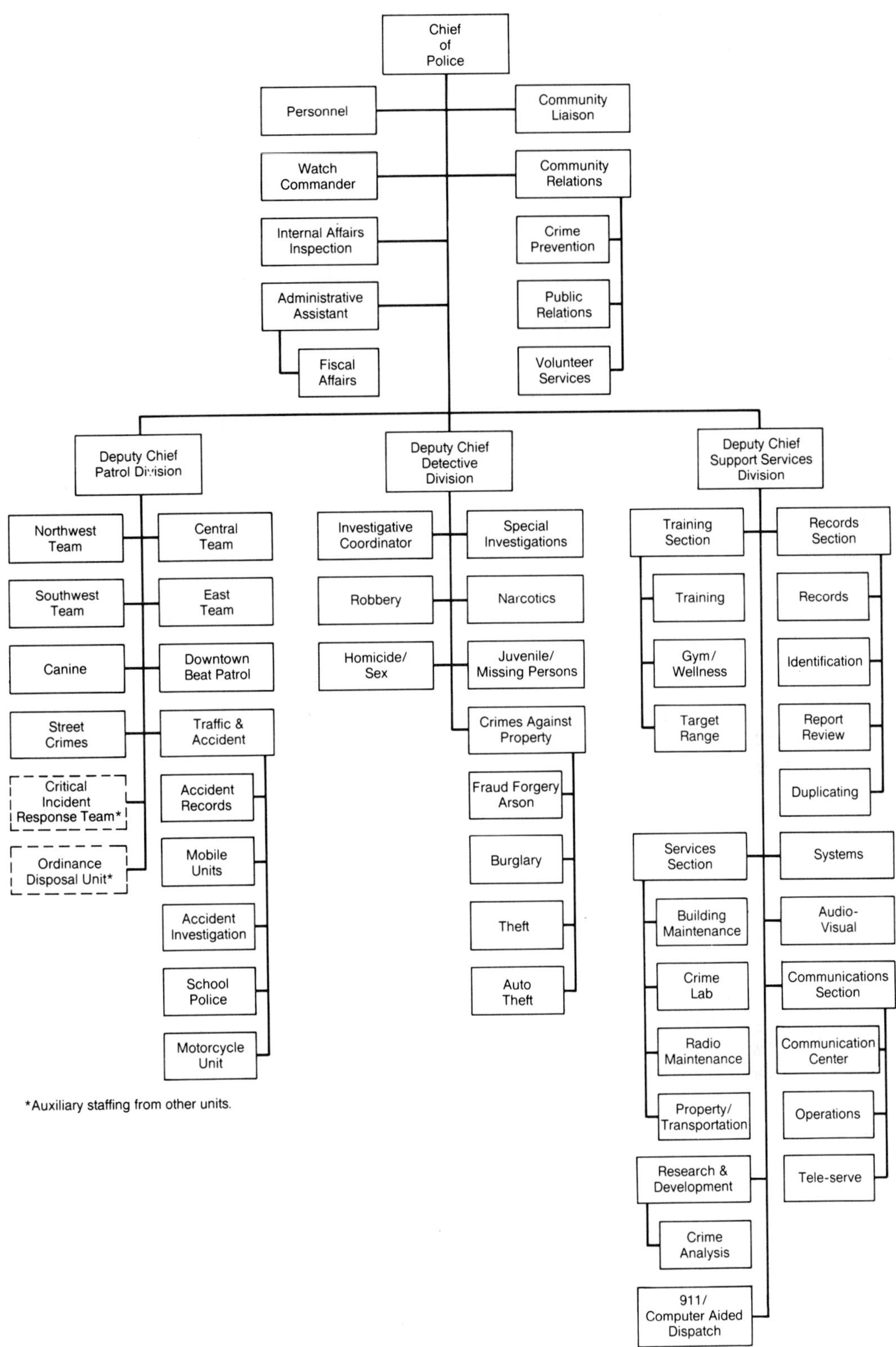

FIGURE 4-7. Line and staff structure in a police department. [Courtesy of the St. Paul, Minnesota Police Department.]

FIGURE 4-8. Units of the San Francisco's First Auxiliary Police Regiment pass in review in 1942. Although times have changed, many police agencies continue to support line officers with highly trained civilians acting in the capacity of auxiliary police officers. [Courtesy of the San Francisco Archives.]

Some of these problems can be eliminated by police organizations using functional design. By forcing specific units to be responsible to a variety of other unit commanders, critical information is assured of reaching other line officers. Sharing is promoted while competing loyalties are diminished.

The major disadvantage of the functional design is that it increases organizational complexity. In Figure 4-9, members of the intelligence division receive instructions from several superiors. This can result in conflicting directions, and thus extensive functionalized structures are seldom found in police agencies. Law enforcement executives should explore the use of the functional design but be ever cautious of the potential confusion that could result if the process is not properly monitored and controlled.

Matrix Structure

One interesting form of organizational design is variously referred to as "matrix" or "grid" structure. In some cases, the style has been inclusively part of "project" or "product" management. The essence of matrix structure is in the assignment of members of functional areas (e.g., patrol, detective, and support services) to

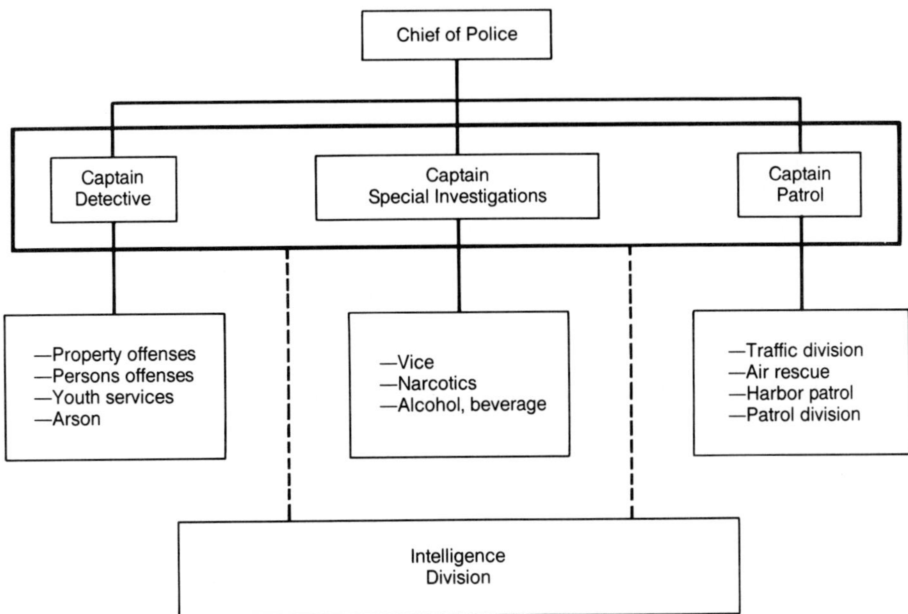

FIGURE 4-9. Functional structure in a police organization.

specific projects (e.g., task forces and crime-specific programs). The most typical situation in which the matrix approach is used is when a community has had a series of sensationalized crimes and the local police department announces it has formed a "task force" to apprehend the violator. One notable example of this occurred in 1981 in Atlanta, Georgia, where a task force comprised of over 300 federal, state, and local law enforcement officers searched for the murderer of young males in that city. As a result of that combined effort, Wayne Williams was arrested and convicted. The advantage of this type of organizational design is in the formation of specific groups of individuals, combining varied talents and levels of expertise in order to fulfill a designated mission or goal. Quite often, the matrix structure is used for relatively short periods of time when specific programs are conducted. After the assignment is completed, individuals return to their respective units.

Figure 4-10 displays the matrix design applied to a police organization. This chart reflects the basic line and staff elements found in most police agencies. However, four specific projects have been initiated that require utilization of personnel from five different units, which further requires each project to organize along the lines suggested by Figure 4-11.

Although the matrix structure greatly increases organizational complexity, it has been successful only in the short-term delivery of police services.

Organizational Structure and Community Policing

Within the last two decades, several studies have questioned the effectiveness of traditional police methods that focus on incident-driven, reactive approaches.[20] As

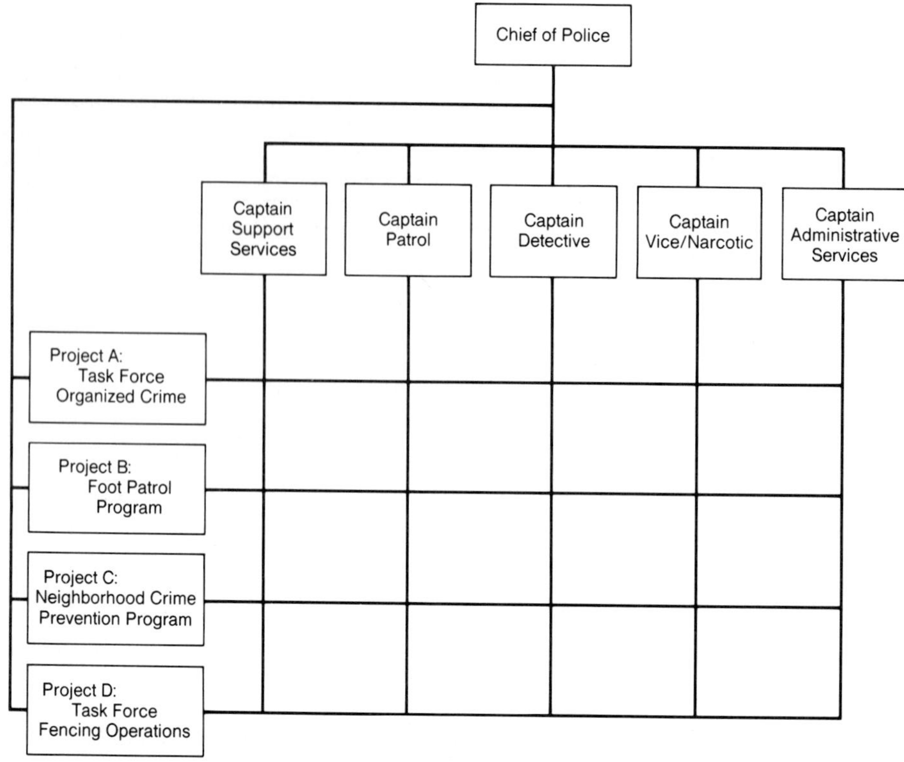

FIGURE 4-10. Matrix structure in a police organization.

a result, community policing methods have been offered that attempt to develop new, progressive strategies aimed at preventing crime and encouraging broad-based, problem-solving techniques. These approaches are being tried in several cities around the country with a mixed set of reviews (refer to Chapter 1).

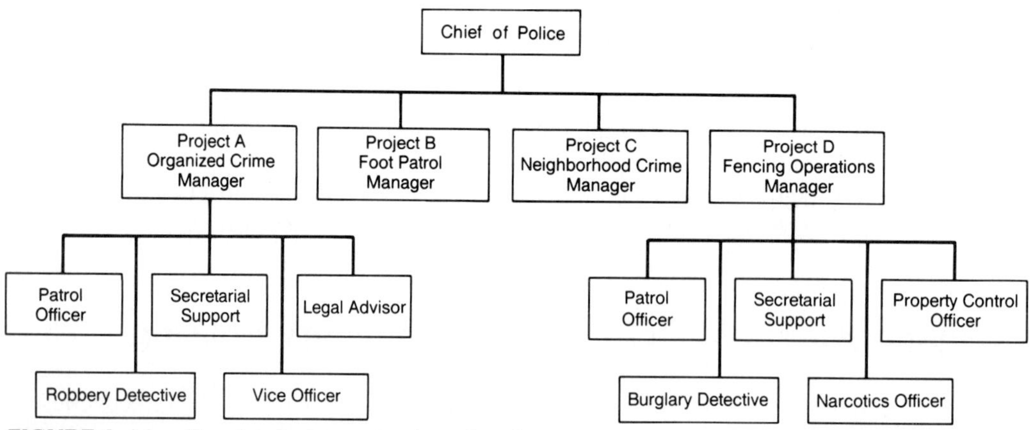

FIGURE 4-11. The detailed organization of projects.

These new styles of policing have called for radical changes in the police mission. As Trojanowicz points out:

> Community policing requires a department-wide philosophical commitment to involve average citizens as partners in the process of reducing and controlling the contemporary problems of crime, drugs, fear of crime, and neighborhood decay, and in efforts to improve the overall quality of life in the community.[21]

This approach includes developing changes in executive philosophy and community perception of the police as well as organizational restructuring with an emphasis on decentralization of police services.[22] To accomplish these changes, departmental structures that emphasize the commitment to continuous community involvement have been suggested.[23]

Certainly, the Houston Police Department has been a national leader in the development of community policing strategies. Reflective of these philosophical changes, the organizational chart of the department provides a new and dynamic look (refer to Figure 4-12). Note that the focus of the department is on service delivery and support rather than the traditional modes of assignment. The police department is viewed more as a community organization than a control agency. As such, the organization is operated similarly to a service corporation that is fully responsible to an executive board comprised of police and community leaders. In

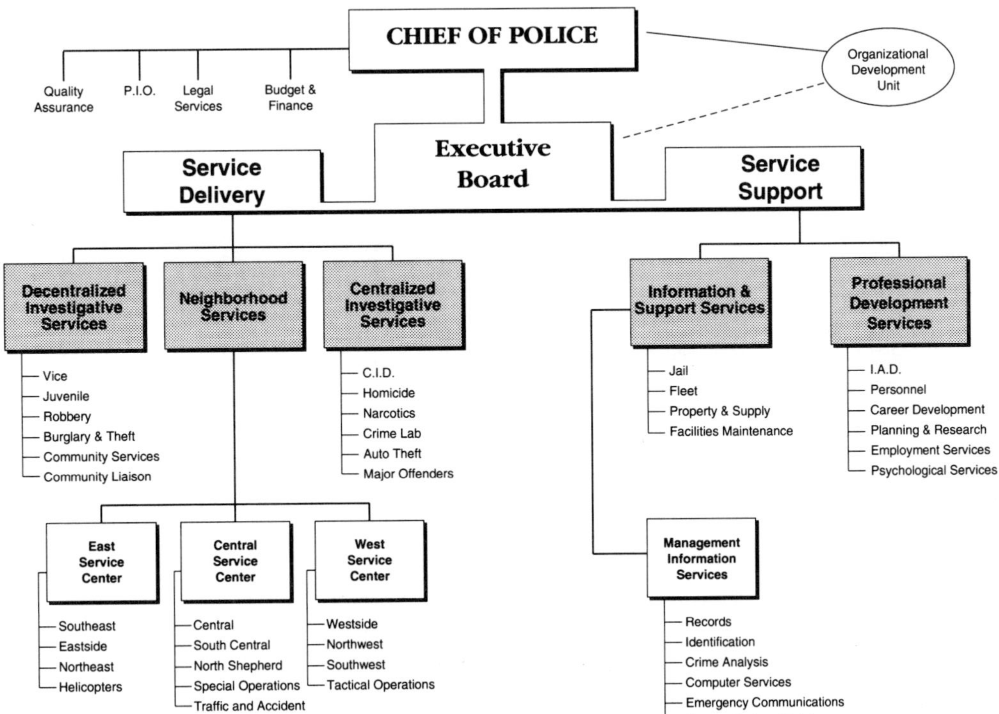

FIGURE 4-12. Organizational chart of the Houston Police Department reflecting an emphasis on service delivery and support through a community-represented "executive board."

this manner, community policing makes individual police officers accountable directly to the people of Houston. The chief of police acts more like a chairman of the board or as a chief executive officer for a major corporation than a traditional police manager.

In smaller cities such as Santa Ana, California, community policing methods also affect organizational structure. In an innovative reorganization called matrix community-oriented policing (MI-COP), the focus is on accomplishing the departmental mission—to ensure the safety and security of all of the people of Santa Ana, California, by providing responsive and professional police service with compas-

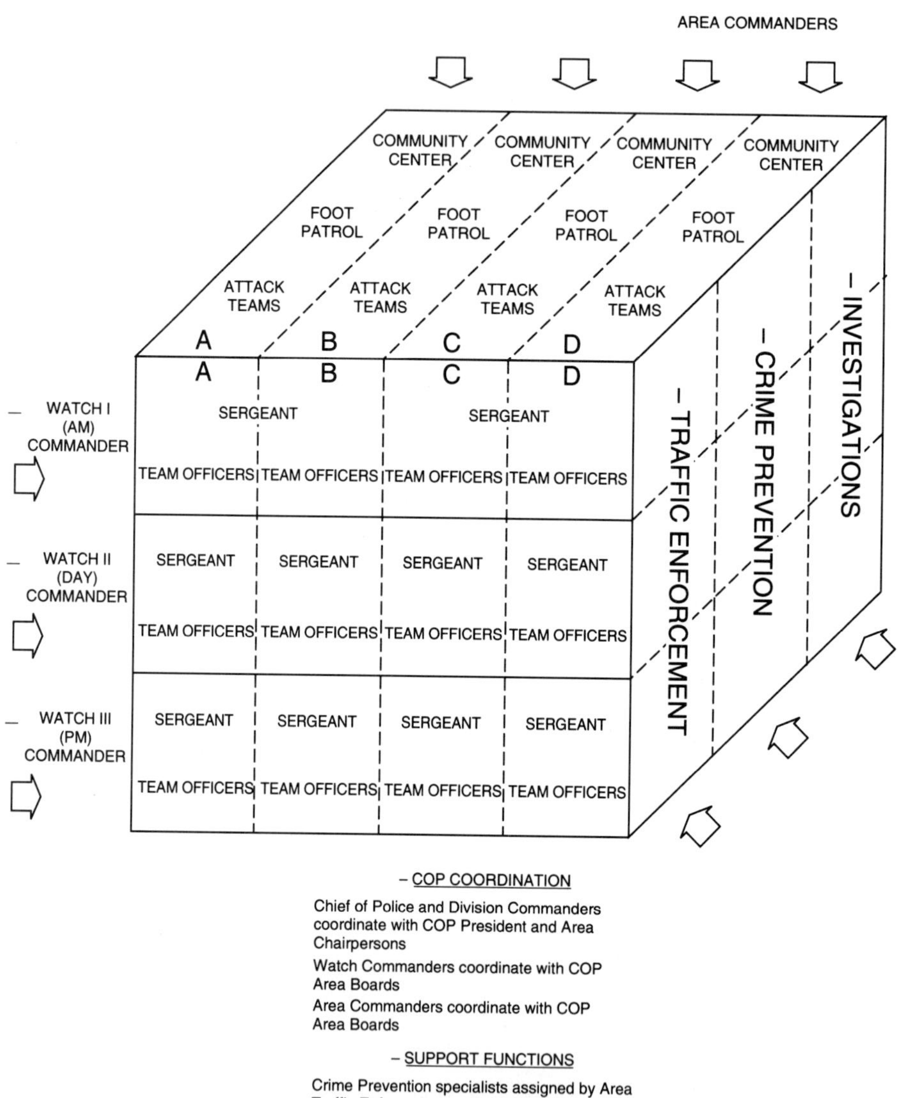

FIGURE 4-13. Matrix community-oriented policing (MI-COP) as presented by the Santa Ana, California Police Department. Note the decentralization of tasks within supervisory and officer ranks.

sion and concern.[24] By arranging the department into specialized forces capable of attacking problems from different perspectives, the entire department is responsible for accomplishing the community policing goals (see Figure 4-13). MI-COP represents a three-dimensional organizational structure approach in which many functions interact to share responsibilities in resolving public safety problems.

Although a number of community policing methods have been adopted across the country, several structural problems have been cited in the literature.[25] For instance, community policing revokes the paramilitary structure of the past 100 years. Traditional structures of police organizations have historically followed the principles of hierarchy that aim to control subordinates. These principles tend to stifle innovation and creativity, promote alienation and loss of individual self-worth, emphasize mediocrity, and diminish the ability of managers to lead (refer to Chapter 3). Community policing requires a shorter and flatter organizational design. Services are decentralized and community based. Necessarily, such a design will be less formalized, less specialized, and less bureaucratic (rule oriented). Cordner[26] suggests that police agencies shift from written rules and regulations (which are primarily used to control officers) to a straightforward, situation-oriented approach. Community policing advocates empowering the individual officer with more discretion and more responsibility than traditional policing; hence, direction from the organization must emphasize shared values, participatory decision making, and a collegial atmosphere. Moreover, the organization of community policing is open and sensitive to the environment, with a built-in need to interact with members of the wider community and be "'results oriented" rather than closed and internally defined. The differences in organizational structure between traditional policing and community policing are outlined in Table 4-3.

Some argue that community policing calls for too radical a change in organizational design, that such changes may be impossible under existing union and civil service constraints. Further, in Chapter 1, we discussed Michel's "iron law of oligarchy" which indicates that modern, large-scale organizations tend toward

TABLE 4-3 Organizational Structure

Traditional policing	Community policing
1. *Bureaucratic:* rigid, formalized—paper based, rule oriented—"by the book policing," standardized.	1. *Nonbureaucratic:* corporate flexible—rules to fit situation—paper where necessary, collegial atmosphere
2. *Centralized:* centralization of all management, support, operational, and authority functions	2. *Decentralization:* of authority and management function to meet operational requirements—organization driven by front end—and community-based demand
3. *Hierarchical:* pyramid with multiple rank levels	3. *Flattened management (rank) structure:* additional rank at operational level
4. *Specialization:* of varied police functions to increase efficiency (C.I.D. functions, crime prevention, etc.)	4. *Generalization:* specialization limited—support generalist officer—patrol based
5. *Closed organization orientation:* distinct from environment, resistant to environmental influence, internally defined agenda, means over ends	5. *Open organization model:* interact with environment, open to change, sensitive to environment, results oriented

Adapted from C. Murphy, *Contemporary Models of Urban Policing: Shaping the Future* (Ontario, Canada: Ministry of the Solicitor General, 1991), p. 2.

specialization and centralization.[27] However, these organizational traits appear to be in conflict with more progressive community policing structures. (See Table 4-3.) Large police departments require a certain amount of specialization to handle diverse tasks efficiently, such as examining various types of physical evidence or handling unique situations, and the amount of hierarchy required to coordinate the various specialized parts produces a tendency toward centralization. This structural conflict causes significant role confusion and ambiguity among officers who are assigned traditional law enforcement duties as well as more contemporary police tasks. As a result of such difficulties, the continued implementation of community policing should provide a dynamic arena for police organizational structure in the future.

Line and Staff Relationships in Police Agencies

The rapid growth in size of many police agencies has been accompanied by a corresponding rapid growth in specialization and a need for the expansion of staff services to provide support for operating units. This expansion and division of responsibility, which occurs in all police departments except those that are a pure line form of organization, is sometimes fraught with difficulty and dissension. If left uncorrected, these conditions will have a serious negative effect on both the quality and the quantity of service a police agency is able to deliver to its citizens. The following represent some of the major causes of conflict between line and staff:

The Line Point of View

One of the basic causes of organizational difficulties, as line operations view them, is that staff personnel attempt to assume authority over line elements instead of supporting and advising them.[28] Line commanders feel that the chief looks to them for accountability of the operation; therefore, staff personnel should not try to control their operation because they are not ultimately responsible for handling line problems. Another commonly heard complaint is that staff personnel sometimes fail to give sound advice because their ideas are not fully thought out, not tested, or "too academic." This attitude is easy for line commanders to develop because of the belief that staff personal are not responsible for the ultimate results of their product and therefore propose new ideas too quickly.

Communications problems sometimes emerge between the staff specialist and line commanders. Staff personnel on occasion fail to explain new plans or procedures and do not give line commanders sufficient time to propose changes. For example, a major staff project was installed in a patrol operation after only a very brief period of time had passed from its announcement until the starting date. Some attempts were made to prepare the personnel for the project by the use of general orders and memos, but this was left to line supervisors to do, and they did not have enough information to fully explain the new program. This resulted in confusion. Individual officers were unsure of what they were to do, so they did little. It took several weeks to recognize the problem and several more weeks to explain, train, and guide the personnel to operate under the new plan. After a three-month delay, the plan began to show results. However, the crime picture for this period was the worst in four years. The chief placed the blame at his precinct commanders' doors. They, in turn, blamed staff for poor preparation and lack of coordination.

Line commanders frequently claim that staff personnel take credit for successful operations and point the finger of blame at the line commander when programs fail. In one department a new report-writing program was installed under staff auspices. This program was designed to improve the statistical data that the staff group would use in preparing the various departmental reports and also to help the patrol commander to evaluate patrol personnel. During the first year of the program several flaws showed up that prompted staff to write a report that stated the patrol supervisors were not checking the reports carefully, and as a result erroneous information was appearing that made evaluation impossible. A retraining program was instituted and the defects were ironed out. The personnel assigned to do the training then wrote a report taking full credit for the improvement. The commander of the patrol division took a rather dim view of this self-congratulatory report because he along with some of his subordinates worked very closely with the training section in formulating the retraining program.

Operational commanders sometimes express the concern that staff personnel do not see the "big picture" because they have only limited objectives that reflect their own nonoperational specialties. For example, the personnel unit of one police department developed a test for the rank of lieutenant. Most of the sergeants who took the examination did poorly. Many became frustrated and angry because they had built up fine work records and believed that the examination procedure failed to measure their potential ability for the rank of lieutenant accurately. The members of the personnel unit who developed the examination procedure were not sympathetic and suggested that the department just did not have the caliber of personnel who could pass a valid examination. The line commanders claimed that the personnel unit did not know enough about the department's needs, and if they would put more effort into helping instead of "figuring out reasons why we're no good, then we'd be better off."

The Staff Viewpoint

Staff personnel contend that line commanders do not know how to use staff. Instead of utilizing their analytical skills, staff personnel feel that line commanders simply want to use them as writers. As an example, in one medium-sized department, the robbery case load was increasing at an alarming rate. When staff was approached to work on the problem, the detective chief told them how he saw the problem, asked them to prepare an order for his signature setting out the changes as he saw them, and refused any staff personnel the opportunity to contact the operating field units to determine what the problems were as they saw them.

Many staff personnel also feel that line officers are shortsighted and resist new ideas. As an example, a department had recently expanded and numerous personnel were promoted, but some of the personnel promoted to administrative and executive positions could not function effectively because they had not been properly trained to assume their new roles and responsibilities. The results were inefficiency and personal conflict. The planning and research officer had much earlier wanted to install a training program for career development for the ranks of lieutenant and above so there would be a trained group to choose from when needed. The planning and research officer blamed the line commanders for being shortsighted and not cooperating earlier to develop career development programs.

Solutions

The problems of line and staff relationships can be corrected. What is needed is (1) a thorough indoctrination and training program and (2) clear definitions as to the task of each.

The line is principally responsible for successful operations of the department and therefore they must be responsible for operational decisions affecting them. Staff, on the other hand, exists to assist the line in reaching objectives by providing advice and information when requested to do so. This does not, however, prohibit staff from volunteering advice it believes is needed.

The use of staff assistance is usually at the option of line commanders but they must recognize that the chief can decide to use staff services to review any operation and that this decision is binding. As an example, a planning and research officer may be ordered by the chief to determine if patrol officers are being properly utilized. The patrol commander is responsible for making effective use of advice received under such circumstances. If the patrol commander disagrees with staff findings, then an opportunity for reply and review by a higher authority should be available.

Staff exists to help line elements accomplish the objectives of the department. To do this effectively, staff must know what line elements are doing. Illustratively, the personnel officer who does not know what tasks police officers must perform cannot effectively prepare selection standards for the hiring of personnel. Both staff and line must exert effort to ensure that staff stays in contact with what is going on in line units.

Line personnel are concerned primarily with day-to-day operating objectives within the framework of departmental goals. Staff can perform a valuable task for them by thinking ahead toward future problems and operations before they arise. The possibility of a plane crash is a subject that staff, in cooperation with line commanders, can anticipate. Thus, time-consuming planning and the development of orders and procedures can be accomplished by staff well before they are needed.

Line commanders should know what the various staff functions are and what they can contribute to the improvement of the line units. In some departments this can be done at meetings by allowing the staff heads to explain what they can do for the line commanders. At the same time line commanders can make known their expectations about staff support. Such discussions lead to closer coordination and to improved personal relationships that are essential for effectiveness. Staff's ideas will be more readily accepted if they demonstrate an understanding of line operations.

Staff activity deals primarily with change. However, people tend to resist change and ideas that threaten the status quo. Change by itself indicates the possibility that the old way is no longer acceptable. Staff should anticipate and dispel resistance to change by the following:

1. Determining to what extent the change proposed will affect the personal relationships of the people involved. Is the change a major one that will affect the social patterns established in the formal and informal organizations? Can the change be broken down into a series of small moves that will have less negative impact than a single large change?
2. Involving those most affected by the change in the early planning stages. When major changes are involved that will modify the relationships between line commanders and the people who work for them, opposition from commanders can be minimized if they participate from the early planning stages. Although it may not be possible for everyone to actually participate, the use of representative groups of employees is often effective in helping to facilitate change.
3. Communicating throughout the entire planning stage. The personnel who will be affected by the change will accept it better if: (a) they believe it will benefit them personally—that it will make their work easier, faster, or safer. The change should be tied in as closely as possible with the individual's personal goals and interests—job, family, future; (b) the personnel have an opportunity to offer suggestions, ideas, and comments concerning the change as it affects them—provided these suggestions are sincerely wanted and are given serious consideration; and (c) they are kept informed of the results of the change.

In order to achieve organizational objectives, a line commander should know how to use staff assistance. The specialized skills of staff people can be used to help achieve these goals more efficiently and economically. By involving staff in the problems of the line, staff personnel can become more effective by learning the line commanders' way of thinking. Line commanders must be able to identify their problems precisely before seeking assistance. They must not vaguely define a problem and then expect the staff unit to do all the work. It is also important for staff to keep other staff informed of decisions that will affect them. As an example, a department was given permission to hire and train 250 new officers, which was double the normal recruit class. The training unit was not advised of this until a week before the class was to start. Subsequently, many problems developed which could have been avoided.

Summary

This chapter elaborated on certain content from Chapter 3 and introduced related concepts. The major concerns in organizing are (1) dividing the jobs, (2) grouping the jobs, (3) forming grades of authority, and (4) equalizing authority and responsibility. Specialization has both advantages and disadvantages. The advantages include placement of responsibility, development of expertise, promotion of esprit de corps, and increased efficiency and effectiveness. Among the disadvantages of specialization are increased friction and conflict, decreased job performance, complication of the command structure, difficulty in finding sufficient qualified leaders, and hampering the development of a well-rounded police program. Organizational design focuses on two spatial levels of differentiation: vertical, based on levels of authority; and horizontal, based on activity. Some of the ways in which horizontal differentiation occurs is through grouping by: clientele, style of service, geography, time, and process. According to Hodge and Anthony, the differentiation process can occur in two basic ways: (1) the bottom-up or synthesis approach and (2) the top-down or analysis approach. Police departments can be considered tall or flat. Tall organizational structures have many different layers which make them more complex and which can impair effective communication. Flat organizations have fewer layers, which is often the result of broadening the span of control, and tend not to suffer from as many communication problems as do the taller departments. Extremely tall organizations are neither needed nor particularly functional, although some amount of hierarchy is needed to coordinate the various parts of a large, complex organization. However desirable theoretically, no major city has made significant and continuing inroads into reducing both the layers of organization and the height of the traditional rank structure.

There are four basic types of structural design that may be found in police agencies: (1) line, (2) line and staff, (3) functional, and (4) matrix. These types can exist separately or in combination. Statistically the line form of organization appears most frequently, but most police officers work in a line and staff structure. Recent advances in community policing and problem-oriented policing are changing traditional perspectives on organizational structure. With a continued emphasis on citizen/community involvement in the police mission and the decentralization of police services, experimental methods offer new means in which to chart responsibility and accountability within an organization. Although there are controversial issues surrounding these innovative designs, their impact on future police organizational structure will be profound.

One of the continuing problems in all but the very smallest police departments is the tension between line commanders and staff specialists. Although the basic causes of these organizational difficulties are varied, there are strategies which can be employed as solutions.

Discussion Questions

1. What are some of the advantages and disadvantages of specialization?
2. Explain the concepts of vertical and horizontal differentiation as applied to organizational design.
3. What are the common ways of grouping activities?
4. What is meant by "tall" and "flat" organizational structures?
5. Identify and explain four basic types of structural design found in police agencies.
6. How have experimental police methods (such as community-oriented policing) influenced organizational structure and design?
7. What are the essential differences between line and staff in police departments?
8. What are some of the major sources of tension in line–staff relationships?

Notes

1. S. P. Robbins, *The Administration Process* (Englewood Cliffs, N.J.: Prentice Hall, 1976), pp. 17–18. This discussion of "Organizing an Overview" was adapted from this source.
2. *The Republic of Plato,* trans. A. Bloom (New York: Basic Books, 1968), p. 47.
3. For example, see Luther Gulick and L. Urwick, eds., *Papers on the Science of Administration* (New York: August M. Kelley, a 1969 reprint of the 1937 edition).
4. O. W. Wilson and R. C. McLaren, *Police Administration,* 3rd ed. (New York: McGraw-Hill, 1972), p. 79.

5. Ibid., p. 81.
6. Ibid., p. 83.
7. N. C. Kassoff, *Organizational Concepts* (Washington, D.C.: International Association of Chiefs of Police, 1967), p. 22.
8. Wilson and McLaren, *Police Administration,* p. 56.
9. Ibid., p. 56.
10. D. A. Tansik and J. F. Elliot, *Managing Police Organizations* (Monterey, Calif.: Duxbury Press, 1981), p. 81.
11. Ibid., p. 81.
12. B. J. Hodge and W. P. Anthony, *Organizational Theory: An Environmental Approach* (Boston, Mass.: Allyn & Bacon, 1979), p. 240.
13. Tansik and Elliot, *Managing Police Organizations,* p. 82.
14. Richard Hall, *Organizations: Structure and Process* (Englewood Cliffs, N.J.: Prentice-Hall, 1972), p. 143.
15. This section is a synopsis of the "Nature and Process of Differentiation" found in Hodge and Anthony, *Organizational Theory,* p. 249.
16. Darlton E. McFarland, *Management: Foundations and Practices,* 5th ed. (New York: Macmillan, 1979), p. 316.
17. McFarland, *Management,* p. 309.
18. B. J. Hodge and H. J. Johnson, *Management and Organizational Behavior* (New York: John Wiley & Sons, 1970), p. 163.
19. Joseph J. Staft, "The Effects of Organizational Design on Communications Between Patrol and Investigation Functions," in U.S. Department of Justice, National Institute of Justice, Research Utilization Program, *Improving Police Management* (Washington, D.C.: University Research Corporation, 1982), p. 243.
20. Several studies focusing on the failures of traditional police methods and advocating experimental styles have appeared in the last twenty years. Refer to G. Kelling, et al., *The Kansas City Preventive Patrol Experiment: A Technical Report* (Washington, D.C.: Police Foundation, 1974); J. Dahman, *Examination of Police Patrol Effectiveness: High-Impact Anti-Crime Program* (McLean, Va.: Mitre Corporation, 1975); J. Schnelle et al., "Social Evaluation Research: The Evaluation of Two Police Patrol Strategies," *Journal of Applied Behavior Analysis,* 4 (August 1975) pp. 232–40; W. Spelman and D. Brown, *Calling the Police: Citizen Reporting of Serious Crime* (Washington, D.C.: U.S. Government Printing Office, 1984); W. Spelman and J. Eck, *Problem Oriented Policing* (Washington, D.C.: National Institute of Justice, 1986); J. Eck and W. Spelman, *Problem Solving: Problem-Oriented Policing in Newport News* (Washington, D.C.: Police Executive Research Forum, 1987); L. Sherman, "Repeat Calls to Police in Minneapolis," *Crime Control Reports,* 4 (Washington, D.C.: Crime Control Institute, 1987); and H. Goldstein, *Problem-Oriented Policing* (New York: McGraw-Hill, 1990).
21. Robert C. Trojanowicz, "Community Policing Is Not Police Community Relations," *FBI Law Enforcement Bulletin,* 59 (October 1990), p. 8.
22. Ibid., pp. 8–10.
23. Robert C. Trojanowicz and Bonnie Bucqueroux, *Community Policing: A Contemporary Perspective* (Cincinnati, OH: Anderson, 1990) p. 8.
24. Clyde Cronkhite, "Santa Ana's Reorganization—Matrix Community Oriented Policing," *Journal of California Law Enforcement,* 22 (April, 1988) pp. 94–99.
25. Several critiques of experimental police methods have been noted in the literature. See Robert W. Taylor and Dennis J. Kenney, "The Problems with Problem Oriented Policing" (paper presented at the Academy of Criminal Justice Sciences Annual Meeting, Nashville, Tennessee, March 1991); Kenneth W. Findley and Robert W. Taylor, "Re-Thinking Neighborhood Policing," *Journal of Contemporary Criminal Justice,* 6 (May 1990), pp. 70–78; Jerome Skolnick and D. Bayley, *Community Policing: Issues and Practices Around the World* (Washington, D.C.: National Institute of Justice, 1988);

Jack Greene and Ralph Taylor, "Community Based Policing and Foot Patrol: Issues of Theory and Evaluation, in *Community Policing: Rhetoric or Reality?,* ed. Jack Greene and Stephen Mastrofski (New York: Praeger, 1988), pp. 216–19; and Stephen Mastrofski, "Police Agency Accreditation: The Prospects of Reform," *American Journal of Police,* 5 May 1986, pp. 45–81.

26. Gary W. Cordner, "Written Rules and Regulations: Are They Necessary," *FBI Law Enforcement Bulletin,* 58 July 1989, pp. 17–21.
27. See Robert Michaels, *Political Parties* (New York: Dover, 1959).
28. Kassoff, *Organizational Concepts,* pp. 31–38.

5 Leadership

Leadership is not a spectator sport.
KOUZES AND POSNER

Introduction

An advertisement asserts that if an organization is having communication problems, it should turn to the telephone company for help, because "the system is the answer." In a similar fashion, for the past two decades police departments, like other organizations, have placed such a strong emphasis on the use of technology (e.g., computers) and on rational management systems (such as special budgeting and decision-making techniques) that leadership has received little attention. When first faced with the "budget crunch," many departments simply tried to use rational analytical tools to decide which programs to cancel or where the budget could be slashed. Faced with reduced resources on the one hand, and a public that needed and demanded quality police services on the other, chiefs of police tried to find ways to improve productivity. This tactic brought the chiefs full circle because leadership reemerged as an important topic. Although technology and rational management techniques unquestionably remain important, the role of leadership in making systems function at a high level has come to the front.

Leadership and Performance

The police leader is responsible for three equally important, but essentially different, broad responsibilities:

1. Fulfilling the mission of the police department
2. Making work productive and helping subordinates to achieve
3. Producing impacts.[1]

A number of factors impinge on how well these responsibilities are met, such as the chief's leadership style, community preferences, the available resources, and even how the chief was selected. Police leaders chosen by a competitive process or who are perceived by subordinates in the department as competent are viewed consistently as having greater expertise and, consequently, have more influence and power.[2] There are, additionally, "habits of minds" that police leaders who meet their three key responsibilities effectively must practice:

1. They know where their time goes and manage it actively. They identify and eliminate things that need not be done at all; they delegate to others things that can be done as well or better by someone else. And they avoid wasting their own time and that of others.[3]
2. They focus on outward contribution. They gear their efforts to results rather than to work. They start out with the question, "What results are expected of me?" rather than with the work to be done, let alone with its techniques and tools.
3. They build on strengths—their own strengths; the strengths of their superiors, colleagues, and subordinates; and the strengths in the situation; that is, on what they can do. They do not build on weakness. They do not start out with the things they cannot do.
4. They concentrate on the few major areas where superior performance will produce outstanding results. They force themselves to set priorities and stay with their priority decision. They know that they have no choice but to do first things first—and second things not at all. The alternative is to get nothing done.
5. They make effective decisions. They know that this is, above all, a matter of system—of the right steps in the right sequence. They know that an effective decision is always a judgment based on "dissenting opinions" rather than on "consensus on the facts." And they know that to make many decisions fast means to make the wrong decisions. What is needed are few, but fundamental, decisions. What is needed is the right strategy rather than razzle-dazzle tactics.

If, as has been suggested, leadership is an intangible, the effects generated by its presence or absence and its character are not. Consider the following examples:

> Police officers, operating a dirty patrol vehicle, approached a motorist they had stopped for a traffic violation. Unkempt in appearance, the officers had a conversation with the person which was correct on the surface, but which had an underlying tone of arrogance.
>
> A sergeant, already 35 minutes late getting off duty, was enroute to the station when a burglary in progress call was given to another unit; he volunteered to help and subsequently was shot to death by two burglars.
>
> The chief of police of a medium-sized city chronically complained to anyone who would listen that his commanders "aren't worth anything" and that he was "carrying the whole department on his back."
>
> A visitor to a city approached an officer walking a beat and asked where the nearest car rental agency could be found; the officer replied, "What the hell do I look like, an information booth?" and walked away. The next day she asked an officer standing on a street corner where the First National Bank Building was. The officer took the woman's arm, escorted her across the street and said, "Lady, you see that big building on the corner where we were just standing? Well, if it had fallen, we'd have both been killed by the First National Bank Building."
>
> Based on limited new information the commander of an investigations bureau re-opened the case file on a convicted "no good" who had already served 14 months for the offense in question. Subsequently, new evidence and a confession resulted in his release and the conviction of another person.

There are many different definitions of what leadership is, each reflecting certain perspectives. For example, leadership may be defined as the characteristics exhibited by an individual or as a function of a position within the police department's hierarchical structure, such as captain. However, a generally accepted definition is that *leadership is the process of influencing organizational members to use their energies willingly and appropriately to facilitate the achievement of the police department's goals.*

The Nature of Leadership, Authority, and Power

The given definition of leadership deserves some analysis. In Chapter 3, the basic rationale for the existence of organizations was given as being that they do those things that people are unwilling or unable to do alone. It therefore follows that police departments, as is true for other organizations, are goal directed. The behavior of its members should be purposeful and in consonance with the department's goals. By "using their energies appropriately," it is meant that morally and legally accepted means are employed in the discharge of duties. The terms *influencing* and *willingly* are related to the concepts of authority and power.

Although these are often treated synonymously, authority and power are allied, but separate, concepts. Authority is a grant made by the formal organization to a position, the incumbent of which wields it in fulfilling his or her responsibilities. The fact that a formal grant of authority has been made does not mean that the person receiving it also is automatically able to influence others to perform at all, let alone willingly, as illustrated in the article, for example, in Box 5-1, "Police Officer Rejects Promotion." Commissioner Lee Brown had the authority to promote Officer James Murphy but not the power to have him accept the promotion.

Some power to induce performance is inherent in positions of authority. But to a significant degree that power, as suggested by Barnard, is a grant made by the led to the leader. The leader whose subordinates refuse to follow is not totally without power, for subordinates may be given verbal or written reprimands or suspensions, or be forced or expelled from the organization, or be fined, imprisoned, or executed, depending upon the specifics involved.[4] The use of this type of power must be considered carefully; failure to invoke it may contribute to a breakdown in discipline and organizational performance; the employment of it may contribute to morale problems, may divert energy from achieving goals, and may have other negative side effects, including calling into question the abilities of the involved leader:

> A uniformed officer riding alone informed the radio dispatcher that he was stopping a possibly drunken motorist. His sergeant, who had only been promoted and assigned to the squad two weeks previously, heard the transmission and told the dispatcher that he would back up the officer. When the sergeant, a nine-year veteran of the force, but who had not served in any "street" assignment for the past six years, arrived, a Marine corporal was about to get into a taxi cab. When questioned by the sergeant, the officer who had stopped the Marine as a possible drunk driver related that the corporal had been drinking, but that it was a marginal case and after talking with him, the corporal agreed to park his car and had called the taxi cab from a nearby pay phone.
>
> The sergeant talked to the Marine and concluded that he had drunk sufficiently to be charged with driving under the influence and directed the officer to arrest him. The officer declined and the sergeant angrily said, "I think you don't want to arrest him because you're an ex-Marine. . . . Arrest him, that's a direct order." The officer refused again, the sergeant got into his car and left, and the Marine departed in the taxi cab.
>
> Later when the sergeant filed charges for refusal to obey the direct order of a superior,

BOX 5-1

Police Officer Rejects Promotion

By Jacques Steinberg

Apparently angered by an investigation of his unit, an officer in one of the New York City Police Department's elite tactical narcotics teams took the unusual step of rejecting his promotion to detective investigator at a public ceremony on Friday.

The officer, James P. Murphy, a member of the Brooklyn North tactical narcotics team, was apparently protesting the department's investigation of allegations that members of the team mistreated prisoners and lied about evidence to shore up shaky arrests. Ten officers have been reassigned, and four of those officers were indicted last month on charges including illegal trespass, falsifying arrest records and perjury, in connection with what prosecutors said was the illegal search of a suspected drug dealer's apartment in 1990.

Officer Murphy, 30 years old and an eight-year veteran of the police force, joined 149 other officers on Friday in an auditorium at police headquarters to receive their promotions. But instead of accepting a salute and a handshake from Police Commissioner Lee P. Brown, Officer Murphy removed his new gold detective's shield from his chest and placed it on the dais.

He then spoke briefly to Robert J. Johnston Jr., the chief of the department, before walking out.

"He said it was on behalf of Brooklyn North T.N.T. and what they've been going through for the past year," Chief Johnston said after the ceremony.

Officer Murphy is not believed to be a subject of the investigation. He could not be reached at his office.

The chief added that in almost 40 years on the force he had seen nothing like Officer Murphy's action.

Officer Murphy was immediately reassigned to an administrative position in the department's organized crime control bureau, a police spokesman, Sgt. Peter Sweeney, said.

One of the 149 officers who accepted promotions at the ceremony was Detective Kathleen Burke, who had pursued a sex-discrimination suit against the department for five years.

But along with her promotion to detective first grade, Detective Burke received something unexpected: words of praise from Commissioner Brown. At the end of the ceremony, the Commissioner told the audience that he wanted to pay "special notice" to Detective Burke.

Source: New York Times, June 2, 1991.

the officer was suspended without pay for two days. The other squad members felt the sergeant was not "streetwise" and had acted in a petty manner. Over time, it became apparent to the sergeant's superiors that he had lost the respect and confidence of the squad and could not regain it. The sergeant was then transferred to a minor staff position where he had responsibility for several functions but actually supervised no one.

Leadership also arises, as demonstrated by the Hawthorne studies, out of the informal side of an organization. Members of a work group give one or more of their members power by virtue of their willingness to follow them. This power may be given on the basis suggested by Weber's charismatic leader; thus, officers may look more to a seasoned and colorful officer in their squad or one who has been decorated several times for heroism than to their sergeant, who represents Weber's rational-legal type of authority. A variant of this situation is a problem more than occasionally in some departments as younger college-educated officers move up in rank rapidly, passing less educated veteran officers. Dismissing them as "test takers," the more experienced officers sometimes use the informal group to vie for leadership with the formally appointed leaders. If, however, the informal leaders support the police department's goals, they can be a significant additive and even help to compensate for mediocre formal leadership.

The Power Motivation of Police Managers

Power is an indispensable dimension of police departments. As we have seen, power is both a grant made from the led to the leader as well as an extension of the formal authority granted to a particular position such as sergeant. Power, however, is not always used for the same purpose; the term *power motivation* refers to the reasons, intentions, and objectives that underlie a police manager's use of power.[5]

Leadership requires that a person have an appreciation of the importance of influencing the outcome of events and the desire to play a key role in that process. This need for impact must be greater than either the need for personal achievement or the need to be liked by others. A police leader's desire for impact may take either of two forms; it may be oriented primarily toward (1) the achievement of personal gain and aggrandizement (a personalized power motivation), or (2) the need to influence others' behavior for the common good of the police department (a socialized power motivation). Additionally, police leaders have some desire to be accepted and liked, which is termed the *affiliation need*. Affiliation needs and aspirations are not power needs because they reflect a greater preoccupation with being accepted and liked than with having an impact on events.

Table 5-1 summarizes the differences between managers who use personalized versus those who use social power. Hall and Hawker have developed an instru-

TABLE 5-1

Police managers with personalized power tend to be:	Police managers with socialized power tend to be:
■ Impulsive and erratic in their use of power	■ Inhibited and self-controlled in their use of power
■ Rude and overbearing	■ Respectful of others' rights
■ Exploitative of others	■ Concerned with fairness
■ Oriented toward strength	■ Oriented toward justice
■ Committed to the value of efficiency	■ Committed to the value of working per se
■ Proud	■ Egalitarian
■ Self-reliant; individualists	■ Organization-minded; joiners
■ Excited by the certitudes of power	■ Ambivalent about power
■ Competitive	■ Collaborative
■ Concerned with exceptionally high goals	■ Concerned with realistic goals
■ Defensive—protective of own sense of importance	■ Nondefensive—willing to seek help
■ Inspirational leaders	■ Builders of systems and people
■ Difficult to replace—leave a group of loyal subordinates dependent on their manager	■ Replaceable by other managers—leave a system intact and self-sustaining
■ Sources of direction, expertise and control	■ Sources of strength for others

Personalized Versus Social Power (from Jay Hall and James Hawker, "Interpreting Your Scores from the Power Management Inventory," © Teleometrics International, The Woodlands, Texas, 1981). Special permission for reproduction is granted by the authors and the publisher, all rights reserved. The Power Management Inventory can be used with a variety of occupations.

ment for measuring personalized power, socialized power, and affiliative needs. In Figure 5-1 the shaded portions of the personalized, socialized, and affiliative columns represents what Hall and Hawker regard, based on research by McClelland and Burnham, as the theoretically ideal profile for managerial success; note that the ideal profile contains a mix of power motivations and affiliative needs. Affiliative needs serve as a check on power motivations, helping to keep them in proper proportions. In the application of Figure 5-1, differences of more than 25 percentile points are required to denote a genuine preference for one approach in comparison to another. The dotted horizontal lines across the personalized, socialized, and affiliative columns reflect the scores of 43 police managers from one medium-sized police agency and are intended as an illustrative rather than as a

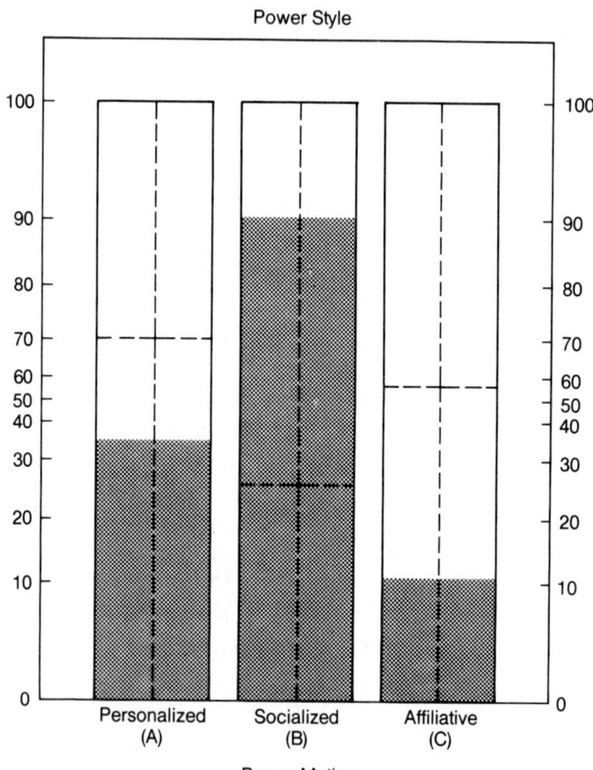

FIGURE 5-1. The Mean Power Management Inventory scores for 43 police managers from one medium-sized department are indicated by the horizontal dotted lines and are contrasted from the ideal scores that are depicted by the shaded areas. The figure is from Jay Hall and James Hawker, "Interpreting Your Scores from the Power Management Inventory," © Teleometrics International, The Woodlands, Texas, 1981, special permission for reproduction of the figure is granted by the authors and the publisher, all rights reserved. The data on the police managers are unpublished and in the files of C. R. Swanson.

generalization about police managers. Among the observations that can be made about the profile of those 43 police managers as a group are (1) the preference for the use of personalized power as opposed to socialized power and (2) a desire to be liked (affiliative needs), which closely approximates their preference for personalized power. This suggests that as a group these police managers are somewhat ambiguous about how to use power. They want to be seen as strong and self-reliant but also liked. Their scores also reflect the absence of a clearly unified approach to the use of power as well as the lack of a crystallized philosophy of management; as a result, they are probably seen as somewhat inconsistent by their subordinates.

The Leadership Skill Mix

As depicted in Figure 5-2 a police department can be divided into three levels and various mixes of three broad categories of skills associated with them.[6] The ranks indicated at each of the three levels of the organization identified in the figure are illustrative only and will vary depending on departmental size and other factors. Additionally, in the discussion of these skills that follows, it should be noted that it is possible to include only a few of the many examples available.

Human Relations Skills

Human relations skills involve the capacity to interrelate positively with other people and are used at all levels of a police department. Examples include motivation, conflict resolution, and interpersonal communication skills. The single

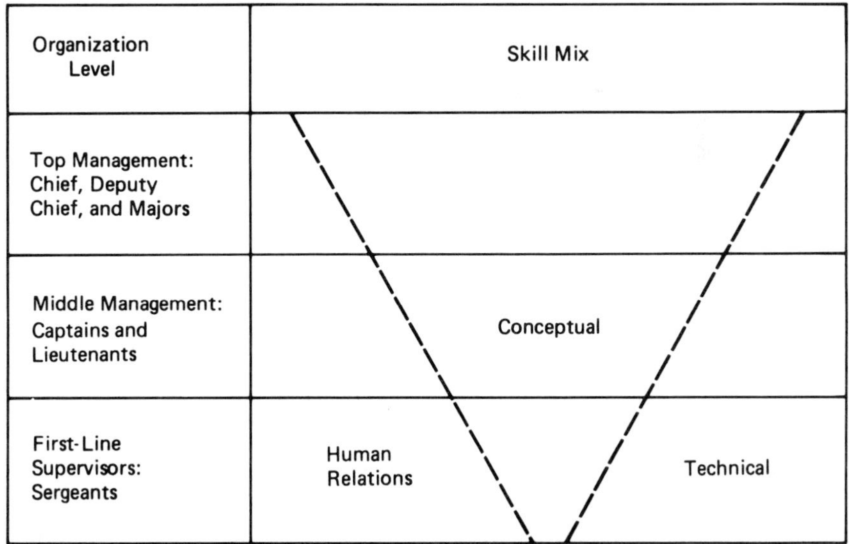

FIGURE 5-2. The leadership skill mix in a police department.

most important human relations skill is communication; without it, nothing can be set in motion, and programs under way cannot be guided.

As one progresses up the rank hierarchy of a police department, typically one becomes responsible for more people but has fewer people reporting directly to him or her. The human relations skills of a police department's top managers remain important, however, as they are used to win political support for the agency's programs and to obtain the resources necessary to operate them. In particular, the chief's human relations skills are critical, as this person is the key representative of the department to the larger environment. The way in which he or she "comes across" is to a certain degree the way in which some significant others—such as the city manager and members of city council—are going to come to regard the police department. The question of the fairness of that fact aside, the practical implication is that the chief must be aware and fulfill the symbolic leadership role.

Within the department, top management must communicate their goals and policies downward and be willing to receive feedback about them. As mid-level managers, lieutenants and captains play an important linking function, passing downward in implementable forms the communications they receive from top management and passing upward certain communications received from first-line supervisors. Because sergeants ordinarily supervise directly the greatest numbers of people, they use human relations with great frequency, often focusing on such issues as resolving interpersonal problems and working to gain or maintain the support of the informal group for departmental goals.

Conceptual Skills

Conceptual skills involve the ability to understand and also to interrelate various parcels of information, which often seem unrelated or the meaning or importance of which is uncertain. Although this skill is utilized at all levels of the police department, the standards for handling the information become less certain and the level of abstraction necessary to handle the parcels becomes greater as one moves upward. Illustrative is the difference between a sergeant helping a detective to evaluate the legal significance of certain evidence and the chief sorting out and interrelating facts, opinions, and rumors about a productive but controversial police program supported and opposed by some combination of political figures, public interest groups, and the news media.

Technical Skills

Technical skills vary by level within a police department. Uniformed sergeants assigned to field duties must be able to help develop and maintain the skills of subordinates in such areas as the identification, collection, and preservation of physical evidence. As one progresses upward toward middle and top management, the range of technical skills narrows, and conceptual skills come to predominate. In that upward progression, the character of the technical skills also changes from being operations oriented to management oriented and gradually includes new elements, such as budgeting, planning, and the kind of decision making that increasingly requires the use of conceptual skills. To elaborate further, one may not be able to tell by the generic label whether a particular skill is, for example, technical or conceptual. A general understanding of the many aspects of financial management (see Chapter 13) is a conceptual skill, but the actual physical preparation of the budget is a technical skill required of middle-management or first-line supervisors, depending on the size and practices of a specific police department.

Theories of Leadership

Theories of leadership attempt to explain the factors associated with the emergence of leadership or the nature of leadership.[7] Included are (1) "great man" and genetic theories, (2) the traits approach, (3) behavioral explanations, and (4) situational theories.

"Great man" theories were advanced by Thomas Carlyle and Georg Wilhelm Friedrich Hegel.[8] Carlyle believed that leaders were unusually endowed individuals who made history. Reversing the direction of causality, Hegel argued that it was the events that produced the "great man." The "born leader" concept is associated with Francis Galton, who espoused that leaders were the product of genetics.[9]

It has also been maintained that leaders possess certain personality traits; for example, Field Marshal Montgomery[10] believed that, although leaders were made, not born, they had certain characteristics such as an infectious optimism, confidence, intellect, and the ability to be a good judge of character. Goode determined that the following traits were important for successful leadership:

1. The leader is somewhat more intelligent than the average of his followers. However, he is not so superior that he cannot be readily understood by those who work with him.
2. The leader is a well-rounded individual from the standpoint of interests and aptitudes. He tends toward interests, aptitudes and knowledge with respect to a wide variety of fields.
3. The leader has an unusual facility with language. He speaks and writes simply, persuasively and understandably.
4. The leader is mentally and emotionally mature. He has come of age mentally and emotionally as well as physically.
5. The leader has a powerful inner drive or motivation that impels him to strive for accomplishment.
6. The leader is fully aware of the importance of cooperative effort in getting things done, and therefore understands and practices very effectively the so-called social skills.
7. The leader relies on his administrative skills to a much greater extent than he does on any of the technical skills which may be associated directly with his work.[11]

Parenthetically, by administrative skills, Goode seems to mean what has been described previously as conceptual skills. Ralph Stogdill analyzed over two hundred studies in his 1948 and 1974 reviews of traits of leadership and following the second review described a leader as being:

> characterized by a strong drive for responsibility and task completion, vigor and persistence in pursuit of goals, venturesomeness and originality in problem solving, drive

> to exercise initiative in social situations, self-confidence, and a sense of personal identity, willingness to accept consequences of decision and action, readiness to absorb interpersonal stress, willingness to tolerate frustration and delay, ability to influence other persons' behavior, and capacity to structure social interaction systems to the purpose at hand.[12]

From an organizational standpoint, the traits approach has great appeal: find out who has these characteristics and promote them, and successful leadership will follow. However, C. A. Gibb[13] has concluded that the numerous studies of traits do not reveal any consistent patterns, and Walter Palmer's[14] research does not provide support for the hypothesis that managerial effectiveness is a product of the personality characteristics of the individual.

Other theories of leadership focus on the behavior of managers as they operate. Whereas trait theories attempt to explain leadership on the basis of what the leader is, behavioral theories try to do the same thing by concentrating on what the leader does.[15] This is referred to as style of leadership, meaning the continuing patterns of behavior as perceived and experienced by others that they utilize to characterize the leader. Various of these approaches are discussed in the section that follows. Although not exclusively, many of the styles reflect elements of scientific management's task-centered and human relations' people-centered orientations.

Situational leadership theories postulate that effective leadership is a product of the fit between the traits or skills required in a leader as determined by the situation in which he or she is to exercise leadership.[16] Illustrative are Frederick Fiedler's contingency model,[17] Robert House's path-goal theory,[18] Robert Tannenbaum and Warren Schmidt's authoritarian-democratic leadership continuum, and Paul Hersey and Kenneth Blanchard's situational leadership theory. The last two are covered in detail in the next section because of their interrelatedness with leadership styles.

Styles of Leadership

General interest in the topic of leadership and the various theories of it have generated both commentary and research on different schemes for classifying styles of leadership. The purpose of this section is to provide a sense of some ways in which this subject has been treated and to discuss certain of the contributions in this area.

Lewin, Lippitt, and White: Authoritarian, Democratic, and Laissez-faire

Although these three styles of leadership had been identified in earlier works, the 1939 publication of Lewin, Lippitt, and White's[19] classical study of boys' clubs has closely identified these approaches with them.

The contrasting approaches of Lewin, Lippitt, and White's styles is detailed in Table 5-2. Briefly, they may be characterized as follows: (1) the authoritarian leader makes all decisions without consulting subordinates and closely controls work performance; (2) the democratic leader is group oriented and promotes the active participation of subordinates in planning and executing tasks; and (3) the laissez-faire leader takes a "hands-off" passive approach in dealing with subordinates.

TABLE 5-2 The Authoritarian, Democratic, and Laissez-faire Leadership Styles

Authoritarian	Democratic	Laissez-faire
1. All determination of policy was by the leader.	1. All policies were a matter of group discussion and decision, encouraged and assisted by the leader.	1. Complete freedom for group or individual decision existed, with a minimum of leader participation.
2. Techniques and activity steps were dictated by the authority, one at a time, so that future steps were always uncertain to a large degree.	2. Activity perspective was gained during discussion period. General steps to group goal were sketched, and when technical advice was needed, the leader suggested two or more alternative procedures from which choice could be made.	2. Various materials were supplied by the leader, who made it clear that he or she would supply information when asked. Leader took no other part in work discussion.
3. The leader usually dictated the particular work task and work companion of each member.	3. The members were free to work with whomever they chose, and the division of tasks was left up to the group.	3. Nonparticipation of the leader was complete.
4. The dominator tended to be "personal" in his or her praise and criticism of the work of each member; remained aloof from active group participation except when demonstrating.	4. The leader was "objective" or "fact-minded" in his or her praise and criticism and tried to be a regular group member in spirit without doing too much of the work.	4. Spontaneous comments on member activities were infrequent unless questioned and no attempt was made to appraise or regulate the course of events.

From Figure 1, p. 32, in *Autocracy and Democracy* by Ralph K. White and Ronald Lippitt. Copyright © 1960 by Ralph K. White and Ronald Lippitt. Reprinted by permission of Harper & Row, Publishers, Inc.; an earlier version of this appears in Kurt Lewin, Ronald Lippitt, and Ralph K. White, "Patterns of Aggressive Behavior in Experimentally Created Social Climates," *Journal of Social Psychology,* 10 (1939), p. 273.

White and Lippitt concluded that, although the quantity of work was somewhat greater under the autocratic leader, autocracy could generate hostility and aggression. The democratically controlled groups were about as efficient as the autocratically controlled ones, but the continuation of work in the former did not depend on the presence of the leader. Under the laissez-faire leader, less work was produced, the work quality was poorer, and the work was less organized and less satisfying to members of the group.[20]

Tannenbaum and Schmidt: The Authoritarian-Democratic Leadership Continuum

In 1958, Tannenbaum and Schmidt[21] published the leadership continuum depicted in Figure 5-3. They believed that the successful leader could choose to be more or less directive depending on certain factors:

1. Forces in the manager, such as his or her value system, confidence in subordinates, leadership inclinations, and need for security in uncertain situations

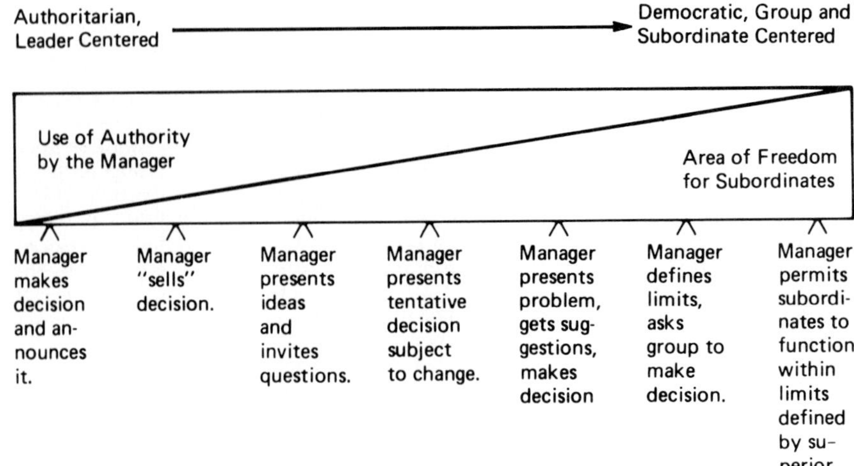

FIGURE 5-3. The authoritarian-democratic continuum. [Reprinted by permission of the *Harvard Business Review*. Exhibit from "How to Choose a Leadership Pattern" by Robert Tannenbaum and Warren H. Schmidt (May–June 1973). Copyright © 1973 by the president and fellows of Harvard College; all rights reserved.]

2. Forces in subordinates, including their needs for independence, readiness to assume greater responsibility and interests, knowledge, and experience
3. Forces in the organization, illustrated by prevailing views and practices, the ability of the group to work together effectively, the nature of the problem, and the pressures of time.[22]

Although their work is often simply presented as styles of leadership, by considering such variables and noting that these forces working together might suggest one leadership style instead of another, Tannenbaum and Schmidt's findings reflect a situational approach to leadership.

Downs: Leadership Styles in Bureaucratic Structures

In 1967, Anthony Downs[23] described four types of leader behavior in bureaucratic structures: (1) climbers, (2) conservers, (3) zealots, and (4) advocates.

Climbers are strongly motivated by power and prestige needs to invent new functions to be performed by their unit, particularly functions not performed elsewhere. If climbers can expand their functions only by moving into areas already controlled by others, they are likely to choose ones in which they expect low resistance. To protect their "turf," climbers tend to economize only when the resultant savings can be used to finance an expansion of their functions.[24]

The bias of conservers is toward maintaining things as they are. The longer a person is in the same job and the older one becomes, the lower one assesses any chances for advancement, and the stronger one becomes attached to job security, all of which are associated with the tendency to become a conserver. Climbers may become conservers when they assess their probability for advancement and expansion to be low. Desiring to make their organizational lives comfortable, conservers dislike and resist change.[25]

The peculiarities of the behavior of zealots stems from two sources: (1) their narrow interest and (2) the missionary-like energy that they focus almost solely on their special interest. As a consequence, zealots do not attend to all their duties and often antagonize other administrators by their lack of impartiality and their willingness to trample over all obstacles to further their special interest. Zealots rarely succeed to high-level positions because of their narrowness and are, consequently, also poor administrators. An exception is when their interest comes into favor and they are catapulted into high office.[26]

Unlike zealots, advocates promote everything under their jurisdiction. To those outside their units, they appear highly partisan, but within their units they are impartial and fair, developing well-rounded programs. Loyal to their organizations, advocates favor innovation. They are also simultaneously more radical and more conservative than climbers. They are more radical in that they are willing to promote programs and views that may antagonize their superiors, if doing so will help their organization. They are more conservative because they are willing to oppose changes from which they might benefit but which would not be in the best overall interest of their organizations.[27]

Traditional Versus Nontraditional Leaders

Traditional versus nontraditional leaders is a simple dichotomy, studies of which have revealed various attributes. As the two studies that follow suggest, however, they are distinguished by the traditionalist's preference for views associated with traditional organizational theory, whereas the nontraditionalists incorporate more thinking from open systems organizational theory.

Cohen: Leadership Styles in the New York City Police Department

Bernard Cohen[28] studied all commanding officers of the New York City Police Department holding the rank of captain or above, a total of 556 managers. Of this number, 535 were white and the balance minorities, including one woman. The analysis of data revealed two separate sets of leaders: tradition oriented and reform oriented.

Tradition-oriented commanders had little education beyond high school, they tended to score low on civil service examinations and tests of executive ability, and their career advancement stemmed primarily from their seniority. Tradition-oriented commanders appeared to identify with the rank and file at the expense of top management, and this downward orientation was associated with a general refusal to accept management goals. As with Downs's conservers, they did not strive to get ahead and were satisfied with the organizational status quo. This leadership style is associated with the use of subjectivity and power, the use of street slang, and the expression of superiority over the "college boys" due to the tradition-oriented leader's "wider practical knowledge."

In contrast, Cohen's reform-oriented commanders were "college boys," having attended college or having earned a college degree. Unlike the tradition-oriented commanders who received higher performance evaluations from their superiors, the reform-oriented commanders as a group got poor evaluations, suggesting a certain degree of independence in expressing their views. Younger, and less senior, this group of leaders experienced career advancement in large measure because of their test scores. Reform-oriented commanders valued education and service to the community, favored severe punishment for brutality, corruption, and civil rights violations, and were less authoritarian than the traditionalists. New organizational goals were supported by the reform commanders, who also aspired to become part of upper levels of management. Altogether, reform-oriented leaders possess some of the qualities of Downs's advocates.

Pursley: A National Study of Police Executive Leadership

In a national study of a sample of police executive leadership, Robert Pursley[29] looked at 58 traditional and 74 nontraditional chiefs of police. The nontraditional chiefs formed a relatively young, highly mobile, and well-educated group whose career development seems strikingly similar to that of young professional city managers; that is, when a good opportunity for advancement existed elsewhere, a move was made. The traditionalists displayed a very significant need to structure and control the work environment and the work-related activities of their subordinates. Their leadership style reflected a tendency toward centralization, a minimum of delegation, and little authority or power to initiate activities at subordinate levels. As opposed to the more authoritarian stance of the traditionalists, the nontraditionalists revealed a greater receptiveness to delegation and a willingness to accept the input of subordinates, traits associated with a more participatory, democratic approach to leadership.

The article in Box 5-2, "Interview with a Reform Chief," focuses on the late Victor Cizanckas, who died of natural causes in 1981 while chief of police in Stamford, Connecticut. A progressive leader who embodied many of the qualities described by both Cohen and Pursley, Cizanckas reveals in the interview a wide range of issues involved in genuine reform.

Van Maanen: Station House Sergeants and Street Sergeants

In a study of a 1,000-officer police department, Van Maanen[30] identified two contrasting types of police sergeants: "station house" and "street." Station house sergeants had been out of the "bag" (uniform) before their promotions to sergeant and preferred to work inside in an office environment once they won their stripes; this preference is clearly indicated by the nickname of "Edwards, the Olympic torch who never goes out" given to one such sergeant. Station house sergeants immersed themselves in the management culture of the police department, keeping busy with paperwork, planning, record keeping, press relations, and fine points of law. Their strong orientation to conformity also gave rise to nicknames as suggested by the use of "by the book Brubaker" to refer to one station house sergeant.

In contrast, street sergeants were serving in the field when they received their

BOX 5-2

Interview with a Reform Chief

Victor I. Cizanckas has been chief of the Stamford, Connecticut, Police Department since May 1977, when he was plucked from the Menlo Park, California, police in an apparent effort to reform the Stamford force.

The 43-year-old lawman began his enforcement career in Menlo Park in 1962 after an eight-year stint with the Marine Corps. He quickly worked his way up through the ranks, becoming chief of the California department in June 1968.

Cizanckas has long been involved in working for change in the criminal justice system. He has served on the California Council on Criminal Justice, the LEAA Manpower Development Committee, and the Advisory Committee of Project STAR (Standards, Training and Requirements).

In addition to his police duties in Stamford, Cizanckas works as a consultant with several public and private research-oriented organizations, including the Police Foundation, LEAA, and ABT Associates.

The holder of an A.A. in police science from the College of San Mateo and a B.S. in sociology from the College of Notre Dame, Cizanckas lectured throughout the United States and has held teaching positions in three colleges while pursuing his policing career.

A keen observer of the police scene, the chief is the author of almost two dozen articles, dealing with topics ranging from law enforcement management to vandalism.

This interview was conducted for Law Enforcement News by Harry O'Reilly and Dorothy H. Bracey.

Len: Could you describe some of the circumstances that greeted you on your arrival in Stamford in 1977?

Cizanckas: There was a challenge here, and there was a national search for a police chief in which I decided to participate and "won." I took the position on May 5, 1977. I was talking to the co-author of my book, Don Hanna, recently, describing what's been going on here for three years, and his comment was that I've had a negative learning experience. I think he's right.

Len: You were brought here with, if I understand it correctly, a mandate from the mayor to clean up the city of Stamford. How does a new police chief go about doing something like that?

Cizanckas: I would suggest to somebody else to do it cautiously; I did not, and it's taken its toll, I think, in many ways on the organization, on the people who work for me and people who have worked for me. Stamford is a unique city; there are just a lot of wonderful people here who are very proud of their city and its history. At the same time, Stamford is—and I use the term advisedly—totally corrupt. Wherever you look, you'll find corruption. It's a very sad set of circumstances. You have what could be one of the best cities in America giving way to an "old boy" system and a matrix, if you will, of, well, not "the Mafia" running the city, but there's Mafia here. It's a system where people serve themselves rather than the community; that's their primary objective. So you have a matrix of relationships that include Mafia, politicians, city workers, and contractors, and the list goes on and on. They've done very well by themselves, to the detriment of the community. I don't know what the total is, but it's millions.

Len: Your mandate definitely did encompass the whole city, though, not just the police department?

Cizanckas: It did encompass the whole city, and I approached it from that point of view. Simultaneously, we had a police department that was, well, political. Promotions, transfers, special assignments were called by a local contractor; that stopped. Tickets were fixed, cases were fixed; that stopped. When you start doing that, you start to take a toll. I collected 500 special police badges and took them away from people. That did not make a lot of friends. A number of department heads are no longer with the city.

BOX 5-2 (cont.)

There's one under indictment being tried right now. They've been fired, indicted, exposed—it goes on and on.
Len: Were the investigations that led to the indictments of other city officials generated through your department?
Cizanckas: Yes.
Len: So that would mean, then, that you had within your department a number of investigators who were trustworthy enough to perform these investigations in their own town and who had to be, of necessity, reform-minded themselves?
Cizanckas: A lot of people were waiting. In any system, no matter how corrupt, there are a lot of decent people, and they're sort of victims themselves. If the mayor or the administrator or police chief says "we're going to do it," they'll watch him for a while, and if they believe he means it and is not part of the system, they'll come through. In the Stamford Police Department itself we're talking about 90 percent honest cops—unfortunately part of an old system, so their reality is the Stamford police reality. They really don't know what's out there. They don't have a measuring stick; they can't set themselves up and say, "Well, we ought to be like this." They want to believe that they're good cops, and that they work for a good police department. When you expose it, there's a terrible price. It hurts them; it just blows them apart. Their pride is hurt, their pride in their job, in what they're dedicated to. It's hard.
Len: How many sworn personnel do you have?
Cizanckas: 243.
Len: Did you bring any of your own people with you when you came here?
Cizanckas: No.
Len: Would you do that again?
Cizanckas: Yes, I would not bring any. Let me explain. I've talked this over with a lot of my friends who are police administrators, and one of the things that has really crippled reform chiefs is they bring in staff, and they talk to each other and no one else. The real task is to find honest cops—they're part of the system, they know the players, and if they become committed you can do it. But if you isolate yourself from the rank and file, it's a disaster. They'll stall every kind of program you can think of, so that's it's not institutionalized and it's not the product of the people who work there. Whatever we've done here is the product of the people who work here, and that's the difference. I believe in that.
Len: What was your initial approach to the press when you first took over the job?
Cizanckas: I decided, after consulting with a lot of my friends, that I would maintain a very high profile, I've had a very high profile here. It's not my preference. I don't need press, and I don't need to read what I do.
Len: I gather from all of this that you emphatically denied the allegations that you came in riding on a white horse to save a department that didn't need saving.
Cizanckas: I came here with a mandate from the mayor—actually a mandate from the population—to clean up what was very bad. It's not over, by a long shot. It continues.

If at the time I had to write a book on Stamford, it would be treated as fiction. It's not real. They tried everything they can to wipe me out, to get me out of here. My own staff has betrayed me, blowing part of my undercover operations to try and embarrass me politically. They've undermined every effort I've put forward, but I've still got honest cops, and they're now in staff.
Len: To be able to function in a climate of negativity like this you've got a nucleus of good, solid police officers who are supportive and honest and helpful, who are with you. How about in terms of the public? What kind of support are you getting from them?
Cizanckas: Absolute. They want good government, most people do, and I have citizen groups, corporation groups, church groups, and I meet with all of them and I keep them advised. But it's a town job.

On that blown undercover operation, I brought somebody in with me and put him as an undercover operator. We opened up a variety store and he took numbers and sports betting. I ran it for 21 months without anyone knowing it. Somebody from my staff betrayed me, and after I was betrayed I had somebody else undercover. I guess if you want to know if I'm winning or losing, the best way is to quote somebody from the other side, talking about the blown undercover, and this was in June. "By blowing this," he's saying, "what he's proving so far is, you know who's winning? There's three rounds so far, and you know how many rounds the chief's got? He's got two rounds already." I had the third when the son of a bitch said that. It's real, but it's unreal.

Len: You have said that the goal of a reform chief is not to lock people up. Could you elaborate on that?

Cizanckas: Too many reform efforts are simply "let's make a few arrests, let's make some press releases, and tell everybody we've got the city cleaned up." That doesn't work. What you're talking about is social change, and it's way beyond arresting a few people. If you want to get into the academic side of it, you're doing organizational development which is changing the mores not only of a police agency but in this case of an entire city. The recurring theme, and something everybody said in this city when I first arrived, but which you have a hard time hearing now is, "one hand washes the other." Over and over again, I just made a lot of speeches about that and said that those people who say it better think about what they're saying, particularly if one hand happened to be very dirty. When you start changing a whole way of life, where if you have a position of power you can get a friend's ticket fixed—that is pervasive corruption, even though people think, well, that comes with their power position, there's no money exchanged but there's a favor. No money may change hands, but you pay a larger price than money. Everything disintegrates; there's no confidence in government, there's no confidence in the people who work for the government, so therefore the kinds of efforts that are necessary to serve the public properly—from every department, not only the police—are substandard.

Len: A number of the reform chiefs of the last decade have also been known as hit-and-run chiefs. Their tenures of office have been relatively short in the departments that they cleaned up. . . .

Cizanckas: You people say that, but you have to take a look at all the chiefs. The tenure of a police chief is relatively short; I think it's about two-and-a-half years now. I've been here three. And most of your reform chiefs usually are beyond three years. I think there's also a life expectancy of a change agent. After a while, you reach the point of diminishing returns. The effort is the same, but the returns are less. Finally, you have hurt so many people and their extended families that you're no longer effective.

Len: So far as the individual is concerned, there is a sort of built-in half life?

Cizanckas: Yes, but who knows when it is? Someday I'll have to make that decision myself.

Len: Have you felt any explicit or implied threats to your own personal safety?

Cizanckas: A very explicit yes. It's very explicit on the tape I quoted from earlier that they were going to throw me out of office, run me out of town. I have been the subject of character assassination—I mean written character assassination, in letters. Everything I'm accused of I told my internal affairs unit to investigate.

My wife gets letters from people who run cemeteries saying, "we'll be happy to take care of your husband." I think that's an implied threat. The head of my internal affairs unit is Italian-American and his mother is old Italian from New York, Little Italy, and she's recovering from her third heart attack in a hospital. They called her to tell her, in Italian, that if her son makes another move he pays the price. That's very explicit. It put her back in intensive care.

It doesn't stop. They attack ministers who are in favor of social reform. . . .

Len: So what you're dealing with is a deeply-rooted clique that involves intermarriage, interrelationships on a business level. . . .

Cizanckas: Business, family, social, and it's very very deep.

Len: And this is almost a kind of Borgia family that's in a power position, calling a lot of shots and wreaking a lot of financial havoc over the town?

BOX 5-2 (cont.)

Cizanckas: That's right. But let me say something. It goes way beyond financial havoc. It affects the quality of life. Deals are made in zoning, deals are made for buildings; everything starts to disintegrate. Deals are made in the Traffic Department. It just goes on and on, and it takes a terrible toll that's way beyond money.
Len: If you have a power nucleus like this, a controlling negative force up here somewhere, and you have the support of the general public, how does someone in your position or in a comparable position localize the small pockets of good people to combat this larger group of power people?
Cizanckas: There's one way, and that's to keep a very high profile. I don't keep anything from the press; I tell them everything, and it drives them crazy. It drives people crazy. I also meet with citizen groups, I meet with corporate executives. I've done three churches on a Sunday and a synagogue on Saturday, to tell them what I'm doing and ask for their support. The bottom line is that people want good government, they will support somebody that's trying to give it to them, and it will work. But it takes a terrible toll, psychologically, intellectually, and emotionally. The question is, how long can you last before you burn out.
Len: It's a human instinct to want to be loved and to be liked and accepted by people, and you can't do that.
Cizanckas: You can't do that; you give it up. When I formed my internal affairs unit . . .
Len: There was no prior internal affairs division?
Cizanckas: Oh no. When I put them together I sat them down and I said to them, "When everybody in this town loves me, when the department is behind me more than 50 percent and everything is going OK, you open a case on me, because I've sold out." I am not going to be loved, I am not going to make friends, and that's a part of it.
Len: You've been able to do some recruiting since you've been here. What were your goals in this?
Cizanckas: The goals have been well-educated, intelligent, decent people, but there's a problem. You have to understand institutions, and let me leave this police department and talk about other police departments. I have seen white, middle-class, liberal, college-educated people with a sociology background enter a police department, and they've never spoken the vernacular, they've never been in the military, they watch their language. Within four weeks they're calling their nightstick a "nigger knocker." That's the nature of organizations. If the organization is bad, it take a very strong personality not to want to belong to that and co-opt one's own values.
Len: That kind of individualism is often looked on as a negative thing, such as with Frank Serpico in New York. You're seen as being so atypical that no one accepts you.
Cizanckas: Absolutely. You're ostracized; you're a freak. They're talking about throwing the internal affairs officers out of the police officers association. The internal affairs officers are good cops who believe in what they're doing. And while they have had some officers found guilty of various things, they've cleared over 70 police officers. The name of the game in this town was that if a police officer made an arrest, the only way to beat the arrest was to make an accusation against the police officer, then he'd fold the case and everybody is happy. What I told attorneys who came to my office when I first arrived was "I'll take your complaint and I'll investigate it, and as soon as your client's case is adjudicated we'll bring the other charge to the commissioner."
Len: You've made a number of changes in the training area relevant to the whole matter of corruption. Could you describe some of these?
Cizanckas: That's part of the gimmick. We teach such "weird" courses as ethics, interpersonal relationships, conflict resolution, professional responsibility, and the list goes on—weird topics for cops.
Len: Do you have your own training establishment?
Cizanckas: When I first came here we had a lot of turnover, and the state police academy could only handle so many, so we designed our own academy, which was certified. It was very different from the state police academy. In fact, our academy has

not been replicated by the state, so we're now using the state academy; they pay all costs. They've included things like Project STAR. It's a greatly expanded curriculum.
Len: Is recruit training done there?
Cizanckas: We do our own, and then we send them there.
Len: You said you had a turnover. Was there a mass exodus from the department?
Cizanckas: Yes, with the announcement of my coming a number of people left, and after my arrival a number of people left.
Len: Naturally, you're going to have to replace these people, or have had to replace them, so can it be assumed then that you have a lot of malleable young people in the lower echelons of your department?
Cizanckas: The problem is I can't reach them; the old guard reaches them first. It's a reality and I admit it, and it's a problem.
Len: On top of that, you can't recruit from all over, most of them are local people, so in many instances they're part of the old regime.
Cizanckas: It's a difficult proposition, as I said earlier. You can take the model recruit, but if you put him in an institution that has a value system that is not positive, not proper, that is corruptive, then that's what he becomes part of. I think one of the saddest case histories we have is the city of Denver in 1961, I think it was. Those police officers who went to prison as burglars did not become police officers to become burglars. Most of them are more purely motivated. They may want a civil service job and security, but they also want to serve. I think that's the greatest example of an institution doing somebody in from peer pressure.

When you talk about change, then you're changing a system, and it's more than making a couple arrests or firing a couple of people. It's a long hard process, but as we talked about earlier, there is a half life for people who do it, because the bottom line is if you're doing it properly there are a lot of people who are very upset with you.
Len: You're one of a few people in the country who have been a police chief executive on both coasts. Have you noted any significant differences?
Cizanckas: There is a major difference. The West Coast police are very professional—in how they write reports, how they handle things. Their educational level is higher. They really know their business. They're also plastic. That's the best way to describe them. I prefer it to what I found here. But on the other side of this, if you take an East Coast cop, and if you're hurt, if you're young, you're old, you're in trouble, they'll take care of you. You can rely on them coming to your house after hours to make sure you're OK. I've seen it. If a husband has a heart attack—I've seen it in many cases—the officer gets off duty, goes to the hospital to comfort the wife. You won't find that in a Western cop. An East Coast cop will drive her home, and when she's home by herself and her husband's in the hospital, they check the house. There's a great dichotomy. I've traveled across the country and I find that to be absolutely true. One of the best experiences I've had was in the city of San Antonio. I do weird things when I go to police chiefs' conferences—I don't go to the conference; I ride around in police cars in every city. I was with a Mexican-American patrol officer and I went out with him. He technically knew his business, I think, but personally. . . . He's not a Western cop, in San Antonio; I'm talking about the West Coast, where we have all the models. Everybody knew this cop by name, they flagged him down to tell him what's going on: "Yesterday there was a hit-and-run," for example, "and so-and-so did it."

There's a middle ground, but how do we accomplish that? I don't know. The morale is highest here when there's a snowstorm. There's no police work going on in the traditional sense. Everybody comes in their old clothes, nobody calls in sick. They're taking doctors and nurses to hospitals, they're taking people who need dialysis treatment to hospitals to be treated, they're taking groceries up to people who are snowed in, taking care of stranded motorists, and they all feel great. My feeling is that the mass media is in large part responsible for the poor police service we get in this country, because they portray a law enforcer Mat Dillon and they don't portray the humanist part of this job.
Len: But you constantly come across things like "don't give us all that social work stuff; we joined this job to fight crime."

BOX 5-2 (cont.)

Cizanckas: Absolutely. But when it's very clear what they're supposed to be doing on a given day, the level of job satisfaction is highest.

There's a great dichotomy between the service officer and the law enforcement officer, and the reality is, as studies show, 80 percent of your time is spent on service calls. But we train for the 20 percent, we emphasize the 20 percent, and we reward for the 20 percent.

The other side of it is that when we have that type of service activity going on, it's one of the few times that a police officer can really judge the success of what he's doing. The rest of it is so ambiguous, it floats around. You know, "Well, I caught a burglar, and what's going to happen to him? He's going to get probation and he'll be back on the street." There's a frustration level that's so high. We even tell them in the academy, "Don't personalize it. If you make your arrest don't worry about it." And the officer says "Yes, I understand all of that. Burglars get probation, but not my burglars." It's a very frustrating job. And let me go beyond the media. Policing is one of the most esoteric professions in the nation. Very few people understand that. The citizen doesn't know what a cop does, because of the media, and they think that by his mere presence on the street he prevents crime. Well he does not. They think that having a cop on every block is going to make the community safe; it's not. And very few police officers really understand what their role in society is. I'll say this also: there are too many police administrators who do not understand what the role of the police officer is. If you have an administrator who makes an assumption about that role, it's not defined in any textbook you have. It's a tough job, and then when you come in from outside like I did, and you start to break the code—you say "we are not perfect, we have some problems"—even though I say 90 percent of my organization is humane, compassionate, they take care of you, if I say one cop is rotten, every other positive thing I say is forgotten and the only thing that's quoted is "he said this guy was a bad guy." And so all defense mechanisms go up and there's a closure of the ranks, and they say "this guy's not a cop, he's not on our side, he's not for us," when the reality is I am very much for them. I like cops. Let me expand on that. I think in too many cases police "reformers," who know what's good for the community, etc., they don't like cops. When you get underneath, they just don't like cops. I like cops; I think they're great, West and East Coast. They're out there doing something, a very demanding job that's little understood by the people they serve. But being a police officer is one of the most exciting professions, and one of the most demanding, both intellectually and physically.

Len: What do you see in your crystal ball for the future of Stamford, in relation to the conditions that existed when you first came here and the current situation?

Cizanckas: In the long run, I think the kind of things that we've done—reorganization, training, a new records room computerization—are really the foundation of any lasting reform, and I think they're finished. But they don't receive much press. The basic things are finished. I think that internally people know what kind of expectations they can have for themselves. So we've reached the point of institutionalizing these things; I don't think it will go back.

Len: And these things are not dependent upon one individual?

Cizanckas: If you do that, then you have not accomplished your mission or responsibility. A lot of people are afraid that things will go back if something happens to me or if I leave. My social scientist "hat" says no, but that's a guess. I hope not.

Source: Harry O'Reilly and Dorothy H. Bracey, "An Interview with Victor Cizanckas, Police Chief of Stamford, Connecticut," *Law Enforcement News,* March 24, 1980, pp. 8–10.

promotions. Consequently, they had a distaste for office procedures and a strong action orientation as suggested by such nicknames as "Shooter McGee" and "Walker the Stalker." Moreover, their concern was not with conformity, but with "not letting the assholes take over the city."

In addition to the distinct differences already noted, station house and street sergeants were thought of differently by those whom they supervised: station house sergeants "stood behind their officers," where street sergeants "stood beside their officers." Each of these two different styles of working as a sergeant also has its drawbacks and strengths. Station house sergeants might not be readily available to officers working in the field, but could always be located when a signature was needed and were able to secure more favors for their subordinates than street sergeants were. Although immediately available in the field when needed, street sergeants occasionally interfered with the autonomy of their subordinates by responding to a call for service assigned to a subordinate and handling it or otherwise, at least in the eyes of the subordinate officer, "interfering."

A consideration of Van Maanen's work leads to some generalizations about the future careers of station house versus street sergeants. The station house sergeant is learning routines, procedures, and skills that will improve future promotional opportunities. Their promotional opportunities are further enhanced by contacts with senior police commanders who can give them important assignments and who can, if favorably impressed, influence future promotions. In contrast, street sergeants may gain some favorable publicity and awards for their exploits, but they are also more likely to have citizen complaints filed against them, more likely to be investigated by internal affairs, and more likely to be sued. Consequently, very aggressive street sergeants are regarded by their superiors as "good cops," but difficult people to supervise. In short, the action-oriented street sergeant who does not "mellow out" may not go beyond a middle manager's position in a line unit such as patrol or investigation.

Price: Male and Female Police Leaders

The infusion of women into policing is basically a post-1972 movement triggered by the enactment of federal legislation covered from different perspectives in Chapters 2, 7, and 10. Although there were women in policing before that time, their numbers were insignificant and they were invariably assigned to special functions such as work with juveniles and vice. Moreover, before 1972 opportunities for the same general assignments as men and for promotion to leadership roles were virtually nonexistent.

Because of the relatively recent entry of women into policing, there has not been sufficient time for large numbers of them to advance to leadership positions and, consequently, there have been few studies of female leaders. In a study comparing 26 women holding the rank of sergeant or above with their male counterparts, Barbra Price[31] found that women were superior at a statistically significant level on selected personality traits associated with leadership. Specifically, Price found that women were more emotionally independent; were more verbally and intellectually aggressive; were more flexible and willing to part from routine and convention; and had scores suggesting a more positive self-image, confidence, and social adequacy. Contrary to popular views, this sample of females was much lower on a measure of submissiveness than male leaders. Their scores also suggested a liberal perspective, and they were more creative and had less inclination toward authoritarian outlooks than did the male police leaders with whom they were compared.

Blake and Mouton: The Managerial Grid

Developed by Robert Blake and Jane Mouton,[32] the Managerial Grid® has received a great deal of attention since its appearance in 1962 in the *Journal of the American Society of Training Directors*. The Grid is part of the survey research feedback stem of organizational development and draws upon earlier work done at Ohio State University and the University of Michigan.[33]

Depicted in Figure 5-4, the Grid has two dimensions: (1) concern for production and (2) concern for people. Each axis or dimension is numbered from 1, meaning low concern, to 9, indicating high concern. The way in which a person combines

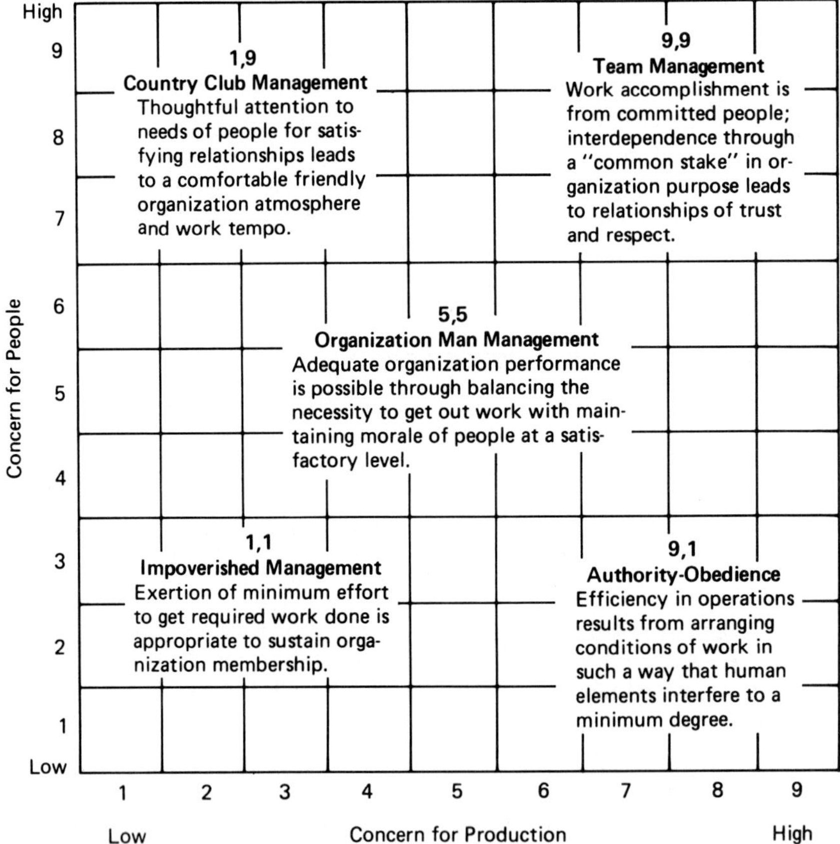

FIGURE 5-4. The managerial grid. [From *The New Managerial Grid* by Robert Blake and Jan Syrgley Mouton. Houston: Gulf Publishing Company, Copyright © 1978, p. 11. Reproduced by permission.]

these two dimensions establishes a leadership style in terms of one of the five principal styles identified on the Grid. The numbers associated with each of the styles reflect the level of concern for each of the two dimensions to the Grid. For example, 9,1 indicates maximum concern for production or the needs of the organization and a minimum orientation toward the needs of people in the organization.

Some of the leadership styles identified previously can be related readily to the Grid. Authoritarian leaders are represented by the 9,1 style; laissez-faire leaders by the 1,1; and democratic leaders by the 5,5. Additionally, the 9,1 and 9,9 styles are consistent, respectively, with the streams of thought summarized in Chapter 3 under the headings of "Traditional Organizational Theory" and "Open Systems Theory."

The leadership style of an individual can be identified by using a questionnaire based on the work of Blake and Mouton. Table 5-3 summarizes the leadership styles identified by 143 police supervisors and managers completing the Grid questionnaire; the police leaders involved came from four different states and represented a state investigative agency, a county police department, and three municipal departments.[34] "Primary style" indicates the style that the police leaders reported as preferring; "backup style" reflects the style the police leaders would use if they were not able to continue using their primary.[35] According to the Grid, one moves from the "best" to the "worst" styles as one moves from a 9,9 through 5,5; 9,1 and 1,9 to the 1,1. The most desirable combination of a primary and backup style is the 9,9 with a 5,5 backup.

A difficulty in using the Grid questionnaire is that the data produced are no more accurate than the perceptions of self of the person completing the instrument. When working in an organizational development context, one way to overcome this is to have each manager complete the instrument and then to have each of his or her subordinates fill out on how they experience the manager.

Hersey and Blanchard: Situational Leadership Theory

Hersey and Blanchard's[36] situational leadership model was influenced greatly by William Reddin's 3-D management style theory. Although many situational vari-

TABLE 5-3 Police Leadership Styles on the Managerial Grid

Backup styles	**Primary styles**					
	9,9	5,5	9,1	1,9	1,1	Totals
9,9		1	12	3	2	18
5,5	19		7	2	1	29
9,1	12	10		3	21	46
1,9	8	0	9		3	20
1,1	6	1	20	3		30
Totals	45	12	48	11	27	143

From Charles Swanson and Leonard Territo, "Police Leadership and Interpersonal Communication Styles," in *Police and Police Work*, ed. Jack R. Greene (Beverly Hills, Calif.: Sage, 1982); with unpublished 1985 data from the files of C. R. Swanson added.

ables are important to leadership—such as the demands of time, the leader, the led, the superiors, the organization, and job demands—Hersey and Blanchard emphasize what they regard as the key variables, the behavior of the leader in relationship to the followers.[37] Although the examples of situational leadership suggest a hierarchical relationship, situational leadership theory should have application when trying to influence the behavior of a subordinate, a boss, a friend, or a relative.[38]

Maturity is defined in situational leadership as the capacity to set high, but attainable, goals, the willingness to take the responsibility, and the education and/or experience of the individual or the group.[39] Age may be a factor, but it is not related directly to maturity as used in situational leadership theory.[40] An individual or group is not mature or immature in a total sense, but only in relationship to the specific task to be performed.[41] This task-relevant maturity involves two factors: (1) job maturity, the ability and the technical knowledge to do the task, and (2) psychological maturity, feelings of self-confidence and self-respect about one's self as an individual.[42]

Figure 5-5 depicts the situation leadership model; the various levels of follower maturity are defined as

- *M1:* The followers are neither willing nor able to take responsibility for task accomplishment.

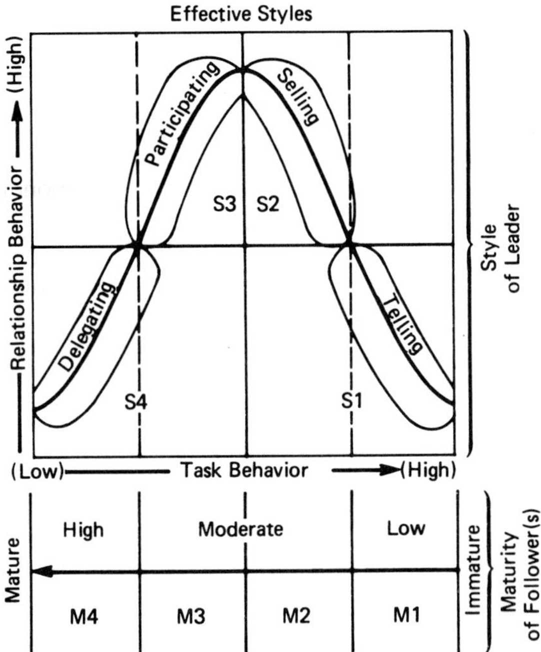

FIGURE 5-5. The situational leadership model. [From Paul Hersey and Kenneth H. Blanchard, *Management of Organizational Behavior: Utilizing Human Resources,* 3rd ed., © 1977, p. 170. Reprinted by permission of Prentice-Hall, Inc., Englewood Cliffs, N.J.]

- *M2:* The followers are willing but not able to take responsibility for task accomplishment.
- *M3:* The followers are able but not willing to take responsibility for task accomplishment.
- *M4:* The followers are willing and able to take responsibility for task accomplishment.[43]

Task behavior is essentially the extent to which a leader engages in one-way communication with subordinates; relationship behavior is the extent to which a leader engages in two-way communication by providing socioemotional support, "psychological strokes," and facilitating behaviors.[44] The definition of the four basic styles associated with these two variable operates like the Managerial Grid and are described in the following terms:

- *S1:* High-task—low-relationship leader behavior is referred to as "telling," because this style is characterized by one-way communication in which the leader defines the roles of followers and tells them what, how, when, and where to do various tasks.
- *S2:* High-task—high-relationship behavior is referred to as "selling," because with this style most of the direction is still provided by the leader. He or she also attempts through two-way communication and socioemotional support to get the follower(s) psychologically to buy into decisions that have to be made.
- *S3:* High-relationship—low-task behavior is called "participating," because with this style the leader and follower(s) now share in decision making through two-way communication and much facilitating behavior from the leader since the follower(s) have the ability and knowledge to do the task.
- *S4:* Low-relationship—low-task behavior is labeled "delegating," because the style involves letting follower(s) "run their own show" through delegation and general supervision since the follower(s) are high in both task and psychological maturity.

The bell-shaped curve in the style-of-leader portion of Figure 5-5 means that, as the maturity level of leader's followers develops from immaturity to maturity, the appropriate style of leadership moves in a corresponding way.[45]

To illustrate, the police leader who has a subordinate whose maturity is in the M2 range would be most effective employing an S2 style of leadership. The probability of success of each style for the four maturity levels depends on how far the style is from the high-probability style along the bell-shaped curve; Hersey and Blanchard describe these probabilities as for

- M1: S1 and S2 2nd, S3 third, S4 low probability
- M2: S2 High S1 and S3 secondary, S4 low probability
- M3: S3 High S2 and S4 secondary, S1 low probability
- M4: S4 High S3 2nd S2 3rd, S1 low probability[46]

Although it is easier said than done, the effective use of Hersey and Blanchard's model depends on police leaders developing or having a diagnostic ability and the flexibility to adapt their leadership styles to given situations.[47]

Transactional and Transformational Leaders

In 1978, James Burns published a book that was simply titled *Leadership*. However modest the title, it was to become a very influential writing. In it, Burns identifies two types of leaders in the behavioral tradition: transactional and transforming.[48]

Most leader–follower relations are transactional—the leaders approach the followers with the idea that they will exchange one thing for another, for example, raises and favorable assignments for good performance or personal loyalty. Each party to the transaction or "bargain" is aware of the resources of the other, and the purposes of both are entwined almost exclusively within the context of this relationship.[49] Transactional leaders emphasize values such as honesty, fairness, acceptance of responsibility, honoring commitments, and getting work done on time.[50] In contrast, transformational leadership occurs when leaders and followers interact in such a way that they are elevated and committed to—and sustained by—some great cause external to the relationship. Transformational leaders emphasize values such as justice, liberty, and equality. A classical example of transformational leadership is the preeminent role played by Martin Luther King, Jr., in the civil rights movement of the 1960s.

Burns's *Leadership* was written at a very broad level from a political science perspective; it was nearly another decade before his concepts began to be applied more narrowly to organizations. A 1984 article in the *Sloan Management Review* by Tichy and Ulrich[51] called for transforming leadership, as did two books the following year: *Leadership and Performance Beyond Expectations* by Bass[52] and *Leaders* by Bennis and Nanus.[53] Despite the importance of these writings, a later book emerged as most influential in galvanizing widespread interest in the transforming leader.

Published in 1987, *The Leadership Challenge: How to Get Extraordinary Things Done in Organizations* by James Kouzes and Barry Posner postulates that successful leaders have made ten behavioral commitments. These commitments are organized under five major headings:

Challenge The Process

1. *Searching out challenging opportunities to change, grow, innovate, and improve*—Outstanding police leaders recognize that they must be change agents and innovators.[54] However, they also know that most innovations do not come from them.[55] Instead, these ideas often come from the officers who do the actual work and from the people who use the department's services.[56] "Leaders listen to the advice and counsel of others; they know that good ideas enter the mind through the ears, not the mouth."[57]
2. *Experimenting and taking risks, and learning from the accompanying mistakes*—"Leaders experiment and take risks. Since risk taking involves mistakes and failure, leaders learn to accept the inevitable disappointments. They treat them as learning opportunities."[58]

Inspire a Shared Vision

3. *Envisioning an uplifting and ennobling future*—In the mold of Burns's transformational style, police leaders look forward to the future with visions and ideals of what can be.[59] "They have a sense of what is uniquely possible if all work together for a common purpose. They are positive about the future and they passionately believe that people can make a difference."[60]
4. *Enlisting others in a common vision by appealing to their values, interests, hopes, and dreams*—Visions seen only by the chief and his or her command staff are insufficient to create an organized movement such as community policing.[61] Police leaders must get

others to see and be excited by future possibilities.[62] One study found that when senior executives were able to communicate their vision of the organization's future effectively, subordinate personnel reported significantly higher levels of

(a) Job satisfaction
(b) Commitment
(c) Loyalty
(d) Esprit de corps
(e) Clarity about the organization's values
(f) Pride in the organization
(g) Encouragement to be productive
(h) Organizational productivity.[63]

Thus, police leaders breathe life into dreams, communicating their visions so clearly that others in the department understand and accept them as their own.[64] They show others how their own values and interests will be served by this long-term vision of the future.[65]

Enable Others to Act

5. *Fostering collaboration by promoting cooperative goals and building trust*—Police leaders develop collaborative and cooperative goals and cooperative relationships with others in the department, knowing that such relationships are the keys that unlock support for their programs.[66] Developing trust in organizations can be a difficult task if the people with whom you work have had their trust abused. One way to build trust is to delegate, for this process is fundamentally a system of trust.[67] Ultimately, you have to be a risk taker when it comes to trust, trusting others first and having faith that they will respond in kind.[68]
6. *Strengthening people by sharing information and power and increasing their discretion and visibility*—In some circles, power is thought to be like a pie; there is only so much and if I have more, then you have less. Kouzes and Posner[69] argue that this view is archaic and retards accomplishments in organizations. Their view is that when people hoard power, others feel less powerful or powerless, leading the less potent to zealously guard their prerogatives and thereby become arbitrary, petty, and dictatorial.[70] According to Kouzes and Posner, it is not centralized power, but mutual respect that sustains extraordinary group efforts; real leaders create an atmosphere of trust and human dignity and nurture self-esteem in others.[71] They make others feel strong and capable,[72] and they empower other officers by such strategies as
   (a) Giving them important work to do on important issues
   (b) Giving them discretion and autonomy over their tasks and resources
   (c) Giving them visibility and recognition for their efforts
   (d) Building relationships for them by connecting them with powerful people and finding them sponsors and mentors.[73]

Model the Way

7. *Setting the example for others by behaving in ways that are consistent with the leader's stated values*—Police officers are astute observers of behavior in organizations and are especially sensitive to differences between what their leaders say is important and their behavior. For instance, if patrol officers are told by their chief that the patrol division is the backbone of the department, but they are the last ones every year to get new cars, then the patrol officers will dismiss the chief's statement as "hype." "Leaders provide the

standard by which other people in the organization calibrate their own choices and behaviors; in order to set an example, leaders must know their values and live by them."[74]

8. *Promoting small wins that reflect consistent progress and build commitment*—Some police chiefs fail because what they propose to do seems overwhelming and this frightens and paralyzes the very people whose support and enthusiasm are essential for success. A wiser strategy is to start with "small wins," doing things that are within the control of the department, that are doable, and that "get the ball rolling." These small wins form the basis for consistently winning, attract followers and deter opposition: it's hard to argue with success. Moreover, each gain preserves past progress and makes it harder to return to the previously prevailing conditions.[75]

Encourage the Heart

9. *Recognize individual contributions to the success of every program*—Having high expectations for themselves and others is a must for police chiefs who wish to be successful; these expectations form the model to which others will adapt their behavior. But simply eliciting the behavior is insufficient. There must be a wide variety of ways police leaders can recognize and reward performance, such as praise, days off, cash awards, and formal award systems. For example, some departments grant officers an extra day off whenever they catch a burglar inside of a building. For a performance-reward system to be effective, three conditions must be met:
   (a) Personnel must know what is expected of them.
   (b) They must receive continuing feedback about their performance so errors can be corrected and solid practices reinforced.
   (c) Only people who meet or exceed standards of behavior should be rewarded, otherwise all rewards are cheapened and the system loses meaning.[76]
10. *Celebrate team accomplishments regularly*—The role of leaders in celebrations is often overlooked. Some police leaders conceive of their role in this area as limited to presiding over annual awards banquets and promotional ceremonies. However, this is a narrow view that is correct only when police department celebrations are limited to such occasions. As used here, *celebrate* simply means to gather people together to savor what they have accomplished and to recognize it jointly. For example, a unit or team who put together a successful grant application could be invited to the chief's home with their spouses for a cookout. Or, investigators who have solved a particularly noteworthy case could, in addition to other recognitions, be the chief's guest at the monthly local chiefs meetings that are common throughout the country. There the chief could publicly introduce them and acknowledge their contributions. For Kouzes and Posner, such activities are both recognition tools and crucial ways of communicating important organizational values.

Transforming police leaders may act in a transactional style around particular issues without abandoning their transformational orientation. In fact, within the organizational setting it is essential that transformational leaders have transactional skills. Few transactional leaders, however, are able to convert to a transforming style because they lack that essential larger and ennobling vision of the future with which to excite potential followers.

The body of literature on transactional and transformational leadership is still evolving. Its most salient contribution is its emphasis on leadership as a primary force in elevating followers to higher levels of performance and purpose and carefully delineating the multiple roles of leaders as visionaries who articulate and teach organizational values.

The Leader and Conflict

Conflict is a condition in which at least two parties have a mutual difference of position, often involving scarce resources, where there is a behavior or threat of behavior through the exercise of power to control the situation or gain at the expense of the other party.[77] Competition differs from conflict in that, in the former, each party is bound to abide by the same rules.[78]

Conflict is a pervasive and perhaps inevitable part of human existence; *it is not inherently "bad" or "good,"* and its consequences depend mainly on how it is managed.[79] *Viewed negatively, conflict is an energy-consuming and destructive phenomenon that divides individuals and groups within the police department, creates tension between representatives of the police department and other agencies, and results in acrimonious and combative exchanges. Viewed positively, conflict can*

1. Stimulate interest
2. Prevent individual, group, and organizational stagnation
3. Be a source of creativity and change as alternative ways of viewing things are aired
4. Give individuals, groups, and organizations a distinctive identity by demarcating them from others
5. Create group and organizational solidarity
6. Be an enjoyable experience of testing and assessing the active use of one's full capabilities.[80]

Although not unique to them, an unfortunate characteristic of many police departments is the view that conflict is destructive so that its positive aspects and potential benefits are overlooked and lost. To tap the useful dimensions of conflict, the police leader must be able to, as outlined in Table 5-4, distinguish between the presence of too much and too little conflict. Additionally, where conflict exists, there is a need to differentiate between pathologically and productively oriented situations. Pathological symptoms in conflict include

1. Unreliable and impoverished communication between the conflicting parties
2. The view that the solution of the conflict will result from the imposition of one view or position over the other
3. A downward spiral of suspicion and hostility that leads to oversensitivity to differences and the minimization of similarities.[81]

Unresponded to, such symptoms are the prelude to hostile infighting, hardening of positions, and protracted opposition. In contrast, productively oriented conflict

1. Is characterized by open and honest communication, which reduces the likelihood of misperceptions and misunderstandings, allows each party to benefit from the knowledge possessed by the other, and promotes a mutual and accurate definition of the issues
2. Encourages the recognition of the legitimacy of the other's interests and of the need to search for a solution that is responsive to the needs of each party
3. Fosters mutual respect and sensitivity to similarities and common interests, stimulating a convergence of positions.[82]

The way in which police leaders will handle conflict is to some extent bound up in their leadership styles. Various methods for resolving conflict are summarized

TABLE 5-4 Symptoms of Too Much and Too Little Conflict

Area of concern	General issue	Symptoms of too much conflict	Symptoms of too little conflict
Attitudes	Awareness of similiarities and differences	Blind to interdependence	Blind to conflicts of interest
	Sophistication about intergroup relations	Unaware of dynamics and costs of conflict	Unaware of dynamics and costs of collusion
	Feelings and perceptions of own and other group	Elaborated stereotypes favorable to own and unfavorable to other group	Lack of consciousness of own group and differences from other group
Behavior	Behavior within groups	High cohesion and conformity; high mobilization	Fragmentization; mobilization
	Conflict management style of groups	Overcompetitive style	Overcooperative style
	Behavior between groups	Aggressive, exploitative behavior, preemptive attack	Avoidance of conflict; appeasement
Structure	Nature of larger system	Separate or underdefined common larger system	Shared larger system that discourages conflict
	Regulatory context for interaction	Few rules to limit escalation	Many rules that stifle differences
	Relevant structural mechanisms	No inhibiting third parties available	No third parties to press differences
	Definition of groups and their goals	Impermeably bounded groups obsessed with own interests	Unbounded groups aware of own interests

From L. Dave Brown, "Managing Conflict Among Groups," in *Organizational Psychology,* 3rd ed., ed. David Kolb, Irwin M. Rubin, and James M. McIntyre (Englewood Cliffs, N.J.: Prentice-Hall, © 1979), p. 383. Reprinted by permission of Prentice-Hall, Inc.

in Table 5-5. The use of denial or withdrawal corresponds to the 1,1 style from the Managerial Grid; suppression or smoothing over with the 1,9; power or dominance with the 9,1; compromise or negotiation with the 5,5; and collaboration with the 9,9. Each of the various methods identified may be appropriate or inappropriate at various times, and to return to an earlier point, good diagnostic ability and flexibility are again central attributes.

Leadership and Organizational Control

Because police leaders are responsible for the performance of their departments, they must be concerned with organizational control and organizational controls. Organizational control is synonymous with organizational direction and is normative, dealing with the future. In contrast, organizational controls consist of measurements of, information about, and analysis of what was and is.[83] Stated more simply, controls pertain to the means, control pertains to an end.[84]

Of necessity, the issues of organizational control and controls permeate police

TABLE 5-5 Methods for Resolving Conflict

Method	Results	Appropriate	Inappropriate	Skills required
Denial or withdrawal	Person tries to solve problem by denying its existence; results in win-lose	When issue is relatively unimportant; when issue is raised at inopportune time	When issue is important; when it will not disappear, but will build to greater complexity	Judgment of what is needed in the situation
Suppression or smoothing over	Differences are played down; results in win-lose	Same as above; also when preservation of relationship is more important than issue	When evasion of issue will disrupt relationship; when others are ready and willing to deal with issue	Empathy
Power or dominance	Authority, position, majority rule, or a persuasive minority settle the conflict; results in win-lose	When authority is granted by one's position; also when group has agreed on method of decision making	When those without power have no means to express their needs and ideas, especially if this lack of opportunity has the potential of future disruption	Decision making; running effective meetings
Compromise or negotiation	Each party gives up something in order to meet midway; results in some loss of each side's position	When both sides have enough leeway to give; when resources are limited; when win-lose stance undesirable	When original position is inflated or unrealistic; when solution must be watered down to be acceptable; when commitment by both parties is doubtful	Attentive listening and paraphrasing; problem solving
Collaboration	Individual abilities and expertise are recognized; each person's position is clear, but emphasis is on group solution; results in win-win	When time is available to complete process; when parties are committed to and trained in use of process	When time is limited; when parties lack training in or commitment to collaborative efforts	Attentive listening and paraphrasing; problem solving

From Lois Borland Hart, *Moving UP: Women and Leadership* (New York: Amacom, © 1980), p. 84. Reprinted with permission of Amacom, a division of the American Management Association. All rights reserved.

departments. Despite the definitions given, practical distinctions between them require some thought. For example, planning, budget preparation, and the written directive system of a police department— consisting of policies, procedures, and rules and regulations—are all control devices in that they all deal with preferred future states, positions, and behaviors. However, when an officer violates a rule and disciplinary measures are invoked, the system of controls is in operation. During the execution of a budget, a midyear review occurs in which performance over the first six months is summarized and analyzed and plans are made for the remaining six months. Thus, this midyear review incorporates features of the system of organizational controls and control. Similarly, quarterly evaluations of police programs incorporate features of the system of controls and control, whereas the final program evaluation report is in the main part of the system of controls. Despite such variations, it is apparent that informed control is a function of the system of controls.

To give the police leader control, controls must satisfy the following specifications:

1. They must be specific and economical.
2. They must be meaningful, relating to significant events.
3. They must use the appropriate indicators.
4. They must be timely.
5. Their limitations must be understood.
6. They must be as simple as possible.
7. They must be directed to those who can take the necessary action.[85]

Perhaps paradoxically, the tighter he or she attempts to control unilaterally, the less control a police leader actually has. A simple illustration of this point is taking a handful of sand and squeezing it forcefully; a great deal trickles out and is lost. Alternatively, the same amount of sand cupped loosely in the hand remains in place. By involving others, by sharing power, the police leader secures the greatest amount of control because individual commitment—the best and most effective type of control—is secured.

Summary

All police managers must be sensitive to their three main responsibilities: (1) contributing to the fulfillment of the department's mission, (2) ensuring that the effort of subordinates is productive and that they are achieving, and (3) producing impacts on their areas of responsibility. Meeting these key responsibilities effectively requires that the police managers practice certain "habits of mind," such as employing their time wisely, building on the strengths that they and their subordinates have, and concentrating on the results to be achieved rather than on the units of work to be accomplished.

Whereas leadership can be seen as the qualities displayed by an individual or as the function of a position, such as major, within a police department, a generally accepted definition is that leadership is the process of influencing the members of an organization to employ appropriately and willingly their energies in activities that are helpful to the achievement of the police department's goals. "Influencing" and "willingly" are related to the concepts of authority and power. In the main, authority is a grant made from above by the formal organization, whereas power is a grant made from below, being confirmed on the leader by the led. However, one should not infer that those who have authority do not also have some power, for the bestowing of authority is accompanied inherently by at least some power.

Leaders at various levels of a police department have different blends of skills that they predominately employ. Human relations, conceptual, and technical are the three major types of skills that are employed in this skill mix. As one advances up the rank hierarchy of a police department, which can be organized under three groupings—first-line supervisors, middle managers, and top managers—the relative emphasis and importance of the three skills shift.

Leadership theories essentially try to establish what variables are related to the emergence of leadership or the nature of leadership itself. Illustrative are (1) great man and genetic theories associated variously with Carlyle, Hegel, and Galton; (2) the traits approach, which has historically enjoyed great appeal; (3) behavioral explanations, which center on what a leader does; and (4) situational statements, which maintain that effective leadership is the result of a good fit between the capabilities of a leader and the demands of a given condition.

The abundance of interest in the subject of leadership has produced alternative ways of classifying leadership styles. Schemes treated in this chapter include (1) authoritarian, democratic, and laissez-faire leaders; (2) the authoritarian-democratic continuum; (3) leader styles in bureaucratic structures; (4) traditional versus nontraditional police leaders; (5) station house versus street sergeants; (6) male versus female leaders in policing; (7) Managerial Grid styles; (8) situational leadership; and (9) transactional and transformational leadership.

A significant element of organizational life with which the police manager must deal is conflict, defined as a situation in which at least two parties have a mutual difference of position and in which one party employs or threatens behavior through the exercise of power to obtain control of the situation at the expense of the other party. Although the presence of conflict is often viewed as being undesirable, the absence of it is certainly unhealthy. Fundamental to any understanding of conflict is that the way in which it is handled is more a determinant of the "goodness" or "badness" of conflict rather than of any inherent characteristic of conflict itself. Leader styles may have certain pronounced preferences or tendencies for the way in which conflict is addressed; for example, the 9,1 style can be related to the use of power or dominance as a method of resolving conflict.

Organizational control and organizational controls are the devices by which the police manager shapes the course and events for the department. Organizational control and organizational direction can be equated usefully, and they are normative, futuristic statements. Measurements of, information about, and analysis of the past and present states are termed *organizational controls*. Organizational control and controls are differentiated further in that the former is a preferred state to be achieved, whereas the latter are the means of achieving that preferred state.

Discussion Questions

1. What is a generally accepted definition of *leadership?*
2. What are the definitions of *authority* and *power,* and how are they related?
3. What distinctions can be made between personalized and social power?
4. Within the skill mix, which skill is most essential to top management? Why?
5. The traits approach to leadership has enjoyed great popularity. What is it and what evidence is there to support it?

6. What differences are there among authoritarian, democratic, and laissez-faire leaders?
7. What issues or forces did Victor Cizanckas discuss that are relevant to reform?
8. Is the research on police leaders by Cohen and Pursley related? If so, how?
9. What evidence is there to support the proposition that women can be effective leaders in policing?
10. What are the two key dimensions and five principal styles of the Managerial Grid?
11. Compare Burns's transactional and transformational leaders.
12. What is conflict and is it good or bad for organizations?
13. Are there any differences between organizational control and controls? If so, what?
14. What specific skills are associated with each of the different methods of resolving conflict?

Notes

1. Peter F. Drucker, *People and Performance: The Best of Peter Drucker on Management* (New York: Harper's College Press, 1977), p. 28.
2. Patrick A. Knight and Howard M. Weiss, "Effects of Selection Agent and Leader Origin on Leader Influence and Group Member Perceptions," *Organizational Behavior and Human Performance,* 26 (August 1980), pp. 17–21. Also, see Thomas Henderson, "The Relative Effects of Community Complexity and of Sheriffs Upon the Professionalism of Sheriff Departments," *American Journal of Political Science,* 19 (February 1975), p. 126.
3. Peter F. Drucker, *The Effective Executive* (New York: Harper & Row, 1966), p. 23 and pp. 36–39. Points 2 to 5 were taken from this source at page 24. Also see Eugene Raudsepp, "Why Managers Don't Delegate," *Journal of Applied Management,* 4:5 (1979), pp. 25–27.
4. The flip side of the coin is the question, "Under what conditions do organizational members voluntarily elect to leave, stay and protest, or simply stay?" An important book addressing these issues is Albert O. Hirschman, *Exit, Voice, and Loyalty* (Cambridge, Mass.: Harvard University Press, 1970).
5. The description of power motivation styles is drawn, with restatement into a police context, from Jay Hall and James Hawker, "Interpreting Your Scores from the Power Management Inventory" (The Woodlands, Tex.: Teleometrics International, 1981).
6. Variants of this model appear in the literature; see, for example, Ronald G. Lynch, *The Police Manager,* 2nd ed. (Boston: Holbrook Press, 1978), Figure 1-2, p. 11; Calvin J. Swank, "Police Management in the United States: A Candid Assessment," *Journal of Police Science and Administration,* 4 (1976), pp. 90–93; Robert Katz, "Skills of an Effective Administrator," *Harvard Business Review,* 33:1 (1955), pp. 33–42.
7. Ralph M. Stogdill, *Handbook of Leadership: A Survey of Theory and Research* (New York: Free Press, 1974), p. 17.
8. Thomas Carlyle, *Heroes, Hero-Worship and the Heroic in History* (New York: A. L. Burt, 1902 and G. W. F. Hegel, The Philosophy of History (Indianapolis: Bobbs-Merrill Company, Inc., 1952).
9. Francis Galton, *Hereditary Genius: An Inquiry into Its Laws and Consequences* (New York: D. Appleton, revised with an American preface, 1887).
10. Field Marshal Montgomery, *The Path to Leadership* (New York: Putnam, 1961), pp. 10–19. To some extent, Montgomery also holds with Carlyle in that the former asserted that the leader must be able to dominate and master the surrounding events.
11. Cecil E. Goode, "Significant Research on Leadership," *Personnel,* 25:5 (1951), p. 349.
12. Stogdill, *Handbook of Leadership,* p. 81, and "Personal Factors Associated with Lead-

ership: A Survey of the Literature," *Journal of Psychology,* 25–26 (January 1948), pp. 35–71.

13. C. A. Gibb, "Leadership," in *Handbook of Sound Psychology,* vol. 2, ed. Gardner Lindzey (Reading, Mass.: Addison-Wesley, 1954).
14. Walter J. Palmer, "Managerial Effectiveness as a Function of Personality Traits of the Manager," *Personnel Psychology,* 27 (Summer 1974), pp. 283–95.
15. Gary Dessler, *Organization and Management: A Contingency Approach* (Englewood Cliffs, N.J.: Prentice-Hall, 1976), p. 158.
16. Stogdill, "Personal Factors," pp. 35–71; Dessler, *Organization and Management,* p. 169.
17. F. E. Fiedler, *A Theory of Leadership Effectiveness* (New York: McGraw-Hill, 1967). Fiedler has worked on a contingency approach to leadership since the early 1950s.
18. Robert J. House, "A Path–Goal Theory of Leader Effectiveness," *Administrative Science Quarterly,* 16 (September 1971), pp. 321–38.
19. See K. Lewin, R. Lippitt, and R. White, "Patterns of Aggressive Behavior in Experimentally Created Social Climates," *Journal of Social Psychology,* 10 (May 1939), pp. 271–99; R. Lippitt and R. K. White, "The Social Climate of Children's Groups," in *Child Behavior and Development,* ed. R. G. Baker, K. S. Kounin, and H. F. Wright (New York: McGraw-Hill, 1943), pp. 485–508; Ralph White and Ronald Lippitt, "Leader Behavior and Member Reaction in Three Social Climates," in *Group Dynamics: Research and Theory,* 2nd ed., ed. Dorwin Cartwright and Alvin Zander (New York: Harper & Row, 1960), pp. 552–53; Ronald Lippitt, "An Experimental Study of the Effect of Democratic and Authoritarian Group Atmospheres," *University of Iowa Studies in Childwelfare,* 16 (January 1940), pp. 43–195.
20. White and Lippitt, "Leader Behavior," pp. 539–45 and 552–53.
21. Robert Tannenbaum and Warren H. Schmidt, "How to Choose a Leadership Pattern," *Harvard Business Review,* 36:2 (1958), pp. 95–101.
22. Ibid., pp 98–101.
23. Anthony Downs, *Inside Bureaucracy* (Boston: Little, Brown, 1967).
24. Ibid., pp. 92–96.
25. Ibid., pp. 96–101.
26. Ibid., pp. 109–10.
27. Ibid., pp. 107–9.
28. Bernard Cohen, "Leadership Styles of Commanders in the New York City Police Department," *Journal of Police Science and Administration,* 8:2 (1980), pp. 125–38. References to Downs's types of leaders has been added.
29. Robert D. Pursley, "Leadership and Community Identification Attitudes Among Two Categories of Police Chiefs: An Exploratory Inquiry," *Journal of Police Science and Administration,* 2:4 (December 1974), pp. 414–22.
30. John Van Maanen, "Making Rank: Becoming an American Police Sergeant," *Urban Life,* 13:2–3 (1984), pp. 155–76. The distinction between station and street sergeants is drawn from Van Maanen's work with some restatement and extension of views. The speculation about future career patterns is the work of the present authors.
31. Barbra R. Price, "A Study of Leadership Strength of Female Police Executives," *Journal of Police Science and Administration,* 2:2 (1974), pp. 219–26.
32. Robert R. Blake and Jane Srygley Mouton, "The Developing Revolution in Management Practices," *Journal of the American Society of Training Directors,* 16:7 (1962), pp. 29–52.
33. The Ohio State studies date from the mid-1940s and identified the dimensions of consideration and structure; the University of Michigan studies date from the late 1940s and identified employee- and production-centered supervisors.
34. These data were gathered from police leaders attending training programs led by Ronald Lynch, Institute of Government, University of North Carolina, and/or Charles

Swanson and Leonard Territo. Because of the way in which the data were obtained, they should be considered as illustrative rather than representative.

35. How long a leader will persist in a given style depends on the strength of preference for the primary over the backup, which is measurable. In this regard, see Jack L. Kuykendall, "Police Leadership: An Analysis of Executives Styles," *Criminal Justice Review,* 2:2 (Spring 1977), pp. 89–100.
36. Paul Hersey and Kenneth H. Blanchard, *Management of Organizational Behavior: Utilizing Human Resources,* 3rd ed. (Englewood Cliffs, N.J.: Prentice-Hall, 1977), p. 105. Also, see William J. Reddin, *Managerial Effectiveness* (New York: McGraw-Hill, 1970).
37. Hersey and Blanchard, *Management of Organizational Behavior,* pp. 160–61.
38. Ibid., p. 161.
39. Ibid., p. 161.
40. Ibid., p. 163.
41. Ibid., p. 161.
42. Ibid., p. 163.
43. Ibid., p. 162.
44. Ibid., p. 168.
45. Ibid., p. 165.
46. Ibid., p. 168.
47. Ibid., p. 159.
48. James McGregor Burns, *Leadership* (New York: Harper & Row, 1978). For an excellent overview on leadership, see Edwin P. Hollander and Lynn R. Offermann, "Power and Leadership in Organizations: Relationship in Transition," *American Psychologist,* 45:2 (1990), pp. 179–89.
49. Ibid., pp. 4, 19–20.
50. Ibid., p. 426.
51. Noel Tichy ad David O. Ulrich, "The Leadership Challenge: A Call for The Transformational Leader," *Sloan Management Review,* vol. 26, no. 1, (Fall 1984), pp. 59–68.
52. B. M. Bass, *Leadership and Performance Beyond Expectations* (New York: Free Press, 1985).
53. Warren Bennis and Bert Nanus, *Leaders* (New York: Harper & Row, 1985).
54. James M. Kouzes and Barry Z. Posner, *The Leadership Challenge: How to Get Extraordinary Things Done in Organizations* (San Francisco: Jossey-Bass, 1987), p. 38. This book does not focus on the police; hence, the present authors have taken the liberty of writing its important lessons into the police context.
55. Ibid., p. 29.
56. Ibid., p. 29.
57. Ibid., p. 29.
58. Ibid., p. 29.
59. Ibid., p. 79.
60. Ibid., p. 79.
61. Ibid., p. 79.
62. Ibid., p. 79.
63. Ibid., p. 108.
64. Ibid., p. 79.
65. Ibid., p. 79.
66. Ibid., p. 131.
67. Ibid., p. 155.
68. Ibid., pp. 159–60.
69. Ibid., p. 162.
70. Ibid., pp. 162–63.
71. Ibid., p. 131.

72. Ibid., p. 131.
73. Ibid., p. 175.
74. Ibid., p. 190.
75. Ibid., pp. 220–21.
76. Ibid., p. 245.
77. Albert E. Roark and Linda Wilkinson, "Approaches to Conflict Management," *Group and Organizational Studies,* 4 (December 1979), p. 441.
78. Ibid., p. 441.
79. Ibid., p. 440; on this point, also see Kenneth Thomas, "Conflict and Conflict Management," in *Handbook of Industrial and Organizational Psychology,* ed. Marvin D. Dunnette (Chicago; Rand McNally, 1976), p. 889.
80. See Lewis A. Coser, *The Functions of Social Conflict* (Glenco, Ill.: Free Press, 1956); G. Simmel, *Conflict* (New York: Free Press, 1955); and M. Deutsch, "Toward an Understanding of Conflict," *International Journal of Group Tensions,* 1:1 (1971), p. 48.
81. Morton Deutsch, *The Resolution of Conflict* (New Haven, Conn.: Yale University Press, 1973), p. 353.
82. Ibid., p. 363.
83. Peter F. Drucker, *Management: Tasks, Responsibilities, Practices* (New York: Harper & Row, 1973), p. 494.
84. Ibid., p. 494.
85. Ibid., pp. 496–505.

6 Interpersonal and Organizational Communication

The difference between the right word and the almost right word is the difference between lightning and lightning bug.
MARK TWAIN

Introduction

Effective communication is essential in all organizations in which people deal with one another. It is very difficult to imagine any kind of activity that does not depend on communication in one form or another. Today's police managers are aware that the efficiency of their personnel depends to a great extent on how well the efforts of individual members can be coordinated. Because coordination does not simply happen, managers must realize that communication is necessary if their subordinates are to obtain the understanding and cooperation required to achieve organizational and individual goals.

A major role of today's manager is that of communicator. Managers at all levels of the police organization spend an overwhelming amount of their time in the process and problems of communication.

Research in recent years has indicated that communication is the number one problem in management, and lack of communication is the employees' primary complaint about their immediate supervisors.[1] The information in this chapter is intended to provide police managers with an overview of both interpersonal and organizational communications and provide specific information that will facilitate and enhance their communication skills.

The Communication Process

An explanation of communication begins with a basic problem—it cannot be examined as an isolated event. Communication is a process, and so it must be understood as the totality of several interdependent and dynamic elements. In the aggregate, communications may be defined as the process by which senders and receivers interact in given social contexts. Another understanding of this definition is that the process of communication requires that we examine the several elements that make up the process; encoding, transmission, medium, reception, decoding, and feedback.[2] Figure 6–1 illustrates this process graphically.

Encoding—Experience cannot be transmitted as experience. In conveying an experience to another person, we do not relive that experience with that person. Even in the most scrupulous reproduction of an experience, every element cannot be duplicated. At the very least, the time period is altered, and intervening experiences have altered us as individuals.

To convey an experience or idea to someone, we translate, or encode that experience into symbols. We use words or other verbal behaviors and gestures, or other nonverbal

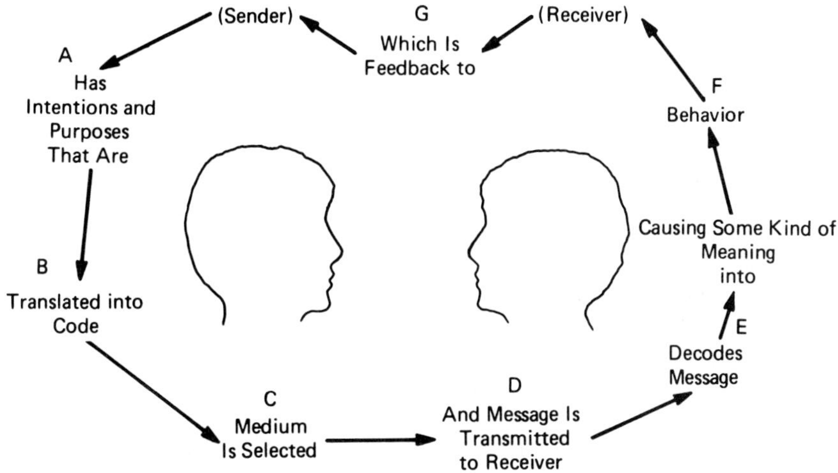

A. The sender has certain intentions, objectives, or purposes.

B. The sender translated these intentions into some code (language, nonverbal gesture, etc.), which becomes the message.

C. The sender then selects a medium (written or spoken words, music, art, etc.).

D. The sender uses the medium to transmit the message to the receiver.

E. The receiver "picks up" the message (listens, reads, watches, etc.) and decodes its meaning.

F. This meaning causes the receiver to behave in some manner.

G. This behavior gives the sender indications, or feedback, as to whether or not the receiver understood the meaning of the message.

FIGURE 6-1. The communication process. [From R. C. Huseman, "The Communication Process," in *Interpersonal Communication: A Guide for Staff Development* (Athens: Institute of Government, University of Georgia, August 1974), p. 22.]

behaviors to convey the experience or idea. These symbols are our code; they stand for certain experiences; they are not experiences themselves.

Transmission—Encoding involves only the decision to use a symbol for some concept. The element of transmission involves the translation of the encoded symbols into some behavior that another person can observe. The actual articulation (moving our lips, tongue, etc.) of the symbol into verbal or nonverbal observable behavior is transmission.

Medium—Communication must be conveyed through some channel or medium. Media for communication may be our sight, hearing, taste, touch, or smell. Some other media are television, telephone, paper and pencil, and radio. The importance of the choice of the medium should not be minimized. All of us are aware of the difference between a message that our superior delivers personally and the one that is sent through a secretary or by a memo. The medium, like the chosen symbol, has an effect on the meaning that the listener eventually attaches to the message in the process of decoding.

Reception—For the receiver, the reception of the message is analogous to the sender's transmission. The stimuli, the verbal and nonverbal symbols, reach the senses of the receiver and are conveyed to the brain for interpretation.

Decoding—The process of interpretation occurs when the individual who has received the stimuli develops some meaning for the verbal and nonverbal symbols and decodes the stimuli. For the receiver, then, decoding is analogous to the process of encoding for the sender. These symbols are translated into some concept or experience of the receiver. Whether the receiver is familiar with the symbols, or whether interference such as any physical noise or physiological problem occurs, determines how closely the message that the receiver has decoded approximates the message that the sender has encoded. The success of the communication process depends on the extent to which the receiver's decoded concept is similar to the concept of the sender. It is for this reason that we hear the phrase, "meaning is in people." Truly, the external verbal and nonverbal symbols that we usually call the message are in fact only stimuli. The actual message is the decoded or interpreted concept of the receiver. This decoded concept is the receiver's meaning for the external stimuli.

Feedback—When the receiver decodes the transmitted symbols, he or she usually provides some response or feedback to the sender. Feedback is a self-correcting mechanism. In our homes, thermostats, self-correcting mechanisms within the heating or cooling unit, will correct the temperature. In communication, responses to the symbols that we have sent act as regulators. If someone appears puzzled, we repeat the message or we encode the concept differently and transmit some different symbols to express the same concept. Feedback that we receive acts as a guide or steering device. Feedback promotes accuracy of communication. Feedback lets us know whether the receiver has interpreted our symbols as we intended. Feedback is, then, a crucial element in guaranteeing that the meaning that the sender intended to convey was in fact conveyed to the receiver.

Communication Barriers

Barriers to communication, or communication breakdowns, can occur at any place in the system. They may be the result of improper techniques on the part of either the sender or the receiver.

Sender-Caused Barriers. The sender hinders communications when

1. The sender is not clear about what is to be accomplished with the message
2. The sender assumes incorrectly that the receiver has the knowledge necessary to understand the message and its intent and does not adapt the message to the intended receiver

3. The sender uses a communication medium not suited for the message; for example, some messages are better transmitted face to face, others in writing or by illustrations
4. The sender does not develop a mechanism for receiving feedback to determine if the message was understood correctly
5. The sender does not interpret feedback correctly or fails to clarify the message on the basis of feedback from the receiver
6. The sender uses language that causes the receiver to stop listening, reading, or receiving
7. The sender analyzes the audience improperly
8. The sender's background experiences and attitudes are different from those of the receiver, and the sender does not take this into account.

Receiver-Caused Barriers. The receiver hinders communication when

1. The receiver is a poor listener, observer, or reader and therefore misinterprets the meaning of the message
2. The receiver jumps to conclusions
3. The receiver hears or sees only certain parts of the message
4. The receiver tends to reject messages that contradict beliefs and assumptions
5. The receiver has other concerns such as emotional barriers, for example, being mentally preoccupied.

Other Barriers. Some other barriers to communication are

1. Noise, temperature, and other physical distractions
2. Distance or inability to see or hear the message being sent
3. Sender–receiver relationship, power structure, roles, and personality differences.

Information Flow and Directionality

Organizational systems of communication are usually created by setting up formal systems of responsibility and explicit delegations of duties, such as implicit statements of the nature, content, and direction of communication that are necessary for the performance of the group. Consequently, formal communication is required by the organization and follows the accepted pattern of hierarchical structure. Delegated authority and responsibility determine the path that communication should take, whether upward or downward. Messages that travel through the formal channels of any organization may follow routine patterns; they may be expected at a given time, or presented in a standard form, and receive a regularized degree of consideration.[3]

Most police managers prefer a formal system, regardless of how cumbersome it may be, because they can control it and because it tends to create a record for future reference. However, motivational factors of the individual and organizations affect the flow of communication. Employees typically communicate with those who help them to achieve their aims and avoid communicating with those who do not assist, or may retard, their accomplishing those goals; they direct their communications toward those who make them feel more secure and gratify their needs and away from those who threaten them or make them feel anxious or generally provide unrewarding experiences; and employees communicate in a manner that allows them to increase their status, belong to a more prestigious group, attain more power to influence decisions, or expand their control. The moving transaction identified as organizational communication can occur at several levels and can result in understanding, agreement, good feeling, and appropriate behavior; the converse may also be true.[4]

Downward Communication

Classical management theories place primary emphasis on control, chain of command, and downward flow of information. Downward communication is used by management for sending orders, directives, goals, policies, procedures, memorandums, and so forth to employees at lower levels of the organization. Five types of such communication within an organization can be identified.[5]

1. Job instruction–communication relating to the performance of a certain task
2. Job rational–communication relating a certain task to organizational tasks
3. Procedures and practices–communication about organization policies, procedures, rules, and regulations
4. Feedback–communication appraisal of how an individual performs the assigned task
5. Indoctrination–communication designed to motivate the employees.[6]

Other reasons for communicating downward implicit in this listing are opportunities for management to spell out objectives, change attitudes and mold opinions, prevent misunderstandings from lack of information, and prepare employees for change.[7] A study conducted by Opinion Research Corporation some years ago revealed surprisingly that large amounts of information generated at the top of an organization did not filter down to the working levels. Studies of the flow of communications within complex organizations repeatedly demonstrate that each level of management can act as an obstacle or barrier to downward communication.[8] In perhaps the best controlled experimental research in downward communication, Dahle[9] proved the efficacy of using oral and written media together. His findings indicate the following order of effectiveness (from most effective to least effective):

1. Oral and written communication combined
2. Oral communication only
3. Written communication only
4. The bulletin board
5. The organizational grapevine.

The research conducted thus far seems to indicate that most downward channels in organizations are only minimally effective. Findings indicate further that attempts at disseminating information downward in an organization should not depend exclusively on a single medium or channel.

Upward Communication

Even though police administrators may appreciate the need for effective upward communication, they may not translate this need into action.[10] It becomes apparent at once that to swim upstream is a much harder task than to float downstream. But currents of resistance, inherent in the temperament and habits of supervisors and employees in the complexity and structure of modern police agencies, are persistent and strong. Let us examine some of these deterrents to upward communication.

Barriers Involving Police Organizations

The physical distance between superior and subordinate impedes upward communication in several ways. Communication becomes difficult and infrequent when superiors are isolated so as to be seldom seen or spoken to. In large police organizations, executives may be located in headquarters or operating centers that are not easily reached by subordinates. In other police agencies, executive offices may be placed remotely or executives may hold themselves needlessly inaccessible.

The complexity of the organization may also cause prolonged delays of upward communication. For example, let us assume that there is a problem at the patrol officer level that must be settled eventually by the chief executive or some other high-ranking officer. A patrol officer tells the sergeant about the problem, and they discuss it and try to settle it. It may take several hours or even a couple of days before all the available facts are compiled. The sergeant in turn brings the problem to the lieutenant, who feels compelled to reexamine all the facts of the problem and perhaps pursue it even further before forwarding it on to the next highest authority. Because each succeeding superior may be concerned that the problem could somehow reflect negatively on his or her ability, delays result that could mean that the problem is not brought to the attention of the chief executive for several weeks. In addition, as the information moves up the organizational ladder, there is a tendency for it to be diluted or distorted, as each supervisor consciously or unconsciously selects and edits information being passed up. The more levels of supervision the information passes through, the more it is filtered and the less accurate it becomes.

Barriers Involving Superiors

The attitude of superiors and their behavior in listening play a vital role in encouraging or discouraging communication upward. If, in listening to a subordinate, a supervisor seems anxious to end the interview, impatient with the subordinate, or annoyed or distressed by the subject being discussed, a major barrier to future communication may be created.

There is always the danger that a supervisor may assume the posture that "no news is good news," when in fact a lack of complaints or criticism may be a symptom that upward communication is operating at a dangerously low level.

Supervisors may also assume, often incorrectly, that they know what subordinates think or feel and also believe that listening to complaints from subordinates, especially complaints about departmental policies or even specific supervisors, is an indication of disloyalty. This attitude tends to discourage employees with justifiable complaints from approaching their superiors.

One of the strongest deterrents to upward communication is a failure of management to take action on undesirable conditions previously brought to their attention. The result is that subordinates lose faith both in the sincerity of management and in the value of communication.

Some executives feel that they are too involved in daily problems and responsibilities to provide adequate time for listening fully to their subordinates' ideas, reports, and criticisms. Nevertheless, many time-consuming problems could be minimized or eliminated if superiors would take time to listen to their employees, for in listening they can discover solutions to present problems or anticipate causes for future ones. The subordinate who has free access to a superior can get answers to many budding problems and thus eliminate the heavier demands that will result when the problems have become much more complex, emotion laden, and possibly even out of control.

Barriers Involving Subordinates

Communication may flow more freely downward than upward because a superior is free to call in a subordinate and talk about a problem at will. The subordinate does not have the same freedom to intrude on the superior's time and is also discouraged from circumventing the chain of command and going over a superior's head or from asking for an appeal from decisions made by superiors. Thus, neither the system available nor the rewards offered to the subordinate for upward communication equal those for downward messages.

Management, on the other hand, can speed the flow of information by the use of written policies, procedures, general orders, meetings, and so forth. There are rarely comparable organizational vehicles available for the upward flow of communications. Further, tradition, authority, and prestige are behind downward communications.

In communicating upward, a subordinate must provide explanations for the desired communication and, in the final analysis, must obtain acceptance from someone with greater status who is also likely to be more fluent and persuasive than the subordinate. The superior probably has worked in a similar position at one time and knows the attitudes, language, and problems at that level. On the other hand, the subordinate who is communicating with a superior rarely understands the responsibilities or difficulties faced by the superior.

Finally, unless superiors are particularly receptive, subordinates generally prefer to withhold or temper bad news, unfavorable opinions, and reports of mistakes or failures. If a manager is defensive about listening to bad news, those who like and respect the manager will withhold information or minimize omissions and errors from friendly motives; others may withhold information from fear, dislike, or indifference.

Horizontal Communication

When an organization's formal communication channels are not open, the informal horizontal channels are almost sure to thrive as a substitute.[11] If there is a disadvantage in horizontal communication, it is that it is much easier and more natural to achieve than vertical communication and, therefore, often replaces vertical channels rather than supplements them. Actually, the horizontal channels that replace weak or nonexistent vertical channels are usually of an informal nature. There are, of course, formal horizontal channels that are procedurally necessary and should be built into the system. Formal horizontal channels must be set up between various bureaus and divisions for the purposes of planning, interwork task coordination, and general system maintenance functions, such as problem solving, information sharing, and conflict resolution.

We can begin by acknowledging that horizontal communication is essential if the subsystems within a police organization are to function in an effective and coordinated manner. Horizontal communication among peers may also furnish the emotional and social bond that builds esprit de corps or a feeling of teamwork. Psychologically, people seem to need this type of communication, and police managers would do well to provide for this need and thus allow peers to solve some of their own work problems together.

Suppose, for example, that patrol sergeant A is having great difficulty communicating certain mutually beneficial information to detective sergeant B because the police department requires strict adherence to the chain of command in transmitting information. As indicated in Figure 6–2A, sergeant A would have to go up through the various hierarchical complexities of the patrol division and back down through the detective division to communicate with sergeant B. The time being wasted and the level-to-level message distortion occurring in the classically managed organization was recognized by Fayol[12] in 1916. Fayol proposed the creation of a horizontal bridge (see Figure 6–2B) that would allow more direct communications between individuals within an organization. The major limiting factor to the use of Fayol's bridge is a loss of network control and the subsequent weakening of authority and random scattering of messages throughout the system. Such random communication channels can lead to diagonal lines of communication, such as direct communication between sergeant A in the patrol division and captain C in the detective division. Diagonal lines of communication are not in and of themselves bad; however, they are very difficult to control from the management point of view.[13]

Despite the need for formal horizontal communication in an organization, there may be tendency among peers not to formally communicate task-related infor-

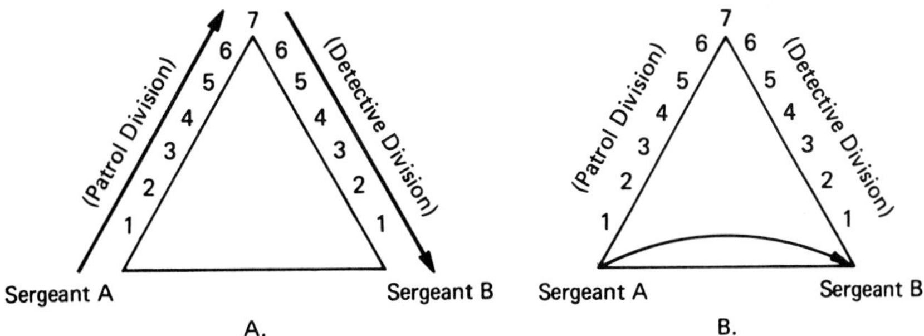

FIGURE 6-2. Horizontal lines of communication: A. Message path from sergeant A to sergeant B following the usual structured channels. B. Message path from sergeant A to sergeant B following Fayol's bridge. [From R. K. Allen, *Organizational Management Through Communication* (New York: Harper & Row, 1977), pp. 78–79. Reprinted by permission of Harper & Row Publishers, Inc.]

mation horizontally. For instance, rivalry for recognition and promotion may cause competing subordinates to be reluctant to share information. Subordinates may also find it difficult to communicate with highly specialized people at the same level as themselves in other divisions.

In the main, then, formal horizontal communication channels are vital as a supplement to the vertical channels in an organization. Conversely, the informal horizontal channels, although socially necessary, can be detrimental to the vertical channels. Informal horizontal channels may not only carry false or distorted information but sometimes tend to replace the vertical channels.[14]

The Grapevine

The best-known system for transmitting informal communication is the grapevine, so called because it meanders back and forth like a grapevine across organizational lines. The grapevine's most effective characteristics are that it is fast, it can be highly selective and discriminating, it operates mostly at the place of work, and it supplements and relates to the formal communication. These characteristics may be divided into desirable or undesirable attributes.

The grapevine can be considered desirable because it gives management insight into employees' attitudes, provides a safety valve for employees' emotions, and helps to spread useful information. Dysfunctional traits include its tendencies to spread rumors and untruths, its lack of responsibility to any group or person, and its uncontrollability. Attributes of the grapevine, its speed and influence, may work either to the good or to the detriment of the organization. The actual operation of the grapevine can be visualized in four ways (see Figure 6–3):[15]

1. The single-strand chain: A tells B, who tells C, who tells D, and so on.
2. The gossip chain: A seeks and tells everyone else, thus being the organizational "Paul Revere."
3. The probability chain: A communicates randomly to D, F, G, and J, in accord with the laws of probability; then D, F, G, and J tell others in the same manner.
4. The cluster chain: A tells three selected others; perhaps one of them tells two others; and one of these tells one other person.

The grapevine is a permanent factor to be reckoned with in the daily activities of management, and no competent manager would try to abolish it. Rather, the astute manager should analyze it and consciously try to influence it.[16]

Interpersonal Styles of Communication: The Johari Window

A cross-cultural study involving respondents from the United States, Japan, and Great Britain revealed that approximately 74 percent of the managers cited communication breakdown as the single greatest barrier to organizational excellence.[17] A fact of organizational life is that, when management is effective and relationships

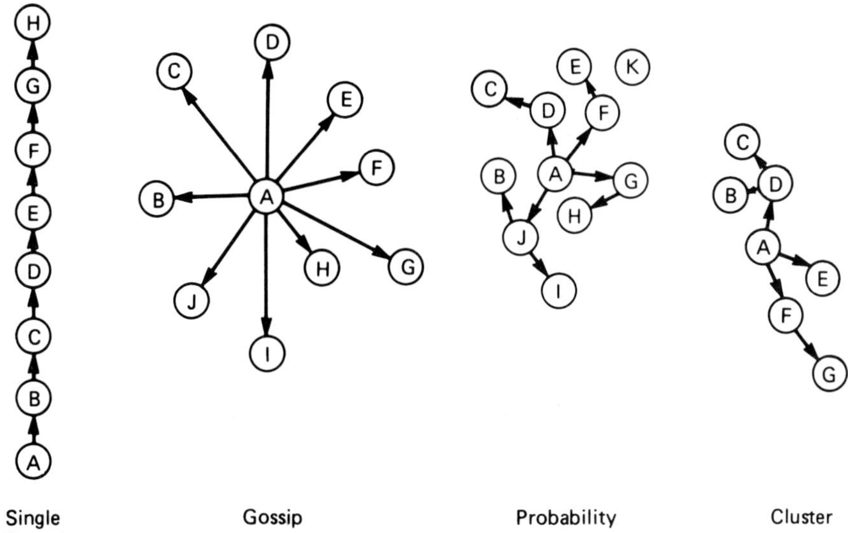

FIGURE 6-3. Types of communication grapevines. [From H. H. Albers, *Organized Executive Action: Decision Making and Leadership* (New York: John Wiley, 1961), p. 343.]

among organizational members are sound, problems of communication breakdown tend not to be heard.[18] It is only when relationships among organizational members are fraught with unarticulated tensions that complaints about communication breakdown begin to be heard.[19] Two important points are implicit in this discussion:

1. The quality of relationships in an organization may dictate to a large extent the level of communication effectiveness achieved.
2. The quality of relationships, in turn, is a direct product of the interpersonal practices of an organization's membership.[20]

The single most important aspect of interpersonal practices is the way in which parties to a relationship communicate with each other. In 1955, Joseph Luft and Harry Ingham developed a communication model for use in their group dynamics training programs; this model has come to be known as the Johari Window, its designation as such arising from the use of portions of the first names of its developers.[21] Subsequently, Jay Hall and Martha Williams modified it to treat the Johari Window as an information flow and processing model. Through the use of a questionnaire developed by Hall and Williams, interpersonal styles of communication are identifiable.[22]

The Johari Window model is depicted in Figure 6–4 and has two key dimensions: exposure and feedback.[23] Exposure means the open and candid expression of the police manager's feelings, factual knowledge, guesses, and the like in a conscious attempt to share; together, these expressions are referred to as information. Untrue, frivolous, and kindred statements do not constitute exposure because they contribute nothing to promoting mutual understanding. Central to

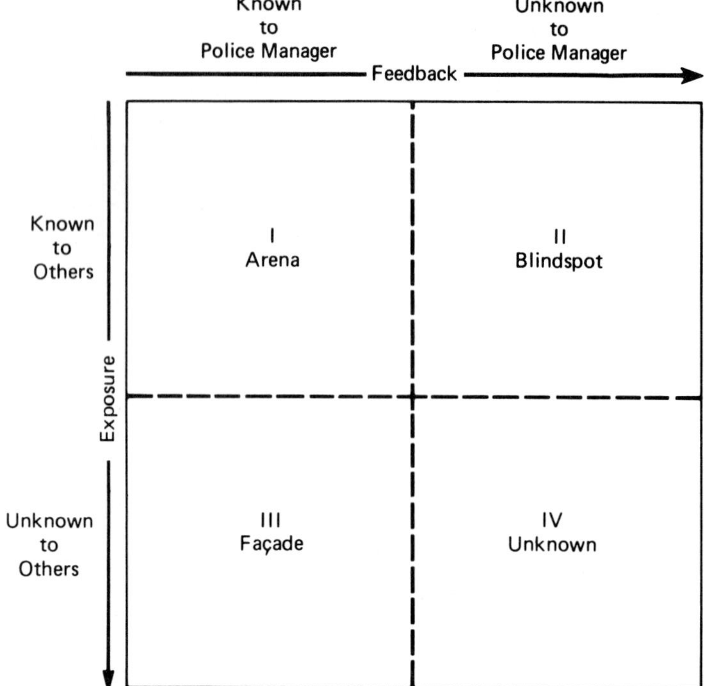

FIGURE 6-4. The Johari Window. [From Jay Hall and Martha S. Williams, "How to Interpret Your Scores on the Personal Relations Survey," © Teleometrics International, The Woodlands, Texas, 1967, with minor modification. Special permission for reproduction is granted by the authors Jay Hall, PhD, and Martha S. Williams, PhD, and publisher, Teleometrics International. All rights reserved.]

the use of exposure by the police manager is the desire to build trust and a willingness to accept a certain amount of risk. The feedback process entails the police leader's active solicitation of information that he or she feels others may have that he or she does not.

Figure 6–4 consists of four quadrants or regions, defined as follows:

1. Region I, termed the arena, is the area of the total space available in which information is shared equally and understood by the police manager and others. This facet of the interpersonal relationship is thought to be the part that controls interpersonal productivity. The underlying assumption is that productivity and interpersonal effectiveness are related directly to the amount of mutually held information in a relationship. Therefore, the larger region I becomes, the more effective, rewarding, and productive becomes the relationship as well.
2. Region II, the blindspot, is that portion of the total space available that holds information known by others but unknown to the police manager. This area represents a handicap to the manager because one can scarcely understand the decisions, behavior, and feelings of others if one lacks the information on which they are based. However, others have a certain advantage to the extent that they have information unknown to the manager.
3. Region III, designated the façade, may also be considered an inhibitor of interpersonal

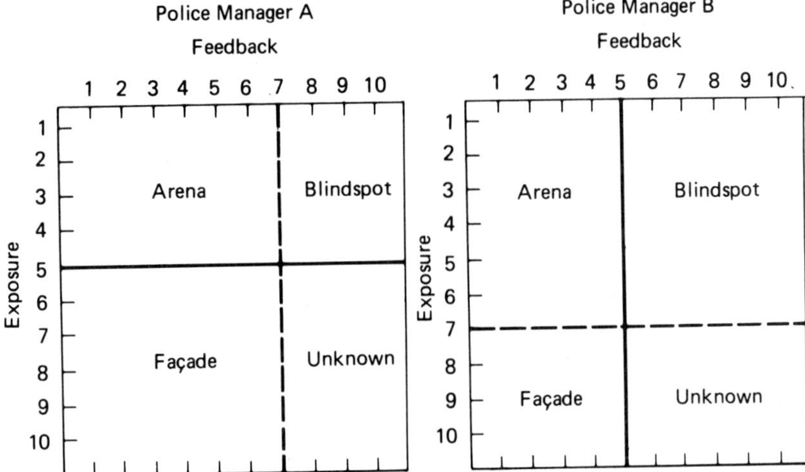

FIGURE 6-5. Illustration of the exchange of exposure and feedback.

effectiveness and productivity, due to an imbalance of information that favors the police manager. This is so because the police manager possesses information that is not known by others. The manager may withhold information that is perceived as potentially prejudicial to the relationship, out of fear, desire for power, or other related reasons. Essentially the façade serves as a protective front, but at the expense of keeping the arena from growing larger. Realistically, every relationship has a façade; the practical question is, How much is actually needed?

4. Region IV, the unknown, is the portion of the total space available that is unknown to both the police manager and others. This area is thought to contain psychodynamic data, unknown potentials, learned idiosyncrasies, and the data base of creativity. However, as interpersonal effectiveness increases and the arena becomes larger, the unknown region shrinks.

As suggested, although the regions shown in Figure 6–4 are of equal size, when they are measured through the use of the Hall–Williams questionnaire, the "Personnel Relations Survey," the regions vary in size. To illustrate, assume as shown in Figure 6–5 that there are two police managers. Manager B actively solicits information from manager A and as a result receives five "parcels" of information. Manager A is giving exposure, and manager B is receiving feedback, as depicted by the solid lines. Subsequently, the roles are reversed, and manager A receives seven parcels of information from manager B, as shown by the dashed lines. On the basis of this hypothetical exchange of feedback and exposure between managers A and B, the size of the quadrants or regions in their respective Johari Windows is established.

Basic Interpersonal Styles of Communication

Figure 6–6 shows the four basic interpersonal communication styles, which may be described in the following terms:

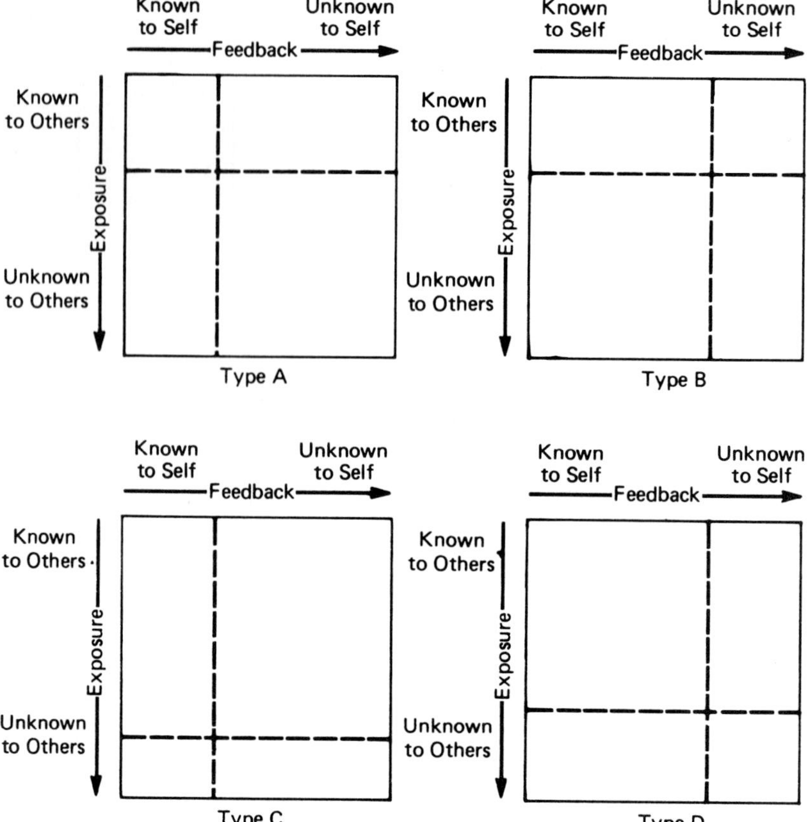

FIGURE 6-6. Interpersonal styles of communication. [From Jay Hall and Martha S. Williams, "How to Interpret Your Scores on the Personal Relations Survey," © Teleometrics International, The Woodlands, Texas, 1967. Special permission for reproduction is granted by the authors Jay Hall, PhD, and Martha S. Williams, PhD, and publisher, Teleometrics International. All rights reserved.]

Type A—This interpersonal style reflects a minimal use of both exposure and feedback processes; it is, in effect, a fairly impersonal approach to interpersonal relationships. The unknown region dominates under this style, and unrealized potential, untapped creativity, and personal psychodynamics prevail as the salient influences. Such a style would seem to indicate withdrawal and an aversion to risk taking on the part of its user; interpersonal anxiety and safety seeking are likely to be prime sources of personal motivation. Police managers who characteristically use this style appear to be rigid, aloof, and uncommunicative. This style may often be found in bureaucratic organizations of some type where it is possible, and perhaps profitable, to avoid personal disclosure or involvement. Persons using this style are likely to receive more than average hostility, because other parties to the relationship will tend to interpret the lack of exposure and feedback solicitation pretty much in terms of their own needs and how this interpersonal lack affects need fulfillment.

Type B—Under this approach, there is also an aversion to exposure, but it is coupled with a *desire* for relationships not found in type A. Thus, feedback is the only process left in promoting relationships, and it is much overused. An aversion to the use of exposure may typically be interpreted as a sign of basic mistrust of others, and it is therefore not surprising that the façade is the dominant feature of relationships resulting from underused exposure coupled with overused feedback. The style appears to be a probing quasi-supportive, interpersonal ploy, and, once the façade becomes apparent, it is likely to result in a reciprocal withdrawal of trust by other parties. This may promote feelings of disgust, anxiety, and hostility on the part of others; such feelings may lead to the user's being treated as a rather superficial person without real substance.

Type C—This interpersonal style is based on an overuse of exposure to the neglect of feedback. It may well reflect ego striving and/or distrust of others' opinions. Individuals who use this style may feel quite confident of the validity of their own opinions and are likely to value authority. The fact is that they are often unaware of the impact they have on others. Others are likely to feel disenfranchised by individuals who use this style; they often feel that such people have little use for their contributions or concern for their feelings. As a result, this style often triggers feelings of hostility, insecurity, and resentment on the part of others. Frequently, others will learn to behave in such a way as to perpetrate the user's blindspot by withholding important information or by giving only selected feedback; as such, this is a reflection of the defensiveness that this style can cause others to experience.

Type D—Exposure and feedback processes are used to a great and balanced extent in this style; candor and openness coupled with a sensitivity to others' needs to participate are the salient features of the style. The arena becomes the dominant feature of the relationship, and productivity may be expected to increase as well. In initial stages, this style may promote some defensiveness on the part of others unused to honest and trusting relationships; but perseverance will tend to promote a norm of reciprocal candor over time such that trust and creative potential can be realized.[24]

Although not one of the basic styles, there is a fifth commonly appearing style, which we designate as type E. The type E style falls between types C and D, using both more exposure and feedback than type C but less than type D. In type E, there is slightly greater reliance on the use of exposure as opposed to feedback (see Table 6–1).

TABLE 6-1 Mean Johari Window Interpersonal Communication Styles for Various Groups of Police Managers

Group	Number in group	Communication with Subordinates	Communication with Colleagues	Communication with Superiors
1	27	E	E	E
2	26	E	C	B
3	21	A	C	C
4	38	B	C	E
5	41	E	C	E
6	40	E	E	E
7	24	E	C	E
8	30	D	D	D
9	19	C	D	C

These data were gathered by Ronald Lynch, Institute of Government, University of North Carolina, and/or Charles Swanson from 1975 to 1985. They include groups of managers from the southeastern United States, New Jersey, and Oregon. Managers from municipal and county police departments and sheriffs' offices are represented.

Police Managers and Interpersonal Styles of Communication

The mean Johari Window scores for 325 police managers are plotted in Figure 6–7. Note that the Johari Window yields the style associated with communicating with three different groups—(1) subordinates, (2) colleagues, and (3) superiors—and

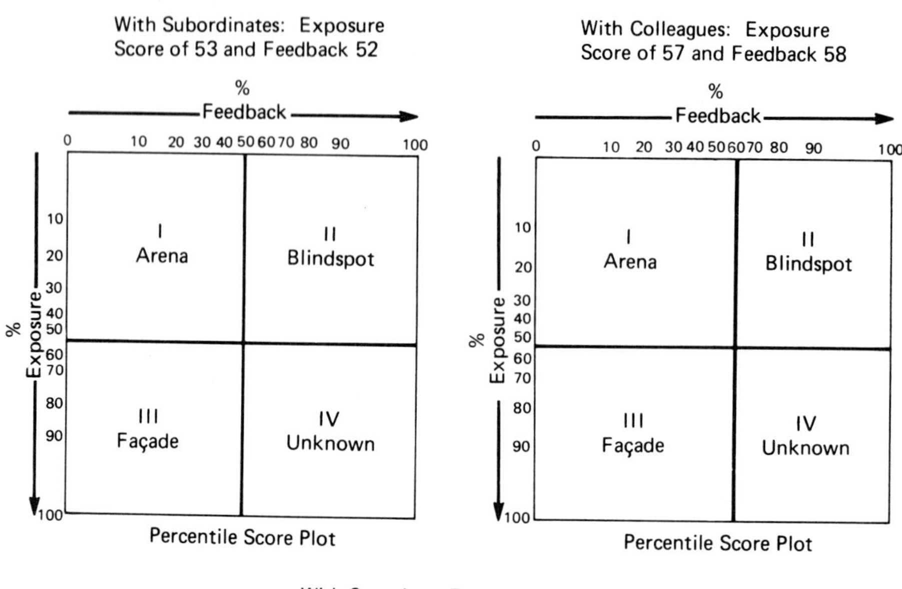

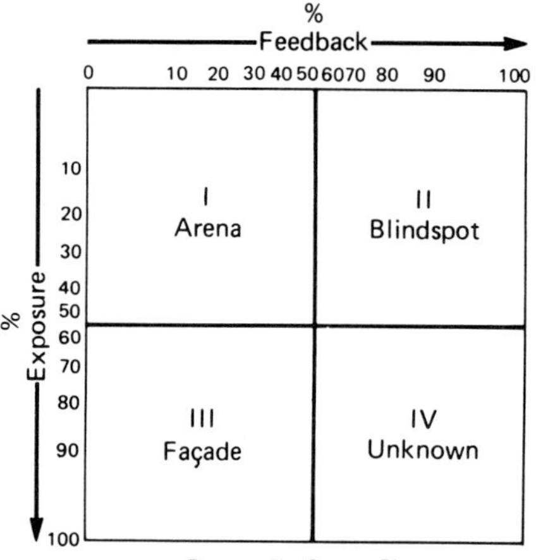

FIGURE 6-7. Mean Johari Window scores for 325 police managers. [The data depicted in these graphs are taken from Jay Hall, "Interpersonal Style and the Communication Dilemma: Utility of the Johari Window Awareness Model for Genotypic Diagnosis," *Human Relations,* 28 (1975), Table 3, p. 730. The graphs on which these data are displayed are taken from Jay Hall and Martha S. Williams, "How to Interpret Your Scores on the Personal Relations Survey," © Teleometrics International, The Woodlands, Texas, 1967. Special permission for reproduction is granted by the authors, Jay Hall, PhD, and Martha S. Williams, PhD, and publisher, Teleometrics International. All rights reserved.]

TABLE 6-2 Relationship of Grid Management and Johari Window Styles

Grid Style	Johari window style
9,9 Team management	Type D
5,5 Organization management	Type E
9,1 Authority-obedience	Type C
1,9 County club management	Type B
1,1 Impoverished management	Type A

Data supporting these correlations may be found in Jay Hall, "Interpersonal Style and the Communication Dilemma: Managerial Implications of the Johari Awareness Model," *Human Relations,* 27 (April 1974), p. 391.

that there is some variance among the scores. This variance is even more striking when examining the styles for eight different groups of police managers summarized in Table 6–1. Given such variance, it is difficult to make a unifying statement, but in general, type E is the most commonly occurring pattern among police managers.

As might be expected, there are correlations between Grid Management styles and Johari Window styles. These relationships are depicted in Table 6–2. To some extent these associations raise a "chicken and egg question" as to whether the choice of grid styles produces the Johari style or whether the reverse is true.

Oral or Written Communication

Suiting the Medium to the Recipient

Although there is a potentially great variety of media available for issuing orders, the individual issuing the orders is generally forced to choose from among a few existing ones that have nothing more than tradition in their favor. When certain media have become established, all subsequent material is made to fit them. If, for example, an organization has a personnel policy manual, it may become the pattern to announce through a routine revision of the manual even those changes that are of immediate and crucial interest to the employees. A change in the design of an application form would not elicit widespread interest, but a new system for computing vacation allowances is bound to interest everyone. Such differences in interest value are important factors in the proper selection of media, but the desired medium must be available in the first place.

Written Communication

There tends to be considerable confidence in the written word within complex organizations. It establishes a permanent record, but a transmittal of information in this way does not necessarily assure that the message will be unambiguous to the receiver. Sometimes, in spite of the writer's efforts, information is not conveyed clearly to the recipient. This may result, in part, because the writer lacks the writing skills necessary to convey the message clearly and unambiguously. For example, the following information was taken from letters received by a county department and illustrates the difficulty some people have in communicating via the written form.

> I am forwarding my marriage certificate and six children. I have seven but one died which was baptized on a half sheet of paper.
>
> Mrs. Jones had not had any clothes for a year and has been visited regularly by the clergy.
>
> Please find for certain if my husband is dead. The man I am living with can't eat or do anything until he knows.
>
> I am very much annoyed to find you have branded my son illiterate. This is a dirty lie as I was married a week before he was born.
>
> In answer to your letter, I have given birth to a boy weighing ten pounds. I hope this is satisfactory.
>
> I am forwarding my marriage certificate and three children, one of which is a mistake as you can see.
>
> Unless I get my husband's money pretty soon, I will be forced to lead an immortal life.
>
> You have changed my little boy to a little girl. Will this make any difference?
>
> I have no children as yet as my husband is a truck driver and works day and night.
>
> I want money as quick as I can get it. I have been in bed with the doctor for two weeks and he doesn't do me any good. If things don't improve, I will have to send for another doctor.

Police administrators increasingly rely on written communication as their dominant medium for communication. The variety of duties that police officers perform, in addition to the officers' wide discretion in handling them, help to account for the proliferation of written directives. The breadth of police duties and functions generates a tremendous number of tasks and situations that are potential topics of written guidelines. When compounded by the need for discretion, simple, straightforward directives are rarely possible. Instead, lengthy directives specifying numerous factors and offering preferred responses for different combinations of those factors are much more common.[25]

The tendency to promulgate rules, policies, and procedures to enhance direction and control has been exacerbated by three contemporary developments. One is the requirement for administrative due process in police discipline, encouraged by court rulings, police officer bill of rights legislation, and labor contracts. More and more disciplinary action against police employees necessarily follows an orderly process and must demonstrate violations of specific written rules. Thus, police departments feel the increasing need to have written rules prohibiting all kinds of inappropriate behavior they want to punish, as well as written procedures outlining the disciplinary grievance processes.

Another development motivating police departments to establish written directives is civil liability. Lawsuits against local governments, police departments, and police managers for the wrongful acts of police officers have become more common in recent years. Written guidelines prohibiting certain acts provide a principal avenue against civil litigation. In essence, police managers try to show that it was not their fault that officers erred. However, written policies and procedures are needed to make this avenue of defense available.

A third stimulus is the law enforcement agency accreditation movement. Although less than 1 percent of all police departments are presently accredited, many are either working toward accreditation or using the accreditation standards as a model for improvement. Agencies pursuing accreditation or simply looking to the program for guidance are clearly and strongly influenced by the possibility of enhancing their own policies and procedures.[26] For a more detailed discussion of the Commission on Accreditation for Law Enforcement Agencies see Chapter 2, Politics and Police Administration: External Influences and Controls.

The trend to rely on written communication as the principal medium for the transmittal of information also occurs quite frequently when dealing with individuals or groups outside the police department. Even in those cases for which the initial contact is made orally, a followup letter or memo is frequently filed in order to create a record of the communication. Such records are becoming routine partly as a result of the realization that they provide the greatest protection against the growing numbers of legal actions taken against police departments by citizens, activists, and interest groups.

Oral Communication

There are some distinct advantages in oral communication to both the sender and the receiver.

The recipient of an oral order is able to probe for exactness wherever the meaning is not entirely clear, provided that the individual is not too unfamiliar with the subject matter. The recipient of the information may ask for a clarifying or confirming statement in writing, or a sketch or chart, or a demonstration of a manual operation. In this situation, both individuals are able to state their case so long as the elements of give and take are preserved.

The person issuing an order, on the other hand, has an opportunity for immediate feedback and can see whether the order has produced understanding or confusion. The person issuing the order can probably discern the recipient's attitude and determine whether it is one of acceptance or rejection, but the attitude of the person issuing the order will also be apparent to the recipient. It appears that an oral medium is highly suitable when it is believed that an instruction will be temporary. For example, a police sergeant instructing an officer to direct traffic at an intersection because of street construction will likely not put that instruction in writing if the problem is one of short duration. However, if the construction will be of long duration, a written order may be forthcoming, specifying that an officer will be assigned to direct traffic at this particular location until further notice. Further, the written order may also specify additional details such as the times the officer is expected to be at the location. Therefore, the method to be employed will sometimes be dictated by the duration of the problem.

Combining Oral, Written, and Electronic Media

Certain advantages are inherent in both oral and written orders and can be exploited according to each individual's situation. There are promising opportunities for using both oral and written form, where one or the other may have been used alone on previous occasions. For example, many police administrators have started using closed-circuit television combined with written communication to transmit information to their officers that may be especially sensitive or controversial. One police chief, upon creating an internal affairs unit, used his closed-circuit television to discuss the reasons that the unit was created and used that opportunity to answer a series of prepared questions that had been forwarded to him by officers who were concerned about the role and scope of this new unit. This televised presentation was given simultaneously with the newly developed procedure that detailed the organizational structure, the scope, and the responsibilities of this new unit.[27] The article in Box 6-1 represents another example of the way closed-circuit television has been used by management to communicate with its personnel.

BOX 6-1

Teleconferencing System History

The City of Glendale, AZ, has grown quickly in the last few years to a population in excess of 130,000 people. This kind of rapid expansion requires equally fast-paced growth in the public safety sector, in order to provide a consistently high level of service to citizens.

To maintain superior response times, the police and fire departments have strategically placed substations throughout the city. Since each department has a headquarters building and three satellite stations (two that are as far as 12 miles away), clear, effective communications became increasingly difficult to sustain. The police department, in particular, was acutely aware of the need to notify police personnel of time-sensitive information accurately and with consistency.

In looking at methods of overcoming communication lag, most of the more popular technology was ruled out because of the expense involved and overall inability to meet our needs. The city encompasses more than 50 square miles, making the challenge of bringing information to all personnel from any point a substantial one.

Teleconferencing

In April 1984, the Glendale Police Department consulted with technicians of a cable communications group concerning the feasibility of using the cable system for direct audio and video communications in a teleconferencing network. The network would consist of three substations as target reception areas, with the headquarters classroom designated as the origination point and mini-studio. Considerations included:

1. Both audio and video upstream (sound and picture),
2. Reliability—would the cable system function regularly to carry our signal 90 to 95 percent of the time,
3. System security—reasonable measures taken to ensure the channel remained uncompromised, and,
4. Ease of operation by those who would use it most, the uniformed officer.

The system met all those needs. It would in fact carry the signal (computer controlled) to any point(s) the department named. The reliability factor of the system to this day averages better than 98 percent; down time is almost nonexistent.

System security was the largest concern. Our requirements were met in two ways—through inherent system design and add-on equipment. First, the system is computer-controlled. Each person who desires to receive cable must have the cable converter (receiver) in their home "authorized" to receive cablecasts. Once every 24 hours, the host computer sends out a signal to all converters to check for authorization. If a particular converter has been tampered with and is receiving an "unauthorized" channel, all cable information to that converter is shut down. The converter is rendered useless and must be serviced by a technician.

Second, the channel allocated for police use has been treated as a "premium" channel, and as such, has a scrambler (HVP-head-end video processor) dedicated to it. The signal is descrambled by the converter, if authorized. An unauthorized converter receiving a scrambled channel receives audio and video that just can't quite be tuned in.

Startup equipment was borrowed from the cable company and the city's Office of Cable Communications. The equipment consisted of a camera, camera control unit, microphone mixer, monitor, microphone, time base corrector, VHS VCR for playback of tapes, and a modulator. A head-end video processor and demodulator was in use at the cable company's "head end." One channel was assigned to the police department for a 3-week test period. Another 3-week test was conducted with the fire department at a later date.

The design allows the primary shift commander to conduct standard briefings. At each substation are a TV monitor and authorized converter. Incoming shift personnel, along with their sergeants, watch the monitor and participate in the briefing through an interactive capability in the network's design. A conference call is initiated in the main classroom with the aid of a speakerphone. As the briefing takes place, personnel watching the monitors hear not only what the shift commander has to say but also comments from those in any of the substations as well. The conference call permits questions and comments to return over standard phone lines to the speakerphone. A microphone at the studio is dedicated to picking up the questions and comments from the speakerphone, sending information to the microphone mixer and subsequently over the network.

The teleconferencing project is an unqualified success measured in terms of the initial objective—disseminating information uniformly and without delay. Turnaround time of reports vital to the police function has been reduced considerably. A prime example involves stolen vehicles. After taking a report of a stolen vehicle, the officer would return to his or her primary duty station to complete the report. Once this was done, it was normally sent to headquarters to be reproduced. Copies were then transported to all substations for distribution to beat officers.

With the advent of teleconferencing, the officer simply relays the information during the next briefing at the duty station. At the conclusion of the scheduled briefing, when the shift commander asks for any comments or information from the substations, the additional briefing information is then transmitted, eliminating the delay usually encountered when information is relayed using traditional methods of paper flow.

Another example which illustrates the versatility of the network involves an undercover officer who has been wired with a body bug during a transaction involving stolen property. An audio/video recording was made from a surveillance vehicle. The officer was dealing with suspects unknown to him. Nicknames of the four involved were all the identifiers he had. The officer played the tape at a briefing, hoping to obtain additional information from beat personnel. In the past, he would have had to go to each substation to reach his intended audience. With the time base corrector and mike mixer, the tape was run at the end of a briefing, mixing the officer's narration with the tape's audio track. Before the tape could be rewound, he received phone calls from fellow officers who knew all four suspects through field interviews.

Once the viability of the network was established, funding for two separate networks,

BOX 6-1 (cont.)

one for police and one for fire, became the central issue. Although police and fire functions occasionally overlap, their major goals and objectives differ. Therefore, it was decided that each would have its own network. Reviews of the license agreement with the cable company revealed a section that would cover costs incurred. The estimate for two systems was approximately $50,000. Although the project could have been done for less, versatility and quality would have suffered.

After specifications were finalized, purchase orders were completed in August 1984. By February 1985, all equipment had arrived and limited teleconferencing was begun. Use of teleconferencing expanded as more and more personnel became trained in the use of the equipment and by June 1, 1985, it was on-line 24 hours a day, 7 days a week.

Teleconferencing Today

Experience over the last 2 years has dictated changes in training methods. Although video is hardly the panacea for all training ills, we have learned to use it to the fullest, without alienating our audience.

Training tapes are now available over the system on a regular basis. Officers in outlying sections no longer need to come to the main facility for most training. Additionally, we no longer need to budget for duplicate video equipment for each substation. On particularly heavy training months, a schedule of tapes available for viewing and the times they may be seen is distributed. Duplication of materials is vastly reduced, as well as travel time to a training facility.

It was learned that the city's Office of Cable Communications had a sophisticated "character generator" (teletext machine) with an unused channel. With help from the cable company, this unused channel was put to use on the teleconferencing network. For technical reasons, we needed a constant video signal for the HVP to lock onto to ensure continued use. The character generator (CG) channel proved immensely useful beyond supplying us with the necessary video signal. We now program nonsensitive briefing information on the CG in the form of "pages of text." The CG is in operation 24 hours a day, paging through information determined to be of briefing value. At times of live briefing, a switching mechanism turns off the CG information as the video camera is turned on. Once the briefing is completed and the camera turned off, the CG returns with the time, date, and continued briefing text. For those personnel who miss a briefing for whatever reason, they need only to watch the CG over a dedicated monitor at a viewing station. Sensitive information is never placed on the CG, nor is it cablecast on the system. Individual squad briefings are used to avoid compromising information.

Because of certain characteristics of the cable system, or selectiveness of converter authorization, staff members can monitor briefings in their homes. For example, a patrol captain who had been away for a period of time could simply turn on his TV at home to pick up the CG information or even "tune in" at the proper time for a current briefing in order to prepare himself for the next day's activities.

Finally, the uniqueness of the system allows for a "live" cablecast from any point in the city that has a cable hookup. With this upstream capability, city disaster coordinators can go "live" to citizens who have cable to bring them information on any emergency or disaster.

Future Teleconferencing

Although we have had but a short time to experiment with this method of bringing information to public safety employees, it has more than met our expectations. As the system is modular, we are able to expand on it at will. Updates to the system are being planned to remain current. One new police building under construction and another on the drawing boards require us to remain creative in meeting future needs.

The amount of money invested so far is just that, an investment. The communication gap has been narrowed considerably. If the police chief wishes to address an important issue and reach the largest number of employees, it is a simple task to have him appear on the network. Officers in the outlying areas feel more a part of the mainstream of the department. Morale increases when personnel believe their views can be seen and heard.

However, the real beneficiaries of this project are the citizens of the City of Glendale. They will profit from an increased level of service. In addition, they will have some of the most well-trained and responsive police officers and firefighters in the Nation—with cable and video technology leading the way!

Source: Mitchell C. Kelsey, "Teleconferencing System History," *FBI Law Enforcement Bulletin,* Nov. 1987, pp. 9–11.

Organizational Communication

Organizational communication is viewed as the process of acquiring and organizing data about the internal workings of the organization as well as about the effects of its actions on the external environment and the impact of the external environment on the organization. The ability of the organization to scan the external and internal environment accurately to assess the variety of involved uncertainty reflects the degree of organizational intelligence. It is this intelligence that then becomes an input to the organizational decision making aimed at defining goals that are compatible with the external environmental conditions, at designing the organizational structure, and in assessing the functions requisite for the accomplishment of these goals. Operationally, the task of organizational communication is performed by employing a tool of information technology, both electronic and human. These two facets of information technology are inseparable and ought to be considered as two sides of the same coin.[28]

The news article in Box 6-2, "Burglar Rapes Woman as Police Bungle Call," illustrates the interrelationship of electronic and human communications and the potential for tragic outcomes if both are not functioning properly and fully interrelated.

BOX 6-2

Burglar Rapes Woman as Police Bungle Call

PITTSBURGH (AP)—An armed burglar overpowered a woman after she called 911 to report an intruder, then raped her twice after watching six officers search outside for evidence of a break-in and leave, authorities said Thursday.

Operators and dispatchers who handled the woman's frantic call to the 911 emergency number apparently failed to tell officers she might be in her apartment with the intruder, and officers didn't ask, authorities said.

"We're not making any alibis for this. This could have been handled better," Louis DiNardo, deputy public safety director, said Thursday.

"There could have been more information relayed to the scene and the officers could have inquired if they needed more information," DiNardo said. "These calls come in so often and they become routine. But they can't be treated routinely."

BOX 6-2 (cont.)

Authorities said the unidentified woman told police she was watching television after 11 p.m. Tuesday when she heard someone trying to break into her second-story apartment.

She dialed 911, gave her address and telephone number, and asked for police, authorities said. An operator asked her to stay on the telephone until police arrived, but the line went dead and the operator thought the woman had hung up, said Public Safety Director Glenn Cannon.

A man had burst into the apartment from a stairwell, overpowered the woman and pulled the wires from the telephone, authorities said.

The woman said he pushed her into the living room, but noticed through a window that police cars had arrived, authorities said. The man asked her how to escape and said he feared being shot by police, authorities said.

The woman said the intruder threatened to harm her and her three sleeping children if she screamed, and then both watched the officers outside until they left, authorities said.

The woman said she was then raped twice at knife point, authorities said.

Cannon said recordings of police communications show dispatchers sent officers to investigate "a possible burglary in progress," but did not tell them the source of the report was the woman herself or that she had had been instructed to stay on the line.

Officers knocked at the front and back doors, checked around the house and found a smashed windowpane in a locked rear door, Cannon said. The officers concluded an intruder could not have entered that way, he said.

They asked a neighbor to call the woman's number but there was no answer, Cannon said. They searched the outside again and then left, he said.

"At that point, they believed they had an unfounded burglary report," Cannon said. "The door seemed secure and no one responded to their knocks. So they left."

The woman said she grabbed her assailant's knife during the second rape and stabbed him at least once, authorities said. The man grabbed a video recorder and fled when a second telephone rang in the apartment, they said.

The caller this time was a neighbor who asked if the woman needed help, police said. The neighbor called police and when officers returned they were met at the door by the victim clutching the knife, authorities said.

Assistant Chief Chester L. Howard said investigators believe the intruder entered through a window in a stairwell.

The woman, who was treated at Magee-Womens Hospital, told The Pittsburgh Press she plans to discuss the incident with her attorney and declined further comment.

DiNardo said city officials took statements Thursday from officers, operators and dispatchers.

"What we know is that there was some additional information at the communications center that could have been passed on to the officers and if that information was passed on, it would have been different," he said.

"The other side of this is does the officer on the scene have an obligation to inquire with communications if there is someone to call back if the victim isn't there. Should the officers question communications? Frankly," he said, "we think both ends of this system need to address that."

Source: Tampa Tribune, February 5, 1988, p. 1A.

Summary

There is considerable evidence to support the premise that, for administrators to be truly effective, they must understand the dynamics involved in both interpersonal and organizational communications. It is not surprising when we learn that administrators who are successful are also effective communicators and have created communicative mechanisms within their organizations that avoid many of the pitfalls discussed throughout this chapter.

To understand the process of communication, we have examined several elements of the process. As a result, we now know that the communication process follows some fairly consistent patterns. For example, the sender has certain intentions, objectives, or purposes, and translates these into some code (language, nonverbal gestures, etc.) that becomes the message. The sender then selects the medium (written or spoken words, music, art, etc.) and uses the medium to transmit the message to the receiver. The receiver in turn "picks up" the message (listens, reads, watches, etc.) and decodes its meaning. This meaning causes the receiver to behave in some manner, which gives the sender indications, or feedback, as to whether or not the receiver understood the meaning of the message.

Further, we have learned that barriers to communication, or communication breakdowns, can occur at any place in the system and may result from either the sender or receiver. Because an information flow is multidirectional (downward, upward, and horizontal), the police administrator must take every possible precaution to assure that barriers are not created in any direction that can disrupt the smooth flow of information throughout the organization.

The use of the Johari window in this chapter has provided readers with an opportunity to examine and evaluate their own interpersonal styles of communication and to assess other styles as well. It is hoped that the insight provides readers with an opportunity to make those adjustments deemed necessary to enhance their interpersonal communication styles.

As we have learned, the police administrator may choose from among a number of ways to communicate. However, there tends to be considerable confidence in the use of written word in complex organizations. This is so, in part, because it establishes a permanent record that can be referred to readily. On the other hand, not all communications can or should be in writing. As we have seen, there are some distinct advantages in oral communication to both the sender and receiver.

Further, there will be those instances in which a police administrator may wish to combine both written and oral communications.

In the final analysis, there can be little argument with the conclusion that effective communication is essential in all organizations. A breakdown in the process of law enforcement not only results in less efficient organization but, as pointed out, may also result in the injury or death of some innocent person.

Discussion Questions

1. Discuss the elements that make up the communication process.
2. Discuss sender-caused barriers, receiver-caused barriers, and other barriers in communications.
3. Discuss the five types of organizational communication that have been identified.
4. Discuss, in rank order, the most effective to the least effective, the means of downward communication, according to Dahle.
5. The physical distance between superior and subordinate may impede upward communication. Why?
6. What are the major desirable and undesirable traits of the organizational grapevine?
7. Discuss the four basic interpersonal styles of communication.
8. What are the advantages in oral communication to both the sender and the receiver?
9. What are the advantages in combining both oral and written orders?
10. Why is effective communications so important in law enforcement?

Notes

1. *Interpersonal Communication: A Guide for Staff Development* (Athens: Institute of Government, University of Georgia, August 1974), p. 15.
2. Much of the discussion in this chapter on the communication process was developed by R. C. Huseman and incorporated into the publication *Interpersonal Communication,* pp. 21–27.
3. P. V. Lewis, *Organizational Communication: The Essence of Effective Management* (Columbus, Ohio: Grid, 1975), p. 36.
4. Ibid., pp. 36–37.
5. Ibid., pp. 37–38.
6. D. Katz and R. L. Kahn, *The Social Psychology of Organizations* (New York: John Wiley & Sons, 1966), p. 239. As cited in Lewis, *Organizational Communication,* p. 38.
7. Lewis, *Organizational Communication,* p. 38.
8. R. L. Smith, G. M. Richetto, and J. P. Zima, "Organizational Behavior: An Approach to Human Communication," in *Readings in Interpersonal and Organizational Communication,* 3rd ed., ed. R. C. Huseman, C. M. Logue, and D. L. Freshley (Boston: Holbrook Press, 1977), p. 11.
9. T. L. Dahle, "An Objective and Comparative Study of Five Methods of Transmitting Information to Business and Industrial Employees" (Ph.D. diss., Purdue University, 1954). As cited in Smith, Richetto, and Zima, "Organizational Behavior," p. 12.
10. Much of the discussion in this chapter on upward communication has been taken from E. Planty and W. Machaver, "Upward Communications: A Project in Executive Development," *Personnel,* 28 (January 1952), pp. 304–19.
11. Much of the discussion in this chapter on horizontal communication has been taken from R. K. Allen, *Organizational Management Through Communication* (New York: Harper & Row, 1977), pp. 77–79.
12. H. Fayol, *General and Industrial Administration* (New York: Pitman, 1949), p. 34. As cited in Allen, *Organizational Management,* p. 78.
13. Allen, *Organizational Management,* p. 78.
14. Ibid., pp. 78–79.
15. K. Davis, "Management Communication and The Grapevine," *Harvard Business Review,* (September–October, 1953), pp. 43–49. As cited by Lewis, *Organizational Communication,* 31:5, p. 41.
16. Lewis, *Organizational Communication,* pp. 41–42.
17. J. Hall, "Interpersonal Style and the Communication Dilemma: Managerial Implications of the Johari Awareness Model," *Human Relations,* 27:4 (1974), p. 381. For a critical review of communication literature, see Lyman W. Porter and Karlene H. Roberts, *Communication in Organizations* (Irvine: University of California Press, 1972).
18. Hall, "Interpersonal Style," p. 382.
19. Ibid., p. 382.
20. Ibid., p. 382.
21. As Joseph Luft describes this, "It is fairly well known now that Johari does not refer to the southern end of the Malay Peninsula. That's Johore. Johari is pronounced as if it were Joe and Harry, which is where the term comes from. . . . Dr. Ingham and I developed the model during a summer laboratory session in 1955 and the model was published in the Proceedings of the Western Training Laboratory in Group Development for that year by the UCLA Extension Office." See Joseph Luft, *Of Human Interaction* (Palo Alto, Calif.: Mayfield, 1969) p. 6.
22. This questionnaire is termed the "Personnel Relations Survey" and is available from Telemetrics International, P.O. Box 314, The Woodlands, Tex. 77380.

23. The description of the Johari window is drawn, largely, with permission and minor modifications, from "How to Interpret Your Scores on the Personnel Relations Survey," © Teleometrics International, The Woodlands, Tex. 77380.
24. The descriptions are taken by permission from "How to Interpret Your Scores," pp. 4–5, with minor modification.
25. G. W. Cordner, "Written Rules and Regulations: Are They Necessary?" *FBI Law Enforcement Bulletin,* 58:5 (1989), p. 18.
26. S. W. Mastrofski, "Police Agency Accreditation: The Prospects of Reform," *American Journal of Police,* 5:3 (1986), pp. 45–81.
27. L. Territo and R. L. Smith, "The Internal Affairs Unit: The Policeman's Friend or Foe," *Police Chief,* 43:7 (1976), pp. 66–69.
28. A. G. Kefalas, "Organizational Communications: A Systems Viewpoint," in *Readings in Interpersonal and Organizational Communication,* ed. Huseman, Logue, and Freshley, p. 42.

7 Human Resource Management

There's only one corner of the world you can be certain of improving and that's your own self.
ALDOUS HUXLEY

Introduction

Most authorities who examine the major issues involved in law enforcement come regularly to the same inescapable conclusion: namely, that the ability of a police department to provide high-quality service to its citizens and to solve its major operating problems will be significantly affected by the quality of its personnel and the ways in which they are managed.

As police departments have attempted to address external problems, such as rising crime rates, and internal problems, such as effectiveness of their operating units, they have undertaken many studies, entertained numerous theories, launched various experiments, and invested heavily in new equipment. In most of these efforts, however, it has been apparent that eventual success depends on the critically important element of human resources. Sound personnel practices, therefore, may well be the single most vital consideration in the quest for effective law enforcement.[1]

The subject of human resource management has gained considerable prominence and visibility within the law enforcement community over the past 30 years. A number of social, political, and economic factors have given impetus to this development, including (1) the civil disorders and rapidly increasing crime rates during the 1960s, which resulted in the creation of two prestigious national commissions and numerous recommendations for improving the police service;[2] (2) expansion of the labor movement within law enforcement, resulting in the revision of personnel policies relating to working conditions, training, discipline, and promotions; (3) the Equal Employment Opportunity Act of 1972, which induced many police departments to change personnel policies that discriminated against minorities and women in both employment and career development; (4) the Civil Rights Act of 1991, which strengthened the Equal Employment Opportunity Act of 1972; (5) the Americans with Disabilities Act (ADA) of 1990, which makes it unlawful to discriminate against persons having or perceived to have disabilities with respect to all employment practices, including recruitment, hiring, promotion, training, layoffs, pay, assignments, transfers, firing, leave, and benefits; (6) the growing willingness of police employees to litigate against practices and actions they feel are unjust; (7) the increased conferring of rights on public employees by the courts; and (8) greater willingness on the part of courts and juries to award large cash settlements to citizens injured by police officers because of some act deemed negligent. Acts of negligence often involve the injury or death of innocent bystanders because of careless use of firearms or police vehicles and are frequently linked to inadequate selection procedures, training, or supervision.[3, 4] These factors make it likely that considerable effort and time will be directed to all areas of human resource management.

Functions of the Police Personnel Unit

In larger departments, a sound personnel management program needs an adequately staffed and financed personnel unit reporting through the chain of command to the police chief. This unit must be specialized and have authority and responsibility to carry out its mission.[5] As a result of such factors as departmental philosophy, historical precedent, the chief executive's preference, intradepartmental power politics, and legislative requirements, broad statements about the functions of a police personnel unit are somewhat difficult to make.[6] However, a personnel unit is generally responsible for the following:

1. Preparing policy statements and standard operating procedures relating to all areas of the administration of human resources, subject to the approval of the chief executive of the agency
2. Advising the chief executive of the department and other line officials on personnel matters
3. Maintaining a performance evaluation system
4. Creating an integrated management information system (MIS), which includes all necessary personnel data such as that pertaining to performance evaluation
5. Maintaining an energetic and results-producing program to recruit qualified applicants
6. Administering a carefully conceived process of selection; that is, administering a valid system for distinguishing those who are to be employed from those who may not be employed
7. Establishing criteria for promotion to the various ranks, along with a method for determining the relative qualifications of officers eligible for such appointments
8. Conducting a multifaceted staff development program for personnel of all ranks from entry through executive level
9. Developing and administering position classification and assignment analysis to assure equal pay for equal work as well as to form the basis for staff assignment and evaluation
10. Developing a plan of adequate compensation, distributed fairly among rank assignments according to difficulty and responsibility of assignments and including provisions for differentials based on special assignments, shifts, or outstanding performance
11. Representing the agency during negotiations with police employee groups and at other meetings with representatives of organized employees, such as at meetings pertaining to grievances and related matters

12. Conducting exit interviews with resigning officers to identify, and subsequently correct, unsatisfactory working conditions
13. Providing advice to managers and supervisors at all levels concerning human resource problems, with special attention to leadership and disciplinary problems, and administering reviews of disciplinary actions and appeals
14. Conducting an ongoing personnel research program
15. Representing the police department to the central personnel office or civil service commission[7]

Few police agencies have viable, adequately staffed, and sufficiently supported personnel units that can maximize the agency's human resources. The most likely reasons for this problem are

1. The failure of police management to determine its human resource objective. What does management really want its personnel arm—or, for that matter, its total personnel strength—to accomplish? Without clear-cut program objectives, it is difficult even for the best personnel administrator to adapt to the police function.
2. The inability or unwillingness of the police administrator to delegate clear-cut authority to accomplish the human resource goals. The absence of clear-cut lines of authority and responsibility is allowed to exist between field supervisors and the personnel staff. In some jurisdictions, civil service laws deny to the police chief, as well as to other line managers, sufficient authority over personnel matters. Without this authority, the personnel director is less than fully effective.
3. The inadequacy of total resources available to the police agency, leading to emphasis on field strength at the expense of personnel administration and frequently other management functions. Although it is politically attractive to the chief to get as many officers into the field as possible, these officers may be underutilized unless there is adequate management direction.
4. The intransigence of some police officials and unions against changes in personnel practices and policies.[8]

Moreover, it is not uncommon to find departmental policy implicitly stating that the human resource is less important than objects of capital expenditure. For example, in a number of cities, there are placards on the dashboards of police vehicles with a statement to the effect, "This car cost the taxpayers of ______ $15,000—treat it with respect or you will be subject to disciplinary measures." Certainly no one would argue that a police officer having a vehicular accident is an unimportant event; accidents result in fewer cars being available for patrol service, thereby reducing coverage, and injuries may occur and liabilities may be created. But, in contrast, consider the sergeant with ten subordinates, each of whom earns $25,000 per year. Let us assume that the chief executive of that department sends the supervisor a memorandum at the beginning of each fiscal year stating, "You are responsible for the management of $250,000 of this organization's resources. Please ensure that the efforts of your subordinates are directed toward achievement of previously agreed-upon objectives." Would not this action, coupled with periodic monitoring, the implementation of any necessary corrective action, and comparison of year's and end results with anticipated outputs, be more beneficial to the public?

Police Personnel Selection

Although there are no hard and fast rules about the precise steps to be followed in the selection process, there has historically been agreement that phases should proceed from the least expensive to the most expensive (see Figure 7-1). However, the ADA of 1990 is altering this traditional sequencing.

The ADA was introduced in Chapter 2, "Politics and Police Administration." The reason that Congress enacted the ADA was to eliminate barriers for individuals with disabilities in employment, transportation, telecommunications, public accommodations, and access to state and local government facilities. Because of the sweeping effect the ADA will have on personnel administration in police agencies, more detailed coverage of it is provided in this chapter. Among the significant provisions of ADA or the interpretative guidelines and policies issued by the Equal Employment Opportunity Commission (EEOC) to implement it are

1. Discrimination in *all* employment practices is prohibited, including job application procedures, hiring, firing, advancement, compensation, training, and other terms and conditions of employment such as recruitment, advertising, tenure, layoff, leave, and fringe benefits.[9] Job application sites must be accessible to those with disabilities. Although discrimination is prohibited, an employer is not required to give preference to a qualified applicant or worker with a disability over other applicants or workers.[10]
2. The ADA makes discrimination against individuals who have a relationship or association with a disabled person illegal.[11] For example, assume that Jane Johnson applies for a position in a police department for which she is qualified and that she has

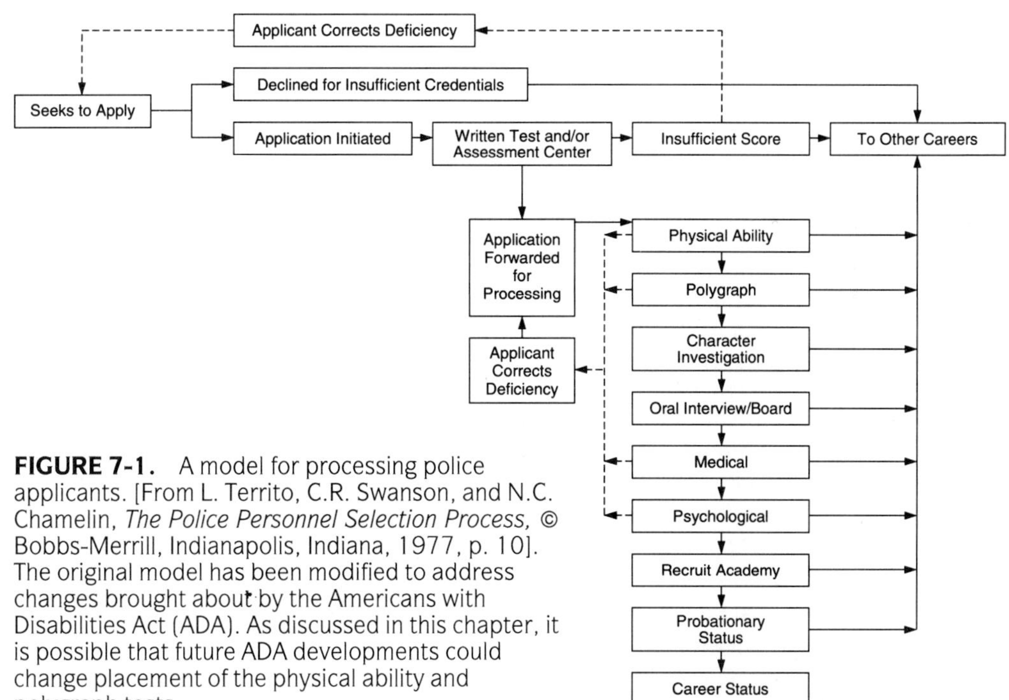

FIGURE 7-1. A model for processing police applicants. [From L. Territo, C.R. Swanson, and N.C. Chamelin, *The Police Personnel Selection Process,* © Bobbs-Merrill, Indianapolis, Indiana, 1977, p. 10]. The original model has been modified to address changes brought about by the Americans with Disabilities Act (ADA). As discussed in this chapter, it is possible that future ADA developments could change placement of the physical ability and polygraph tests.

a disabled husband. It is illegal for the department to deny her employment solely on the basis of its unfounded assumption that she would take excessive leave to care for her spouse. Another illustration of a protected relationship or association is provided by a police officer who does volunteer work with dying acquired immunodeficiency syndrome (AIDS) patients. A chief of police who was uncomfortable with the officer's volunteer work and adversely affected any of the terms and conditions of the officer's employment would be in violation of the ADA. Similarly, police departments and other employers are prohibited from retaliating, for example, by transferring to undesirable precincts or hours of duty, against applicants or employees who assert their rights under ADA.

3. The ADA expressly excludes certain conditions from protection,[12] including current illegal drug use, homosexuality, bisexuality, transvestitism, exhibitionism, voyeurism, gender identity disorder, sexual behavior disorder, compulsive gambling, kleptomania, pyromania, and psychoactive substance disorders resulting from current use of illegal drugs. However, former drug users who have successfully completed a rehabilitation program are covered by the ADA. Arguably, however, despite this provision, law enforcement employment could possibly be denied to former drug users because such applicants' prior conduct raised material questions about their judgment, criminal associates, willingness to abide by the law, and character.[13]
4. A person is defined by the ADA as disabled if that person has a physical or mental impairment that substantially limits one or more major life activities, has a record of such impairment, or is regarded or perceived as having such an impairment, even if they do not actually have it. Generally, a person is disabled if the person has any physiological disorder, condition, disfigurement, anatomical loss, or mental or psychological disorder that makes the individual unable to perform such functions as caring for him- or herself, performing manual tasks, walking, seeing, hearing, speaking, breathing, learning, or working to the same extent as the average person.[14] A person is not "substantially limited" just because he or she is unable to perform a particular job for one employer or is unable to perform highly specialized professions requiring great skill or talent.[15] Protection against handicap discrimination does not include being able to work at the specific job of one's choice.[16]
5. A qualified individual with a disability is a person who meets legitimate skill, experience, education, or other requirements of an employment position that he or she is seeking and who can perform the "essential functions" of that position with or without reasonable accommodations.[17] Job descriptions will be considered highly indicative of what the essential functions of a job are, and they should be drafted with considerably greater care than that used by some personnel and police departments in the past. The "essential functions" provision states that an applicant will not be considered to be unqualified simply because of an inability to perform minor, marginal, or incidental job functions.[18] If an individual is able to perform essential job functions except for limitations caused by a disability, police departments and other employers must consider whether the individual could perform these functions with a reasonable accommodation. A reasonable accommodation is any change or adjustment to a job or work environment that permits a qualified person with a disability to enjoy benefits and privileges of employment equal to those of employees without disabilities.[19] Reasonable accommodations may include
    (a) Acquiring or modifying equipment and devices
    (b) Job restructuring
    (c) Part-time or modified work schedules
    (d) Reassignment to a vacant position
    (e) Adjusting or modifying examinations—such as physical ability tests, training materials, or policies

(f) Providing readers and interpreters

(g) Modifying the physical work environment.[20]

Illustrations of this last point include installation of elevators, widening doorways, relocating work stations, and making break rooms accessible or relocating the break room so that the employee with the disability has opportunity to interact with other police employees. Failure to provide reasonable accommodation to a known physical or mental limitation of a qualified individual is a violation of the ADA unless it creates an undue hardship on the employer's operations.[21] Undue hardship means that the accommodation would be unduly costly, extensive, substantial, or disruptive, or would fundamentally alter the business of the employer.[22] Although some police departments may raise the "unduly costly" defense, the EEOC scrutinizes such claims carefully. Particularly when the accommodation needed for modified equipment, remodeled work space, or the development of new policies and examinations is a small fraction of the overall budget, claiming undue hardship may be viewed by the EEOC as a pretext for discrimination against applicants and employees with disabilities. Among the remedies federal courts have invoked in other types of civil rights cases in which the defendants claimed an inability to pay, is requiring jurisdictions to borrow money to finance the ordered remedies. The requirement to make a reasonable accommodation is generally triggered by a request from an individual with a disability.[23] Without this request, police agencies are not obligated to provide one.[24]

6. The ADA does not encourage, prohibit, or authorize testing for illegal drugs in the work force.[25] Drug testing is not a medical examination under the ADA. Solely from an ADA perspective, police and other employers can continue to do pre-employment drug screening of applicants and random tests of probationary and other employees.
7. Police applicants and employees often have medical conditions that can be controlled through medication or auxiliary means. Examples are persons whose diabetes or high cholesterol is mitigated through appropriate medication. Even though their medical conditions have no significant impact on their daily lives, such individuals are covered by the ADA.[26] The ADA does not cover employees whose impairments are temporary (e.g., a broken arm), do not substantially limit a major life activity, are of limited duration, and have no long-term effects.[27]
8. No medical inquiries can be made of an applicant, nor can any medical tests be required or conducted, *before* a job offer is made, although the offer can be made contingent upon passing the medical test. Questioning applicants about their ability to perform job-related functions is permitted as long as the questions are not phrased in terms relating to a disability.[28] It is unlawful to ask applicants if they are disabled or the extent or severity of a disability.[29] It is permissible to ask an applicant to describe or demonstrate how, without reasonable accommodation, the applicant will perform job-related functions.[30]

Because the ADA did not go into effect until mid-1992, guidelines from the EEOC and case law will evolve rapidly and become important sources from which administrators can draw important lessons to guide their practices and decisions. Although much is not known about the ADA at this early 1992 writing, there are a number of ways this new federal law is going to change employment practices, including

1. Application forms must be altered to eliminate all medical inquiries.
2. Job descriptions must be carefully reviewed and in many instances revised to ensure that the "essential functions" of each class of positions (e.g., patrol officer or investigator) are clearly specified.
3. All medical information must be kept in separate confidential files and access to them

limited to supervisors and managers who need to know about a particular employee in order to make a reasonable accommodation, to safety and first aid personnel to whom disclosure of a disability or medical condition would be appropriate, and to government officials investigating compliance with the ADA.

4. Training will have to be provided to clerks, supervisors, and managers, background investigators, and other officials to ensure that rights of applicants and employees are not violated with respect to the ADA. For example, personnel who accept applications will have to be taught that inquiries as to whether the applicant has a disability or about the nature or the severity of a disability are unlawful.
5. The sequence of events in the selection process will have to be reordered. For example, because no medical or psychological examinations can be given before a job offer is made, these examinations will come at the end of the selection process. Also, if the EEOC or the courts determine that even rudimentary-screening medical inquiries conducted by nonmedical personnel before physical agility tests (e.g., "Do you have a history of dizziness or fainting?") and before polygraph tests (e.g., "Are you taking any type of medication?") are impermissible medical inquiries, then substantial changes will be required. One possibility is for the agility and polygraph tests to come at the end of the selection process, after a conditional employment offer has been made. Alternatively, the agility test could remain about where it is in the selection process, but departments using medical screening inquiries could require signed waivers of liability from applicants before allowing them to participate in the physical agility testing. Such a practice, however, would require the careful examination of each jurisdiction's attorneys, risk experts, and insurers.
6. New forms, such as a written letter offering employment contingent on passing medical examinations, must be designed.
7. The average cost of processing police applicants will increase because more expensive steps such as the character investigation will have to precede less expensive steps such as medical and psychological examinations. Other costs associated with implementation of the act include development of more carefully crafted job descriptions, identifying and providing reasonable accommodations, and litigation.

In summary, there are many uncertainties about how to interpret and apply the ADA. It is clear, however, that its evolution will generate high concern, new costs, and substantial litigation. Police administrators must monitor ADA developments closely to avoid committing unlawful acts.

The Initial Application

A prospective applicant will ordinarily make a preliminary visit to the police department, civil service commission, or central personnel office to obtain employment information. The results of such a visit should be several. The individual should come away with sufficient knowledge to make an informed decision concerning a career in policing. This will be gained through literature prepared especially for that purpose and by access to someone who can respond to questions accurately and in detail. If an individual clearly does not meet the minimum standards for employment, he or she should be so advised, along with possible remedial action, if any, that could be taken to qualify for consideration. Often overlooked by even seasoned personnel officers is the harm that can be done by treating an obviously unqualified prospective employee brusquely. Such action does little to mediate the person's disappointment and may cause the story of the treatment to be circulated among the individual's friends, reinforcing old stereotypes of the police and, in effect, dissuading other people from making application.

Among local units of government, most individuals will be required to visit the central personnel office, which serves all departments of city government, and submit an application. Alternately, it is not uncommon to find a civil service commission, consisting of a board of three to five prominent citizens, existing independently of the central personnel office. In such situations, the board would typically direct a professional staff that would perform most of the actual work. Historically,[31]

> The independent Civil Service Commission has often been limited to control over examinations for entry, promotions, and to the judicial function of hearing appeals from disciplinary actions.[32]

Where central personnel offices and civil service commissions exist concurrently in the same jurisdiction, the authority for matters not historically within the purview of the commission are retained by the central personnel office which constitutes no smaller number of functions or amounts of power. In some jurisdictions the central personnel office has virtually disappeared, supplanted by the civil service commission.

Regardless of which arrangement prevails, the person seeking to make an application will have to demonstrate the meeting of certain criteria before the application is accepted; among these are citizenship, attainment of minimum age, and related factors. The candidate's application form is one of the most important sources of information about a candidate for a law enforcement agency. The data included in this form will provide much of the focus for the personnel investigator's line of inquiry, as it includes specifics related to the following: personal data; marital status and former martial status, including divorces, annulments, or widowhood; educational background; military service; foreign military services; foreign travel; employment record; financial history; criminal and juvenile record; motor vehicle operator record; family background; references; and willingness to undergo a polygraph examination.[33]

Where satisfactory proof of any of the basic criteria cannot be established, the application would be declined for insufficiency. An individual may later seek to reinstitute an application by correction of deficiencies or by obtaining and presenting additional documents.[34]

The Entrance Examination: The Written Test and/or Assessment Center

In 1972, Congress amended Title VII of the Civil Rights Act of 1964 and the EEOC was charged with the responsibility of administering its provisions. Title VII made it illegal to impermissibly discriminate against any person on the basis of race, sex, color, religion, or national origin in employment decisions. An example of a permissible discrimination is refusing to hire a man to model women's lingerie; in this situation hiring only women would constitute a bona fide occupational requirement (BFOQ). "Employment decisions" is defined broadly and includes hiring, demotion, transfer, layoff, promotion, and firing decisions. Any procedure or requirement used in making these decisions is a test and comes under the scrutiny of the EEOC. Thus, application forms, interviews, oral boards, written tests, probationary ratings, assessment centers, performance evaluations, education, background investigations, physical fitness or ability tests, and other logically related matters are all subject to EEOC review for a determination as to whether there has been an unlawful act of discrimination.

Initially the EEOC focused on entry-level requirements and testing because in many organizations there had been little progress in hiring minorities. In more recent years, the EEOC has directed greater attention to promotions and other personnel decisions as greater numbers of minorities have been hired and are affected by such decisions. A key concern of the EEOC is whether written tests and assessment center evaluations are job related and predictive of future job performance. A 1990 survey of employment practices in police agencies revealed that 91.9 percent of the departments responding to a survey used a written or cognitive test to determine eligibility for hiring.[35] Such written tests are relatively inexpensive, easy to administer, and can be quickly scored. Smaller jurisdictions may lease their examinations from firms specializing in such services, whereas larger cities and counties typically use one that has been developed by their own testing specialists, who often have been educated as industrial-organizational psychologists. Typically, written entrance tests are given as an "assembled examination"—all of the candidates eligible to take it are brought together at the same time. In large cities such as New York and Chicago 25,000 or more applicants may take the written entrance examination simultaneously at public schools and other designated public properties designated as examination sites.[36]

In contrast, assessment centers are used by 22.6 percent of police agencies; local departments are somewhat more likely to use them than state police agencies.[37] Greater information on assessment centers is presented later in this chapter. Briefly, assessment centers provide a series of behavioral tests or simulations in which candidates are given information and placed into mock situations where they are observed by teams of trained raters or assessors. The raters look for and evaluate the performance of candidates with respect to behaviors that are important to successful job performance as an entry-level police officer, such as oral communication skill. Assessment centers are very expensive in comparison to written tests. The design of the simulations or mock situations—referred to as exercises—requires a great deal of thought, raters must be trained, the number of candidates each team of four to six assessors can reliably rate each day ideally should not be greater than six, scheduling is complex, the process is labor intensive due to the time devoted by the assessors, and the cost per candidate is considerably higher as compared to the use of written tests. Despite some apparent disadvantages of assessment centers, some jurisdictions prefer them because they provide information about candidates' actual behavior, they yield more detailed information than written tests, and minorities tend to pass them at higher rates than those usually associated with written tests. A few jurisdictions use written tests on a pass-fail basis to screen candidates going to assessment centers, which ensures each prospect's minimum level of cognitive ability and thus makes the assessment center more cost effective.

The method by which a test can be shown to be associated with subsequent performance on the job is through a process of validation, the starting point for which is a job analysis. A job analysis reveals what the important tasks are for a position such as police officer as well as what specific knowledge and skills are needed to perform the job well.[38] Validation is a detailed undertaking whose thorough treatment is not possible here. However, some general statements are both proper and necessary. When the question is asked "Is this test valid?" what is really being asked is whether it is appropriate (valid) to make a decision about a person's ability to perform a particular job based on that person's score on a particular test.

A test that discriminates against a group of prospective or current employees and cannot be shown to be valid is impermissible discrimination under EEOC guidelines. However, if a police department or other employer can show that different test scores are associated with different levels of performance on the job, then even if the test discriminates against some identifiable group, including minorities, the courts are likely to find that it is a permissible discrimination, unless some other test would adequately meet the employer's needs and produce less of a discriminatory impact.[39]

Under EEOC guidelines, discrimination in testing occurs when there is a substantially different rate of selection in hiring, promotion, or other employment decision that works to the disadvantage of members of a race, sex, or ethnic group. This different rate of selection is termed "adverse impact" and is impermissible unless the test or other practice has been validated. As a rule of thumb, adverse impact occurs when the selection rate for any sex, race, or ethnic group is less than four fifths (80 percent) of the selection rate for the group with the highest selection rate.[40] Table 7-1 illustrates how the so-called "four fifths rule" is applied; in that hypothetical case adverse impact is demonstrated and will be judged to be impermissible if the test has not been properly validated.

The four fifths rule does not allow up to 20 percent discrimination; it is not a legal definition, but a means of keeping attention focused on the issue. Regardless of the amount of difference in selection rates, other unlawful discrimination may exist and may be demonstrated through appropriate means. To use an extreme example, assume that the president of the local minority employees's association is very militant and vocal about his opposition to the current chief of police's policies. Further assume that the president's daughter applies for a job with the police department. All other applicants taking the written test mark their answers

TABLE 7-1 Hypothetical Group of Candidates for Employment as Police Officers

	White	Black	Totals
Took test	400	100	500
Passed	120	10	130
Failed	280	90	370
Passing rate	30%[a]	10%[b]	26%

[a] 120 (white passed) ÷ 400 (total white candidates = 30% white selection rate

[b] 10 (black passed) ÷ 100 (total black candidates) = 10% black selection rate

Adverse Impact Calculation:
10% (black selection rate) ÷ 30% (white selection rate) = 33.3% or less than 80% (four fifths)

in ink, but the daughter is required to use a pencil. Later, the daughter is told that she failed the test because she left half of the answer sheet blank. An examination of that sheet reveals that half of her answers were erased and that the majority of the erasures involved correct responses. In this situation, an impermissible discrimination would be shown even if there was no adverse impact on minorities overall.

"Reverse Discrimination"

Under EEOC guidelines all discrimination is prohibited and there is no recognized "reverse discrimination" theory. Yet, when the courts mandate preferential hiring and promotional opportunities for minorities to correct for past employment practices, problems arise. Majority individuals, who are typically white males, label the preferential treatment as "reverse discrimination" and at odds with the merit principle. Moreover, as reflected in the article "Officers Charged in Variety of Crimes: Relaxed Recruiting Cited in Miami Police Scandals" (see Box 7-1), relaxing standards to achieve important social goals may at least occasionally create problems in the operation of the police department.

One of the regrettable side effects of trying to overcome years of blatant discrimination is the occasional tension between majority officers, who except for the need to meet a court mandate would have been promoted, and those who receive the preferential treatment. Despite the clear necessity to correct for long-standing discrimination in the work place, the use of such practices is difficult for the average officer to support. They feel that the "rules of the game" have been unfairly changed, that such preferential treatment needlessly endangers the public if the less able are hired or selected to lead. Even when a clearly superior minority officer, who would be promotable under any system, is selected ahead of them, their sense of anger may lead them to denigrate the minority officer's very real and substantial capabilities. Criticism of preferential consideration of minorities to correct long-standing abuses in hiring and promoting has come from different quarters, including the U.S. Commission on Civil Rights. Although such developments made civil rights leaders uneasy about the prospect of less support for their movement, it was two 1989 decisions by the Supreme Court that both frightened and angered them, leading many to charge that the clock on civil rights was being turned backward. Both decisions were discussed in Chapter 2 "Politics and Police Administration," but a brief restatement of them is appropriate here. In *Wards Cove Packing* v. *Antonio* the Court held that minorities could not be favored in hiring decisions and that the plaintiffs must disprove the claims of the employer—in this instance it was an Alaskan salmon cannery—that the adverse impact on minority hiring was based on factually neutral considerations.[41] In *Martin* v. *Wilks* the Court held that majority employees in the Birmingham, Alabama, Fire Department could challenge a consent decree because they had not been parties to the negotiations that had the effect of abrogating their rights.[42] Together these decisions made challenging employment decisions and practices more difficult for minorities, while facilitating challenges from majority employees of consent decrees favorable to minorities. Thus, to no small extent the Civil Rights Act of 1991 can be viewed as an attempt to strengthen the 1972 Title VII law administered by the EEOC as well as an effort to limit the impact of or to negate court decisions

BOX 7-1

Officers Charged in Variety of Crimes: Relaxed Recruiting Cited in Miami Police Scandals

MIAMI (AP)—The arrest of Miami police officers last week on murder and drug-trafficking charges is the latest scandal to hit what law enforcement officials call the department's "Mariel generation," officers hired at a time when standards were relaxed.

The officers were accepted during the effort to strengthen the force after the 1980 "freedom flotilla" boatlift brought 125,000 Cuban refugees from Mariel, Cuba, including more than 5,000 criminals from the island's prisons.

In all, a dozen current and former Miami officers recruited to fight the ensuing crime wave in South Florida have been arrested, suspended or fired this year for crimes ranging from drug possession to first-degree murder.

And more officers are under investigation for a series of "home invasions," in which armed men seeking drugs or cash enter homes and terrorize occupants, said Lew Wilson, assistant chief of the Southern Region of the Florida Department of Law Enforcement.

Police officials say that rapid expansion of the force, coupled with pressure to increase minority hiring in the early 1980s, led the department to relax its standards, letting in candidates who might otherwise have been rejected.

"After the boatlift, we had to put people on the streets," department spokesman Reginald Roundtree said. He estimated that the department's 1,065 officers include at least 400, of various ethnic backgrounds, who were hired in the first years after the boatlift.

But Roundtree emphasized that most of the Mariel generation are "very good, competent police officers."

"There is nothing wrong with minority hiring," said Sgt. James Cox, president of the Police Benevolent Assn. "But you have to hire the best, even you have to go recruit at colleges."

Roundtree said the department has stopped hiring while it reviews its recruiting standards. A review committee set up in October is expected to deliver its report at the beginning of the new year.

Cox, a 27-year veteran, said increased temptation also is to blame for the scandals in the nation's No. 1 entry point for smuggled drugs.

He recalled that when he was on the vice squad 10 years ago, "street policemen never saw kilos of cocaine and people carrying hundreds of thousands of dollars. The biggest thing we ever had was a boatload of marijuana."

Last week's arrests and charges were the most serious to hit the department this year.

Three officers were arrested Friday and charged with the first-degree murder of three suspected drug dealers on July 28. The victims' bodies were found floating in the Miami River.

The officers charged with the murder and two other officers, including one who recently resigned, also were charged with trafficking in cocaine. The ex-officer was still at large Saturday.

In an unrelated case Thursday, two officers were arrested and charged with trafficking in cocaine seized by the police.

Two other Miami officers were arrested earlier this month on cocaine charges. Two more were relieved of duty in connection with the investigation of the Oct. 9 theft of $150,000 from a police safe.

An officer and a retired officer were arrested in August and accused of selling weapons to undercover agents.

Source: Los Angeles Times. Dec. 29, 1985, Part I, p. 19.

unfavorable to civil rights interests. Although the 1972 Title VII law did not allow for the award of punitive damages, the Civil Rights Act of 1991—also administered by the EEOC—does so on the following bases: (1) for employers who have more than 14 and fewer than 101 employees in each of 20 calendar weeks in the current or preceding year (referred to as the base period), up to $50,000; (2) for employers who have more than 100 and fewer than 201 employees for the base period, there is a cap or limit of $100,000 in punitive damages; (3) for employers who have more than 200 and fewer than 501 employees during the base period, $200,000; and (4) in the case of employers who have 500 or more employees during the base period, the maximum punitive damage award is $300,000.[43] Unquestionably this punitive damage provision is a significant development. Employers will abandon many questionable practices, employees will be more likely to litigate, and plaintiffs will be less likely to be satisfied with only the traditional EEOC remedies previously available to them, such as hiring or promotion, back pay, and orders to cease using the employment practices successfully challenged. However, as noted in Chapter 2, "Politics and Police Administration," under the Civil Rights Act of 1991 the punitive damage provision cannot be applied to a government, government agency, or political subdivision.

As a concluding note, in early 1992 a federal district court in Missouri ruled in *High* v. *Broadway Industries, Inc.*, that the Civil Rights Act of 1991 should not be applied retroactively because there is no expression of congressional intent to do so; the EEOC's policy guidelines currently agree with this holding.[44] Similarly, in *Mojica* v. *Gannett Co.* a federal judge vacated a $125,000 punitive award to a women who had been allowed to amend her complaint to request punitive damages under the 1991 Civil Rights Act.[45] Although it appears that the 1991 Civil Rights Act may not be applied retroactively to cases that predate its enactment, at the writing of this text in early 1992 the issue is not a matter of settled law. The nation's largest independent federal employees union—National Treasury Employees Union (NTEU)—has sued the EECO over its announced policy position of refusing to apply the 1991 Civil Rights Act retroactively.[46]

Physical Ability Testing

A 1990 study reported that 80.3 percent of responding police agencies presently use qualifying physical strength and/or ability tests.[47] However, before the enactment of Title VII in 1972, the principal physical requirement used in police officer selection was based on standards of height and weight. It is now recognized that these standards adversely affected the employment of women and some ethnic groups with small body size and are no longer rigidly used as hiring criteria because police departments consistently failed to, or were unable to, show the importance of these factors in job performance.[48] Interestingly, however, in *Robinson* v. *City of Lake Station* (1986) physical size was found to be a legitimate factor in hiring for the position of garbage packer.[49] It was noted the position required extensive lifting, changing oversized truck tires, and occasionally pushing trucks out of mud and snow.

As police departments moved away from rigid reliance on height and weight standards during the 1970s, many of them decided to use physical agility tests. Some departments adopted military-type obstacle courses or components of them.

In general, police departments found it difficult to defend the use of this type of test when women—who typically failed the test at significantly higher rates than males—challenged it under EEOC provisions. For example, one department used a course that required applicants to scale a six-foot-high-fence. Women who had been eliminated from further employment consideration successfully challenged the practice and won when their attorney pointed out that a city ordinance forbade the construction of fences of greater than five feet in height, creating a *prima facie* showing that the test was not job related. In *Harless* v. *Duck* (1980), a federal district court struck down a police department's use of a physical agility test that included the following components: (1) 15 pushups, (2) 25 situps, (3) a six-foot standing broad jump, and (4) a 25-second obstacle course.[50] The court ruled that although a job analysis showed the need for some physical activity on the job, it did not specifically define the amount of physical strength or extent of physical exertion required. Moreover, it was noted that the test was developed intuitively, there was justification for the exercises chosen, and there were no benchmark scores. In contrast, in *Evans* v. *City of Evanston* (1989), women challenging a firefighters' physical agility test lost when the defendants were able to show that a job analysis had been done, the test faithfully imitated tasks firefighters are called on to perform in their work, and the test had been pretested on firefighters to determine scoring.[51]

By the 1990s, police departments were more inclined to describe their physical agility testing as physical fitness or ability tests (see Box 7-2). This shift represents more than a terminology change. It represents a content shift away from obstacle course–style testing toward measuring applicants' job-related anaerobic level (strength) and aerobic (cardiovascular) fitness, often over the distance of a 12-minute run. In *Zamlen* v. *City of Cleveland* (1988), unsuccessful female applicants to the fire department brought suit claiming that the physical ability test favored men in that it emphasized anaerobic (strength) components and neglected aerobic (cardiovascular) fitness, the latter test being one in which many women do excel.[52] However, the court held that the lack of aerobic content was alone insufficient grounds to invalidate the test. *Zamlen* is also noteworthy because the court found that a city is not required to announce the exact physical tasks on the physical ability test if the job announcement describing the physical components is fairly representative and puts applicants on notice to prepare for the test. In *United States* v. *City of Wichita Falls* (1988), a physical assessment test measuring the general fitness of applicants was used as a screening device for entry into the police academy.[53] Female applicants who had failed the test were unsuccessful in challenging it because male applicants' scores were compared to benchmark scores for males and female applicants' scores to female benchmark scores.

Based on current information, police departments wanting to create a defensible physical ability test should follow certain steps: (1) review the decisions in prior litigation carefully, (2) have a detailed job analysis done by competent authority using sound methodology, (3) employ an exercise physiologist to link the physical tasks identified by the job analysis with specific physical abilities (e.g., upper-body strength) and then specify which physical test is best suited to assess an applicant's capability, (4) pretesting the physical ability procedure to develop benchmark scores that are gender specific and properly associated with acceptable job performance levels, (5) announce the components of the test in detail well before the test itself so that candidates know what to prepare for and have the

BOX 7-2

City Police Applicants Face Tougher Physicals

By John Branton *The Columbian*

Wanted: New Vancouver police officers. Men in their 20s who cannot do 38 sit-ups in a minute and run 1.5 miles in 12 minutes and 51 seconds need not apply.

The Vancouver police have new tougher physical-fitness standards for future officers, Chief Rod Frederiksen said Wednesday. In the past, the department has had strength and agility tests that were less demanding.

The new standards, which vary for men and women and for different age groups, are based on the 40th percentile of the so-called "Cooper test," developed by the Institute for Aerobics Research in Dallas, Texas.

A score at the 40th-percentile would mean that, on average, 60 percent of the population could do better. But although the 40th percentile sounds easy, it has proved too rich for many would-be cops' blood.

In fitness tests earlier this year at the Washington state police academy, as many as 71 percent of newly hired police officers failed the same standards, said Garry Wegener, assistant director for the Washington State Criminal Justice Training Commission.

"People are showing up for the academy overweight and out-of-shape," Wegener said. "Maybe it's the TV generation, or the Pizza Hut generation."

Frederiksen said the new standards are needed to find officers who are more fit and detect health problems that could surface later.

"I don't think it's an unreasonable test," he said. "It's one I think I could pass right now. I think we're clearly communicating to people before the test that this is a requirement, that they should get into shape."

The new standards will be used in the department's next recruitment effort, which starts later this month. The department has two openings and will advertise a newly approved "lateral entry" hiring process designed to attract officers who already have at least two years of police experience.

The fitness test will be administered to applicants in June, and those who fail will be out of the running, Frederiksen said. The new standards also are to apply to later recruitment efforts, including those involving inexperienced officers, he said.

Besides the running, push-ups and sit-ups, the test has a fourth component that measures body flexibility.

New fitness standards will affect new officers, but the department so far has no provision to see that officers stay fit, Frederiksen said. He said he might later suggest a salary-incentive plan that would reward officers who can continue to perform well for their age group.

Source: Columbian (Vancouver, Washington), May 2, 1991.

time to do so, (6) administer the test in a consistent manner, (7) preserve all records of the test for the period of time dictated by applicable records retention laws or policies, and (8) be prepared for requests for reasonable accommodation under the ADA.

The Polygraph Test in Pre-employment Screening

The federal Employee Protection Act of 1988 prohibits the use of the polygraph in most private-sector pre-employment screening, but all governmental bodies are exempt from this restriction.[54] However, a few state courts have prohibited even the police from using the polygraph in screening applicants.[55] Such state court decisions take precedent over the federal law. Nationally, 56.6 percent of studied police agencies reported using the polygraph in employment screening; municipal police departments were more likely (73.1 percent) than state police agencies (44.4 percent) to use it.[56] Typically most departments (83 percent) conducted their own examinations rather than contracting with a source outside of the department.[57]

The term *polygraph* refers to the multiple-pen subsystem that records the instrumental responses on a roll of paper. Contemporary polygraph equipment measures, simultaneously, three physiological responses: breathing patterns, blood pressure, and pulse and skin resistance to external current. The results of a polygraph should never be the sole basis for disqualifying an applicant. Areas that appear to be problems during the polygraph test should be the focus of additional sensitivity during the background investigation. Law enforcement agencies using the polygraph in the pre-employment screening process have indicated that there are many practical benefits derived from its use.

First, law enforcement agencies found that, when it was widely publicized that they were going to begin to use the polygraph to examine applicants, there were fewer numbers of undesirable applicants applying for positions with their agencies. This was supported by the decreasing percentage of applicants who were being eliminated at the conclusion of their background investigations.

Second, although it was difficult to prove empirically, there were some indications that the polygraph reduced the rate of turnover. This was accomplished by determining whether an applicant was seriously interested in pursuing a law enforcement career or was merely trying to find temporary employment. It is unreasonable to expect any young person to make a career commitment at the time of employment, but clear-cut cases of using the agency as a "temporary meal ticket" should be dealt with accordingly.

Third, by publicly announcing that it uses the polygraph to screen all law enforcement applicants, the law enforcement agency is letting its community know that it is determined to hire only those persons whose character and morals are above reproach.

When to Administer the Polygraph Examination

Although historically the polygraph has been used quite early in the screening process, the ADA, as discussed earlier in this chapter, may cause it to be used at later stages, thus eliminating some advantage to its use. Many law enforcement agencies using such instruments in their pre-employment screening process do so immediately after the applicant has passed all written and/or assessment center testing and the FBI fingerprint record check has been returned to the agency from Washington, D.C. Investigators responsible for conducting character investigations are at a distinct advantage if they know as much about the applicant's background as possible before conducting their investigations. The polygraph examination may just possibly give them some important additional information that might not otherwise have been available when they started their investigation.

Any investigator who has had to conduct large numbers of character investigations will be the first to admit that occasionally an undesirable applicant slips through the administrative screen. The use of the polygraph will not eliminate this problem completely, but it will help minimize the chance of such an applicant's being employed.

The Character Investigation

All police agencies conduct character investigations because, with the exception of observing the probationary officer's actual performance under varied field conditions, the single most important element of the process is the character investigation. The basic course of action in the character investigation is to review and verify all responses made by the applicant as to his or her education, military service, prior employment history, and related matters, as well as to check the references listed and develop other references.

An editor once stated that the three basic rules for great journalists were "check your facts, check your facts, and check your facts." These three basic rules also apply to conducting the character investigation; making assumptions or failing to independently verify "facts" will result in an increase in negligent hirings. This creates, as is discussed in Chapter 10, "Legal Aspects of Police Administration," a liability problem because people who should not have been employed are hired. A case history illustrates this point:

> On his initial employment form an applicant to a large city department reported that he had served a tour of duty in the Coast Guard. Among the documents he showed the department's personnel investigators were the original copy of an honorable discharge as well as DD 214 (Armed Forces of the United States Report of Transfer or Discharge). The investigators believed the discharge and DD 214 to be authentic. Still, they obtained an authorization for release of military records and medical information from the candidate. This release was then sent to the appropriate military records center. Meanwhile, the candidate's character investigation went on with respect to other factors. The candidate reported on his application form that following his discharge from the Coast Guard, he and his wife had spent 5 months traveling the country on money they had saved, thus there was no employment history during that time. When the military record information arrived, it was learned that he had, in fact, been honorably discharged, but in less than 30 days had reenlisted and 2 months into that tour of duty, he got drunk, badly beat up his wife, and assaulted military authorities who were sent to his quarters on base to handle the domestic disturbance. Subsequently, he was dishonorably discharged from the service. When questioned about it, he readily admitted to these facts and added that he was betting that either the department wouldn't check or that the record of the second enlistment wouldn't yet be in his permanent personnel file if the department did check.

Such incidents have made many agencies realize that character investigations are very specialized and very demanding, and that a failure to properly conduct them will eventually produce results ranging from very serious to catastrophic.

Oral Interviews and Oral Boards

Oral interview refers to a one-on-one interview between the applicant and some authority in the hiring process, such as the chief of police. In smaller jurisdictions the interview may actually take the place of a written test or assessment center. In other instances, although there may be a written test or an assessment center, the police chief may simply want a chance to see and talk with candidates before they are hired. In general, such interviews tend to be unstructured, free flowing, and either not scored or graded on a pass-fail basis. If legally challenged, unstructured interviews are difficult to defend because unskilled questioners may ask legally impermissible questions and because different candidates may be asked widely varying questions—a lack of standardization.

In contrast to interviews, oral boards, usually involve a face-to-face contact between a three-member panel and the police applicant. Panel members may be police officials, representatives of the civil service or merit board, community members, or combinations of these people. A standard set of job-related questions is drawn up ahead of time, and panel members are trained in the use of the written evaluation form, which they incorporate into their consideration of each candidate. Such well-planned, systematic, structured systems are more reliable, have greater defensibility, and are better predictors of future job performance than unstructured interviews.[58]

As a related point, many police promotional systems have an oral board component. Research by Gaines and Lewis,[59] however, has shown the difficulty in their successful operation.

Medical and Psychological Testing of Police Applicants

Although all police departments medically test candidates before employing them, only 56.5 percent require applicants to undergo psychiatric or clinical psychology evaluations.[60] Psychiatric assessment of police candidates was pioneered in 1938 in Wilmington, Delaware, and Toledo, Ohio.[61] A 1956 study found that only 15.6 percent of cities had adopted this practice, but by 1971 this figure had increased to 39 percent.[62] By 1988, the use of psychiatric or psychological evaluation by police departments had climbed to over 50 percent[63] (see Box 7-3).

Stress, "Liability-Prone," and Negligent Admission/Retention

Excessive stress can lead to aggressive and unconventional behavior, as well as mental and physical dysfunctions on the job.[64, 65] Police work is a well-known high-stress occupation (see Box 7-4). Stress can be a significant factor in causing serious and expensive problems, but the stress tolerance level of officers or applicants can be a significant factor in preventing problems. (The topic of police stress is discussed in greater detail in Chapter 8, "Stress and Police Personnel.") People have different ways of coping with stress. Some individuals are emotionally "liability prone." These individuals have an increased propensity to develop serious behavioral, psychological, and physical problems. They may become a serious threat to themselves, their fellow officers, the welfare of the community, and the agency budget.

Apart from the obvious moral obligation that law enforcement agencies have to ensure that their officers do not abuse their powers, inappropriate police behavior is expensive. The cost of investigating and processing personnel complaints is high. Disciplinary actions often include suspension, which reduces manpower. In addition, lawsuits and civil claims are costly in both dollars and manpower and are devastating to agency morale. The courts have identified "negligent admission"

BOX 7-3

Tests Cut Some Cop Candidates
Psychological Data Cuts 21 Candidates

By Bill Briggs *Denver Post Staff Writer*

Psychological tests aimed at weeding out potentially dangerous or risky Denver Police Department hires knocked out 16 percent of the agency's current crop of applicants.

Of the 131 would-be cops who had cleared two major hurdles in the hiring process—the written and fitness exams—21 were found to have personality flaws serious enough to eliminate them from the job chase, according to figures released yesterday.

"These are good folks and they're doing well, but not everybody can be a police officer," said psychologist John Nicoletti, who interviewed the applicants.

The psychological exams, which cost between $100 and $150 per applicant, were beefed up two years ago to include face-to-face interviews to ensure that no mentally imbalanced people were handed a badge and a gun in Denver. But the tighter process has further reduced the shrinking pool of possible black hires in the department. Black recruits again posted the highest failure rate among the major ethnic groups, as they did during the recent written and fitness tests. All three tests were given this summer.

Civil service commission figures show that 33 percent of the 53 black applicants did not pass the test.

In contrast, 13 percent of the 61 white applicants flunked and none of the 12 remaining Hispanic recruits was deemed mentally unfit for the job. However, once again civil service officials could offer no explanation for the failure rates.

"That's just the way the numbers fell," said Ed Gietl, executive director of the commission. Gietl and Nicoletti denied any problem exists in the testing process, saying that each of the exams has been found racially sensitive.

Some civil leaders, including City Councilman Ted Hackworth, have charged that the police department's recruitment effort was flawed from the start and did not target the highest-caliber people.

The latest test results cut the remaining pool of possible black hires to 41. But two other black applicants recently were shipped off with military reserve units to Saudi Arabia, trimming the number to 39.

While civil service officials remain confident they will meet their goal of placing 18 blacks in the 40-seat November police academy, Gietl now says he cannot guarantee the spring academy will meet the same court-ordered quota.

Each of the 131 recruits was mentally dissected in the series of psychological tests. They were graded one through four, with one indicating the most stable and four being the least. Anyone scoring three or four was cut.

"The threes might be able to do the job, but hiring them involves a lot of risk," Nicoletti said. "They might have a problem with authority. They may have a tendency to overreact in stressful situations.

"Four means there are some major concerns. They take (the emotional problems) to real extremes. They may have major problems getting along with people or be real abusive," Nicoletti said. "We really don't see that many fours."

The psychological screening detects whether recruits have a tendency to take excessive risks, if they have addictive personalities, how they handle stress, how they get along with others and whether they can take orders, among other things.

What's the perfect personality for a cop?

According to Nicoletti, they should be mildly independent, but not so much that orders aren't followed; have a high energy level; and have a positive attitude toward people, but not to the point of being naive.

Source: Denver Post (Colorado), Sept. 7, 1990.

BOX 7-4

Ex-Officer Gets Injury Pension For Job Stress

By Selwyn Raab

After four years of legal arguments and anguish, Paul J. Hipple is being compensated for an emotional breakdown he suffered while working as an undercover police officer in New York City.

Responding to a renewed plea by Mr. Hipple, one of the city's most highly decorated offices, a city pension board has reversed an earlier decision and granted him a line-of-duty disability pension instead of the ordinary early retirement one.

Jeffrey L. Goldberg, a lawyer who specializes in police pension matters and who represented Mr. Hipple, said in an interview that the ruling was "a landmark for the city in recognizing for the first time that accumulated stress from hazardous police work is a viable claim for accident disability." Mr. Goldberg said Los Angeles was the only other large city in the nation that has granted disability pensions to police officers for stress-related psychiatric disabilities.

Payment Increased by $11,000

As a result of the decision by the Police Department's Pension Board of Trustees, Mr. Hipple's payment will increase to $28,000 from $17,000 a year. The money, Mr. Hipple said yesterday, was secondary to the "vindication that my work for the department has finally been recognized."

"It's like getting an honorable instead of a dishonorable discharge," he added.

Mr. Hipple, who is 40 years old, retired as a police officer in 1985 after police doctors found he was psychiatrically disabled. In seeking a disability pension, he claimed that his breakdown had been caused by prolonged stress and repeated injuries, most of them suffered in 15 years as an undercover investigator and decoy.

In his 16-year career on the police force, Mr. Hipple participated in the arrests of more than 1,500 suspected muggers, armed robbers, drug dealers and rapists. He was awarded 44 departmental citations for excellent or meritorious work.

But in 1985 the pension board declined to grant him a disability pension, saying he had failed to show that the breakdown was caused by a specific on-the-job injury, as city law requires. The board said stress was present in all police jobs and was an insufficient ground for a disability pension.

Questions Raised by Unions

Mr. Hipple filed a lawsuit against the city in an effort to obtain the disability pension, but it was rejected in October, when the Court of Appeals, the state's highest court, refused to hear an appeal on it. Earlier, judges in lower state courts had ruled that they lacked the authority to overturn the pension board's administrative decision.

After the ruling by the Court of Appeals, Mr. Goldberg resubmitted Mr. Hipple's request to the pension board, which had denied his original request on a 6-to-6 vote. The board has six representatives from city agencies, while police officers' unions, which supported Mr. Hipple's first request, have six votes.

In explaining why the board reversed itself, Inspector Philip J. Bowden, the executive director of the city's Police Pension Fund, said union representatives had "raised questions that a thorough analysis of the facts had not been undertaken" in the 1985 decision.

The new Police Commissioner, Richard J. Condon, also had "expressed an interest that the right thing be done in the Hipple case," Inspector Bowden said.

The decision by the board to grant a disability was approved unanimously on Nov. 16, and Mr. Goldberg said he was formally notified about it this week. Mr. Hipple is now entitled to three-quarters of the salary he had earned in his last year as an officer.

BOX 7-4 (cont.)

Mr. Goldberg said Mr. Hipple's pension for post-traumatic stress syndrome was unprecedented for the city's police force.

Inspector Bowden said he was unable to recall any other disability pension being granted in the last 10 years by the police Pension Board for disabilities from post-traumatic stress syndrome, like Mr. Hipple claimed. But, he emphasized that it would be impossible to verify that Mr. Hipple's case was the first without a review of records that would take months.

Mr. Hipple and Mr. Goldberg said they believed the pension board had been reluctant to award the pension to Mr. Hipple in 1985 because it might have established a costly precedent for the granting of other stress-related pensions.

When he was notified about the increased pension this week, Mr. Hipple was at his home in Bronxville, recovering from open-heart surgery that he underwent in June. Mr. Hipple, who said he is unable to work full time because of his heart ailment, said yesterday that he is planning to write a book about his life as a police officer.

Source: New York Times, Nov. 25, 1989, p. 25.

and "negligent retention" of officers as legal liabilities (see Chapter 10, "Legal Aspects of Police Administration"). Most police departments can trace a major portion of their unfavorable incidents to a relatively small number of officers. It is in the area of identifying applicants whose behavior will be costly to the agency that psychological screening efforts can be most effective.

Strategies—"Select In" or "Screen Out"

Too often, police administrators are led to believe in a "select in" strategy, which suggests that psychological evaluations can aid in selecting the best candidate for police work. This is not quite true. Psychological input can be helpful in deciding which individuals within an agency or department are suitable for specific assignments, such as Special Weapons and Tactics (SWAT), hostage negotiation, or bomb squads, but the most effective use of psychological evaluation is to "screen out" or identify those applicants who may not be emotionally suitable or may be a high risk for law enforcement.

The former strategy—select in—implies a precision and level of accuracy that psychologists do not possess and psychological procedures do not produce. In addition, this strategy ignores the possibility that future events, such as personal problems, could severely impact applicants initially judged to be acceptable and cause them to become high-risk employees at a later time.

Unsuitable applicants do not always appear to be inappropriate. Applicant pools approximate the normal curve—some individuals will appear to be excellent candidates, some will be obviously unacceptable, and the great majority will be somewhere in the middle. Applicants in this middle range who, in the judgment of a psychologist, demonstrate the risk of engaging in liability-resulting behavior should be screened out. This decision is not always clear, but in admitting individuals to law enforcement, judgmental decisions should be made with caution.

Other mechanisms should exist in the screening process to minimize possible decision errors. Included should be an appeal or review process conducted at a higher administrative level.

How to Select and Best Use a Psychological Consultant. It would be ideal for law enforcement agencies to have a full-time mental health professional as part of the staff. In this case, the professional should be involved in an orientation period long enough to provide familiarity with police management, police officers' tasks, and criteria for successful job performance. Because the majority of police agencies do not have or cannot afford full-time mental health professionals, outside consultants are used for a variety of psychological services, including the psychological screening of applicants. Outside consultants may be psychologists, psychiatrists, management consultants, and, on occasion, physicians. Most often, a licensed professional or certified consultant is required.

An important consideration in choosing a professional for a department is the person's ability to relate to the police organization and to become knowledgeable in police consultation. Police agencies are approached by professionals from all areas and backgrounds who wish to become associated with an agency or propose a project on a fee-for-service or contract basis. In rural areas and small towns, police organizations sometimes develop working arrangements with university professors. In some cases, research academicians look upon police officers as subjects for data gathering and fail to understand the needs of police officers and administrators.

Academic persons working in applied areas or professionals who have done research in areas of police psychology are sometimes better prepared to begin consultation in law enforcement. It is, however, important that such professionals also possess training in the area of identifying clinical or personality issues that could impair police officers' performance. Consultants who are not familiar with the job should approach the consultation task initially as a student, and police agencies should insist on exposing them to relevant areas of police work.

The sheriff or chief of police will often be the primary contact for the consultant. The psychological screening information is usually transmitted directly to him or her or to another previously designated representative. In most cases, the decision to hire is made by the chief of police after background results, medical results, psychological results, and, in some cases, polygraph results are available. Some agencies prefer either a yes or a no response as to whether an applicant is suitable for police work. This response may be verbal, followed by a written report. Some police administrators prefer to meet with the consultant to discuss each applicant. However, in most cases, a detailed written report including the background as reviewed by the consultant, the results of any psychological tests administered, interview data, and a summary and recommendation is submitted to the department.

The consultant should function as part of a team that includes all those involved in processing applicants. It is strongly desirable for the consultant to meet with all persons in the system, including the training officers who will eventually complete the screening process by either recommending recruits for permanent status, probation, or termination. The consultant should know the training officer's perspective and be aware of any past psychological problems of the recruits. The training officer should know on what basis the psychologist will recommend marginal applicants be accepted with the hope they will develop as suitable officers during probation.

Consultants should be willing to explain and defend screening decisions should it become necessary. When an applicant appeals disqualification, the consultant should be available to appear before a civil service board or in court, if necessary.

In many cases, a psychologist or other professional will be hired solely to provide preemployment psychological screening. After the agency develops confidence in him or her, the consultant may be called on to perform psychological "fitness for duty" evaluations on officers who have demonstrated patterns of excessive-force complaints or highly unusual liability-prone behavior. Also, officers applying for special assignments, such as bomb squad technicians or hostage negotiators, may be evaluated to ensure that the persons chosen are the best suited for the job. In these cases, the officer's personnel file and work history provide valuable information regarding past performance. Information on the number and nature of complaints against the officer, sick time taken, and performance under stress provides valuable input for the psychological consultant.

In all cases, it is important to remember that the decision as to who will be selected for employment and which officers will receive specialized assignments remains in the hands of the administration. The psychologist or consultant only provides specialized information and judgments that will be taken into consideration along with other important factors. In some instances, police administrators may choose officers who have not been recommended by the psychologist. Often, in these instances, the psychological consultant can identify areas of needed development and can suggest to the administration ways of supporting individual development.

Screening Components. Police administrators and managers are often concerned with the validity of psychological tests. Psychological instruments and procedure were developed through scientific and statistical investigation, but the relevance of any single statistical score to a well-integrated psychological judgment is often overemphasized. Good decisions require information. The three best sources of information in evaluating law enforcement applicants are

1. Psychological tests
2. Background information and
3. An in-depth or clinical interview by a psychologist knowledgeable in law enforcement.

All information developed in the preemployment stages could reasonably be used by a clinical psychologist. Typically, most psychologists choose the Minnesota Multiphasic Personality Inventory (MMPI), the Sixteen Personality Factor Questionnaire (16PF), or the California Psychological Inventory (CPI). Extensive information exists on these instruments and their use in law enforcement screening;[66] however, psychologists may vary in the psychological tests they use depending on their training and experience.

Some psychological tests, such as the MMPI and the 16PF, can be computer scored, but a psychologist must review and interpret the results on an individual basis. Because most computer interpretations of the MMPI are based on the assumption that the test applicant is a mental patient or an outpatient in psychotherapy, negative or pathological information is likely to be emphasized. The MMPI can be extremely useful in screening, but it must be interpreted by a professional who is knowledgeable in both the test's subtleties and law enforcement.

The Psychologist as an Expert Judge

In the psychological screening approach, the psychologist plays a critical role in integrating psychological test results, background information, and interview data in order to arrive at a judgment of unsuitability. This is a "clinical" or expert judgment, not a statistical or scientific outcome. Studies have been done relating various kinds of biographical or psychological test score information to criterion variables, such as disciplinary actions, number of arrests made, commendations, sick time taken, on-the-job automobile accidents, and so on. These studies are helpful in suggesting which tests and criteria may be of potential benefit, but to rely totally on test scores and correlations would be inappropriate. It is the psychologist who is familiar with law enforcement who renders a clinical judgment that brings expertise and credibility to the screening process.

The psychological consultant, who is properly trained and working as support for management, can maximize the success and professionalism of the screening and selection process. But psychologists cannot predict the future. Assuming they know the intricacies of a police officer's job, they can develop relevant information regarding an individual's emotional functioning in a law enforcement position and render a judgment about an individual's suitability. Psychological screening minimizes the admission of inappropriate applicants and is consistent with the safeguards and precautions that the law and common sense dictate.

The Recruit Academy, Probationary Period, and Career Status

Widespread use of the police academy to train police rookies for their new responsibilities is a comparatively recent development. A survey of 383 cities by the Wickersham Commission in 1931 showed that only 20 percent of the municipalities provided police academy training.[67] At the time the use of the police academy was limited almost exclusively to the larger cities. In many jurisdictions new officers were simply equipped and told to go out and "handle things" or, at most were assigned to work briefly with a veteran officer who "showed them the ropes."

Following World War II, there was increased recognition of the need to prepare newly hired personnel for police work, but, being a matter of local discretion, it remained largely undone. In 1959 California pioneered state-wide legislation that statutorily established police minimum standards, including entry-level training or academy training. New Jersey, Oklahoma, and Oregon followed suit in 1961, and by 1975 44 states had done likewise. Today all states have legislation regulating entry-level police training. This training requirement is usually expressed as a minimum number of recruit academy hours. The national average number of hours that must be minimally provided is approximately 450. Minnesota uses a somewhat different approach. All of its applicants must have a two-year college degree, including a small core of police courses, and then complete a skills-based training program of approximately 12 weeks.

It is important to note that although state statutes require a minimum number of hours, many jurisdictions choose to exceed that amount considerably, based on the basis of their own needs and philosophies. Police academy training is provided under a variety of arrangements. A state academy may offer the basic course, often referred to as mandate training; individual police agencies, usually the larger ones, operate their own academies; and regional academies provide training for police agencies in a multicounty area. Combinations of these arrangements exist in most states, and variations are possible. For example, for many years larger agencies that operated their own academies allowed smaller agencies to send recruits to their academies whenever they had unused seats. This practice initially was free under the "good neighbor" doctrine, but over time fiscal pressures have led to the use of fees.

Police academy training is frequently followed by placing new officers in the care of a field training officer (FTO). The FTO carefully monitors the development of the rookie under actual job conditions; often the rookie is rotated between shifts and FTOs to be further evaluated. FTO evaluations can be crucial in determining whether an officer stays with the department or is "washed out." Some agencies have adopted officer retention boards to review all evidence on each probationary officer and to recommend to the agency head whether an officer should be granted career (or permanent) employee status or released.

Education

Law enforcement administrators as well as a broad segment of our nation's social and political leaders agree that the once-satisfactory entry standard of a high school education is no longer an acceptable minimum level. This position has been supported by three national commissions: the Wickersham Commission, 1931; the President's Commission on Law Enforcement and the Administration of Justice, 1967; and the National Advisory Commission on Criminal Justice Standards and Goals, 1973. The National Advisory Commission study recommended that

> Every police agency should, no later than 1982, require as a condition of initial employment the completion of at least 4 years of education (120 semester hours or a baccalaureate degree) at an accredited college or university.[68]

It is apparent that neither has this higher education standard been met nor is there reason to believe that it will be met any time in the immediate future. This can be explained in part by considering that, in jurisdictions in which civil service commissions establish entrance requirements, the chief executive is limited in being able to change educational standards.[69] However, even with the absence of such a requirement, many police agencies report that they are attracting an ever-increasing number of applicants who have either completed some college work or are college graduates.[70]

It has been argued by some that police work, especially at the local level, does not require a formal education beyond high school because such tasks as directing traffic, writing parking tickets, conducting permit inspections, and performing clerical tasks do not require higher education. In addition, it has been suggested that a highly intelligent and well-educated person would soon become bored with these mundane and repetitive tasks and either resign or remain and become either an ineffective member of the force or a malcontent. However, in more progressive police agencies, such routine tasks have been turned over to civilian personnel or paraprofessionals and other governmental agencies. Thus, police officers are left with their more essential tasks, which include social control in a period of increasing social turmoil, preservation of our constitutional guarantees, and exercise of the broadest range of discretion—sometimes involving life-and-death decisions—of any government service. The need for police officers who are intelligent, articulate, mature, and knowledgeable about social and political conditions is apparent.[71]

A number of agencies employing personnel who have college backgrounds have made some favorable reports about their performance as compared with those officers who did not have such a background. For example, one West Coast police department initiated a preemployment requirement of a four-year college degree.[72] The chief of that department reported that

> Having employed four-year college graduates for over three years, we have found our crime rate down and yet we spend less for personnel. We have more applicants for patrolman jobs than we can use even though we have not advertised for applicants in over three years. We find we have an unusually low turnover in personnel and morale is high. We have few disciplinary problems because the men are more mature and do not feel they have to prove themselves. We have fewer citizen complaints because the men are not as threatened by abusive language and thus do not overreact. I foresee some of these men going on to other disciplines in public service and new professional public servants taking their place. The public through these men, will receive a better understanding of police problems, and better service will result.

A study of the New York City police revealed

> As a group, the men with at least one year of college education who remained in the force were found to be very good performers. They advanced through civil service promotion, but not disproportionately through the detective route of advancement, and they had fewer civilian complaints than average. The men who obtained college degrees, either before or after appointment to the force, exhibited even better on-the-job performance. They advanced through preferential assignments and civil service promotions, they had low incidence of all types of misconduct except harassment, on which they were average, they had low sick time and none had their firearms removed for cause.[73]

These findings were similar to the results of a Chicago Police Department study, which revealed that the highest-rated group of tenured officers were those with significantly higher education.[74] Other researchers have found that college-educated police officers are not only significantly less authoritarian than are noncollege-educated police officers but also less authoritarian than college graduates in other fields.[75]

Although much of the literature on this subject of higher education tends to extol the benefits to be gained by police departments that hire college graduates, some observers have taken a more cautious approach.[76, 77, 78, 79] There is evidence to suggest that the transition of going from an agency with none or few personnel with college backgrounds to one with many has created some difficulties for both the older, less educated personnel and the newer, better educated personnel. Several complaints heard consistently from the older, less educated personnel: namely, the new employees have unrealistic expectations and believe that they should be given preferential treatment in assignments and promotions because of their higher than average formal education, and they have an elitist attitude and believe that they are "better" than those who are less formally educated.

In addition, college-educated officers have expressed a number of difficulties they have encountered: (1) rejection by noncollege-educated peers; (2) command officers' failure to encourage continuing education; (3) no reward system that encouraged education; (4) not being placed in specialized positions where their training and education could be most useful; (5) a slow promotional system; (6) no pay differential for their educational achievements; (7) little emphasis on a college education as long as the traditionalists were running the police organization; and (8) the absence of a mandatory retirement at an early age to make available openings in the higher ranks.[80]

Employment of Minorities

Police officers cannot be effective in an environment they do not understand. Moreover, when the racial composition of a police department does not approximate the racial makeup of the community's labor pool, then white officers may be seen by minorities as an army of occupation rather than as protectors. This perception invariably produces a downward spiral in community relations, distorts communications, increases suspicion and misunderstanding, and historically culminates with a violent episode that calls for reform of police hiring practices.

There are two major practices used by police administrators to make the police more effective when dealing with minority populations. The first is to conduct the necessary training to understand other cultures and to speak their language, a substantial logistical problem in large cities that have many different and well-defined ethnic groups such as Russians, Laotians, South Vietnamese, Nungs, Chinese, Poles, Arabs, and Hispanics. The second is to recruit minorities from these ethnic groups and to use them both to work with those populations and to train other police officers. However, the assignment of officers to work exclusively with their respective ethnic populations makes a department vulnerable to the charge that such practices neglect the development of a well-rounded police officer and that career advancement is therefore sacrificed. This perception subsequently makes future recruiting harder and may also reduce the credibility of minority officers in these areas. Thus, police departments must effectively recruit from all groups represented in their cities' populations, assign them for maximum effectiveness, but be very diligent about promoting their overall development. As a rule of thumb, police departments that recruit most successfully in minority areas have minorities in leadership as well as entry-level positions.

Employment of Women

Not too many years ago, it was common for police administrators to dismiss the notion that women could adequately perform functions normally falling within the exclusive domain of male officers—such as patrol work, nonfamily-related crime investigations, riding a motorcycle, and so forth. Legislative, administrative, and judicial action have long since resolved the question of whether or not women should be permitted to perform these functions, and women have put to rest the questions about their ability to handle these tasks. There is ample empirical evi-

FIGURE 7-2. Patrol officer Douglas Wilson, San Antonio, Texas, Police Department, and a few of his friends. [Photo courtesy of the San Antonio Police Department.]

dence to support the proposition that carefully selected and carefully trained females can be as effective as police officers as carefully selected and carefully trained males. Not all women are suited for police work, nor are all men. This, however, is not meant to suggest that women have been universally and enthusiastically accepted by their male counterparts, but their employment opportunities and career advancement have improved immeasurably during the past two decades.

The first women to be assigned to operating units that were traditionally comprised exclusively of men usually experienced the most serious difficulty. These women faced certain psychological pressures that were encountered by the women who followed them years later. For example, the first female police officers performed their duties in an atmosphere of disbelief on the part of their supervisors and peers in their ability to deal physically and emotionally with the rigors of street work, particularly patrol functions. It must be remembered that peer acceptance is one of the greatest pressures operating within the police organizations.[81] The desire to be identified as a "good officer" is a strong motivating force, and a failure to achieve that goal in one's own eyes as well as in the eyes of one's peers can have a devastating and demoralizing effect.

For the rookie female officer, attaining the approval of her peers can be an even more frustrating task than it is for her male counterpart. As is true for her male counterpart, she must overcome her doubts about her own ability to perform her duties effectively, but unlike her male counterpart, she must also overcome the prejudice stemming from societal influences depicting the female as the "weaker sex."[82] Also, unlike her male counterpart, she often receives little support from her family, friends, and perhaps even her husband or other close male companions. Thus, additional pressures are imposed on women choosing careers in law enforcement that are not imposed on men.

In 1989, the Police Foundation conducted a comprehensive national study to determine the status of women in policing (see Box 7-5). The survey findings

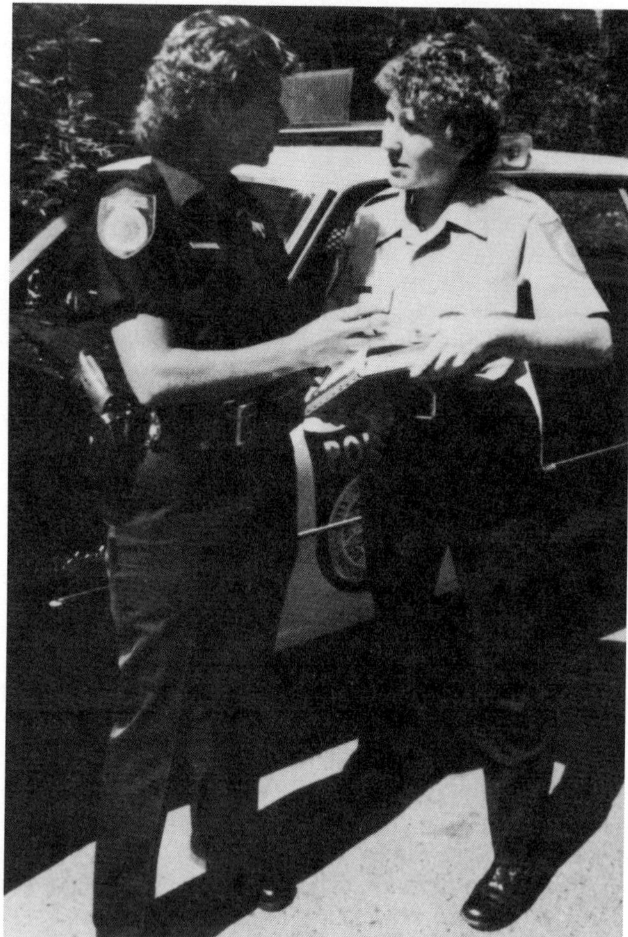

FIGURE 7-3. Officer instructing cadet on the proper way to complete a report form. [Photo courtesy of the Sacramento, California Police Department.]

BOX 7-5

Progress Steady but Slow for Women in Blue

By Marina Pisano *Express-News Staff Writer*

Women, children and typewriters—dealing with them was the only role open to "policewomen," as they were called, for the first 62 years of their history in police work.

That all began to change in 1972 with passage of the Equal Employment Opportunity Act. Today, female police officers patrol beside men all along the increasingly dangerous front lines of law enforcement.

Women are doing their jobs capably, according to a recently released, in-depth report from the Washington-based Police Foundation called "The Status of Women in Policing." Despite early doubts about the performance level of physically smaller females, they can cut it, the report says. Women have benefited from a shift of emphasis in policing to self-defense skills, exercise, diet and general fitness rather than height, weight and upper-body strength considerations alone.

The report, based on data gathered in a national survey of municipal and state police departments and through intensive case studies done in five large cities—none in Texas—demonstrates that slow quantitative progress has been made as well.

Representation of women nationally climbed from 4.2 percent of the sworn police officers in municipal departments in 1978 to nearly 9 percent in 1986. Local percentages vary widely. The San Antonio Police Department figures aren't as high. Women make up only 5.7 percent of the city's 1,568-member force.

On the other hand, Texas provided a dramatic example of the progress women have made early this year when Elizabeth Watson was sworn in as chief of the Houston Police Department, the first woman ever to be named top cop in a major American city.

As Hubert Williams, president of the Police Foundation, observes during an interview about the report, "What we've seen is an evolution, not a revolution. Attitudes have changed, but not radically. Biases still linger. We find in some of the critical-point, tactical units that there's still a reluctance to put women in those positions.

"What we're dealing with is a police culture that for more than 100 years reflected a masculine culture. And cultures take time to change," Williams says.

SAPD Officer Anna M. Zuniga confirms that, adding, "I think the regional culture plays a big role in this. The good ol' boy system is still going strong down here. Women in the South haven't progressed as far as they have up North."

"There are more enlightened and educated police officers out there. But you still find the jokes and the harassment. It does get pretty salty at times," Williams says, adding, "I don't think sexual harassment is being properly addressed in some departments. It shouldn't be tolerated."

One recommendation in the Police Foundation report is that agencies adopt and vigorously enforce a clear policy prohibiting sexual harassment. Williams says that policy hinges on a strong commitment by department leaders.

Similar commitment is needed to recruit, train, integrate and retain women in policing. "And women (officers) ought to be involved in any planning process to attract and increase the numbers," he stresses.

Spurred by a strong affirmative action mandate from the city council two years ago, the Dallas Police Department boosted the number of sworn female officers to 13.2 percent. Women make up 8 percent of DPD supervisory officers. That's higher than the national average for female supervisors in city police departments—3 percent—and much higher than SAPD's figure—1.3 percent.

The status report strongly recommends that departments encourage the promotion of women by keeping the system as open and fair as possible. Once promoted to sergeant or lieutenant, women often hit old attitudes, Williams says. "Some men don't like taking orders from women. And women don't have many mentors or role models in those higher positions. Men tend to exclude them from their networks."

BOX 7-5 (cont.)

Zuniga says professional organizations such as the International Association of Women Police can help. "Anytime I have a question, I can pick up the phone and ask someone who has gone through the same thing. It makes a big difference. That's why I think the conference is so important—networking."

The international group is holding its 29th annual training conference in San Antonio next September—its first in Texas. Conference director Zuniga hopes to register 1,000 participants and present super-role model Watson as a speaker, along with Pam Walt, Dallas' deputy chief of police.

For Williams, a troubling aspect of the study is the high, non-retirement turnover rates among female officers. "We're not keeping them. Part of that is because the job is glorified in the media. They come in with unrealistic expectations. But the high turnover is also due to family considerations. Women do more of the caring for children. They can't handle the long hours and late shifts."

To ease work-family stresses on both sexes, the report calls for flexible hours, part-time shifts at peak call periods and parental leave policies.

As Williams points out, Chief Watson again is providing a great model for women in blue. "She's not only the first woman chief, but just a couple of weeks ago she became the first chief to give birth to a baby. It will be interesting to see how she handles that."

Source: San Antonio Express-News (Texas), Dec. 29, 1990.

suggest that there has been some positive change in the status of women in policing during the past decade. The proportion of female officers has increased in police departments in each population category and geographic region. By the end of 1986, women made up nearly 9 percent of officers in municipal departments in cities over 50,000.[83] The pace of change is, nonetheless, relatively slow; women still constitute only 3.3 percent of the supervisory level, thus continuing to face the problems experienced by "tokens," such as performance pressures, heightened boundaries against "outsiders," and entrapment in stereotyped roles.

About 20 percent of both current applicants and recruits are female, which suggests that once women apply, there does not seem to be systematic discrimination against them. Wide variation exists, however, among departments, in both application and acceptance rates, which points to the fact that some agencies attract women and others do not, leaving considerable room for more effective recruitment efforts. Such efforts are particularly important because women have higher turnover rates than men; thus, more women must enter policing just to maintain current sex ratios. From a policy perspective, the following points are important to police departments seeking to attract and retain women:

- Because affirmative action policies have substantially changed the composition of larger departments, such policies should be maintained.
- Voluntary affirmative action hiring policies should focus on enlargement of the recruit pool, which will permit selection of more well-qualified women while avoiding imposition of court-ordered changes in hiring procedures that cause a backlash of resentment.
- To increase the rate of female promotion, departments need to alter promotion standards to eliminate criteria irrelevant to identifying supervisory ability or potential and adopt policies and procedures clearly stating that promotions are based on merit.

- Increasing the number of women in recruitment and training assignments as well as in high-visibility supervisory posts will create more role models for both potential recruits and women already on the job.
- Active, vigorous enforcement of existing sexual harassment policies may reduce turnover rates.
- The adoption of a policy permitting pregnant women to remain on the job in non-contact assignments and allowing new mothers to take leave beyond the brief period needed for physical recovery would have a salutary effect.

Employment of Homosexuals

One of the more controversial police hiring practices was started by the San Francisco Police Department several years ago when it actively recruited homosexuals. This practice is now being followed by other police departments around the country, and in other cases police administrators simply do not make an issue of an applicant's sexual orientation during the pre-employment screening process. However, the decision not to make inquiries into this area could create a dilemma for police departments after an applicant is hired, especially if the police department is in a state that prohibits the commission of homosexual acts. Administrators in such states will have to determine how they wish to reconcile their decisions not to make inquiries into an applicant's sexual orientation (see Box 7-6 on pp. 258–259).

Performance Evaluation

The process of performance evaluation is one that is too often disliked and misunderstood by both the individuals doing the evaluation and those being evaluated. This occurs many times because the purposes of the performance evaluation are simply not understood and the police department provides no clearly defined, unambiguous policy or procedure.[84]

Purpose of Evaluation

Employee Performance. Appraisals serve as an aid in motivating employees to maintain an acceptable level of performance. In this sense, performance refers to more than just measurable units of work. Law enforcement is too complex an undertaking to base appraisals solely on how a person fulfills assigned tasks. In addition to an evaluation of how an officer performs physically, the appraisal must also address itself to aspects that are difficult to quantify, such as attitudes and traits, but are of utmost importance to the successful accomplishment of mission.

Career Development. Personnel evaluations, if administered properly, pinpoint strengths that can be developed and weaknesses that should be corrected, thereby furnishing administrators with a developmental and remedial device of considerable worth. Those employees who consistently maintain a level of performance above the standards set by the department can, based upon their eval-

BOX 7-6

LAPD Gays' Hope: Mainstream Acceptance

Gay and lesbian police officers in Los Angeles hope that changing attitudes in other big-city police departments and a lawsuit filed by a gay former Los Angeles police sergeant, who contends he was threatened and harassed off the force by fellow officers, will change the department's view of their sexual orientation and allow them to be accepted into the law enforcement mainstream.

In the 1970's, then-Police Chief Edward M. Davis clashed with Civil Service Commission officials over the commission's vote to bar discrimination against homosexuals in police hiring practices. At the time, Davis had warned that admitting gays to the force would "completely destroy" officer morale and that citizens would "lose confidence and respect for their law enforcement agency" if homosexuals were hired. [See LEN, October/November 1975.]

While the board dismissed Davis's claims and ordered the Police Department to hire homosexuals, no recruiting campaign aimed at gays has ever been undertaken by the department. Perhaps more importantly, say gay and lesbian officers interviewed by the Los Angeles Times, the attitudes of their fellow police officers have remained unchanged and are characterized by animosity at best, forcing them to maintain the secrecy that they have tried to leave behind.

"I know these people play rough here," said a 24-year-old LAPD recruit who requested anonymity. "Something could happen to me. There are people, some hard-core people, who would stop at no lengths to get rid of me. I mean, it's one thing to handle the court system, but something else to have your own brother officers against you."

A lesbian officer with six years on the force said she also maintains a secret life and avoids department gatherings such as picnics because she can't allow her lover to accompany her. "The walls have ears," she said. "Nothing happens that your sergeant and your lieutenant and your captain don't know about."

Recent developments indicate, however, that the walls may be falling around the Los Angeles Police Department. A statewide study released in June by the California Commission on Peace Officer Standards and Training, which certifies police officers, identified the gay community as a key pool for recruiting police officers if the department hopes to bolster sagging recruitment efforts. On the national level, the International Association of Chiefs of Police (IACP) last year rescinded its decades-old policy of opposing the hiring of homosexual officers.

"That policy was one that no longer reflected the views of our organization," said Phil Lynn, manager of the IACP's National Law Enforcement Policy Center.

Other big-city California departments have left their Los Angeles brethren in the dust in formulating recruitment policies geared toward gays. Many feel that hiring homosexuals can alleviate tensions between police and their gay constituents, whose relationship has been strained in recent years, particularly in San Francisco, where a demonstration by AIDS activists last fall ended in violence and led to the dismissal of an assistant police chief.

At least 20 percent of the sworn work force of the San Francisco County Sheriff's Department is gay or lesbian. A lesbian lieutenant supervises a 70-officer bailiff security office, the department's budget supervisor is a lesbian, and several gay sergeants are watch commanders. A gay sheriff's aide was handily voted into office as president of the local Deputy Sheriffs Association a few years ago.

In San Diego, Police Chief Bob Burgreen has assigned an officer to work as a special liaison with the gay community there. The department also spearheaded a campaign to hire more homosexual officers this year.

Members of the Golden State Peace Officers Association, run for and by gay and lesbian officers, travel the state teaching local departments about the value of recruiting among the homosexual community.

On the East Coast, the Gay Officers Action League (GOAL) has a very visible presence within the New York City Police Department. Recruiting drives aimed at gays have become commonplace, and the manpower-starved department is actively recruiting gays and lesbians to act as police auxiliaries in an effort to stem the incidence of anti-gay violence that has increased sharply in the city this year.

Los Angeles Police Chief Daryl F. Gates, not one to shy from controversial views, has said he would not condone harassment among his troops, but neither will he compromise on the issue of a recruiting drive that targets gays and lesbians. "In the factors that go into being a police officer, sexual preference is irrelevant. It should stay irrelevant. And it will stay irrelevant while I have anything to say about it. I guarantee that," he said.

Police administrators say that not one man or woman on the force of approximately 8,400 officers is openly gay. But local gay activists say that as many as 10 percent of the force is gay or lesbian. Most fear ridicule or retaliation from their fellow officers and remain in the closet, and most know too well the experience of Mitchell Grobeson, a former LAPD sergeant who was open about his homosexuality. His candor cost him dearly, he says.

In a landmark lawsuit filed in September 1988 against the City of Los Angeles, the Police Commission and Chief Gates, as well as several fellow officers and supervisors, Grobeson contends he was the target of ridicule and derision by his fellow officers. He said he was referred to as a "faggot" at roll calls; received an "AIDS survival kit" with a picture of gay actor Rock Hudson, who died of the disease, that was signed "To Mitch, Love Rock Baby," and suffered other indignities. Most seriously, said Grobeson, officers would not come to his aid in potentially life-threatening situations. Ultimately, Grobeson left the force after a five-year career.

In an interview at the time he filed the suit, Grobeson said that Los Angeles police officers perceived gays as the bottom of society's heap. "There's a police mentality that there is a whole group of second-class citizens who don't have the rights that other people have. . . . At the very bottom of that list of second-class citizens are gays," he said.

Recently, Grobeson said he was optimistic that he would prevail in his legal fight against the department and that attitudes would change. "It's going to happen," he said. "It has to happen. Otherwise, the number of lawsuits will be so exorbitant to the City of Los Angeles that it will be too costly for the department not to."

Source: Law Enforcement News, Sept. 30, 1990, p. 7.

uations, be assigned to more responsible duties. Conversely, officers who are unable to meet reasonable standards can be given the guidance, supervision, and training necessary to save a career before it flounders.

Supervisory Interests. Systematic evaluations encourage supervisors to take a personal interest in the officers under their command. Within this context, appraisals can have a humanizing effect on supervision by holding commanders responsible for the performance of subordinates. Ideally, the program will foster mutual understanding, esprit de corps, solidarity, and group cohesiveness.

Salary Decisions. With the current managerial emphasis on rewards won on merit, personnel evaluations serve as a basis, often the only one, for pay increases. Officers with satisfactory appraisals will probably receive raises on time, whereas increases for those who fall below standards may be temporarily withheld. In industry, superior employees often receive early pay raises, an idea that may be of some value in police work, where it has not been used to any extent.

Selection Practices. When entry-level procedures are valid, most individuals selected for employment will make positive contributions to the department. If, however, many rookie officers in an agency are unable to perform adequately, something may be seriously wrong with the selection process. Personnel appraisal allows administrators to maintain a continuing check on entrance standards to determine if they are relevant or in need of modification. Furthermore, promotional examinations can be validated if supervisory and command evaluations are accurate.

Performance evaluations are sometimes used by employees as a legal defense to countermand allegations of misconduct by their departments.

An Evaluation Policy

Naturally, it must be a first management priority to install an evaluation system that has a good chance of delivering. If a defective system is put into operation, nothing can be done to make it work. Once top management has drafted the right instrument, reasonable steps can be taken to see that it is utilized correctly. A policy declaration should be enacted that clearly informs personnel of all aspects of the plan. Ideally, the policy should address itself to a discussion of the topics that follow.

Coverage. Everyone on a police department beneath the chief executive should be evaluated formally by a superior. In the case of the highest level of management, the chief serves as the evaluator. One of the major reasons for appraising upper-echelon administrators is to motivate cooperation with the acceptance of the plan on the part of supervisory and line personnel. Nothing could be more subversive to the program than to institute a selective system of appraisal that eliminated certain individuals or classes of positions.

Preparation. Formal classroom instruction must be scheduled periodically for evaluators, especially line sergeants, who probably have the most challenging and rewarding job. At least four hours of yearly training is appropriate, with more when possible. The evaluation instrument should be accompanied by a written directive that explains, in detail, the elements of the process, including a step-by-step description of each factor on the form.

In addition to supervisory preparation, employees (i.e. patrol officers and civilian workers) must be prepared formally, although it should be more in the nature of an orientation than a classroom training session. Each prospective employee should be furnished with the policy pronouncement, a sample form, and a copy of the supervisory instructions regarding its use. An appropriate medium for the orientation is roll call training, reinforced by a training bulletin.

Frequency. The frequency with which employees should be evaluated varies. In recruit school, there may be value in appraising rookies formally on a weekly or, at the very least, monthly basis. Probationers, be they patrol officers or supervisors, should be evaluated quarterly. Yearly evaluations are appropriate for permanent employees. In special cases, these time frames may be narrowed in the interest of the department. For example, when a major deficiency has been noted on an officer's evaluation sheet, a special evaluation should be made before the next scheduled appraisal deadline.

Responsibility for Evaluation. Personnel evaluation is one responsibility that cannot be delegated except in the most extraordinary instances. Some scholars have taken the opposite tack, asserting that appraisals must be taken out of the chain of command because the close working relationship between a supervisor and his or her subordinates may stand in the way of a rater's objectivity. Another consideration is that the bond of camaraderie can be shattered by formal assessments. This may be so, but there is no suitable option available in police operations, so the responsibility for evaluations will continue to rest in the hand of supervisors directly in the chain of command of those to be appraised.

Use of Results. There is a wide divergence of opinion on just how the results of an appraisal should be used. Evaluations can form a basis for (1) the development of an employee's full potential, (2) making salary decisions, (3) determining training needs, (4) invoking discipline, and (5) determining promotability. On this last point, there has been widespread criticism that most appraisal systems do not predict, with any degree of accuracy, the ability of officers to succeed at the next level or rank. An officer's evaluations may show how good an officer he or she is, but do not adequately gauge potential as a sergeant. To end this problem, the International Association of Chiefs of Police has recommended that regular performance evaluations should be completed to assess an officer's in-grade progress, while a special form, called the promotional potential rating, should be completed after a candidate passes a promotional examination. Although the idea appears sound, it may be too late to wait until an individual passes a promotional exam to implement it.

Forms Control. A command decision must be made regarding the items to be included on evaluation forms, the needed number of different types of forms, and their distribution. The first point will be taken care of when the system is installed. However, there is always the temptation to design one form for everyone on the agency and to personalize it by changing the color and the name at the top to fit individual needs cosmetically. Of course, this practice is faulty, for there are differing qualities needed to fulfill the varied positions in a department. This is not to say that every level of rank in an agency should have a unique evaluation form. But those sworn positions that differ dramatically from all others deserve a special report form.

It appears that major police departments should draft unique forms for (1) officers attending recruit school, (2) probationary employees, (3) permanent nonsupervisory personnel, and (4) supervisors and middle managers. The appropriate evaluation form for top managers is a letter or memorandum from the chief of police. The purpose of the probationary report is different from the rest and as such should have a strong negative orientation because the major concern is to identify those persons who are incapable of effective performance.

There should be at least four copies of each report form so that both the evaluator and his or her subordinate can receive a copy, one can be filed in the appropriate division, and the last can be transmitted to the subject officer's personnel folder. Regardless of the system used, there should be ample space for a comment, in the form of a brief essay, by the rater. It is wise to implement an appellate process that equates roughly to grievance machinery, although no allowance need be made for extradepartmental appeals.

Focus on Results, Not on Personal Traits. When objectives are not set and results not defined, means tend to become more important than ends, style replaces substance, and a preoccupation with procedure replaces the willingness to focus on performance as the basis of evaluation. Emphasis should be placed on job performance, not on personal characteristics.

Focus on Strengths, Not on Weaknesses. A 10 percent improvement in what an officer does best will provide a far bigger yield than will a 10 percent improvement in what an employee does worst. More important, it is far easier to achieve. It is best to build into the evaluation process an emphasis on what employees do right, not on what they do wrong.

Salary Administration

Salary administration is one of the most critical components in the personnel administration function. The ability of a police agency to compete with business and industry in attracting the most highly qualified personnel will be directly affected by the wages and other benefits offered. Thus, one finds that considerable administrative time and effort are expended in developing and updating pay plans and salary schedules to assure that the police agency is in a sound competitive position in the labor market.[85]

When a pay plan is being developed, it must be remembered that it must accomplish several objectives, namely (1) to pay salaries that are equitable in relation to the complexity and responsibility of the work performed and to maintain internal equity in the relation of pay and employees; (2) to maintain a competitive position in the employment market and thereby attract and retain competent employees; (3) to provide data needed in budgeting, payroll administration, and other phases of financial and personnel management; (4) to stimulate personnel management and reward high-level performance; and (5) to provide an orderly program of salary policy and control.

Closely related to the development of the pay plan is the need for accurate information on existing employee benefits and trends regarding new benefits. Employee benefits include all payments in cash or in kind in excess of the base rate for time worked. For purposes of impact analysis, employee benefits can be classified into four basic categories: (1) income supplement (tax break) benefits, including issuance of uniforms, clothing allowance, paid medical and life insurance; (2) income supplement (trade-offs) benefits, including overtime pay, stand-by pay, and shift pay differentials; (3) good life benefits, including paid vacations, holidays, and recreational facilities; and (4) protection benefits, including sick leave and other paid leave, retirement pensions, and workmen's compensation.

Recent trends show considerable interest in a shorter workweek, early retirements, more paid holidays, longer vacations, payment for unused sick leave, and broader paid medical coverage for dental and eye care. Collective bargaining and rising expectations of employees are likely to increase the demands for new and improved fringe benefits. Every effort should be made to use employee benefits as a tool for attracting and retaining the best employees. Cost information on employee benefits is needed, not only to plan and implement a total compensation program but also to permit thorough explanations to employees and the public. Some police departments have prepared an information sheet for their employees that outlines the various fringe benefits enjoyed by their employees. Along with the dollar value of these benefits, this type of information is useful because it assists both the interested applicant and the employee in assessing more accurately actual earnings resulting from employment with the agency.

Salary Schedule

No standard salary structure can be applied universally in police departments, simply because of the structural diversity and variations in classifications that exist among them. There are, however, some standards that experience suggests should be applied in designing the policy salary schedule. For example, there must be enough ranges to permit salary differentiation among all the job classes in the classification plan and room enough in the total span of salaries to provide for significant differences in salary between successive ranks. The generally accepted rule of thumb is that pay grades should be at least 5 percent apart. Thus, if a law enforcement agency chooses to have various grades of patrol officers, a 5 percent differentiation should exist in addition to longevity considerations. Differentials between major ranks (i.e., sergeant, lieutenant, captain, etc.) should be at least 10 percent and preferably 15 percent.[86]

A sample salary schedule is presented in Table 7-2. Notice that the range from minimum to maximum is broad enough to allow not only salary growth within a given pay range but also recognition through merit increases or pay-for-knowledge compensation systems (e.g., successful completion of a series of courses and designation as a Master Patrol Officer).

Assessment Centers

All organizations, whether public or private, share common personnel problems. The most significant of these involve the identification of talent, the development of human resources within the organization, and compliance with various legal requirements with regard to the selection and promotion of personnel. Many organizations have learned the hard way that effective performance at one level does not necessarily predict effective performance at a higher level.[87]

The task of selecting people for entry-level or promotional positions in law enforcement has produced various techniques over the years, few of which have been strong in their predictive aspects. The traditional methods of selection in police agencies are easy to attack for their inadequacies, but it is another matter to develop an economical, ethically sound selection system that can produce better results. One attempt at finding a more reliable way in which to predict future performance is through an assessment center.[88]

What Is an Assessment Center?

An assessment center is a method, not a place; it is a multiple assessment strategy. It involves multiple evaluation techniques, including various forms of job-related

TABLE 7-2 Sample Salary Schedule

RANK	STEP / GRADE	A	B	C	D	E	F	G	H	I	J	K	L	M	N	O	P	Q	R
	10	10.99	11.26	11.55	11.83	12.13	12.43	12.74	13.06	13.39	13.72	14.07	14.42	14.78	15.15	15.53	15.92	16.31	16.72
		1,904.76	1,952.38	2,001.19	2,051.22	2,102.50	2,155.06	2,208.94	2,264.16	2,320.77	2,378.79	2,438.26	2,499.21	2,561.69	2,625.74	2,691.38	2,758.66	2,827.63	2,898.32
		22,857.14	23,428.57	24,014.29	24,614.64	25,230.01	25,860.76	26,507.28	27,169.96	27,849.21	28,545.44	29,259.08	29,990.55	30,740.32	31,508.82	32,296.54	33,103.96	33,931.56	34,779.85
Police Officer	11	11.54	11.83	12.12	12.43	12.74	13.05	13.38	13.72	14.06	14.41	14.77	15.14	15.52	15.91	16.30	16.71	17.13	17.56
		2,000.00	2,050.00	2,101.25	2,153.78	2,207.63	2,262.82	2,319.39	2,377.37	2,436.81	2,497.73	2,560.17	2,624.17	2,689.78	2,757.02	2,825.95	2,896.60	2,969.01	3,043.24
		24,000.00	24,600.00	25,215.00	25,845.38	26,491.51	27,153.80	27,832.64	28,528.46	29,241.67	29,972.71	30,722.03	31,490.08	32,277.33	33,084.27	33,911.37	34,759.16	35,628.13	36,518.84
Corporal	12	12.12	12.42	12.73	13.05	13.37	13.71	14.05	14.40	14.76	15.13	15.51	15.90	16.29	16.70	17.12	17.55	17.99	18.43
		2,100.00	2,152.50	2,206.31	2,261.47	2,318.01	2,375.96	2,435.36	2,496.24	2,558.65	2,622.61	2,688.18	2,755.38	2,824.27	2,894.87	2,967.25	3,041.43	3,117.46	3,195.40
		25,200.00	25,830.00	26,475.75	27,137.64	27,816.08	28,511.49	29,224.27	29,954.88	30,703.75	31,471.35	32,258.13	33,064.58	33,891.20	34,738.48	35,606.94	36,497.11	37,409.54	38,344.78
Detective	13	12.72	13.04	13.37	13.70	14.04	14.39	14.75	15.12	15.50	15.89	16.28	16.69	17.11	17.54	17.97	18.42	18.88	19.36
		2,205.00	2,260.12	2,316.63	2,374.54	2,433.92	2,494.76	2,557.12	2,621.05	2,686.58	2,753.74	2,822.59	2,893.15	2,965.48	3,039.62	3,115.61	3,193.50	3,273.33	3,355.17
		26,460.00	27,121.50	27,799.54	28,494.53	29,206.89	29,937.06	30,685.49	31,452.63	32,238.94	33,044.91	33,871.04	34,717.81	35,585.76	36,475.40	37,387.29	38,321.97	39,280.02	40,262.02
	14	13.36	13.69	14.03	14.38	14.74	15.11	15.49	15.88	16.27	16.68	17.10	17.53	17.96	18.41	18.87	19.35	19.83	20.32
		2,315.25	2,373.13	2,432.46	2,493.27	2,555.60	2,619.49	2,684.98	2,752.10	2,820.91	2,891.43	2,963.72	3,037.81	3,113.75	3,191.60	3,271.39	3,353.17	3,437.00	3,522.93
		27,783.00	28,477.57	29,189.51	29,919.25	30,667.23	31,433.91	32,219.76	33,025.26	33,850.89	34,697.16	35,564.59	36,453.70	37,365.05	38,299.17	39,256.65	40,238.07	41,244.02	42,275.12
Sergeant	15	14.03	14.38	14.74	15.10	15.48	15.87	16.26	16.67	17.09	17.52	17.95	18.40	18.86	19.33	19.82	20.31	20.82	21.34
		2,431.01	2,491.79	2,554.08	2,617.93	2,683.38	2,750.47	2,819.23	2,889.71	2,961.95	3,036.00	3,111.90	3,189.70	3,269.44	3,351.18	3,434.96	3,520.83	3,608.85	3,699.07
		29,172.15	29,901.45	30,648.99	31,415.21	32,200.60	33,005.61	33,830.75	34,676.52	35,543.43	36,432.02	37,342.82	38,276.39	39,233.30	40,214.13	41,219.48	42,249.97	43,306.22	44,388.88
	16	14.73	15.09	15.47	15.86	16.26	16.66	17.08	17.50	17.94	18.39	18.85	19.32	19.81	20.30	20.81	21.33	21.86	22.41
		2,552.56	2,616.38	2,681.79	2,748.83	2,817.55	2,887.99	2,960.19	3,034.20	3,110.05	3,187.80	3,267.50	3,349.18	3,432.91	3,518.74	3,606.70	3,696.87	3,789.29	3,884.03
		30,630.76	31,396.53	32,181.44	32,985.98	33,810.62	34,655.89	35,522.29	36,410.35	37,320.60	38,253.62	39,209.96	40,190.21	41,194.96	42,224.84	43,280.46	44,362.47	45,471.53	46,608.32
Lieutenant	17	15.46	15.85	16.25	16.65	17.07	17.49	17.93	18.38	18.84	19.31	19.79	20.29	20.80	21.32	21.85	22.39	22.95	23.53
		2,680.19	2,747.20	2,815.88	2,886.27	2,958.43	3,032.39	3,108.20	3,185.91	3,265.55	3,347.19	3,430.87	3,516.64	3,604.56	3,694.67	3,787.04	3,881.72	3,978.76	4,078.23
		32,162.30	32,966.35	33,790.51	34,635.27	35,501.16	36,388.69	37,298.40	38,230.86	39,186.63	40,166.30	41,170.46	42,199.72	43,254.71	44,336.08	45,444.48	46,580.59	47,745.11	48,938.74
	18	16.24	16.64	17.06	17.48	17.92	18.37	18.83	19.30	19.78	20.28	20.78	21.30	21.84	22.38	22.94	23.51	24.10	24.70
		2,814.20	2,884.56	2,956.67	3,030.59	3,106.35	3,184.01	3,263.61	3,345.20	3,428.83	3,514.55	3,602.42	3,692.48	3,784.79	3,879.41	3,976.39	4,075.80	4,177.70	4,282.14
		33,770.41	34,614.67	35,480.04	36,367.04	37,276.21	38,208.12	39,163.32	40,142.41	41,145.97	42,174.61	43,228.98	44,309.70	45,417.45	46,552.88	47,716.71	48,909.62	50,132.36	51,385.67

Courtesy of Stephen E. Condrey, Carl Vinson Institute of Government, University of Georgia, Athens, 1992.

simulations, and may include interviews and psychological tests. Common job simulations include in-basket exercises, management tasks, group discussions, simulations of interviews with subordinates, fact-finding exercises, oral presentation exercises, and written communications exercises.[89]

The essentials of the assessment center method are described best in the definition presented in the standards and ethical statement endorsed by the Third International Congress on the Assessment Center Method held in Quebec, Canada, several years ago. The following is excerpted from this statement.

> To be considered as an assessment center, the following minimal requirements must be met:
>
> 1. Multiple assessment techniques must be used. At least one of these techniques must be a simulation. A simulation is an exercise or technique designed to elicit behaviors related to dimensions of performance on the job by requiring the participant to respond behaviorally to situational stimuli. Examples of simulations include group exercises, in-basket exercises and fact-finding exercises.
> 2. Multiple assessors must be used. These assessors must receive training prior to participating in a center.
> 3. Judgments resulting in an outcome (i.e. recommendation for promotion, specific training or development) must be based on pooling information from assessors and techniques.
> 4. An overall evaluation of behavior must be made by the assessors at a separate time from observation of behavior.
> 5. Simulation exercises are used. These exercises are developed to tap a variety of predetermined behaviors and have been pretested prior to use to insure that the techniques provide reliable objective and relevant behavioral information for the organization in question.
> 6. The dimensions, attributes, characteristics or qualities evaluated by the assessment center are determined by an analysis of relevant job behaviors.
> 7. The techniques used in the assessment center are designed to provide information which is used in evaluating the dimensions, attributes or qualities previously determined.[90]

In summary, an assessment center consists of a standardized evaluation of behavior based on multiple inputs. Multiple trained observers and techniques are used. Judgments about behavior are made, in part, from specially developed assessment simulations.

These judgments are pooled by the assessors at an evaluation meeting during which all relevant assessment data are reported and discussed, and the assessors agree on the evaluation of the dimensions and any overall evaluation that is made.

What Is Not an Assessment Center?

In an attempt to prevent misuse of the term *assessment center*, the Third International Congress on the Assessment Center Method identified activities that do not constitute the process:

1. Panel interviews or a series of sequential interviews as the sole technique.
2. Reliance on a specific technique (regardless of whether or not this is simulation) as the sole basis of evaluation.

FIGURE 7-4. A candidate is filmed during an Assessment Center simulated press conference. [Photo courtesy of the Fairfax County, Virginia Police Department.]

3. Using only a test battery comprised of a number of pencil/paper measures, regardless of whether the judgments are made by a statistical or judgmental pooling of scores.
4. Single assessor or assessment.
5. The use of several simulations with more than one assessor when there is no pooling of data, i.e., each assessor prepares a report on performance in an exercise, and the individual reports (unintegrated) are used as the final product of the center.
6. A physical location labeled as an "assessment center" which does not conform to the requirements above.[91]

Historical Development of Assessment Centers

The first modern-day experiments with assessment centers were conducted by the Germans in World War I. Their objective was to select persons suited for intelligence assignments that required certain unique characteristics.[92] Simulation exercises were reactivawted in World War II by German and British military psychologists to aid in the selection of military officers. In the United States, the Office of Strategic Services (OSS) used similar procedures for selecting intelligence agents. Candidates taking part in the OSS testing program participated in a wide range of paper-and-pencil tests, interviews, and simulations over a period of several days. The simulations were intended to reflect aspects of field intelligence work under wartime conditions, and some were, therefore, designed to be highly stressful.[93]

In the private sector, assessment centers have been employed since 1956, when they were introduced by the American Telephone & Telegraph Company. To date, over 100,000 people have been assessed by Bell companies alone. The use of such centers has grown particularly over the past six to eight years, and it is estimated that there are presently over 300 assessment centers in operation in private business, including those of Standard Oil of Ohio; International Business Machines; General Electric; and Sears, Roebuck.[94] More recently, as their value has become clear, assessment centers have been modified for use in the public sector by such organizations as the Internal Revenue Service, the Social Security Administration, and the U.S. Army. Adapted to a wide variety of settings and organizations, these centers in both public and private agencies have been employed for the assessment of first-line supervisors as well as middle- and upper-level management positions and for identification of career development and training needs.[95]

Development of Simulation Exercises

The first step in developing the simulation exercises used in an assessment center is to identify the behaviors that are important to successful job performance. For example, if the assessment center is being conducted to identify those who are qualified to advance from the rank of lieutenant to captain, then it is necessary to determine which behaviors (skills) are required to perform a captain's duties properly. Ideally, these skills would be identified as the result of a carefully conducted job analysis. Because of the technical skill, cost, and time required to perform a job analysis, many departments substitute a less rigorous job analysis consisting of a few interviews with job incumbents or a senior police commander's list of requisite skills. Care should be taken, however, with such substitutes, because an improperly conducted or inadequate job analysis leaves a testing process open to possible legal challenge on the basis that it lacks validity.

Continuing with the example of a captain's assessment center, the skills identified as essential for effectiveness are termed *dimensions*. Illustrations of dimensions include

1. Decisiveness
2. Judgment
3. Oral communication
4. Stress tolerance
5. Written communication
6. Planning
7. Flexibility.

Once the dimensions are identified, simulation exercises that provide a context in which to evaluate the candidates' skill degrees must be developed. The common denominator in all exercises is that candidates competing for promotion assume the role that they would actually have to perform if selected for advancement. Among the most common types of exercises are

1. The in-basket, in which candidates assume the role of a newly promoted captain who comes to the office and finds an accumulation of paperwork that must be dealt with.

Included in the accumulated material may be such things as new regulations, requests for transfers, complaints against officers, letters from citizens, reports on shooting incidents, requests from officers to attend special training schools or to have special days off, notification from the training bureau that certain officers must be at the pistol range on particular days for their annual qualification firing, and other similar types of information. The length of time for in-basket exercises varies from 90 minutes to as much as four hours.

2. A leaderless group discussion (LGD), in which captain candidates are told that as recent promotees to the rank of captain, they have been appointed by the chief to a committee to study a particular problem in their department and they should come up with specific recommendations to solve it. Among the problems often given in this exercise are how to improve community relations, how to defend the department's budget against proposed reductions, and how to cut down on the number of on-duty traffic accidents by officers. Ideally, there are four to five candidates in an LGD exercise, which may last from 45 to 90 minutes. Since 1985, a number of large corporations have stopped using LGDs because they do not resemble actual work situations: someone is always in charge. Some consultants have followed this practice. Despite these developments, many police departments continue to use LGDs, a matter they would probably be wise to reevaluate.
3. An oral presentation, in which the candidates play the role of a departmental representative giving a speech on a topic of their own choice to a civic club or giving out information at a press conference as their department's sole representative. In these exercises or variants of them, the candidates typically have a short time to prepare the speech or to study information given to them about the upcoming press conference. Not including the approximately 30 minutes allowed for preparation, each candidate then presents information for 10 to 30 minutes.
4. The written problem analysis, in which candidates are asked to analyze a problem in their department and to send a memo to the chief containing their rationale, alternatives considered, and recommended course of action. The problem may be an actual one in their agency or one that is specially written for the exercise. Depending on how complex the problem is, this exercise may last from 45 minutes to two hours.
5. An individual role play, in which the candidate first studies specially prepared materials on some departmental operation, issue, or problem and then meets with someone—or several people at the same time—for the purpose of eliciting information and making decisions. The preparation time given to candidates runs from 20 to 45 minutes and the meetings from 15 minutes to as much as an hour, although 20 minutes is more typical.

Even when candidates have been given a detailed orientation to the assessment center process, they often become confused, thinking that they are being evaluated on the basis of a particular exercise. Moreover, they may become very upset if they think they "blew" an exercise. However, as depicted in Table 7-3, candidates are being assessed on the basis of their cumulative performances on each dimension. Thus, candidates' final standings are not based solely on how they did on the in-basket or any other single exercise, but rather on how well they performed on each dimension as it was repeatedly assessed over a number of exercises. Some candidates, thinking that they have failed an exercise, lose their confidence and fail to do well in those remaining. Their failure to manage themselves is regrettable from two perspectives: (1) whatever troubled them about their performance on an exercise might not have been a dimension that was assessed on that exercise, and (2) even if it had been assessed, they might have done so well in other exercises on that dimension that they were still competitive.

TABLE 7-3 Illustration of a Dimension-Exercise Matrix

Dimension	In-basket	Leaderless group discussion	Oral presentation	Written problem analysis	Individual role play
		Exercises			
1. Decisiveness	X	X	X	X	X
2. Judgment	X	X	X	X	X
3. Written communication	X	0	0	X	0
4. Oral communication	0	X	X	0	X
5. Planning	X	0	X	X	X

X = assessed

0 = not assessed

It is part of the assessment center process for candidates to experience and manage their own feelings. However, candidates occasionally get very angry with assessment center directors who do not comfort or encourage them.

Advantages of the Assessment Center

The assessment center technique offers a number of advantages over written tests and other management identification techniques. A number of important managerial abilities, such as planning and organizing, establishing priorities, leadership, relevant analytical skill, sensitivity to the needs of subordinates, management control, stress tolerance, and communications effectiveness, are very difficult to measure adequately with the use of written tests alone. Also, because of the job relevance and the involved procedures, assessment center results are generally readily accepted by individuals who object to traditional testing procedures. Some of the more significant advantages to the assessment center method are:[96]

1. The exercises are simulations of on-the-job behaviors.
2. A large amount of information is generated by each participant in a relatively short time.
3. A variety of methods is used.
4. The exercises are constant for all participants.
5. There is a consensus of judgment among the assessors for each participant.
6. The observers typically have no personal involvement with the participants.
7. The observers are well trained in evaluation procedures.
8. The observers are able to devote full attention to the task of assessing.
9. Information obtained can be used effectively to develop personnel. Individuals are provided with specific behaviorally referenced indicators of strengths and weaknesses, and developmental programs can be planned to strengthen weaknesses so that an individual may be promotable in the future.
10. Assessors receive valuable training in behavioral observation techniques, and this training carries over to their regular job performance.

Assessors

The role of the assessor is not to make promotion decisions. The assessors are to analyze behavior, make judgments about behavior, organize the information in a report, and make the report available to the individual making the promotion decision.[97]

As typically found in business organizations, assessors are managers who are one and sometimes preferably two levels higher than the position for which people are applying. This is based on the assumption that prior experience in the job facilitates judgment of the candidate's aptitude for the position and is far enough away from the candidate to be assessed to ensure greater objectivity than their immediate supervisors might exercise. Also not to be overlooked is the credibility of the assessment center concept when upper-level officers are involved.[98] Depending on the number of candidates to be assessed and the time allotted for assessment, anywhere from three to six assessors may be needed.

Because the assessors may not be thoroughly familiar with the mechanics of operating the center and the instruments, a prime concern is training each assessor in the skills of being a keen observer of human behavior. A natural starting point in training is for prospective assessors to participate in the exercise themselves so they may experience the behavior they will be observing. Training in interviewing, observation of specific behavior, and precise analysis are also very important. Such training will very likely have to be provided by a professional who has extensive experience in this area of management. However, a large number of assessors may be trained at one time and the expense spread over considerable time as the assessors are used over the years whenever assessment centers are convened.[99, 100]

Cost and Validity

In principle, assessment center methodology has merit, although the practical question of its cost makes it appear less attractive. Comparisons of "per candidate" costs in industry are not very instructive because, for example, companies treat assessors' costs differently. Two general observations are that assessment centers for police usually cost more than conventional testing procedures, and, beyond the conventional wisdom that "one gets what one pays for," it is difficult to show the cost benefits.[101] Yet there are two things to keep in mind concerning the cost of assessment centers. First, the center generates valuable information on which promotion decisions will be made.[102] Second, and just as important, the real costs in promotion decisions (and entry selection decisions, too) are not the direct cost of the instruments and the salaries of the personnel participating in the process but, rather, the costs to the organization of decision to promote individuals and elevate individuals to positions in which they do not perform well. These hidden and indirect costs can be staggering over a prolonged period of time. Put very simply, good police supervisors make fewer mistakes. Money spent in selecting those who have the capacity to become effective supervisors pays off in superior organization performance.[103]

Civil service agencies know of assessment center validity research, and they usually find that the procedure is objective, especially when written examinations are included as part of the center.[104]

In analysis of over a dozen studies concerning the validity of assessment centers, Byham concludes

> This research and most other research indicate that assessment centers are better at predicting ratings of management potential and actual advancement than performance at first level. This is probably covered by the increasing importance of the management components of jobs as individuals rise in an organization. It is the management component that is most commonly and accurately measured in an assessment center.[105]

Recovering the Cost of Training Police Officers

Cities and counties often encounter the problem of providing new officers with recruit training only to watch them later depart for other opportunities, often with larger police or sheriff's departments. The original police employer suffers the loss of a trained employee in addition to the cost of training someone to take his or her place. These repetitive costs add up to substantial losses.

One response by smaller local agencies has been to hire only officers who are already trained. Although in many instances this practice works well, it contains a substantial risk in that some of these officers have questionable incidents in their backgrounds, incidents that may be overlooked in the interest of economy. Also overlooked by some jurisdictions is the increased liability risk: one police department of eight "recycled officers" had committed so many acts for which the city had been successfully sued that the insurer told the city it was withdrawing all insurance coverage.

A growing number of jurisdictions have reduced repetitive costs through the use of training contracts, which may be used for both entry-level and specialized or advanced courses. The total cost of providing the training, including an officer's compensation and the course tuition, is calculated. These costs are identified in a contract between the jurisdiction and the officer, in which as a condition of attending the course, the officer agrees that if he or she voluntarily leaves before a specified term, he or she will repay a corresponding amount. In the case of entry-level training, the police or sheriff's department contract may require the officer to repay one twenty-fourth of the training cost for each month absent from a 24-month base period. For example, an officer under this arrangement who left after 12 months would have to repay 50 percent of the cost of the initial training. If the base period for repayment was 36 months and the officer left after 12 months, then 12/36ths of the agreed-upon period of service would have been completed and the officer would owe 66 percent of the training cost to the initial employer. A Georgia court held that such contracts are valid and enforceable (see Box 7-7 on next page).

Employing Civilians in Police Work

Civilians are being employed by police departments in significant numbers in an increasing variety of activities. Moreover, the trend toward greater and more varied use of civilians is likely to continue. It appears that there are four major motivating factors leading to this greater use of civilian personnel: (1) the need to control costs yet improve service to citizens; (2) the appropriateness of using civilians for both

BOX 7-7

Court Orders Police Officer to Reimburse Department for Training Costs

On February 23, 1990, the Georgia Court of Appeals ruled on the case of *City of Pembroke v. Alfonso Hagin.* Factually, Mr. Hagin was hired by the City of Pembroke as a police officer and was directed to sign an agreement wherein the City agreed to pay the costs of training on the condition that the officer remain employed by the City for a period not less than twelve months after graduation from the program. By signing the agreement, the officer promised to repay the City the sum of $1,800 representing a portion of the total expenses of attending the training program in the event he voluntarily terminated his employment before the twelve-month period expired. Officer Hagin resigned before the twelve-month period expired and accepted employment with another law enforcement agency. The City sued to recover the $1,800.

The Court of Appeals concluded that this agreement was legal and binding upon Mr. Hagin and, thus, required him to repay the $1,800 to the City of Pembroke. The court concluded that the agreement was reasonably related to the City's interest in protecting its investment in training a new officer.

This case is important since numerous law enforcement agencies have voiced concern about paying for the training of officers and then, once the officers are trained, they are lured into a different, higher paying job.

Source: Mission, March–April–May 1990, p. 5.

low-skilled "routine" tasks and specialized functions such as budget, personnel, and computer system analysis; (3) federal and state encouragement of the use of civilians; and (4) specific programs aimed at increasing the use of civilians.[106]

Cost pressures can be traced back to the urban population boom after World War II. Although the rapidly growing cities needed more services, particularly in law enforcement, a growth in police personnel was often deterred by tight city budgets and job competition from the private sector. In many departments, non-sworn personnel began to replace sworn officers in specialized jobs, and the trend has continued at a steady pace ever since.[107] The use of civilians has also been encouraged by leaders in law enforcement as well as from national commissions studying the practices of American law enforcement agencies. The most recent commission report recommended that

> Every police agency should assign civilian personnel to positions that do not require the exercise of police authority or the application of the special knowledge, skills, and aptitudes of the professional police officer.[108]

The Urban Institute conducted a survey of 13 police departments in an effort to determine what types of functions were being performed by civilians and what types of overall benefits and problems have resulted from the process. Table 7-4 identifies the tasks being performed by civilians within these 13 agencies. The findings of this study are as follows.

1. Officers are relieved of such routine tasks as fingerprinting, dispatching cars, and handling prisoners.
2. Costs are reduced.

TABLE 7-4 Tasks Performed by Civilians

Identification	Detention
Fingerprint Technician:	Receives inmates and others awaiting trial
Takes fingerprints	Transports inmates
Lifts latent prints	Searches, fingerprints, and photographs inmates
Classifies, searches, verifies prints	Responsibility for well-being of inmates:
Communicates with other agencies	Allowing telephone calls
Operates microfilm reader	Health
Performs clerical function of above actions	Property safekeeping
Photography Technician:	Feeding
Takes photographs	Rehabilitation
Gathers physical evidence at crime scene	Educational programs
Performs field identification of disaster victims	Recretational programs
Makes plaster and rubber casts	Screens visitors
Processes film	Security check of facilities
Prepares slides	Provides court security
Prepares pictorial evidence	Enforces discipline from inmates
Takes motion pictures	Processes release
Operates video equipment	Operates computer
Operates drying, enlarging, and copying equipment	Checks Identification Department
Mixes chemicals	Analyzes Intoxometer
Stores and safeguards developing equipment	Serves as witness in court
Minor camera repair	Investigates in facility:
Instructs officers in use of equipment	Accidents
Other:	Deaths
Operates mobile crime investigations	Contraband evidence
Uses Intoxometer for breath tests	Irregular incidences
Receives, catalogs, and preserves property	Preserves evidence
Prepares property for disposition	Plans, coordinates, supervises work assignments of inmates
Operates teletype	Trains and instructs other correctional officers
Packages and mails evidence	Prepares records and reports
Gathers physical evidence of persons	Recommends new and revised policies and procedures
Prepares courtroom evidence	Communications
Testifies in court	Receives and/or transmits information
Develops and maintains training program	Gives general information to citizens
	Maintains location of all police units
	Determines if situation requires police action
	Notifies other emergency units
	Operates switchboard
	Monitors interdepartmental radio
	Performs clerical functions of above actions
	Trains new communications personnel

From A. J. Schwartz et al., *Employing Civilians for Police Work,* Washington, D.C.: U.S. Government Printing Office, July 1975, pp. 1–5.

3. More uniformed personnel are available for more active law enforcement duties.
4. Service to the community is improved.

These findings are corroborated by the fact that almost half the 13 departments have used civilians in communications, identification, or detention work for three to 12 years—and even longer in another fourth of those departments. Further, all 13 cities intend to continue employing civilians. Police managers held very positive views toward civilians. They felt that the civilians were well qualified, exercised initiative, and helped to improve civilian–officer relations in general.

Most problems described by police managers were related to management issues, particularly civilians' low pay, lack of knowledge of police work, and inadequate training. The managers also expressed some concern about civilian tardiness, lack of dedication, excessive use of sick leave, and personality conflicts.

Officers in charge of civilians also expressed a very high opinion of the job performance of civilians. The 33 officers polled said that 75 percent of the tasks performed were very well done, 22 percent were fairly well done, and 3 percent were not so well done.

Seventy-two percent of those officers reported further that the civilians' work was very beneficial to the department, and 28 percent felt that their work was of some benefit; none reported very little or no benefit. Eighty-five percent felt more civilians should be hired. They thought civilians were most helpful by relieving officers for more critical duties; by assisting officers in various ways, including writing reports, fingerprinting, and handling prisoners; by providing information for action by the officers, and in communicating with the public.

One third of the officers in charge said that civilians had not caused problems for officers; but of those who acknowledged problems, 71 percent were attributed to deficiencies in management practices, 19 percent to personality conflicts, and 10 percent to a lack of dedication on the part of the civilians.

Officers suggested that civilians might be more helpful if departmental management practices were improved by providing additional training, permitting them greater responsibility and reducing their workload.

Police Service Officer

The Santa Ana, California, Police Department has taken the civilianization process even further by creating the position of police service officer (PSO). For years, the Santa Ana Police Department had used nonsworn personnel to supplement enforcement officers. The scope of their duties, however, was limited and traditionally restricted to parking control and desk assignments. A management decision was made to create the PSO position, which greatly expanded the duties of nonsworn personnel to encompass virtually every aspect of police service except those specifically restricted to sworn officers due to job hazards and required job skills. The rationale for this decision was that a large percentage of police calls were service oriented rather than enforcement related and that many of the services being provided by sworn police officers could be handled by nonsworn PSOs. Box 7-8 details the tasks presently being performed by the PSOs of the Santa Ana Police Department.

Cost Consideration

In transferring jobs from officers to civilians, a common goal is to reduce costs. Nineteen percent of the police managers interviewed listed cost saving as an objective, and 58 percent identified it as a realized benefit. Similar views were expressed by officers in charge of civilians and by the civilians themselves. Based on cost data and estimates provided by departments, there have been significant savings. But these savings often are offset partially by less obvious costs.

BOX 7-8

Police Service Officer Assignments

Front Desk

- Answer incoming calls regarding information and police matters.
- Assist citizens who come to the front desk.
- Take reports over the phone or in person on petty thefts, grand thefts, vehicle burglaries, habitual runaways, annoying or obscene calls; information reports on malicious mischief, lost property, patrol checks, supplemental reports.
- Female PSO's assist police officers in pat-down searches of female prisoners.
- Sign off traffic citations.

Community Oriented Policing (C.O.P.) Program

- Scheduling and handling C.O.P. meetings.
- Organize and distribute C.O.P. bulletins, Crime Warning Bulletins, Crime Alert Bulletins and Area Crime Resume.
- Maintain Area crime statistics.
- Coordinate residential burglary seminars and home security inspections with the Community Service Officers.
- Assist other police agencies in setting up a community watch program in their city.
- Recruit and train block captains.
- Maintain an updated block captains' information list.
- Maintain an on-going relationship with block captains and community watch members.
- Serve as an advisor to the area executive board and city-wide executive board.
- Assist in organizing special citywide C.O.P. events such as C.O.P. Track Meet, Golf Tournament, Block Captains' Picnic, etc.

Patrol

- Mark abandoned vehicles and store them.
- Handle all types of crime reports which are not in progress.
- Handle minor non-emergency calls to assist citizens.
- Handle recontacts on crime reports to obtain further information.
- Accident reports—injury and non-injury.
- Crime Scene Investigation.

Civilian Accident Investigator

- Traffic accidents—injury and non-injury; if the C.A.I. is the closest to an injury accident or a no-detail accident, they respond Code 3.
- Render first aid, give mouth to mouth resuscitation and/or CPR when necessary.
- If it is a hit and run accident, perform CSI (Crime Scene Investigation) and follow up on leads in an attempt to locate the suspect.
- Lay flare patterns and do traffic control when needed.

BOX 7-8 (cont.)

Community Police Offices

- Answer telephones and handle citizen inquiries.
- Take reports over the phone or in person on petty thefts, grand thefts, vehicle burglaries, habitual runaways, annoying or obscene phone calls; information reports on malicious mischief, lost property patrol checks and supplementals.
- Sign off citations for non-moving violations.
- Maintain list of referral numbers for citizens who come in or call for such assistance.
- Keep a monthly pin map showing problem areas, specifying burglaries of residential, commercial or vehicles; also armed robberies are pinned.

Career Criminal Apprehension Program (C-CAP)

- Analyst/Trainee (Crime Analysis)
- Processing and submitting criminal information and data for computer entry.
- Daily compilation and dissemination of "Daily Investigative Supplemental," consisting of outstanding warrants, stolen vehicles, wanted persons, field interviews and photo requests to patrol and areas of the department.
- Monitoring outstanding warrant/stolen vehicle log.
- Daily pin-mapping of residential burglary cases, by area and team grids.

Juvenile Investigation

- Log all bike thefts and all impounds (recoveries and founds) in logs and compare both logs for possible matching.
- This PSO is assigned all bicycle theft reports.
- Processes Child Abuse Registry reports as a resource to the investigators and assigns case numbers to them.

General Investigation—Theft/Pawn Detail

- Handles petty theft reports of gasoline and some shoplift cases from department stores.
- Assists outside agencies and citizens making pawn inquiries.
- Files and reviews all reported pawn slips for completeness and for known sellers of stolen property.
- Checks on traceable (serialized) pawns and office equipment repair records.
- Notifies other agencies when stolen property has been located.
- At least once a week, walks through in uniform all pawn shops and secondhand businesses.
- Investigates all applications filed for Second-hand Business Licenses and Security Guard Licenses.

General Investigation—Crimes Against the Elderly Detail

- The PSO assigned to this detail is responsible for crime prevention programs for seniors; which includes scheduling and presenting meetings and seminars on a variety of crime prevention subjects.

- Assists in follow-up of certain cases, including victim assistance and referral.
- Prepares and distributes Crime Warning Bulletins for seniors.
- Maintains crime statistics.

General Investigation—Crimes Against Persons Detail

- Responsible for investigation of lewd and annoying phone calls, indecent exposures and misdemeanor assaults.
- Maintains mug files.
- Responsible for the placement and maintenance of VARDA (robbery and burglary) alarms.

Special Investigation—Vice Detail

- Handles and/or coordinates investigations regarding the issuance of permits and licenses by the Chief of Police and the City Manager. (These include dance permits, bingo, massage, escort services, modeling, and ABC licenses.)
- Performs premise inspections with regard to these licenses and permits.
- Maintains liaison with other city departments to insure proper and timely reports and inspections as needed.
- Responsible for all record keeping and correspondence related to these licenses and permits, as well as liaison with the City Council.
- Under direction of supervisor, performs background investigations as related to municipal code and vice enforcement.
- Assists as needed with vice investigations.

Court Liaison

- Prepares and packages DUI cases involving injury or accident for review by the D.A.
- Files these cases with the Central Court.
- Types complaints for DUI's with no accident or injury involved, approves the complaints and files them.
- Prepares and packages warrant cases for D.A. review and files them in Central Court.
- Walks through warrants on misdemeanor cases.
- In absence of sworn court liaison officer, the PSO assigned to this position prepares and packages all in-custody cases.

Media Relations

- With department's sworn public information officer (lieutenant), this PSO serves as liaison between news media and the police department.
- Responsible for publicity of departmental programs and events.
- Assists in organizing special events.
- Maintains records of media coverage.
- Responsible for preparation of some departmental brochures and other publications.

Community Crime Resistance

- Provides training workshops to block captains.

BOX 7-8 (cont.)

- Responsible for preparation and layout of a bi-monthly departmental publication and assisting with a publication of the C.O.P. Block Captains' Association.
- Serves as liaison between the police department and the C.O.P. Block Captains' Association.

Reserves' Office

- Recruitment of Reserve applicants.
- Assists with all phases of screening/selection process.
- Conducts and/or coordinates all background investigations on potential Reserve Officers.
- Maintains statistical data and confidential personnel files for Reserves.
- Arranges for monthly training and updates on laws and pertinent information for Reserves.
- Ensures P.O.S.T. requirements are continually met as changes occur.
- Once a Reserve is appointed, assigns to an area in keeping with the Team Policing concept. Assists with "call-ups" in emergency/disaster situations and coordinates assignments of Reserves where and as needed on a special basis.
- Serves as liaison between Reserve Officers and other departmental sections/personnel.
- Responsible for monthly communication with all Orange County Reserve Coordinators for updates, etc.
- Coordinates recruitment, screening and placement of Civilian Volunteers, who perform a wide variety of services for the department, based on their expertise, experience and technical skills.

Traffic Safety Officer

- The PSO assigned to this position is responsible for the total administration of the adult crossing guard program, which includes the hiring of adult crossing guards, training, supervision, liaison between schools, children and the guards, and scheduling. This PSO is also responsible for ordering and maintaining supplies and working out specific traffic problems which affect locations manned by adult crossing guards.
- This PSO is also responsible for the School Safety Patrol, which includes liaison with schools, ordering and maintaining supplies and coordinating field trips.
- Bicycle safety programs are a responsibility of this position. This includes presenting films and lectures, ordering and distributing literature, providing obstacle courses for coordination of bicycle rider, bicycle licensing, and inspection of bicycles for defects.
- Presents films, lectures and literatures on pedestrian safety.
- Responsible for mechanical inspection of each tow truck, catering truck, ice cream truck, taxi and produce truck, then attaches city sticker.
- Performs background research for tow truck and taxi company permits.
- Writes citations for Santa Ana Municipal Code vehicle violations and California Vehicle Code parking violations.

Source: Santa Ana, CA Police Dept.

There are large local variations. For the 13 cities as a whole, the average civilian salaries ranged from 22 to 25 percent less than that of patrol officers. But within the cities, civilian salaries ranged from 10 to 34 percent less than patrol officer salaries. Savings in overhead costs—generally meaning fringe benefits—also seem to be substantial in some cities but negligible or nonexistent in others.

Although variations in employee benefits and in budgeting and accounting procedures make detailed comparisons difficult, police managers have provided estimates of overhead costs for officers and civilians. In general, differences have diminished during the last ten years as cities, and particularly the larger departments, have begun providing similar benefits for police and civilian employees. Even so, overhead costs were estimated at 15 percent of salary for civilians and at 25 percent for officers—a difference of about 10 percent of salary. Thus the total savings—considering salaries plus benefits—from hiring civilians would be 29 percent rather than 23 percent when only salaries are considered.

Complaints of any kind from officers about civilians were few and minor as compared with the reported benefits. These evident savings are, however, partially offset by less evident costs. Police managers have generally ignored or de-emphasized these hidden costs. It has been the officers in charge and their civilian employees who have stressed the intangibles. Although none considered the problems serious enough to outweigh the benefits, the problems do have cost ramifications.

When basic needs—such as competitive salaries, adequate supervision, and training—are not met, long-term costs result. These include

1. Lack of job knowledge (a major problem identified by managers, officers, and civilians)
2. Officer anxieties about the reliability of civilians and the degree to which officers can depend on them in emergencies
3. Higher civilian attrition rates (causing start-up costs to be repeated more often in jobs filled by civilians than in those filled by sworn officers)
4. Costs of job supervision
5. Abuse of sick leave, tardiness, or other costs attributable to undesirable practices
6. Officer concern that the use of civilians threatens job security, particularly when they fill jobs traditionally available to officers for light duty in case of physical disability.

In weighing the cost advantages of using civilians, these negative factors should be considered. Although the actual dollar cost of these intangibles is difficult to assess, individual departments should be able to estimate such costs based on past experience with civilian personnel and refine this estimate after gaining more experience.

Alternative Career Tracks

The financial rewards and professional status in most police departments are directed toward those individuals who become managers. The individual who has served as a patrol officer for twenty years and has retired, regardless of accomplishments, is frequently considered by peers to have been "not very successful." However, by the very pyramiding nature of the existing organization structures of most police departments, 85 to 90 percent of all police officers will never rise above rank of patrol officer, and it is not in the best interest of any organization to have a reward system that raises the expection of so many to an unrealistic level.

One can find among the ranks of any police department many individuals who have neither the interest nor the aptitude to become managers, yet these same individuals feel compelled to pursue managerial positions because it provides the only major organizational alternative to achieving some degree of professional stature and monetary reward.

It is apparent that some new organizational models must be considered that can provide realistic and cost-effective alternatives. Among the alternatives is a dual career track system which allows police officers to follow either the nonmanagerial professional police officer track or the professional police management track.

Such a system would greatly reduce the difficulties associated with the single track system because it would provide a realistic and viable alternative. Within the framework of such a model, the individual could remain with the patrol ranks in a nonmanagerial capacity yet still enjoy some of the professional and monetary rewards offered by the organization.

There is clearly no single best model to accomplish this objective and if a decision is made to develop an alternative career track, its final bureaucratic configuration will be affected by the size of the agency, philosophy of top management, and most certainly budgetary considerations.

In an effort to provide the reader with a broad-brush picture of some of the alternative plans, we have examined three agencies which have alternative career tracks. Namely, the Palatine Police Department, Palatine, Illinois; Palm Beach County Sheriff's Office, Palm Beach, Florida; and Altamonte Springs Police Department, Altamonte Springs, Florida.[110]

Palatine Police Department

The Palatine Police Department implemented its "Dual Career Ladder Program" in 1981.[111] In order to be eligible to apply for advancement in the program, an officer had to have at least six years of service at the patrol officer level. A Dual Career Ladder Review Board was organized to assess the applicant's credentials for making recommendations to the chief of police regarding the applicant's suitability for advanced positions in the dual career ladder. It was determined that the review board would only serve in an advisory capacity to the chief, who would make the final selection of applicants. The Dual Career Ladder Review Board consisted of a representative from each of the ranks in the police department with appointments to the board being made by the chief. The selection process involves a comprehensive assessment of the officer's credentials with particular emphasis given to job performance and demonstrated proficiency in job-related knowledge and skills areas. A comprehensive examination is administered to dual career applicants to determine whether they can demonstrate basic proficiencies in those knowledge and skill areas that are considered fundamental for officers within the agency.

The profile of fundamental knowledge and skill areas developed by the Dual Ladder Task Force Advisory Committee for the basic police officer's knowledge and skill assessment included the following: criminal law/constitutional law; firearms proficiency/use of force; physical fitness proficiency; arrest, search and seizures; patrol procedures; investigative procedures; report writing; juvenile law and procedures; crime prevention; accident investigation; evidence processing; court testimony/case preparation; DUI processing; prisoner processing; specialized equipment operations; local ordinances; emergency medical treatment; drugs and controlled substances; defensive driving; traffic enforcement; interviewing and interrogation; crisis intervention; civil and criminal liability; situations/incident perception and judgment; department rules and regulations/policies and procedures.

Advanced Police Officer Knowledge and Skill Assessment. Just as there are knowledge and skill areas that are fundamental to every police officer, there are also knowledge and skill areas that require advanced training, study, and experience in order to utilize effectively the knowledge or skill in job-related situations. These advanced areas involve specialties which the department must depend on periodically. The department philosophy is that a police officer is a generalist who is also expected to function effectively when called on to perform in these specialized areas. The Dual Career Ladder program involved a formal attempt to encourage and reward officers who had developed specializations. The purpose of the advanced police officer knowledge and skill assessment was to certify that the officer possesses a working competency in these speciality areas.

The following list represents the skill areas that would be taken into consideration: firearms instructor; technical accident investigation; selected traffic enforcement; field training officer; overweight vehicle enforcement; drugs and controlled substance identification and case investigation; interviewing and interrogation; special weapons attack/hostage negotiations; foreign language fluency; advanced DUI processing; defense tactics; officer friendly/bike safety; juvenile law enforcement procedures; crime prevention; evidence technician; investigative procedures; certified police instructor.

In order to progress along the advanced positions of the Dual Career Ladder program, the officers were required to demonstrate a working competency in the advanced areas as specified below.

Advanced Officer—Two Advanced Areas

Police I—Four Advanced Areas

Police II—Six Advanced Areas

Police III—Eight Advanced Areas

It was recommended that officers serve at least one year in each of the positions before being eligible for the next higher rank.

Educational Requirements

Advanced Officer—30 semester hours toward the attainment of a degree in an appropriate field of study.

Police Officer I—AA/AS/AAS in an appropriate field of study or 60 semester hours toward the attainment of a degree.

Police Officer II—90 semester hours toward the attainment of a bachelor's degree in an appropriate field of study.

Police Officer III—bachelor's degree (B.A. or B.S.) in an appropriate field of study.

Dual Career Ladder Bonus Pay. The bonus pay for advancement in each of these Dual Career Ladder positions is as follows.

Advanced Officer—$1,100
Police Officer I—$1,775
Police Officer II—$3,000
Police Officer III—$4,000

Dual Career Ladder Insignia. As a symbol of achievement, each DCL position has an attendant insignia to be worn by the officer.

Palm Beach County Sheriff's Office

Within this agency, the Dual Career Ladder program created four additional levels of Deputy Sheriffs based on individual qualifications which are achieved without regard to assignment.[112] The motivation in creating this program was to recognize and reward the deputies who had completed various training and college courses. It was also intended to promote long-term dedicated employees by offering career alternatives and guidelines.

Basic Selection Criteria. Sworn personnel of this agency are evaluated in four areas before they can be considered for participation in the Dual Career Ladder program. They are: time in grade; job skills; education; and performance evaluations.

Time in Grade—This qualification provides on-the-job experience in each professional level in the career path program. All time accrued as a certified deputy with the Palm Beach County Sheriff's Office is considered as time in grade, including broken time. Time with any other law enforcement agency is not considered as time in grade. Any candidate who meets the appropriate qualification may enter the career path program at any level.

Skills—This requires the successful completion of advanced law enforcement-related skills. Skills qualifications are earned beyond on-the-job experience. For example, each 80-hour block of career development courses completed is equal to one skill (two 40-hour blocks must be combined for one skill).

Job Assignment Skills—All specialized skills earned by virtue of assignment requiring the advanced training will count as one skill only. Such assignments include but are not limited to: traffic homicide investigator; crime scene investigator; reinforcement; and canine.

Certified Skills—Only valid state and/or Palm Beach County Sherrif Office certifications for the following skills will be considered: law enforcement-related instructor; field training officer; and licensed paramedic. Corrections deputies certified as firefighters may also count this as a skill. Crisis intervention may count as a skill if the deputy has attended certified training classes and regularly works with such facilities on a volunteer basis. A deputy who is proficient in a second foreign language may count this as one skill. Extra police skills such as membership in the emergency field force (EFF) or the special response team (SRT) count as one skill.

Education—A year of college or equivalent continuing education units is required for advancement to each successful level. Continuing education units (CEU) are those units issued for each 10-hour block of classroom instruction offered by an accredited college or university. CEUs are not equal to the same number of college hours or career development courses. Only classes certified as continuing education units count toward this requirement.

Performance Evaluations—The only requirement for this element is an overall above-average performance evaluation by the deputy's supervisor for the previous two years.

Summary of Criteria

Career Deputy I—Must be in grade for at least six years, have at least one year of college, or eight CEUs, and have an above-average performance evaluation.

Career Deputy II—Must have at least 10 years time in grade, two years of college or 16 CEUs, and have an above-average performance evaluation.

Career Deputy III—Must have at least 14 years time in grade, three years of college or 24 CEUs, and have a performance evaluation of above average.

Career Deputy IV—Must have at least 18 years of service in grade, four years of college or 32 CEUs, and have an above-average performance evaluation.

Salary Considerations—Each time a deputy moves up on grade he or she receives a 5 percent step increase in pay.

Altamonte Springs Police Department

This department has created three ranks above that of a basic patrol officer, namely: patrol officer second class; patrol officer first class; and master patrol officer.[113]

Qualifications for a patrol officer second class—Qualifications required to compete for this position are: a minimum of three years service as a full-time sworn officer with the department irrespective of unit assignment. For the preceding 12 months, the officer must have maintained an overall performance evaluation rating of "exceeds expectations" or better. No individual category of the performance evaluation may be rated "needs improvement" or "satisfactory." In the case of an officer who has been transferred within the above time frame, his or her evaluation qualification will be based on 12-month time frame prior to any transfer, and for the preceding 12 months, the officer may not have been awarded formal discipline.

Testing process for patrol officer second class—A written test covering selected statutes, city and departmental policies and regulations and governmental structure; and an in-basket exercise requiring demonstration of a required skill, common knowledge, and abilities appropriate to the position. Each component of the examination is administered separately, and a passing score of 75 percent must be achieved before continuing to the next component; an overall score of 75 percent is required to be considered for promotion.

Patrol Officer First Class—Qualifications for this position are: a minimum of three years in service as a patrol officer second class with the department irrespective of the assignment. Same performance evaluation criteria as for Patrol Officer Second Class.

Testing process for patrol officer first class—Except for a role playing exercise requiring demonstration of skills, knowledge, and abilities appropriate for this position, the testing procedure and performance evaluation expected are the same for this position as for the Patrol Officer Second Class.

The Master Patrol Officer—The qualifications for this position are: a minimum of three years of service as a patrol officer first class with the department irrespective of the unit assignment. The performance evaluation expectations are essentially the same for this rank as for others discussed thus far, except instead of using the preceding 12 months as a benchmark, they use 18 months. The testing model for this position is essentially the same as for Patrol Officer First Class.

Unlike the other agencies discussed thus far, this department imposes limitations on the number of personnel that can fill these positions. For example, for patrol officer second class, the number of authorized personnel can only be equal to one-half the number of sworn officers not assigned to the command track. The number of sworn officers is determined by the approved budget of the police department. For the position of patrol officer second class, the number of authorized positions is equal to one-half the number of patrol officers second class. The number of master patrol officers is equal to one-quarter the number of patrol officer first class positions.

It should be noted that patrol officers who choose to become involved in the Dual Career Ladder program for any of these agencies do not preclude themselves from applying for supervisory positions.

Retirement Counseling

Many police officers seem to experience considerable difficulty when they retire.[114] Consider the example that Joseph Wambaugh, in his book *The New Centurions*, relates: "It's your friend Andy Kilvinsky, Gus: your wife said that she was called tonight by a lawyer up in Oregon. Kilvinsky left you a few thousand dollars. He's dead, Gus. He shot himself."[115] This all too often is the result of retirement from police service. The stress of change becomes too much for the individual to cope with, and the path of least resistance is followed. There is stress connected with retirement. One study revealed that retirement is ranked tenth of 43 items in difficulty of adjustment (see Box 7-9).[116]

One police psychologist identified this problem by describing police officers as people who face stress as a group. "Similar to the military, police work is a way of life and retirement may present special problems. While many officers talk about putting in their 20 few make plans for that magic day."[117]

A unique problem associated with police officer retirements relates to the relatively young age at which police officers are eligible to retire. Many police pension plans provide for retirement after 20 to 25 years of service. Therefore, many police officers are between 43 and 48 years of age when they retire. This, for most American males, is the prime of their working lives. Very few people look forward to the prospect of starting a second career, and police officers are no exception. Very few can actually retire completely, in part because their pensions are inadequate to meet their financial obligations. Also, many are not psychologically prepared to sit around idly for the rest of their lives. Thus, many do continue working at some second career after retirement. Interestingly, even police departments that have comprehensive career development training programs never consider the need for retirement planning as a part of that program.

Program Development

The Kansas City, Missouri, police department developed a 20-hour preretirement planning lecture series for law enforcement personnel with 23 or more years of service and civilian personnel with 20 or more years of service.[118]

BOX 7-9

Retiring Law Officers Are Likely Candidates for Suicide, Experts Say

By Rosalva Hernandez *Tribune Staff Writer*

LARGO—Recently retired law enforcement officers, stripped of the only identity they have known for years, lose touch with friends and have few outside interests to occupy them, psychologists say.

"A police officer, particularly an administrator or sheriff's officer, their personal psychological identify is tied to their work and they become their work," said Dr. David Stenmark of the University of South Florida's psychology department, who has worked extensively with police agencies.

He also knew Warren K. McNeely. McNeely, a 23-year veteran of the Pinellas County Sheriff's Office, Friday shot and killed his ex-wife, Flora Jean; and daughter, Patricia Kay, before turning the weapon on himself—four months after handing in his sheriff's deputy badge.

McNeely, who earned $66,000 a year as a chief at the Sheriff's Office, was anxiously awaiting word from the Largo Police Department on whether he would get a $14,872 dispatcher's job.

McNeely's profile was an almost textbook example of a person likely to commit suicide, said Dr. Vincent Skotko, psychologist for the Pinellas County Sheriff's Office.

"You take someone who has risen to a high rank and commands over hundreds of people and has that power of office and then he's going to become a security officer at a warehouse?" Skotko asked. "There's just no comparison."

Skotko said the general profile of a suicide victim is a white male over age 40 who may have retired or lost a job, who uses alcohol, and who has access to firearms. What didn't fit in McNeely's case was shooting his family, he said.

Suicide is the 10th leading cause of death in the country, Skotko said. It is in seventh place in Florida and is the leading cause of death in the Tampa Bay area, based on its large elderly and retired population, Skotko said.

Skotko and Stenmark said there are no definitive statistics on police suicides, but they agreed the circumstances surrounding an officer's retirement can figure into a suicide. "Their personality and their lifestyle becomes their identity," Stenmark said. "And if your identity is your work and you no longer do that work, who are you? I know McNeely was very intimately identified with his work."

Stenmark said he had talked with McNeely last year about stress management and pre-employment psychological testing for his Sheriff's Office employees.

McNeely's death came almost exactly two years after the suicide of John F. "Jack" Brady, another top officer under former Sheriff Gerry Coleman.

Brady shot himself in the head in a St. Petersburg motel room April 21, 1987, as his Sheriff's Office overtime payments were being scrutinized by the federal Labor Department. In a suicide note, Brady blamed a constant neck pain from an old gunshot wound and his resulting dependence on painkillers.

Source: Tampa Tribune, April 15, 1989.

Offered on an off-duty status over eight successive Tuesdays, each two-and-one-half-hour evening lecture addressed a specific topic of importance to a potential retiree. Department representatives and outside personnel with expertise in the various areas of retirement planning were invited to lecture on preretirement options and alternatives. A retirement planning resource handbook was provided for each participant to supplement verbal presentations.

Because the transition from employment to retirement can have a major impact on family life, spouses of department members were encouraged to participate in the program. Scheduling the lecture series in the evening hours made it more convenient for working spouses to attend.

Vocational psychologists believe that it is vital for the officer's spouse to be involved in the preretirement plan.[119] This is especially true for police officers who retire at a young age. Both partners must be made to realize the importance for the officer to develop long-term plans rather than to begin planning for retirement a few months ahead of time. It is also important to prepare the spouse for some of the changes that will occur when the officer is no longer an officer.

To make certain that department members were aware of the newly developed preretirement lecture series, a department memorandum not only acknowledged the new employee benefit program but also assured those individuals who were targeted for the first presentation that they were not being singled out for retirement but rather were part of the initial group of department employees who would be invited to participate in the program.

Based on the experiences of other organizations that had developed preretirement programs, the promoters of the Kansas City program realized that getting a good turnout was essential in the implementation of an initial program. Because of many people's negative image of retirement, preretirement programs, in their early stages, often are not particularly popular or well attended. To combat this negative image and promote greater participation, preretirement orientation meetings were held to acquaint department personnel with the new program on a volunteer basis. The one-hour orientation meetings were scheduled on department time on all three shifts. The employee's commander/supervisor determined the best time for employee attendance based on division/unit workload. The orientation program included: a 16-mm 19-minute color documentary entitled "A Week Full of Saturdays," developed by Benefits Media, Inc., Rutherford, New Jersey. Rated excellent by numerous authorities in the retirement field, the documentary was used as a motivational opener to encourage personnel to participate in the lecture series. The documentary discusses such topics as financial planning, second careers, housing considerations, and retirement attitudes.

A 20-minute verbal presentation on the importance of preretirement planning was offered. Included in the presentation were demographic statistics on aging, the fears/myths of retirement, and the eight topic areas to be covered in the lecture series. This was followed by a 20-minute discussion period for questions and answers.

Following the distribution of the department memorandum and the scheduling of orientation meetings, an article announcing the lecture series was included in the "Police News" (the department in-house publication), and a personal invitation from the chief of police was mailed to individual homes encouraging all eligible members and their spouses to participate in the program.

As a result of program publicity, 28 department members (civilian and sworn law enforcement) and 26 spouses registered to attend the preretirement lecture series.

Program Content

Each evening of the lecture series was dedicated to a specific retirement topic. The eight-evening program included the following topics:

FIGURE 7-5. Major Arthur Barnett, commander of the Administrative Analysis Division and president of the Department's Credit Union, discusses the topic of investment planning at a session of the preretirement planning lecture series. [Photo courtesy of the Kansas City, Missouri Police Department.]

Assessment of Concerns. A specialist in gerontology from Lincoln University, who had served as an observer to the White House Commission on Aging, discussed transitional barriers facing potential retirees and positive steps that can be taken to ensure a successful retirement. A panel comprised of past retired department members then shared with participants their personal experiences "prior to" and "after" their retirement from the department.

Pension System/Social Security. A department administrator from the KCPD retirement program served as a lecturer on pension system policies and benefits. Following his presentation, a branch manager of the Social Security Administration explained how contributions are calculated, the procedure in requesting "a statement of earnings," built-in "cost of living" adjustments, and the "financial soundness" of the Social Security system.

Physical/Mental Health. A licensed counseling psychologist stressed to the participants that "mental health" was just as important an issue in preretirement planning as second careers, legal affairs, or financial planning. One's emotional and mental health have an impact on one's family, friends, and retirement alternatives. A professor from the Division of Geriatrics, School of Medicine, University of Missouri at Kansas City, then discussed the importance of nutrition, exercise, and aging versus sexuality. He stressed that how one exercises, eats, and thinks impacts his or her health and longevity.

Second Careers. As indicated in the 170-page report, "Aging in the Eighties," published by the National Council on Aging, 79 percent of the survey respondents stated they would engage in some type of postretirement paid work. In addressing this topic, the associate director for career development at Rockhurst College discussed self-career analysis, transferrable job skills, and reentering the job market. A representative of the KCPD personnel division then discussed résumé writing, job interviewing, and the roles of employment agencies and executive consulting firms in second-career placement.

Consumer/Housing Considerations. A family economics and management specialist from the University of Missouri explained how to get the most out of one's retirement dollar in a time of inflation and rising cost of living. Following her presentation, a local area realtor discussed residential versus apartment, condominium, and mobile home living. Cost factors in buying and selling property, renting, and relocating to other parts of the country were also discussed.

Legal Affairs. Because of the technical decisions facing potential retirees regarding legal considerations, a trust officer from a local bank was invited to address the topic of legal affairs. His in-depth presentation on wills, personal and living trusts, estate planning, probate, power of attorney, and tax shelters alerted participants to the need for legal planning in order to guarantee their independence, security, and financial peace of mind.

Insurance Options. A representative of the KCPD retirement system discussed the department's "carry-over" plans for health and life insurance. Even though retirees presently pay for their own individual/family health care coverage, the department provides retiring members with an opportunity to participate in a "group rate" plan. A chartered life underwriter then discussed life insurance, cash refunds, and variable annuities.

Investment Planning

The final evening of the lecture series was devoted to developing a money management plan to provide financial security in retirement. A financial advisor from a local investment firm and the president of the KCPD credit union discussed stocks, bonds, money market certificates, the Keough Act, and Individual Retirement Accounts.

Evaluation

In order to evaluate the success of the lecture series, a questionnaire was developed to measure the participants' knowledge of retirement issues. Administered before and at the conclusion of the program, an overall 20 percent increase in knowledge was realized. In addition to the questionnaire, the participants were requested to evaluate the content, materials, and lecture series presentations. Over 95 percent of the participants rated the lecture series as "very helpful" and would encourage other department members to participate in future sessions. Participants' comments ranged from "an excellent program," "extremely helpful," "long overdue," to "guest lecturers provided timely, in-depth presentations of tremendous personal benefit."

The preretirement lecture series demonstrated to the participants that the department had a deep and abiding interest in their welfare beyond their active service. Based on the participants' enthusiastic response, the program will be offered on a regular basis in the future.

Summary

There can be little argument that human resource management is one of the most important areas in police administration today because the quality of the service that a police department can deliver to its citizens can never exceed the quality of its personnel.

In this chapter we have examined some of the major components of police human resource management, drawn upon the latest state-of-the-art information from a wide variety of disciplines, and suggested ways in which police administrators can improve the overall effectiveness of their agencies within the confines of the resources available to them.

We began by discussing the functions of the police personnel unit and outlined the basic responsibilities of the unit. Some of these responsibilities included preparing policy statements and standard operating procedures in all areas of human resource administration; creating integrated management information systems; developing recruitment programs; developing selection, promotion, and career development programs; developing position classifications and pay plans; representing the agency during negotiations with police employee groups; conducting exit interviews; providing advice to management on human resource problems; and representing the police department to the central personnel office or civil service commission.

We then proceeded to discuss the process employed in selecting police officers—certainly one of the most important components of human resource management. Although there are no hard and fast rules about the precise steps to follow in the selection process, there is general agreement that the phases should proceed as follows: acceptance of the initial application, administration of the written test and/or assessment center, physical agility test, polygraph, character investigation, oral interview board, and medical and psychological screening.

The issue of identifying the best level or most appropriate type of formal education for police officers is a rather thorny issue with considerable diversity of opinion among both practitioners and criminal justice educators. However, it does seem abundantly clear that police officers entering law enforcement during the decade of the 1990s will be far better educated than were their older counterparts. There will likely be benefits that accrue to the agencies they join, but there will also be some difficulties, especially in law enforcement agencies that are tradition bound and conservative in their organizational structure and dominant management styles.

On the subject of the recruitment of minorities and women, we concluded that the successful recruitment of minorities will be enhanced if the police department initiates a strong minority recruitment program, shows a commitment to internal equal opportunity, uses carefully selected minority officers in the recruiting process, and actively pursues promising individuals. Although police departments generally have not had great difficulty in recruiting good female applicants, administrators should be sensitive to some of the extra problems that females face upon entering law enforcement. This is especially true when a police department has had either no women or very few women employed as uniformed patrol officers. A failure to address some of the problems discussed in this chapter could result in a disproportionately high turnover rate of female officers.

As one of the more controversial components of human resource management, performance evaluation is often disliked and misunderstood by both the individuals doing the evaluation and those being evaluated. This occurs many times because their purposes are simply not understood by many of the people involved. The major purposes of performance evaluation are to aid employees in maintaining acceptable levels of behavior, to assist in career development, to encourage supervision to take a personal interest in officers under their command, to make salary decisions, and to evaluate the selection procedure.

Salary administration is one of the most critical components in the personnel administration junction. The ability of a police agency to compete with business and industry in attracting the most highly qualified personnel will be directly affected by the wages and other benefits offered. When a pay plan is being developed, it must accomplish the following: be equitable in relation to the work performed, maintain a competitive position in the employment market, provide data needed in budgeting, reward high-level performance, and provide an orderly program of salary policy and contract.

The task of selecting people for entry-level or promotional positions in law enforcement has produced various techniques over the years, none of which is strong in its predictive aspect. One attempt at finding a more reliable way to predict future performance is through an assessment center. An assessment center is a method, not a place; it is a multiple assessment strategy that involves multiple techniques, including various forms of job-related simulations, and may include interviews and psychological tests. Some of the more significant advantages to the assessment center method are use of simulations of on-the-job behaviors; a large amount of information is generated by each participant in a relatively short time; a variety of methods is used; the exercises are consistent for all participants; there is a consensus of judgment among the assessors for each participant; the observers are well trained in evaluation procedures; the observers are able to devote full attention to the task of assessing; information obtained can be used to develop personnel effectively; and assessors receive valuable training in behavioral observation techniques, which carries over to their regular job performance.

On the topic of civilians in police work, the literature indicates that civilians are being employed by police departments in rapidly growing numbers and in an increasing variety of activities, and it seems that this trend is likely to continue. There are four generally accepted reasons for this: namely, the need to control costs yet improve service to citizens; use of civilians for low-skilled and specialized tasks, thus freeing police officers to assume police functions; encouragement by the federal and state governments; and development of specific programs aimed at increasing the use of civilians. In our discussion of alternative career tracks, we examined some of the shortcomings of the traditional organization, one of which is raising the expectations of its officers to an unrealistic level. It is apparent that most police organizations in this country give a disproportionate amount of the financial awards and status to those individuals who become managers. Thus the system has built into it features that make the managerial positions far more attractive than the nonmanagerial positions. But some 85 to 90 percent of able police officers will never rise above the rank of patrol officer. Alternatives for financial reward and status must be created. The model suggested in this chapter presents one alternative.

Finally, we discussed an often neglected area of personnel administration: retirement counseling. There tends to be general agreement that many police officers experience considerable difficulty when they retire. Part of this is explained by the relatively young age at which they retire and the need to pursue a second career, often with little preparation, because they cannot realistically meet their financial obligations on their pensions. In addition, one police psychologist has noted that, as with the military, police work is a way of life and police officers frequently encounter difficulty when separated from those facets of police work that fill so many of their psychological needs. Because of these problems, it has been recommended that police departments institute preretirement counseling programs to start the employee thinking about retirement plans and adjustments and to create a setting in which questions, criticisms, and desires on the part of the worker can be voiced freely.

Discussion Questions

1. Since the late 1960s, the subject of human resource management has gained considerable prominence and visibility within the law enforcement community. What are some of the major social, political, and economic factors that have given impetus to the movement?
2. Why did Congress enact the Americans with Disabilities Act of 1990?
3. What are some of the significant provisions of the Americans with Disabilities Act?
4. What is the major purpose of the preemployment written examination?
5. What two decisions were made by the U.S. Supreme Court in 1989 that caused civil rights leaders to become uneasy, and what was the essence of these two decisions?
6. What are the significance of *Robinson* v *City of Lake Station* (1986) and *Evans* v *City of Evanston* (1989) as they relate to physical ability testing?
7. The law enforcement agencies using the polygraph in the preemployment screening process have indicated there have been many practical benefits derived from its use. What are these benefits?
8. What are the three best sources of information in evaluating applicants?
9. What psychological tests are typically used to screen police applicants?
10. What function does the Field Training Officer (FTO) serve in relation to new officers?
11. In one recent study, college-educated police officers talked about difficulties encountered on the job. What were these difficulties?
12. What two major practices are used by police administrators to make police more effective in dealing with minority populations?
13. Why are the pressures imposed on females entering law enforcement frequently greater than those on their male counterparts?
14. What are the major purposes of performance evaluations?
15. Pay plans must accomplish several objectives. What are they?
16. What does an assessment center consist of?
17. There are several options available to municipalities that might seek to recover the financial investment made in training new police officers. What are they?
18. What were the major topics discussed in the retirement counseling program of the Kansas City, Missouri Police Department?

Notes

1. O. G. Stahl and R. A. Staufenberger, eds., *Police Personnel Administration* (Washington, D.C.: Police Foundation, 1974), p. 111.
2. For a detailed analysis of these findings and recommendations, see The President's Commission on Law Enforcement and the Administration of Justice. *Task Force Report on the Police* (Washington, D.C.: U.S. Government Printing Office, 1967); *Report of The National Advisory Commission on Civil Disorder* (New York: New York Times, 1968).
3. W. W. Schmidt, "Recent Developments in Police Civil Liability," *Journal of Police Science and Administration*, 4:3 (1976), pp. 197–202.
4. D. M. Walters, "Civil Liability for Improper Police Training," *Police Chief*, 38:11 (1971). pp. 28–36.
5. W. D. Heisel and P. V. Murphy, "Organization for Police Personnel Management," in *Police Personnel Administration*, ed. O. G. Stahl and R. A. Staufenberger (Washington, D.C.: Police Foundation, 1974), p. 1.

6. L. Tenito, C. R. Swanson, Jr., and N. C. Chamelin, *The Police Personnel Selection Process* (Indianapolis, Ind.: Bobbs-Merrill, 1977), p. 3.
7. Heisel and Murphy, "Organization for Police Personnel Management," pp. 8–11.
8. Ibid., pp. 1–2.
9. U.S. Equal Employment Opportunity Commission, *The Americans with Disabilities Act: Your Responsibilities as an Employer* (Washington, D.C.: U.S. Government Printing Office, 1991), p. 2.
10. Ibid., p. 3.
11. U.S. Equal Employment Opportunity Commission and U.S. Department of Justice, *The Americans with Disabilities Act: Questions and Answers* (Washington D.C.: U.S. Government Printing Offic, July 1991), p. 7.
12. Jeffrey Higginbotham, "The Americans with Disabilities Act," *FBI Law Enforcement Bulletin*, 60:8 (1991), p. 26.
13. Ibid., pp. 26–27.
14. Ibid., p. 26.
15. Ibid., p. 26.
16. Ibid., p. 26.
17. Higgenbotham, "Americans with Disabilities Act: Questions and Answers," p. 4.
18. Ibid., p. 2.
19. Ibid., p. 3.
20. U.S. Equal Employment Opportunity Commission, *Americans with Disabilities Act: Your Responsibilities as an Employer*, p. 4.
21. Ibid., p. 5.
22. Ibid., p. 5.
23. U.S. Equal Employment Opportunity Commission, *Americans with Disabilities Act: Questions and Answers*, p. 4.
24. Ibid., p. 4.
25. Ibid., p. 6.
26. Jody M. Litchford, "The Americans with Disabilities Act," *Police Chief*, 58:1 (1991), p. 11.
27. U.S. Equal Employment Opportunity Commission, *Americans with Disabilities Act: Your Responsibilities as an Employer*, p. 10.
28. Ibid., p. 10.
29. Ibid., p. 6.
30. Ibid., p. 6.
31. Territo, Swanson, and Chamelin, *Police Personnel Selection Process*, p. 10.
32. Heisel and Murphy, "Organization for Police Personnel Management," p. 5.
33. Territo, Swanson, and Chamelin, *Police Personnel Selection Process*, pp. 12, 13.
34. Ibid., p. 12.
35. Philip Ash, Karen Slora, and Cynthia F. Britton, "Police Agency Selection Practices," *Journal of Police Science and Administration*, 17:4 (1990), p. 262.
36. Ibid., p. 263.
37. Ibid., Table 4, p. 265.
38. U.S. Equal Employment Opportunity Commission, "Adoption of Questions and Answers to Clarify and Provide a Common Interpretation of the Uniform Guidelines on Employee Selection Procedures," *Federal Register*, Mar. 2, 1979, p. 12007.
39. Ibid., p. 12003.
40. Ibid., p. 11998.
41. 43 *FEP Cases* 130 (1989).
42. 57 *Law Week* 4616 (1989).
43. Civil Rights Act of 1991, Title 1, Section 1977A.
44. *Employee Relations Weekly*, 10:2 (1992), p. 34.
45. Ibid., p. 34.

46. Ibid., p. 39.
47. Ash, Slora, and Britton, "Police Agency Selection Practices," p. 264.
48. Walter S. Booth and Chris W. Horwick, "Physical Ability Testing for Police Officers in the 80s," *Police Chief*, 1:1 (1984), pp. 39–41.
49. 630 F.Supp. 1052 (1986).
50. 619 F.2nd 611, U.S. *cert den*, 449 U.S. 872 (1980).
51. 881 F.2nd 382 (1989).
52. 686 F.Supp. 631 (1988), U.S. *cert den*, 111 Supreme Court Reporter 1388 (1990).
53. 704 F.Supp. 709 (1988).
54. Ash, Slora, and Britton, "Police Agency Selection Practices," p. 265.
55. Ibid., p. 265.
56. Ibid., p. 265.
57. Ibid., p. 265.
58. Robert M. Guion, "Personnel Assessment, Selection, and Placement," in *Handbook of Industrial and Organizational Psychology*, vol. 2, ed. Marvin D. Dunnette and Leaetta M. Hough (Palo Alto, Calif.: Consulting Psychologists Press, 1991), p. 347.
59. L. K. Gaines and Bruce Lewis, "Reliability and Validity of Oral Interviews in Police Promotions," *Journal of Criminal Justice*, 10:5 (1982), pp. 403–20. Also see Stephen Falkenberg, L. K. Gaines, and Terry Cox, "The Oral Board Interview: What Does It Measure?," *Journal of Police Science and Administration*, 17:1 pp. 32–39.
60. Ash, Slora, and Britton, "Police Agency Officer Selection Practices," p. 265.
61. Ibid., p. 265.
62. Ibid., p. 265.
63. Ibid., p. 265.
64. Susan Saxe and Joseph Fabricatore, "Use of Psychological Consultants in Screening Police Applicants," *FBI Law Enforcement Bulletin* (August 1982). This discussion was adapted from this source, pp. 8–11.
65. W. D. Haynes, *Stress-Related Disorders in Policemen* (San Francisco: R & E Research Associates, 1978): R. H. Rahe and E. K. E. Gunderson, *Life Stress and Illness* (Springfield, Ill.: Charles C. Thomas, 1974); M. Reiser, "Stress, Distress and Adaptation in Police Work," *Police Chief* 41:1 (1976).
66. J. Gottesman, *The Utility of the MMPI in Assessing the Personality Patterns of Urban Police Applicants* (Hoboken, N.J.: Stevens Institute of Technology, 1975); S. J. Saxe and M. Reiser, "A Comparison of Three Police Applicant Groups Using the MMPI," *Journal of Police Science and Administration*, 4:4 (1976); J. Fabricatore, F. Azan, and H. Sibbe, "Predicting Performance of Police Officers Using the 16 Personality Factor Questionnaire," *American Journal of Community Psychiatry*, 6:1, (1978); R. H. Blum, *Police Selection* (Springfield, Ill.: Charles C. Thomas, 1964).
67. The President's Commission on Law Enforcement and Administration of Justice, *Task Force Report: The Police* (Washington, D.C.: U.S. Government Printing Office, 1967), p. 137.
68. National Advisory Commission on Criminal Justice Standards and Goals, *Report on the Police* (Washington, D.C.: U.S. Government Printing Office, 1973), p. 369.
69. *The National Manpower Survey of the Criminal Justice System*, volume 2, *Law Enforcement* (Washington, D.C.: U.S. Government Printing Office, November 1972), p. 20.
70. Ibid., p. 20.
71. National Advisory Commission, *Report on the Police*, p. 370.
72. D. P. Geary, "College Educated Cops—Three Years Later," *Police Chief*, 37:8 (1970), p. 62.
73. B. Cohen and J. M. Chaiken, *Police Background Characteristics: Summary Report* (Washington, D.C.: U.S. Government Printing Office, November 1972), p. 20.
74. E. M. Baehr, J. E. Furcon, and E. C. Froemel, *Psychological Assessment of Patrolman*

Qualifications in Relation to Field Performance (Washington, D.C.: U.S. Government Printing Office, November 1968), p. 212.

75. A. B. Smith, B. Locke, and W. F. Walker, "Authoritarianism in Police College Students and Non-Police College Students," *Journal of Criminal Law, Criminology, and Police Science*, 59:3 (1968), pp. 440–43.
76. D. L. Carter, "Issues and Trends in Higher Education for Police Officers," in *Issues and Trends in Criminal Justice Education*, ed. G. D. Copus. Criminal justice monograph, (Huntsville, Tex.: Sam Houston State University, 8:5, 1978), pp. 9–19.
77. S. Gross, "Higher Education and Police: Is There a Need for a Closer Look?" *Journal of Police Science and Administration*, 1:4 (1973), pp. 477–83.
78. J. D. Jamison, "Issues and Trends in Criminal Justice Education: The Philosophy of Curriculum Development," in *Issues and Trends in Criminal Justice Education*, ed. Copus, pp. 2–8.
79. C. R. Swanson, Jr., "An Uneasy Look at College Education and the Police Organization," *Journal of Criminal Justice*, 5 (1977), pp. 311–20.
80. R. C. Tojanowicz and T. G. Nicholson, "A Comparison of Behavioral Styles of College Graduate Police Officers vs. Non-College Going Police Officers," *Police Chief*, 43:8 (1976), p. 58.
81. B. Washington, "Stress Reduction Techniques for the Female Officer," in *Job Stress and The Police Officer*, ed. W. H. Kroes and J. J. Huneil (Washington, D.C.: U.S. Government Printing Office, December 1975), p. 36.
82. Ibid., p. 36.
83. Susan E. Martin, "A report on the status of women in policing," *Police Foundation Reports*, May 1989, p. 7.
84. W. Bopp and P. M. Whisenand, *Police Personnel Administration*, 2nd ed. (Boston: Allyn & Bacon, 1980). Much of the discussion on performance evaluation was taken from this source.
85. J. N. Matzer, Jr., *Personnel Administration: A Guide for Small Local Governments* (Washington, D.C.: Civil Service Commission). Much of the information in this chapter dealing with salary administration was taken from this source.
86. C. F. Lutz and J. P. Morgan, "Jobs and Rank," in *Police Personnel Administration*, Bopp and Whisenand, p. 39.
87. R. J. Filer, "Assessment Centers in Police Selection," in *Proceedings of the National Working Conference on the Selection of Law Enforcement Officers*, ed. C. D. Spielberger and H. C. Spaulding (Tampa, Fla.: University of South Florida, March 1977), p. 103.
88. R. Reinke, *Selection Through Assessment Centers: A Tool for Police Departments* (Washington, D.C.: Police Foundation, 1977), p. 1.
89. Filer, "Assessment Centers," pp. 103, 104.
90. Ibid., pp. 105, 106.
91. Third International Congress on the Assessment Center Method, *Standards and Ethical Considerations for Assessment Center Operators* (Quebec, Canada, May 1975), p. 3.
92. D. P. Slevin, "The Assessment Center: Breakthrough in Management Appraisal and Development," *Personnel Journal*, 57 (April 1972), p. 256.
93. M. D. Dunnette and S. J. Motowidlo, *Police Selection and Career Assessment* (Washington, D.C.: U.S. Government Printing Office, 1976), p. 56.
94. D. A. Kent, C. R. Wall, and R. L. Bailey, "A New Approach to Police Personnel Selection," *Police Chief*, 44:6 (1974), p. 73.
95. Ibid., p. 73.
96. Filer, "Assessment Centers," pp. 105, 106.
97. W. J. Kearney and D. D. Martin, "The Assessment Center: A Tool for Promotion Decisions," *Police Chief*, 42:1 (1975), p. 32.

98. Ibid., p. 32.
99. Ibid., p. 32.
100. The following are some police departments that have utilized assessment centers: Chattanooga (Tenn.) Police Department, intermediate commander; Ft. Worth (Tex.) Police Department, patrol officers; Kansas City (Mo.) Police Department, sergeant and captain; Minneapolis (Minn.) Police Department, detective; New York City Police Department, high-level commanders; Portland (Ore.) Police Department, intermediate commander; Rochester (N.Y.) Police Department, investigator; Savannah (Ga.) Police Department, chief of police; Washington (D.C.) Police Department, patrol officer and detective.
101. Reinke, *Selection Through Assessment Centers*, p. 4.
102. Kearney and Martin, "Assessment Center," p. 33.
103. Ibid., p. 33.
104. Reinke, *Selection Through Assessment Centers*, p. 5.
105. W. C. Byham, "The Assessment Center as an Aid in Management Development, "Training and Development Journal, 25:12 (1971), p. 15.
106. A. U. Schwartz et al., *Employing Civilians for Police Work* (Washington, D.C.: U.S. Government Printing Office, July 1975), p. 1.
107. Ibid., p. 1.
108. National Advisory Commission, *Report on the Police*, p. 258.
109. Schwartz et al., *Employing Civilians for Police Work*, pp. 8–10.
110. The information used in this discussion of Alternative Career Tracks was provided by Richard B. Walker of the Hillsborough County Sheriff's Office in Tampa, FLorida. His original research on this topic was done in conjunction with an Area Project completed in partial fulfillment for his master's degree in the Department of Criminology at the University of South Florida, Tampa, Florida. It was his hope that such a plan would eventually be adopted by his agency.
111. Palatine Police Department General Order 81-1R, *Dual Career Ladder Program*, effective Feb. 28, 1986. All information discussed about this agency was obtained directly from this general order.
112. Palm Beach County Sheriff's Office Dual Career Ladder/Career Path Program. All information discussed about this agency was obtained directly from this document.
113. Altamonte Springs Police Department Policy and Procedure *Operational Career Track.* April 4, 1983. All information discussed about this agency was obtained directly from this document.
114. K. E. Johnson, "Retirement Counseling, *FBI Law Enforcement Bulletin*, 47:6 (June 1978), pp. 28-31. Much of the discussion on retirement counseling was taken from this source.
115. J. Wambaugh, *The New Centurions* (Boston: Little, Brown, 1970), p. 297.
116. B. S. Dohrenwend and B. Dohrenwend, *Stressful Life Events, Their Nature and Effects* (New York: John Wiley and Sons, 1974), p. 50.
117. H. E. Russell and A. Beyel, *Understanding Human Behavior for Effective Police Work*, (New York: Basic Books, 1976), p. 292.
118. N. A. Caron and R. T. Kelly, "The Kansas City Police Department Pre-Retirement Lecture Series," *Police Chief*, 50:1 (January 1983), pp. 47-49.
119. E. H. Moore and G. Strub, *The Nature of Retirement* (New York: Macmillan, 1959), p. 198.

8 Stress and Police Personnel

If, under stress, a man goes all to pieces, he will probably be told to pull himself together. It would be more effective to help him identify the pieces and to understand why they have come apart.

R. RUDDOCK

Introduction

Historically, U.S. business and industry have been slow to identify and provide for the needs of workers. Largely because of the labor union movement, the U.S. worker has achieved a variety of benefits, ranging from increased wages to comprehensive medical care and retirement programs. The inclusion of mental health compensation as a significant management issue has evolved through a combination of union pressures and simple economics. A healthy, well-adjusted worker means increased efficiency and higher production for the corporation. As a consequence, job-related stress "has moved from the nether world of 'emotional problems' and 'personality conflicts' to the corporate balance sheet. . . . Stress is now seen as not only troublesome but expensive."[1]

Government and public service sectors generally lag behind industry and business in employee benefit innovations, and the mental health issue is no exception. However, the private sector's recent concern with the wide-ranging effects of job-related stress on workers is beginning to be shared by criminal justice authorities—or at least by those in law enforcement. More and more literature on stress factors in policing is becoming available to the law enforcement executive for use in developing programs designed to reduce stress among police personnel.[2]

What Is Stress?

Despite the volumes of research published on stress, the phenomenon remains poorly defined. Hans Selye, the researcher and theorist who pioneered the physiological investigation of stress, defines stress in the broadest possible terms as *anything that places an adjustive demand on the organism.* Identified as "the body's nonspecific response to any demand placed on it," stress may be either positive (*eustress*) or negative (*distress*).[3] According to this distinction, many stressful events do not threaten people but provide them with pleasurable challenges. The excitement of the gambler, the thrill of the athlete engaged in a highly competitive sport, the deliberate risk taking of the daredevil stunt man—these are examples of stress without *distress.* For many people, this kind of stress provides the spice of life.

Basowitz and his associates define stress as those stimuli that are likely to produce disturbances in most people. The authors postulate a continuum of stimuli that differ in meaning and in their anxiety-producing consequences:

> At one end are such stimuli or cues, often highly symbolic, which have meaning only to single or limited numbers of persons and which to the observer may appear as innocuous or trivial. At the other end are such stimuli, here called stress, which by their explicit threat to vital functioning and their intensity are likely to overload the capacity of most organisms' coping mechanisms.[4]

The authors also distinguish between pathological, neurotic, or harmful anxiety and the normal, adaptive, or healthy form of anxiety. In the first instance, anxiety is defined as a conscious and painful state of apprehension unrelated to an external threat. This kind of anxiety may render an individual incapable of distinguishing danger from safety or relevant information and cues from irrelevant ones. Ultimately one's psychological and physiological functioning can become so reduced that death occurs. As the authors state, anxiety in this severe form is generally derived from "internal psychological problems and therefore is chronically present, leading to more serious, long-lasting somatic and psychological changes."[5] In the second instance, anxiety is defined as a state of increased alertness that permits maximum psychological and physiological performance. A state of fear, according to this formulation, is a simple form of anxiety characterized by the life-threatening or harmful nature of the stimuli. Unlike the more severe, harmful forms, simple forms of anxiety are temporal and beneficial to the individual. Of course, distinctions among the various levels of anxiety are difficult to make. For example, a person may react to a minimally threatening stimulus as though his or her life were in imminent danger. The fear response may have been appropriate and the overreaction inappropriate (perhaps indicative of psychological disturbance). Anxiety, then, can be defined as the individual's ability to cope with, or respond to, threatening situations.

Biological Stress and the General Adaptation Syndrome

Selye has formulated what he calls the general adaptation syndrome (GAS) to describe on the biological level how stress can incapacitate an individual. The GAS encompasses three stages of physiological reaction to a wide variety of *stressors*—environmental agents or activities powerful enough in their impact to elicit a reaction from the body. These three stages are (1) alarm, (2) resistance, and (3) exhaustion.

The alarm stage, sometimes referred to as an *emergency reaction,* is exemplified on the animal level by the so-called "fight or flight" syndrome. When an animal encounters a threatening situation, its body signals a defense alert. The animal's cerebral cortex flashes an alarm to the hypothalamus, a small structure in the midbrain that connects the brain with body functions. A powerful hormone called ACTH is released into the bloodstream by the hypothalamus and is carried by the bloodstream to the adrenal gland, a part of the endocrine, or ductless gland, system. There ACTH triggers the release of adrenin, which produces a galvanizing or energizing effect on the body functions. The heart pounds, the pulse races, breathing quickens, the muscles tense, and digestion is retarded or inhibited. The adjustive function of this reaction pattern is readily apparent, namely, preparing the organism biologically to fight or to run away. When the threat is removed or diminished, the physiological functions involved in this alarm, or emergency reaction, subside, and the organism regains its internal equilibrium.

If the stress continues, however, the organism reaches the resistance stage of the GAS. During this stage, bodily resources are mobilized to deal with the specific stressors, and adaptation is optimal. Although the stressful stimulus may persist, the symptoms that characterized the alarm stage disappear. In short, the individual seems to have handled the stress successfully.

Under conditions of prolonged stress, the body reaches a point where it is no longer capable of maintaining resistance. This condition characterizes the exhaustion stage. Hormonal defenses break down, and many emotional reactions that appeared during the alarm stage may reappear, often in intensified form. Further exposure to stress leads to exhaustion and eventually to death. Even before this extreme stage has been reached, however, excessive hormonal secretions may result in severe physiological pathology of the type that Selye calls "diseases of adaptation," for example, ulcers, high blood pressure, and coronary susceptibility.[6]

Psychological Stress

While life-threatening situations have understandably received considerable attention from researchers and theorists, there are many other circumstances in which the stress involved threatens something that the individual deems valuable: self-esteem, authority, and security, for example. The human being's highly developed brain, accumulated knowledge, and ability to perceive and communicate through the medium of symbols lead him or her to find unpleasant or pleasant connotations in an incredible number of situations and events. Human beings react not only to tangible, physical stresses but also to symbolic or imagined threats or pleasures.[7] The effects of the stimulus can vary widely, depending on a person's culture, personal and family background, experiences, and mood and circumstances at the time. The objective nature of an event is not nearly as significant as what the event means to a particular individual at any given time. People are able to influence the nature of stress through their ability to control and anticipate events in the environment. As anticipation can simplify stress, the lack of it does so even more. The unanticipated event often has the greatest impact on an individual and leaves the most persistent aftereffects.[8]

Reactions to Stress

Most people adjust their behavior to daily stress according to their adaptive range. At the high end of the range, when a person encounters an extremely demanding situation, his or her first reaction is usually anxiety, a varying mixture of alertness, anticipation, curiosity, and fear. At the low end of the range, when confronted with a stressful situation, an individual experiences a condition of overload. The ability to improvise deteriorates, and behavior is likely to regress to simpler, more primitive responses. Regardless of personality type, people under high stress show less ability to tolerate ambiguity and to sort out the trivial from the important. Some authorities report that people become apathetic and inactive when stress is either minimal or absent. As stress increases slightly, the person becomes attentive and more active. When stress increases further, the individual becomes either interested and curious or wary and cautious. Greater stress then results in emotional states of unpleasant anxiety or pleasant expectation. When stress becomes extreme, anxiety may increase until it threatens to overwhelm the individual. At this point, panic, accompanied by paralysis, flight, or attack, may occur. Under high levels of emotion, an individual becomes less discriminating and tends to make either disorganized or stereotyped responses, to lose perceptual judgment, and to idealize and overgeneralize.[9] As one police psychologist puts it, "People under stress make mistakes." In policing where job-related stress is involved, the kind of mistakes that are likely to occur can result in potentially irreparable, even fatal, consequences[10] (see Box 8-1 on pp. 300–302).

Stress in Law Enforcement

Police work is highly stressful—it is one of the few occupations in which an employee is asked continually to face physical dangers and to put his or her life on the line at any time. The police officer is exposed to violence, cruelty, and aggression and is often required to make extremely critical decisions in high-pressure situations.

Stress has many ramifications and can produce many varied psychophysiological disturbances that, if sufficiently intense and chronic, can lead to demonstrable organic diseases of varying severity. It may also lead to physiological disorders and emotional instability, which can manifest themselves in alcoholism, a broken marriage, and, in the extreme, suicide. Three-fourths of the heart attacks suffered by police officers are from job-related stress, studies have shown. As a result, courts have ruled that a police officer who suffers a heart attack while off duty is entitled to worker's compensation.[11] Thus, even a superficial review of the human, organizational, and legal impacts of stress-related health problems should sensitize every administrator toward the prevention, treatment, and solution of these problems.

Job Stress in Police Officers

In law enforcement, stressors have been identified in various ways.[12] Researchers such as Kroes,[13,14] Eisenberg,[15] Reiser,[16,17,18,19] and Roberts[20] have all conducted extensive studies into law enforcement occupational stress, and although they do not group these stressors in identical categories, they tend to follow similar patterns. Most of the law enforcement stressors can be grouped into four broad categories: (1) organizational practices and characteristics, (2) criminal justice

BOX 8-1

Science Probes Biological Basis to Stress Syndrome
Post-traumatic Disorder Tied to Terror, Adrenaline Surges

Scientific research is finding that single instances of overwhelming terror can alter the chemistry of the human brain, which can make people more sensitive to adrenaline surges—a major factor in post-traumatic stress disorder (PTSD) that affects crime victims, combat veterans and police officers. Experts say the recent findings could offer new hope that those suffering from PTSD can be treated through medication.

But a pair of experts who have dealt with the syndrome as it affects police officers told LEN that while the research is valuable, the importance of psychological debriefing and followup counseling should not be overlooked.

The New York Times reported this month that scientists have discovered the first direct evidence pointing to a biological basis for PTSD because research suggests that specific sites in the brain undergo chemical changes in response to devastating emotional trauma triggered by horrific events. The situations involved are catastrophic events—those threatening life or safety or those over which the person has no control. In the case of police officers, the kinds of events that could trigger such chemical reactions include using deadly force against suspects, being the target of an armed suspect, witnessing the on-duty death of a patrol partner or simply experiencing the day-to-day morass of social ills that police officers often confront.

It is estimated that one out of every 10 Americans has suffered some degree of symptoms associated with PTSD, according to a study presented at a recent meeting of the American Psychiatric Association.

"It does not matter if it was the incessant terror of combat, torture or repeated abuse in childhood, or a one-time experience, like being trapped in a hurricane or almost dying in an auto accident," said Dr. Dennis Charney, a Yale University psychiatrist and director of clinical neuroscience at the National Center for Post-Traumatic Stress Disorder. "All uncontrollable stress can have the same biological impact."

Researchers say that the more intense the traumatic incident, and the longer it lasts, the more likely it is to result in post-traumatic stress. They have also found that some people who experienced traumatic events never develop the syndrome, and for others, symptoms may not appear immediately. Symptoms can last indefinitely, or can clear up spontaneously or through psychotherapy.

Animal studies, in which laboratory subjects are subjected to stress they could not escape while researchers measured their brain activity, have shown several distinct changes in brain activity that have been indirectly confirmed in humans. The changes occur in these ways:

—The part of the brain that regulates the secretion of two hormones that mobilize the body for an emergency—called the locus ceruleus—becomes "hyper-reactive," and begins to secrete too much of the chemicals, even in situations of little or no threat.

—Scientists also note increases in the secretion of corticotropin-releasing factor, or CRF, which is one of the main hormones that mobilizes the body's response to emergency. The hormone is regulated by the link between the hypothalamus, located in the brain's emotion center, and the pituitary gland. The increased secretions alert the body for emergencies that are not there in reality, say scientists.

—The opioid system of the brain, which can blunt the feeling of pain, is hyperactive. Researchers say this can explain why sufferers of PTSD experience emotional numbing and an inability to experience feelings of warmth and tenderness, which are two of the hallmarks of the disorder.

The revelations about brain activity resulting from a traumatic event have increased the hope for a possible medicinal treatment for PTSD. Experts note that traditional psychiatric drugs have a hit-or-miss effect, but say that the knowledge of brain activity in relation to PTSD can narrow down the search for pharmacological solutions, a search that is well under way.

"Understanding the brain basis of post-traumatic stress can help us design medication that reverses these changes," said Dr. Matthew Friedman, the executive director of the National Center for Post-Traumatic Stress Disorder. But Friedman cautioned against advocating a totally medicinal approach to treating the disorder. That, he said, is only part of the answer.

"You can use a drug to turn down the volume of physiological symptoms, so people feel less driven, anxious, can sleep better and have fewer nightmares. But there are other problems, such as alienation, emotional numbness, guilt and moral pain that you need psychotherapy for," Friedman told the Times.

Two experts on how PTSD affects police officers, contacted by LEN for their comments on the findings, agreed.

"Medication is not the total answer," said Richard Pastorella, a New York City police officer assigned to the NYPD Bomb Squad who was severely injured in a 1982 terrorist bombing that left him blind and maimed. Pastorella, himself a sufferer of PTSD, formed a counseling group, the Police Self-Support Group, in which police officers wounded in the line of duty counsel their fellow officers.

"You must also attack the problem through psychologists or psychiatrists. It's a two-pronged attack; it can't be done alone," he asserted.

Pastorella, who is studying for a master's degree in psychology at John Jay College of Criminal Justice, said there are three levels of PTSD that vary in intensity. The most severe form, such as that suffered by Vietnam combat veterans, is rarely affected by drugs or psychotherapy, he maintained. Persons suffering from the most severe form of PTSD most likely "will never be totally free of the disorder," said Pastorella.

But other forms of PTSD can be offset by critical-incident stress debriefing, which must be performed as soon after the traumatic incident as possible.

"If you can get to that individual and allow that individual to unload, to get rid of that shock, to talk about the experience with a mental health professional or a peer counselor present, it will lessen the possibility of the onset of post-traumatic stress disorder. That's the beauty of critical-incident stress debriefing," said Pastorella, who added that a vital part of such debriefing involves a counselor explaining the sufferer's interpretation of the incident back to him.

Police officers suffer a more "cumulative" form of PTSD, said Pastorella, because of the nature of the duties they perform everyday, such as handling fatal highway accidents, responding to violent domestic disputes and reports of child abuse or crimes against the elderly, as well as the "life-and-death" decisions they are sometimes forced to make.

"These are awesome responsibilities. [Police officers] see death, literally, on a daily basis. That, on a day-in, day-out basis, probably would make them great candidates for post-traumatic stress disorder—depending upon the individual's personal makeup prior to becoming a police officer. That has a great effect, also," he said.

A medical solution to PTSD to alleviate symptoms "is the same thinking behind making any problem go away," said Dr. Daniel Blumberg, a psychologist, who with Dr. Michael Mantell, treats San Diego-area police officers suffering from PTSD symptoms.

"A lot of people would like to take a pill to relieve symptoms and make PTSD go away," much like they would take a pill to treat any other ailment, said Blumberg. But medication can help to alleviate the intense anxiety police officers often experience after a traumatic incident, which in turn can enable them to address other PTSD symptoms, he added.

Blumberg prescribes a "preventive" approach to PTSD through intensive bouts of stress-management training that can prevent PTSD symptoms from developing. "You train officers to know, well ahead of a crisis, what they are likely to go through in a crisis," said Blumberg. Such training is no guarantee that PTSD will not develop, but Blumberg said that well-trained supervisors can be effective in assessing when an officer might expect critical incidents to occur.

BOX 8-1 (cont.)

Blumberg also advocates the use of group or individual debriefings for officers immediately following traumatic incidents, and said that supervisors should "strongly push their officers" to take advantage of debriefings.

Police psychologists often are stigmatized in law enforcement agencies and that can dissuade police officers in need of psychological aid from seeking it out, noted Blumberg. That kind of thinking needs to be changed, he said.

"Many of the administrators continue to maintain a belief that if you use a psychologist, there's something wrong with you. And that just keeps people away," he said.

Source: Law Enforcement News, June 15/30, 1990, pp. 1, 13,

system practices and characteristics, (3) public practices and characteristics, and (4) police work itself.

One group of researchers interviewed one hundred Cincinnati patrol officers about the elements of their job that they felt were stressful. Foremost on their list of items were the courts (scheduling appearances and leniency), the administration (undesirable assignments and lack of backing in ambiguous situations), faulty equipment, and community apathy. Other items listed but not with so great a frequency were changing shifts, relations with supervisors, nonpolice work, other police officers, boredom, and pay.[21]

A survey of twenty police chiefs in the southeastern United States confirmed these findings. These chiefs, when asked about situations they felt were stressful

FIGURE 8-1. Police and demonstrators collide during a protest march against the Rodney King verdict. [Photo copyright © 1992 Linda Rosier, Impact Visuals.]

for line personnel, listed lack of administrative support, role conflicts, public pressure and scrutiny, peer group pressures, courts, and imposed role changes.[22]

While working with the San Jose Police Department, one researcher was able to identify numerous sources of psychological stress that were basically reflections of his personal observations and feelings while performing the functions of a patrol officer for approximately two years. Some of these sources of psychological stress were poor supervision; absence or lack of career development opportunities; inadequate reward reinforcement; offensive administrative policies; excessive paperwork; poor equipment; law enforcement agency jurisdiction; isolationism; unfavorable court decisions; ineffectiveness of corrections to rehabilitate or warehouse criminals; misunderstood judicial procedures; inefficient courtroom management; distorted press accounts of police incidents; unfavorable attitude by the public; derogatory remarks by neighbors and others; adverse local government decisions; ineffectiveness of referral agencies; role conflict; adverse work scheduling; fear of serious injury, disability, and death; exposure to people suffering and in agony, both physically and mentally; and consequences of actions, their appropriateness, and possible adverse conditions.[23]

Stress Indicators

Several years ago, Sewell[24] developed a law enforcement critical life event scale, which he administered to sessions of the FBI National Academy, each of which contained 250 officers from departments throughout the country. Sewell also chose a county police department in Virginia for comparison and analysis. The law enforcement critical life event scale developed by Sewell established a ranking system whereby officers would rate events from most to least stressful. Sewell's research indicated that the events requiring the greatest amount of readjustment were those relating to the categories of violence, threat of violence, personnel matters, and ethical concerns (see Table 8-1).

One of the great values of the study conducted by Sewell is that it tends to identify many of the same sources of psychological stress and similar reactions to it by police officers regardless of the geographical location or the organizational differences. The existence of these similarities is quite important, for it increases the possibility of creating programmatic solutions that have a high degree of applicability for a variety of law enforcement agencies that may on the surface seem to be dissimilar.

The Psychological Services Unit of the Dallas, Texas, Police Department has set forth in Table 8-2 its assessment of job-related stresses, the immediate response to stress, and the long-term response to stress. The unit has also developed a useful and practical guide to assist police supervisors in detecting the fifteen most prevalent warning signs of stress (see Table 8-3).

Alcoholism and Police Officers

Alcoholism in government and industry is not only widespread but also extremely costly—a fact established most convincingly by many independent researchers.

TABLE 8-1 Law Enforcement Critical Life Events Scale

Event	Value
1. Violent death of a partner in the line of duty	88
2. Dismissal	85
3. Taking a life in the line of duty	84
4. Shooting someone in the line of duty	81
5. Suicide of an officer who is a close friend	80
6. Violent death of another officer in the line of duty	79
7. Murder committed by a police officer	78
8. Duty-related violent injury (shooting)	76
9. Violent job-related injury to another officer	75
10. Suspension	72
11. Passed over for promotion	71
12. Pursuit of an armed suspect	71
13. Answering a call to a scene involving violent non-accidental death of a child	70
14. Assignment away from family for a long period of time	70
15. Personal involvement in a shooting incident	70
16. Reduction in pay	70
17. Observing an act of police corruption	69
18. Accepting a bribe	69
19. Participating in an act of police corruption	68
20. Hostage situation resulting from aborted criminal action	68
21. Response to a scene involving the accidental death of a child	68
22. Promotion of inexperienced/incompetent officer over you	68
23. Internal affairs investigation against self	66
24. Barricaded suspect	66
25. Hostage situation resulting from a domestic disturbance	65
26. Response to "officer needs assistance" call	65
27. Duty under a poor supervisor	64
28. Duty-related violent injury (non-shooting)	63
29. Observing an act of police brutality	62
30. Response to "person with a gun" call	62
31. Unsatisfactory personnel evaluation	62
32. Police-related civil suit	61
33. Riot/crowd control situation	61
34. Failure on a promotional examination	60
35. Suicide of an officer	60
36. Criminal indictment of a fellow officer	60
37. Improperly conducted corruption investigation of another officer	60
38. Shooting incident involving another officer	59
39. Failing grade in police training program	59
40. Response to a "felony-in-progress" call	58
41. Answering a call to a sexual battery/abuse scene involving a child victim	58
42. Oral promotional review	57
43. Conflict with a supervisor	57
44. Change in departments	56
45. Personal criticism by the press	56
46. Investigation of a political/highly publicized case	56
47. Taking severe disciplinary action against another officer	56
48. Assignment to conduct an internal affairs investigation on another officer	56

TABLE 8-1 (cont.)

Event	Value
49. Interference by political officials in a case	55
50. Written promotional examination	55
51. Departmental misconduct hearing	55
52. Wrecking a departmental vehicle	55
53. Personal use of illicit drugs	54
54. Use of drugs by another officer	54
55. Participating in a police strike	53
56. Undercover assignment	53
57. Physical assault on an officer	52
58. Disciplinary action against partner	52
59. Death notification	51
60. Press criticism of an officer's actions	51
61. Polygraph examination	51
62. Sexual advancement toward you by another officer	51
63. Duty-related accidental injury	51
64. Changing work shifts	50
65. Written reprimand by a supervisor	50
66. Inability to solve a major crime	48
67. Emergency run to "unknown trouble"	48
68. Personal use of alcohol while on duty	48
69. Inquiry into another officer's misconduct	47
70. Participation in a narcotics raid	47
71. Verbal reprimand by a supervisor	47
72. Handling of a mentally/emotionally disturbed person	47
73. Citizen complaint against an officer	47
74. Press criticism of departmental actions/practices	47
75. Answering a call to a sexual battery/abuse scene involving an adult victim	46
76. Reassignment/transfer	46
77. Unfair administrative policy	46
78. Preparation for retirement in the near future	46
79. Pursuit of a traffic violator	46
80. Severe disciplinary action to another officer	46
81. Promotion with assignment to another unit	45
82. Personal abuse of prescription drugs	45
83. Offer of a bribe	45
84. Personally striking a prisoner or suspect	45
85. Physical arrest of a suspect	45
86. Promotion within existing assignment	44
87. Handling a domestic disturbance	44
88. Answering a call to a scene involving the violent non-accidental death of an adult	44
89. Change in supervisors	44
90. Abuse of alcohol by another officer	44
91. Response to a silent alarm	44
92. Change in the chief administrators of the department.	43
93. Answering a call to a scene involving the accidental death of an adult	43
94. Move to a new duty station	43
95. Fugitive arrest	43
96. Reduction in job responsibilities	43
97. Release of an offender by the prosecutor	41

(continued)

TABLE 8-1 (cont.)

Event	Value
98. Job-related illness	41
99. Transfer of partner	40
100. Assignment to night shift duty	40
101. Recall to duty on day off	39
102. Labor negotiations	39
103. Verbal abuse from a traffic violator	39
104. Change in administrative policy/procedure	38
105. Sexual advancement toward you by a citizen	37
106. Unfair plea bargain by a prosecutor	37
107. Assignment to a specialized training course	37
108. Assignment to stakeout duty	37
109. Release of an offender on appeal	37
110. Harassment by an attorney in court	37
111. Administrative recognition (award/commendation)	36
112. Court appearance (felony)	36
113. Annual evaluation	35
114. Assignment to decoy duty	35
115. Assignment as partner with officer of the opposite sex	35
116. Assignment to evening shift	35
117. Assignment of new partner	34
118. Successful clearance of a case	34
119. Interrogation session with a suspect	33
120. Department budget cut	33
121. Release of an offender by a jury	33
122. Overtime duty	29
123. Letter of recognition from the public	29
124. Delay in a trial	28
125. Response to a "sick or injured person" call	28
126. Award from a citizens group	27
127. Assignment to day shift	26
128. Work on a holiday	26
129. Making a routine arrest	26
130. Assignment to a two-man car	25
131. Call involving juveniles	25
132. Routine patrol stop	25
133. Assignment to a single-man car	25
134. Call involving the arrest of a female	24
135. Court appearance (misdemeanor)	24
136. Working a traffic accident	23
137. Dealing with a drunk	23
138. Pay raise	23
139. Overtime pay	22
140. Making a routine traffic stop	22
141. Vacation	20
142. Issuing a traffic citation	20
143. Court appearance (traffic)	19
144. Completion of a routine report	13

Reproduced from the *Journal of Police Science and Administration,* 11:1 (1983), pp. 113, 114, by permission of the International Association of Chiefs of Police, Inc., 1110 North Glebe Road, Suite 200, Arlington, Virginia 22201.

TABLE 8-2 Short-Term/Chronic Stress Reaction

Job-related stressors	**Immediate responses to stress**			
	Personality	Health	Job Performance	Home Life
Administration Job conflict Second job Inactivity Shift work Inadequate resources Inequities in pay and job status Organizational territoriality Job overload Responsibility for people Courts Negative public image Conflict values Racial situations Line of duty/crisis situations Job ambiguity	Temporary increases in: Anxiety Tension Irritability Feeling "uptight" Drinking rate	Temporary increases in: Smoking rate Headaches Heart rate Blood pressure Cholesterol level	Job tension "Flying off the handle" Erratic work habits Temporary work decrement	"Spats with spouse" Periodic withdrawal Anger displaced to wife and children Increased extramarital activity
	Long-term responses to stress			
	Personality	Health	Job performance	Home life
	Psychosis Chronic depression Alienation Alcoholism General malaise Low self-esteem Low self-actualization Suicide	Chronic disease states: Ulcers High blood pressure Coronary heart disease Asthmatic attacks Diabetes	Decreased productivity Increased error rate Job dissatisfaction Accidents Withdrawal Serious error in judgment Slower reaction time	Divorce Poor relations with others Social isolation Loss of friends

Adapted from W. H. Kroes, *Society's Victim—The Policeman,* Psychological Services Unit, Dallas Police Department (Springfield, Ill.: Charles C Thomas, 1976), p. 66.

Some 6.5 million employed workers in the United States today are alcoholics. Loss of productivity because of the disease of alcoholism has been computed at $10 billion.[25]

Although precise figures are not available to substantiate a high incidence of alcoholism among police, department officials have reported informally that as many as 25 percent of the officers in their respective departments have serious alcohol abuse problems.[26]

Alcohol problems among police officers manifest themselves in a number of ways. Some of these are a higher than normal absentee rate before and immediately following the officer's regular day off, complaints of insubordination by supervisors, complaints by citizens of misconduct in the form of verbal and physical abuse, intoxication during regular working hours, involvement in traffic accidents while under the influence of alcohol on and off duty, and reduced overall performance.

It has been suggested further that policing is especially conducive to alcoholism. Because police officers frequently work in an environment in which social drinking is commonplace, it is relatively easy for them to become social drinkers. The nature of police work and the environment in which it is performed provides the stress stimulus.[27]

Traditionally, police departments adhere to the "character flaw" theory of alco-

TABLE 8-3 Fifteen Most Prevalent Stress Warning Signs

Warning signs	Examples
1. Sudden changes in behavior. Usually directly opposite to usual behavior.	From cheerful and optimistic to gloomy and pessimistic
2. More gradual change in behavior but in a way that points to deterioration of the individual	Gradually becoming slow and lethargic, possibly with increasing depression and sullen behavior
3. Erratic work habits	Coming to work late, leaving early, abusing compensatory time
4. Increased sick time due to minor problems	Headaches, colds, stomach aches, etc.
5. Inability to maintain a train of thought	Rambling conversation, difficulty in sticking to a specific subject.
6. Excessive worrying	Worrying about one thing to the exclusion of any others
7. Grandiose behavior	Preoccupation with religion, politics, etc.
8. Excessive use of alcohol and/or drugs	Obvious hangover, disinterest in appearance, talk about drinking prowess
9. Fatigue	Lethargy, sleeping on job
10. Peer complaints	Others refuse to work with him or her
11. Excessive complaints (negative citizen contact)	Caustic and abusive in relating to citizens
12. Consistency in complaint pattern	Picks on specific groups of people (youths, blacks, etc.)
13. Sexual promiscuity	Going after everything all of the time—on or off duty
14. Excessive accidents and/or injuries	Not being attentive to driving, handling prisoners, etc.
15. Manipulation of fellow officers and citizens	Using others to achieve ends without caring for their welfare

Reproduced by permission of the Psychological Services Unit, Dallas Police Department, 1980.

holism. This philosophy calls for the denunciation and dismissal of an officer with an alcohol problem because recognizing him or her as a symptom of underlying problems reflects on the department. What is not considered is that alcoholism may result from the extraordinary stress of the job and that eliminating the officer does not do away with the source of stress.[28]

Departmental Programs

There is no single "best way" for a department to assist its officers with a drinking problem, but some agencies have enjoyed a fair degree of success for their efforts. For example, the Denver Police Department is now utilizing its closed-circuit television system to teach officers who are problem drinkers and encourage them to join the in-house program. A major portion of the in-house program is designed to persuade the problem drinker, after he or she has digested a sufficient amount of the educational aspect, to enter the Mercy Hospital CareUnit® and achieve the status of a recovering alcoholic.[29]

One researcher has concluded that it is the responsibility of the individual police agency and its administrators to recognize and accept the fact of alcoholism as a disease and to create a relaxed atmosphere and an in-house program for the dissemination of information relative to this problem. As indicated earlier, the objective of such a program is ultimately to persuade individual officers to enter a care unit for treatment. The combination of unsatisfactory performance, excessive costs, and the almost certain progressive deterioration of the individual officer to the point of unemployability, if the illness goes unchecked, creates a situation that conscientious chiefs of police should neither tolerate nor ignore.[30]

An essential point to remember is that, if drinking affects an officer's health, job, or family, immediate action is essential—the officer is probably an alcoholic.

Reports by the Denver Police Department indicate that the organization has benefited in specific ways since the implementation of their alcohol abuse program. Some of these specific benefits have been

1. Retention of the majority of the officers who had suffered from alcoholism
2. Solution of a set of complex and difficult personnel problems
3. Realistic and practical extension of the police agency's program into the entire city government structure
4. Improved public and community attitudes by this degree of concern for the officer and the officer's family and by eliminating the dangerous and antisocial behavior of the officer in the community
5. Full cooperation with rehabilitation efforts from the police associations and unions that may represent officers
6. The preventive influence on moderate drinkers against the development of dangerous drinking habits that may lead to alcoholism. In addition, an existing in-house program will motivate some officers to undertake remedial action on their own, outside the scope of the police agency program.[31]

Drug Use by Police Officers

During the last five years, drug abuse by police officers has garnered a great deal of attention.[32] A national study of 2,200 police officers found that 10 percent had serious drug problems.[33] As a result of this condition, police administrators have had to grapple with such issues as

- What positions will the employee unions or other employee organizations take if drug testing is proposed?
- Who should be tested for drugs? Entry level officers? Regular officers on a random basis? All officers before they are promoted? Personnel assigned to high-profile units such as bomb disposal and special tactics and response?
- When does a supervisor have "reasonable suspicion" of a subordinate's drug use?
- Who should collect urine or other specimens and under what conditions?
- What criteria or standards should be used when selecting a laboratory to conduct the police department's drug testing program?
- What disciplinary action is appropriate when officers are found to have abused drugs?
- What duty does an employer have to rehabilitate employees who become disabled as a result of drug abuse?[34]

The courts have provided guidelines that address some of these questions.

Guidelines for Testing Law Enforcement Personnel

Courts are currently in agreement that law enforcement personnel may be tested for drug use on the basis of reasonable suspicion. This suspicion provides a necessary connector between a positive drug test result and job impairment. This connector, however, is missing when testing is based on systematic random testing. The Supreme Court seems to indicate that interests of deterrence may justify systematic random testing. It is unclear, however, that positive test results based on systematic random testing are in themselves sufficient to satisfy procedural due process requirements if the employee is terminated solely as a result of positive test results.[35]

Given the above, adherence to the following guidelines seems appropriate in testing law enforcement personnel for drug use.

When to test

- Testing is appropriate as a condition of employment.
- Testing is appropriate if conducted pursuant to a scheduled physical examination.
- Testing is appropriate following a serious motor vehicle accident or the discharging of a firearm.
- Testing is appropriate if based on individualized reasonable suspicion that the employee is engaged in an improper association with the use of drugs.
- Systematic random testing is permissible if tested officers are required to perform their police functions if they witness illegal conduct while off duty.

How to test

- The individual administering the test should not directly observe the employee urinating.
- The administering individual should be in close enough proximity, however, to develop any reasonable suspicion of tampering. If such suspicion ensues, direct observation is appropriate.
- Upon receipt, each urine sample should be divided into two separate samples. The first sample is subjected to a test designed to determine if drugs are present in the urine. If a positive result is obtained, a second and more sophisticated test is administered to determine the quantity of the drug in the system.
- If a positive test results from the second analysis, the employee should be provided an opportunity to have the second sample reconfirmed at a laboratory of his or her choosing.
- The laboratory contracted to conduct urinalysis testing should be subjected to blind testing. The results of the blind testing should be made available to any employee subjected to testing from that laboratory.

What to do with the results

- Test results may be used for disciplinary action.
- Test results should not be turned over to any other agency, including criminal prosecutors, without the employee's written consent, unless the test was obtained on the basis of a valid warrant and probable cause.

- A positive test result based on reasonable suspicion of on-duty drug impairment may result in employment termination.
- A positive test result based on systematic random testing may result in employment termination only if the officer is required to perform police functions while off-duty or additional objective evidence of improper drug use is uncovered.

Police Management Response

Setting aside the question of whether or not employment termination is a legal response to positive drug test results, another question arises as to whether termination is the "smart" management response. One police administrator suggests that it is.[36] The argument is that police officers who fear the loss of their jobs are more likely to avoid drugs and, further, that if the public is aware of even one drug abuser in a particular police department, it is apt to discredit that particular organization as well as the entire profession. The suggestion has been made, however, that there may be room for several exceptions.

Often a comparison is made between the effects of alcohol and the impairment of drug abuse. Drug abuse is usually illegal, however, whereas alcohol use is not. Accordingly, a more proper comparison may be the treatment given to police arrested for criminal violations. Some criminal convictions lead to termination, but minor charges such as disorderly conduct often do not. Perhaps a similar factual inquiry is appropriate when determining the response to a positive employee drug test. Just as the officer arrested in a neighboring jurisdiction for drunk driving may not lose his or her job, a police officer abusing prescription drugs in response to a particular job stress need not automatically be discharged. Here, an appropriate action might involve giving that officer an opportunity to seek assistance. Further, perhaps those employees who voluntarily step forward to seek assistance should receive special consideration. It is reasonable for police departments to assist its employees actively in overcoming drug abuse.

Anabolic Steroids

When police administrators consider the use of illegal drugs by their personnel, they typically think of the traditional illegal drugs such as marijuana, cocaine, heroin, amphetamines, barbiturates, and so forth. However, drugs that are abused more than many people realize are anabolic steroids.

Background

The use of anabolic steroids by athletes began in the late 1940s.[37,38] It is estimated that 80 to 99 percent of male body builders[39] and perhaps as many as 96 percent of professional football players have used these drugs, as have many other athletes.[40] Sixty-eight percent of interviewed track and field athletes had used steroids in preparation for the 1972 Olympics in Munich.[41] Since then, the International Olympic Committee has banned all anabolic drugs, and the top six performers in each Olympic event are now tested for nontherapeutic drugs of all types. Despite such developments, steroid use is widespread. The Mayo Clinic has estimated that more than one million Americans are regular steroid users.[42]

The law enforcement community is not exempt from this new form of drug abuse. For example, the U.S. Bureau of Customs was investigating the smuggling of anabolic steroids into this country. Their investigation led them to certain health clubs in North Carolina, where it was determined that state patrol officers were illegally using anabolic steroids. The North Carolina State Patrol joined the investigation, and subsequently three troopers were terminated. In Miami Beach, a physical training sergeant noticed that one of his charges was "bulking up" too fast. This female also displayed street behavior that led a department supervisor to recommend that she be assigned to nonstreet duties. It was subsequently established that she had been using anabolic steroids. In addition to using steroids themselves, officers in New York have been convicted of selling anabolic steroids.

Adverse Health Impact

There are recognized medical uses of anabolic steroids. Among the conditions for which anabolic steroids may be therapeutically appropriate are deficient endocrine functioning of the testes, osteoporosis, carcinoma of the breast, growth retardation, and severe anemia.[43]

The use of anabolic steroids, as summarized in Table 8-4, is associated with a number of potential outcomes that are adverse to an individual's health. These risks are even greater when anabolic steroids are taken under the direction of a self-appointed " 'roid guru" or when self-dosing, because the typical usage under these and related circumstances is ten to one hundred times greater than typical medical dosages.[44] Further complicating the nontherapeutic use of steroids is self-treatment with preparations not legally available in the United States and veterinary preparations such as Boldenone (Equipose®), for which it is difficult to estimate dosage equivalency,[45] virtually assuring dosages well beyond those recognized as medically appropriate.

Unknown, or less well known, to anabolic steroid abusers than the previously noted risks are certain affective and psychotic symptoms. Charlier[46] maintains that "aggressive behavior is almost universal among anabolic steroid users. There are

TABLE 8-4 Adverse Effects of Anabolic Steroids

Men	Women	Both Sexes
▪ Breast enlargement ▪ Testicular atrophy with consequent sterility or decreased sperm count ▪ Impotence ▪ Enlarged prostate	▪ Breast diminution ▪ Clitoral enlargement ▪ Facial hair growth ▪ Deepened voice ▪ Menstrual irregularities ▪ Excessive body hair ▪ Baldness	▪ Increased aggression known as " 'roid rage" ▪ Increased risk of heart disease, stroke, or obstructed blood vessels ▪ Acne ▪ Liver tumors, jaundice, and peliosis hepatitis (blood-filled cysts) ▪ Pre-teens and teenagers, accelerated bone maturation leading to permanent short stature

From *FDA Drug Bulletin,* 17:3 (1987), p. 27, with modification.

documented case histories of severe depression, visual and auditory hallucinations, sleep disorders, thoughts of suicide, outbursts of anger, anorexia, psychomotor retardation, and irritability.[47] In a survey of health club athletes who used steroids, 90 percent reported steroid-induced aggressive or violent behavior.[48] Pope and Katz conducted a study of 39 male and two female anabolic steroid abusers whose psychiatric histories were generally unremarkable. Yet five subjects had psychotic symptoms and others had manic episodes or periods of major depressions:

> One 23-year-old man bought a $17,000 automobile. . . . when he stopped taking anabolic steroids he realized he could not afford the payments and sold the car. A year later, while taking steroids again, he impulsively bought a $20,000 sports car. . . . another subject bought an old car and drove it into a tree at 40 miles per hour while a friend videotaped him. . . . a third subject believed his mind was influencing the pictures on television and promised a friend he would show God to him.[49]

Although not physically addicting, steroids can cause a psychological dependence. Goldstein[50] discusses three stages of drug abuse: initial stage of exploration, continuing stage of regular usage, and cessation from use. People are attracted to steroid use for a variety of reasons, all of which center on developing a more domineering physique. Initial users are generally "turned on" to the drugs by other abusers or seek them out at health clubs or gyms, where such drugs are commonly abused. The continuation stage occurs after initial use, when subjects have experienced some success with the drug. Thereafter, subjects become obsessed with their larger physiques, increased strength, or sexual appeal. Exercise becomes easier whenever steroids are used, and pain and a lack of strength appear when the drugs are discontinued. This process may continue until subjects are confronted with difficulties that result from their drug dependency. Cessation of usage will come only when the subjects become disinterested or are confronted with their problems.

Anabolic Steroids: The Legal Environment

The Drug Enforcement Administration has the major responsibility for enforcing the federal Controlled Substances Act (CSA), which is intended to minimize the quantity of drugs available for illegal use. The CSA places a substance into one of five schedules based on such factors as potential for abuse and whether there is a recognized medical use of the substance. Most over-the-counter (OTC) and prescription drugs do not fall within one of the CSA schedules and responsibility for enforcement efforts relating to them rests with the Food and Drug Administration (FDA) and state agencies. The FDA determines whether a substance falls within the OTC or prescription category; each state then has the legal power to determine who can legally prescribe and dispense OTC and prescription substances. Signed into law on November 18, 1988, the federal Anti-Drug Act of 1988—also referred to as the Omnibus Drug Abuse Initiative—created a special category of anabolic steroids within the prescription class, and all violations involving the sale or possession with intent to distribute anabolic steroids are now felonies.

Even before the passage of the Anti-Drug Act, it was illegal to possess anabolic steroids without a prescription in all 50 states. Thus, all officers in this country using anabolic steroids without a prescription have committed an illegal act. By November 1, 1989, at least 28 bills focused on anabolic steroids had been introduced in the state legislatures of Alaska, California, Connecticut, Georgia, Hawaii, Idaho, Illinois, New York, North Dakota, Oklahoma, Oregon, Pennsylvania, Rhode Island, and Washington. In general, these proposed laws would make prosecution of anabolic steroid–related crimes less cumbersome and call for more severe penalties.

Awareness of the nature and impact of illegal anabolic steroid use is beginning to be seen in litigation, an effect that is likely to expand quickly. "Anabolic steroid–induced rage" has been used as a defense in sexual assault cases; in one instance the judge accepted this argument as a mitigating factor when sentencing a defendant in a sexual assault. Liability is one of the most critical issues regarding steroid usage. It is only a matter of time before it will be alleged in a state tort or federal civil rights lawsuit that "but for the failure of the police department to conduct a proper background and drug screening, the anabolic steroid–induced violent assault on my client would never have occurred" (negligent selection) or that "but for the failure of the police department to properly train its supervisors on how to identify the manifestations of anabolic steroid abuse, then the physical trauma to Mrs. Johnson would not be an issue before this court today" (failure to train and failure to supervise). Although there are almost limitless liability scenarios, there is only one inescapable conclusion: if administrators do not confront this issue quickly, harm will be done to citizens, officers, families, and public treasuries.

Administrative Concerns and Anabolic Steroids

Regarding administrative attitudes toward steroid use, people in the internal affairs, public information, and command positions, as well as staff psychologists, of thirty police departments across the country were interviewed. With few exceptions, the response was "that's not a problem in this department and we've never had a problem with it." Yet replies of that nature are deceiving. For example, a departmental representative who had stated in the morning that steroid abuse was not a problem called back in the afternoon, saying "I've been thinking . . . one of our retired officers runs a gym frequented by our officers and some of them have gotten very muscular awfully quick." Police officials readily recognize cocaine or marijuana abuse as a police personnel problem, but for the most part they still are not aware of the seriousness of steroid abuse. If this situation is not soon corrected, departments will be confronted with increasing numbers of steroid-related problems.

As a practical matter, however, the agendas of most police departments are already crowded with pressing issues. Drug-testing programs are costly to develop and implement and may be opposed by police unions or elected officials who want their support. Even where in place, however, general drug tests will not detect the presence of anabolic steroids; a separate test is required, representing an additional cost for which to budget. Moreover, present information about police officer use of anabolic steroids is fragmented and impressionistic. Thus, full agendas, other priorities, difficulties in implementing drug-testing programs, politics, cost, and the lack of available information combine to limit the amount of organizational attention that will be given to police officer use of steroids in the near future.

Suicide and Police Officers

Suicide as a problem for police officers can best be understood by examining the differences between younger and older officers. Suicide among young police officers is not particularly common, but when it does occur, it is frequently associated with divorce or other family problems. Among older police officers, suicide is more common and may be related to alcoholism, physical illness, or impending retirement.[51] Although hard data are not readily available, there is some speculation that suicides immediately after retirement may not be uncommon. Some researchers have suggested that police officers do not retire well. This fact is widely known within police departments, and it is not surprising to see newly retired officers becoming depressed and allowing their physical condition to deteriorate. As occurs with individuals in other occupations, police officers do not plan realistically for retirement. However, unlike workers in some other occupations, police officers are generally deeply involved with their work until the actual moment of retirement. It is a shock to be estranged suddenly from a job that has occupied a major portion of one's life and has provided the source of so many social activities as well.[52]

These losses can have devastating effects on retiring or retired police officers, but unfortunately most police departments, unlike many major industries, have not yet addressed themselves to this problem, which has no doubt led to an undetermined number of police suicides.

One study concluded that the data that are available indicate that male police officers are more likely to kill themselves than are men in other occupations.[53] For example, the suicide rate for members of the New York City Police Department from 1960 to 1967 was 21.7 per 100,000 per year. The rate from 1950 to 1965 was 22.7. This is higher than the suicide rate of 16.7 for all males in the United States during this period.[54]

In reported suicide rates for males in various occupations in the United States in 1950, police officers had the second highest rate of thirty-six occupations at 47.6 per 100,000 per year. Only self-employed manufacturing managers and proprietors had a higher suicide rate. Clergymen had the lowest rate (10.6).[55]

Six possible clues have been outlined to help comprehend the high police suicide rates: (1) police work is a male-dominated profession, and males have demonstrated a higher successful suicide rate; (2) the use, availability, and familiarity with firearms by police in their work provide them with a lethal weapon that when used affords the user little chance of survival; (3) there are psychological repercussions of constantly being exposed to potential death; (4) long and irregular working hours do not promote strong friendships but do strain family ties; (5) there is constant exposure to public criticism and dislike for "cops"; and (6) judicial contradictions, irregularities, and inconsistent decisions tend to negate the value of police work.[56]

Some authorities believe that aggressive behavior stems not from internal drive but rather from societal frustration. In a sense they say that suicide and homicide are different manifestations of the same phenomenon. As acts of aggression, suicide and homicide cannot be differentiated with respect to the source of the frustration generating the aggression. Moreover, when the aggression legitimized by the aggressor is directed outward (other oriented) because of societal frustration, homicide results. Suicide or self-oriented aggression, a consequence of frustration, becomes a residual category or aggression for which outward expression against others is deemed illegitimate.[57]

In one study conducted several years ago of suicides of 12 Detroit police officers, Danto found that the group consisted of

> young men, married and for the most part, fathers, [who] came with backgrounds of unskilled employment prior to their police appointment, or military service, high school education or better, and some stable family life as measured by parents who were married and who had created families. The majority of the officers were white and had not been employed as police officers for many years. Many had received citations and commendations, as well as some reprimands. For some, service ratings were not good.
>
> The officers who committed suicide did so during the late hours of evening and early hours of morning. Most were either home or near loved ones or family when they died. They used firearms and fatally shot their heads and abdomens. Carbon monoxide was the second most common cause of death and many of the suicides, regardless of method, occurred in an automobile. Significant, perhaps, was that none of the officers was found in their uniforms at the time of their deaths.
>
> Marital trouble appeared to be the most important precipitating stress. Many of the officers had received psychiatric consultation and treatment prior to their suicide; a few had asked for help directly.
>
> The officers of the Detroit Police Department who committed suicide were different from the New York Police Department suicides. The Detroit group was younger, had less service time with the department, had a lower suicide rate within a police department, and less physical illness and police medical consultation histories, and fewer were single. In some respects they were similar: many had a history of alcohol abuse and dependency, had picked primarily firearms as their suicide method, and had suffered marital disharmony prior to their deaths.
>
> Neither study proves that the police officer is any more prone to choose his profession because of its opportunities to express aggression than anyone else in society. The rising suicide and homicide rates for nonpolice persons should attest to that. Furthermore, since women have become more violent in terms of crime, homicide and suicide, we know that we are dealing with a more general trend than a masculine assertion or aggression conflict. I do not feel that the police officer of today is more aggressive than most of the civilian population he serves.
>
> By far and away the most upsetting problem for the suicidal police officer is his marriage. This marital discord is reflected both in the fact that the officer sometimes committed suicide following the murder of a significant person, but also killed himself in a location near to persons for whom he cared very deeply. To some extent, problems may be connected to his work because his hours are erratic, constantly subject to change, and the officer is subjected to danger which is beyond the reach of most civilian minds. Not only does his spouse have trouble accepting his working hours and risk of danger and injury, but she finds herself left out of his life as far as the police department is concerned. She is in competition with the department for her husband's interests and she finds that the military structure of the police department is such that her husband has become the property of the department. He is told how he will dress, where he will live (in terms of residency restrictions within the city), what hours he will work, what duty he will pull, and what danger he must face. He finds himself like a knot being pulled in a tug-of-war between the police department on one side and his wife and family on the other. For the officer who commits suicide it may be that he chooses death as a final exercise of control over his life, control that he feels others have removed from him. In this respect he may resemble the cancer patient who, when near death, commits suicide as his last expression of determination to decide his time and means of death, fearful that illness will rob him of that potency.
>
> It would appear that the police officers in both police departments committed suicide in response to important personal problems.[58]

It has been suggested that the police suicide phenomenon should be viewed from a psychological basis that emphasizes both the unique and multideterminant aspects of an individual's behavior as well as the societal influences on that behavior. The human being is a frustrated and status-oriented social animal not isolated from peers. In many ways the American police officer is like a health professional. Officers frequently come in contact with the behaviorally different and socially ill citizens of our cities as part of their life's work. Likewise, when they are suffering unrelenting anguish, they often fear the loss of their jobs (perhaps realistically so because of parochial attitudes toward mental health held by their department) if they seek treatment. Yet the closest analogy, unfortunately, linking the police and health professionals is the reluctance of their respective colleagues to get them involved in treatment, in spite of their colleagues' awareness of their difficulties, because they may feel it is none of their business. A troubled police officer, like a health professional, is of no use to the public or to the profession if the officer does not seek treatment.[59]

Postshooting Trauma

For many years the FBI has compiled information concerning law enforcement officers who were killed in the line of duty. Until recently, however, there was little information regarding officers who killed in the line of duty either in their efforts to apprehend criminals or while defending themselves or others. The evidence is starting to mount that officers face very real and serious psychological and emotional side effects from these events.

Responses from police officers who killed someone in the line of duty vary. In some cases, officers experience incredible guilt, feeling immobilized and perhaps even believe they have compromised their religious beliefs.[60] The other extreme is comprised of individuals who experience no guilt, as in the case of one officer who said to a police psychologist, "Doc, isn't it alright if I don't feel guilty? If I had another gun, I would have shot him six more times."

Patterns of Reaction

The effects of a shooting are often varied among police officers, but interviews with officers who have experienced such incidents suggest that the following is a very common pattern.

Denial. The police officer does not believe the incident occurred and stands over the body in disbelief with shotgun or pistol in hand. The officer has not consolidated the entire event into his or her thinking system and there is momentary psychological shock. The activity leading up to the shooting has required the use of a reflexive behavior rather than a step-by-step thinking process. This disbelief or denial subsides rather quickly as the police officer becomes aware of a dead body in front of him or her or a wounded subject needing help.

Gathering Facts. The police officer realizes that there is a need to present all of the facts relating to the sequence of events and the shooting must be justified. The officer is also beginning to prepare for what will be an investigation by the homicide squad, internal affairs, and/or the administration. Police officers are trained to think in very factual terms when reporting such incidents. It is therefore

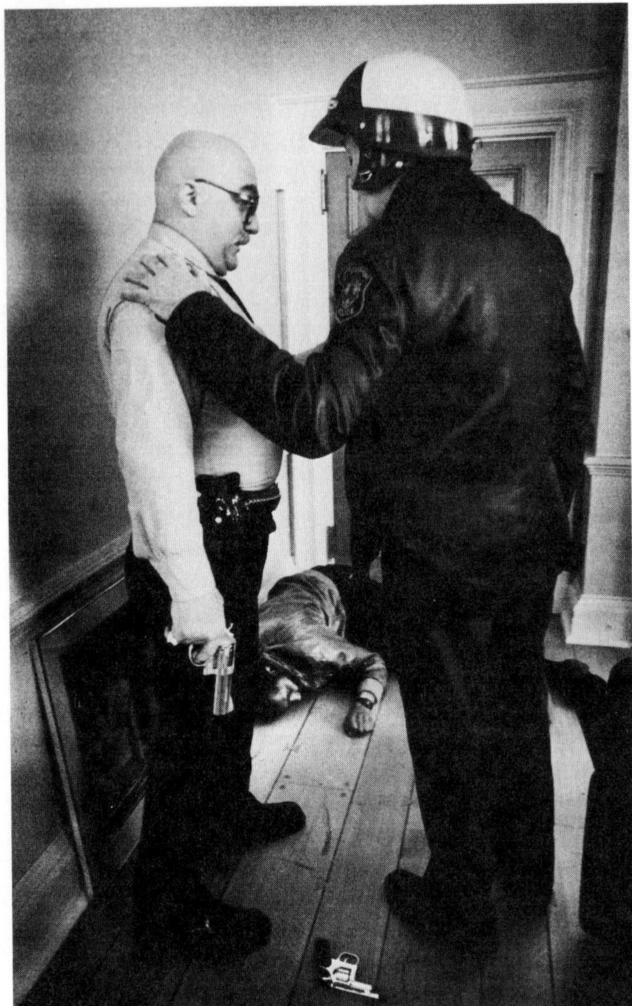

FIGURE 8-2. Pittsburgh police officer, left, is comforted by a fellow police officer after shooting a suspect after the man shot and wounded his wife. [Photo courtesy John Kaplan, Pittsburgh, Pa. Press.]

suggested that it will probably not be wise for the police psychologist to speak to the police officer at that very moment. It would be best first to provide the officer with an opportunity to give the investigators all the available factual information.

Reporting Facts. The police officer presents the facts to the investigators hoping for support and vindication. If the officer receives this support, then the officer becomes less defensive. Up to this point the police officer is acting according to previous training. Fact gathering and reporting incidents are daily tasks for a police officer. The stages the officer enters next are beyond the scope of most training programs and are frequently psychologically threatening. It is at this point that the police officer is in need of stress management. The officer should be aware that he

FIGURE 8-3. Wife of a Cincinnati police officer at her husband's funeral. The officer and his partner were killed by a robbery suspect. Friends of the slain officer also show the impact on them. [Photo courtesy of the *Cincinnati Post* (Ohio).]

or she will be entering the following stages and should be assured that his or her responses are normal ones.

Physical Anxiety. The officer will experience a high amount of stress even if the officer is assured that the action taken was a correct one. The officer continues to respond to this experience in a fight/flight response. Having fought to save his or her own life by shooting another person, the officer begins to experience a response more akin to the flight response. The officer would like to get away from the situation and find some relief. The officer finds that he or she is unable to relax and wonders whether there is something physically wrong. This may manifest itself in the inability of the officer to sleep, and in frequent pacing, inability to sit still, and so forth. All police officers involved in a shooting incident should engage in some type of physical activity within 24 hours. Depending upon the officer's life-style, this could be a sedentary activity such as fishing, or active exercise, such as playing racquetball or baseball. This activity relieves the anxiety tension and continued state of preparedness in which the physical body of the police officer remains.

Peer Group Support. A rather significant phenomenon in the data accumulated is that police officers are often back at the police station wishing to speak to fellow officers within 48 hours of the incident. They are obviously seeking some peer reassurance. Some departments will give the police officer two or three days off with pay, yet the officer may insist on going back to the station and speaking with fellow officers. It is believed that this return to the station is necessary and healthy and reassures the officer that despite having taken someone's life, there are those who support the behavior.

Moral Questioning. After two or three days the police officer begins to think of the moral implications of the behavior. Within a few days the very strong value systems possessed by most police officers dramatically affect the officer's self-evaluation as a human being. It is at this point that a psychologist can be most helpful. Besides experiencing moral anxiety the officer may become concerned with his or her psychological state and wonder whether he or she is going to "lose it." The officer may be unable to speak to anybody about these problems and not know how to broach the subject. The situation gets rapidly out of hand and some police officers who have not had posttraumatic shooting counseling have expressed that they have died "a thousand deaths" since the shooting period. They continue to have nightmares about the incident and continue to expect some sort of high-level punishment of a religious nature. Their peers who deal with many of the same types of events are frequently unavailable. The macho image so important in the police culture does not often encourage the mutual sharing of emotionally wrenching experiences, and a police officer who has experienced a fatal shooting incident unfortunately will quite often not easily share those feelings. Officers also find they are not able to speak to their spouses or families. Even though the families may be supportive there is some suggestion that they do not form the same type of solid framework of peer group relationships as does the police culture, and the officer may believe that since they are not police officers they cannot understand his or her feelings. Thus the police officer quickly and unfortunately excludes important persons in his or her life, thus bringing about his or her own isolation and quite possibly ultimate immobilization.

Counseling. The most effective way to get a police officer into stress management counseling after such an incident is to establish a policy making such counseling mandatory. By making counseling mandatory, the decision-making responsibility is immediately taken from the police officer who is already suffering from extreme stress. Although there may be some momentary resistance toward such an order, it is up to the psychologist to bring relief to the police officer. The end result is usually the appreciation of the officer for having had such a counseling session.

The first counseling session is conducted with only the officer, who is immediately assured of total confidentiality. No information is given to other people. Because the officer is being investigated by the department, the psychologist could easily be seen as another departmental inquiring force who is building a case against the officer if things have not been done according to department policy.

In many of these incidents an effort is made to have the police officer come back to the second session with his or her spouse. Again there is hesitation by the police officer who did not really want to involve the spouse. It is quite typical for a spouse to attempt to persuade the officer to transfer to a different kind of police work or even encourage the officer to get out of police work entirely. Now the officer has not only the stress of the incident, his or her own psychological stress and moral anxiety, but also the concern for his or her spouse and family. Thus the police officer is presented with incredible responsibility and decision making, a process for which the officer has probably not been trained.

The police officer and spouse are then given the option of attending future sessions. If it is believed that further support is needed, very strong encouragement is given to the officer and spouse to return. One study revealed that some 70 percent of all persons involved in such programs had returned for advice not only on police-related matters but also for other personal problems. It is also significant that this group of police officers has been very active in referring other police officers to the psychologist.[61]

Stress and the Police Administrator

As any individual who has risen through the ranks of a police agency realizes, the types of problems and pressures encountered as an administrator are quite different from those encountered as a patrol officer. For either position, however, the end results of the stress can be equally menacing to the person performing the job.

The High Price of Success

One management expert has suggested that upward mobility in almost any type of bureaucracy tends to impose unique stresses on individuals. These stresses occur in part because an individual often must sacrifice family relationships for career goals and because each promotion brings with it more responsibilities for the individual over wider-ranging areas and increased numbers of subordinates. In addition, young men and women who ascend the organizational ladder rapidly tend to generate considerable envy from their peers who believe that they have been passed over unfairly for promotion. Sometimes this envy manifests itself in negative interpersonal contacts between the superior and his or her less successful subordinates.[62]

Upward mobility regardless of age carries with it certain risks. The higher one rises in the organization, the harder the fall if one should err. The errors that occur in the higher levels of police organizations are likely to be bigger, more costly, and more painful personally than are those in the lower ranks. Because his or her errors are more obvious to a wider range of people, the individual becomes increasingly concerned about being viewed as incompetent. A person may also feel isolated as peers become subordinates and once-gratifying relationships with them become modified or perhaps even dissolved.

Moreover, at a certain point in the upward climb, usually close to the top, many executives experience a specific disappointment. Once having achieved a certain position, they discover that they still have the same frailties, inadequacies, and self-doubts except that now their younger and less experienced subordinates look to them for the answers to complex problems. Looking upward from the lower rungs of the hierarchy, subordinates often tend to view distant supervisors as omnipotent. They have a powerful impact on the organization and always seem to know what they are doing. When the younger person reaches these levels, he or she soon realizes that the giants were really human after all and that one does not acquire omnipotence merely from having achieved a certain position.[63]

Sources of Stress for Managers

Preliminary research has already begun to identify sources of stress on the police manager. Kroes, Hurrell, and Margolis, for instance, found that "many police administrators and supervisors were experiencing stress problems that were different from those experienced by officers, yet equally menacing."[64] Conducting interviews of 12 captains and 13 lieutenants on the Cincinnati Police Department, they found that these administrators sensed their major stress as coming from administration (e.g., lack of higher echelon support), equipment/manpower (e.g., inadequacy of equipment or manpower), community relations (e.g., public apathy/ignorance and citizen complaints/demands), and courts (e.g., court scheduling problems and judicial leniency). Work ambiguity and work overload were the respondents' major concerns, with community relations, relations with superiors and subordinates, and work conflict also classified as "bothersome." Additionally, several of these administrators identified "taking disciplinary actions against subordinates" and "new administrative assignments" as specific stressors that concerned them. Finally, the researchers concluded

> The most significant stressors seemed to be a result of the administrator being in the position of the "man in the middle" while complex demands were being made upon him from the community, his superiors, and subordinates.[65]

In their study of 20 police chiefs and sheriffs at a National Development Institute, Hillgren, Bond, and Jones separated sources of stress into inherent line (events encountered as part of the routine job function) and administrative organization (problems resulting from the police agency or the criminal justice system) stressors. In this study, police executives were randomly divided into three groups and instructed "to consensually identify stressors believed to be affecting their line personnel and which they perceived to weigh heavily on them as chief administrators.[66]

Two of the findings in this study were particularly important. First, as other researchers have indicated, the source of much police officer stress, even for the "bosses," begins within the police agency and its policies and procedures. Second, there is a "marked similarity between the sources of stress identified by police officers for themselves, and those identified by chief administrators for themselves,"[67] a finding similar to that in the research of Kroes, Hurrell, and Margolis. With these studies as a starting point, a number of specific sources of stress for police administrators can be identified.

Dependence on Others. The position of the law enforcement officer often requires extreme independence and the ability to rely on oneself; at the most common level, one depends on only one's partner for backup and support. The position of administrator, however, requires learning to depend on subordinates and support staff to accomplish its defined mission. Especially in large departments, it is mentally and physically impossible for senior administrators to know and do everything; they must instead develop a dependence on others, which runs contrary to their basic training as police officers. Perhaps Harry Truman's commentary on the presidency best captures the essence of being a police chief: "I sit here all day trying to persuade people to do the things they ought to have sense enough to do without my persuading them. . . . That's all the powers of the President amount to!"

Concerns for Personnel and Their Needs. In performing his or her daily activities, the street officer and the detective are each concerned about equipment, supplies, and support that directly and individually pertain to them. Although they may feel some ties with other officers, the concern over the needs of others is not a major priority. For the administrator, however, the focus changes. Instead of being concerned over one shotgun, one case, one patrol vehicle, and one partner, the administrator must be concerned for the well-being and resource needs of the multiple officers under his or her command.

Lack of Resources. In recent years many governmental agencies have seen the era of "cut-back management." Many departments operate within the constraints of increasing demands for police services with fewer personnel and fiscal resources to respond to mounting street crime and citizen concerns. The lack of available resources, including salary and benefits, and competition with other governmental agencies over limited revenue obviously hamper the ability of the administrator to do the job and can cause a significant degree of stress.

Increased Community Demands and Pressures. Again, the last several years have seen an increase in demands for police activities, particularly as concern about real or perceived crime in the street increases. Especially in our larger cities, community pressures to assure professionalization of police, prevent discriminatory and abusive practices, and provide a prompt and complete response to citizens have increased the public's expectations of administrators.

Impact of the External Bureaucracy. The police manager, especially the agency's chief administrator, must also react to controls, regulations, demands, and even paperwork imposed by outside sources such as courts, prosecutors, or the state or federal government that are difficult to influence and often impossible to predict. The many mandates from outside the department often place the police manager in a position that allows little flexibility of response and discourages managerial creativity and productivity.

Political Nature of the Job. The very nature of law enforcement is, of course, political. Police officers at all levels always have been placed in positions where they must deal with competing demands within a complex political environment. For the administrator, the political nature of the job is magnified by the number of high-profile cases, the number and power of special interest groups, and the number of members of the local governing body. Especially wherever administrators are not protected by civil service status, the political nature of their jobs can, of course, even result in termination.

Sedentary Nature of the Job. Law enforcement is an action-oriented profession. Street officers in particular perceive themselves to be the "glory guys," able to take quick and effective action against the criminal "hordes." For an officer promoted through the ranks, the sedentary nature of an administration position can take its toll. For example, instead of being a radio car operator who immediately tackles community disorder, the officer becomes a "desk jockey" who handles papers and is less able to respond in a physical manner to discharge the adrenalin inherent in stressful situations. The result is heart attack, ulcers, and other diseases associated with a lack of cardiovascular exercise and a stressful vocation.

Lack of Preparation for the Job. Traditionally in law enforcement, professional development has been devoted primarily to street officers and investigators to prepare them for the day-to-day operational tasks they must confront. Especially in small departments, little effort has been given to prepare administrators and supervisors for the demands of their positions, and too many administrators still perceive themselves as "top cops" instead of modern managers. The position of police administrator requires a significant degree of training and flexibility to meet changing job requirements. Without effective preparation and development, administrators, like their operational counterparts, are ineffective and incapable of meeting the demands placed on them.

Conflict with Employee Organizations. Over the last 25 years, there has been a significant increase in the number of employee organizations representing law enforcement officers as their collective bargaining units. As a result of unfair management activities in the past and the lack of career protection for law officers, these organizations have grown in strength and power as they have proved their effectiveness. Especially for newly appointed chief executives, there is often a conflict between their desire to be agents of change, and the organization, which tries to protect the status quo, too often in the mistaken belief that the chief will again become too powerful. The conflict within and between ranks can become a major source of stress.

Difficulty of Effecting Lasting Change. A major frustration for administrators is their perception of their inability to effect lasting change in an organization. With the limited tenure of police administrators and with the demands of the political environment, change is slow to occur, and its actual effect may not be known for years. By then, some administrators' frustrations have built to the point that they have left for other horizons. Although a problem for many professionals, the long lead time necessary to put changes into effect is especially disappointing for law enforcement administrators, whose prior training and experience have instilled in them a need to be decisive and act quickly.

Separation from the Subculture. For most officers, the involvement with and camaraderie of peers are critical parts of the law enforcement experience. The ability to associate off duty with those who have shared similar life experiences and who generally view the profession in a similar manner contributes to the maintenance of the police subculture. Upward progression in the administrative hierarchy, however, reduces the number of direct peers. Because of the responsibilities associated with their rank and assignment, many managers find fewer officers with whom they can comfortably and in confidence share their experiences, concerns, emotions, and problems. Likewise, comrades from a manager's days in patrol or investigations may be reticent to discuss fully their opinions of administrative actions or to include managers in their social or even professional activities. The lack of someone to talk to—a sudden limitation on the "brotherhood of the badge"—can be one of the greatest shocks of promotion.

Dealing with the Manager's Stress

The important first step in successfully dealing with managerial stress is recognizing the problem. Many managers fail to notice tension, pressure, and anxiety; others accept that it is part of the police manager's way of life. In either case, stress can psychologically, and more likely, physiologically, take its toll. To confront stress effectively, as in dealing with any administrative problem, administrators must acknowledge its existence and effect and then plan a program to manage it.

Second, the development of a unique program of stress resolution and management for administrators is critical. Although many administrators have hurried to improve the capability of their officers to deal with the stress of law enforcement, only a few have recognized the need for their own stress management programs. Such programs should include components that emphasize the importance of proper diet and nutrition, physical fitness and exercise, and psychological fitness in handling the stress of police management.[68]

As part of the program of stress management, it is important that an administrator learn to use leisure activities to relieve stress. Recreational outlets, including sports, hobbies, and social functions, are alternatives to the stressful life of a manager. Periods of rest and relaxation, including regular vacations, are imperative to allow the body an opportunity to recharge and prepare for stress in the days to come.

Third, preparation for management positions is as critical a step in professional development as it is for investigators and technicians. The training of supervisors and managers, whether in a classroom or through on-the-job experience, should begin before promotion. Creativity in training, including the use of temporary administrative duty assignments, intradepartmental management internships, and interdepartmental exchange programs, can offer new and perhaps more effective methods of career development and preparation for future managers.

Fourth, perhaps one of the greatest frustrations experienced by any manager is the feeling that he or she has no control over time. Time management is, in effect, no more than successful self-management. Although many of the demands on a manager's time may be imposed by others, the majority of time constraints are his or her own. Successful time management simply requires a manager to organize, prioritize, and structure time in order to get things done more effectively and efficiently.[69]

Finally, as officers progress up through the ranks, they must develop new peer groups with whom to discuss problems and share confidences. The problems one manager must confront have often been experienced by others, and it is helpful to draw from others' experiences to learn from their successes and failures. Although not a complete substitute for the camaraderie of "working cops," professional associations at the local, state, and national levels offer police administrators an opportunity for communication, discussion, and fellowship that they may otherwise lack.

Midlife Crisis and the Middle-Aged Manager

Behavioral scientists have coined the phrase "midlife crisis" to describe some of the physical and psychological changes some people may undergo between the ages of 35 and 45. For example, statistics provided by life extension examiners indicate that specific symptoms—such as extreme fatigue, indigestion, and chest pains—rise sharply among young executives just moving into top management.[70] One-third of the symptoms found in the 30- to 40-year-old management groups can be traced to an organic cause, the examiners report.[71]

Although some explanations for this increase in symptoms are no doubt a product of the aging process itself, there are more pressing psychological forces. The British psychoanalyst Elliot Jaques[72] contends that a peak in the death rate between 35 and 40 is attributable to the shock that follows the realization that one is inevitably on a descending path. This produces what for most people is a transitory period of depression. Depression increases a person's vulnerability to illness. There is much medical evidence that physical illness is likely to occur more frequently and more severely in people who feel depressed.

Middle-aged managers going through midlife crises may find themselves running after lost youth with vain cosmetic efforts, dressing in a manner comparable to younger people. Carried to its extreme forms, the midlife crisis can be self-destructive to individuals and to the organization. Thus police organizations must take the middle-aged period seriously in their thinking, planning, and programming.

One of the needs for coping with midlife crisis is the opportunity to talk about it; therefore, a part of supervising and appraisal counseling should be devoted to some of the issues and concern of their conditions. Department educational programs should inform both managers and their spouses about this period of life and its unique pressures.

Stress and the Police Family

A law enforcement career is much more than a job or an occupation for the individual; it is a way of life for the officer and his or her family. A police officer's life becomes one of shared priorities between family and the outside world in which he or she functions on an official basis. Problems and frustrations encountered on the job might be brought home to the family. Conversely, the frustrations, tensions, and hostilities engendered by an unsatisfactory home life might be vented on the public.

Administrators are starting to recognize that the spouse and family are significant contributors to the success or failure in a law enforcement career. Marital and family strife, discord, and unresolved emotional problems affect a police officer's development, motivation, productivity, and effectiveness in ways that we are only beginning to appreciate and understand.

The excessive psychological pressures on officers to maintain self-control on the job drain their energies and can leave them totally depleted and unable to cope with problems at home. The spouse and family who need and expect some time and attention in working out their own problems are confronted with a person who simply lacks the emotional resources to deal with one more stressful situation. Whether the problem is large and important or small and trivial is irrelevant to the emotionally depleted officer; the officer is unable to deal with it.[73]

Problems in Police Marriages

Marriages of law enforcement personnel are susceptible to certain kinds of stresses inherent in the nature of policing. Erratic work schedules, job pressures, and the necessity for 24-hour availability are a few factors that can drive a wedge between officers and their spouses. There is considerable evidence that police officers as an occupational group have one of the highest divorce rates in the country, and divorce seems to be especially prevalent among young police officers.

Some authorities point out that

> In large departments, it is easy to find numbers of patrol officers who are on their third marriage before age 30. There is no particular mystery with regard to the breakup of marriages existing prior to entry into police service. Many police officers are married

FIGURE 8-4. New York City policeman receiving award with his family present. [Photo courtesy of New York City Patrolmen's Benevolent Association.]

within a few years after finishing high school and typically neither spouse had any realistic notion of what police service would mean in terms of its effect on family life. Police agencies that provide any orientation or counseling for spouses are increasing in number but they are still the exception rather than the rule.[74]

Earlier in this century, law enforcement personnel ranked thirtieth in divorce rates out of 39 job categories.[75] Some occupations or professions ranked higher than police were physicians, lawyers, teachers, and salesmen. One explanation provided by Durner[76] and others is that law enforcement officers during this earlier period constituted large numbers of Irish, Polish, and Italian Catholics. Thus it seems reasonable to assume that traditional condemnation of divorce by the Roman Catholic church kept the divorce rate from being a reliable indicator of the success or failure of law enforcement marriages. Some authorities have suggested that divorce rates are merely the tangible expression of a far greater problem, dissatisfaction in marriage, whether or not it ends in divorce. Expressed dissatisfaction among married people is identified as a more accurate indicator of the number of people who are living in a state of marital discord and aggravation than is the actual divorce rate.

In the case of the police officer, an unhappy marriage becomes a social disability because of the officer's role as a controller of society. There is an urgent need to identify and overcome difficulties leading to marital dissatisfaction in police officers, for the plight of the officer's marriage affects everyone: the officer, his or her family, his or her offspring, and society as a whole. Generally, a long period of poor communication, confrontation, and frustration precedes the actual dissolution of a marriage.[77]

Job-Induced Problems

We spoke earlier of job-related pressures that are inherent in the law enforcement career. Unusual working hours, scattered weekends, excessive overtime, court appearances, and the constant presence of a gun in one's everyday life are enough to cause significant stresses and problems in a marital relationship. Most of these are obvious pressures to which most couples are able to adjust. There are stresses, however, that can have long-range and lasting effects on a relationship. Many of them create problems that have never been encountered, or even imagined by the couple until they are forced to cope with them following the marriage ceremony. In many instances, these stresses take their toll over an extended period of time, and neither party attends to the warning signals or is able to pinpoint the actual source of the difficulties.

Changing Work Schedules. Extensive disruption occurs in the family routine as a result of changing work schedules and may have an adverse effect on home life. Not enough time is spent with the children; weekends and holidays with the family are missed; the spouse dislikes and resents being home alone at night; and social events with friends and family are difficult to plan. Working overtime merely accentuates the problems of shift work and leaves even less time to spend with the family. The most important factor in all these missed opportunities is the lack of shared experience among husband and wife and children. The end result can be a loss of interest in one another and a resulting breakdown in communications.

Emotional Exhaustion. The inability to function effectively and deal successfully with people's problems confronts the police officer daily. This constant barrage of unsolvable problems, along with the various negative situations with which the officer constantly comes in contact, leads to frustration and psychological exhaustion. By the time the officer gets home, all his patience has been expended. Problems at home either seem insignificant or, at the other extreme, may serve to infuriate the officer. An outburst of displaced aggression may then be released on the family. In any event, the family is the loser.

Negative Public Image. How other people behave toward us is a well-known determinant of social behavior. Most police believe that what they do is important, but they are also very conscious of what they believe the public opinion of them is. Perceived public animosity and disrespect impose the negative label of "cop" on the officer. Such a label has adverse effects not only on the officer but also on his close friends and family relations.

Overprotecting the Spouse and Family. One police psychologist points out that "because of the trauma and degradation they observe every day, law enforcement officers tend to become overprotective of their families."[78] The job teaches and actively encourages an individual to become extremely observant and to develop suspiciousness as a part of his working personality. Often, without realizing it, the police officer carries over these characteristics, which are highly functional on the job, into his personal relationships to the degree that he or she becomes overly concerned about his or her spouse's and family's welfare. Wanting to know where the family is, what they are doing, and who they are with at all times can impose irksome restrictions on them. What the officer views as concern and love for his or her family can often be misinterpreted by the spouse and children as a lack of trust and confidence on the part of an authoritarian who is not around most of the time.

Hardening of Emotions. To function adequately on the job, law enforcement officers often find it necessary to suppress their feelings. There is little room on the job for anger, disgust, tears, or sadness. Emotional suppression enables police officers to avoid deep personal involvement in the upsetting and occasionally traumatic incidents with which they have to deal on a daily basis. The "hardening" process helps police officers to perform unpleasant and distasteful but necessary tasks without any outward display of emotions. Unfortunately, it is impossible for the police officer to shed this stoic image with the uniform. Most officers bring this stoicism home to spouse and family who must try to relate to their impassiveness. Often, the spouse is unable to see, or even remember, the formerly cherished personal qualities of his or her partner, which are now hidden because the career demands it.

Sexual Problems. Sexual problems between the officer and his spouse may be either a symptom or a cause of emotional conflict and estrangement—and often are both. Intimacy is an early casualty of the pressures that the officer experiences. Once the harmony between marital partners has been shattered, it becomes exceedingly difficult to restore. The consequence is a vicious circle in which frustration creates anxiety and self-doubt, which in turn results in further frustration. As one group of police psychologists point out,

> Sexual promiscuity can also be a problem when the parties, out of frustration, seek release outside of marriage. Some of the sexual problems emanate from factors relating to police work. For instance, the officer who works nights, whose spouse works days, and both have different days off, encounter the basic problems of scheduling their sex life. In addition, if they also have children at home, the problem is exacerbated. Too frequently the couples do not put forth the effort to understand and tolerate these difficulties and to work out a compromise solution. Instead, they engage in open hostility toward each other and this creates feelings which in time can result in one or both partners seeking sexual partners elsewhere. This course of action, if discovered by the non-offending spouse, frequently results in the dissolution of the marriage.[79]

Infidelity on the part of the officer or spouse is a common source of domestic discord. Infidelity appears to be far more common among male officers than among their wives. In those cases, where the wife finds out about her husband's extramarital affairs, confronts him, and threatens to leave him, he usually undergoes severe depression and attitudinal and personality changes, which can result in serious problems for him both on and off the job.

Identity Problems. Traditional roles of men and women in marriage have undergone rapid changes in the past several years. Many women, no longer content to live in a world circumscribed by child rearing and housework, are asserting their fundamental rights to seek a broader set of opportunities outside the home for personal growth and self-actualization. They set great store on their individuality—on their separate selves.

In the case of male officers, marital problems may also result when the officer's wife believes that she has outgrown her husband and her social station as a police officer's wife. One case cited by a police psychologist concerned an officer's wife whose job involved circulating in highly sophisticated circles where her husband felt he did not belong: "This caused a serious strain in their relationship and they eventually sought counseling. If the officer's wife views his position as being one which does not have the degree of status or prestige she views as important to her own self-concept, then difficulties may emerge in the relationship.[80]

Problems with the Children. Children of police officers may encounter negative reactions and rejections from both peers and schoolteachers because of their father's or mother's occupation. Juvenile problems also seem to become prevalent when the children of police families reach adolescence. Although many of these problems are between the children and their parents, serious delinquency is not uncommon and may involve school truancy, vandalism, alcohol and drug abuse, rebelliousness, and various other kinds of misconduct.

Psychologists interpret the delinquent actions of police officers' children as the rejection of the authority represented by their parents' occupation. According to one group of police psychologists,

> Many times it is apparent that the officer is overprotecting his [or her] children and creating such an inhibiting home environment that they rebel. This phenomenon is far more common with adolescents who may feel trapped and stifled by their parent's protectiveness and act out in a manner that reinforces the parent's reason for overprotecting them.[81]

Once again, we see the familiar pattern of the vicious circle: the tighter the control, the more rebellious the juvenile becomes.

Marital Problems as an Administrative Concern

Until recently, law enforcement administrators have viewed marital problems among police personnel as a private matter involving only the officer and spouse. Fortunately, police executives are now beginning to view marital difficulties as an administrative problem. In acknowledgment of the magnitude and importance of marital problems and their far-reaching effects on job performance, some administrators have devised programs for solving, or at least reducing, marital problems within their organizations. As yet, however, these programs have not been implemented in the majority of departments. There is an urgent need to identify and overcome difficulties leading to marital discord and conflict among law enforcement personnel. The following are suggested programs for spouses of police officers that should help administrators reach this goal.

Orientation Programs for Spouses. An orientation program for police spouses should make them more aware and understanding of the many activities of the police agency. It should provide a comprehensive view of operations within the department, levels of command, and the day-to-day duties performed by law enforcement officers. This program should also enable the spouse to ask top police administrators questions concerning the department's function, the officer's job role, and off-duty requirements such as attending political rallies, doing volunteer work, and giving presentations at luncheon meetings. There should also be an honest effort given to presenting a realistic view of the law enforcement field and of the problems encountered on the job.

Interview Programs with the Spouses of Police Applicants. As part of the investigation of a police applicant, an interview could be conducted with the spouse at home to help determine the compatibility of the couple and their life-style to a law enforcement career. This interview should be only one determinant in the selection of law enforcement personnel, because most pressures in law enforcement careers that result in marital problems are very difficult to foresee. From this interview, police administrators can gauge the willingness of the spouse to assume the burdens of a law enforcement marriage. Similarly, the spouse benefits by being able to ask questions about the job that her husband possibly cannot or will not answer.

Ride-Along Programs. Law enforcement agencies should implement a ride-along program to provide spouses with first-hand observation and knowledge of the law enforcement officer's occupational role. This type of program also helps to familiarize the spouse with the police organization and its procedures.

Programs in Firearm Usage and Safety. Programs should be designed to introduce spouses to basic gun usage techniques and safety precautions because many people are frightened by the presence of firearms in their home. Instruction in the proper use and care of handguns should be given to reduce this stress situation for many couples. The spouse should be given opportunities to actually fire a weapon. Such programs provide the additional benefits of reducing the risk of a family member being injured accidentally.

FIGURE 8-5. Basic problems encountered in law enforcement marriages and solutions, as well as methods to improve communications, are among the subjects discussed by the department psychologist with spouses. [Photo courtesy of the Los Angeles County Sheriff's Department.]

An Exemplary Program

Dr. John Stratton, psychologist for the Sheriff's Department of Los Angeles County, has written about a program for spouses that was developed within this agency. Of the over four-hundred spouses participating in the program, it was evaluated as follows: excellent, 62 percent; very good, 33 percent; good, 5 percent; fair, 0 percent; and poor, 0 percent.

Although the spouses viewed all segments of the program as valuable, they mentioned some aspects that they felt were especially beneficial, namely, that the department values the spouse as an important contributor, that their fears about firearms were allayed because they learned safety techniques and how to fire a gun, and that they were given the opportunity to experience patrol in realistic situations as opposed to what they generally saw on television and in the movies.

The following are some written responses from spouses who attended the program:

> It helped me realize that I was not the only one having problems. It rather relieved the tension that had been building up inside. It was nice to air out problems that others had in common with you.
>
> It lessened the fear that I have for this type of law enforcement work. The more you know about something, the less you will usually fear it.
>
> The friendships that developed among the spouses were really great. It helped make spouses more enthusiastic toward their husbands' work, which in turn makes it easier to understand problems that might be involved with their work. Also I know that I now don't feel "apart" or "distant" from my spouse's work experience.

There are obviously no simple solutions to the complex marital and family problems that afflict law enforcement personnel. The kinds of programs suggested are based on the premise that spouses who understand their mates' work, the nature of its responsibilities, and the types of personality and behavioral changes it may cause will be more supportive, patient, and understanding, thus increasing the possibility of a successful marriage.

Although these programs are extremely beneficial, they should be supplemented by marriage, family, and personal counseling services obtained from specialists employed by the agency or by referral to professionals in the community.

The majority of these spouse orientation programs were originally intended for wives of police officers since law enforcement was until recent years a male-dominated profession. However, such programs are equally valid for the male partners of female officers, and many agencies now have both male and female spouses participating in spouse orientation programs.

Employee Assistance Programs

In recent years an increasing number of police departments have developed Employee Assistance Programs (EAPs) to assist police officers with many of the stresses associated with police work.[82] Although offering programs to help employees to deal with personal or work-related problems clearly demonstrates management's concern for the health and welfare of the officers, part of the motivation is pragmatic in nature.

Enlightened police managers are aware that if employees are lost for reasonable and correctable reasons, the cost in experience lost and training new employees far outweighs the cost of prevention and health programs. Thus the concept of EAPs is a viable way of dealing with many of the problems experienced by police officers in their work.

EAP Criteria

An effective EAP should provide 24-hour availability for officers affected by traumatic incidents such as shootings, the death or wounding of an officer, exposure to mutilated victims, the death of a family member, or extended personal illness. Such programs typically deal with such stress-related factors as financial problems, alcohol or drug abuse, and retirement planning, and spouses' concerns are also encouraged. Some of these can be treated through counseling, seminars, workshops or other formalized programs. Group therapy with others who have experienced the same problems has proved extremely beneficial.

In establishing an EAP, several considerations must be addressed.

Confidentiality and Credibility. The credibility of those providing the assistance and the guarantee of confidentiality are essential for any program designed to provide assistance to employees. If the helper is believed to report negative information to the administration or is seen as one hired to get rid of problem employees, the program is doomed to failure.

Voluntary Versus Involuntary. People can be ordered to attend counseling, but they can't be forced to be involved in it or to be honest and open with the counselor. Although some people have benefited when forced to attend counseling sessions or alcoholism meetings, a program that people seek out on their own is generally more effective.

Status of the EAP and Its Staff. The importance placed on the EAP, the caliber of the staff, and the existence of independent ethical and professional standards are the key considerations in establishing an effective program.

Location and Accessibility of the EAP. These factors are crucial. For providing services to employees, a location away from headquarters generally seems the most beneficial. Some EAPs are set up in regular professional buildings, whereas others are set up in residential areas nearby. To be really functional in a law enforcement environment, an EAP must be accessible on a 24-hour basis and allow direct access to the employee assistance personnel.

Division of Administrative Versus Treatment Preventive Services. Employee assistance programs are geared to provide assistance to employees with personal problems or job-related matters. Any problems related to job performance are an administrative area and should not be addressed by EAP personnel. If the counselors' advice is ignored or doesn't change behavior, and the employee continues to perform poorly, administrative measures should be taken by supervisory and management personnel.

Additional Programs. Programs that contribute to employees' overall health, such as required yearly or biannual physical examinations, blood pressure screening and physical fitness programs that provide incentives for good physical health, benefit them both physically and emotionally. Providing information in the department's in-house newspaper or magazine on fitness and maintaining good emotional health can be very helpful.

Spouse orientation programs such as those discussed earlier are a very valuable component of any EAP. All of the EAPs discussed call for a firm commitment from both the individual and the police department. Any efforts toward increasing one's effectiveness in coping with stress are less successful in the absence of close cooperation between the individual officer and the department.

Enhancement of Awareness and Self-Esteem

There are a number of specific means that can be employed in reducing stress. On individual levels officers can decrease the impact of stress by increasing their understanding of the problems they are facing; that is, they should know the type of stressors they will likely encounter in their work and the physical and emotional effects these stressors may have on them. Self-understanding leads to increased knowledge of others, a deeper comprehension of one's own motivations, habits, idiosyncrasies, and hangups and also diminishes the stress involved in interpersonal conflict. In addition, the self-assurance that comes with knowledge and understanding is a vital asset to the police officer. True self-confidence, not bravado, is required to react quickly, decisively, and effectively.

Psychologists use such terms as "ego strength" and "frustration tolerance" to refer to an individual's overall capacity for handling stressors of various kinds, especially those involving threats to self-esteem. Persons with high self-esteem are less prone to anxiety; when they experience frustration, they are more likely to deal realistically and directly with the source of their frustration than to divert their energies to substitute or alternative targets. Persons with low self-esteem, on the other hand, are less likely to deal constructively with frustration and stress.

> A person with low self-esteem not only has to attempt to solve the frustrating problem with which he is faced, but must also prevent any further loss of self-esteem. The latter task sometimes gets to be more important than the problem-oriented one, and the low [person] defends himself by hostility, withdrawal, excessive assertiveness in the use of power or insulting behavior. As the threat increases his anxiety, his thinking may become rigid and his solution of the problem at hand becomes less effective. On the other hand, the high self-esteem person is less diverted by a need to protect his self-esteem and can work more directly on the problem at hand. He approaches it with more confidence because his past experience has shown him that he can and does solve problems effectively. He can act directly on the problems and has little need to withdraw from them.
>
> Self-esteem is not a fixed quality in a person. No matter how secure a person is, there are going to be times when he feels blue, when he questions himself, when things happen that shake him up. A person's self-esteem may hover at lower levels on some days and higher on others. In fact, with extreme changes in life situations, a person's self-esteem can take remarkable nose dives or it may soar. New assignments, arrests, and case solutions can all have an influence on a police officer's esteem.[83]

Although one's self-esteem tends to increase from heightened understanding and mastery of specific job skills, it can also be improved by more direct methods of intervention. For example, one police stress control program makes use of training and rational self-assertion and also gives officers exposure to *cognitive restructuring:*

> The cognitive restructuring exercises are methods in which individuals are taught how their thinking process effects their emotional feelings and behavior. The negative or irrational self-statements which maintain the individual at a high level of anxiety are identified, and techniques to alter stress-inducing thoughts are initiated. . . . the aim of this instruction is to offer practical strategies for controlling disturbing self-talk without necessarily seeking professional assistance.[84]

A combination of assertiveness training and cognitive restructuring is also part of the program in "anxiety management training" that clinical psychologist Richard M. Suinn[85] has developed for helping type A individuals (those who are especially prone to heart attacks) learn to cope more effectively with stressful situations.

Physical Fitness: Exercise and Diet

Physical exercise can play an important part both in reducing stress and in increasing one's ability to cope with stressful situations. Although dedication and an unavoidable amount of discomfort are involved, especially in the early stages of a physical conditioning program, the results can be extremely rewarding to the individual. It is important that exercise become a part of a broader program aimed at improving overall physical fitness.

Although all types of physical exercise are beneficial, the greatest value is derived from aerobic exercises, those that involve the sustained exchange of oxygen. Aerobic exercises, in particular, benefit the cardiovascular system. Jogging, swimming, bicycling, tennis, and similar activities also improve muscle tone and physical strength.

Studies conducted by the Dallas Police Department, Los Angeles County Sheriff's Department, and the Aerobic Clinic of Dallas show the comparatively inferior condition of the average police officer. In the Dallas study, the participants in the experimental group who engaged in a consistent program of physical exercise demonstrated a 42 percent decrease in sick days. The control group showed a 5 percent increase in sick time.

After the physical training program, officers in the experimental groups averaged .91 commendations per man as compared with .67 commendations per man before the program. Complaints against officers for a six-month period before physical training were .24 per officer. After the program was completed, complaints dropped to .12 per officer. Overall job performance in the experimental group, as rated by the supervisors, increased by 15 percent.

Some of the areas showing improvement in the experimental group were job enthusiasm, self-control, job attitude, human relations skills, police image, and total performance. Of these, the two most affected by the training program were police image and self-control. One can conclude that the more physically fit officers are and feel, the more self-assured and happy they are with themselves.

Diet is another area that contributes significantly to physical well-being and is important in any stress management program. "Officers' diets, because of job demands and shift changes, are often nutritionally deficient. Eating the proper amount and type of food aids health, reduces the effects of stress, and enables the officer to perform effectively.[86]

Biofeedback and Relaxation Training

Because most people do not know how to relax, relaxation methods should be included in stress management programs. Techniques for relaxation are many and varied, ranging from such uncomplicated methods as listening to soothing instrumental music or practicing simple muscle relaxation to sophisticated approaches such as self-hypnosis, transcendental meditation, and biofeedback. Generally, some combination of these approaches is more successful and convenient than the use of a single method.

Deep muscle relaxation, as defined by Axelberd and Valle, is a procedure "whereby the person learns to identify tension in various muscles in his body and to reduce this tension by successively tensing and relaxing the affected muscle(s). The goal of this technique is to improve circulation and relieve the tension that could lead to more serious disorders.[87] The person is instructed just to tense his or her hands, biceps, face, shoulders, chest, stomach, legs, and feet and then to relax them and focus on the feeling that follows the muscle tensing. Breathing exercises are taught in conjunction with the deep muscle relaxation to increase the oxygen supply to the parts of the body involved in the exercise. Although not as vigorous as the aerobic exercises, deep muscle relaxation and breathing exercises are highly effective in the reduction of muscle tension, improving circulation, and diminishing the work that needs to be performed by the heart.[88]

These exercises may be augmented by the use of biofeedback, a technique that delivers both sociological and psychological benefits. Biofeedback training provides individuals with information about their bodies' function during ongoing physical conditions. Equipment is used to measure such variables as peripheral temperature, muscle tension, perspiration, and even brainwaves. Once a subject has been instructed in the use of biofeedback, he or she can learn to achieve some control over various physiological responses, particularly when the exercise in biofeedback is undertaken together with listening to tapes that aid in deep relaxation.

Peer Counseling

Because there is evidence that many stress-related factors are linked directly to organizational policies and practices, police agencies should endeavor to reduce, modify, or eliminate those factors under their control. Some authorities suggest that the easiest way for administrators to identify those organizationally related job stressors is to use the consultant services of rank-and-file officers.

> The officer on the street has built up a wealth of experience and intimately knows the stressors which impinge upon him. By getting a group of experienced officers together to talk about stress problems, the most significant stressors can be identified. Once the major stressors are known, ideas need to be developed on how they may be eliminated. Since organizational change may be necessitated, the full cooperation of management is necessary in this process. It is also especially important to allow individual officers to participate in any decisions about eliminating a stressor which directly affects their job. Should it be found that a particular stressor is "impossible" to eliminate, rotation may be helpful. That is, personnel could be rotated on and off assignments so that they are not trapped for long periods of time in an assignment which could cause a damaging degree of stress. In a practical sense these techniques involve training and stress awareness, insights into self and others, and specific skill training.[89]

In particular, the Boston Police Stress Program has made a pioneering effort in the use of peer counseling and has enjoyed considerable success in handling troubled officers with drinking, marital, family, and on-the-job problems.

Implications of Higher Education for Law Enforcement Stress

Following the 1967 President's Commission and the passage of the Omnibus Crime Control Act, law enforcement officers found themselves being encouraged and enticed to enroll in college by educational incentive pay, the Law Enforcement Education Program (LEEP), and the G.I. Bill. Many officers initially enrolled in courses for the monetary benefits; some were collecting money under both LEEP and the G.I. Bill. Many found they could not afford *not* to go to school, for the more credits they earned, the more money they received through education pay incentive programs.[90]

Diminished Family Time

Although officers soon learned that going to school was financially rewarding, many also learned there was a personal cost involved. For these officers who worked their duty shifts, attended classes, studied, and wrote term papers during their off hours found they had less and less time to devote to their families.

Program Quality

Colleges and universities quickly realized there was a demand for criminal justice higher education programs and money to be made. Initially, however, these programs lacked quality in curricula and course content. A limited pool of qualified faculty led some colleges to turn to law enforcement and hire instructors from their training academies. Many of the courses conducted in those early years were even held in law enforcement facilities. Officers in these programs often became frustrated in attending what they perceived as nothing more than a glorified training academy.

Carter, Sapp, and Stephen,[91] in their study on police education, contended that qualitative limitations of criminal justice programs were not a function of "profiteering" by colleges as much as they were the combined effect of a dramatic growth in demand and a lack of planning and direction for program development by colleges and universities.

Animosity Toward the College-Educated Officer

Another source of frustration for the officer pursuing a higher education was the animosity demonstrated toward him or her by the "street-educated" officer. This became a particular problem when a more highly educated subordinate attempted to make a suggestion to a more experienced officer who had not attended college. Resentment abounded between the "college boy" with no common sense and the seasoned veterans who had received their education through "hard knocks" in the streets.

Expectations of Spouse and Friends

Many officers found that once they had received college degrees, their spouses and friends would ask, "Now that you have a degree, when are you going to quit law enforcement and get a *good* job?" Spouses often perceived the officers' spending long hours in classes and studying on their off-duty time simply as preparation for leaving law enforcement and finding a new and more lucrative occupation. As a result, the officer who thought he or she had a good job and, in fact, loved police work, began to have anxiety attacks over whether this was no longer the right occupation.

Misconceptions About Job Future

Many officers also had false expectations about being promoted when they received their college degrees. When the promotion was not forthcoming, they perceived the selection process to be unfair because it did not take into account their education. If they received the promotion, some members of the agency looked on them as "prima donnas," assuming they got promoted strictly on the basis of their education, as opposed to ability.

Lack of Input into Policy and Decision Making

The more education law enforcement officers have, the more "say" they want to have in how the department is run. The greatest source of stress, then, for college-educated officers is their lack of input into policy and decision making. Phelps,[92] in discussing the increase in educated police officers, commented: "A professional does not like to accept the status quo. In the absence of movement toward a work climate which seeks employee participation in administrative decisions affecting their work, the costs in anxiety and hostility may be intense."

The lack of employee participation into policy and decision making has been identified in Chapter 11 as an organizational stressor in law enforcement work. Its negative impact is only compounded with increased education. The officer who has worked hard, obtained an education, and attempts to apply the knowledge on the job becomes extremely frustrated when there are no opportunities to be heard or when suggestions fall on deaf ears and he or she is ignored.

Increased Boredom on the Job

The potential for boredom and frustration exists for all law enforcement officers. However, its impact is more than likely intensified in the college-educated officer, who has higher expectations and greater ambitions.

Superiors' Attitudes

Other concerns about college-educated officers were expressed by police administrators in Carter, Sapp, and Stephens's 1989 report, *The State of Police Education*. Administrators responding to a survey reportedly perceived college-educated officers as more likely to question orders, to request more frequent reassignment, to have lower morale and more absences, and to become more easily frustrated with bureaucratic procedures. The following are specific comments of survey respondents:

> Statistically, the more educated a police officer becomes (from a formal education framework), the higher the probability that he or she will leave law enforcement.
>
> Officers with advanced degrees sometimes feel frustrated from lack of challenges and advancement opportunities in law enforcement. Also, their creative abilities are not utilized in a manner that would be fulfilling to the officer.
>
> The only disadvantage of college-educated officers is meeting their employment needs (job satisfaction, sense of accomplishment). Sometimes they have a tendency to become bored because of not being challenged enough.
>
> Older deputies seem to sometimes resent young officers with a strong educational background in that they seem to feel that there is no substitute for experience.

Some Education-Related Stressors Now Resolved

Fortunately, many of the stressful or negative aspects of a college education for law enforcement officers are no longer relevant. Criminal justice programs have evolved from the glorified training academies conducted in the basements of police departments to outstanding academic programs at the nation's leading universities.[93] Gone also, to a large extent, is the animosity in the ranks between the "haves" and the "have nots"—a result of the attrition of the older, uneducated officer.

Have Administrators Failed to Keep Pace with the Educated Work Force?

The real issue to be addressed is whether law enforcement administrators have kept pace with officers' changing needs since the 1967 President's Commission on Law Enforcement and Administration of Justice and the 1973 National Advisory Commission on Criminal Justice Standards and Goals made recommendations to elevate educational requirements for the police. Specifically, *how have administrators changed their work environments and their management and leadership styles to adapt to the subsequent increase in the educational level of law enforcement officers?* In the face of a more educated and enlightened work force, it is clearly apparent that today's administrator can no longer cling to authoritative and paramilitaristic ways of management.

To reiterate, the issue is not whether education is good or bad for the law enforcement profession—it is, of course, good. The issue, rather, is whether law enforcement administrators have adapted their management styles to utilize the educated officer effectively and whether they can continue to do so in the future.

"Enlightened" Management: The Goal of Today's Administrator

The need to change the law enforcement work environment to a more enlightened one is in part substantiated by Carter, Sapp, and Stephens.[94] Discussing the concern of retaining college-educated personnel, these authors remarked that while salary benefits are important, job satisfaction and occupational challenges are also important variables. They contended that if, in addition to reasonable compensation, the officer derives satisfaction from his or her assignments and has a good work environment, the probability of losing that officer is reduced.

The authors described their visits to selected police agencies that had implemented higher education requirements for entry and promotions. Following a visit to the San Diego, California, Police Department, the authors concluded

> Overall, the San Diego Police Department command staff views personnel from what McGregor (1964) called a "Theory Y" perspective; i.e., employees are viewed as motivated, competent, and dedicated individuals who are committed to the goals of the organization. As such, the department does not take a concise position in regard to employee motivation, direction and control. Rather the police department provides a communal working environment and attempts to facilitate employee self-motivation.

Following a visit to another agency—the San Jose, California, Police Department—the study found that this organization attributed its low attrition rate, high number of applicants, lack of problems with the educational requirement, and limited problems attracting minority applicants to two primary factors: working conditions and a good salary and benefits package. Commenting on the good working conditions, interviewed personnel stated that the cooperative and supportive environment within the department, along with the training and field support, makes the San Jose Police Department "a good place to work."

It is clear that law enforcement administrators of the 1990s who want to eliminate the management practices and organizational factors identified as sources of stress (and intensified by increased education) must follow the lead of agencies run by enlightened management. Quite simply, they must make their departments "good places to work."

Summary

Our objective throughout this chapter has been to present clear and straightforward discussions of major subjects in the area of stress that can be read with profit and interest by a person who does not necessarily possess a scientific background and training. We have tried to provide the reader with an orientation and introduction to the general topic of stress and some of its principal effects in terms of psychological, physiological, and social consequences and to acquaint the reader with some of the basic concepts and terminology relating to stress that are beginning to attain wider currency among law enforcement personnel. It is quite apparent that some stress factors are unique to policing; others are comparable to the sorts of stress encountered in other occupations and professions. However, the latter's meaning and significance for the present account lie in how they interact with the unique stress factors in policing to create special problems in coping effectively with the total stress situation.

There is little doubt that some unmistakable trends are developing in the study and prevention of stress-related problems in police work. It appears that in the future we will witness a greater number of law enforcement administrators directing their professional efforts and organizational resources toward the creation of services that can deal effectively with job-related health and personal problems. The organizational changes that result will manifest themselves in a number of ways. We can expect to see an increasing number of law enforcement agencies implementing psychological and psychiatric assessment of police applicants. This will be done in part to screen out the emotionally unstable applicant.[95] Further, we will witness a dramatic increase in the number of law enforcement agencies that will make available to their personnel and their families in-house professional mental health specialists as well as referral services to community-based mental health specialists. We will also see a greater number of in-service training courses on this subject for both patrol officers and supervisors to assist them in recognizing and coping with job stress and the physical and psychological conditions associated with it.

This trend toward greater organizational sensitivity is indeed a welcome change and certainly long overdue. It is hoped that it will result in the reduction of alcohol- and drug-related problems, suicide, marital and other family problems, and premature retirements. In the final analysis, the police officer, his or her family, and the organization will be the beneficiaries.

Discussion Questions

1. What is the general adaptation syndrome?
2. How do most people react to stress?
3. Most law enforcement stressors can be grouped into four broad categories. What are these categories?
4. Of what value is the study conducted by Sewell, which resulted in the development of the critical life event scale?
5. Alcohol-related problems among police officers manifest themselves in a number of ways. What are they?
6. What are some of the specific benefits reported by the Denver Police Department since it implemented its abuse program?
7. What types of guidelines have been provided by the courts for the drug testing of law enforcement personnel?
8. There are a number of recognized medical uses of anabolic steroids. What are they?
9. How do suicide patterns among younger and older police officers differ?
10. What are the typical phases officers go through in postshooting trauma?
11. It has been suggested that upward mobility in almost any type of bureaucracy tends to impose unique stresses on individuals. Why is this so?
12. What can the manager do to deal with job related stress successfully?
13. How do behavioral scientists define midlife crisis?
14. Marriages of law enforcement personnel are susceptible to certain kinds of stresses inherent in policing. What are some of them?
15. What are some of the specific means employed to cope with and reduce stress?
16. What should an effective EAP provide to its personnel?
17. What were some of the personal costs officers paid by enrolling in college courses when LEEP monies and the G.I. Bill were readily available to them?
18. What types of expectations do spouses and friends sometimes have once police officers receive their college degrees?

Notes

1. K. Slogobin, "Stress," *New York Times Magazine,* November 20, 1977, pp. 48–55.
2. For a comprehensive treatment of literature on police stress, see L. Territo and H. J. Vetter, eds., *Stress and Police Personnel* (Boston: Allyn & Bacon, 1981). Much of the discussion in this chapter was drawn from this source.

3. H. Selye, *Stress Without Distress* (Philadelphia: Lippincott, 1974), p. 60.
4. H. Basowitz, *Anxiety and Stress* (New York: McGraw-Hill, 1955), p. 7.
5. Ibid., p. 4.
6. Selye, *Stress Without Distress,* pp. 35–39.
7. J. C. Coleman, "Life Stress and Maladaptive Behavior," *The American Journal of Occupational Therapy,* 27:3 (1973), p. 170.
8. O. Tanner, *Stress* (New York: Time-Life Books, 1978).
9. For a comprehensive treatment of defensive behavior patterns, see J. M. Sawrey and C. A. Tilford, *Dynamics of Mental Health: The Psychology of Adjustment* (Boston: Allyn & Bacon, 1963), pp. 40–67.
10. J.G. Stratton, "Police Stress: An Overview," *Police Chief,* 45:4 (April 1978), p. 58.
11. "Compensation for Police Heart Attacks Allowed," *Crime Control Digest,* 9:10 (1975), p. 3.
12. Stratton: "Police Stress," p. 58.
13. W. H. Kroes, B. L. Margolis, and J. Hurrell, "Job stress in Policemen," *Journal of Police Science and Administration,* 2:2 (1974), pp. 145–55.
14. W. H. Kroes, *Society's Victim—The Policeman* (Springfield, Ill.: Charles C. Thomas, 1976).
15. T. Eisenberg, "Labor–Management Relations and Psychological Stress," *Police Chief,* 42:14 (1975), pp. 54–58.
16. M. Reiser, "Stress, Distress, and Adaptation in Police Work," *Police Chief,* 43:1 (1976), pp. 24–27.
17. M. Reiser, R. J. Sokol, and S. J. Saxe, "An Early Warning Mental Health Program for Police Sergeants," *Police Chief,* 39:6 (1972), pp. 38–39.
18. M. Reiser, "A Psychologist's View of the Badge," *Police Chief,* 37:9 (1970), pp. 24–27.
19. M. Reiser, "Some Organizational Stress on Policemen," *Journal of Police Science and Administration,* 2:2 (1974), pp. 156–65.
20. M. D. Roberts, "Job Stress in Law Enforcement: A Treatment and Prevention Program," in *Job Stress and the Police Officer: Identifying Stress Reduction Techniques,* ed. W. H. Kroes and J. Hurrell (Washington, D.C.: U.S. Department of Health, Education, and Welfare, 1975), pp. 226–33.
21. Kroes et al., "Job Stress in Policemen," pp. 145–55.
22. S. A. Somodevilla, et al., *Stress Management in the Dallas Police Department* (Dallas: Psychological Services Unit, Dallas, Texas, Police Department, 1978), p. 6.
23. Eisenberg, "Labor–Management Relations," pp. 54–58.
24. J. D. Sewell, "The development of a critical life events scale for law enforcement," *Journal of Police Science and Administration,* 1:1 (1983), pp. 109–16.
25. L. Dishlacoff, "The Drinking Cop," *Police Chief,* 43:1 (1976), p. 32.
26. Kroes and Hurrell, "Stress Awareness," in *Job Stress and the Police Officer,* p. 241.
27. Ibid., p. 241.
28. Ibid., p. 241.
29. Dishlacoff, "The Drinking Cop," p. 39.
30. Ibid., p. 39.
31. Ibid., p. 39.
32. On this point, see Mary Niederberger, "Random Drug Test for Police Opposed," *Pittsburgh Press,* April 6, 1989; Rob Zeiger, "14 Fired Officers Returned to Duty," *Detroit News,* July 22, 1988; Shelly Murphy, "Court Upholds Drug Tests for Hub Cops," *Boston Herald,* May 13, 1989; Marilyn Robinson, "Drug Use Cuts Police Recruits by Nearly 50%," *Denver Post,* July 15, 1983; and David Schwab, "Supreme Court Back Drug Tests for South Jersey Police Officers," *Newark Star-Ledger,* April 4, 1989.
33. J. J. Hurrell and R. Kliesmet, *Stress Among Police Officers* (Cincinnati, Ohio: National Institute of Occupational Safety and Health, 1984), p. 12.
34. *Newlun v. State Department of Retirement Systems,* 770 P.2d 1071 (Wash. App. 1989).

Relatedly, *McElrath* v. *Kemp,* 27 Govt. Emp. Rel. Rep. (BNA) 605 (D.D.C. 1989), deals with an alcoholic employee who had relapses after being treated and was terminated, but was reinstated later.

35. H. J. Redway, "Drug Testing Police Personnel: A Discussion Paper" (Washington, D.C.: Police Executive Research Forum, 1989). This discussion was adapted from this source.
36. D. E. Nowicki, "Police Officer Drug Abuse: An Issue of Public Safety," *Police Chief,* 53:3 (1986), pp. 71–73.
37. C. Swanson, L. Gaines, and B. Gore. "Use of Anabolic Steroids," *FBI Law Enforcement Bulletin,* 60:8 (1991), pp. 19–23. This discussion of anabolic steroids was adapted from this source.
38. R. F. Doerge, ed., *Wilson and Grisvold's Textbook of Organic Medicinal and Pharmaceutical Chemistry* (Philadelphia: Lippincott, 1982), pp. 679–84.
39. Schuckitt, "Weight Lifter's Folly: The Abuse of Anabolic Steroids," *Drug Abuse and Alc Newsletter,* 17:8 (1988); and Hecht, "Anabolic Steroids: Pumping Trouble," *FDA Consumer* (September 1984), pp. 12–15.
40. Couzens, "A Serious Drug Problem," *Newsday,* Nov. 26, 1988.
41. Doerge, *Wilson and Grisvold's.*
42. Couzens, "Serious Drug Problem."
43. A. G. Gilman et al., *Goodman and Gilman's The Pharmacological Basis of Therapeutics* (New York: Macmillan, 1985), pp. 1440–58.
44. Harrison G. Pope and David L. Katz, "Affective and Psychotic Symptoms Associated with Anabolic Steroid Use," *American Journal of Psychiatry,* 145:4 (1988), p. 488.
45. *Ibid.*
46. Charlier, "For Teens, Steroids May Be Bigger Issues than Cocaine Use," *Wall Street Journal,* Oct. 4, 1988.
47. Pope and Katz, p. 487–490.
48. Cowart, "Physician–Competitor's Advice to Colleagues: Steroid Users Respond to Education, Rehabilitation. *JAMA,* Volume 257, Number 4, 1987, pp. 427–428.
49. Pope and Katz, *Affective and Psychotic Symptoms,* pp. 489, 487.
50. Goldstein, p. 4.
51. J. A. Schwartz and C. B. Schwartz, "The Personal Problems of the Police Officer: A Plea for Action," in *Job Stress and the Police Officer,* ed. Kroes and Hurrell, p. 136.
52. Ibid., p. 136.
53. D. Lester, "Suicide in Police Officers," *Police Chief,* 45:4 (1970), p. 17.
54. P. Friedman, "Suicide Among Police," in *Essays in Self-Destruction,* ed. E. Schneidman (New York: Science House, 1967).
55. S. Labovitz and R. Hagedorn, "An Analysis of Suicide Rates Among Occupational Categories," *Sociological Inquiry,* 41:1 (1971), pp. 67–72.
56. Z. Nelson and W. Smith, "The Law Enforcement Profession: An Incidence of Suicide," *Omega,* 1:4 (1970), pp. 293–99.
57. A Henry and J. Short, *Suicide and Homicide* (Glencoe, Ill.: Free Press, 1954), p. 15.
58. B. L. Danto, "Police Suicide," *Police Stress,* 1:1 (1978), pp. 32–36, 38, 40.
59. M. F. Heiman, "The Police Suicide," *Journal of Police Science and Administration,* 3:3 (1975), pp. 267–73.
60. Walter Lippert and Eugene R. Ferrara, "The Cost of Coming Out on Top: Emotional Responses to Surviving the Deadly Battle," *FBI Law Enforcement Bulletin* (December 1981), pp. 6–10. This discussion of Postshooting trauma was adapted from the source.
61. Ibid., pp. 6–10.
62. H. Levinson, "On Being a Middle-Aged Manager," *Harvard Business Review,* 47 (July–August 1969), pp. 55–57.
63. H. Levinson, *Executive Stress* (New York: Harper & Row, 1970), pp. 95–97.
64. J. D. Sewell, "The Boss as Victim: Stress and the Police Manager," *FBI Law Enforcement Bulletin* 57:2 (1988), pp. 15–18. The discussion was adapted from this article.

65. William H. Kroes, Joseph J. Hurrell, and Bruce Margolis, "Job Stress in Police Administrators," *Journal of Police Science and Administration,* 2;4 (1974), p. 381.
66. *Ibid.,* p. 287.
67. James S. Hillgren, Rebekah Bond, and Sue Jones, "Primary Stressors in Police Administration and Law Enforcement," *Journal of Police Science and Administration,* 4:4 (1976), p. 447.
68. *Ibid.*
69. For suggestions on effective programs, see, for example, Harry Levinson, *Executive Stress* (New York: Mentor Executive Library, 1975); Alfred Goodloe, Jane Bensahel, and John Kelly, *Managing Yourself: How to Control Emotion, Stress, and Time* (New York: Franklin Watts, 1984); Executive Health Examiners, *Stress Management for the Executive* (New York: Berkley Books, 1985); James D. Sewell, "Stress Management for the Police Manager," *Florida Police Chief,* 12:3 (1986), pp. 56–65; and James T. Chandler, "The Demoted Police Executive," *Law and Order,* 33:8 (1985), pp. 29–31. R. Alec MacKenzie, *The Time Trap* (New York: McGraw-Hill, 1975) is one of the classic works on successful time management.
70. Levinson, "On Being a Middle-Aged Manager." Much of the discussion of midlife crisis was taken from this source, pp. 51–60.
71. "Clinical Health Age 30–40," *Business Week,* March 3, 1956, p. 56.
72. E. Jaques, "Death and the Mid-life Crisis," *The International Journal of Psychoanalysis,* 46 (October 1965), p. 502.
73. For a further discussion, see J. G. Stratton, "Pressure in Law Enforcement Marriages," *Police Chief,* 42:11 (1975), pp. 44–47; B. Weber, "The Police Wife," *Police Chief,* 43:1 (1976), pp. 48, 49; C. Maslach and S. E. Jackson, "Burned-Out Cops and Their Families," *Psychology Today* (May 1979), pp. 59–62.
74. J. A. Schwartz and C. B. Schwartz, "The Personal Problems of the Police Officer" in *Job Stress and the Police Officer,* ed. Kroes and Hurrell, p. 134.
75. J. P. Lichtenberger, *Divorce: A Study in Social Causation* (New York: Columbia University Press, 1969), p. 96.
76. J. A. Durner et al., "Divorce: Another Occupational Hazard," *Police Chief,* 42:11 (1975), p. 48.
77. Ibid., p. 50.
78. Stratton, "Pressure in Law Enforcement Marriages," p. 45.
79. Somodevilla et al., *Stress Management,* p. 12.
80. Ibid., pp. 13, 14.
81. Ibid., p. 13.
82. J. G. Stratton, "Employee Assistance Programs: A Profitable Approach for Employers and Organizations," *Police Chief,* 52:21 (1985), pp. 31–33. The discussion of EAPs was adapted from this article.
83. International Association of Chiefs of Police, *Training Key #257* (Gaithersburg, Md: 1978), p. 3.
84. M. Axelberd and J. Valle, *Stress Control Program for Police Officers of the City of Miami Police Department.* From Concept Paper #1, City of Miami, Florida, Police Department, November 14, 1978.
85. R. M. Suinn, "How to Break the Vicious Cycle of Stress," *Psychology Today,* 10 (December 1976), pp. 59, 60.
86. Stratton, "Police Stress," p. 76.
87. Axelberd and Valle, *Stress Control Program,* p. 10.
88. Ibid., p. 10.
89. Kroes and Hurrell, *Job Stress and the Police Officer,* p. 243.
90. R. M. Ayres, George S. Flanagan, and M. B. Ayres, *Preventing Law Enforcement Stress: The Organizations Role* (Alexandria, Va.: The National Sheriff's Association, 1990). The discussion of the implications of higher education on law enforcement stress was adapted from this source (pp. 18–21).

91. D. L. Carter, A. D. Sapp, and D. Stevens, *The State of Police Education: Policy Direction for the Twenty-First Century* (Washington, D.C.: Police Executive Research Forum, 1989).
92. L. Phelps, "Police Tasks and Related Stress Factors from an Organizational Perspective," in *Job Stress and the Police Officer,* ed. Kroes and Hurrell, pp. 146, 156.
93. Examples of outstanding programs are the following: Michigan State University's School of Criminal Justice, East Lansing, Michigan: John Jay College of Criminal Justice, New York, New York; Sam Houston State University's College of Criminal Justice, Huntsville, Texas; and The University of Louisville's School of Justice Administration, Louisville, Kentucky.
94. Carter, Sapp, and Stevens, *State of Police Education,* p. 21.
95. For a comprehensive treatment of this topic, see L. Territo, C. R. Swanson, Jr., and N. C. Chamelin, *The Police Personnel Selection Process* (Indianapolis, Ind.: Bobbs-Merrill, 1977), Chapter 5, "Psychological and Psychiatric Assessment of Police Applicants."

9 Labor Relations

"You, a lowly policeman is going to tell me how to run my department! . . . Get out!" and you had to go; he hated me. . . .

RANK-AND-FILE ORGANIZATION LEADER JOHN CASSESE ON AN EARLY MEETING WITH NEW YORK CITY POLICE COMMISSIONER KENNEDY.

Introduction

No single force in the past 50 years has had as much impact on the administration of police agencies as collective bargaining by officers. Police unions represent a major force that must be reckoned with by police managers. This chapter deals with the powerful phenomenon of collective bargaining under the following headings: (1) the unionization of the police, (2) the impact of unions, (3) the basis for collective bargaining, (4) police employee organizations, (5) establishing the bargaining relationship, (6) conducting negotiations, (7) grievances, (8) job actions, (9) use of surveillance, and (10) administrative reaction to job actions. This coverage provides a broad overview with supporting details, sufficient to understand the topic and also to create an appreciation for both its complexities and subtleties.

The Unionization of the Police

From 1959 through the 1970s, a number of events combined to foster public sector collective bargaining. These significant forces were (1) the needs of labor organizations, (2) the reduction of legal barriers, (3) police frustration with the perceived lack of support for their "war on crime," (4) personnel practices in police agencies, (5) salaries and benefits, (6) an increase in violence directed at police, and (7) the success of the groups in making an impact through collective action.[1]

The Needs of Labor Organizations

The attention of labor organizations was devoted almost entirely to the private sector until the 1960s. However, as the opportunity to gain new members became increasingly constrained because of the extensive organization of industrial workers, unions cast about for new markets and statistics such as these impressed them:

> Public service is the most rapidly growing major sector of employment in the United States. In the last 30 years public employment has tripled, growing from 4.2 million to 13.1 million employees. Today nearly one out of five workers in the United States is on a government payroll.[2]

Thus, as with any organization that achieves its primary objective, labor groups redefined their sphere of interest to include public employees. Concurrently, there were stirrings among public employees to use collective action to improve their lot.

The Reduction of Legal Barriers

Although workers in the private sector had been given the right to bargain collectively under the federal National Labor Relations Act of 1935, it was another quarter of a century before the first state enacted even modest bargaining rights for public employees. Beginning with the granting of public sector collective bargaining rights in Wisconsin in 1959, many of the legal barriers that had been erected in the wake of the Boston police strike of 1919 began to tumble. Other states that also extended such rights to at least some classes of employees at an early date included California (1961) and Connecticut, Delaware, Massachusetts, Michigan, Oregon, Washington, and Wyoming, all in 1965. Many other states followed this lead, particularly from 1967 to 1974.[3] President John F. Kennedy granted limited collective bargaining rights to federal workers in 1962 by Executive Order 10988. The courts, too, were active in removing barriers; for example, in *Atkins* v. *City of Charlotte* (1969), the U.S. district court struck down a portion of a North Carolina statute prohibiting being or becoming a union member as an infringement on the First Amendment right to free association.[4] While *Atkins* involved firefighters, the federal courts reached similar conclusions involving Atlanta police officers in *Melton* v. *City of Atlanta* (1971)[5] and a Colorado deputy sheriff in *Lontine* v. *VanCleave* (1973).[6]

Police Frustration with Support for the War on Crime

Historically, the police have felt isolated in their effort to control crime. This stems from two factors: perceived pubic hostility and the impact of the due process revolution.

The police perceive a great deal more public hostility than actually exists. Illustrative of this is a survey of one big-city department, which found that over 70 percent of the officers had an acute sense of citizen hostility or contempt.[7] In contrast, a survey conducted by the National Opinion Research Center revealed that 77 percent of the respondents felt that the police were doing a "very good" or "pretty good" job of protecting people in their neighborhoods, and a 1965 Gallup poll showed that 70 percent of the public had a great deal of respect for the police.[8] These data notwithstanding, the police saw the public as hostile, and the most persuasive "evidence" of this emerged in the attempts to create civilian review boards, which carried several latent messages to police officers. First, it created anger with its implied allegation that the police could not, or would not, keep their own house in order. Second, it fostered the notion that politicians were ready to "throw the police to wolves" and thus were part of "them."

Particularly among street-level officers, the reaction of the police to the whirlwind of Supreme Court decisions, discussed in Chapter 2, was one of dismay at being "handcuffed" in attempts to control crime. It tended to alienate the police from the Supreme Court and to contribute toward a general feeling that social institutions that should support the police effort in combatting crime were, instead, at odds with it.

Personnel Practices

Past practices become precedent, precedent becomes tradition, and tradition, in turn, becomes the mighty anchor of many organizations. By the late 1960s, the tendency to question the appropriateness of certain traditions was pervasive. Police rank-and-file members were no exception. This tendency was heightened by the increased educational achievement of police officers. Although management's general performance was often judged to be suspect, traditional personnel practices were the greatest concern, as these directly affected the individual officer.

Among the practices that were most distasteful to rank-and-file members were the requirement to attend, unpaid, a thirty-minute roll call immediately before the eight-hour tour of duty; uncompensated court attendance during off-duty time; short-notice changes in shift assignments; having to return to the station from home for minor matters, such as signing reports, without pay or compensatory time for such periods; favoritism in work assignments and selection for attendance at prestigious police training schools; and arbitrary disciplinary procedures. Gradually, the gap between officers and management widened. Officers began turning to employee organizations to rectify collectively the shortcomings of their circumstances. Subsequently, the solidarity of police officers was to prove of great benefit to employee organizations.

In addition to providing material for ferment through illegal, ill-conceived, abrasive, or insensitive general personnel practices, police managers often unwittingly contributed to the resolve and success of police unions by their treatment of leaders of police employee associations. In Atlanta, the chief of police transferred the president of the Fraternal Order of Police 51 times in 45 days for his outspokenness,[9] and in Boston, Dick MacEachern, founder and president of the then fledgling Police Patrolmen's Association, was transferred repeatedly from precinct to precinct and Mayor White subsequently refused to sign MacEachern's disability pension for the same reason.[10] Such actions provide free publicity, create a martyr (an essential for many social movements), put the leaders in contact with people they ordinarily would not meet, increase group cohesiveness, and provide compelling confirmation in the minds of rank-and-file members why they need and should join a union.

Salaries and Benefits

As did other government workers in the 1960s, police officers felt that their salaries, fringe benefits, and working conditions were not adequate. In 1961, mining production workers were averaging $111 a week in earnings, lithographers $114, tire and inner-tube producers $127, and telephone line construction workers $133,[11] whereas the pay of police officers averaged far less. Even by 1965, the salary range for patrol officer in the larger cities, those with more than 100,000 in population, was only between $5,763, and $6,919.[12] The rank-and-file members believed increasingly that, if what was fairly theirs would not be given willingly, they would fight for it. In New York City, the Patrolmen's Benevolent Association (PBA) was believed to have been instrumental, from 1958 to 1969, in increasing entry-level salaries from $5,800 to $11,000 per year; obtaining longevity pay, shift differential pay, and improved retirement benefits; and increasing the death benefit from $400 to $16,500.[13] In 1968, the Boston PBA, in negotiating its first contract—which required mediation—obtained increased benefits for its members, such as an annual increase of $1,010, time and a half for all overtime including court appearances, and twelve paid holidays.[14]

Violence Directed at the Police

In 1964, there were 9.9 assaults per 100 officers; in 1969, this figure rose to 16.9. Before 1968, the killing of police officers by preplanned ambushes was unheard of; in that year, there were seven such incidents.[15] The escalating violence had considerable psychological impact on the police, who saw themselves as symbolic targets of activists attacking institutional authority. Rank-and-file members began pressing for body armor, special training, the placement of special weapons in police cars, and sharply increased death benefits.

The Success of Other Groups

During the 1960s the police witnessed mass demonstrations on college campuses, which used many of the tactics associated with the civil rights movement. Among the campus demonstrations that were highly publicized were the University of California at Berkeley (1964–1965), the University of Chicago (1965), Columbia University (1968), and San Francisco State College (1969). By 1970, campus demonstrations reached the point that, within ten days of President Richard Nixon's announcement to invade enemy sanctuaries in Cambodia, a total of 448 campuses were either shut down or otherwise affected by campus unrest.[16]

The analogy was not lost on the police: if concerted action could impact foreign policy, it could also be a potent force in winning benefits for the police. Moreover, the police began supplying their own success models. In 1966, Mayor Lindsay of New York City appointed an independent Civilian Review Board. In resistance, the PBA filed a petition to have the issue put to a citywide referendum and in the ensuing publicity campaign spent an estimated $250,000 to $1,000,000 to defeat the measure, not a small feat as both Senators Robert Kennedy and Jacob Javits had allied themselves with the mayor.[17]

The Impact of Unions

Despite the fact that police unionism as a viable force has had a history of less than 30 years, its impact has been considerable. Traditionally, public officials in general and law enforcement executives in particular have opposed the idea of police unions. A 1944 publication of the International Association of Chiefs of Police (IACP) concluded that police unions could accomplish nothing.[18] In a 1967 address to the State House at Annapolis, Maryland, Baltimore Police Commissioner Donald Pomerleau concluded that "a police union is not compatible with police responsibility."[19]

When such objections are distilled and analyzed, what often remains is the fear that police unions will result ultimately in reduced executive prerogatives (see Box 9-1 on pp. 352–353). There can be little serious question that such fears have a reasonable and factual basis. As co-equal to management at the bargaining table, police unions represent a new power center that has in many instances effectively diminished management's unilateral and sometimes ill-considered exercise of control. In some matters administrators have simply made bad bargains, giving away prerogatives vital to the ability to manage properly. Far more difficult to assess are the consequences to the times that police executives have failed to act, or have acted differently, in anticipation of the union's stand.

Police unions have impacted on public policy decisions in many ways. For example, in various cities they have thwarted the use of civilian review boards and advocated the election of "law and order" candidates (see Box 9-2 on pp. 354–355); resisted the replacement of two-officer cars with one-officer cars; litigated to avoid layoffs; lobbied for increased budgets, especially for raises; caused the removal of chiefs and other high-ranking commanders; and advocated the elimination of radar guns from patrol vehicles because of potential adverse health risks associated with their use.

Police labor organizers often maintain that there is only one color that counts, the color of the uniform. Despite this low-pitched plea for solidarity among rank-and-file members, police employee associations and unions are believed by some observers to have contributed to racial tensions. In 1990, the president-elect of the Boston Police Patrolmen's Association told a forum on crime and violence that "if black men want to go out and fornicate and don't want to take care of their nests . . . then we have a problem." The comment set off a firestorm of reaction from both blacks and whites.[20] Other instances that have served to heighten racial tensions include the opposition of police unions to civilian review boards and the use of their support to help elect white candidates running against blacks. Such incidents have created the feeling among blacks that white-dominated employee organizations are insensitive to issues affecting minorities. Consequently, blacks have tended to form their own organizations to address issues of importance to them.

It is incautious to make categorical statements about the impact of unionism on police professionalization, as it has had both positive and negative effects. Until the mid-1960s, police professionalization was conceived of as including all sworn officers. To the extent to which unionism drives a wedge between those at the lower reaches of the department and management, it negates police professionalization as it has been conceived of for many years. In addition, professionals traditionally do not participate in labor movements. However, as many professional groups, such as the American Association for the Advancement of Science,

BOX 9-1

Labor Conflict Handcuffs Police

Wall of Mistrust Keeps Union, Administration Apart

By Susan Schulman *News Staff Reporter*

Two years ago, the administration of the Buffalo Police Department proposed a mentor program for young officers to improve on-the-job training.

Three years ago, the department proposed drug testing of police officers.

Six years ago, the department proposed using some one-officer cars to increase patrols in the city.

None of these things ever occurred.

The police union knocked down each idea.

Relations between the police union and city administration are in shambles in Buffalo. The two sides have built up a wall of mutual distrust that has kept union and management far apart on most issues and has left the department unable to move forward in many areas.

"The management and operations of the Buffalo Police Department are suffused by labor-management conflict," states a report issued recently by the International Police Chiefs Association. "The level and intensity of conflict is resulting in a continuing and inexcusable waste of resources, disorientation of the focus of department management, and has established, in many quarters, a siege mentality.

"Unless there is a greater understanding, sacrifice and a new spirit of partnership and statesmanship, the department will not move forward constructively to the degree demanded by current and future conditions," the report concludes.

The union-management relationship in Buffalo has been uneasy for years, but possibly never so much as in the past three, since Lt. Robert P. Meegan Jr. became president of the union, the Police Benevolent Association.

Management sees Meegan as an obstructionist.

Most cops on the street see Meegan as their hero.

Since taking office in 1988, Meegan has battled the Griffin administration almost every step of the way, trying to break down what the union perceives as the patronage-dispensing machine the mayor established in the department.

For years, the union claims, Griffin rewarded police officers who worked on his political campaigns with plum assignments, giving them cushy inside jobs or prestigious posts in the detective office.

Griffin has found loopholes in the Civil Service law to promote his political supporters and has demoted officers who have worked on the campaigns of his opponents, the union charges.

And Griffin made sure that when overtime was doled out, it went to the officers of his choice, the union claims.

Under Meegan, the union has fought back by strictly enforcing seniority provisions of its collective bargaining agreement.

Any time the department authorized a transfer, promotion or overtime pay that wasn't based on seniority, the union filed a grievance.

In the past 39 months, more than 900 grievances have been filed.

And, in ruling after ruling, arbitrators agreed that the union contract requires that seniority be the key factor in selecting qualified applicants for a job—even highly sensitive jobs such as chief of homicide, intelligence or other detective units.

From the union's perspective, the rulings have taken some of the politics out of the Police Department.

"We've removed quite a bit of the politics, not all of it," said Meegan. "Seniority is a relatively new standard in the department. It used to be political: Buy tickets or be a poll watcher and they'll give you a job."

From the point of view of management, which consistently has denied its decisions are politically influenced, the rulings have undermined its ability to place people they

BOX 9-1 (cont.)

trust in high-level positions that often require strong working relationships with the department's top brass.

"Seniority has been a big thing." Police Commissioner Ralph V. Degenhart said. "We have to assign people to very vital positions according to seniority rather than ability."

But seniority isn't the only issue splitting the two sides.

"They have grieved practically anything and everything we tried to do through the years," Degenhart said. "They were against drug testing, refused to change to straight shifts."

Like most unions, the PBA often puts the interest of its membership above that of the department as a whole.

When, for example, the Griffin administration proposed that police officers work straight shifts, the union fought it, since many members established part-time jobs around the existing shift schedule. Under that schedule, officers sometimes work two eight-hour shifts in one 24-hour period.

Similarly, the union has fought the administration's attempts to consolidate precincts and introduce some one-officer patrol cars, in part because of its concern that those changes would allow the department to function with fewer officers, thereby reducing the size of the union.

But many times, the union's objections have been based on the PBA belief that the Griffin administration isn't bargaining in good faith, that the administration wants to take away existing union benefits without offering enough in return.

The union would be glad to talk about one-officer cars and shift changes, among other issues, Meegan said, if the administration would offer things in return, including higher pay and better equipment.

Other times, the problem isn't money. It's the union's basic distrust of the Griffin administration.

When Degenhart proposed drug testing, the union said it supported the idea. But the PBA espoused testing as part of the Civil Service process, before officers are appointed.

When the department attempted drug testing of officers, the union questioned whether the testing would be used to punish officers not allied with Griffin.

"We never opposed drug testing," Meegan said. "We said test individuals before they join the force. Stop it before it starts. But when they said they wanted to test people once they came on, we said, 'What do they want to do—test the non-political favorites?' "

In 1988, the union's belief that the Griffin administration is intent on rewarding its political favorites also was the downfall of an on-the-job training program Degenhart proposed for new recruits.

Under the plan, veteran officers would receive an extra stripend to work with new officers during their first eight weeks on the job. Other police departments have similar programs.

Meegan agreed the program was needed but objected that the department's proposal for selecting the training officers was subject to political influence. When police management declined to negotiate the plan with the union, Meegan called on his union members not to participate in the program. The program died.

In its report, the Police Chiefs Association recommends that the city and PBA renegotiate their contract, with the goal of restoring some of management's authority.

"Until management becomes unbridled, leadership will suffer," the report concluded. "The agency cannot move successfully into the 1990s until management rights are restored."

Union officials say they are reluctant to do that but have said they will show some flexibility on any issue—except seniority—if the Griffin administration does the same.

Degenhart, meanwhile, is taking a guardedly optimistic view.

"We don't trust them, and obviously they don't trust us," he said. "As the report says, you have to live together or die together. For the safety of the citizens, we have to live together, it would appear. I'm for that."

Source: Buffalo News, (New York), April 1, 1991.

BOX 9-2

Police Group Flexes Its Political Muscle

By Jeff Collins *Times Herald Staff*

Dallas police, who have incorporated genetics, sociology and psychology into their work, are learning to master another field this year: political science.

During the past few months, the Dallas Police Association has been deeply involved in local politics, not just to defeat a police review board proposition officers opposed, but also to elect candidates they support.

Political observers say the group emerged this year more organized, more savvy and better financed than at any other time in its 30-year history. And with crime and police morale a major issue in this year's city elections, the 2,200-member officers group has become one of the city's most influential political players.

DPA officials say with a war chest of nearly $130,000, they managed to trounce Proposition 1, which would have strengthened the police review board. And in all but three of the City Council races, candidates they endorsed won; two candidates—Jim Garner and Mary Poss—won a place in Saturday's runoff election, and only one—former Sheriff Don Byrd—lost.

"You absolutely can't deny the impact of their endorsements. Next to the newspaper endorsements, it was the most sought-after endorsement this year," said Lisa LeMaster of Fairchild/LeMaster Inc., a political consulting firm involved in several local campaigns.

"I think there's a difference this year in what they did following their endorsements than what they did in the past. In the past, they made the endorsement, but there was no followup," LeMaster added. "This year, they had billboards, they had special mailings, they were willing to sign letters for their candidates."

Said political consultant John Weekley, "It all comes down to votes, [and] they did the kinds of things that produce votes. They had mailings and phone calls and visited people, and they got out the votes."

Noting the DPA raised nearly $30,000 just for City Council races, Weekley said, "That makes them a major player in the [political action committee] department. Especially now, because there are fewer PAC's that contribute to local campaigns."

Most of the money raised by the DPA's political action committee, the Committee for Professional Law Enforcement, was donated by rank-and-file police officers, DPA officials said. Of the $100,000 raised to fight Proposition 1, about $25,000 was donated by the DPA board, with officer and public donations making up most of the balance.

The DPA has come a long way, from the days when officers campaigned for air-conditioned squad cars and the right to wear short-sleeve uniforms. Today, the group uses public relations consultants, slick pamphlets and phone banks to reach a specially targeted audience.

DPA officials say they began planning for the election as early as last September.

Former association President J.K. Ramsey said rank-and-file police officers started to become politically aware in 1986, after the slaying of officer Gary Blair and the acquittal of a man accused of helping Blair's killer. The department had been under criticism for its use of deadly force, and the Blair killing sparked an open confrontation between officers and some city leaders.

"I think it was a result of the frustration that's felt by the officers," said Ramsey, a retired sergeant. Police felt that the chief, the city manager and the City Council had been "turning a deaf ear [on them], so this became a defense mechanism."

Other leaders say officers are learning the key to winning greater sympathy from the City Council is to elect more friendly candidates. As a banner posted over the phone bank at DPA headquarters states, "Our futures are in these phones."

Council members "do have an impact on our lives, and the only chance for a change is to play the same game they do and to become more politically active," said Cpl. W.J. Craig, treasurer for the Committee for Professional Law Enforcement.

Nonetheless, police politics has a controversial side.

For years, Dallas city leaders sought to prevent the DPA from making political endorsements, citing a city charter provision prohibiting political endorsements and campaign contributions by city employees.

Eventually, police won the right to participate in local campaigns, waging a seven-year court battle and defying orders against political endorsements in 1983.

Candidates and their consultants still question the right of the organization to join council races.

Though not allowed to campaign in uniform, off-duty officers are clearly identifiable in their DPA T-shirts and gimme caps as they campaign door-to-door, talking to voters or leaving literature stating that "this was left by a member of the Dallas Police Association."

"They're definitely using the power and prestige of the Dallas Police Department to back candidates," said Allyn, who worked this year for two candidates not endorsed by the DPA. "It allows candidates—in my opinion, unfairly—to wear a badge."

Source: Dallas Times Herald (Texas), May 16, 1989.

the American Society of Civil Engineers, the American Nurses Association, and the American Association of University Professors (whose members have traditionally been considered professionals), come to act more like unions, there may be some redefinition of the relationship between a profession and unionism. The differences between labor and management have also served to foster a high degree of professionalization in the administration of police departments to deal with the existence and demands of unions.

Where the objectives of the union and the police administrator are the same, the union can be a powerful ally. Even when they are not the same, the union may line up behind a chief and provide support if the cost to the union is not too great. In such instances it may be simply a case of a display of police solidarity, the fact that the union likes a city manager or mayor even less than it likes the chief, the desire to improve the union's image by supporting something from which there is no apparent gain, or for some other reason. Also, when the union exercises its considerable political muscle, it can defeat important policy and program initiatives by the police chief, such as halting the use of one-officer cars as an alternative to two-officer units. It is here that the union confronts the police executive at a basic point: the control of the police department. One chief left a unionized department to take a similar position in another state that did not allow public sector collective bargaining. Over a period of time the city formerly employing him had given up control over many administrative matters as a substitute for demands made by the union for economic gains. As the chief himself put it: "I realized I had to get out because the union could do two things I couldn't; it could stop the department and it could start it." Although an extreme example, it does bring clearly into focus the issue of who controls the department for what purpose. Moreover, it squarely raises the issue of accountability: if police chiefs control increasingly less of their departments, to what extent can they be properly held accountable? Finally, presuming that a chief wants to administer for the common good, for the safety of the general public, but cannot do so, then for whose benefit is the department being operated?

The Basis for Collective Bargaining

Because each state is free to choose whether to provide for public sector collective bargaining and what that structure will be, there is considerable diversity with respect to the practices, policies, and legal provisions relating to bargaining by government employees. Presently, more than 80 percent of the states have adopted one or another legislative framework permitting collective bargaining.[21]

Two long-time holdouts from extending collective bargaining rights to public employees, Ohio and Illinois, adopted such legislation in 1984,[22] although bargaining rights in Illinois were not given to law enforcement officers until 1986. In general, the states without public bargaining laws are concentrated in the deep South; Florida is the only state in that region that is an exception. In some states, the collective bargaining law applies only to state or to local government employees, and coverage under the laws may differ with respect to the size of cities and counties and the occupational group such as police officers, teachers, and firefighters. In states that have comprehensive laws permitting the practice of collective bargaining by all government employees, the administration of the statute is often the responsibility of a state agency that functions as a labor commission and that may be designated as the Public Employees Relation Commission (PERC) or Public Employees Relation Board (PERB).

Just because there is no state statute permitting collective bargaining does not mean that it does not take place. In the absence of state legislation, bargaining may take place under terms of verbal or written agreements, executive orders, legislative resolutions, or local ordinances. These forces may also serve as a potent

Instructor from the Management Science Unit, Federal Bureau of Investigation Academy, addressing police executives at a labor relations seminar sponsored by the Massachusetts Criminal Justice Training Council. [Photo courtesy of the Federal Bureau of Investigation.]

adjunct to state law in shaping the practice of bargaining. Where bargaining has gone on for some time despite the absence of some state provision for it, it does not mean that this will continue to be the case. In Virginia in 1974, for example, the attorney general ruled that, because there was no express statutory authority for it, units of government could not enter into collective bargaining agreements with their employees, thereby ending what had been a practice.

Employee Organizations

Knowledge of the various police employee organizations is essential to an administrator because these organizations tend to have their own philosophies and orientations. It is somewhat difficult to identify police employee organizations and those for whom they bargain accurately because one organization will succeed another and groups of police officers will choose to drop their affiliation with one union in favor of another.[23] Consequently, any such description is not unlike a photograph in that it depicts situations at a given time. In general, organizations that seek to organize police officers may be divided into three broad categories: subdivisions of industrial unions, independent government employee associations, and independent police-only associations.

Industrial Unions as the Parent Organization

The American Federation of State, County, and Municipal Employees (AFSCME) is the largest all-public-employee organization with an industrial union as parent. Although police officers are bargained for separately, they belong to locals comprised of a variety of public employees. AFSCME's greatest police strength has traditionally been in Michigan, Connecticut, and Maryland. AFSCME is an American Federation of Labor–Congress of Industrial Organizations (AFL–CIO) affiliate.

Among federal workers, the American Federation of Government Employees (AFGE) is AFSCME's counterpart and is also an AFL–CIO affiliate. AFGE was founded in 1932, four years before AFSCME received its AFL–CIO charter. It has represented personnel from a number of federal agencies, including the Drug Enforcement Administration, the Border Patrol, protective officers with the General Services Administration, and deputy federal marshals. As is true for AFSCME, AFGE is an all-public-employee union.

The Service Employees International Union (SEIU) has been involved in organizing police officers two ways. The first was through a subordinate organization, the National Union of Police Officers (NUPO); the second has been to charter directly autonomous police locals. SEIU, unlike AFSCME and AFGE, is a mixed union admitting both private and public sector employees. NUPO was formerly designated the International Brotherhood of Police Officers but had to change its name because an organization by that name already existed. SEIU strength historically has been primarily in Michigan, Louisiana, Missouri, South Carolina, and the Virgin Islands.

The International Brotherhood of Teamsters, Chauffeurs, Warehousemen, and Helpers of America (IBT or Teamsters) has had some interest in organizing the police for about two decades. The IBT places police officers either in mixed locals or in all-public-employee locals, such as Local 310 of the State of Minnesota, which includes state, county, and municipal employees. The Teamsters' greatest success in organizing police officers has historically been in rural, suburban, and western areas of the country, although it has had recent success in the Sunbelt states.

Independent Government Employee Associations

The National Association of Government Employees (NAGE) was founded in 1961 and organizes police officers through its subordinate arm, the International Brotherhood of Police Officers (IBPO). IBPO was founded in 1964 in Rhode Island and became affiliated with NAGE in 1970. While IBPO's main strength is in New England, it also has locals in Texas, Utah, and California.

The Assembly of Government Employees (AGE) has almost no impact on police labor relations. Founded in 1952, AGE organizes on a government-wide basis with most of its affiliates being at the state level, such as the 12,000-member Colorado State Employees Association. However, some number of police officers do belong, although they are believed to be only a very small percentage of the 700,000 members claimed by AGE.

Independent Police Associations

Independent police associations limit their membership to police personnel and may be national, statewide, or local. For twenty years following its founding in 1953, the International Conference of Police Associations (ICPA) was an association of associations with the purpose of exchanging information about police employee organizations. In 1973, however, ICPA decided to become a police union and to charter locals. By 1978, it represented about 182,000 officers in some 400 locals with heavy membership in New York, Illinois, New Jersey, and California.

At the ICPA's July 1978 convention in Toronto, Canada, the question of affiliation with the AFL–CIO split the member organizations evenly. Subsequently, at the ICPA's winter 1978 meeting in Phoenix, Ed Kiernan, Robert Gordon, and 28 ICPA regional vice presidents resigned to form the International Union of Police Associations (IUPA). As president of the newly formed IUPA, Ed Kiernan submitted an application for a charter to the president of the AFL–CIO, George Meany. A review committee, composed of Jerry Wurf of AFSCME, Paul Hall of SEIU, and Howard McClennan of the International Association of Firefighters (IAFF), was appointed by Meany and in January of 1979 reported favorably on the matter. On February 20, 1979, the AFL–CIO Executive Board voted to extend a charter to the IUPA. In 1985 IUPA claimed 13,000 members nationwide.

The ICPA's loss of key executives and defection of member unions to the AFL–CIO left it weakened. Additionally, those associations that had elected not to follow Kiernan's lead were left with the ICPA's burden of $300,000 of outstanding debts; as the remaining local police associations began to resign from the ICPA to avoid being left "holding the bag," the ICPA became doomed as an organization.[24]

Representatives of police associations from such places as New York, Detroit, St. Louis, and New Jersey subsequently formed the National Association of Police Officers (NAPO) with the intent that it should have a national, police-only, independent character, making it a successor to the ICPA in all significant respects.

The Fraternal Order of Police (FOP) has historically resisted labeling as a union. As a practical matter, however, where it represents police officers as a bargaining agent (e.g., Tulsa, Akron, and Philadelphia), it is a union. Founded in 1915, the FOP is not militant, largely because the lodge leadership positions tend to be dominated by low-ranking officers with long years of service. At least occasionally, this creates some dissatisfaction with younger, more militant officers who sometimes form rival organizations. In general, FOP membership is concentrated in the northeastern and southern states.

Some state police associations are independent, such as the Massachusetts Police Association and the Florida Police Benevolent Association; others, such as the Police Conference of New York, were formerly affiliates of the now nonexistent ICPA. Typically, state associations are not involved directly in negotiations. Instead, they provide services to their substate affiliates such as legal counseling, disseminating information, lobbying, and conducting wage and benefit surveys.

Because of the activeness of IUPA and IBT, the success of these groups in displacing independent police locals, and the advantages of affiliation of some type, we may expect the future to bring some erosion in the number of independent police locals.

Establishing the Bargaining Relationship

The Process

Assuming the existence of some legal provision for collective negotiations, the process of establishing a bargaining relationship is straightforward, although fraught with the opportunity for disputes. The mere fact that most members of a police department belong to a single organization does not mean that it automatically has the right to represent its members for the purposes of collective bargaining.[25] Those eligible to be represented may in fact select an organization to which they already belong for this purpose, or they may select another one. This choice must be made, however, in ways that conform to the legislation providing for collective bargaining if the employee organization hopes to gain certification by the PERC.

The union will begin an organizing drive (see Box 9-3), seeking to get a majority of the class or classes of employees it seeks to represent to sign authorization cards of which Figure 9-1 is typical. Once a majority, defined as 50 percent plus one of the employees eligible to be represented by the union, have signed cards, the union notifies the police department. If management believes that the union has obtained a majority legitimately and that it is appropriate for the class or classes of officers to be grouped together as proposed by the union, it will recognize the union as the bargaining agent of the officers it has sought to represent. Once recognized by the employer, the union will petition the PERC or other body responsible for administering the legislation for certification. In such cases, the

BOX 9-3

Police Still Bent on Union

By John Buzbee *Staff Writer*

Organizers of a Teamsters local union for the Kansas City Police Department said Friday that their movement had gained steam in recent weeks, but spokesmen were unsure when they'd be able to apply for a Teamsters chapter.

"We're not going away, whether it's a month, six months or a year," said John Dawson, a sergeant in the Detention Unit and spokesman for the group.

Dawson and other officers organizing the group said they had concerns about promotions, assignments and fairness in disciplinary actions.

Police spokesman Sgt. Gregory Mills has said that support for the union movement was born of frustration over recent disciplinary action against several officers for excessive use of force.

But the organizers said they had been working on a union before the disciplinary action increased dissension in the department.

They also said that they were not primarily concerned with wages and benefits and that their chapter bylaws would include a no-strike clause.

Organizers say they are worried about what they perceive as nepotism and favoritism in the department, which they say influences personnel decisions. Officers are sometimes shifted to different jobs in different locations on different shifts with little notice, they said.

"Your days off are changed and your whole life is changed," said another spokesman, Shelley Reese, a patrol officer on the overnight shift in the Central Patrol Division. "Those people who have families and kids, they're in a world of a bind. All we're asking for is common understanding and courtesy."

The concerns are not unique to police departments. But because police officers' jobs are stressful to begin with, such problems only make it worse, the organizers said.

The Kansas City chapter of the Fraternal Order of Police has voiced concerns recently about equipment and on-the-job stress in the department. FOP officers questioned the credibility of the Teamsters, which organizes a variety of workers in addition to police.

Dawson acknowledged that the Teamsters had a questionable reputation with some officers, but he said they were the most scrutinized union in the nation because of past problems.

The organizers hope to receive confidential cards from about half of the department's thousand officers and sergeants expressing interest in forming a union. Once they receive enough cards, they will hold a vote among those who expressed interest.

If more than half vote to go ahead with the union, the group will apply to the Teamsters for a local union chapter composed only of Kansas City police officers. Officers from other departments could form their own chapters in the local, organizers say.

At first, the group would be essentially a club with no bargaining rights or official recognition as representatives of the officers. But the group would speak out for the officers and work to change state laws that prohibit officers from bargaining collectively for salary and fringe benefits, the organizers said.

Source: Kansas City Star (Missouri), Oct. 7, 1990.

PERC does not check the authorization cards, but only the appropriateness of the grouping of the officers. If the grouping is deemed appropriate by the PERC or similar administrative body, then the employee organization is certified as the bargaining representative.

If the employee organization is not recognized by management, it can petition

INTERNATIONAL UNION OF POLICE ASSOCIATIONS

AUTHORIZATION FOR REPRESENTATION

Name ______________________ Telephone__________

Address ______________________

City ______________________ State________ Zip Code ________

Name of Department ______________________

Job Title ______________________

I hereby authorize the International Union of Police Associations, affiliated with the AFL-CIO, to represent me as my Bargaining agent in matters of wages, hours and other conditions of employment.

Signature ______________________ Date __________

FIGURE 9-1. A typical authorization card.

PERC for an election; the petition must be accompanied by signed and dated representation cards from 30 percent of the group of employees the union seeks to represent. A secret vote is then held at the direction of the PERC, with the ballot including the union or unions that are contesting the right to represent the officers along with the choice of no union. The union that receives a majority of the votes from among the officers who both are eligible to be represented by the employee organization and who actually cast ballots is then certified. Alternately, a majority of those casting ballots may vote for no union. In the even that no majority is achieved, a runoff election is necessary.

The Opportunity for Conflict

In establishing the bargaining relationship, there is ample opportunity for disputes to develop. Management may undertake a campaign to convince officers that they are better off without the union at the same time that the union is mounting its organizing drive. The employee organization may wish access to bulletin boards, meeting space, and mailing lists to publicize the advantages of unionizing to the officers, all of which management may not wish to provide. The decision as to what is an appropriate grouping of officers for the purposes of collective bargaining, technically referred to as *unit determination,* is profoundly significant and one about which management and the union may have sharp differences.

Questions such as the following may arise: Are lieutenants part of management and therefore not eligible for representation by the union for purposes of collective bargaining? Should civilian radio dispatchers be part of the same bargaining unit as uniformed officers? Should detectives be in a bargaining unit by themselves? These decisions are important because they may affect the operation of the police department; determine, to some degree, the dynamics of the employee organization; impact upon the scope of bargaining; affect the stability of the bargaining relationship; or even be decisive in the outcome of a representation election.[26]

Both the union and management are pragmatic when it comes to defining the appropriate bargaining unit. In general, both may prefer a broad unit, the union, because the numbers will give it strength while management resists the proliferation of bargaining units because each one that is recognized officially must be bargained with separately. Here, too, despite a similar orientation, disputes may arise. The union may know that it has the support of only one category of employees, for the purposes of illustration, detectives, and seeks to represent them as a single bargaining unit. Management may feel that particular union is too militant and, consequently, favors, as a part of a hidden agenda, the inclusion of detectives in a wider unit as a means of promoting the election of a more moderate union that is also seeking to represent employees.

What constitutes an appropriate unit may be defined by state law. For example, in Massachusetts the appropriate unit for the state police is all ranks up to and including sergeant; in Nebraska all ranks subordinate to the chief may be placed in one unit.[27] The most common method of unit determination, however, is for the PERC or similar administrative body to make decisions on a case-by-case basis, applying certain criteria stipulated in the legislation.[28] Among the criteria often identified are the desires of the employees, the "community of interests" shared by employees, the need to avoid creating too many bargaining units, the effects on efficiency of operations, and the history of labor relations in the police department.

Legislation establishing the right to bargain collectively enumerates certain unfair labor practices for management and employee organizations. Certain of these may come into play during the union's organizing period, particularly if management mounts a countering campaign.

> It is an unfair labor practice, sometimes referred to as an "improper practice" or "prohibited practice," for a public employer to:
>
> (1) interfere with, restrain or coerce public employees in the exercise of their enumerated rights;
> (2) dominate or interfere with the formation or administration of an employee organization;
> (3) discriminate in regard to hire or tenure of employment or any term or condition of employment to encourage or discourage membership in any employee organization;
> (4) discharge or otherwise discriminate against an employee because he had filed charges or given testimony under the act; and
> (5) refuse to bargain in good faith with the duly designated bargaining agent.
>
> Similarly . . . it is an unfair labor practice for an employee organization to:
>
> (1) restrain or coerce employees in the exercise of their enumerated rights;
> (2) cause or attempt to cause an employer to interfere with, restrain or coerce employees in the exercise of their enumerated rights;
> (3) restrain or coerce employers in the selection of their representatives for the purposes of collective bargaining or the adjustment of grievances; and
> (4) refuse to bargain in good faith.[29]

The interpretation of these provisions would be a function of the PERC; for example, a police union may claim that the employer is engaging in an unfair labor practice by having its managers conduct a surveillance of the union's meeting place during organizing rallies. After conducting a preliminary investigation, the PERC, if substantiating evidence were found to support the claim, would order a hearing. In this example, assuming the necessary presentation of evidence, the PERC would issue a cease-and-desist order requiring the police department not to engage in such activities, which clearly is an unfair labor practice by the employer.

Negotiations

Selection of the Management and Union Teams

Figure 9-2 depicts a typical configuration of the management and union bargaining teams. The union's chief negotiator will usually not be a member of the bargaining unit; rather he or she will be a specialist brought in to represent it. This ensures a certain level of expertise, wider experience, an appropriate degree of objectivity, and an autonomy that comes from knowing that, once the bargaining

Management Team

Chief's Representative	Assistant City Manager	Director of Labor Relations	Assistant Finance Director	Assistant Personnel Director	**Title**
Team Member (resource)	Team Member (secretary)	Chief Negotiator	Team Member (resource)	Team Member (research)	**Role**

Bargaining Table

Role	Team Member (research)	Chief Negotiator	Team Member (secretary)	Team Member (research)
Title	Patrol Officer	Professional Labor Relations Specialist	Union President	Detective

Union Team

FIGURE 9-2. The management and union bargaining teams. [From Charles W. Maddox, *Collective Bargaining in Law Enforcement* (Springfield, Ill.: Charles C Thomas, 1975), p. 57, by permission and with modification.]

is over, he or she will not be working daily for the people sitting across the table. It is not automatic that the union president will be a member of the bargaining team, although customarily some union officer is, and often it is the president. Accompanying the union's chief negotiator and president will be two or three team members who have conducted in-depth research on matters relating to the bargaining issues and who will have various types of data, facts, and documents—such as wage and benefit surveys, trends in the consumer price index, and copies of recent contracts for similarly sized jurisdictions—with them. Although there will only be several union research team members at the table, they will have had assistance in gathering their information from others in the union. Unless the union's chief negotiator is an attorney, there will seldom be an attorney sitting at the table with the union's team.

The composition of management's negotiating team is also depicted in Figure 9-2; the chief negotiator may be the director of labor relations for the unit of government involved or a professional labor relations specialist. Some jurisdictions prefer the latter because, if there are acrimonious occurrences, once the bargaining is over the director of labor relations can step back into the picture and assume a relationship with the union that is unscarred by any incidents. The chief of police should not appear at the table personally, but a key member of the command staff who has his confidence should. The appearance of the chief at the table makes the task of leadership more difficult; to appear there on equal footing with the union's bargaining team on one day and then to step back atop the organizational hierarchy on the next requires greater adjustments by both the chief and the union members than the creation of any benefits associated with his presence are worth. Although not depicted in Figure 9-2, an assistant city attorney may also sit with the management team.

The issues, the way in which they are presented, and the flexibility that both sides have will impact strongly on how the bargaining sessions will go. Perhaps equally important are the decisions made as to who will represent each side in what role at the table. It is not uncommon in evolving or newly established bargaining relationships to find that both parties put great effort into preparing for negotiations but make the selection of their representatives without the same thought. Zealots, those with "axes to grind," and firebrands are poor choices, as are those with sarcastic, acrid, or abrasive personalities. The purpose of bargaining is to produce a bilateral written agreement to which both parties will bind themselves during its lifetime. This is not only a profoundly important task, but one that is sufficiently difficult—witness the collapse of the mayor of Toledo, Ohio, in 1979 following an all-night bargaining session with representatives of 3,500 striking city employees—without including people on either side who have an agenda other than negotiating in good faith or whose personalities create yet another obstacle. For these reasons, management must exercise careful consideration in deciding who will represent the police department at the table and, if necessary, influence the selection of the city's other representatives.

The Scope of Bargaining

The scope of bargaining refers to the decision as to what aspects of the employment relationship should, or should not, be subject to joint determination at the bargaining table.[30] Management prefers a narrow scope of negotiations because it means less shared power; the union's preference is for the widest possible scope. An analysis of police contracts reveals that only 9 percent had the "strongest" management rights clauses, suggesting that administrators have not been vigorous in preserving their managerial prerogatives by limiting the participation of labor organizations in the decision-making process.[31] The applicable state statute may categorize matters within the scope of bargaining as being either mandatory or nonnegotiable, with other matters not specifically identified considered permissible.

The level of specificity in the wording of the scope of bargaining provision varies from state to state. For example, in Alaska, California, Connecticut, Kentucky, and Florida, the mandatory scope of bargaining provided for statutorily, essentially includes the "terms and conditions of employment, including wages and hours," whereas Nevada's statute covering local government employees enumerates over twenty specific factors within the mandatory scope of negotiations, such as the total number of days' work required of an employee in a work year.

As a rule of thumb, the scope of bargaining typically makes policy decisions by management a reserved preserve. However, "since virtually every proposal submitted by either party at the bargaining table affects policy and employment conditions—the turf of management on the one hand and employees on the other—it is often a difficult task to identify which proposals fall into the reserved policy category."[32] When the courts have been called on to decide the issue, they have recognized the impracticability of drawing a hard and fast line between "terms and conditions of employment," which are bargainable, and "policy determinations," which are ordinarily not.[33] In accommodating these two considerations, one often-cited case held that, although management is not required to negotiate a policy decision, it must negotiate with respect to the impact of the policy decision on the conditions of employment.[34] Thus, the policy decision to use civilians in office work positions to free the more costly time of sworn officers for field duties or to replace two-officer cars with one-officer cars is not negotiable, but its impact is—and may meet stiff opposition from the employee organization as in Boston—although some civilianization has occurred without significant union opposition in such places as New York City, New Haven, Baltimore, Dayton, and Hartford.[35]

Preparing for Negotiations

Management can ill afford to simply wait until the employee organization prepares its demands and presents them; effective action requires considerable effort on management's part before it receives the union's proposal. Management's negotiating team must be selected; agreement with the union obtained on the site where the actual negotiations will take place; the bargaining schedule established in conjunction with the union; and various types of data and information gathered, tabulated, and analyzed. Although final preparations for negotiating will begin several months before the first bargaining sessions, the preparation process is a continuous one; management should begin preparing for the next year's negotiations as soon as this year's are completed. The demands not obtained by the union in the past year may be brought up again in this year's bargaining sessions, and management should be prepared for this.

Various types of records should be kept and summaries made of such factors as the union membership; types and outcomes of grievances; the costs of settling grievances; the numbers, kinds, and consequences of any contract violations by the employee organization; the subject matters brought before the union–management committee during the life of the expiring contract and the disposition of them; and the themes reflected in the union's newsletter. Additionally, just as the employee organization's bargaining team is doing, the management team must be familiarizing itself with changes in the consumer price index and provisions of recent contracts in similarly situated jurisdictions and conducting its own wage and benefit survey or cooperating with the union on one.

From all these and other sources, it is essential that management do three things. First, it must develop fairly specific anticipations as to what the union will be seeking and the relative importance of each demand to the union. Second, it must develop its position with respect to the anticipated preliminary demands that it believes the union will present. Third, it must develop the objectives that it seeks to achieve during the forthcoming process of bilateral determination. If it is not already an institutionalized practice, arrangements should be made to have the union submit its demands in writing some agreed-upon number of days before the first scheduled round of negotiations. These demands may be submitted either in the form of a proposed contract or as a "shopping list," which simply lists the demands being made. The presentation of the demands in writing before the first bargaining session allows for a more productive use of the time allotted for the first negotiating session.

If management has done a good job, there will be relatively few surprises when the proposed contract is submitted. Surprises do not indicate that management's preparation was wasted; the knowledge gained through the process of anticipating the union's demands add to the negotiating team's depth of understanding and overall confidence, key ingredients of bargaining table success. It is difficult to know precisely when management's bargaining team is prepared, but a lack of preparation is detected easily and is capitalized on by the employee organization.

The Negotiating Sessions

The publicity and attending atmosphere preceding the negotiating sessions focus considerable attention on them and may be barometers of, or influence, the way in which they unfold. However, prebargaining publicity is also part of attempts to influence public opinion, to impress the public or rank-and-file members with the city's or union's resolve, and to create a façade behind which both sides may maneuver for advantage. Thus, one should not be too encouraged or discouraged about the content of such publicity; it should be considered and evaluated, but not relied on solely as an informational source.

The number of bargaining sessions may run from one to several dozen, lasting from 30 minutes to 10 or more hours, although half-day sessions are more common, depending on how close or far apart the union and management are when they begin to meet face to face. Traditionally, any means of making verbatim transcripts, such as the use of a stenographer or tape recorder, have generally been excluded from the bargaining sessions, as it was believed that they tended to impede the progress of negotiations because people would begin speaking for the record.

In a related vein, the enactment of Florida's "sunshine law" opened up many previously closed governmental meetings to the general public, including bargaining sessions, and stirred up some controversy. Advocates of the legislation argued that it opened government up to the people and would make it both more responsive and responsible. With respect to its application to collective negotiations, critics of the law maintained that the real bargaining would be done secretly, that the scheduled public bargaining sessions would be merely a ritualistic acting out of what had been agreed on privately, and that real negotiating would be difficult because both sides would tend to "play to the audience." This last point is underscored by one negotiator's wry observation that bargaining under the sunshine law was like "a Roman circus with kibitzers."[36]

At the first meeting, friendly conversation may be passed across the table or there may be merely strained greetings before the formal session begins. Much like the prenegotiations publicity, this may, or may not, be reflective of how the session will go. Friendly conversation may suggest that rapid and amicable bargaining will follow, but, instead, no mutually acceptable positions are reached because the friendly conversation has veiled only thinly the hostility or aggressiveness of one or both sides, which quickly comes to the fore. On the other hand,

Representatives of the Florida Police Benevolent Association at the bargaining table with State of Florida officials during the negotiations for members of the State Law Enforcement Supervisors Unit. [Photo courtesy of the Florida Police Benevolent Association.]

strained greetings may reflect the heavy responsibility that each party to the negotiations feels, and quick progress may follow.

In the initial session, the chief negotiator for each party will make an opening statement; management's representative will often go first, touching on general themes such as the need for patience and the obligation to bargain in good faith. The union's negotiator generally will follow this up by voicing support for such sentiments and will outline what the union seeks to achieve under the terms of the new contract. Ground rules for the bargaining may then be reviewed, modified as mutually agreed on, or developed. The attention then shifts to the terms of the contract that the union is proposing and the contract is examined thoroughly in a "walkthrough" during which time management seeks to learn what the union means by particular wording. This is a time-consuming process but of great importance because both parties need to share a common understanding of what it is they are attempting to commit each other to or there will be frequent unresolved conflicts and many complex and expensive grievances filed during the lifetime of the contract. For purposes of illustration, the union may have proposed that "vehicles will be properly maintained to protect the health and safety of officers." Discussion of this proposal may reveal that their expectations are much more specific:

1. This is to apply to all vehicles, including marked, semimarked, and unmarked.
2. Each patrol vehicle, whether marked, semimarked, or unmarked, will be replaced at 60,000 miles.
3. All vehicles will be equipped with radial tires.
4. Plexiglas® protectors will be installed between the front and rear seats.
5. Shotguns in locking mounts accessible from the front seat will be provided for in all marked and semimarked cars.
6. First-aid kits of a particular type will be placed in all vehicles.

Another illustration is reflected in Table 9-1; assuming that the union is seeking a two-year contract and wants a 20 percent raise during the lifetime of the contract, there are several ways that the cost of that raise might be spread. Management must find out what the union is bargaining for in very specific terms and then cost it out so that the administration knows the budgetary implications of its commitments and counterproposals beforehand.[37] The walkthrough may take several sessions to complete; during this time, little bargaining is being done, as management is basically attempting to obtain clarity about what the union's expectations are.

For bargaining purposes, the union will have categorized each clause in the proposed contract as being (1) "expendable," meaning that under certain circumstances it will be withdrawn as a symbol of good faith; (2) a "trade-off," indicating that it will be dropped as total or partial payment for obtaining some other benefit; (3) "negotiable," meaning that the benefit needs to be obtained in one form or another; and (4) "nonnegotiable," meaning that the benefit is wanted exactly as proposed.[38] Management will study the information gained from the walkthrough for several days, and then both parties will return to the table. Management then responds to the union's proposal by indicating which clauses it (1) "accepted," (2) "accepted with minor modification," (3) "rejected," and (4) wishes to make its own proposals and counterproposals to. Management cannot simply reject a

TABLE 9-1 Alternative Ways to Costing Out a 20% Raise over a Two-Year Contract

1. 10% increase each year of contract	
Year 1 cost: 10% of 980,000	= $98,000
Year 2 cost: 10% of year 1 wages, $1,078,000	= 107,800
plus continuation of year 1	= 98,000
	$303,800
2. 15% increase in year 1; 5% in year 2	
Year 1 cost: 15% of $980,000	=$147,000
Year 2 cost: 5% of year 1 payroll of $1,127,000	= 56,350
plus continuation of year 1	= 147,000
	$350,350
3. 20% in year 1; nothing in year 2	
Year 1 cost: 20% of $980,000	=$196,000
Year 2: no new increase but continuation of year 1 raise	=$196,000
	$392,000

clause out of hand; to do so would not constitute bargaining in good faith. Instead, it must give a reason for the rejection that is reasonable, such as an actual inability to pay.

Having been told formally of management's position on the contract proposed, the bargaining begins, concentrating on the items on which agreement can be reached immediately or fairly rapidly. Such an approach helps to foster a spirit of mutualism that can be useful in dealing with the issues about which there are substantial differences. As bargaining enters the final stages, the issues that must be dealt with usually become fewer but also more difficult in terms of securing agreement about them.

At such points, "side trips" may threaten to make the sessions unproductive. These side trips may involved wild accusations, old recriminations, character assassinations, or discussion of a specific clause in philosophical or intellectual terms as a means of not dealing with the concrete realities that may be threatening and anxiety provoking for one or both parties. At these times a caucus or even a slightly longer space of time than ordinary until the next session may give enough time for tempers to calm or for more perspective to be gained.

Ultimately, unless a total impasse is reached, agreement will be obtained on the terms of a new contract. The union's membership will vote on the contract as a whole. If approved by the membership, the contract then goes before the necessary governmental officials and bodies, such as the legislative unit that appropriates the funds, for its approval.

Bargaining Impasse Resolution

Even parties bargaining in good faith may not be able to revolve their differences by themselves and require the invocation of some type of impasse resolution technique. The essence of all bargaining impasse resolution techniques is the insertion of a neutral third party who facilitates, suggests, or compels an agreement. Of present concern are the three major forms of impasse resolution: mediation, fact-finding, and arbitration. All, several, or only one of these techniques may be provided for in a particular jurisdiction. In Massachusetts and Iowa, for example, all the techniques are provided for by state statute. In Tennessee, covered workers have access only to mediation and fact-finding, whereas issues involving Rhode Island state police officers go to arbitration if an agreement is not reached in 30 days.[39]

Mediation

"Mediation arises when a third party, called the mediator, comes in to help the adversaries with the negotiations."[40] This person may be a professional mediator, a local clergyman whom both parties respect and have confidence in, or some other party. The mediating will most often be done by one person, although three- and even five-member panels may be used.

In most states mediation may be requested by either labor or management, although in some states both parties must request it, and in others the PERC can intervene on its own initiative. The mediator may be appointed by the parties to the negotiations or by a governmental body. Meeting with labor and management either jointly and/or separately,[41] the task of the mediator is to build agreement about the issue or issues involved by reopening communications between the two groups. An analysis of various experiences suggests that 50 to 70 percent of the issues going to mediation are resolved successfully.[42]

The mediator will remove himself or herself from a case when (1) an agreement is reached, (2) one of the parties to the negotiations requests his or her departure, (3) the agreed-on time comes to use the next step in the impasse resolution procedure, or (4) the mediator feels that his or her acceptability or effectiveness is exhausted.[43] Because the mediator is without any means to compel an agreement, a chief advantage to the process is that it preserves the nature of collective bargaining by maintaining the decision-making power in the hands of the involved parties. Balancing this advantage, however, is the belief that the effectiveness of mediation depends on a certain level of sophistication by those conducting the negotiations, and where this condition does not exist, the mediator may spend more time simply educating the two parties than in helping them resolve their differences.[44]

Fact-Finding

The designation of this technique as fact-finding is something of a misnomer; one study found that about half the respondents were sure of the facts and another 28 percent were only in "slight doubt" with respect to them.[45] Much of the work in fact-finding is the interpretation of facts and the determination of what weight to attach to them.

Appointed in the same ways as are mediators, fact-finders also do not have the means to impose a settlement of the dispute. Fact-finders may sit alone or as part of a panel, which often consists of three people. If a panel is used, a common procedure is for management and labor each to appoint a representative, and those two pick the third person, who is designated as the neutral. If the two appointed members cannot agree on the third, then the PERC, the American Arbitration Association (AAA), or other body or official as provided for in the applicable state law will do so. In some states the representatives that management and labor placed on the panel have no part in the selection of the neutral, it being a decision of the PERC. Rarely does a panel consist of three neutrals, due to the cost. If a single fact-finder is used, the parties may agree on one: he or she may be appointed by a body such as the PERC; or a group such as the AAA supplies a list of names and labor, and then management and the union take turns striking off names from a list of seven until only one remains, that person being then appointed as the fact-finder.

The fact-finding hearing is quasi-judicial, although less strict rules of evidence are applied. Both labor and management may be represented by legal counsel, verbatim transcripts are commonly made, and each side generally presents its position through the use of a single spokesperson along with some exhibits. Following the closing arguments, the fact-finder will prepare the report containing his or her recommendations that must be submitted in a specified number of days, such as within 30 days of appointment or 10 days following the close of the hearings. A finding of one study was that 89 percent of the disputes submitted to fact-finding are resolved,[46] although other research found that the fact-finder's recommendations were the basis for settlement of 60 to 70 percent of the issues.[47]

In the majority of instances, the fact-finder's recommendations will be made public at some point. However, the report should first be given to the two parties for their use for some specified period of time so that they might carry out further negotiations free of distractions. Although there is some minor debate as to whether fact-finders should even make recommendations, the majority position is described aptly by the view that fact-finding without recommendations is "as useful as a martini without gin."[48]

Arbitration

In most respects—including the selection and appointment of arbitrators and as a process—arbitration parallels fact-finding; it differs chiefly in that the "end product of arbitration is a final and binding decision that sets the terms of the settlement and with which the parties are legally required to comply."[49] The arbitrator's jurisdiction may apply to all matters or may be limited, as in cases involving municipal employees in Maine, in that it is binding only with respect to noneconomic issues. Although the term "advisory arbitration" is occasionally encountered, it is a contradiction of terms because arbitration is compulsory and binding; "advisory arbitration" is, instead, another term that is used occasionally to describe the process of fact-finding.[50] Arbitration may be compulsory or voluntary:

> It is compulsory when mandated by law, regulation and/or Executive Order and is binding upon the parties even if one of them is unwilling to comply. On the other hand it is voluntary when the parties undertake of their own volition to use the procedure. Voluntarism could be the result of a statute which permits, rather than requires, the parties to submit disputed issues to binding arbitration on their own initiative. It could also arise from the parties' own initiative with respect to future contract impasses pursuant to a permanent negotiation procedure.[51]

Even when entered into voluntarily, however, arbitration is compulsory and binding upon the parties who have agreed to it.

Although some states now permit strikes under certain conditions, the more prevalent public policy choice has been no strikes, particularly with respect to providers of services viewed as critical, most notably correctional, police, fire, and hospital workers.[52] Simultaneously, the final step provided for in resolving most bargaining disputes has been some provision short of arbitration. The net result was that labor was denied the use of its ultimate tactic, the strike, and also had no neutral "final court of appeal" in which to resolve a bargaining impasse. The inherent unfairness of this situation became easier to deal with as public sector collective bargaining began gaining acceptance, and by 1985 the number of states providing arbitration for public employee bargaining disputes numbered 24.[53] Although compulsory arbitration tended initially to be provided for only those occupational groups viewed as providers of critical services, there has been some movement to broaden the coverage to include other or all types of employees.[54]

One form of bargaining impasse arbitration that began to emerge about 1973 is final offer selection (FOS); presently less than a dozen states provide for some form of it. In FOS, each party submits its last offer, and the arbitrator or arbitrators select, without modification, one of them as being final and binding. Although FOS may be done on an item-by-item basis, as was done, for example, in the case of police and firefighters in Massachusetts and Michigan, it is usually done on a package or whole-contract basis.[55] Ohio's 1984 public bargaining law gave all employees except public safety personnel the right to strike, with a ten-day mandatory advance notice. As an alternative to the use of a strike, public safety personnel in Ohio were given item-by-item FOS.

Although court cases have challenged the use of arbitration on the basis of its being an unlawful delegation of power, the courts have generally upheld its use.[56] Moreover, even in considering the ability to pay, several courts have held that the employer must make available the funds necessary to implement an agreement that has been reached by the parties.[57]

In one unusual situation, a contract was also found to take precedence over a city's charter:

> The Michigan Supreme Court backed up a line of Michigan Employees Relations Commission decisions, in *Detroit Police Officers Association v. City of Detroit and Michigan Employment Relations Commission* (1974), and held that a residency requirement cannot be imposed upon the police even if a voter referendum amended the city charter to establish such a requirement. The court explained that "residency is a mandatory subject of bargaining under PERA (the state bargaining law) and collective bargaining cannot be avoided through the enactment of a city ordinance.[58]

Grievances

Why Grievances Are Inevitable

There is a notion that, once the bargaining is completed and an agreement signed, the most difficult part of labor relations has been passed through and easy times are ahead. Such a notion is natural. Bargaining is high drama, with a great deal of attention focused on it by the news media and the community. The production of an agreement acceptable to both the union and management is in fact a significant achievement. Beyond it, however, is the day-to-day administration of the contract during its lifetime. Because the contract outlines the duties and rights of each party in its dealings with the other, it is ironically not only the basis for accord, but also for conflict:

> It would, of course, be ideal for all concerned, including the public, if in the negotiation of the agreement both parties were able to draft a comprehensive document capable of foreseeing and forestalling all potential disputes which might arise during its life. Unfortunately, such crystal-ball vision is usually lacking, particularly when the parties are pressured to obtain agreement in a period of negotiation tensions and time deadlines. It is not humanly possible in a new collective bargaining relationship to draft such a perfect document.
>
> Therefore it is inevitable that questions will arise concerning the interpretation and application of the document drafted in the haste and pressure of contract negotiations. What is the meaning of a particular clause of the agreement? How does it apply, if at all, to a set of facts which occurred after the agreement was signed? These questions are not at all uncommon in any contractual relationship.[59]

The Definition of a Grievance

Whereas in common usage a grievance is a complaint or expression of dissatisfaction by an employee with respect to some aspect of employment, what can be grieved formally is usually defined within the contract itself. Grievances may be limited to matters discussed specifically in the contract, primarily contract related, or anything pertaining to the job, as is seen in these clauses from three different agreements:

1. A grievance is defined as a complaint arising out of the interpretation, application or compliances with the provisions of this agreement.
2. For the purpose of this agreement the term "grievance" shall mean the difference of dispute between any policeman and the Borough, or a superior officer in the chain of command, with respect to the interpretation, application, claim or breach, or violation of any of the provisions of this agreement, or with respect to any equipment furnished by the Borough.
3. A grievance, for the purposes of this article, shall be defined as any controversy, complaint, misunderstanding or dispute arising between an employee or employees and the City, or between the Brotherhood and the City.

The Grievance Procedure

The grievance procedure is a formal process that has been the subject of bilateral negotiations and that is detailed in the contract. It involves the seeking of redress of the grievances through progressively higher levels of authority and most often culminates in binding arbitration by a tripartite panel or a single neutral.[60] A typical sequence of steps would include the following:

> Grievances shall be presented in the following manner and every effort shall be made by the parties to secure prompt disposition of grievances:

> *Step 1.*
> The member shall first present his grievance to his immediate supervisor within five (5) days of the occurrence which gave rise to the grievance. Such contact shall be on an informal and oral basis, and the supervisor shall respond orally to the grievance within five (5) working days.
>
> *Step 2.*
> Any grievance which cannot be satisfactorily settled in Step 1 shall be reduced to writing by the member and shall next be taken up by his division commander. Said grievance shall be presented to the division commander within five (5) working days from receipt of the answer in Step 1. The division commander shall, within five (5) working days, render his decision on the grievance in writing.
>
> *Step 3.*
> Any grievance not satisfactorily settled in Step 2 shall be forwarded, in writing, within five (5) working days, to the Chief of Police, who shall render his written decision on the grievance within five (5) working days.
>
> *Step 4.*
> If the grievant is not satisfied with the response of the Chief of Police, he will forward his written grievance within five (5) working days to the City Manager, who will have ten (10) working days to reply, in writing.
>
> *Step 5.*
> If the grievance has not been settled to the satisfaction of the grievant in Step 4, the matter will be subject to arbitration. An arbiter will be selected, without undue delay, according to the rules of the American Arbitration Association. The arbiter will hold an arbitration hearing. When the hearing has ended, the arbiter will be asked to submit his award, in writing, within fifteen (15) days. His decision shall be final and binding on both parties.[61]

Because the union must share equally the cost of arbitration with management, the decision to take a grievance to the last step is customarily the prerogative of the union rather than the individual officer who is grieved.

Not only are the steps of the grievance procedure enumerated in the agreement, but also such matters as the manner of selecting the tripartite panel or the single neutral, along with their duties and powers. If the panel is used, management and the union each appoints one member and those two appoint the third; where the two cannot agree on the neutral, the contract may provide for the referral of the choice of a chairperson to a designated agency[62] such as the AAA, the Federal Mediation and Conciliation Service, or a state agency. Where a single arbitrator is used, a variety of techniques are employed in selection, ranging from agreement on the person by the union and management on a case-by-case basis, to the appointment of a permanent arbitrator during the lifetime of the contract, to having an outside agency submit a list of qualified arbitrators from which management and the union take turns eliminating names until only one remains or they agree to accept any of some number remaining, such as three.

The arbitration hearing is quasi-judicial with more relaxed rules of evidence than are found in either criminal or civil proceedings. Witnesses may, or may not, be sworn, although they generally are. Ordinarily, because the arbitrator is a creature of the parties to the proceeding, he or she will be guided by them on the decision of whether to swear witnesses but will require an oath where the parties cannot agree on the matter. The burden of proof is on the grieving party, except in discipline cases where it always is on the employer. The parties may be represented by legal counsel at the hearing, and the format will generally be obtaining agreement of what the issue is, the opening statements by each side (with the grieving party going first), examination and cross-examination of witnesses, and closing arguments in the reverse of the order in which the opening statements were made.

Arbitration Issues and Decision Making

There is great variety as to what ends up before an arbitrator, and one has only to review *Labor Arbitration in Government,* a monthly summary of awards and fact-finding recommendations, to appreciate the diversity of issues. For example, the Boston Police Superior Officers Federation argued unsuccessfully that the transfer of primary authority for enforcing sick leave regulations from the commanding officers of districts to staff inspection was a violation of their contract,[63] and in Auburn, New York, a member of Security and Law Enforcement Employees Council 82 under indictment maintained that the city had deprived him of the opportunity to obtain double pay for working holidays by keeping him on the payroll but not actually permitting him to work. The city negated the grievant's claim by pointing out that, because criminal proceedings were pending against the officer, it could do no more than maintain him on the payroll, but on a nonduty status, during that period.[64]

Despite the many different types of matters that can be and are grieved, the largest single category of cases, about 90 percent of the total, brought to an arbitration hearing are those involving discipline against the officer. Although some arbitration decision making is not difficult because one side chooses to take a loosing case to arbitration, because of its symbolic importance, the need to appear supportive of union members, or to be seen as strongly supporting one's managers, other decisions are complex as they seek to obtain equity in a maze of conflicting testimony, ambiguous contract language, changes from past practices, credibility of evidence, and valid and persuasive cases by both parties that emphasize the relative importance of different factors. Arbitrators often employ checklists in conducting the hearings to ensure that all relevant points are covered. In a discipline case, the list might include the following:

1. Was the rule that management sought to enforce, along with the possible consequences of noncompliance, properly promulgated, so that the grieving officer was aware of what was expected and that discipline would in all probability result from disobedience?
2. Did the police department make a fair and objective investigation into the alleged wrongdoing and all of its surrounding circumstances?
3. Does the invoked penalty meet the test of being even-handed?
4. Does the evidence support the employer's conclusion that a disciplinary offense was committed?
5. If the evidence does support the police department's conclusion, was the imposed penalty appropriate with respect to the notion of progressively more serious discipline and/or justified by the gravity of the offense?[65]

If an employee is found to have done what he or she was accused of, the arbitrator may then consider certain factors that might mitigate the severity of the penalty, including the officer's years of service to the department; the provocation, if any, that led to the alleged offense; the officer's previous disciplinary history, including the numbers, types, and recency of other violations; the consistency with which the applicable rule is enforced; and the penalties applied for similar offenses by other officers.[66]

Table 9-2 summarizes the actions ordered by arbitrators in police grievance cases; the percent column adds up to more than 100 percent because of multiple responses; e.g., an officer could be reinstated and given back pay or reinstated with a reprimand or suspension.

One study of police grievances that were arbitrated reveals that the officer involved in the grievance was assigned to uniformed patrol 84 percent of the time, another police officer was involved in the incident slightly more than half the time (56 percent of the cases), the grieving officer's supervisor supported him or her 14 percent of the time, and in exactly three-quarters of the cases the involved officer had a clear disciplinary record.[67] Given that police unions must be selective in terms of the cases they take to arbitration, the results are not too surprising: the union won 77 percent of the grievances.

A key advantage to arbitration is the speed with which issues are heard and a decision made as compared with seeking resolution of the dispute in court. The deadline for issuance of the award may be established by statute; the parties; by some governmental authority, such as PERC; the arbitrator, if he or she is acting as an independent and his without other guidance; or the body appointing the arbitrator.[68] The AAA requires arbitrators to render their decision in writing within 30 days of (1) the conclusion of the hearing; (2) the receipt of the hearing transcript, if one has been made; or (3) the receipt of posthearing briefs.[69] In general, except in such instances as fraud or bias by the arbitrator, the hearing officer's decision, where binding arbitration is provided for, will not be reviewed by the courts.

Job Actions

"Job action" is a label used to describe several different types of activities in which employees may engage to express their dissatisfaction with a particular person,

TABLE 9-2 Actions Ordered by Arbitrators in Police Grievance Cases

Action ordered	Percent
Officer awarded back pay	39.1
Department to change practices, such as discipline	32.8
Reinstatement of officer	29.7
Officer suspended	21.9
Discharge of officer	10.9
Reprimand issued to officer	6.3

Source: Helen Lavan and Cameron Carley, "Analysis of Arbitrated Employee Grievance Cases in Police Departments," *Journal of Collective Negotiations in the Public Sector,* 14:3 (1985), from Table 1, p. 250.

event, or condition or to attempt to influence the outcome of some matter pending before decision makers, such as a contract bargaining impasse. Job actions carry the signal "we are here, organized, and significant, and the legitimacy of our position must be recognized."

Through job actions, employees seek to create pressure that may cause the course of events to be shifted to a position more favorable or acceptable to them. Such pressure may come from a variety of quarters, including the city manager, elected officials, influential citizens, merchant associations, political party leaders, and neighborhood groups. Under such pressure, administrators may agree to something that they might not under more relaxed circumstances. When ill-advised agreements are made, they may be attributable at a general level to pressure but on a more specific plane to such factors as stress, miscalculations, the desire to appear responsive to some superior or constituency, or the mistaken belief that the implications of a hastily conceived and coerced agreement can be dealt with effectively later. Four types of job actions are recognizable: the vote of confidence, work slowdowns, work speedups, and work stoppages.

The Vote of Confidence

The vote of confidence, which typically produces a finding of no-confidence when taken, has been used sparingly in law enforcement. It is the method by which rank-and-file members formally signal their displeasure with an administrator and his or her policies. Although votes of confidence have no legal standing, they may have high impact because they are a public and often highly publicized statement. No-confidence votes have played roles in forcing the removal of Chief Robert Digrazia in Montgomery County, Maryland, and perhaps in the retirement of Chief Harold Bastrup in Anaheim, California.[70] Other chiefs receiving votes of no-confidence in the past include Harry Caldwell in Houston; John Rhoads in Prince Georges County, Maryland; and Carl Calkins in Long Beach, California.

Although votes of no-confidence may produce changes in the leadership of a police department, it is by no means certain that it will. Moreover, such votes may be interpreted as a sign that a chief is making much needed improvements. Following the vote on Houston's Chief Caldwell, Dale Harris of the Chamber of Commerce said that the vote was to be expected because management was being very aggressive and "exposing a lot of past corruption."[71] Houston City Councilman Louis Macey echoed this stance by observing that "you've got a chief now who is clamping down, making the police officers, at least in the public view, toe the line."[72]

Work Slowdowns

A work slowdown means that, although officers will continue to provide all the usual services, less initiative is used and work is done at a measured pace so that each unit of work takes longer to complete, causing productivity to drop. As productivity decreases, certain benefits are lost and work begins to accumulate. Pressures begin to mount as more and more people begin to perceive the loss of those benefits and experience the delivery of services on an untimely basis. These people then begin using whatever avenues are open to them to try to establish a normal state of affairs by, for example, calling the mayor, complaining to the chief of police, or writing to the members of the city council (see Box 9-3).

The California Highway Patrol has used a slowdown in the writing of traffic citations to create pressure by cutting revenue; in Phoenix, Arizona, officers slowed down investigations by following regulations meticulously;[73] and in Long Beach, California, members of the Police Officers Association (POA) implemented their notion of "professionalism" to protest a 5.4 percent raise, when they had asked for 10.8 percent; the POA's professionalism resulted in fewer arrests being made due to the "thorough investigation" of cases and the writings of lengthy reports on those investigations.[74] Slowdowns have also occurred in other cities, including Columbus, Georgia; Compton, California; and Louisville, Kentucky. In Louisville, 36 officers were suspended when, minutes after the contract in force expired, 32 police cars were disabled by flat tires and the radio system was deliberately jammed.[75]

Work Speedups

As the term suggests, the work speedup is an acceleration of activity resulting in a large increase in the productivity of one or more types of police services. The purpose is to create pressure through overproduction. To stimulate contract negotiations, New York City transit police ticketed three times the average number of subway riders for usually ignored violations such as smoking and littering in the hope that angered riders would demand the contract be finalized so that things would return to normal.[76] Other cities, such as Chicago, have had "ticket blizzards"—periods of abnormally high issuances of traffic citations. In Holyoke, Massachusetts, a city of 50,000 persons, police officers handed out 2,000 parking tickets, ten times the normal amount, in less than a week to protest stalled negotiations with the city; not to be outdone, Mayor Ernest Proulx ordered "meter maids" to ticket all illegally parked cars belonging to officers and barred officers on the night shift from using the parking lot behind City Hall.[77] Strict law enforcement tactics, resulting in increased productivity with its attending pressures, have also been used in Fairfax and Arlington counties, Virginia, to protest announced pay raise limitations or to protest pay raises offered.[78]

Work Stoppages

Work stoppages may involve the virtually total withholding of production in one or a limited number of areas of police service or may involve the ultimate job action, the strike, which represents a total withholding of the services of labor.

Examples of work stoppages, in the narrow context, include police officers in Cincinnati, Ohio, refusing to give traffic citations and officers in Phoenix, Arizona, declining to write parking tickets or issue traffic citations for minor violations and refusing off-duty jobs directing traffic around construction sites.[79] In San Diego, members of the POA campaigning for a 22.5 percent pay increase wore black arm

BOX 9-3

Ticket Slowdown, Threat of Layoffs Shake NYPD

New York City police officers, protesting an impasse in contract negotiations, staged a work slowdown that reduced by nearly 60 percent the number of tickets and summonses usually issued, and cost the city about $1.5 million in lost revenues.

An angry Police Commissioner Lee P. Brown responded by ordering sergeants and lieutenants to ride along with officers to make sure they wrote summonses.

Brown also threatened to invoke New York state's Taylor Law, which forbids job actions by government employees, in order to end the slowdown that began April 1. If invoked, the law could have cost the officers two days' pay for each day of the slowdown. Brown also said any officer who ignored their ticket-writing duties could also be brought up on departmental charges. He also warned supervisors they too could face punishment if they allowed the slowdown to continue.

No disciplinary charges had been made in connection with the work slowdown as of April 10, according to a police spokesman, Capt. Robert Cividanes.

"The public expects, and we expect, police officers to police the city. I'm sure that police officers will act like professionals and do their job," Brown said.

The action came as contract talks between the city and the Patrolmen's Benevolent Association (PBA), which represents 21,000 rank-and-file officers, reached an impasse over salary and vacation days. The last contract, which expired in July, granted officers an 18-percent pay hike over three years. But in current negotiations, officials of the financially strapped city offered a 2.5-percent increase over the next three years. A Federal mediator was called in to break the deadlock.

PBA officials maintained they did not order or support the slowdown but some police officers interviewed by the New York Times said they had heard about the action from union delegates. Some said they went along with the tactic rather than be perceived as disloyal to the powerful union. One officer said he would write tickets "if I see something." but, he quickly added, "I haven't seen anything."

Police spokesman Capt. Steven Davis said that on April 9, officers wrote 5,161 parking tickets, compared to 10,599 issued on an average day in March. On the same day, tickets for moving violations decreased to 1,895 from the 4,683 issued on an average March day. Summonses for parking and moving violations are off by an overall average of 54 percent, or about 80,000 tickets, Davis added. The total of fines from tickets normally issued in the first 10 days of April, if paid, would be nearly $1.5 million.

That is money that the cash-starved city can ill afford to let slip away. City officials have already notified police administrators that they must cut $20 million from the Police Department budget for fiscal year 1992. To meet that demand, the New York Daily News reported, police officials are considering laying off 800 civilians—over 10 percent of the civilian workforce. Such a move, which would require sworn officers to take over duties currently performed by civilians, would threaten Brown's highly publicized plan to civilianize the department so that more officers can be deployed to community-oriented patrols.

The department is examining a variety of ways, including the elimination of less-crucial police units, to make the budget cut without laying off staff, said Joseph Wuensch, deputy police commissioner for management and budget. "All options are on the table," he told the Daily News, adding that layoffs of civilians would be a "last alternative."

The Police Department has 7,068 civilian employees, about 2,220 of whom are assigned to precincts. Brown has said he would like to increase the number of civilian employees to 10,000.

Source: Law Enforcement News, **April 15, 1991, p.5.**

bands during a moratorium on traffic citations that lasted ten days; during this period an average of 15 citations per day were issued as compared with the normal daily average of 880.[80]

Although only eleven states—Alaska, Hawaii, Idaho, Illinois, Minnesota, Montana, Ohio, Oregon, Pennsylvania, Vermont, and Wisconsin—have granted at one time or another the limited right to strike to some employees, nationally there are numerous illustrations of police officers striking, including New Orleans; San Francisco; Montebello, Monterey, and Vallejo, California; Pontiac, Michigan; Baltimore; Memphis; Lorain, Cleveland, Youngstown, Warren, and Steubenville, Ohio; Tucson; Detroit; Tuskegee, Alabama; Skokie, Illinois; Albuquerque; Biloxi, Mississippi; New Bern, North Carolina; and sheriffs' deputies in Santa Barabara and Salinas, California, and Jefferson County, Alabama.

Strikes may take a variety of forms such as "sick out" or "blue flu" (see Box 9-4) as has happened in Honolulu; Gennesse County, Michigan; and San Jose, California. In Winthrop, Massachusetts, the entire day shift called in sick;[81] in Harvey, Illinois, 21 officers were separated from the service by the chief when they were absent from their jobs for 10 days;[82] and in Joplin, Missouri, officers were afflicted with the "bluebonic plague." Strikes thinly veiled as resignations have occurred in Poplar Bluff, Missouri, where 21 officers resigned en masse;[83] in Ontario, Oregon, where 13 officers quit their jobs; in Lafayette, Georgia, where the entire 25-member police department resigned because town officials didn't grant them a 4 percent across-the-board pay increase;[84] and in Oklahoma City. In Oklahoma City, a land area larger than Los Angeles, all but 16 of 597 officers quit, many throwing their badges on the desk of City Manager Howard McHahan, including one officer recuperating from wounds received while attempting to make an arrest, who was carried into the city manager's office on a stretcher.[85]

Although strikes or other job actions are often for reasons that are on the face immediately identifiable as economic, such as a pay raise, others are less clearly so. The Birmingham police struck when the city announced plans to change the carrier of the city's health insurance coverage from one company to another.[86] Birmingham's policy was to give preference for doing business with the city to companies located within the city, and when Blue Cross–Blue Shield made public its plans to move out of the city, another insurance carrier, whose coverage was not as attractive to the police, was selected. The strike by the police, joined by other city employees, however, forced the city to abandon such a shift for at least one year. A mixture of both economic and social factors may cause the rank and file to act also. In Newark, New Jersey, officers threatened a blue flu if attempts were made to make them abide by the city's residency requirement, a move seen by the police as working an economic hardship on them, along with having significant impact on their families.[87]

The Political Context of Job Actions

Although job actions frequently center on economic factors, they may be initiated for reasons that exist almost purely in the political context of police work. Cincinnati officers struck to protest the death of Melvin Henze, the fourth Cincinnati officer to die in the line of duty in 10 months.[88] The officers flung the keys to their cruisers at a statue honoring the department's dead and walked off the job. The

BOX 9-4

Frustrated Police Officers Plan 'Blue Flu' for July 2

Will One-Day Show of Solidarity Divide Force, Alienate Public?

By Mike Carter *Tribune Staff Writer*

Salt Lake City police officers, feeling they have been betrayed by city government, are planning a one-day "blue flu" for the Independence Day weekend.

A police union meeting Thursday night lent impetus to a movement that likely will result in officers calling in sick starting with the graveyard shift next Saturday morning—the beginning of what traditionally is one of the busiest weekends of the year.

Police administration and city government officials hope to be able to avert the action, but acknowledge the officers' frustrations.

While some officers believe a "blue flu" is necessary to underscore their plight and demonstrate union solidarity, others believe any action will only serve to divide the department and alienate the administration, city government and the public.

Salt Lake Police Association President N. Eldon Tanner, who says the union neither "condemns nor condones" the action, believes the action will have a tearing effect throughout the department.

"It will hurt everyone—the officers, the administration, city government and the public. There are no winners," he said.

But officers believe the walkoff is necessary to underscore their frustration with a lack of manpower and the failure to secure a pay raise for the third year running, the union president said.

Some officers do not believe the union will be able to muster enough support to pull together an effective slowdown. That assessment stems partially from allegations that captains in the plainclothes and traffic divisions have threatened their detectives with transfer if they call in sick.

Mr. Tanner roundly condemned those tactics.

"The administration forgets who it is dealing with," he said. "Police officers are the masters of threats and intimidation. It's how they get half their job done. They're using the wrong tactics."

But it is partially for that reason the sick call-in will not take place until the graveyard shift beginning midnight Friday. Detectives generally have weekends off.

One officer, who requested anonymity, said a call-in by "80 or 90 percent" is necessary for success. "Anything less and we'd lose," he said.

Because of the lack of participation by detectives, and the decision by some patrolmen not to participate in the action, some union members predict a turnout of 30 percent or less.

Mr. Tanner said Friday that he personally opposes a blue flu. Other union members, however, said Mr. Tanner has voiced support for the action in union meetings and elsewhere. They say he publicly opposes the blue flu only because the union could face decertification if it supported a walk-off.

Regardless, Mr. Tanner said he has no doubt members of the SLPA will take some action in the near future.

"I've heard this coming weekend . . . and other dates kicked around," he said. Another possible target date for a blue flu is the Pioneer Day weekend, he added.

"This is a grassroots movement," he said. "This is the officer out on the street . . . but I have my opinion that, if the union were to call for an action, you would see 85- or 90-percent of the police officers walk" off the job, he said. "But I think what you are going to see is some uniform officers go out."

He agrees a big turnout is necessary for any job action to succeed. "If they are going to do it, they are going to have to be disciplined . . . The association will step up and back them," he said.

BOX 9-4 (cont.)

Mr. Tanner said union attorney Clint Balmforth addressed officers at the Thursday meeting, outlining their options and possible repercussions.

Officers hope to draw attention to a plight they say has sent department morale to "rock bottom" lows in the past months. Failure of the union to secure a pay hike, combined with the lowest number of officers on the streets in more than a decade, have spurred union members to seek the work slowdown.

Rumors of the impending job action by officers have led to a contingency plan enacted by police administration that includes canceling vacations for supervisors and an unprecedented chief's memorandum condemning any possible strike and reminding them that any such action is against department policy.

"The citizens of Salt Lake City have come to rely upon the integrity of their police personnel," the memo says. "Conduct yourselves accordingly."

What the memo implies, but doesn't spell out, is that anyone calling in sick Friday afternoon exposes himself to policies governing unauthorized time off. Officers may be required to turn in notes from their doctors and must have their take-home cars and any other police equipment available for department emergencies.

Department administrators—those with the rank of sergeant or above—are scheduled to fill in for missing patrolmen.

Action Chief of Police Ed Johnson said he is confused over what the blue flu is all about and doesn't know what union members expect to accomplish.

One of the main frustrations union members have voiced over and over is diminished manpower. At about 286 sworn officers, the department is down considerably from its authorized manpower of 320 officers.

The chief said he will address that problem Sept. 1 when the department hires 25 new officers.

"What do they want me to do?" Chief Johnson said. "They want more people, I'm hiring more people.

". . . I sympathize with them, but I think this is all just their frustration talking," the acting chief said. "This is going to hurt me, it is going to hurt you, the public. I find it hard to believe these men and women will let the public down."

Union members also are angered at not receiving a cost-of-living and merit raises this year.

But contract negotiations are over for this fiscal year, notes Mike Zuhl, chief of staff to Mayor Palmer DePaulis.

Mr. Zuhl noted that the mayor has met with union officials and they are talking about language in next year's contract already.

Mr. Zuhl again pointed at decreasing revenues and other city departments which also are suffering in tight financial times. He said it is "unfortunate" that officials are dealing with misinformation alleging the mayor is trying to break the union or doesn't see public safety as a priority.

"I can understand how they feel that way. They feel overworked, underappreciated and underpaid right now.

"We have to share some of the blame, and we do," Mr. Zuhl said. "But we need to look ahead," he said. "Any action they take won't really help the situation. It won't put more officers on the street. And it will probably alienate the public."

Source: The Salt Lake City Tribune (Utah), June 25, 1988.

president of the Fraternal Order of Police, Elmer Dunway, told officers not to return to work until after a city council meeting at which police wives and others intended to press for improved weapons, body armor, and the institution of two-officer patrol units. Cincinnati police officers had also complained that lenient judges and parole boards were releasing criminals "to prey upon society" in a city

FIGURE 9-3. Policemen on strike, Albuquerque, New Mexico. [Photo copyright © Michael Douglas, The Image Works.]

where law enforcers are "grossly undermanned." Within weeks of the strike the Cincinnati City Council voted to give police officers .357 caliber magnum handguns with hollow-point expansion bullets, a move that pleased the officers and their families but drew criticism from black community leaders. Also, hundreds of Prince Georges County, Maryland, police officers stayed home from work, without a strike vote, to voice their bitterness at circumstances surrounding the manslaughter conviction of Terrence Johnson for the slaying of two Prince Georges County police officers. The officers felt that the media had misrepresented them and that the county citizens had abandoned them by virtue of what the officers saw as a lenient verdict.[89]

The Use of Surveillance in the Labor–Management Relationship

One of the most controversial tactics in the labor–management relationship is the use of surveillance to obtain information to influence the decision-making process. It may be used by police unions, police associations in states without collective bargaining rights, small informal groups of police employees, and employers (see Box 9-5).

Police officers have well-developed skills that make this tactic particularly effective when those being observed have relationships or habits that would bring discredit on them if publicly disclosed. In a state that did not have a public sector collective bargaining law, a new chief was brought into the Whiteville Police Department from another state. Having previously run a unionized department,

BOX 9-5

City-Hired Private Eye Snoops on Police Union in Labor Strife

A California police union embroiled in a labor dispute has filed an $8-million claim against the City of West Sacramento over the city's hiring of a private investigator to keep tabs on union members.

The claim was filed Nov. 6 on behalf of the union's 76 members and is now being reviewed by city officials prior to being filed in court, said Martin Flatley, president of the West Sacramento Police Officers Association.

Flatley told LEN the union took the action shortly after learning that an investigator from the Glendale-based firm of D.Y. Jones & Associates had been hired to monitor the whereabouts of its members. The action was taken, according to city officials, in case union members tried to avoid court orders forcing them to abandon labor protests such as sickouts and slowdowns.

"We weren't doing anything criminally wrong," Flatley said. "There were never any accusations or any assumptions that would indicate we would do anything other than exercise our constitutional rights, and for that, the city goes out and hires an investigator to surveill us. We found that highly offensive. If this is common practice—which some people seem to think it is—we want it stopped."

Flatley said the union believed the city brought in the investigator to intimidate union members and to gather information for possible "administrative actions" against those involved in the ongoing labor dispute. Earlier last month, the city unilaterally implemented a one-year contract that granted officers a 17-percent increase in salaries and benefits after union members refused to accept it.

"It's been a pretty bitter struggle, and if they could find anything of any substance, they might be able to take action against the members as far as any violation of any general orders in the department," said Flatley. "Then they would utilize that to try to frighten, coerce, intimidate [union members] to get them back in line."

City officials defended the action, reasoning that the union had attempted slowdowns and sickouts before during labor contract disputes. Mayor Ray Jones said city officials had heard reports that union members planned "to leave the city en masse" to protest the city's implementation of the contract.

City Manager Joe Goedan "had determined that everything they said they were going to do, they had done up to that point. He, the city attorney and the Chief of Police determined that it would be best to know the whereabouts of the officers so they could serve a court order in the event that they were to take off to Lake Tahoe or wherever," Jones told LEN.

Police Chief Barry Kalar, who described the dispute as "very acrimonious," said he agreed with the plan after being assured that everything being done was legal. "There was no invasion of privacy involved. It was protecting the public interest. Quite frankly, I feel it was an appropriate decision based on the information that was available at the time," Kalar said.

The investigator followed some union members for a few days, according to Kalar and Jones. The surveillance covered "a brief period of time" and targeted "no specific individual," said Kalar. City officials withdrew the investigator from the assignment after the union announced its claim against the city.

Flatley said questions remain over how much access the investigator was given to personnel files and other confidential information. "The city, in the beginning, took the position that no confidential information was given out," he said. "We found that rather ridiculous because we know you can't conduct an investigation unless you have some of that information."

The union has not determined what types of information about police officers were released to the investigator and his firm, and is concerned about what may ultimately be done with it. "We don't know who has that information now. It is a private company and there's no control on those people to maintain the confidentiality that's mandated by law in the state of California," Flatley said.

The city can enact a unilateral labor contract for only one year and negotiations are due to resume in March, said Flatley. Jones said a "two-track resolution" to the dispute is being urged—having union officials and City Manager Goedan sit down together to iron out differences and having police officers air their grievances in meetings with City Council members. Flatley said the disagreements remain over the loss of full medical coverage and salary disparities between sworn and unsworn members.

Source: Law Enforcement News, Dec. 31, 1991, p. 4.

this chief thought he could have total control of the Whiteville officers due to the absence of a union in their department with which to contend. Initially the department was very cool to the chief because he was the first outsider brought in to run it. Within six months, however, everyone had warmed to him because he purchased new equipment the officers had long wanted.

Unfortunately, this "honeymoon" was short-lived, coming to a swift and bitter end when the chief moved to reorganize the department. During the prior chief's administration, Whiteville had wanted to give officers a raise, but under the existing pay plan many officers were "topped out" and would have had nowhere to go for promotion. At this point the city's classification and compensation plan should have been redone, but the city went for the quick fix: raises were given to everyone, including the topped out officers, who were promoted "in place" without changes in their assignments or responsibilities. Corporals were made sergeants without any supervisory responsibilities, sergeants became lieutenants, and so on. Approximately 70 percent of the department ended up with some type of rank.

To implement his new organizational structure, the new chief wanted to "roll back" people to their former ranks. Although the chief did not attempt to reduce the pay of these people, the response from the department was fairly immediate, widespread, and vocal. The "outsider" issue was resurrected as personnel protested that because the community had become accustomed to seeing them with their new ranks it would appear that they were being demoted and would thus be viewed as less reliable police officers. The "roll back" took place and departmental personnel litigated. When a chief from a nearby jurisdiction committed suicide, a copy of the newspaper article covering it was edited to read as if it had happened to Whiteville's chief and was placed on department bulletin boards. T-shirts showing the chiefs face, circled and crossed out, which were referred to as the "chief buster" shirts, were defiantly worn around the department by some of the officers.

A small group of officers resorted to the use of surveillance to get information with which to drive the chief out of the department. While his wife was out of town, the chief reportedly "hosted" the visit of a woman from another state. Several days later, a copy of material appeared in the city manager's office, allegedly containing photographs of the chief picking the woman up in his departmental car in another jurisdiction, copies of the chief's credit card imprint at a hotel, logs of when the chief and the woman entered and left the hotel, the times lights went on and off in the woman's room, and other details. Ultimately, the chief left the department, but not before he unwisely called a departmental meeting in which he explained that he had sought marital counseling, exposing himself to even further disregard.

In light of these events, the very real threat of surveillance tactics within police departments, however sparingly they may be used, becomes clear. Police administrators must keep their personal lives on an exemplary plane or risk public exposure of professionally crippling information.

Administrative Reaction to Job Actions

Anticipatory Strategies

There are no simple answers for what police administrators should do in the face of a job action. A short period of ignoring a work slowdown may see its natural dissipation, or it may become more widespread and escalate. Disciplinary action may effectively end a job action, or it may simply serve to aggravate the situation further, causing the job action to intensify and become more protracted. In choosing a course of action, one must read the environment, assess the situation, review alternatives, decide on a course of action, implement it, monitor the impact, and make adjustments as necessary. In short, it is a decision-making process, albeit a delicate one.

The best way in which to handle job actions is for both management and the union to take the position that they have mutual responsibilities to avoid them. This may, however, not be uniformly possible; a union leadership that is seen to be too cooperative with management may, for example, be discredited by rank-and-file members and a sickout may occur. Negotiations that do not meet expectations, however unrealistic, of militant union members may produce a walkout. In general, the following can be expected to reduce the possibility of a job action:[90]

1. The appropriate city officials, both appointed and elected, union leaders, and management must be trained in the tenets and practices of collective bargaining, particularly as they relate to mutual trust and the obligation to bargain in good faith.
2. Formal and informal communications networks should be used freely within city government, the police agency, and the union for the transmission of messages between them. The timely sharing of accurate information is essential to good labor relations in that it reduces the opportunity for misinformation or noninformation to create distance and build barriers.
3. On a periodic basis, key managers from the police department, along with the staff and its labor relations unit, should meet with union leaders and the representatives, including elected officials, of the city who are responsible for the implementation of its labor relations program. This serves to strengthen existing communications networks, it establishes the possibility to open new networks, and it is a continuing affirmation of the mutualism that is central to the process of collective bargaining.
4. Well before any job actions occur, management must develop and publicize the existence of a contingency plan that contemplates as many of the problems as reasonably can be foreseen with respect to each type of job action. For example, in planning for a strike, one must consider such things as how the rights and property of

nonstrikers will be protected.[91] What security measures are to be invoked for government buildings and property? What are the minimum levels of personnel and supplies required? What special communications arrangements are necessary? Does the city's insurance extend to coverage of potential liabilities to employees and property? What legal options exist and who has authority to invoke them under what circumstances? What coordination arrangements are needed with other police departments and governmental agencies? What effect will various strike policies have on labor relations after the strike? How will nonstriking officers and the public react to various strike policies? May a striking employee injured on the picket line be placed on sick leave? Do striking employees accrue leave and retirement credit for the time they were out?

5. In attempting to determine the possibility of various job actions, the philosophy, capabilities, strengths, weaknesses, and propensities of the union, its officers, negotiators, legal counsel, and its members must be assessed. That, along with an estimate of the financial resources of the union, will be useful in anticipating the actions in which it is likely to engage and toward which planning can be directed. Although the hallmark of good planning is that it provides for future states of affairs, management is most likely to underestimate the union's capabilities, and the planning bias should, therefore, be toward an overstatement of what is possible.

During the Job Action

Using a strike as an illustration, police managers must appreciate its long-range implications. The striking officers are engaging, as is the employer, in a power struggle that has an economic impact on both parties. The union is not attempting to divest itself of its employer, and for both legal and practical reasons, the employer cannot unilaterally rid itself of its relationship with the union; at some point in the very near future, it is most likely that they will resume their former relationship.[92] Considering this, managers must be temperate in their private and public remarks regarding striking officers; emotionally laden statements and cynical characterizations regarding strikers may provide a degree of fleeting satisfaction, but at some cost to the rapidity with which antagonisms may be set aside and the organization restored to its normal functioning. The union leadership and the rank-and-file membership have the same obligation; in the face of either management or the union not fulfilling their obligation, it becomes even more important that the other side be restrained in their remarks, or the ensuing trail of recriminations and biting comments will lead only to a degeneration of goodwill and the production of hostility, both of which will have negative effects on future relations.

Managers should strive to maintain a fair and balanced posture on the subject of the strike, and their dominant focus should be on ending it. Additionally,

1. No reaction to a strike or other job action should be taken without first anticipating the consequences of a reaction from the union and the officers involved. For example, the decision to seek an injunction ordering the officers to terminate the action and return to work could result in the officers disobeying the order and forcing a confrontation with the court issuing the order. A public statement that all officers involved in the action will be fired places the chief in the difficult position after the conflict is terminated of either firing participating officers or, in the alternative, losing face with his employees.
2. All management responses to a strike should be directed toward terminating it only, and not toward an ulterior purpose, such as trying to "bust" the union. There have been job

> actions in which the employer's sole objective was to destroy the union, an objective that frequently results in aggravated hostility between the employer and the union, the chief and officers participating in the action and among the officers themselves. The long-range effect of this approach is to injure the morale of the police department, affecting the quality of police services and ultimately the level of service to the public.[93]

The degree of support that nonstriking employees, the media, the public, and elected and appointed officials will give management in the event of a strike is a product not only of the soundness of management's position but also of how effective management is in communicating. For a department whose work force is depleted by a walkout, personnel are a scarce resource and not to invest it in communications efforts is a natural temptation tinged heavily by the reality of other needs that must also be considered. To be borne in mind, however, is the perspective that the effective use of some personnel in communications efforts may shorten the strike.

It is essential during a strike that communications be rapid, accurate, consistent, and broadly based. Nonstriking employees may be kept informed by the use of the daily bulletin, briefings, or other devices. Letters may be sent to the homes of striking officers informing them of the applicable penalties for their actions, the status of negotiations, and management's present position with respect to these issues. Facsimile letters for this and other actions should already have been prepared as part of the development of the contingency plan.

Personal appearances by police managers before neighborhood groups, professional associations, civic clubs, and other similar bodies can be useful in maintaining calmness in the community, in providing one means of informing the public of special precautionary measures that they can take to protect themselves, and in galvanizing public opinion for management's position. Care must be taken to ensure that in this effort the needs of lower socioeconomic groups are not overlooked; they are not likely to be members of the Kiwanis or the local bar association, and special attention must be given as to how they too will be informed and their needs listened to.

In the Aftermath

At some point either the strike will collapse or an agreement will be reached, or both sides will agree to return to the bargaining table upon the return of personnel to the job. Often, a tense atmosphere will prevail for some time. Nonstrikers will resent any threats made and any damage to their personal property. Those who walked out will view those who continued to work as not having helped to have maintained the solidarity necessary for effective job actions. Union member dissatisfied with what the strike did or didn't produce may engage in petty harassments of nonstrikers, display thinly veiled contempt for management, or surreptitiously cause damage to city property. Management's posture during the strike can in part reduce the tensions inherent in the poststrike adjustment period, but it cannot eliminate the need for responsible action by the union or overcome the intransigence of a subversely militant union.

As soon as an agreement ending the strike is reached, a joint statement with the union should be released announcing the settlement and highlighting its key features, and letters should be sent to the homes of all officers urging them to put aside the matter and to return to the business of public service with renewed commitment. All personnel in the department should take particular care not to discriminate between those who struck and those who did not.

Among the other items of business that must be handled after a strike relate to whether strikers are to be disciplined, although the union will typically insist on amnesty for all striking officers as a precondition to returning to the job; what disciplinary measures are to be taken against those who destroyed private or public property during the course of the strike; what measures are to be taken against those who undertook various actions against officers who did not walk out; and the securing of a union commitment not to act in any way against nonstrikers and to actively discourage such actions by union members.

Some of what management does during and after a strike may be provided for by legislative enactment, which either requires or makes possible certain decisions. In Indiana, striking public employees cannot be paid for the days they missed during the walkout. In Texas, striking officers may be fined up to $2,000, cannot receive a pay increase for one year, and are placed on probation for two years, and the courts may fine the union $2,500 to $20,000 per day during the strike.

As a final note, there has been some experimentation with reconciliation meetings of parties to promote goodwill. Experience has demonstrated that, in most cases, the wounds are so fresh and the feelings so intense that it simply creates the opportunity for an incident; in one notable instance, a reconciliation party resulted in two hours of strictly staying in groups of strikers and nonstrikers and ultimately in a mass fight at the buffet table.[94]

Summary

From 1959 through the 1970s seven forces were at work contributing to the evolution of collective bargaining by public sector employees, including (1) the needs of labor organizations, (2) the reduction of legal barriers, (3) police frustration with a perceived lack of support in the war on crime, (4) insensitive personnel practices, (5) inadequate salaries and fringe benefits, (6) a sharp upswing in violence directed at the police, and (7) the success of other groups in using collective action to attain their objectives.

Unions have successfully fought the hiring of lower salaried civilians to replace police officers working inside at routine desk and clerical jobs. Although the officers would not have lost their jobs, they would have been returned to street duty, where they would have to endure the extremes of weather and other unpleasant conditions. Unions have also displayed political muscle in defeating the institution of civilian review boards, electing pro-police candidates to office, altering the disciplinary processes of their departments, halting the use of one-officer cars as an alternative to two-officer cars, and obtaining more powerful weapons for the police to use—even in the face of opposition by minorities—and other actions. All of these actions confront police executives at a basic point: the control of the police agency.

Over 80 percent of the states have adopted legal provisions permitting the practice of public sector collective bargaining. In states with comprehensive laws, there is usually an agency that functions as a labor commission and may be titled a Public Employees Relations Commission (PERC).

Police employee organizations that represent their members for bargaining purposes are called unions. These organizations vary as to their philosophy and orientation and may be any of the following: (1) subdivisions of industrial unions, (2) independent government employee associations, and (3) independent police-only associations.

Merely because a majority of officers belong to a police employee organization does not mean that the association bargains for the officers. An appropriate number of signed authorization cards must be obtained from the group of officers that the union seeks to represent, and the grouping of the officers—the unit—must be determined to be appropriate by the PERC. Under certain conditions, an election by secret ballot may be required and any of three outcomes may arise: (1) the union or a particular union from among several competing unions may gain a majority vote, (2) there may be a runoff election, or (3) the officers eligible for union membership may vote for no union.

During the time that a bargaining relationship is being established, there are frequent chances for conflict to occur. These may represent conflicts over access to bulletin boards, meeting space, or more substantial matters. Of particular concern to both management and the union is that each party observe the other's rights and not engage in unfair labor practices.

Considerable effort is expended before management and the union arrive at the bargaining table; the members of the respective bargaining teams must be selected with care; the issues to be presented must be identified and researched; a site must be selected; and common procedures must be agreed on by both parties, among other matters.

Bargaining can be tough work, with progress difficult to come by. Even when there has been a general spirit of mutualism among the negotiating parties, a single hotly contested item can grind progress to a halt. In these situations, a cooling-off period may be sufficient to get negotiations back on track, or it may be necessary to resort to one of the major forms of resolving bargaining impasses.

The achievement of a written contract obtained through bilateral negotiations is a noteworthy accomplishment, one often heralded in the media. However, the hard work is not over. For a year or whatever period the contract covers, the parties to the agreement must daily live under the terms that they have mutually agreed will regulate their relationship. Despite the best of intentions and efforts and the existence of well-intended and reasonable people, it is inevitable that differences are going to occur as to what a particular clause means, allows, requires, or prohibits. When presented formally, these differences are called grievances and ultimately may be settled by arbitration.

When unionized officers are displeased with such things as the progress of negotiations or when they want to influence or protest a decision, they may engage in job actions such as (1) votes of confidence, (2) work slowdowns, (3) work speedups, and (4) work stoppages. Although strikes by police are almost always illegal, numerous examples of them exist. The administrative handling of job actions is an issue requiring sensitivity and good judgment. The best posture regarding job actions is one in which management and the union agree that they have a joint obligation to avoid them; however, management as a practical matter must plan for the worst scenario, and its bias should be to overestimate the negatives in the situation to be faced. In contrast, management's public pronouncements must be statesmanlike.

Discussion Questions

1. There are three broad categories of police unions. What are they?
2. What is unit determination and why is it important?
3. What parties in what roles sit at the bargaining table?
4. Of what significance is the scope of bargaining?
5. With respect to the scope of bargaining, what do the terms *mandatory, non-negotiable,* and *permissible* mean?

6. What is a walkthrough?
7. How are expendable, trade-off, negotiable, and non-negotiable union proposals distinguished?
8. What are the three major types of impasse resolutions?
9. Are grievances inevitable in labor relations?
10. What are the major forms of job actions?
11. What can chiefs of police do to reduce the possibility of job actions by unionized officers?

Notes

1. These themes are identified and treated in detail in Hervey A. Juris and Peter Feuille, *Police Unionism* (Lexington, Mass: Lexington Books, 1973).
2. C. M. Rehmus, "Labor Relations in the Public Sector," Third World Congress, International Industrial Relations Association, in *Labor Relations Law in the Public Sector,* ed. Russell A. Smith, Harry T. Edwards, and R. Theodore Clark, Jr. (Indianapolis, Ind.: Bobbs-Merrill, 1974), p. 7.
3. The Public Service Research Council, *Public Sector Bargaining and Strikes* (Vienna, Va.: Public Service Research Council, 1976), pp. 6–9.
4. 296 F.Supp. 1068, 1969.
5. 324 F.Supp. 315, N.D. Ga., 1971.
6. 483 F.2d 966, 10th Circuit, 1973.
7. President's Commission on Law Enforcement and Administration of Justice, *Task Force Report: The Police* (Washington, D.C.: U.S. Government Printing Office, 1967), p. 144.
8. Ibid, p. 145.
9. Charles A. Salerno, "Overview of Police Labor Relations," in *Collective Bargaining in the Public Sector,* ed. Richard M. Ayres and Thomas L. Wheeler (Gaithersburg, Md.: International Association of Chiefs of Police, 1977), p. 14.
10. Rory Judd Albert, *A Time for Reform: A Case Study of the Interaction Between the Commissioner of the Boston Police Department and the Boston Police Patrolmen's Association* (Cambridge, Mass.: M.I.T. Press, 1975), p. 47.
11. From various tables, U.S. Department of Labor, *Employment and Earnings,* 8:4 (October 1961).
12. Bureaus of the Census, *Statistical Abstract of the United States,* 1975 (Washington, D.C.: U.S. Government Printing Office, 1975), p. 162
13. John H. Burpo, *The Police Labor Movement* (Springfield, Ill.: Charles C. Thomas, 1971), p. 34.
14. Albert, *A Time for Reform,* p. 29. Several recent studies have reported that market forces other than unions explain better the rise in public employees' salaries than does union activity.
15. These data were extracted from the Federal Bureau of Investigation's *Uniform Crime Reports* (Washington, D.C.: U.S. Government Printing Office, 1965 and 1970).
16. William W. Scranton, chairman, *Report of the President's Commission on Campus Unrest* (Washington, D.C.: U.S. Government Printing Office, 1970), p. 18.
17. Sterling D. Spero and John M. Capozzola, *The Urban Community and Its Unionized Bureaucracies* (New York: Dunellen, 1973), p. 183.
18. International Association of Chiefs of Police, *Police Unions and Other Police Organizations* (Washington, D.C.: International Association of Chiefs of Police, 1944), pp. 28–30.
19. From the March 16, 1967 statement of Commissioner Donald Pomerleau on the unionization of the Baltimore Police Department at the State House, Annapolis, Maryland.

20. Joe Sciacca, "Cop Union Chief's Comment Draws Fire," *Boston Herald*, Dec. 12, 1990.
21. David Lewin, "The Climate for Public Sector Labor Relations in the 1970's: A Changing of the Guard," the 1977 meeting of the American Society for Public Administration.
22. James K. McCollum and Roger S. Wolters, "Public Sector Bargaining Legislation in Illinois and Ohio, 1983," *Journal of Collective Negotiations in the Public Sector*, 14:2 (1985), pp. 161–72.
23. Portions of this section, revised and with additional information, are drawn from Charles R. Swanson, "A Topology of Police Collective Bargaining Employee Organizations," *Journal of Collective Negotiations in the Public Sector*, 6:4 (1977), pp. 341–46.
24. "Labor News," *Police Magazine*, 2:3 (May 1979), pp. 46–47.
25. William J. Bopp, *Police Personnel Administration* (Boston: Holbrook Press, 1974) p. 345.
26. See Richard S. Rubin et al., "Public Sector Unit Determination Administrative Procedures and Case Law," Midwest Center for Public Sector Labor Relations, Indiana University Department of Labor Contract J-9-P-6-0215, May 31, 1978.
27. Government Employee Relations Report, "State and Local Programs" (Washington, D.C.: The Bureau of National Affairs, 10-21-85), pp. 77, 89. (Hereafter GERR.)
28. In this regard, see Stephen L. Hayford, William A. Durkee, and Charles W. Hickman, "Bargaining Unit Determination Procedures in the Public Sector: A Comparative Evaluation," *Employee Relations Law Journal*, 5:1 (Summer 1979), p. 86.
29. These points are drawn from the private sector National Labor Relations Act, Section 7 amended, which has served as a model for the portion of many public sector laws pertaining to unfair labor practices. Also, see Russell A. Smith, Harry T. Edwards, and R. Theodore Clark, Jr., *Labor Relations Law in the Public Sector* (Indianapolis, Ind.: Bobbs-Merrill, 1974), p. 108.
30. Paul Prasow et al., *Scope of Bargaining in the Public Sector—Concepts and Problems* (Washington, D.C.: U.S. Department of Labor, 1972), p. 5. For a more extended treatment of the subject, see Walter Gershenfeld, J. Joseph Loewenberg, and Bernard Ingster, *Scope of Public-Sector Bargaining* (Lexington, Mass.: Lexington Books, 1977).
31. Steven A. Rynecks, Douglas A. Cairns, and Donald J. Cairns, *Police Collective Bargaining Agreements* (Washington, D.C.: National League of Cities and Police Executive Research Forum, 1978). For a dissenting view, see Steven C. Kahn, "The Scope of Collective Bargaining in the Public Sector: Quest for an Elusive Standard," *Employee Relations Law Journal*, 1 (Spring 1979), p. 562.
32. Kahn, "Scope of Collective Bargaining," p. 562.
33. Ibid., p. 565.
34. *West Irondequoit Teachers Ass'n.* v. *Helsby*, 35 N.Y. 2d 46, 87 LRRM 2618 (1974).
35. Hervey A. Juris and Peter Feuille, *Police Unionism* (Lexington, Mass.: Lexington Books, 1973), p. 133.
36. Donald Slesnick, "What Is the Effect of a Sunshine Law on Collective Bargaining: A Union View," *Journal of Law and Education*, 5 (October 1976), p. 489.
37. On costing out contracts, see Marvin Friedman, *The Use of Economic Data in Collective Bargaining* (Washington, D.C.: Government Printing Office, 1978).
38. Charles W. Maddox, *Collective Bargaining in Law Enforcement* (Springfield, Ill.: Charles C. Thomas, 1975), p. 54.
39. There are also other types of statutory regulations affecting the police; illustratively, in Nevada, Ohio, and New Jersey the police cannot join or belong to a union with nonpolice members; on this and related points see GERR, pp. 3–139 for a state-by-state summary of collective bargaining laws.
40. Arnold Zack, *Understanding Fact-Finding and Arbitration in the Public Sector* (Washington, D.C.: Government Printing Office, 1974), p. 1. A well-regarded work on this topic is William E. Simkin's *Mediation and the Dynamics of Collective Bargaining* (Washington, D.C.: Bureau of National Affairs, 1974).

41. Ibid., p. 1; most characteristically the mediator meets with labor and management separately.
42. Thomas P. Gilroy and Anthony V. Sinicropi, "Impasse Resolution in Public Employment," *Industrial and Labor Relations Review,* 25 (July 1971–1972), p. 499.
43. Zack, *Understanding Fact-Finding,* p. 1.
44. Gilroy and Sinicropi, "Impasse Resolution," p. 499.
45. William R. Word, "Fact Finding in Public Employee Negotiations," in *Collective Bargaining: Non-Profit Sector,* ed. Charles S. Bunker (Columbus, Ohio: Gird, 1973), p. 217.
46. James L. Stern, "The Wisconsin Public Employee Fact Finding Procedure," *Industrial and Labor Relations Review,* 20 (October 1966–1967), pp. 3–29.
47. Gilroy and Sinicropi, "Impasse Resolution," p. 501.
48. Robert G. Howlett, "Fact Finding: Its Values and Limitations—Comment," Arbitration and the Expanded Role of Neutrals, Proceedings of the twenty-third annual meeting of the National Academy of Arbitrators (Washington, D.C.: Bureau of National Affairs, 1970), p. 156.
49. Zack, *Understanding Fact-Finding,* p. 1.
50. Ibid., p. 1.
51. Ibid., p. 1.
52. J. Joseph Loewenberg et al., *Compulsory Arbitration* (Lexington, Mass.: Lexington Books, 1976), p. 152.
53. In 1985 these states were Alaska, Connecticut, Delaware, Hawaii, Illinois, Indiana, Iowa, Maine, Michigan, Massachusetts, Minnesota, Montana, Nevada, New Hampshire, New Jersey, New York, Ohio, Oregon, Pennsylvania, Rhode Island, Texas, Vermont, Washington, and Wyoming. In some of these states arbitration is available to all public employees, whereas in others only to special categories of workers, such as police officers, prison guards, workers in mental health facilities, and fire department employees. In three of these states—Delaware, Maine, and New Hampshire—the general rule is that wages, salaries, pensions, and insurance are not subject to arbitration, although even these three states show variation. New Hampshire does not permit arbitration on cost items, whereas Delaware allows arbitration on everything except wages and salary. See GERR, pp. 3–139.
54. Loewenberg et al., *Compulsory Arbitration,* p. 152.
55. Council of State Governments and the International Personnel Management Association, *Public Sector Labor Relations* (Lexington, Ky.: Council of State Governments, 1975), p. 38. In Iowa, the arbitrators may take the last offer of either party or the fact-finder's recommendation.
56. One exception is *City of Sioux Falls* v. *Sioux Falls Firefighters Local 813, 535,* GERR B-4 (1973), a Fourth Judicial Circuit Court of South Dakota decision.
57. Council of State Governments, *Public Sector Labor Relations,* p. 31. The state courts were those of Rhode Island and Kentucky and involved teachers and firefighters, respectively.
58. Ibid., p. 28.
59. Arnold Zack, *Understanding Grievance Arbitration in the Public Sector* (Washington, D.C.: U.S. Government Printing Office, 1974), p. 1.
60. A 1978 study of police contracts found that 75 percent provided for binding arbitration of grievances at the last step; 4 percent advisory arbitration, the equivalent of fact finding; 10 percent determination by some management person; with the balance being miscellaneous such as final determination by the civil service commission or binding arbitration entered into voluntarily. See Rynecki, Cairns, and Cairns, *Police Collective Bargaining Agreements,* p. 19.
61. Maddox, *Collective Bargaining,* p. 109.
62. Zack, *Understanding Grievance Arbitration,* p. 4.

63. "Special Orders Create New Sickness Reporting Mechanism," *Labor Arbitration in Government*, 9:1 (January 1979), p. 3.
64. "Premium Holiday Pay While Not on Active Duty Status," *Labor Arbitration in Government*, 9:2 (February 1979), p. 8.
65. Maurice S. Trotta, *Arbitration of Labor–Management Disputes* (New York: Amacon, 1974), p. 234, with changes.
66. Ibid., p. 237, with changes.
67. See Helen Lavan and Cameron Carley, "Analysis of Arbitrated Employee Grievance Cases in Police Departments," *Journal of Collective Negotiations in Public Sector*, 14:3 (1985), pp. 250–51.
68. Zack, *Understanding Grievance Arbitration*, p. 32.
69. Ibid., p. 32.
70. David Marc Kleinman, "Zinging It to the Chief," *Police Magazine*, 2:3 (1979), p. 39.
71. Ibid., p. 44.
72. Ibid.
73. *Crime Control Digest*, 10:25 (1976), pp. 3–4.
74. *Crime Control Digest*, 5:28 (1971), p. 7.
75. *Crime Control Digest*, 10:30 (1976), pp. 7–8.
76. *Crime Control Digest*, 6:43 (1972), p. 10
77. *Atlanta Constitution and Journal*, April 13, 1977, p. B-19.
78. *Crime Control Digest*, 10:27 (1976), p. 8.
79. *Crime Control Digest*, 10:25 (1976), pp. 3–4.
80. *Crime Control Digest*, 4:11 (1970), p. 13.
81. *Crime Control Digest*, 4:5 (1970), p. 13.
82. *Crime Control Digest*, 3:20 (1969), pp. 8–9.
83. *Crime Control Digest*, 4:5 (1970), p. 13.
84. *Atlanta Constitution*, May 16, 1979, p. C-1.
85. *Crime Control Digest*, 9:43 (1975), p. 8.
86. *Atlanta Journal*, May 4, 1979, pp. A-1, A-26.
87. *Crime Control Digest*, 6:6 (1972), p. 4.
88. *Washington Post*, May 9, 1979, p. A-7.
89. *Washington Post*, April 3, 1979, pp. C-1, C-3.
90. On September 29, 1976, Richard M. Ayres presented a paper, "Police Strikes: Are We Treating the Symptom Rather than the Problem," at the 83rd International Association of Chiefs of Police Meeting, Miami Beach, Fla. Although it is not quoted here, some of his themes may be identifiable and his contribution in that regard is acknowledged.
91. This list of questions with some modification and additions is drawn from Charles C. Mulcahy, "Meeting the County Employees Strike," in *Collective Bargaining in the Public Sector*, eds. Ayres and Wheelen, pp. 426–30. Also see Carmen D. Saso, *Coping with Public Employee Strikes* (Chicago: Public Personnel Association, 1970).
92. Harold W. Davey, *Contemporary Collective Bargaining* (Englewood Cliffs, N.J.: Prentice-Hall, 1972), p. 195.
93. John H. Burpo, *Labor Relations Guidelines for the Police Executive* (Chicago: Traffic Institute, Northwestern University, 1976), p. 14, with modifications and additions.
94. Lee T. Paterson and John Liebert, *Management Strike Handbook* (Chicago: International Personnel Management Association, 1974), p. 42.

10 Legal Aspects of Police Administration

Law is order, and good law is good order.
ARISTOTLE

Introduction*

One of the primary characteristics of our nation's law is its dynamic nature. Rules of law are promulgated in three basic ways: by legislation, by regulation, and by court decision. Statutes and ordinances are laws passed by legislative bodies, such as the U.S. Congress, state legislatures, county commissions, and city councils. These lawmaking bodies often produce legislation that establishes only a general outline of the intended solution to a particular problem. The legislation authorizes a particular governmental agency to fill in the details through rules and regulations. Such rules and regulations have the full force of the law.

When the solution to a legal dispute does not appear to be specifically provided by an existing statute, rule, or regulation, a judge may rely on prior decisions of that or other courts which have previously resolved disputes involving similar issues. Case decisions can be reversed or modified by a higher level court or by passage of new legislation. Sometimes judges must develop their own tests or rules to resolve an issue fairly through creative interpretation of a statute or constitutional provision.

Clearly, the fluid nature of our lawmaking system renders it impossible to offer a definitive statement of the law that will remain true forever or perhaps even for very long. The task of stating rules of law is complicated further by the vast

*Jack Call and Donald D. Slesnick were the co-authors of this chapter in the first edition; Slesnick and Janet E. Ferris were the co-authors in the second edition; and the authors of *Police Administration* have assumed responsibility for it in this edition.

number of legislative bodies and courts in this country. Statutes and judge-made law may vary considerably from state to state and from one court to another. However, interpretations of the U.S. Constitution and federal law by the U.S. Supreme Court are binding on all other courts, be they state or federal, and, therefore, are given special attention in this chapter.

The reader should view the material that follows as instructive background rather than as an authoritative basis for action. Police administrators should always seek qualified legal counsel whenever they face a problem or a situation that appears to possess legal ramifications. A primary objective of this chapter is to make police administration more capable of quickly determining when they face such a problem or situation.

Liability for Police Conduct

One of the most troubling legal problems facing police officers and police departments in recent years has been the expanded impact of civil and criminal liability for alleged police misconduct. It is commonplace to hear police spokespersons complain that law enforcement officers are widely hampered by the specter of being undeservedly sued for alleged improper performance of duty. Although one may argue that the magnitude of police misconduct litigation may be overstated, the amount of litigation appears to be increasing, and is apparently accompanied by a movement toward larger monetary damage awards.

Basic Types of Police Tort Actions[1]

Law can be divided into two parts: the criminal law and the civil law. Police officers and other criminal justice practitioners are generally more familiar with criminal law because they deal with it on a daily basis. Each "piece" of the law addresses a specific type of action. For instance, criminal law focuses on crimes, whereas civil law applies to torts.

Barrineau defines *crime* as a public injury, an offense against the state, punishable by fine and/or imprisonment. It is the violation of a duty one owes the entire community; the remedy for a breach of such duty is punishment (fine or imprisonment) imposed by the state. Crimes are exemplified in the FBI Crime Index (murder, assault, robbery, rape, burglary, larceny, auto theft, and arson), wherein each crime is composed of specific elements and has an affixed penalty.

On the other hand, a *tort* is a private injury inflicted on one person by another person for which the injured party may sue in a civil action. Such action may bring about liability that leads to an award of money damages. Tort actions encompass most personal injury litigation. The injured party initiates the lawsuit and is called the *plaintiff*. The sued person is called the *defendant* and is often referred to as the *tort feasor*.[2] Examples of tort actions that are brought against police officers are allegations of criminal violations such as assault and battery (police brutality). (See Box 10-1 for an editorial on the highly publicized Rodney King case.) However, most commonly they are civil actions brought about by false arrest, false imprisonment, invasion of privacy (through illegal search and seizure), negligence, defamation, and malicious prosecution.[3]

BOX 10-1

The Legacy of Rodney King: An Editorial

By Charles C. Keeton *The University of Texas at Tyler*

On March 3, 1991, a speeding car's driver refused to pull over in Los Angeles. A car-mounted posse, formed by officers of the L.A.P.D. and the California Highway Patrol, pursued the vehicle for miles. The small Hyundai finally stopped. The driver, Rodney King, released the steering wheel and exited the car, laughing, grabbing his buttocks, and dancing as he did so. Though ordered to, King failed to prostrate himself for a search. Consequently, four L.A.P.D. officers beat him. He was later treated for numerous skull fractures, a broken ankle, and missing teeth.

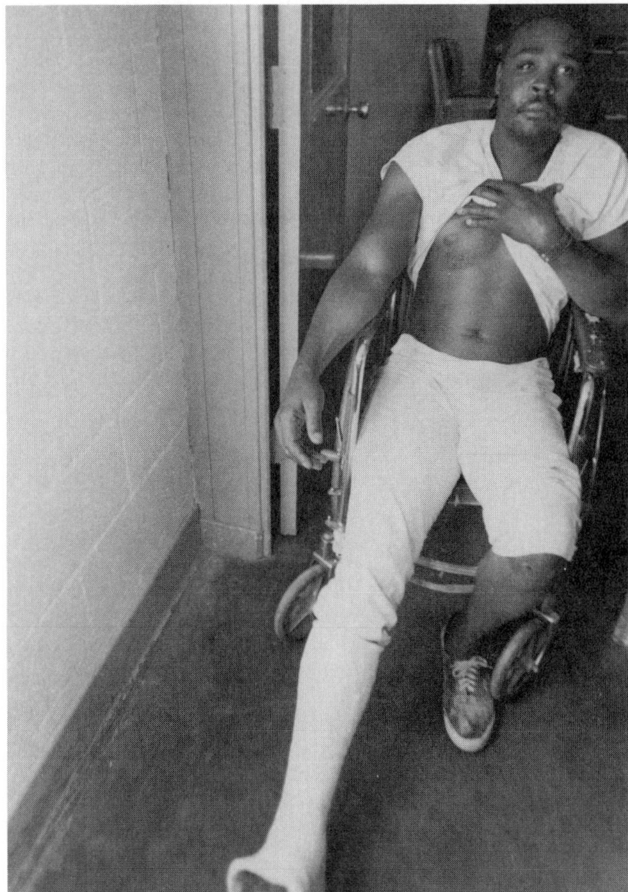

FIGURE 10-1. Rodney King in the Los Angeles County jail 48 hours after his arrest on March 3, 1991. [Photo courtesy Roger Sandler, Los Angeles, CA.]

Unknown to the officers, George Holliday, a local resident, peered at them through his home video camera, and when he saw how they treated King, he pressed a button marked "Record." Soon after this, the nation witnessed what happened to Rodney King.

Then, we reacted. But we were not strangers to violent scenes. Videotape had allowed us to eat supper and watch our troops fire tracers and bombs and missiles into people. Still, our responses to Desert Storm and the Rodney King beating were as different as the phases of a bipolar psychosis—mania and depression. Facing General

BOX 10-1 (cont.)

Schwartzkopf and the troops, we beamed euphorically. Facing Chief Gates and the L.A.P.D., we screamed despondently:

"Brutality!"

Brutality? The word, derived from the Latin *brutus,* connotes the state of being nonhuman. And after the Los Angeles beating, such terms peppered the descriptions of several metropolitan police agencies. Consider *Newsweek* as an example. Under the heading, "An Ugly Pattern," this magazine in its April 1, 1991 issue highlighted similar abuses by police in Houston, TX, Teaneck, NJ, and San Francisco, CA. Other periodicals offered such data simultaneously with information about "The War on Drugs."

Curious, isn't it? Video technology pictured one uniform as shining and another as soiled. After all, both groups committed violent acts; both were told to prosecute a war. So, when evening news viewers watched smart-bombs blast Baghdad and Basra, they gobbled their stew. Yet when the same viewers saw the Rodney King beating on their screen, they shoved back their plates and dropped their forks.

Meanwhile, fascination mingled with outrage as the scene unfolded. Nightsticks, gripped like baseball bats in the officers' hands, slammed over and over into King. From his shirt, a taser gun dart connected him to another officer's hand; high-voltage jolts of pain generated convulsive jerks in King's torso, while the lead from the taser alternately looped and stretched like a leash restraining a jumping animal. Of course, it grew hard to discern which weapons caused the most jerks: the nightsticks or the taser. Both rocked his body. Obviously, however, King did not resist arrest. He only grimaced, his face an anguished and swollen mask.

Looking on, officers in uniforms and badges stood everywhere. Only four, however, battered King. The rest—more than 20—remained by their squad cars and *watched.*

Many later claimed that they disagreed with what happened to King. But during the incident, not one stepped up to place an insistent, calming hand on a participant's shoulder. Not one from this crowd yelled:

"Stop!"

Stop is a simple word. It may have prevented King's injuries; it may have kept four L.A.P.D. officers from facing felony charges. Why didn't any of the other officers intervene?

The media printed many explanations. Most reporters listed some pressures unique to police work, and for decades now, these perceived sources of stress have remained unchanged. The list includes: (1) police are overworked; (2) they are too tightly restrained to deal with crime effectively; and (3) they are frustrated by liberal courts. Admittedly, the list describes challenges faced by police. However, each time an investigation's naked light bulb glares upon police agencies, they wince, roll out the list, and shade themselves. Thus, they avert harsh public scrutiny.

Theories, if accepted as personal justifications, harm people. For example, recidivists often speak about their childhoods in sociology's jargon. When interviewed about their antisocial behavior, they blink, answer in clipped quotes of Merton, and hide themselves. Thus, they avoid personal responsibility. Yet a psychologist could teach them that they are now responsible adults, that the scars of childhood trauma can heal, and that they can, above all, change.

Change happens anyway and history says so.

The civil rights movement during the sixties initiated change and shocked many police officers. To aggravate them further, activists paired *police* and *brutality* into a cliché. Words also became laws prohibiting abuse by racist officials. Neighborhoods took a stand, some peacefully and some not so peacefully.

Remember Watts? This neighborhood still stands and, from what we saw during the King beating, so does racism. Like an ugly, indestructible skeleton, it raised its hideously hard skull again. It sneered at us, the words of those who tried to kill it hanging like shredded hunks of rotten meat upon its age-bleached whiteness.

But racism, although it looms as grotesque as this figure, is an abstract quality. Thus, it can't be easily found and wiped out. We can't blast or beat or bomb or bury what we can't physically see. No laser-guided smart bomb can even target it.

Viewers, however, inferred it as a motivation: King is an African-American, and the officers are white. Transcribed computer communications between officers later supported their reasoning. From these transcripts, racial slurs and boasts about the beating appeared in the news. Further, other African-Americans have won law suits costing Los Angeles millions.

So, police maladjustment and racism motivated the beating of Rodney King. Yes, but blame falls elsewhere, too. The L.A.P.D. Chief led his department straight to the Rodney King beating. Daryl Gates, the stubborn tough-guy, has never swayed in his public stance, despite any criticism, bad press, or lawsuit. Although Holliday didn't see the Chief's face in his view-finder, he definitely saw the image of Daryl Gates beating Rodney King.

Cops love tough guys like Gates. They stand and cheer when he argues for their rough and rumble ways or when he defends them as warriors against anarchy and decadence. They proudly watch him don his broad-brimmed white hat, relishing the extra shade it provides from public scrutiny. And into this shade, or more accurately this murky shadow, they withdraw.

Hiding in their own subculture, feeling alternately safe and scared, they nourish another cause of the Rodney King beating—cop folklore.

Policing's oral tradition contradicts everything written. It praises tough cops, whose exploits are passed on as legends. Visit cops where they live, and if they like and trust you, they will talk about their heroes. They will smile and speak reverently of the cop's cop, a hard man, who like the fictional "Dirty Harry" never put up with wise guys. To this day, as the legend goes, you can breath the name of any cop's cop on the streets and watch the snitches snivel and the crooks cringe. They were all rough and they were all right.

They were all cops and they all broke the law.

Unfortunately, many officers emulate them still; it may always be so. In fact, our society supports this folklore. You see, we love the legends of the cop's cop, too.

Thus, we elect politicians who also love the legends. They instruct the police to "crack down," as if this action will heal our society. We buy newspapers and magazines that sensationally claim that police are fighting a war and losing. We flock to movies about a cop's cop, who always wins through violence. Upon hearing about an obnoxious criminal, we say: "They ought to beat the hell out of that crook." We incite our police with our words and our deeds.

And when they prove that they believe us, we indict them.

Then we casually call bombs "smart" and our police *brutus*. There are plenty of explanations for what happened to Rodney King. But no justification exists—for any of us.

The legacy of Rodney King goes well beyond the four Los Angeles police officers who stopped him on March 3, 1991. In addition to the high-speed chase, the clubbing and beating with batons, and the shooting of King with an electric stun gun, came a six-minute audiotape of radio communications made during the incident. The radio tapes did not back up police accounts that King's car traveled at speeds over 115 miles per hour. Most embarrassing, however, were the racial epithets made about King. Police officers were shown not only to be brutal but also untrustworthy and bigoted.

The roots of the King case go well beyond a single incident. They tell more about the history of the Los Angeles Police Department and the stewardship of Chief Daryl Gates than of four officers gone astray. Over the years, the popular media have portrayed the L.A.P.D. as a model of dedicated professionals steeped in rigorous training and para-military efficiency. But with 8,300 officers serving an increasingly multiracial

BOX 10-1 (cont.)

population of 3.4 million, the L.A.P.D. has the lowest officer-to-resident ratio of the nation's six largest police departments. To compensate, the Los Angeles Police Department fostered a "rough and ready" attitude characterized by the use of SWAT teams, helicopter pursuits, motorized battering rams, and other force tactics not normally the focus of other police–community efforts. The estimated $10 million in excessive use of force judgments against the city (in 1991) reflected this attitude and subsequent philosophy.

The April 29, 1992 acquittal verdict of the four officers in the King case sparked nothing more than an existing tinder box where tension between the police and the community had been growing for years. The resulting riots left 55 people dead, 2,383 people injured, and 13,379 jailed. Property damage totaled over $1 billion. And again, the legacy of Rodney King rested more in damage to reputation than in physical loss as National Guard troops, soldiers, Marines, and other federal peace-keepers were called in to "restore order."

Across the country, police agencies and their communities are still trying to answer the difficult questions as to what happened in L.A. Yet, the incidents of brutality and excessive force on the part of the police continue to rise, resulting in more felony charges, disciplinary actions, and civil lawsuits against police officers and their agencies.

Sources: (1) *Newsweek*, "L.A.'s Violent New Video," Leerhen and Wright, 28 March 1991), "Los Angeles Aftershocks," Baker, Wright, Joseph, and Katel, 1 April 1991, "After Police Brutality: L.A.'s Identity Crisis," 5 May 1991; (2) *The New York Times*, "Judge Is Barred From Trial of Officers in Beating," 23 August 1991; (3) *Time*, "America's Ugliest Home Video, Painton and Cole, 25 March 1991, "Law and Disorder," Booth, Monroe, and Reingold, 1 April 1991, "Gates: The Buck Doesn't Stop Here," 1 April 1991, "More Hardball Ahead," 8 April 1991; (4) *Vanity Fair*, "Gates's Hell," Danner, August 1991.

There are three general categories of torts that cover most of the suits against police officers: negligence torts, intentional torts, and constitutional torts.[4]

Negligence Torts

Our society imposes a duty on individuals to conduct their affairs in a manner that does not subject others to an unreasonable risk of harm. This responsibility also applies to criminal justice practitioners. If a police officer's conduct creates a danger recognizable as such by a reasonable person in like circumstances, the officer will be held accountable to others injured as a result of his or her conduct. In negligence suits, defendants will not be liable unless they foresaw, or should have anticipated, that their acts or omissions would result in injury to another. The key in negligence suits is *reasonableness*. Was the conduct or action reasonable in the eyes of the court? Examples of negligence involving police officers often arise from pursuit driving incidents in which the officers violate common traffic laws, such as speeding, running a stop sign, or failing to control their vehicles, which results in the injury or death of another person.

Intentional Torts

An intentional tort is the voluntary commission of an act that to a substantial certainty will injure another person. It does not have to be negligently done to be actionable. Therefore, an intentional tort is really a *voluntary* act such as assault, false arrest, false imprisonment, and/or malicious prosecution.

Constitutional Torts

The duty to recognize and uphold the Constitutional rights, privileges, and immunities of others is imposed on police officers and other criminal justice practitioners by statute, and violation of these guarantees may result in a specific type of civil suit. Most of these suits are brought under Title 42, U.S. Code, Section 1983, in federal court.[5]

In our system of government, there are court systems at both federal and state levels of government. However, federal courts are intended to be courts of somewhat limited jurisdiction and generally do not hear cases involving private, as opposed to public, controversies unless a question of federal law is involved or the individuals involved in the lawsuit are residents of different states. Even then, the suit may usually be decided in a state court if both parties to the controversy agree to have the dispute settled there. As a result, historically most tort suits have been brought in state courts.

Title 42, U.S. Code, Section 1983

A major trend in the area of police misconduct litigation is the increase in the number and proportion of these suits that are being brought in federal court. The most common legal vehicle by which federal courts can acquire jurisdiction of these suits is commonly referred to as a "1983 action." This name derives from the fact that these suits are brought under the provisions of Section 1983 of Title 42 of the U.S. Code. This law, passed by Congress in the aftermath of the Civil War and commonly referred to as the Civil Rights Act of 1871, was designed to secure the civil rights of the recently emancipated slaves. It prohibits depriving any person of life, liberty, or property without due process of law. Specifically, Section 1983 states

> Every person who, under color of any statute, ordinance, regulation, custom, or usage of any State or Territory, subjects, or causes to be subjected, any citizen of the United States or any other person within the jurisdiction thereof to the deprivation of any rights, privileges, or immunities secured by the Constitution and laws, shall be liable to the party injured in an action at law, suit in equity, or other proper proceeding for redress.[6]

After ninety years of relative inactivity, Section 1983 was resuscitated by the U.S. Supreme Court in the landmark case, *Monroe* v. *Pape* (1961).[7] In this case, the Court concluded that when a police officer is alleged to have acted improperly, for example, in conducting an illegal search, that officer can be sued in federal court by alleging that he or she deprived the searched person of his or her constitutional right under the Fourth Amendment to be free from unreasonable searches and seizures. A critically important element of Section 1983 is that the violation must have occurred while the officer was acting "under color of State law," that is, while the officer was on duty and acting within the scope of employment as a sworn police officer.[8]

Bivens *Action*

Section 1983 is the primary civil rights statute involved in litigation against municipal and state police officers. However, the statute rarely applies to federal agents (such as officials of the FBI, Secret Service, Drug Enforcement Administration, etc.) because its terms require that the plaintiff be acting under "color of State law." Federal officials can be sued under one of two complaints—a *Bivens* action against individuals, but not the United States for violations of constitutional rights, and a tort action against the United States under the Federal Tort Claim Act (FTCA).[9] The actions can be combined in one lawsuit.

Essentially, a *Bivens* action is a judicially created counterpart to a Section 1983 tort action. The Supreme Court has permitted suits against federal officials (not, however, against the United States) for violations of constitutional rights that would otherwise be the subject of a Section 1983 action against a state or local officer. Its name is derived from the landmark case, *Bivens* v. *Six Unknown Federal Narcotics Agents* (1971), wherein the U.S. Supreme Court held that a cause of action for violation of the Fourth Amendment (search and seizure clause) can be inferred from the Constitution itself.[10] Hence, federal courts have jurisdiction to hear federal question cases involving suits against federal employees in their individual capacities.[11]

The preceding discussion demonstrates that three basic types of tort actions may be brought against police for misconduct: traditional state law torts, Section 1983 torts, and *Bivens* torts. This classification is important in that the type of tort action brought will determine who can be sued, the kind of behavior that will result in liability, and which immunities might be available to the defendants.

Who Can Be Sued

At common law, police officers were held personally liable for damage caused by their own actions that exceeded the boundaries of permissible behavior. This rule applied even though the officer might have been ignorant of the boundary established by the law. Unjust as many of such results may often seem, the rule establishes one of the traditional risks of policing.

A more difficult question concerns whether the supervisors of the officer and/or the governmental unit by which he or she is employed can be sued for that individual's misbehavior. Generally, an effort to impose liability on supervisors for the tortious conduct of their employees is based on the common law doctrine of respondent superior. That doctrine, also called vicarious liability, developed along with the growth of industrial society, and reflected a conscious effort to allocate risk to those who could afford to pay for the complained of damages.[12]

Although American courts have expanded the extent to which employers can be sued for the torts of their employees, they have traditionally been reluctant to extend the doctrine of vicarious liability to police supervisors and administrators.[13] There appear to be two primary reasons for this reluctance.

The first is that police department supervisors and administrators have limited discretion in hiring decisions.[14] The second reason is that police officers are public officials whose duties are established by the governmental authority that created their jobs rather than by their supervisors or police administrators.[15] Therefore, police supervisors do not possess as much ability to control the behavior of their employees as their counterparts in private industry.

The court decisions that have refused to extend vicarious liability to police supervisors or administrators do not go so far as to insulate them from liability for acts of their subordinates in all cases. If the supervisor authorized the misbehavior, was present at the time of the misbehavior and did nothing to stop it, or otherwise cooperated in the misconduct, he or she can be held partially liable for the officer's tortious behavior.[16] However, these situations are not classic examples of vicarious liability; rather, they are instances in which it can be said that the supervisor's own conduct is, in part, a cause of the injury giving rise to the lawsuit.[17]

Nevertheless, the growing area of negligence as a Section 1983 cause of action has caused concern within police supervisory ranks. The courts have supported several negligence theories applicable to police supervision and management. The following is a discussion of important negligence cases and subsequent legal development in this area:[18]

Negligent Hiring. The law enforcement administrator and the local government entity have a duty to "weed out" those obviously unfit for police duty. Further, the courts have held that an employer must exercise a reasonable standard of care in selecting persons who, because of the nature of their employment (such as policing), could present a threat of injury to members of the public.[19]

Negligent Assignment, Retention, and Entrustment. Police administrators who know, or should have known, of individual acts or patterns of physical abuse, malicious or threatening conduct, or similar threats against the public by officers under their supervision must take immediate action. If an internal investigation sustains an allegation of such serious conduct by an officer, appropriate action by a police chief could be suspension—followed by assignment to a position with little or no public contact—or termination. A police chief failing to take decisive action when required could be held liable for future injuries caused by the officer. In addition, entrustment of the "emblements of office" (e.g., a badge, a gun, a nightstick) subjects a municipality and appropriate administrators of a municipal agency to liability whenever injury results from the known misuse of such emblements. In other words, administrators and supervisors have a duty to supervise errant officers properly.[20]

Negligent Direction and Supervision. The administrator and/or supervisor have the duty to develop and implement appropriate policies and procedures. Therefore, a written manual of policies and procedures is an absolute must. This manual must provide clear instruction and direction regarding the position of police officer, be widely disseminated, and be accompanied with training so that all officers understand the significance of the manual.[21] Further, the courts have held that supervisors must "take corrective steps" where evidence indicates that official policy is being abridged and/or the public is being placed at an "unreasonable risk" due to the actions of a police officer. Inaction on the part of the police supervisors and/or administrators is enough to establish negligence.[22] For example, the failure of a police sergeant to order the termination of a high-speed pursuit of a minor traffic violator through a congested downtown business area that results in serious personal injuries or deaths to members of the public is sure to bring litigation based on an allegation of failure to supervise.

Negligent Training. The local unit of government and the administrator or supervisor of a police department have an affirmative duty to train their employees correctly and adequately. In a recent landmark case (*City of Canton* v. *Harris*), the Supreme Court limited the use of inadequate police training as a basis for Section 1983 actions. The Court held that inadequate police training may form the basis for a civil rights claim "where the failure to train amounts to deliberate indifference to the rights of persons with whom the police come in contact." Therefore, it is

FIGURE 10-2. As described in Chapter 1, community policing places additional responsibility on the supervisor to instruct and direct officers during routine incidents. Neighborhood disturbances are often characterized by high emotion and potentially violent confrontations, which may require the presence of a supervisor at the scene. The failure to provide such direction and/or supervision can result in a negligence tort action. [Photo courtesy of the Lexington–Fayette Urban County, Kentucky, Police Department.]

incumbent on the plaintiff to prove that the training program is inadequate as to the expected duties of an officer and that the deficiency of training is closely related to the ultimate injury[23] (see Box 10-2).

The two areas of negligence that have been the greatest sources of litigation under Section 1983 in recent years have been negligent supervision and negligent training. Incidents arising out of the use of deadly force have certainly raised significant questions regarding training and will be covered later in this chapter.

A second difficult question with respect to who may be sued for damages caused by police misconduct concerns the liability of the police department and the governmental unit of which the department is a part.[24] To answer this question, it is necessary to briefly consider the concept of sovereign immunity.

Under common law in England, the government could not be sued because the government was the king, and, in effect, the king could do no wrong. Although this doctrine of sovereign immunity was initially adopted by the American judicial system, it has undergone extensive modification by court decisions and acts of legislative bodies.

The courts were the first to chip away at the doctrine as it related to tort action in state courts. Most of the courts taking this action did so on the basis that the doctrine had been created initially because the times seemed to demand it, and thus the courts should abrogate the doctrine because modern times no longer justified it. Kenneth Culp Davis,[25] a commentator on administrative law, reported that 18 courts "had abolished chunks of sovereign immunity" by 1970, 29 had done so by 1975, and 33 by 1978.

BOX 10-2

Written Policies Best Defense Against Police Liability Exposures

By Michael Schachner

ATLANTA–Police departments can best manage potential liability by implementing written policies and procedures and then training officers to adhere to them, according to a liability management consultant.

Police chiefs and municipal risk managers also must make a greater effort to supervise and guide subordinates to control police liability exposures, he said.

In light of recent highly publicized cases of police brutality, like the Rodney King case in Los Angeles (*BI*, March 25), law enforcement officers now are under a tremendous amount of scrutiny regarding the use of force, observed G. Patrick Gallagher, director of the Institute for Liability Management in Leesburg, Va.

"Jury sensitivity toward police violence is way up, while police credibility is down. Supervisors must do more to look over their subordinates—not overlook their actions," Mr. Gallagher said during a session at the 12th annual Public Risk Management Assn. conference in Atlanta earlier this month.

"The police chief and risk manager can't manage liability if they can't manage their people. The greatest exposure to liability exists when the police chief knows what's going on but doesn't do anything," he explained.

Mr. Gallagher said that while police work is a "tough line of business where the adrenaline gets pumping," supervisors of line officers must implement a systematic approach to instructing officers about the proper use of force, one which addresses liability and increases effectiveness. Any approach also must detail disciplinary measures the department will take against officers who violate policy.

"As a leader, you need to guide with a plan and vision," Mr. Gallagher said.

That plan should include:

- A complete program of policies and procedures. "You have to have these. There are no short cuts," Mr. Gallagher asserted.

  Policies are usually formal written rules. They are formal when issued by the police chief, but they become informal when modified by supervisors, he noted.

  "You need policies for every little thing you do," agreed Richard Shaffer, police chief for the city of Harrisburg, Pa., in another session during the PRIMA conference. "Whether it be in the use of firearms, foot pursuit or vehicle operation, you must have written policies governing the procedures."

- Training. "You have to train your people in departmental policies. Officers do go through the academy, but they don't come out with an understanding of your department's policies," Mr. Gallagher said.

  "For example, a shooting case can become a problem—not because the officers lacked the skills to fire their weapons properly, but because they weren't trained as to when to shoot," he explained.

  "You can't have police on the street with a gun or performing a high-speed chase when they haven't completed proper training courses. We wouldn't have pilots flying airplanes under the promise that they'll soon be attending flight school," Mr. Gallagher said.

- Supervision and discipline. Officers who commit egregious acts do not feel that they will be held personally responsible, Mr. Gallagher said.

  "Often, the police department doesn't feel pain or loss in a lawsuit. Change your policy so that the officers know that they'll be held directly responsible for what they do on the street," he advised.

  Supervision and discipline, "combined with policy and training, is your defense in court," Mr. Gallagher said.

BOX 10-2 (cont.)

"If you have clearly written policies, training and supervision, you can control a case. You can't control a robbery or a high-speed car chase at 2 a.m., but if you have done everything else, it forces the plaintiff to fight you based on the incident only, rather than on five fronts."

"If you have policies and training, the chief, the department and the city are much better protected," Mr. Shaffer agreed.

- Review and revision. Risk managers and police department heads must pay close attention to police liability lawsuits filed locally or nationally, court decisions and any new state or local statutes that affect law enforcement and adjust their policies and procedures accordingly, Mr. Gallagher urged.
- A legal adviser, who does not necessarily have to be the city attorney.

Mr. Gallagher recommended that the public entity responsible for a law enforcement body employ a full-time specialist knowledgeable about police work who would advise the chief and city attorney after an incident, handle post-incident press relations and be a liaison between the department and a plaintiff.

"This specialist should be able to offer advice, but not necessarily legal counsel. Many city attorneys just don't understand police work," Mr. Gallagher said.

A problem in implementing the program often develops, though, because many risk managers cannot establish a partnership with the police chief and the department's other ranking officers, according to Mr. Gallagher.

"Hopefully, the relationship between the police department and the risk manager is good," Mr. Shaffer said. "But if the chief is not open to communication, then the risk manager should go straight to the mayor, who is likely the only one who'll be able to change the police chief's mind," he said.

"But don't start out by trying to stuff your risk management program down the throat of the police chief," Mr. Shaffer warned. "You have to remember that cops aren't risk managers—they're police officers, and they don't know your lingo and speech."

In developing a liability management program, departments should study the programs in place at similar police departments around the country and use them as models, Mr. Gallagher advised.

"Try to identify five departments that you would call leaders. Examine their leadership, training courses and values and employ them for yourself. There are plenty of very good police departments out there—they just have to be identified," Mr. Gallagher said.

Source: Business Insurance, May 27, 1991, p. 3.

Davis noted that the trend toward abrogation of sovereign immunity by judicial action was on the wane by 1976 and that the state legislatures had become the primary movers toward limiting or eliminating the doctrine. As a result of combined judicial and legislative action, by 1978 only two states still adhered fully to the traditional common law approach that government was totally immune from liability for torts occurring in the exercise of governmental functions.[26]

Lawsuits brought in federal courts against state and local officials are analyzed somewhat differently. The courts first examine the claim asserted by the plaintiff in the case, and will then determine whether the relief requested can be imposed against the defendants named in the action. For governmental officials and governmental entities named as defendants, the plaintiff's ability to succeed will depend on which immunities are available to those defendants. These immunities will be applied to determine whether governmental defendants remain in the lawsuit and whether damages can be assessed against them.

In federal lawsuits against a state, or state officials sued in their official capacities, the courts have concluded that the Eleventh Amendment to the United States Constitution precludes awards of monetary relief.[27] The courts have arrived at this result by deciding that the essence of the Eleventh Amendment is its protection of state treasuries against damage awards in federal court. The U.S. Supreme Court recently extended this principle to bar the recovery of attorneys' fees against state officials sued in their official capacity under 42 U.S.C. 1983.

The Eleventh Amendment does not, however, preclude courts from ordering state officials to do certain things in the future,[28] even if such orders will require the expenditure of substantial sums from the state treasury.[29] The rationale behind such orders is that federal courts can require that the actions of state officials comport with the federal constitution. The U.S. Supreme Court decided in 1984 that the federal constitution does not allow those courts to consider allegations that a state official violated state law; such claims must be addressed in state courts.

Individuals pursuing damage claims under Section 1983 against local government officials, and state officials who are sued in their individual rather than official capacities will have to overcome the defense available to such parties of "qualified, good-faith immunity." Such official immunities are not creatures of Section 1983; they arose from traditional, common law protections that were historically accorded to government officials. Basically, the good faith immunity doctrine recognizes that public officials who exercise discretion in the performance of their duties should not be punished for actions undertaken in good faith. Imposing liability on public officials in such situations would inevitably deter their willingness to "execute . . . [their] office with the decisiveness and the judgment required by the public good."[30]

Over the years, the courts have struggled to develop a test for "good faith." In 1975, the U.S. Supreme Court articulated such a test that considered both the official's state of mind when he committed the act in question (the subjective element) and whether the act violated clearly established legal rights (the objective element).[31]

However, seven years later the Supreme Court decided that the subjective element of the text should be dropped, leaving only the standard of "objective reasonableness."[32] Now, a court must determine only whether the law at issue was "clearly established" at the time the challenged action occurred. Furthermore, if the plaintiff's allegations do not show a violation of clearly established law, a public official asserting good faith immunity will be entitled to dismissal of the lawsuit before it proceeds further.[33]

The immunities available to state and local officials are generally designed to protect individuals from liability arising out of the performance of official acts. With the Eleventh Amendment providing similar protection to the states, the question of the immunity of a local government was raised. Initially, the U.S. Supreme Court concluded that Congress had not intended to apply 42 U.S.C. 1983 to municipalities, thereby giving municipalities what is called "absolute," or unqualified immunity from suit.[34] Upon reexamination of this issue in the 1978 case *Monell* v. *Department of Social Services,*[35] the Court decided that Congress had intended for Section 1983 to apply to municipalities and other local government units. The Court further concluded that although certain other immunities were not available to a municipality in a Section 1983 lawsuit, the municipality could not be held liable solely because it employed an individual who was responsible for Section 1983 violations. The Court made it clear that local government entities will be liable under Section 1983 only when that government's policies or official procedures could be shown to be responsible for the violation of federally protected rights.

Unfortunately, the *Monell* decision did not fully articulate the limits of municipal liability under Section 1983. The result has been considerable litigation to establish when a deprivation of federally protected rights actually results from enforcement of a municipal policy or procedure, and at what point an official's actions can be fairly treated as establishing the offending policy.[36]

More recently, the Supreme Court has held that "single acts of police misconduct" do not, by themselves, show that a city policy was involved in the alleged tortious act.[37] A lower federal court has since acknowledged that it may be questionable whether an alleged policy of inadequate training or negligent hiring will suffice to impose liability on a municipality for the unconstitutional actions of its police officers.[38]

Scope of Liability

In general, state tort actions against police officers provide a greater scope of liability than do the Section 1983 and *Biven* suits. That is, in tort actions under state law, a greater range of behavior is actionable.

The types of torts under state law that commonly are brought against police officers may be categorized as intentional or negligence torts. An intentional tort is one in which the defendant knowingly commits a voluntary act designed to bring about certain physical consequences. For example, the tort of assault is the purposeful infliction on another person of a fear of a harmful or offensive contact. If X points an unloaded pistol at Y, who does not know the pistol is unloaded, X has created in Y an apprehension that Y is about to experience a harmful contact from a bullet. X voluntarily lifts the pistol and points it at Y, fully expecting that it will cause Y to be apprehensive about being hit by a bullet. Thus, X is liable to Y for the intentional tort of assault.

The tort of negligence involves conduct that presents an unreasonable risk of harm to others which, in turn, is the proximate cause of an actual injury. Whereas in an intentional tort the consequences following an act must be substantially certain to follow, in the tort of negligence the consequences need only be foreseeable. When X drives through a stop sign, even though unintentional, and hits the side of Y's car, X's behavior presents an unreasonable risk of harm to others and is the proximate cause of the damage to Y's car. Although X would have been negligent for "running the stop sign" even without hitting the other car, he or she would not have committed the tort of negligence in that no injury was caused (see Box 10-3).

Recently, the Supreme Court limited the scope of liability in reference to negligence as an element of deprivation of constitutional rights in Section 1983 and *Bivens* actions. In *Daniels* v. *Williams* (1986), the petitioner sought to recover damages as a result of injuries sustained in a fall caused by a pillow negligently left on the stairs of the city jail in Richmond, Virginia. The Court held that the peti-

BOX 10-3

Agency and Officer Liability—a Case Example

In some instances juries may determine that both the law enforcement agency and the officer should be liable for the actions of the officer. The following case illustrates this point.

A police officer on routine patrol observed a motorcycle fail to stop for a stop sign. There were two men on the motorcycle. The officer pulled in behind the motorcyclist and activated his emergency equipment. The motorcyclist pulled over and stopped. The officer approached the driver and advised he stopped him for failing to stop at the stop sign. The driver took exception to the officer's observations and very sarcastically and profanely denied that he failed to stop. The officer became angry at the attitude of the driver and ordered both men to get off the motorcycle. They complied with his instructions. The verbal confrontation between the officer and the men escalated, and the officer proceeded to strike the driver across the head with a metal flashlight, knocking him to the ground. The passenger at that point became angry, very loud, and also profane, at which point the officer struck this individual several times across the head with the flashlight, knocking him to the ground. Both men eventually had to be taken to the hospital for their injuries. The driver had sustained permanent brain damage as a result of being struck in the head with the flashlight. The men were both charged with disorderly conduct, assault and battery on a police officer, and resisting arrest.

The officer completed his report and provided statements to the internal affairs unit that the men had physically threatened him and he was merely defending himself. There were no eyewitnesses to this incident other than the officer and the two arrested men.

As a result of their investigation, the internal affairs unit determined that the charges made by the two men could not be substantiated, and the police chief ruled in favor of the officer. Prior to this incident, neither of the men on the motorcycle had any police record.

At the criminal trial, both men were found not guilty. A civil action was initiated against the officer and his department by the two men. At the civil trial it was learned that this same officer had been investigated on numerous occasions for excessive force, and his actions had resulted in at least ten people being hospitalized in the past seven years because of the force he used in making arrests. In every case his department cleared him of any wrongdoing.

Upon hearing the evidence, the jury concluded, based in great part upon the officer's previous record, that he used excessive force in this case and his department, by their previous inaction, had condoned his actions and were guilty of negligent retention.

The jury returned a defense verdict which imposed $100,000 in punitive damages against the officer for his excessive and unnecessary use of force, and $250,000 against his agency for failing to take proper action against this officer, by either counseling, disciplining, reassigning, or dismissing him.

tioner's constitutional rights were "simply not implicated by a negligent act of an official causing *unintentional* loss or injury to life, liberty, or property."[39] This case has had a profound impact on limiting Section 1983 and *Bivens* actions to intentional torts; hence, the sheer volume of such cases has significantly decreased in past years. It is important to note, however, that the Supreme Court "has not changed the rule that an intentional abuse of power, which shocks the conscience or which infringes a specific constitutional guarantee such as those embodied in the Bill of Rights," still implicates serious liability.[40]

As noted earlier in this chapter, many lawsuits against police officers are based on the intentional torts of assault, battery, false imprisonment, and malicious prosecution.[41] Suits against police officers for intentional torts can be brought as state tort actions, Section 1983 suits, or *Bivens* suits. Although suits against police officers for negligence torts can be brought as state tort actions, the issue is not so clear-cut with regard to Section 1983 and *Bivens* suits.

Generally damages assessed in civil litigation for negligence are ordinary (compensatory) damages that are paid by the employing governmental entity (or its liability insurance carrier) on behalf of the defendant officer. Therefore, as a general rule, the individual employee is not required to pay ordinary damages that result from a civil negligence suit. This is so because normally when governmental employees are performing their duties within the scope of employment, they are deemed to be the agents or representatives of the employing agency, and therefore not personally liable for their acts. However, where punitive damages are assessed for conduct that is grossly negligent, wanton, or reckless, individuals who have been responsible for such acts are personally liable, and, generally speaking, these assessments are not absorbed by the employing governmental entity nor by liability insurance. Thus, law enforcement employees who act in reckless, wanton, or grossly negligent manners will be subject to, and personally liable for, punitive damage awards.

FIGURE 10-3. When police officers use wholesale "round-up" procedures on gang members without probable cause to arrest or search, they may run the risk of being sued under the Section 1983 tort claims of harassment, false imprisonment, and malicious prosecution. [Photo courtesy of the *FBI Law Enforcement Bulletin,* 1990.]

Immunities

In this constantly changing area of the law, the U.S. Supreme Court has established a rule that police are entitled to "qualified" immunity for acts made in good faith that can be characterized as "objectively reasonable." In *United States* v. *Leon*[42] the Court focused on the objectively ascertainable question of whether a reasonably well-trained officer would have known that the act committed was illegal. Subsequently, the Court following that logic held that if police personnel are not "objectively reasonable" in seeking an arrest warrant, they can be sued personally for many damages despite the fact that a judge has approved the warrant. In fact, the Court stated that a judge's issuance of a warrant will not shield the officer from liability if a "well-trained officer in [his] position would have known that his affidavit failed to establish probable cause and that he should not have applied for the warrant."[43] Thus, whereas public officials exercising discretion (for example, judges and prosecutors) have absolute immunity for their unreasonable acts, the only person in the system left to sue for damages for a wrongdoing will be the police officer unless his or her acts can be attributed to the policy or procedural custom established by the employing governmental agency.

Trends in Tort Liability for Police Supervisors and Administrators

Although there has been a traditional reluctance to hold police supervisors or administrators liable for the misbehavior of their subordinate officers, some courts have been increasingly willing to extend liability to these officials where the plaintiff has alleged negligent employment, improper training, or improper supervision.[44]

Under the first of these, negligent employment, a police official may be held liable for his failure to conduct a thorough investigation of a prospective employee's suitability for police work where he or she hires an applicant with a demonstrated propensity "toward violence, untruthfulness, discrimination or other adverse characteristics."[45] Of course, under this theory, the injuries suffered by the plaintiff would have to have been the result of the negative trait that had been demonstrated by the individual before employment as an officer. If the negative trait is not demonstrated until after employment, a party injured by the officer may be able to sue a police official successfully for negligently retaining the officer or otherwise failing to take appropriate remedial action. In some circumstances, the official may not be able to dismiss an officer who has demonstrated unfitness, but he or she still might be found liable if he or she negligently assigns the unfit officer to duties where the public is not protected adequately from the officer's particular unfitness. Finally, the official is potentially liable for negligently entrusting a revolver to an officer who has a history of alcohol or drug abuse or misuse of a weapon.

Suits alleging that police officials improperly trained a police officer have been particularly successful where firearms were involved in inflicting the injury. Courts have stressed that the "law imposes a duty of extraordinary care in the handling and use of firearms."[46] and that "public policy requires that police officers be trained in the use of firearms on moving and silhouette targets and instructed when and how to use them."[47] Suits alleging lack of necessary training are also becoming increasingly successful in cases involving the use of physical force to overcome resistance, the administration of first aid, pursuit driving (see Box 10-4 on page 414), and false arrest.[48]

Another emerging theory of recovery against police officials is an allegation of failure to properly supervise or direct subordinate officers. This type of suit is typically brought where officials have failed to take action to rectify a recurring problem exhibited in the conduct of police operations by subordinates.[49] An interesting recent development in this area concerns the situation in which the police department issues a written directive that establishes a policy more stringent than the law requires. In several cases involving such a situation, the courts have held that the written directive establishes a standard of conduct to which police officers must conform or face the possibility of civil liability for their actions.[50]

The last area to which courts have given recent increased attention concerns cases in which it is alleged that the police officer failed to provide needed medical

FIGURE 10-4. Police officers responding to hostage and/or barricaded suspect situations often require specialized training in crisis negotiations as well as use of firearms. In this case, a man was taken hostage at a local television station while the suspect shouted demands from the control room. After hours of skilled negotiations on the part of local detectives, the hostage was released without harm, avoiding potential liability stemming from the incident. [Photo courtesy of the Phoenix, Arizona, Police Department, 1991.]

care to people with whom the officer came in contact.[51] Although the incidents giving rise to such allegations can occur in a variety of situations, they seem to occur with greatest frequency when the plaintiffs have been in custody or have been mistakenly thought to be intoxicated when they actually were suffering from a serious illness. There are four theories of recovery on which these cases are based: (1) failure to recognize and provide treatment for injury, (2) failure to provide treatment upon request, (3) failure to provide treatment upon recognition of an injury, and (4) negligent medical treatment. Suits in the first three categories may allege either negligent conduct or intentional behavior. Some courts have held that police officers do not have a duty to care for injured persons with whom they come in contact,[52] although such a holding is not likely to occur when the injured person is in their custody.

Administrative Discipline: Due Process for Police Officers

The Fifth and Fourteenth amendments to the U.S. Constitution state that "no person shall be . . . deprived of life, liberty, or property, without due process of law."

Liberty and Property Rights of Police Officers

There are two general types of situations in the disciplinary process in which an employee of a law enforcement agency can claim the right to be protected by the guarantees of due process.[53] The first type involves those situations in which the disciplinary action taken by the government employer threatens liberty rights of the officer. The second type involves a threat to property rights.

Liberty rights have been defined loosely as those involving the protection and defense of one's good name, reputation, and position in the community. It has, at times, been extended further to include the right to preserve one's future career opportunities as well. Thus, where an officer's reputation, honor, or integrity are at stake because of government-imposed discipline, due process must be extended to the officer.[54]

It should be noted that the use of the "liberty rights" approach as a basis for requiring procedural due process has proven extremely difficult. The Supreme Court further restricted the use of this legal theory by holding that it can be utilized only when the employer is shown to have created and publicly disseminated a false and defamatory impression about the employee.[55]

The more substantial and meaningful type of due process guarantee is that pertaining to the protection of one's property. Although the general concept of property extends only to real estate and tangible possessions, the courts have developed the concept that a person's property also includes the many valuable intangible belongings acquired in the normal course of life such as the expectation of continued employment. However, not all employees are entitled to its protection.

BOX 10-4

Police Chases Killed 300 Nationwide Last Year

By Amy Snider
Staff Writer

More than 70 people died last year nationwide because they got in the way of police chases, according to the National Highway Traffic Safety Administration.

Five more victims were riding in police cars.

In all, 300 people were killed in chases last year, a few more than the 296 who died in 1988.

Missouri had seven fatalities in 1988, or 2.4 percent of the nation's total, compared with eight fatalities in the state in 1989, or about 2.7 percent of the nation's total.

Kansas recorded no fatalities from police chases in 1989 and one in 1988, or 0.3 percent of the nation's total.

Chases have been fading from police protocol for the past decade, said Hubert Williams, president of the Police Foundation in Washington, D.C.

"I think they're changing in almost every major city," Williams said.

He said departments were changing policies for a lot of the same reasons: lawsuits filed when innocent people are injured or killed, insurance costs, safety concerns for officers and expensive patrol cars often damaged during chases.

"A high-speed car is equivalent to a gun. It's a dangerous instrument," Williams said. "Police must be justified in using any weapon."

Most new policies take away control from the officers, he said, and give the decision-making control to a neutral, emotionally distant radio dispatcher or supervisor.

"The elements of policies may be different from city to city, but the underlying theme is to make the officers accountable," Williams said.

Williams' ideas are reflected in Louisiana, where a lawsuit, filed after a fatal police chase, has contributed to across-the-board policy changes.

"There was really no one incident that made us decide to look at our policies," said Cpl. Jeff Wesley, public affairs officer for the Baton Rouge Police Department.

But Wesley conceded that the 1989 accident was a contributing factor.

In that accident police were following a pickup truck. The truck passed a sheriff's car, and the sheriff turned on his car lights and sirens and began the chase.

"At that point, we didn't have much choice but to do the same," Wesley said.

The pickup truck ended up running a red light and crossing into an intersection of a busy highway from a side street. The pickup hit another car broadside and killed two persons. A lawsuit is pending, Wesley said.

The new chase policies will be a big change, giving officers involved in the chase less decision-making power.

"We didn't have a specific chase policy," Wesley said. "Generally it was left up to the discretion of the officer and his supervisor."

Source: Kansas City Star (Missouri), Oct. 5, 1990, p. 2.

The courts have consistently held that an employee acquires a protected interest in a job only when it can be established that there exists a justifiable expectation that employment will continue without interruption except for dismissal or other discipline based on just or proper cause. This expectation of continued employment is sometimes called "tenure" or "permanent status."

In 1972, the Supreme Court issued two landmark decisions on tenure.[56] In one of these cases, the plaintiff was a state university professor who had been hired under a one-year contract, and had been dismissed at the end of that year without notice or a hearing. The Court held that the professor was not entitled to notice or a hearing because under the circumstances the professor had no tenure because he had no justifiable expectation of continued employment after his contract expired. Therefore, he had no vested property interest protected by the Fourteenth Amendment. The other case also involved a state university professor employed on a one-year contract, but this professor had taught previously in the state college system for ten years. Under these circumstances, the Court held that the professor had acquired de facto tenure (a justifiable expectation of continued employment) and, therefore, possessed a vested property interest protected by the Fourteenth Amendment.

Because property rights attach to a job when tenure has been established, the question of how and when tenure is established becomes crucial. Public employment has generally used certain generic terms, such as "annual contract," "continuing contract," and "tenure" in the field of education or "probationary" and "permanent" in civil service systems to designate the job status of employees. However, court decisions indicate that it is the definition of these terms as established by the employer rather than the terms themselves that determines an employee's legal status. Thus, the key to the establishment of the rights of an employee is the specific wording of the ordinance, statute, rule, or regulation under which that person has been employed.[57]

Merely classifying job holders as probationary or permanent does not resolve the property rights question. Whether or not a property right to the job exists is not a question of constitutional dimension; rather, the answer lies in a careful analysis of the applicable state and local laws that might create legitimate mutual expectations of continued employment.[58]

Federal courts have been inclined to read employment laws liberally so as to grant property rights whenever possible. For example, the Fifth Circuit Court of Appeal found that a city employment regulation that allows termination "only for cause" created a constitutionally protected property interest.[59] A federal district court held that a Florida statute (Section 112.532) known as the "Law Enforcement Officers' and Correctional Officers' Bill of Rights," created a property interest in employment because of its disciplinary notice provisions.[60] That approach is consistent with those of other jurisdictions in which state statutes have been interpreted to give property interests in a job to local government employees.[61]

Once a liberty or property right has been established, certain due process guarantees attach to protect the employee. The question becomes "What process is due?"[62]

The question of due process for police officers falls into two categories: procedural and substantive. The former, as its name implies, refers to the legality of the procedures used to deprive police officers of status or wages, such as dismissal or suspension from their job. Substantive due process is a more difficult and elusive concept. We will simply define substantive due process as the requirement that the basis for government disciplinary action is reasonable, relevant, and justifiable.

Procedural Due Process

Kenneth Culp Davis has identified twelve main elements of a due process hearing:

> (1) timely and adequate notice, (2) a chance to make an oral statement or argument, (3) a chance to present witnesses and evidence, (4) confrontation of adverse witnesses,

(5) cross-examination of adverse witnesses, (6) disclosure of all evidence relied upon, (7) a decision based on the record of evidence, (8) a right to retain an attorney, (9) a publicly-compensated attorney for an indigent, (10) a statement of findings of fact, (11) a statement of reasons or a reasoned opinion, (12) an impartial deciding officer.[63]

The courts have not examined all the trial elements in the context of the police disciplinary process. However, there are cases that have held that police officers must be informed of the charges on which the action is based,[64] given the right to call witnesses,[65] confronted by the witnesses against them,[66] permitted to cross-examine the witnesses against them,[67] permitted to have counsel represent them,[68] have a decision rendered on the basis of the record developed at the hearing,[69] and have the decision made by an impartial hearing officer.[70]

A question that has proven particularly troublesome for the courts is whether or not due process requires that an evidentiary hearing be held before the disciplinary action being taken. In *Arnett* v. *Kennedy*, a badly divided Supreme Court held that a "hearing afforded by administrative appeal after the actual dismissal is a sufficient compliance with the requirements of the Due Process Clause."[71] In a concurring opinion, Justice Powell observed that the question of whether a hearing must be accorded before an employee's removal "depends on a balancing process in which the government's interest in expeditious removal of an unsatisfactory employee is weighed against the interest of the affected employee in continued public employment."[72] In *Mathews* v. *Eldridge*, the U.S. Supreme Court set forth the competing interests that must be weighed to determine what process is due: (1) the private interest that will be affected by the official action; (2) the risk of an erroneous deprivation of such interest through the procedures used, and the probable value, if any, of additional or substitute procedural safeguards; and (3) the government's interest, including the function involved and the fiscal and administrative burdens that the additional or substitute procedural requirement would entail.[73]

In 1985, the Court further clarified the issue of pretermination due process in *Cleveland Board of Education* v. *Loudermill*.[74] The Court found that public employees possessing property interests in their employment have a right to "notice and an opportunity to respond" before termination. The Court cautioned that its decision was based on the employee's also having an opportunity for a full post-termination hearing. Therefore, assuming that a public employee will be able to challenge the termination in a full-blown, evidentiary hearing after the fact, pretermination due process should include an initial check against mistaken decisions: essentially, a determination of whether there are reasonable grounds to believe that the charges against the employee are true and support the proposed action. The Court went on to describe an acceptable pretermination procedure as one that provides the employee with oral or written notice of the charges against him or her, an explanation of the employer's evidence, and an opportunity to present his or her side of the story. The Court reasoned that the governmental interest in the immediate termination of an unsatisfactory employee is outweighed by an employee's interest in retaining employment and the interest in avoiding the risk of an erroneous termination.[75]

Thus, it is clear that those public employees who can legitimately claim liberty or property right protections of due process for their jobs are guaranteed an evidentiary hearing. Such a hearing should be conducted before disciplinary action was taken unless the predicipline protections just mentioned were provided, in which case the full-blown hearing could be postponed until afterward.

For those administrators with a collective bargaining relationship with their employees, where minimal procedural safeguards are provided in contractual grievance-arbitration provisions, that avenue of relief may very well provide an acceptable substitute for constitutionally mandated procedural rights.[76]

Substantive Due Process

As mentioned earlier, due process requirements embrace substantive as well as procedural aspects. In the context of disciplinary action, substantive due process requires that the rules and regulations on which disciplinary action is predicated be clear, specific, and reasonably related to a valid public need.[77] In the police environment, these requirements present the greatest challenge to the commonly found departmental regulations against conduct unbecoming an officer or conduct that brings discredit upon the department.

The requirement that a rule or regulation be reasonably related to a valid public need means that a police department may not intrude into the private matters of its officers in which it has no legitimate interest. Therefore, there must be a connection "between the prohibited conduct and the officer's fitness to perform the duties required by his position."[78] In addition, the conduct must be of such a nature as to adversely affect the morale and efficiency of the department or have a tendency to destroy public respect for and confidence in the department.[79] Thus, it has been held that a rule prohibiting unbecoming conduct or discrediting behavior cannot be applied to the remarks of a police officer that were highly critical of several prominent local figures but were made to a private citizen in a private conversation in a patrol car, and were broadcast accidentally over the officer's patrol car radio.[80]

The requirements for clarity and specificity are necessary to ensure (1) that the innocent are not trapped without fair warning, (2) that those who enforce the regulations have their discretion limited by explicit standards, and (3) that where basic First Amendment rights are affected by a regulation, the regulation does not operate unreasonably to inhibit the exercise of those rights.[81]

The courts' applications of these requirements to unbecoming conduct and discrediting behavior rules have taken two courses. The first course, exemplified by *Bence* v. *Breier*, has been to declare such regulations unconstitutional because of their vagueness. In its consideration of a Milwaukee Police Department rule that prohibited "conduct unbecoming a member and detrimental to the service," the court found that the rule lacked

> inherent, objective content from which ascertainable standards defining the proscribed conduct could be fashioned. Like beauty, their content exists only in the eye of the beholder. The subjectivity implicit in the language of the rule permits police officials to enforce the rule with unfettered discretion, and it is precisely this potential for arbitrary enforcement which is abhorrent to the Due Process Clause.[82]

The second course taken by the courts has been to uphold the constitutionality of the regulation because, as applied to the officer in the case at hand, it should have been clear to him that his behavior was meant to be proscribed by the regulation. Under this approach, the court is saying that there may or may not be some circumstances in which the rule is too vague or overbroad, but the rule is constitutional in the present case. Thus, it should be clear to any police officer that fleeing from the scene of an accident[83] or making improper advances toward a young woman during the course of an official investigation[84] constitutes conduct unbecoming an officer or conduct that discredits the police department.

Many police departments also have a regulation prohibiting neglect or dereliction of duty. Although on its face such a rule would seem to possess some of the same potential vagueness and overbreadth shortcomings characteristic of the unbecoming conduct rules, it has fared better in the courts because the usual disciplinary action taken under neglect-of-duty rules nearly always seems to be for conduct for which police officers could reasonably expect disciplinary action. The courts have upheld administrative sanctions against officers under neglect-of-duty rules for sleeping on the job,[85] failing to prepare for planned demonstrations,[86] falsification of police records,[87] failure to make scheduled court appearances,[88] failure to investigate a reported auto accident,[89] and directing a subordinate to discontinue enforcement of a city ordinance.[90] The courts have refused to uphold disciplinary action against a police chief who did not keep eight-to-four office hours,[91] and against an officer who missed a training session on riot control because of marital problems.[92]

Damages and Remedies

In determining an employee's entitlement to damages and relief, the issue of whether the employer's disciplinary action was justified is important. For example, when an employee's termination was justified, but procedural due process violations occurred, the employee can recover only nominal damages in the absence of proof of actual compensable injuries deriving from the due process violation. Upon proof of actual injury, an employee may recover compensatory damages, which would include damages for mental and emotional distress and damage to career or reputation.[93] However, injury caused by the lack of due process when the termination was justified will not be compensable in the form of back pay.[94]

Constitutional Rights of Police Officers

Free Speech

The First Amendment of the U.S. Constitution prohibits Congress from passing any law "abridging the freedom of speech." It has been held that the due process clause of the Fourteenth Amendment makes this prohibition applicable to the states, counties, and cities as well.[95]

Although freedom of speech is one of the most fundamental of all constitutional rights, the Supreme Court has indicated that "the State has interests as an employer in regulating the speech of its employees that differ significantly from those it possesses in connection with regulation of the speech of the citizenry in general."[96] Therefore, the state may place restrictions on the speech of its employees that it could not impose on the general citizenry. However, these restrictions must be reasonable.[97] Generally, disputes involving infringement of public employee speech will be resolved by balancing the interests of the state as an employer against the employee's constitutional rights.[98]

There are two basic situations in which a police regulation or other action may be found to be an unreasonable infringement on the free speech interests of an officer. The first is when the action is overly broad. A Chicago Police Department rule prohibiting "any activity, conversation, deliberation, or discussion which is derogatory to the Department" was ruled overly broad because it prohibited all criticism of the department by police officers, even if the criticism occurred in private conversation.[99] The same fate befell a New Orleans Police Department regulation that prohibited statements by a police officer that "unjustly criticize or ridicule, or express hatred or contempt toward, or . . . which may be detrimental to, or cast suspicion on the reputation of, or otherwise defame, any person."[100]

A second situation in which a free speech limitation may be found unreasonable is in the way in which the governmental action is applied. The most common shortcoming of police departmental action in this area is a failure to demonstrate that the statements by the officer being disciplined adversely affected the operation of the department.[101] Thus, a Baltimore police regulation prohibiting public criticism of departmental action was held to have been applied unconstitutionally to a police officer who was president of the police union and who had stated in a television interview that the police commissioner was not leading the department effectively and that "the bottom is going to fall out of this city."[102] In this case, no significant disruption of the department was noted. However, when two officers of the Kinloch, Missouri, Police Department publicly complained of corruption within city government, the Court held that the "officers conducted a campaign . . . with complete disregard of chain of command motivated by personal desires that created disharmony among the 12-member police force."[103] Because the allegations were totally unfounded and were not asserted correctly through channels instituted by state "whistle-blower" procedures, the dismissals were upheld.

A more recent basis for enforcing employees' First Amendment freedom of speech is that of public policy. The Eighth Circuit held that discharging an employee who violated the police department's chain of command by reporting misconduct to an official outside of the city violated the employee's First Amendment rights. The court reasoned that the city's interest in maintaining discipline through the chain-of-command policy was outweighed by the public's vital interest in the integrity of its law enforcers, and by the employee's right to speak out on such matters.[104] However, the same court upheld a department's refusal to promote a fire captain who, as union president, had issued a letter to the public in which he accused the chief of destroying the department.[105]

It appears that one's right to speak openly about the policies of a police department may well depend on four important factors: (1) the impact of the statements on the routine operations of the department, (2) the truth of the statements, (3) the manner in which the statements were made regarding existing policy orders involving chain-of-command and state whistle-blower regulations, and (4) the position occupied by the officer. For instance, statements made by dispatchers, clerks, and first-line officers in a large department that have relatively little impact may be given much more tolerance than supervisory or command personnel complaining of departmental policy, because the degree of influence, validity, and credibility significantly increases with rank.

Other First Amendment Rights

A basic right of Americans in our democratic system of government is the right to engage in political activity. As with free speech, the government may impose reasonable restrictions on the political behavior of its employees that it could not impose on the citizenry at large. It is argued that if the state could not impose some such restrictions, there would be a substantial danger that employees could be pressured by their superiors to support political candidates or causes that were contrary to their own beliefs under threat of loss of employment or other adverse action against them for failure to do so.[106]

At the federal level, various types of partisan political activity by federal employees are controlled by the Hatch Act. The constitutionality of that act has been upheld by the U.S. Supreme Court.[107] Many states have similar statutes, which are usually referred to as "little Hatch" acts, controlling political activity by state employees. The Oklahoma version of the Hatch Act, which was upheld by the Supreme Court,[108] prohibited state employees from soliciting political contributions, joining a partisan political club, serving on the committee of a political party, being a candidate for any paid political office, or taking part in the management of a political party or campaign. However, some states, such as Florida, specifically prohibit local governments from limiting the off-duty political activity of their employees.

Whereas the Supreme Court decisions might appear to have put to rest all controversy over the extent to which the government can limit political activity by its employees, that has not been the case. In two more recent cases, lower courts have placed limits on the authority of the state in limiting the political activity of state employees.

In Pawtucket, Rhode Island, two firemen ran for mayor and city councilman, respectively, in a nonpartisan election, despite a city charter provision prohibiting all city employees from engaging in any political activity except voting and privately expressing their opinions. In granting the firemen's requests for an injunction against the enforcement of this provision, the court ruled that the Supreme Court precedents did not apply to the Pawtucket charter provision because the statutes upheld in the prior decisions had prohibited only partisan political activity.[109] In a very similar case in Boston, however, the court upheld the police departmental rule at issue there on the basis that whether the partisan-nonpartisan distinction was crucial was a matter for legislative or administrative determination.[110]

In a Michigan case, the court declared unconstitutional two city charter provisions that prohibited contributions to or solicitations for any political purpose by city employees because it was overly broad.[111] That court specifically rejected the partisan-nonpartisan distinction as crucial, focusing instead on the office involved and the relationship to that office of the employees whose political activity was at issue. For example, the court saw no danger to an important municipal interest in the activities of a city employee "who is raising funds to organize a petition drive seeking a rate change from the Public Service Commission."[112.]

Thus, whereas the Supreme Court has tended to be supportive of governmental efforts to limit the political activities of government employees, it is clear that some lower courts intend to limit the Supreme Court decisions to the facts of those cases. Therefore, careful consideration should be given to the scope of political activity to be restricted by a police regulation, and trends in the local jurisdiction should be examined closely.

The cases just discussed dealt with political activity, as opposed to mere political affiliation. May a police officer be relieved of his or her duties because of his or her political affiliations on the basis that those affiliations impede his or her ability to carry out the policies of superiors with different political affiliations? The Supreme Court addressed this question in a case arising out of the sheriff's department in Cook County, Illinois.[113] The newly elected sheriff, a Democrat, had discharged the chief deputy of the process division and a bailiff of the juvenile court, both of whom were nonmerit system employees, because they were Republicans. The Court ruled that it was a violation of these employees' First Amendment rights to discharge them from non-policy-making positions because of their political party memberships.[114]

Nonpolitical associations are also protected by the First Amendment. However, it is common for police departments to prohibit officers from associating with known felons or other persons of bad reputation on the basis that "such associations may expose an officer to irresistible temptations to yield in his obligation to impartially enforce the law, and . . . may give the appearance that the community's police officers are not themselves honest and impartial enforcers of the law." Sometimes the prohibition is imposed by means of a specific ordinance or regulation, whereas in other instances the prohibition is enforced by considering it conduct unbecoming an officer. Of course, if the latter approach is used, the ordinance or regulation will have to overcome the legal obstacles discussed earlier, relating to unbecoming conduct or discrediting behavior rules.

As with rules touching on the other First Amendment rights, rules prohibiting associations with criminals and other undesirables must not be overly broad in their reach. Thus, a Detroit Police Department regulation that prohibited knowing and intentional associations with convicted criminals or persons charged with crimes except in the course of an officer's official duties was declared unconstitutional because it proscribed some associations that could have no bearing on an officer's integrity or the public's confidence in an officer. The Court cited as examples an association with a fellow church member who had been arrested on one occasion years ago, and the befriending of a recently convicted person who wanted to become a productive citizen.[115]

The other common difficulty with this kind of rule is that it is sometimes applied to situations in which the association has not been demonstrated to have had a detrimental effect on the performance of the officer's duties or on the discipline and efficiency of the department. Thus, one court has held that a police officer who was a nudist but was fully qualified in all other respects to be a police officer could not be fired simply because he was a practicing nudist.[116] On the other hand, another court upheld the firing of a police officer who had had sexual intercourse at a party with a woman he knew to be a nude model at a local "adult theater of known disrepute."[117] The court viewed this behavior as being of such a disreputable nature that it had a detrimental effect on the discipline and efficiency of the department.

The First Amendment's protection of free speech has been viewed as protecting means of expression other than verbal utterances.[118] That issue as it relates to an on-duty police officer's personal appearance has been addressed by the Supreme Court decision in *Kelley* v. *Johnson,*[119] which upheld the constitutionality of a regulation of the Suffolk County, New York, Police Department that established several grooming standards for its male officers. The Court in *Kelley* held that either a desire to make police officers readily recognizable to the public or a desire to maintain an esprit de corps was a sufficiently rational justification for the regulation.

Searches and Seizures

The Fourth Amendment to the U.S. Constitution protects "the right of the people to be secure in their persons, houses, papers, and effects, against unreasonable searches and seizures. . . ." This guarantee protects against actions by the states as well as by the federal government.[120] Generally, the cases interpreting the Fourth Amendment require that before a search or seizure can be effectuated, the police must have probable cause to believe that a crime has been committed and that evidence relevant to the crime will be found at the place to be searched. Because of the language in the Fourth Amendment about "persons, houses, papers, and effects," for years the case law analyzed what property was subject to the amendment's protection. However, in an extremely important case in 1967, the Supreme Court ruled that the amendment protected individuals' reasonable expectations of privacy and not just property interests.[121] Interestingly, twentieth-century technology has brought forth a number of key Fourth Amendment issues regarding privacy, especially involving private communications and wire taps. In a case involving a police officer suspected of gambling, the Supreme Court held that the use of a pen register did not require the same constitutional safeguards as those surrounding a wire tap. The pen register uses a "trap and trace" device that records phone numbers and the duration of each call but does not capture any type of communication between parties. The Court reasoned that no warrant or probable cause was needed as the Fourth Amendment was applicable to captured communication only, and that there was no reasonable expectation to privacy regarding the actual phone number.[122]

The Fourth Amendment usually applies to police officers when at home or off duty as it would to any other citizen. However, because of the nature of the employment, a police officer can be subjected to investigative procedures that would not be permitted when an ordinary citizen was involved. One such situation arises with respect to equipment and lockers provided by the department to its officers. In this situation the officer has no expectation of privacy that merits protection.[123] The rights of prison authorities to search their employees was at issue in a 1985 Iowa case. There the court refused to find a consent form signed as a condition of hire to constitute a blanket waiver of all Fourth Amendment rights.[124]

Another situation involves the ordering of officers to appear at a lineup. Requiring someone to appear in a lineup is a seizure of his or her person and, therefore, would ordinarily require probable cause. However, a federal appeals court upheld a police commissioner's order to sixty-two officers to appear in a lineup for the purpose of identifying officers who had allegedly beaten several civilians. The court held that in this situation "the governmental interest in the particular intrusion (should be weighed) against the offense to personal dignity and integrity." Because of the nature of the police officer's employment relationship, "he does not have the full privacy and liberty from police officials that he would otherwise enjoy."[125]

To enforce the protections guaranteed by the Fourth Amendment's search and seizure requirements, the courts have fashioned the so-called "exclusionary rule," which prohibits the use of evidence obtained in violation of the Fourth Amendment in criminal proceedings. However, in a series of recent cases, the Supreme Court has redefined the concept of "reasonableness" as it applies to the Fourth Amendment and the exclusionary rule. In *United States* v. *Leon* and the companion case of *Massachusetts* v. *Sheppard*, the Court held that the Fourth Amendment "requires officers to have reasonable knowledge of what the law prohibits" in a search.[126] In essence, *Leon* and *Sheppard* began to develop the concept of "totality of circumstances" confirmed in *Illinois* v. *Gates*, that is, that evidence cannot be suppressed when an officer is acting "under good faith" whether or not a warrant issued is good on the surface.[127] These cases have far-reaching implications in civil actions against police officers, in that officers enjoy the benefits of qualified immunity when they are acting in good faith and under the belief that probable cause does exist.[128] Indeed, the Court has held that only a clear absence of probable cause will defeat a claim of qualified immunity.[129]

Finally, the exclusionary rule and the above mentioned cases have an important bearing on disciplinary hearings involving the police. In *Sheetz* v. *Mayor and City Council of Baltimore*, the Court held that illegally seized drugs in the possession of an officer could be used in an administrative discharge proceeding against that officer.[130] The Court reasoned that only a bad faith seizure would render the evidence inadmissible because the police are not motivated to seize illegally for the purpose of use in an administrative discharge proceeding; hence, the exclusionary rule was not applicable and the officer's firing was upheld.

Right Against Self-Incrimination

On two occasions the Supreme Court has addressed questions concerning the Fifth Amendment rights of police officers who are the subjects of investigations. In *Garrity* v. *New Jersey*,[131] a police officer had been ordered by the attorney general to answer certain questions or be discharged. He testified and the information gained as a result of his answers was later used to convict him of criminal charges.

The Fifth Amendment protects an individual from being compelled "in any criminal case to be a witness against himself."[132] The Supreme Court held that the information obtained from the police officer could not be used at his criminal trial because the Fifth Amendment forbids the use of coercion of this sort to extract an incriminating statement from a suspect.

In *Gardner* v. *Broderick*,[133] a police officer had declined to answer questions put to him by a grand jury investigating police misconduct on the grounds that his answers might tend to incriminate him. As a result, the officer was dismissed from his job. The Supreme Court ruled that the officer could not be fired for his refusal to waive his constitutional right to remain silent. However, the Court made it clear that it would have been proper for the grand jury to require the officer to answer or face discharge for his refusal so long as the officer had been informed that his answers could not be used against him in a criminal case and the questions were related specifically, directly, and narrowly to the performance of his official duties. The Court felt that this approach was necessary to protect the important state interest in ensuring the police officers were performing their duties faithfully.

In their ruling, the Supreme Court set forth a basic standard for disciplinary investigations of police officers. Referring to *Garrity*, the Court ruled that although a police agency can conduct an administrative investigation of an officer, it cannot in the course of that investigation compel the officer to waive his or her privilege against self-incrimination. As it has been interpreted, *Garrity* requires that before a police agency can question an officer regarding an issue that may involve disciplinary action against the officer for refusal to answer questions, the agency must

1. Order the officer to answer the questions
2. Ask questions that are specifically, directly, and narrowly related to the officer's duties
3. Advise the officer that the answers to the questions will not be used against the officer in criminal proceedings[134] (see Box 10-5).

If the officer refuses to answer appropriate questions after being given these warnings and advisement, then he or she may be disciplined for insubordination.

As a result of these cases, it is proper to discharge police officers who refuse to answer questions that are related specifically and directly to the performance of their duties and who have been informed that any answers they do give cannot be used against them in a criminal proceeding.[135]

Historically, it was not uncommon for police departments to make use of

BOX 10-5

Disciplinary Interview Advice of Rights

The following is a sample warning given to police officers during a disciplinary setting. Note that the "advice of rights" statement is *not* the warning mandated in criminal cases under the *Miranda* decision. In a disciplinary interview, *Miranda* has no application.

I wish to advise you that you are being questioned as part of an official investigation of the Police Department. You will be asked questions specifically directed and narrowly related to the performance of your official duties or fitness for office. You are entitled to all the rights and privileges guaranteed by the laws and the constitution of this state and the Constitution of the United States, including the right not to be compelled to incriminate yourself (and to have an attorney of your choice present during questioning). I further wish to advise you that if you refuse to testify or to answer questions relating to the performance of your official duties or fitness for duty, you will be subject to departmental charges which would result in your dismissal from the Police Department. If you do answer, neither your statements nor any information or evidence which is gained by reason of such statements can be used against you in any subsequent criminal proceeding. However, these statements may be used against you in relation to subsequent departmental charges.

Source: Police Discipline and Labor Problems Workbook (Chicago, Ill.: Americans for Effective Law Enforcement, Inc., 1989), pp. 2–8.

polygraph examinations in the course of internal investigations. The legal question that has arisen most frequently is whether an officer may be required to submit to such a procedure under threat of discharge for refusal to do so. There is some diversity of legal authority on this question, but the majority of courts that have considered it have held that an officer can be required to take the examination.[136]

An Arizona court overturned a county merit system commission's finding that a polygraph examination could be ordered only as a last resort after all other investigative efforts had been exhausted, and held that

> a polygraph is always proper to verify statements made by law enforcement officers during the course of a departmental investigation as long as the officers are advised that the answers cannot be used against them in any criminal prosecution, that the questions will relate solely to the performance of official duties, and that refusal will result in dismissal.[137]

On the other hand, a more recent decision of the Florida Supreme Court held that the dismissal of a police officer for refusing to submit to a polygraph test constituted "an unjust and unlawful job deprivation." Further, the court recognized that granting to public employers a carte blanche authority to force employees to submit to unlimited questioning during a polygraph test would conflict with the employee's constitutional right of privacy, and would abrogate his or her protection against self-incrimination.[138]

Further, the use of the polygraph test to screen job applicants for police jobs has fallen under severe criticism. In 1987, a federal judge declared the test to be both unconstitutional and unreliable and ordered the city of Philadelphia to reconsider the applications of individuals denied positions due to their failure to pass a polygraph.[139]

As a result of these cases and the resulting ambiguity concerning polygraph testing and the Fifth Amendment, most jurisdictions have limited the use of the polygraph by statute and/or administrative regulation. Also, most agencies have developed extensive internal policies to limit the use of the polygraph and to expressly detail circumstances in which the test may be used to corroborate officer statements.

Other Grounds for Disciplinary Action

Conduct Unbecoming an Officer

By far the largest number of police disciplinary cases arise under rules prohibiting conduct unbecoming an officer. These rules have traditionally been vague and overbroad in order to control officers both on and off duty.[140] Most "conduct unbecoming" regulations have been challenged for being unconstitutionally vague.[141] The basis of this claim rests in the concept of reasonableness as applied to the misconduct.[142] In a leading case, the California Supreme Court held that the permissible application of a "conduct unbecoming" regulation turns on whether the officer could reasonably anticipate that his or her conduct would be the subject of discipline:

> We construe "conduct unbecoming" a city police officer to refer only to conduct which indicates a *lack of fitness* to perform the functions of a police officer. Thus construed, [the rule] provides a sufficiently specific standard against which the conduct of a police officer in a particular case can be judged. Police officers . . . will normally be able to determine what kind of conduct indicates unfitness to perform the functions of police officer.[143]

A wide variety of conduct has been held to fall appropriately within the scope of a "conduct unbecoming" regulation. It is important to note that the regulation must reasonably warn the officer of what type of conduct would be considered unbecoming and that said conduct would tend to affect the officer's performance of his or her duties adversely or cause the department to fall into public disrepute.[144] Some of the activities that commonly fall within the scope of a "conduct unbecoming" regulation and that have been upheld by the courts include associating with crime figures or persons with a criminal record,[145] verbal abuse and swearing,[146] off-duty drinking and intoxication,[147] criminal conduct,[148] dishonesty,[149] fighting with co-workers,[150] insubordination,[151] and a number of improprieties involving sexual activity.

FIGURE 10-5. The routine traffic stop has been the setting for activities that commonly fall within the scope of "conduct unbecoming" an officer. Complaints often allege verbal abuse, swearing, unprofessional conduct, and/or sexual harassment by police officers. Some agencies have placed hidden cameras and microphones in police vehicles, in part to defend themselves against such allegations. [Photo courtesy of the *FBI Law Enforcement Bulletin,* 1990.]

Sexual Conduct

The cases in this area tend to fall into two general categories: cases involving adultery and cases involving homosexuality.

Most cases of the 1970s and 1980s were in general agreement that adultery, even though committed while the policeman was off duty and in private, created a proper basis for disciplinary action.[152] The courts held that such behavior brings adverse criticism on the agency and tends to undermine public confidence in the department. However, one case involving an Internal Revenue Service agent suggests that to uphold disciplinary action for adultery, the government would have to prove that the employing agency was actually discredited; and further stated that the discreditation would not be presumed from the proof of adulterous conduct.[153]

More recently, the Supreme Court justices appeared to be divided on the issue of extramarital sexual activity in public employment. In 1984, the Sixth Circuit held that a Michigan police officer could not be fired solely because he was living with a woman to whom he was not married (a felony under state law).[154] In 1985, the Supreme Court denied review of that decision over the strong objection of three justices who felt the case "presented an important issue of constitutional law regarding the contours of the right of privacy afforded individuals for sexual matters."[155]

In those cases involving sexual improprieties that clearly affect an officer's on-the-job performance, the courts have had far less controversy. In a series of cases, the court has consistently supported the disciplinary action attached to the department's "conduct unbecoming" regulation, including cases in which officers were cohabiting or in which the sexual activities were themselves illegal (e.g., public lewdness, child molestation, sexual activity with prostitutes, and homosexuality).[156] In fact, the courts have upheld internal regulations barring the employment of spouses, due in part to the concern for an officer's work performance (see Box 10-6).

The issue of homosexual activity as a basis for discharge was recently presented to the Supreme Court. Oklahoma had a law permitting discharge of schoolteachers for engaging in "public homosexual activity."[157] The lower court held the law to be facially overly broad and therefore unconstitutionally restrictive. The Supreme Court affirmed the decision.[158] Another federal court held that the discharge of a bisexual guidance counselor did not deprive the plaintiff of her First or Fourteenth Amendment rights. The counselor's discussion of her sexual preferences with teachers and other personnel was not protected by the First Amendment. Her equal protection claim failed because she did not show that the heterosexual employees would have been treated differently for communicating their sexual preferences.[159]

In an equally important federal case involving thirteen lesbian deputies terminated from the Broward County, Florida, Sheriff's Department, the Court held that homosexuals are not a suspect class accorded strict scrutiny under the equal protection clause, and, therefore, the dismissal did not deprive the plaintiffs of any constitutional or equal protection right.[160]

Finally, the courts have upheld the right of the states to make laws prohibiting sodomy and thus developing the argument that homosexuality is a criminal violation that may be a viable basis for discharging a police officer. In a 1987 case, a

BOX 10-6

Officer Who Wed Colleague Denied Reinstatement

PASADENA—A former Pasadena police officer who lost her job for marrying a fellow officer was denied reinstatement Wednesday by the Pasadena Civil Service Commission.

"I'm disappointed, but I wasn't really surprised," Kerri Burch Fry said. "I don't understand why it's OK to have other people in the department (who are) related but not married officers."

Mrs. Fry, 27, was forced to resign after she married a fellow officer with whom she already had a child. She had asked the service commission to reinstate her to the police department where she had worked for six years.

Unemployed now, she said she plans to appeal the commission's ruling.

She was dismissed earlier this month under a department nepotism policy. Under that policy, if two officers marry, the one having the least seniority automatically must resign.

Mrs. Fry is married to Lt. Jack Fry, 35, who has been with the department for 12 years.

During the hearing Wednesday, Mrs. Fry contended the police administration punished her for taking wedding vows although officials had known of the couple's past live-in relationship and the baby she had months before their marriage.

"It condones officers living together. They knew we lived together and had a child, but we did the right thing and got punished for it. Our child has a right to bear her father's name," she said.

Mrs. Fry said city nepotism laws are discriminatory because they are selectively enforced by department leaders.

Mrs. Fry's husband voluntarily took the stand under an arrangement that prohibited questioning from attorneys.

Pointing to his wife, Officer Fry said: "I've put my life on the line for this department. I can't understand why this lady here can't do the same thing and still be married—why we can't have a personal life.

"It's telling me, 'We trust you to lay your life on the line but we don't trust you to marry somebody who has that same dedication.' "

Police Chief Lee Gilbert testified that the no-spouses law prevents potential favoritism between spouses and other management problems.

"It would be a management nightmare for me to manage 10 to 15 married couples, worrying about deploying them and keeping them separate," he said.

"The conflict of interest is obvious. We're a relatively small department."

Source: Dallas Morning News, Aug. 18, 1989, p. 26A.

federal court of appeals upheld the FBI's policy of not hiring homosexuals on the grounds that agents must be able to work in any state in the country, half of which have criminal laws prohibiting homosexuality or sodomy.[161]

Residency Requirements

A number of local governments have established requirements that all or certain classes of their employees live within the geographical limits of the jurisdiction. These residency requirements have been justified by the governments imposing them as desirable because they increase employees' rapport with, and understanding of, the community. When police officers were concerned, it has been asserted that the presence of off-duty police has a deterrent effect on crime and results in chance encounters that might lead to additional sources of information (see Box 10-7).

Before 1976, challenges to the legality of residency requirements for public employees dotted the legal landscape. The challenges had persisted in spite of the U.S. Supreme Court's denial of an appeal from the decision of the Michigan Supreme Court that Detroit's residency requirement for police was not irrational.[162] In 1976, the Supreme Court in *McCarthy* v. *Philadelphia Civil Service Commission* ruled that Philadelphia's residency requirement for firemen did not violate the Constitution.[163]

Since the *McCarthy* decision, the legal attacks on the residency requirements have subsided. The cases now seem to be concerned with determining what constitutes residency. The most obvious means of attempting to avoid the residency requirement (by establishing a second residence within the city) appears doomed to failure unless the police officer can demonstrate that he or she spends at least a substantial part of his or her time at the in-city residence.[164] A strong argument has been made that, in areas where housing is unavailable or prohibitively expensive, a residency requirement is unreasonable.[165] In upholding the

BOX 10-7

Where New York's Finest Should Live

New York City's plan to hire thousands of police officers adds urgency to an old proposal: Require police recruits to live in the city. Deployment strategies for the expanded force make the case stronger than ever.

Other cities, notably Chicago, require police officers to live inside the city limits. There are sound practical arguments for the policy. In emergencies, resident officers can be called up more rapidly. Law enforcement can benefit from the presence of police on subways and streets as they go to work and back. A residency rule would likely increase minority representation on the force. And it would insure that officers living in the city, and those who choose to retire here, would spend their pay and retirement benefits in New York.

There's a more important, less tangible argument, however. Police officers who live in suburbs experience the city mainly as a place of violence and trouble—and some learn to loathe the communities they are sworn to protect. There's a good chance those who live in the city, sharing a commitment to it, won't be so demoralized.

That concern is more important given Police Commissioner Lee Brown's plans to deploy newly hired officers on community patrol. Beyond simply responding to calls for help, such officers are expected to involve themselves with neighborhoods, assess crime problems and lead efforts to address them. Daily retreat to the suburbs seems inconsistent with that job description.

Opponents of the requirement, which needs Albany's approval, worry that recruits might not be able to afford the city, especially as their families grow older. These concerns may become less germane as real estate prices fall. In any case, recruiters are likely to find plenty of willing candidates during the current recession. Mr. Brown plans an aggressive search among men and women leaving military service. And the city recently raised the age limit for applicants from 29 to 35.

The arguments for a residency requirement outweigh the arguments against. The issue deserves a place on Albany's agenda.

Source: New York Times, May 27, 1991, p. 18(L).

application of such requirements, courts have focused on the issues of equal enforcement and the specificity of the local residency standard.[166]

Religious Belief or Practice

In part, Title VII of the Civil Rights Act of 1964 prohibits religious discrimination in employment. The act defines religion as including "all aspects of religious . . . practice, as well as belief, unless an employer . . . is unable to reasonably accommodate to an employee's . . . religious . . . practice without undue hardship on the conduct of the employer's business."[167] Title VII requires reasonable accommodation of religious beliefs, not accommodation in exactly the way the employee would like. Title VII also does not require accommodation that spares the employee any cost whatsoever.[168] For example, an Albuquerque fireman who was a Seventh-Day Adventist refused to work the Friday night or Saturday day shifts because they fell on what he believed to be the Sabbath day. Although department policy would have permitted the fireman to avoid working these shifts by taking leave with pay, taking leave without pay, or trading shifts with other firemen, he refused to use these means and insisted that the department find other firemen to trade shifts with him or simply excuse him from the shifts affected by his religious beliefs. The department refused to do either. Under these circumstances, the court ruled that the department's accommodations to the fireman had been reasonable and that no further accommodations could be made without undue hardship to the department. Therefore, the fireman's discharge was upheld. However, as the court itself emphasized, decisions in cases in this area depend on the particular facts and circumstances of each case. Recently, the courts have held that the termination of a fundamentalist Mormon police officer for practicing plural marriage (polygamy), in violation of state law, was not a violation of his right to freely exercise his religious beliefs.[169]

Moonlighting

Traditionally, the courts have supported the authority of police departments to place limits on the outside employment of their employees.[170] Police department restrictions on "moonlighting" range from a complete ban on outside employment to permission to engage in certain endeavors, such as investments, rental of property, teaching of law enforcement subjects, and employment designed to improve the police image. The rationale in support of moonlighting prohibitions is that "outside employment seriously interferes with keeping the [police and fire] departments fit and ready for action at all times"[171] (see Box 10-8).

However, in a Louisiana case, firemen offered unrefuted evidence that moonlighting had been a common practice before the city banned moonlighting; during the previous sixteen years, no firemen had ever needed sick leave as a result of injuries suffered while moonlighting; there had never been a problem locating off-duty firemen to respond to an emergency; and moonlighting had never been shown to be a source of fatigue that was serious enough to impair a fireman's alertness on the job. Under these circumstances, the court ruled that there was not

BOX 10-8

Off-Duty Job Can Create Problems for Police

By Lisa Olsen *Staff Writer*

At Lynnhaven Mall in Virginia Beach, nearly half the security staff carries government-issued guns, badges and the clout of full arrest powers. They're off-duty cops.

In Smithfield, people who need their grass cut or snow shoveled can call 4 Seasons Lawn Care, a company owned and operated by the town's police chief.

In Chesapeake, city officials spent only $7,500 to gut and renovate a police precinct building in 1988. They saved money by hiring four off-duty officers for the five-month job.

Moonlighting has become an institution for Hampton Roads police officers, who often seek second or third jobs to supplement starting salaries that range from about $17,000 to $21,000 a year. More than half the officers in Hampton Roads work second jobs. But it can be dangerous for them and the public they serve, state and national experts say.

A second job does more than add to income, they say: It contributes to stress, burnout and the risk of accidents or injury. It also creates troubling conflict-of-interest questions that often aren't addressed by police policies.

"It's certainly dangerous for the officer who has to take a second job to make ends meet and is still expected to be alert and prepared," said Robert E. Colvin, a former police officer and the executive director of the Virginia State Crime Commission.

Police departments in Virginia Beach, Norfolk, Chesapeake and Hampton limit part-time work to 20 hours a week, but there are no such limits in Portsmouth, Smithfield, the Sheriff's Department in Isle of Wight County, and in Newport News and Hampton.

"Probably everyone at one time or another has worked part time during their career," said Robert P. Haynes, police spokesman for Norfolk. "At one time in their career, it has been part of their routine. Almost 100 percent."

Security work provides the majority of part-time jobs held by police, but Hampton Roads officers do everything from practicing law to washing cars.

Most police departments restrict officers from working in bars or in liquor stores, but other rules are less common. In most cases, police chiefs or other supervisors routinely approve jobs, although many policies prevent officers from taking work that could interfere with police work or present a conflict of interest.

At least three Hampton Roads police officers use their training in accident investigations to work as expert witnesses, although they work only outside the cities where they are employed.

Top police officials often authorize moonlighting by officers, but they rarely have second jobs themselves. Smithfield Police Chief Claiborne A. Havens is an exception. Havens, who owns a lawn care business with his wife, employs several of his officers to cut lawns.

Part-time work has become such an institution that several Hampton Roads police departments, especially in fast-growing Chesapeake and tourist-driven Virginia Beach, regularly take calls from businessmen asking for off-duty officers to take security posts.

"I know at the Oceanfront, a lot of hotels use (off-duty police officers) in the summertime," said Master Police Officer Lewis B. Thurston, a Virginia Beach department spokesman. Thurston works off-duty at Lynnhaven Mall.

That practice has led to shootings, heated debates and lawsuits elsewhere in the country, said Dr. James J. Fyfe, a criminal justice professor at American University in Washington and a former New York City police officer.

"The big ethical dilemma," Fyfe said, "is whether police officers should be permitted to work as hired guns.

"I have a problem with that because I think if a police officer carries a gun and wields his power in the public interest and is expected to be fair and objective, it seems to me

BOX 10-8 (cont.)

to be a bit twisted if he works in a hotel or a bar as a security guard. . . . It seems to me he's using his enforcement power and wearing his guns for private interest and he can't be objective."

Off-duty officers who work without radio contact or patrol cars are more vulnerable to attack than on-duty officers and can become aggressive more quickly under pressure, said Virginia Beach lawyer Kenneth W. Stolle, a former police officer.

Stolle worries about the consequences.

"If (the officer) gets hurt, is he eligible for compensation? If someone else gets hurt, who do they sue?" Stolle asked. "It's a no-win situation. The police departments don't want to force the officers not to work. At the same time, there is a lot of liability attached to what they do."

A Virginia Supreme Court decision said that a city or county can be held responsible for the actions of an off-duty officer when he or she is enforcing the law and using police powers.

Virginia Beach was sued for $300,000 in 1987 by a man who had been shot by an off-duty officer moonlighting as a store security guard. However, the officer was fired after an investigation, and the city did not have to pay.

Fyfe said moonlighting, especially as security guards, can lead to more police shootings. In a study of 2,900 police shootings in New York City from 1971 to 1975, he found that about 20 percent involved off-duty officers who were moonlighting or simply off-duty. Of those, half were found to be "bad shootings"—cases where officers did not follow policy. After that study, New York City prohibited its officers from taking second jobs, Fyfe said.

Shootings, though, are not nearly as common as sheer exhaustion among moonlighting officers.

Haynes, of Norfolk, once worked part time in radio and television news, a job that pushed his work week to 70 or 80 hours.

"I'm an example of one who burned out," he said. "As much as I love it, I'm not going to do that anymore."

Source: Norfolk Pilot (Virginia), Aug. 13, 1990.

a sufficient basis for the prohibition on moonlighting and invalidated the ordinance.[172]

It is important to note that in several cases involving off-duty officers moonlighting (as private security guards or store detectives), the same legal standards imposed on sworn officers acting in the capacity of their jobs apply. The court has held that off-duty officers act "under color of State law" and are subject to Section 1983 liability while working in a private security or "special patrolman" capacity.[173] Therefore, it follows that police agencies and departments may be liable under the same ramifications, opening up a new wave of future litigation involving police officer off-duty employment.

Misuse of Firearms and Deadly Force

Because of the obvious dangers associated with the use of handguns and other firearms, it is not surprising that police departments customarily regulate the use of such weapons by their officers. The courts have held that such regulation need only be reasonable and that the burden rests with the disciplined police officer appellant to demonstrate that the regulation is arbitrary and unreasonable.[174] Moreover, the cases suggest that the courts are inclined to grant great latitude to police department administrators in determining when their firearm regulations have been violated.[175]

Police firearm regulations tend to address four basic issues: (1) requirements for the safeguarding of the weapon, (2) guidelines for carrying the weapon while on and off duty, (3) limitations on when the weapon may be used (use of deadly force), and (4) training in the use of the firearm and deadly force.

There is little case law dealing with regulations concerning the safeguarding of an officer's weapon. However, a New York court has held that an officer could not be disciplined for neglecting to safeguard his weapon when the evidence showed that the weapon had been stolen during a burglary of the officer's room while he was asleep.[176]

FIGURE 10-6. Officers enter a suspected drug house during a search warrant execution. Police firearms regulations should provide direction during those incidents in which the probability for the use of deadly force may be high. [Photo courtesy of the Derry, New Hampshire Police Department and the *FBI Law Enforcement Bulletin,* 1990.]

Regulations concerning the firing of a weapon are difficult to construct with precision.[177] Applying these regulations to actual situations is equally difficult. An important caution relates to an earlier discussion of the fact that some courts in damage suits have held police officers subject to a higher standard of care than the law itself would require, because the department's regulations established a higher standard. Although police departments should not necessarily refrain from establishing exacting requirements as to when their officers can fire their weapons, police administrators should be aware of the possible effect such action could have in civil damage actions.[178]

Therefore, departmental policies and procedures are important in lawsuit prevention. It is necessary not only to develop and maintain written guidelines regarding the use of firearms, but also to follow such directives.[179] These guidelines must adhere to state and federal laws. For instance, departmental policy with regard to shooting at a fleeing felon must not violate state common-law standards on the use of deadly force.[180] Most state laws authorize use of deadly force only in self defense and as a last resort, which requires reasonable belief on the part of the police officer that his or her life, or the life of an innocent person, is in immediate danger.

The events surrounding the use of deadly force by police officers have accounted for some of the most expensive damages awarded to plaintiffs. As noted earlier, the negligent failure to properly train is a cause of action under Section 1983. In a series of cases, the courts have indicated that simply meeting state-mandated minimum standards may not be enough; in addition, the training must be correct.[181] Further, the department must provide evidence that

1. The training was necessary, as validated by a task analysis
2. The persons conducting the training were, in fact, qualified to conduct such training
3. The training did, in fact, take place and was properly conducted and documented
4. The training was "state-of-the-art" and up to date
5. Adequate measures of mastery of the subject matter can be documented
6. Those who did not satisfactorily "learn" in the training session have received additional training and now have mastery of the subject matter
7. Close supervision exists to monitor and continually evaluate the officer's program of training.[182]

Although the court has provided these standards with particular emphasis on the use of firearms and deadly force, they apply to all areas of police practice and procedures. For instance, training involving the proper use of handcuffs, the police baton, flashlights, tear gas, stun guns, restraint and choke holds, and arrest procedures is critically important not only in defending against lawsuits but also in providing professional police service to the community[183] (see Box 10-9).

Testing in the Work Environment

Alcohol and Drug Testing

It is common for police departments to require that their officers not be under the influence of any intoxicating agent while on duty. Even in the absence of such

FIGURE 10-7. Police use of deadly force requires extensive training in firearms techniques that can be validated and documented by qualified personnel. [Photo courtesy of the Lexington–Fayette Urban County, Kentucky Police Department, 1990.]

specific regulation, disciplinary action has been upheld when it was taken against an officer who was suspected of being intoxicated while on duty by charging him with neglect of duty or violation of a state law.[184]

Regulations that prohibit being under the influence of an intoxicating or mind-altering substance have been upheld uniformly as reasonable because of the hazardous nature of a police officer's work and the serious impact his or her behavior or misbehavior is sure to have on the property and safety of others. The necessity to require a clear head and rational action, unbefuddled by alcohol or drugs, is clear.[185] A Louisiana court upheld a regulation that prohibited an officer from consuming alcoholic beverages on or off duty to the extent that it caused the officer's behavior to become obnoxious, disruptive, or disorderly.[186]

Effective enforcement of regulations against an officer's being under the influence of drugs or alcohol will occasion situations when a police supervisor or administrator will order an officer to submit to one or more tests to determine the presence of the prohibited substance in the subject's body. It has been held that a fireman could be ordered to submit to blood sampling when reasonable grounds existed for believing that he was intoxicated, and that it was permissible to discharge the fireman for his refusal to comply with the order.[187] More recently the

BOX 10-9

D.C. Police Union Links Poor Training to Brutality

Stress, Relaxed Standards Also Are Cited

By Patrice Gaines-Carter *Washington Post Staff Writer*

Gary Hankins, the head of the D.C. Fraternal Order of Police, said yesterday that "tremendous stress" caused by a rising crime rate, the lowering of standards for new recruits and inadequate training might explain why some incidents of police brutality occur.

Although Hankins condemned the March 3 police beating of an unarmed black motorist in Los Angeles, he said during a nationally televised interview, "I'm afraid that unless we begin to pump the proper resources, both education and financial resources, into law enforcement, you're going to have more and more aberrations until they become the norm."

Citing a new FOP survey of D.C. police officers, Hankins said that of the 750 respondents, "three-quarters of them . . . felt the training academy was not adequate in training them. Better than 70 percent say their ongoing in-service training is inadequate. Over 70 percent say they don't have proper equipment."

Hankins's comments, during an appearance on the CBS News program "Face the Nation" were similar to criticisms raised last year after a 14-month investigation of the D.C. police department by the General Accounting Office.

The GAO study found that requirements for graduation from the District's academy in Southwest Washington have varied widely from year to year. The report focused on the period from 1982 to 1988 and said improvements had been made at the academy since Isaac Fulwood Jr. became chief of the department.

But the GAO also found that records were so poor and incomplete that the agency could not adequately evaluate whether police were being trained properly.

Hankins said yesterday that new recruits are more likely to pass exams because the tests have been revised to make them easier.

But Lt. Reginald L. Smith, a department spokesman, said the recruits pass because they are more likely to be "college-educated and have more technical knowledge."

Critics of the department, including the FOP, say one reason the force periodically has lowered academy graduation standards is that the department has felt pressure from the wave of drugs and violence to get officers on the street.

The department several years ago abandoned a residency requirement for recruits. In September 1988, the academy director recommended that five recruits be fired, but then Police Chief Maurice T. Turner Jr. allowed them to graduate. Each had failed five or more exams.

Fulwood has since tightened the limit, saying recruits who fail three exams will be expelled.

Also, academy training is now set at 22 weeks, Smith said. The GAO had reported that training varied from seven weeks in some years to 24 in others.

Smith said, "In the ongoing training process, there is room for improvement." He noted that some refresher courses for police officers have been temporarily halted.

Smith agreed with Hankins that police officers are under considerable pressure. He too insisted that such stress was no justification for violence.

Smith said the stress comes more "from the kinds of things that police officers have to deal with today—more violence, more people with weapons and more powerful weapons—than from being any less academically or professionally equipped."

Source: Washington Post, March 25, 1991, p. A8.

courts have also been asked to review police department policies that require officers to submit to urinalysis for the purpose of determining the presence of drugs or alcohol. In *United States* v. *Jacobsen*, the Supreme Court defined the concept of search and seizure:

> A "search" occurs when an expectation of privacy that society is prepared to consider reasonable is infringed. A "seizure" of property occurs when there is some meaningful interference with an individual's possessory interests in that property.[188]

According to the Supreme Court, removing urine from an individual's body is a search within the meaning of the Fourth Amendment. Consequently, when a government agency tests an employee's urine, due process must be applied, which involves providing probable evidence of illegal activity. In the case of public employer drug testing, the search is justified from the beginning, when "reasonable grounds exist for suspecting that the search will turn up evidence of work-related drug use."[189]

A reasonable search depends on a "balancing test" set forth by Justice Sandra Day O'Connor:

> A determination of the standard of reasonableness applicable to a particular class of searches requires balancing the nature and quality of the intrusion on the individual's Fourth Amendment interests against the importance of the governmental interest alleged to justify the intrusion. In the case of searches conducted by a public employer, we must balance the invasion of the employee's legitimate expectations of privacy against the government's need for supervision, control, and the efficient operation of the work place.[190]

In *Lovvorn* v. *Chattanooga*, mandatory drug testing without probable cause was proposed for firefighters departmentwide. The firefighters claimed this violated their Fourth Amendment rights. The Supreme Court applied the above mentioned balancing standard between the reasonable privacy expectations of the firefighters and the governmental need to safeguard the public sector work place. The Court stated

> The act of urinating is one of the most private of all activities. The subjective expectations of privacy felt by many individuals when urinating is undoubtable one that society is prepared to consider reasonable. There are few other times where individuals insist as strongly and universally that they be let alone to act in private.[191]

The court also found that even though the city of Chattanooga was interested in the safety of visitors, public employees, and residents, the job of firefighter did not harbor the same possibility of catastrophic harm if an employee used drugs as did the job of air traffic controller or nuclear plant employee. Therefore, drug tests could be mandated *only* when evidence indicated a specific drug problem. Similar court rulings have appeared in cases involving police officers.[192] The prevailing view appears to be that totally random, unscheduled urine testing is unacceptable, but that particular officers can be required to submit to urinalysis if there exists a "reasonable suspicion" that the officer has been using a prohibited substance.[193] The results of such compulsory tests are appropriate evidence for introduction in administrative discharge proceedings.[194] Decisions involving other governmental employees and similar kinds of personal intrusions (e.g., strip searches of prison guards) seem to support the view that random testing is unreasonable under the Fourth Amendment[195] (see Box 10-10).

In an attempt to skirt the issue of mandatory or random testing, some departments have incorporated drug testing as a "usual and customary" part of a required medical examination. For instance, the Philadelphia Police Department requires a medical examination for all individuals attempting to secure employment under the following conditions: (1) when an officer is first hired; (2) when an officer is transferred to a "sensitive" position (i.e., vice and narcotics division, SWAT, and hostage negotiation teams); (3) when an officer is promoted to a higher rank; and (4) when an officer returns to duty after an extended period of time (i.e., long illness or disability, or suspension). Drug abuse is viewed as a medical malady and subject to disclosure similar to the findings of other tests that show spinal problems, poor vision, hearing loss, and the like. Hence, drug testing can be viewed as a routine part of the medical examination for pre-employment to a new position.

In Arlington, Texas, all police officers are required to take an annual medical examination as well as perform acceptable physical agility tests that "qualify" them for continued employment. The department links these tests to "insurability" through policies and regulations. Officers with physical disabilities (including alcohol and drug addiction) cannot be insured through the city of Arlington. An important note regarding both the Arlington and Philadelphia police departments is the attitude expressed about officer drug abuse. Each department views the problem as a medical issue; therefore, extensive programs for counseling and rehabilitation have been established. Although these regulations have *not* been court

BOX 10-10

AG Says Random Drug Tests for Police Violate Privacy

AUSTIN (AP)—Random drug testing of law enforcement officers would violate the Texas Constitution's guarantee of privacy unless a "compelling governmental objective" is shown, said an attorney general's opinion released Thursday.

"We need not address the issue of random testing under the federal Constitution . . . we believe that the Texas Constitution prohibits the practice," the opinion said.

Harrington said the opinion "applies even stronger" to other public employees. He said that is because courts have made a distinction between them and public safety officers, who may have little direct supervision and come into contact with drugs through their work.

Although such testing isn't widespread, Harrington said, the opinion is helpful to promote uniformity and is "a very consistent interpretation of the law."

The opinion, dated Dec. 27, was signed by then-Attorney General Jim Mattox. He was replaced by Dan Morales, who was sworn into office on Wednesday.

The opinion was requested by Jimmie McCullough, Robertson County attorney, who asked about the authority of a sheriff's department to require its deputies and jailers to submit to random drug testing by means of urine samples.

McCullough, who also serves as district attorney, said the idea had been considered because a large number of people in the area have been prosecuted for drug offenses.

Source: Tyler Morning Telegraph (Texas), Jan. 4, 1991, p. 1.

tested, it appears reasonable that a comprehensive look at the issue of drugs in the workplace will support drug testing as a routine part of a medical examination.

Terms and Conditions of Employment

Wage and Hour Regulations

The Fair Labor Standards Act (FLSA) was initially enacted by Congress in 1938 to establish minimum wages and to require overtime compensation in the private sector. In 1974, amendments to the act extended its coverage to state and local government employees and established special work period provisions for police and fire. However, in 1976 the U.S. Supreme Court ruled that the extension of the act into the realm of traditional local and state government functions was unconstitutional.[196] Almost a decade later, the Supreme Court surprisingly reversed itself, thus bringing all local police agencies under the coverage of the FLSA.[197] Shortly thereafter, Congress enacted the Fair Labor Standards Amendments of 1985 (effective April 15, 1986), which set forth special wage and hour provisions for government employees in an effort to reduce the monetary impact of the overtime requirements on state and local governments.

Generally, all rank-and-file law enforcement officers are covered under the FLSA. Exemptions include elected officials, their personal staffs, and those employees in policy-making positions. The law requires that overtime be paid to police personnel for all work in excess of 43 hours in a seven-day cycle or 171 hours in a 28-day period. Employers are allowed to establish or negotiate a work/pay period as they see fit within those boundaries. (The FLSA sets minimum standards that may be exceeded by offering greater benefits.) The appropriate wage for overtime hours is set at 1½ times the employee's regular rate of pay. This may be given in money or compensatory time. Public safety officers may accrue a maximum of 480 hours of "comp" time, which, if not utilized as leave, must be paid off upon separation from employment at the employee's final regular rate or at the average pay over the last three years, whichever is higher.

Of special interest to police agencies is that off-duty work and special details for a separate independent employer voluntarily undertaken by the employee are not utilized for calculating overtime payment obligations. Thus, specific hourly rates may still be negotiated for such work.

Because the new provisions discussed previously were only recently placed into effect, it is exceedingly difficult to offer definitive guidance to police administrators as to the precise application and interpretation of the 1985 amendments. Therefore, readers should seek legal guidance to ensure that wage and hour regulations are appropriately implemented and enforced.

Age-Based Hiring and Retirement Policies

State and local governments have adopted a variety of personnel policies to ensure that police officers are in adequate mental and physical condition in order to perform the normal and the unexpected strenuous physical activities of the job satisfactorily and safely. Based on the assumption that increasing age slows responses, saps strength, and increases the likelihood of sudden incapacitation because of breakdowns of the nervous and/or cardiovascular systems, many police departments and state law enforcement agencies have established mandatory hiring and retirement ages.

During the 1970s the courts allowed employers much latitude in enforcing retirement age requirements, finding such standards to be rationally related to a legitimate state interest in seeing that officers were physically prepared to protect the public's welfare.[198] In more recent decisions, however, the Supreme Court has significantly restricted the employer's ability to require that an employee be terminated upon reaching a certain age.

The Age Discrimination In Employment Act (ADEA) is a federal law that prohibits discrimination on the basis of age against employees who are between the ages of forty and seventy, unless age is shown to be a "bona fide occupational qualification (BFOQ) reasonably necessary to the normal operation of the particular business."[199] The Supreme Court has held that the BFOQ exemption is meant to be an extremely narrow exception to the general prohibition of age discrimination contained in the ADEA.[200] For an employer to demonstrate successfully that its age-based mandatory retirement rule is valid, it must first prove the existence of a job qualification reasonably necessary to the essence of its operation. Second, the employer must show that it has reasonable cause, based on fact, for believing that substantially all persons in the prohibited age group would be unable to perform the job duties safely and efficiently, or that it is impractical or impossible to accurately test and predict the capabilities of individuals in the excluded group.[201]

In another 1985 decision, the Supreme Court stated that stereotypical assumptions about the effects of aging on employee performance were inadequate to demonstrate a BFOQ. Instead, the Court held that employers are required to make a "particularized, factual showing" with respect to each element of the BFOQ defense.[202]

The federal courts have considered an ADEA challenge to a New York state law setting a maximum age of twenty-nine for those applying for jobs as police officers. The court concluded that age 29 was not a BFOQ and ruled that the requirement was a violation of the law. The court noted that the employer has the same burden of proof to justify an age-based hiring standard as it does to justify an age-based retirement requirement.[203]

Sexual Harassment

The increasing number of women joining the law enforcement poses a challenge to law enforcement managers and executives. As in many other professions, women joining the law enforcement ranks are sometimes stereotyped by those who believe that they are not capable of being good police officers. Moreover, the addition of women to a male-dominated profession, where notions of machismo may prevail, can create a situation in which women are singled out and made to feel unwelcome solely because of their gender, regardless of their work performance.[204]

FIGURE 10-8. Employment discrimination on the basis of age and/or race is prohibited by federal law. [Photo courtesy of the Longview, Texas Police Department.]

The challenge to law enforcement managers and executives is to break down the inaccurate stereotypes attached to women and eliminate any notion of disparate treatment of employees based on gender. Although common sense and good management practice dictate these must be done, the law requires it.[205] Under Title VII of the 1964 Civil Rights Act, commonly referred to simply as Title VII, when an employer causes, condones, or fails to eliminate unfair treatment of women in the workplace, liability may be found.[206]

Sexual Harassment: A Definition

It is somewhat difficult to provide a precise definition of conduct that constitutes sexual harassment; it is apparently more easily recognized than defined. Sexual harassment falls within the broader, prohibited practice of sex discrimination and may occur when an employee is subjected to unequal and unwelcome treatment based solely on the employee's sex.

Specific guidance on the types of conduct that would constitute sexual harassment is provided in the Equal Employment Opportunity Commission's (EEOC's) *Guidelines on Discrimination Because of Sex.*[207] These guidelines, although not carrying the force of law, "constitute a body of experience and informed judgment to which courts and litigants may properly resort for guidance."[208] The guidelines describe sexual harassment as follows:

> Unwelcome sexual advances, requests for sexual favors, and other verbal or physical conduct of a sexual nature constitute sexual harassment when (1) submission to such

> conduct is made either explicitly or implicitly a term or condition of an individual's employment; (2) submission to or rejection of such conduct by an individual is used as the basis for employment decisions affecting such individuals; or (3) such conduct has the purpose or effect of unreasonably interfering with an individual's work performance or creating an intimidating, hostile, or offensive working environment.[209]

In general, sexual harassment can take two forms. First, sexual harassment exists when an employee is requested or required to engage in or submit to a sexual act as a term or condition of a job benefit or assignment. Second, sexual harassment may arise when the comments, conduct, or actions of the employer, supervisors, or co-workers create an unwelcome and hostile work environment for an employee, based on gender. Both denigrate the workplace and must be prevented.

Sexual Harassment: Theories of Liability

Because by general definition sexual harassment falls into two categories, it is not surprising that courts have imposed liability on employers and co-workers for participating in, condoning, or permitting sexual harassment at work under two parallel theories. These two theories upon which liability may be found have been referred to as *quid pro quo liability* and *hostile environment liability*.[210]

Quid pro quo liability is established when a sexual act is the condition precedent before an individual is hired or promoted or becomes the recipient of any other job benefit. The converse is also true. Quid pro quo liability can be found where the refusal to engage in a sexual act is the reason for the refusal to hire, the firing, a denied promotion, or a withheld job benefit. Unlike the hostile working environment theory, the plaintiff in a quid pro quo case must show that the sexual demand was linked to a tangible, economic aspect of an employee's compensation, term, condition, or privilege of employment.[211]

The second legal theory on which sexual harassment can be predicated is the hostile working environment. Individuals who must work in an atmosphere made hostile or abusive by the unequal treatment of the sexes are denied the equal employment opportunities guaranteed to them by law and the Constitution.[212] As the Court of Appeals for the 11th Circuit said:

> Sexual harassment which creates a hostile or offensive environment for members of one sex is every bit the arbitrary barrier to sexual equality at the workplace that racial harassment is to racial equality. Surely, a requirement that a man or woman run a gauntlet of sexual abuse in return for the privilege of being allowed to work and make a living can be as demeaning and disconcerting as the harshest of racial epithets.[213]

The elements of a hostile environment case were most clearly spelled out in *Henson* v. *City of Dundee*.[214] To prevail in such a suit, the court noted that a plaintiff must establish four elements. First, as in all Title VII cases, the employee must belong to a protected group, which requires only "a simple stipulation that the employee is a man or a woman."[215] Second, the employee must show that he or she was subject to unwelcome harassment. Third, the harassment was based on sex, and but for the employee's gender, the employee would not have been subjected to the hostile or offensive environment. Fourth, the sexual harassment affected a term, condition, or privilege of employment.

It can easily be seen that the greatest attention is focused on the last three factors. If a plaintiff can establish each of those elements, with membership in a protected group being a given, then a claim of sexual harassment has been stated and liability may attach. Because these three factors form the core of the sexual harassment claim, each will be discussed in turn.

Unwelcome Sexual Harassment

In 1986, the Supreme Court had the occasion to address the issue of what constituted unwelcome sexual harassment. In *Meritor Savings Bank* v. *Vinson,*[216] a bank employee alleged that following completion of her probationary period as a teller-trainee, her supervisor invited her to dinner and, during the course of the meal, suggested they go to a motel to have sexual relations. The employee first declined but eventually agreed because she feared she might lose her job by refusing. Thereafter, over the course of the next several years, the employee alleged that her superior made repeated demands of her for sexual favors. She alleged she had sexual intercourse forty to fifty times with her superior, was fondled repeatedly by him, was followed into the women's restroom by him, and was even forcibly raped on several occasions. In defending the suit, the defendant-bank averred that because the employee had voluntarily consented to sexual relations with her superior, the alleged harassment was not unwelcome and not actionable.

The Supreme Court disagreed. The Court stated that "the fact that sex-related conduct was 'voluntary,' in the sense that the complainant was not forced to participate against her will, is not a defense to a sexual harassment suit brought under Title VII."[217] Sexually harassing conduct is unwelcome if the "employee did not solicit it or invite it, and the employee regarded the conduct as undesirable or offensive."[218]

The determination of whether specific conduct, even if "voluntary," constitutes unwelcome sexual harassment is a fact-bound inquiry.[219] Each case brings different facts and parties, leading to potentially different results. However, the courts have provided some guidance as to the types of facts that are relevant in determining whether the conduct considered in a sexual harassment suit was unwelcome.

For example, in *Meritor Savings Bank* v. *Vinson,*[220] the Supreme Court noted

> While "voluntariness" in the sense of consent is not a defense to such a claim, it does not follow that a complainant's sexually provocative speech or dress is irrelevant as a matter of law in determining whether he or she found particular sexual advances unwelcome. To the contrary, such evidence is obviously relevant.[221]

Thus, the Supreme Court ruled that to some extent,[222] the employee's own conduct is at issue when he or she files suit alleging sexual harassment. The nature of relevant employee conduct extends to the employee's participation in office vulgarities and sexual references,[223] the employee's nonwork conduct where a moral and religious character particularly sensitive to sexual jokes is claimed,[224] and proving that the employee actually initiated the sexual advance or innuendo.[225] Also relevant to the issue of "unwelcome" conduct is whether and when the employee complained. At least two courts have ruled that a failure to report instances of alleged sexual harassment, where the opportunity and mechanism to do so existed, was proof that the conduct later complained of was not genuinely offensive or unwelcome.[226]

Whether the conduct is unwelcome is a "totality of circumstances" analysis. Conduct alleged to be sexual harassment must be judged by a variety of factors, including the nature of the conduct; the background, experience, and actions of the employee; the background, experience, and actions of co-workers and supervisors; the physical environment of the workplace; the lexicon of obscenity used there; and an objective analysis of how a reasonable person would react to and respond in a similar work environment.[227] However, rather than risk making an incorrect ad hoc determination of whether conduct is or is not unwelcome in each instance of alleged sexual harassment, police managers should be prepared to take appropriate action when conduct directed against employees because of sex first appears to be offensive and unwelcome.

Harassment Based on Sex

As stated earlier, the second major element of a Title VII claim of hostile environment sexual harassment requires that the harassment be directed against an employee based on the employee's gender. Conduct that is offensive to both sexes is not sexual harassment because it does not discriminate against any protected group.[228] "The essence of a disparate treatment claim under Title VII is that an employee . . . is intentionally singled out for adverse treatment on the basis of a prohibited criterion."[229]

The prohibited criterion here is, of course, an employee's gender. In quid pro quo cases, this requirement is self-evident. The request or demand for sexual favors is made because of the employee's sex and would not otherwise have been made. However, discrimination based on gender is not always as clear in a hostile environment case. "In proving a claim for a hostile work environment due to sexual harassment, . . . the plaintiff must show that but for the fact of her [or his] sex, [the employee] would not have been the object of harassment."[230]

The term *sexual harassment* usually brings to mind sexual advances or acts, comments, and jokes relating to sexual activities. However, whereas sexual harassment includes all those types of conduct if they are unwelcome, the concept itself is broader. Any unwelcome conduct aimed at an employee that would not have occurred but for the employee's sex is sexual harassment. For example, in *Hall* v. *Gus Construction Co.*,[231] three female employees of a road construction firm filed suit alleging sexual harassment by fellow male employees. The conduct the women complained of included the use of sexual epithets and nicknames, repeated requests to engage in sexual activities, physical touching and fondling of the women, the exposure of the men's genitals, "mooning," the displaying of obscene pictures to the women, urinating in the women's water bottles and gas tank of their work truck, refusal to perform necessary repairs on the work truck until a male user complained, and refusal to allow the women restroom breaks in a town near the construction site. The defendant construction company argued that some of the conduct—such as the urinating in water bottles and gas tanks, the refusal to perform needed repairs on the truck, and the denial of restroom breaks—could not be considered as sexual harassment because the conduct, although perhaps inappropriate, was not sexually oriented.

The court disagreed. It concluded that the "incidents of harassment and unequal treatment . . . would not have occurred but for the fact that [the employees] were women."[232] Intimidation and hostility toward women because they are women can obviously result from conduct other than explicit sexual advances. Additionally, there is no requirement that the incidents, sexually oriented or not, be related to or part of a series of events. Sexual harassment can be based on repeated, though unrelated, events.[233]

Police managers and executives should be aware that any type of unwelcome conduct that is directed at an employee because of that person's gender may constitute sexual harassment. The lesson, as before, is to be alert and stifle any conduct that threatens disparate treatment because of the employee's sex.

Harassment Affecting a Condition of Employment

Title VII prohibits discrimination based on sex with respect to "compensation, terms, conditions, or privilege of employment."[234] Although it can readily be seen how the quid pro quo theory of a sexual harassment claim is sex discrimination with regard to compensation, terms, conditions, or privileges of employment, how can a sexually hostile environment affect a condition of employment, if no economic or tangible job detriment is suffered?[235]

The answer is simple. One of the conditions of any employment is the psychological well-being of the employees.[236] Where the psychological well-being of employees is adversely affected by an environment polluted with abusive and offensive harassment based solely on sex, Title VII provides a remedy. "The language of Title VII is not limited to 'economic' or 'tangible' discrimination. The phrase 'terms, conditions or privileges of employment' evinces a congressional intent 'to strike at the entire spectrum of disparate treatment of men and women' in employment."[237]

However, this is not to say that any conduct, no matter how slight, directed against an employee because of sex constitutes a hostile working environment. "For sexual harassment to be actionable, it must be sufficiently severe or pervasive to alter the conditions of the victim's employment and create an abusive working environment."[238] Isolated incidents[239] or genuinely trivial ones[240] will not give rise to sexual harassment liability. Not every sexual epithet or comment will affect the conditions of employment to a sufficient degree to create a hostile environment in violation of Title VII. Nonetheless, law enforcement management must realize that Title VII obligates it to provide a workplace where the psychological health of its employees is protected against sexual harassment.

Grounds for Sexual Harassment Claims

Generalizations about the kinds of conduct that translate into a legal finding of sexual harassment are difficult because each case is a fact-oriented determination involving many factors. However, an analysis of the cases indicates that at least three broad categories of conduct can be identified that, if found, generally lead to a legal finding of sexual harassment.

First, invariably when allegations of quid pro quo sexual harassment are proved, liability follows.[241] That such is the case is not surprising. Demands for sex acts in exchange for job benefits are the most blatant of all forms of sexual harassment. In addition, whenever a job benefit is denied because of an employee's refusal to submit to the sexual demand, a tangible or economic loss is readily established. The primary difficulty in a quid pro quo case is in carrying the burden of proof and establishing that the alleged event(s) actually occurred. Because such incidents usually occur in private conversations, the cases often involve a one-on-one contest of testimony.[242] However, if the employee sufficiently proves the event(s) happened, courts readily conclude that sexual harassment existed.

Second, courts frequently conclude sexual harassment exists where the alleged conduct was intentionally directed at an employee because of the employee's gender, was excessively beyond the bounds of job requirements, and actually detracted from the accomplishment of the job. When the conduct becomes so pervasive that the offending employee's attention is no longer focused on job responsibilities and significant time and effort is diverted from work assignments to engage in the harassing conduct, courts will generally conclude that sexual harassment exists.

This principle can be illustrated by examining two law enforcement–related cases. In *Vermett* v. *Hough*,[243] a female law enforcement officer alleged sexual harassment by her co-workers. One specific act alleged to have been offensive to her was a male officer placing a flashlight between her legs from behind. The court ruled that the conduct was nothing more than "horseplay"[244] and a stress-relief mechanism in a high-pressure job. The "horseplay" was viewed by the court to be more indicative of the female's acceptance as a co-worker than sexual harassment. Moreover, horseplay was an occasional part of the police station behavior but not on an inordinate basis.

The second case, *Arnold* v. *City of Seminole*,[245] illustrates the other side of the coin—out-of-control office joking leading to sexual harassment. In *Arnold*, a female officer chronicled a series of events and conduct to which she was subjected because she was female. Among the offensive conduct that created a hostile working environment were the following: (1) a lieutenant told her he did not believe in female police officers; (2) superior officers occasionally refused to acknowledge or speak to her; (3) obscene pictures were posted in public places within the police station with the female officer's name written on them; (4) epithets and derogatory comments were written next to the officer's name on posted work and leave schedules; (5) false misconduct claims were lodged against her; (6) work schedules were manipulated to prevent the female officer from being senior officer on duty, thus denying her command status; (7) she was singled out for public reprimands and not provided the required notice; (8) members of the female officer's family were arrested, threatened, and harassed; (9) other officers interfered with her office mail and squad car; (10) attempts to implicate the female officer in an illegal drug transaction were contemplated; and (11) the female officer was not provided equal access to station house locker facilities. Based on this amalgam of proof, which far exceeded any colorable claim of office camaraderie, the court ruled that the female officer had indeed been subjected to an openly hostile environment based solely on her sex.

A note of caution is in order. The line between innocent joking that contributes to esprit de corps and offensive sexual harassment can be a fine one. Police managers should be cognizant of such conduct and be prepared to take immediate and corrective action at the first moment it appears to be in danger of exceeding acceptable bounds.

The third category of sexual harassment generally arises from conduct or statements reflecting a belief that women employees are inferior by reason of their sex or that women have no rightful place in the work force. For example, where a supervisory employee stated, among other things, that he had no respect for the opinions of another employee because she was a woman, sexual harassment was found.[246] Similarly, a supervisor who treated his male employees with respect but treated his women employees with obvious disdain, used the terms *babe* and *woman* in a derogatory fashion, and indicated his belief that women should not be working at all was found to have sexually harassed his female employees.[247]

Although the law alone cannot realistically dispossess people of their personal prejudices, it can require that they not exhibit them in the workplace. Police managers have the responsibility to see that they do not.

Liability for Sexual Harassment

One of the primary goals of Title VII is to eliminate sexual harassment from the workplace.[248] However, to the extent it does not, civil liability remedies are available against both the employer and the offending co-workers. Both are matters of concern for law enforcement managers.

The Supreme Court in *Meritor Savings Bank* v. *Vinson*[249] made it clear that an employer would not be held liable simply because sexual harassment occurred in the workplace. Rather, the Court ruled that employer liability would be guided by agency principles, although it declined "to issue a definitive rule on employer liability."[250]

The lower courts have consistently applied agency principles to effect a remedy for sexual harassment. Three such principles can be identified. First, where a supervisory employee engages in quid pro quo sexual harassment, that is, the demand for sex in exchange for a job benefit, the employer is liable. As one court explained:

> In such a case, the supervisor relies upon his apparent or actual authority to extort sexual consideration from an employee. . . . In that case the supervisor uses the means furnished to him to accomplish the prohibited purpose. . . . Because the supervisor is acting within at least the apparent scope of the authority entrusted to him by the employer when he makes employment decisions his conduct can fairly be imputed to the source of his authority.[251]

Second, in cases where a plaintiff has successfully proved that sexual harassment by supervisory employees created a hostile working environment, courts will hold the employer liable. The Fourth Circuit Court of Appeals noted this to be the rule:

> Once the plaintiff in a sexual harassment case proves that harassment took place, the most difficult legal question typically will concern the responsibility of the employer for that harassment. Except in situations where a proprietor, partner or corporate officer participates personally in the harassing behavior, the plaintiff will have the additional responsibility of demonstrating the propriety of holding the employer liable under some theory of respondent superior.[252]

Third, if the sexually hostile working environment is created at the hands of co-workers, the employer will be liable only if he or she knew or reasonably should have known of the harassment and took no remedial action. It is the burden of the offended employee to "demonstrate that the employer had actual or constructive knowledge of the existence of a sexually hostile working environment and took no prompt and adequate remedial action.[253] Actual knowledge includes situations in which the unwelcome, offensive conduct is observed or discovered by a supervisory or management-level employee[254] and supervisory employees are personally notified of the alleged sexual harassment.[255] Constructive knowledge arises when the sexually harassing conduct is so widespread or pervasive that knowledge is imputed to the employer.[256] "Absence of actual notice to an employer does not necessarily insulate that employer from liability[257] (see Box 10-11).

These three principles suggest the manner in which sexual harassment liability can be prevented. Law enforcement managers and executives must not engage or participate in any conduct that constitutes sexual harassment. In addition, when such conduct comes to their attention, corrective action must be taken. Further, management has an affirmative obligation to monitor the workplace to ensure sexual harassment does not become a widespread practice.

Although the remedies available under Title VII are directly against the employer only and are limited by statute to primarily equitable relief,[258] not including compensatory damages,[259] other remedies may also be available to impose liability against employers or co-workers for sexual harassment claims. In addition to the relief available under Title VII, a plaintiff may seek monetary damages for a violation of federal civil and constitutional rights[260] as well as for state tort violations.[261] The important point to be noted is that liability may not be appropriate where no sexual harassment exists or where the employer takes swift remedial action.[262] The primary goal of law enforcement managers and executives should be to prevent the occurrence of any type of sexual harassment. If it does exist, sexual harassment must quickly be confronted and stopped. If this is done, no liability will attach.

Policy Recommendations

Because the potential for sexual harassment allegations and lawsuits exists in any workplace where men and women are co-workers, law enforcement must be prepared to respond if it occurs at the police station. Perhaps the best way to do so is to establish clear policy and procedure in the manner of the following.

First, the policy must identify that conduct which constitutes sexual harassment. It should include by definition both the request or demand for sexual favors in exchange for job benefits and any unwelcome sexual advances, physical contact, verbal contact, or other conduct directed against an employee by any other employee or supervisor because of the employee's sex that creates a hostile working environment. Consideration should also be given to a training program that emphasizes and reinforces the definition of sexual harassment so that a common understanding of all employees is achieved. Second, the policy and procedure must prohibit the offensive conduct and provide for appropriate remedial and punitive measures that will be taken if the policy is violated.

A mandatory and accessible grievance procedure should also be established so that police management can become aware of any sexual harassment and move

BOX 10-11

Seven Who Sued

Seven former Detroit police officers have sued the city for sexual harassment. Here are details:

Since 1975, the Detroit Police Department has nearly tripled the number of women in its ranks, having the highest percentage in the country, at 20 percent. Several female officers have complained of sexual harassment within the department as part of precinct esprit de corps. Some have successfully sued.

- February 1981: Karen Gluski, now 47, sued after receiving obscene notes and 21 transfers in 19 months at the 7th Precinct in retaliation for testifying in a 1975 federal sex discrimination suit against the department. The state Court of Appeals upheld her $87,000 jury award in 1987.
- May 1984: Cheryl Preston, now 36, sued when her 15th Precinct commander offered to stop death threats and slurs from other cops if she had sex with him. Preston had a nervous breakdown. In 1987, a jury awarded her $900,000. The Court of Appeals upheld a $225,000 award against the commander, but ordered a new trial on the city's portion. The case is pending.
- July 1987: Carol Dornan, now 41, sued after repeated harassment, including the 5th Precinct ranking officer who kissed her after showing her an erotic book, then suggested that they have an affair. A Wayne Circuit Court jury awarded her and her husband, a retired police officer, $157,000 in September 1989. The city is appealing.
- November 1987: Janette Dyer, now 35, sued when harassment began after she won Officer of the Year in 1984 at the 5th Precinct. Her performance evaluation was lowered, she was assigned tough tasks without backup and was moved to an office where male cops boasted about sex exploits. Dyer had two nervous breakdowns. The city settled in July 1990 for $942,000.
- November 1988: Gloria Hanna, now 41, sued after 5th Precinct officers flashed nude magazines at her, put rubber dildos in her locker and made racial and ethnic slurs. The city settled in July 1990 for a reported $350,000.
- August 1990: Toninicole Lynette Smith, 24, sued, claiming she was the target of a 7th Precinct betting pool with the winner being the first officer to have sex with her. Two senior officers said they would help her if she had sex with them. Her case is pending.
- October 1990: Suzanne Walcheck, 39, sued over an alleged barrage of lewd conduct at the 4th Precinct and the Tactical Services Section, including one officer who sketched his "trademark"—a penis and testicles—everywhere. Another officer, she says, targeted her with vivid obscenities during roll call. Her case is pending.

Source: Adapted from "Sexually Harassed, Female Cops Say," in *Detroit News,* Dec. 9, 1990, pp. A11–A15, B1.

quickly to resolve it. Care must be taken, however, not to establish a single-chain grievance procedure. Rather, multiple persons should be authorized to receive sexual harassment complaints so that an employee is not stifled by a requirement to report the harassment to the very person who may be the offender. Consideration should also be given to having persons of both sexes named as grievance counselors so that no unnecessary discomfort is required of an employee who alleges sexual harassment that would be embarrassing to discuss with a member of the opposite sex.

Third, the policy and procedure should establish a mechanism for the thorough and timely investigation of sexual harassment complaints. All employee allegations of sexual harassment should be treated seriously because each complaint constitutes actual knowledge of a potential problem in terms of an employer's civil liability. Lastly, law enforcement management must effectively resolve each instance of sexual harassment. The importance of this last requirement cannot be overstated. Besides the self-evident need to do so for sound management principles alone, the Supreme Court has noted that "the mere existence of a grievance procedure and a policy against discrimination"[263] will not by itself insulate an employer from liability. The grievance procedure must effectively resolve problems.[264]

Summary

In recent years there has been a significant increase in the amount of litigation involving police agencies and their officers. A substantial portion of this litigation has stemmed from efforts by citizens to receive compensation for injuries allegedly caused by department policy and the actions of police department employees. Such suits are brought as state tort actions, Section 1983 claims, or *Bivens*-type suits. In state tort actions, the plaintiff alleges that his or her injury was caused by conduct that constitutes a tort under state law, such as assault, battery, false imprisonment, or false arrest. A Section 1983 claim is brought under a federal statute that permits relief from infringements of rights created by the Constitution or by federal law by persons acting under color of state law. A *Bivens*-type suit also provides relief from infringements of constitutional rights and serves primarily to fill some "holes" left by Section 1983.

All three types of suits have limitations on who can be sued. The police supervisor and administrator are generally not liable solely by virtue of their status as the employer of the officer whose conduct caused the injury, unless the supervisor or administrator specifically authorized or cooperated in the officer's conduct that led to the injury. However, in an increasing number of cases, supervisors and administrators have been found liable for the misbehavior of their subordinates when plaintiffs were able to demonstrate that the former were negligent in the employment, training, or retention of their subordinates.

The governmental body that employs the officer accused of culpable behavior was traditionally shielded from liability by the doctrine of sovereign immunity. In recent decades, the protection of sovereign immunity in state tort actions has been eroded substantially by legislative and judicial action, but it remains an important restriction on the amount of recovery that can be obtained against the government.

Plaintiffs seeking recovery for injuries caused by police conduct are also limited by the judicial extension of immunity to public employees. In suits based on federal law, an absolute immunity is extended to prosecutors, and to judicial and quasijudicial officials. A qualified immunity is extended to other officials while they are acting in a discretionary capacity, in good faith, and in a reasonable manner. However, a defendant is not acting in good faith if his or her conduct violates settled law. In state tort actions, absolute immunity is still usually extended to public officials in their exercise of discretionary functions.

Disciplinary actions against police officers raise issues concerning procedures that are required by the due process guarantees of the U.S. Constitution. Due process protections apply when property interests or liberty interests of a public employee may be affected by disciplinary action. Supreme Court cases suggest that in determining when property and liberty interests evoke due process guarantees, the Court will carefully examine whether the local government intended to create a protected interest in the public employee.

When due process is mandated, procedural protections are required by the Constitution in taking disciplinary action against a police officer. Court decisions have extended to the police officer rights to be given notice of the charges, to call witnesses, to be confronted by and cross-examine adverse witnesses, to have counsel, and to have a decision based on the record of a hearing conducted by an impartial party. The evidentiary hearing may be postponed until after the disciplinary action is taken when risk-reducing protections, such as written notice of and opportunity to rebut the reasons for the action, are afforded the employee.

Due process also requires that disciplinary rules be clear, specific, and reasonably related to a valid job requirement. Accordingly, a disciplinary rule must address conduct that has an impact on an officer's fitness to perform his or her duties, adversely affects departmental morale or efficiency, or undermines public confidence in the department. The rule must be clear enough to give fair warning, to control the discretion of administrators, and to avoid a "chilling effect" on the exercise of constitutional rights by officers. Many departments prohibit conduct "unbecoming an officer" or "tending to bring discredit upon the department." The application of due process protections to rules of this nature has resulted in some rules being declared unconstitutional for vagueness. Other courts have upheld the constitutionality of such rules because in various disciplinary situations, it should have been clear to the officer that the rule was intended to prohibit his or her conduct.

Sometimes disciplinary rules attempt to prohibit conduct of police officers that is protected by the Constitution. Rules infringing upon the free speech of officers may be upheld if the legitimate interest of the governmental employer is found to be more important than the officer's free speech interest. However, such rules frequently run afoul of the Constitution because they are too broad, or because the department failed to demonstrate that the officer's speech produced an unjustifiable adverse effect on the department's ability to perform.

Rights regarding political participation are also protected by the First Amendment to the Constitution. However, the federal Hatch Act and similar state laws that prohibit nearly all partisan political activity by public employees have been upheld by the Supreme Court. Nevertheless, courts have struck down prohibitions that extended to nonpartisan political activity or political activity, which seemed only remotely related to an important governmental interest. Dismissals of non-policy-making public employees for reasons of political party affiliation have been held illegal.

In other areas affected by the First Amendment, courts have generally upheld rules prohibiting police officers from associating with criminals or other undesirables so long as the rule is not too broad, and it can be demonstrated that the association has a detrimental effect on the department's operation. With regard to freedom of expression, the Supreme Court has upheld the establishment of grooming standards for police officers.

Courts have held that the Fourth Amendment protection against unreasonable searches and seizures does not prevent a department from searching lockers and equipment issued to officers, or from ordering officers to appear in a lineup when there is a strong governmental interest at stake.

The constitutional right against self-incrimination does not prohibit a police department from ordering an officer to answer questions directly related to the performance of his or her duties. Although there is some disagreement among courts considering the question, most courts have also held that officers may be required to take polygraph examinations under the circumstances just described.

Other issues regarding disciplinary action against police officers include

1. "Conduct unbecoming," which has been defined as a lack of fitness to perform the functions of a police officer, including associating with crime figures, fighting, dishonesty, off-duty drinking, insubordination, and a wide array of other inappropriate activity.
2. Adultery has generally been upheld as a proper basis for disciplinary action.

3. Homosexuality. The key seems to be whether the employee's homosexuality impairs the efficiency of the agency, and only flagrant displays of homosexual conduct have generally been found to have such an effect.
4. Residency. A department can require its officers to live within the geographical limits of its jurisdiction.
5. Religious preference. A department must reasonably accommodate the religious practices of its officers without imposing an "undue hardship" on itself or other employees.
6. Moonlighting may be prohibited.
7. Regulations relating to the use of weapons issued to officers will be upheld so long as they are reasonable.
8. Regulations prohibiting intoxication or impairment of an officer's ability to perform while on duty as a result of the influence of drugs or alcohol carry a strong presumption of validity. Police officers can probably be ordered to take blood, breathalyzer, or urinalysis when there is a reasonable suspicion of abuse or influence.

In administrative matters unrelated to the disciplinary process, the Supreme Court has held that police departments must comply with the minimum wage and overtime requirements of the Fair Labor Standards Act. Persons between the ages of forty and seventy may not be discriminated against in employment decisions unless age is a bona fide occupational qualification reasonably necessary to the operation of the department's business.

The best way for law enforcement administrators to prepare to respond to potential incidents of sexual harassment allegations and lawsuits in the workplace is to establish a clear policy and procedure in the following manner: First, the policy must identify that conduct that constitutes sexual harassment. Second, the policy and procedure must prohibit the offensive conduct and provide for appropriate remedial and punitive measures that should be taken if the policy is violated. Third, the policy and procedure should establish a mechanism for the thoroughly and timely investigation of all sexual harassment complaints. Finally, law enforcement management must effectively resolve each incident of sexual harassment.[265]

Discussion Questions

1. What are the two vehicles by which federal courts can acquire jurisdiction of tort suits that have traditionally been brought in state courts?
2. What is the difference between a crime and a tort?
3. Explain the three general categories of torts. How do they differ?
4. What does "acting under color of State Law" mean? How does this statement relate to Section 1983 actions?
5. What is a *Bivens* action?
6. List and discuss the negligence theories applicable to police supervision and management.
7. What are procedural and substantive due process?
8. What are the twelve elements of a due process hearing?
9. In what three ways are the rules of law promulgated?
10. What are liberty rights and property rights?
11. Discuss some of the grounds for disciplinary action often brought against police officers.
12. List some of the important aspects of training in a deadly force case that a department might offer to defend against a negligence suit.

13. What is the "balancing test," as referred to in alcohol and drug testing in the workplace?
14. What policy recommendations have been made in order to reduce the potential for sexual harassment allegations and lawsuits against police departments?

Notes

1. Much of this section is taken, with some addition, from H. E. Barrineau III, *Civil Liability in Criminal Justice* (Cincinnati, Ohio: Anderson, 1987), pp. 3–5.
2. Ibid., p. 3.
3. False arrest is the arrest of a person without probable cause. Generally, this means making an arrest when an ordinarily prudent person would not have concluded that a crime had been committed or that the person arrested had committed the crime. False imprisonment is the intentional illegal detention of a person. The detention that can give rise to a false imprisonment claim is any confinement to a specified area and not simply incarceration in a jail. Most false arrests result in false imprisonment as well, but there can be a false imprisonment after a valid arrest also, as when the police fail to release an arrested person after a proper bond has been posted, the police unreasonably delay the arraignment of an arrested person, or authorities fail to release a prisoner after they no longer have authority to hold him. "Brutality" is not a legal tort action as such. Rather, it must be alleged as a civil (as opposed to a criminal) assault and/or battery. Assault is some sort of menacing conduct that puts another person in reasonable fear that he or she is about to have a battery committed upon him or her. Battery is the infliction of harmful or offensive contact on another person. Harmful or offensive contact is contact that would be considered harmful or offensive by a reasonable person of ordinary sensibilities. See Clarence E. Hagglund, "Liability of Police Officers and Their Employers," *Federation of Insurance Counsel Quarterly*, 26 (Summer 1976), p. 257, for a good discussion of assault and battery, false arrest, false imprisonment, and malicious prosecution as applied to police officers.
4. Although a fourth category (strict liability tort action) does exist in the wider body of law, such a general category is rare in police officer litigation. Therefore, for the purposes of this book, strict liability actions are not discussed. Under strict liability, one is held liable for one's act irrespective of intent or negligence. The mere occurrence of certain events will necessarily create legal liability. A good example of such cases is often found in airplane disasters in which the air transportation company is strictly liable for the passengers' health and well-being regardless of other factors.
5. The definitions of *negligence, intentional torts* and *constitution torts* are taken from Barrineau, *Civil. Liability*, p. 5.
6. Title 42, U.S. Code Section 1983.
7. See *Monroe* v. *Pape*, 365 U.S. 167, (1961). The plaintiff and his family sued thirteen Chicago police officers and the city of Chicago, alleging that police officers broke into their home without a search warrant, forced them out of bed at gunpoint, made them stand naked while the officers ransacked the house, and subjected the family to verbal and physical abuse. The Court held that the definition of "under color of State law" for Section 1983 purposes was the same as that already established in the criminal context, and also concluded that because Section 1983 provides for a civil action, the plaintiffs need not prove that the defendants acted with a "specific intent to deprive a person of a federal right" (365 U.S. at 187). The Court also held that municipalities (such as the city of Chicago, in this case) were immune from liability under the statute. [Citations to case opinions give the volume number in which the opinion is located, followed by the name of the reporter system, the page number, the court if other than the Supreme Court, and the year in which the opinion was rendered.]

8. The resuscitation of Section 1983 hinges on the misuse and abuse of power imbued to individuals acting as police officers. All municipal and county law enforcement officers take an oath to uphold and enforce the laws of a specific state in which their municipality resides. Therefore, municipal police officers fall squarely within the confines of Section 1983. "Misuse of power, possessed by virtue of state law and made possible only because the wrongdoer is clothed with the authority of state law, is action taken 'under color of' state law." *United States* v. *Classic*, 313 U.S. 299 at 326, 61 S.Ct. 1031 at 1043 (1941) as quoted in *Monroe* v. *Pape*. Thus, private citizens cannot be sued under Section 1983 unless they conspire with state officers. (See *Slavin* v. *Curry*, 574 F.2nd, 1256 [5th Cir. 1978].)
9. Most tort actions against the U.S. government must be brought under the FTCA. The FTCA is a partial waiver of sovereign immunity, with its own rule of liability and a substantial body of case law. Federal employees can be sued for violation of constitutional rights and for certain common law torts. For more information, refer to Isidore Silver, *Police Civil Liability* (New York: Matthew Bender, 1987), Section 1.04, from which this material is taken.
10. See *Bivens* v. *Six Unknown Federal Narcotics Agents*, 403 U.S. 388, 91 S.Ct. 1999, 29 L. Ed., 3d 619 (1971). Also, refer to Silver, *Police Civil Liability*, Section 8.02.
11. Silver, *Police Civil Liability*, Section 8.02.
12. See William L. Prosser, *Handbook of the Law of Torts*, 4th ed. (St. Paul: West, 1971), p. 69, for a good discussion of the philosophical basis for and development of the doctrine of vicarious liability.
13. Wayne W. Schmidt, "Recent Developments in Police Civil Liability," *Journal of Police Science and Administration*, 4 (1976), p. 197, and the cases cited therein.
14. [T]he courts have very generally drawn a distinction between a sheriff and a chief of police, holding that the deputies of the former are selected and appointed by the sheriff and act purely as his representatives, but that police officers are generally not selected exclusively by the chief of police, and are themselves officers and do not act for the chief of police in the performance of their official duties," *Parish* v. *Meyers*, 226 p. 633 (Wash. 1924).
15. *Jordan* v. *Kelly*, 223 F.Supp. 731 (1963), p. 738.
16. Ibid., p. 739.
17. Schmidt, "Recent Developments," p. 197.
18. Although this list does not include all types of negligence theories regarding Section 1983 action against police supervisors and managers, it does provide a starting point in the understanding of this issue. This part has been adapted from Barrineau, *Civil Liability*, pp. 59–60.
19. See *Peter* v. *Bellinger*, 159 N.E.2nd 528 (1959); *Thomas* v. *Johnson*, 295 F.Supp. 415 (1968); *McKenna* v. *City of Memphis*, 544 F.Supp. 425 (1982); *McGuire* v. *Arizona Protection Agency*, 609 P.2nd 1080 (1980); *Di Cosal* v. *Kay*, 19 N.J. 159, 450 A.2nd 508 (1982); *Ponticas* v. *KMS Investments*, 331 N.W. 2d 907 (1983); and *Welsh Manufacturing Div. of Textron, Inc.* v. *Pinkertons, Inc.*, 474 A/2md 426 (1984).
20. See *Moon* v. *Winfield*, 383 F.Supp. 31 (1974); *Murray* v. *Murphy*, 441 F.Supp. 120 (1977); *Allen* v. *City of Los Angeles* (No. C-9837) LA Sup.Ct. (1975); *Stengel* v. *Belcher*, 522 F.2d 438 (1975); *Dominguez* v. *Superior Court*, 101 Cal. App.3d 6 (1980); *Stuessel* v. *City of Glendale*, 141 Cal. App.3d 1047 (1983); and *Blake* v. *Moore*, 162 Cal. App.3d 700 (1984).
21. See *Ford* v. Breiser, 383 F.Supp. 505 (1974); *Dewel* v. *Lawson*, 489 F.2d 877 (1974) *Bonsignore* v. City of New York, 521 F. Supp. 394 (1981); *Webster* v. *City of Houston*, 689 F.2d 1220 (1982: Rehearing July, 1984); and *District of Columbia* v. *Parker*, 850 F.2d 708 (1988).
22. See *Marusa* v. *District of Columbia*, 484 F. 428 (1973); *Brandon* v. *Allen*, 516 F.Supp. 1355 (1981); *Webster* v. *City of Houston*, *suprs*; and *Grandstaff* v. *City of Borger*, 767 F.2d 161 (1985).

23. See *City of Canton* v. *Harris*, 109 S.Ct. 1197 (1989); *Merritt* v. *County of Los Angeles* 875 F.2d 765 (1989); and *Owens* v. *Haas*, 601 F.2d 1242 (1979).
24. Prosser, *Handbook of the Law of Torts*, pp. 977–78.
25. Kenneth Culp Davis, *Administrative Law of the Seventies* (Rochester, N.Y.: Lawyers Cooperative, 1976), pp. 551, p. 207, 1978 Supplement.
26. In most states in which abrogation of sovereign immunity has occurred, the abrogation has not been total. In some states, the abrogation is an unconditional waiver of sovereign immunity, but the waiver extends only to certain activities, to cases in which the employee had a particular state of mind, to liability not to exceed a designated monetary amount, or to only a particular level of government. In some states, the waiver of sovereign immunity is effective only if the government unit being sued is insured for the potential loss. Yet another approach taken by some states is not to allow government units to be sued but to require indemnification of public employees who have been sued successfully. (For an example, see *Florida Statutes*, Chapter 768.28.)
27. *Hans* v. *Louisiana*, 134 U.S. 1 (1890); *Edelman* v. *Jordan*, 415 U.S. 651 (1974); *Scheuer* v. *Rhodes*, 416 U.S. 232 (1974).
28. *Alabama* v. *Pugh*, 438 U.S. 781 (1978).
29. *Davis* v. *Scherer*, 104 S.Ct. 3012 (1984).
30. *Scheuer* v. *Rhodes*, 416 U.S. 232, 240 (1974).
31. *Wood* v. *Strickland*, 420 U.S. 308 (1975).
32. *Harlow* v. *Fitzgerald*, 457 U.S. 800 (1982).
33. *Mitchell* v. *Forsyth*, 105 S.Ct. 2806 (1985).
34. *Monroe* v. *Pape*, 365 U.S. 167 (1961).
35. 436 U.S. 658 (1978).
36. See, for example, *Rookard* v. *Health and Hospitals Corp.*, 710 F.2d 41 (Cir. 1983).
37. *Oklahoma City* v. *Tuttle*, 105 S.Ct. 2427 (1985), but see *Pembaur* v. *Cincinnati*, 475 U.S. 469 (1986).
38. *Fundiller* v. *City of Cooper City*, Case No. 84-5104, (11th Cir. 1985).
39. *Daniels* v. *Williams*, 106 S.Ct. 662 (1986).
40. *New* v. *City of Minneapolis*, 792 F.2nd, 724, 725–26 (1986). See also *McClary* v. *O'Hare*, 786 F.2nd, 83 (1986).
41. Hagglund, "Liability of Police Officers," p. 257.
42. *United States* v. *Leon*, 468 U.S. 897 (1984).
43. *Malley* v. *Briggs*, No. 84-1586 (S.Ct. 1986).
44. Schmidt, "Recent Developments."
45. Ibid., p. 198.
46. *Wimberly* v. *Patterson*, 183 A.2d 691 (1962), p. 699.
47. *Piatkowski* v. *State*, 251 N.Y.S. 2d 354 (1964), p. 359.
48. Schmidt, "Recent Developments," p. 199.
49. *Fords* v. *Breier*, 383 F.Supp. 505 (E. D. Wis. 1974).
50. *Lucas* v. *Riley*, Superior Court, Los Angeles County, Calif. (1975); *DeLong* v. *City of Denver*, 530 F.2d 1308 (Colo. 1974); *Grudt* v. *City of Los Angeles*, 468 P.2d 825 (Cal. 1970); *Dillenbeck* v. *City of Los Angeles*, 446 P.2d 129 (Cal. 1968).
51. *AELE Law Enforcement Legal Defense Manual*, "Failure to Provide Medical Treatment," Issue 77-6 (1977).
52. Ibid., and cases therein.
53. See, generally, Joan Bertin Lowy, "Constitutional Limitations on the Dismissal of Public Employees," *Brooklyn Law Review*, 43 (Summer 1976), p. 1; Victor G. Rosenblum, "Schoolchildren: Yes, Policemen: No—Some Thoughts About the Supreme Court's Priorities Concerning the Right to a Hearing in Suspension and Removal Cases," *Northwestern University Law Review*, 72 (1977), p. 146.
54. *Wisconsin* v. *Constantineau* 400 U.S. 433 (1970); *Doe* v. *U.S. Department of Justice*, 753 F.2d 1092 (D.C. Cir. 1985).

55. *Codd* v. *Velger*, 97 S.Ct. 882 (1977). See also *Paul* v. *Davis*, 424 U.S. 693 (1976), which held that injury to reputation alone does not constitute a deprivation of liberty. Also see *Swilley* v. *Alexander*, 629 (F.2d 1018 (5th Cir. 1980), where the court held that a letter of reprimand containing untrue charges that was placed in an employee's personnel file infringed on his liberty interest.
56. *Board of Regents* v. *Roth*, 408 U.S. 546 (1972); *Perry* v. *Sindermann*, 408 U.S. 593 (1972).
57. *Arnett* v. *Kennedy*, 416 U.S. 134 (1974); *Bishop* v. *Wood*, 426 U.S. 341 (1976). See Robert L. Rabin, "Job Security and Due Process; Monitoring Administrative Discretion Through a Reasons Requirement," *University of Chicago Law Review*, 44 (1976), pp. 60, 67, for a good discussion of these cases; also *Bailey* v. *Kirk*, No. 82-1417 (10th Cir. 1985).
58. See Carl Goodman, "Public Employment and the Supreme Court's 1975–76 Term," *Public Personnel Management*, 5 (September–October 1976), pp. 287–89.
59. *Thurston* v. *Dekle*, 531 F.2d 1264 (5th Cir. 1976), vacated on other grounds 438 U.S. 901 (1978).
60. *Allison* v. *City of Live Oak*, 450 F.Supp. 200 (M.D. Fla. 1978).
61. See, e.g., *Confederation of Police* v. *Chicago* 547 F.2d 375 (7th Cir. 1977).
62. *Parratt* v. *Taylor*, 451 U.S. 527 (1981).
63. Davis, *Administrative Law*, p. 242.
64. *Memphis Light, Gas & Water Division* v. *Craft*, 436 U.S. 1 (1978); also *Okeson* v. *Tolley School Dist.*, 760 F.2d 864 (8th Cir. 1985).
65. In re Dewar, 548 P.2d 149 (Mont. 1976).
66. *Bush* v. Beckman, 131 N.Y.S. 2d 297 (1954); *Gibbs* v. *City of Manchester*, 61 A. 128 (N.H. 1905).
67. *Morrissey* v. *Brewer*, 408 U.S. 471 (1972).
68. *Goldman* v. *Kelly*, 397 U.S. 254 (1970). See also *Buck* v. *N.Y. City Bd. of Ed.*, 553 F.2d 315 (2d Cir. 1977). *cert den*, 438 U.S. 904 (1978).
69. *Morrissey* v. *Brewer*.
70. *Marshall* v. *Jerrico, Inc.*, 446 U.S. 238 (1980) and *Hortonville J.S.D. No. 1* v. *Hortonville Ed. Assn.*, 426 U.S. 482 (1976); and *Holley* v. *Seminole County School Dist.*, 755 F.2d 1492 (11th Cir. 1985).
71. 416 U.S. 134 (1974), p. 157.
72. Ibid., pp. 167–68.
73. 424 U.S. 319, 335 (1975).
74. 105 S.Ct. 1487 (1985).
75. Ibid., at 1494.
76. *Gorham* v. *City of Kansas City*, 590 P.2d 1051 (Kan. S.Ct. 1979) and *Winston* v. *U.S. Postal Service*, 585 F.2d 198 (7th Cir. 1978).
77. *Bence* v. *Breier*, 501 F.2d 1185 (7th Cir. 1974).
78. *Perea* v. *Fales*, 114 Cal. Rptr. 808 (1974), p. 810.
79. *Kramer* v. *City of Bethlehem*, 289 A.2d 767 (1972).
80. *Rogenski* v. *Board of Fire and Police Commissioners of Moline*, 285 N.E.2d 230 (1972). See also *Major* v. *Hampton*, 413 F.Supp. 66 (1976), in which the court held that an IRS rule against activities tending to discredit the agency was overbroad as applied to a married employee who had maintained an apartment for illicit sexual liaisons during off-duty hours.
81. *Grayned* v. *City of Rockford*, 408 U.S. 104 (1972), pp. 108–9.
82. *Bence* v. *Breier*, p. 1190.
83. *Rinaldi* v. *Civil Service Commission*,. 244 N.W. 2d 609 (Mich. 1976).
84. *Allen* v. *City of Greensboro, North Carolina*, 452 F.2d 489 (4th Cir. 1971).
85. *Petraitis* v. *Board of Fire and Police Commissioners of City of Palos Hills*, 335 N.E. 2d 126 (Ill. 1975); *Haywood* v. *Municipal Court*, 271 N.E. 2d 591 (Mass. 1971); *Lewis* v.

Board of Trustees, 212 N.Y.S. 2d 677 (1961). Compare *Stanton* v. *Board of Fire and Police Commissioners of Village of Bridgeview*, 345 N.E.2d 822 (Ill. 1976).

86. *DeSalvatore* v. *City of Oneonta*, 369 N.Y.S. 2d 820 (1975).
87. *Marino* v. *Los Angeles*, 110 Cal. Rptr. 45 (1973).
88. *Guido* v. *City of Marion*, 280 N.E.2d 81 (Ind. 1972).
89. *Carroll* v. *Goldstein*, 217 A.2d 676 (R.I. 1976).
90. *Firemen's and Policemen's Civil Service Commission* v. *Shaw*, 306 S.W. 2d 160 (Tex. 1957).
91. *Martin* v. *City of St. Martinville*, 321 So. 2d 532 (La. 1975).
92. *Arnold* v. *City of Aurora*, 498 P.2d 970 (Colo. 1973).
93. *Carey* v. *Piphus*, 435 U.S. 247 (1978).
94. *County of Monroe* v. *Dept of Labor*, 690 F.2d 1359 (11th Cir. 1982).
95. *Gitlow* v. *New York*, 268 U.S. 652 (1925).
96. *Pickering* v. *Board of Education*, 391 U.S. 563 (1968), p. 568.
97. *Keyishian* v. *Board of Regents*, 385 U.S. 589 (1967).
98. *Pickering* v. *Board of Education*.
99. *Muller* v. *Conlisk*, 429 F.2d 901 (7th Cir. 1970).
100. *Flynn* v. *Giarusso*, 321 F.Supp. 1295 (E.D. La. 1971), p. 1299. The regulation was revised and later ruled constitutional in *Magri* v. *Giarusso*, 379 F.Supp. 353 (E.D. La. 1974). See also *Gasparinetti* v. *Kerr*, 568 F.2d 311 (3d Cir. 1977).
101. *In re Gioglio*, 248 A.2d 570 (N.J. 1968); *Brukiewa* v. *Police Commissioner of Baltimore*, 263 A.2d 210 (Md. 1970); *Kannisto* v. *City and County of San Francisco*, 541 F.2d 841 (9th Cir. 1976). Compare *Magri* v. *Giarusso; Hosford* v. *California State Personnel Board*, 141 (Cal. Rptr. 354 (1977); *Simpson* v. *Weeks*, 570 F.2d 240 (8th Cir. 1978).
102. *Brukiewa* v. *Police Commissioner*.
103. *Perry* v. *City of Kinloch*, 680 F.Supp. 1339 (1988).
104. *Brockell* v. *Norton*, 732 F.2d 664 (8th Cir. 1984).
105. *Germann* v. *City of Kansas City, Mo*., 766 F.2d (8th Cir. 1985).
106. *Broadrick* v. *Oklahoma*, 413 U.S. (1973) and *Reeder* v. *Kansas City Bd. of Police Comm*., 733 F.2d 543 (8th Cir. 1984).
107. *United Public Workers* v. *Mitchell*, 330 U.S. 75 (1947); *U.S. Civil Service Commission* v. *National Association of Letter Carriers*, 431 U.S. 548 (1973).
108. *Broadrick* v. *Oklahoma*.
109. *Magill* v. *Lynch*, 400 F.Supp. 84 (R.I. 1975).
110. *Boston Police Patrolmen's Association, Inc*. v. *City of Boston*, 326 N.E.2d 314 (Mass. 1975).
111. *Phillips* v. *City of Flint*, 224 N.W. 2d 780 (Mich. 1975). But compare *Paulos* v. *Breier*, 507 F.2d 1383 (7th Cir. 1974).
112. *Ibid*., p. 784.
113. *Elrod* v. *Burns*, 427 U.S. 347 (1976). See also *Ramey* v. *Harber*, 431 F.Supp. 657 (W.D. Va. 1977) and *Branti* v. *Finkel*, 445 U.S. 507 (1980).
114. *Connick* v. *Myers*, 461 U.S. 138 (1983); *Jones* v. *Dodson*, 727 F.2d 1329 (4th Cir. 1984).
115. *Sponick* v. *City of Detroit Police Department*, 211 N.W. 2d 674 (Mich. 1973), p. 681, but see *Wilson* v. *Taylor*, F.2d 1539 (11th Cir. 1984).
116. *Bruns* v. *Pomerleau*, 319 F.Supp. 58 (D. Md. 1970). See also *McMullen* v. *Carson*, 754 F.2d 936 (11th Cir. 1985), where it was held that a Ku Klux Klansman could not be fired from his position as a records clerk in the sheriff's department simply because he was a Klansman. The Court did uphold the dismissal because his active KKK participation threatened to cripple the agency's ability to perform its public duties effectively.
117. *Civil Service Commission of Tucson* v. *Livingston*, 525 P.2d 949 (Ariz. 1974).
118. See, for example, *Tinker* v. *Des Moines School District*, 393 U.S. 503 (1969).
119. 425 U.S. 238 (1976).

120. *Mapp* v. *Ohio*, 367 U.S. 643 (1961).
121. *Katz* v. *United States*, 389 U.S. 347 (1967).
122. *Smith* v. *Maryland*, 442 U.S. 735 (1979) and *Chan* v. *State*, 78 Md. App. 287, 552 (1989). The "expectation to privacy" clause was developed in *Katz* v. *United States*, 389 U.S. 347 (1967), a case that involved warrantless electronic surveillance of a public telephone booth. The Court said that "the Fourth Amendment protects people, not places. What a person knowingly exposes to the public, even in his own home or office, is not subject of Fourth Amendment protection. But what he seeks to preserve as private, even in an area accessible to the public, may be constitutionally protected. . . . There is a two-fold requirement, first that a person have exhibited an actual expectation of privacy, and second that the expectation by one society is prepared to recognize as reasonable/legitimate."
123. See *People* v. *Tidwell*, 266 N.E.2d 787 (Ill. 1971).
124. *McDonnell* v. *Hunter*, 612 F.Supp. 1122, 23 GERR 1078 (S.D. Iowa 1985).
125. *Biehunik* v. *Felicetta*, 441 F.2d 228 (1971), p. 230.
126. *United States* v. *Leon*, 104 S.Ct. 3405 (1984) and *Massachusetts* v. *Sheppard*, 104 S.Ct. 3424 (1984).
127. *Illinois* v. *Gates*, 462, U.S. 213 (1984).
128. The concept of the "good faith–reasonable belief" defense as either a qualified or an absolute immunity has significant case history. See Isadore Silver, *Police Civil Liability*, chapters 4 and 7.
129. See *Floyd* v. *Farrell*, 765 F.2d 1 (1985) and *Malley* v. *Briggs*, 475 U.S. 335, 106 S.Ct. 1092 (1986).
130. *Sheetz* v. *Mayor and City Council of Baltimore, Maryland*, 315 Md. 208 (1989).
131. *Garrity* v. *New Jersey*, 385 U.S. 493 (1967).
132. The states are bound by this requirement as well. *Malloy* v. *Hogan*, 378 U.S. 1 (1964).
133. *Gardner* v. *Broderick*, 392 U.S. 273 (1968).
134. These procedural rights in police disciplinary actions have often been referred to as the "Garrity Rights." They were developed through a series of cases, see *Lefkowitz* v. *Turley*, 414 U.S. 70 (1973), and *Confederation of Police* v. *Conlisk*, 489 F.2d 891 (1973). Further, as the rights appear here, see Will Aitchison, *The Rights of Law Enforcement Officers*, (Portland, Ore.: Labor Relations Information System, 1989), p. 118.
135. See *Gabrilowitz* v. *Newman*, 582 F.2d 100 (1st Cir. 1978). Cases upholding the department's authority to order an officer to take a polygraph examination include *Eshelman* v. *Blubaum*, 560 P.2d 1283 (Ariz. 1977); *Dolan* v. *Kelly*, 348 N.Y.S. 2d 478 (1973); *Richardson* v. *City of Pasadena*, 500 S.W. 2d 175 (Tex. 1973); *Seattle Police Officer's Guild* v. *City of Seattle*, 494 P.2d 485 (Wash. 1972); *Roux* v. *New Orleans Police Department*, 223 So. 2d 905 (La. 1969); *Coursey* v. *Board of Fire and Police Commissioners*, 234 N.E. 2d 339 (Ill. 1967); *Frazee* v. *Civil Service Board of City of Oakland*, 338 P.2d 943 (Cal. 1959); and *Hester* v. *Milledgeville*, Case No. 85-8010 (11th Cir. 1985). Cases denying the department's authority include *Molino* v. *Board of Public Safety of City of Torrington*, 225 A.2d 805 (Conn. 1966). *Stape* v. *Civil Service Commission of City of Philadelphia*, 172 A.2d 161 (Pa. 1961), and *Farmer* v. *City of Fort Lauderdale*, 427 So. 2d 187 (Fla. 1983), *cert den*, 104 S.Ct. 74 (1984).
136. *Eshelman* v. *Blubaum*, p. 1286.
137. *Farmer* v. *Ft. Lauderdale*.
138. *Faust* v. *Police Civil Service Commission*, 347 A.2d 765 (Pa. 1975); *Steward* v. *Leary*, 293 N.Y.S. 2d 573 (1968); *Brewer* v. *City of Ashland*, 86 S.W. 2d 669 (Ky. 1935); *Fabio* v. *Civil Service Commission of Philadelphia*, 373 A.2d 751 (Pa. 1977).
139. *Anderson* v. *City of Philadelphia, Pennsylvania*, 668 F.Supp. 441 (1987).
140. See Aitchison, *The Rights of Law Enforcement Officers*, pp. 58–62.
141. See *Bigby* v. *City of Chicago*, 766 F.2d 1053 (1985); *McCoy* v. *Board of Fire and Police*

Commissioners (*Chicago*), 398 N.E.2d 1020 (1979); *Davis* v. *Williams*, 588 F.2d 69 (1979); *Parker* v. *Levy*, 417 U.S. 733 (1974); *Bence* v. *Brier*, 501, F.2d 1185 (1974); and *Gee* v. *California State Personnel Board*, 85 Cal. Rptr. 762 (1970).

142. Whether or not reasonable men would agree that the conduct was punishable so that an individual is free to steer a course between lawful and unlawful behaviors is the key to "reasonableness." Refer to *Cranston* v. *City of Richmond*, 710 P.2d 845 (1986), and *Said* v. *Lackey*, 731 S.W. 2d 7 (1987).
143. *Cranston* v. *City of Richmond*, supra.
144. See *City of St. Petersburg* v. *Police Benevolent Association*, 414 So. 2d 293 (1982), and *Brown* v. *Sexner*, 405 N.E.2d 1082 (1980).
145. *Richter* v. *Civil Service Commission of Philadelphia*, 387 A.2d 131 (1978).
146. *Miller* v. *City of York*, 415 A.2d 1280 (1980), and *Kannisto* v. *City and County of San Francisco*, 541 F.2d 841 (1976).
147. *McIntosh* v. *Monroe Police Civil Service Board*, 389 So. 2d 410 (1980), *Barnett* v. *New Orleans Police Department*, 413 So. 2d 520 (1982), and *Allman* v. *Police Board of Chicago*, 489 N.E.2d 929 (1986).
148. *Philadelphia Civil Service Commission* v. *Wojtuski*, 525 A.2d 1255 (1987), *Gandolfo* v. *Department of Police*, 357 So. 2d 568 (1978), and *McDonald* v. *Miller*, 596 F.2d 686 (1979).
149. *Monroe* v. *Board of Public Safety*, 423 N.Y.S. 2d 963 (1980).
150. *Redo* v. *West Goshen Township*, 401 A.2d 394 (1979).
151. *Brase* v. *Board of Police Commissioners*, 487 N.E.2d 91 (1985).
152. *Major* v. *Hampton*, 413 F.Supp. 66 (1976).
153. *City of North Muskegon* v. *Briggs*, 473 U.S. 909 (1985).
154. 53 U.S.L.W. 3909.
155. *National Gay Task Force* v. *Bd. of Ed. of Oklahoma City*, 729 F.2d 1270 (10th Cir. 1984).
156. See *Whisenhund* v. *Spradlin*, 464 U.S. 964 (1983) and *Kukla* v. *Village of Antioch*, 647 F.Supp. 799 (1986); cohabitation of officers; *Coryle* v. *City of Oil City*, 405 A.2d 1104 (1979); public lewdness; *Childers* v. *Dallas Police Department*, 513 F.Supp. 134 (1981) and *Fout* v. *California State Personnel Board, supra*: child molesting; *Fugate* v. *Phoenix Civil Service Board*, 791 F.2d 736 (1986): sex with prostitutes; *Doe* v. *Commonwealth Attorney*, 425 U.S. 901 (1976), *Smith* v. *Price*, 616 F.2d 1371 (1980), and *Bowers* v. *Hardwick* 478 U.S. 1986): sodomy as a state law prohibiting homosexuality.
157. *Bd. of Ed.* v. *National Gay Task Force*, 53 U.S.L.W. 4408, No. 83-2030 (1985).
158. *Rowland* v. *Mad River Sch. Dist.*, 730 F.2d 444 (6th Cir. 1984).
159. *Dronenburg* v. *Zech*, 741 F.2d 1388 (D.C. Cir. 1984).
160. *Todd* v. *Navarro*, 698 F.Supp. 871 (1988).
161. *Padula* v. *Webster*, 822 F.2d 97 (1987).
162. *McCarthy* v. *Philadelphia Civil Service Comm.*, 424 U.S. 645 (1976).
163. *Miller* v. *Police of City of Chicago*, 349 N.E. 2d 544 (Ill. 1976); *Williamson* v. *Village of Baskin*, 339 So. 2d 474 (La. 1976); *Nigro* v. *Board of Trustees of Alden*, 395 N.Y.S. 2d 544 (1977).
164. *State, County, and Municipal Employees Local 339* v. *City of Highland Park*, 108 N.W. 2d 898 (1961).
165. *Hameetman* v. *City of Chicago*, 776 F.2d 636 (7th Cir. 1985).
166. 42 U.S.C. §200e(j).
167. *Pinsker* v. *Joint Dist. No. 28J*, 554 F.Supp. 1049 (D. Colo. 83).
168. *United States* v. *City of Albuquerque*, 12 EPD 11, 244 (10th Cir. 1976). See also *Trans World Airlines* v. *Hardison*, 97 S.Ct. 2264 (1977).
169. *Potter* v. *Murray City* 760 F.2d 1065 (10th Cir. 1985).
170. *Cox* v. *McNamara*, 493 P.2d 54 (Ore. 1972); *Brenckle* v. *Township of Shaler*, 281 A.2d 920 (Pa. 1972); *Hopwood* v. *City of Paducah*, 424 S.W. 2d 134 (Ky. 1968); *Flood* v.

Kennedy, 239 N.Y.S. 2d 665 (1963). See also *Trelfa* v. *Village of Centre Island*, 389 N.Y.S. 2d 22 (1976). Rules prohibiting law enforcement officers from holding interest in businesses that manufacture, sell, or distribute alcoholic beverages have also been upheld. *Bock* v. *Long*, 279 N.E.2d 464 (Ill. 1972); *Johnson* v. *Trader*, 52 So. 2d 333 (Fla. 1951).

171. Richard N. Williams, "Legal Aspects of Discipline by Police Administrators," Traffic Institute Publication No. 2705 (Evanston, Ill.: Northwestern University, 1975), p. 4.
172. *City of Crowley Firemen* v. *City of Crowley*, 264 So. 2d 368 (La. 1972).
173. See *Rojas* v. *Alexander's Department Store, Inc.*, 654 F.Supp. 856 (1986), and *Reagan* v. *Hampton*, 700 F.Supp. 850 (1988).
174. *Lally* v. *Department of Police*, 306 So. 2d 65 (La. 1974).
175. See, for example, *Peters* v. *Civil Service Commission of Tucson*, 559 P.2d 698 (Ariz. 1977); *Abeyta* v. *Town of Toas*, 499 F.2d 323 (10th Cir. 1974); *Baumbartner* v. *Leary*, 311 N.Y.S. 2d 468 (1970); *City of Vancouver* v. *Jarvis*, 455 P.2d 591 (Wash. 1969). But compare *Thompson* v. *Lent*, 383 N.Y.S. 2d 929 (1976), and *Glover* v. *Murphy*, 343 N.Y.S. 2d 746 (1973).
176. *Glover* v. *Murphy*, Compare *Taylor* v. *Police Board of Chicago*, 378 N.E.2d 1160 (Ill. 1978).
177. *Peters* v. *Civil Service Commission of Tucson* contains a portion of such a regulation that illustrates this point. See Lay Gerald Safer, "Deadly Weapons in the Hands of Police Officers, On Duty and Off Duty," *Journal of Urban Law*, 49 (1971), p. 565, for a good discussion of possible statutory approaches to the question of when police officers should be permitted to use deadly force.
178. *Chastain* v. *Civil Service Board of Orlando*, 327 So. 2d 230 (1976), p. 232.
179. Barrineau, *Civil Liability*, p. 83.
180. See *Brown* v. *City of Clewiston, Florida*, 848 F.2d 1534 (1988);' *Tennessee* v. *Garner*, 471 U.S. 1, 105 (1985); and *Monell* v. *New York City Department of Social Services*, 436 U.S. 658 (1978).
181. See *Popow* v. *city of Margate*, 476 F.Supp. 1237 (1979); *Billings* v. *Vernal City*, U.S. District Court of Utah C77-0295 (1982); *Sager* v. *City of Woodlawn Park*, 543 F.Supp. 282 (1982); *Labb* v. *Labb*, 679 F.Supp, 508 (1988); and *City of Canton* v. *Harris*, 109 S.Ct. 1197 (1989).
182. Barrineau, *Civil Liability*, p. 84.
183. The cases and/or suits against police officers and agencies involving improper use of handcuffs, police batons, flashlights, stun guns, tear gas, and restraint/choke holds that have resulted in plaintiffs' serious injury or death are too numerous to list. For a cursory examination of the subject matter, see Silver, *Police Civil Litigation*, Section 8.
184. *Reich* v. *Board of Fire and Police Commissioners*, 301 N.E.2d 501 (Ill. 1973).
185. *Krolick* v. *Lowery*, 302 N.Y.S. 2d 109 (1969), p. 115, *Hester* v. *Milledgeville*, 598 F.Supp. 1456, 1457, n2 (M.D. Ga. 1984).
186. *McCracken* v. *Department of Police*, 337 So. 2d 595 (La. 1976).
187. *Krolick* v. *Lowery*.
188. *United States* v. *Jacobsen*, 466 U.S. 109 (1984).
189. *National Federation of Federal Employees* v. *Weinberger*, 818 F.2d 935 (1987). See also related cases *National Treasury Employees Union* v. *Von Raab*, 816 F.2d 170 (1987), and *Lovvorn* v. *City of Chattanooga, Tennessee*, 846 F.2d 1539 (1988).
190. *O'Connor* v. *Ortega*, 480 U.S. 709 (1988).
191. *Lovvorn* v. *City of Chattanooga, supra*.
192. See *Capua* v. *City of Plainfield*, 643 F.Supp. 1507 (1986), *Fraternal Order of Police* v. *Newark, New Jersey*, 524 A.2d 430 (1987), and *Taylor* v. *O'Grady*, 669 F.Supp. 1422 (1987).
193. *City of Palm Bay* v. *Bauman*, 475 So. 2d 1322 (Fla. 5th DCA 1985).
194. *Walters* v. *Secretary of Defense*, 725 F.2d 107 (D.C. Cir. 1983).

195. *Security of Law Enforcement Employees, District Counsel 82* v. *Carly*, 737 F.2d 187 (2d Cir. 1984); *Division 241 Amalgamated Transit Union* v. *Suscy*, 538 F.2d 1264 (7th Cir. 1976) *cert. den*, 429 (U.S. 1029 (1976); *McDonnell* v. *Hunter*, 612 F.Supp. 1122 (S.D. Iowa 1984), aff'd 746 F.2d 785 (8th Cir. 1984).
196. *National League of Cities* v. *Usery*, 526 U.S. 833 (1976).
197. *Garcia* v. *San Antonio Transit*, 105 S.Ct. 1005 (1985).
198. *Massachusetts Board of Retirement* v. *Murgia*, 427 U.S. 307 (1976).
199. 29 U.S.C. 623(f).
200. *Western Airlines* v. *Criswell*, 105 S.Ct. 2743, 2751 (1985), and *Dothard* v. *Rawlinson*, 433 U.S. 321, 329 (1977).
201. *Usery* v. *Tamiami Trail Tours, Inc.*, 531 F.2d 224 (5th Cir. 1976).
202. *Johnson* v. *Mayor and City Council of Baltimore*, 105 S.Ct. 2717, 2722 (1985).
203. *Hahn* v. *City of Buffalo*, 770 F.2d 12 (2d Cir. 1985).
204. Jeffrey Higgenbotham, "Sexual Harassment in the Police Station," *FBI Law Enforcement Bulletin*, 57 (September 1988), pp. 22–28. This discussion of sexual harassment was adapted from this article.
205. 42 U.S.C. S2000e-2(a)(1) makes it "an unlawful employment practice for an employer . . . to discriminate against any individual with respect to his compensation, terms, conditions, or privileges of employment, because of such individual's . . . sex."
206. See, e.g., 41 U.S.C. SS2000e-5 and 2000e-6.
207. 29 C.F.R. S1604.11 (1987).
208. *General Electric Co.* v. *Gilbert*, 429 U.S. 125, 141–42 (1976).
209. 29 C.F.R. S1604.11(a).
210. *Katz* v. *Dole*, 709 F.2d 251 (4th Cir. 1983).
211. *Henson* v. *City of Dundee*, 681 F.2d 897 (11th Cir. 1982). See also *Vermett* v. *Hough*, 627 F.Supp. 587 (W.D. Mich. 1986).
212. *Supra* note 1. See also U.S. Constitution, Amendment 14.
213. *Henson* v. *City of Dundee, supra* note 7, at 902.
214. 682 F.2d 897 (11th Cir. 1982).
215. *Id.* at 903.
216. 106 S.Ct. 2399 (1986).
217. *Id.* at 2406.
218. *Id.*
219. *Moylan* v. *Maries County*, 792 F.2d 746 (8th Cir. 1986).
220. *Meritor Savings Bank* v. *Vinson*, 106 S.Ct. 2399, 2406 (1986).
221. *Id.*
222. *Id.* at 2407.
223. The Supreme Court noted that a trial court must exercise its discretion to decide whether the relevance of the evidence is outweighed by the danger of unfair prejudice, but may not establish a *per se* rule excluding such evidence. *Id.*
224. See *Loftin-Boggs* v. *City of Meridian*, 633 F.Supp. 1323 (S.D. Miss. 1986), aff'd, 824 F.2d 921 (5th Cir. 1987), *cert den*, 108 S.Ct. 1021 (1988).
225. *Laudenslager* v. *Covert*, 45 F.E.P. Cas. 907 (Mich. Ct. App. 1987).
226. *Highlander* v. *K.F.C. National Management Co.*, 805 F.2d 644 (6th Cir. 1986).
227. See *Silverstein* v. *Metroplex Communications*, 678 F.Supp. 863 (S.D. Fla. 1988); *Neville* v. *Taft Broadcasting Co.*, 42 F.E.P. Cas. 1314 (W.D.N.Y. 1987). However, in *Meritor Savings Bank* v. *Vinson, supra* note 12, the Supreme Court refused to hold that the failure of an employee to use an employer's grievance procedure automatically insulated the employer from liability. That issue was "plainly relevant" but not conclusive. 106 S.Ct. at 2409.
228. *Rabidue* v. *Osceola Refining Co.*, 805 F.2d 611 (6th Cir. 1986); see also 29 C.F.R. S1604.11(b).
229. See, e.g., *Henson* v. *City of Dundee, supra* note 7. See also *Bohen* v. *City of East*

Chicago, Ind., 799 F.2d 1180 (7th Cir. 1986) (conduct equally offensive to men and women is not a violation of equal protection).

230. *Henson* v. *City of Dundee*, *supra* note 7, at 903.
231. *Id.* at 904.
232. 842 F.2d 1010 (8th Cir. 1988).
233. *Id.* at 1014.
234. *Vermett* v. *Hough*, 627 F.Supp. 587 (W.D. Mich. 1986).
235. 42 U.S.C. S2000e-2(a)(1).
236. See *Meritor Savings Banks* v. *Vinson*, 106 S.Ct. 2399, 2404 (1986). The existence of a tangible effect on a condition of employment is inconsequential. No economic or tangible job detriment need be suffered.
237. *Rogers* v. *EEOC*, 454 F.2d 234 (5th Cir. 1971), *cert den*, 406 U.S. 957 (1972); *Meritor Savings Bank* v. *Vinson*, 106 S.Ct. 2399, 2405, (1986). See also *Broderick* v. *Ruder*, 685 F.Supp. 1269 (D.D.C. 5/13/88) (sexual activities in the workplace between other employees can affect the psychological well-being of an employee and create a hostile environment).
238. *Meritor Savings Bank* v. *Vinson*, 106 S.Ct. at 2404 (citations omitted).
239. *Id.* at 2406.
240. See *Fontanez* v. *Aponte*, 660 F.Supp. 145 (D. Puerto Rico 1987); *Sapp* v. *City of Warner Robins*, 655 F.Supp. 1043 (M.D. Georgia 1987); *Strickland* v. *Sears, Roebuck & Co.*, 46 F.E.P. Cas. 1024 (E.D. Va. 1987); *Petrosky* v. *Washington-Greene County Branch*, 45 F.E.P. Cas. 673 (W.D. Pa. 1987).
241. Se *Moylan* v. *Maries County*, *supra* note 15; *Katz* v. *Dole*, *supra* note 6.
242. See, e.g., *Arnold* v. *City of Seminole*, 614 F.Supp. 853 (E.D. Oklahoma 354-18 1985). See also discussion at footnote 48 and accompanying text, *infra*.
243. See *Lake* v. *Baker*, 662 F.Supp. 392 (D.D.C. 1987).
244. 627 F.Supp. 587 (W.D. Michigan).
245. *Id.* at 599.
246. 614 F.Supp. 853 (E.D. Oklahoma 1985).
247. *Porta* v. *Rollins Environmental Services*, 654 F.Supp. 1275 (D.N.J. 1987), aff'd, 845 F.2d 1014 (3d Cir. 1988).
248. *DelGado* v. *Lehman*, 665 F.Supp. 460 (E.D. Va. 1987).
249. See *Arnold* v. *City of Seminole*, 614 F.Supp. 853, 872 (E.D. Oklahoma 1985). See also 29 C.F.R. S1604.11(f).
250. *Supra* note 12.
251. 106 S.Ct. at 2408.
252. *Henson* v. *City of Dundee*, 682 F.2d 897, 910 (11th Cir. 1982).
253. *Katz* v. *Dole*, 709 F.2d 251, 255 (4th Cir. 1983) (emphasis added).
254. *Id.* at 255.
255. *Hall* v. *Gus Construction Co.*, 842 F.2d 1010, 1016 (8th Cir. 1988).
256. *Sapp* v. *City of Warner Robins*, 655 F.Supp. 1043, 1050 (M.D. Ga. 1987). See also *Hall* v. *Gus Construction Co.*, *supra* note 51, at 1016.
257. See, e.g., *Arnold* v. *City of Seminole*, *supra* note 42; *Hall* v. *Gus Construction Co.*, *supra* note 51; *Henson* v. *City of Dundee*, *supra* note 10.
258. *Meritor Savings Bank* v. *Vinson*, *supra* note 12, at 2408.
259. See 42 U.S.C. S2000e-5(g).
260. See, e.g., *Arnold* v. *City of Seminole* 614 F.Supp. 853, 871 (E.D. Oklahoma 1985).
261. See, e.g., *Johnson* v. *Ballard*, 644 F.Supp. 333 (N.D. Ga. 1986); *Bohen* v. *City of East Chicago, Ind.*, *supra* note 25; *Brown* v. *Town of Allenstown*, 648 F.Supp. 831 (D.N.H. 1986); *Hunt* v. *Weatherbee*, 626 F.Supp. 1097 (D. Mass. 1986).
262. See, e.g., *Brown* v. *Town of Allentown*, *supra* note 57; *Priest* v. *Rotary*, 634 F.Supp. 571 (N.D. Cal. 1986); *Owens* v. *Tumage*, 46 F.E.P. Cas. 528 (D.N.J. 1988).
263. See, e.g., *Sapp* v. *City of Warner Robins*, *supra* note 52; *Strickland* v. *Sears, Roebuck*

& Co., 46 F.E.P. Cas. 1024 (E.D. Va. 1987); *Smemo-Rosenquist* v. *Meredith Corp.*, 46 F.E.P. Cas. 531 (D. Ariz. 1988).

264. *Meritor Savings Bank* v. *Vinson*, 106 S.Ct. 2399, 2408 (1986). See also *Vermett* v. *Hough*, *supra* note 7; *Katz* v. *Dole*, *supra* note 6.

265. The co-authors of this chapter in the first two editions have extensive legal experience. Donald D. Slesnick II practices public sector labor and employment law in Miami, Florida. His clients include fifteen police personnel collective bargaining units. Before entering private practice a decade ago, he served as director of Personnel and Labor Relations of the Metro-Dade County Public Safety Department, director of Employment Relations and Legislative Affairs of the Dade County School Board, and general labor counsel of the Florida Police Benevolent Association. Slesnick is a past chairman of the Florida Bar Labor and Employment Relations Law Committee, and is currently the co-chairman of the American Bar Association's State and Local Government Collective Bargaining Committee. Janet E. Ferris currently serves as general counsel of the Florida Department of Law Enforcement, a post she has held since 1982. Previously, she was an assistant state attorney in Broward County, Florida, and an assistant attorney general of the State of Florida. After assisting the state legislature in the composition of the Racketeer Influenced and Corrupt Organizations (RICO) Act, she was appointed as the first chief of the attorney general's civil RICO section. Ms. Ferris is a regular lecturer to various professional law enforcement and legal associations and at the Organized Crime Institute.

11 Planning and Decision Making

People who rise in management are expected with each successive promotion to concern themselves with events further in the future.
ALVIN TOFFLER

Introduction

Decision making is a complex process that includes not only procedures for reaching a sound decision on the basis of pertinent knowledge, beliefs, and judgments but also procedures for obtaining the required knowledge, ideas, and preconditions. Moreover, in the case of important decisions, these procedures may involve many minor decisions taken at various stages in the decision-making process. For example, a chief's decision to automate the records division by purchasing a computer and software usually follows a series of decisions. First, the chief decides that the present manual system is not adequate. Second, a decision is made to evaluate the number of systems available on the open market. This decision probably accompanied the decision to address the city council for additional funding with which to purchase the necessary equipment. And finally, the chief resolves that records division personnel must be retrained to operate in an automated system. These minor decisions were only part of the overall process in arriving at a major decision. Thus, the decision to take a certain action, if sound, should be based on the judgment that this action probably will have more desirable results than any other action, and this judgment may be based on conclusions as to the probable consequences of alternative decisions.[1]

Decision making also involves the application of our knowledge, our experience, and our mental and moral skills and powers to determine what actions should be taken to deal with a variety of problem situations. Moreover, this decision-making process includes the application of logic for testing conclusions and the use of ethics for testing judgments.[2] For instance, an individual officer's decision to arrest a violent, drunk husband at a family disturbance will usually be based on the officer's past knowledge that if the current situation is left unattended, the probable result will be a criminal act involving assault, wife or child abuse, or even murder. Ethically, the officer is bound to deter crime and as such will take the necessary course of action to prevent the physical harm of any family member.

Decision making is a responsibility that all police officers come to accept routinely. These decisions may be as ordinary as deciding whether to write a motorist a traffic citation or as complex as a split-second decision whether to shoot at someone. The quality and types of decisions made by police managers in their policy formulation and by the street-level officer in invoking arrest action will be based, in part, on the personality characteristics of the individual making the decision, the recruiting and career development practices of the police department, and, equally important, the type of community being served. For example, one merely has to read the works of Wilson[3] and Skolnick[4] to conclude that enforcement decisions that appear to be quite adequate for one community may be totally unacceptable for another; that recruitment practices that would be acceptable to one community would be objected to by another. Thus, there is no single model that police administration can follow to make the best decisions all the time. However, certain principles, when understood and applied carefully, can result in good decisions being made much of the time. Although sometimes not understood as such, planning is basically part of the decision-making process, and as such will be treated accordingly.

Planning

Police administrators sometimes do not appreciate the importance of planning because of their pattern of career development. It is ironic that the pattern of career development for typical police managers carries with it seeds that sometimes blossom into a negative view of planning. Having spent substantial portions of their careers in line divisions, such as patrol and investigative services, police managers may see planning as "clerical" or "not real police work." Further, because many agencies have a "planning and research" unit, there is a natural tendency to believe that planning should occur only in that area by individuals assigned to that task. However, planning is an integral element of good management and good decision making.[5] Management needs to anticipate and shape events; it is weak if it merely responds to them.[6] The police manager whose time is consumed by dealing with crises is symptomatic of a department with no real planning or decision-making process. Police departments are sometimes said to be practicing "management by crisis"; in fact, it is "crisis by management"[7] That is, the lack of attention given by police managers to planning creates an environment in which crises are going to occur with regularity. This is so because management by crisis produces a present-centered orientation in which considerations of the future are minimal. In contrast, planning can be expected to

1. Improve analysis of problems
2. Provide better information for decision making
3. Help to clarify goals, objectives, and priorities
4. Result in more effective allocation of resources
5. Improve inter- and intradepartmental cooperation and coordination

6. Improve the performance of programs
7. Give the police department a clear sense of direction
8. Provide the opportunity for greater public support
9. Increase the commitment of personnel.

In short, competent planning is a sure sign of good police administration and the first step in accurate decision making.[8]

Definitions of Planning

There are no simple definitions of planning. The word *planning* became common terminology in the vocabulary of criminal justice, with the introduction of the Omnibus Crime Control and Safe Streets Act of 1968. However, what appeared to be missing in that now-famous document was an examination of what planning actually involved, or what it meant in the operation of criminal justice organizations. Hudzik and Cordner[9] have defined planning as "thinking about the future, thinking about what we want the future to be, and thinking about what we need to do now to achieve it." Stated more succinctly, planning involves linking present actions to future conditions. Planning is defined by Mottley as

> A management function concerned with visualizing future situations, making estimates concerning them, identifying the issues, needs and potential danger points, analyzing and evaluating the alternative ways and means for reaching desired goals according to a certain schedule, estimating the necessary funds and resources to do the work, and initiating action in time to prepare what may be needed to cope with changing conditions and contingent events.[10]

There is also the assumption that planning is oriented toward action, which means that thinking is only a part of planning; the real purpose is determining what an organization should do, and then doing it. And finally, planning is associated with empirical rationalism: planners gather and analyze data and then reach an objective conclusion.

Planning Approaches

A variety of approaches are employed in the planning processes. Each is unique and can be understood as a *method* of operationalizing the word *planning*. There are basically five major approaches to planning: (1) synoptic, (2) incremental, (3) transactive, (4) advocacy, and (5) radical.

Synoptic Planning

Synoptic planning or the rational-comprehensive approach is the dominant tradition in planning. It is also the point of departure for most other planning approaches, which, in general, are either modifications of synoptic planning or reactions against it. Figure 11-1 represents the typical synoptic model. It is based on "pure" or "objective" rationality and attempts to assure optimal achievement of desired goals from a given situation.[11] This model is especially appropriate for police agencies as it is based on a problem-oriented approach to planning. It relies heavily on the problem identification and analysis phase of the planning process and can assist police administrators in formulating goals and priorities in terms that are focused on specific problems and solutions that often confront law enforcement. For instance, police administrators are more apt to appreciate a planning model centered around problem-oriented goals and priorities (such as the reduction of burglaries in a given residential area) than around more abstract notions (such as the reduction of crime and delinquency).[12] Then, too, police departments are designed for response, and it is easier to mobilize individual officers and gain cooperation between police units if concrete goals and objectives are set in reaction to a given problem.

Synoptic planning consists of 11 progressive steps. Each step is designed to provide the police manager with a logical course of action:[13]

Prepare for Planning

Hudzik and Cordner[14] point out that the most important aspect of planning is that it takes place in advance of action. Therefore, the task of planning should be a detailed work chart that specifies (1) what events and actions are necessary, (2) when they must take place, (3) who is to be involved in each action and for how long, and (4) how the various actions will interlock with one another.[15]

Police managers need to understand that when a course of action and its con-

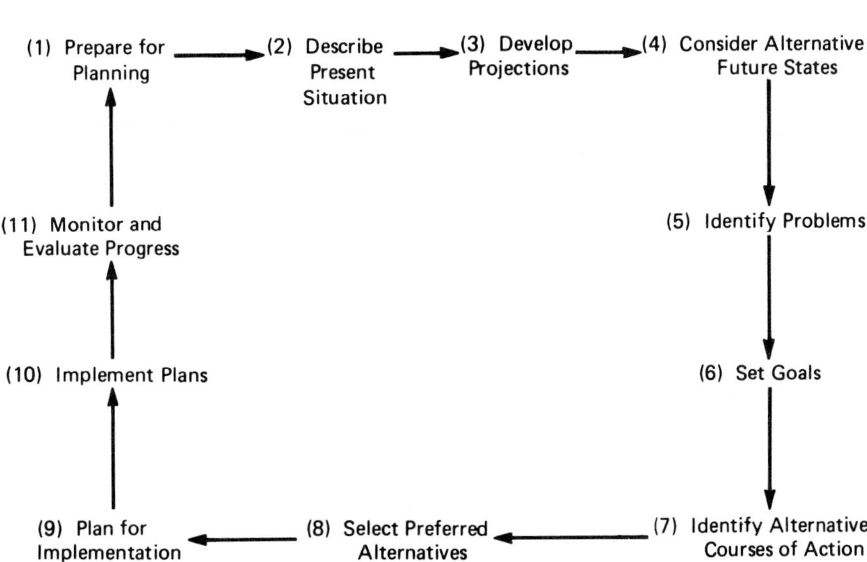

FIGURE 11-1. The synoptic or traditional planning model. [From Robert Cushman, *Criminal Justice Planning for Local Governments* (Washington, D.C.: U.S. Government Printing Office, 1980), p. 26, with minor modification.]

sequence seem "patently clear," a grand planning event may be unnecessary and inefficient. However, when consequences are not clear, or when undiscovered courses of action may be better, the value of planning increases greatly.[16] This assumes that decision making is ongoing and that planning attempts to predict or at least partially control the future.[17] Police managers, then, must be prepared to address the vast array of possibilities that may arise from a given course of action. It is during this stage that the police chief organizes the planning effort with a central theme—what are we trying to accomplish and what type of information is required to understand the problem?

Describe the Present Situation

This step is often forgotten or overlooked by police administrators because of the desire to immediately eliminate the problem. Planning must have a means for evaluation, and without an accurate beginning data base there is no reference point on which to formulate success or failure. Weiss[18] states that a primary purpose of planning is in evaluation, or comparing "what is" with "what should be." To this end, police chiefs following this model must describe the current situation; describe crime and criminal justice system functions (What exactly do police, courts, and corrections do?); and analyze community characteristics associated with crime (Is the community conservative or liberal? Does any religious or political agenda affect the situation?).

Develop Projections and Consider Alternative Future States

Projections should be written with an attempt to link the current situation with the future, keeping in mind the desirable outcomes. One projection should at least dwell on the status quo. What will happen if the police do nothing? In some instances, it may be best to eliminate police presence. For example, a police chief may decide that the best course of action is to reduce police visibility. This tactic has been successful where a high probability for violence between a group of people and the police exists—such as rock concerts, outlaw biker parades, and demonstrations. It is important for the police executive to project the current situation into the future to determine possible, probable, and desirable future states while considering the social, legislative, and political trends existing in the community. What may work in one city may not work in another. For instance, a parade of gay activists marching in San Francisco may be a somewhat common occurrence, whereas the same type of activity in another city may be received differently.

Identify and Analyze Problems

The discovery of problems assumes that a system to monitor and evaluate the current arena is already in place. The final step in the synoptic model addresses this concern. However, closely related to the detection and identification of issues is the ability of the police manager to define the nature of the problem; that is, to be able to describe the magnitude, cause, duration, and expense of the issues at hand. This provides a clear conceptual picture of the present conditions confronting the chief in which to develop means for dealing with the problem. It is here that the chief develops a detailed understanding of the problem and ensuing issues. At this point, the planning process allows for estimations of the gap between the probable future and desired outcomes—or how serious and complex the problem really is. A complete understanding of the problem leads to the development of means to deal with the issues.

Set Goals

A goal is an achievable end state that can be measured and observed. Making choices about goals is one of the most important aspects of planning.[19] However, without the previous steps, goal setting has little meaning. It makes no sense to establish a goal that does not address a specific problem. Remembering that police departments are "problem-oriented," choices about goals and objectives should adhere to the synoptic model.

Hudzik and Cordner point out that several kinds of choices must be made concerning goals:

> Several kinds of choices must be made. First, choices must be made about preferred states or goals. An important and sometimes ignored aspect of this choice involves the choice of the criteria for measuring goal attainment. This is often hard, much harder than setting the goal itself. For example, the goal of a juvenile treatment program may be to reduce recidivism among those treated. Yet, in measuring goal attainment several questions arise. First, what constitutes recidivism? Technical or status violation? Arrest for criminal violation? Conviction on a criminal violation, and only for those crimes against which the juvenile program may have been directed? Also, over how long a period will recidivism be monitored? A year? Two years? Five years? Ten Years? It is not that those questions cannot be answered, but securing agreement on the appropriate criteria becomes a major difficulty.[20]

The following steps attempt to link set goals with desired outcomes through the establishment of specific means.

Identify Alternative Courses of Action

Alternatives are means by which goals and objectives can be attained. They may be policies, strategies, or specific actions aimed at eliminating a problem. Alternatives do not have to be substitutes for one another or perform the same function. For instance, improving officer-survival skills through training, modifying police vehicles, issuing bulletproof vests, utilizing a computer-assisted dispatch program, and increasing first-line supervision may all be alternatives in promoting officer safety.

It is important that the activities (the means) that a police department engages in actually do contribute to the achievement of goals (the ends). If the means are not connected to the ends, then a police agency could expend a great deal of resources in activities that keep personnel busy, but do not contribute to fulfilling key objectives or responsibilities.

Means-Ends Analysis. Depicted in Figure 11-2 is a means-ends analysis chart. This is one method of trying to ensure that the police department's programmatic efforts and expenditures do make an appropriate contribution toward arriving at the desired state. Means-ends analysis charting is also a very effective method in which alternatives can be identified in the planning process.

The following procedure is used to develop a means-ends analysis chart:

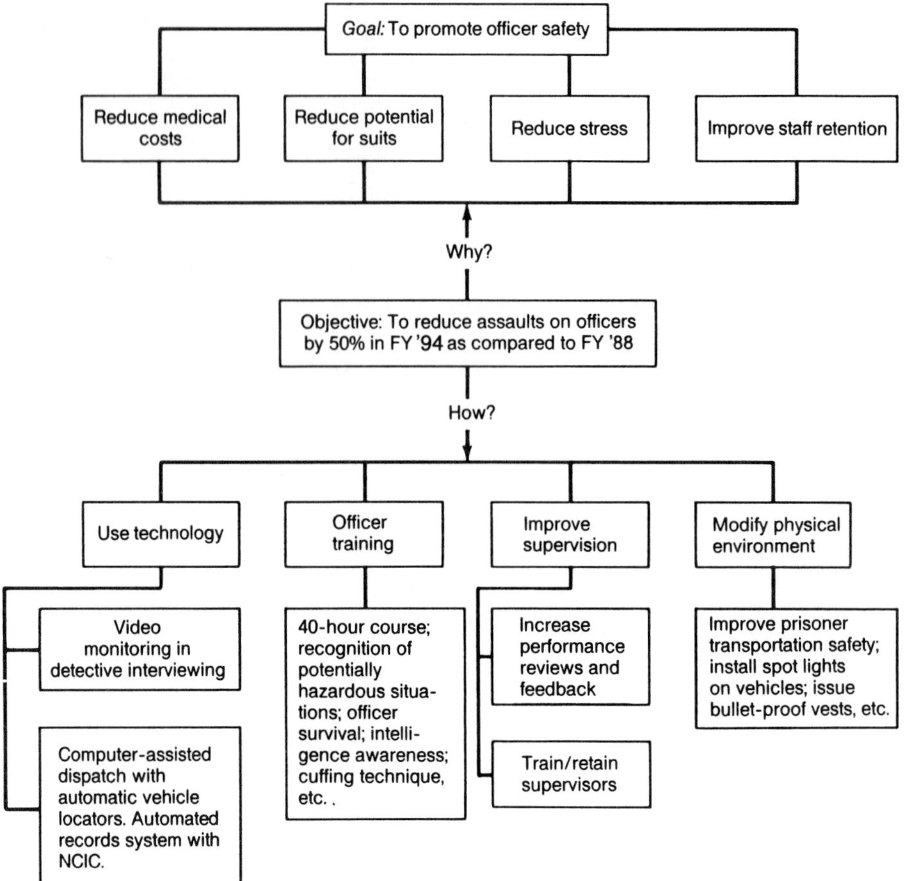

FIGURE 11-2. Means-ends analysis chart.

1. At the center of a page, state the objective you are trying to achieve. In the case of Figure 11-2, this is stated as "to reduce assaults on officers by 50 percent in fiscal year (FY) 1994 as compared to fiscal year 1993." Note that an objective differs from a goal in that an objective can be achieved within one year.
2. Identify the "whys" of trying to attain the objective. Place these statements above the objective on the work page. Figure 11-2 identifies four such "whys," namely reduce medical costs, reduce potential for civil suits, reduce officer stress, and improve officer retention.
3. Identify and select the "hows" to obtain the objective. Referring again to Figure 11-2, four major "hows" or means are specified: use technology, increase officer training, improve supervision, and modify the physical environment.

The police manager should realize that the means-end analysis chart does not select alternatives; that is discussed in the following step of the synoptic planning model. However, means-ends analysis is an excellent method of brainstorming that assists the police chief in identifying alternative courses of action designed to achieve specific goals and objectives.[21]

Select Preferred Alternatives

The selection process for deriving a preferred course of action or alternative is often fraught with complexity. The issue has been researched for several decades by scholars in business management, public administration, systems science, and criminal justice in order to assist decision makers in this process. Three basic techniques to select alternatives are discussed here: (1) strategic analysis, (2) cost-effectiveness analysis, and (3) must-wants analysis.

Strategic Analysis. The first study addressing the selection of preferred courses of action originated at the U.S. Naval War College in 1936 and has been popular in police management circles.[22] Since that time, the model has been refined into a more systematic and objective treatment.[23] The process is shown as a diagram in Figure 11-3. In order to visualize how the technique can be applied and selections made, it will be helpful to use an example currently confronting law enforcement managers, for example, the issue of automating a records division with particular reference to the improvement of officer-generated reports by use of lap computers.

Given a set of possible alternatives or courses of action, the number of alternatives can be reduced in the following ways:

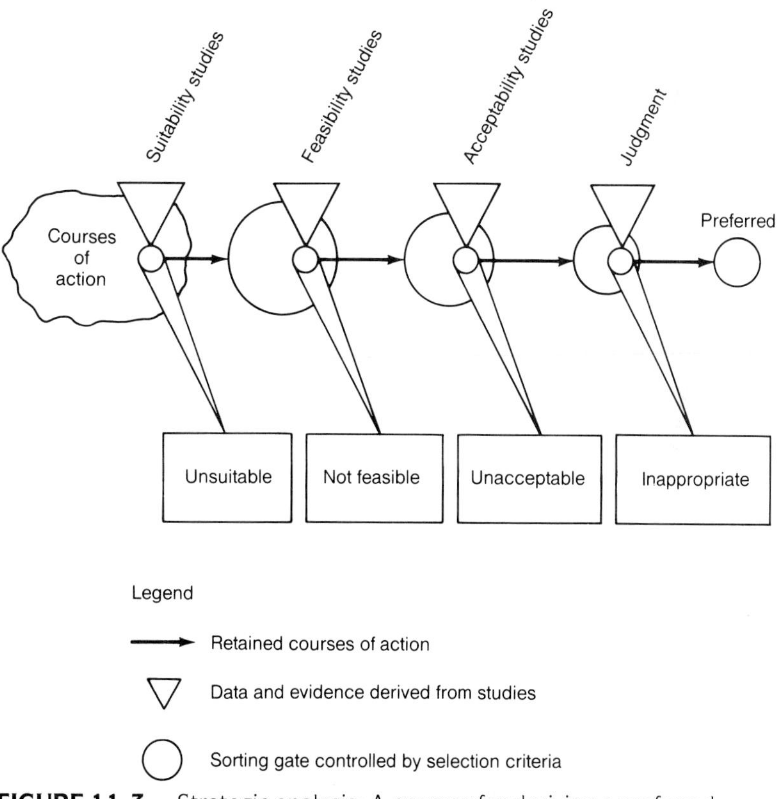

FIGURE 11-3. Strategic analysis: A process for deriving a preferred course of action. [*Source:* C. M. Mottley, "Strategic Planning," *Management Highlights,* 56, September 1967.]

First, through making suitability studies of all alternatives. That is, each course of action is evaluated in accordance with general policies, rules, and laws. For example, in some jurisdictions it is illegal to maintain an automated records system that contains arrest and conviction data of juveniles in order to safeguard the juvenile's reputation. A manual records system is deemed more secure because access can be totally controlled.

Second, the retained and suitable alternatives are subjected to feasibility studies. These include the appraisal of the effects of a number of factors weighed separately and together. Continuing with the example, the feasibility of an automated records system would be judged on the basis of meeting (1) the existing standards of operation (e.g., Will an automated records system do everything the manual system can do?); (2) the conditions of the operational environment (e.g., Is the police department facility large enough to accommodate a computer? Is it air-conditioned? Does it have proper electrical outlets?); (3) the restrictions imposed by the state of the art (e.g., Is the desired software compatible with the existing computer system?); and (4) limitations on the resources available (e.g., Is the cost for an automated records system beyond police funding approval? Can the records division personnel be retrained and how much will that cost?).

Third, the retained courses of actions (those judged to be suitable and feasible) are then analyzed in acceptability studies. Four principal factors are combined and enter into this evaluation: (1) the cost of each alternative, (2) the performance, (3) the effect of the alternative on the entire system, and (4) the time involved in implementation and setup. These factors are applied to each alternative to reveal critical limits and trade-offs. Finally, a judgment is rendered that selects the preferred course of action.

Cost-Effectiveness Analysis. This technique is sometimes called cost-benefit or cost-performance analysis. The purpose of this form of selection is that the alternative chosen should maximize the ratio of benefit to cost. The concept is based on economic rationalism: calculations are made "scientifically" through the collection of data and the use of models in an attempt to maximize benefits and minimize costs. A model is a simplified representation of the real world that abstracts the cause-and-effect relationships that are essential to each course of action or alternative.[24] Using the example of automating a records division, each course of action would be analyzed in an attempt to compare the cost in dollars of each segment of the system (mainframe, software, lap computers) with the benefits (increased officer safety, more efficient crime analysis, and subsequent apprehension that diminishes property loss and injury). In the analysis of choice the role of the model (or models, for it may be inappropriate or absurd to attempt to incorporate all the aspects of a problem into a single formulation) is to estimate for each alternative (or course of action) the costs that would be incurred and the extent to which the objectives would be attained.[25] The model may be as complex as a set of mathematical equations to a purely verbal description of the situation, in which intuition alone is used to predict the outcomes of various alternatives. Figure 11-4 is the structure of cost-effectiveness analysis.

It is important to note that each alternative is weighed against a criterion: the rule or standard by which to rank the alternatives in order of desirability. This provides a means to analyze cost against effectiveness.[26] Unlike strategic analysis, alternatives are not dismissed from the process but ranked in order of preference.

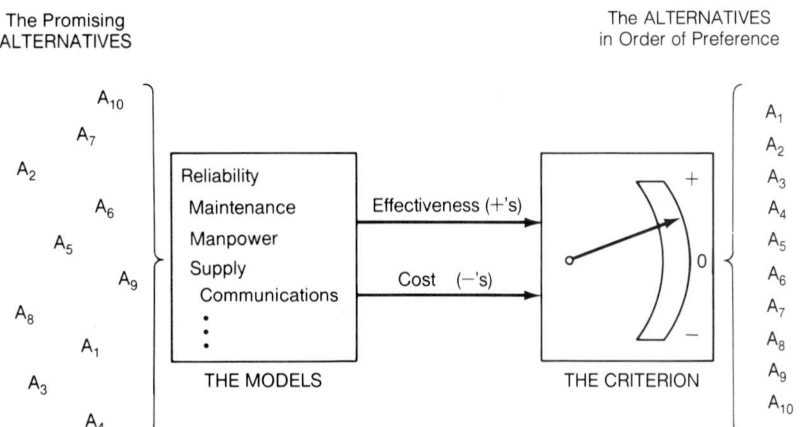

FIGURE 11-4. The structure of cost-effectiveness analysis. [*Source:* E. S. Quade, "Systems Analysis Techniques for Planning-Programming-Budgeting," in F. J. Lyden and E. G. Miller, *Planning, Programming, Budgeting: A Systems Approach to Management* (Chicago, Ill.: Markham, 1972), p. 250.]

Must-Wants Analysis This method of selecting a preferred course of action combines the strengths of both strategic and cost-effectiveness analyses. Must-wants analysis is concerned with both the subjective weights of suitability, feasibility, and acceptability as well as the objective weights of costs versus benefits.

In this method of selection a "must-wants chart" is developed to assist the police administrator. Returning to the example of automating a records division and improving officer-generated reports by the use of laptop computers. Figure 11-5 provides a chart for evaluating three alternative brand-name laptop computers, namely the Compaq SLT 386s/20, the Zenith TurbosPort 386e, and the Toshiba T3100SX.

The must-wants chart is constructed in the following manner:

1. "Musts" are placed at the top of the page. These are conditions that are set by the police chief and that absolutely have to be met in order for an alternative (in this case a specific laptop computer) to continue to be a viable choice. Failure of any alternative to meet a must condition immediately eliminates it from further consideration. In Figure 11-5, note that Alternative B, the Zenith TurbosPort 386e, did not conform to the must of having a minimum expandable random access memory (RAM) exceeding four megabytes (MB) and was eliminated.
2. "Wants" are conditions, performances, characteristics, or features that are desirable but not absolutely necessary. They are listed below the musts and the corresponding data for each want are completed for each alternative that was not discarded at the previous step.
3. Weight (the column marked "wt." in Figure 11-5) reflects the subjective importance of the want as determined by the police chief. Weight has a scale of 1 (lowest) to 10 (highest).
4. Score (the column marked "sc." in Figure 11-5) is the evaluation of the actual existence of wants by the chief. A scale of 1 to 10 is also used in this column. The score is set by the administrator to reflect an assessment of the subjective or actual existence of the

MUSTS	Alternative A: Compag SLT 386s/20	Alternative B: Zenith TurbosPort 386e	Alternative C: Toshiba T3100SX
Total purchase price not to exceed $7,500.	$6,799	$7,483	$6,998
Maintenance contract not to exceed $500/yr.	yes	yes	yes
Minimum 80386 processing	yes	yes	yes
Minimum 40 MB hard disk	yes	yes	yes
Minimum random access memory (RAM) expandale to over 4MB	yes	NO NO GO	yes
Receivable within 30 days	yes		yes
Local area dealership within 20 miles of police department	yes		yes

WANTS	wt.		sc.	wt × sc.		sc.	wt × sc.
Minimum total price	7	$6,799	8	56	$6,998	6	42
Lowest maintenance contract per year	4	$450	7	28	$490	5	20
High microprocessing speed	7	20 MHz	8	56	16 MHz	6	42
High random access memory (RAM) capacity	8	14 MB	9	72	13 MB	8	64
High installed RAM	6	6 MB	9	56	3 MB	5	30
No wait states	5	0	10	50	1	7	35
High hard disk capacity (options)	6	120 MB	6	36	80 MB	4	24
Excellent keyboard functioning/response	9	very good	7	63	excellent	9	81
Good keyboard layout	4	very good	8	32	excellent	9	36
Large, well-defined keys	7	good	6	42	very good	8	56
Excellent screen visibility with high resolution mode (VGA)	10	twisted LCD	10	100	gas plasma	8	80
Good graphics capability	2	good	6	12	good	6	12
Standard 3.5″ diskette drive	8	yes	5	40	yes	5	40
Internal modem option based on price	3	$599 extra	3	9	$349 extra	7	21
Included software (DOS 4.01)	3	no	2	6	yes/plus	10	30
IBM compatible	10	yes	5	50	yes	5	50
Lightweight	4	13.8 lbs.	7	28	14.6 lbs.	5	20
Durable and long-wearing cover	5	yes	7	35	yes	8	30
Performance total, wants objectives				771			723

FIGURE 11-5. Must-wants chart for selecting a laptop computer. [*Source*: "Power Portables: The Next Wave," *PC Magazine,* 9 (October 16, 1990), pp. 99–176. The "results" in the illustration of must-wants analysis are hypothetical and should not be used as a basis of action.]

want. In this example, the want of "excellent screen visibility with high resolution" is a subjective evaluation, while "IBM compatible" can be objectively determined. In general, the scoring of wants should be based on a limited number of factors because too many could distort the choice of an option.

5. The weight and score for each want are multiplied (wt. × sc. in Figure 11-5) and summed. The sum of each wt. × sc. column is called the performance total for wants objectives.
6. The second part of the must-wants chart, shown in Figure 11-6, is called the "possible adverse consequences worksheet." On this worksheet, statements concerning possible detriments or negative outcomes are listed for each alternative. The probability and seriousness of each comment is subjectively scored. The probability of an adverse consequence happening is scored on a scale from 1 (very unlikely) to 10 (certain to happen). Seriousness is scored on the same type of scale, with 1 representing "extremely unserious" and 10 denoting "'very serious." The final scores are summed and used in the last choice, the selection step.
7. Some advocates of using the must-wants chart recommend that the totals of the possible adverse consequences worksheet be considered only advisory, whereas others recommend that the performance totals for each alternative be mathematically reduced by the value of the possible adverse consequences score. if this latter approach is used,

Alternative A: Compaq SLT 386s/20				**Alternative C: Toshiba T3100 SX**			
	Probability	Seriousness	P × S		Probability	Seriousness	P × S
Relatively low power supply (20 watts)	6	4	24	Relatively slow disk speed	8	6	48
No system shutdown on battery failure	8	8	64	Slightly lower battery life than other tested models	8	9	72
Unable to display simultaneous images on its own screen and on an external VGA monitor	7	2	14	Lacks expansion slots	6	8	48
Function keys are complicated, requiring additional officer training	10	8	80	Slightly heavier than other models	7	6	42
Totals			182				210

FIGURE 11-6. Possible adverse consequences worksheet—laptop computers.

the alternative with the highest total points should be chosen. Referring to Figure 11-7, Alternative A would be selected with a total point score of 589.

Despite the "rational" and "objective" appearance of the must-wants analysis approach, there are a number of subjective scores, weights, and probabilities in the chart. The "bottom line" values in Figure 11-7 (589 and 513) were calculated on subjective measures. The real value in must-wants analysis is in the methodology. The chief must not become a captive of the device and follow the results mechanistically. He or she should use a must-wants chart to consider and weigh the intangibles that are not easily quantifiable between alternatives. The value of must-wants analysis is not in the end product, but rather in the sharpening of differences or similarities between alternatives or courses of action.

As with must-wants charts, the other two approaches (strategic and cost-effectiveness analyses) are methods of selecting a preferred alternative or choosing a desired course of action. In the final analysis, the judgment of the police chief plays a key and indisputable role, one that cannot be taken lightly or afford to be ill-informed about the alternative courses to be made.

Plan and Carry-Out Implementation

Once a preferred course of action is selected, the next step in the synoptic planning model is to implement the chosen alternative. Implementation requires the chief to execute plans that fulfill the objectives or goals of the process. The classic work on implementation was conducted by Pressman and Wildavsky[27] in Oakland, California. In that study, the authors contend that the process of implementation alone can produce complexities in the future. An example of this phenomenon is observed in any organization undergoing change. The very process of change often causes anxieties within personnel, disputes over responsibilities, and restructuring of the organization. Organizational change is discussed in Chapter 15. But as an illustrative point, consider again the case of automating a police records division. Certainly, the automation process will cause most of the records clerks to reassess their value as workers. Some may think that the computer will eliminate their position, whereas others will resist being retrained because they have little or no previous familiarity with computers. Then too, who will manage the new computerized center? What will happen if the software has minor "bugs" or faults? Who will fix the hardware if it breaks? Thus, a whole series of new issues and questions arises from the implementation of a computer into a police department.

	Ericsson Portable alternative A	Hewlett-Packard PLUS alternative C
Musts:	All met	All met
Wants performance total:	771	723
Possible adverse consequences total:	−182	−210
	589	513

FIGURE 11-7. The final step in must-wants analysis—selecting an alternative. The alternative with the highest point value should be chosen.

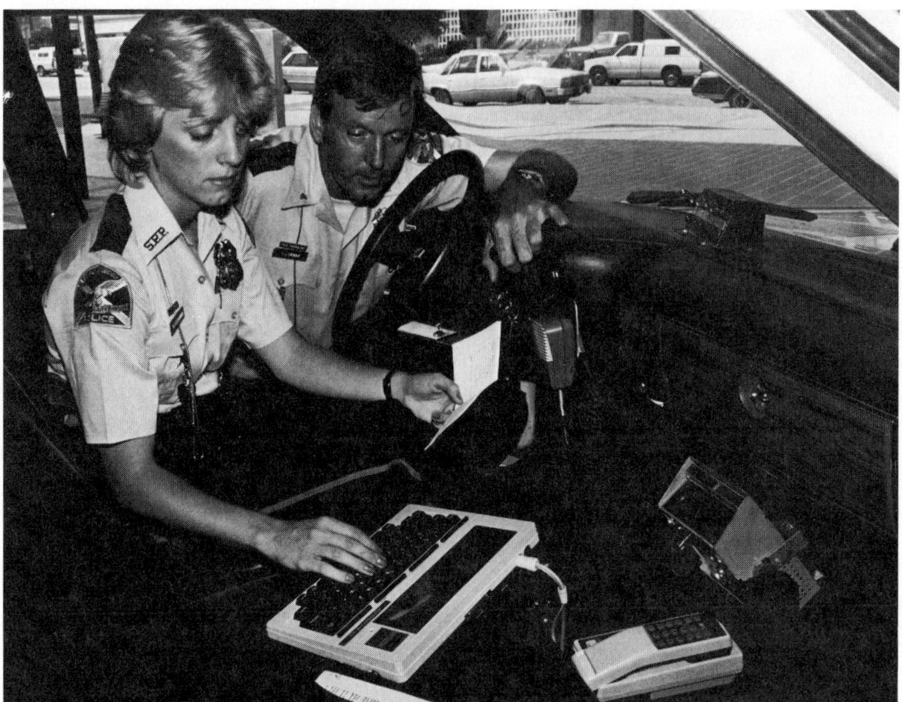

FIGURE 11-8. Officers using a lap computer via a cellular telephone hook-up in a marked police vehicle. [Courtesy of St. Petersburg, Florida, Police Department and GTE Mobilnet, Inc.]

In any event, the police administrator must be aware that implementation requires a great deal of tact and skill. It may be more important "how" an alternative is introduced to a police department than "what" it actually is.

Monitor and Evaluate Progress

The final step of the synoptic planning model is evaluation: Were the objectives achieved? Were the problems resolved? The answer to these questions should be obtained through a system that monitors the implementation process.

Evaluation requires comparing what actually happened with what was planned for—and this may not be a simple undertaking.[28] Feedback must be obtained concerning the results of the planning cycle; the efficiency of the implementation process; and the effectiveness of new procedures, projects, or programs. This is an important step of synoptic planning—trying to figure out what, if anything, happened as a result of implementing a selected alternative. It is for this reason that baseline data are so critical (Step 2—Describe the present situation). Hudzik and Cordner[29] point out that evaluation completes the cycle of rational planning. The issue of identifying problems must be considered again. Does the original problem still exist or was it solved? Is there a new problem?

Summation of the Synoptic Planning Approach

Considerable attention has been given to synoptic planning because it is the most widely used approach in police management. Most other approaches have been derived from the model just described. Synoptic planning basically comprises four activities: preparing to plan, making a choice between alternatives, implementation, and evaluation. The eleven-step approach is a refinement of this cyclical process.

The approaches to follow are other methods commonly used in business forecasting or social planning. Although these approaches are not used as extensively in police management as the synoptic approach, they too deserve some attention.

Incremental Planning

Incremental planning levels a series of criticisms at synoptic planning, including its tendency toward centralization, its failure to appreciate the cognitive limits of police executives (decision makers), and unrealistic claims of rationality. Incrementalism concludes that long-range and comprehensive planning are not only too difficult, but inherently bad. The problems are seen as too difficult when they are grouped together and easier to solve when they are taken one at a time and broken down into gradual adjustments over time. The incremental approach disfavors the exclusive use of planners who have no direct interest in the problems at hand and favor a sort of decentralized political bargaining that involves interested parties. The incrementalists feel that the real needs of people can best be met this way and the "tyranny of grand design" avoided.[30]

Transactive Planning

Transactive planning is not carried out with respect to an anonymous target community of "beneficiaries" but in face-to-face interaction with the people who are to be affected by the plan. Techniques include field surveys and interpersonal dialogue marked by a process of mutual learning. For example, in planning a crime-prevention program in a particular neighborhood, the police might go to certain randomly selected houses to talk to residents about unreported crime, their concerns and fears, and the rise in residential burglary rates. The residents receive crime prevention techniques and a more secure feeling knowing that the police are concerned about their neighborhood. The police department also receives benefits; intelligence information is gathered about strange persons or cars in the area, a more aware citizenry is likely to detect and report crimes, and a more supportive public attitude concerning the police is developed.

Advocacy Planning

Advocacy planning grew up in the 1960s in the adversary procedures modeled by the legal profession. This approach is usually associated with defending the interests of the weak—the poor and politically impotent, for example—against the strong. Beneficial aspects of this approach include greater sensitivity to unintended and negative side effects of plans.

Radical Planning

Radical planning has an ambiguous tradition with two mainstreams that sometimes flow together. The first mainstream involves collective action to achieve concrete results in the immediate future. The second mainstream is critical of large-scale social processes and how they permeate the character of social and economic life at all levels, which, in turn, determine the structure and evolution of social problems.

Types of Plans

From an applications perspective, the planning process yields an end product—the plan. These can be categorized by use and are delineated into four groups:[31]

1. Administrative or management plans include formulation of the department's mission statement, goals, and policies; the structuring of functions, authority, and responsibilities; the allocation of resources; personnel management; and other concerns whose character is that they are prevalent throughout the entire agency. An administrative plan from the Anchorage, Alaska, Police Department appears as the appendix to this chapter. Note that this plan is expressed as a general order. General orders are issued to cover standing or long-term situations. In contrast, special orders are issued to cover unique nonrecurring events, such as a visit by the president of the United States, which last for only a limited and specific period of time. Parenthetically, the announcement of promotions, transfers, and other such actions are made known in personnel orders.
2. Procedural plans, in line with many but certainly not all management plans, are ordinarily included as part of a police department's written directive system, a copy of which is assigned to every officer and is updated periodically. Procedural plans are the guidelines for the action to be taken under specific circumstances and detail such matters as how evidence is to be sent or transported to the crime laboratory, the conditions under which male officers may search arrested females and the limits thereto, and how to stop and approach traffic violators.
3. Operational plans are the work programs of the line units (such as patrol and detectives) as established by an analysis of the need for services.
4. Tactical plans involve planning for emergencies of a specific nature at known locations. Some tactical plans are developed in anticipation of such emergencies as the taking of hostages at a prison or a jailbreak and are subject to modification or being discarded altogether in peculiar and totally unanticipated circumstances. Other tactical plans are developed for specific situations as they arise, such as how to relate to a demonstration in the park or a march on city hall. Although well-operated police agencies invest considerable effort in developing tactical plans that may seldom or never be used, their very existence stimulates confidence among field officers and lessens the likelihood of injury to officers, the public, and violators.

Effective Plans

Regardless of how plans are classified, the bottom line is that organizations with a formal and continuous planning process outperform those without one. This discrepancy in performance increases as the larger environment becomes more turbulent and the pace and magnitude of change increase.[32] This is the type of environment that police administrators have faced in recent years and is illustrated by Proposition 12 in California, which severely limited police expansion; fuel shortages and the attending swift rise in fuel prices; the unionization of police officers and job actions, such as strikes and demonstrations; the escalation of litigation by the public and police department employees; and times of fiscal restraint producing cutbacks in the availability of resources.[33]

Considering these and other circumstances, police administrators must not only have a planning process and plans but also must be able to recognize characteristics of effective plans.

1. The plans must be sufficiently specific so that the behavior required is understood.
2. The benefits derived from the achievement of the goals associated with the plan must offset the efforts of developing and implementing the plan, and the level of achievement should not be so modest that it is easily reached.
3. Involvement in their formulation must be as widespread as is reasonably possible.
4. They should contain a degree of flexibility to allow for the unforeseen.
5. There must be coordination in the development and implementation of plans with other units of government whenever there appears even only a minimal need for such action.
6. They must be coordinated in their development and implementation within the police department to ensure consistency.
7. As may be appropriate, the means for comparing the results planned for versus the results actually produced must be specified before implementation. For tactical plans, this often takes the form of an analysis, referred to as the "after-action report."

Planning and Decision Making

As stated previously, planning is the first integral part of decision making. Planning is primarily concerned with coming to understand the present situation (problem) and widening the range of choices (alternatives or courses of action) available to the police chief (decision-maker). Therefore, planning is aimed at providing information (a plan) whereas decision making is aimed at the use of this information to resolve problems or make choices.[34]

Decision Making

The literature dealing with decision making in the police management field is not very extensive, and most of it is devoted to methods of applying the decision-making process. Whereas in theory it should be easy to divide decision-making processes into discrete, conceptual paradigms, in reality, it is extremely difficult to separate one approach from another.

However, three models derived from decision-making theory appear to be basic in most of the literature. They are (1) the rational model, (2) the incremental model, and (3) the heuristic model.

The Rational Model

The traditional theory of management assumes that people are motivated predominantly by "economic incentives" and will, therefore, work harder given the opportunity to make more money. The "economic actor" concept also prevails in early decision-making theory. In Chapter 3, the scientific management approach developed by Taylor was presented. Within this concept, the economic person is presumed to act in a rational manner when faced with a decision-making situation. The assumptions for this rational behavior are (1) that a person has complete knowledge of all alternatives available to him or her, (2) that a person has the ability to order preferences according to his or her own hierarchy of values, and (3) that a person has the ability to choose the best alternative for him or her. Money is usually used as a measure of value for the decision maker. It is considered only natural that a person will want to work harder if that person can maximize the return of money by so doing. But these assumptions are difficult for a person to achieve in real life. Just by looking at the first assumption—that a person has knowledge of all available alternatives and their consequences in any given decision situation—we can see how impossible it would be to fulfill these requirements in most circumstances.

There is some evidence to suggest that administrative rationality differs from the "economic actor" concept of rationality because it takes into account an additional spectrum of facts relative to emotions, politics, power group dynamics, personality, and mental health. In other words, the data of social science are facts just as much as the carbon content of steel, but they are difficult and, in many cases, impossible to quantify with a high degree of accuracy.[35]

Police administrators bring to administrative decision making their own personal value system that they inject into the substance of decision making while clothing their decision with a formal logic of the "good of the organization." They clothe the decision with the official mantle of the department's logic and respectability while their eyes remain fixed on more personal goals. But this does not lead to chaos, because there is frequently a large element of commonality in personal value systems as related to organizational goals.[36] For example, the police executive who develops and directs a specialized unit to solve a series of murders will be accomplishing a law enforcement goal: to apprehend criminals. Although the executive's personal motives are to gain public success of his or her unit, the personal objectives are in line with the organizational goals. Thus, conflict does not arise, unless the personal values begin to compete with the department's mission.

In an earlier chapter the work of Gulick and Urwick was discussed as a description of administrative behavior focusing on the work of the chief executive. Part of their theory includes the act of making rational choices by following prescribed elements of work (PODSCORB). Their contribution set the stage for the rational model of decision-making by suggesting that executives follow orderly and rational steps before making decisions. Subsequently, Simon[37] responded to these assumptions in his article "The Proverbs of Administration," in which he outlined several requirements for a scientifically based theory of administration. Simon's article was then included in his *Administrative Behavior* (1947).[38]

Simon explains that rational choices are made on a "principle of efficiency." His model of rationality contends that there are three essential steps in decision making; (1) list *all* of the alternative strategies, (2) determine and calculate *all* of the consequences to each strategy, and (3) evaluate *all* of these consequences in a comparative fashion.[39] Whereas Simon is given credit for the development of this approach, its comprehensive expansion can be observed in the literature of several other theorists. Drucker's concept of the "Effective Executive," Iannone's "style" in *Supervision of Police Personnel,* and Sharkansky's decision-making model in *Public Administration* all exhibit an expansion of Simon's original work.[40] The rational model, now often referred to as the rational-comprehensive model, sets forth a series of formalized steps toward "effective" decision making. These steps can be generally observed and listed as follows:

1. Identify and define the problem
2. Ascertain *all* information regarding the problem
3. List *all* possible alternatives and means to solving the problem
4. Analyze the alternatives and assess the facts
5. Select the appropriate alternatives; find the answer

It is important to observe the elaboration on Simon's original method. The decision-making model assumes an ideal condition whereby the decision-maker is aware of *all* available information related to the problem and has an unlimited amount of time in which to explore and narrow down proposed alternatives by a "rational" and comparative process. Unfortunately, actual practice rarely allows for the ideal.

Highly criticized for being too idealistic and irrelevant to the administrative functions of a police organization, the rational decision-making model has been subjected to harsh criticisms. Many of these criticisms were noted as limitations by proponents of the method. For instance, Sharkansky[41] provided a detailed discussion of "roadblocks" to the fulfillment of the rational-comprehensive model in practical administration. He documented constraints of all available data and emphasized contingencies in the human ability to make decisions. Additionally, Simon elaborated on the concept of a "rational man." Noting that man was "bounded" by a triangle of limitations, he stated

> On one side, the individual is limited by those skills, habits, and reflexes which are no longer in the realm of the conscious . . . on a second side, the individual is limited by his values and those conceptions of purpose which influence him in making decisions . . . and on a third side, the individual is limited by the extent of his knowledge that is relevant to his job.[42]

It is apparent that Simon understood not only the decision-making process but also the "human" factors associated in the term of *rationality.* A prerequisite to "effective" decision making is an acute awareness of the social, environmental, and organizational demands placed on the administrator. Simon[43] accurately stresses that one's ability to make rational decisions is bounded by the limitation of his or her knowledge of the total organization. From this critical observation, Simon formulates a modified rational-comprehensive idea entitled "bounded rationality."[44] The emphasis, of course, is on man's inherent limitations to make decisions. Refer to Figure 11-9.

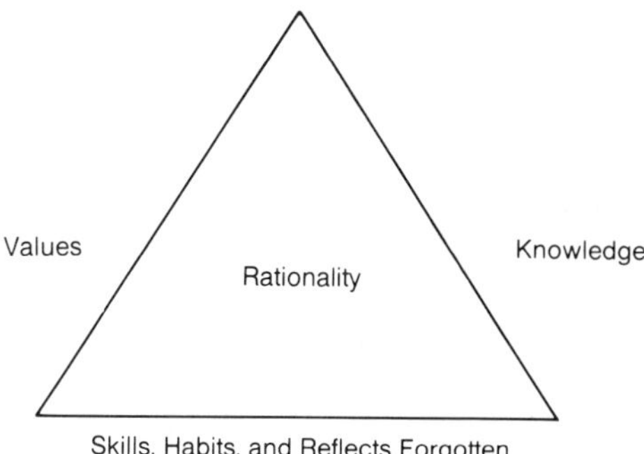

FIGURE 11-9. Simon's concept of bounded rationality.

The Incremental Model

Another important approach concerning the modification of rational decision making is the "incremental" and "muddling through" theories explored by Lindblom.[45] Based on his study of governmental institutions in the United States, Lindblom states that the decision-making process is so fragmented and so complex, incorporating the interaction of various institutions, political entities, pressure groups, and individual biases, that rationality can have only a marginal effect. That is, for the police administrator there are a set of limiting political factors (such as the mayor's wish to be reelected), that prevent the decision-making process from being truly rational. For elected sheriffs, the political agendas may be so strong that purely rational decision making is inhibited.

Lindblom asserts that decision making is serial, that it is limited by time and resources as it gropes along a path where means and ends are not distinct, where goals and objectives are ambiguous, and where rationality serves no purpose. Contending that police managers and administrators "play things safe" and opt to move very slowly (incrementally) in decision making, Lindblom[46] proposes that managers "muddle through" problems rather than analytically choosing decisions. In Lindblom's view, decision making that occurs through a series of incremental steps provides the police administrator (and hence the public) with a number of safeguards against error:

> In the first place, past sequences of policy (decision) steps have given him knowledge about the probable consequence of further similar steps. Second, he need not attempt big jumps toward his goals that would require predictions beyond his or anyone else's knowledge, because he never expects his policy (decision) to be a final resolution of a problem. His decision is only one step. . . . Third, he is in effect able to test his previous predictions as he moves on to each further step. Lastly, he often can remedy a past error fairly quickly—more quickly than if policy (decision) proceeded through more distinct steps widely spaced in time.[47]

Lindbolm's ideas have support, if not in theory, at least in practice, as many police managers find them to be "a description of reality."[48]

The Heuristic Model

In another opposing concept to rationality and logic, Gore[49] identifies the crucial element of humanism in decision making. He presents a "heuristic model" appropriately referred to as "the gut level approach" when considering the police organization. The seasoned patrol officer frequently refers to an unknown quality or phenomenon known as "moxie" or the ability to be "street-wise." This unknown dimension is captured in Gore's decision-making method for police administrators. In an antithesis to the rational model, Gore identifies a process by which a decision is the product of the maker's personality. Gore views the heuristic process "as a groping toward agreements seldom arrived at through logic . . . the very essence of those factors validating a decision are internal to the personality of the individual instead of external to it."[50] Whereas the rational method is concrete, formalized by structure and calculations, the heuristic concept is nebulous, characterized by "gut feelings reaching backward into the memory and forward into the future."[51]

For Gore, decision making is basically an emotional, nonrational, highly personalized, and subjective process. Therefore, the facts validating a decision are internal to the personality of the individual instead of external to it. The key word in this statement is *validating*; it is intended to convey a sense of personal psychological approval or acceptance. The optimum situation is to select that decision alternative that creates the least anxiety or disruption to the individual's basic needs, wants, and desires. In effect, every "objective" decision should be modified or adjusted to meet the emotional needs of the various members of the police department who will be affected by the decision. The passage from which this statement was taken provides additional insight into Gore's heuristic decision-making scheme:[52]

> Whereas the rational system of action evolves through the identification of causes and effects and the discovery of ways of implementing them, the heuristic process is a groping toward agreement seldom arrived at through logic. The very essence of the heuristic process is that factors validating a decision are internal to the personality of the individual instead of external to it. Whereas the rational system of action deals with the linkages between a collective and its objectives and between a collective and its environment, the heuristic process is orientated toward the relationship between that private core of values embedded in the center of the personality and its public counterpart, ideology. The dynamics of personality are not those of logic but rather those of emotion.[53]

In other words, although logic and reason may be the basic intellectual tools needed to analyze a given problem or to structure a series of solutions to a given situation, logic and reason may not prove to be completely effective in establishing intraorganizational agreement in connection with any given decision.[54]

Applauded for its contribution to the decision-making process, Gore's approach is also highly criticized as being too simplistic and nonscientific. Souryal[55] writes that "Gore's analysis is too unreliable . . . it could complicate an existing situation, promote spontaneity, discredit the role of training and delay the advent of professionalism" in police organizations. This is an unfair assessment of the method. Gore views heuristic applications as adjuncts or alternatives to rational models. Further, some type of credibility must be assessed to that vague, unknown, and nonmeasurable entity we call "experience," "talent," or the "sixth sense." It was these elements that Simon had so much trouble with in calculating his "bound and limited" argument regarding the rational model. In any event, Gore's contributions remain as an opposite to decision making based solely on figures, formulas, and mathematical designs.

Alternative Decision-Making Models

A more recent attempt to outline various approaches to the decision-making process is Allison's[56] account of the 1962 Cuban Missile Crisis. He contends that the rational decision-making model, although most widely used, is seriously flawed. Allison presents two additional models (the organizational process model and the government politics model) to explain decision making during crisis events that police and other government agencies often face. The organizational process model is based on the premise that few government decisions are exclusively the province of a single organization. In other words, police agencies are dependent on information and advice from other governmental units (like the mayor's office, the FBI, and the district attorney's office) to make major decisions that affect public policy. The government politics model purports that major government policies are rarely made by a single rational actor, such as the chief of police. Rather, policy and general decision making is the outcome of a process of bargaining among individuals and groups to support those interests. Implicit in both of the models is that the decision-maker requires direction from his or her internal staff as well as support from other governmental agencies in the making of important decisions. This is especially true during crisis situations.[57]

Other alternative models to decision making have evolved from the systems approach to management as described in Chapter 3. These techniques are vastly influenced by large, complex systems of variables. The application, collection, and analysis of data from decision making within the organization is called "operations research."[58] In response to a need for a management–science that addressed complex problems involving many variables, such as government planning, military spending, natural resource conservation, and national defense budgeting, operations research employs the use of mathematical inquiry, probability theory, and gaming theory to "calculate the probable consequences of alternative choices" in decision making.[59] As a result, techniques such as Program Evaluation and Review Technique (PERT) and Planning, Programming, and Budgeting Systems (PPBS) were developed for use in managerial planning, forecasting, and decision making.[60] By their very nature, these techniques must structure the system for analysis by quantifying system elements. This process of abstraction often simplifies the problem and takes it out of the real world. Hence, the solution of the problem may not be a good fit for the actual situation.

PERT is a managerial attempt to convert the disorganized resources of people, machines, and money into a useful and effective enterprise by which alternatives to problem solving can be assessed. This process is conducted by a cost-effective analysis or an estimation for each alternative of the costs that would be incurred and the extent to which the objectives would be attained, which is similar to those discussed in the synoptic model.

Another model, the decision tree, is illustrated in Figure 11-10. In this model, the probabilities for various outcomes are calculated for each branch of the tree. In the example used in Figure 11-10, the first branch of the trunk has three possible outcomes: (1) arrest at the scene by a patrol officer, (2) no arrest at the scene, and (3) arrest at the scene by a detective. Note in Figure 11-10 that the probabilities for those three events total 1.0, which is the mathematical value for certainty; all possible outcomes for that branch of the example are accounted for. The next higher branch of the example decision tree deals with the various types of evi-

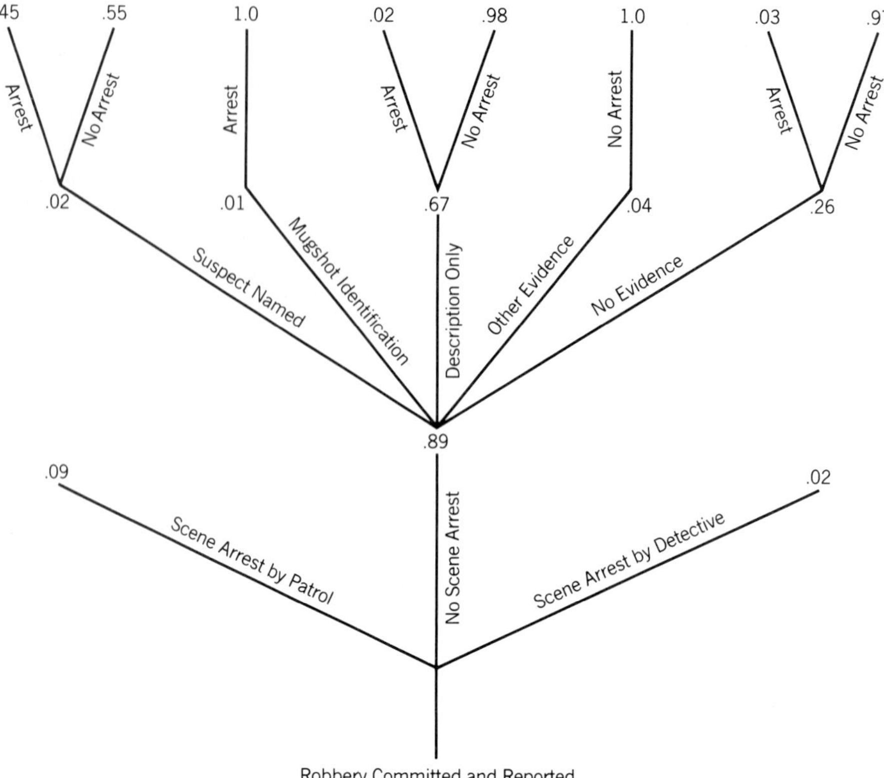

FIGURE 11-10. Decision tree of hypothetical probabilities of various outcomes in a robbery investigation.

dence obtained from investigation and the final branches deal with the probability of arrest associated with the gathering of each type of evidence. Decision trees are very useful in analyzing situations and for reference when series of decisions that flow from one event are involved. For example, decision trees would be useful to the commander of a detective bureau in formulating policy and guidelines on when to continue or inactivate an investigation based on the types of evidence which were involved in order to make best use of investigative resources. In this regard, decision trees can be seen as a tool of operations research. If an administrator is facing a decision for which there are no actual data, a decision tree can still be useful in analyzing the situation and the "probabilities" can be the administrator's own subjective estimations based on past experience.

These approaches are highly sophisticated elaborations of the rational model utilizing quantitative techniques. The weakness of the methods are in their practicality to real-world situations in which time and resources are not directly structured to gather intelligence about every problem and possible alternative. Further, these models assume that human biases will not enter the decision-making process. The most critical aspect of the approaches appears to be in their overriding insistence that decision making is not a human activity but the product of some scientific, computerized, and unimpressionable robot that digests quantitative information.

Wildavsky[61] has continually warned that the application of decision making to costs, benefits, resources, and budgets frequently results in the adoption of meaningless data and places unwarranted stimuli into the process.

Types of Decisions

Regardless of the model, a number of types of decisions exist. (For a case study in decision making, see Box 11-1.) Each type may represent a different method, or several types may be arrived at from the same technique. The more important aspect here is that decisions can be recognized and classified for study and review:

- A *decision by avoidance* is made by not making a decision about an idea that has been proposed; the idea is therefore disposed of and the police manager's inaction results in a continuation of things as they are. The key thing about this style is that not making a decision is effectively a decision against change and a decision for the status quo.
- *Individual, authority-based decisions* leave room for some real conferring, whereas authoritarian decisions do not. It is useful here to observe that decisions made on the basis of expert power are authoritative, but are not authoritarian.
- The *statistical average* of the individual decisions involves passing out forms, individually ranking alternatives without discussion, averaging the individual rankings to identify statistical average, and selecting the one ranked highest. This approach reduces the effect of extreme decisions. However, the lack of discussion reduces the amount of information commonly shared and understood.
- *Minority decisions* are those in which a vocal minority dominates discussions and ultimately the selection of the decision itself.
- *Majority rule decisions* are based on a majority vote. Although consistent with democratic practices, up to 49 percent of the people voting may feel no commitment to the selected course of action and this approach could badly split a police command staff into two roughly even and warring camps.
- *General consensus decisions* involve genuine discussion and sometimes spirited debate. General consensus decisions are based on collective agreement; they are not the same as majority rule or total agreement decisions in that the final decision forged is one that has the support of all those who participated in the process even though they might not favor every specific of the decision. A key advantage of this and the next type of decision is that by allowing active participation, people develop a sense of "ownership" about the decision and are, therefore, much more likely to support it.
- *Total agreement decisions,* in which every individual agrees on every point, are statistically possible, but as a practical matter they occur only infrequently. On very key issues it might be important to obtain genuine total agreement, particularly because of the commitment it brings; however, attaining total agreement is extremely time consuming and costly, and therefore is used sparingly. Sound decision making requires that when a group is immediately in total agreement about a course of action, some time could be profitably spent examining the unspoken (and therefore unexplored) underlying rationale and assumptions that might have produced total agreement—but be totally wrong.[62]

To this point, we have concentrated mainly on individual decision making. However, police administrators rarely act alone. They are surrounded by deputy chiefs, bureau commanders, and division captains who provide input into the

BOX 11-1

A Case Study in Decision Making: "Attention, MOVE. This Is America"

In the early morning hours of May 13, 1985, the Philadelphia Police Department engaged the radical cult MOVE—a name that apparently meant nothing. Police Commissioner Gregore Sambor bellowed over a police bullhorn: "Attention, MOVE. This is America. You have to abide by the laws of the United States." What followed was one of the most devastating police battles in the history of law enforcement. After a day-long siege, Police Commissioner Sambor made the decision to drop two one-pound charges of Du Pont Tovex—a TNT-related blasting agent used in mining—atop MOVE's rooftop bunker. The bomb apparently sparked a fire, fueled by stored gasoline inside the house. The impending result reduced most of two tree-lined city blocks to smouldering rubble. Over $7 million in damages: 61 houses destroyed, 250 people homeless, and 11 MOVE members, including 5 children, killed during the episode.

What events led to the decision that ended in such a tragedy? Why would the police even consider a bomb as a viable alternative? How did the police commissioner arrive at this course of action? These questions and others provide an interesting basis in which to analyze police executive decision making.

First, consider the synoptic planning approach. Was there an accurate and detailed description of the problem? Apparently not, as police testified that they were unaware of the stored gasoline and the number of children in the house. Did police executives exhaust the number of possible alternatives? Possibly. Police tactics included the use of tear gas, water cannons, attempted SWAT assaults, and selective sniper fire. However, each attempt was futile against the MOVE fortified house.

From the rational decision-making model, one could assume that Police Commissioner Sambor might have considered retreat. All else had failed and back-up plans were deemed not feasible. For example, hostage negotiators were not utilized because of the violent past history of the group; and the intended plan to use a crane to knock down fortifications was abandoned as city streets were too narrow. Certainly, police could have fallen back and attempted to arrest suspects at a later time, when the heat and emotion of urban confrontation was less.

Looking at the incremental model, what events precipitated the police strike? The incident was the second violent confrontation between Philadelphia police and MOVE. The first incident occurred in August, 1978, when police attempted to evict the leader and founder of the group MOVE, Vincent Leaphart (calling himself John Africa) from a house less than five miles away from the current situation. During that confrontation, one police officer was killed and twelve other police and firemen were injured. As a result, nine MOVE members including John Africa were convicted of murder and sentenced to prison. Within a week previous to the current incident, MOVE leaders had demanded the release of their jailed "brother" as the condition for ending their continued confrontation with police. When the city refused, MOVE threatened to blow up the entire residential block. With that risk, the Mayor (Wilson Goode), Police Commissioner Sambor, and other government officials justified the May 13th police strike. Moving in at dawn, police hoped to take the MOVE group by surprise. After some ten hours of siege, police used a helicopter to drop the bomb in hopes that the charge would blow a hole in the roof through which tear gas and water could be dispersed. However, the bomb sparked a fire. If the decision was made from a series of incremental steps, why wasn't the fire department standing by for a fire contingency? The fire department responded a full 40 minutes after the house was engulfed in flames. Why weren't ambulances called to nearby locations to reduce their response time? After all, previous contact with MOVE had resulted in violence. The decision had not been made rationally or incrementally.

In all probability the decision to use a bomb on the May 13th MOVE incident came heuristically—at the "gut level" of Police Commissioner Gregore Sambor, himself a 35-year police veteran. The decision was not without some rationality: the bomb was

BOX 11–1 (cont.)

supposed to be nonincendiary and an air strike from above would not further endanger police officers on the ground. The decision to use explosive entry devices after some 90 minutes of a full-fledged fire fight with MOVE dissidents, wherein over 7,000 rounds of police ammunition was expended. As expressed by one officer, "We wanted action but we never expected this."

The purpose of this case study is not to criticize the Philadelphia Police; hindsight is always 20–20. The important element here is for students and police executives to realize that decision making *always* involves planning for the unexpected. No one decision-making model guarantees success, and what works one time may not work the next.

Source: Marci McDonald, "Attention, MOVE. This Is America," *MacLeans,* May 27, 1985, pp. 28–29.

working structure of a police department. Their actions in the decision-making arena are critically important to the success or failure of a specific decision, and therefore require exploration.

Group Decision Making

Research on group problem solving reveals that this approach has both advantages and disadvantages over individual problem solving. If the potential for group problem solving can be exploited, and if its deficiencies can be avoided, it follows that group problem solving can attain a level of proficiency that is not ordinarily achieved. The requirement for achieving this level of group performance seems to hinge on developing a style of leadership that maximizes the group's assets and minimizes its liabilities. Because members possess the essential ingredients for the solution, the deficiencies that appear in group solutions reside in the processes by which group solutions are developed. These processes can determine whether the group functions effectively or ineffectively. With training, a leader can supply these functions and serve as the group's central nervous system, thus permitting the group to emerge as a highly efficient entity.[63]

Group Assets

A number of advantages are found in group decision making. They are

Greater Total Knowledge and Information. There is more information in a group than in any of its members; thus, problems that require utilization of knowledge (both internal and external to the police agency) should give groups an advantage over individuals. If one member of the group (e.g., the police chief) knows much more than anyone else, the limited unique knowledge of lesser informed individuals could serve to fill in some gaps in knowledge.

Greater Number of Approaches to a Problem. Most police executives tend to get into ruts in their thinking, especially when similar obstacles stand in the way

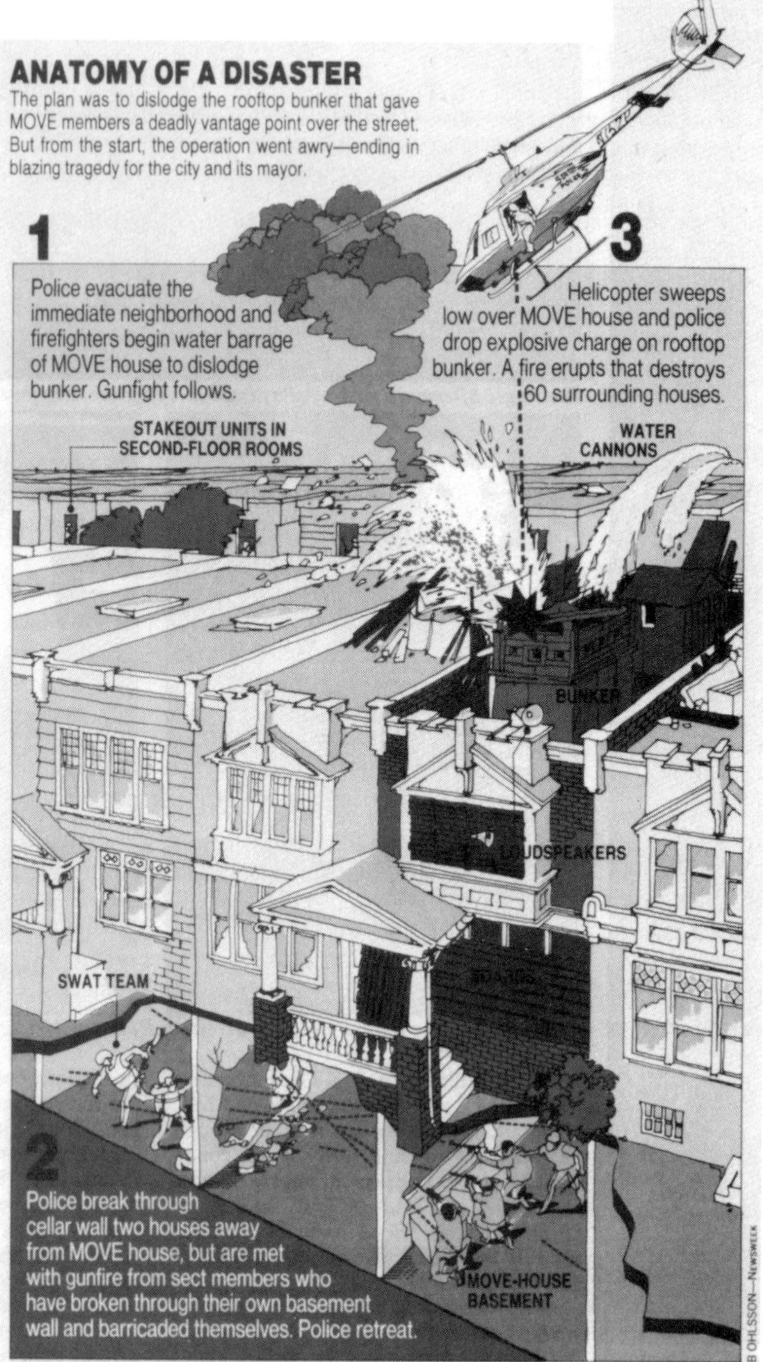

FIGURE 11-11. The anatomy of a disaster. Incremental steps in Philadelphia's attempt to evict MOVE. [Courtesy of *Newsweek*, May 27, 1985.]

FIGURE 11-12. Philadelphia's Osage Avenue and environs after the decision to bomb MOVE headquarters. [Photo courtesy Tannenbaum/SYGMA.]

of achieving a goal, and a solution must be found. Some chiefs are handicapped in that they tend to persist in their approach and thus fail to consider another approach that might solve the problem in a more efficient manner. Individuals in a group have the same failing, but the approach in which they are persisting may be different. For example, one police administrator may insist that the best way to cope with the increasing number of robberies of local convenience stores in a community is to place the businesses under surveillance by specially trained police officers who are equipped with sufficient firepower to either arrest or shoot the robbers if necessary. Another police administrator might insist that the best way to reduce the number of robberies is through the implementation of crime-prevention programs designed to employ procedures that would make the businesses in question either less attractive or less vulnerable to robberies (e.g., keep the amount of cash available down to a minimum, remove large signs from the front of the store windows that block the view of passing patrol cars and other motorists). It is sometimes difficult to determine which approach or approaches would be most effective in achieving the desired goal. But undue persistence or allegiance to one method tends to reduce a decision group's willingness to be innovative.

Participation in Problem Solving Increases Acceptance. Many problems require solutions that depend on the support of others to be effective. Insofar as group problem solving permits participation and influence, it follows that more individuals accept solutions when a group solves the problem than when one person solves it. When the chief solves a problem alone, then he or she still has the task of persuading others. It follows, therefore, that when groups solve such problems, a greater number of persons accept and feel responsible for making the solution work. A solution that is well accepted can be more effective than a better

FIGURE 11-13. A common group decision-making technique: the decision table. [Photo courtesy Tyler, Texas Police Department.]

solution that lacks acceptance. For example, the decision to establish a crime-prevention program in a ghetto neighborhood must have support from the level of chief to individual beat officer. Although other measures to reduce crime (like increasing the number of patrol officers or stricter enforcement of juvenile gang activity) might have a more substantial impact, it is important to remember that most of the program participants must support the effort.

Better Comprehension of the Decision. Decisions made by an individual but that are to be carried out by others must be communicated from the decision maker to the decision executors. Thus, individual problem solving often requires an additional state—that of relaying the decision reached. Failures in this communication process detract from the merit of the decision and can even cause its failure or create a problem of greater magnitude than the initial problem that was solved. Many police organizational problems can be traced to inadequate communication of decisions made by superiors and transmitted to officers who have the task of implementing the decision. The chances for communication failures are reduced greatly when the individuals who must work together in executing a decision have participated in making it. They not only understand the solution because they saw it develop, but also are aware of the several other alternatives that were considered and the reasons they were discarded. The common assumption that decisions supplied by superiors are reached arbitrarily, therefore, disappears. A full knowledge of goals, obstacles, alternatives, and factual information tends to open new lines of communication, and this communication in turn is maximized when the total problem-solving process is shared.

This maxim is especially important concerning law enforcement because officers assigned to regular "beats" or "districts" often provide the administrator with additional information or new dimensions to the problem. Additionally, almost any new program aimed at reducing crime in a specific area (neighborhood crime prevention or neighborhood watches) must necessarily include the patrol officer for implementation and success.

Group Liabilities

Notwithstanding the benefits of group decision making, a number of liabilities are worth mentioning as a precautionary measure:

Social Pressure. Social pressure is a major force for increasing conformity. The desire to be a good member and to be accepted may become more important than whether or not the objective quality of a decision is the most sound. Problems requiring solutions based on facts, independent of personal feelings and wishes, can suffer in group problem-solving situations.

It has been shown that minority opinions in leaderless groups have little influence on the solution reached, even when these opinions are the correct ones. Reaching agreement in a group often is confused with finding the right answer, and it is for this reason that the dimensions of a decision's acceptance and its objective quality must be distinguished.

Individual Domination. In most leaderless groups, a dominant individual emerges and captures a disproportionate amount of the influence in determining the final outcome. Such individuals can achieve this end through a greater degree of participation, persuasive ability, or stubborn persistence (wearing down the opposition). None of these factors is related to problem-solving ability, so that the best problem solver in the group may not have the influence to upgrade the quality of a solution (which the individual would have had if left to solve the problem alone). The mere fact of appointing a leader causes this person to dominate a discussion. Thus, regardless of the individual's problem-solving ability, a leader tends to exert a major influence on the outcome of a discussion. In police circles, the influence of the chief's opinion is undeniable. All too often, the chief dominates the group process so much that participation is squelched. The chief needs to be aware of his or her influence and make a cognitive effort to listen rather than dominate.

Conflicting Secondary Goals: Winning the Argument. When groups are confronted with a problem, the initial goal is to obtain a solution. However, the appearance of several alternatives causes individuals to have preferences, and, once these emerge, the desire to support a particular position is created. Converting those with neutral viewpoints and refuting those with opposing viewpoints now enter the problem-solving process. More and more, the goal becomes having one's own solution chosen rather than finding the best solution. This new goal is unrelated to the quality of the solution and, therefore, can result in lowering the quality of the decision.

Factors That Can Serve as Assets or Liabilities

Depending on the skill of the discussion leader, some elements of group decision making can be assets or liabilities:

Disagreement. Discussion may lead to disagreement and hard feelings among members or it may lead to a resolution of conflict and hence to an innovative solution. The first of these outcomes of disagreement is a liability, especially with regard to the acceptance of solutions; the second is an asset, particularly where innovation is desired. A chief can treat disagreement as undesirable and thereby reduce both the probability of hard feelings and innovation. The skillful police administrator creates a climate for disagreement without risking hard feelings because properly managed disagreement can be a source of creativity and innovation. The chief's perception of disagreement is a critical factor in utilizing disagreements. Other factors are the chief's permissiveness, willingness to delay reaching a solution, techniques for processing information and opinions, and techniques for separating idea elicitation from idea evaluation.

Conflicting Versus Mutual Interests. Disagreement in discussions may take many forms. Often, participants disagree with one another with regard to the solution, but when the issues are explored, it is discovered the solutions are in conflict because they are designed to solve different problems. Before there can be agreement on a solution, there must be agreement as to the problem. Even before this, there should be agreement on the goal as well as on the various obstacles that prevent the goal from being reached. This is where the synoptic planning model can be an invaluable tool. Once distinctions are made among goals, obstacles, and solutions (which represent ways of overcoming obstacles), the opportunities for cooperative problem solving and reduced conflict are increased.

Often, there is also disagreement regarding whether the objective of a solution is to be of the highest quality or merely acceptable. Frequently a stated problem reveals a group of related, but separate problems, each requiring a separate solution so that a search for a single overall solution is impossible. Communications are often inadequate because the discussion is not synchronized, and each person is engaged in discussing a different aspect of the problem. Organizing the discussion to systematically explore these different aspects of the problem increases the quality of solutions. The leadership function of guiding such discussions is quite distinct from the function of evaluating or contributing ideas.

When the discussion leader helps separate different aspects of the problem-solving process and delays the inclination of the group to come to a quick but not well-thought-out solution, both the quality of the solution and acceptance of it improve. When the leader hinders or fails to facilitate the isolation of these processes, there is a risk of deterioration in the group process. The leader's skill thus determines whether a discussion drifts toward conflicting interests or whether mutual interests are located. Cooperative problem solving can only occur after the mutual interests have been established, and it is interesting how often they can be found when a discussion leader makes this a primary task.

Risk Taking. Groups are more willing than individuals to reach decisions that involve risk. Taking risks is a factor in the acceptance of change, but change may represent either a gain or a loss. The best protection against the latter outcome seems to be primarily a matter of the quality of a decision. In a group situation, this depends on the leader's skill in utilizing the factors that represent group assets and avoiding those that make for liabilities.

Time Requirements. In general, more time is required for a group to reach a decision than for an individual to reach one. Insofar as some problems require quick decisions, individual decisions are favored. In other situations, acceptance and quality are requirements, but excessive time without sufficient returns also presents a loss. On the other hand, discussion can resolve conflicts, whereas reaching consensus has limited value. The practice of hastening a meeting can prevent full discussion, but failure to move a discussion forward can lead to boredom and fatigue, and group members may agree to anything merely to put an end to the meeting. The effective utilization of discussion time (a delicate balance between permissiveness and control on the part of the leader), therefore, is needed to make the time factor an asset rather than a liability. Unskilled leaders either tend to be too concerned with reaching a solution and, therefore, terminate a discussion before the group's agreement is obtained, or tend to be too concerned with getting input, allowing discussion to digress and become repetitive.

Who Changes. In reaching consensus or agreement, some members of a group must change. In group situations who changes can be an asset or a liability. If persons with the most constructive views are induced to change, the end product suffers, whereas if persons with the least constructive points of view change, the end product is upgraded. A leader can upgrade the quality of a decision because the leadership position permits the individual to protect the person with the minority view and increase the individual's opportunity to influence the majority position. This protection is a constructive factor because a minority viewpoint influences only when facts favor it.

In many problem-solving discussions, the untrained leader plays a dominant role in influencing the outcome, and when the person is more resistant to changing personal views than are the other participants, the quality of the outcome tends to be lowered. This negative influence of leaders was demonstrated by experiments in which untrained leaders were asked to obtain a second solution to a problem after they had obtained their first one. It was found that the second solution tended to be superior to the first. Because the dominant individual had influenced the first solution and had won the point, it was not necessary for this person to dominate the subsequent discussion that led to the second solution. Acceptance of a solution also increases as the leader sees disagreement as producing ideas rather than as a source of difficulty or trouble. Leaders who see some of their participants as troublemakers obtain fewer innovative solutions and gain less acceptance of decisions than do leaders who see disagreeing members as persons with ideas.

Brainstorming

Brainstorming is a special case or type of group decision making developed initially in advertising to help trigger creativity. The idea behind brainstorming is to bring a group together and to establish an environment in which individuals within the group can present any idea that seems to apply even remotely to the subject being considered with the understanding that criticism will be withheld unless it can somehow improve on the original idea.[64] The practitioners of brainstorming have been able to determine some specific procedures that improve the effectiveness of the brainstorming sessions. Karass points out that

1. The sessions should last 40 minutes to an hour, although brief 10- to 15-minute sessions may be effective if time is limited.

2. Generally, the problem to be discussed should not be revealed before the session.
3. The problem should be stated clearly and not too broadly.
4. A small conference table that allows people to communicate easily should be used.[65]

This approach can be useful in dealing with many public policy or administrative problems. When the major problem is one of discovering new ways of dealing with a situation, brainstorming may prove useful. One of the most difficult aspects of brainstorming, however, is creating a situation in which it can occur. Most of the "rules of the game" are based on an implicit level of trust between individuals that sometimes does not exist in a politically volatile organization. This kind of trust must be developed for the procedure to be successful; thus, people tend to become freer and better able to use the process as they have repeated experiences with it.[66]

Personality Characteristics of Decision Making

It has been suggested by Katz and Kahn that among the more important personality dimensions of policymakers that may affect their decisions are (1) their orientation to power versus their ideological orientation, (2) their emotionality versus their objectivity, (3) their creativity versus their conventional common sense, and (4) their action orientation versus their contemplative qualities.[67]

Ideology versus Power Orientation

A police department dominated by a power-driven chief will find its policy decisions moving in the direction of survival and aggrandizement of the chief rather than toward the healthy development of the total department. The following actual case illustrates how this may occur.

> A newly appointed police chief selected from outside his department made a decision to implement team policing in one section of the city. The experiment enjoyed some success, and as a result the chief was beginning to gain national recognition via articles in police journals, guest speaker appearances at national conferences and so forth. There was considerable speculation within the ranks of his police department that the chief was using the police department as an experimental laboratory to test the team policing concept and also as a staging area of self-aggrandizement in the hopes of eventually moving to some larger police department.
>
> The team policing project had been in operation for approximately six months when the chief made a decision to implement it throughout the entire city. The decision was made, in fact, because this would have been the first time team policing had been tried on such a large scale in the United States and would most certainly have thrust the police chief into the national spotlight.
>
> The chief's entire command staff was opposed to the move because there were still some personnel and operational problems that had not been worked out in the experimental team policing area. In addition, there was considerable resistance to the concept among rank-and-file personnel. There was sufficient evidence to support all these concerns. A confrontation occurred between the police chief and his entire command staff. The command staff threatened to resign en masse if the chief tried to implement the plan. The city manager became embroiled in the confrontation and decided to

support the command staff. The chief was fired, and with his dismissal the entire team policy project was abandoned.

In the final analysis, the chief's quest for self-aggrandizement and his own personal ambitions were perceived by his command staff and many rank-and-file officers as not being congruent with the organizational welfare or with their own personal welfare.

However, in some instances, the power interest of the police executive and organizational welfare coincide. The questions to be answered are: How pertinent are the contributions of the leader to the organization, and what is left for the department when the top leader has moved on?

A police department may have a remarkable chief executive whose brilliant rise in the agency has been accompanied by new organizational developments and substantial benefits to the organization, and when this does occur, such a person may be classified as having an ideological orientation. In reality, however, few organization leaders are ideological crusaders or power-driven survivalists or self-aggrandizers. Most decision makers represent combinations of these value orientations and often use practical compromises to achieve power.

Emotionality versus Objectivity

All individuals are to some extent susceptible to interjecting emotional components into the decision-making process. To a great extent, the degree to which either one's emotions or one's objectivity intervene will depend on the characteristics of the decision makers and the variables involved in the situation calling for a decision. However, some decision makers seem to possess a higher degree of chronic emotional biases with accompanying momentary emotional impulses than do others. For example, time after time in World War II, Hitler made military decisions reflecting his need to project the image of Germans as supermen. His armies, though outflanked, were never to withdraw but were to fight to the death. The Germans suffered unnecessary losses on the Russian front, in Egypt, and finally on the Western front because decisions were made not only on the basis of objective military strategy and tactics but also on the basis of Hitler's unconscious need to avoid any display of weakness.

Some personality characteristics are capable of activating defense mechanisms in the decision-making process. These psychological characteristics can block or distort the analysis of the problem or the assessment of consequences. Experimentation has shown that defense mechanisms can change the perception of incoming information. Threatening and unpleasant facts are often denied, ignored, or distrusted. Police executives whose defensiveness results in their avoiding certain types of unpleasant information may be reinforced in their blindness by subordinates who keep such facts from them.

Creativity versus Common Sense

Some individuals are gifted in originality; they are able to see new relationships and to impose new structure on old facts. Others may have a marked ability in making commonsense judgments requiring the evaluation of many relevant factors and the accurate prediction of likely outcomes. Although not logically antithetical, these two abilities do not often occur in the same person. Some individuals by virtue of their enthusiasm, originality, and creativity do not examine the flow of their ideas with searching criticism. Such an attitude would inhibit the creative process. On the other hand, the person seeking to make a balanced judgment and concerned with giving the appropriate weight to competing plausible notions is unlikely to produce a new solution. Occasionally, the two abilities are combined in a person who can move from a phase of creativity to a phase of criticism.

In general, the power to make policy is in the hands of people of good judgment rather than with creative police managers. The police chief with good judgment can single out subordinates to perform the innovative function. Creative police managers can supplement their talents by surrounding themselves with individuals of good sense, yet still have the problem of making the final judgment. It is understandable, then, that the most original minds in any organization are rarely found in top positions. The complexities of organizational life, with its many conflicting demands on the police chief, require critical and judgmental abilities at this level.

Action Orientation versus Contemplation

Another personality characteristic relevant to organizational functioning is the capacity for action, the ability to act on judgments. Many people have excellent ideas; not nearly as many translate their ideas or even make their decisions into the required implementing actions. Many individuals make that translation in what is called the "action paragraph," acting only when the situation compels it or when they are otherwise forced to perform. As a result, the opportunity for action is sometimes lost entirely.

Impact of Personality Traits on Decision Making

In the final analysis, an understanding of personality characteristics is essential if one is to understand the decision-making process. An individual's intellect, reasoning powers, emotions, and biases enter into most decisions, and even when decisions appear to be based almost entirely on hard data, the data that are selected for inclusion in the decision-making process are influenced to some degree by emotion and feeling.[68]

In fact, it is rarely possible to make decisions that are completely free from inherent discrimination of some kind. Biases may be introduced into the process in many ways, and, whether through ignorance or carelessness, many decision makers appear to overlook the bias of their methods. They tend to use the decision-making process with which they are most comfortable or familiar without any real concern for their fairness. This practice may produce conflict in circumstances when the chief is called on to defend a decision from attack by advocates of a rejected course of action who contend that their disadvantaged position had resulted from biased or unfair decisions.[69]

Holland's study of decision making and personality concluded that

> Intelligent persons can think their own thoughts. Moreover, a measure of critical introspection is imperative in a well-lived life. They must recognize outward signs of anxiety, depressions, peculiar habits and mechanisms and view these as symptoms of causes which lie in a repressed drives or counter drives. Most highly civilized people are shocked when they recognize powerful negative emotions in themselves. Yet we all have hostilities and fears and we can learn to discharge these without damage. Administrators can admit punitive, egotistical drives for power and omnipotence and deal with these wisely, with a sense of amusement at themselves or even recognize irrational, perfectionistic compulsions as signs of their own overdeveloped conscience. They can get their centers of gravity back in their own hands and away from the primitive impulses and counteracting inhibitions.[70]

Common Errors in Decision Making

Analysis of the decision-making process indicates that certain types of errors occur at a higher frequency than others. Nigro and Nigro[71] have indicated that these are: (1) cognitive nearsightedness, (2) the assumption that the future will repeat the past, (3) oversimplification, (4) overreliance on one's own experience, (5) preconceived notions, (6) unwillingness to experiment, and (7) reluctance to decide.[72]

Cognitive Nearsightedness

The human tendency is to make decisions that satisfy immediate needs and to brush aside doubts of their long-range wisdom. The hope is that the decision will prove a good one for the future also, but this actually is to count on being lucky. The odds for such good fortune to occur consistently across all decisions are poor.

Attempting to find a solution which is a "quick fix" may create infinitely greater difficulties in the future. An example of this phenomenon is observed in barricaded hostage situations, in which the chief wants to assault the location immediately with a SWAT team. In crisis situations such as this, time has always proven to be an ally of the police.[73] Unfortunately, the complicated environment in which police officials function sometimes creates pressure to act on relatively narrow considerations of the moment. Also related to cognitive nearsightedness is the "narrow view" or the consideration of only one aspect of a problem while neglecting all other aspects of that problem.

Assumption That the Future Will Repeat Itself

In making decisions, police officials must try to forecast future conditions and events. Human behavior controls many events; in relatively stable periods of history, the assumption can safely be made that employees, client groups, and the public in general will behave much as they have in the past. The present period is, however, far from stable; many precedents have been shattered, and police officers along with other public employees can behave in sometimes surprising ways. Very rarely do dramatic changes occur without some warning signals. Early trends frequently can serve as valuable indicators of future behavior, but the police administrator must make the effort to be aware of these trends and develop strategies to cope with them.

Oversimplification

Another tendency is to deal with the symptom of a problem rather than with its true cause because the actual cause may be too difficult to understand. It is also easier for those participating in a decision-making process to understand a simpler solution: it is more readily explained to others and therefore more likely to be adopted. Although a less-involved solution may actually be the better one, the point is that the decision maker looking for an acceptable answer may take the first simple one, no matter how inferior it may be to other, somewhat more complicated, alternatives.

Overreliance on One's Own Experience

In general, law enforcement practitioners place great weight on their own previous experience and personal judgment. Although the experienced police executive should be able to make better decisions than the completely inexperienced one, a person's own experience may still not be the best guide. Frequently, another police executive with just as much experience has a completely different solution and is just as certain that his or her solution to a problem is the most satisfactory one. In fact, past success in certain kinds of situations may be attributable to chance rather than to the particular action taken. Thus, there is frequently much to be gained by counseling with others whose own experience can add an important and uniquely different dimension to the decision-making process.

Preconceived Notions

In many cases, decisions allegedly based on facts actually reflect the preconceived ideas of the police executive. This appears to be dishonest, and it is dishonest if the facts are altered to justify the decision. However, in many cases, individuals are capable of seeing only those facts that support their biases. Administrative decisions might be better if they were based on social science findings, but such findings are often ignored if they contradict the ideas of the police chief.[74] In administrative policymaking, conclusions are often supported by a structure of logic that rests dangerously on a mixed foundation of facts and assumptions.[75] Decision makers may appear as if they are proceeding in an orderly way from consideration of the facts to conclusions derived logically from them, when, in fact, what sometimes occurs is that the conclusion comes first and then the facts are found to justify them.

Unwillingness to Experiment

The best way in which to determine the workability of a proposal is to test it first on a limited scale. However, pressure for immediate large-scale action often convinces the police chief that there is not time to proceed cautiously with pilot projects, no matter how sound the case for a slow approach. Sometimes police executives are reluctant to request funding and other needed support from the small-scale implementation of new programs for fear that such caution may raise doubts about the soundness of the programs. In all fairness to the cautious police administrator, sometimes this assessment has merit.

Reluctance to Decide

Even when in possession of adequate facts, some people will try to avoid making the decision. Barnard speaks of the natural reluctance of some people to decide:

> The making of a decision, as everyone knows from personal experience, is a burdensome task. Offsetting the exhilaration that may result from a correct and successful decision is the depression that comes from failure or error of decision in the frustration which ensues from uncertainty.[76]

The Future Police Decision Makers

Harland Cleveland, former U.S. Assistant Secretary of State, has developed a profile of what he believes will be required for future executives in both the public and private sectors to be effective decision makers. He states that

> The new style public-private horizontal systems will be manned by a new breed of men and increasingly women. I call them the public executives, people who manage public responsibilities whether in public or private organizations. They will climb ladders of specialized achievement, into positions that require them to "get it all together." Their administrative style will have to be adjusted to an environment which is still described by drawing square and static diagrams on two dimensional charts; it will feel more like a continuous chemical reaction in a liquefied solution. From this analysis of the executive a jungle of close decisions, openly arrived at"—I have tried to derive a description of the kind of person who will climb into our aristocracy of specialized achievement to try his or her hand at general management. My estimate is that before the end of this decade we will need a million of them at any one time in the United States alone.[77]

Apart from the physical capacity to operate under the pressure of executive responsibility, Cleveland believes that the following predictions can be made with some assurance about executive style in complex systems:

1. The future executive will be more intellectual than the executive of the past and capable of plunging into the complex staff work in which the options are analyzed and the real decisions made. If the executive is not personally plowing through the analysis, then the executive is not making decisions but is merely presiding while others decide. The obligation to think will be the one executive function that cannot be delegated.
2. The future executive will be a low-key individual with a soft voice and a high boiling point. On this point much of the evidence is already in. Even in the administration of infantry divisions, fighter squadrons, and warships at sea, the people who are running things find less and less need for a loud voice or a parade ground manner. If they want to reach large numbers of people, they ask for an electronic amplifier. If they have

orders to give subordinates, they are increasingly likely to call a meeting and act by consensus—or at least to formulate the command as a suggestion.

3. The executive of the future will show more talent for many-sided consensus than for two-sided debating and will develop a taste for ambiguity. Individuals who say that they cannot get on with their part of a job until the lines of authority and responsibility are clarified may simply not yet have learned that ambiguity is an important part of systems management, and, in fact, responsibilities may be intentionally blurred for the benefit of the organization. Individuals who understand and promote the principle of constructive ambiguity are likely to be executives for the world of tomorrow.
4. The future executive will have the optimism of the doer and the determination to organize the future in a different way. Gloom and reluctance are often the hallmarks of expertise; the sum of specialized advice is usually to proceed cautiously and to do nothing. [78]

Effective police executives of the future will reflect these same qualities. Additionally, police managers must be aware that their organizations are drastically influenced by a continuously changing relationship between the police department and the community. This relationship should be viewed as a source of knowledge about how to make appropriate changes.

Summary

Decision making is an integral part of the responsibilities of all administrators, yet it is clear that some individuals are more effective at it than others. We have attempted to examine the decision-making process in a way that would assist readers in evaluating and enhancing their own decision-making skills.

FIGURE 11-14. During future crisis situations, police executives will be forced to make decisions influencing a wide range of organizational, community, and political issues. [Photo courtesy of the San Diego Police Department.]

Planning was discussed as an integral first step in the decision-making process. Special attention was given to the synoptic planning model and three methods of selecting a preferred course of action: strategic analysis, cost-effectiveness analysis, and must-wants analysis. Other planning approaches mentioned were the incremental, transactive, advocacy, and radical techniques. Various types of plans were identified as well as the characteristics of effective plans.

The major strengths and weaknesses of major decision-making models were discussed, including rational decision making, incremental decision making, and heuristic decision making. Attention was also given to certain alternative decision making models and types of decisions.

In the discussion of group decision making, it was learned that this approach has some very distinct advantages and disadvantages. The advantages of group decision making include a greater knowledge and information from the group than from any of its members; a greater number of approaches to a problem likely to be considered; an increase in the potential for acceptance by individual members; and a better understanding of the decision. The liabilities of group decision making include the desire to be a good group member and to be accepted, which tends to silence disagreement and favors consensus; the potential of individual domination from a person who does not possess the greatest problem-solving ability; and conflicting secondary goals, such as the desire to win an argument rather than to obtain the best possible solution.

The ways in which one's own personality characteristics can affect the types of decisions one makes was examined. These characteristics include orientation to power versus ideology, emotion versus objectivity, creativity versus conventional common sense, and action versus contemplation. There are also certain decision-making errors that occur with a higher frequency than others: cognitive nearsightedness, assumption that the future will repeat the past, oversimplification, overreliance on one's own experience, preconceived notions, unwillingness to experiment, and reluctance to decide. The chapter concluded with a section on the future police decision makers.

Discussion Questions

1. Discuss the synoptic planning approach. Describe three methods of selecting a preferred course of action.
2. Compare and contrast five planning approaches.
3. What are the differences between administrative, procedural, operational, and tactical plans?
4. Discuss Simon's concept of "bounded rationality."
5. Explain Lindblom's theory of incremental decision making.
6. How does Gore view the decision-making process?
7. According to Katz and Kahn, what are some of the more important personality dimensions of policymakers that will affect their decisions?
8. Analysis of the decision-making process indicates that certain types of errors occur at a higher frequency than others. What are they?

Notes

1. G. S. Fulcher, *Common Sense Decision-Making* (Evanston, Ill.: Northwestern University Press, 1965), p. 4.

2. Ibid., pp. 4–5.
3. J. Q. Wilson, *Varieties of Police Behavior* (Cambridge, Mass.: Harvard University Press, 1978). In this study, Wilson considers how the uniformed officers of eight communities deal with such offenses as assault, theft, drunkenness, vice, traffic violators, and disorderly conduct. He also analyzes the problems facing the police administrator both in deciding what patrol officers ought to do and then in getting the officer to do it, how patrol officers in various cities differ in performing their functions, and under what circumstances such differences are based on explicit community decisions.
4. J. H. Skolnick, *Justice Without Trial* (New York: John Wiley & Sons, 1966). This book is based on the author's actual participation as a detective plus comparative community and case material. He discusses key issues such as the organization of the police in America; the effects of police bureaucracy on criminal justice, narcotics, and vice investigation; the informer payoff and its consequences; and the relation between the police and black citizens. His findings are analyzed in light of organizational and legal controls over the police and their effect on the decision-making processes with law enforcement.
5. Israel Stollman, "The Values of the City Planner," in *The Practice of Local Government Planning*, ed. Frank S. So et al. (Washington, D.C.: International City Management Association, 1979), p. 13.
6. Ibid., p. 13.
7. Robert C. Cushman, *Criminal Justice Planning for Local Governments* (Washington, D.C.: U.S. Government Printing Office, 1980), p. 8; five of the elements identified are provided by Cushman, and the others have been added.
8. Ibid., p. 8.
9. John Hudzik and Gary Cordner, *Planning in Criminal Justice Organizations and Systems* (New York: Macmillan, 1983), p. 1.
10. Charles M. Mottley, "Strategy in Planning," in *Planning, Programming, Budgeting: A System Approach to Management,* 2nd ed., ed. J. F. Lyden and E. S. Miller (Chicago, Ill.: Markham, 1972), p. 127.
11. The term *pure* or *objective rationality* is taken from the alternative planning models identified by Tony Eddison, *Local Government: Management and Corporate Planning* (New York: Harper & Row, 1973), pp. 19–23.
12. Cushman, *Criminal Justice Planning,* p. 4.
13. The synoptic model is thoroughly discussed in R. C. Cushman, *Criminal Justice Planning*. Some of the following information relating to the model is paraphrased from that work.
14. Hudzik and Cordner, *Planning in Criminal Justice,* p. 10.
15. Ibid., p. 24.
16. Ibid., p. 10.
17. Ibid., p. 10.
18. Carol Weiss, *Evaluation Research: Methods of Assessing Program Effectiveness* (Englewood Cliffs, N.J.: Prentice-Hall, 1972), p. 7.
19. P. Davidoff and T. A. Reiner, "A Choice Theory of Planning," *Journal of American Institute of Planners* (May 1982), pp. 103–115.
20. Hudzik and Cordner, *Planning in Criminal Justice,* p. 14.
21. R. G. Lynch, *The Police Manager* (Boston, Mass.: Holbrook, 1975), p. 144.
22. U.S. Naval War College, *Sound Military Decisions* (Newport, R.I.: U.S. Naval War College, 1942).
23. The following discussion of strategic analysis is taken from Charles M. Mottley's "Strategic Planning," *Management Highlights,* Release 56, Office of Management Research, U.S. Department of the Interior (September 1967), pp. 103–119.
24. E. S. Quade, "System Analysis Techniques for Planning-Programming-Budgeting," in *Planning, Programming, Budgeting,* ed. Lyden and Miller, p. 249.

25. Ibid., p. 249.
26. Ibid., p. 249.
27. J. L. Pressman and Aaron Wildavsky, *Implementation* (Berkeley, Calif.: University of California Press, 1973).
28. Hudzik and Cordner, *Planning in Criminal Justice*, p. 196.
29. Ibid., p. 196.
30. The last portion of this paragraph is taken, with some restatement, from Stollman, "Values of the City Planner," pp. 14–15.
31. A number of sources identify plans according to their use; see O. W. Wilson, *Police Planning*, 2nd ed. (Springfield, Ill.: Charles C. Thomas, 1962), pp. 4–7; Vernon L. Hoy, "Research and Planning," in *Local Government Police Management*, ed. Bernard L. Garmire (Washington, D.C.: International City Management Association, 1977), pp. 374–75.
32. Stanley S. Thune and Robert J. House, "Where Long-Range Planning Pays Off," *Business Horizons*, 13 (August 1970), pp. 81–90.
33. For information on managing organizational decline and cutback, see Elizabeth K. Kellar, ed., *Managing with Less* (Washington, D.C.: International City Management Association, 1979); Jerome Miron, *Managing the Pressures of Inflation in Criminal Justice* (Washington, D.C.: U.S. Government Printing Office, 1979).
34. Hudzik and Cordner, *Planning in Criminal Justice*, p. 195.
35. J. M. Pfiffner, "Administrative Rationality," *Public Administration Review*, 20:3 (Summer 1960), p. 126.
36. Ibid., p. 128.
37. Herbert A. Simon, "The Proverbs of Administration," *Public Administration Review*, (Winter 1946), 6, pp. 53–67.
38. Herbert A. Simon, *Administrative Behavior* (New York: Macmillan, 1961; a reprint of 1947 edition), p. 39.
39. Ibid., p. 40.
40. For a complete discussion of the rational-comprehensive model, see Peter F. Drucker, *The Effective Executive* (New York: Harper & Row, 1967); N. F. Iannone, *Supervision of Police Personnel* (Englewood Cliffs, N.J.: Prentice-Hall, 1970); and Ira Sharkansky, *Public Administration* (Chicago: Markham, 1972).
41. See Sharkansky, *Public Administration*, p. 44, and Sam S. Souryal, *Police Administration and Management* (St. Paul, Minn.: West, 1977), p. 315.
42. Simon, *Administrative Behavior*, p. 40.
43. Ibid., p. 40.
44. See Paul M. Whisenand and R. Fred Ferguson, *The Managing of Police Organizations*, 2nd ed. (Englewood Cliffs, N.J.: Prentice-Hall, 1978), pp. 202–3, for a discussion of Simon's "bounded-rationality" concepts.
45. Charles F. Lindblom, *The Policy-Making Process* (Englewood Cliffs, N.J.: Prentice-Hall, 1968).
46. Ibid., p. 209.
47. Charles F. Lindblom, "The Science of Muddling Through," *Public Administration Review*, 19 (Spring 1959), p. 86.
48. Jack Kuykendall and Peter Unsinger, *Community Police Administration* (Chicago: Nelson-Hall, 1975), p. 132.
49. William J. Gore, *Administration Decision-Making: A Heuristic Model* (New York: John Wiley & Sons, 1964).
50. Ibid., p. 12.
51. Souryal, *Police Administration*, p. 318.
52. L. G. Gawthrop, *Bureaucratic Behavior in the Executive Branch* (New York: Free Press, 1969), pp. 98–99.
53. Gore, *Administrative Decision-Making*, p. 12.

54. Gawthrop, *Bureaucratic Behavior*, p. 99.
55. Souryal, *Police Administration*, p. 319.
56. Graham T. Allison, *Essence of Decision: Exploring the Cuban Missile Crisis* (Boston, Mass.: Little, Brown, 1971).
57. Some of this discussion was excerpted from an excellent review of Allison's book by Robert B. Denhardt, *Theories of Public Organization* (Monterey, Calif.: Brooks/Cole, 1984), pp. 81–85.
58. John Ott, "The Challenging Game of Operations Research," in *Emerging Concepts of Management*, ed. Max S. Wortmann and Fred Luthans (London: Macmillan, 1970), p. 287.
59. Ibid., p. 287.
60. Peter P. Schoderbeck, "PERT—Its Promises and Performances," in *Emerging Concepts*, ed. Wortmann and Luthans, p. 291, and E. S. Quade, "Systems Analysis Techniques for Planning-Programming-Budgeting, "*RAND Report*, p. 3322 (Santa Monica, Calif.: RAND Corporation, 1966), p. 7.
61. Aaron Wildavsky, *Speaking Truth to Power: The Art and Craft of Police Analysis* (Boston, Mass.: Little, Brown, 1979), p. 84.
62. This information appears in the *Jail Management Seminar Notebook*, located in the Jail Center at the National Institute of Corrections Library, Boulder, Colorado. No author or source is indicated. We continue to search for a citable source.
63. N. R. F. Maier, "Assets and Liabilities in Group Problem Solving: The Need for Integrated Function," *Psychology Review* 74:4 (1967), pp. 239–48. Much of the information in this chapter dealing with the discussion of group decision making was obtained from this source.
64. Gortner, *Administration in the Public Sector* (New York: John Wiley & Sons, 1977), p. 124.
65. C. S. Whiting, "Operational Techniques of Creative Thinking," *Advanced Management Journal*, 20:28 (1955), pp. 24–30.
66. Gortner, *Administration in the Public Sector*, p. 124.
67. Much of the discussion on these four personality dimensions of decision makers that follows has been drawn extensively from D. Katz and R. L. Kahn, *The Social Psychology of Organizations* (New York: John Wiley & Sons, 1966), chapter 10, "Policy Formulation and Decision-Making," pp. 290–94.
68. A. J. DuBrin, *Fundamentals of Organizational Behavior* (New York: Pergamon Press, 1974), p. 76.
69. A. Easton, *Decision-Making: A Short Course for Professionals*, Lessons I (New York: John Wiley & Sons, 1976), p. 35.
70. H. K. Holland, "Decision-Making and Personality," *Personnel Administration*, 31:3 (1968), pp. 28–29.
71. Much of the information in this chapter dealing with the discussion of common errors in decision making was obtained from F. A. Nigro and L. G. Nigro, *Modern Public Administration* (New York: Harper & Row, 1977), pp. 226–32.
72. Katz and Kahn, *Social Psychology*, p. 285.
73. Robert W. Taylor, "Hostage and Crisis Negotiation Procedures: Assessing Police Liability," *TRIAL Magazine*, 19:4 (1983), pp. 64–71.
74. See, for example, A. Leighton, *Human Relations in a Changing World* (Princeton, N.J.: Princeton University Press, 1949), p. 152.
75. Ibid., p. 152.
76. C. Barnard, *The Functions of the Executive* (Cambridge, Mass.: Harvard University Press, 1938), p. 189.
77. H. Cleveland, "The Decision Makers," *Center Magazine* (September–October 1973), p. 14.
78. Ibid., pp. 14–15.

Appendix

Municipality of Anchorage
Anchorage Police Department
General Order No. 91-3

DATE: October 25, 1991
TO: All Personnel
FROM: Duane S. Udland, Deputy Chief of Police
SUBJECT: Victim's Rights Act of 1991, Confidentiality Requirements

The Victim's Rights Act of 1991 (A.S. 12.61.100–150) became effective September 15, 1991. This Act restricts public access to certain information contained in our files, our press releases, and in court documents.

Protected Information That May Not be Released:

1. The *residence address, business address, or telephone number of any victim or witness* to any crime. (This applies to crimes only, not to violations or infractions that carry no jail time.)
2. The *name of the victim* of the following crimes:
   Kidnapping involving physical or sexual assault
   Sexual Assault—First, Second and Third degree
   Sexual Abuse of a Minor—First through Fourth degrees
   Incest
   Unlawful Exploitation of a Minor
   Indecent Exposure
3. NOTE: This Act should not be construed to limit the release of the name of any kidnapping victim needed to facilitate the recovery of the missing victim or to conduct the necessary investigation of the crime.

Effective immediately, the following policies will be followed in regards to the release of information:

Release of Records to the Public:

1. Police reports will only be released by the Records Section and Crime Prevention Unit personnel in accordance with their unit procedures.
2. Police reports or other records, such as papers, photographs, court files, or notebooks, may **only** be released to the public **after** they have been examined for the presence of protected information and that information has been deleted or made unreadable.
3. Other Law Enforcement agencies, Municipal Prosecutors, and District Attorneys may request and obtain complete copies of any police report. If the identity of the person requesting the report is not known to the employee, proper identification will be required.
4. According to the Alaska Department of Law, the release of police reports to insurance

companies does not constitute a release of protected information and is not restricted under the Act.

Media Releases:

1. Press releases may **not** contain any protected information. Personnel providing authorized releases will insure that they do not contain the names of Sexual Assault, Sexual Abuse of a Minor, Incest, Indecent Exposure or Kidnapping victims; and that **no** victim or witness addresses or phone numbers are given.
2. Although the Act does not apply to verbal communications, it is the policy of the Anchorage Police Department that protected information will not be released in any form.

Required Court Certification

The Court System now requires that a Certification Form be attached to all paperwork being filed in any criminal case, including all criminal complaints, misdemeanor citations, and search warrants. Most often, the prosecutor's office will handle this requirement. Occasionally, officers will submit paperwork directly to the court system and will then secure this form through the Clerk of the Court's office. This applies to **crimes only**, not to violations or infractions that carry no jail time.

Law enforcement officers can sign the forms in good faith, and will be in compliance with the Victim's Rights Act of 1991, if the complaint or other court document does not contain:

1. the address or telephone number of any victim or witness (other than the defendant), unless the address is used to identify the place of the crime. **This applies in all cases.**
2. the name of the victim, but instead uses initials to identify the person. If the victim is a minor, you must also use initials to identify the minor's parent or guardian. **This applies in sex and kidnapping cases only.**
3. In some cases, it may be necessary to use some protected information in search warrant applications or criminal complaints. In those instances, the court clerk's office should be notified, and they will have to take the necessary precautions to guard against the disclosure of the court files.

12 Information Systems and Applications

"A tool is but the extension of a man's hand, and a machine is but a complex tool. And he that invents a machine augments the power of a man and the well-being of mankind."
HENRY WARD BEECHER, 1857

Introduction

In the last fifteen years, there has been a tremendous increase in computer automation in law enforcement. This technological trend has brought about dramatic changes in police personnel, roles, and services, and for the most part these changes have resulted in increased police efficiency and effectiveness.

Unlike years past, computers are no longer very expensive first-time investments requiring outside subsidies or matching federal grants for their purchase. Today's computers provide even the smallest departments with the capability of becoming automated at a cost they can afford. Further, the networking or "tying together" of small computers can surpass the memory capacity that was previously available in large and expensive mainframe computers.

The information society so accurately predicted by futurists of the 1960s is now an American reality in which "individual and organizational survival is dependent on the ability to access information."[1] Law enforcement agencies are vast information-processing organizations. All too often, managers and the general public think of police work in terms of physical security, patrol cars, weaponry, crime control, and traffic enforcement. In fact, most police work involves the collection, manipulation, structuring, collating, and dissemination of information, so much so, that an automated records and communication system is no longer viewed as a luxury but a necessity.[2]

Understanding Computer Systems[3]

Ideally, a computer system is designed to solve problems. Unfortunately, all police agencies do not have the same set of problems that can be solved with the same type of computer solution. For instance, an agency with a jail management problem requires a different type of solution than an agency that requires a better communications system.

Various problems, then, require different types of computer systems. Problems that require large, volume processing of records will require powerful computers called *mainframes*. These machines have traditionally been the "number crunchers" of government and business computing. They require highly trained personnel (computer programmers and systems analysts) and an air-conditioned environment in which to operate. Most mainframe computers act as a central host for over 100 terminals. Mainframe computing is an expensive venture, in terms of both immediate cash outlay and ongoing maintenance. Prices for mainframes range from $500,000 to $10 million. In the criminal justice arena, mainframe computers are often used in large police agencies and courthouses, where extensive record-keeping functions are required.

Another type of computer system not quite as powerful as the mainframe is called a *minicomputer*. These machines support between 10 and 100 terminals and are usually found in small to medium-size departments. Minicomputers are often used in large departments for specific tasks such as maintaining accounting and budget records or operating the computer-aided dispatch (CAD) system. CAD systems are discussed later in this chapter. Minicomputers cost between $10,000 and $1 million. They, too, require highly trained personnel and special air-conditioned environments in which to operate.

The advances in computer technology within the last 10 years have given rise to less expensive, yet powerful machines commonly referred to as *microcomputers* or *personal computers* (PCs). No longer novel, PCs play a key role in both business and government. Today's workplace is dominated by managers and users who interact with computers through small PCs. These machines are relatively inexpensive, costing between $1,000 and $10,000, and provide a high level of computing power for the low price. They do not require highly trained programmers or systems analysts to operate, and they can be placed just about anywhere within the work environment.[4] However, PCs have limitations; for example, they cannot replace the volume processing capabilities of larger mini and mainframe machines. Figure 12-1 displays the advantages and limitations of the PC.

Hardware and Software Compatibility

Computer hardware is a term used to describe the components of a computer system such as input/output devices, data storage devices, and the central processing unit (CPU).[5] Hardware is the actual physical mechanisms of a computer, whereas *software* is the directive programming and operational systems that provide instruction to the CPU and other hardware devices. Software (computer programs) is the common communication medium between the user and the computer.[6] During the planning process, it is critically important to match these

Advantages	***Limitations***
1. Flexibility and portability	1. Different files at different locations often result in multiple, inconsistent data files and data management problems
2. Inexpensive high-power computing capability	2. Size of appliction programs limited by main memory
3. Availability of high-quality graphics and color monitor resolution	3. End user responsible for backing up files, installing new software, and interpreting error messages
4. Wide range of software products giving computer power to the end user	4. PC vendors are new with less reliable record than established mainframe vendors
5. Full control of applications by end user	5. PC technology is changing very fast, making relatively new models out-of-date
6. Low hardware and software maintenance	

FIGURE 12-1. The advantages and limitations of the personal computer. (*Partial source:* E. M. Awad, *Management Information Systems: Concepts, Structure, and Applications* (Menlo Park, Calif.: Benjamin/Cummings, 1988), p. 59.)

two integral components—hardware and software—to provide smooth and efficient operation and subsequent goal achievement.

A Microcomputer System

Data are processed and stored in a computer system through the presence or absence of electronic signals in the computer's circuitry or in the media that it uses, which is called a *binary*, or "two-state," representation of data. The smallest element of data is a *bit*, or binary digit, which can have a value of either one or zero. A *byte* is a grouping of bits that the computer operates on as a single unit. It typically consists of eight bits and is used to represent one character of data.

Figure 12-2 emphasizes that a microcomputer is a complete system that uses a variety of devices (or peripherals) to perform the system functions of input, processing, output, and data storage. These four functions form the PC system.[7]

Input. Components used to enter data into the microcomputer system are referred to as input devices. They include keyboards, a mouse, touch screens, light pens, and optical scanners—by no means a complete list of the available input devices, but rather the most common devices found in the office environment. Their main purpose is to transform information into a binary format.

Processing. The "brain" of the microcomputer system is a silicon chip called the *microprocessor*. This chip serves as the CPU and control device for the entire microcomputer system. The most common microprocessors are the Intel 8088, 80286, and 80386 chips, used by IBM and IBM-compatible PCs, and the Motorola 68000, 68020, and 68030, used by Apple Macintosh computers. Their processing speed is typically measured in *megahertz* (MHz), or millions of cycles per second. New advances in the computer chip industry have produced "super-chips," such as the Intel 80486 and 80586, which integrate the capabilities of the 80386 chip with high-speed math coprocessing.

FIGURE 12-2. The input, processing, output, and storage components of a microcomputer system. [Photo courtesy of the Craig, Colorado Police Department.]

Output. Output devices transform digital data in the microcomputer into a form that is readable by humans or other machines. For example, when data are entered into the system via a keyboard, the computer reads the keyboard characters as digital data for manipulation by the microprocessor. For the user to see the characters on a printed page, the output device converts the digital data back to characters. Output devices include monitors, printers, and plotters.

Storage. Microcomputers need to be able to store data and programs for an indefinite period of time. Storage devices provide long-term media to save programs and data for quick access. There are two types of storage devices commonly used in the microprocessing environment: *disk drives* and *tape drives*.

Disk storage devices include the common *floppy diskette*, which is available in three sizes: 8 inches, 5¼ inches, and 3½ inches in diameter. Floppy diskettes are somewhat like stereo records in that they are logically divided into concentric rings and data are stored or accessed by an arm that moves back and forth across their surfaces. Floppy diskettes are inexpensive, removable storage media that can be reused many times before they wear out.

Hard disks or drives function similarly to floppy diskettes, except that they are dramatically faster, hold much more data, and are normally not removable from the microcomputer system. Whereas floppy diskettes store from approximately 360 kilobytes (thousands of bytes) to about 1.5 megabytes (millions of bytes), the hard disk sizes start at 10 megabytes (MB) and exceed 1 gigabyte (GB) (billions of bytes) of data!

Optical disk drives, also known as CD-ROMs (cartridge disk read only memory) and laser disk drives, are a new type of data storage device that falls within the category of a hard disk. These disk platters hold vast amounts of data and are almost always rated in GBs.

The second type of storage device is a *magnetic tape drive* (or simply tape drive), which usually serves as a backup or secondary storage device on microcomputer systems. Tape drives protect data and programs against accidental loss as a result of power failure, system errors, fatal disk errors, theft or other catastrophes, as well as providing a medium for archiving data.

Local Area Networks

A local area network (LAN) is designed to connect PCs within a limited physical or geographical area. In the past five years, LAN development has received enormous attention because of the dramatic increases in speed, processing power, and data storage now offered by PCs. By linking PCs together via a LAN, public agencies (like the police) can enjoy the benefit of shared information and volume processing, previously unavailable except through expensive mainframe computer operations (see Box 12-1). Further, LAN users receive additional benefits such as flexibility, user-friendly applications, electronic mail, and shared computer peripherals (printers, plotters, etc.) previously unknown to the data processing environment. The best of all news, of course, is that recent surges in LAN and PC development have forced prices down, providing managers with a less expensive information processing option.

There are three common LAN cable layouts or topologies: star, bus, and token passing. Each design focuses on the use of a powerful PC with a large hard disk capacity called a *file server*. This processing unit is the heart of the network and contains the network control programs that distribute shared data files and software applications to less powerful PCs or terminals on the network (commonly called nodes or work stations).

Star Network. The star design is the oldest and simplest configuration of network topology. It employs the use of terminals (not stand-alone PCs) linked by a separate line to a host computer. Acting somewhat like a traffic cop giving stop and go directions, the host computer poles the "slave" terminals for data transmission.

There are a number of disadvantages to this design. Because it links slave terminals via a separate line, a star configuration is severely limited to the number of free and open slots existing in the host unit. Further, the design employs slave terminals, not stand-alone PCs, as work stations. Therefore, when the network fails, the entire system goes down. Unfortunately, even individual terminal failure often causes entire system failure in the star configuration. For the most part, the star design represents an obsolescing technology because it is relatively slow and cumbersome. The only advantage to the star network is that it provides multiple usage from one computer at an inexpensive rate.

BOX 12-1

Help Is on the Way—Sent by a LAN

Police, Fire Departments Track Incidents via Micro Nets

By Sheridan R. Hansen

"I've just been robbed!" a Provo, Utah, gas station attendant says into the mouthpiece, his voice relaying fear through the telephone wires.

With the crime scene address already on the computer screen, the police dispatcher responds, "Did he use a gun or a knife?"

"A knife."

"Which way did he go?"

"Heading south, down Freedom Boulevard."

With that much information, the dispatcher keeps the robbery victim on the line, at the same time sending all police units in the area to the location.

"What did he take?" the dispatcher continues. "What did the suspect look like?" The dispatcher's questions go on until the victim has provided all the important details.

Provo Police officers have access to five laptop computers which allow them to type reports immediately following an incident. Back at the station, the report is downloaded to the network. [Photo courtesy of the *LAN Times* and the Provo, Utah Police Department.]

A Paperless Revolution

Help always came quickly from Provo's police and fire departments, but never as fast as it comes now. The city's local area network has revolutionized Provo's pen-and-paper system into a fast, computerized emergency response program.

Before the network was installed 2½ years ago, all information from emergency calls was written on a card and then given to an officer or firefighter. Now that data is automatically entered on the screen and employees can refer to the specific call's file when filling out their own incident reports.

BOX 12-1 (cont.)

When a resident makes an emergency call, the call automatically comes to the city's police dispatch unit; from there, dispatchers send police, fire, or emergency medical equipment to the scene.

LANs in both the fire and police departments run Novell NetWare v2.12 on a 386 IBM-clone file server. The police department has 16 workstations, along with five Tandy laptop computers for use in the field. The fire department has five workstations. All workstations are IBM PC AT and XT clones.

Provo is also in the process of installing a new 386 to operate the city's Enhanced-911 emergency system. The sophisticated emergency dispatching system automatically brings up an address to match the phone number. The city plans to use Via/Sys Inc.'s geographic database records system along with the Enhanced-911 system to track the history of a specific address. For example, firefighters and police officers can locate emergency exits in businesses and public buildings, fire hydrant locations, fire inspection records, types of hazardous materials found in area businesses, and if there is a history of domestic violence. The program, Computer Aided Dispatch, will also be able to provide records of previous criminal activity of any suspect brought in.

Provo Police Dispatcher Brenda Nielson answers an emergency call at dispatch headquarters. [Photo courtesy of the *LAN Times* and the Provo, Utah Police Department.]

As It Happens

The police LAN is already in operation with another Via/Sys Inc. program, ACRIS (Advanced Crime Reporting and Information Systems), software specifically designed for law enforcement agencies. Once installed, Computer Aided Dispatch will merely be another feature of ACRIS. At the present time, ACRIS provides a records management system to gather information at the time an incident occurs.

According to Mark Stiegemeier, president of Via/Sys Inc., it is important to have a good response system in a law enforcement agency. Via/Sys recommends that police departments run ACRIS software on NetWare.

BOX 12-1 (cont.)

"NetWare is reliable and easy to install and administer," Steigemeier said. "Many cites can't afford to have a complete data processing center. NetWare is so easy we can readily use a working police officer as a network supervisor." It may sound too good to be true, but Steigemeier says living proof that the network is uncomplicated comes when a police sergeant who knows nothing about computers can be trained to supervise a network. The documents are easy to understand, he said.

Via/Sys software is in use in 70 different law enforcement agencies in 9 different states. Stiegemeier said. Half of all the agencies in Utah use the Via/Sys software together with Novell NetWare. Two out of the 70 agencies use Via/Sys on 3Com operating system software because of product availability and support.

According to Sam Metcalf, supervisor of the Provo Police LAN, the software programs have standardized reports and improved record keeping. The more reliable records available from the LAN have also helped the police carry accurate information through the court system.

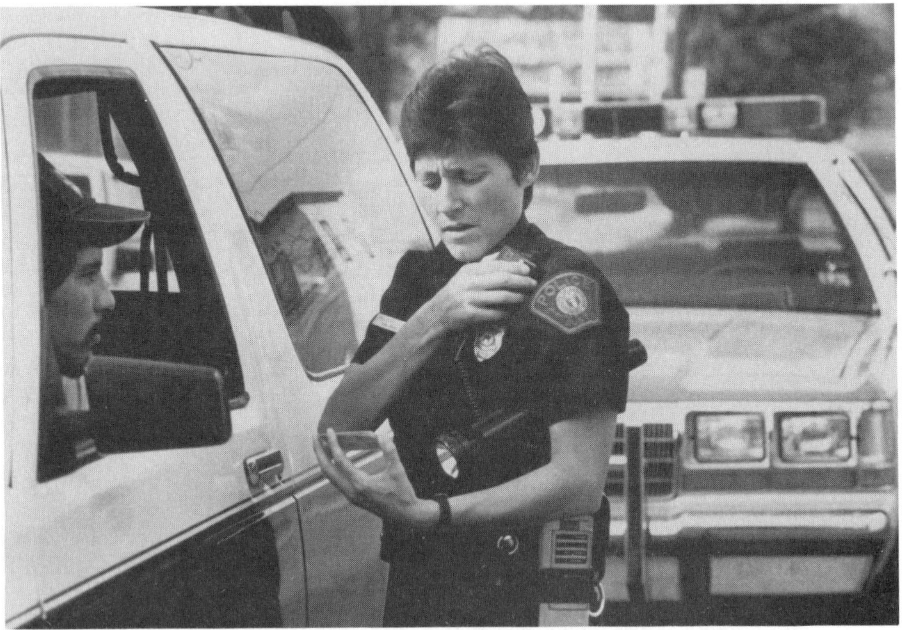

LANs provide an efficient dispatch system, making routine traffic stops a safer procedure. [Photo © Daemmrich/The Image Works.]

A Safer System

For Dana Ferre, dispatch shift coordinator at Provo Police, the network has made a big difference in the city's emergency dispatching system.

"I've dispatched for 10 years, and the network has made the officer's job 10 times safer and our job much more efficient. Before, I remember writing everything out. But you can type so much faster and more efficiently."

The network keeps track of the officers' locations and what they are doing. For example, if an officer makes a traffic check and is out of contact with the dispatcher for more than 10 minutes, the officer's name is automatically highlighted on the dispatcher's screen. The dispatcher can then make contact to ensure that everything is in order.

BOX 12-1 (cont.)

Caught Red-Handed

The system is also capable of tracking gun registrations, pawn tickets from area shops, and an individual's criminal history. Sande Krieger, records supervisor for Provo Police, uses the system to track all arrests and the nature of the arrests. If an officer wants to find out the number of robberies, rapes, or accidents, and where they occurred within a certain time period, the officer can get the information in a matter of minutes. This information is compiled in monthly and yearly reports that are sent to the state Bureau of Criminal investigations.

The network has also given the police department easier access to the state crime computer. Through a modem, officers can use any one of five computers designed to access the state computer. They can request the criminal history of a suspect or make inquiries on vehicle registrations with a simple keystroke, said Tim Deardeuff, supervisor of the city's information systems LAN.

The police department's laptop computers have also opened a new door in filing incident reports, he said. An officer can sit in his car and get the report done right after an incident. Once the officer is back in the station, the information can be downloaded to the network.

Putting Out Fires

The software used in the fire department is also a record-keeping system, but it was developed by Provo City employee T. J. Humphries, supervisor of the fire department network.

Like ACRIS, Humphries' record-keeping program is primarily used in filing incident reports and makes it easier and quicker for fire employees to complete the paperwork that comes with the job.

Better record keeping has been a plus for the fire department, but Humphries said the program also allows the department to detect records for weed abatement and for the location of hazardous materials in the city.

To keep firefighters updated on the last information, fire stations located throughout Provo are able to communicate with the network through a communications server, Humphries said.

Time Brings Improvements

Most city employees have been satisfied with the network, even though Deardeuff said there were times when the LAN supervisors faced a number of problems with NetWare v2.1 and had no idea what was going on. Once the network was upgraded to v2.12, most of the problems, which seemed to be related to heavy LAN traffic, went away, showing that networks seem to get better with age.

So for the person on the other end of the line, don't worry. You can be assured that help is on the way faster than ever in Provo City.

Source: LAN Times, April 1989, pp. 54–55. Copyright 1990 McGraw-Hill, Inc. All rights reserved. Reprinted with permission.

Bus Network. This form of design uses coaxial wire called bus cable. It can be likened to an electrical one-lane highway with two-way traffic. Personal computers are linked to a powerful file server via this cable and are restricted only by the amount of "traffic" using the "highway." Heavily used systems requiring intensive data base operations and processing tend to restrict the allowable number of work stations on one file server.

Technically, the network utilizes carrier sense, multiple access with collision detection (or CSMA/CD) to avoid "traffic jams," or data collisions. The standard bus topology is called Ethernet and has been adopted by a number of computer vendors. It is very reliable and relatively inexpensive. Ethernet incorporates standalone PCs, not slave terminals, as work stations. It represents the largest number of installed networks in present-day business.

Token Passing Network. In this topology, PCs are linked together to form a ring. Data lines connect each unit to adjacent ones only. Therefore, no dependence on a central file server is necessary. Data routing is relatively simple. Each PC work station must wait for a coded, electrical signal (called a token) to pass by. The PC senses the token's arrival and attaches information to it that moves down the data transmission line to the point of delivery.

Token passing topology is very reliable. Because there is no dependence on a central device, a single break in the network will not cause entire system failure. However, adding new terminals requires the reconfiguration of the entire loop. Cabling, installation, and the software itself are expensive.

Figure 12-3 provides a schematic view of each LAN topology.

Wide Area Networks

A wide area network (WAN) is a network that can interconnect different types of computers (or other networks) over a large geographical area via telephone or dedicated media such as microwave or fiber optic cable. Most WANs use a *modem* for communication between computers. A modem is an abbreviation of *mo*dulator/*dem*odulator. It converts a digital message from a computer to an analog signal so that data can be transmitted via standard telephone linkages, a process called modulation. On the receiving end, analog signals are decoded back to digital data for computer processing, called demodulation. This entire process occurs very quickly and is usually measured in a *baud* rating (bits per second). The standard baud ratings are 300, 900, 1200, 2400, 9600, and 19,200 baud.

An excellent use of modems in law enforcement can be observed when querying the National Crime Information Center (NCIC), located in Washington, D.C. The officer or dispatcher enters a query from a remote location, for instance, Seattle, Washington. This query from the input computer is modulated to an analog signal (through a local modem) and sent via telephone to the NCIC mainframe. Another modem at the receiving end demodulates the signal back to a digital format, and the NCIC's computer processes the query. If a "hit" is discovered, the information is transformed in the reverse and sent back to Seattle.

Planning for Computerization

The term *planning* is a loosely defined and poorly understood concept. Stated simply, planning is a process that attempts to link information from the past with probable future events. The decision to purchase an automated records system

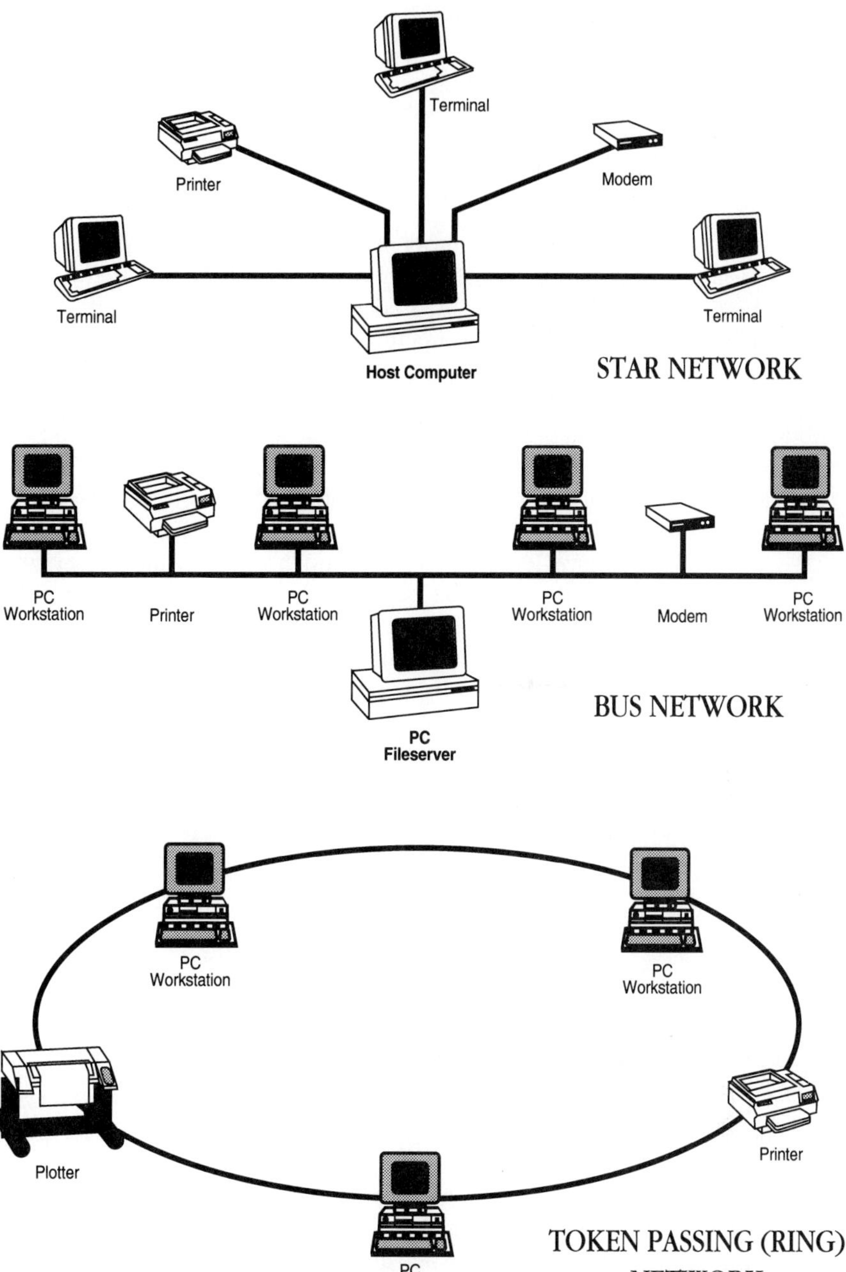

FIGURE 12-3. Common topologies of local area networks (LANs): star, bus, and token-passing. [Graphics courtesy of Dr. Matt Prosser, Tyler, Texas.]

requires careful and proper planning considerations. Many police chiefs have been faced with the dilemma of implementing such a system without having the necessary information and knowledge on which to base correct decisions.

Technological Expertise

Law enforcement administrators make the mistake of relying on information pertaining to computers that they or others in their department have gained on a novice basis. Often some member of their agency recently purchased a home computer and now feels competent to automate the police records division. The pitfalls of this approach are obvious as the complexities and extensiveness of such a project may well be beyond the capabilities of such personnel. For the most part, police chiefs are general managers, and as such they should seek specialized advice. There are a number of sources from which this help can be obtained.

One source is the outside consultant. Most cities have a number of consulting firms that specialize in office automation. Although these consultants may have the technological knowledge to ascertain and evaluate a number of computer systems, they may not understand the needs of the police organization. Ideally, the consultant should have police experience, preferably at a supervisory or management level, in addition to extensive technological knowledge. Realizing that this type of consultant may be hard to find, especially in nonmetropolitan areas, the police chief may have to rely on a number of specialty journals or seminars in order to obtain an objective evaluation of current, state-of-the-art computer systems.

Another source of valuable information for the police chief may be in the local university or community college. Higher educational facilities often have a department of criminal justice or law enforcement with a faculty member specializing in the area of automation and technology. Such persons are able to provide the valuable and critically important technological expertise that is necessary during the computerization process.

Needs Assessments

One of the major problems observed in the planning process for computerized systems in law enforcement is the lack of a valid needs assessment. A needs assessment is basically a statement that gives the goals and objectives for the system to be purchased. What specific functions will the computer perform? This question appears to be basic; however, it is frequently overlooked in the planning process. Certain variables—such as the size of the department, the number of calls received in a year, the budget allocation for spending, and the like—provide valuable insights and limitations on the type and size of computer that would be necessary to perform the functions required within a police department. Many chiefs make the mistake of buying computers with capabilities that either far exceed or fail to match their needs. The result is having a greater deal of capability that is not used or having a system that is inadequate to perform the tasks for which it was purchased. Also, contrary to popular belief, the computer cannot do everything. Automation is not a cure-all for problems within the department's information-processing system.

During the needs assessment stage, a consultant or outside source can also serve a very useful function. Many times, the outside reviewer can provide valuable points that otherwise would have been overlooked by the internal administrator or manager. The old proverb "not being able to see the forest because of the trees" often is true during the needs assessment stage. Obviously, the chief can become so involved in the department that he or she will fail to consider a number of important points.

Software Applications

A number of computer systems are limited to specific operating systems and computer languages. Compatibility refers to the capability of a computer hardware system to run a software package. Literally thousands of software packages are available that singularly or in combination provide a number of functions directly related to law enforcement. Records management, data analysis, graphics, telecommunications, and word processing are application programs that currently exist in the software market. Most of these software packages require little customizing or adapting for police usage.

In addition to these general purpose programs, a number of software packages are specifically designed for use in law enforcement. One of the first attempts to maximize compatibility between computer hardware systems by means of a shared software package evolved through the cooperation of the Bureau of Justice Statistics, the U.S. Department of Justice, and the International Association of Chiefs of Police. The main program, called POSSE (Police Operations Systems Support—Elementary) (see Figure 12-4), is a relatively low-cost computer system that stores a variety of management reports. The main program interfaces with three other limited-use data-management systems:

- CASS (Crime Analysis System Support) is a generalized, automated crime analysis system that provides crime suspect/correlations, crime patterns, target profiles, forecasting, and resource allocation studies.
- IMIS (Investigate Management Information System) is a criminal investigation monitoring system that provides feedback on workload, performance, case status, and support budget requests.
- FMIS (Fleet Management Information System) is a fleet management system that assesses vehicle and equipment class performance, monitors fuel consumption, and provides support for budget requests.

The POSSE system represents just one of a number of software packages designed to service law enforcement agency needs. Most packages incorporate a series of subprograms that manipulate stored data into some type of meaningful report. A good example is the Uniform Crime Report (UCR) schedules that are routinely made by police agencies on a monthly basis. Stored data regarding the number of offenses is tabulated, and a report is generated that is then submitted in accordance with FBI guidelines. Most of the features available in specifically designed software packages fall into one of three broad-based categories: (1) operations (data base information), (2) management and administration (data base management), and (3) communication and training (data base sharing).

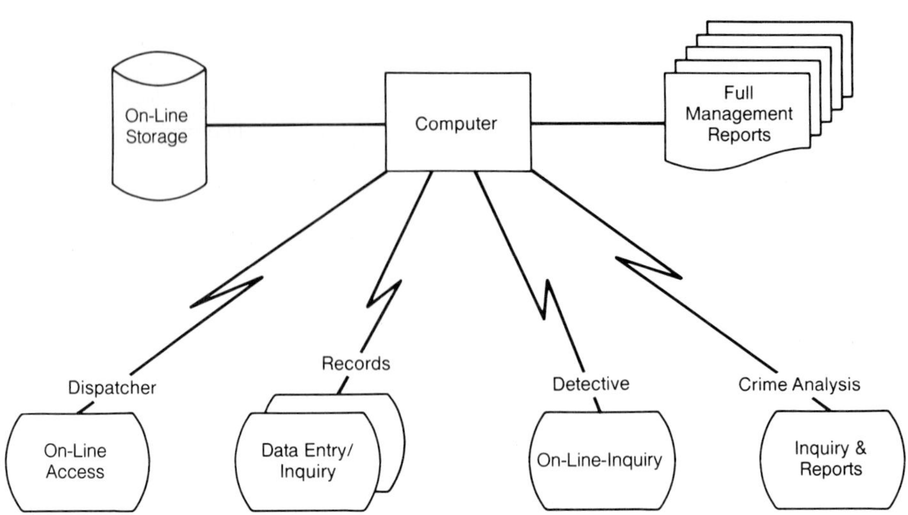

FIGURE 12-4. Diagram of the typical POSSE computer system. [Courtesy Hadron System Products Group (formerly Simeon Incorporated), Fairfax, Virginia.]

Operations

Law enforcement agencies are excellent examples of information-processing systems. The information may be as mundane as tracking a parking ticket through the system or as complex as an analysis of crime trends in an area.[9] Traditionally, most agencies have captured information on original police reports and stored it in vast warehouse rooms called "Records Division." Police records usually include information about persons, locations, vehicles, offenses, incidents, and so on that establishes a large, centralized data base. The problem with nonautomated systems is that specific information cannot be retrieved immediately nor can such information be statistically manipulated without many hours of hand tabulation. The hours expended in such efforts and the large volume of report forms to be analyzed necessitate computerization.

Automated Records Systems

An automated records system enables police agencies to maintain large data bases with an immediate search and retrieval capability. In this manner, law enforcement personnel have almost instantaneous access to individual criminal histories, outstanding warrants, traffic information, field contacts, investigations, and the like. Further, these systems usually provide data summaries and displays that allow police analysts to recognize patterns in reported incidents and to match suspects, vehicles, and weapons with criminal activities (see Figure 12-6).

These systems can be either very simple (store, sort, and retrieve) or extremely complex with a variety of added features. Some of the more advanced systems incorporate

- *Special hazard denotations*—Small one- or two-word messages that are highlighted or flash in order to catch the operator's attention. A common hazard message is "Armed and Dangerous" when describing a particular suspect.
- *Address verification files*—subprograms that automatically search the entered address and confirm its location, giving dispatch directions and names of residents.
- *Phonetic files*—subprograms designed to list sound-alike names with different spellings. For instance, the last name "Martinez" may be queried under the phonetic spellings of "Martenes," "Martins," or "Martines." Obviously such an automated file would be invaluable concerning names of different nationalities pronounced the same way although spelled differently.
- *Monikers files or AKA files*—This system can list an alias for a given individual or query an individual by the name entered. The nickname "Scarface" may be the only name heard by a victim or witness. By entering the moniker, the identities and criminal histories of all persons known as "Scarface" are obtained.

One of the more innovative and interesting projects that is directly related to improving automated records systems is "live reporting."[10] Police officers produce reports by telephoning a record specialist who directly enters the information into the computer. In this manner, the system produces professionally typed reports

FIGURE 12-5. In 1939, the San Francisco Police Department announced that it would use a "mechanical brain" to analyze crime. The cards were punched in the machine in the foreground, sorted in the machine on the left, and "analyzed" and printed by the last machine. Current computer and software technology advancements have gone far beyond this once state-of-the-art capability. [Photo courtesy of the San Francisco Archives.]

WANTED/HAZARD

LEADS NAME DISPLAY

LEADS NUMBER: 46					UPDATE DATE:	2/11/92
NAME: BROWN, LEROY JAMES					FBI: 12345AB123	
					FDLE: 987654XXX	
MONIKERS: BAD LEROY					HCSO: 999999210	

SEX:	M	RACE:	W	DOB:	7/08/50	ANTI-SOCIAL-TRAITS
HGT:	6'5"	WGT:	240	SSNO:	123-45-6789	RESISTS ARREST
EYES:	BLU	HAIR:	BRN	PHONE:	555-1234	

	OPERATORS LICENSE	ST	YR
SCARS-MARKS-TATTOOS	ABCD—123456	AZ	92
JAGGED SCAR ON CHIN			

	ASSOCIATED VEHICLES	LIC PLT	ST
LAST KNOWN ADDRESS	80 CHOP HARLEY MC	M-1234	AZ
100 N. PLAZA WAY	85 RED CADILLAC 2DR	ABC-123	AZ

* * * * * * * * * * * * * * *

FIGURE 12-6. The Law Enforcement Automated Data System—LEADS front name page. An excellent example of an automated records system. Note the special hazard denotation and moniker file. [Courtesy COMSEC, Inc., Tyler, Texas.]

and serves as the primary source of management information that is accessible instantaneously from remote locations. Additionally, with the advent of programmable, battery-powered, notebook-sized computers that weigh less than four pounds, with a full-sized keyboard, a built-in telephone modem, and preprogrammed word processing and communications, some police departments, such as those in St. Petersburg and Ocala, Florida, are pioneering the use of portable computers for writing formatted police reports in the field.[11]

These new techniques greatly enhance existing automated records systems by (1) reducing time spent by uniform police officers in preparing reports, thus increasing officer, and supervisor "street time"; (2) providing instant "on-line" management information and instant retrieval of reports from any remote location, such as the precinct or detective office; (3) reducing office space used to maintain hard copies in filing cabinets or vaults by storing reports in computer memory; (4) improving the quality, accuracy, and timeliness of crime analysis, management reports, and UCR by electronically processing, aggregating, distributing, and filing these documents; and (5) improving the quality, legibility, and accuracy of police reports.[12]

Crime Analysis

The statistical analysis of data and the organization of information into manageable summaries provide law enforcement with meaningful tools in which to com-

FIGURE 12-7. Crime-specific targeting in a residential neighborhood. [Photo courtesy of Maricopa County Sheriff's Office, Phoenix, Arizona.]

bat crime. The crime problem has continued to grow in terms of quantity, sophistication, and complexity, thereby forcing police officers and investigators to seek additional help in enforcement techniques. The purpose of crime analysis is to organize massive quantities of raw information, from data bases utilized in automated records systems, and to forecast specific future events from the statistical manipulation of these data. In theory, crime analysis provides a thorough and systematic analysis of data on which to make rational decisions regarding past, present, and future actions.[13]

Crime analysis is not limited solely to reported crime information. Attention has also been given to the statistical analysis of intelligence information. Kinney[14] reports that criminal intelligence analysis can support investigators, decision makers, and policymakers in their attempt to prevent and control crime.

Some of the more common crime analysis techniques are

- *Crime-Specific Analysis*—A tabular or graphic display of reported crimes within a given pattern of time and/or location (see Figure 12-7). It is often used to detect robberies or burglaries that cluster in specific locations during various time periods.
- *Link Analysis*—A graphic portrayal of associates between individuals or organizations, charted from available information to a given point in time. This is invaluable in putting many identities in proper relational perspective. It is most frequently used as an investigative and briefing aid.[15]

- *Telephone Toll Analysis*—Computerized reports derived from court ordered long-distance telephone billings of suspects in illegal narcotics trafficking. Reports indicate number and frequency of calls that are displayed in numerical, chronological, and geographical order. Link Analysis can be used to show the relationship between billing numbers and the numbers called.[16]
- *Visual Investigative Analysis (VIA)*—Charting that depicts key events of criminal activity in chronological order. VIA is used to show the degree of involvement of subjects. This method is especially convincing in conspiracy cases and can also be used as a planning tool to focus the resources of an investigative effort.[17]
- *Case Analysis and Management System (CAMS)*—Computerized case management in which large amounts of data are compiled and indexed for each retrieval of specific items. This system is used to clarify relationships and to calculate the probability of associations.[18]

Although not all of these techniques are fully automated, the basic procedures follow a flow-chart configuration that provides a sound basis for software design. Combining these techniques with a statistical package (such as SPSS/X, ABSTAT, SAS, or STATPRO) produces a strong capability for forecasting and prediction.

Geographic Information Systems (GIS)

The last five years have given rise to the integration of automated data base operations, crime analysis, and high-level mapping. The merger of these powerful programs is commonly referred to as *geographic information systems* (GIS).[19] Traditionally, map data and tabular data describing pieces of land such as police beats have been stored separately, but computer technology now provides the opportunity to merge the two yet preserve their independent natures. Unfortunately, only a few police departments have implemented GIS technologies on a mainframe, mainly due to expense and the developmental newness of the product. However, several microcomputer-based mapping programs are making significant advances in the crime analysis field.

The new technology of desktop mapping allows the display of geographic information (spatial data) on computer monitors—topography, natural resources, transportation hubs, highways, utilities, political boundaries, and police beats. Geographic information systems combine these spatial representations with almost any other type of data an analyst wishes to enter. Textual and tabular data (attribute data) such as population density, crime locations, traffic patterns, demographic profiles, and voting patterns can be displayed and manipulated against map backgrounds. From this type of analysis, it is possible to overlay multiple map sets so that police researchers and executives can pictorially view the interrelationships among several variables. Thus, GIS technologies differ from previous types of crime analysis techniques and/or information systems in that their primary purpose is *not* purely cartographic, with emphasis on display and graphics, but rather the analysis, manipulation, and management of spatial data.

General information system technologies have far-reaching implications not only in police operations as defined by crime analysis, but also as management and communications tools (see Box 12-2). Police agencies can use GISs in dis-

BOX 12-2

To Catch a Thief: High-Tech Cops Using Crime Information Systems

Police departments have been particularly receptive to automated mapping technology for crime analysis because the systems lend themselves to documenting crimes by location, time, modus operandi and other factors.

By Laura Lang

In television shows and movies, "good guys" often stood before large wall maps, solving crimes by using push-pins to indicate where they took place. Or taking it a step further, they would color-code the pins to provide details for cracking cases, such as times, incidence sequence, or modus operandi (M.O.).

Push-pins were used by police in the real world too, but their use in crimesolving was limited since they could only effectively show one variable. For instance, if different colored pins were used to show rapes, murders, and robberies in one area, they couldn't also indicate the time of day or day of the week that the crimes occurred. Worse, in real life the pins often fell out of the wall or were inadvertently jumbled.

But today, the same officers who once squinted at wall maps probably hover around computer terminals as crime variables are overlaid with sophisticated "crime information systems." These programs use computer maps linked to databases for analysis, manipulation, visual management and presentation of statistical information based on geographic locations.

Crime information systems far exceed the value and versatility of manual push-pin maps. They can show robberies on a block and overlay others factor such as assaults or murders in the same area. And since they are closely tied to the database, they can be used to search for area residents with criminal records or similar crimes in adjacent areas.

In Syracuse, NY, the Police Department installed a PC-based desktop mapping system, from MapInfo Corp., Troy, NY, about 18 months ago to geocode and automatically display selected crime incidents—and crime-related data from their files—on street maps.

MapInfo includes built-in base maps of the U.S. and the world as well as national five-digit ZIP code centroids. Other maps are sold *a la carte,* so departments can buy maps for their city and surrounding areas as needed.

According to Don Large, commanding officer in the Information Systems Division at the Syracuse Police Department, when they first used the system for crime analysis they took criminal trends of burglaries for 1988 and put out geographic maps of patrol areas with geographic "pin maps" of information attached.

"In one mapped area we deployed investigators with the information, and within two days we caught several suspects in progress who were committing burglaries, and ended up clearing 35 burglaries," explained Large.

"MapInfo made the information digestible both in printed and visual form so the patterns were easier to recognize," he added.

Syracuse's system runs on five networked 386s, the mapping system is resident on one of the PCs. They access a county-wide 14-agency law enforcement system on a mainframe and download information into dBase IV for crime analysis as it is needed.

"Because criminals have set patterns, they can effectively be recorded and analyzed by police departments using desktop mapping/crime information systems. Seen graphically, the crimes are easier to predict and plan for—and that's the real benefit they offer," agreed Laszlo Bardos, MapInfo's director of marketing.

BOX 12-2 (cont.)

About a dozen vendors market crime information programs, ranging from "low end" desktop mapping packages like MapInfo which is priced under $1,000 to "high end" geographic information systems (GIS) running on PCs, workstations, minicomputers or mainframes which might cost up to $90,000 and allow users to integrate databases with map graphics for analysis, display, editing, and to generate reports and thematic maps.

Information Control

Police departments have been particularly receptive to automated mapping technology for crime analysis, vendors say, because the systems lend themselves well to documenting crimes by location, time, M.O. and other factors.

After a brief training period, these programs are used by police investigators and detectives who make use of existing records for crime analysis and trending.

"Police departments collect enormous amounts of data, but unless (the data) can be turned into usable information, it's useless," said Bud Emerson, commander of the Systems Development Division of the Minneapolis Police Department.

In Minneapolis, an UltiMap Crime Information System (UltiMap Corp., Minneapolis, MN) is used to improve crime trend analysis and response, according to Emerson. UltiMap integrates automatic mapping and facilities management (AM/FM), GIS, and computer-aided design (CAD) technologies for engineering applications.

"The system is far more flexible than what we used to use in helping our officers to analyze crime statistics," Emerson said. "This system will help us turn our mass of data into useful information to help us improve the way we deliver police services and determine what our services should comprise."

The workstation-based Crime Information System is directly linked to the department's existing computerized police records system (CORPS), resident on a Unisys A10 mainframe computer.

The department created its own base map database, and then classified their crimes by codes (i.e., theft, homicide, robbery) and by coded ranges within the categories such as type of business and exact location and time of the crime.

Using UltiMap's customized crime analysis on-screen menus, the database is searched by multiple parameters, geocoded, electronically displayed in picture form, plotted as patterns or incidences on maps, or output to tabular reports.

According to UltiMap President Jerry W. Robinson, an advantage of a full-fledged GIS over a low-end desktop mapping system is that the central database can be shared with other departments within the city (such as Planning or Public Works), and the system linked to other data sources.

"Since our (UltiMap) system is based on Apollo workstations, we provide users with a lot of processing power right on their own desks. They also have strong networking capabilities to communicate with other workstations in the network and to share information with other users," Robinson said.

"Typically, low-end desktop mapping systems wouldn't have those features," he added.

Vehicle Dispatch

In some departments, crime information systems are used for dispatching squad cars and other emergency vehicles. By typing in an address, a map can be brought up on-screen, and the program indicates the best way for the vehicles to travel to the location. In addition, the software can supply a history of the address, such as if a similar call has come in before or if the house is under suspicion for illegal activities.

The Tonawanda, NY, Police Department has used MapInfo for the past two years for dispatching emergency vehicles, said Mark Winters, a lieutenant who helped select and install the system. "We wanted to set up a way to locate and get to residences quickly for emergency dispatch, and this system has been a tremendous aid," he said.

BOX 12-2 (cont.)

In Tonawanda, every call that comes into 911 for police or ambulance response is entered by dispatchers into the MapInfo system, which links to a database of home owners and other statistical data for every residence in the city.

The program is set up so the operator can bring up a map in about seven or eight seconds of the immediate area around an address, showing all fire hydrants and cross-streets, with the residence circled and the owner's name at the bottom of the screen.

In some cases, a code will also appear on-screen to alert dispatchers to special information attached to that address, such as if a handicapped person were living at the house and special requirements such as where the person sleeps and if he needed to be kept on an oxygen machine, or if chemicals or fire arms have been known to be kept on the premises.

With the information displayed on screen, the dispatcher can refer to the graphics as emergency vehicles are directed to the call. Taking this a step further, Winters predicted that in a few years laptop computers will be taken along in emergency vehicles so the same map being viewed by the dispatcher can also be shown on the display in the car to show the response team where they're going and what to expect graphically.

In a related use, if a hazardous chemical is spilled and residents need to be evacuated from an area, the map can be brought up and used to plot out the area that needs to be cleared. The names of home owners are immediately available, to expedite contacting and moving people.

Tonawanda's system is used on 286-based PCATs on a Novel network. There are 16 terminals attached to the network, but only one terminal can access the map at any given time. Since the main use of the system is for dispatching, the map database is normally accessed by the dispatcher. When the dispatcher isn't using the database, however, it may be used by other department members for crime analysis or other tasks.

The police department uses its own software to track complaints and convert the data in that file into MapInfo plot maps of the city for crime statistics. "This is especially useful for burglaries since we can pinpoint incidents across the city at any specific time or other factor," Winters said. "We can locate that residence, and bring up the text file to review what was stolen and who owns the residence."

"We can give the maps to the patrols to see where burglaries are and at what times so we can best cover the areas."

Winters added, "This software has been an unbelievable bonus for us, and it's extremely flexible. Even if someone walks into the station and just asks directions to a residence, we can use the maps to show them on screen where the address is."

It took the department about a month to set up their databases with information including owners of residences, locations of fire hydrants and indicators on handicapped residents.

The project utilized two full-time officers and several members of the auxiliary police. The initial maps supplied by MapInfo were double-checked to make sure the addresses and locations were accurate and added information—such as fire hydrant locations—was included. But Winters was quick to point out, "This has been a fully functional and effective system from the start.

"I can see this technology catching on with departments all over the country. It really saves us a lot of time and there's no limit to the applications we'll be able to add," he noted.

According to Syracuse's Don Large, "We were one of the first departments to use crime information systems, so we've been contacted by many other departments interested in buying and implementing the technology.

"We have found it a cost-efficient way to work. Of course, there are more expensive, elaborate mapping systems, but for investigative purposes desktop mapping was the most responsive technology for our needs," he explained.

BOX 12-2 (cont.)

"We see police departments as a very big market since they need a way to better manage spatial information," said UltiMap's Robinson. "It helps them to improve their services to the community."

Added Bardos, "Police departments have been quick to jump into desktop mapping technology. It's making their work more efficient since they can double-team during heavy crime hours and (in heavy crime) areas, or be well-prepared when called to a dangerous address where crimes frequently occur.

"The technology is making their jobs easier and greatly benefits the community they're serving."

Source: Government Technology, October 1989, pp. 1, 21–22.

patching police units by providing directions to locations; address histories; and locations of nearby fire and waste hazards, fire hydrants, alarm boxes, high power lines, water lines, and the like. Police managers can use GISs to provide graphic analysis of specific crime patterns, evaluate new policing strategies, and even track individual officer performance by area. Not surprisingly, GISs have emerged as powerful tools helping police executives make better-informed decisions (see Figure 12-9 on pp. 532–533).

Investigations and Case Management

The RAND study of detectives identified a number of functions performed by investigators.[20] The study questioned whether many of these functions (such as preparing cases for prosecution, apprehending suspects, engaging in intensive investigations when there are no suspects, conducting pro-active investigations, and performing administrative tasks and paperwork related to these functions) should be performed at all by detectives.[21] The study concluded that these functions could be performed better (more effectively) and at a lower cost (more efficiently) by patrol officers and clerical personnel.[22] The present process of investigation was concluded to be so chaotic and complex that all of the functions could not be adequately performed by a single individual.

In direct response to this study and in an attempt to coordinate activity between investigators and prosecutors, a number of automated case management systems were designed. These systems assign cases to individual detectives and then monitor the progress of the investigation from case opening to final disposition. Although most such systems are internal to police agencies, some, like the Prosecutor's Management and Information System—PROMIS—attempt to coordinate activities between law enforcement and prosecution.[23] The computerization of the assembly-line production of case investigation and prosecution reduces fragmentation of responsibility and control. Further, the automation of such a process allows evaluation at various points or stages in the assembly line by means of the application of a uniform set of criteria. In this manner, more important cases (based on the gravity of the crime and the suspect's prior record) can receive special attention while assuring an even-handed treatment of cases of less seriousness.[24]

Artificial Intelligence and Expert Systems

Another type of information system having direct applications in law enforcement is *artificial intelligence* (AI). Most definitions of AI vary to emphasize the interdisciplinary nature of the subject. Artificial intelligence is a science and a technology based on disciplines such as computer science, biology, psychology, linguistics, mathematics, and engineering. The goal of AI is to develop computers that can think, as well as see, hear, walk, talk, and feel.[25] Basically, artificial intelligence can be defined as a shift from mere data processing to an intelligent processing of knowledge. The model for such development is the human body and brain. Artificial intelligence focuses on four major areas of research:

- *Natural language applications*—systems that translate ordinary human commands into language that computer programs can understand and execute; computer programs that read, speak, and understand human languages
- *Robotic applications*—machines that move and relate to objects as humans do; programs that focus on developing visual, tactile, and movement capabilities in machines
- *Computer science applications*—development of more advanced, fifth-generation computers and the replication of physical brain functioning such as that found in human cell–computer interfacing and neural networks
- *Cognitive science applications*—programs that mimic the decision-making logic of the human brain, such as that found in expert systems, knowledge-based systems, and logic systems.

Figure 12-8 provides a schematic view of the major application domains of AI.

It is this last area of cognitive science applications involving expert systems that police managers find most promising. Basically, expert systems attempt to sup-

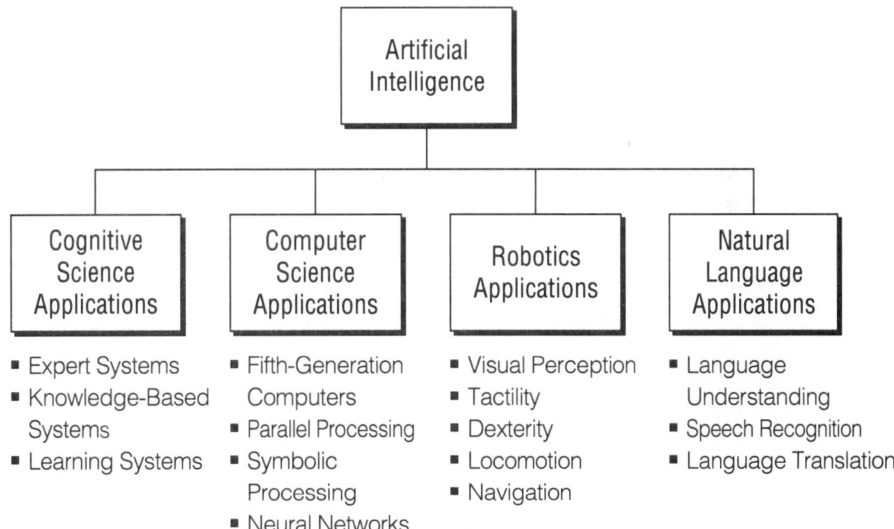

FIGURE 12-8. The major application domains of artificial intelligence [*Source:* J. A. O'Brien, *Management Information Systems: A Managerial End User Perspective.* (Homewood, IL: Irwin, 1990), p. 357.]

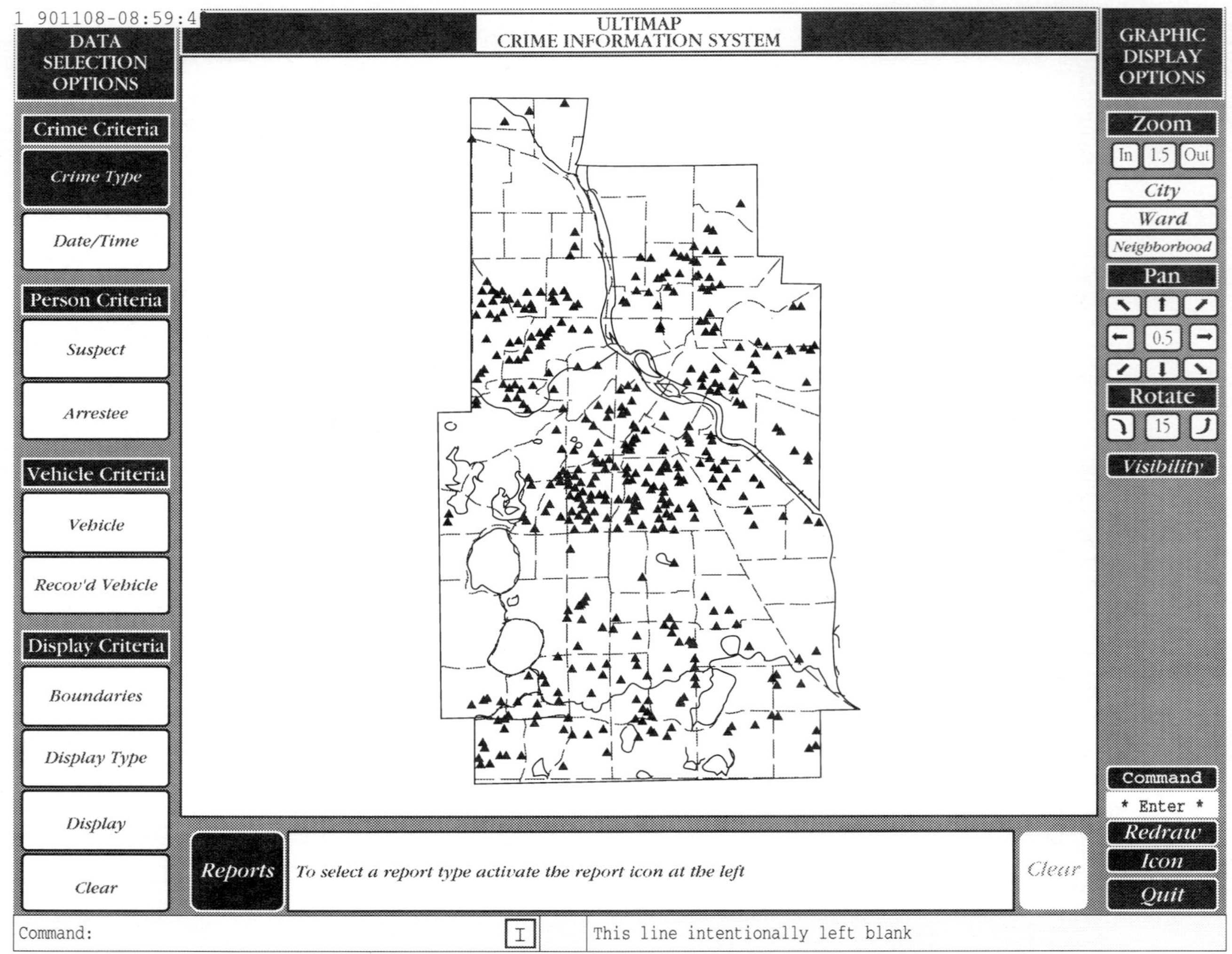
1 901108-08:59:4
DATA SELECTION OPTIONS
ULTIMAP
CRIME INFORMATION SYSTEM
GRAPHIC DISPLAY OPTIONS
Crime Criteria
Crime Type
Date/Time
Person Criteria
Suspect
Arrestee
Vehicle Criteria
Vehicle
Recov'd Vehicle
Display Criteria
Boundaries
Display Type
Display
Clear
Zoom
In
1.5
Out
City
Ward
Neighborhood
Pan
0.5
Rotate
15
Visibility
Command
* Enter *
Redraw
Icon
Quit
Reports
To select a report type activate the report icon at the left
Clear
Command:
I
This line intentionally left blank

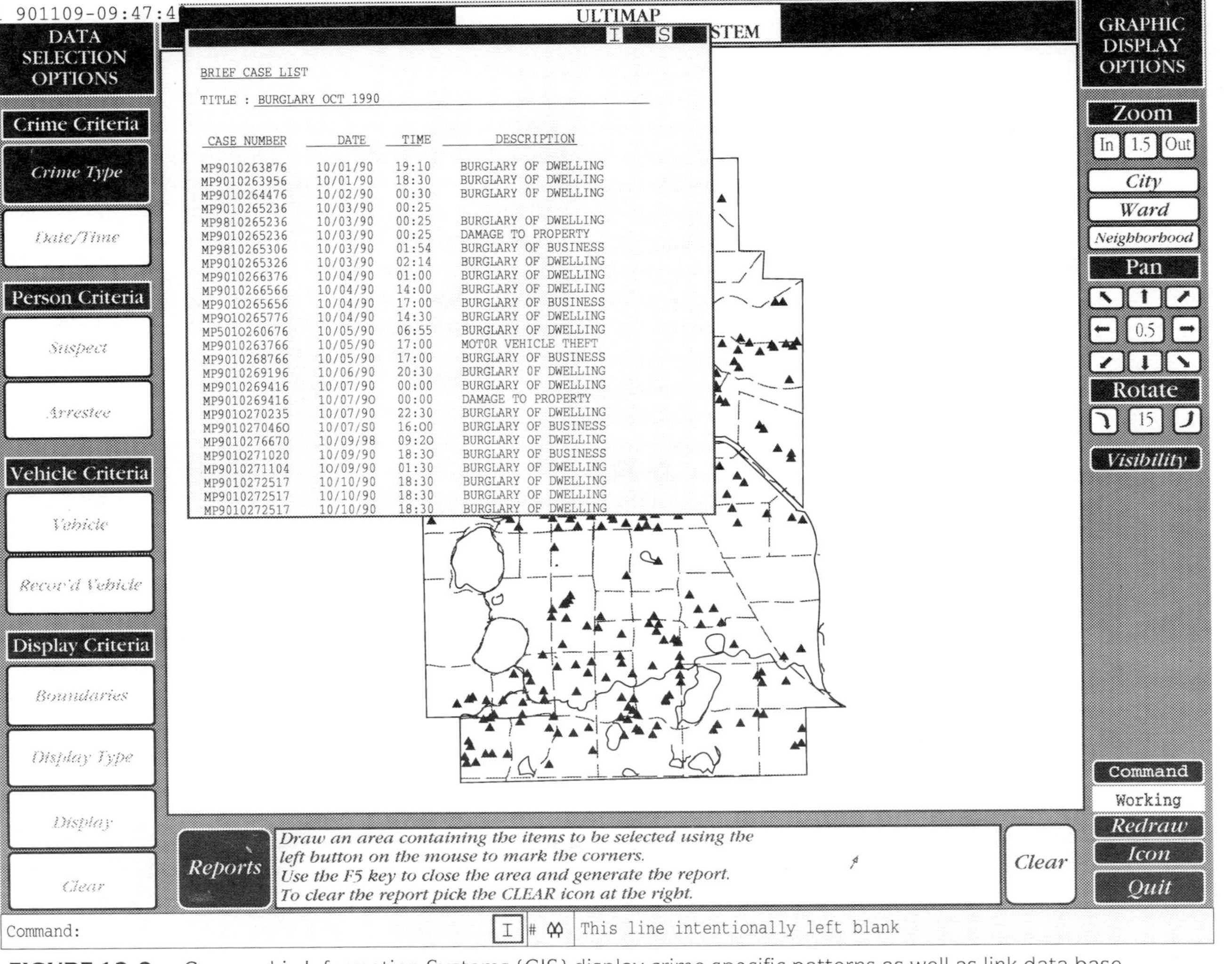

FIGURE 12-9. Geographic Information Systems (GIS) display crime specific patterns as well as link data base information with on-line mapping capabilities. In these selections, note the distribution of burglaries within neighborhood boundaries and the capability of directly accessing all relevant information pertaining to specific cases. (Courtesy of the Minneapolis Police Department, Systems Development Division.)

plant rather than supplement human efforts in arriving at solutions to complex problems. For instance, the state of Washington is using a case analysis expert system to provide suspect profiles in the Green River homicide investigation.[26] The Baltimore, Maryland, Police Department uses an expert system to assist in solving burglary cases (see Box 12-3). The system correlates past suspect methods of operation with current burglary events to determine potential trends. About 25 specific items of information relating to a burglary are entered into the AI system, which provides a list of possible suspects, ranked in order of probability.[27] The Los Angeles Sheriff's Department uses a comprehensive database called CHIEFS to aid in homicide investigations (see Box 12-4). Other expert systems are being developed within the FBI's Behavioral Science Unit in Quantico, Virginia, to support investigations of organized crime, narcotics, arson, and terrorism.[28]

On a more mundane level, expert systems are also being used to assist local police managers with complex planning and task scheduling. However, their greatest benefit may be in changing the way organizations behave by promoting a different perspective on problem solving. In law enforcement, this approach requires creative and innovative police executives who challenge traditional assumptions concerning the police function and mission. Indeed, with the development of expert systems that attempt to combine textbook guesses about a specific problem, executives need no longer rely on their own intuition or inspiration. What may have worked well in the past may appear foolish when contrasted to solutions based on expert systems.[29]

The future of expert systems and other AI applications holds great promise for law enforcement as the price and power of computer hardware improve and the sophistication of software development increases. The trend is clear. Police ad-

FIGURE 12-10. One of the application domains at artificial intelligence (AI) (robotics) produces robots often used in law enforcement for special operations such as bomb disposal. [Photo courtesy of the Denver, Colorado Police Department.]

BOX 12-3

BaltCo PD Ready to Roll

Artificial Intelligence, Real Results

The Baltimore County Police Department's Residential Burglary Expert System (REBES) is now fully operational after four years of preparation and testing, but even as police planners work out "bugs" in the system, some successes have already been noted and plans are afoot to adapt the technology to other law enforcement applications.

The heart and soul of REBES is a software package that incorporates rule statements about burglaries gleaned from the knowledge of detectives. Closed burglary cases—with information about arrestees—are entered into REBES, and when new burglaries are committed, the expert system can combine the two bases of information to provide investigators with a list of possible suspects.

Capt. Ernest Crist of the agency's Planning Management Unit said that REBES, which became operational last June, is now being evaluated for any "bugs." The next phase of evaluation, slated for later this year, will involve comparing current clearance rates to those achieved before REBES went on line.

Doing What They Hoped

Already, however, REBES is doing what its developers hoped it would all along: help point investigators to possible suspects. "We've seen a number of successes to this point," said Crist. "We consider a success a case which we've entered into the REBES system, and the system has produced a list of suspects with the perpetrator on the list somewhere."

REBES matches data elements of crime scenes—supplied by data-coding sheets completed by crime-scene technicians—with criminal characteristics of the nearly 600 past offenders whose histories are stored in the system. Once the case data is entered into the computer, it will match them against certain"if . . . then" rules that give some clue to the criminal's modus operandi. For example, if a technician notes that the suspect rifled through a medicine cabinet during the burglary, the expert system may infer that the suspect is a drug abuser. The system then looks for suspects with histories of drug abuse.

"Then it will produce a list and the list will rank the data elements in the case. If we have a suspect in there [and] if there were four data elements in the case, and he matched three of the four, he will get a 75 percent ranking," explained Crist. Detectives then check out the suspect.

In the next two years, Baltimore County police planners expect to apply REBES technology to robbery and also to aid in formulating strategies to solve substance-abuse problems, said Crist. "Some problems respond strictly to law enforcement intervention. Other problems require a combination of treatment, education and law enforcement. Some problems may only respond to treatment strategies. So we're trying to collect some data now on which problems respond to which strategies, and then we'll write rules and put them in to the system and ultimately, when we recognize a drug problem in the area, we'll have a system to recommend those strategies to us."

Helping Each Other Along

Start-up work on Baltimore's REBES, the first in the nation, began in 1987 when the Jefferson Institute, a Washington, D.C.–based criminal justice research organization, received a grant from the National Institute of Justice to develop the prototype. The technical work was performed by Edward Ratledge, a systems engineer with the University of Delaware.

The Bureau of Justice Assistance has since provided funds to launch similar artificial-intelligence projects in Tucson, Ariz., Rochester, N.Y., Charlotte, N.C., and Tampa, Fla. According to Joan Jacoby, director of the Jefferson Institute, Tucson's expert

BOX 12-3 (cont.)

system is close to operational, and the others will soon follow suit. The projects were staggered so that, "as each jurisdiction gained experience in one phase of working with the expert systems, they could help the next jurisdiction along."

Police agencies utilizing expert systems have banded together to form the Law Enforcement Expert Systems Association (LEESA), which promotes a free exchange of information between agencies about the technology. Crist serves as LEESA's co-chairman, and the group will hold its second annual meeting in October in Tampa, one of the BJA demonstration sites for expert systems.

While more testing and evaluation are needed, Jacoby said she believes expert systems will play a very visible role in law enforcement in coming years. Agencies now using them "are probably at least five years ahead of themselves," she said. "This technology is just so new that five years from now, people will say, 'Oh yeah, we've got expert systems. Everybody's got them.' Right now, they're breaking all of the new ground. They're on the cutting edge of even the advanced technology."

Source: Law Enforcement News, April 30, 1991, p. 17.

ministrators will be using more AI-based technology as decision support systems in both operations and management.

Management and Administration

One of the most important benefits stemming from the use of computers in law enforcement is the monitoring and improvement of officer productivity, a task long associated with management and administration. The assumption is that managers, when given precise information regarding personnel resources and capabilities, should be better equipped to make correct decisions. These types of computerized systems that serve the needs of managers and administrators throughout an organization are termed "decision support systems."[30] Although a number of computer-based decision support systems are available to the law enforcement manager, the most critical involve productivity and personnel evaluations.

Productivity and Personnel Evaluation

Most automated records systems provide data sheets or summaries of officer activity over a given period of time. These usually include the number of arrests (felony and misdemeanor) made by each officer, the number of tickets written by each traffic unit, and other related standard indicators. A common problem associated with such tabulations is that they lead to a wrong assumption: By increasing the amounts reported in each category of officer activity, there is a proportionate increase in the quality of police service. Unfortunately, the concepts of police productivity and quality of service are often misinterpreted.[31] As Hernandez[32] has pointed out, "In order to effectively deal with the concept of police productivity, one must come to grips with identifying the mission, goals and objectives of the police agency."

With this in mind, decisions and actions should be based on the appraisal of the

BOX 12-4

L.A. Police Computers Match Clues with Cases

The Los Angeles Sheriff's Department (LASD) is the umbrella law-enforcement agency for the 4,070 square miles of Los Angeles County. The department serves as the police force for contract cities and unincorporated areas, and works with other agencies to manage the law enforcement and public safety for a population of nearly 7.5 million county residents.

The LASD Homicide Bureau includes 94 law-enforcement officials who investigate several thousand homicides and related cases each year. Until recently, crime analysis—the science of spotting significant connections between apparently unrelated crimes—depended on luck, intuition and good memories.

Since 1986, however, the Homicide Bureau has used a superminicomputer and relational-like data-management software, both from Prime Computer, Natick, Mass., to automate crime analysis and speed homicide investigations. Employing these advanced tools, LASD deputy Joe Raffa developed the CHIEFS database, which now contains the details of more than 8,000 homicide investigations dating back to 1976.

Carefully constructed database searches, conducted by Maxine Allen, one of the bureau's crime analysts, have revealed unsuspected similarities between past crimes and current cases. Armed with this information, investigators often can move their cases farther and faster than was possible before.

"CHIEFS is a crime-analysis tool that saves investigators weeks, or even months, searching through index cards, looseleaf binders and files," says Allen. "Decisions are based on more complete and accurate information than ever before."

Lt. Ed Knutson, who oversees automation projects for the detective division, adds, "As the department grows, and the nature of investigative work becomes more complex and more mobile, there is very little time to just sit around talking about cases.

"Today's suicide weapon may have been a murder weapon two months ago," he says, "but until we automated our crime analysis, we had no consistently reliable way to put those two pieces of information together and make the right connections between clues and cases."

Allen is one of 25 crime analysts operating within the various LASD stations. She designs and conducts 15 to 20 database searches a month for the Homicide Bureau and monitors the quality and integrity of new information being added to the database each day.

New cases pour in daily from other law-enforcement agencies in the county, from the daily caseload sheets submitted by LASD investigators and from subsequent case reports. These are filed and updated, with reports provided on the numbers and types of homicides being investigated by each station during a period. Previously, as much as two days were needed to search by hand through files to compile a similar report.

Veteran investigators, accustomed to keeping most of the facts of a case in their heads, are accepting the small adjustments required of them, according to Allen.

"There is no question that CHIEFS lets investigators focus more quickly on the most-useful information instead of spending days or weeks just trying to figure out what that information is," Allen says.

Source: American City and County, June 1988, p. 78.

best available data inseparably linked with overall agency needs and goals. By far the most exhaustive study assessing police productivity with computerized data-based systems is that conducted by Danziger and Kraemer.[33] Their study indicated that the productivity of professional workers and managers who undertake semistructured tasks and are dependent on a rich information environment is greatly enhanced by computer technology.[34] Further, they associate "enhanced productivity" with "case-oriented" objectives and performance measures—a critical point for evaluation.[35]

One of the more useful software packages in this area is CAPE—Computer Assisted Personnel Evaluation. The CAPE system includes a series of performance-evaluation manuals designed to assess the various job classifications in law enforcement such as officer, investigator sergeant, and lieutenant. Manuals, which were developed and tested in various law enforcement agencies, consist of a series of five-point behaviorally anchored rating scales that describe the specific duties of each separate job classification. There are more than 400 separate scales grouped into 15 different job categories from which a department may select for use in evaluating any job classification.[36] Although CAPE is specifically designed for promotion and selection appraisals, minor modifications would allow the program to assess productivity measures.

Fiscal Management and Analysis

Historically, the computer process entered the business world through the automation of payroll and billing. Payroll was an easy task for computers and high-speed printers. Then too, the rigid bookkeeping regulations required in accounting practices lend themselves well to the automation process.

In the public sector, and more specifically concerning law enforcement, a number of software packages are available to facilitate the budget process. Police agency budgets are part of an overall municipal or state budget, which is enacted and controlled by that government. Many of the administration and record-keeping functions of a police budget are the responsibility of another department of that government. However, most police agencies do keep an ongoing accounting of expenditures and for this purpose a number of software packages perform in-house accounting tasks adequately.

TABLE 12-1 Flagstaff budget worksheet, fiscal year 1991–1992

Police					
Account	Current year	Expended thru 12/31	Estimate 1/1–6/30	Total estimate this year	Estimate next year
Salaries	2,063,803.00	1,016,897.71		1,016,897.71	
Overtime	226,025.00	101,341.64	125,659.00	227,000.00	250,000.00
Pension contributions	76,319.00	38,473.63		38,473.62	
Social Security	161,878.00	77,290.01		77,290.01	
Industrial accident insurance	43,597.00	22,714.35		22,714.35	
Clothing allowance	23,000.00	13,141.37	13,000.00	26,141.00	42,480.00
Group insurance	43,770.36	24,384.27		24,387.27	
Shop labor	700.00	4,017.75	400.00	4,417.00	1,000.00

Spreadsheet budgeting using Lotus 1–2–3 (courtesy Flagstaff, Arizona Police Department).

"Spreadsheet" programs are especially well-suited for budget development (see Table 12-1). The spreadsheet is a powerful tool designed mainly for handling quantitative information in a two-dimensional table (rows and columns). Beyond basic statistical analysis and mathematical tabulation, some spreadsheet programs provide sophisticated financial modeling capabilities designed specifically to assist top executives in decision making.

General Management Functions and Microcomputers[37]

With the recent advent of low-cost microcomputers, many law enforcement agencies are discovering new ways of keeping records and expediting paperwork. From a clerical standpoint, the introduction of word-processing programs has totally revolutionized the secretarial role. Word processing greatly speeds report writing and editing when compared to traditional typewriting, dictation, or handwriting. Erasure is fast and easy and allows the user to compose and edit simultaneously, producing a faster, better written copy without several drafts.[38] Further, most word-processing programs can be customized to handle standardized departmental forms and reports.

Another important set of software programs useful for law enforcement falls in the general description of "data base management." This is a term used to describe the range of programs functioning as computerized file clerks in an electronic file cabinet.[39] Through the use of general purpose data base management programs like Clipper, DBASE IV, or Paradox, law enforcement agencies can build their own applicational files. As Benton, Stoughton, and Silberstein explain:

> Personnel management is an obvious choice for a data-base program. Each employee would be included, along with such pertinent information as employment type (civilian, sworn peace officer, supervisory, line, probationary, permanent, etc.), salary, overtime, authorized absences. By maintaining such a data base, the department would be free to perform a variety of analyses at any time. For example, a supervisor could locate potential leave abuses or identify the need for increased staffing by looking at a sick leave or overtime used by each unit or by individuals on a monthly or quarterly basis. Scheduling staff for training, tracking the end of probationary status, or remembering when to conduct personnel reviews are just some of the many management functions aided by a locally available data-base system.
>
> Inventory control of equipment, vehicles, stolen property and evidence could also benefit from a data-base file system. There are commercial packages specially designed for inventory records or the department can create its own.[40]

Jail and Prisoner Management

Although jail and prisoner management is not the responsibility for many local and state law enforcement agencies, it is often a major function for county sheriffs. An example of a common software package designed for this task is JAMS-II-Jail Administration Management System.[41] JAMS-II simplifies jail record keeping and offers administrators up-to-the-minute information on the inmate population. JAMS-II, as well as other jail and prisoner management software, performs the following functions:

- *Booking*—Automatically generates a booking number and captures all the information necessary to complete the booking record. A detailed account of personal property and cash removed from the inmate is maintained and a paper copy of the booking record is generated.
- *Updating*—Changes and records corrections quickly and efficiently. Updating functions include inmate releases, cell moves, and changes in holds, warrants status, medical status, visiting and phone privileges, charge disposition, scheduled court appearances, and sentence calculation/outdates.
- *Record inquiry*—Retrieves selected portions of an inmate record and displays them on an operator's terminal. Staff may display current information or historical records, and a paper copy may be printed.
- *Daily log/audit trail*—Collects and prints the shift log of activities. The log includes all bookings, releases, and tallies for the shift. Every system transaction is logged to an audit file that may be printed or stored for processing later. The audit file contains the operator ID number, date and time of usage, record accessed, and transaction.
- *Medical accounting*—Maintains medical information for each inmate. The medical module is protected from unauthorized use by a special security feature.
- *Classification/pretrial release*—Supports inmate classification and pretrial release programs, and supplies information for indigence and bail/release recommendations.
- *Inmate cash accounting*—Accounts for inmate cash, allowing the jail to keep track of cash on hand, commissary purchases, other cash expenditures, as well as cash deposits.
- *Billing*—Produces billing reports and agency invoices which detail the particulars of inmate housing.

Communications and Manpower Allocation Design

In the last 25 years, computer automation has not been the only rapidly growing industry affecting law enforcement. Another major advancing technology during this same time period has been that of radio communications (see Figure 12-11). The portable radio is as common now in police work as the "billy club" was a century ago. The advent of computer and communication technologies has provided the individual police officer with increased levels of safety and given police executives additional tools with which to manage the work force.[42]

CAD System Overview

The development of computer-assisted dispatch (CAD) plans, which combine modern communication and automated record systems, has enabled police managers to improve the allocation or use of uniformed officers assigned to patrol duties. A number of CAD system software packages are available in the law enforcement market. Most packages offer dispatch speed and flexibility well beyond any manual system. Uniformed officers are dispatched based on the type of incident and the location. When this information is entered, the CAD system responds with detailed information about that location, such as verification of address, best access route, dangers near the location (e.g., known dangerous felons and biker hangouts), immediate past police or emergency service history (within the last 24 hours), and any other information that previously was entered. Additionally, most systems maintain a dynamic status review for available person-

ASPRIN* Communication Plot

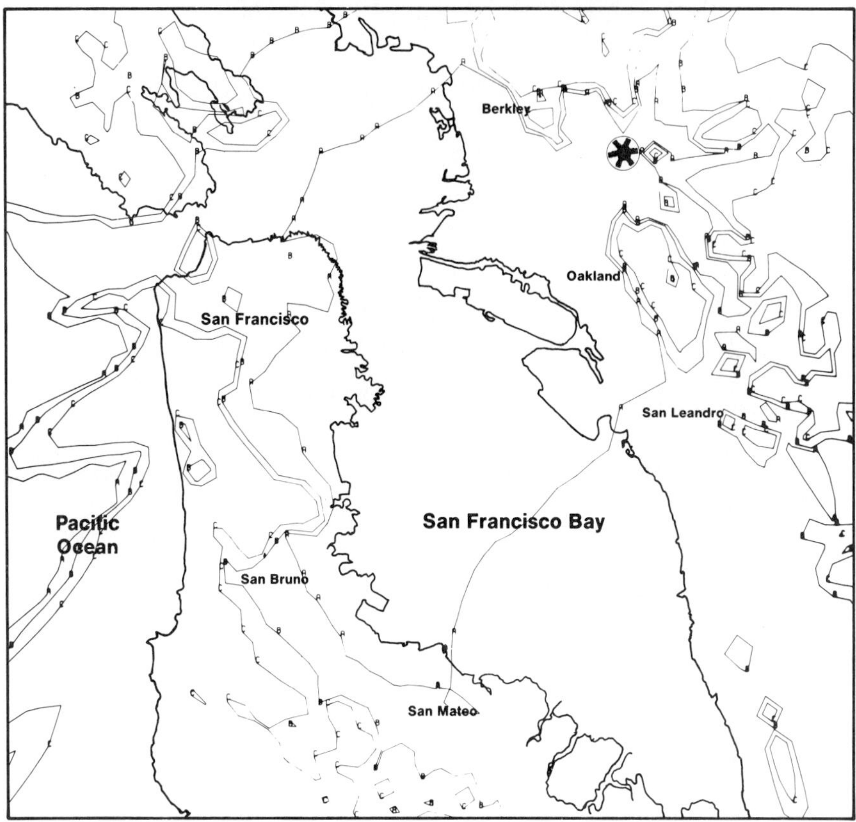

Talk-In 850 MHz Reliability A = 95%
B = 80%
C = 50%

FIGURE 12-11. Automated system prediction for radio-integrated networks (ASPRIN). This schematic represents the latest in computer-communication linkages applied to law enforcement applications. The chart measures communication reliability based on geographical setting in the San Francisco Bay area. In this manner, police communication devices can be strategically placed to increase radio and CAD reception reliability. [Courtesy of ElectroCom Automation, Inc., Arlington, Texas.]

nel and suggest the closest available unit to the location. In systems incorporating automatic transponders within patrol vehicles, units are visually monitored and assigned in coordination with the computer suggestion. Enhanced CAD systems utilize mobile digital terminals (MDTs) placed within each patrol car. Dispatching can then be conducted electronically from the host computer to each MDT, eliminating most of the mundane and routine voice communication of the past (see Figure 12-12).

Mobile digital terminals and CAD systems provide a number of important advantages for the individual police officer as well as the law enforcement agency:

- Officers are free to query names and license plates directly through records and warrant files without interfering with radio communications or requiring the time of a dispatcher.

FIGURE 12-12. Computer-assisted dispatch (CAD) system utilizing mobile digital terminals (MDTs) in patrol vehicles. Terminals in police cruisers provide officers with rapid access to such information as motor vehicle registrations and outstanding warrants. The system also permits transmission of sensitive information without the danger of it being monitored as in the case of voice radio transmissions and public scanners. [Photo courtesy of Scott Boatright, Fairfax County, Virginia Police Department.]

Thus, CAD systems provide an interface or direct computer-to-computer linkage between local systems and county, state, and/or federal criminal justice information systems, such as the NCIC.

- Document control numbers and initial report formats can be directly entered into the automated records system, thereby eliminating certain clerical functions.
- Exact addresses can be displayed with nearest cross streets, map coordinates, and in some cases even floor plans.
- Coordination of all emergency agencies to include fire and ambulance services can be visually monitored by the officer and the dispatch center.
- Response time is dramatically decreased as the complete dispatch process from call-in to arrival time is fully automated.
- Automatic processing of incident information via a preformatted incident form is completed.
- Geo-coding is utilized to identify responsible agencies; assign the nearest unit; capture reported, dispatched, arrival, and completion times; and verify address locations.
- The status of patrol units and personnel is constantly maintained, which enhances officer security and safety.
- CAD systems enable the accumulation of large amounts of data over time that can be used in basic crime analysis and allocation planning to assign personnel when and where crime is highest or calls for service are heaviest.
- To have officers available when and where services are needed.

For the most part, CAD systems and manpower allocation design models have been parallel in development. The most intricate plans combine the immediate database from a CAD system with an ongoing allocation format. To understand this unique convergence of advancing computer and communication technology with allocation modeling, it is important to assess various developments.

Allocation Design—Early Developments

The analysis of police patrol allocation in the United States began with the work of August Vollmer in Berkeley, California, during the early 1900s. Vollmer established a list of police functions that still appears in the literature on municipal policing.[43] With little variation, that list of police functions consists of crime prevention, crime repression, apprehension, criminal investigation, public service, maintenance of peace and security, regulation of noncriminal activities, traffic control, and provision of emergency services. According to Vollmer, these combined functions are the police mission. He was the first to associate these functions with a territorial unit of work or the "beat." Vollmer's contribution to patrol allocation can be viewed in two perspectives. First, he placed a priority emphasis on the study of beat construction by formulating a standard for allocation: patrol officers should be distributed by area in proportion to the amount of work to be done.[44] Second, Vollmer initiated the advancement of technological innovations in patrol assignments, especially in the use of communications.

In 1920, Fosdick expanded on Vollmer's earlier thoughts. Noting that patrol deployment must change and alter with new political, economic, employment, residential, and crime-occurring conditions, Fosdick proposed that the type and mode of patrol must adapt to new situations.[45] He was the first to recognize a relationship between a changing community environment and the need for a patrol strategy or allocation design.

Smith's *Police Systems in the United States* (1929), recognized still another important aspect of patrol deployment. Indicating that patrol had been traditionally "distributed on an equal, or nearly equal, basis throughout the 24 hours of the day," despite marked increases in workload and crime occurrences, Smith was the first to advance the use of crime analysis in allocation design.[46] For the first time, patrol distribution was related to activity and crime documentation by police records. This was an important step for allocation design, as managers recognized the need to deploy personnel in an effort to maximize patrol activity during those times of highest crime and workload occurrence.

The Hazard Model

In 1941, O. W. Wilson, then Chief of Police at Wichita, Kansas, established the "relative need" approach to police deployment. Emphasizing the redistribution of patrol forces based on a set of "proportionate need factors," Wilson called for the application of law enforcement to the locations, during the times and toward the particular criminal violations that represented the greatest demands on the police.[47]

Elaborating on his original work, Wilson[48] formulated a deployment scheme that was based on allocation by hazard. The formula was first initiated in the Los Angeles Police Department in 1953 and, with relatively minor changes, is still in use today. Each type of crime is given a weighted hazard score, and by prioritizing

BOX 12-5

When It Comes to Expert Systems, No Agency Is Too Small to Lead the Pack

When one thinks of police departments that have made great strides in adapting computer technology to tackle everything from record-keeping to crime-fighting, those located in major cities like New York, Los Angeles, Houston or San Jose, Calif., might first come in mind.

True, these cities are relying increasingly on computers to perform a variety of tasks, but not-so-large departments are taking the high-tech plunge as well. In fact, the 20-member Alliance, Neb., Police Department now ranks among the leaders in computer-driven law enforcement with its growing use of so-called "expert systems," or artificial intelligence.

An expert system has the ability to manipulate data and infer conclusions from a set of rules that are based on information supplied by detectives. By combining the calculating speed and power of a computer with the street smarts, experience and intuitive abilities of a police officer, the expert system aids investigators by collecting, storing and analyzing data that can match information taken from crime scenes with characteristics of known criminal suspects or which can point to new leads. One of the most well-known expert systems is the Residential Burglary Expert System that has been on line at the Baltimore County, Md., Police Department for just under a year.

In-House Tutoring

The Alliance Police Department uses its expert system to score cases so that the agency can best allocate its limited resources to solve the most common crimes occurring in its jurisdiction, said the department's services manager, Lieut. Tim Kees. In this manner, the expert system serves as a "tutor" for officers, prompting them to investigate facets of a crime that might otherwise be overlooked.

"What I want [the expert system] to do is get a minimum of work done to a case—consistently—by everyone," Kees told LEN. "It asks questions on the solvability factors of a crime, which I've come up with and which are fairly general. I'm not looking to match it to a suspect so much as to say, 'If you've answered this question one way, then here is a tutor. Here is the next thing you want to do with this case.' And that way, I guarantee a certain amount of investigative work [on the case] is done by everyone."

Alliance's expert system, which is still being developed by Kees and which he expects will be in use by all of the officers next month, asks investigators 25 "generic" questions about crimes, with a particular focus on those that occur most frequently—burglary, theft and vandalism—in the town of 10,000 in Nebraska's western panhandle. "We have a volume of those [crimes] and it's an area that could use some consistency," Kees pointed out. "There's no sense in doing one for homicide when we average one or two homicides a year. There's no sense for me to waste my time on that because all of the department's resources would be allocated toward that anyway."

25 Questions to Ponder

Officers who respond to crime scenes write their reports on laptop computers that are standard equipment in the department's squad cars. The information is downloaded into a computer containing the expert-system software. Officers then answer the 25 questions flashed to them by the expert system. "For instance, in a burglary, one question would be, 'Was the neighborhood checked on?' The answer may be, 'Yes,' 'No,' or 'Partially.' If they answered 'No' to a neighborhood check, then the tutor part of it would say, 'You should do a neighborhood check,' " said Kees.

Once the officers finish answering the questions—and carrying out other areas of investigation suggested by the expert system—the system will compute a score to indicate the crime's solvability. Case managers can then decide what and how much of the agency's resources should be allocated to solving the crime.

BOX 12-5 (cont.)

The expert system will prompt officers to carry out any facet of an investigation they may have overlooked, and the extra legwork may increase the probability that a crime will be solved. "I have a very young department—a bunch of go-getting people without a lot of years of experience. Hopefully, the expert part of the system has the data in there to help them come to some sort of collective minimum standard," said Kees.

Goodbye to Paper-Pushing

The expert system is just one of many computerized functions in the Alliance Police Department. In addition to the crime reports that are routinely prepared on portable laptop computers, virtually all of the department's record-keeping is processed by computer and stored in data bases, eliminating paperhandling and making the resulting information easily accessible to the department's investigators, managers and crime analysts.

"I just think that the blend between law enforcement and computers is good because all we do is process information," observed Kees.

The department is also equipped with a computer-aided dispatch (CAD) system that records all calls for service—34,000 were received by the department last year—on a computer. It also classifies the types of calls which helps the department compile its crime statistics for submission to the FBI's Uniform Crime Reporting Program. The CAD system also generates numbers that are unique to each case so that no case number is ever issued twice.

The CAD system "is the essential data base for all of the calls for service. It stamps the dates and times, who the dispatcher was, who the officer assigned to the call was, what the disposition was, what the exact nature of the call was, where it was, and then, what we did with it," said Kees.

"It's the starting point of all the systems," he added. The agency's daily media report and blotter, and its case-management report also originate out of the CAD system. It is also linked to a Rolodex-like data base that can tell officers certain information about local businesses to which they may be called, warning them, for instance, if there are flammable or toxic materials at the site. The CAD system is also linked to a data base known as the "tactical pre-plan" which compiles information about individuals or locations that could pose special dangers to officers responding to calls.

"A Ground-Zero Start"

Prior to going on line with the CAD system, finding information was a chore, Kees recalled. Previously, he said, "You had to go through 11,000 index cards if you wanted something." To find out about a certain call for service, employees would have to "physically thumb through" the cards to get the information. "Now we just hit the 'find' [button] and have it in a couple of seconds," he added. "We can never go back to a paper system now."

The Alliance Police Department began computerizing about three and a half years ago and has spent about $20,000 of its regular police budget to come this far. "It was a ground-zero start," said Kees, which required a little training for everyone. While Kees would not say that the result has been a high clearance record of solved cases, he acknowledged that computerization has been a tremendous boon to the department's crime fighting capabilities. "When information becomes more accessible quickly, it gives the officers and the detectives better resources to work from. . . . So they're left to tune into the factors that will solve crime and they spend more of their time doing that."

The advanced state of the Alliance Police Department's use of computer technology has forged a reputation that is known well beyond the borders of Nebraska. "For their size and for what they're doing, it's really just sort of spectacular," said Joan Jacoby, director of the Jefferson Institute, a research organization that helped the Baltimore County Police Department design and install its own expert system. "When you look at

BOX 12-5 (cont.)

that department, it's hard to separate their own personal interest in computers from their professional interest because they're just tied, one on one."

Kees was a bit more modest about the agency's achievements in computerization. "Any size department can do this. It just takes a little bit of effort. More to the point, if we can do it, anybody can do it. We're just a normal department. With a little bit of work and a little bit of support, we've done a pretty darn good job and I think what we'd like to do is encourage everybody else to do the same thing."

Source: Law Enforcement News, April 30, 1991, p. 1.

the incidence of crime, a total weighted sum for each region is calculated. The patrol force is then allocated accordingly.

Allocation Design: Post-1960 Developments

In the early 1960s, Phoenix, Arizona modified the hazard model somewhat for its own use. The Phoenix model includes considerations of any delay in responding to a call for police service, travel time to the location of the call, and the amount of time actually used in providing whatever police services are needed.[49] Currently, Phoenix is able to provide police, fire, and emergency medical service cars with mobile graphics on their MDTs. These graphics can display, for example, a diagram of a building, including the floor plan and the location of stairwells and other related features (see Figure 12-13).

Crowther,[50] in 1964, suggested a series of computer programs for the allocation of patrol personnel in St. Louis. The St. Louis model allows for the patrol force to be distributed on the assumption that up to 15 percent of calls for police service may not be responded to immediately. Instead, calls are placed in line or queue and handled as patrol units come back in-service from other calls.

The Law Enforcement Manpower Resource Allocation System (LEMRAS) is very similar to the St. Louis model.[51] A key variation is the LEMRAS method for prioritizing calls. Calls for services are categorized by event codes. These codes are then assigned to one of three priority levels that designate the length of time the call will beheld in queue. For example, a "cold" burglary may be placed in priority three, where as a robbery in progress is assigned a priority one. Calls are then dispatched in order of decreasing priority. Thus, all priority one and two calls would be dispatched before any priority three call, thereby decreasing the delay for any high-priority incident.

In 1969, Larson[52] designed a simulation model that bases the allocation of the patrol force on factors such as expected time of travel to the location of a call in relationship to the geographical characteristics of the city, the number of patrol cars on duty, and the demands for service in specific rectangular sectors.[52] Larson's model, in contrast to LEMRAS, uses more than three priority levels for calls placed in line or queue.

Developed in 1975, the Patrol Car Allocation Method (PCAM) is based heavily on Larson's program.[53] PCAM does not attempt to equalize the calls for service work load across watches or shifts. Instead, its goal is to deploy officers so that dispatch delays and response times can be optimized.

The Shoup–Dosser[54] or split force model was first proposed in 1964, although

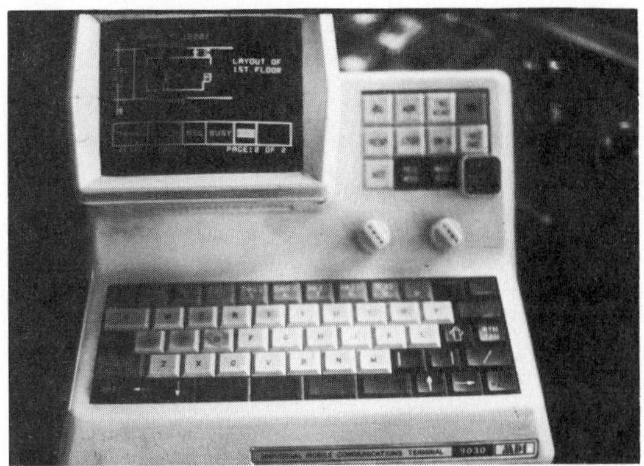

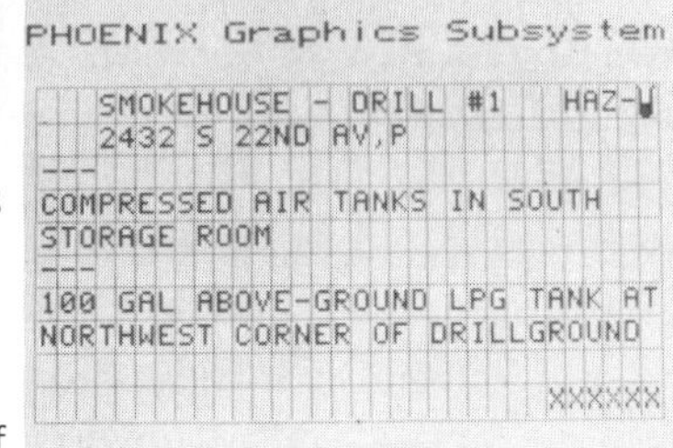

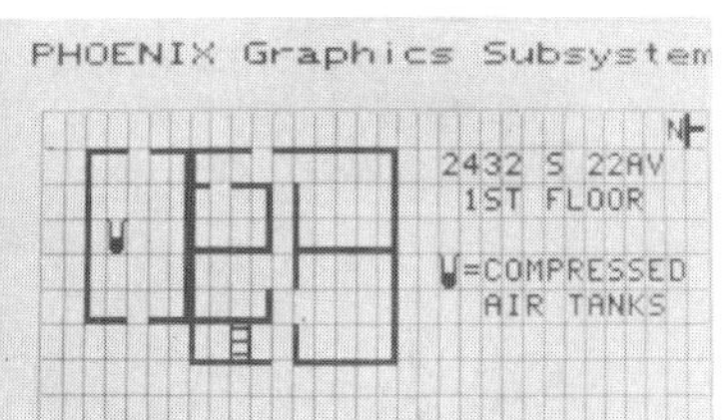

FIGURE 12-13. The Phoenix Graphics System is one of the most advanced MDT systems available to police, fire, and other emergency service agencies. Each vehicle is equipped with an MDT displaying both a written description and a visual diagram of the building queried. [Photo courtesy of the Phoenix, Arizona Fire Department.]

actual use of it was not made until later. It is based on the assumption that police officers have a direct and quantifiable effect on the crime rate within each geographical area. The ideal situation for this model is to have enough officers at any given moment to match the demand for police service, while at the same time having enough of a preventive patrol force distributed to minimize criminal activity. Thus, the patrol force is split into response and preventive duties.

The hypercube queuing model was developed in 1977 by Larson.[55] It assists police managers in the design of individual patrol beats. The goal of the model is to provide maximum relevant information about the ability of patrol units to answer service calls in the various patrol beats. A key objective of this is equalization of the work load between patrol units.

Deployment Plans in General

The preceding material covers the major evolutions in police patrol allocations/CAD models. Only those studies and models that are well known have been analyzed. There are numerous other designs, however, that are rarely mentioned in the literature.[56]

One of the pronounced shortcomings of police patrol allocation designs, in general, lies in the area of evaluation. The evaluation of patrol deployment plans has not been well developed and has failed to make use of experimental design.[57] What is required to further the advancement of patrol deployment is a carefully designed experiment that measures the effect of innovations in police strategies and schemes. For example, very few of the noted patrol allocation designs have ever been implemented to measure what the police actually did.[58] Instead, they attempted to measure the effect of increased or decreased response times, elapsed times, police presence, work load, calls for service, and the like. Further, only recently have social scientists begun to review and critique patrol allocation plans.

Training

In the 1960s and even into the early 1970s, an enormous amount of excitement was generated over the potential of the computer as a tool to aid learning. It was confidently predicted that computer-assisted instruction (CAI) would soon be an integral part of classroom procedures.[59] William and Betty Archambeault[60] have defined CAI as "the use of the computer to aid instruction which places the learner in a conversational or interactive mode with a computer that has a preprogrammed study or instructional plan."

The advent of the microcomputer has sparked even more fascination with the possibilities of CAI. These small, relatively inexpensive machines now make it possible for most school districts to at least experiment with CAI. Similar applica-

FIGURE 12-14. State-of-the-art computerization automatically maintains data which are used in developing more precise manpower deployment plans. The data are often collected at advanced communication centers, which help dispatchers send assistance as quickly as possible. Note the integration of an enhanced 911 telephone system with a geographic information system portraying on-line maps of the city. [Photo courtesy of Scott Boatright, Fairfax County, Virginia Police Department.]

tion of computer use has been tested in industry. Computer-based training (CBT) has emerged as an alternative delivery style for employee skill acquisition and improved retention of learned material.[61] The use of computers in both education and training has provided the basis for extensive research and development by many multinational corporations. Bell Laboratories' Richard Davis predicted that in 1990 about 10 percent of all industrial training would use computers in some form, and that this figure would increase to 50 percent by the year 2000.[62]

In the area of law enforcement training, computer-based education has recently developed as a viable and realistic entity. The application of PLATO (programmed Logic for Automated Teaching Operations) in various courses at the Police Training Institute, University of Illinois, was the first to raise considerable interest in the field.[63] Today, three general recognized types of CAI programs are utilized in law enforcement training—tutorial, drill and practice, and simulation.

Tutorial CAI

In tutorial programs, instruction takes place solely between the student and the computer. Based on the traditional "Socratic" method of teaching, the computer presents a logical progression of facts, information, and questions.[64] This type of program mimics the lecture-style format in classroom instruction utilizing written versus oral communication. Feedback is provided to student answers, and the program allows for review in a related field when incorrect responses are recorded.

Drill and Practice CAI

Drill and practice CAI software is designed to work in cooperation with an instructor to intensify and review previously taught material. After a period of instruction by the course teacher, the student is tested on the material by the drill and practice program. The computer presents a question that in turn is answered by the student. The computer checks the answer and returns appropriate feedback if correct. If the answer is incorrect, a group of review questions pertaining to the studied material is presented. The procedure continues in this manner until the correct responses have been recorded.

Simulation CAI

Simulation CAI program packages are much more advanced than the previously mentioned types of software. Like drill and practice, they are designed to be used in conjunction with an instructor. However, simulation CAI provides the opportunity not only to respond to given questions but also to apply previously learned problem-solving skills to a specific "real-life" situation.[65] Simulation CAI utilizes audio and visual elements to present a realistic scenario for the student. In each presented "game" or situation, the student must make decisions and judgments based on a variety of behavioral instincts and/or intellectual skills. For instance, the Federal Law Enforcement Training Center (FLETC) at Glynco, Georgia, has designed a simulation courseware involving "shoot, don't shoot" exercises. A laser disc is employed to score accurate "shots" fired by students while encountering different environments. Shooting proficiency and decision-making skills are evaluated through computer-assisted target analysis (CATA) programs.[66] Simulation CAI has an immense potential in law enforcement training from personnel selection and promotion (e.g., real-life situations and video scenes require an individual to apply agency policy) to top executive development and testing (e.g., individuals must play a game in which decision trees lead to effective outcomes during crisis events such as terrorist attacks, floods, earthquakes, and the like).[67] In general, simulation CAI courseware can be utilized in any area in which individuals must learn specific values and rationales from a behavioral science and apply them to a dynamic and ever-changing environment.

CAI Effectiveness

Most of the research attempting to evaluate the effectiveness of CAI on general police training has been very positive. Wilkenson[68] has shown that adults prefer to learn, or actually learn better when the following conditions exist:

FIGURE 12-15. Simulation CAI: IRS agents-in-training utilize portable computers to assist in audit and fraud investigations. [Photo courtesy of Federal Law Enforcement Training Center, Glynco, Georgia.]

- Courses are presented in a single-concept manner with heavy emphasis on the application of the concept to relevant real-world problems
- New material is presented at a pace that permits mastery of one idea at a time with frequent summarization
- Projects are self-directed and the pace of study is controlled by the learner
- The study environment eliminates risk taking, such as asking questions in public
- The material is presented in a manner that promotes learning in the fastest and easiest way possible.

General CAI courseware appears to meet many of these conditions and as such has been found to reduce learning time and improve learning skills for students within law enforcement training arenas.[69]

The Impact of Automation on Law Enforcement

The socioeconomic impact of the computer revolution has received considerable attention by futuristic writers. Most noteworthy are the observations of Naisbitt,[70] who asserts that power is directly related to "information control." Those individuals who have information knowledge can create an economic value and reality. One can support Naisbitt's argument by observing the well-documented increase in white-collar and service jobs as manufacturing jobs have declined. Fundamental shifts in an industrial society will occur, but not necessarily along the lines that economists, planners, political scientists, and bureaucrats usually monitor. Toffler[71] suggests that civilization has grossly fragmented or "'de-massified" into a number of idiosyncratic and socially diverse institutions that he calls the techno-sphere, the socio-sphere, the info-sphere, the bio-sphere, the power-sphere, and the psycho-sphere. He argues that the more mass society fractures and the more economy becomes differentiated, then the more information must be exchanged to maintain integration in the system. This has brought about the revolution of the Third Wave or the dependence on technology and information sharing.[72] Toffler, as well as many others, has dedicated considerable time and effort in attempting to assess the impact of this change on society and world civilization in general.[73]

Paradoxically, there is little empirical research focusing on the impact of automation on the police, an institution that often reflects societal attitudes and perspectives.[74] (The article in Box 12-6 is a good example, however, of the impact of automation on one city's police department.) Sykes has pointed out that the reform movement toward professionalism during the last 20 years required the use of computerization of records and reports. He writes:

> Police professionalism primarily stressed efficiency and technical competence in crime control. Implicitly this assumed a centralized, systematic information-gathering process. Automation became a necessary complement in the effort to supervise, evaluate, and maintain more direct administrative control over line officers in terms of this professional role. Information gathering and processing so essential for efficient crime control, due to technical innovations in silicon chip technology, now assumes more significance than in the past.
>
> . . . If the "professional" focus in policing as a crime-control activity fosters the need for more efficient information gathering, coding, storing and processing for use by the criminal justice system automation of management information provides more complete data on personnel and other resources to be used in decision-making by police

BOX 12-6

Richmond PD Polices Images and Rescues Jobs During Drug War

Officers' report-writing time cut by 15% as departmental savings soar.

By Tod Newcombe

Faced with a surge in violent crime brought on by increased drug use, the city of Richmond, CA, had few choices in responding to the problem. It could either hire more police officers, a traditional but budget-busting response, or squeeze more efficiency out of the current ranks.

"We chose more efficiency," says Lieutenant Michael Tye, a 22-year veteran of the Richmond Police Department. The department has installed a LAN-based imaging system that will capture just about every element of information that is involved with a crime—from the officer's report to crime scene diagrams and photographs, mug shots, and even full-motion video.

According to Tye, project leader of the department's automation plan, the system will cut every officer's time spent creating reports by a minimum of 15%. The net result will be the equivalent of having another six to ten officers.

Huge Savings Projected

The annual cost to put a police officer on the street can reach $70,000, including salary, benefits, car and equipment. This means the department could recover/save anywhere from $300,000 to $1 million in personnel and related costs. Even more important is officers having more time to spend out in the community.

"Our focus is on improving productivity through more efficient handling of information, beginning with the officer in the field writing his report and going all the way to the district attorney for filing of charges," notes Tye.

Later this spring when the new LAN-based imaging system is operational, the multiple forms of information will be linked through indexing and then automatically routed to the appropriate investigators for their evaluation and disposition. Later this year, the information will be available to the district attorney for court action, and, if necessary, to neighboring cities via a wide area network.

Wang Laboratories (Lowell, MA) is helping the Richmond Police Department integrate the application, which consists of a Novell (Orem, UT) LAN linked to 18 Wang industry-standard PCs, including a Wang EC 486/33C as a server, running Microsoft (Redmond, WA) Windows 3.0. The system is supported by magnetic and optical disk storage.

Data Management Design (DMDI, Reston, VA) is developing the document imaging and information application, using its new workflow product, Client/Server-Comprehensive Information Management System (CS-CIMS). CS-CIMS incorporates image tools from Wang's OPEN/image-Windows. It is an open system workflow tool that can help police departments manage and route their paperwork appropriately.

"The LAN architecture was chosen for its flexibility," explains Tye. "We wanted to have the ability to change pieces of the system readily—for instance upgrading server processors—as the technology improves. We also have a large number of installed PCs in the department and plan to tie them into the LAN eventually."

The Richmond Police imaging application actually begins in the field where the department's 183 officers gather information from incidents or crime scenes. Until recently, all officers had written their own reports, often consuming 25 to 35% of their time.

After the department rejected laptop computers, it turned to a technology first used in the 1950s—a call-in system that allows officers to dictate their reports over the phone to a digital database service staffed by a pool of clerks. According to Tye, the service has had two major benefits: "We've seen an immediate reduction in time spent by officers

BOX 12-6 (cont.)

and detectives preparing reports. At the same time, there's been an increase in the amount of information coming in over the phones."

Approximately 60% of the information gathered in the police reports is also entered into the department's existing Tiburon/PSW3 (Fremont, CA) Records Management System (RMS), which operates on a DEC VAX minicomputer. Currently 11 police clerks key in the data for the RMS, which is integrated with the computer-aided dispatching system and also accesses county, state and federal databases via a wide area network.

The new LAN system will remove the redundant data entry by eliminating manual input for the RMS through an electronic link, being finalized by DMDI, between the police report and the RMS. The LAN-based system will recognize certain data elements in the RMS, such as names, crime locations, vehicles, methods of operation and any statistical information. It will then automatically place the data into the electronic police report (also called an electronic report form).

Each police report form is assigned an index number. Information that cannot be converted into text or data, such as alcohol test results, crime scene diagrams and photos, will be scanned, stored on optical disk and linked to the appropriate police report via the same index number.

Another major improvement is the routing of the report forms. In the past, photocopies were regularly made of every piece of information and routinely routed to more people than necessary.

CS-CIMS will recognize certain fields in the text of the police report forms and automatically route the information on the LAN to the appropriate personnel.

"This is a multi-application solution that eliminates about forty percent of the clerical staff's previous work which involved typing, copying, routing and filing," says Tye. "As a result, our support staff can do more than before, and our staffing levels are the same as in 1976 despite the increase in crime."

Photographs and video are separate elements of the overall database. Applied Media Technologies (Walnut Creek, CA) is developing an application that links photos and full-motion video to the electronic report forms. According to Tye, "If a witness to a robbery recalled the suspect had a gold tooth, an investigator could search the database for all photo images of suspects with a gold tooth and present them as an 'electronic lineup' for viewing by witnesses or victims."

Source: Imaging World, May 1992, pp. 18–19. (See Figure 12-16 for a schematic diagram of the Richmond, California Police Department's Information System.)

managers. Information on workloads, scheduling, performance, budgeting, and program evaluation will substantially enhance the ability of police executives to know what is happening within their organizations and allegedly provides the data necessary to use resources in a more organizationally responsible manner. In plain terms, the automation of police agencies is almost an inevitable reform given the emphases of the professional movement with its complementary efforts to develop sophisticated police management.[75]

Police Role

The increased demand for information for criminal justice agencies and police management needs may alter the existing role of individual police officers. Bittner[76] has provided a colorful and dramatic image of the "soldier-bureaucrat," an individual totally controlled by administrative tasks, unable to perform rudimen-

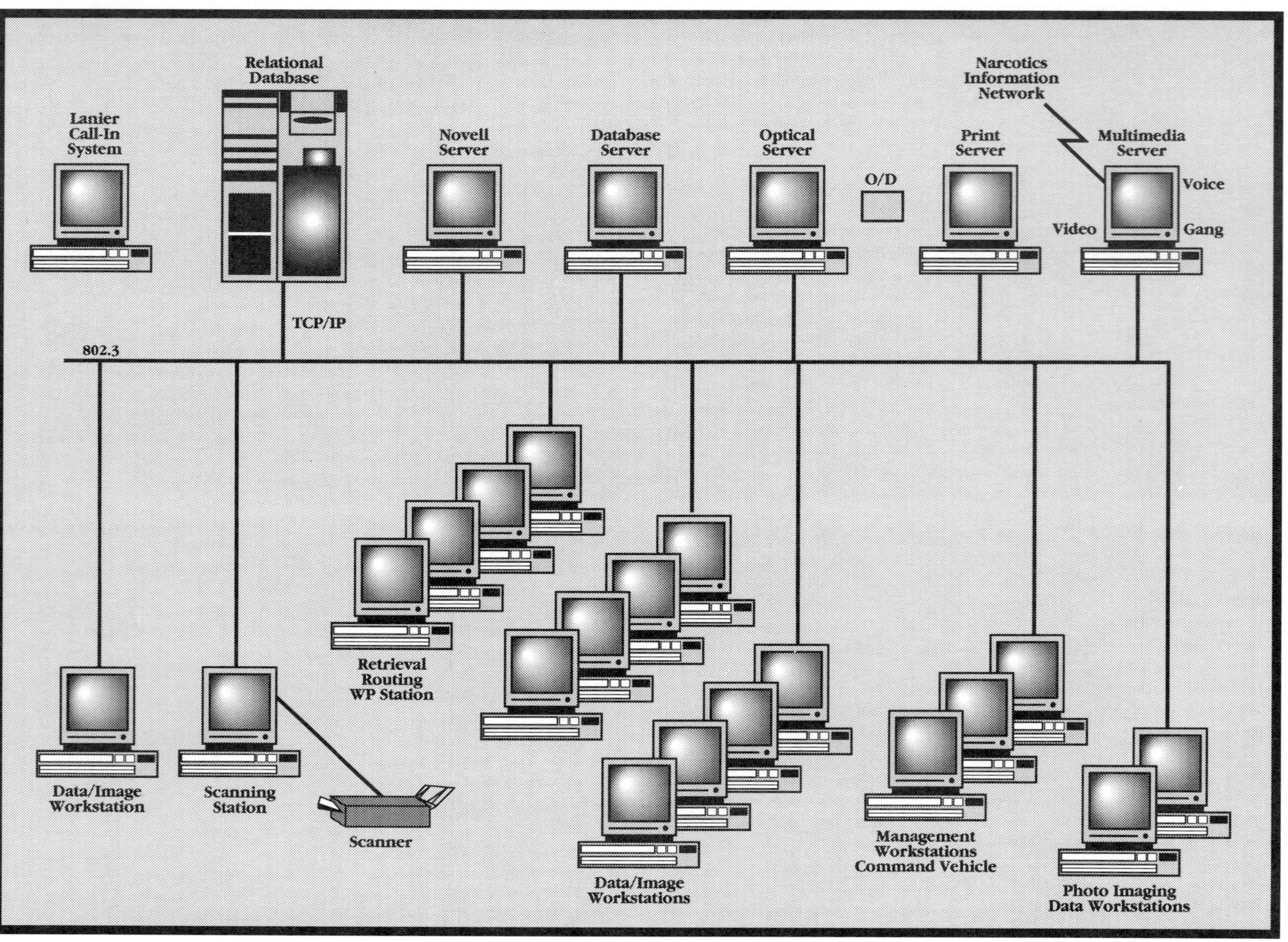

FIGURE 12-16. Schematic diagram of the Richmond, California Police Department Information System.

tary duties and make discretionary judgments. Sykes[77] suggests an even darker scenario as the "line officer, metaphorically speaking, could become an appendage of the machine."

In essence, have computerization and the subsequent need for information provided unnecessary shifts in the police role? If so, an interesting issue may arise. Who controls whom? Does the officer generate a report that becomes bits of information for processing or does the computer (regulated by management) demand that certain bits of information be processed?

The scenario as described by Bittner and Sykes is not unrealistic, especially when one evaluates the changing emphasis on recruit entrance requirements. Many police departments require a college degree or at least two years of higher education as a result of the professionalization movement. Today's agencies prefer that entering law enforcement candidates have a familiarity with computers and computer applications in criminal justice; hence, the subtle shifting of education (for police recruits) from broad-based social and behavioral science programs to a more technically oriented background. This type of education is contradictory to the original rationale for recommending higher education among police officers. The 1967 President's Commission on Law Enforcement and Administration of Justice,[78] after exhaustive review of the preceeding ten years (which were characterized by massive unrest, turbulence, and violence) recommended that police officers be schooled in basic human relations and social/behavioral sciences in an effort to reduce racial bias and social prejudices. We need officers who can relate to people and not machines. Is the pendulum swinging back to narrow, technically oriented programs for police officers? If so, is this the type of officer that the community really wants?

Some proponents might argue "yes" as the automation explosion has developed a new type of crime and criminal. The uneducated, blundering "con" of the past has been replaced by a sophisticated, technically smart thief who utilizes the computer as an instrument of crime. The increasing cases of computer fraud, credit card manipulation, and automation theft have provided police with new arenas for investigation that they are ill prepared to handle. However, these are jobs for specialized investigators, not line officers.

Today's police officers still require the ability to relate to various people under strained conditions in often hostile environments. Peacekeeping involves extralegal intervention into human situations that call for judgment and skill in relating to people.[79] For this challenge, police officers must understand their role in the community as aided by, and not controlled by, the technological marvels of automation.

Summary

The advent of computerized systems has drastically affected law enforcement organization, personnel, and services. The vast amount of data and information collected by police agencies demand an efficient system that offers immediate retrieval capabilities. Further, the issue of police accountability for actions and expenditures requires the tabulation of information into meaningful summaries and statistics in which managers can measure and justify operational decisions.

The implementation of a computerized system requires exhaustive planning, often involving technical areas beyond the scope of the law enforcement executive. Police administrators should rely on technological expertise in the development of accurate and precise needs assessments. These organizational evaluations should attempt to match perfectly the computer hardware and software system capable of meeting the department's goals and fiscal limitations. The most important consideration in adopting such a system is a thorough understanding of the computer applications available for law enforcement. These applications fall into three categories: (1) operations (data base information), (2) management and administration (data base management), and (3) communication and training (data base sharing).

For the operation of any police agency, an automated records system will increase management efficiency. Added statistical analysis of crime data will yield meaningful tools necessary to judge and evaluate officer productivity. In addition, new techniques in geographic information systems (GISs) (mapping) and the advent of artificial intelligence (AI) (expert systems) increase the meaning and usefulness of crime data to both patrol and investigation. General management functions for microcomputers include word processing, automated budgeting, personnel management, scheduling, inventory systems, and various data base filing systems.

We have seen great advances not only in computer technology but also in the radio communication industry. The combination of these two technologies has given law enforcement a substantial increase in efficiency. The development of computer-assisted dispatch (CAD) systems that provide immediate data for patrol allocation design has allowed patrol deployment to be based on sophisticated mathematical and game theories instead of mere intuition. Computers have also entered the training arena, opening new horizons in increased skill levels and improved effectiveness. Computer-assisted instruction (CAI) has been reviewed by three general program types—tutorial, drill and practice, and simulation.

Notwithstanding the dramatic effect that computer automation has had on law enforcement agencies and organizations, we still must be ever cognizant of the role of the individual line officer. Policing is a human task requiring exceptionally good judgment and skill in relating to people. Although technological advances have promised to increase the efficiency and effectiveness of the police, the true test for successful law enforcement will always rest on the sensitivity and professionalism of the individual officer.

Discussion Questions

1. Why is automation no longer viewed as a luxury but rather a necessity for most police agencies?
2. What are the advantages and limitations of a PC?
3. Discuss some of the most important considerations in planing for a computerized system.
4. Discuss the four system functions of a microcomputer. Name a peripheral that might be associated with each function.
5. What is a LAN? Discuss the three LAN cable layouts or topologies.
6. Explain the terms *hardware, software,* and *compatibility*.
7. What is an automated records system and how does it increase police efficiency? Explain some of the features found on an advanced records system.

8. What is a GIS? How does such a system enhance law enforcement services?
9. What are the four major application domains of AI? Which application holds the most promise for law enforcement, and why?
10. What is a "spreadsheet" program?
11. What is a CAD system? Discuss some of the important advantages developed with a CAD system.
12. What is and who developed the "hazard model" of patrol allocation design?
13. Explain the three types of CAIs: tutorial, drill and practice, and simulation.
14. Discuss the negative as well as the positive impacts of automation on law enforcement.

Notes

1. W. G. Archambeault and G. J. Archambeault, *Computers in Criminal Justice Administration and Management* (Cincinnati, Ohio: Anderson, 1984), p. 4.
2. Robert W. Taylor, "Managing Police Information," in *Police and Policing: Contemporary Issues,* ed. Dennis J. Kenney (New York: Praeger, 1989), p. 258.
3. Much of the material and information included in the following four sections was excerpted and modified from the SEARCH Group, Inc., *The Criminal Justice Microcomputer Guide and Software Catalogue* (Washington, D.C.: U.S. Department of Justice, 1988).
4. Elias M. Awad, *Management Information Systems: Concepts, Structures, and Applications* (Menlo Park, Calif.: Benjamin/Cummings, 1988), pp. 58–62.
5. Archambeault and Archambeault, *Computers in Criminal Justice,* p. 16.
6. Ibid., p. 27.
7. Refer to SEARCH Group, *Criminal Justice Microcomputer Guide,* and James A. O'Brien, *Management Information Systems: A Managerial End User Perspective* (Homewood, IL: Irwin, 1990), pp. 138–42.
8. G. Robertson and S. Chang, "Crime Analysis Support System," *Police Chief,* 47 (August 1980), pp. 41–43.
9. R. E. Bensmiller, *Local Crime Information Computer* (Whitsett, Tex.: Bensmiller Computer Service, 1982), p. 1.
10. D. A. George and G. H. Kleinknecht, "Computer Assisted Report Entry—CARE," *FBI Law Enforcement Bulletin,* 54 (May 1985), pp. 3–7.
11. For more detailed information, refer to internal policies and directives from the City of St. Petersburg, Florida, Police Department and the City of Ocala, Florida, Police Department. Both agencies are experimenting in the use of "lap" computers for the generation of police reports.
12. George and Kleinknecht, "Computer Assisted," p. 3.
13. J. B. Howlett, "Analytical Investigative Techniques," *Police Chief,* 47 (December 1980), p. 42.
14. J. A. Kinney, "Criminal Intelligence Analysis: A Powerful Weapon," *International Cargo Crime Prevention,* (April 1984), p. 4.
15. D. M. Ross, "Criminal Intelligence Analysis," *Police Product News* (June 1983), p. 45.
16. Ibid., p. 45.
17. Ibid., p. 45.
18. Ibid., p. 49.
19. For background material on the development of GISs, refer to Roger F. Tomlinson and A. Raymond Boyle, "The State of Development of Systems for Handling Natural Resources Inventory Data," *Cartographica,* 18 (1988), pp. 65–95: Donna Peuguet and John O'Callaghan, eds., *Design and Implementation of Computer-Based Geographic*

Information Systems (Amherst, N.Y.: IGU Commission on Geographical Data Sensing and Processing, 1983); and Robert C. Maggio and Douglas F. Wunneburger, "A Microcomputer-Based Geographic Information System for Natural Resource Managers," unpublished manuscript, Texas A&M University, Department of Forest Science, College Station, Tex. 1988.
20. J. Chaiken, P. Greenwood, and J. Petersilia, "*The RAND Study of Detectives*," in *Thinking About Police: Contemporary Readings*, ed. C. Klockars (New York: McGraw-Hill, 1983), pp. 167–84.
21. Ibid., p. 178.
22. Ibid., p. 179.
23. Institute for Law and Social Research, Inc., *Prosecutor's Management and Information System (PROMIS), New Orleans* (Ann Arbor, Mich.: Inter-University Consortium for Political and Social Research, 1984).
24. Ibid., p. i.
25. O'Brien, *Management Information Systems*, p. 356.
26. W. Coady, "Automated Link Analysis: Artificial Intelligence–Based Tools for Investigator," *Police Chief*, 52 (1985), pp. 22–23.
27. Edward C. Ratledge and Joan E. Jacoby, *Handbook on Artificial Intelligence and Expert Systems in Law Enforcement* (Westport, Conn.: Greenwood, 1989), chapter 8.
28. R. Krause, "The Best and the Brightest," *Law Enforcement Technology*, 3 (1986), pp. 25–27.
29. For more detailed information on this subject, refer to Robert W. Taylor, "Managing Police Information," in *Police and Policing: Contemporary Issues*, ed. Dennis J. Kenney (New York: Praeger, 1989), pp. 257–70.
30. Refer to Peter G. W. Keen and Michael S. Morton, *Decision Support Systems: An Organizational Perspective* (Reading, Mass.: Addison-Wesley, 1978), and S. L. Alter, *Decision-Support Systems: Current Practices and Continuing Challenges* (Reading, Mass.: Addison-Wesley, 1980).
31. Lucious Riccio, "Police Data as a Guide for Measuring Productivity," in *The Future of Policing*, ed. Alvin Cohn (Beverly Hills, Calif.: Sage, 1978).
32. Ernie Hernandez, Jr., *Police Handbook for Applying the Systems Approach and Computer Technology* (El Toro, Calif.: Frontline Publications, 1982), p. 19.
33. James N. Danziger and K. L. Kraemer, "Computerized Data-Based Systems and Productivity Among Professional Workers: The Case of Detectives," *Public Administration Review*, 45 (January/February, 1985), pp. 196–209.
34. Ibid., p. 206.
35. Ibid., p. 206.
36. G. W. Smith and M. W. Lehtinen, "Better Personnel Evaluation—With Computers," *Law Enforcement News*, (1985), p. 7.
37. Much of this section is condensed from an excellent article that applies open market software to police applications by W. Benton, D. Stoughton, and J. Silberstein, "A Fast and Easy Way to Build a Software Library," *Law Enforcement News*, 11:3 (1985), pp. 6–12.
38. Ibid., p. 6.
39. Ibid., p. 6.
40. Ibid., p. 7.
41. JAMS-II is a program developed by SEARCH under grants awarded by the Bureau of Justice Statistics. SEARCH, the National Consortium for Justice Information and Statistics, is a nonprofit corporation governed in the interest of the criminal justice community by appointees of the governors of the states. For over ten years SEARCH has been a pioneer in the exploration of information technology for law enforcement, courts, and corrections. Much of the information regarding JAMS-II is taken from the SEARCH Group, Inc., brochure on the software package.

42. P. K. Wormeli, "Hi-Tech: Changing the Nature of Policing," *Law Enforcement News*, 11:3 (1985), p. 1.
43. G. E. Misner and R. Hoffman, *Police Resource Allocations* (Berkeley: University of California Press, 1967), p. 7.
44. August Vollmer, "The Police Beat," in *Police Patrol Readings*, ed. Samual G. Chapman (Springfield, Ill.: Charles C. Thomas, 1964), p. 189.
45. Frank E. Walton, "Selective Distribution of Police Patrol," in *Police Patrol Readings*, ed. Chapman, p. 177.
46. Ibid., p. 177.
47. Ibid., p. 178.
48. O. W. Wilson, *Police Planning* (Springfield, Ill.: Charles C. Thomas, 1958), p. 81.
49. RAND Corporation, "Methods for Allocating Police Patrol Resources," in *Issues in Police Patrol*, ed. Thomas J. Sweeney (Kansas City, Mo.: Kansas City Police Department, 1973), p. 244.
50. Robert F. Crowther, *The Use of a Computer System for Police Manpower Allocation in St. Louis, Missouri, Part I, Manpower Requirements for Calls Answering Services* (Terre Haute: Indiana University Press, 1965), pp. 1–2. Also see Thomas McEwan, *Allocation of Patrol Manpower Resources in the St. Louis Police Department* (St. Louis: Metropolitan Police Department, 1966), pp. 6–48.
51. RAND Corporation, "Methods of Allocating," p. 247.
52. See Richard C. Larson, *Urban Police Patrol Analysis* (Cambridge, Mass.: MIT Press, 1972).
53. Jan Chaiken and Peter Dormant, *Patrol Car Allocation Method: Users Manual* (Santa Monica, Calif.: RAND Corporation, 1975).
54. Carl S. Shoup and Douglas Dosser, "Standards For Distributing a Free Governmental Service: Crime Prevention," *Public Finance*, 19 (1964).
55. Richard C. Larson, *Hypercube Queuing Model: Users Manual* (New York: RAND Corporation, 1977).
56. For a detailed explanation of less cited patrol allocation models, refer to Gregory L. Campbell, *A Spatially Distributed Queuing Model for Police Sector Design* (Cambridge, Mass.: MIT Press, 1972); Richard Mudge, *A Description of the New York City Police Department RMP Allocation Model* (New York: Rand Institute, 1974); Peter Kolesar, *A Simulation Model of Police Patrol Operations* (New York: Rand Institute, 1974); Wayne Bennett and John DuBois, *The Use of Probability Theory in the Assignment of Police Patrol Areas* (Washington, D.C.: U.S. Government Printing Office, 1970); Kenneth Chelst, *An Interactive Approach to Police Sector Design* (Cambridge, Mass.: MIT Press, 1974); Spencer B. Smith, *Superbeat: A System for the Effective Distribution of Police Patrol Units* (Chicago: Illinois Institute of Technology, 1973).
57. Wilson and Boland, "Effect of Police on Crime," p. 383.
58. Ibid., p. 383.
59. Refer to a number of the early works on CAI by D. Coulson, "Factors in Learning," *Journal of Educational Psychology*, 14 (1962), pp. 133–47; J. W. Loughary, ed., *Man–Machine Systems in Education* (New York: Harper & Row, 1966); and J. C. Meridith, *The CAI Author and Instructor* (Englewood Cliffs, N.J.: Educational Technology Publications, 1971).
60. Archambeault and Archambeault, *Computers in Criminal Justice*, p. 118.
61. P. H. Seldon and N. L. Schultz, "What the Research Says About CAI's Potential," *Training*, 14 (1982), pp. 61–65.
62. Ibid., p. 62.
63. Paul Palumbo, "Firearms Training: Computer-Assisted Target Analysis," *Police Chief*, 50 (May 1983), pp. 67–69.
64. C. J. Flammang and R. O. Walker, "Training: A Rationale Supporting Computer Assisted Instruction," *Police Chief*, 49 (August 1982), pp. 60–62.

65. Archambeault and Archambeault, *Computers in Criminal Justice*, p. 125.
66. Palumbo, "Firearms Training," p. 67.
67. Archambeault and Archambeault, *Computers in Criminal Justice*, p. 125.
68. Tom Wilkenson, "The Use of Computers in Police Training," *Police Chief*, 51 (April 1984), p. 49.
69. R. O. Walker and C. J. Flammang, "Instructional Applications of Computer-Based Education in Police Training," *Journal of Police Science and Administration*, 9 (Spring 1981), pp. 224–28.
70. John Naisbitt, *Megatrends: Ten New Directions Changing Our Lives* (New York: Warner Books, 1982).
71. Alvin Toffler, *The Third Wave* (New York: William Morrow, 1980).
72. Ibid.
73. Refer to the works of Alvin Toffler, *The Eco-Spasm Report* (New York: Bantam Books, 1975); A. Toffler, *Future Shock* (New York: Random House, 1970); E. Cornish, *The Study of the Future* (Washington, D.C.: World Future Society, 1977); G. T. Molitor, "The Information Society: The Path to Post-Industrial Growth," *Futurist* (April 1981), pp. 23–30; Naisbitt, *Megatrends*. For references that relate directly to futuristics and the police, refer to William L. Tafoya, *Futuristics: New Tools for Criminal Justice Crime Prevention, Parts I, II, and III*, unpublished manuscript (Quantico, Va.: FBI Academy, Management Science Division, 1986).
74. For an excellent review of the impact of automation on police reform, refer to G. W. Sykes, "The Functional Nature of Police Reform: The 'Myth' of Controlling the Police," *Justice Quarterly* (March 1985), pp. 53–65, and Sykes, "The Impact of Automation on Police Organization: The New Reformers?," a paper presented at the Annual Conference of the Academy of Criminal Justice Sciences, Las Vegas, Nev. (March 1985). Much of the discussion in this book regarding the impact of automation on police was derived from Sykes's work.
75. Sykes, "The Impact of Automation," pp. 3–4.
76. Egon Bittner, *The Functions of the Police in Modern Society* (Washington, D.C.: U.S. Government Printing Office, 1971).
77. Sykes, "The Impact of Automation," p. 6.
78. President's Commission on Law Enforcement and Administration of Justice, *Task Force Report: The Police* (Washington, D.C.: U.S. Government Printing Office, 1966).
79. Sykes, "The Impact of Automation," p. 11.

13 Financial Management

Not least among the qualifications of an administrator is his ability as a tactician and gladiator in the budget process.
FREDERICK C. MOSHER

Introduction

The historical importance of financial management to this country's very existence is unmistakable; the issue of taxation without representation was part of the disagreement with England that led ultimately to the American Revolution. The present importance of financial management in government is readily established by examining the content of daily newspapers.[1] Stories may note the arrest and indictment of an official for embezzling public funds, the defeat or passage of a bond referendum to construct a jail, an auditor's report that describes the police department's accounting procedures for handling funds for informants and narcotics purchases as "woefully inadequate," the closing of a school or precinct station because funds were no longer available to operate it, or the efforts of local officials to obtain the state legislature's approval to levy new taxes or to increase the levels of existing ones.

In Chapter 12 the view that some police managers have of planning was discussed. Relatedly, some police administrators see budgeting and financial management in a similar vein. The mistaken view that financial management is "only detailed clerical work" and therefore unattractive and unimportant deserves some attention here.

First, financial management does involve some detailed effort. The product of that effort is attended by the possibility of uncomfortable or potentially severe consequences for misjudgment or oversight. For example, the dramatic rise in gasoline prices in 1979 and 1980, which far exceeded what was judged to be likely, resulted in some police agencies having to limit the numbers of miles patrolled daily, the purchasing of smaller cars, the cost of driver training programs to increase fuel economy, and the need to return to the legislative body for additional funds. In this last regard, the Maryland State Police had to request an additional $525,000 in one year, and Detroit's city-wide annual budget for gasoline was found to have been inadequate by some $2,000,000.[2] As can be seen from reading the article "No Fueling—Illinois Orders Troopers to Go Bargain-Hunting for Gasoline" in Box 13-1, police budgets have continued to be adversely affected

BOX 13-1

No Fueling—Illinois Orders Troopers to Go Bargain-Hunting for Gasoline

Illinois State Police officials have eased most of the strict gasoline conservation measures imposed in January, but the state's 2,000 troopers are still being urged to shop for fuel bargains and avoid gas stations that tack on surcharges for credit-card purchases.

"We sort of declared victory and went home on that one," said State Police spokesman Bob Fletcher of the conservation measures that were in effect until early this month.

Under the voluntary guidelines, imposed after the escalation of the Persian Gulf crisis caused fuel prices to skyrocket, troopers were asked to turn off their engines for 15 minutes each hour and drive their patrol vehicles only 80 miles per eight-hour shift. Officials also requested that troopers perform a certain amount of "stationary patrol" during each shift, during which time engines would be cut off. District commanders were given discretion as to how strictly they would order troopers to comply with the gas-saving measures, Fletcher said.

State Police officials issued the guidelines after discovering that as of January the agency had already used $4.2 million of the $7.2 million allotted for gasoline and vehicle maintenance for this fiscal year. Rising prices at gas pumps were blamed by officials for the cost overrun. "It was an anomaly caused by the war—nothing you could plan for or budget for," said Fletcher.

New funds would not be available until the start of the new fiscal year in July, Fletcher noted, so officials decided to "dust off" conservation measures developed during the energy crisis of the early 1970's to prevent the State Police from literally running out of gas.

"We found ourselves in the proverbial bind," Fletcher told LEN. "We had projected the year for purchasing gasoline at about $1.09 a gallon. And suddenly saw prices rising to a buck and a quarter, a buck and a half in some locales. . . . It became obvious that unless we took some measures, we would easily come up short for the year."

Fletcher maintained that the conservation measures did not affect the agency's enforcement capabilities. "We monitored that all the way through and we discovered that performance remained at the same level as last year—if not going up," he said.

With the end of the war with Iraq, and an easing of gasoline prices, the State Police has found itself "in a better position," said Fletcher. "I don't believe there's a district in the state that's still using the other conservation measures—the ones that restricted mileage."

Troopers are still being encouraged to shop wisely, he added.

Source: Law Enforcement News, April 15, 1991, p. 1.

into the 1990s by dramatic increases in the price of gasoline that were not foreseeable. The best budget preparation process in the world cannot anticipate global events such as the Persian Gulf Crisis, and thus, little harm is done to the reputation of an agency when a budgetary shortfall occurs. However, when items are not included in a budget request through oversight, considerable embarrassment is created. Illustrative of such an oversight was the failure of a sheriff to request any ammunition in his annual budget, which required him to go before the county commissioners considerably red-faced to specially request it. Lest one think that such events happen only in small departments, one state police agency forgot to request the $4 million in funds it needed to provide recruit training for newly hired troopers, resulting in a one-year hiring freeze.

A second factor related to viewing financial management as unattractive work is that it offers little of the excitement, attention, or perhaps even glamour that directing a noteworthy major investigation does. However, success in obtaining and shepherding resources increasingly involves the need for creativity and is a potentially rich source of job satisfaction. As to financial management not being "real police work," the validity of that statement diminishes as one advances up the hierarchy, incurring at each successive level a set of new responsibilities that renders operational prowess less relevant.

Politics and Financial Management

During the 1970s, financial assistance from the federal government increased the budgets of state and local units of government. In the following decade this process was reversed and financial pressure on state and local governments increased. The economic turndown of the late 1980s that continued into the 1990s did not uniformly affect all states—there have been pockets of relative prosperity, but the tandem of the cutback of federal assistance and a recession has often meant the loss of jobs and reduced governmental services to the public. Within this context, public officials have had to make difficult choices.

In early 1991, Mayor David Dinkins announced that he expected to lay off 16,000 city workers, including 3,600 police officers, in an attempt to close an expected budget gap of $2.6 billion over the following 18 months.[3] On the other coast in posh Beverly Hills, that affluent city faced the prospect of eliminating 100 jobs due to the lingering recession.[4] The Suffolk County, New York, Police Department was faced with demoting 129 lieutenants, sergeants, and detectives due to a revenue shortfall of $103 million dollars unless employees agreed to defer salary increases or to a "payroll lag" that would eliminate one payday in 1991.[5] In that same year in Massachusetts, there was a freeze on hiring new state troopers, and existing troopers had to forego pay raises.[6] In Albany, New York, union officials charged that the freeze on overtime for police and firefighters was resulting in too few public safety workers being on duty, creating a safety risk.[7] The Detroit Police Officers Association sought an emergency order in Wayne County Circuit Court, charging that the layoff of 300 officers would endanger the safety of Detroiters.[8] The Boston Police Department planned to sell its helicopter and use the $600,000 in revenue to buy cruisers;[9] Denver, also, has divested itself of its two police helicopters.[10] Teterboro, New Jersey, Borough Manager Michael Tedesco proposed in 1991 that the eight-member, $465,000-a-year police department be eliminated altogether.[11] In some instances budget restrictions have meant that jurisdictions cannot afford to pay officers to go to court and testify, resulting in dismissed charges (see Box 13-2).

Budgeting is inherently a political process. Anything done through government entails the expenditure of public funds.[12] If politics is regarded in part as a conflict over whose preferences shall prevail in the determination of policy, the outcome

BOX 13-2

Shrinking Funds for Police Force Court Case Dismissals

By Don Aucoin and Kevin Cullen *Globe Staff*

A growing number of district court cases in Massachusetts are being dismissed because financially strapped cities and towns cannot afford to pay police officers to show up for trial, according to police and court officials.

While most of the cases that have been thrown out so far are misdemeanors and noncriminal traffic offenses, there have been instances of more serious cases such as drunken driving being dismissed. And many officials warn that the state's fiscal crisis creates a risk that even felonies will be dismissed.

"It has the potential of becoming a very serious problem," said Judge Samuel F. Zoll, chief justice of the district courts.

Zoll, like others interviewed, said there are few statistical data on how many cases are being dismissed. But officials say anecdotal evidence is growing.

Some police officers warn that the resolve the state brought to the prosecution of drunken driving cases over the past decade is being steadily weakened.

"Such a good job was being done by law enforcement on drunk driving, and now, it is back the way it was," said Weymouth police officer Kevin Mahoney.

Last month, court appearances by 60 Framingham police officers were canceled by the police chief because of a lack of money, according to Paul Nicoli, head of the patrolman's union. Several drunken driving cases were among the more than 40 cases that officers were not able to testify on, he said.

A judge is usually required to dismiss a case if the arresting officer is not present to testify. Paul L. Doherty, executive director of the Massachusetts Chiefs of Police Association, said the incidence of dismissals "ties in with communities that are being hit by layoffs."

For instance, Weymouth, Chelsea and Brockton, where police officers have been laid off, have little money to pay officers overtime to testify in court.

In revenue starved Brockton, where 31 police officers were recently let go, "We have even seen some felonies dismissed already" because the former officers were not available to testify, said Kevin Creedon, clerk-magistrate of the Brockton District Court. "And believe me, in the coming months there will be a large number of cases dismissed."

Many of the cases the laid-off officers were involved in will come to trial this summer, and court officials will have to serve summonses to the homes of the officers, who may have found new jobs, rather than the police station, Creedon said. In the courtroom, defense attorneys will be ready to pounce, demanding a dismissal if the arresting officer does not appear, he predicted; even if a judge grants a continuance, "when it comes up a second time and the officer still can't be there, the judge will have to dismiss that case."

Brockton's dilemma is mirrored in Chelsea. Robert O'Leary, assistant clerk magistrate of Chelsea District Court, said he has dismissed numerous traffic complaints and other minor cases or been forced to route appeals to already-backlogged judges because police officers often don't show up to testify on noncriminal cases.

"I've seen some judges have to take 20 or 30 minutes deciding on a speeding ticket," O'Leary said. "And meanwhile there's no time for trials on felonies . . . The whole system is a farce and a sham. They've got these officers writing tickets and they know if there's a hearing it will be dismissed" because officers are often unable to attend.

Chelsea Police Chief Frank Sobolewski said money will always be found so officers can testify on drunken driving cases, but for lesser infractions, such as running a traffic light, "if it's a $50 citation and I end up paying the officer $75 to go, it doesn't make any sense." He said the department's $70,000 annual allocation for court appearances is nearly depleted.

In Weymouth, Mahoney said the police force has shrunk in recent years to 94 officers

BOX 13-2 (cont.)

from 113, so "they just don't bring you over to court anymore" to testify on minor offenses.

Mahoney said he has testified twice this year on arrests he has made, compared to 50 appearances by this time last year.

"If you receive a speeding ticket for $300, the officer would never appear in court and you'd win," said Mahoney. "In this department you can beat any citation."

The irony, according to police officers, is that the cases their departments can't afford to pursue are the very ones that raise critically needed revenue for their towns.

"A lot of revenue is going out the door," said O'Leary, noting that a failure by police to testify during one recent afternoon in the Chelsea court left $4,000 in possible fines uncollected.

Nicoli, of the patrolmen's union, said that fines from speeding tickets and other motor vehicle infractions last year added almost $800,000 to Framingham's coffers.

Zoll said he learned about the trend in recent meetings with judges and clerks from district courts across the state.

"The isolated stories I've heard about have not included any of the more serious stuff, but there is the potential for that," said Zoll.

Ned Merrick, the legislative agent for the Massachusetts Police Association, which represents officers in 310 cities and towns, says the dismissals "are a natural phenomenon" as the criminal justice system retools in the face of drastic budget cuts. Merrick says police prosecutors are being called on to absorb some of the duties formerly handled by assistant district attorneys who have been laid off or forced to concentrate on only felony cases.

"I don't have any hard figures, but common sense tells you if there is no money for overtime, they aren't going to court," said Merrick, referring to police officers. "It's not fair to tell a guy to work midnight to 8, then say he has to go to court instead of home to bed, without compensating him."

Merrick said some officers are attending court without compensation, especially in serious cases, but that cities and towns should devise a formal alternative compensation program if money is not available. One option is more vacation time.

"Contractually, some alternatives may be prohibited," said Merrick, "but I think collective bargaining groups would be willing to work with their communities."

While the state's budget problems became serious as far back as 1988, officials say the problem of dismissals is only now emerging because a July 1989 Supreme Judicial Court ruling bought some time. The SJC ruled that police officers who cite drivers for civil motor vehicle violations do not have to be in court when a motorist initially challenges the citation before a clerk-magistrate. The officer must be present at any subsequent hearing or appeal, or the complaint is dismissed.

Police chiefs say that ruling allowed them to cut overtime and temporarily avert the crisis.

Source: Boston Globe, May 16, 1991.

of this struggle is recorded in the budget.[13] Thus, the single most important political statement that any unit of government makes in a given year is its budget. Essentially the budget process confronts decision makers with the gambler's adage, "put your money where your mouth is."[14] Because often increasing demands are made on resources that are declining, stable, or outstripped by the claims made on them, the competition for appropriated funds is keen and often fierce as the police and other departments seek to make the best case they can for their own budget. Beset by competing demands from each department of government, assailed by informal "arm twisting," influenced by media reports of public opinion on various subjects, confronted by special-interest groups with different priorities, and in consideration of their own values and judgments, those who appropriate the funds are making a highly visible and often controversial political decision when they enact a budget. Because legislatures allow public officials, such as city managers and police chiefs, some discretion in how they execute a budget, they too are making political decisions whose impact may evoke strong reactions.

Although its political orientation is inescapable, a budget is more than an indicator of who won and who lost, who was able to form effective coalitions and work out acceptable compromises and who was not able to perform this feat, and whose policies are in ascendancy and descendancy; it is also a key managerial tool.[15]

State and Local Financial Management

The States' Role in Local Finance

There are numerous examples of private sector organizations that have had severe financial problems, including Chrysler, Lockheed, and Penn Central. Historically, local governments have also not been without a certain degree of financial frailty. In the last 150 years, over 6,000 units of local government have defaulted on their financial obligations, although about two-thirds of these came during the decade that followed the economic crash of 1929.[16] States simultaneously contribute to, and attempt to help, local government avoid financial difficulties. They contribute to the problem by mandating programs that require the expenditure of local funds. Examples of such mandated programs include the training of peace officers, proscribing levels of police service, and establishing special disability and retirement benefits for police.[17] Our national government also contributes in a similar fashion; for example, it is estimated that programs legislated by the federal and state government cost Iowa cities $50 to $60 million annually.[18]

As the sovereign and superior governmental entity for the geographic areas they encompass, the states have constitutional responsibilities over local government.[19] Under the legal doctrine known as Dillion's rule,[20] no local government may organize, perform any function, tax citizens, or receive or spend money without the consent of the state. With an eye toward helping local government avoid financial woes, state laws, which vary, may control (1) the revenue structure of local governments and methods of tax collection; (2) budgeting, accounting, and financial reporting practices; (3) cash collection, deposit, and disbursement procedures; and (4) procedures for incurring debt, the types of debts that may be issued, and the level of debt that is allowable.

A general model of how states assist local government is depicted in Figure 13-1; such efforts require the state to commit significant resources, another sign of the importance attached to them. In New York, for example, the financial activities of the 9,100 units of local government are monitored and supervised by three state agencies, the most significant being the Department of Audit and Control, which employs 420 people and expends $7.5 million annually in this effort.[21]

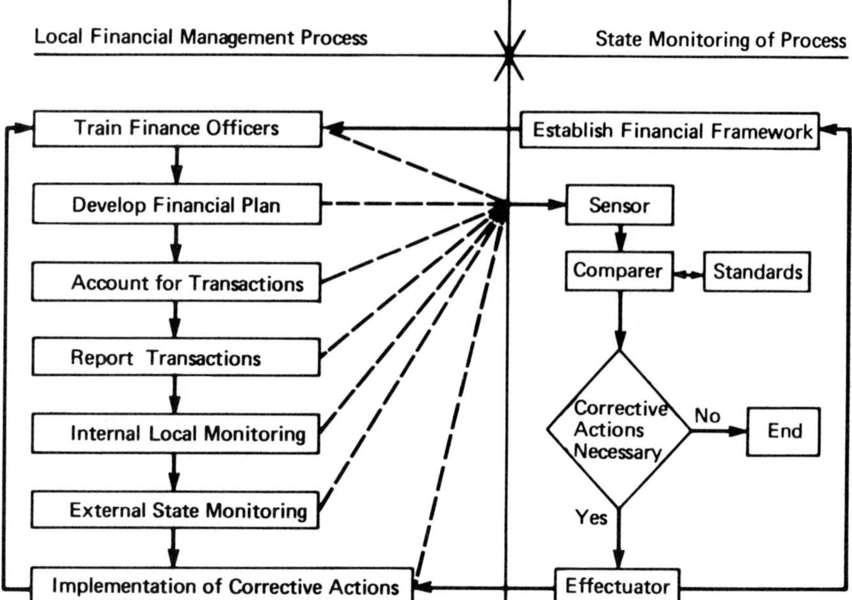

FIGURE 13-1. A general model of a state fiscal monitoring system. [From Paul Moore and Alan G. Billingsley, "Financial Monitoring of Local Governments," *State Government,* 52 (Autumn 1979), Exhibit 1, p. 157.]

Local Administration

In addition to whatever requirements are established by the federal and state governments, the practice of local financial management is also shaped by a number of other forces, including the city charter, ordinances, executive orders, regulations, and practices. Of considerable impact is the political structure of the unit of government. In city manager and strong mayor cities, these figures play dominant roles in their respective systems in the development of what is termed an executive budget. In weak mayor systems, the city council is the dominant force in the development of what is termed a legislative budget. Under this arrangement, a city council budget committee has responsibility for preparing the budget. A budget staff frequently serves this committee by providing administrative support. The heads of the various departments, including the police, and their budget staffs deal directly with the council budget committee and its staff in formulating the budget. Under the declining commissioner plan, three to seven elected officials serve as both members of the local legislative branch of government and as heads of one or more departments of city government. One of the commissioners receives the title of mayor, but it is largely ceremonial, akin to a weak mayor system. Under the commissioner plan, the budget preparation process may follow any of several patterns: (1) the commission as a whole may be the dominant force, (2) the commission may have a budget officer attached directly to it, or (3) the preparation of the budget may be guided by a budget officer assigned to the commissioner of finance, but who serves at the pleasure of the commissioners as a whole to ensure responsiveness to them.

Definitions of a Budget

The word *budget* is derived from the old French *bougette,* meaning a small leather bag or wallet.[22] Initially, it referred to the leather bag in which the chancellor of the exchequer carried the documents to English Parliament stating the government's needs and resources.[23] Later, it came to mean the documents themselves. Currently, *budget* has been defined in many ways, including a plan stated in financial terms, an estimate of future expenditures, an asking price, a policy statement, the translation of financial resources into human purposes, and a contract between those who appropriate the funds and those who spend them.[24] To some extent, all these are true and help us to understand something about budgets but they lack the feature of being comprehensive.

Even more comprehensive definitions of a budget reflect different notions. The definitions that follow represent, successively, the budget as a management tool, the budget as a process, and the budget as politics:

> The budget is a comprehensive plan, expressed in financial terms, by which a program is operated for a given period of time. It includes: (a) the services, activities, and projects comprising the program; (b) the resultant expenditure requirements; and (c) the resources usable for their support.[25] In Sunnyvale, California, each year a ten-year budget is adopted using the term Resource Allocation Plan (RAP), which reflects a strong planning orientation in the use of that city's fiscal resources.
>
> The budget is a unified series of steps taken to implement a government's policy objectives. It involves the development of a documented work program . . . the careful linkage of the program with a formal, comprehensive financial plan, and the carrying out of the entire scheme through an administrative arrangement.[26]
>
> The budget is a device for consolidating the various interests, objectives, desires and needs of our citizens.[27]

Budgets may also be defined as operating and capital. An operating budget is usually for one year and is for items that have a short life expectancy, are consumed in the normal course of operations, or are reincurred each year. Included in operating budgets are batteries, paper, duplicating and telephone expenses, as well as salaries and fringe benefits. There is a great deal of diversity in how different jurisdictions treat their capital budgets. "Capital project" or "capital improvement plan" (CIP) is often used to denote expenditures to buy land or to construct or for a major renovation of public facilities. Normally three to five years are needed to complete the development of, and paying for, a CIP. Depending on the guidelines that a jurisdiction uses, vehicles, furniture, and other equipment may or may not be included in the CIP. If not included in the CIP, such objects as police vehicles, radios, desks and chairs, binoculars, and microcomputers may be included in the operating budget under the heading of "capital item," "capital outlay," or just simply "capital." Table 13-1 illustrates a capital budget for a police department.

Operating and capital improvement budgets are normally acted on separately by the legislative body to which they are presented for consideration. Moreover, in some places such as Tucson, Arizona, the distinction between operating and capital budgets is reflected, as shown in Figure 13-2, in organizational specialists to deal with each of these two different types of budgets.

TABLE 13-1 The Las Vegas Metropolitan Police Department's 1991–1992 Capital Budget Request

Acct. No.	Bureau/section	Office furnishings	Office equipment	Radio equipment	Vehicles	Other equipment	Total
3111	Staff	1,000	0	0	0	0	1,000
3112	Planning	1,350	0	0	0	0	1,350
3113	Internal Affrs	0	0	0	15,509	959	16,468
3114	Fiscal Affrs	3,500	1,695	0	0	0	5,195
3115	PEAP	600	0	0	0	600	1,200
3116	Community Srvc	300	0	0	0	0	300
3131	Intelligence	1,550	0	0	76,628	0	78,178
3139	SED	12,675	0	0	108,563	0	121,238
3141	North Area	0	0	39,575	533,899	0	573,474
3142	Traffic	2,600	0	0	167,304	45,000	214,904
3143	Search/Rescue	350	0	0	19,200	0	19,550
3144	SWAT/K9	1,000	0	0	119,636	0	120,636
3146	Res. Off.	0	0	0	209,799	720	210,519
3147	Special events	0	0	2,300	0	0	2,300
3148	South Area	6,600	0	39,575	441,389	8,970	496,534
3149	West Area	8,280	1,200	41,375	403,803	8,950	463,608
3151	Detective	2,400	1,310	0	235,035	500	239,245
3152	Vice	1,990	0	0	35,600	7,286	44,876
3153	Narcotics	7,185	0	1,555	93,944	1,034	103,718
3161	Personnel	7,351	495	0	15,509	0	23,355
3162	Training	1,544	0	0	0	2,952	4,496
3163	Crime Prevent	4,415	0	0	15,509	0	19,924
3164	Supply	4,194	1,055	0	13,500	20,956	39,705
3165	Prof Standards	2,300	0	0	0	0	2,300
3171	Records	5,750	6,480	0	0	0	12,230
3172	Info Srvc	1,800	7,239	0	0	0	9,039
3173	Communications	0	0	25,000	30,000	9,550	64,550
3174	Fingerprint	1,400	5,609	0	0	0	7,009
3175	Criminalistics	6,905	495	0	76,089	20,166	103,655
3176	Forensic Lab	800	0	0	15,145	7,000	22,945
	TOTAL	87,839	25,578	149,380	2,626,061	134,643	3,023,501

Source: Las Vegas, Nevada Police Department.

The Budget Cycle and Roles

Some governments require all their departments to budget for a two-year period called a biennium. The Kentucky State Police represents an agency that practices biennium budgeting. Most governments, however, budget for a shorter time, called a fiscal year (FY). A fiscal year is a twelve-month period that may coincide with a calendar year, although commonly its duration is from July 1 of one year until June 30 of the next; in the federal government, it is from October 1 of one year until September 30 of the following year. A budget that took effect on July 1, 1993, and

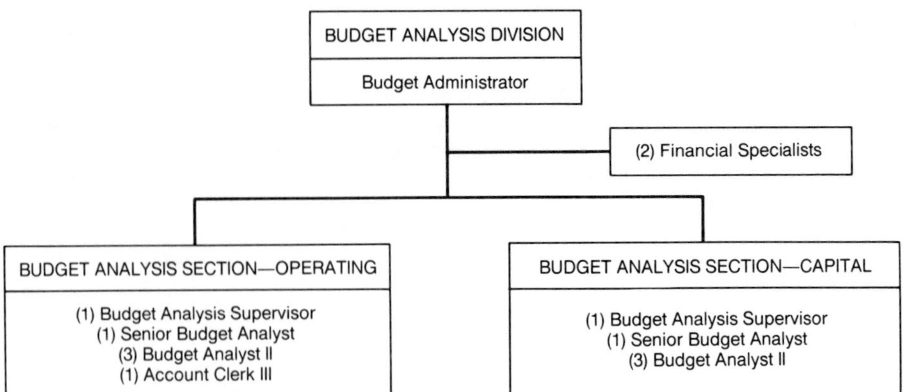

FIGURE 13-2. Organization of the City of Tucson, Arizona, Budget Analysis Division.

terminated on June 30, 1994, would be described as the FY 1994 budget. Both biennium and annual or fiscal year budgeting systems have fundamental strengths and weaknesses. The biennium approach fosters long-range planning and analysis, but it is more likely to be affected by unforeseen contingencies because of its longer time horizon. Fiscal year budgets provide for a more frequent scrutiny of programs, but they may be costly in that they emphasize thinking in small increments of time to the neglect of more sweeping considerations such as economic trends.

The budget cycle consists of four sequential steps that are repeated every year at about the same time in a well-organized government: (1) budget preparation (2) budget approval, (3) budget execution, and (4) the audit. Fiscal years and the budget cycle overlap. For example, while a police department is executing this year's budget, it will at various times be faced with an audit of last year's and the preparation of next year's. Within each of the steps, a number of things occur that affect the dynamics of budgeting and with which the police manager must be familiar to be effective.

Budget Preparation

Given that the executive budget predominates, whether in the form of the president's, a governor's, a strong mayor's, or a city manager's, this discussion of the elements of the budget cycle will assume for purposes of illustration a city manager form of government.

Long before the police department or any other unit of city government begins the preparation of its annual submission, a great deal of effort has gone on, principally within the department of finance or other similarly titled unit. Figure 13-3 depicts the general and detailed organization of such a body.

Included in this preliminary effort are revenue forecasts, determinations of how much money from existing departmental budgets will not be expended, analyses of how population shifts will affect demands for various types of public services, and the development of the city's budget preparation manual. Budget preparation manuals tend to focus on the technical aspects of budget, such as responsibilities, definitions, and instructions on completing forms.

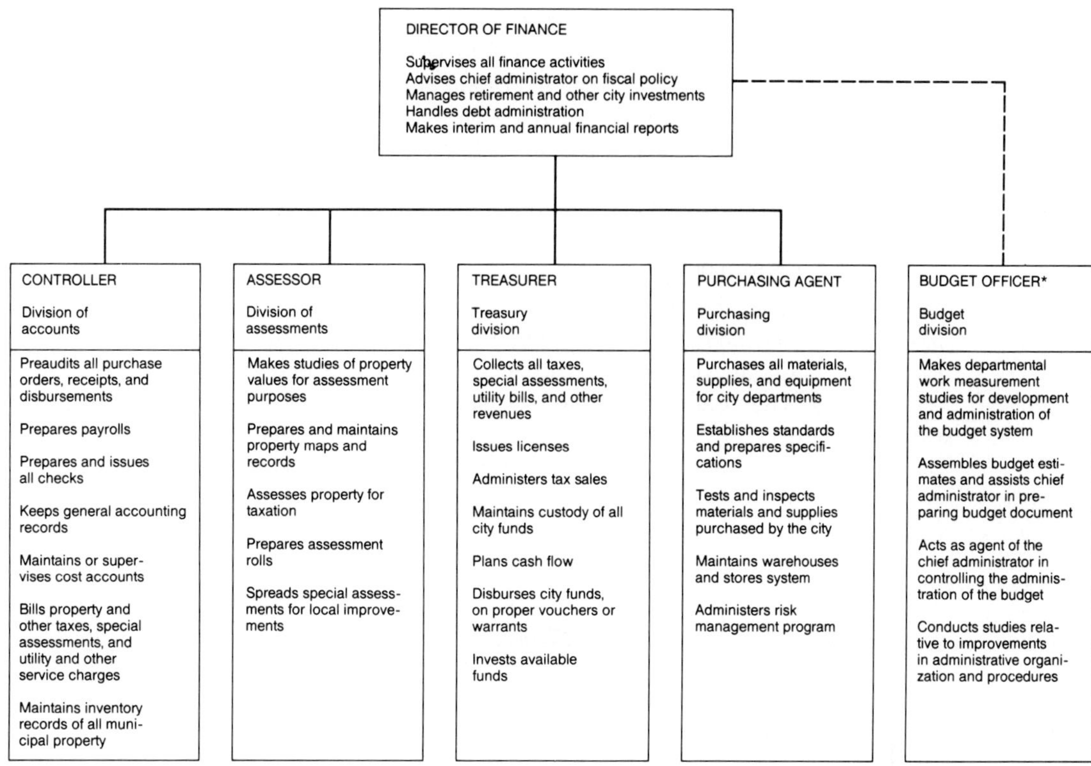

*The dotted line between the director of finance and the budget officer indicates that the latter is often primarily responsible to the chief administrator, being physically located in the finance department to prevent the duplication of records. In many cities the finance director handles the budget.

FIGURE 13-3. A functional organizational chart of a municipal department of finance. [*Source:* Leonard I. Ruchelman, "The Finance Function in Local Government," in *Management Policies in Local Government,* J. Richard Aronson and Eli Schwartz, eds. (Washington, D.C.: International City Management Association, 1987), Figure 1-5, p. 22.]

Ordinarily accompanying the budget preparation manual is a memorandum from the city manager that discusses the general fiscal guidelines to be followed by the departments in preparing their budget requests. The content of this memorandum essentially reflects the data generated by the preliminary effort discussed previously, supplemented by whatever special information or priorities the city manager may have.

In some jurisdictions the city manager will formally or informally go before the city council to get members' views as to their priorities in terms of spending levels, pay raises, new hirings, and programs. This does not constitute a contract between the city manager and the council; rather, it is an exchange of information that is binding on neither but that can eliminate time-consuming and costly skirmishes later. In other jurisdictions, the council may unilaterally issue a statement of their expectations, or the city manager and department heads may have to try to establish the council's expectations through reading their statements to newspapers or informal contacts with individual council members.

An important element of the budget preparation manual is the budget preparation calendar, which is the time schedule a city follows from the time it begins to prepare a budget until the budget is approved. From the standpoint of a chief of police, there are actually two budget preparation calendars: the one established by the department of finance's budget officer and the one the police department develops that duplicates the timetable of the city's overall budget preparation but that also establishes a timetable and set of responsibilities within the police department. Table 13-2 shows an internal budget preparation calendar for a large police department.

Upon receipt of the city's budget preparation manual and the city administrator's fiscal policy memorandum, the chief of police will have the planning and research unit, assuming that this is where the department's fiscal responsibility is located as budgeting is most fundamentally a planning process, prepare the internal budget calendar and an internal fiscal policy memorandum. This material establishes the chief's priorities within the context of the directions he or she has been given, just as the city manager's fiscal policy memorandum does for the city.

TABLE 13-2 A Budget Preparation Calendar for a Large Police Department

What should be done	By whom	On these dates
Issue budget instructions and applicable forms	City administrator	November 1
Prepare and issue budget message, with instructions and applicable forms, to unit commanders	Chief of police	November 15
Develop unit budgets with appropriate justification and forward recommended budgets to planning and research unit	Unit commanders	February 1
Review of unit budget	Planning and research staff with unit commanders	March 1
Consolidation of unit budgets for presentation to chief of police	Planning and research unit	March 15
Review of consolidated recommended budget	Chief of police, planning and research staff, and unit commanders	March 30
Department approval of budget	Chief of police	April 15
Recommended budget forwarded to city administrator	Chief of police	April 20
Administrative review of recommended budget	City administrator and chief of police	April 30
Revised budget approval	City administrator	May 5
Budget document forwarded to city council	City administrator	May 10
Review of budget	Budget officer of city council	May 20
Presentation to council	City administrator and chief of police	June 1
Reported back to city administrator	City council	June 5
Review and resubmission to city council	City administrator and chief of police	June 10
Final action on police budget	City council	June 20

Source: National Advisory Commission on Criminal Justice Standards and Goals, *Police* (Washington, D.C.: U.S. Government Printing Office, 1973), p. 137.

The budget preparation manual with the city manager's and chief's cover memorandums attached is then distributed to the police department's major units where the budget building actually takes place.

Just how far down the organizational hierarchy involvement in this process goes is related somewhat to the size of the police department. In small departments where there is little or no functional specialization, the chiefs may actually prepare the budgets alone or with minimal input from their watch commanders. In some instances, most often when the city manager has a high need for control, small department chiefs may have little or no input into preparing the budget request for their departments and may never actually see the budget under which their departments operate. In police departments sufficiently large for functional specialization, the lowest supervisory ranks in the smallest organizational entities should be involved in preparing the budget request for their own operation; when their request is completed, it is submitted to the next largest organizational entity in the police department's structure, where it is reviewed, returned for any adjustments, resubmitted, and becomes part of the request initiated by that next largest organizational entity. This process is repeated until each of the largest organizational entities, normally designated as bureaus, has a budget request that covers its entire operations for the forthcoming fiscal year.

The planning and research unit will then review the bureau budget requests for compliance with technical budgeting instructions and the priorities of the chief and the city manager. Here and elsewhere, there is often a great deal of communication between the police department's designated liaison with the city budget officer regarding waivers from certain requirements, clarification of guidelines, and other related matters. After any necessary adjustments are made by the bureaus, the planning and research unit will prepare a consolidated budget for the entire police department and submit it to the chief with its recommendations. Following this, the chief will have a series of meetings with the staff of the planning and research unit and the bureau commanders to discuss the department's budget.

In these meetings, the interplay of the stakes, the issues, personalities, internal politics, value differences, personal agendas, and other variables create an atmosphere that is tense and sometimes heated. The chief both mediates and contributes to conflicts. One key way in which the chief contributes to mediating and promoting conflict is by using the budget as a means of rewarding "the faithful" and disciplining "the disloyal." In a very real sense, a chief can harm a subordinate's interests more than he or she can help them; programs can be cut back, assigned low priorities, and eliminated with a greater likelihood of success than can initiating requests for additional personnel, special equipment, and funds to support travel to conferences.

Also considered during these meetings between the chief and key staff members are questions of overall budget strategy. Such questions include what priorities to assign different programs, how to best justify requests, and how large a request to make. Police administrators must be able to justify the contents of their department's budget proposal. Any portion of a request for which a persuasive defense cannot be made fosters the belief in budget analysis that more, perhaps much more, of the request can be cut. This, in turn, invites even closer scrutiny and some cuts that go beyond "trimming the fat" and go to "cutting muscle and bone." However, if the city's central budget office operates in the role of "cutters" and "defenders of the public treasury," to some extent the practical question is not whether to "pad the budget," but rather where and how. This may take the form of requesting funding for one or a few programs that are justifiable, but can essentially serve as "sacrificial lambs" while at the same time not endangering the rest of the request. The alternative is to present a budget from which the chief can tolerate no cuts and hope that at some other point of consideration the essential cut funds will be restored. There is a fine point involved here; if the chief is seen as someone who simply routinely pads the budget, he or she will lose the respect and confidence of those involved in the budgetary process. If, however, the chief is skillful in these maneuvers, his or her reputation may be enhanced as being an effective advocate for the department, a programmatic innovator, and a realist who can be flexible in budget negotiations. Based on such considerations and input, the chief makes decisions and directs the planning and research unit to develop the police department's budget request that is going to be submitted to the city manager. This document is then forwarded to the city manager with a cover letter from the chief of police. This cover letter (one appears in the Appendix to this chapter) highlights the detailed budget request, calls attention to new initiatives and past successes, and may warn of consequences if funds are not forthcoming or appropriated.

The city manager will, in turn, treat the police department's budget in the same manner as the unit budgets were treated within the police department. The city manager's budget office will consolidate the requests from the various departments, the heads of which will meet with the city manager and the budget officer to discuss their requests. Subsequently, the city manager will direct the city's budget officer to make certain changes, often cuts, and prepare a draft of the citywide budget that the city manager will recommend to the council. This recommended budget will then be sent to the council with a cover letter not unlike the one the chief sent the city manager, except that it will be in the broader perspective of the city's needs and may call attention to such variables as the legal requirement for a balanced budget, that is, one in which expenditures do not exceed revenues.

Budget Approval

Having received the city manager's recommended budget, the city council will commence its consideration, which begins with an analysis of the budget by the council's budget officer, if it has one. Subsequently, the city manager will appear before the council to answer whatever questions the members have. At some point, the heads of each department and their key staff members may appear before the council as the budget request for their department is being considered (see Box 13-3). The appearance of representatives of the individual departments may be opposed by the city manager who sees such appearances as a threat to his or her power, fiscal policies, or other matters, because it presents the opportunity for department heads to get cuts made by the city manager restored to the police budget.

BOX 13-3

City Council Takes Close Aim at Police Budget

By Rebecca Theim and Coleman Warner *Staff Writers*

Frustration with New Orleans' escalating crime problem pervaded City Council budget hearings Monday, as council members undertook a haphazard review of the Police Department's budget.

The tedious three-hour review came on the next-to-last day of budget hearings and focused on how the department would use its share of a property tax increase of up to 10 mills voters approved last month for improved police and fire protection. Ratification of the tax is up to the council, which has the option of rejecting the millage or imposing only a portion of it.

"People want to see police out there," Councilman Lambert Boissier told police department officials. "I want to support you and give you what you need to do that, but I want to see police on the streets."

Tempers flared during Monday's hearing while Councilwoman Peggy Wilson sharply questioned Superintendent Warren Woodfork about the Police Department's budget. The exchange seemed to highlight Woodfork's frustration with the growing crime problem and his critics.

"I've been with this Police Department for 27 years," Woodfork said, his voice rising. "I've never had a 9-to-5 job. I created the felony action squad, I devised innovative programs. A whole lot of things came from Warren Woodfork."

Woodfork said that while residents' calls have increased 66 percent in the past 10 years, the number of police officers has decreased, from 1,532 to 1,403.

At any time, between 20 percent and 30 percent of the Police Department's car fleet is out of service and being repaired, Woodfork said, and many patrol cars have been driven more than 100,000 miles.

Radios are old and often do not work, he said.

Under a plan proposed by Woodfork, the $7.5 million the Police Department's 5-mill share would generate would be used to hire 260 employees, including 200 officers, 30 civilian employees, 20 communications specialists and 10 police technicians to handle routine tasks so officers could be on the streets; and buy 400 police cars, 600 police radios and $1.5 million in additional fuel.

Paradoxically, the new police and fire tax complicates the council's job of balancing the budget.

To ensure that the public safety millage increases police and fire protection money and is not swallowed into general budget needs, city officials are barred from reducing police and fire budgets below 1990 levels if they intend to collect the tax.

Leaving the police and fire budgets intact means that other city departments must bear the brunt of across-the-board cuts.

Boissiere and Councilman Jim Singleton also asked Woodfork about complaints that large numbers of New Orleans patrol cars are seen outside the parish after hours. Woodfork denied that marked patrol cars are taken out of the parish except on official business. He acknowledged that roughly 27 percent of police officers live outside New Orleans. Although a city ordinance requires police officers to live in New Orleans, many lived outside of the city when the law was passed and were exempted.

In addition, the law is poorly written and confusing, Woodfork said, raising questions about whether an officer has to live in the city, or merely needs a New Orleans mailing address.

The council called a second hearing to ask more questions of Woodfork and other criminal justice officials. Residents also may ask about the city's crime-fighting effort at the hearing, Monday at 5:30 P.M. in the council chamber.

In addition, the public may ask about budgets proposed by other city departments during a special hearing Friday at 9:30 A.M., also in the council chamber.

Budget hearings will continue today at 9:30 A.M. and will focus on the Fire Department, the chief administrative office and the Job Partnership Training Act.

Source: Times-Picayune (New Orleans, Louisiana), Nov. 13, 1990.

For example, in San Jose, California, the police department's budget requested no new personnel in accordance with the city administrator's restrictions.[28] However, when presenting the budget request to the council, police officials included a frank description of conditions, using simple and carefully selected graphics. Immediately subsequent to this presentation, the San Jose City Council added 90 new positions to the police department's budget. This incident also gives rise to considering how a police administrator can be effective in obtaining funds from appropriators. In the case of San Jose, the positions given to the police department required reducing the budgets of several other departments. The following represent some things believed to be important to being successful in getting appropriations:[29]

1. Have a budget that is carefully justified.
2. Anticipate the environment of the budget hearing; find out by examining news reports and through conversations the priorities of the council members. Talk to department heads who have already presented their budgets to learn what types of questions are being asked. Analyze local, regional, and national papers to identify criticisms being made of the police and current issues and innovations. For example, reports that the Savannah, Georgia, Police Department modified 25 cars to operate on propane might lead city council members in other localities to ask "What are the advantages and disadvantages of using propane as a fuel in police vehicles?"[30]
3. Determine which "public" will be at the police department's budget hearing and prepare accordingly. As the issues change from year to year, so will the portion of the community that is sufficiently aroused to participate in these proceedings. A child killed by a vehicle while crossing an unguarded intersection, a series of violent robberies in the downtown area, the rapes of several elderly women, and incidents of "gay bashing" are likely to mobilize such groups as the parent–teacher association, the chamber of commerce and the merchants association, the Grey Panthers, and Queer Nation.
4. Help shape the environment by planting questions with sympathetic council members, the answers to which put the police department in a favorable light.
5. Make good use of graphics in the form of pie charts (Figure 13-4) and histograms (Figure 13-5). In Figure 13-5 note how dramatically the increase in vehicle trade-in mileage is displayed, particularly the increase between FY 1981 and FY 1987. In budget presentations the use of carefully selected colors adds to the impact of graphics. In using graphics it is important to be selective and not "go overboard"; short case histories of police successes are natural and potent adjuncts to graphics.
6. Rehearse and critique the presentation several times using role playing; the use of videotaping is especially helpful in this regard.
7. Have the physical layout checked before the presentation so it is known where electrical outlets are, where the screen should be situated, and if an extension cord is needed for any audiovisual equipment.
8. The chief of police must have, or develop, a reputation for being an able and economical administrator.
9. Take advantage of unusual situations to dramatize the need for special police equipment or additional personnel.
10. Be a political realist.

After the police and all other departments have appeared before it, the city council will give directions to the city manager. These directions may take any of

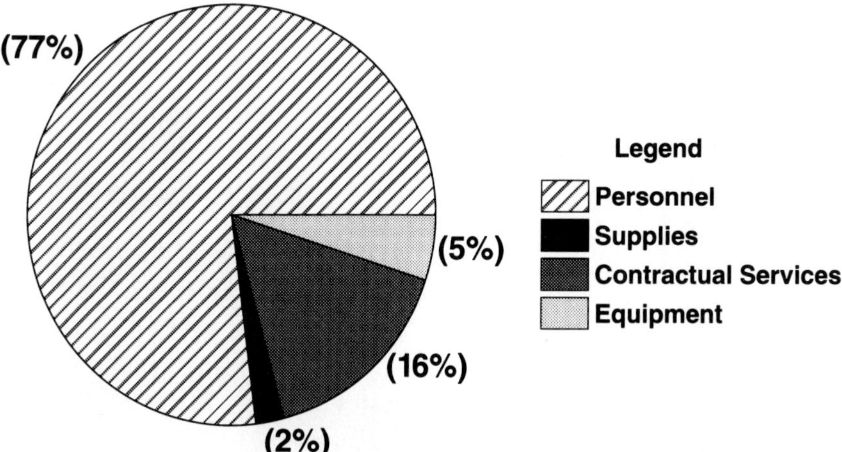

FIGURE 13-4. A pie chart of the Indianapolis Police Department's fiscal year 1991 budget of $62,790,758 by major object of expense.

several forms, such as cutting the overall city budget request by $1.5 million with, or without, any guidance as to where the cuts are to be made or directing that certain programs cut by the manager be reinstated, again with or without guidance in where to find the funds. When all adjustments are made to the satisfaction of the city council, the budget is adopted by the passage of an ordinance by a simple majority vote.

Table 13-3 shows the budget approval process for the Fayetteville, North Carolina, Police Department's FY 1992 budget as it relates to major expenditure categories. The "1989–1990 Prior Year Actual" heading indicates actual expenses for the FY 1990 budget. The "1990–1991" heading has two supporting columns: (1) "This Year Budget," which reflects the budget as approved by FY 1991, and (2) "12 Months Estimated Actual," which reflects that although Table 13-3 is the budget request process for the FY 1992 budget, the Fayetteville Police Department was still operating under the FY 1991 budget, and, therefore, this column shows an assessment of what the actual expenditures have been so far (actual expenses) plus a projection of expenditures over the balance of FY 1991 (estimated). By examining the two supporting columns under "1990–1991," members of city council have some important feedback as to how their approved budget for the police department is actually working. The "1991–1992" heading has three supporting columns: (1) the budget amount "Proposed by Department," (2) the amount "Recommended by City Manager," and (3) the amount ultimately "Approved by City Council." Across most budget categories, the city manager cut the amount requested by the police department, and these reductions were accepted by council. By examining the bottom line of Table 13-3, we can see that in terms of the "Department Total," the city manager recommended, and council accepted, a reduction of approximately $1.1 million in the amount requested by the police department. Later in this chapter, budget for-

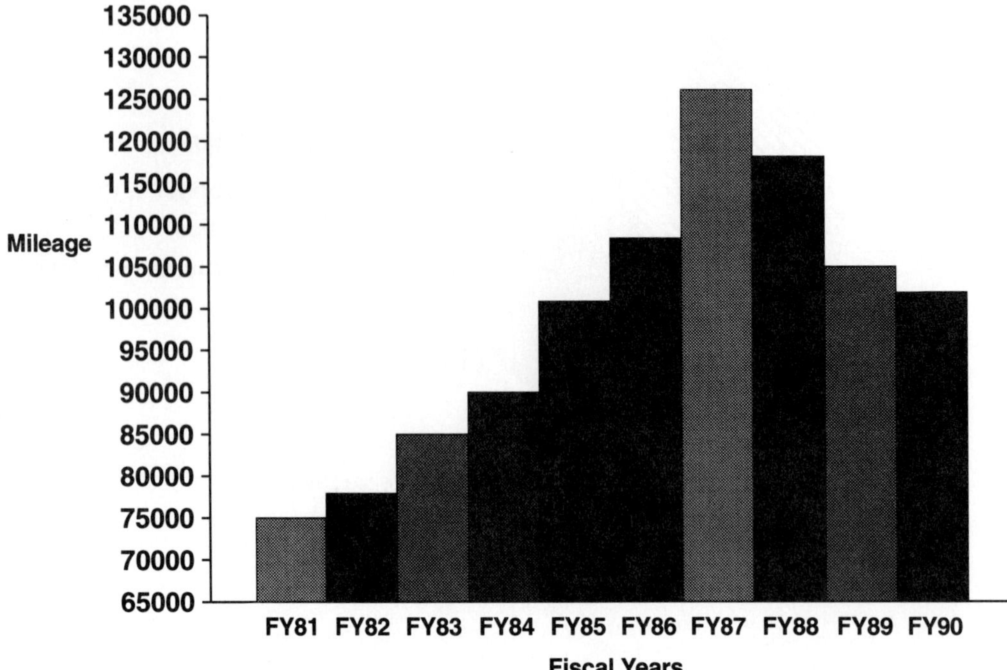

FIGURE 13-5. A histogram of the mileage on Illinois State Police vehicles at trade-in between fiscal year 1981 and fiscal year 1990. Note the dramatic increase, which peaked in fiscal year 1987.

mats are discussed. For the present it is sufficient to note that Table 13-3 reflects an object or expenditure budget format.

Budget Execution

The budget execution function has four objectives:

1. To provide for an orderly manner in which the police department's approved objectives for the fiscal year are to be achieved.
2. To ensure that no commitments or expenditures by the police department are undertaken, except in pursuance of authorizations made by the city council.
3. To conserve the resources of the police department that are not legitimately required to achieve the approved objectives.
4. To provide for a suitable accounting, at appropriate intervals, of the manner in which the chief's stewardship over entrusted resources has been discharged.[31]

These objectives are supported by three different mechanisms: (1) a system of allotment, (2) accounting controls, and (3) management controls.[32]

TABLE 13-3 The Budget Approval Process for the Fayetteville, North Carolina, Police Department, Fiscal Year (FY) 1992

	1989–1990	1990–1991		1991–1992		
Classification of Expenditure	Prior Year actual	This Year budget	12 Months estimated actual	Proposed by department	Recommended by city manager	Approved by city council
Salaries	$6,461,944	$7,275,057	$7,205,052	$7,751,940	$7,375,622	$7,321,098
Fringe Benefits	1,379,048	1,607,525	1,623,689	1,770,566	1,710,089	1,702,010
Other Svc and supplies	102,010	94,245	90,602	127,260	82,200	82,201
Total Personnel Svc	7,943,022	8,976,827	8,919,343	9,649,766	9,167,911	9,105,309
Utilities	1,994	2,950	2,950	7,292	7,292	7,292
Supplies	103,820	128,126	122,855	142,945	125,100	125,100
Prog Supplies/ Services	8,037	15,945	15,074	13,700	11,100	11,100
General Maintenance	52,855	75,597	75,495	92,055	86,400	86,400
Vehicle Operations	530,534	593,728	648,973	1,107,539	701,568	701,568
Communi- cations	60,823	60,995	62,725	67,690	63,500	63,500
Travel and Training	26,961	14,781	15,638	33,590	27,000	27,000
Dues and Subscrip- tions	9,962	12,693	12,693	10,680	8,600	8,600
Insurance	0	0	0	0	0	0
Other Services	195,692	355,579	354,255	485,421	485,421	485,421
Total Operating Svc	990,678	1,260,394	1,310,658	1,960,912	1,515,981	1,515,981
Accounting/ Audit Svc	0	0	0	0	0	0
Legal Services	0	0	0	0	0	0
Medical Services	35,612	23,310	24,310	64,825	18,000	18,000
Architect Services	0	0	0	0	0	0
Consulting Services	1,937	22,200	22,200	33,150	25,000	25,000
Other Contract Svc	3,670	17,170	17,170	25,700	25,700	25,700
Total Prof/ Contract Svc	41,219	62,680	63,680	123,675	68,700	68,700
Land	0	0	0	0	0	0
Building	0	0	0	4,500	0	0
Improvements	0	0	0	0	0	0

TABLE 13-3 (cont.)

	1989–1990	1990–1991		1991–1992		
Classification of Expenditure	Prior Year actual	This Year budget	12 Months estimated actual	Proposed by department	Recommended by city manager	Approved by city council
Office Equipment	172,566	6,521	4,638	29,786	12,000	12,000
Other Equipment	49,657	51,389	53,580	67,480	50,000	50,000
Vehicles	26,600	555,765	569,091	34,465	13,000	13,000
Heavy Equipment	0	0	0	0	0	0
Non-Inventory Assets	292	0	0	0	0	0
Total Capital Outlay	249,115	613,675	627,309	136,231	75,000	75,000
Total Other Charges	279,252	238,529	182,977	364,200	269,000	269,000
Department Total	9,503,266	11,152,105	11,103,967	12,234,784	11,096,592	11,033,990

Source: Fayettville, North Carolina Police Department.

The Allotment System

Once an appropriations ordinance has been enacted by the city council, money can be expended legally by that unit of government. Once this has happened, it is theoretically the responsibility of the city's finance office to break each department's approved budget up into allocations for specific periods of time. When actually used, this procedure—referred to ordinarily as the allotment system—usually employs a three-month period known as a quarter. However, because the spending patterns of the various departments do not fall into neat "quarters" and vary widely, establishing the actual needs of each department is a time-consuming process. Therefore, despite the attention that allotment systems receive in the literature, many units of government have elected to rely on other mechanisms, such as budget status reports, as a means of monitoring spending and exercising control.

Accounting Controls

A police department's budget officer, acting on behalf of the chief, will have a system of accounts to ensure that expenditures do not exceed the available resources. Separate budget ledgers are established for the major cost centers involved. Figure 13-6 illustrates the use of cost centers. Expenditures must be authorized by means of appropriate forms and supporting documents. The police department's budget officer wields considerable power in this regard, and occasionally his or her decisions will be appealed to the chief.

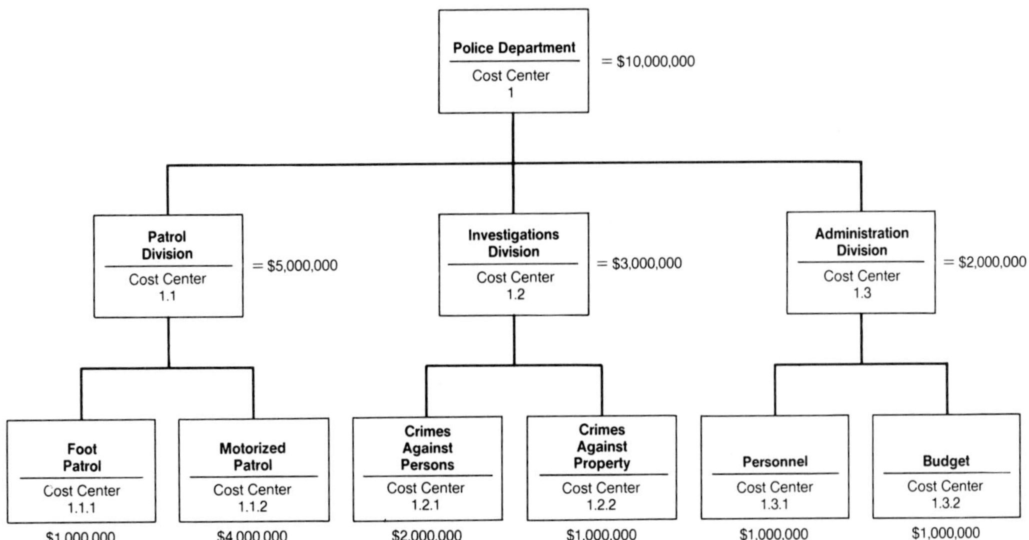

FIGURE 13-6. Illustration of the use of cost centers in a police department. [*Source:* Kent John Chabotar, *Measuring the Costs of Police Services* (Washington, D.C.: U.S. Department of Justice, National Institute of Justice, 1982), p. 25.]

Here a certain dilemma exists that must be dealt with on a case-by-case basis: if the chief supports too many appeals, the budget officer loses some effectiveness and the chief may find him- or herself deluged with appeals; if no appeals are supported, the police department may lose some effectiveness because of the lack of equipment or may lose the chance to capitalize on some unusual opportunity.

Periodic reports on accounts are an important element of control in that they serve to reduce the likelihood of overspending. Additionally, they identify areas in which deficits are likely to occur. Although police agencies budget for unusual contingencies, deficits may occur because of rises in gasoline prices, extensive overtime, natural disasters, or other causes. Table 13-4 is a budget status report; from the standpoint of managerial use, it incorporates several deficiencies:

1. The "% Used" column reflects only the total in the "Expenses to date" column without consideration of the amount obliged, but for which no disbursements have been made. This leads to a misimpression as to the amount of funds actually available for use.
2. There is no provision for comparing the percentage of the budget used with the percentage of the budget year that has lapsed to make some judgment about the coinciding of expenditures with the passage of time.

The advent of electronic data processing has facilitated the accounting control function by making information available to police managers on a more timely basis.

Management Controls

The last element of budget execution is management controls, without which financial controls are incomplete. Management controls reach down and through-

TABLE 13-4 A Police Department's Budget Status Report, December 31, 1992

Line item	Amount budgeted	Expenses to date	Amount obligated	Balance to date	% Used
Salaries	$1,710,788	$848,161.05	$ 0.00	$862,626.95	49.58%
Training	15,000	5,374.47	6,098.00	3,527.53	35.83
Professional services	1,000	828.40	115.00	56.60	82.84
Travel	4,500	2,077.55	834.06	1,588.39	46.17
Dues and subscriptions	1,021	383.83	164.11	473.06	37.59
Communications	19,557	8,669.28	1,273.01	9,614.71	44.33
Utilities	35,000	17,213.81	1,420.36	16,365.83	49.18
Office supplies	21,000	7,988.76	3,274.99	9,736.25	38.04
Printing	7,000	3,725.43	1,854.75	1,419.82	53.22
Repairs to equipment	55,129	25,979.00	3,363.11	25,786.89	47.12
Real property maintenance	4,500	2,946.50	374.28	1,179.22	65.48
Equipment leasing	2,600	1,438.71	352.39	808.90	55.34
Riot agents	1,000	0.00	0.00	1,000.00	0.00
Ammunition	2,500	524.07	745.00	1,230.93	20.96
Investigation fee	4,000	2,057.46	538.00	1,404.54	51.44
Xerox	7,000	2,370.36	625.60	4,204.04	33.86
Fuel and lubricants	108,000	42,103.88	10,000.00	55,896.12	38.99
Janitorial supplies	4,000	1,082.73	808.46	2,308.81	27.07
Uniforms	31,500	10,004.56	3,955.75	17,539.69	31.76
Protective equipment	6,530	1,007.18	1,118.31	4,404.51	15.42
Intoximeter	800	220.53	82.60	496.87	27.57
Cash match	812	0.00	0.00	0.00	0.00
Pistol team	1,500	803.96	681.10	14.94	53.60
Swat team	3,000	66.74	600.00	2,333.26	2.22
Capital teams	84,173	13,713.62	63,685.82	6,773.56	16.29

out a police department to regulate the use of resources. Often, the character of these controls is prospective in that they prevent financial obligations from being incurred. Examples include a chief's placing a freeze on hiring or requiring that, when a specific percentage of expenditures in budget categories is reached, his or her approval is required for any additional expenditures or obligations. Management controls are also retrospective in that a chief may have to initiate corrective action.

Illustrative of this would be preparing a budget amendment request to take surplus funds from one account to cover an account in which a deficit exists. Transfer of funds requests go from the police department to the city's budget officer, through the city manager, and to the city council for their approval if they exceed any latitude given to the city manager by the council for budget administration.

Management controls may also be both retrospective and prospective; the midyear review affords the chief and his command staff the opportunity to examine financial performance and progress toward departmental objectives during the first half of the fiscal year and to plan and take any necessary corrective action for the remaining period. Monitoring actions will occur on a more frequent basis, such as monthly or quarterly, but the midyear review represents a major milestone.

The Audit

The term *audit* refers to the act of verifying something independently.[33] The basic rationale for an audit has been expressed in the following way:

> A fundamental tenet of a democratic society holds that governments and agencies entrusted with public resources and the authority for applying them have a responsibility to render a full accounting of their activities. This accountability is inherent in the governmental process and is not always specifically identified by legislative provision. This governmental accountability should identify not only the object for which the public resources have been devoted but also the manner and effect of their application.[34]

Audits are concerned with three broad areas of accountability: (1) financial, which focuses on determining whether the financial operations of the police department are conducted properly, whether its reports are presented accurately, and whether it has complied with the applicable laws and regulations; (2) management, which concerns whether the police chief and his subordinate managers are utilizing resources in an efficient and economical manner, along with the identification of any cases of inadequate, inefficient, or uneconomical practices; and (3) program, which determines whether the benefits and objectives that the city council intended to arise and achieve from the operation of the police department during the fiscal year were actually created and attained, along with the causes of any nonperformance.[35]

Figure 13-7 depicts the participants in the audit process; those in the role of auditors vary—for example, they may be part of a state's system of monitoring local finances or, if that provision does not exist, they may be representatives of private sector firms that complement the city's internal audit function. Auditors look for

1. Unauthorized transfers of funds between accounts
2. Failure to compile and submit financial reports punctually
3. Year-end accounting manipulations that move liabilities from one fiscal year to the next
4. The use of commingled accounts to disguise the use of grant funds for unauthorized purposes
5. Improper computations
6. The disbursements of funds without adequate documentation
7. The use of bond proceeds for projects other than those authorized

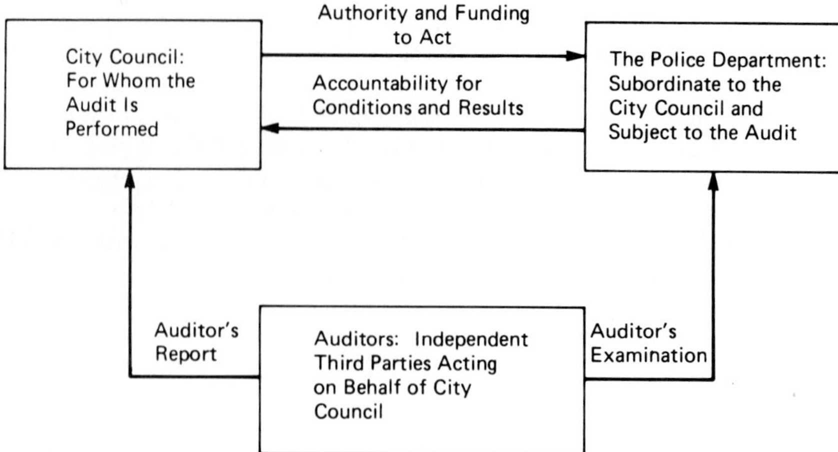

FIGURE 13-7. Participants in the audit process. [From Lennis M. Knighton, "Four Ways to Audit Effectiveness," *Governmental Finance,* 8 (September 1979), p. 9, with modification.]

8. Expenditures in excess of appropriations
9. The lack of compliance with established bidding procedures.[36]

Before the audit report is submitted, it will be discussed with the chief of police, and any errors of fact or representation in the report will be adjusted. Matters relating to differences of opinion or judgment between the auditors and the chief are usually the subject of a letter from the chief to the city council. After reviewing the auditor's report, the city council may request the formal appearance of the chief to discuss the report or direct the city manager to cause any corrective action required to be initiated.

Although audits may reveal weaknesses and thus are a source of potential professional embarrassment, police managers should welcome them because of the advantages they hold for improved information for decision making, the potential to increase the police department's effectiveness and efficiency, and the opportunity to correct deficiencies that might otherwise lead to the loss of grant funds or other negative consequences.

Budget Formats

At the turn of this century, there was nothing that resembled the budget cycle just described. The situation in California was portrayed by Governor Young as follows:

> When I first entered the legislature in 1909 there was little short of chaos as far as any orderly provisions for state expenditures were concerned. There had been no audit of state finances for over twenty years. The finance committees of the two houses were scenes of a blind scramble on the part of the various institutions and departments of the state in an endeavor to secure as large a portion as possible of whatever money might

> happen to be in the treasury. Heads of institutions encamped night after night at the committee rooms, each alert for his own interest regardless of the interests of other institutions.[37]

Not only were other states similarly situated, but conditions were not any better in local governments at that time; cities had not yet recovered from the havoc wrought by political rings stealing and squandering enormous sums of public money in earlier years, and waste and extravagance flourished.[38] There were no systematic procedures for handling fiscal matters, there was no comprehensive or long-term financial planning, the total cost of operating a city's government was often unknown or suspect, and one could not tell in advance if the year would end with a surplus or deficit.[39] The practices of the federal government were not sharply differentiated from those of the state and local governments of that time. In 1885, eight committees of the House of Representatives had authority to recommend appropriations; later, this was increased to 10. The Senate was not far behind with appropriating authority given to eight of its standing committees.[40] The assertion of Senator Aldrich in 1909 that the Congress had enacted $50 million of wasteful appropriations gave dramatic publicity to the need for reform.[41]

The center of power in budgeting at the turn of the century was with the legislative body; the following factors characterize legislative budgeting at that time:

1. There was no central official who was empowered to review or revise departmental estimates or to make recommendations to the legislature.
2. Most frequently each department's requests were submitted separately, often at different times.
3. Each agency classified accounts in its own way.
4. Departmental requests were often presented as a lump sum without supporting detail.
5. Requests were not related in any way to revenues anticipated.
6. Each department bargained separately with the appropriations committees.
7. There was little or no supervision of department spending.[42]

Illustrative of several of these points is that when President Taft prepared a budget for the national government for the 1914 fiscal year and submitted it to Congress, it was coldly received and practically ignored.[43] However, strong forces were at work that led to budgeting reforms at all levels of government. The most significant development was the advent of the executive budget, in which every department submitted its estimates to the chief executive of the unit of government involved or a designated representative, creating centralized control. Centralized control hastened, if not made possible, standardized budget cycles, budget formats, and other tools.

The forces that contributed to budgeting reforms include the writings about municipal corruption by such "muckrakers" as Ida Tarbell, Ray Baker, and Lincoln Steffens;[44] the 1899 Model Municipal Corporation Act, which proposed a budget system under the direct supervision of the mayor; the influence of the scientific management movement; the formation of the New York Bureau of Municipal Research in 1906, which brought together such luminaries as Frederick Cleveland, William Allen, and Henry Bruère, who undertook an immediate study of New York City's budgeting and published in 1907 the influential *Making a Municipal*

Budget,[45] the good government and city manager movements during the second decade of the century; and the 1916 issuance of a model city charter by the National Municipal League. It is interesting to note that the rise of the executive budget, with its centralized control and standardized budget cycles and formats developed in the cities, spread to the states between 1915 and 1925[46] and only appeared in the federal government in 1921 with the passage of the Budget and Accounting Act.

The flow of these events is important from two key perspectives; first, it accounts for the control orientation of the first budget format widely adopted; second, it underpins the notion that each prevailing budget format is understood and appreciated best as a product of the period in which it evolved.

Six different budget formats are covered in the sections that follow. Some have enjoyed a period of dominance, but these periods are difficult to identify precisely because the rhetoric of the budget literature and actual practices do not always coincide. The *line-item budget* remains the single most commonly employed budget format and is associated generally with the period 1915 to just after World War II. *Performance budgets* came into vogue following World War II until about 1960. The *planning-programming budget system* was a dominant theme in the literature from 1960 to 1971, but it was never practiced widely outside of the federal government. *Programmatic budgets* evolved during the early 1970s, and variants of it presently abound. *Zero-based budgets* gained attention in the literature in the early 1970s, but they have not been adopted widely by state and local governments. *Hybrid budgets* have always existed, and in actual practice most budgets incorporate features of several different formats.

When attempting to decide which type of a budget a police department uses, the test is not which label is applied—because labels are often used almost indiscriminately—but rather what the emphasis of the format is.

The Line-Item or Object-of-Expenditure Budget

The line-item or object-of-expenditure budget[47] is the oldest and simplest of budget types. It is the basic system on which all other budget types rely because of its excellence as a control device. As suggested by Table 13-5, the line-item budget derives its identity from its character; every amount requested, recommended, appropriated, and expended is associated with a particular item or class of items; it is therefore described as an input-oriented budget. A budgetary format keyed to objects of expenditure fosters control in a number of ways:

1. Control is comprehensive because no item escapes scrutiny.
2. There are multiple points at which control can be exercised.
3. Control is exact in that expenditures for very specific items can be regulated.[48]

The structure of a line-item budget typically involves the use of about four major categories, each of which has a number of standardly defined categories that are used throughout city government. In police departments large enough for functional specialization, there will be an overall budget and the budget will be broken down into smaller line-item budgets for the various organizational entities such as

TABLE 13-5 The 1991 Object of Expenditure Budget for the Knox County, Maine, Sheriff's Office Budget Summary

Appropriation number	Account title	Approved for 1991
3000	Personal services	$617,122
3500	Employee benefits	214,932
4000	Contractual services	116,592
5000	Commodities	34,574
7000	Capital outlay	10,150
	GRAND TOTAL	$993,370

Personal Services Detail
01-611-3000

	Position title	Number of Employees	1990 Budget	Number of Employees	1991 Budget
3105	County officer, sheriff	1	$ 30,420.00	1	$ 31,333.00
3110	Chief deputy	1	$ 20,042.00	1	$ 27,664.00
3115	Patrol administrator	1	$ 24,274.00	1	$ 25,822.00
3116	Patrol supervisor	1	$ 10,554.00	2	$ 39,688.00
3120	Regular employee/secretary	1	$ 17,223.00	1	$ 18,284.00
3145	Administrative officer	1	$ 18,949.00		
3145	Patrol deputies	5	$108,254.00	6	$112,529.00
9145	Detective & detective supervisor	2	$ 42,422.00	2	$ 45,420.00
3150	Dispatcher-supervisor	1	$ 17,000.00	1	$ 19,844.00
3150	Dispatchers	3	$ 47,445.00	4	$ 63,401.00
3152	Overtime/holidays	16	$103,400.00		$118,155.00
3205	Part-time employees		$ 17,655.00		$ 23,510.00
3205	Part-time secretary				
3211	Full-time deputy, Vinalhaven*	1	$ 7,500.00	1	$ 17,535.00
3211	Part-time deputy, North Haven*	1	$ 7,500.00	1	$ 7,500.00
3212	Employee meetings		$ 7,000.00		
3120	Civil process officer	1	$ 15,122.00	1	$ 15,580.00
3120	Youth aide officer	1	$ 17,015.00	1	$ 20,863.00
3125	BIDE officer**	0	$ 0.00	1	$ 29,994.00
	TOTALS		$511,775.00		$617,122.00

* 1991 entire salary noted

** Reimbursed by State

patrol, investigation, and crime prevention. These smaller budgets serve further to facilitate control and serve as the basis of allocations within the police department. Workload indicators for past years and the forthcoming budget year may also be included as part of a line-item budget. Typically such things as numbers of (1) arrests by various categories, (2) calls for service, (3) traffic and parking citations,

Employee Benefits Detail

No.	Detail Title	Amount
3500	EMPLOYEE BENEFITS	
3502	Life insurance	
3503	F.I.C.A.	$ 47,210.00
3504	Blue Cross/Blue Shield	$105,000.00
3505	Workers' compensation	$ 51,222.00
3506	Unemployment insurance	$ 4,000.00
3507	Retirement lability	$ 0.00
3508	Administrative costs	$ 0.00
3509	Resignation benefits	$ 1,500.00
3510	Vacation	$ 0.00
3512	ICMA retirement	$ 6,000.00
	TOTAL	$214,932.00

Contractual Service Detail

No.	Detail Title	Amount
4000	PROF. FEES & SPEC. SERVICES	
4050	Attorney & computer consultant	$10,000.00
4055	K 9 Program	$ 0.00
4100	TRAVEL	
4105	Automobile mileage	$ 875.00
4110	Meals	$ 880.00
4115	Lodging	$ 880.00
4120	Other (tolls, ferry, etc.)	$ 200.00
4125	Airline	$ 320.00
4200	COUNTY-OWNED VEHICLES	
4205	Gas, oil, grease	$30,000.00
4210	Repairs	$12,650.00
4216	Boat fuel	$ 0.00
4217	Boat repairs	$ 0.00
4300	UTILITIES	
4305	Electricity	$ 1,430.00
4310	Sewage	$ 64.00
4311	Water	$ 183.00
4315	Telephone	$ 7,198.00
4400	RENTALS	
4415	Equipment-pagers	$ 0.00
4420	Car leases-1991	$22,554.00
4420	Boat lease-1991	$ 2,301.00
4600	REPAIRS & MAINTENANCE	
4610	Buildings & structures	$ 477.00
4630	Copy machine (contract & parts)	$ 1,360.00
4635	Heating	$ 220.00
4640	Painting	$ 100.00
4645	Plumbing	$ 150.00

Contractual Service Detail (cont.)

No.	Detail Title	Amount
4656	Radios	$ 3,270.00
4660	Rubbish removal	$ 330.00
4665	Typewriters	$ 500.00
4675	Computers	$ 250.00
4685	Radar	$ 800.00
4700	FIXED CHARGES	
4715	Vinalhaven & North Haven	$ 4,500.00
4800	OTHER OPERATING	
4820	Dues	$ 400.00
4836	Postage	$ 700.00
4840	Printing	$ 2,000.00
4900	OTHER	
4905	Criminal investigating	$ 5,000.00
4940	Training	$ 7,000.00
	TOTAL	$116,592.00

Commodities Detail

No.	Detail Title	Amount
5200	FUEL	
5205	Heating fuel	$ 1,454.00
5300	SUPPLIES	
5310	Automotive	$ 6,600.00
5315	Cleaning & disinfecting	$ 330.00
5325	Maintenance	$ 660.00
5335	Office	$ 5,500.00
5340	Photographic	$ 880.00
5345	Toner, fuser oil, copy paper	$ 1,350.00
5350	Public education	$ 250.00
5355	Public relations	$ 100.00
5375	Training (ammo.)	$ 3,520.00
5385	Computer	$ 0.00
5400	CLOTHING & CLOTHING MATERIALS	
5405	Uniforms	$10,000.00
5406	New employees	$ 3,000.00
5500	BOOKS & PERIODICALS	
5505	Books, subscriptions, etc.	$ 385.00
5510	Statutes and reference books	$ 495.00
5600	OTHER	
5610	Tools and implements	$ 50.00
	TOTAL	$34,574.00

Capital Outlay

No.	Detail Title	Amount
7000	CAPITAL	
7310	Radios (2)	$ 3,700.00
7320	Handguns (2)	$ 550.00
7345	Vehicle equipment	$ 1,000.00
7345	Light bars (3)	$ 3,000.00
7345	Radar set (1)	$ 1,400.00
7350	Typewriter (1)	$ 500.00
	TOTAL	$10,150.00

(4) accident investigations, and (5) criminal investigations, along with other indicators, such as miles patrolled, will be included.

The line-item budget has five rather straightforward advantages: (1) it is easy to construct; (2) because incremental changes in the appropriations are made annually on the basis of the history of expenditures, the likelihood of the police department having a budget that is grossly inadequate is reduced; (3) it is easy to understand; (4) it is easy to administer; and (5) control is comprehensive. On balance, there are also some clear disadvantages to this budget format: (1) the emphasis on control results in an orientation toward the input to the detriment of managing toward results; (2) long-range planning is neglected; (3) any correlations between the input and results occur at only a very gross level, such as numbers of arrests made; and (4) it has limited utility with respect to evaluating performance.

As a final note, the line-item budget format tends to favor continuation of the police department's status quo—a disadvantage to the reform chief but an advantage to one who has less energy and drive.

The Performance Budget

The key characteristic of a performance budget is that it relates the types and volume of work to be done to the amount of money spent.[49] As an efficiency-oriented tool, the performance budget can be described as input-output centered. The single most important consequence of performance budgeting is that it increases the responsibility and accountability of police managers for output as opposed to input.[50] As a management-oriented system, the performance budget incorporates the following features:

1. A cost structure consisting of the various programs under each of which related functions or activities are clustered
2. A detailed system of workload and unit cost measures
3. A line-item component for fiscal control.

Although the origin of the performance budget is not universally agreed upon, public sector milestones in the advocacy of its elements and its use and places of adoption are identifiable. This lack of agreement is perhaps best accounted for by the fact that performance budgeting did not spring into use fully developed but rather evolved over time.

In 1912 the Taft Commission on Economy and Efficiency, which opposed the line-item format, recommended one element associated with performance budgeting—the organization of expenditures around the types of work being done. From 1913 to 1915, the Borough of Richmond, New York City, experimented with a cost data budget,[51] and during the 1920s, periodic mention of this type of budget appeared in the literature.[52] As early as 1939, the Municipal Finance Officers Association advocated a model emphasizing activities grouped under functions. The U.S. Department of Agriculture worked with project and activity budgeting in 1934, and about the same time the Tennessee Valley Authority employed a budget classification of programs and accomplishments.[53] Shortly following the adoption of the city manager form of government in Richmond, Virginia, in 1948, a performance-type budget was implemented.[54]

These various developments received both attention and impetus with the report of the first Hoover Commission in 1949, which called for adoption of a format referred to specifically as a "performance budget." This recommendation was reinforced by the report of the second Hoover Commission in 1955, which applauded the progress made and called for even greater use. In 1950, the federal Budget and Accounting Procedures Act, although not specifically using the term *performance budgeting,* gave further encouragement to its use. Cincinnati began experiments with performance budgeting in about 1950,[55] Maryland adopted it in 1952,[56] and Boston followed in 1955.[57] During the 1950s and very early 1960s, a number of cities experimented with it, including San Diego, Cleveland, Phoenix, Rochester, and Los Angeles.[58]

The advantages of the performance budget include (1) a consideration of outputs; (2) the establishment of the costs of various police efforts; (3) an improvement in the evaluation of programs and key managers; (4) an emphasis on the responsibility of police managers for output; (5) an emphasis on efficiency; (6) the increased availability of information for managerial decision making; (7) the enhancement of budget justification and explanation; and (8) an increased responsibility of police managers, which leads to some decentralization and thus greater participation.

The disadvantages of the performance budget include (1) its expense to develop, implement, and operate given the extensive use of cost accounting techniques and the need for additional staff; Figure 13-8 shows the complexity of using cost accounting to determine total costs; (2) the difficulty and controversies surrounding choosing appropriate workload and unit cost measures; (3) the tendency to generate data more suitable for police managers than for policymakers; (4) its emphasis on efficiency rather than effectiveness; (5) its failure to lend itself to long-range planning; (6) the questionable need, according to police managers, for much of the data; and (7) its frequent inability to relate community needs systematically to police workload and unit cost measures.

The Planning-Programming Budgeting System (PPBS)

In principle, PPBS or PPB was born and died in the federal government, and its use in state and local government was always negligible. Understanding of it is, how-

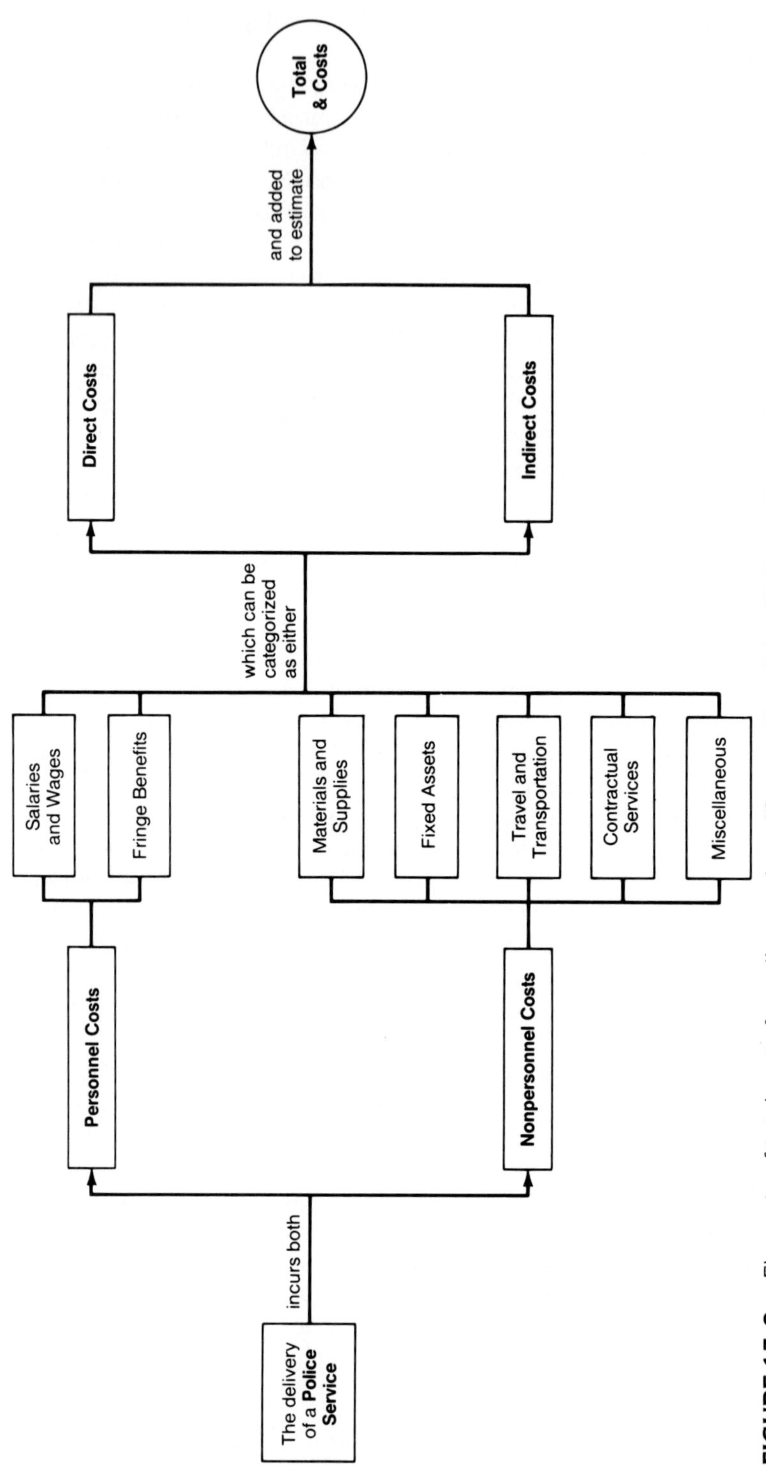

FIGURE 13-8. Elements of total costs for police services. [*Source:* Kent John Chabotar, *Measuring the Costs of Police Services* (Washington, D.C.: U.S. Department of Justice, National Institute of Justice, 1982), p. 20.]

ever, important in that it is a significant segment of the literature of budgeting and represents part of the stream of thinking and practice devoted to improving budgeting.

To some extent every budget system incorporates planning, management, and control processes.[59] However, only one of these processes can predominate. Although PPBS treated the three basic budget processes as compatible and complementary, they were not regarded as co-equal; PPBS was predicated on the primacy of planning.[60] This future orientation of PPBS was to transform budgeting from an "annual ritual" into "formulation of future goals and policies"[61] on a long-range basis. Thus, the singularly unique function of PPBS was to implement policy choices by allocating the resources necessary for their accomplishment. The characteristics of a classical PPBS system include

1. A program structure
2. Zero-based budgeting, to be discussed in detail later in this chapter
3. The use of cost-budget analysis to distinguish between alternatives
4. The use of a budgetary time horizon, often five years
5. The systematic relating of the three basic budgetary processes by a crosswalk system to provide a diversified and comprehensive information base.

General Motors documents reveal that in 1924 it was using a basic PPBS method to identify major objectives, to define programs essential to these goals, and to allocate resources accordingly.[62] The RAND Corporation was a major contributor to the development of PPBS in a series of studies dating from 1949.[63] By the mid-1950s a few states such as California, Illinois, Kentucky, Washington, North Carolina, and Pennsylvania were utilizing elements of a PPB system. It remained, however, for Secretary Robert McNamara to introduce PPBS into the Department of Defense for the system to emerge fully in government. In 1965 President Johnson issued a directive calling for its use in the federal government. The "Five-Five-Five" project, fully operational in 1967, sought to test a "true" PPB system in five states, counties, and cities.[64]

A 1971 survey revealed that only 28 percent of the cities and 21 percent of the contacted counties had implemented a PPB system or significant elements of it.[65] Also in 1971, the death of PPBS was announced in the federal government by a memorandum from the Office of Management and Budget. The general interest in PPBS faded rapidly as did its practice in the few states and local governments that had adopted it.

Implied and partial explanations of the demise of PPBS are sprinkled throughout the literature and include "fantastic terminological tangles used with a false sophistication" and the absence of a precise definition of PPBS.[66] Because PPBS was born and died in the federal government, analysis of its demise there is most appropriate. The most lucid and complete dissection of PPBS becoming an "unthing" in federal agencies is provided by Schick,[67] who attributes the following factors as leading to its death:

1. PPBS failed because it did not penetrate the vital routes of putting together and justifying a budget. Always separate, but never equal, the analysts had little influence over the form or content of the budget.
2. Many analysts failed to comprehend the connection between their work and budgeting.

Because they came to PPBS with little administrative or budgetary experience, they did not recognize that the fate of analysis hinges on its use in budgeting.

3. The government-wide application of the Department of Defense's PPBS gave little consideration to the preferences or problems of individual departments.
4. For all its talk about an integrated planning and budgetary system, the Bureau of the Budget kept the two apart, quarantining its tiny PPBS operation from the powerful budget review staffs and promulgating separate PPB and budget instructions.
5. PPBS had become a threat to budgeters and an embarrassment to reformers, reminding the latter of their failure to deliver and the former of the inadequacies of their process.
6. PPBS was introduced without much preparation, inadequate support, and a leadership with too few resources to invest in its behalf.
7. There was neither an adequate number of analysts nor sufficient data, and PPBS did not have enough time to make up the deficit.
8. The implementors of PPBS were arrogantly insensitive to budgetary traditions, institutional loyalties, and personal relationships.
9. PPBS was conceived almost exclusively from an executive perspective, as if Congress did not exist.
10. PPBS failed to penetrate because budgeters did not let it in and PPBS'ers did not know how to break down the resistance.

The explanation that PPB failed because of agency subversion is rejected by Schick, who feels that most departments gave it a try.[68] Another explanation rejected by Schick is that offered by Thompson, who contends that the emphasis on rationality and analysis is at odds with the American political process.[69] Among the police departments that employed a PPBS at one time are those in Phoenix, Arizona; Dayton, Ohio; Dade County, Florida; and San Diego, California.

The Programmatic or Results Budget

Programmatic or *program budget* is a term that has been used to describe a variety of practices. In the 1950s and 1960s, it referred to, along with functional or activity budgets, simply using programs as cost centers with little additional data. During the 1960s and early 1970s, it was a popular shorthand used to refer to a PPB system. In the contemporary sense, it refers to budgets that emphasize the results achieved or outcomes produced.

While the literature of budgeting and the practice of federal budgeting was being dominated by PPBS from 1960 to 1971, the practice of local governmental budgeting was quietly undergoing change. Performance budgeting, with its emphasis on workload and cost measures, did not disappear entirely, and there was considerable interest in the achievement of policy aspects of PPBS. The result was the evolution of a budget type that incorporated features from the performance and PPBS formats and is referred to as a results, outcomes, objectives, or programmatic—in the contemporary sense—budget. In general, a programmatic budget typically includes

1. A statement of need as established by legal mandates, executive orders, the population to be served, or other related indicators
2. A program structure

3. The identification of objectives to be achieved within each of the identified programs
4. A brief work plan
5. Limited and carefully selected workload and cost measures for each of the identified programs
6. A line-item component for fiscal control.

Additionally, multiyear projections may be included, although the practice is probably more honored in its breach than in its observance.

Table 13-6 illustrates a portion of a programmatic budget for a sheriff's office. A

TABLE 13–6 A Portion of the San Diego County Sheriff's Department's Programmatic Budget

PROGRAM: Law Enforcement Services — DEPARTMENT: Sheriff
PROGRAM #: 12002 — ORGANIZATION #: 2400
MANAGER: J. M. Brown, Assistant Sheriff — REFERENCE: 1990–91 Proposed Budget - Pg. 13-8

AUTHORITY: Government Code 26600-26602 requires the Sheriff to preserve the peace, to make arrests, to prevent unlawful disturbances, which come to his attention, to investigate public offenses which have been committed. The County Charter (Section 605) requires the Sheriff to provide the County efficient and effective police protection and to perform all the duties required of him by law. The Government Code (51301 and 51304) authorizes intergovernmental agreements for the provision of law enforcement services.

	1987–88 Actual	1988–89 Actual	1989–90 Actual	1989–90 Budget	1990–91 Budget	% Change
DIRECT COST						
Salaries & Benefits	$41,512,575	$41,641,397	$46,234,364	$45,118,731	$50,544,436	12.0
Services & Supplies	1,996,220	2,025,442	2,118,259	2,452,496	2,340,084	(4.6)
Other Charges	0	0	0	0	0	0.0
Operating Transfers	0	0	30,000	0	0	0.0
Fixed Assets	1,887,228	320,133	220,358	220,358	25,970	(88.2)
Vehicle/Comm. Equip.	153,050	263,600	709,300	709,300	717,500	1.2
TOTAL DIRECT COST	$45,549,073	$44,250,572	$49,312,281	$48,500,885	$53,627,990	10.6
PROGRAM REVENUE	(17,732,912)	(19,453,886)	(22,139,289)	(23,017,800)	(24,784,950)	7.7
NET GENERAL FUND CONTRIBUTION	$27,816,161	$24,796,686	$27,172,992	$25,483,085	$28,843,040	13.2
STAFF YEARS	832.00	847.83	946.00	942.00	985.75	4.9
POSITIONS	843	870	947	943	995	(89.4)

TABLE 13–6 (cont.)

PROGRAM DESCRIPTION

Although the Sheriff is responsible to the electorate for public safety throughout the entire County including all incorporated cities his primary law enforcement services are delivered in the unincorporated area and the incorporated cities that contract for the Sheriff's law enforcement and traffic services. Currently the contract cities are Del Mar, Imperial Beach, Lemon Grove, Powey, Santee, San Marcos, Vista, Encinitas, and Solana Beach. Nine other cities maintain their own police departments. The Sheriff's primary service area encompasses about 90% of the County's 4,300 square miles and approximately 702,237 residents. The County's flourishing tourist industry, the beaches, parks, mountains, and deserts, and such major events as the Del Mar Fair and the Del Mar Races, annually attract hundreds of thousands of visitors to the Sheriff's primary service area. This influx of visitors adds considerably to the normal service requirements of the resident population.

As the chief law enforcement officer the Sheriff is also required by law to coordinate law enforcement mutual aid among all law enforcement agencies in the County and to provide back-up support services to all of the police departments and other law enforcement agencies within San Diego County.

The Sheriff's Law Enforcement Services Program is directed by an Assistant Sheriff. Regular law enforcement in the primary service area is delivered by Sheriff's stations and substations located at Encinitas, Vista, Fallbrook, Valley Center, Powey, Ramona, Julian, Pine Valley, Alpine, Santee, Lemon Grove, and Imperial Beach. In the most remote rural areas law enforcement is delivered by Resident Deputy Sheriffs residing in or near the communities of Warner Springs, Ranchita, Sorrego Springs, Jacumba, and Boulevard.

The Sheriff's direct law enforcement delivery system is supported by a centralized Communications Center where all 911 calls for police, fire, and ambulance emergencies in the Sheriff's primary service area are responded to. The Communications Center also receives other telephonic calls for service, provides radio dispatch of Sheriff's units throughout the County, and provides communications services to other County functions such as emergency medical, trauma centers, fire dispatch, coroner, road department, and County Administration.

Specialized investigative support to the Sheriff's stations and substations as well as to municipal police departments, when necessary, is provided through three investigative divisions. The Central Investigations Division encompasses specialized units for the investigation of homicides, kidnapping, and other very serious violent crimes, as well as arson cases or bomb cases, fraud cases, and forgery cases. The same division also includes the Sheriff's Regional Crime Lab which conducts crime scene searches and forensic examinations involving the use of sophisticated scientific instrumentation for analysis of criminal evidence. The Juvenile Services Division is responsible for the investigation of crimes against children, such as child abuse, and for follow-up investigation, case clearance, property recovery, and diversion/referral disposition decisions on all arrested juveniles. The division also operates as part of the Sheriff's Juvenile Diversion Program. The Sheriff's Special Investigations Division is responsible for covert or semi-covert investigations of gambling, prostitution, child pornography, narcotics violations and trafficking, street gang activities, and criminal intelligence.

1990–91 OBJECTIVES

1. To implement the final phase of training in the Sheriff's Communications Center in order to increase communications dispatch service, efficiency, and timeliness.
2. To ensure the overall crime rate (FBI index offenses) in the Sheriff's direct service area remains below the county-wide average.
3. To successfully file 85% of felony arrests as determined by District Attorney issuances.
4. To provide an increased level of law enforcement services to the unincorporated area of the County, contract cities and County residents as a whole.
5. To foster a service-wide attitude of crime prevention, victim assistance, professional conduct, delivery of quality police services.

TABLE 13–6 (cont.)

Performance Indicators	1987–88 Actual	1988–89 Actual	1989–90 Actual	1989–90 Budget	1990–91 Budget
ACTIVITY A: Law Enforcement Operations—Contracts					
% OF REFERENCES: 32%					
WORKLOAD					
Calls for Service	115,201	127,532	138,420	138,420	150,270
Crime Reports	29,199	30,383	31,792	31,792	33,051
Field Interviews	12,084	14,027	11,483	11,483	11,930
Arrests	13,845	12,658	13,027	13,027	12,359
Citations Issued	69,296	65,303	54,129	54,127	47,742
EFFICIENCY					
Response Time (Priorities 1-2 from CAD)	8.2	8.7	8.7	8.7	9.0
EFFECTIVENESS					
Not applicable					
ACTIVITY B: Law Enforcement Operations—Unincorporated					
% OF RESOURCES: 29%					
WORKLOAD					
Calls for Service	83,160	93,757	98,490	98,490	107,132
Crime Reports	23,672	25,094	24,567	24,567	25,339
Field Interviews	7,869	9,304	6,906	6,906	7,063
Arrests	8,638	8,218	8,075	8,078	7,751
Citations Issued	11,523	12,080	9,995	9,995	9,671
EFFICIENCY					
Response Time (Priorities 1-2 from CAD)	12.1	11.9	11.4	11.4	11.1
EFFECTIVENESS					
Not applicable					
ACTIVITY C: Law Enforcement Support					
% OF RESOURCES: 28%					
WORKLOAD					
Calls for Service	603,000	623,000	629,000	648,000	640,000
Crimonological Examinations	49,000	51,357	52,547	53,411	53,200
Crime Investigations	6,641	6,178	6,324	6,548	6,467
Assists	7,500	2,200	3,560	4,000	4,500
EFFICIENCY					
Productivity Index (Total Workload/staff years)	2,346	2,253	2,354	2,184	2,190
EFFECTIVENESS					
Not applicable					

TABLE 13–6 (cont.)

Performance Indicators	1987–88 Actual	1988–89 Actual	1989–90 Actual	1989–90 Budget	1990–91 Budget
ACTIVITY D: Juvenile Services					
% OF RESOURCES: 6%					
WORKLOAD					
Calls for Service	20,000	18,786	20,687	20,000	21,000
Investigations	3,000	3,570	4,333	3,700	4,500
Evidentiary Examinations	384	250	226	375	250
Juvenile Intervention	13,200	7,944	12,546	14,000	13,549
EFFICIENCY					
Not applicable					
EFFECTIVENESS					
Not applicable					
ACTIVITY E: Street Gangs					
% OF RESOURCES: 2%					
WORKLOAD					
Crime Investigations	240	22	55	60	65
Arrests	130	12	45	40	48
Gang Activity Interventions	65	10	28	25	29
Number of Gang Members Documented	2,720	3,264	4,000	4,460	4,700
EFFICIENCY					
Not applicable					
EFFECTIVENESS					
Not applicable					
ACTIVITY F: Street Narcotics					
% OF RESOURCES: 1%					
WORKLOAD					
Number of Investigations	335	36	347	450	400
Number of Arrests	284	75	161	400	200
Search Warrants	84	36	0	104	150
EFFICIENCY					
Not applicable					
EFFECTIVENESS					
Not applicable					

TABLE 13–6 (cont.)

Performance Indicators	1987–88 Actual	1988–89 Actual	1989–90 Actual	1989–90 Budget	1990–91 Budget
ACTIVITY G: Crime Prevention					
% OF RESOURCES: 1%					
WORKLOAD					
Neighborhood Watch Groups	3,096	3,274	3,513	3,600	3,800
Program and Presentations	1,620	5,868	3,534	6,400	4,000
Security Inspections	3,462	2,517	4,618	2,750	5,100
EFFICIENCY					
Not applicable					
EFFECTIVENESS					
Residential burglary rate is one (1) burglary per 39 housing units in unincorporated areas. Within the Sheriff's neighborhood watch areas the rate is one (1) per 11,021 housing units.					
ACTIVITY H: CAL-ID					
% OF RESOURCES: 1%					
WORKLOAD					
Total Cases Completed	0	2,880	2,353	3,000	2,500
Person Crimes Fingerprint Searches	0	134	183	140	183
Property Crimes Fingerprint Searches	0	2,746	2,170	2,860	2,175
Total Case Hits	0	277	226	300	230
Person Crimes Fingerprint Identification	0	17	25	18	25
Property Crimes Fingerprint Identification	0	260	201	282	210
EFFICIENCY					
Not applicable					
EFFECTIVENESS					
CAL-ID has been partially staffed since July 1988					

review of the six elements identified previously as typically being included as part of the structure of the programmatic format and of Table 13-6 reveals that all six elements are present. Note, however, that, whereas some of the elements are clearly immediately identifiable (e.g., there are workload and cost measures and a line-item component for fiscal control), other elements, although present, are less immediately identifiable. For example, no overall program structure is presented, but it can be properly inferred from the "Program: Law Enforcement

Services" budget portion that there is a larger structure that encompasses other programs such as detention and investigations.

The advantages of the program budget include (1) an emphasis on the social utility of programs conducted by the police department; (2) a clear relationship between policy objectives and expenditures; (3) organizational behavior that is directed at the attainment of specific objectives; (4) its ability to provide a good basis for justifying and explaining the budget; (5) its facilitating citizen understanding of police programs and objectives; (6) its establishing a high degree of accountability; and (7) its format and the wide involvement in formulating objectives, which lead police officers at all levels of the department to understand more thoroughly the importance of their roles and actions.

The disadvantages of this budget type include (1) its cost in terms of time and dollars to develop, implement, and administer; (2) the fact that police managers may be resistant to increased accountability; (3) difficulties associated with developing appropriate objectives and performance measures; (4) the fact that the city council may rely on the line-item portion of the budget to make adjustments in appropriations, negating the policy value of this format and causing serious problems in the execution of programs; and (5) the fact that police managers responsible for the various programs may not have been or may not be interested in developing the skills necessary for directing large-scale and complex programs.

Zero-Based Budgets

The concept of a zero base is not new. It is one of the elements associated with PPBS, and the FY 1964 budget submitted by the U.S. Department of Agriculture was a zero-based budget. An analysis of that experience revealed that it produced only $200,000 in changes in the department's budget while consuming at least 180,000 person-hours of effort.[70]

Based on Peter Phyrr's use of a zero-based budget (ZBB) at the Texas Instruments Company, Jimmy Carter, then Governor of Georgia, implemented it in that state during the early 1970s. After election to national office, Carter announced that ZBB would be implemented in the federal government for FY 1979. Other governmental adopters have included New Mexico; Montana; New Jersey; Texas; Arlington County, Virginia; Wilmington, Delaware; and Orange County, Florida. Some agencies, such as the Portland, Oregon, Police Bureau, at one time used variants that incorporate many of the features of a ZBB.

As popularly understood in the most literal sense, ZBB implies preparing a budget without any reference to what was done before.[71] This interpretation has been widely condemned as naïve and impractical;[72] such an application would unproductively utilize enormous amounts of energy, and the product would be likely to confuse, if not overwhelm, decision makers. As actually practiced, ZBB involves the use of marginal analysis techniques to see how various levels of funding affect the delivery of services. The heart of ZBB is a four-step analytical process:

1. *Establishment of budget decision units.* The decision unit (DU) represents the smallest entity for which a budget is prepared in the police department. Every DU has an identified manager empowered to make all decisions regarding the budget submission.

As a practical matter, DUs tend to coincide with the police department's organizational structure.

2. *Budget unit analysis.* The police manager responsible for the DU must conduct a detailed appraisal of the purpose and operations of the unit before any consideration of costs. This critical examination includes asking the zero-base question of what consequences would there be if this DU were eliminated, clarifying objectives, describing current operations, analyzing for potential productivity improvements, and specifying the measures that can be used best to justify and monitor the DUs' workload and performance.[73]
3. *Service-level analysis.* The manager responsible for the DU must next define the service priorities and structure them into a series of incremental packages of activities, resources, and projected performances. Called "decision packages" in some ZBB systems and "service levels" in others, these incremental packages are the building blocks for the budget request ultimately submitted by the police department. The first package is designated as the base, the minimum service level, and is the deepest possible programmatic and economic reduction short of the total elimination of the DU. The second package provides an additional level of service above the base; the third package provides an increment of service above the second package; and so forth.
4. *Ranking.* After the lower level DU managers in the police department have prepared the decision packages, they are placed in a priority ranking by the department's command staff in a group session. Table 13-7 reflects the priority ordering for 37 packages used by the Portland Police Bureau in developing its fiscal 1981 request. Note that the first five choices represent the base for certain key areas of the organization but that the sixth choice, an incremental increase in precinct operations services, was given a slightly higher priority than the base for special operations. The priority list, also referred to as a ranking table, is important because once a level of funding is selected, the "line is drawn," meaning that lower priority packages are not funded. In the case of the Portland Police Bureau's fiscal 1981 requests, packages 23 to 37 fell below the line.

The advantages of a ZBB include (1) a fresh approach to planning by requiring police managers to ask the question, "Why are we doing this?"; (2) the duplication of effort is identified and eliminated; (3) emphasis can be given to priority programs; (4) marginally effective and nonproductive programs can be rationally eliminated; (5) there is better information for managerial decision making;[74] (6) the evaluation of the police department's performance and that of its subordinate managers is strengthened; (7) it improves communications between different levels of the police department; (8) budget information and justification are improved; (9) it fosters better linkages between police operational planning and budgeting; and (10) police managers are involved in budgeting in a more substantive way.[75] The disadvantages include (1) the number of decision packages may become overwhelming—the fiscal 1973 use of ZBB in state government in Georgia, for example, contained an estimated 10,000 of them; (2) the process of developing the system and each annual budget request requires the use of considerable resources; (3) the process is weakened considerably by poorly prepared decision packages; (4) police managers may not be very motivated to undertake critical self-examinations; and (5) the system may implicitly foster a belief that increased funds are the only way in which to increase services, causing police managers to neglect other means of improving productivity.

The ZBB represents the last major innovation designed to improve budgeting. In 1980, some knowledgeable observers of the budgetary scene predicted that ZBB would experience the same sort of mercurial fall that PPBS did. Although ZBB

TABLE 13–7 Portland, Oregon, Police Bureau Package Ranking and Summary*

(1) Rank		(2) Package name/number/description	(3) Full-time positions 1980–81	(4) Approved budget 1979–80	(5) Discretionary request 1980–81	(6) Total request 1980–81
1	PO-1	Precinct operations base	372.38	$10,735,358	$12,112,450	$12,150,118
2	SER-1	Services base	17.38	819,008	757,399	807,116
3	INV-1	Investigations base	204.76	5,862,717	6,307,822	6,356,935
4	REC-1	Records base	76.06	1,459,476	1,461,595	1,595,200
5	MGT-1	Management base	20.93	545,964	740,111	740,527
6	PO-2	Current service level	28.84	663,261	713,371	713,371
7	SO-1	Special operations base	11.27	445,500	427,424	447,676
8	TRA-1	Traffic base	65.90	2,397,426	2,663,063	2,664,588
9	CPD-2A	Locks project	6.06	234,282	2,406	231,351
10	SER-2	Current service level	13.08	324,770	359,831	371,645
11	REC-2	Current service level	8.14	128,795	137,645	137,645
12	REC-3	CRISS conversion	4.00	—	86,447	86,447
13	INV-2	Current service level	7.50	218,586	217,212	220,467
14	CPD-1	Crime prevention base, target level	11.32	804,371	392,396	571,179
15	TRA-2	Current service level	10.22	318,810	317,638	317,638
16	SER-3	Affirmative action, court coordinator, word processor	5.00	—	83,988	83,988
17	MGT-2	Current service level (word processor)	1.16	—	32,144	32,144
18	MGT-3	Legal advisor	1.00	—	16,508	16,508
19	PO-4	Horses, horse patrol (6)	7.00	—	225,853	225,853
20	REC-4	Shelving	—	—	127,000	127,000
21	PO-6	Reserves	—	—	9,154	9,154
22	INV-5	Cameras, bureau request	—	—	2,004	2,004
		Total request	872.00		27,079,161	$27,794,384
23	PO-3	Annexation	12.00		270,240	270,240
24	INV-3	CJO	2.00		53,333	53,333
25	CPD-2B	GF transition	—		175,844	175,844
26	REC-5	Property room	—		5,000	5,000
27	INV-4	Paraprofessional	2.00		34,551	34,551
28	TRA-3	Prior current service level	10.00		251,211	251,211
29	REC-6	Current years planned service level	8.00		105,903	105,903
30	SER-4	Evaluation system, background checks	2.00		76,159	76,159
31	SER-5	LET, instructors	8.00		151,889	151,889
32	REC-7	Purge record files	6.00		83,495	83,495
33	INV-7	Prior current service level	7.00		159,508	159,508
34	INV-6	New ID technicians	4.00		66,034	66,034
35	MGT-4	Command coordinator	1.00		32,921	32,921
36	REC-8	New files	—		24,000	24,000
37	PO-5	Horses, horse patrol(2)	2.00		49,187	49,187
		Total all packages	936.00		$28,618,436	$29,333,659

* The Portland Police Bureau no longer uses ZBB, but for illustration purposes its FY 1981 ZBB format is shown.

Source: Courtesy of Portland, Oregon Police Bureau.

has not been officially pronounced as deceased, by 1986 it was infrequently practiced as described herein. Moreover, the Portland, Oregon, Police Department no longer practices it as shown in Table 13-7. Portland adopted ZBB during a time of financial pressure; as these pressures declined there was more resistance from managers throughout the city who did not want to go through the ZBB process. As a consequence, Portland moved to a budget with a program structure and no performance indicators. Subsequently, police managers found that they did not have the data to resist budget cuts—one estimate is that as a result of budget cuts after abandoning ZBB, the police department's response time to calls gradually increased by approximately two minutes. The legacy of ZBB is that many departments that use a line-item or some other format have incorporated the use of decision packages into the budget request process. For example, in Fort Worth, Texas, a decision package (DP) is a narrative and financial description of a service or a program that is part of the police department's budget request. In Fort Worth there are four types of DPs:

1. Reduction or elimination of an existing service or program
2. Continuation of an existing service or program
3. Expansion of an existing service or program
4. Addition of a new service or program.

Thus, although increasingly less practiced, ZBB has contributed to the evolution of budgetary practices and the DP continues to be part of the language and practice of financial management.

Hybrid Budgets

Although it is important to understand the orientations of different budgeting systems, their emphases, and their relative advantages and disadvantages, budget systems can be discussed with a great deal more purity than they exist in actual practice. Most police budget systems are a hybrid of several approaches that are blended together to meet the particular needs of a unit of government. Given the different approaches, the relative emphasis that can be placed on them, and the sheer frequency of hybrid budget systems, one should not be startled when examining a police department's budget to find that it is not clearly one type or another. Nor should judgments be made too quickly about the "rightness" of what has been done. To understand and appreciate it in context, one must understand the needs, resources, and priorities that led to its implementation, another manifestation of the political nature of financial management.

Strategies for Supplementing the Police Budget

Police departments can employ a variety of tactics to reduce the cost of delivering services, such as using volunteers and replacing officers with less costly civilian positions whenever possible. This section focuses on strategies for supplementing the department's budget by (1) obtaining grants from federal agencies and general foundations, (2) implementing donation programs, (3) taking advantage of forfeiture laws, (4) initiating user fees, (5) enacting police tax legislation, and (6) applying for Internal Revenue Service rewards and reimbursements.[76]

Federal and General Foundation Grants

Over the past 20 years, grant-awarding organizations—such as the now defunct Law Enforcement Assistance Administration (LEAA), the Highway Traffic Safety Administration, and to a lesser extent general foundations—have been important sources of funding external to the normal budgeting process of police departments. Some recipients of grants, despite provisions to prohibit such employment, have substituted the money for resources that otherwise would have been appropriated or expended by the involved unit of government.

Grants have been used for a variety of endeavors, including the purchase of vehicles, riot equipment, and communications centers; for training; to create regional crime laboratories, frequently emphasizing the examination of narcotics evidence; and to develop special efforts in such areas as crime prevention, alcohol safety–accident prevention, family crisis intervention, and programs for rape victims and the elderly. Many police agencies became adept at getting grants by locating potential grantors in the *Federal Directory of Domestic Aid Programs* and elsewhere and by preparing well-conceived, responsive proposals.

The reasons for pursuing grants have been varied. Occasionally, it was done simply to get the city manager "off the back" of the chief or to provide evidence that the chief was a good administrator. In other instances, law enforcement agencies accepted grants urged on them by the funding source for experimental or demonstration projects. In such cases, at least some police agencies had little commitment to the "pet project" of the grantor but accepted the grant in the belief that it would create goodwill at the time when the grantor was considering some future proposal from that police department or in the belief that enough equipment or other resources would remain as a useful residue from the project, regardless of its other merits. Often missing in the various machinations involved in getting the money was a strong management analysis of certain factors:

1. What problem or need, if any, will go unmet in the absence of the grant funds?
2. What would be the probable qualitative and quantitative impact of not meeting the problem or need?
3. What would be the qualitative and quantitative impact on police services of using the grant funds?
4. If a multiyear grant, what are the consequences and probabilities of midproject termination or reduced funding?
5. How many sworn and civilian employees will be added to the total personnel complement who may have to be continued on the payroll at the end of the project?
6. Will any equipment or facilities be acquired that nongrant funds ultimately will have to maintain?
7. What obligations are incurred with respect to continuing the effort initiated following the termination of the grant period?
8. Must the police department provide some matching contribution to the project? If so,

how much? Can it be an in-kind match, such as providing space, or must the match be in equal funds? If actual funds are required, will they come from the police department's budget or from a special municipal fund established for just such purposes?

9. What operational or financial procedures have to be changed to meet grant requirements?
10. What ongoing programs will be brought under new state or federal regulations as a result of receiving the grant, in what way, and at what costs?
11. What will be the cost of the administrative overhead outside of the police agency necessary to support the administration of the grant?[77]

None of this is intended to ignore the existence of many exemplary projects that have improved the delivery of police services to the public. However, even in some number of excellent projects, there have been side costs, and the potential for these hidden side costs increases inversely with the amount of management planning done when considering whether to take grant funds offered or whether to apply for grant funds. It is also important to note that some police chiefs have deliberately chosen not to raise certain of the identified issues—to the chagrin of their city managers and sometimes at risk of their own jobs—to initiate badly needed programs that could not be funded through the normal budget process.

Donation Programs

Police Donation programs may be characterized as single issue or ongoing. Single-issue programs seek to obtain funds for a particular purpose and may be fairly small or large in the level of support they are seeking. Illustratively, the Erie County, New York, sheriff's office got $5,000 from a local bank to renovate an old van for use in a crime-prevention program. More expansive was the raising of $1 million in Chicago over a period of 18 months to buy bulletproof vests for officers. In terms of ongoing donations, in 1971 the New York City Police Foundation was formed as a nonprofit, tax-exempt organization independent of the city with the following goals:

1. Enhancement of police-community relations
2. Improvement of police service
3. Funding of police projects
4. Combating police corruption.

The projects undertaken by the New York City Police Foundation have been diverse and include providing police scholarships, creating a program to reduce officer hypertension, and establishing a bomb squad. In one recent year this foundation raised $1 million for worthy initiatives. In 1979, the Baltimore County Police Foundation was established for similar efforts.

Forfeiture Laws

The essence of forfeiture laws is twofold: (1) criminals should not be allowed to profit financially from their illegal acts, and (2) the assets of criminals that are subject to seizure can be put to work against them by funding additional law enforcement initiatives (see Box 13-4).There is a wide variety of state statutes regarding forfeitures, but they generally cover cash and property from four categories of crime:

1. Narcotics
2. Transportation of contraband goods
3. Organized crime, racketeering, and unlawful gambling
4. Targeted crimes (e.g., in North Carolina vehicles used in serious drunk-driving cases may be forfeited).

Upon seizing airplanes, cash, cars, boats, guns, or other property subject to their state's forfeiture law, law enforcement officers may initiate forfeiture proceedings by making a request to the prosecutor or by retaining a lawyer for that purpose. Care is taken to protect the rights of others who were not involved in the crime and who have a financial interest in the forfeited property, such as a lender who has a lien on an airplane. Four patterns exist regarding the way forfeited property is handled:

1. All benefits from the forfeiture go to the unit of government's general fund.
2. The police may keep all property, typically using cars for undercover operations and aircraft for surveillance, but if the property is later sold, the proceeds of the sale go to the unit of government's general fund.
3. The police may keep or sell the property, but if it is sold, the police can keep up to only some ceiling amount, such as $20,000, and any excess goes into a trust fund to which the department can apply for specific uses.
4. All property and cash can be kept by the police department.

User Fees

User fees can be very controversial when used by police departments (see Box 13-5). The public accepts being charged a nominal fee to obtain a copy of an accident report and the cost of police permits for parades and special events such as rock concerts. However, cities that have tried to charge for such public services as unlocking car doors to get keys accidentally left inside the vehicle have often had to retreat in face of public outcry. Perhaps the largest and least controversial sources of user fees have been charges to hook up alarms to the police monitor or to a computer-aided dispatch (CAD) system, as well as charges to monitor the alarms and the cost of responding to false alarms. Typically user fees end up in the unit of government's general fund, but although not directly strengthening the police budget, they do put managers in a more advantageous position during the budget review process.

Police Taxes

As a reaction to Proposition 13 limitations, some jurisdictions—Palos Verdes, California, for example—have adopted referendums to institute a special police tax.

BOX 13-4

Seized Assets Underwrite the War on Drugs

Crime: The millions of dollars are buying new equipment and increased manpower for law enforcement. However, the bounty is accompanied by problems, mostly political.

By Ronald I. Soble *Times Staff Writer*

A motor home complete with sleeping quarters and a microwave oven has been pressed into service by the Santa Monica Police Department as a mobile command post.

A new intelligence center constructed under the El Segundo City Hall is coordinating the war on drugs in Los Angeles County's coastal cities.

A sprawling Orange County ranch once used to process marijuana could be converted into a regional training center for narcotics officers, while two helicopters are on the Riverside County sheriff's shopping list.

None of this is being financed by taxpayer dollars. It is being underwritten by narcotics traffickers snagged in the war on drugs.

Crime pays—for the copes, too. Since the mid-1980s, federal and state asset forfeiture laws have generated millions of dollars in cash—plus booty used by traffickers such as cars, planes and boats—which has been turned over to local law enforcement agencies.

Nowhere is this more apparent than in Southern California, which in the last few years has eclipsed southern Florida as the nation's leading distribution center for cocaine.

In fiscal 1990, which ended last Sept. 30, the federal government returned more than $56 million in seized drug cash and property to law enforcement agencies in Southern California.

Separately, $49 million in cash and property was returned in 1989–90 to police, sheriff's agencies and district attorney offices through a similar California program.

Reaping such bounties from the drug war is not without its problems, mostly political.

In Los Angeles, a tug of war exists between the Police Department and City Council over how to spend millions of dollars in seized drug money. The City Council wants the cash to put more officers on the street, while the Police Department says it needs the money for its narcotics unit to escalate its all-out war on drug dealers.

In San Diego, a political battle over the cash windfall became so intense that the former sheriff defied county supervisors, opening a separate drug assets account so he could spend the money as he saw fit.

In Orange County, one of the biggest drug-related forfeiture cases occurred after the 1987 raid of Daniel James Fowlie's marijuana smuggling operation. Fowlie's 213-acre spread, Rancho del Rio, located in a remote corner of southeast Orange County, was seized and returned by the federal government to the county.

Orange County Sheriff Brad Gates has coveted the ranch as a regional narcotics enforcement training center. County supervisors did not see it that way, and recently decided to put it up for sale. Gates hopes that private supporters will find the cash to keep his plan alive. "We're not through, yet," he said.

Aside from political bickering, there is another problem with the asset forfeiture program, according to the Glendale Police Department's Lt. Michael Post, who heads that agency's narcotics unit.

The sheer size of some of the forfeitures, he said, has captured the attention of many lawmakers to the point where they expect the revenue stream to continue indefinitely.

Post said he has seen evidence of other police departments "under pressure to be revenue producers" to the point where they use shortcuts to seize drug cash but do not follow up on their investigations in an effort to arrest the dealers.

"That's not what we're on God's Earth to do," he said. "We're supposed to be sure that the end user on the street doesn't have any product to buy."

BOX 13-4 (cont.)

At the federal level, agencies such as the Drug Enforcement Administration and U.S. Customs determine how much seized cash and property should be returned to local law enforcement based on their participation in federal drug investigations.

The same principle applies to a California program under which county prosecutors decide how much seized cash or property local law agencies receive, also based on their participation in drug busts.

Because some of the nation's largest drug seizures have occurred in Southern California in the last few years, local police agencies have received heavy cash infusions. In February, customs officials handed out $16.5 million to two dozen Southern California law enforcement agencies for their participation in a number of drug cases.

The West Covina Police Department received almost $3 million, its share of eight federal-local task force seizures in the West Covina and Pasadena areas.

The Los Angeles County Sheriff's Department received a similar amount for participation in drug and money laundering cases in Los Angeles and Orange counties.

The smallest amount, $30,000, was handed over to the Santa Monica Police Department for helping to seize drug cash at Los Angeles International Airport.

The record drug bust in Sylmar in September, 1989—the result of a joint investigation conducted by the DEA and a number of local police agencies—uncovered about $12 million in cash, in addition to more than 21 tons of cocaine. The $12 million has been distributed to several Los Angeles area police agencies.

What is believed to be the biggest cash seizure in Southern California has yet to be distributed by Washington: more than $100 million in assets confiscated in 1989 in a money laundering operation centered in the downtown Los Angeles jewelry district.

Aside from cash, a potpourri of items, such as sports cars, houses and boats, also have been returned to local police.

In one instance, Glendale police last year seized a 1986 black Ferrari 328 GTS worth more than $60,000, and put it on the auction block. Instead of asking for cash bids, the agency wanted vehicles they could use for surveillance.

"We got five new mid-sized vehicles for it," said Post. In addition, he said, before the Ferrari was auctioned, "we put a patrol light bar on top of it and used it as a prop at [police] recruiting fairs."

More often than not, police will forgo keeping the flashy cars once driven by drug dealers and auction them off for their cash value.

California Deputy Atty. Gen. Gary W. Schons, who is in charge of the state's drug assets forfeiture program, said the reason for that is that high-profile autos stand out like sore thumbs in undercover work. "It's not like 'Miami Vice,' " he said.

Officials from several small police agencies say asset sharing has been a boon allowing them to purchase sophisticated equipment that normally would be rejected out of hand because of local budget constraints.

Capt. Jim Lewis of the Rialto Police Department in San Bernardino County said his agency has used drug cash to purchase exotic items such as night-vision binoculars. "Let's face it," he said, "this type of equipment never flies in the city's budget. It's kind of nice because you need sophisticated equipment you wouldn't get otherwise."

But high-tech is not high on everyone's list. "We don't go after a lot of gadgets," said Cmdr. John Distelrath, who is in charge of investigations for the West Covina Police Department. Instead, he said, much of his agency's emphasis is on attacking the drug problem at its roots in West Covina's elementary and high schools.

"It's our feeling that's what the asset sharing program is for," he said.

Local law enforcement officials interviewed by The Times had high praise for the asset forfeiture program in helping to underwrite the war on drugs.

"The beauty of the program is that assets can be removed from narcotics traffickers and returned to the local law enforcement level," said San Diego County Sheriff's Capt. Joseph G. Celluci, who manages his agency's forfeiture program.

"The program has certainly given us some money we wouldn't have had otherwise,"said Paul E. Myron, chief of the detective division of the Los Angeles County Sheriff's Department and manager of the agency's forfeiture program.

SEIZED ASSETS

Funds returned to local police agencies based on participation with federal government in successful investigations of illicit narcotics operations. Figures for Treasury also include property:

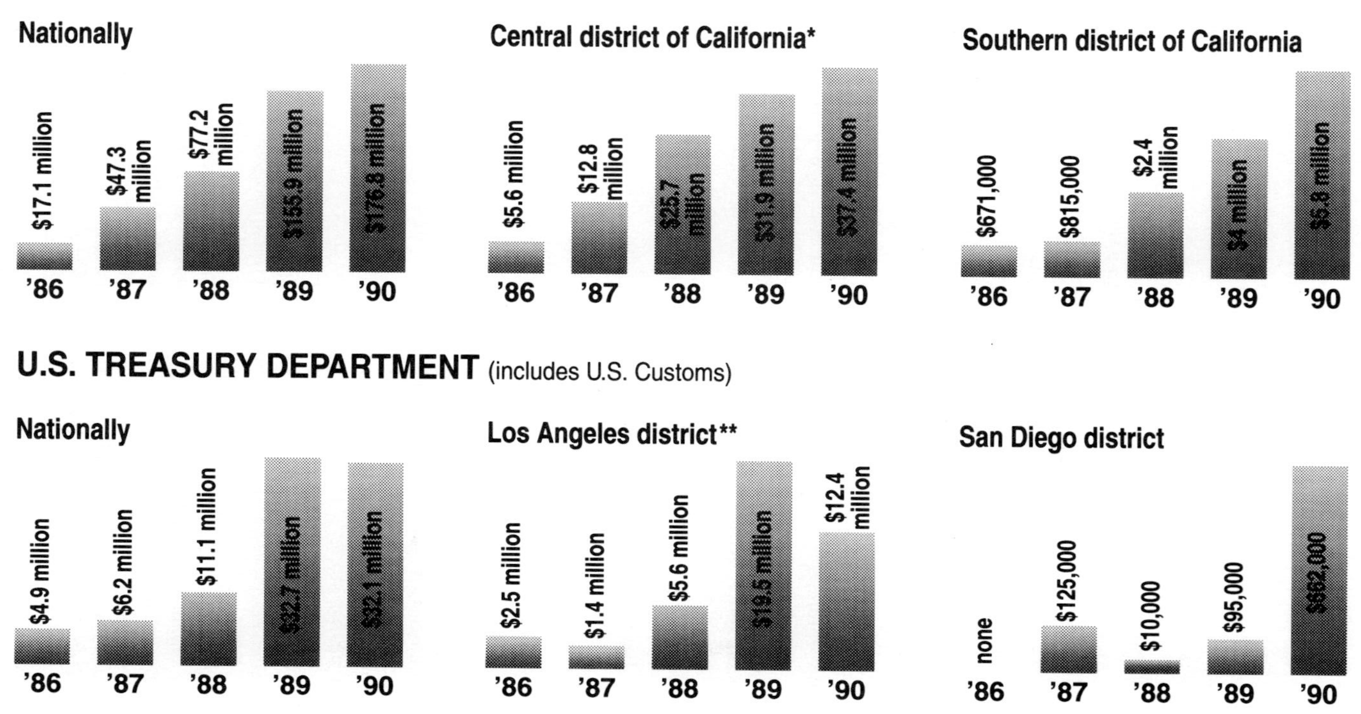

NOTE: Graphs are not in proportion to each other.

*Includes Los Angeles, Orange, Ventura, Riverside, Santa Barbara, San Bernardino, and San Luis Obispo counties.

**Includes Orange, San Bernardino, Riverside, Ventura, and Kern counties and the Las Vegas area.

BOX 13-4 (cont.)

About $41 million returned to the Los Angeles County sheriff in the last six years has paid for two dozen more narcotics detectives, drug education programs for students and first-time drug offenders, underwritten the purchase of computers, and even provided a seized boat, which the department uses to patrol Pyramid Lake, Myron said.

Smaller agencies, such as the Riverside County Sheriff's Department, saved the cash turned over to them by the federal government. As a result, said Lt. T. J. Smith, the county saved $1.7 million to purchase two helicopters to help patrol the 7,000-square-mile county.

Since Congress authorized the return of drug assets to local law enforcement agencies in 1984, the program has come under fire from more than one federal agency.

In a report issued last June, the U.S. General Accounting Office, Congress' investigative arm, criticized both U.S. Customs and the Justice Department for inadequate management of the program.

"The bottom line is that neither agency has a good way of measuring the effectiveness or efficiency of its operations," the GAO concluded.

Three months later, the Justice Department's inspector general also complained about the program's management. Cited were the DEA and the FBI for not processing forfeited cash and property in a timely manner.

The DEA and FBI explained that many of the problems resulted from personnel shortages, but that that has been corrected and backlogs are minimal.

Once the money reaches the local police, it often can become a political football with law enforcement and politicians squabbling over how to spend it.

On paper, the Los Angeles Police Department, operating in a city awash with cocaine traffickers, should be hip deep in cash generated by drug busts. But the department has been generally unable to purchase state-of-the-art equipment and greatly expand its force of narcotics officers.

Much of the problem, said Cmdr. L. C. Kramer, head of the narcotics group, has to do with the City Council.

Between 1984 and 1990, the Police Department received approximately $41 million from its participation in federal and state drug investigations. Yet, only about $8 million has been returned directly to Kramer's unit. The balance—approximately $33 million—was used by the council to hire more officers, a legal expenditure since the cash can be used for any legitimate law enforcement purpose.

"It's terribly frustrating," Kramer said in an interview. "We have a dire need for equipment to keep pace with the crooks."

A spokesman for Councilman Zev Yaroslavsky, chairman of the council's Budget and Finance Committee, said lawmakers believe that it is more important to expand the police force than to pour the cash into specific channels of narcotics enforcement. "While I sympathize with Kramer, I don't think he's being very realistic about the available money," said Katharine Macdonald.

The San Diego County Sheriff's Department produced a similar controversy between county supervisors and recently retired Sheriff John Duffy. Since 1984, the agency has received almost $5 million through the federal program.

Last year, Duffy caused a major controversy by failing to deposit more than $300,000 seized in drug raids into the county treasury, as required by local law. Instead, he set up a separate account after a decision by supervisors prohibiting him from spending the money without their approval. Duffy, who was sheriff for 20 years, maintained that he had the right to determine how the money should be spent for law enforcement.

Duffy would never talk much about the controversy before he retired earlier this year. "He's been making mystifying decisions for 20 years," reflected one of his assistants.

With millions of dollars still flowing into local law enforcement coffers, is the end of the war on drugs in sight?

Myron, of the Los Angeles County Sheriff's Department, believes that using illicit drug cash to underwrite narcotics education programs is a big step toward snuffing out the ubiquitous dealers. But years of hard work remain, he said.

"It will take a generation to take effect," he said.

Source: Los Angeles Times, April 16, 1991.

BOX 13-5

County Fees for Inmate Bookings Create Uproar

Budgets: A new state law allows those charges and one for collecting property taxes. The bills are now coming due.

By Shawn Hubler *Times Staff Writer*

The high-desert town of Adelanto in San Bernardino County is a small and gritty place with 13 police officers, a one-cell jail and more tumbleweeds than people. Yet each year, more than 1,500 arrests occur there—one for every 10 residents.

So when Police Chief Philip Genaway heard about a new state law allowing the county to bill him $122.90 for every person his officers booked into the county jail, his reaction was sharp. One crisp November day, he announced he was letting four suspected burglars "go free" because he couldn't fit them into his jail and couldn't afford the county's booking fees.

In truth, the police chief didn't really let the four go. He just freed them "pending further investigation" and rearrested them after he had made his point and made room in the city jail.

But the protest foreshadowed what has become a roiling political battle over the latest byproduct of California's budget crunch—a new set of fees that has pitted counties against cities (particularly their police departments and schools) over who will shoulder the burden of the state's fiscal woes.

Last July, in the wee hours of a heated budget debate, the Legislature stripped the counties of more than $700 million in state funding to help make up for a $3.6-billion state deficit. To help the counties recoup the loss, state lawmakers gave them the authority to begin charging local governments for two services: property tax collection and the jailing of criminal suspects for the day or two before they make their initial court appearance.

The law went into effect Jan. 4, but counties were allowed to charge the fees retroactive to last July.

Mired in red ink and fearful of an impending recession, all but three of the state's 58 counties adopted one or both of the fees in some form.

The booking fees, which range from $36.03 per prisoner in rural Nevada County to $154 a head in San Diego and Orange counties, are expected to raise $40 million statewide for cash-strapped counties.

With the bills now coming due, communities throughout California are in an uproar. Last month, 200 city and police officials turned out in Sacramento to give a legislative committee an earful at a hearing on proposed revisions to the fees.

And last October, 3,000 municipal officials demonstrated against the assessments in Anaheim, waving protest signs and demanding that the fees be repealed.

While continuing to protest the fees, cities have begun to brace for their anticipated effect. School districts are planning deeper-than-ever budget cuts and police officials say they are scaling back drastically on the number of people—from shoplifters to drunk drivers, check forgers and prostitutes—they book into county jail.

"Crime almost pays," a disgusted Chief Genaway said recently. "It's gotten so you almost have to have a financial officer standing by for every arrest."

Some county officials say the police are overstating the problem and the lengths to which they will go to avoid the fees. Police concede that some of the suspects who are ticketed and released—after promising to return for the court appearance—would no doubt bail out of jail shortly after their arrests anyway.

And both sides agree that most of those who are released are not accused of violent crimes.

So beyond the issue of safety, both sides said, is the question of fairness.

BOX 13-5 (cont.)

"We all have to share in this deficit," said David Oppenheim of the County Supervisors Assn. of California. "It's not fair for one level of government to absorb all the pain, and the counties have been the whipping boys for a long time."

Countered Santa Ana Mayor Dan Young: "The counties are just doing what the state has already done—they're passing the buck."

The furor over the two new fees has spawned at least nine legislative bills seeking to repeal one or both of them and a 10th measure seeking to toughen them.

Several lawsuits involving booking fees are also in the works, and a suit challenging the property tax fee was filed in January on behalf of the school districts, who say the levies could cost them up to $150 million this year.

Though concern has been expressed about the impact of both fees, by far the biggest political outcry has been over the booking fees.

Cities say that they are cutting back by the hundreds on the number of defendants they book into county jail, preferring instead to issue tickets and trust the accused to show up later in court. (Until their first court appearance, arrestees are the responsibility of the city.)

Oppenheim, of the county supervisors' group, said jail bookings are down by as much as 40% from last year in some parts of the state. It is unclear how much of that is due to the booking fees.

Even with the decreased bookings, city officials say the fees will mean millions of dollars in unexpected costs this year, most of which will come out of police budgets.

At the Los Angeles Police Department, for example, the bill from the county is expected to arrive this month to the tune of an estimated $800,000, none of it budgeted for, said Cmdr. Matthew V. Hunt, who manages the LAPD's jail system.

The LAPD's facilities for women inmates are limited, Hunt said. So the department books about 1,700 suspects a month into the county jails, 95% of them female and each of them now worth $108.71 to the county in booking fees.

For the last three months, the LAPD has sought to save money by detaining women defendants in a converted holding tank in the Rampart station near downtown. But the tank fills up fast, particularly on weekends when the vice squads conduct prostitution sweeps, LAPD officials said. Despite its best efforts, LAPD often ends up having to send women to county jail after all.

"Frankly, I don't know where the money's going to come from," said Hunt. "Maybe we'll give the county an IOU."

Like Los Angeles, most cities operate their own jails, but those facilities are far too small to handle the overflow crowds that would be booked there. For years, they have relied on the county jails to handle the spillover. But in urban areas, such as Los Angeles and Orange counties, the county jail system is overcrowded as well.

Consequently, county jail officials welcome the booking fees, saying it not only helps replenish county coffers, but makes cities think twice about using valuable jail space.

City police complain, however, that booking fees only make it that much more difficult to keep criminals off the street.

For example, Sgt. Ernest Tull of the San Bernardino vice squad says he now routinely arrests women for prostitution only to ticket them, release them and catch them soliciting on his way home. Police officials in other communities say they too have had such repeat business.

Compton Police Chief Terry Ebert, whose city has one of the highest crime rates in the state, says his officers are now booking only about 20 people per month into the county jail, compared to more than 50 per month before the fees. But he suspects—although it is too soon to tell—that a sizable number of the people his officers ticket and release will break their promises to show up in court.

Unlike the suspects who are released after being cited, police believe those who must bail themselves out have a stronger incentive to return to court—money.

BOX 13-5 (cont.)

"It's a lousy way to run a railroad," said Oxnard Police Chief Robert Owens. "And it's a terrible way for the state to balance its budget."

In response to concerns expressed by the cities, several counties—including Orange—have sought to soften the blow by postponing imposition of the fees until next fiscal year.

Others have forgone their option to make the fees retroactive. Los Angeles County has exempted smaller cities, such as Bellflower and Hawaiian Gardens, that contract with the Sheriff's Department for law enforcement.

These and other factors contribute to the feeling by some county officials that the problem has been overblown.

"The overwhelming majority [of the arrestees cited and released] are misdemeanants," said Michael Corbett, a legislative representative for the county supervisors' group.

"They are check writers, forgers, simple assaults, not robbers or felons. And in many instances what's being done [the cite and release] is not much more than has already been done in other counties because of [jail] overcrowding."

Oppenheim said that, from the county standpoint, the new fees are overdue. When Proposition 13 was passed in 1978, freezing property tax assessments, the counties lost most of their ability to raise revenue. As the costs of collecting property taxes, administering jail bookings and other services continued to rise, he said, counties were forced to cut other services to cover the loss.

Cities, meanwhile, had more independence and were able to raise taxes and fees to cover their costs.

But cities say their situation is far more bleak than Oppenheim acknowledges.

They, too, have been brought up short by the recession, and are scrambling to stay out of the red. A recent survey of 200 communities by the League of California Cities, for example, found that 31% already had cut staff or services to balance their budgets even before the new fees hit.

While the city vs. county funding debate continues, school districts and police are warning local taxpayers about the drawbacks of the current solution—warning that the new fees will translate into less adequate classrooms and less rigorous law enforcement.

"This," said San Bernardino Mayor Bob Holcomb, "is government at its worst."

Source: Los Angeles Times, March 18, 1991.

In Palos Verdes, Referendum A allowed a tax of up to $300 per year based on property value to support police services.

Internal Revenue Service Rewards and Reimbursements

Police Departments may be able to supplement their budgets with two types of funds available from the Internal Revenue Service (IRS): (1) rewards and (2) reimbursement for investigations, under certain conditions.

Realizing that it often arrested racketeers who had not properly reported their income, the Atlanta Police Department approached the IRS about collecting the 10 percent informers fee on unpaid taxes. Subsequently, the city council passed an ordinance allowing the Atlanta Department of Public Safety to apply for rewards on behalf of the city, to be deposited in a special account earmarked for law enforcement activities. Atlanta has already filed 31 claims. The IRS does not divulge the identities of agencies who have received such awards, their amounts, or other related information.

Internal Revenue Code 7624 allows the Internal Revenue Service the discretion to reimburse state and local agencies for certain types of investigations. After February 16, 1989, state and local law enforcement agencies which provide information that substantially contributes to the recovery of at least $50,000 in federal taxes on illegal drug dealing or related money laundering may receive reimbursement for their investigative efforts. The reimbursement cannot exceed 10 percent of the unpaid taxes recovered. If more than one agency is involved, the IRS must equitably allocate that 10 percent amount among the various agencies involved. An agency is not eligible for the reimbursement if it will receive or has received reimbursement under a federal or state forfeiture program or under state revenue laws. A key requirement for agencies seeking reimbursement is that they must indicate their intent to do so when they first provide the information to the IRS.

Summary

Some police executives view financial management as an unattractive responsibility. Successful police executives know that money is the fuel on which police programs operate. The unwillingness to invest a high level of energy in acquiring and managing financial resources pre-establishes the conditions for mediocre or worse performance by the police department.

Government activities inherently involve public funds; thus financial management is a political process. Illustrative of the entwining of politics and financial administration are state provisions for monitoring and controlling certain aspects of local government finance; the budget preparation instructions given to the various departments by the mayor, city manager, or finance director; the internal dialogue within a police department when deciding how much to request; the development of the city's consolidated budget; the appropriations decision by the city council; and decisions made in the course of executing the budget.

Typically, local government budgets for a 12-month period are referred to as a fiscal year. In properly administered governments, there is a sequence of four steps that are termed the budget cycle and that are repeated at approximately the same time each year: (1) budget preparation, (2) budget approval, (3) budget execution, and (4) the audit.

Numbers are the basic language in which budgets are expressed; the way in which those numbers and any accompanying narrative are organized is termed the budget format. The oldest, simplest, and most universally employed budget is the line item, because of its ease of construction and the potential for control that it offers. In fact, because of its control feature, it is the base on which all other formats rest. Each budget format can be associated loosely with a time in which it was a dominant force; sometimes this domination was far greater in the literature than in actual practice. Nonetheless, from the line item forward, each format can be viewed as an attempt to improve and reform the practice of financial management.

In addition to the use of volunteers and the substitution of less costly civilian positions for sworn positions whenever feasible, police executives can strengthen their budgets by (1) federal and general foundation grants, (2) donation programs, (3) forfeitures, (4) user fees, (5) police taxes, and (6) IRS rewards and reimbursements.

Discussion Questions

1. How can politics and financial management be related usefully?
2. What is the budget cycle and what are the major steps in it?
3. How do the federal and state governments shape the practice of local financial management?
4. What is a fiscal year? What are some examples of different fiscal years?
5. Are there some things that police managers can do to enhance the likelihood of getting their departmental budgets enacted? If so, what are they?
6. If you were a police manager undergoing an audit of the department's last fiscal year budget, what are some things you would expect to see examined?
7. What are the advantages and disadvantages of the following budget formats?
   a. Line item
   b. Performance
   c. PPBS
   d. Programmatic
   e. ZBB
8. What is the significance of hybrid budgets?
9. You are the recently appointed director of planning and research for the department, and the chief of police has just sent for you. The chief tells you that the department may apply for a grant from a federal agency. The chief is seeking your advice as to whether or not to apply. What kinds of perspectives would you encourage the chief to consider?
10. Identify and discuss six strategies for supplementing the police budget.

Notes

1. This idea and several of the examples in the next sentence are taken from Felix A. Nigro and Lloyd G. Nigro, *Modern Public Administration,* 5th ed. (New York: Harper & Row, 1980), p. 337.
2. See National Highway Traffic Safety Administration, "The Impact of Fuel Costs on Law Enforcement" (Washington, D.C.: Mimeographed, February 1, 1980), 11 pp. For a view of some models on police financial stress, see Charles H. Levine, "Police Management in the 1980s: From Decrementalism to Strategic Thinking," *Public Administration Review,* 45 (November 1985), pp. 691–700.
3. Josh Barbanel, "Dinkins Is Expected to Lay Off 16,000 to Close Budget Gap," *New York Times,* Jan. 16, 1991, p. B14.
4. Kenneth J. Garcia, "Even Beverly Hills Feels the Squeeze of Recession," *Los Angeles Times,* June 13, 1991, p. A1.
5. "Suffolk County Cops Facing Demotions, Payless Payday," *Law Enforcement News,* 16:322 (1990).
6. "Mass. SP Transfers Personnel to Offset Manpower Drain," *Law Enforcement News,* 16:322 (1991).
7. Jay Jeohnowitz, " 'Not Enough Cops' Police Union Leader Says," *Times Union* (Albany, N.Y.), Aug. 2, 1990.
8. Angle Cannon, "DPOA Sues to Bar 300 Police Layoffs," *Detroit Free Press,* March 29, 1991.
9. David Armstrong, "Copter Sale Expected to Net $600G for Cruisers," *Boston Globe,* Nov. 23, 1990.
10. Marilyn Robinson, "Cost Load Too Heavy for Cop Copters," *Denver Post,* Jan. 22, 1991.
11. Robert Hanley, "Tax Haven in Jersey in Bind, Plans to Drop Police," *New York Times,* Feb. 12, 1991, p. A13.

12. Roland N. McKean, *Public Spending* (New York: McGraw-Hill, 1968), p. 1.
13. Aaron Wildavsky, *The Politics of the Budgetary Process,* 2nd ed. (Boston: Little, Brown, 1974), p. 4.
14. S. Kenneth Howard, *Changing State Budgeting* (Lexington, Ky.: Council of State Governments, 1973), p. 13.
15. Harold F. Gortner, *Administration in the Public Sector* (New York: John Wiley & Sons, 1977), p. 315.
16. Advisory Commission on Intergovernmental Relations, *City Financial Emergencies* (Washington, D.C.: U.S. Government Printing Office, 1973), from Table 2-1, p. 10.
17. Advisory Commission on Intergovernmental Relations, *State Mandating of Local Expenditures* (Washington, D.C.: U.S. Government Printing Office, 1978), from Table IV-4, p. 55.
18. "Inflation, Limits, Mandates, Strain Budgets," *Iowa Municipalities,* 34:7 (1979), p. 3. Also see George E. Hale and Marian Lief Palley, "The Impact of Federal Funds on the State Budgetary Process," *National Civic Review,* 67:10 (1978), pp. 461–64, 473.
19. The information in this paragraph is taken from John E. Peterson, C. Wayne Stallings, and Catherine Lavigne Spain, *State Roles in Local Government Financial Management: A Comparative Analysis* (Washington, D.C.: Government Finance Research Center, 1979), pp. 1, 5. The Government Finance Research Center is a nonprofit professional service organization that serves as the research arm of the Municipal Finance Officers Association.
20. The rule is described in Peterson, Stallings, and Spain, *State Roles,* p. 4, as follows: "Dillion's Rule, first espoused by John F. Dillion, a justice of the Supreme Court of Iowa, from 1862 to 1869, and later accepted by courts in many other states and the U.S. Supreme Court, establishes the full legal superiority of the state over local governments." Dillion himself stated the rule as follows: "It is a general and undisputed proposition of law that a municipal corporation possess and can exercise the following powers, and no others: First, those granted in express words; second, those necessarily or fairly implied in or incident to the powers expressly granted; third, those essential to the accomplishment of the declared objects and purposes of the corporation—not simply convenient, but indispensable. Any fair, reasonable, substantial doubt concerning the existence of power is resolved by the courts against the corporation, and the power is denied." In states that have a constitutional provision conferring home rule powers on cities, Dillion's Rule is used by the courts in interpreting the scope of home rule powers.
21. Paul Moore and Alan G. Billingsley, "Financial Monitoring of Local Governments," *State Government,* 52 (Autumn 1979), p. 155.
22. A. E. Buck, *The Budgets in Governments of Today* (New York: Macmillan, 1945), p. 5.
23. See James C. Snyder, "Financial Management and Planning in Local Government," *Atlanta Economic Review* (November–December, 1973), pp. 43–47.
24. Wildavsky, *Politics of the Budgetary Process,* pp. 1–4.
25. Orin K. Cope, "Operation Analysis—The Basis for Performance Budgeting," in *Performance Budgeting and Unit Cost Accounting for Governmental Units* (Chicago: Municipal Finance Officers Association, 1954), p. 8.
26. James W. Martin, "An Economic Criteria for State and City Budget Making," *Public Administration Review,* 24 (March 1964), p. 1.
27. Fritz Morstein Marx, "The Bureau of the Budget: Its Evolution and Present Role, II," *American Political Science Review,* 39 (August 1945), p. 871.
28. This case is taken from William P. Gloege, "Successful Police Department Budgeting," *Police Chief,* 44:5 (1977), pp. 58–59.
29. These strategies, with some change, are essentially those identified by Wildavsky, *Politics of the Budgetary Process,* pp. 63–123.
30. Margret Minis, "Savannah Will Modify Police Cars for Propane," *Atlantic Journal and Constitution,* June 1, 1980, p. 4-B.

31. Lennox L. Moak and Kathryn W. Killian, *A Manual of Techniques for the Preparation, Consideration, Adoption, and Administration of Operating Budgets* (Chicago: Municipal Finance Officers Association, 1973), p. 5, with changes.
32. These three types of controls are identified in J. Richard Aronson and Eli Schwartz, eds., *Management Policies in Local Government Finance* (Washington, D.C.: International City Management Association, 1975), pp. 86–87, and are drawn on with changes here.
33. Lennis M. Knighton, "Four Keys to Audit Effectiveness," *Governmental Finance,* 8 (September 1979), p. 3. Also see Kenneth S. Caldwell, "Operational Auditing in State and Local Government," *Governmental Finance,* 3–4 (May 1974–1975), pp. 36–43.
34. The Comptroller General of the United States, *Standards for Audit of Governmental Organizations, Programs, Activities, and Functions* (Washington, D.C.: General Accounting Office, 1972), p. 1.
35. These three types of accountability are drawn, with modification, from U.S. Comptroller General, *Standards of Audit.*
36. Peter F. Rousmaniere, ed., *Local Government Auditing* (New York: Council on Municipal Performance, 1979), from Tables 1 and 2, pp. 10, 14.
37. A. E. Buck, *Public Budgeting* (New York: Harper and Brothers, 1929), p. 12.
38. Ibid., p. 12.
39. Ibid., p. 12.
40. Jesse Burkhead, *Government Budgeting* (New York: John Wiley & Sons, 1956), p. 11.
41. Ibid., p. 17.
42. Allen Schick, *Budget Innovation in the States* (Washington, D.C.: Brookings Institution, 1971), pp. 14–15.
43. Buck, *Budgets in Governments,* p. 40.
44. Burkhead, *Government Budgeting,* p. 13.
45. Ibid., p. 13.
46. In 1913, Ohio became the first state to adopt the executive budget.
47. Budget purists would argue that there are technical differences between line-item and object-of-expenditure budgets. In common usage and practice, however, they are synonymous.
48. Schick, *Budget Innovation,* p. 23; Schick lists a total of 10 ways in which the line-item budget fosters control, but these three sum them up adequately.
49. Malchus L. Watlington and Susan G. Dankel, "New Approaches to Budgeting: Are They Worth the Cost?" *Popular Government,* 43 (Spring 1978), p. 1.
50. Burkhead, *Government Budgeting,* p. 155, with change.
51. Herbert Emmerich, chairman, "Symposium on Budget Theory," *Public Administration Review,* 213 (Winter 1950), p. 26.
52. See, for example, A. E. Buck, "Measuring the Results of Government," *National Municipal Review* (March 1924), pp. 152–57.
53. Burkhead, *Government Budgeting,* p. 134.
54. Robert B. Elmore, "Performance Budgeting in Richmond, Virginia," *Municipal Finance,* 28:2 (1955), p. 77.
55. Vernon E. Koch, "Cincinnati's Budget Developments," *Public Administration Review,* 20:20 (Spring 1960), p. 79.
56. John A. Donaho, "Performance Budgeting in Maryland," *Municipal Finance,* 28:12 (1955), p. 69.
57. Joseph P. Lally, "Performance Budgeting in Boston," *Municipal Finance,* 28:2 (1955), p. 80.
58. Burkhead, *Government Budgeting,* p. 137.
59. Allen Schick, "The Road to PPB: The Stages of Budget Reform," *Public Administration Review,* 26 (December 1966), p. 244.
60. Ibid., pp. 245–46.
61. Ibid., p. 244.

62. David Novick, ed., *Program Budgeting* (New York: Holt, Rinehart and Winston, 1969), p. xxvi.
63. Ibid., p. xxiv.
64. For information on this project, see Council of State Governments, *State Reports on Five-Five-Five* (Chicago: Council of State Governments, 1968). The involved states were California, Michigan, New York, Vermont, and Wisconsin; the counties were Dade (Florida), Davidson (Tennessee), Los Angeles (California), Nassau (New York), and Wayne (Michigan); and the cities were Dayton, Denver, Detroit, New Haven, and San Diego.
65. International City Management Association, *Local Government Budgeting, Program Planning and Evaluation* (Urban Data Service Report, May 1972), p. 7. Also see Selma J. Mushkin, "PPB in Cities," *Public Administration Review,* 29:2 (1969), pp. 167–77.
66. These two examples are drawn from Roger H. Jones's "Program Budgeting: Fiscal Facts and Federal Fancy," *Quarterly Review of Economics and Business* (Summer 1969), p. 45.
67. Allen Schick, "A Death in the Bureaucracy: The Demise of Federal PPB," *Public Administration Review,* 33 (March–April 1973), pp. 146–56.
68. Ibid., p. 148.
69. Ibid., p. 149.
70. Joseph S. Wholey, *Zero-Base Budgeting and Program Evaluation* (Lexington, Mass.: Lexington Books, 1978), p. 8.
71. Graeme M. Taylor, "Introduction to Zero-Base Budgeting," in *Experiences in Zero-Based Budgeting,* ed. Joseph L. Herbert (New York: Petrocelli, 1977), p. 3.
72. Ibid., p. 3.
73. The descriptions of budget unit and service-level analysis are drawn with some changes from J. Robert Krebill and Ronald F. Mosher, "Delaware Budgets for Productivity," *State Government,* 53 (Winter 1980), pp. 20–21.
74. Robert F. Littlejohn, "Zero-Base Budgeting," *Police Chief,* 45 (December 1978), p. 35.
75. Points 6 through 9 are restatements of matter found in Taylor, "Introduction to Zero-Base Budgeting"; the article also appeared in *Bureaucrat,* 6 (Spring 1977), pp. 33–55.
76. The information on donation programs, forfeitures, user fees, police taxes, and IRS rewards is drawn from Lindsey D. Stellwagen and Kimberly A. Wylie, *Strategies for Supplementing the Police Budget* (Washington, D.C.: U.S. Department of Justice, National Institute of Justice, 1985), with some restatement.
77. Some of these eleven points are identified by Wayne Stallings in "Improving Budget Communications in Smaller Local Governments," *Governmental Finance* (August 1978), p. 24.

Appendix

A Budget Transmittal Letter

Ocala Police Department
P.O.Box 1270, Ocala, Florida 32878
June 11, 1991

The Honorable Jack Clark
Mayor
City of Ocala
Ocala, Florida

Dear Mayor Clark:

This letter summarizes the Fiscal Plan of the Ocala Police Department for 1991-92, to include our program priorities. Our budget for the coming year is being submitted for $8,234,797 which is a 9.1% increase over the present budget. We realize the concern for fiscal restraint and when you review the budget detail you will see that 6% of the proposed 9.1% increase is for police vehicles. Should these vehicles be funded from the Fleet Replacement Fund instead of the General Fund, our request (which also includes substantial increases in City allocations) would be only 3.18% over our current budget. The Police Department Budget has been providing allocations to the Fleet Replacement Fund for five years, so it should contain adequate revenues to purchase our vehicles.

Mayor, we are sensitive to the current economic conditions and in reviewing the Department's program priorities, you will notice we have not asked for additional sworn officers due to their expense. This does not however, preclude our need for additional street officers and investigators. Ocala's increase in businesses, traffic, community events, transients and the increased intensity and complexity of investigations has continued to impact on the additional need for these officers.

The following program priorities in our fiscal plan have been submitted to the City Manager's staff as part of the budget process. The Fiscal Plan we have submitted, however, does not include salary increases as this will be added later by the City Manager.

Fiscal Summary

Our proposed budget consists of the following three fiscal components:

▪ Personal Services	$5,999,921	73%
▪ Operating Services	$1,748,131	21%
▪ Capital Outlay	$ 486,745	6%

The Personal Services requests are 2% over this year's approved budget. These requests are discussed later in this letter.

The Operating Services requests of $1,748,131 is 17% over the current budget. Most of the requests in this category are minimal and can be attributed to increased rates on supplies and services that we use routinely as basic items to operate the Department.

This increase also includes the following fixed allocated costs that are established and added to our budget each year by City Staff for which we have no control and which continue to increase substantially:

		Changes this Year	
▪ Data Processing	$ 149,355	up	$ 39,828
▪ Insurance, fire	$ 2,041		
▪ Insurance, auto	$ 34,234		
▪ Insurance, liab.	$ 82,010	up	$ 15,305
▪ Insurance, Risk Mgmt.	$ 35,822	up	$ 7,836
▪ Auto User Charges	$ 767,363	up	$ 62,257
▪ Utilities	$ 55,000	up	$ 3,000
▪ Building Maint.	$ 30,298	dn	$ 4,210
▪ Tower Allocation	$ 187	dn	$ 4,748
Total	$1,156,310	UP	$127,688

These figures reflect that 66% of our Operating Services requests are in fixed allocations. Increases in these same allocations amount to 50% of the 17% increase in Operating Services costs being requested. Another allocation, yet to be added to the new budget proposal, will be an allocation for the employee clinic. This amount will be over and above allocations listed above.

Our Capital Outlay request of $486,745 includes $446,600 to purchase 29 police vehicles. These vehicles are the primary support units for the officers on the street. As you are aware, we have been replacing fewer and fewer vehicles from the fleet each year and we are driving emergency vehicles with greater road mileage and lengthy service records which places our officers at increased risk and greater vulnerability for potential equipment hazards and malfunctions.

The personnel of the Ocala Police Department are dedicated employees who strive constantly to provide excellent service to the citizens of Ocala. Likewise, they continue to confront greater challenges in the nature and seriousness of the crimes committed in our jurisdiction. The tragedy that recently occurred to Officer Clarence Shuler has certainly brought to the forefront the lurking dangers that confront our employees each and every day. While we recognize the factors of circumscription effecting our economy we also have organizational needs that are very necessary. Our top four program priorities are just such needs. While not asking for street officers, we need to support our present officers with key support personnel. Accordingly, by funding our priorities we will support the service needs of our officers.

The following program budget requests are discussed in order of priority.

Priority One—Provide Two Communications Technicians—$ 41,498

This request will provide the two Technicians that were cut by the Department from last years request. These positions were presented as part of last year's budget proposal for six Technicians. We requested the four approved and Council seemed receptive to approving the other two Technicians this year. The Communications Center is the center of Police Operations and serves as the primary resource center to the officers and the public when they dial 9-1-1. Funding these positions will fully staff the Communications Center and provide dispatchers for the two primary radio channels that are being implemented on July 15th, 1991. Because of its responsibilities, this unit must be operational twenty-four hours-a-day, seven days a week.

The Communications Center will meet their staffing needs with the addition of these two Technicians which will also enable them to fully implement our two primary radio channels and our Officer Inquiry channel.

Priority Two/Three—Provide Two Clerical Assistants for District Operations—$ 29,168

Currently the District offices have one secretary for the entire District. She must do all secretarial work for the Major, Captains, Sergeants and Investigators. These two Clerical Assistant positions will provide secretarial support to the Investigators, Sergeants and other officers needing clerical support. These officers are having to do more of their own typing and we need to relieve them of this work so they can spend more time on the streets.

Priority Four—Provide One Equipment Service Worker—$ 17,509

We have one person to coordinate repairs and service for the entire police fleet of vehicles and all radio maintenance for both mobile and portable radios. This person has been overworked for the past five years. We are fortunate that we have an extremely dedicated employee in this position. The stress of the workload however is impacting his physical well-being. We have to pull personnel from other law enforcement duties to assist him daily because of his workload. By not having a second Equipment Service Worker we have been unable to process many repairs and services in a timely manner without pulling personnel from other duty assignments.

We have asked for this position for the past four years and it has not been funded. The funding of this position is long overdue. The proper coordination of our equipment services and repairs is paramount to an effective operation.

Priority Five/Six/Seven/Eight/Ten and Eleven—Police Vehicle Replacement—$354,200

The Department's fleet is being replaced with fewer vehicles each year. We obtained the City Council's concurrence several years ago to replace a third of our fleet each year. The experience of many national fleet management directors has been to replace police emergency vehicles between 60-70,000 miles. This usually occurs during the third year, which seems to be the most cost effective period for police vehicles. Over the past several years the City has been replacing fewer and fewer police emergency vehicles. We are now driving emergency vehicles that have close to 100,000 miles. More miles, means more maintenance; more maintenance, means more down-time; and more down-time, means insufficient numbers of vehicles for overlapping assignments of officers during high incidents of crime.

Our fleet vehicles should be funded from the Fleet Replacement Fund. Part of the Equipment Service Charge allocated to our Department's Budget is placed in this fund each year for replacement of each vehicle. Our vehicles are listed by the City as having a four year life and the replacement cost is allocated on a four year replacement basis yet we find fewer vehicles being replaced each year.

Priority Nine—Upgrade Evidence Technicians—$ 6,076

We have a very good evidence program at the Ocala Police Department. Evidence technology is a very complex, diverse and technical profession. As such, we need personnel with basic levels of skill, but we also need personnel with intermediate and advanced levels of skill who can be our experts in evidence technology, as well as our trainers and coaches for our junior technicians. This upgrade proposal will allow us to phase in over the next two years, the three proposed grade levels for our evidence technicians. In other words, after three years we will have Evidence Technicians classified and rated in three levels of skill and experience rather than the current single level. This "skill level" approach is a common practice for other Departments across the United States. It is designed to both encourage and support the advancing experience of these technicians who are critical for collecting, preserving and processing evidence at crime scenes. We need to compensate these personnel for their experience, training and outstanding job performance so we don't lose them to other agencies. Funding of this proposal will assist us greatly in maintaining the experience level of our Technicians and to encourage further advancement of their skills. Most criminal cases can be won or lost on the strength of physical evidence and we want to maintain the highest degree of skill we can to support our investigative efforts.

I am including a complete listing of each Capital Outlay and personnel request for your review, along with a copy of the detailed budget that has been submitted to the City.

Lee McGehee
Chief of Police

14 Productivity, Quality, and Evaluation of Police Services

We have no choice but to learn to manage the service institutions (such as the police) for performance and productivity.
PETER F. DRUCKER

Introduction

Productivity, quality, and evaluation of police services research are rational enterprises.[1] Productivity seeks to specify the relationship between inputs to the police organization (such as money allocated in the department's budget) to outputs (such as number of traffic accidents investigated and other such indicators). Quality management is an organization-wide effort to reduce errors and to improve the quality of services to the community. Program evaluation seeks to assess the extent to which goals are realized (for example, has the number of violent crimes reported to the police decreased in the past year?). The assumption is that by providing pertinent facts, productivity measures and program evaluations assist decision makers. However, evaluation is a rational enterprise that takes place in a political context. This chapter explores this area and provides various perspectives on the interrelatedness of productivity and program evaluation within police administration.

Productivity

There are three basic reasons that all of us should be concerned about productivity:

1. Our *real* wages go up, over the long run, as fast as our productivity increases. And real wages are the dollars left in our pay envelopes after deducting what inflation eats up. Only real wages give us more purchasing power.
2. We can get more leisure time only as our productivity improves. By increasing output per man-hour, we can get more of the goods and services we want while working the same or less.
3. Productivity gains give us, as a nation, choices we may not have had before. As productivity goes up, we can spend the increased output in a variety of ways. We can pay for a cleaner environment, more education, earlier retirement, universal health care or government services, or any combination of these. The United States has been fortunate over the past 200 years in that the choices we could make to improve our lives have constantly expanded. By increasing our productivity, we can assure that this will continue to be the case for ourselves and for future generations.[2]

Although the costs of operating local government have increased, there has not been a proportional rise in the resources available to pay for those increases.[3] Citizens have resisted higher taxes and are defeating badly needed bond issue proposals. When bond issues are defeated, new schools, hospitals, jails, courthouses, fire stations, and police buildings go unbuilt, leaving the professionals who work in these settings to labor under increasingly crowded conditions with old and dated equipment. At least nine states have imposed tax ceilings on their localities because of continued citizen pressure for tax relief.[4]

In light of such pressures it is not surprising that people increasingly rely on private security services. This sector of our economy now employs two and a half times the number that public law enforcement does and outspends it by 73 percent.[5] (See Figure 14-1). These pressures are also associated with a strong interest in total consolidation of entire governmental units. For example, in Georgia the Consolidated Government of Columbus–Muscogee County represents the combination of the former municipalities in that county with the county to form a single governmental entity. It has produced a governmental unit with a full range of services and an unusually low per capita expenditure for their delivery. The Unified Government of Athens–Clarke County, Georgia, is another example of total governmental consolidation, having been approved by local referendum in 1990. At the state level there has been periodic discussion of members of the Georgia General Assembly of consolidating some of that state's 159 counties into a smaller number of governmental units in order to provide a full range of services to citizens at a lower cost, which would presumably be achieved through an economy of scale effect. Short of total governmental consolidation is functional consolidation, that is, a single department jointly funded by the county and its constituent cities that delivers all of a particular type of service. For certain types of services such as parks and recreation, this arrangement often can be accomplished without undue controversy. However, when more highly visible departments such as the police are involved, functional consolidation can become highly controversial (see Box 14-1).

Defining Productivity

Specialists have not always agreed on the precise definition of productivity, but it is generally assumed to be a ratio of "output" to "input." A somewhat longer definition is that

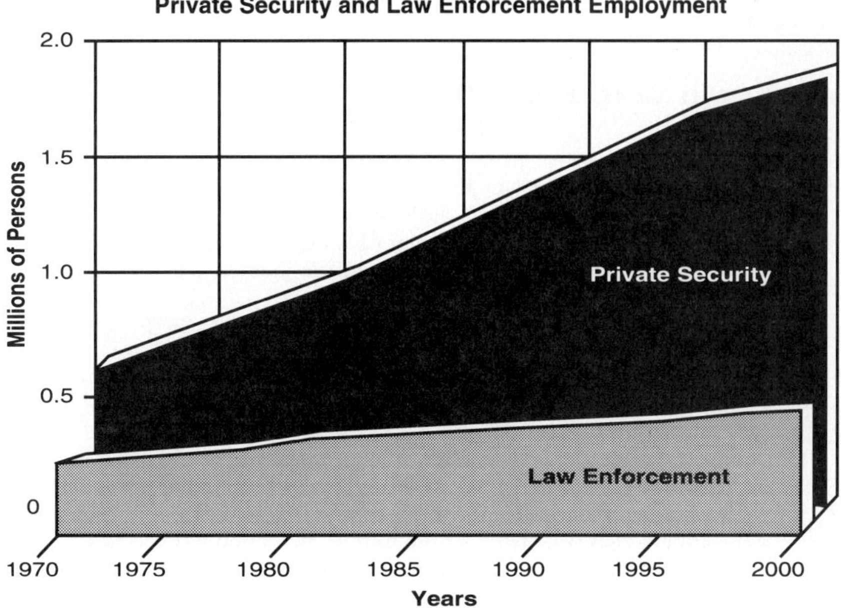

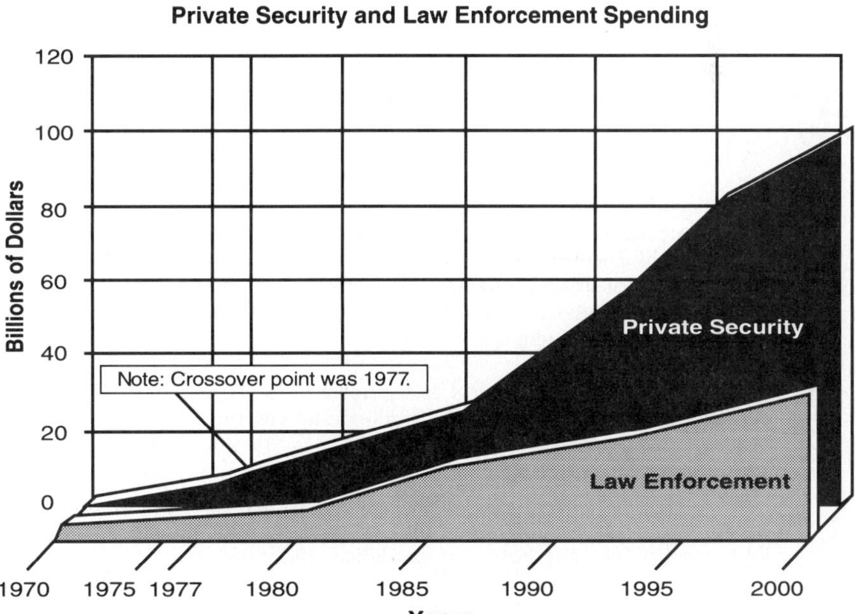

FIGURE 14-1. Trends in employment and spending for private security and public law enforcement. [*Source:* William C. Cunningham, John J. Strauchs, and Clifford W. Van Meter, *Private Security: Patterns and Trends* (Washington, D.C.: National Institute of Justice, Research in Brief), August 1991, p. 3.]

BOX 14-1

Power Key in Merger of Police

By Robert Behre

It's not about saving money. It's not about personalities. And it's not about consolidating city and county police forces.

The Nov. 6 referendum on whether Charleston County should abolish its police force and give its duties and employees to Sheriff Al Cannon is about power—the power to set police policy.

In less than four weeks, voters will pick between the current system where an appointed police chief reports to an administrator and county council or a new system where the sheriff calls the shots and answers to the voters every four years.

Will taxpayers pay more?

Placing the county police under the sheriff's department will result in some added expense, according to a Post-Courier cost analysis by Katherine Duffy & Associates.

The new cost—about $321,416 for the first year and $131,162 each year after—mostly stems from added personnel, a raise for the sheriff and pay increases to put his deputies on equal footing with county police, the study showed.

Those personnel costs, plus the cost of new badges, new car markings and new forms will be about $406,408, while taxpayers will save about $84,992, including the elimination of the police chief's salary, the study found.

However, Cannon said he strongly disagrees with Ms. Duffy's estimate.

Car markings, badges and forms would be replaced as the current ones wore out, he said. And he already has fought for added personnel and salary adjustments before the merger was proposed.

Cannon estimated the county may save about $100,000 because of increased efficiency, though exact figures are hard to come by.

"Under a merger, you would have 36 different deputies available to assist other on-duty officers. How do you compute what the value of that is? That's an enhancement over the current situation," he said.

Still, either the $100,000 savings or $321,410 in new costs are relatively small—less than 2 percent of what the sheriff's department budget would be under the merger.

"I don't think the cost is a factor, either way," Ms. Duffy said. "I think the issue is definitely one of structure—where the control is and who ultimately has it."

If the sheriff were to add the county police to his responsibilities of running the jail and collecting delinquent taxes, his budget would grow from $6.94 million to $16.64 million.

And the sheriff would control 26.5 percent of the county budget, 35.8 percent of all county employees and 37 percent of all county vehicles.

The impact on police

Cannon has vowed not to demote, dismiss or displace any police employees strictly because of the merger. The sheriff's department and the county police force do different jobs, and Cannon said those jobs would stay the same.

Not quite.

Even if police report to work at the same time, do the same jobs, and take home the same size paycheck, the rules of their employment will have changed.

A county policeman currently has a grievance procedure in cases of disagreements with his superior. Under a sheriff, employees work at the sheriff's pleasure—he can hire and fire who he wants.

Cannon said employees do not need a grievance procedure as long as they receive fair treatment—and he intends to give that. He also said personnel policies would not change, and sheriffs, like police chiefs, still must comply with state and federal employment laws.

BOX 14–1 (cont.)

However, it's unclear how many police officers believe their jobs will be as secure under Cannon. County Administrator Ed Fava has asked all police employees not to comment publicly on the proposed merger.

Acting police chief Thomas Dawson recently declined comment on the merger referendum, but his concern is evident in an Aug. 14 memo.

"Deputies serve at the discretion of the sheriff. Since new sheriffs typically replace staff level officers upon taking office, the county may consequently lose experienced officers as a result of the proposed merger," Dawson's memo said.

Would crime rates fall?

The public debate over the merger has touched on costs, personnel, authority and other issues, but much less has been said about whether law enforcement will improve.

And apparently, there is room for improvement.

A University of South Carolina study showed that Charleston ranked in the bottom half of the state in the amount of crimes that occurred versus the amount of crimes that were anticipated.

However, that study did not rate the job done by police forces within the county nor did it differentiate in the seriousness of the crimes, according to Dr. James G. Fraser, director of USC's College of Criminal Justice.

The bottom line, Fraser said, is voters have few objective standards to compare law enforcement agencies.

"The general public is woefully undereducated about the cost of providing police service and how to judge whether it's good or not . . . and I don't know that professionally, we've provided them much help in understanding that," he said.

Cannon has said he plans no major policy changes within the police department and employees would continue to do their jobs "except with the added stability of reporting to a sheriff."

Fraser said he was familiar with the police-sheriff referendum, but added that voters have few facts on which to base their decision.

"I would end up making the choice based on personalities, and I would go with the sheriff. He's an experienced law enforcement professional. He's well educated, and he's a man of principle. I believe any person as strong-minded as Al Cannon may be the best antidote to the problems that have plagued Charleston County," Fraser said.

However, there is no guarantee Cannon will be on the job much longer—he faces re-election in 1992.

"The danger is—what you've got to be careful is—you cannot compare personalities. It has to be a more broad-based view than Al Cannon versus Tommy Dawson as chief of police," County Councilman Andrew Savage said.

A political question

Placing the police force under the sheriff would change the political landscape of county law enforcement probably for a long time.

Council no longer would have direct input into how the police force is run, although council still would decide how much money the sheriff's department receives.

Ant that likely will set up interesting battles between council members and the sheriff, especially at budget time.

"It's already been an interesting relationship," Cannon said. "While some council members are very supportive and recognize the need to modernize and update the sheriff's office, others have faulted me on that."

The qualifications to run for sheriff are much more lax than those for a county police chief.

A sheriff candidate must be at least 21 years old; reside in the county; be a registered voter; have no criminal record; and have at least a high school education or five years experience in law enforcement.

BOX 14-1 (cont.)

Meanwhile, County Council has set far more stringent requirements for police chief candidates, including extensive administrative and law enforcement experience. Still, council members said they have made mistakes in picking police chiefs—some have lasted less than a year.

The Nov. 6 referendum is binding, and if voters decide to give the sheriff more responsibility, "it should be considered almost permanent."

Restructuring the sheriff's department likely will require another referendum, Ms. Duffy said.

Councilman Betsy Kerrison said the changes are serious and lasting, but there has not been enough study to know if these changes are right.

"We're concerned with public safety and we're concerned with taxpayer's money. I don't know what the answer is, but I don't think you go off half-cocked with something when you really don't know what you're doing."

However, Cannon said there's no mystery behind the merger—sheriffs run the police force in 44 of South Carolina's 46 counties. Meanwhile, council has spent enough of its time trying to fix up the police force, he said.

"If you set Hurricane Hugo aside, no other issue has occupied more of the county administrator's and County Council's time than working on problems in the county police department," he said, adding that under a merger, "council will experience some increased efficiency."

Lingering questions

Regardless of what voters decide, council members said they still will face new decisions on law enforcement, where a lot is happening.

The sheriff collects delinquent taxes, and Charleston had a higher percentage of overdue taxes than any other large county in the state last year. Meanwhile, council is planning a new jail and a new public safety building.

Under a merger, Cannon's plate would be full, and council should continue to look at ways to improve the system, Councilman Charles Wallace said.

"Should the merger take place, there will still be a lot of work to be done, involving everyone, as to how best make this work. I don't necessarily think that everything that's in place has to stay in place," Wallace said.

Cannon said he is open to talking about taking the jail or delinquent taxes away from the sheriff's department.

"If they can demonstrate with any degree of certainty that they could do it more efficiently than I could do it right now, I'd certainly be willing to talk to them," he said.

Another continuing question will be the merger's impact on efforts to consolidate city and county police departments—an idea almost all council members look favorably upon.

Cannon said the merger will be an indirect boost to consolidation efforts because he is accountable to voters in cities as well as unincorporated areas. And he said his department already works with police.

But council members said overall consolidation will not occur until city and county leaders agree to share turf.

Source: News and Courier (Charleston, S.C.,), Oct. 14, 1990.

> Productivity improvement is among the practical approaches government is taking to achieve its objectives of effectiveness, efficiency and economy. The concept of productivity improvement focuses on whether the right things are being done and whether they are being done without wasting valuable resources.[6]

The National Commission on Productivity has determined that police productivity can be improved in the following four ways:

1. Improve current police practice to its optimum level to achieve better performance without causing a proportionate increase in cost. Put simply, this means doing the necessary tasks of police work, but doing them as efficiently as possible.
2. Allocate the resources to those activities that give the highest return for each additional dollar that is spent. This involves a number of decisions focusing on police services. Are the police not only doing things right, but also doing the right thing?
3. Increase the probability that a given objective will be met. For instance, the most successful criminal apprehension programs assign police personnel when and where crime is the highest or calls for police service are the heaviest. This can be achieved through careful analysis of data to pinpoint the likely times and places of crime occurrence, thereby increasing the probability that a suspect will be apprehended.
4. Make the most of personnel talents. Many times the individual talents of police officers are overlooked by rigid organizational procedures. This not only squanders public resources but also suffocates individual potentials and desires.[7]

Efficiency and Effectiveness

In its application to the public sector (especially police), the notions of productivity have centered largely on two basic concepts: efficiency and effectiveness.

> Efficiency measures determine the level of resources—human, financial, and environmental—that are required to provide a given level of service; effectiveness measures determine the impact and quality of the service being provided. Efficiency measures describe how much of a given service is being provided and the costs associated with that service level; effectiveness measures describe the results—both positive and negative—that the provision of the service has on the client or community.[8]

In this definition, the qualitative dimension of service is considered as part of the measures of effectiveness, although another perspective is that quality is itself a separate dimension, a matter discussed more fully later in this chapter. Stated more simply, effectiveness is the ability to get a job done, including meeting the standards set for quality control. Efficiency, on the other hand, is determined by what resources (inputs) are needed in producing outputs.

Effectiveness and efficiency must both be present if there is to be an improvement in productivity. Measurements such as hours of work, individual response time to calls, and number of arrests are necessary to *monitor* effectiveness and efficiency. Measurements comparing specific time periods, such as last calendar year versus the present calendar year, are essential to indicate whether improvement has been achieved.

Implementing a Productivity Program

Whether a police productivity improvement program is large or small, simple or complex, experience has demonstrated that there is a basic checklist of conditions that must be satisfied for it to be developed and implemented successfully. Police leaders must have

1. The courage and determination to initiate and sustain the program.
2. The analytical capacity to determine what needs to be done, what can be done, and how to do it.
3. The active support or, failing that, at least the neutrality of relevant others, such as the city or county manager, the legislative body, the interested public, and the union.
4. The ability to overcome resistance from other departments of government, such as personnel or central purchasing, who may resist the writing of new job and equipment specifications because they impinge on established control practices.
5. Overall, the cooperation of the people within the police department. Even if large numbers of personnel are committed, lesser numbers of well-situated people opposing the program can mean failure.
6. The organizational control system and controls to facilitate and reinforce the changes to be made.
7. Competent persons responsible for the changes.[9]

A key and positive way of reinforcing the changes to be made is a widespread system of incentives that makes efforts to improve productivity have some "pay-off" to those involved. Police administrators may be guaranteed that some portion of the savings generated by productivity improvements will be made available to them for new or expanded programs.[10] For example, in Plainville, Connecticut, police officers with perfect attendance for 90 days were given an extra day off, a measure that reduced the use of sick says considerably.

Basically, productivity improvements can be made in two ways: (1) increasing the level of output while holding the level of resources used constant, or (2) maintaining or increasing the level of output with a decrease in the level of resources used. Productivity improvement does not mean working harder; it means working "smarter." The efforts to do so show rich diversity as in the following cases:

- Covington, Kentucky, recruited 40 taxicab drivers to help them reduce crime. At a cost of $300 for a two-hour training session and decals to identify participating drivers, the department added "eyes and ears." The program is credited with the prevention of crimes by identifying suspicious persons, and the arrests of suspects during the commission of their crimes.[11]
- Handicapped citizens in West Valley City, Utah, complained that able-bodied people were using handicapped parking spots at stores and malls. The police did not have enough personnel to increase enforcement; therefore, the department recruited, organized, and trained handicapped residents to patrol and issue citations for such violations.[12]
- The Pomona, California, Police Department contracted with a private security company to provide parking enforcement. The result was a doubling of the number of issued citations and a 35 percent reduction in the cost of the effort.[13]
- In Virginia Beach, Virginia, extensive use is made of trained volunteers: the Marine Patrol Program uses pairs of uniformed officers and volunteers to patrol the 51 square miles of water in its jurisdiction, and volunteers care for the equipment, trailers, grounds, barn, and horses; in the sex crime, robbery squad, and felony assault divisions, two volunteers update arrest files by collecting data from offense reports, maintain photographic files, cross-reference files, and assemble "mug books"; and in the homicide squad they make computer data entries and perform crime trend analyses, and related tasks.[14]

- Indianapolis, Indiana, pioneered the practice of assigning patrol cars to individual officers, a practice that came to be referred to as "personal" or "take-home" police cars. Subsequently, a number of agencies such as the Visalia, California, Police Department experimented with this practice.[15] Visalia's approach differs importantly from the Indianapolis system in that Visalia's officers are allowed to use their car only for police business or travel between their home and the police station. Patrol cars may not be used to transport family members or for other personal uses. Furthermore, the privilege of commuting in a patrol car is available only to those officers who reside within the boundaries of the unified school district, a geographic area that extends slightly beyond the city limits.

  Systems that feature take-home patrol car plans usually defend their program on the strength of enhanced police visibility, increased deployment flexibility, and expanded enforcement activity. Motorists and other persons alter (i.e., improve) their behavior upon sighting the police vehicle. The take-home plan increases the frequency of that occurrence. Deployment flexibility is increased by the availability of a greater number of police vehicles that can be called into service for emergencies or special events. Expanded enforcement occurs when off-duty officers nevertheless perform police duties while traveling in patrol cars.

  In 1988, the Visalia Police Department prepared an analysis of the first seven and one-half years' experience with the personalized patrol vehicle program. That report noted many of the benefits in visibility and flexibility that have been claimed by take-home systems elsewhere, but focused primarily on economic impacts relative to costs that would have been incurred by continuation of standard line vehicle policies. Under a standard system of continuous use of patrol cars and frequent replacement, the city estimated that its costs for purchase, maintenance, fuels and supplies for the patrol fleet would have totaled $2.27 million. Actual costs for a much larger fleet of personalized patrol vehicles and their maintenance, fuels, and supplies totaled $1.56 million over the seven and a half year period, for a savings of more than $700,000. How were such substantial savings possible? Individual officers demonstrated a new sense of responsibility for their vehicle. They took better care of it, were less likely to abuse it, and made sure that prescribed preventive maintenance occurred. As a result, overall maintenance costs were reduced and individual vehicles lasted longer—even longer than originally expected. By 1988, 14 of the original cars were still in service and not expected to be replaced until 1989. By 1990, the department's rule of thumb was to officially anticipate a five-year life for personalized patrol vehicles, but to actually expect an additional five years of secondary use or backup service.

- The Police Executive Research Forum (PERF) has replicated the Stanford Research Institute burglary case-screening model. The replica involved 12,001 cases from 26 different police departments and proved 85 percent accurate in determining which cases would benefit from follow-up investigations. From it, two implicit findings emerge: (1) the success or failure of the follow-up investigation is more a function of the characteristics of the case than the follow-up investigation itself, and (2) the application of the model eliminates a great deal of nonproductive investigative effort.[16]

- The first major audit of the Philadelphia Police Department in 14 years found that the police averaged 16.8 sick days per year and that a strictly enforced sick leave policy (one that required a doctor's note for absences) could save the city $6 million annually.[17]

- Flint, Michigan; Orange, California; and New York City represent a few of the jurisdictions that have tied productivity to the collective bargaining process. In general, such efforts offer incentives for improvements or seek to renegotiate contractual provisions—such as a requirement that all cars are manned by two officers—that may be blocks to increased productivity.

- The Glendale, Arizona, Police Department makes extensive use of nonsworn employees for many duties handled by sworn police officers in other jurisdictions.[18] In fact, approximately one-third of the department's 300 employees are nonsworn. Not only do nonsworn employees serve in integral capacities in the communications bureau and the department's general management ranks, but they also handle the vast majority of the department's traffic accident investigation duties. The city's rationale for such extensive use of nonsworn employees is simple: by carefully selecting appropriate tasks and allowing specialization, nonsworn employees can perform selected jobs as well as or better than sworn personnel and at a lower cost. The use of nonsworn traffic accident investigators saves the city more than $70,000 each year, for cumulative savings in excess of $1 million since the program was initiated (see Box 14-2).
- In Prince George's County, Maryland, local officials estimated that they responded to an average of 50 false alarms per day, which cost the county $547,500 annually. The county passed a law requiring owners of burglar alarms to purchase $10 initial permits and pay a $5 annual renewal fee. Failure to register results in a $200 penalty. Families with registered alarms are allowed only three accidental or false alarms each year. A $35 fine is imposed for additional false alarms. As a result of the permit requirements, false alarms have been reduced by about 20 percent.[19]

From these illustrations, it can be seen that productivity improvement efforts are possible in both large and small police departments and that they may involve a variety of strategies. As suggested by the National Commission on Productivity and Work Quality, a shift in the style of management employed by a police department may itself be a productivity improvement measure. In terms of sequential steps, the implementation of a productivity improvement effort involves

1. Selecting a program, subprogram, or activity for concentrated study, such as a neighborhood crime watch program.
2. Determining the true objectives of the program; to increase crime prevention awareness within specific neighborhoods and thereby reduce reported street crime.
3. Choosing the appropriate analytical procedures for eliciting information, such as interviewing victims or surveying officers.
4. Designing several program improvement options; for example, new technology, improved procedures, increasing employee motivation, contracting out service, and so on.
5. Forecasting direct and indirect impacts of program options, such as decreased fear of crime and safer and more secure public feeling.
6. Implementing the program—putting the selected program option into effect. This includes developing strategies for overcoming individual, organizational, and institutional barriers.
7. Evaluating the program—determining how well the new or adjusted program works when compared with the original program.[20]

Management Style and Productivity

The overall strategy involved in implementing a productivity improvement program may take one of three forms: (1) centralized, (2) nondirective, and (3) decentralized.[21] Phoenix, Arizona; Milwaukee, Wisconsin; and San Diego, California,[22] all operate from a centralized perspective with their Department of Budget and Research, Bureau of Budget and Management, and Financial Management

BOX 14-2

Glendale, Arizona: Nonsworn Traffic Accident Investigators

Begun on a pilot basis in 1975, the program initially drew employees from Glendale's public works department who volunteered for training and reassignment as accident investigators. For eight years the program was based in the general services department before moving in 1983 to the police department. The program evolved gradually from being a role player in the traffic accident investigation program to its status as the dominant actor today.

The program began with six investigators on shifts staggered to cover the hours of 6:00 A.M. to 11:30 P.M. seven days a week. Initially, nonsworn investigators worked only minor accidents; accidents involving serious injury or criminal offenses were handled by sworn police officers. Even with these limitations, however, the pilot program proved to be successful and was established on an ongoing basis. The program's demonstrated success, coupled with new state legislation expanding the authority of "unarmed traffic investigators," allowed nonsworn investigators to assume a larger and larger share of the traffic accident investigation responsibilities.

By 1990, the corps of nonsworn investigators had grown to 10 and served along with 10 sworn motorcycle officers in the traffic services bureau of the Glendale Police Department. The nonsworn investigators unit had grown in size and in authority, but perhaps the most impressive growth rate associated with the unit was the dramatic increase in its workload. The number of reported accidents in Glendale grew from approximately 1,200 in 1976 to approximately 5,000 per year by 1990, an increase of more than 300 percent. Nonsworn accident investigators, now providing coverage around the clock, handle approximately 80 percent of all traffic accidents.

The operational success of the program is evidenced by the notable expertise of the nonsworn investigators and the unit's ability to handle a dramatically increased workload without commensurate increases in personnel. The unit includes advanced accident investigators, investigators skilled in reconstruction techniques, and investigators qualified to provide expert testimony. C. Scott Loper, manager of police traffic services, identifies three factors as being instrumental to program success:

1. Specialization. The development of specialties allows employees to become expert in their individual capacities. Specialization has also proven to be attractive to former police officers who have moved into nonsworn traffic accident investigator positions because they prefer that aspect of police work.
2. Appropriate status and equipment. The investigators are part of an important unit within the police department and are appropriately uniformed and equipped. Although they are not armed, investigators wear uniforms that differ only slightly from those worn by sworn officers, and they drive fully marked police cars. They do not, however, engage in patrol or other nontraffic functions.
3. Extensive training. New investigators must complete eight weeks of training. The first three weeks consist of accident investigation technology, report writing, traffic laws, police radio procedures and use, court procedures and testimony, and first aid. The next five weeks are spent in on-the-job training with current investigators.

Unit costs for traffic accident investigations in Glendale reflect an approximate $18 differential between those conducted by sworn officers and investigations conducted by nonsworn personnel. A portion of the difference is attributable to the lower salary paid to nonsworn investigators, and part is attributable to the greater speed at which highly specialized employees can complete an investigation. With 80 percent of the city's 5,000 accidents handled by nonsworn investigators, the result is an annual savings of more than $70,000.

Source: David N. Ammons, Model Programs in Local Governments: A Report on Site Visits (Athens: Carl Vinson Institute of Government, University of Georgia, 1991), pp. 3–5.

Department, respectively, taking the lead role. In a highly centralized system, the productivity staff might have responsibility for

1. Establishing and imposing performance targets and timetables on the operating agencies
2. Identifying the programs or activities for which productivity improvements will be developed
3. Analyzing programs and activities
4. Designing and scheduling productivity improvement projects
5. Managing the implementation of productivity improvement projects
6. Operating a central information and control system on all productivity improvements
7. Negotiating or controlling negotiations with employee unions on productivity improvements.[23]

The case for a centralized system is that it unites trained analysts with elected officials and ties productivity improvements to the power of the budget. Against it is the inherent danger of resistance from the police or other departments when change is experienced or perceived as being imposed. Tacoma, Washington, used a nondirective approach in that, although the city manager "made no bones" about his interest in productivity improvements, he left it to the department heads to decide a course of action. For those who sought improvements, he provided substantial assistance in eliminating bureaucratic obstacles and obtained expert help, and was otherwise actively supportive. No pressure was placed on the "laggards" save the example set by the city manager and the responsive department heads; over time, increasingly more departments joined the effort. Decentralization places responsibility for improvements with the heads of operating agencies, and although there is a reduction in central control, there is also less tension from imposed change and a closer linkage between the analysts and operations—improving both—because they are housed within each department of government.

Total Performance Management

Total performance management (TPM) is a comprehensive approach to improving productivity. Its underpinnings reaffirm from yet another perspective Douglas McGregor's observation that theory and practice are inseparable. Figure 14-2 summarizes TPM, which combines elements of industrial engineering—with roots back to scientific management—and the use of behavioral science techniques such as survey research feedback. The use of TPM requires

1. The collection of data from customers and employees to provide information about both positive and negative aspects of performances, along with data about productivity
2. "Playing back" the data in summarized forms to both managers and employees
3. Managers and employees who develop action plans to build on strengths and eliminate or reduce weaknesses.

From the types of data gathered and how they are used, certain key aspects of TPM can be seen: it assumes that customers can and will provide valuable information

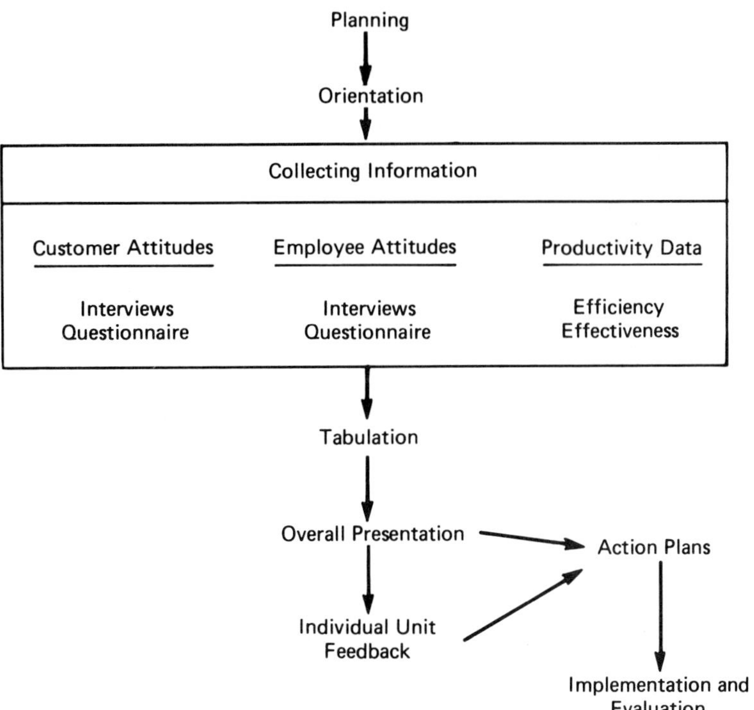

FIGURE 14-2. Total Performance Management. [From National Center for Productivity and Quality of Working Life, "Total Performance Management: Some Pointers for Action" (Washington, D.C.: U.S. Government Printing Office, 1978), p. 6.]

about services received; employees are an important source of data and creativity; and at the core of any productivity improvement program is some amount of relevant data on which decisions can be made.

Total performance management was developed by the General Accounting Office of the United States in cooperation with the National Center for Productivity and Quality of Working Life. The first application of TPM was in a small editorial unit of a federal agency, about whose careless work and missed deadlines other units of the agency had been complaining.[24] Impressive results were obtained from this first small-scale initial experimentation, including a 45 percent decline in the time required to respond to requests for services, higher quality, higher work-force morale, and increased customer satisfaction.[25] Several California jurisdictions, including Sunnyvale, San Diego, Los Angeles County, and Manhattan Beach, have experimented with TPM.[26] For the most part, these initial experiments with TPM have been encouraging, reflecting similar results in increased productivity and morale.

Conditions that suggest the wider use of some variation of TPM in the future include (1) the fact that TPM lends itself to a centralized implementation strategy, which many city leaders may prefer; (2) it is systems oriented; (3) it provides an opportunity for employees to participate in defining and shaping the solutions to problems; and (4) elements of it are already being practiced in many places—the city of Charlotte, North Carolina, for example, has surveyed citizens on their perception of police performance at least since 1976. A number of jurisdictions and agencies have gone beyond TPM to quality management, discussed later in this chapter. In this regard, TPM can be seen as an important part of the history of management practices which led to quality management.[27]

Management by Objectives

A management approach that is a natural adjunct to productivity programs and that enhances them is management by objectives (MBO) or some alternative designation of it, such as policing by objectives (PBO).[28] The concept of MBO is widely attributed to Peter Drucker in *The Practice of Management* (1954). In general, the use of MBO in government can be described as a late-1960s, early-1970s movement. Its adoption has not been universal, and as late as 1978, some major police departments were only beginning its implementation.[29]

MBO can be defined as having a result, as opposed to an activity, orientation to managing whose underlying philosophical bias is participative management. Drucker elaborates on this philosophical bias by describing MBO as a common and explicit understanding between managers and their subordinates regarding what their contributions to the organization will be over a definite period of time.[30] Where MBO has been tried by police departments and has failed, its lack of success most often has been caused by using it as a purely technical management system implemented without a shift from reliance on traditional organizational theory precepts to the use of bridging or open systems theories, which stress the importance and worth of officers at all levels of the department. Stated in terms of leadership orientations, the MBO system implemented under a 9,1 (authority obedience) orientation incurs a greater risk of failure than under the 5,5 (organization man management) or 9,9 (team management) approaches.

The underlying rationale of MBO has been stated as "the better a manager understands what he hopes to accomplish (the better he knows his objectives), the greater will be his chances for success."[31] In a sense, MBO provides the manager with a blueprint that guides him or her toward the objective he or she has set. Others suggest, "if one knows where he is going, he finds it easier to get there, he can get there faster, and he will know when he arrives."[32]

Figure 14-3 summarizes the major steps commonly involved in the MBO process. The formulation of long-range goals and strategic plans is preceded by the development of the police department's *mission statement,* which is the broadest, most comprehensive statement that can be made about the overall purpose of the police department.[33] The mission statement recognizes either explicitly or implicitly legislatively mandated roles, professional tenets, community preferences, and related sources.

Goals are end states or conditions that take one or more years to achieve. Complex goals (e.g., designing, obtaining approval for, procuring, and placing a new jail communications system into operation) may take three to five years. Goals may also be stated in such a fashion that the pursuit of them is continuous (e.g., "to promote officer safety and performance by providing a variety of basic and in-service training experiences"). Because of the time-horizon associated with goals, they are supported by more immediately achievable (and subsequently measurable) objectives.

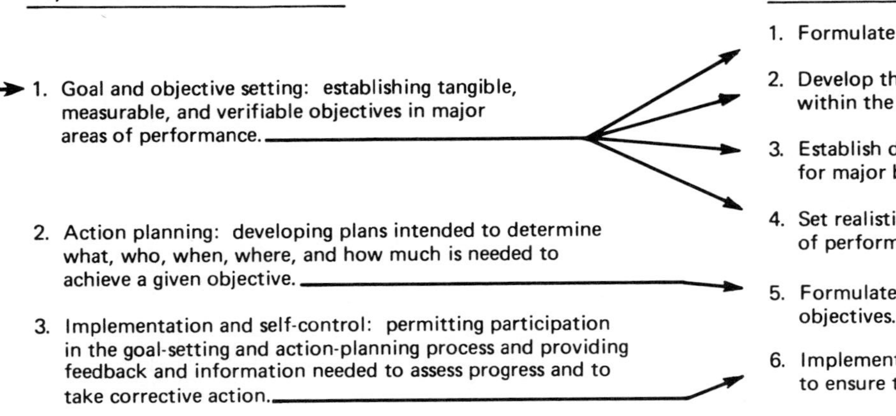

FIGURE 14-3. The MBO process. [From Anthony P. Raia, *Managing by Objectives* (Glenview, Ill.: Scott, Foresman, 1974), p. 16. Copyright 1974 Scott, Foresman Co. Reprinted by permission].

Objectives are end states that can be achieved in one year or less. Well-stated objectives have three characteristics:

- Target specific
- Quantified
- Identified time frame.

The following statement of an objective illustrates the use of these three characteristics: Objective One—to have 100 percent of all sergeants complete 120 hours of supervisory training during FY 1995. These characteristics are important because they provide a basis for determining whether or not the organization accomplished what it set out to do. These characteristics also help explain one underlying reason for resistance to planning in general and goal and objective setting in particular; formal statements of expectations are generated, impacting on *responsibility* and *accountability,* the very essence of program evaluation.

The achievement of the identified objectives is then reinforced by the development of an action plan, as shown in Figure 14-4. The specificity of the action plan

GOAL	To provide a management environment that facilitates achieving department goals while providing for the career needs of its employees.	
OBJECTIVE	To develop and place into operation by August 4, 1994 a new telecommunications center.	TARGET DATE August 4, 1994
DIVISION	Administration	PERSON RESPONSIBLE M. E. Deen
ACTION PLAN		TARGET DATE
	Development and Construction of Ocala Police Department Communications Center to Be Operational by August 4, 1994.	
A.	Equipment selection to include equipment options	Jan. 31, 1994
B.	Develop equipment specifications	Feb. 25, 1994
C.	Site plan and specifications completed	Feb. 25, 1994
D.	Bids released on communications equipment and construction	March 3, 1994
E.	Bids received by city of Ocala purchasing office	Mar. 28, 1994
F.	Bids awarded for equipment and construction by city council	Apr. 1, 1994
G.	Communications equipment ordered from successful bidder	Apr. 2, 1994
H.	Construction begins on communication center	Apr. 14, 1994
I.	Delivery and installation of communications equipment	Jul. 23, 1994
J.	Construction work in center completed	Aug. 1, 1994
K.	Communications center operational	Aug. 4, 1994
PREPARED BY	M. E. Deen	DATE PREPARED Jan. 31, 1993.
APPROVED BY		DATE APPROVED

FIGURE 14-4. An Action Plan. [*Source:* The Ocala, Florida Police Department.]

allows for (1) monitoring; (2) taking corrective action as needed, as the basis of evaluating; and (3) improved planning and decision making. In Ocala, Florida, a zone awareness program allowed the individual officer assigned to each geographic area to develop, in cooperation with his or her supervisor, objectives for policing the area.[34] Progress toward achieving the objectives was monitored, adjustments were made as needed, and in bimonthly meetings the officer's performance was evaluated and new objectives prepared. Thus, MBO can be a tool for evaluating not only programs but also individual performance.

Obstacles and Benefits

Management by objective systems can fail for a variety of reasons. Stein[35] conducted a study in which the attitudes of lower-level and midlevel management personnel using MBO were examined. The results of the study revealed a number of problems associated with the MBO system. The three most critical problems were

1. Difficulty in defining objectives that were both meaningful and measurable
2. Insufficient followup, monitoring, and updating of the program
3. Lack of commitment by management to the purposes and concepts of MBO.[36]

Further, it should be remembered that the implementation of MBO requires large-scale organizational change. However, a fully developed and properly implemented MBO system may require two to five years of sustained effort in large organizations before it takes hold. A review of the research on MBO reveals that it has the potential to

1. Increase goal specificity
2. Increase awareness of goals
3. Contribute to improved planning
4. Result in greater specificity in identifying and defining problems
5. Produce better resource allocation
6. Have a favorable effect on productivity
7. Improve superior–subordinate relationships
8. Increase the receptivity of superiors to new ideas and suggestions
9. Make greater use of subordinates' ability and experiences
10. Improve interpersonal and organizational communications
11. Increase motivation and job satisfaction among employees
12. Increase objectivity in evaluating performances[37]

From these points, one could conclude, as one chief wryly did, "that MBO will do everything but take out the garbage." Given its potential utility, why aren't fully developed MBO systems being used in every police department? There may be no single answer, but from experience some observed reasons are that (1) it is easier to maintain the status quo than to enter into the change process; (2) some police leaders are unable or unwilling to part with highly centralized control; (3) MBO has been oversold in that, as compared with its benefits, not as much attention has been given to the reality that it takes sustained hard work to achieve changes; it cannot simply be dropped into the police department like a set of spark plugs into a car; (4) some managers do not really want to know the answer to the question, "How well am I (or are we) doing?"; (5) reports of failures in the use of MBO have discouraged some potential adopters; and (6) the costs involved in developing the system and training personnel in both the technical and the behavioral aspects of it are high.

Additionally, research also suggests that MBO may have certain dysfunctional consequences if not implemented properly: (1) over time, officers may become indifferent to it as "just another management procedure"; (2) when participation in objective setting does not reach the lower levels of the organization, it is likely to fail, making future innovations more difficult to implement; (3) it can create excessive paperwork with an emphasis more on building a paper record than on achieving results; and (4) easily quantifiable objectives may be substituted for more important, but more difficult to measure, ones.[38] Despite such barriers, the use of MBO should, and is likely to, increase within police departments.

Productivity Measurement

Whereas the concept of productivity is deceptively simple, trying to employ it meaningfully in policing presents challenges. The fact that such challenges exist does not, however, mean that productivity improvement efforts (PIEs) should not be undertaken. At present, productivity measurement in policing is still in a relatively early stage; some number of performance measures (PMs) are crude because the technology is developing. However, the legacy of the resource scarcity over the past decade has been a heightened concern for "getting the most for the buck," resulting in a continued movement toward the use of more formal PIEs and PMs. Relatedly, the most fundamental obligation that managers seeking public appropriations have is to demonstrate that they have exercised careful stewardship over the resources previously entrusted to them. Failing a demonstration of that, on what grounds can police managers reasonably expect effectively to advance a case for any additional funding?

A key issue in using PMs is developing a definition of output. If part of the role of the police is preventing crime, how, for example, do you measure how many crimes the police prevented? A related problem is establishing that there is some relationship between police effort and outcome. To illustrate, if reported crime decreases or increases, it may be the result of a reduction in, or an increase in, public confidence that the police cannot or can do something about crime. This shift in public confidence may occur quite independently of anything that the police may or may not do; such a shift may be caused by rumors, statements by political candidates, or the errors in news reports that occasionally happen under the pressure of deadlines. Additionally, if specific police programs aimed at particular crime problems do not yield results, the police may be tempted to discourage the filing of complaints or assign the complaints to another crime category. In a city with a rash of robberies, the uniformed officers may be told at roll call to "make sure you really have a robbery; some of those reports coming in as robberies are actually larcenies, and it's causing extra paperwork in getting them classified properly." The words spoken notwithstanding, the real message is "we're taking a lot of heat about these robberies and one way or another we've got to reduce them."

Other problems relating to measuring productivity include the following: (1) an increase in police productivity may be accompanied by a reduction in the quality of output; (2) the achievement of a given productivity level does not mean that the level of services being provided is consistent with community desires or needs; (3) there is difficulty in developing adequate and appropriate measures for staff functions such as personnel and training; and (4) achieving the desired level of productivity in one area may make it difficult to achieve the desired level in another.

In some cases, the crime control and community relations functions may come into conflict. For example, assume that a police department assigns officers in teams to various high-crime neighborhoods. All members of the team are dressed to blend into the street life where they are assigned and one or more serve as decoys. When offenders attempt to victimize the decoys, the other team members close in and make an arrest. After seven months, the arrest and conviction rates for serious offenses are five times higher among team officers as compared with the rates for conventionally deployed officers. However, in the course of these special operations, six minority citizens have been shot to death and two others wounded as they attempted to commit violent felonies involving the decoys as victims. As a result, the minority community is aroused, and their relations with the police are reaching new lows. Thus we have two desirable goals that are in conflict, namely improved community relations and the reduction of violent street crime.

MBO, Productivity, and Quality Improvement Efforts

Figure 14-5 depicts the integration of an MBO system and a productivity improvement effort. Although an MBO system and PIE effort have some overlapping features—which is why MBO is a natural adjunct to a productivity program—there are some differences. The starting place for an MBO system is the mission statement, which is a global orientation, whereas the starting place for a PIE is selecting a program, a subprogram, or an activity for concentrated study.

Three separate types of performance measures are identified in Figure 14-5: (1) efficiency, used to denote the efficiency of the service delivery system rather than the individual worker; (2) quality; and (3) effectiveness. Typically, when a productivity system is introduced, the measures of efficiency and effectiveness draw the early attention. Subsequently, concern for what will happen or what is happening to the quality of service delivery emerges and measures are adopted or developed to deal with this concern.

To illustrate, in 1950, W. Edwards Deming was invited by the Union of Japanese Scientists and Engineers to speak to leading industrialists who were concerned about breaking into foreign markets.[39] At that time Japan used typical management and efficiency measures and had a deserved reputation for poor quality goods. Deming convinced them that Japanese quality could be the best in the world if they adopted his methods, which center on 14 points (see Box 14-3).[40] "The industrialists took Deming's philosophy to heart and the rest is history."[41] Each year Japanese industry presents on television the coveted Deming prize to the company that has achieved the greatest gains in productivity. Its past winners

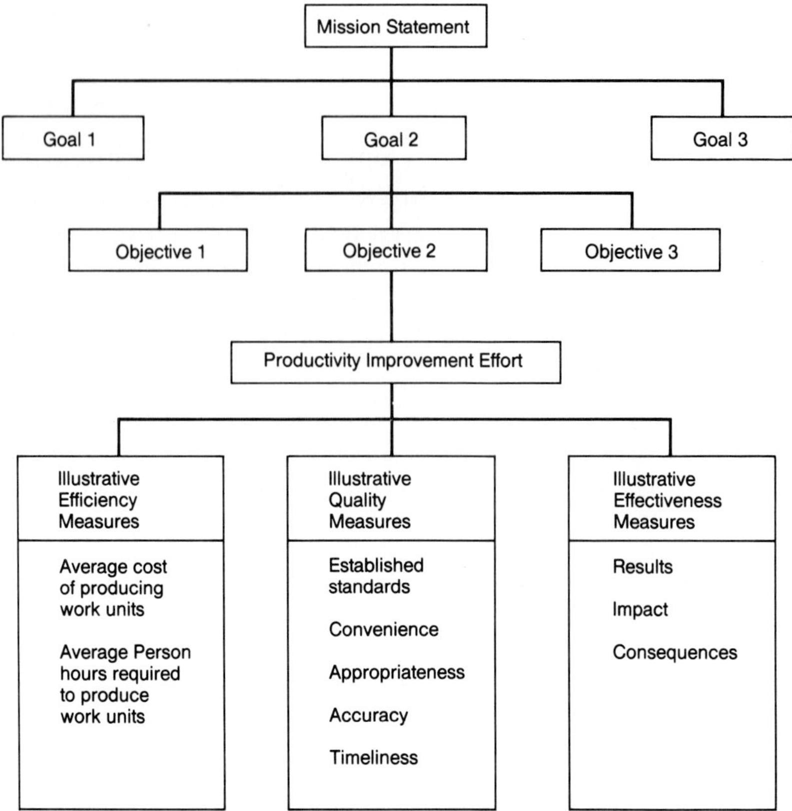

FIGURE 14-5. The integration of an MBO system and a productivity improvement effort. [Portions of this figure are drawn and modified from Brian Usilaner and Edwin Scott, "Productivity Measurement," in *Productivity Improvement Handbook for State and Local Government,* ed. George J. Washnis (New York: John Wiley & Sons, 1980), p. 93.]

have included Nissan, Hitachi, and Toyota.[42] In 1985, Texas Instruments became the first American recipient of a Deming award.[43] Events such as these sparked considerable private and public sector interest in this country. Quality circles (QCs)—discussed in Chapter 3, "Organizational Theory"—quickly sprang up everywhere. However, by the early 1990s some observers viewed the QCs as "quick fixes" that were based on the faulty assumption that by training workers at the lower levels of the organization, quality would take care of itself. In contrast, Deming's view of quality is that it permeates every aspect of the organization (total quality management, or TQM) and its suppliers and also pulls in the consumer's views and wants. Thus, in some American industrial settings, QCs have matured into self-directed work teams that are different from QCs in that they operate within an environment that has an overall quality strategy and culture in place.[44] In 1987, President Reagan signed the Malcolm Baldrige National Quality Improvement Act. Named after a former secretary of commerce, the act mandated the creation of a quality award for manufacturing, service, and small businesses, with a limit of two awards per year in each of those categories.[45] The National Institute

BOX 14-3

Deming's 14 Quality Points

1. Create constancy of purpose toward improvement of product and service, with a plan to improve competitive position and stay in business.
2. Adopt the new philosophy. We are in a new economic age. We can no longer live with commonly accepted levels of delays, mistakes, defective materials and defective workmanship.
3. Cease dependence on mass inspection. Require, instead, statistical evidence that quality is built in to eliminate the need for inspection on a mass basis.
4. End the practice of awarding business on the basis of price tag. Instead, depend on meaningful measures of quality, along with price.
5. Find problems. It is management's job to work continually on improving the system.
6. Institute modern methods of training on the job.
7. Institute modern methods of supervision.
8. Drive out fear so that everyone may work effectively for the company.
9. Break down barriers between departments.
10. Eliminate numerical goals, posters, and slogans that seek new levels of productivity without providing methods.
11. Eliminate work standards that prescribe numerical quotas.
12. Remove barriers that rob employees of their pride of workmanship.
13. Institute a vigorous program of education and retraining.
14. Create a structure which will push on the prior 13 points every day.

Source: Howard S. Gitlow and Shelly J. Gitlow, *The Deming Guide to Quality and Competitive Position* (Englewood Cliffs, N.J.: Prentice-Hall, Inc. 1987), p. 20.

of Standards and Technology (NIST) was responsible for the development of standards that organizations could use to evaluate their quality improvement efforts. NIST developed a seven-category, 1,000-point scoring system and a three-level judging process to evaluate applicants for a Baldrige Award (see Box 14-4).[46] Past Baldrige winners include Xerox, Cadillac, Motorola, and the first awardee in the service category, Federal Express. Among the criticisms of the Baldridge Award is that it doesn't predict financial success for a company and that it really doesn't recognize superior quality because Cadillac has yet to distinguish itself in stellar ratings of automobiles such as the J. D. Powers survey.[47] However, in 1990 the General Accounting Office reported that there was a cause-and-effect relationship between the TQM practices embodied in the Baldrige Award and corporate performance as measured by employee relations, customer satisfaction, or profitability.[48] Among the police departments making a substantial commitment to quality is the department in Madison, Wisconsin, as discussed in Chapter 1, "The Evolution of American Policing" and illustrated in Figure 1-10, which identifies the department's principles of quality leadership.

Figure 14-6 illustrates the relationship of objectives and PMs. Naturally, in a

BOX 14-4

Scoring the 1991 Baldrige Award

1.0 Leadership (100 points)
1.1 Senior Executive Leadership (40)
1.2 Quality Values (15)
1.3 Management for Quality (25)
1.4 Public Responsibility (20)
2.0 Information and Analysis (70 points)
2.1 Scope and Management of Quality Data and Information (20)
2.2 Competitive Comparisons and Benchmarks (30)
2.3 Analysis of Quality Data and Information (20)
3.0 Strategic Quality Planning (60 Points)
3.1 Strategic Quality Planning Process (35)
3.2 Quality Goals and Plans (25)
4.0 Human Resource Utilization (150 points)
4.1 Human Resource Management (20)
4.2 Employee Involvement (40)
4.3 Quality Education and Training (40)
4.4 Employee Recognition and Performance Measurement (25)
4.5 Employee Well-Being and Morale (25)
5.0 Quality Assurance of Products and Services (140 points)
5.1 Design and Introduction of Quality Products and Services (35)
5.2 Process Quality Control (20)
5.3 Continuous Improvement of Processes (20)
5.4 Quality Assessment (15)
5.5 Documentation (10)
5.6 Business Process and Support Service Quality (20)
5.7 Supplier Quality (20)
6.0 Quality Results (180 points)
6.1 Product and Service Quality Results (90)
6.2 Business Process, Operations, and Support Service Quality Results (50)
6.3 Supplier Quality Results (40)
7.0 Customer Satisfaction (300 points)
7.1 Determining Customer Requirements and Expectations (30)
7.2 Customer Relationship Management (50)
7.3 Customer Service Standards (20)
7.4 Commitment to Customers (15)
7.5 Complaint Resolution for Quality Improvement (25)
7.6 Determining Customer Satisfaction (20)
7.7 Customer Satisfaction Results (70)
7.8 Customer Satisfaction Comparison (70)
1,000 Total Points

Source: National Institute of Standards and Technology

productivity context, intervening between the objectives and the PMs would be whatever PIEs had been determined to be needed. Figure 14-6 also illustrates the need for a productivity system to define the terms it uses; for example, in the first objective, does the average cost include vehicle costs and travel time or only the cost of actual person-hours spent at the call's location? In addition, it should be observed that some of the objectives identified in Figure 14-6 might be considered subobjectives of objectives, even as objectives are subdivisions of goals. If an

Objective: To reduce the average cost of uniformed officers responding to domestic disturbance calls by 10 percent in fiscal 1995 as compared with fiscal 1994

Performance Measure:

$$\frac{\text{Average cost of sample FY '94 calls—Average cost of sample FY '95 calls}}{\text{Average cost of sample FY '94 calls}} \times 100 = \_\_\_\_\_\_ \%$$

Objective: To provide a minimum of 40 hours of appropriate training to not less than 80 percent of sworn personnel during fiscal 1995

Performance Measure:

$$\frac{\text{Number of officers receiving at least 40 hours training}}{\text{Number of total actual strength officers}} \times 100 = \_\_\_\_\_\_ \%$$

Objective: To maintain the accuracy of data entered into the computer system at 95 percent during fiscal 1995

Performance Measure:

$$\frac{\text{Total number of entries made in sample period without error}}{\text{Total number of entries made in sample period}} \times 100 = \_\_\_\_\_\_ \%$$

Objective: To ensure that in fiscal 1995 all cases investigated, prepared, and submitted to the judicial system by the Investigation Division are of sufficient quality that 65 percent of those cases pass the first judicial screening.

Performance Measure:

$$\frac{\text{Number of cases that pass first judicial screening}}{\text{Total number of cases submitted}} \times 100 = \_\_\_\_\_\_ \%$$

Objective: To decrease the fiscal 1995 accident-related police vehicle collision repair costs by 10 percent as compared with fiscal 1994

Performance Measure:

$$\frac{\text{Collision repair costs for FY '94—collision repair cost for FY '95}}{\text{Collision repair costs for FY '94}} \times 100 = \_\_\_\_\_\_ \%$$

Most of these illustrations are taken, with modification, from the Portland, Oregon, Police Bureau's 1980–1981 Alternative Service Level Budget Submission.

FIGURE 14-6. Illustrative objectives and performance measures.

objective is written fairly broadly, it is likely to incorporate a number of subobjectives, roughly three to five. These subobjectives may separately or in some combination deal with the three measures of service delivery: efficiency, quality, and effectiveness. However, one should not expect all objectives or subobjectives to be accompanied routinely by all three types of PMs.

Program Evaluation

As in the case of many other basic concepts, evaluation is one that everyone seems to understand and agree on until they begin to define it.[49] Then, a great deal of difference begins to emerge. Most definitions seem to look at evaluation from one or more of three perspectives:

1. As a process, which focuses on how evaluation is done, the steps and procedures involved in designing and conducting an evaluation

2. As a product, meaning the findings or judgments that are made as a result of doing an evaluation
3. In terms of its purpose, the end use of evaluation, such as for planning, policymaking, and decision making.[50]

These three perspectives can be grouped together logically to form a view of evaluation as a process, which results in a product, which has a purpose.[51] This section is not intended to provide information about how to do evaluation, on which there is ample literature, but rather about how to examine evaluation from an administrative point of view.

Types of Program Evaluation

In its broadest context, *program* refers to an activity or group of related activities undertaken by a unit of government to provide a service to the public.[52] A program may be contained in a single agency, such as the police department, or spread among several agencies, such as emergency medical services. Again in the broadest context, *program evaluation* refers to the systematic assessment of an activity or group of related activities. Under the umbrella heading of program evaluation, three different types are recognizable.[53]

1. *Process evaluation.* This type of evaluation is not concerned with the ultimate usefulness or appropriateness of the program activities but, rather, with only how well they are being performed. It looks at, for example, whether intermediate hiring quotas are being reached or if the police department's budget is being expended at the projected rate. Process evaluation goes beyond program monitoring in that, in addition to describing what is happening, it determines "why or why not" these things are happening. Although often not recognized as such, process evaluation is an ongoing activity in police departments and is part of the way in which organizations are controlled. Illustrative are the periodic receipt and analysis of budget status reports and the system of administrative inspections that are conducted to determine if established policies and procedures are being followed, to identify deviations, and to recommend any needed corrective actions.
2. *Program evaluation.* This type of evaluation asks whether or not a program has met its ultimate objectives. It is concerned with the intended consequences of a police department's various programs. Police departments, although often not recognizing it, do more program evaluation than they realize. For example, the one-group pretest versus post-test design is represented in the following way:

$$O_1 \quad X \quad O_2$$

This design consists of a first observation (O_1), where a measurement is made; a treatment (X), such as a productivity improvement program; and a second observation (O_2). The difference between the two measurements is then considered to be a function of the treatment. However, this design is methodologically simple and subject to influences other than the treatment. To use an earlier example, a reduction in reported crime may not be due to anything that the police are doing but, instead, be a function of some event that occurred between O_1 and O_2, such as rumors sweeping the community that reduce confidence in the ability of the police to deal with crime, leading to a reduction in reported crime. The issue is not what the limitations of the one-group pretest versus post-test design are; rather, it is what forms of program evaluation the police should be and are engaged in.

3. *Impact evaluation.* This type of evaluation is the most difficult and costly to perform. It goes beyond the issue of how well the program was operated and whether it met its objectives to ask the question, "In both a positive and negative sense, what differences did the operation of this program make?" Of the three types of evaluation, impact is used least by police departments. The importance of impact evaluation is established easily, however, by returning to the example of the decoy teams discussed in the productivity section. Assume that the process evaluation of that program was positive and that the program evaluation revealed that it was exceeding its stated objectives. The use of an impact evaluation could, however, provide a measure of the discontent and anger existing in the minority community. These data could then serve as a basis to eliminate or modify the program, be helpful in reducing the level of tension by giving minorities a formal means of expressing their views, and provide a priority focus for community relations efforts.

The Police Administrator and Evaluation

There is an old saw that says, "Regardless what patients do regarding their appointment with a psychiatrist, some useful meaning can be gained by the psychiatrist." If patients are early, they are anxious; if they are on time, they are compulsive; if they are late, they are resistant. In a similar vein, historically police administrators have relied, to their own advantage, on reported crime as the evaluative measure of their department's performance. If crime was falling, cuts in personnel were resisted so that the "favorable position" could be maintained; if crime was increasing, additional officers were "required" to "turn the situation around." There is a sense in which program failure is essential for many organizations in that the effective solution of the problems they address would eliminate the purpose and, therefore, the very need for the organizations.[54] Recognizing this, the appropriators of funds and others began raising the question as to whether they should continue to support organizations that benefit from their own failure.[55]

Crime is a complex social issue on which the police have a negligible or marginal impact at best; the elimination of crime and consequently the need for the police are unlikely to happen. However, city managers, directors of departments of finance and management, and city councils are increasingly disinclined to accept the self-serving manipulations of some police chiefs to justify their budgets and characterize the performance of their departments. Consequently, there is an increasing use of some sort of performance standard or MBO system as a measure of program evaluation. Impetus was given to developing more sophisticated evaluation measures from 1970 to 1975 as productivity emerged as a national issue, a movement reinforced by the requirement for an evaluation component in the numerous LEAA grants that were awarded to the police.[56]

Despite these and related pressures, some chiefs resisted using—where they existed—their planning and research units for much more than tabulating statistics for the annual report and performing crime analysis for the line bureaus. Among the reasons for this posture were the following:

1. Police administrators did not understand, or would not acknowledge, the advantages to be gained from comprehensive program evaluation.
2. The policy preferences and positions of police administrators are translated into

programs, and they were not very motivated to do anything that could discredit their stances.
3. The allocation of resources to the staff function of program evaluation was often viewed as a lower priority than the allocation of resources to line functions.
4. A distrust of evaluation existed that was coupled with a preference for relying on subjective judgments gained through years of experience.
5. Disfavorable evaluations were feared as a powerful tool for "outsiders" to criticize the administrator personally or the department, whereas favorable evaluations would not be accorded very much weight.
6. Initiating evaluation and then using the results involves a commitment to being change oriented, and sheer organizational inertia was a frequent barrier.

The resistance of some chiefs notwithstanding, by the mid-1970s there was widespread acknowledgment in more forward-thinking police departments that, whatever the merits of MBO as a decentralized, but coordinated, means of evaluation, it was not a substitute for formal program evaluation methodologies.

Making Evaluation Work

The previously cited projects have yielded considerable debate similar to other controversial studies focusing on the impact of computerization on the police, the effectiveness of women officers, and the general role or function of uniformed police. It has become apparent that with respect to evaluations, there are two types of police administrators:

1. "Trapped" administrators believe in the efficiency, rightness, or perhaps the inevitability of their programs. If evaluations demonstrate a lack of effectiveness in the programs advocated by these administrators, they are likely to dismiss the evaluations as irrelevant, too academic, or invalid, or to simply shelve and ignore them. This posture creates problems for evaluation staffs and inhibits the intelligent development and execution of police programs.
2. "Experimental" administrators are not committed to a particular program, but to the concept of improving individual programs and the police department as a whole. If new or old programs are found as experimental administrators to be lacking, they are shelved or modified in attempts to find more successful ways. Experimental police administrators might be disappointed if evaluations show ineffectiveness, but unlike the trapped administrators they are not disorganized nor do they fail to act on the results. The experimental administrators are pragmatic and more interested in finding solutions than in justifying a particular course of action.[57]

Returning to the material covered in Chapter 5 on leadership, many of the attributes of the experimental administrator can be associated with the reform-oriented and nontraditional leadership styles. Additionally, by comparing the attributes of trapped and experimental police administrators, it is seen that the administrator is the key to whether evaluation will be a useful management tool. In order to make evaluation "pay off," police administrators must:

1. Adopt a genuinely supportive stance toward evaluation. Such a stance is reflected in the quality of staff selected for assignment to the evaluation function; in the resources made

available to the evaluation effort; in according evaluation a place in the police organizational structure, which suggests its importance to the administrator; in the willingness to be involved in the evaluation process; and in ensuring a good relationship between the evaluation unit and the line bureaus.

2. Be willing to learn the key concepts in evaluation. There is a considerable amount of informative, but not overly technical, written material for police administrators, and they must avail themselves of it and other opportunities to learn, including attendance at workshops.[58]
3. Require informative evaluation. To "inform" means that the "information" being transmitted is understood. This requires not only that police administrators learn something of the key concepts and language of evaluation but also that they require evaluators to learn the key concepts and language of management.
4. Be assertive when dealing with researchers. The expectations and informational needs of administrators must be made known specifically to the evaluators. When evaluators present concepts or procedures with which administrators are unfamiliar, they should require an explanation in terms that can be understood by the administrators. Nothing should be accepted "on faith."
5. Remember George Bernard Shaw's observation that every profession has its "conspiracy against the laity." Evaluation reports are often laced with dozens of complex statistical tables that are easily understood by evaluators but not by administrators. Evaluation, however, is a logical and not a statistical process. Complex statistical notations should be eliminated altogether, except perhaps as appendices, and the results stated in straightforward language. Reports that do not do so should be returned to the evaluators for redrafting.
6. Be able to describe the evaluation procedures and results to other nonresearchers, such as city managers, budget analysts, civic club members, and city councils or county commissions. Although administrators may have gained some sophistication in evaluation, they must guard against the use of "research jargon." Their purpose is not to display mastery but to win supporters for police programs.
7. Lose no chance internally or externally to praise the evaluation staff, their products, and their contributions.
8. Personally adopt and foster an environment supportive of experimentation.
9. Understand that much evaluative research is flawed and can be criticized but that the defects are seldom so great that all the information is useless. This means that police administrators must be willing to accept a certain element of risk in making policy and program decisions.[59]

The Insider–Outsider Evaluator Question

Police administrators have several options with respect to who conducts the evaluation of experimental programs: (1) the police units conducting the activity may also perform the evaluation; (2) the evaluation may be done by the police department's planning and research unit; (3) another department of government, such as finance and management, may take responsibility; or (4) a contract may be executed with a research institute, a consultant, or some other related independent provider of services. These various possibilities raise certain questions, such as "Is it appropriate for the police unit conducting an experimental program to evaluate itself?" Whereas the need to separate those who are carrying out an experimental program and those who evaluate it is apparent, the question of how

FIGURE 14-7. Santa Fe, New Mexico policeman talks to senior citizens about "Neighborhood Watch" safety program. [Photo by Mimi Forsyth, Monkmeyer Press Photo Service.]

much separation there should be gives rise to the "insider–outsider" evaluator question.

Among the views that should be considered when a police administrator is trying to decide whether to use the department's planning and research unit or an outsider to evaluate an experimental program are

1. The public and public officials may have more confidence in an autonomous outsider.
2. The outsider may have greater competence.
3. Outsiders may be perceived as being more objective.
4. An outsider may have a prestigious name that can be an asset in promoting the experimental program.
5. Outsiders may "sweeten" the results obtained by the program to gain favor and possible future business.
6. "Insiders" have greater knowledge of the operation of their particular department.
7. Insiders may see more practical ramifications to the results of the program than outsiders.
8. Insiders may suppress negative findings out of departmental loyalty or fear of personal and professional consequences to them.
9. Insiders may be more responsive to the legitimate directives of police administrators.
10. Insiders may have a "special axe to grind" and withhold or distort findings that reflect favorably on the program or on particular individuals.[60]

When such factors as cost, departmental staff capacity, and the availability of competent outsiders are added, the most advantageous way in which to proceed may still not be clear. In such matters, the identification of the issues is often a great deal easier to come by than is the answer. In other cases, there may be no decision to make other than who the external evaluator will be, because some grants are conditioned by the requirement of—and money is provided for—an independent evaluator who is external to the unit of government being used.

Summary

Productivity has two fundamental components: effectiveness and efficiency. Stated simply, effectiveness means that the police reached the objective they sought to achieve. In considering efficiency the question is, "How much of our resources were required to achieve this objective?" More recently, considerations of productivity have also included the dimension of quality. The creation in 1987 of the Malcolm Baldrige Award has given enhanced visibility and impetus to total quality management, or TQM. Successful productivity management programs are generally found to have met a basic checklist of conditions that include such variables as some analytical capacity and the ability to overcome any resistance.

Productivity programs may be—in terms of implementation—centralized, decentralized, or nondirective. Regardless of the implementation strategy, productivity programs require doing more with current resources, or maintaining or increasing output in the face of decreased resources. Total performance management is a comprehensive approach to productivity improvement that combines the features of industrial engineering and behavior science techniques. A natural adjunct to a productivity improvement program is an MBO (management by objectives) system. The measurement of productivity raises difficult challenges such as establishing some relationship between what the police do and the change in resulting conditions, and how to ensure that an increase in productivity does not have the unintended consequences of reducing the quality of service.

The evaluation of police programs is an absolute necessity. Three types of evaluation can be employed: (1) process, (2) program, and (3) impact. The police routinely, often without recognizing it, do process evaluation, and performance measures are often nothing more than a variant on some type of program evaluation design such as the one-group pretest versus post-test comparison. Police administrators can and must take certain steps to ensure useful evaluations. The issue of inside versus outside program evaluators raises a number of questions that must be considered in light of the specifics of the situation involved, as does the issue of "insiders versus outsiders" in organizational change, discussed in the next chapter.

Discussion Questions

1. For what three reasons should all of us be concerned about productivity?
2. What four ways can police productivity be imposed, according to the National Commission on Productivity?
3. Define the words *efficiency* and *effectiveness.*
4. What is the Malcolm Baldrige Award? Is it having any effect on organizations?
5. You have been assigned the responsibility for developing a productivity improvement effort. What sequential steps will you follow in developing and implementing it?
6. What is TPM? What is its relationship to Quality Management?

7. Discuss the key elements of MBO.
8. Describe the difference between a QC and a self-directed work team.
9. What are the three major obstacles in implementing an MBO program?
10. Describe the three types of program evaluation.
11. Distinguish between trapped and experimental administrators.
12. What measures must a police manager take to make program evaluation meaningful?
13. What issues arise when attempting to decide whether to use the police department's internal unit or an outsider to evaluate an experimental program?

Notes

1. Much of this section has been modified from Carol H. Weiss, "Evaluation Research in the Political Context," in *Handbook of Evaluation Research,* vol. 1, ed. E. Struening and M. Guttentag (Beverly Hills, Calif.: Sage, 1975), pp. 13–25.
2. U.S. Civil Service Commission, *Ten Questions and Answers on Productivity* (Washington, D.C.: U.S. Civil Service Commission, 1977), p. 3. Also see Daniel A. Blumberg, "Higher Productivity: The Only Lasting Answer to Spiraling Inflation," *Financial Planning Today,* 4 (July 1980), pp. 159–65.
3. Mark E. Keane, "Why Productivity Improvement?" in *Productivity Improvement Handbook for State and Local Government,* ed. George J. Washnis (New York: John Wiley & Sons, 1980), p. 10.
4. Ibid., p. 10.
5. William C. Cunningham, John J. Strauchs, and Clifford Van Meter, *Private Security: Patterns and Trends* (Washington, D.C.: National Institute of Justice, Research in Brief), Aug. 1991, p. 1.
6. *Personnel News,* 40 (September 1974), p. 1.
7. National Commission on Productivity, *Report of the Advisory Group on Productivity in Law Enforcement on Opportunities for Improving Productivity in Police Services* (Washington, D.C.: U.S. Government Printing Office, 1973).
8. Keane, "Why Productivity Improvement?," p. 8.
9. Frederick O'R. Hayes, "Leadership and Politics of the Productivity Process," in *Productivity Handbook for State and Local Government,* pp. 19–23, with some changes and additions.
10. Edgar G. Crane, Jr., "Productivity in State Government," *Productivity Improvement Handbook,* p. 55.
11. International City Management Association (ICMA), *Service Delivery in the 90s: Alternative Approaches for Local Governments* (Washington, D.C.: International City Management Association, 1989), p. 52.
12. Ibid., p. 62.
13. Ibid., p. 88.
14. Ibid., pp. 158–59.
15. This account is taken from David N. Ammons, *Model Programs in Local Governments: A Report on Site Visits* (Athens: Carl Vinson Institute of Government, University of Georgia, 1991), pp. 15–16.
16. "SRI Model Gets High Marks as a Solvability Predictor," *Law Enforcement News,* 6:3 (1980), pp. 1, 6.
17. "First Audit of Philly Police in 14 Years Shows Abuse of Sick Leave, Areas to Trim," *Crime Control Digest,* 14:11 (1980), pp. 4–5.
18. Ammons, *Model Programs,* p. 3.
19. ICMA, *Service Delivery in the 90s,* p. 69.

20. Keane, "Why Productivity Improvement?" pp. 9–10.
21. The discussion of these three strategies is drawn from Frederick O'R. Hayes, "Implementation Strategies to Improve Productivity," in *Productivity Improvement Handbook,* pp. 26–27.
22. For information on San Diego's Financial Management Department's work on police productivity, see *Productivity Improvement Program: Police Investigations Bureau* (San Diego, Calif.: Financial Management Department, 1979).
23. Hayes, "Implementation Strategies," p. 26.
24. National Center for Productivity and Quality of Working Life, *Total Performance Management: Some Pointers for Action* (Washington, D.C.: U.S. Government Printing Office, 1978), p. 2.
25. Ibid., p. 3.
26. "Performance Management Yields Morale Benefits," *Public Administration Times,* 2:7 (1979), p. 10; Sherry A. Suttles, "TPM: Long Beach Tackler Performance," *Western City* (February 1979), p. 1.
27. See Budget and Evaluation Department, *Police Field Patrol Activities: An Evaluation* (Charlotte, N.C.: Budget and Evaluation Department, August 6, 1976).
28. Other terms that describe an MBO-type system include "cohesive management system" and "priority program planning system," both of which were used by the New York City Police Department in 1974 and 1975.
29. Drucker is commonly credited with coining the term and probably should be accorded recognition more for publicizing than for innovating the involved operations.
30. Peter Drucker, *Management: Tasks, Responsibilities, Practices* (New York: Harper & Row, 1973, p. 438). Also see George S. Odiorne, *Management by Objectives* (New York: Pittman, 1965), pp. 55–56. For an excellent synopsis on the empirical evidence on MBO, see Mark L. McConkie, "Classifying and Reviewing the Empirical Work on MBO: Some Implications," *Group Organization Studies,* 4:4 (1979), pp. 461–75.
31. Charles D. Hale, *Fundamentals of Police Administration* (Boston: Holbrook, 1977), p. 333.
32. Rodney H. Brady, "MBO Goes to Work in the Public Sector," *Harvard Business Review,* 51 (March–April 1973), pp. 65–74.
33. Ronald G. Lynch, *The Police Manager,* 2nd ed. (Boston: Holbrook, 1978), p. 154.
34. "Zone Awareness Program" (Ocala, Fla.: Ocala Police Department), mimeographed, p. 10.
35. C. D. Stein, "Objective Management Systems: Two to Five Years After Implementation," *Personnel Journal,* 54 (October 1975), p. 525.
36. Ibid., p. 525.
37. McConkie, "Classifying and Reviewing," pp. 467–71.
38. Ibid., pp. 471–72.
39. Howard S. Gitlow and Shelly J. Gitlow, *The Deming Guide to Quality and Competitive Position* (Englewood Cliffs, N.J.: Prentice-Hall, 1987), p. 7.
40. Ibid., p. 7.
41. Ibid., p. 7.
42. Ibid., p. 7.
43. Ibid., p. 7.
44. *Productivity,* 12:7 (July 1991), p. 10.
45. David A. Garvin, "How the Baldrige Award Really Works," *Harvard Business Review,* (November–December 1991), p. 81.
46. Ibid., p. 81.
47. Ibid., pp. 82, 84.
48. Ibid., p. 84.
49. Jack Reynolds, *Management-Oriented Corrections Evaluation Guidelines* (Washington, D.C.: U.S. Government Printing Office, 1979), p. 3.

50. Ibid., p. 3.
51. Ibid., p. 3.
52. Harry P. Hatry, Richard E. Winnie, and Donald M. Fisk, *Practical Program Evaluation for State and Local Government Officials* (Washington, D.C.: Urban Institute, 1973), p. 8.
53. U.S. Department of Housing and Urban Development, *A Guide for Local Evaluation* (Washington, D.C.: U.S. Government Printing Office, 1976), pp. 1–2, with minor modification.
54. James F. Rooney, "Organizational Success Through Program Failure: Skid Row Rescue Missions," *Social Forces,* 58 (March 1980), p. 904.
55. Ibid., p. 904.
56. This is not to suggest that the evaluations were done very well. In a sample for 42 completed evaluations done in four states between 1973 and 1975, one study found serious deficiencies. For example, only 19 percent of the projects adequately set forth the evaluation research design and methodology used, and 55 percent did not present the projects' hypotheses or relate them to the projects' intended goals and objectives. See U.S. Comptroller General, *Evaluation Needs of Crime Control Planners, Decision-Makers, and Policy Makers* (Washington, D.C.: U.S. Government Printing Office, 1978), p. 49. Illustrative of other evidence regarding the need for improved police program evaluation was a major 1974 study funded by the National Science Foundation, which was generally critical of what existed. See Saul I. Gass and John M. Dawson, *An Evaluation of Policy Related Research: Reviews and Critical Discussions of Policy Related Research in the Field of Police Protection* (Bethesda, Md.: Mathematica, 1974).
57. For a description of the trapped and experimental administrators, see Donald T. Campbell, "Reforms as Experiments," in *Quasi-Experimental Approaches,* ed. James A. Caporaso and Leslie L. Rose, Jr. (Evanston, Ill.: Northwestern University Press, 1973), p. 224; Stuart Adams, *Evaluative Research in Corrections* (Washington, D.C.: U.S. Government Printing Office, 1975), pp. 19–20.
58. For example, see Lawrence P. Clark, *Designs for Evaluating Social Programs* (Croton-on-Hudson, N.Y.: Policy Studies Associates, 1979); Guy D. Boston, *Techniques for Project Evaluation* (Washington, D.C.: U.S. Government Printing Office, 1977); Weiss, *Evaluation Research,* pp. 6–9, on the differences and similarities between evaluation and other types of research; Douglas K. Stewart, *Evaluation for Criminal Justice Agencies: Problem-Oriented Discussion* (Washington, D.C.: U.S. Government Printing Office, 1978); National Criminal Justice Reference Service, *How Well Does It Work: Review of Criminal Justice Evaluation* (Washington, D.C.: U.S. Government Printing Office, 1978); Donald T. Campbell and Julian C. Stanley, *Experimental and Quasi-Experimental Designs for Research* (Chicago: Rand McNally, 1963).
59. These points are restatements, with some additions, of material found in Michael P. Kirby, *The Role of the Administrator in Evaluation* (Washington, D.C.: Pretrial Services Resource Center, 1979), pp. 11–12.
60. On these points, see Carol H. Weiss, *Evaluation Research* (Englewood Cliffs, N.J.: Prentice-Hall, 1972) pp. 20–21; Charles S. Bullock III and Harrell R. Rodgers, Jr., "Impediments to Policy Evaluation: Perceptual Distortion and Agency Loyalty," *Social Science Quarterly,* 57 (December 1976–1977), pp. 506–19.

15 Organizational Change and the Future

There is nothing more difficult to take in hand, more perilous to conduct, or more uncertain of success, than to lead in the introduction of a new order of things.
MACHIAVELLI, THE PRINCE

Introduction

In the dynamic society surrounding law enforcement agencies today, the question of whether change will occur is not relevant. Instead, the issue is how police executives cope with the barrages of changes that confront daily those who attempt to keep their agencies viable, current, and responsive to community needs. Although change is a fact of life, police executives cannot be content to let change occur as it will. They must be able to develop strategies to plan, direct, and control change.[1]

To be effective in the change process, police executives must have more than good diagnostic skills. Once they have analyzed the demands of their environment, they must be able to adapt their leadership style to fit the demands and develop the means to change some or all of the other situational variables.[2]

This chapter has been organized to facilitate an examination of some of the critical dimensions of planned change. A police executive contemplating the implementation of change, especially on a large scale, will increase the likelihood of success if certain fundamental principles, discussed here, are followed.

Why Change Occurs

The initiation of large-scale organizational change in American law enforcement tends to follow similar patterns. Often, a new police chief will be appointed either from within or from outside of the law enforcement agency as a prelude to a planned, large-scale reorganization desired by a city manager, mayor, or some other influential person or groups in the community. Before the appointment of the police chief, it is likely that one or more of the following events has transpired, giving impetus to the plan changes:

1. A new mayor is elected or a new city manager appointed who wants to replace the current chief with a new chief of his or her own choice.
2. The police department has been judged to be generally deficient in its crime-fighting capabilities by a study, the local media (see Box 15-1), by interest groups within the community, or by a commission of citizens created specifically to make a careful assessment of the capabilities of the department.
3. Police minority relations are at an all-time low, in part because of repeated alleged acts and misconduct by the police in dealing with members of the minority community.
4. The police department has a poor public image because of its low recruiting standards and failure to provide adequate training for its officers.
5. The previous police chief and or other high-ranking police officials have been indicted for accepting payoffs relating to gambling, prostitution, liquor violations, or narcotics violations.
6. The former police chief, who was an elderly person and who had served for many years as the bulwark of traditionalism, recently retired.
7. The ranks of the police department and the community agree that morale among the police officers is dangerously low, as reflected in an abnormally high attrition rate, excessive use of sick time, incidence of injury to prisoners, high numbers of resisted arrests, increasing citizen complaints of officer misconduct, poor supervisory ratings, and generally poor performance of personnel throughout the organization.
8. The chief's personal style has become an issue in the community. In the extreme situation, part of the platform of a mayoral candidate is the pledge that if elected to office his or her first action will be to fire the chief of police. In one instance where this happened, the highly visible chief in a medium-size department went to the scene of an incident where an armed man had barricaded himself in. When the man suddenly ran from the house firing at the officers, the chief and others shot the man dead. This incident raised questions as to how the chief could rule on the use of force if he had taken part in it and why he had taken part in it when there were so many well-armed officers present. On the heels of other highly publicized incidents involving this chief, this spelled the end for him, and the mayor forced the chief out shortly after taking office.
9. The life cycle of the department may dictate the need for a change in leadership. The previous reform- or change-oriented chief may have pursued his or her programs so rapidly or insensitively that the department is in open revolt. In such instances the new chief is told to stabilize the situation and to "lay off" making substantial changes, unless they involve dismantling some of those instituted by the prior chief. Too, a lack of any change may cause a chief to be toppled. In one community there was widespread support for a bike patrol on the beach and in the downtown area. The chief opposed the idea and dragged his heels, creating barriers for implementation at every opportunity. This single issue led to his replacement, and ultimately a new chief activated the bike patrol very rapidly with great success.

The newly appointed police chief has likely been given a mandate to move forward with speed to rectify the difficulties in the department and is, more often than not, excited and enthusiastic about the prospect of implementing ideas formulated through years of professional growth and experience. It may appear that

BOX 15-1

Police Rip Globe Series; Flynn Picks Panel

By John Ellement and Michael Rezendes *Globe Staff*

Mayor Flynn unveiled a special panel to examine the management of the Boston police yesterday just an hour after the department's command staff said that The Boston Globe was malicious and demeaning last month in the series of stories about the police.

At City Hall, Flynn named attorney James D. St. Clair, who represented former President Nixon during the Watergate scandal, to head the eight-member panel that will begin by reviewing the Globe series, a police rebuttal to the series, and two other studies of Police Department operations.

Noting that polls are finding an increasingly volatile climate on Boston's streets, Flynn appeared reluctant to embrace either the conclusions of the Globe series or a detailed police response released yesterday. He said his primary objective in appointing the panel is to shore up confidence in the Police Department.

"I've said in the past on a number of occasions that there are always ways to improve the effectiveness and efficiency of all city departments," Flynn said. "It is in the best interests of us all to take the necessary steps to restore full confidence in our police department."

Flynn said the St. Clair committee was "primarily a response to the Globe series." St. Clair also served as special prosecutor in 1982 when then-Boston Police Commissioner Leo J. Sullivan resigned due to charges of corruption.

At police headquarters yesterday, Commissioner Francis M. Roache and Superintendent Joseph V. Saia Jr. sharply criticized the Globe and reporter Todd Locy for reporting and publishing a four-part series in April under the collective title of "Boston Police: Bungling the Basics."

The series examined 736 murder, robbery and armed robbery cases from 1988, 1989, and part of 1990 and found that poor investigative work had contributed to a low arrest rate, a high degree of plea bargaining and lighter sentences for those who pleaded guilty to crimes.

One part of the series drew on Uniform Crime Reports, which are statistics collected by the FBI, to conclude that the department fared poorly in solving major crimes when compared with departments in 29 other major cities.

Roache said the series forced him to criticize one media outlet for the first time in his "six years, seven months and three days" as commissioner.

"While there will always be room for continued improvement, I will not stand by and see the members of the department unfairly treated by unfounded criticism," Roache said.

In a statement released yesterday afternoon, Globe Editor John S. Driscoll defended the series. He said the Globe "fully reviewed" its findings with the department's command staff before the series was published.

"We find nothing in the response provided yesterday by the Boston police to contradict our belief that our reporting was anything but a thorough, accurate and fair assessment of the problems and challenges facing the Boston Police Department," Driscoll said.

For the police "to issue a lengthy rebuttal at this time is rewriting history," he said.

Roache left it to Saia to deliver specific criticisms, which he often did while pointedly attacking Locy. Saia said the section of the series that examined plea bargaining practices "demeaned the Boston Police Department."

He also charged that individual criminal cases the Globe used as representations of larger department problems failed to support the thesis of the series. "Every case was inaccurate or misleading," he said.

The Globe had attempted before publishing the series to review the cases with Superintendent Paul F. Evans, who said during an interview that he was not prepared to discuss specific cases.

BOX 15-1 (cont.)

In its 15-page rebuttal entitled "Setting the Record Straight," the department criticized the series in the following areas:

■ The use of Uniform Crime Reports as a barometer of the department's performance. In the first-day story, the Globe published a chart and a companion 1,200-word sidebar comparing Boston's success in solving major crimes with 29 other major cities.

Based on its analysis of the data from 1985 to 1989, the Globe found the department ranked 28th in solving major crimes—murder, aggravated assault, burglary, larceny and motor theft.

But Saia said the Globe reported "inaccurate, incomplete, UCR data" even though the department had provided the newspaper with data it had never supplied to the FBI. He also said the Globe was warned by the FBI not to use the data to make comparisons.

Driscoll's statement said the assertion that the newspaper was warned by the FBI against using the statistics was "untrue."

The newspaper had reported in the series that when the additional statistics provided by the Police Department were added to the Uniform Crime Reports, the department's overall performance in solving major crime improved to 16th among the 30 cities.

Saia read from a letter by J. Wilson Harper to Driscoll. Harper, the head of the FBI's crime reports section, said the Globe made "speculative and invalid conclusions" based on the statistics.

However, in a telephone interview last week, Harper acknowledged he had not read the entire series and that he wrote his letter after his staff had reviewed only part of the first day of publication. However, he insisted the Globe erred in using the Uniform Crime Report numbers as it did.

In addition to those statistics, the newspaper made wide use of a review of 738 prosecutions brought in the Suffolk County courts.

■ The Globe reported that weak investigation of major crimes by police often led Suffolk District Attorney Newman A. Flanagan's office to plea bargain cases allowing defendants to receive lesser prison sentences.

The Globe reviewed 98 first-degree murder charges brought during the 2½-year period examined and found that 54 of the cases were bargained down to manslaughter, which carries a far less severe prison sentence. In the story, Flanagan was quoted as saying that "The cards are dealt us by the law enforcement agencies . . ."

But Saia said the Globe erred in blaming the police for plea bargaining, which he said is done by prosecutors and defense lawyers.

Driscoll said the Globe's examination focused on plea bargaining in murder cases and that the review by the Globe raised legitimate questions about the quality of investigative work done by the department.

■ The Globe reported that the department lacked the skills and equipment needed to develop forensic evidence and that contributed to acquittals or dismissals of major criminal cases.

In one case cited by the newspaper, the chairwoman of a jury said the panel voted against convicting a man charged with murder because the prosecution failed to provide physical evidence linking the defendant to the crime.

But Saia said no physical evidence, such as a gun or spent bullet shells, was found at the scene in that case. He also said the defendant was not arrested until two years after the crime was committed, rendering a gunpowder test useless.

The department also said its forensic team examined more than 3,700 pieces of evidence in 1990 and that it spends $2.5 million for the 53-person staff, which includes 34 officers.

Driscoll said the response from the department did not address the key question of how the police used those individuals. "Their defense of investigative and technical capabilities . . . address quantity and not issues of quality."

He did not say whether the review of police management would be completed before the Sept. 24 preliminary mayoral election. He said reports may be released periodically.

BOX 15-1 (cont.)

The St. Clair panel is the third commission Flynn has named to examine the department in the last two years.

Other members of the panel are: Peter Madden, special adviser to State Street Bank; Norman Rosenblatt, dean of the College of Criminal Justice at Northeastern University; Barbara Salisbury, administrative dean at Harvard University's Kennedy School of Government; William Coughlin, executive director of the Artery Business Committee; Apolo Catala, head of the Massachusetts Association of Hispanic Attorneys; John Driscoll Jr., head of the Boston Bar Association; and Daniel Dennis, managing partner of Daniel Dennis & Co.

Source: Boston Globe, May 8, 1991.

the chief is operating from a position of considerable strength and need not be too concerned with those who might try to thwart the change process. However, such an assumption could be very risky. Although there will be factions in the department and in the community that fully support the change effort, there will be powerful factions within the police department and within the community that will attempt to block any changes that appear to endanger their interests.

No chief can afford to overlook the impact that each type of group can have on the planned changes. In developing a strategy for change, certain elements must be built into the plan to identify and enhance the cooperation and support received by a group that desires change and to enhance the possibility of winning over the groups that may be neutral or only moderately opposed to the planned changes. Also, the plan must have a number of highly developed strategies to counteract or neutralize those individuals or groups that will make every possible effort to reduce the success of the planned changes.

The risks involved in implementing large-scale changes are considerable, but, surprisingly, many police executives either fail to take notice of these risks in their preplanning strategies or grossly underestimate them. This phenomenon has too often resulted in both goals and objectives falling far below expectations or failing to come to fruition at all. In other instances, the change effort encounters so many difficulties and obstacles, and so much opposition that the chief is eventually forced to resign or is fired.

The Change Agent

Throughout this chapter, the term *change agent* will be used to describe an individual or group from within or outside the police department whose role involves the stimulation, guidance, and stabilization of change. Within the context of planned organizational change, the role of the change agent is to assist in resolving organizational problems.[3] The specific person or group playing the role of change agent will vary. In some cases, the change agent will be the police chief or some person within the agency designated by the chief to assume responsibility for implementing change. In other cases, the change agent may be some individual or group of consultants hired from outside the organization to conduct a comprehensive study of all or certain segments of the organization and to produce a comprehensive report with specific recommendations for enhancing the operation of the police department. On occasion, outside consultants will also assist in implementing the recommended changes.

When a police agency does seek outside assistance, it frequently contracts with a private firm whose members possess high levels of experience, skills, techniques, and knowledge about how to improve the level of performance of law enforcement agencies.[4] Such consultants often possess academic credentials at the graduate level and considerable prior experience as law enforcement practitioners, administrators, or educators.

Framework for Change Agent's Role

The change agent's organization model determines what information is collected for diagnosing an organization's problems.[5] The most important things examined during diagnosis also tend to be the things that are worked on most often to create change in the organization. The relationship between diagnosis and change approaches has been proposed by Noel Tichy,[6] who studied 91 types of change agents. Figure 15-1 is a model designed by Tichy for studying the role of change agents.

There are five basic components to the model, all of which interact with one another. First are the *background characteristics* of the change agent. These typically include the agent's educational training, income, religion, age, sex, relationships to clients, and so forth. Second is the *value component*. This is the agent's evaluative orientation toward change, such as attitudes toward important social changes, political orientation (liberal, moderate, conservative), social-change goals (increased range of individual freedom and choice, improved satisfaction of members, equalization of power between organization members, and so forth),

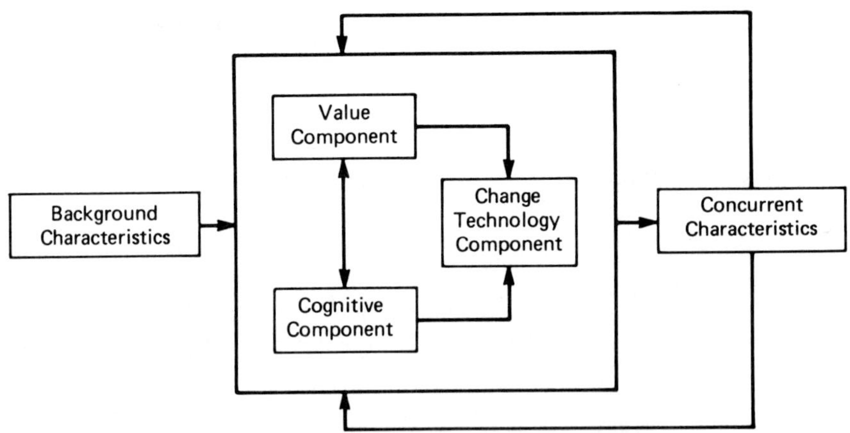

FIGURE 15-1. Framework for change agent's role. [From Noel M. Tichy, "Agents of Planned Social Change: Congruence of Values, Cognitions, and Actions," *Administrative Science Quarterly,* 19 (1974), p. 165.]

and the goals that he or she feels change agents should have. This component represents behavior expected of a change agent. The third basic component is the agent's *cognitive component*—concepts about means of affecting change. The fourth is the agent's *technology component*. This refers to the tools and skills the change agent has used to effect social change. To make use of his or her knowledge (cognitive component) and to act on his or her other values (value component), each change agent has a set of techniques, such as sensitivity training, operations research, survey feedback, and team development that can be applied to a situation. Finally, the *concurrent characteristics* refer to the actual behavior of the change agent. The relationship among the five components of the model assumes that stress exists in the change agent when the value component and concurrent characteristics or the cognitive component and actions are not in agreement with each other.

Types of Change Agents

Based on consistent differences in the patterns of these five components of the model in Figure 15-1, four different types of change agents have been identified. These are (1) people change technology (PCT), (2) analysis from the top (AFT), (3) organization development (OD), and (4) outside pressure (OP). Because the OP type (e.g., Ralph Nader, Betty Furness) is rarely used by managers to bring about changes, only the three other types of change agents will be discussed.

People Change Technology (PCT)

Change agents who use PCT work to achieve change in the ways in which employees behave. These agents are concerned with improving motivation, job satisfaction, and productivity. One PCT agent described her role as being

> to help individuals and organizations focus on goals, obstacles that stand in the way of goal attainment, individual motivation patterns and requirements of the task, organizational goal attainment, emphasis on individual, and organizational self-development.

Tactics favored by the PCT change agent are role clarification, change in reward structure, change in decision-making structure, technological innovation, job training, and team development. Use of these tactics should lead to job enrichment, behavioral modification, need achievement training, management by objectives, and the like. The basic assumption of PCT change agents is that, if individuals change their behaviors, the organization, too, will change, especially if enough (or the right) individuals in the organization change.

Data gathered by Tichy indicate that PCT change agents usually hold academic positions with doctorates and range in age from 35 to 40. Their political orientation is liberal, and they express a moderate degree of social criticism. The linkage between political orientation and values indicates that their primary value is to improve system efficiency, increase output, and equalize the power and responsibility with the organization.

Analysis From the Top (AFT)

Change agents who use the AFT approach rely primarily on the operations research model. These agents work on improving decision making and maintaining and controlling employee performance. One AFT agent described his role as being

> to work with groups concerned with problems of design and operation of system, to aid in resolving their problems. Normally, the work involves technological remodeling and analysis.

Tactics favored by the AFT change agent are changes in the decision-making structure, role clarification, technological innovation, job training, and changes in the reward structure. Use of these tactics should lead to changes in the decision-making structure of the organization, technological innovations, and job training in areas such as computerized information processing systems and development of new tasks. AFT change agents assume that, if the organization's impersonal technical and structural processes are changed, the organization's efficiency will increase.

AFT change agents are likely to be older than PCT change agents (ranging in age from 40 to 50), are not associated with an academic institution, and do not have a doctorate. They are moderates in political orientation and are not critical of society.

Organization Development (OD)

Change agents who use OD techniques work to improve the organization's problem-solving capabilities by helping people learn to help themselves. This involves assisting members of the organization to work out their interpersonal problems and communications, conflicts of interest, career plans, and the like. Organization development change agents rely on team development, role clarification, confrontation meetings, change in decision-making structure, and sensitivity training to achieve their goals. A basic goal of the OD change agent is to increase democratic participation in decision making by all members. In this way, the organization can develop problem-solving mechanisms so that key executives can work with each other.

The background characteristics of the OD change agents include a median age of 40 to 50 and primarily Protestant religious beliefs, with a high proportion holding advanced academic degrees. Their political affiliation tends to be liberal to moderate. They do not advocate radical changes in organizations to achieve their objectives.

Basic Qualifications of Change Agents

The selection of change agents and or leaders for teams is a crucial element in the process of organizing for change. The capabilities and performances of the team leader have often been the critical factors in the success or failure of many programs of planned change.[7]

There are a number of qualities and qualifications that the change agent must possess to be successful, the single most important one being technical competence in the specific tasks of the change project. Dangers exist in bringing in persons from an unrelated or marginally related field.[8]

Another factor related to technological qualifications is the ability of the agent to develop solutions and recommendations for change that can be applied realistically within the framework of the skills and resources available within the organization. Thus, an understanding of the way in which police departments operate and are organized is essential to persons involved as change agents.

Planning skill is another important capability a change agent should possess. Particularly important is the ability to plan for the unexpected by allowing flexibility through alternative or contingency planning and the maintenance of reserved resources. Although the change agent should be able to function well in a crisis, efforts should be made to avoid crisis management as a characteristic mode of management.[9]

The ability of the change agent to work well with members of the organization who are not involved directly to the change plan is crucial. Indifference to persons and organizations outside the change team can create major problems.[10] Empathy with members of the larger organization can sensitize change agents to delicate areas in which extra caution is necessary; if an intervention in those areas is under consideration, it will increase the likelihood that change will be well received.[11]

Change Agent Errors

Just as change agents can enhance the effectiveness of change programs by developing certain traits, they can limit the effectiveness of the program or team by committing certain errors. One serious error that a change agent can make is to become tied prematurely to a particular set of strategies and tactics. This problem is more severe when the commitment is made publicly and is compounded when individuals critical of the change process were not consulted before making the public statement about a change that will directly affect them or their areas of responsibility.

Planning for change should involve the identification of relevant groups affected by the change team's efforts, their interdependencies, and their need to feel involved in goal-setting and strategy design processes. Typically, the importance of cooperation is overlooked because a change agent may underestimate the value of the contribution that members of the organization can make in helping to structure and focus the change process. Sometimes the change agent is under the mistaken assumption that members of the police department do not want to participate actively in various aspects of change programs directed at them and/or they are unable to provide useful information through participation.[12]

Another error is inadequate planning for the initiation of the change process. The sudden creation of a formal commission, the quick institutionalization of a change team, the hasty hiring of a consultant, or some other rapid implementation of a formal change program may create immediate resistance. The change agent must not overlook the informal system, a problem likely to occur when the change agent is overly confident of his or her perception of the changes needed.

The change agent must also consider the roles played by individuals and groups outside the police department. This may include members of the local political community, citizen action groups, unions, and even spouses. The change agent must consider how the advocated change will affect these groups and what their perceived needs for change are, as well as what their expectations may be regarding the behavior of the change team and the consequences of the intervention.[13]

Change agents sometimes fail to identify or even recognize influential individuals or groups that may be willing to provide support for the change effort. Such persons or groups may be developed into strong advocates of the change if provided with adequate information in the appropriate manner. If an influential person or group is favorably disposed toward innovation, reinforcing information should be provided routinely, particularly if the advocated change is controversial and resisting groups are trying to alter the influential party's feelings and beliefs.[14]

Internal Versus External Change Agents

When a decision has been made to reorganize a police department, one of the most important concerns is determining who will undertake the task. Should personnel from within the organization be selected? Should outside consultants be employed? Should a combination of sources from both groups be pooled in a cooperative effort? A number of useful guidelines can help to answer these questions.

Internal Change Agent: Pros and Cons

Certain positive features associated with selecting a change agent from within an agency make this an attractive alternative. The internal change agent will have valuable insights into both the formal and the informal organization and will be aware of the potential sources of support for certain types of change as well as from which segments of the organization resistance is most likely to come. Such knowledge can prove quite useful in developing strategies for planned change. Because the change agent is a part of the organization, he or she will likely share certain values and attitudes with members of the organization with whom the agent will be working that will facilitate communications in all directions.[15] If the internal change agent has a reputation within the organization as a competent professional with unquestioned integrity, this, too, will enhance the change effort.

One drawback to using an internal agent is the possible lack of acceptance of the person by the organization as an "expert." Colleagues who remember when the change agent was "just a wet-behind-the-ears rookie" or who have personal jealousies or animosities directed at the agent will make it difficult for the internal agent to establish credibility. Some important questions may be raised when internal change agents are used. For example, what possible personal or professional gain does the individual hope to acquire? Is the change agent overly concerned about the ways in which the changes will negatively impact on agency personnel that he or she knows personally? Does the internal change agent have some preconceived notions about the direction the change should take, thus limiting the range of viable alternatives that might be considered realistically?

Finally, individuals from within the agency acting as change agents will possibly have to be relieved of their present responsibilities, thus shifting the burden of their work to someone else. The extent to which this will impact on the organization depends on the amount of time involved in the change process, the amount of work to be shifted to subordinates, and the abilities of the subordinates.

External Change Agent: Pros and Cons

The externally selected change agent has from the outset certain important advantages over the internal change agent. Individuals from outside the organization employed as change agents are selected because of their knowledge, experience, and professional reputation. Thus, when entering the police agency, they already enjoy considerable credibility as "experts" in their field. This legitimacy tends to bestow on the change agent a high degree of respect and deference. This, in turn, facilitates cooperation from key members of the organization, at least in the early stages of the change process. The external change agent has, more often than not, a broad range of experience with planned change and can complete the task both effectively and expeditiously.

One of the important disadvantages faced by the external change agent is the absence of knowledge to identify with accuracy the major forces within the organization that can help or hinder the change process. For example, is a group of police officers within the agency fearful of certain changes and are these officers prepared to mobilize support in the community to resist such changes? Is the police union potentially supportive of some changes but opposed to others? Who are the informal leaders in the organization? Is the reorganization effort just a ploy by a city manager, mayor, or city council to embarrass the police chief into a forced resignation or dismissal?

Because external change agents rarely have to actually implement the changes they recommend, have no long-term commitment to any single agency, and may be unfamiliar with the factors outside their designated realm, they may make recommendations that are difficult or impossible for the agency to implement. It is not unheard of for a consulting firm to make some recommendations that cannot be implemented legally, especially if the consulting firm representatives are not familiar with the state laws, local ordinances, civil service regulations, or state-mandated police officers' standards. Other recommendations may be impossible to implement because of serious budgetary limitations related to a community's tax base or because agency personnel lack the experience or expertise to do so.

It could be argued that it is precisely because the external change agent does not have to be concerned about certain extraneous elements that the external change agent can make a fair and objective assessment. However, the external change agent, to be of maximum benefit to the police department, must be able to assist in improving the organization within the framework of its ability to change. There are those who would suggest that the closer someone comes to actually having to be responsible for implementing change, the less idealistic and more realistic that person becomes. Thus, some police departments actually require as a part of the contractual agreement with a consulting firm that the representatives of the firm remain with the agency for some reasonable period of time to implement the more difficult changes.

Locating External Change Agents

The police chief or city manager contemplating the possibility of seeking outside assistance to provide an in-depth study of the police department is frequently faced with the dilemma of locating and then selecting the individual or firm that will provide this service. Although there is no central directory containing the names of individuals or firms providing this type of service, contact with the State Criminal Justice Planning Agency is a good starting point, as this agency often underwrites grants to fund such projects. The state planning agency will be able to provide information relating to police departments that have used consulting services and the names of firms providing such services. Police agencies using a particular consultant can then be contacted and their assessments of the consultants solicited. The consultant's final report to each police department should, if possible, be reviewed. Contacts should be made with the firm providing the service and a request made for a list of their former law enforcement clients. These departments, too, may be contacted and an assessment of the firm requested. After these contacts are made, a reasonably accurate picture of the quality and cost of services a consulting firm can deliver will emerge.

Methods of Organizational Change

Organizational change can be initiated in numerous ways, but approaches can be grouped into two broad categories: (1) those that focus on changing the individuals working in the organization and (2) those that focus on changing specific organizational structures. Effective programs of organizational change usually involve the simultaneous use of both approaches and a variety of intervention techniques.[16]

Changing Individuals

In general, future behavior is predicted by past behavior; that is, circumstances being equal, people will go on doing what they have always done. If an individual has been compliant, that person will continue to be compliant; if self-seeking, the individual will continue to be self-seeking. This picture is neither cynical nor pessimistic, it is simply realistic.[17]

Of course, individuals can change their attitudes and their behaviors. Certain conditions typically are associated with such change, and, by knowing what these conditions are, a person can increase the likelihood of affecting a desired change in behavior.[18] Lewin[19] suggests that change occurs in three phases: (1) the unfreezing of an old pattern of relationships, (2) the changing to a new pattern through change induced by a change agent, and (3) the refreezing of a new pattern of relationships.

Unfreezing

A key motivator in the unfreezing phase of change is a feeling of discomfort with old behavior.[20] If a person feels no discomfort, no logic or force or threats will motivate the person to change. Certain techniques, however, can be employed to induce an individual to change.

The first step in a change program is to "unfreeze" or rearrange the environmental context that supports the individual's current behavior. Some of the mechanisms that might be used include removing reinforcement for the current behavior, inducing guilt or anxiety about the current behavior, making the individual feel more secure about change by reducing threats or barriers to change, removing the individual from the environment that supports current behavior, or physically changing the environment in which the person is behaving.

The following is an example provided by Reitz:

> a program designed to change a manager's leadership style could provide him with feedback that his current style is ineffective and inappropriate. It could involve changing his office location to make him more or less accessible to his employees. It could remove him from the situation and provide a "safe" climate in which he can experiment with alternative behaviors by sending him to a training program conducted away from the premises.[21]

Changing to a New Behavior Pattern

After the unfreezing of old behaviors, individuals seeking change must try an alternative behavior and determine its consequences.[22] There are two important elements necessary in this phase of the process. First, the change agent must be sensitive to the fact that experiences of success with a new behavior are so important that the behavior in the beginning should take place under controlled conditions. A change agent who wishes to establish problem-solving behavior, for example, should have individuals or groups participate in simulations or experiential learning situations that have predictable outcomes. By knowing that an exercise will demonstrate successful utilization of problem-solving skills, the change agent reinforces the knowledge, attitudes, and skills necessary to deal with more complicated, nonexperiential situations; success in an initially controlled training environment begets success in real-life situations.

Second, if an individual's regular environment is antithetical to the successful trial of a new behavior, the individual should, if it is practical, be removed from the existing environment until the new behavior is learned.[23]

Refreezing

Refreezing is the stabilization and integration of the changed behavior. It is accomplished most effectively by providing the individual with a social and physical environment that will support the changed behavior.[24]

One authority has identified a number of subprocesses for the refreezing phase:

> If the new attitude has been internalized while being learned, this has automatically facilitated refreezing because it has been fitted naturally to the individual's personality. If it has been learned through identification, it will persist only so long as the target relationship with the original influence model persists unless new surrogated models are found or social support and reinforcement is obtained for expression of the new attitude.[25]

Changing Organizational Structures and Systems

An alternative to attempting to change people who make up an organization is to change the structure of the organization itself or the systems and practices that guide its activities. Sometimes, the organizational change simply amounts to somebody pushing boxes around in an organizational chart, with nobody else knowing or caring much about it. In other instances, this approach to change can profoundly influence the patterns of activity that take place within organization boundaries, with important consequences for the long-term growth and health of the organization.[26]

In law enforcement agencies, changing organizational structures is not an unusual way in which to implement change. Naturally, the extent of any reorganization will be affected by a number of variables, including the availability of funds to create new positions; the support for change from the city manager, mayor, or other local officials; and the reasons for the reorganization in the first place.

A reorganization can be a very powerful tool for implementing change. It can be used to designate new priorities in the areas of enforcement, improve the quality and quantity of police service, or improve police minority relations.

Radical Versus Gradual Change

The objectives for any police chief contemplating change should be to do so in a manner that offers the greatest possibility of success, does not result in a reduction of the quality or quantity of service to the public, does not polarize the organization into warring factions, and does not result in the police chief being forced to resign or being fired. To achieve these goals, gradual changes are sometimes more effective than radical changes.

Conventional wisdom about change states that the way in which to change an organization is to bring in a new top executive, give the individual his or her head (and maybe a hatchet as well), and let the individual make the changes that he or she deems necessary. And, in fact, organizations (especially in times of crises) often use exactly that strategy to achieve change—sometimes unwittingly, sometimes not. What the conventional wisdom overlooks are the long-term consequences of unilateral, top-down change. It may often be the case, for example, that short-term problems are solved quickly, radically, and dramatically by executive action but that the "human problems" of the organization, which very well might have been causal in generating the short-term problem in the first place, are substantially worsened in the process.[27]

The problem with radical and unilateral change, then, is the possibility of creating a negative balance of the human resources of the organization, which can result in a severe backlash in the organization over the long term. The complementary problem for changes that are made very gradually and participatively is that, after years of meetings and planning sessions and endless questions, nothing very striking or interesting has actually happened in the organization, and in a spirit of resignation, organization members slowly abandoned their change activities and settled back into their old ways.[28]

Finding an appropriate pace for change to take place—neither too quickly and radically nor too slowly and gradually—is one of the most critical problems of planned organizational change. Trying to set the right pace often poses special problems for organizational consultants—especially those who are based outside the organization. On the one hand, if they suggest or induce change that moves too quickly or radically vis-à-vis a given organization, they risk losing their association with the organization and, therefore, any chance they might have to influence the effectiveness of the organization.[29] As one experienced observer notes in a list of "rules of thumb for consultants," the first task of the consultant is to "stay alive," one means of which is to take the level and pace of one's consulting activities in reasonable congruence with the current state of the organization.[30] Similarly, others counsel consultants explicitly about being careful not to introduce interventions that are too intense or deep for the change organization to handle.[31,32]

The other side of the issue is, of course, that the consultant or change expert can be "seduced" by the existing values in the client system and ultimately find himself or herself co-opted by that system or even implicitly colluding with it in activities that restrict genuine change. For this reason, it is often useful for consultants to work in groups, so that they can maintain an independent point of reference that contrasts to that of the client organization. By this means, additional insurance is provided that the consultant will be more likely to adhere to professional values concerning change recommendations.

In summary, the tension between the readiness of (and capabilities of) the organization for change and the values and aspirations of the professional change consultant is a continuing problem for which no easy resolutions are available or appropriate. Somehow, the consultant must introduce material to the organization that is sufficiently discrepant from the status quo to provide impetus for change—but not so deviant as to be rejected out of hand by the organizational managers. That, as most practicing organizational interventionists know very well indeed, is a fine line to walk.[33]

As suggested earlier in this chapter, a police chief is sometimes appointed specifically to effect reform and thus may be under pressure to make changes (sometimes radical ones) quickly. Drastic changes, whether implemented or only planned, however, make the chief vulnerable to attack.

Resistance to Change

Over and above the general predisposition against change in the social climate of most organizations, specific proposals for change are almost certain to encounter rigorous obstacles in the form of organized resistance from individuals and groups both within and external to the organization.[34] Rather than being attributable to personality characteristics, the causes of resistance may be rooted in a past experience or past reinforcement history of those facing change. Lower level members of organizations in particular might have had direct experience that has led them to associate change with negative consequences.[35] If, for example, the last organizational change undertaken by a police department resulted in patrol officers having to work more evening hours to accommodate increased calls for service and increased crimes, and if this change disrupted the officers' off-duty personal lives and also failed to provide salary or other compensating differentials, then some officers will very likely be predisposed to believe that change, although perhaps beneficial to the organization, is not beneficial to them (see Box 15-2).

Most people who perceive, rightly or wrongly, that a proposed change will adversely affect them can usually be counted on to resist the change as mightily as they can.[36] In any case, most members of an organization have a vested interest in the status quo. They have adapted to the organization's environment and know

BOX 15-2

Cops, Chief at Odds over Reorganization

Department Shuffle Requires Demotions

By Martine Costello *Register Staff*

New Haven—Police Chief Nicholas Pastore has a vision to rebuild and revolutionize the Police Department by chipping away at the highest ranks and putting his money into cops on the street.

Pastore says his plan to swap 10 majors and commanders for 24 sergeants, lieutenants and captains would carve out new career paths and streamline his department.

But some union leaders say the plan to demote the department's top brass to the rank of captain—with pay cuts up to $4,000—is a humiliating blow. They argue Pastore could accomplish the same thing by leaving jobs unfilled as the veteran officers retire.

Two of the officers affected are considering legal action if Pastore tries to enact his plan. A third said the changes are making him consider more seriously whether to retire.

Pastore, disappointed with how the department operated under the direction of the majors and commanders, said the reorganization is long overdue.

"Just because they have the highest rank, it doesn't mean they're the best qualified," Pastore said. "It's not to demean those who've been here, it's to change the direction."

Pastore said the changes are a necessary part of his community-based police program, which relies heavily on patrol officers and middle-level supervisors on the streets.

The traditional police hierarchy, where high-ranking officers sit behind desks and give orders, becomes expendable.

The move would redirect more than $600,000 in salaries from the 10 commanders and majors and three other high-paying positions into the middle ranks, Pastore said.

He would add one assistant chief to replace the current staff of three majors and four commanders. The other three posts are vacant. Commanders are union members; majors have petitioned to be in the union.

"Simply stated, I don't need 10 positions at that level. I need one," Pastore said. "We were too top-heavy."

The proposed changes are part of a string of bold initiatives that have rattled the department since Pastore became chief in February 1990.

But the reorganization plan, which Pastore offered as part of his 1991–92 budget proposal, is the first suggested wholesale change of his administration.

"I have a different way of doing things," Pastore said. "What chief wouldn't make changes?"

While the changes offer unprecedented career opportunities for the rank-and-file, some union members are upset they would come on the heels of demotions.

"It is great they are opening up the Police Department, but it's not the way we wanted it, on the demotions of others," said Sgt. Louis Cavalier, the union president. The union will file a grievance when Pastore enacts his plan, he said.

Several officers interviewed were hesitant to comment publicly on the controversial plan, but said they were encouraged by the possibility of more career advancement.

Pastore denies his proposal causes any humiliation to the majors and commanders, since the officers will still carry the third-highest rank in the department.

Cavalier said Pastore could as easily put the commanders and majors on the street, and take advantage of their supervisory experience.

But Pastore said there are other officers in the department better qualified for the job, who will be able to embrace the department's new philosophy of community-based policing.

"I came here with the obvious conclusion that things haven't worked very well in the past," Pastore said.

BOX 15-2 (cont.)

"There are well-qualified sergeants and lieutenants and captains who will be involved in running the department," he said.

Pastore's plan is now before the Board of Finance.

Cmdr. James O'Neill, one of the officers facing a demotion, said Pastore has not included commanders and majors in decision-making, and has not taken advantage of their years of experience.

Pastore assigned O'Neill to be in charge of the department's garage.

"I think most of us would have been glad to try to work with him (Pastore) and would have made some serious contributions to his plan," O'Neill said.

He is planning to sue the Police Department and Pastore if the chief enacts his plan.

"He has no trust in us," O'Neill said.

Maj. Thomas P. Muller, who said he went from supervising 300 officers to about six after Pastore took the helm, said the chief is trying to get back at him because of a court case he pursued in the early 1980s that led to Pastore's demotion.

Pastore in 1982 was demoted from director—a position higher than a captain, which was created by former Chief Edward U. Marrone—to his previous rank of lieutenant.

It was one of 17 demotions that came after Muller and Cmdr. Leonard L. Gallo won a court case on the grounds that any rank from sergeant up should require a civil service exam.

"He (Pastore) views me as a guy who de-seated him from a promotion," Muller said. Muller also is considering legal action, he said.

Pastore adamantly denies Muller's allegation, but acknowledges he is dissatisfied with how the department was running over the past seven or eight years while Muller was in charge of operations.

"I'm looking for improvements. I'm trying to draw some lessons from the past," Pastore said.

He said he appreciates officers who work hard—no matter what their rank is.

"The way to ingratiate yourself to the chief is to work hard," Pastore said. "That's what I recognize: competency. And I don't care what rank it is."

Maj. Walter Connor said the plan is making him more seriously consider retiring, though he will wait to see whether Pastore actually enacts it.

"It's the chief's plan, I'm not included in it. It's something he perceives he wants to do," Connor said. "Every chief does it. And somebody always falls by the wayside. And in this case, it's me."

Efforts to reach Gallo, who works the midnight shift, were unsuccessful.

The other commanders and majors declined to comment or were unavailable.

Muller argues the 10 high-ranking posts are an essential part of the chain of command.

"A chain of command is essential in any organization, especially a paramilitary organization," Muller said. "Picture the Army or the Navy with no chain of command."

But Pastore said that a military approach is precisely what he's trying to change. "I don't want an Army or a Navy—that's what I want to get away from," he said. "I'm not into the military . . . concept."

The department would go from 45 to 57 sergeants, 12 to 18 lieutenants and 6 to 12 captains, Pastore said. He also would hire about 20 more patrol officers to raise department ranks to 425.

The net increase on the street would be 35 officers, Pastore said.

"It will give new recruits more opportunities," he said.

Civilians would fill two other high-paying positions of superintendent, which carry no rank, at a lower salary. A third high-paying position of chief investigator would be eliminated.

Superintendent of maintenance Ronald Lankton would go back to his previous rank of patrol officer, with a pay cut of about $9,000 a year. The other superintendent and chief investigator posts are vacant.

Source: New Haven Register (Connecticut), March 24, 1991.

how to cope with it; they have developed behavioral patterns that enable them to obtain satisfactory outcomes and to avoid unpleasant outcomes. Change means uncertainty; there is no assurance that a new scheme will be as satisfactory as the old one, even though the old one might have been flawed.[37] Thus, people sometimes resist innovations even when they cannot identify any results harmful to them simply because they grow anxious about consequences they cannot foresee that might injure their interests.

Occasionally, resistance to change is presented by individuals or groups even when it is known that their interests will not be compromised. These people may be obstructionists in the hope of exerting concessions or other advantages in return for their support or acquiescence.[38]

Some individuals may resist change because of the heavy psychic costs associated with change. According to Kaufman,

> The advocates of change naturally concentrate so heavily on the benefits to be derived from their recommendations that they sometimes lose sight of the personal effort and agony of people who have to accommodate the new patterns. Over and above advantages lost and penalties inflicted by opponents, beyond the humiliation of becoming a raw novice at a new trade after having been a master craftsman at an old one, and in addition to the expensive retraining and tooling, is the deep crisis caused by the need to suppress ancient prejudices, to put aside the comfort of the familiar, to relinquish the security of what one knows well. Put aside the social and financial incentives to stand fast: after those are excluded, it is still hard for most of us to alter our ways. The psychic costs of change can be very high, and therefore go into the balance sheet on the side of keeping things as they are. In addition, the psychic costs of pressing for an innovation are substantial. If the change is adopted and fails, the embarrassment and loss of stature and influence can be chilling to contemplate; the costs and benefits of the old ways are at least known. If battle is joined on behalf of change the proponents are likely to be opposed from all sides. Some critics will accuse the advocates of being too timid in the struggle, while others will portray the campaign as evidence of hunger for power; some will complain of the innovator's readiness to experiment wildly at the expense of those they serve, while others ridicule them for unwillingness to try something more daring than marginal adjustments. To win allies the proposed reforms must be amended and weakened and compromised until the expenditure of efforts seems hardly worthwhile. Meanwhile the drama of the struggle often arouses expectations among the beneficiaries out of all proportion to the realities of the improvement; instead of winning the applause and gratitude, the innovators often reap denunciation from those they thought they were helping as well as from their adversaries in the controversy. And anyone with experience in such a contest is aware that he or she may end up with obligations to supporters whose purposes he or she does not share and with fleeting credit but lasting enmities. On balance, then, the members or contributors to an organization are presented with much stronger incentives to act warily than daringly. Precedent serves as a valuable guide because it clearly defines the safe path; in a mine field wise men step exactly in the footprints of predecessors who have successfully traversed the hazardous area.
>
> The collective benefits of stability and the calculated opposition to change thus weigh heavily against innovation even when the dangers of inflexibility mount.[39]

Finally, it is often overlooked that police departments have a number of features that make them quite resistant to change. For example, the behavioral expectations for police officers, especially of those in medium-size and larger agencies, are usually specified in great detail and are divided very specifically. Every component must perform according to a set pattern, or there is a danger that the entire operation will be disrupted. Officers are therefore screened and groomed for the positions they will occupy; they are socialized and fitted into the ongoing system.

Officers are chosen not only for skills and aptitudes but also for attitudes and personality traits. Their values and perceptions are then shaped by the organization. Officers learn their training manual, master the methods of their department, and forge understandings with their fellow officers until the whole system becomes second nature to them. Directives, orders, commands, instructions, inspections, reports, and all other means of organizational control, however irksome they might once have been, are gradually accepted as each officer's own premise of thought and action, until compliance with them is no longer reluctant or indifferent obedience, but an expression of personal preference and will.[40] Change after such indoctrination can be traumatic indeed.

Success and Failure Patterns in a Planned Change

A great deal can sometimes be learned by studying the success and failure patterns of organizations that have undertaken planned change. To discover whether there were certain dimensions of organizational change that might stand out against the background of characteristics unique to one organization, Greiner and others conducted a survey of eighteen studies of organizational change. Their findings were as follows:

> Specifically, we were looking for the existence of dominant patterns of similarity and/or difference running across all of these studies. As we went along, relevant information was written down and compared with the other studies in regard to (a) the conditions leading up to an attempted change, (b) the manner in which the change was introduced, (c) the critical blocks and/or facilitators encountered during implementation, and (d) the more lasting results which appeared over a period of time.
>
> The survey of findings shows some intriguing similarities and differences between those studies reporting "successful" change patterns and those disclosing "less successful" changes—i.e., failure to achieve the desired results. The successful changes generally appear as those which:
>
> Spread throughout the organization to include and affect many people.
>
> Produce positive changes in line and staff attitudes.
>
> Prompt people to behave more effectively in solving problems and in relating to others.
>
> Result in improved organization performance.
>
> Significantly, the less successful changes fall short of all of these dimensions.

Success Patterns

Using the category breakdown just cited as the baseline for "success," the survey reveals some very distinct patterns in the evolution of change. In all, eight major patterns are identifiable in five studies reporting successful change, and six other success studies show quite similar characteristics, although the information contained in each is somewhat less complete. Consider

1. The organization, and especially top management, is under considerable external and internal pressure for improvement long before an explicit organization change is

contemplated. Performance and/or morale are low. Top management seems to be groping for a solution to its problems.

2. A new administrator, known for the ability to introduce improvements, enters the organization, either as the official head of the organization, or as a consultant who deals directly with the head of the organization.
3. An initial act of the new person is to encourage a reexamination of past practices and current problems within the organization.
4. The head of the organization and all immediate subordinates assume a direct and highly involved role in conducting this reexamination.
5. The new person, with top management support, engages several levels of the organization in collaborative, fact-finding, problem-solving discussions to identify and diagnose current organization problems.
6. The new person provides others with new ideas and methods for developing solutions to problems, again at many levels of the organization.
7. The solutions and decisions are developed, tested, and found creditable for solving problems on a small scale before an attempt is made to widen the scope of change to larger problems and the entire organization.
8. The change effort spreads with each success experience, and as management support grows, it is gradually absorbed permanently into the organization's way of life.

The likely significance of these similarities becomes more apparent when we consider the patterns found in the less successful organization changes. Let us briefly make this contrast before speculating further about why the successful changes seem to unfold as they do.

Failure Forms

Apart from their common "failure" to achieve the desired results, the most striking overall characteristic of seven less successful change studies is a singular lack of consistency—not just between studies, but within studies. Where each of the successful changes follows a similar and highly consistent route of one step building on another, the less successful changes are much less orderly.

There are three interesting patterns of inconsistency:

1. The less successful changes begin from a variety of starting points. This is in contrast to the successful changes, which begin from a common point—i.e., strong pressure both externally and internally. Only one less successful change, for example, began with outside pressure on the organization; another originated with the hiring of a consultant; and a third started with the presence of internal pressure, but without outside pressure.
2. Another pattern of inconsistency is found in the sequence of change steps. In the successful change patterns, we observe some degree of logical consistency between steps, as each seems to make possible the next. But in the less successful changes, there are wide and seemingly illogical gaps in sequence. One study, for instance, described a big jump from the reaction to outside pressure to the installation of an unskilled newcomer who immediately attempted large-scale changes. In another case, the company lacked the presence of a newcomer to provide new methods and ideas to the organization. A third failed to achieve the cooperation and involvement of top management. And a fourth missed the step of obtaining early successes while experimenting with new change methods.

3. A final pattern of inconsistency is evident in the major approaches used to introduce change. In the successful cases, it seems fairly clear that *shared* approaches are used—i.e., authority figures seek the participation of subordinates in joint decision making. In the less successful attempts, however, the approaches used lie closer to the extreme ends of the power distribution continuum. Thus, in five less successful change studies, a *unilateral* approach (decree, replacement, structural) was used, while in two other studies a *delegated* approach (data discussion, T-group) was applied. None of the less successful change studies reported the use of a *shared* approach.[41]

Police Futures Research

Historically there has been great interest in forecasting the future, and there are a number of intriguing examples. Condorcet (1743–1794), a French philosopher, foresaw that all European colonies in the New World would become independent; social insurance would be provided for the aged, widowed, and orphans; education would become public and universal; women would receive equality with men; advances in medicine would eliminate infectious and hereditary diseases; and scientific knowledge would expand and improve technology.[42] Malthus (1766–1834) believed that unchecked human population growth would outstrip food supply, the result of which would be famine, disease, and poverty.[43] A Harvard sociologist, Sorokin (1889–1968), identified the basic characteristics and long-range trends of Western civilization, which he characterized as increasingly this-worldly, secular, materialistic, pragmatic, utilitarian, and hedonistic.[44] In 1967, Daniel Bell foretold of a "post-industrial society" to be created by a decline in "blue-collar" workers and a rise in "white-collar" employees.[45] What Condorcet, Malthus, Sorokin, and Bell share is having accurately forecast future events.

Despite the existence of a body of literature that one way or another reflects concern about social, technological, and economic change, the police have traditionally remained remarkably uninterested in futures research. There are a number of possible reasons for this disinterest: (1) a time horizon, for many law enforcement agencies, no longer than the next budget cycle; (2) a "hot stove" approach to managing, meaning that "we'll handle today's crisis now and worry about tomorrow when it gets here"; and (3) a lack of any perceived need to consider what conditions may be like in 10 to 20 years.

In 1973, the California Commission on Peace Officer Standards and Training (POST) completed Project Star, a study of the impact of social trends on crime and criminal justice, the first major comprehensive futures study involving the police in this country.[46] After momentary excitement about Project Star, interest in law enforcement circles about futures research rapidly waned, although there was, in one form or another, intermittent interest among police scholars as evidenced by occasional publications.[47] Since roughly 1980, there has been growing interest among law enforcement executives in futures research. To no small degree this interest has been fueled by the growing imperative to make sense out of a turbulent and sometimes chaotic environment and the highly visible work of William Tafoya (see Box 15-3), who developed the nation's first graduate- and doctoral-level futures courses geared specifically to law enforcement. Echoing this development are several state agencies, such as California's POST, which now include a futures research component in their training curricula for law enforcement ex-

BOX 15-3

FBI Futurologist Foresees an Era of Lawlessness

By Dan Freedman
Washington Bureau, Scripps-Howard

WASHINGTON—When behavioral scientist William Tafoya gazes into the future, he sees America in 1999 wracked by civil disturbances that go way beyond the riots that engulfed many U.S. cities in the 1960s.

Relying on what he describes as a scientifically valid survey method of forecasting trends, Tafoya rolls out the following scenario:

- By the end of the decade, crime will overwhelm law enforcement officials, reducing them to little more than taking preliminary reports.
- By 2005, economic deprivation—the gap between the haves and the have-nots—will be the leading factor in even more crimes.
- By 2035, private security companies will take over the majority of police functions, and law enforcement agencies won't be able to reassert themselves until 2050.

Tafoya's projections would be hardly surprising or controversial were he a pop futurologist riding the TV talk-show circuit or a Democratic pollster forecasting life in America after successive Republican administrations.

But Tafoya is an FBI agent and an instructor in behavioral sciences at the bureau's academy in Quantico, Va.

What's more, the FBI's traditionally conservative and guarded hierarchy not only tolerates Tafoya, but it also is accepting many of his conclusions and disseminating them publicly.

"We've provided our top level officials on several occasions with background and briefing materials," said John Henry Campbell, chief of the behavioral sciences unit, in which Tafoya works. FBI executives have referred to Tafoya's work in talks on what law enforcement faces into the next century.

Campbell added that Tafoya made several projections five years ago for 1990 that have come to pass, including increases in bias-related crime and in computer crime.

Nevertheless, Tafoya, 46, cultivates something of a rebel image, the smiling, white-haired and shirt-sleeved gadfly in a house of blue-suited, poker-faced agents.

"I've always thought it's OK in organizations to have rebels, to have people who think in unconventional terms that challenge the status quo," Tafoya said. "I've been fortunate to have superiors who also think it's OK."

In addition to teaching at Quantico, Tafoya is on loan to the Capitol Hill agency, the Congressional Clearinghouse on the Future, helping lawmakers chart the potential for future social unrest.

Working at a cramped desk Tafoya is anxious to convince skeptics that his work is neither sorcery nor sophistry.

"Some people look at it as crystal-ball gazing and it's going to be a while before it's accepted," he said. But he insists: "My research is grounded in science."

Author Alvin Toffler, whose 1970 best-seller "Futureshock" turned futurology into a pop culture staple, says of Tafoya: "He's a very serious guy with a very broad view of what law enforcement is all about, that it's not just cops and robbers. The world is getting to be a much more messy place. Tafoya's projection of turbulence makes a lot of sense."

Toffler added that the FBI's acceptance of Tafoya represents a "recognition that the world has changed, that the old ways, the old definitions aren't going to hold."

Source: San Antonio Light (Texas), April 29, 1990.

ecutives. In 1991, the Society of Police Futurists International (PFI) was organized, another indicator of the broadening prominence of police futures research.

The Futures Research Unit

Futures research is a discipline devoted to addressing potential changes in our society.[48] The use of the plural *futures* reflects a basic premise of this type of research: the future is not predetermined or predictable and can be influenced by individual and organizational choices.[49] Through the use of environmental scanning—analytically examining the right data with the appropriate forecasting methods—the futures research unit produces forecasts and policy options that allow law enforcement administrators to improve the odds of a preferable future from among the many existing alternatives.[50] One of the forecasting methods frequently used is the Delphi Technique. The Delphi was developed by the RAND Corporation in the mid-1950s and involves pooling the individual judgments of panel members selected on the basis of their expertise. Forecasts developed with a properly conducted Delphi Technique have had 85 percent or higher accuracy.[51] Unlike a prediction, which describes an event ahead of time and does not allow for error or probability, a forecast is a probabilistic statement of what may occur at some future time.

Establishing a Futures Research Unit

A futures research unit (FRU) is not redundant if a law enforcement agency already has a planning unit because their missions are different and a great deal of planning, such as structuring a grievance procedure, is conducted without any real forecasting.[52] Moreover, futures research is also distinguishable from planning in that it assesses trends, countertrends, shifting values, and other indicators and attempts to provide an understanding of what they mean, where a department is going, and what should be done. In terms of organizational structure arrangements, the FRU can be placed within an existing planning component or made a separate unit altogether. The dynamics within individual agencies will dictate which approach to use.

To a substantial degree, any success the FRU has is indicative of access to and support from the agency's chief executive, reporting arrangements, and the quality of personnel selected for or by it. The FRU staff must be capable of using a variety of forecasting methodologies; be computer literate and statistically proficient due to the many types of data to be analyzed; and be self-starters who are imaginative, flexible and inquisitive, relishing challenges.[53] To the greatest possible extent FRU personnel should come from the ranks of the police department, as opposed to being civilian experts, giving them one less issue with which to deal while on the road to gaining credibility.

As a minimum, all FRU members should have their own personal computers, have access to internal and external data bases, and be provided with appropriate forecasting and data base management software. Ideally, all computers would be networked to facilitate electronic mail (e-mail) and the sharing of information.[54]

Selecting the right leader for a FRU is a crucial decision. Essentially the FRU is an organizationally sponsored center for creativity, and creative people can be difficult to manage. Tradition-bound leaders who require inflexible working hours, strict observance of rules and regulations, and reverence for their positions may find the situation unsatisfactory and possibly hamper performance. Moreover, creative individuals do not perform best in traditional, hierarchical organizational structures. Companies that manage creativity and innovation will work at fostering and nurturing these attributes.[55] The best choice for police departments may be to locate the FRU away from headquarters at sites where the FRU can develop its own work culture. In this way the culture of the larger organization remains intact while an environment is designed that maximizes productivity and impact.

Although FRUs are still evolving, often within the umbrella of a planning or planning and research unit, there are already a number of law enforcement agencies with futures capabilities, including the police departments in Madison, Wisconsin; Seattle, Washington; Portland, Oregon; Alexandria, Virginia; Tulsa, Oklahoma; Santa Ana, California; and the San Diego County, California, Sheriff's Office. In such jurisdictions law enforcement executives know that futures research can help them understand how the conditions, events, and trends of today will impact on what may happen tomorrow. With such information, new programs can be initiated, personnel trained, equipment procured, the organizational structure modified, policies and procedures developed, and other measures instituted in thoughtful anticipation of, rather than in a crisis reaction to, the shifting environment.

Summary

The objectives of any police executive contemplating change should be to do so in a manner that offers the greatest possibility of success, does not result in a reduction of the quality and quantity of service to the public, and does not polarize the organization and the community into warring factions. In this chapter, we have examined some of the major components of the change process to accomplish these objectives.

We started by examining some of the most common reasons for initiating change within a law enforcement agency. They tend to evolve from issues related to the crime fighting capabilities of a police department, poor police–minority relations, poor public image, corruption, retirement of a long-tenured police chief, and poor morale.

The person or persons who actually assume the role of change agent will vary. In some cases, it may be the police chief or some other person designated by the chief from within the organization. In other cases, the change agent may be some individual or group of consultants hired from outside the organization.

To better understand planned organization change, Tichy has created a model that is comprised of five major components: (1) the background characteristics of the change agent, such as education, income, religion, and service; (2) the value component, which includes the change agent's attitude toward important social changes, political orientation, and own special goals; (3) the agent's cognitive component, that is, concepts about means of effecting change; (4) the agent's technological component, such as the tools and skills used to effect change; and (5) the concurrent characteristics, that is, the actual behavior of the change agent. Based on this model, four types of change agents have been identified: (1) people change technology (PCT), which works to achieve change in the way employees behave; (2) analysis from the top (AFT), which relies primarily on the operations research model and works on improving decision making and maintaining and controlling employee performance; (3) organization development (OD), which works to improve the organization problem-solving capabilities by helping people to learn to help themselves and involves assisting members of the organization to work out their interpersonal problems and communication, conflict of interest, and career plans; and (4) outside pressure (OP), which is rarely used by managers to bring about change.

Change agents must possess a number of basic qualifications: technical competence, ability to develop realistic solutions, planning skills, and the ability to work well with members of the organization.

The most common change agent errors are becoming tied prematurely to a particular set of strategies and tactics; failing to identify relevant groups affected by the change team's efforts; failing to recognize the relevant groups' interdependence; failing to fulfill their need to be involved in goal setting and the strategy design process; planning inadequately for the initiation of the change process; failing to plan adequately for the initiation of the change process; and failing to consider the roles played by individuals and groups outside the police department.

Once the decision is made to implement change within the law enforcement agency, consideration must be given to using internal change agents, external change agents, or a combination of both types. Internal change agents have the benefit of valuable insights into both the formal and informal organization as well as the potential sources of support or opposition. However, internal change agents sometimes experience difficulty in establishing credibility. Further, their motives may be questioned, and, if the change process is a lengthy one, someone will have to assume their regular duties.

External change agents frequently have the advantage of considerable knowledge and experience, which provides assurance that the planned change will be completed effectively and expeditiously. In addition, they also enjoy considerable credibility as experts in the field. The one important disadvantage faced by external change agents is their lack of knowledge to identify accurately the major forces within the organization that can help or hinder the change process.

The actual methods by which organizational change can be initiated may vary, but generally they can be grouped into two broad categories: (1) those that focus on changing the individuals working within the organization and (2) those that focus on changing specific organizational structures.

One major problem faced in implementing change is that of determining a pace that is neither too quick or radical nor too slow and gradual. Setting the right pace often poses special problems, especially for outside consultants. On the one hand, if outside consultants suggest or introduce change too quickly or radically, they risk losing their association and therefore any chance they might have had to influence the effectiveness of the organization; on the other hand, the consultant or change agent can be "seduced" by existing values in the client system and ultimately find himself or herself co-opted by the system or even implicitly colluding with it in activities that restrict genuine change.

An understanding of why people resist change is absolutely essential to the successful accomplishment of a change process. Over and above the predisposition against change in the social climate of most organizations, specific proposals for change are almost certain to encounter rigorous obstacles in the form of organized resistance from individuals and groups both within and external to the organization. This resistance by individuals may be attributable to certain personality characteristics, but it is more likely to be rooted in some unfavorable past experience with the change process. Most people who perceive that change will affect them adversely can be counted on to resist it. Also, police departments frequently have a number of features that make them quite resistant to change. These include highly defined behavioral expectations that are uniform in the training and supervision of officers and a host of rules, regulations, policies, and procedures that are viewed as the organizational gospel. Thus, the officers' values and perceptions may be shaped by all these factors for many years, and sudden change can be perceived as threatening.

Although there are no guarantees that any particular pattern of planned change will succeed or fail, a great deal can be learned from the experience of organizations that have undergone change. Greiner and others conducted a survey of eighteen organizations that had undertaken planned change and noted the following success and failure patterns. Success patterns were spread throughout the organization to include and affect many people, produce positive changes in line and staff attitudes, prompt people to behave more effectively in solving problems, and result in improved organization performance. The failure patterns included a lack of consistency in the planned change, wide and seemingly illogical gaps in the sequence of planned change, failure to achieve cooperation and involvement of top management, and failure to use a shared approach.

The likelihood of implementing successful organizational change will be enhanced considerably if certain aspects of the change process are handled appropriately. Failure to consider many of the factors discussed will likely result in both the goals and the objectives of police executives falling far below their expectations or perhaps failing to come to fruition at all. In addition, a poorly planned and poorly timed change effort could result in the mobilization of certain powerful groups within the police agency and in the community joining together to force the police executive's resignation or dismissal.

There are numerous examples of the historical interest in forecasting the future, including the work of Condorcet, Malthus, Sorokin, and Bell. However, the police have traditionally been uninterested in futures research for a variety of reasons. The first major comprehensive futures study of U.S. police was Project Star, completed in 1974 by the California Commission on Peace Officer Standards and Training. Despite the ensuing publicity, there was little interest in police circles in futures research until the 1980s, in large measure due to the nationally visible work of Tafoya. One indication of the growing interest in futures is the creation in 1991 of the Society of Police Futures International. Futures research is a discipline devoted to addressing potential changes in our society and uses various forecasting tools, including the Delphi Technique. By knowing how the events and conditions of today may manifest themselves in the future, law enforcement administrators have greater lead time to make adaptive changes. Recognizing the contributions that can be made, some agencies such as those in Seattle, Washington; Tulsa, Oklahoma; Madison, Wisconsin; and Alexandria, Virginia, have created futures research capabilities in their police departments. When law enforcement executives contemplate creating a futures research unit, a number of factors must be considered, such as placement in the organizational structure, personnel, equipment, leadership, and physical location.

Discussion Questions

1. What types of events frequently give impetus to planned change within a police department?
2. Briefly discuss the four different types of change agents that have been identified.
3. What are the basic qualifications of a change agent?
4. What are some of the most serious change agent errors?
5. What are the pros and cons of internal change agents?
6. What are the pros and cons of external change agents?
7. According to Lewin, change in individuals occurs in three phases. What are they?
8. If changing the organizational structure of a law enforcement agency is determined to be the means employed to change the organization, certain factors must be considered. What are they?
9. Successful change patterns in organizations generally achieve certain results. What are they?

10. There are a number of interrelating patterns of inconsistency among those organizations experiencing less successful changes. What are they?
11. Define and discuss futures research.
12. What factors should be considered when an FRU is created?

Notes

1. P. Hersey and K. H. Blanchard, *Management of Organizational Behavior: Utilizing Human Resources,* 3rd ed. (Englewood Cliffs, N.J.: Prentice-Hall, 1977), p. 273.
2. Ibid., p. 273.
3. G. N. Jones, *Planned Organizational Change* (New York: Praeger, 1969), p. 19.
4. Ibid., pp. 19–20.
5. D. Hellriegel and J. S. Slocum, *Organizational Behavior,* 2nd ed. (New York: West, 1979), pp. 564–68. Much of this discussion on the topic framework for change agents' role and accompanying references were taken from this source.
6. N. Tichy, "How Different Types of Change Agents Diagnose Organizations," *Human Relations* (November 9, 1975), pp. 771–79; N. Tichy and J. Nisberg, "Change Agent Bias: What They View Determines What They Do," *Group and Organization Studies,* 1:3 (1976), pp. 286–301.
7. G. Zaltman and R. Duncan, *Strategies for Planned Change* (New Yo.:k: John Wiley & Sons, 1977) p. 190.
8. Ibid., p. 190.
9. Ibid., p. 191.
10. Ibid., pp. 192–93.
11. Ibid., p. 193
12. Zaltman and Duncan, *Strategies for Planned Change,* pp. 204–05.
13. Ibid., pp. 205–06.
14. Ibid., pp. 206–07.
15. E. M. Rogers and D. K. Bhowmik, "Homophily–Heterophily: Relational Concepts for Communications Research," *Public Opinion Quarterly,* 34:4 (Winter 1970–1971), p. 529.
16. L. W. Porter, E. L. Lawler III, and J. R. Hackman, *Behavior in Organizations* (New York: McGraw-Hill, 1975), p. 439.
17. A. C. Filley, *Interpersonal Conflict Resolution* (Glenview, Ill.: Scott, Foresman, 1975), p. 126.
18. Ibid., p. 126.
19. K. Lewin, "Group Decision and Social Change," in *Readings in Social Psychology,* ed. E. E. Maccoby, T. M. Newcomb, and E. C. Hartley (New York: Holt, Rinehart and Winston, 1958), pp. 197–212.
20. H. J. Reitz, *Behavior in Organizations* (Homewood, Ill.: Richard Irwin, 1977), pp. 546–47.
21. Ibid., p. 547.
22. Filley, *Interpersonal Conflict Resolution, p. 133.*
23. Ibid., pp. 133–34.
24. W. G. Bennis et al., *Interpersonal Dynamics* (Homewood, Ill.: Dorsey Press, 1968), pp. 338–66.
25. E. H. Schein, "Management Development as a Process of Influence," *Industrial Management Review,* 2:11 (1961), p. 10.
26. Porter, Lawler, and Hackman, *Behavior in Organizations,* p. 446.
27. R. R. Blake and J. S. Mouton, *Building a Dynamic Corporation Through Grid Organization Development* (Reading, Mass.: Addison-Wesley, 1969), pp. 8–9.

28. Porter, Lawler, and Hackman, *Behavior in Organizations,* p. 479.
29. Ibid., p. 479.
30. H. A. Sheppard, "Changing Relations in Organizations," in *Handbood of Organizations,* ed. J. G. March (Chicago: Rand-McNally, 1965), as cited in Porter, Lawler, and Hackman, *Behavior in Organizations,* p. 479.
31. R. Harrison, "Choosing the Depth of Organization Intervention," *Journal of Applied Behavioral Science,* 6 (November 1970), pp. 118–202.
32. E. H. Shein, *Process Consultation: Its Role in Organizational Development* (Reading, Mass.: Addison-Wesley, 1969), as cited in Porter, Lawler, and Hackman, *Behavior in Organizations,* p. 479.
33. Porter, Lawler, and Hackman, *Behavior in Organizations,* p. 480.
34. H. Kaufman, *The Limits of Organizational Change* (Tuscaloosa: University of Alabama Press, 1971), p. 10.
35. Reitz, *Behavior in Organizations,* p. 545.
36. Kaufman, *Limits of Organizational Change,* p. 11.
37. Rietz, *Behavior in Organizations,* p. 545.
38. Kaufman, *Limits of Organizational Change,* p. 11.
39. Ibid., pp. 13–15.
40. Ibid., pp. 16–18.
41. L. E. Greiner, "Patterns of Organization Change," *Harvard Business Review,* 45:3 (1967), pp. 124–25. This article is part of a larger study on organizational development involving Greiner and his colleagues, L. B. Barnes and D. P. Leitch, that was supported by the Division of Research, Harvard Business School.
42. California Commission on Peace Officer Standards and Training (POST), *The Impact of Social Trends on Crime and Criminal Justice: Project Star* (Cincinnati, Ohio and Santa Cruz, Calif.: Anderson and Davis, 1976), p. 12. For additional information on Condorcet's forecasts, see Burnham P. Beckwith, *The Next 500 Years* (New York: Exposition Press, 1967), pp. 6–7.
43. Ibid., p. 12.
44. Ibid., pp. 12–13. Also see Pitirim A. Sorokin, *Social and Cultural Dynamics* (Boston: Extending Horizon Books, 1957).
45. Ibid., p. 13. This idea is fully elaborated in his "Notes on the Post-Industrial Society," *The Public Interest,* 6 (Winter 1967), pp. 25–35 (Part 1), and 7 (Spring 1967), pp. 102–18 (Part 2).
46. POST, *Impact of Social Trends: Project Star.*
47. For example, see John E. Angell, "Organizing Police for the Future: An Update on the Democratic Model," *Criminal Justice Review* (Fall 1976), pp. 35–51, and Gerald Caiden, *Police Revitalization* (Lexington, Mass.: Lexington Books, 1977).
48. John Henry Campbell, "Futures Research: Here and Abroad," *Police Chief,* 57:1 (1990), p. 30.
49. Ibid., p. 30.
50. Ibid., p. 30.
51. William Tafoya, "Rioting in the Streets: Deja Vu?," in *Bias Crimes: The Law Enforcement Response,* ed. Nancy Taylor (Chicago: Office of International Criminal Justice, University of Illinois at Chicago, 1991) p. 7.
52. Campbell, "Futures Research," p. 30.
53. Ibid., p. 31.
54. Ibid., p. 31.
55. Ibid., p. 33.

Index

C

Q

R

T